Introductory Foods

Twelfth Edition

Marion Bennion

Barbara Scheule
Kent State University

PEARSON

Prentice
Hall

Upper Saddle River, New Jersey 07458

Library of Congress Cataloging-in-Publication Data

Bennion, Marion
    Introductory foods / Marion Bennion, Barbara Scheule—12th ed.
        p. cm.
Includes bibliographical references and index.
    ISBN 0-13-110001-7
    1. Food.   2. Cookery.   I. Scheule, Barbara.   II. Title.
    TX354 .B46 2004
    641.3–dc21

                                                        2003009369

Publisher: Stephen Helba
Executive Editor: Vernon Anthony
Assistant Editor: Linda Cupp
Director of Production and Manufacturing: Bruce Johnson
Manufacturing Manager: Ilene Sanford
Managing Editor: Mary Carnis
Production Editor/Liaison: Janice Stangel
Manufacturing Buyer: Cathleen Peterson
Creative Design Director: Cheryl Asherman
Cover Design Coordinator: Christopher Weigand
Cover Design: Kevin Kall
Cover Illustration/Photo: The cover photos are fresh produce and cream sauce
    ingredients. Courtesy of Getty Images.
Composition/Full-Service Project Management: Bruce Hobart/
    Pine Tree Composition, Inc.
Printer/Binder: Courier Companies, Inc.

Credits and acknowledgments borrowed from other sources and reproduced, with permission, in this textbook appear on appropriate page within text and on page xvi.

Pearson Education Ltd., London
Pearson Education Singapore, Pte. Ltd
Pearson Education, Canada, Ltd
Pearson Education—Japan
Pearson Education Australia PTY, Limited
Pearson Education North Asia Ltd
Pearson Educación de Mexico, S.A. de C.V.
Pearson Education Malaysia, Pte. Ltd
Pearson Education, Upper Saddle River, New Jersey

10 9 8 7 6 5 4
ISBN 0-13-110001-7

Contents

FEATURE BOXES xiii

PREFACE xv

INTRODUCTION

CHAPTER 1   Food Choices and Sensory Characteristics 1

FACTORS AFFECTING PATTERNS OF EATING   1
SENSORY CHARACTERISTICS OF FOOD   12
OBJECTIVE EVALUATION OF FOOD   20
CHAPTER SUMMARY   22
KEY TERMS   23
STUDY QUESTIONS   23
REFERENCES   24

CHAPTER 2   Food Economics and Convenience 29

TRENDS IN FOOD USE   29
CONSUMER FOOD WASTE   33
SOME FACTORS INFLUENCING FOOD COSTS   34
AVAILABILITY AND USE OF CONVENIENCE FOODS   42
BUYING FOOD   50
CHAPTER SUMMARY   51
KEY TERMS   52
STUDY QUESTIONS   52
REFERENCES   53

CHAPTER 3   Food Safety 57

PREVENTING FOODBORNE ILLNESS   57
CHARACTERISTICS OF MICROORGANISMS   67

FOODBORNE INFECTIONS AND INTOXICATIONS   69
CHAPTER SUMMARY   90
KEY TERMS   91
STUDY QUESTIONS   92
REFERENCES   93

CHAPTER 4   **Food Regulations and Standards**   **99**

FOOD AND DRUG ADMINISTRATION   99
DEPARTMENT OF AGRICULTURE   110
ENVIRONMENTAL PROTECTION AGENCY   114
CENTERS FOR DISEASE CONTROL AND PREVENTION   114
FEDERAL TRADE COMMISSION   116
OTHER FEDERAL AGENCIES   116
STATE AND LOCAL AGENCIES   116
INTERNATIONAL STANDARDS   117
CHAPTER SUMMARY   117
KEY TERMS   118
STUDY QUESTIONS   119
REFERENCES   120

P R I N C I P L E S   O F   C O O K E R Y

CHAPTER 5   **Back to Basics**   **123**

WEIGHTS AND MEASURES   123
RECIPES   129
SMALL EQUIPMENT AND TOOLS   132
CHAPTER SUMMARY   137
KEY TERMS   138
STUDY QUESTIONS   138
REFERENCES   139

CHAPTER 6   **Heat Transfer in Cooking**   **141**

EFFECTS OF COOKING FOOD   141
HEAT INVOLVED IN CHANGE OF STATE   142
THERMOMETER SCALES   145
TYPES OF HEAT TRANSFER   145
MEDIA FOR HEAT TRANSFER   150
CHAPTER SUMMARY   152
KEY TERMS   153
STUDY QUESTIONS   153
REFERENCES   154

CHAPTER 7   **Microwave Cooking**   **155**

FOOD-RELATED USES OF MICROWAVES   156
ACTION OF MICROWAVES IN HEATING   159

ADVANTAGES OF MICROWAVE COOKING   161
LIMITATIONS OF MICROWAVE COOKING   162
PACKAGING MATERIALS AND COOKING UTENSILS   164
GENERAL COOKING SUGGESTIONS   166
CHAPTER SUMMARY   168
KEY TERMS   169
STUDY QUESTIONS   169
REFERENCES   170

CHAPTER 8   Seasoning and Flavoring Materials   **171**
BASIC SEASONINGS   172
FLAVOR ENHANCERS   174
SPICES AND HERBS   176
FLAVOR EXTRACTS   181
VEGETABLES AND FRUITS AS FLAVORINGS   183
ALCOHOL   183
CHAPTER SUMMARY   184
KEY TERMS   185
STUDY QUESTIONS   185
REFERENCES   185

CHAPTER 9   Food Composition   **187**
WATER   188
CARBOHYDRATES   194
LIPIDS OR FATS   201
PROTEINS   206
SOLUTIONS AND DISPERSIONS   213
CHAPTER SUMMARY   215
KEY TERMS   217
STUDY QUESTIONS   218
REFERENCES   220

FATS,   FRYING,   AND   EMULSIONS
CHAPTER 10   Fats, Frying, and Emulsions   **221**
FAT CONSUMPTION AND NUTRITIVE VALUE   221
PROPERTIES OF FATS   224
PROCESSING AND REFINING OF FATS   226
DETERIORATION OF FAT AND ITS CONTROL   233
FRYING   236
BUYING FATS   242
COOKING LOW FAT   243
FAT REPLACERS   243
EMULSIONS   246

SALAD DRESSINGS   247
CHAPTER SUMMARY   252
KEY TERMS   254
STUDY QUESTIONS   255
REFERENCES   256

S W E E T E N E R S ,   C R Y S T A L L I Z A T I O N , S T A R C H ,   A N D   C E R E A L   G R A I N S

CHAPTER 11   Sweeteners and Sugar Cookery   **259**

TRENDS IN SWEETENER CONSUMPTION   259
NUTRITIVE VALUE   260
PROPERTIES OF SUGARS   261
CRYSTALLINE FORMS OF SUGAR   264
SYRUPS, MOLASSES, AND HONEY   267
ALTERNATIVE SWEETENERS   269
SUGAR ALCOHOLS (POLYOLS)   274
BULKING AGENTS   275
SUGAR COOKERY   276
CLASSIFICATION OF CANDIES   279
THE CONFECTIONERY INDUSTRY   288
CHAPTER SUMMARY   289
KEY TERMS   291
STUDY QUESTIONS   291
REFERENCES   292

CHAPTER 12   Frozen Desserts   **295**

COMMERCIAL ICE CREAM PROCESSING   296
"LIGHT" FROZEN DESSERTS   297
TYPES OF FROZEN DESSERTS   299
NUTRITIVE VALUE   300
CHARACTERISTICS OF FROZEN DESSERTS   300
PREPARATION OF FROZEN DESSERTS   301
CHAPTER SUMMARY   307
KEY TERMS   309
STUDY QUESTIONS   309
REFERENCES   310

CHAPTER 13   Starch   **311**

SOURCES OF STARCH   311
COMPOSITION AND STRUCTURE   312
HYDROLYSIS OF STARCH   317
EFFECT OF HEAT ON STARCH   317
GEL FORMATION AND RETROGRADATION   320

STARCH COOKERY   321
CHAPTER SUMMARY   326
KEY TERMS   327
STUDY QUESTIONS   328
REFERENCES   329

CHAPTER 14   Pasta and Cereal Grains   **331**

CONSUMPTION   331
STRUCTURE AND COMPOSITION   332
NUTRITIVE VALUE AND ENRICHMENT   334
COMMON CEREAL GRAINS   336
BREAKFAST CEREALS   342
COOKING OF RICE   346
PASTA   348
CHAPTER SUMMARY   352
KEY TERMS   354
STUDY QUESTIONS   354
REFERENCES   355

B A K E R Y   P R O D U C T S

CHAPTER 15   Batters and Doughs   **357**

INGREDIENTS   357
CLASSIFICATION OF BATTERS AND DOUGHS   374
GENERAL METHODS FOR MIXING BATTERS AND DOUGHS   374
STRUCTURE OF BATTERS AND DOUGHS   376
DRY FLOUR MIXES   376
BAKING AT HIGH ALTITUDES   377
CHAPTER SUMMARY   378
KEY TERMS   380
STUDY QUESTIONS   380
REFERENCES   381

CHAPTER 16   Quick Breads   **383**

POPOVERS   383
CREAM PUFFS AND ÉCLAIRS   385
PANCAKES   387
WAFFLES   389
MUFFINS   389
NUT BREADS, COFFEECAKES, AND FRIED
   QUICK BREADS   393
BISCUITS   393
SCONES   395
CHAPTER SUMMARY   395

KEY TERMS   397
STUDY QUESTIONS   397
REFERENCES   398

CHAPTER 17   Yeast Breads   **399**

CHARACTERISTICS OF YEAST BREAD   401
INGREDIENTS   402
MIXING AND HANDLING   407
FERMENTATION AND PROOFING   411
COMMERCIAL PROCESSES   413
BAKING BREAD   415
ROLLS   416
WHOLE-GRAIN AND VARIETY BREADS   417
STALING OF BREAD   421
CHAPTER SUMMARY   422
KEY TERMS   425
STUDY QUESTIONS   425
REFERENCES   426

CHAPTER 18   Cakes and Cookies   **429**

SHORTENED CAKES   429
UNSHORTENED CAKES   439
COOKIES   445
CHAPTER SUMMARY   450
KEY WORDS   452
STUDY QUESTIONS   452
REFERENCES   453

CHAPTER 19   Pastry   **455**

CHARACTERISTICS OF PLAIN PASTRY   455
INGREDIENTS IN PLAIN PASTRY   458
TECHNIQUES OF MIXING   458
ROLLING PASTRY   459
BAKING   461
OTHER TYPES OF PASTRY AND CRUSTS   463
CHAPTER SUMMARY   466
KEY TERMS   466
STUDY QUESTIONS   467
REFERENCES   467

FRUITS, VEGETABLES, AND SALADS

CHAPTER 20   **Vegetables and Vegetable Preparation**   **469**

COMPOSITION AND NUTRITIVE VALUE   469
BIOTECHNOLOGY AND VEGETABLE PRODUCTION   478
SELECTION   479
STORAGE   482
VEGETABLE PREPARATION   485
PARTIALLY PROCESSED VEGETABLES AND FRUITS   506
POTATOES   507
DRIED LEGUMES   509
PLANT PROTEINS AND VEGETARIAN DIETS   511
CHAPTER SUMMARY   518
KEY TERMS   521
STUDY QUESTIONS   521
REFERENCES   523

CHAPTER 21   **Fruits and Fruit Preparation**   **529**

COMPOSITION AND NUTRITIVE VALUE   529
COLOR   532
FLAVOR   533
CHANGES DURING RIPENING   535
SELECTION OF FRESH FRUITS   537
STORAGE OF FRESH FRUITS   546
FRUIT JUICES   547
DRIED FRUITS   549
CANNED FRUITS   551
FROZEN FRUITS   551
PREPARATION   551
CHAPTER SUMMARY   555
KEY TERMS   558
STUDY QUESTIONS   558
REFERENCES   559

CHAPTER 22   **Salads and Gelatin**   **561**

SALADS   561
GELATIN AND GELS   570
CHAPTER SUMMARY   578
KEY TERMS   579
STUDY QUESTIONS   579
REFERENCES   580

DAIRY PRODUCTS AND EGGS

CHAPTER 23   Milk and Milk Products   **581**

CONSUMPTION TRENDS   581
COMPOSITION AND PROPERTIES OF MILK   582
SANITATION AND MILK QUALITY   588
MILK PROCESSING   590
TYPES OF MILK PRODUCTS   591
CREAM   601
CHEESE   604
CHAPTER SUMMARY   618
KEY TERMS   621
STUDY QUESTIONS   621
REFERENCES   623

CHAPTER 24   Eggs and Egg Cookery   **627**

COMPOSITION AND NUTRITIVE VALUE   627
STRUCTURE   629
EGG QUALITY   630
PRESERVATION AND PROCESSING   638
EGGS IN FOOD PREPARATION   640
EGG SUBSTITUTES   656
CHAPTER SUMMARY   657
KEY TERMS   659
STUDY QUESTIONS   659
REFERENCES   661

MEAT, POULTRY, AND SEAFOOD

CHAPTER 25   Meat and Meat Cookery   **663**

CONSUMPTION OF RED MEAT   663
COMPOSITION AND NUTRITIVE VALUE   664
STRUCTURE OF MEAT   667
CLASSIFICATION   670
POSTMORTEM CHANGES AND AGING   671
FACTORS AFFECTING TENDERNESS   673
BUYING OF MEAT   676
CURED MEATS   696
SAFE STORAGE AND PREPARATION OF MEATS   699
COOKING MEAT   701
SOUP STOCK   719
GRAVY   720
CARVING MEAT   721
SOY PROTEINS AND MEAT PROCESSING   723
CHAPTER SUMMARY   723

KEY TERMS   727
STUDY QUESTIONS   727
REFERENCES   729

CHAPTER 26   Poultry   **735**
CONSUMPTION   735
PROCESSING   735
COMPOSITION AND NUTRITIVE VALUE   736
CLASSIFICATION AND MARKET FORMS   737
BUYING POULTRY   738
STORAGE AND HANDLING   742
COOKING POULTRY   746
CHAPTER SUMMARY   750
KEY TERMS   752
STUDY QUESTIONS   752
REFERENCES   752

CHAPTER 27   Seafood   **755**
COMPOSITION AND NUTRITIVE VALUE   755
CLASSIFICATION AND MARKET FORMS   757
SHELLFISH   759
FISH PRODUCTS   763
AQUACULTURE   765
SELECTION, HANDLING, AND STORAGE   765
WASTE   768
PREPARATION   768
CHAPTER SUMMARY   771
KEY TERMS   772
STUDY QUESTIONS   772
REFERENCES   773

B E V E R A G E S

CHAPTER 28   Beverages   **775**
CARBONATED BEVERAGES   775
SPORTS OR ISOTONIC BEVERAGES   777
NONCARBONATED FRUIT BEVERAGES   777
ALCOHOLIC BEVERAGES   778
COFFEE   778
TEA   787
COCOA AND CHOCOLATE   791
NUTRITIVE VALUE OF CHOCOLATE BEVERAGES   794
BLOOM   794
STORAGE   795

CHAPTER SUMMARY   796
KEY TERMS   798
STUDY QUESTIONS   798
REFERENCES   799

FOOD   PRESERVATION

CHAPTER 29   Food Preservation and Packaging   **801**

CAUSES OF FOOD SPOILAGE   802
GENERAL METHODS OF FOOD PRESERVATION   802
PACKAGING OF FOOD   809
CHAPTER SUMMARY   818
KEY TERMS   819
STUDY QUESTIONS   820
REFERENCES   820

CHAPTER 30   Food Preservation by Freezing and Canning   **823**

FREEZING   823
CANNING   834
CHAPTER SUMMARY   843
KEY TERMS   845
STUDY QUESTIONS   845
REFERENCES   846

APPENDIX A   Weights and Measures   **849**

SYMBOLS FOR MEASUREMENTS   849
EQUIVALENTS   849
SOME INGREDIENT SUBSTITUTIONS   850
STANDARD CAN SIZES   850
METRIC CONVERSIONS   851
COMMON MEASUREMENTS USED IN FOOD PREPARATION   851
APPROXIMATE NUMBER OF CUPS IN A POUND
   OF SOME COMMON FOODS   851
WEIGHTS AND MEASURES FOR SOME
   FOOD INGREDIENTS   851

APPENDIX B   Temperature Control   **852**

OVEN TEMPERATURES   852
THERMOMETERS FOR OTHER USES   852
CONVERTING FAHRENHEIT
   AND CELSIUS TEMPERATURES   852

APPENDIX C   Nutritive Value of Selected Foods   **854**

APPENDIX D   Glossary   **862**

INDEX   **867**

Feature Boxes

Multicultural Cuisine

ETHNIC FOODS IN AMERICA—
   SO WHAT IS THE TYPICAL MEAL?   4
EXPLORE ETHNIC FLAVORS—EXCITE YOUR TASTEBUDS!   178
SOUPS—LESS TRADITIONAL AND MORE DIVERSE?   323
PASTA—REFLECTING GLOBAL TASTES?   352
EVOLUTION OF THE SANDWICH   400
IT'S A SMALL WORLD!   605
BISON   672

Healthy Eating

OVERWEIGHT CHILDREN AND ADOLESCENTS—
   A NATIONAL EPIDEMIC?   10
NUTRACEUTICALS OR FUNCTIONAL FOODS—
   A LUCRATIVE AND CHALLENGING MARKET?   44
SALAD DRESSINGS—A WAY TO MORE FLAVOR
   AND NUTRITION   249
FORMULATED FOODS FOR DIABETICS   270
CONFECTIONS—INDULGING OR HEALTH-PROMOTING?   288
WHOLE-GRAIN FOODS—HOW MANY SERVINGS TODAY?   333
DESIGNER FIBERS—INTO THE MAINSTREAM?   362
SUGAR OR SUCRALOSE? TIPS FOR BAKING   449
FRUITS—"FEEL GOOD" FOODS?   533

Hot Topics

PROBIOTICS—FRIENDLY BACTERIA?   70
GENETIC ENGINEERING OF FOODS—
   A BLESSING OR A CURSE?   88

A SINGLE FOOD SAFETY AGENCY—IS THIS THE ANSWER?   112
ORGANIC FOODS—EXPLODING SALES   115
PLANT STEROL ESTERS—NATURAL PHYTONUTRIENTS   229
THE CHANGING OLDE ICE CREAM SHOPPE   296
ACRYLAMIDE—A CARCINOGEN IN FOODS?   464
DRY BEANS—INTO THE MAINSTREAM?   512
ARE FRESH FRUITS AND VEGETABLES SAFE?   566
FOCUSING ON EGGS!   637
MYCOPROTEIN—FROM FUNGI?   665
SCIENTISTS AND CHICKENS—PARTNERS?   739
FUTURE FISH—ARE THEY HERE NOW?   758

Preface

Advances in food preparation and processing, along with shifting demographics and expanding knowledge of nutritional needs, mandate a text that is periodically updated and revised to reflect the most recent changes in technology. This 12th edition of *Introductory Foods* has been written and revised to give beginning college students an understanding of the basic fundamental principles of food preparation and to alert them to many innovations in science and technology related to foods. It is designed to be used in a first course in food preparation.

The organization of chapters in the book has changed from the 11th edition. The first four chapters contain introductory material about food choices, sensory analysis, economics, food safety, and regulations. The next five chapters provide a foundation in the principles of cooking. These first nine chapters contain basic principles that the student may refer to throughout the entire course. The brief discussion of carbohydrates, fats, and proteins in Chapter 9 may be used as a review for students who have had chemistry courses or as an introduction for those who have not studied chemistry. The remaining chapters are divided into eight sections: *Fats, Frying, and Emulsions; Sweeteners, Crystalization, Starch, and Cereal Grains; Bakery Products; Vegetables, Fruits, and Salads; Dairy Products and Eggs; Meat, Poultry and Seafood; Beverages;* and *Food Preservation.* The chapters in this book are independent, in that you may choose to present them in any order that best fits the structure of your own course. Cross-references to other chapters are indicated periodically in the written text.

This edition has been substantially updated to cover many recent developments in food safety and regulation, food consumption data, biotechnology, technological innovations in food processing and the discussion of new food products. Over 400 new references have been added throughout the text to provide students with current information in food technology, consumer trends, and scientific findings. Feature boxes are added for the first time throughout this 12th edition under three themes: *Multicultural Cuisine, Hot Topics,* and *Healthy Eating.* In these features, topics such as ethnic foods in America, nutraceuticals, genetic engineering, organic foods, ethnic flavors, plant sterol esters, probiotics, whole-grain foods, acrylamide, bison, mycoproteins, and fruits are discussed with an emphasis on timely food-related issues and trends. Also new to this edition are chapter summaries and key term lists. We believe students will find these supplements useful in their review of the chapters.

More than 150 new illustrations have been added to depict recipes and foods popular in today's society while maintaining those photographs that demonstrate specific food preparation techniques. The number of color pages have doubled and allowed the addition of several new color photographs.

ACKNOWLEDGMENTS

Appreciation is extended to Barbara Scheule's former colleagues in the Dining Services at Kansas State University who shared their knowledge of food science, always with a focus on food quality. In addition, the faculty and students at Kent State University are recognized for their support and encouragement throughout this revision. Dr. Scheule's family is thanked for their patience, understanding, and helpfulness.

Breanna Harris is recognized for the many hours spent seeking new photographs and illustrations for this edition. Her hard work and persistence permitted the addition of many wonderful new photographs. We also are grateful to everyone who generously shared photographs for use in this text.

Our editors, Vernon Anthony and Linda Cupp, are recognized for their guidance and helpful advice on this edition. We express our appreciation for the insightful and constructive comments and suggestions that were offered by the reviewers of this edition: Kim Lukhard, East Carolina University; Janelle M. Walter, Ph.D., Baylor University; Amy Eades, Eastern Illinois University; and Barbara D. Liles, University of North Carolina-Greensboro. The input of these reviewers has been invaluable.

The following figures are courtesy of *On Cooking: A Textbook of Culinary Fundamentals, Third Edition* by Labensky, Hause, and Labensky, published by Prentice Hall copyright © 2003, Pearson Education, Inc.: Figures 5-1, 5-2, 5-5, 5-6, 5-7, 5-9, 5-10, 5-11, 5-12, 5-13, 6-2, 6-4, 6-8, 6-10, 8-2, 8-3, 8-4, 10-4a, 10-4b, 10-8, 10-9, 11-10, 12-1, 13-7, 13-8, 13-9, 15-7, 15-8, 15-9, 16-3, 16-5, 16-9, 17-6, 17-8, 17-9, 17-14, 18-5, 19-5, 19-9, 20-8, 20-12, 20-13, 21-9, 21-10, 21-11, 21-12, 22-1, 22-4, 22-7, 22-11, 23-9, 23-12, 24-8, 24-10, 24-11, 24-14, 25-29, 27-7, 27-8, 28-4, & Plate XXV (lamb loin).

M. B
B. S

Food Choices and Sensory Characteristics

1

The food choices that we make and the development of our behavior and habits concerning food are influenced by many interacting factors, including availability, income, culture, concerns about health, social values, religion, and even genetics [19, 65]. Yet, for most persons and in ordinary circumstances, foods must be **palatable** or have **appetite** appeal if they are to be eaten. A palatable food is one that is both acceptable to an individual and agreeable to his or her taste. Various **sensory** impressions or sensations, including odor, appearance, taste, and mouthfeel or touch, are involved in our judgment of palatability and food quality.

Learning to prepare foods with great appetite appeal includes learning to discriminate and evaluate the quality of food through the intensity of the sensations received when food is sampled. Individuals vary in their capacities to experience flavors and odors, but sensitivities to pleasurable encounters with food may be heightened as more is learned about food characteristics and quality.

A taste or liking for a variety of foods may be acquired. In fact, many American consumers have today developed an ethnically diverse palate as they learn to appreciate and demand a medley of foods from around the globe. Indeed, as you learn to like new foods you will receive ample rewards from increased enjoyment and enhanced aesthetic experiences. Eating a wide variety of foods is also an excellent practice from a nutrition and health point of view. You are, then, encouraged to develop a discriminating taste as you begin to learn basic reasons why foods behave as they do during preparation and/or processing.

palatable pleasing to the taste

appetite a desire or craving either for food in general or for some specific food

sensory having to do with the senses (sight, taste, smell, hearing, touch); connected with receiving and transmitting sense impressions

FACTORS AFFECTING PATTERNS OF EATING

Social and Cultural

Family and Social.   Humans, as biological beings, require food to sustain life. Humans eat to satisfy hunger and to meet a basic drive for food. But a person is also a social being. Humans have learned to live and work together and have organized themselves into societies. As infants grow and develop, they are incorporated into this society through a variety of experiences, and some of these experiences involve food. Children learn food provides comfort when hungry and is a pleasurable dimension of family activities, celebrations, and time with friends (Figure 1-1). Adults share meals with friends, family, and coworkers as part of their social interactions.

Figure 1-1
Two children enjoy each others' company while enjoying a healthy snack. (Photo by Keith Weller, Courtesy of U.S. Department of Agriculture)

Our pattern of eating includes the available foods deemed acceptable and the time periods and settings in which these foods are consumed. The family structure and interactions among family members are important influences on the development of our food habits. Several studies have shown an association between children's food preferences and the food practices of their parents [1, 18, 62]. Peers, schools, daycare providers and the media also influence eating patterns of children and adolescents [1, 18, 62, 20].

The food patterns of 21st century families are being influenced by time restraints. Nearly 70 percent of women with children under 18 are working outside the home [8]. Food preparation time is further limited by a variety of extracurricular family activities. Families are coping with this time challenge through increased meals eaten out [8], food consumed in the car [30, 57], the purchase of **home meal replacement** and convenience foods [28], and the simplification of menus to include fewer sidedishes [8]. Meals purchased outside the home account for 47 percent of total food expenditures [12] and is estimated to reach 53 percent of the food dollar by 2010 [45].

Regular, shared meals have been declining under the pressures of modern society. Nevertheless, the family meal plays an important role in human communication—communicating love, values, and information. It can be especially effective in increasing the well-being of children. Even in our changing society, older ideals about the importance of family meals have persisted [8]. Nearly 80 percent of the time, Americans eat dinner at home [39]. A movement toward a more simplified life and a stronger sense of family may be occurring, bringing with it a return to family dinners [55].

home meal replacement prepared foods purchased to be consumed at home that have similar characteristics to food that may be prepared in the home. Roasted chickens purchased in a foodservice establishment or a grocery store are an example of a home meal replacement food.

Cultural.   Cultural forces shape our food behaviors. The **culture** in which we develop determines, to a large extent, our food patterns or habits. Foods are eaten in combination with other foods in ways that are determined and perpetuated by our culture. Food patterns differ markedly from one culture to another. Grasshoppers or roast dog may be delicacies in some parts of the world,

culture a way of life in which there are common customs for behavior and in which there is a common understanding among members of the group

whereas in other areas it would be unthinkable for humans to consume these products. Eggs are a staple breakfast food in certain cultures, whereas in others they are taboo, at least for some members of the group. Not everyone in a cultural group eats exactly alike, however. Within a culture, individual preferences differ and subgroups develop. Families tend to develop their own distinctive food patterns, and even individuals within a family have personal food preferences. Differences among cultural groups may be found not only in what specific foods are eaten but also in the number of meals eaten each day, the way the food is served, and the utensils used in the service.

The influence of **ethnic** groups is also seen in geographical areas where individuals from these cultures predominate. Food habits learned in other geographical areas of the world tend to continue, when possible, as an individual or group moves to a new location. In the United States, some of the regional food preferences can be traced to the influx of immigrants into the region. Each culture passes on its food habits and patterns by training children from infancy in their unique patterns [23, 13]. In the United States, cultural food habits are modified as **acculturation** with the "American diet" occurs [74, 73].

The study of foods should help you understand and appreciate the food patterns of other cultures or ethnic groups as well as different taste preferences among various regions of the United States [14, 38]. America is becoming increasingly more global in its tastes for food, resulting from a more diverse population, increased travel, and rapid communication [66]. Each ethnic group (e.g., Mexican, Japanese, Italian, Armenian) has developed a **cuisine** with its distinctive combination of flavorings for basic foodstuffs. When you eat out, you often are looking for a culinary experience involving different and sometimes exotic foods. A large percentage of restaurants are ethnic in character and have become popular in the United States [14]. The food industry is accepting the challenges presented by **demographic** changes in the Americas and Western Europe, with new menu items featuring Japanese, Thai, Vietnamese, Korean, Middle Eastern, Carribean, Jamaican, and Mediterranean foods [60]. Advances in food technology are enabling the food industry to commercially produce many ethnic foods for both domestic and world markets. We have open to us, therefore, a great variety of food choices. Fascinating experiences await the adventurer who learns to enjoy, and to prepare, the foods of many different cultures.

ethnic pertains to basic divisions of mankind into groups that are distinguished by customs, characteristics, language, and so on

acculturation the adaptation of a cultural group that has moved into a new area or country to practices common in the new location

cuisine a style of cooking or manner of preparing food

demographic having to do with the statistical study of populations

Religious Beliefs. Food has significance in relation to many religious beliefs. Among the sets of rules governing different aspects of religious life are food laws. These may set strict guidelines dictating the types of food to be consumed, the procedures for processing and preparing foods, the complete omission of certain foods, and the frequency of eating other foods. To take advantage of the large markets available in religious communities, the food industry must serve the needs of these various groups.

The kosher dietary laws, *kashruth*, are observed to varying degrees by members of the Jewish faith [52, 38]. These laws include a prohibition against eating blood and thus dictate rules concerning the slaughter of animals and their further processing [34]. Milk products and meat products must be kept separate. Only certain species of animals are considered to be suitable for consumption. Pork and shellfish, among others, are prohibited. Kosher laws also extend to ingredients that are used in food processing. Even many non-Jewish

---

Multicultural Cuisine

Ethnic Foods in America—So what is the typical meal?

The U.S. Census Bureau estimates that in 2050 the Hispanic population will be nearly one-fourth of the total population of the United States, or potentially 96.5 million people [3]. Asians and Pacific Islanders also are anticipated to grow in number to 34 million. The non-Hispanic white population is still expected to be the largest ethnic group with 206 million, while non-Hispanic blacks are estimated to be 54 million. Only time will tell if the immigration and birth rate patterns will hold to materialize these predictions. Meanwhile, however, how do ethnic trends influence what we eat?

In the decade ahead, Mexican, Chinese, Caribbean, and Thai foods are expected to have the fastest development [59]. Latin cuisine is gaining in popularity as well [58]. The flavors and ingredients from South American and Caribbean cuisines characterize Latin food. Latin food can be hot due to the use of chilies or refreshing with citrus fruits and assorted vinegars. Look for *empanadas*—a beef dish, Peruvian blue potatoes, *postones*—fried plantain, mango fruits, *dulce de leche* ice cream—based on a South American sweet caramel-like milk product, and many other Latin-inspired dishes.

---

individuals choose kosher products because they see them as clean, high-quality foods.

Islam also prescribes a set of food laws [11, 38]. Foods that are lawful for Muslims to consume are called "halal" [34]. As a general principle, most foods are permitted; however, some prohibitions are specified. Prohibited foods include swine and all their by-products, intoxicants of all types, birds of prey, land animals without ears such as snakes, flowing or congealed blood, and animals killed in a manner that prevents their blood from being fully drained from their bodies. Thus, there are strict requirements for the slaughtering of animals. Food products may be certified by the Islamic Food and Nutrition Council of America.

Hindu dietary practices emphasize the avoidance of foods that may interfere with the development of the body or mind [38]. Although not required, many Hindus are vegetarian. The consumption of cows is prohibited because cows are considered sacred. Pork also is frequently avoided by Hindus. When fish or meat is consumed, it must first be sanctified.

Several religions advocate vegetarianism, although vegetarianism may be chosen for ecological, health, or other reasons as well. Chinese Buddhists advocate vegetarianism because they believe in compassion [31]. A vegetarian diet is recommended by the Seventh-Day Adventist Church but is not required for membership [7].

lacto-ovo vegetarians those who consume milk, eggs, and products derived from them as well as vegetable foods

vegans those who exclude from their diet all products that are not of plant origin

In the United States, approximately 2.5 percent of the population, or 4.8 million people, are vegetarians [29]. The majority of these are **lacto-ovo vegetarians.** The remainder are strict vegetarians or **vegans** [24]. The food industry has made available products of special interest to vegetarians, including high-quality plant-protein foods prepared from wheat and soy, soy milk, and cereal products free of animal fats. Vegetarian entrees are being offered with increasing frequency in many foodservice establishments. (Vegetarianism is discussed further in Chapter 20.)

Nutrition and Health

An interest in healthful lifestyles, including recognition of nutrition as an important part of the health improvement process, is flourishing among Americans. National nutrition objectives are included in the U.S. Public Health Service's broad-based initiative *Healthy People 2010: National Health Promotion and Disease Prevention Objectives* [70]. Dietary guidelines for Americans, first published in 1980 by the U.S. Departments of Agriculture (USDA) and Health and Human Services, is now in the 5th edition [69, 15]. The 2000 Dietary Guidelines focus on the promotion of general health and the prevention of certain chronic diseases through three themes: aim for fitness, build a healthy base, and choose sensibly (Figure 1-2). New in the 2000 Dietary Guidelines are recommendations for exercise and food safety, in addition to greater specificity for the dietary guidelines.

Figure 1-2
Dietary guidelines for Americans.
(Courtesy of U.S. Department of Agriculture)

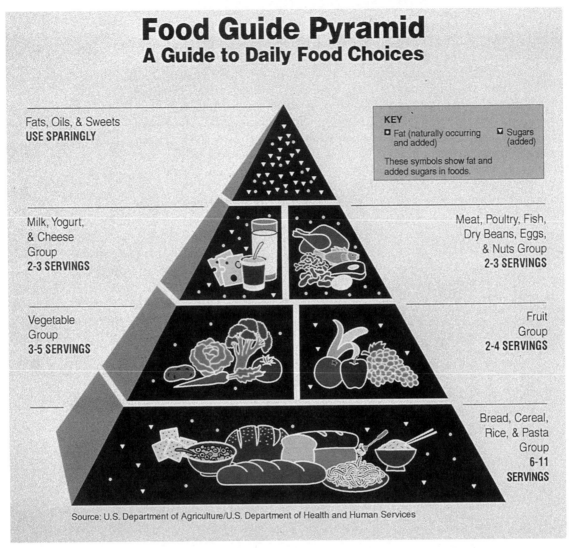

Figure 1-3
The Food Guide Pyramid. (Courtesy of U.S. Department of Agriculture)

The Food Guide Pyramid was introduced by the USDA in 1992 to graphically illustrate the dietary guidelines [67, 15]. This pyramid (Figure 1-3) places at the top those food groups that should be used sparingly. As one descends the pyramid, the daily servings from the food groups are suggested in increasing amounts. The bread, cereal, rice, and pasta group forms the base of the pyramid, with six to eleven daily servings recommended. Although the number of servings of some food, such as the bread, cereal, rice and pasta group, may at first glance seem high, a careful examination of the portion sizes reveals that one serving of bread is one slice of bread, one-half of a hamburger bun, or one-half cup of pasta (Table 1-1). Thus, the amount of spaghetti that may be served at home or in a restaurant as one portion may actually represent 3–4 servings from the bread, cereal, rice, pasta group! A food guide pyramid for children also has been developed (Figure 1-4).

The food pyramid provides a helpful guide for consumers to use when planning a healthful diet. During the decade of the 90's, Americans improved

Bread, cereal, rice, and pasta

1 slice of bread	1/2 cup cooked cereal, rice or pasta
1 oz ready-to-eat cereal	
1 tortilla	3–4 small crackers
1 4" pancake	1/2 English muffin or bagel

Vegetables

1 cup raw leafy vegetables	7–8 carrot sticks
1/2 cup cooked or canned vegetables	1 medium potato
	3/4 cup vegetable juice

Fruit

1 medium apple, orange, banana	1/2 cup chopped, cooked, or canned fruit
3/4 cup fruit juice	1/2 grapefruit
1/4 cup dried fruit	1/2 cup berries

Milk, yogurt, and cheese

1 cup milk	8 oz plain or flavored yogurt
1 1/2 oz natural cheese	2 oz process cheese

Meat, poultry, fish, dry beans, eggs, and nuts

2–3 oz cooked lean meat, poultry, or fish
The following each count as 1 oz of meat:
1 egg
2 Tbsp peanut butter
1/2 cup cooked dry beans, peas, or lentils
1/3 cup nuts

Source: Reference 67.

Table 1-1

Sample Serving Sizes for Food Groups in the Food Guide Pyramid.

their diets by reducing their fat intake [15]. However, the American diet still reveals an unbalanced pyramid (Figure 1-5) and the incidence of obesity among both adults and children is rising. Americans are encouraged to choose more fruits, green and yellow vegetables, low fat dairy foods, and whole grain breads and cereals. The fruits most frequently now chosen include orange juice, bananas, fresh apples and apple juice. Iceberg lettuce, fresh or frozen potatoes, and potato chips make up 52 percent of the vegetables in our diets. Thus, a wider selection of fruits and vegetables in our diets would be beneficial.

A decrease in the consumption of foods with added fats, added sugars, and refined breads and grains would further help to balance the American diet pyramid [51]. Carbonated beverages have been implicated as one of the important sources of added sugar in the American diet. The consumption of carbonated beverages has increased significantly over the years. Figure 1-6 depicts the change in beverage milk and soft drink consumption from 1945 to 1998 [49]. Other sources of added sugar in the diet include cakes, candies, cookies, pastries, pies, and sweet snacks.

In 1990, the Nutrition Labeling and Education Act resulted in the provision of standardized nutrition labels on nearly all processed foods. These labels

Figure 1-4
*The Food Guide Pyramid for 2–6
year old children.* (Courtesy of U.S.
Department of Agriculture)

do appear to be used by consumers seeking to make informed choices about the foods purchased [15]. (Additional information on nutrition labeling is discussed in Chapter 2.)

Information about nutrition and the effects of various diets on health may encourage those responsible for food purchasing and preparation to adjust food patterns in accordance with public health suggestions on diet. In general, food prepared and consumed at home is lower in fat and sodium and higher in fiber, iron, and calcium than food eaten away from home [41]. As Americans eat a greater percentage of their meals "out," the impact of these food choices on the total diet is significant. **Quick service restaurants** accounted for 2 percent of childrens' caloric intake in the mid to late 1970's, but increased to 10 percent by the mid 1990's [42]. The inclusion of nutrition information in restaurants and other food outlets has been suggested as one way to encourage people to choose a healthful diet when eating out [70, 51, 21].

quick service restaurants
foodservices who provide limited, but fast service. Menu selections are limited and include foods that may be quickly prepared and served.

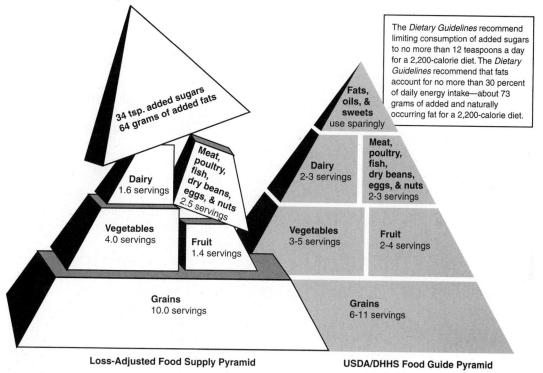

The *Dietary Guidelines* recommend limiting consumption of added sugars to no more than 12 teaspoons a day for a 2,200-calorie diet. The *Dietary Guidelines* recommend that fats account for no more than 30 percent of daily energy intake—about 73 grams of added and naturally occurring fat for a 2,200-calorie diet.

Loss-Adjusted Food Supply Pyramid

USDA/DHHS Food Guide Pyramid

Figure 1-5
The unbalanced American diet. (Reference 51)

Economic and Marketplace Factors

Food Availability. Geography of an area and variations in climate influence the types of food that can be and usually are grown. Historically, this fact has had a profound influence on the availability of particular foods and, in turn, on the eating patterns of people in the area. Examples are the widespread use of

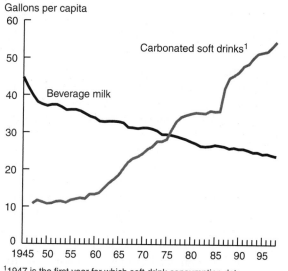

Figure 1-6
Milk consumption compared with soft drink consumption. (Reference 49)

[1]1947 is the first year for which soft drink consumption data are available.

Healthy Eating

Overweight Children and Adolescents—A national epidemic?

The percentage of adolescents who are overweight has tripled in the past two decades [71]. At the start of the 21st century, 13 percent of school age children and 14 percent of adolescents were overweight. Seventy percent of overweight adolescents are likely to become overweight adults who are at high risk for heart disease, diabetes, high blood pressure, and some forms of cancer.

The causes of overweight among the young were identified in a Surgeon General's Call to Action paper as lack of physical activity and unhealthy eating patterns. Genetics and lifestyle were listed as contributing factors [71]. Meanwhile, researchers have found that away-from-home foods provide more of the diet components that should be reduced and less of the nutrients that are under consumed [41]. A *Washington Post* article argues that practices of the food industry are contributing factors to childhood obesity [9]. The authors note that the average child sees 10,000 food advertisements per year and is the subject of multiple food-related promotions. In this article the food lobby and fast food are linked with obesity in children.

Some have gone so far as to suggest that high fat foods and foods of limited nutritional value should be taxed at a higher rate than other foods. What do you think should be done to reduce the rate of obesity in our population?

pinto beans and chili peppers in the southwestern United States and the extensive use of seafood in coastal areas. With the development of rapid transportation and modern food-handling facilities, however, the influence of geography and climate on our food habits has decreased greatly. For example, 40 percent of the fresh fruit consumed by Americans is imported and during the winter months especially, many imported vegetables may be found in American grocery stores [50]. We now have available in U.S. supermarkets, on a regular basis, fresh fruits from tropical areas and live seafood, even though we may live far from the tropics or the ocean.

Economics.   Whether we consume the variety of foods available to us in supermarkets and restaurants depends, to a considerable extent, on our purchasing power. Economics is a powerful factor in limiting or expanding our dietary patterns, although these changes may be transitory in some cases. When food budgets are restricted because of financial problems, less expensive foods must comprise a larger share of the menus offered. When budgets are liberal, more convenience items and snack foods are often purchased, and "eating out" occurs more frequently. These trends can be observed nationally when the country is in recession or in a period of economic prosperity [12].

Income and household size are the most important factors determining where and how Americans spend their food dollars [6]. Low income families spend 48 percent of their income on food, whereas middle income and high income households spend 13 percent and 8 percent, respectively. High income households spend a larger share of their food dollar on eating out. Overall, a household size of four people spent $1,549 per person for food in 1998 [6].

food security access to enough nourishment, at all times, for an active healthy life

Some households in America do not enjoy **food security** [54, 70]. In 1999, 3.8 percent of children lived in homes where food insecurity was a concern [54].

There are a number of nutrition assistance programs available to help families, such as food stamps and the National School Lunch Program [46]. The United States Department of Agriculture (USDA) calculates costs for four levels of food plans [68]. Understanding food preparation and food quality is an advantage whether working with limited or generous household food budgets.

Technological Development

The food-processing industry is sharing in the many ideas, innovations, and technological developments that are bringing about major changes in our society. The industry's growth and continued development keep an ever-increasing supply of new and convenient foods on the market and affect the purchasing habits of the consumer and the types of meals served both at home and in food-service establishments. Advertising through television, radio, newspapers, and magazines ensures that the consumer not only is aware of the new types of foods available but also is enticed to try them. The development of technological expertise in transportation and in food preservation extends the seasons of food availability. Irradiation may be used to decrease bacterial contamination on poultry and meat and increase the shelf life of fresh fruits. **Aseptic packaging** decreases processing time and results in more flavorful food products. Flavor specialists are designing systems to improve the delivery of flavor for many foods. New-generation refrigerated foods offer fresh and flavorful entrees that may be stored under refrigeration for several weeks before reheating and service. Food safety issues such as *Salmonella* in eggs and emerging bacteria in fresh fruit juices are being approached by new methods [36, 56, 44].

aseptic packaging the food and package are sterilized separately; then the sterilized container is filled with sterilized food in an environment in which sterility is maintained

Sous vide [2] refers to one method of producing refrigerated foods that involves vacuum sealing fresh food in impermeable plastic pouches, cooking at length at low temperatures in circulating water, then chilling and holding at refrigerated temperatures. This method of food processing was developed in France and has the potential to consistently deliver superior cuisine on a large scale to the foodservice industry [53]. There are concerns, however, that sous vide foods could pose a potential public health hazard in terms of microbiological safety if proper controls are not maintained throughout the processing and delivery operations.

sous vide literally means "under vacuum"

Conventional breeding and selection of plants and animals over the centuries has been used to improve food supplies. Now, with a group of genetic tools that falls under the heading of **biotechnology,** the variety, productivity, and efficiency of food production can be targeted in less time and with greater predictability and control than was possible with traditional methods [25]. Genetic engineering may be used to increase crop yields and disease resistance and to produce faster-maturing, drought-resistant varieties. Biotechnology could be used to improve the nutritional quality of the food supply and reduce the use of chemicals [5]. However, in spite of the benefits, biotechnology has not been without controversy [32]. There is a need, however, for public education about biotechnology so that people will acquire a base of knowledge with which to make judgments about these new tools as they make choices in food purchasing [10].

biotechnology the collection of industrial processes or tools that involve the use of biological systems, i.e., plants, animals, and microorganisms

Refrigeration and freeze processing within the modern home allow patterns of cooking and eating that cannot exist in still technologically developing societies in which methods for keeping foods fresh are not readily available. Different types of cooking equipment, including the microwave oven, have markedly affected patterns of eating. Even the social aspects of food may be influenced by developments in food technology as we need to rely less on other family members to prepare the food we eat. Almost anyone in the household can retrieve an entree from the freezer and quickly heat it in the microwave oven.

Emotional and Psychological Effects

With all of today's technological influences, it is important that the meanings of food, other than the biological and economic ones, be considered (Figure 1-7). Food means security, hospitality, and even status. Infants learn about security when mothers respond to their crying by giving them food. Familiar foods bring back memories of home and family and make one feel secure. Feeling full and physically satisfied and knowing that there is more food available for other meals bring security. Food is a symbol of hospitality and is used to show that one cares about others and is a friend. Gifts of food are given in times of both happiness and sorrow.

SENSORY CHARACTERISTICS OF FOOD

Sensory characteristics are important factors in determining whether we will first taste, then eat, and enjoy the food. Those involved in food preparation, both in the home and in commercial establishments, must take into careful account the appearance, flavor, and texture of the dishes prepared. Humans assess their food using the five senses: taste, smell, sight, touch, and hearing. Understanding these sensory characteristics is essential in the study of food.

Appearance

Appearance creates the first impression of food. Such qualities as color, form, size, and design or arrangement contribute to what may be called "eye appeal" of foods. Without an attractive and appealing appearance, foods may be rejected without being tasted. For the commercial vendor of prepared foods, the appearance of the food is extremely important, because this is the first opportunity to impress the potential buyer with the quality and desirability of the product.

The freshness of a food is often indicated by its appearance. In some cases its safety may also be evaluated, as with the appearance of mold on fruits or vegetables. Certain food products have nutritional advantages but may not always have an attractive appearance. For example, nonfat milk often appears thin and bluish in color as compared to whole milk. A method of improving the color and perceived creaminess of nonfat milk has been developed with the application of a milk-coagulating enzyme used in cheese making. The resulting nonfat milk product is improved in appearance but retains its original nutritional advantages and flavor [47].

Flavor

flavor a blend of taste, smell, and general touch sensations evoked by the presence of a substance in the mouth

olfactory having to do with the sense of smell

tactile having to do with the sense of touch

pungency a sharp, biting quality

Millions of flavor sensations are experienced in a lifetime. **Flavor** is an important attribute of a food. Perceived flavor results from an integrated response to a complex mixture of stimuli or sensations from the **olfactory** center in the nasal cavity, the taste buds on the tongue, **tactile** receptors in the mouth, and the perception of **pungency**, heat, cooling, and so on when a food is placed in

Figure 1-7
Mexican women chat while they roast chili peppers. (Photograph by Kay Franz)
A brother and sister can get to know each other over ice cream cones. (Photograph by Roger P. Smith)
Eating spaghetti requires real concentration. (Photograph by Chris Meister)

taste sensations perceived through stimulation of taste buds on the tongue; primary tastes are sweet, salty, sour, and bitter

odor a smell, pleasant or unpleasant, perceived through stimulation of the olfactory center

taste bud a group of cells, including taste cells, supporting cells, and nerve fibers

papillae small, nipplelike projections of various shapes on the surface of the tongue

taste receptor tiny ends of the taste cells that come in contact with the substance being tasted

taste pore a tiny opening from the surface of the tongue into the taste bud

the mouth [33]. The process involved in this integration that produces flavor is not well understood because of its complexity. The flavor of real food systems can be affected by every step in the production process, from selection of ingredients to processing to packaging and storage of the final product [40]. However, much of what we call flavor is a blending of **taste** and **odor.** The term *aroma* is usually applied to a pleasant odor. Other sensory factors also affect our total experience with food, including its visual appearance and even the sounds of crunching crisp foods such as raw carrots and celery and the sizzle of fajitas when they are brought to the table.

Taste and Odor. Sometimes the words *flavor* and *taste* are used synonymously. In a strict sense, however, taste is only one part of flavor. Taste involves the sensations produced through stimulation of the **taste buds** on the tongue. It is generally accepted that there are only four primary taste sensations: sweet, sour, bitter, and salty; but that which we often call taste involves, to a considerable extent, the sense of smell along with the taste sensations.

Taste buds are found in small elevations, called **papillae,** on the surface of the tongue (Figure 1-8). The actual taste sensations are produced when bitter, salty, sweet, or acid substances in a solution contact **taste receptors** in the **taste pore** leading to the taste bud. Figure 1-8 also shows a diagram of a taste bud. A

Figure 1-8
Drawing of the tongue, showing papillae on the surface. Taste buds are located on the sides and at the base of many of the papillae. Taste buds near the tip are more sensitive to sour, and those near the back are more sensitive to bitter.

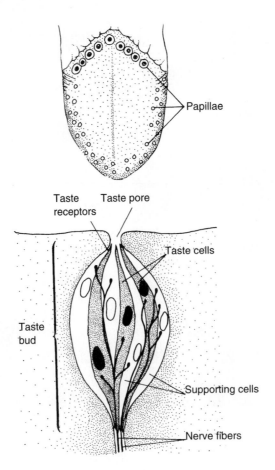

Diagram of an individual taste bud containing tiny taste receptors that come in contact with the substance being tasted, taste cells, and nerve fibers that carry the message from the taste bud to the brain for interpretation.

message is sent to the brain from the taste cells via nerve fibers with endings in the taste cells. The brain interprets and identifies the specific taste.

The olfactory center is found at the top of the nasal cavity, as shown in Figure 1-9. To stimulate the olfactory center, substances must be in gaseous form. The gaseous molecules enter the nose as food is placed in the mouth and are drawn toward the olfactory center, where they stimulate nerve endings. Nerve impulses are thus sent to the brain to be interpreted. The sense of smell is estimated to be about 10,000 times as sensitive as the sense of taste in detecting minute concentrations, and it can differentiate hundreds, or possibly thousands, of distinct odors.

Temperature may affect the blending of primary tastes and other factors contributing to flavor. Within the temperature range at which most foods are eaten, from ice cream to hot chocolate, are marked changes in the apparent intensity of some of the primary tastes. The same amount of sugar seems sweeter at higher temperatures than at lower temperatures. Just the reverse seems to be true of salt. Furthermore, extremes of temperature may create pleasant sensations or cause actual pain or injury to body tissues. Some substances such as menthol feel cool; certain receptors in the mouth and throat are sensitized so that they exaggerate the feeling of coolness. Conversely, some foods such as chili peppers contain molecules that irritate the mucous membranes lining the mouth and produce a hot or biting sensation. The compound primarily responsible for the "hotness" of chili peppers is capsaicin. To the uninitiated, this hot sensation is often so strong that it is painful.

Countless numbers of molecules contribute to our perception of odor or aroma and taste. One single flavor may be produced from the interaction of many different chemical molecules. Did you know, for example, that more than 200 different compounds are used to make artificial banana flavor? Many of the odorous substances in foods occur in such vanishingly small concentrations that it is difficult to show that they are even present. With the development of

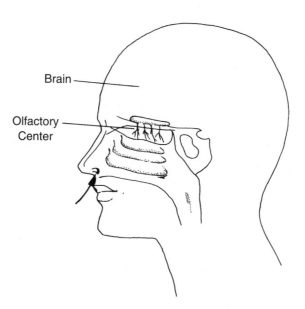

Figure 1-9
Gaseous molecules enter the nose and stimulate the olfactory center, from which nerve fibers send messages to the brain concerning the odor of food.

Brain

Olfactory Center

Figure 1-10

The geographic origin of a spice may be identified by examining the gas chromatographic tracing of its flavor components. Each peak on the tracing represents a different flavor substance. Oregano grown in Greece contains various flavor components in different amounts than the oregano grown in Mexico. (Courtesy of the R. T. French Company)

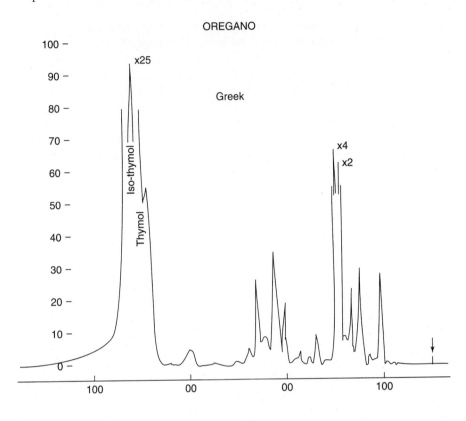

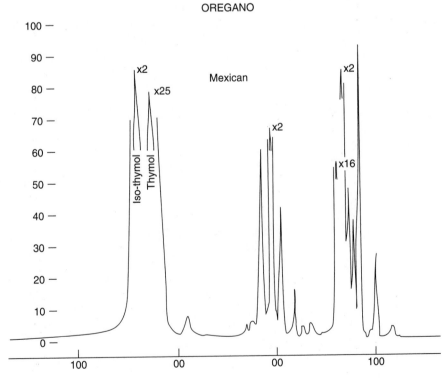

analytical tools such as the gas chromatograph, tracings from which are shown in Figure 1-10, the chemist has been able to separate, isolate, and identify many of the molecules that are responsible for aroma and taste in such foods as onions, strawberries, and beef. Analytical tools used to great advantage by the flavor researcher are high-performance liquid chromatography, (HPLC) and the electronic nose [37, 43]. HPLC is especially useful for studying **nonvolatile** and/or **labile** flavor components (see Figure 1-11). Among other things, it can be used to test for adulteration of flavoring materials from natural sources. The electronic nose is a chemical sensing system that offers the advantage of the rapid detection of volatiles (Figure 1-12).

    Continuing research about flavor is important in order to learn more about its chemistry and how the flavor of food is perceived by humans. As food markets continue to expand on a global basis, more knowledge is needed concerning the diverse tastes of people from different cultures. If flavor research is to be applied in a real-life setting, then cultural, economic, and environmental factors must be integrated with information about the chemical components of odor and taste [35].

Types of Flavors.   The flavors of some foods are readily perceivable in the raw "natural" state, whereas cooking other foods produces flavors from nonflavor substances called flavor **precursors.** For example, strawberries, peaches, and other fresh fruits contain a natural, unique flavor bouquet composed of many volatile substances that stimulate the nasal olfactory center in combination with sweet and acid components that stimulate the taste buds. Raw vegetables, meats, and fish also present their own characteristic flavors. The flavor of raw meat and fish is appreciated by some people, whereas others prefer the change in flavor that is produced when these foods are cooked. Incidentally, raw meat and fish are made safer by proper cooking to destroy any pathogenic organisms that may be present.

    The chemical changes that occur during heating in the presence of air are apparently quite complex and are not completely understood for most foods.

nonvolatile lacking the ability to readily change to a vapor or to evaporate

labile unstable

precursor something that comes before; in flavor study, it is a compound that is nonflavorful but can be changed, usually by heat or enzymes, into a flavorful substance

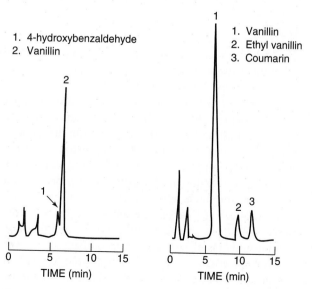

Figure 1-11
High-performance liquid chromatography (HPLC) may be used in testing vanilla for adulteration. The tracing on the left is from a true vanilla-bean extract and the one on the right is from a sample that has been adulterated with coumarin, a substance banned as a flavor source in the United States. (From Kenney, B. F. "Applications of high-performance liquid chromatography for the flavor research and quality control laboratories in the 1990s." *Food Technology 44,* 76(9), 1990. Copyright © Institute of Food Technologists)

yeast fermentation a process in which enzymes produced by the yeast break down sugars to carbon dioxide and alcohol, and also produce some flavor substances

enzymatic reactions those that are *catalyzed* by enzymes, which are special proteins produced by living cells; a catalyst changes the rate of a reaction without itself undergoing permanent change

synthetic compounds those produced by chemically combining two or more simple compounds or elements in the laboratory

Figure 1-12
A piece of equipment named the electronic nose is used to pick up and record the aromas of various foods. (Courtesy of Cyrano Sciences)

texture arrangement of the parts of a material showing the structure; the texture of baked flour products such as a slice of bread may be fine and even or coarse and open; the texture of a cream sauce may be smooth or lumpy

For example, flavors produced when meat is cooked in water are different from those produced when it is roasted in an oven, where it is surrounded by dry heat. Some flavor precursors are present in the lean portion of meats such as beef, pork, and lamb, whereas other precursors are present in their fat. The tantalizing odors that develop during the baking of bread are additional examples of flavor substances produced by heating. Many of the volatile substances that waft from the oven where bread is baking are initially the products of **yeast fermentation.** Crust formation occurs as the outer layers of the bread are dehydrated and subjected to very high temperatures. Browning of the crust contributes to both an attractive appearance and a pleasant flavor.

Flavors may also be produced during processing by **enzymatic reactions,** as is cheese flavor, or by microbial fermentation, as is butter flavor. Flavor substances that occur naturally or that are generated during heating, processing, or fermentation are considered to be "natural" flavors [33].

Biotechnology can be used to generate natural flavor substances from enzymatic or microbial reactions. These and other natural flavors may be added to fabricated foods to improve or create desirable flavor bouquets. Since there are not enough natural flavorings to flavor all of the foods that are produced by the food industry, these natural flavors are simulated as closely as possible through the production of **synthetic compounds.** Synthetic compounds that are added to foods either individually or as part of a mixture are considered in the United States to be "artificial" or "synthetic" flavors. Both natural and artificial flavorings are combined in many foods.

Knowledge of flavor chemistry and ways of simulating natural flavors is especially important as the world population increases and global markets expand [35]. Foods must be flavored so that they are accepted by consumers in their unique cultural environment. To apply the science of flavor successfully to the development of new products and the improvement of old ones, the flavor researcher must first identify the substances that are responsible for the acceptable flavor and the mechanism by which people eating the food experience flavor. Then new food-flavor ingredients can be developed and foods can be processed in a manner that results in the most desirable flavors [26, 40].

Texture

The physical properties of foods, including **texture,** consistency, and shape, involve the sense of touch or feeling, also called the *tactile* sense. When food is contacted, pressure and movement receptors on the skin and muscles of the mouth and tongue are stimulated. Sensations of smoothness, stickiness, graininess, brittleness, fibrous qualities, or lumpy characteristics may be detected [63]. The tingling feeling that comes from drinking a carbonated beverage is an attribute of texture. Terms describing extremes of texture and consistency may include dry or moist, solid or fluid, thick or thin, rough or smooth, coarse or fine, tough or tender, hard or soft, and compact or porous.

The sound made when a food is eaten is also part of palatability and the enjoyment of eating. We often evaluate crispness by the sound it makes and by its tactile sensations in the mouth. Try to imagine how crisp carrot and celery sticks would "taste" without the accompanying sound of crunching.

Texture includes those qualities that we can feel with the fingers, the tongue, the palate, or the teeth [47]. It is an important attribute that affects consumer attitudes toward and preferences for different foods. Textural characteristics of food have both positive and negative connotations for the consumer [64]. Those textures that are universally liked are crisp, crunchy, tender, juicy, and firm. Those generally disliked are tough, soggy, crumbly, lumpy, watery, and slimy. Texturizing agents are often used by the food processor to impart body, to improve consistency or texture of a food, or to stabilize an **emulsion** [48]. Such agents, of which there are many, optimize the quality of a food product so that consumers will find it acceptable.

emulsion a system consisting of one liquid dispersed in another with which it is immiscible or not mixable, as oil and water

Sensory Evaluation of Food

When the quality of a food is judged or evaluated by the senses (taste, smell, sight, touch, and hearing), it is said to be a sensory evaluation. Because food is prepared for the primary purpose of being eaten and enjoyed through the senses, sensory evaluation is most appropriate. No machine has yet been devised that can totally substitute for the human senses in evaluating the quality of human food. However, the human instrument used in sensory evaluation is very complex, and many problems need to be managed as data are collected and analyzed. Computers are generally used to analyze data from sensory evaluations and may also be used to collect information firsthand [4].

Flavor perceptions are difficult to characterize verbally. For example, think about how a strawberry tastes; then try to describe it to someone else. In food research, small groups of trained individuals, called judging panels or sensory panels, are commonly used to determine differences among food samples [17]. These panels often consist of five to fifteen individuals who have had training and experience in testing the particular food products being evaluated.

Sensory evaluation of foods and flavors has a long history in the food industry. It is an important part of quality assurance for the food processor. A variety of scoring, ranking, or difference tests are used by sensory panels. It may sometimes be desirable to do a complete analysis of all flavor components, such as sweet, buttery, burnt, fragrant, grainy, and metallic, in a particular food. Such a **flavor profile** of the food, giving a picture of its palatability, may be determined by a panel of trained judges working together (Figure 1-13). Aroma and taste are studied separately to complete the total flavor analysis.

flavor profile an outline of the major flavor components and their intensities that are blended to form the overall flavor sensation created by a food

Because any food product will likely contain many flavor components of differing degrees of volatility, these flavor components will impact the olfactory center at different times. Thus, aroma, taste, and texture may change as we eat and drink, especially for foods, such as chocolate, that melt in the mouth. These dynamic aspects of taste may be examined by using a time–intensity curve. The intensity of the flavor may be weak, moderate, strong, or someplace in between. Through the use of a computer mouse, the taster may record the changing intensity of a particular flavor attribute over a 30-second to 2- or 3-minute period [72]. Combining time–intensity curves for the various flavor components in a particular food may produce what has been called a dynamic flavor profile [16].

As new food products are developed, food manufacturers need to know if they can capture a large enough share of the market to warrant the cost of development and marketing. Many new products are introduced and fail each year. Sensory-evaluation professionals and marketing personnel may conduct consumer tests to obtain information on product quality and preference. Consumers and producers may not always agree on quality or preference. Trained sensory panels and consumer panels both involve people. However, trained panels are usually more objective than consumer panels. By correlating the two

Figure 1-13
A sensory panel is used to evaluate the taste of foods. (Courtesy of CCFRA)

Figure 1-14
A hedonic scale for children has easy to interpret faces.

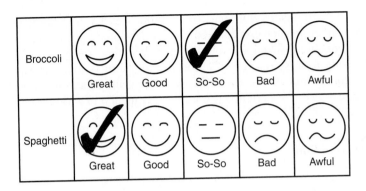

panels, the consumer can be better understood and the likelihood of product success enhanced [27]. Consumer input is important from the very beginning of the development process [61].

The character of a taste or aroma may be described using a wide variety of terms. Often the terms used to describe the flavor of a food indicate that the flavor is similar to that of some other familiar food product. For example, prepared cereal may be described as being nutty, starchy, haylike, floury, oily, or buttery. The primary tastes—sweet, sour, salty, and bitter—are relatively easy to describe. Other terms used to describe flavors in foods include caramel, stale, rancid, metallic, cardboardlike, musty, fragrant, flowery, fruity, sharp, pungent, tart, chalky, branny, burnt, spicy, astringent, sulfury, diacetyl (butterlike), malty, effervescent, earthy, chemical, putrid, yeasty, fishy, grassy, bland, toasted, and **aftertaste.** You may enjoy the challenge of finding new descriptive words for flavor evaluation.

In some cases, particularly in consumer preference testing that involves large groups of people, a **hedonic** scale is used without a description of the flavor components. A hedonic scale for children is shown in Figure 1-14. An example of a scale for adults follows.

aftertaste a taste that remains in the mouth after a food has been swallowed

hedonic having to do with pleasure; a hedonic scale indicates how much a person likes or dislikes a food

_____ Like extremely well   _____ Dislike slightly

_____ Like very much   _____ Dislike moderately

_____ Like moderately well   _____ Dislike very much

_____ Like slightly   _____ Dislike extremely

_____ Neither like nor dislike

OBJECTIVE EVALUATION OF FOOD

objective evaluation having to do with a known object as distinguished from existing in the mind; in food science, measurement of the characteristics of food with a laboratory instrument such as a pH meter to indicate acidity or a viscometer to measure viscosity or consistency

Objective evaluation of food involves the use of laboratory instruments to determine certain characteristics that may be related to eating quality. Devices and the objective measurements that may be made in the laboratory include a viscometer to measure viscosity (thickness or consistency) of a tomato paste or a starch-thickened pudding, a gelometer to measure the firmness or strength of a gelatin gel or a fruit jelly, a pH meter to measure the acidity of lemon juice, a colorimeter to measure the color of red apples, a compressimeter to measure the compressibility or softness of a slice of bread, and a shear or cutting apparatus to measure the tenderness of a sample of meat (Figure 1-15). These types of tests do not directly involve the human senses and thus are not part of sensory evaluation.

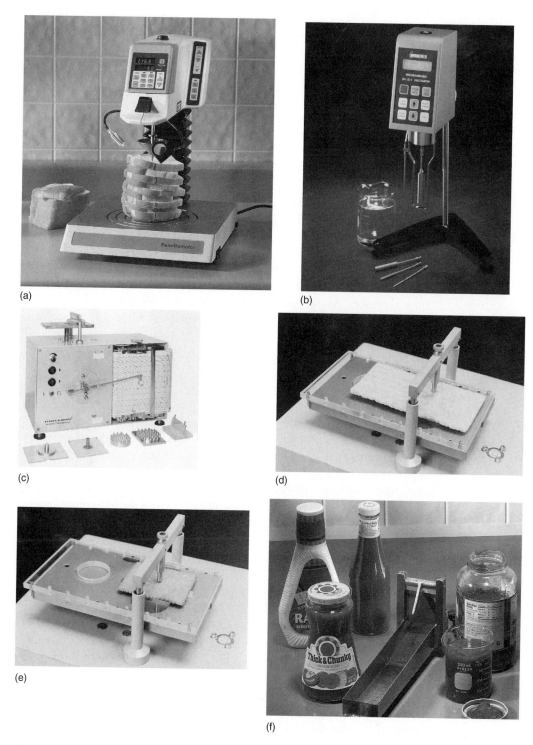

(a)

(b)

(c)

(d)

(e)

(f)

Figure 1-15

A variety of instruments are used in the objective measurement of food quality. (a) A micro processor–based digital penetrometer measures such characteristics of foods as the softness of bread. (Courtesy of Cole-Parmer Instrument Co., 888-409-3663)
(b) A Brookfield viscometer. (Courtesy of Brookfield Engineering Labs, 240 Cushing Street, Stoughton, Massachusetts)
(c, d, and e) The Brabender® Struct-O-Graph® may be used for testing mechanical parameters of foods that describe texture and structure. For example, textural characteristics of crackers and cookies may be measured. (Courtesy of C.W. Brabender Instruments, Inc., South Hackensack, New Jersey)
(f) The viscosity of food products such as sauces, salad dressings, and salsas may be measured by use of a consistometer. (Courtesy of Cole-Parmer Instrument Co., 888-409-3663)

The use of judging panels to evaluate food is often time consuming and expensive. Therefore, the use of laboratory instruments that give useful information with less time and expense is desirable when the information thus collected correlates well with sensory characteristics. Objective tests can usually be reproduced with reasonable precision. In the overall evaluation of the quality of a food product, sensory and objective methods complement each other [22].

CHAPTER SUMMARY

- The food choices we make and the development of our behavior and habits concerning food are influenced by many factors, including social, cultural, family, and religious traditions. Additionally, interest or concern with health and nutrition, food availability, economic resources, and technological developments have an impact on what we eat.

- The food selections of 21st century families are increasingly influenced by time restraints. More convenience foods and foods prepared outside the home are being consumed. Nevertheless, family meals are still a priority for most families.

- An understanding of ethnic, cultural, and religious traditions is an important aspect of the study of foods.

- Guidance has been provided for healthy eating habits through the USDA 2000 Dietary Guidelines and the USDA Food Guide Pyramid. American diets have improved through the lowering of fat intake, yet our consumption of foods reveals an out of balance pyramid. More fruits and vegetables in our diets as well as a wider variety of foods consumed in these two categories is recommended. The consumption of foods with fewer added fats and sugars also is encouraged.

- The geography of an area has historically influenced the foods consumed in that region. Today, transportation and preservation methods have permitted a wide variety of foods to be served nearly anywhere.

- Income and household size are important factors determining where and how Americans spend their food dollars. Less affluent people spend a greater proportion of their income on food and spend less money on eating out as compared to those with greater financial resources.

- The food industry continues to develop innovative products, new packaging and improved preservation methods to enhance the quality and availability of foods. Aseptic packaging, sous vide, irradiation, and other biotechnology developments all have an impact on the type and quality of food we consume.

- Sensory characteristics often determine whether we will first taste, then eat and enjoy food. Appearance creates the first impression and includes such qualities as color, form, size, and design. Much of what we call flavor is a blending of taste and odor. There are four primary taste sensations: sweet, sour, bitter, and salty. The sense of smell is estimated to be about 10,000 times as sensitive as the sense of taste in detecting minute concentrations and differentiating hundreds of distinct odors. Texture includes the qualities that we feel with the fingers, the tongue, the palate, or the teeth and is accompanied by the sound that biting into a crisp food creates.

- The analysis or evaluation of food can be accomplished using human sensory test panels or through objective measurements with laboratory instruments. A combination of both of these types of tools provides the most complete understanding of the sensory qualities of a food.

KEY TERMS

palatable	pungency
appetite	taste
sensory	odor
home meal replacement	taste bud
culture	papillae
ethnic	taste receptor
acculturation	taste pore
cuisine	nonvolatile
demographic	labile
lacto-ovo vegetarians	precursor
vegans	yeast fermentation
quick service restaurants	enzymatic reactions
food security	synthetic compounds
aseptic packaging	texture
sous vide	emulsion
biotechnology	flavor profile
flavor	aftertaste
olfactory	hedonic
tactile	objective evaluation

STUDY QUESTIONS

1. Why is it important for the student of food science to be able to evaluate the palatability and quality of foods?

2. What is meant by *palatability?*

3. Discuss how family, society, and culture may affect the kind of eating patterns that an individual develops.

4. How may religious practices have an impact on the foods consumed?

5. Identify several regional or ethnic food patterns, then discuss how these foods are becoming integrated into home and restaurant menus.

6. Summarize the recommendations for health found in the USDA Food Guide Pyramid and the USDA Dietary Guidelines.

7. Identify several food choices that could be changed in the typical American diet for our usual food consumption patterns to more closely meet the recommendations of the USDA Food Guide Pyramid and the USDA Dietary Guidelines.

8. Explain how economic, marketplace, and technological changes have an impact on food selection and availability.

9. Define and distinguish among the terms *flavor, taste,* and *odor.*

10. List the four primary tastes.

11. Briefly describe how the heating of food produces the sensations of taste and smell in humans. Give examples of (a) flavors that occur preformed in foods, and (b) flavors that are produced by heating.

12. Discuss what effect the temperature of a food has on your perception of its flavor.

13. Of what practical importance to humanity is research on flavor chemistry?

14. Discuss recent technological developments affecting flavor chemistry and their potential influence on the future of food processing.

15. Give an example of how the appearance of a food may influence your evaluation of its flavor or other quality characteristics.

16. Which human sense perceives the texture and consistency of a food?

17. Food quality may be evaluated by sensory or objective methods. (a) Provide examples of each type of evaluation and (b) describe several situations or conditions under which quality evaluation of specific food products may be desirable or necessary.

REFERENCES

1. American Dietetic Association. (1999). Position of the American Dietetic Association: Dietary guidance for healthy children aged 2–11 years. *Journal of the American Dietetic Association, 99*, 93–101.

2. Baird, B. (1990). Sous vide: What's all the excitement about? *Food Technology, 44*(11), 92.

3. Beale, C. L. (2000). A century of population growth and change. *Food Review, 23*(1), 16–22.

4. Billmeyer, B. A., & Wyman, G. (1991). Computerized sensory evaluation system. *Food Technology, 45*(7),100.

5. Blackburn, G. L. (2001). Feeding 9 billion people—A job for food technologists. *Food Technology, 55*(6), 106.

6. Blisard, N. (2000). Food spending by U.S. households grew steadily in the 1990's. *Food Review, 23*(3), 18.

7. Bosley, G. C., & Hardinge, M. G. (1992). Seventh-Day Adventists: Dietary standards and concerns. *Food Technology, 46*(10),112.

8. Bowers, D. E. (2000). Cooking trends echo changing roles of women. *Food Review, 23*(1), 23–29.

9. Brownell, K. D., & Ludwig, D. S. (2002, June 9). Fighting obesity and the food lobby. *Washington Post.* Retrieved June 16, 2002, http://www.washingtonpost.com/wp-dyn/articles/A15232-2002jun7.html

10. Bruhn, C. M. (1992). Consumer concerns and educational strategies: Focus on biotechnology. *Food Technology, 46*(3), 80.

11. Chaudry, M. M. (1992). Islamic food laws: Philosophical basis and practical implications. *Food Technology, 46*(10), 92.

12. Clausen, A. (2000). Spotlight on national food spending. *Food Review, 23*(3), 15–17.

13. Costacou, T., Levin, S., & Mayer-Davis, E.J. (2000). Dietary patterns among members of the Catawba Indian nation. *Journal of the American Dietetic Association, 100*, 833–835.

14. Cousminer, J., & Hartman, G. (1996). Understanding America's regional taste preferences. *Food Technology, 50*(7), 13.

15. Crutchfield, S. R., & Weimer, J. (2000). Nutrition policy in the 1990's. *Food Review, 23*(3), 38–43.

16. DeRovira, D. (1996). The dynamic flavor profile method. *Food Technology, 50*(2), 55.

17. Ennis, D. M. (1990). Relative power of different testing methods in sensory evaluation. *Food Technology, 44*(4), 114.

18. Escobar, A. (1999). Factors influencing children's dietary practices: A review. *Family Economics and Nutrition Review,12*(3–4), 45–55.

19. Falciglia, G. A., & Norton, P. A. (1994). Evidence for a genetic influence on preference for some foods. *Journal of the American Dietetic Association, 94*, 154.

20. Gable, S., & Lutz, S. (2001). Nutrition socialization experiences of children in the Head Start program. *Journal of the American Dietetic Association, 101*, 572–577.

21. Gerrior, S., & Bente, L. (2001). Food supply nutrient and diet guidance, 1970–1999. *Food Review, 24*(3), 39–46.

22. Giese, J. (1995). Measuring physical properties of foods. *Food Technology, 49*(2), 54.

23. Hampl, J. S., & Sass, S. (2001). Focus groups indicate that vegetable and fruit consumption by food stamp–eligible Hispanics is affected by children and unfamiliarity with non-traditional foods. *Journal of the American Dietetic Association, 101*, 685–687.

24. Hardinge, F., & Hardinge, M. (1992). The vegetarian perspective and the food industry. *Food Technology, 46*(10), 114.

25. Harlander, S. K. (1991). Biotechnology: A means for improving our food supply. *Food Technology, 45*(4), 84.

26. Hoch, G. J. (1997). Flavor technology report: Reaction flavors. *Food Processing, 58*(4), 57.

27. Hollingsworth, P. (1996). Sensory testing and the language of the consumer. *Food Technology, 50*(2), 65.

28. Hollingsworth, P. (2001). Supermarket trends. *Food Technology, 55*(3), 20.

29. Hollingsworth, P. (2001). Veggie burgers swerve into the mainstream. *Food Technology, 56*(1), 18.

30. Hollingsworth, P. (2002). One-handed cuisine and other business trends to watch. *Food Technology, 56*(4), 18.

31. Huang, Y., & Ang, C. Y. W. (1992). Vegetarian foods for Chinese Buddhists. *Food Technology, 46*(10), 105.

32. Institute of Food Technologist's Expert Report on Biotechnology and Foods. (2000). Benefits and concerns associated with recombinant DNA biotechnology-derived foods. *Food Technology, 54*(10), 61–80.

33. Institute of Food Technologists' Expert Panel on Food Safety & Nutrition. (1989). Food flavors. *Food Technology, 43*(12), 99.

34. Jackson, M. A. (2000). Getting religion: For your products, that is. *Food Technology, 54*(7), 60–66.

35. Karahadian, C. (1995). Impact of global markets on sensory testing programs. *Food Technology, 49*(2), 77.

36. Katz, F. (1997). Technology trends. *Food Technology, 51*(6), 46.

37. Kenney, B. F. (1990). Applications of high-performance liquid chromatography for the flavor research and quality control laboratories in the 1990s. *Food Technology, 44*(9), 76.

38. Kittler, P. G., & Sucher, K. P. (2001). *Food and Culture.* 3rd ed. Wadsworth: United States.

39. Langen, S. (2002). Consumers want easy meals. *Food Technology, 56*(1), 10.

40. Leland, J. V. (1997). Flavor interactions: The greater whole. *Food Technology, 51*(1), 75.

41. Lin, B. H., Guthrie, J., & Frazao, E. (1999). Nutrient composition of food away from home. In: Frazao, E., ed. *America's Eating Habits: Changes and consequences.* Washington, DC: USDA, ERS, AIB-750.

42. Lin, B. H., Guthrie, J., & Frazao, E. (2001). American children's diets not making the grade. *Food Review, 24*(2), 8–17.

43. Madsen, M. G., & Grypa, R. D. (2000). Spices, flavor systems, and the electronic nose. *Food Technology, 54*(3), 44–46.

44. Mermelstein, N. H. (2001). Pasteurization of shell eggs. *Food Technology, 55*(12), 72–73, 79.

45. National Restaurant Association. (2002). *Restaurant Industry Pocket Factbook.* Retrieved June 14, 2002, from http://www.restaurant.org/pdfs/pocket_factbook_200-2.pdf

46. Oliveira, V. (2000). Decline in nutrition assistance expenditures continued in 1999. *Food Review, 35*(2), 35.

47. Pszczola, D. E. (1997). Feelin' good: Ingredients that add texture. *Food Technology, 51*(11), 82.

48. Pszczola, D. E. (1997). Lookin' good: Improving the appearance of food products. *Food Technology, 51*(11), 39.

49. Putnam, J. (2000). Major trends in the U.S. food supply. *Food Review, 23*(1), 8–14.

50. Putnam, J., & Allshouse, J. (2001). Imports' share of U.S. diet rises in late 1990's. *Food Review, 24*(3), 15–22.

51. Putnam, J., Kantor, L. S., & Allshouse, J. (2000). Per capita food supply trends: Progress toward dietary guidelines. *Food Review, 23*(3), 2–14.

52. Regenstein, J. M., & Regenstein, C. E. (1979). An introduction to the kosher dietary laws for food scientists and food processors. *Food Technology, 33*(1), 89.

53. Rhodehamel, E. J. (1992). FDA's concerns with sous vide processing. *Food Technology, 46*(12), 73.

54. Rogers, C. C. (2001). A look at America's children and their families. *Food Review, 24*(2), 2–7.

55. Sloan, A. E. (1996). Family dinners: A re-emerging tradition. *Food Technology, 50*(4), 32.

56. Sloan, A. E. (1996). The top 10 trends to watch and work on. *Food Technology, 50*(7), 55.

57. Sloan, A. E. (1999). Bite-size goes big time. *Food Technology, 53*(7), 30.

58. Sloan, A. E. (2000). La cucina latina. *Food Technology, 54*(9), 24–25.

59. Sloan, A. E. (2001). Ethnic foods in the decade ahead. *Food Technology, 55*(10), 18.

60. Sloan, A. E. (2001). More on ethnic foods: Move over, BBQ, Cajun, and Caesar. *Food Technology, 55*(11), 18.

61. Stone, H., McDermott, B. J., & Sidel, J. L. (1991). The importance of sensory analysis for the evaluation of quality. *Food Technology, 45*(6), 88.

62. Story, M., Neumark-Sztainer, D., & French, S. (2002). Individual and environmental influences on adolescent eating behaviors. *Supplement to the Journal of the American Dietetic Association, 102*(3), S40–S51.

63. Szczesniak, A. S. (1963). Classification of textural characteristics. *Journal of Food Science, 28*, 385.

64. Szczesniak, A. S. (1990). Texture: Is it still an overlooked food attribute? *Food Technology, 44*, (9), 86.

65. Terry, R. D. (1994). Needed: A new appreciation of culture and food behavior. *Journal of the American Dietetic Association, 94*, 501.

66. Uhl, S. (1996). Ingredients: The building blocks for developing "new" ethnic foods. *Food Technology, 50*(7), 79.

67. U.S. Department of Agriculture. (1992, August). *The food guide pyramid.* Home and Garden Bulletin No. 252.

68. U.S. Department of Agriculture. (2000). Official USDA food plans: Cost of food at home at four levels, U.S. average, May 2001. *Family Economics, 13*(1), 122.

69. U.S. Department of Agriculture and U. S. Department of Health and Human Services. (2000). *Nutrtion and your health: Dietary guidelines for Americans, 5th edition.* Home and Garden Bulletin No. 232.

70. U.S. Department of Health and Human Services. (2000). 19—Nutrition and overweight. *Healthy People 2010.* Retrieved May 17, 2002, from http://www.health.gov./healthypeople/document/tableofcontents.htm

71. U.S. Surgeon General's office. (2001). The Surgeon General's call to action to prevent and decrease overweight and obesity. Retrieved June 14, 2002, from http://www.surgeongeneral.gov/topics/obesity/calltoaction/fact_adolescents.htm

72. van Buren, S. (1992). Analyzing time—intensity responses in sensory evaluation. *Food Technology, 46*(2), 101.

73. Weicha, J. M., Fink, A. K., Wicha, J., & Herbert, J. (2001). Differences in dietary patterns of Vietnamese, White, African-American, and Hispanic adolescents in Worchester, Mass. *Journal of the American Dietetic Association, 101,* 248–251.

74. Yi-Ling, P., Dixon., Z, Himburg, S., & Huffman, F. (1999). Asian students change their eating patterns after living in the United States. *Journal of the American Dietetic Association, 99,* 54–57.

Food Economics and Convenience

2

Economics has been defined as the efficient use of resources to achieve a desired goal. Food economics, then, is our wise use of all available resources to obtain food that is acceptable, enjoyable, and healthful to an optimal extent. To achieve our goal we use not only money but also time, energy, knowledge, skills, equipment, and even our values or philosophy.

We are all consumers. Throughout our lives we exchange money for goods and services. The responsibility for spending an individual's or a family's income is tremendous, and the cost of food is usually an appreciable expenditure for a household. In high-income countries such as the United States, Japan, and Western Europe, the average share of the total budget for food is 13 percent. However, in low-income countries such as Bangladesh, 47 percent of the total budget is used for food [46]. Likewise, among United States families, the highest income families spend more for food than low-income families (Figure 2-1) [3]. In any case the responsibility for food purchasing is a major one, and the choices made can have significant impact on resources available for other expenses. For those involved in purchasing food for a foodservice establishment, financial responsibility is even greater.

Today's consumers occupy a key position in the economic world. Consumerism has become popular. To increase the power of separate individuals, groups of consumers have become organized, and the influence of many of these groups is being felt in the world of food marketing. Consumers are also making an impact on legislation related to food safety, nutritional quality, and cost.

To be most effective in the economic world, both the individual consumer and the professional in foods and nutrition need some knowledge of trends in food consumption. An understanding of some of the factors that affect the cost and quality of food is also important.

TRENDS IN FOOD USE

What do people eat? And how much? Answers to these questions are important to those who work in the various fields of food and nutrition. Information on food consumption of populations and of individuals may be collected in different ways using various sources.

Figure 2-1

Per capital food spending by income quintile, 1998. Low income house-holds spend about 37 percent less per person on food as compared to high-income households. (Reference 3)

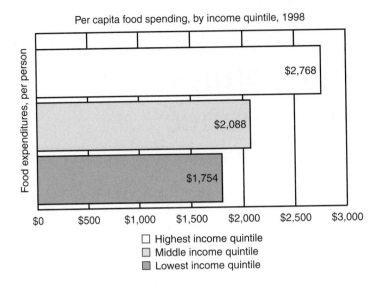

Per capita food spending, by income quintile, 1998

Food Disappearance Data

One method of obtaining information on the food consumption or food use of populations is to measure directly (or to estimate through sampling and statistical procedures) the quantities of food that "disappear" into the nation's food distribution system. First, to calculate the total available food supply, three components are measured: total food production, total imports of food, and beginning-of-the-year inventories. From this total of available food is subtracted food that was exported, used by nonfood industries, used for seed by farmers, and year-end inventories. Food consumption calculated in this manner is called a *residual component*—what is left over when other uses are subtracted from the available total supply. Therefore, the data are subject to various errors resulting from sampling, incomplete reporting, and techniques that may be used in estimating. These limitations should be kept in mind when the information is interpreted and used. The Economic Research Service of the U.S. Department of Agriculture (USDA) has periodically collected data for up to 350 commodities, such as beef, eggs, wheat, and various fruits and vegetables, since 1909 [42,40].

Food consumption, on a per capita basis, is calculated from the primary figures using various conversion factors which account to some degree for further processing, trimming, shrinkage, or loss that occurs during marketing. The data are national averages for the entire population and do not differentiate such factors as age, sex, ethnic background, region, or income level. Nutrient content is calculated from the food consumption data [41].

According to these figures for food use, the American diet has changed considerably over the past decade or two [41]. Americans consumed 196 pounds of meat (red meat, poultry, and fish) per person in 1998, reflecting a 19-pound increase over 1970 levels. Consumption of red meat has fallen, while poultry and fish use has increased (Figure 2-2). Egg use has declined from 309 eggs per person per year in 1970 to 234–244 eggs per person in the 1990's. Cheese consumption has increased by 147 percent since 1970, while per capita consumption of beverage milks declined by 23 percent. Soft drinks may be displacing beverage milk in the diet. The trend in beverage milk is toward lowfat and skim milks rather than whole milk.

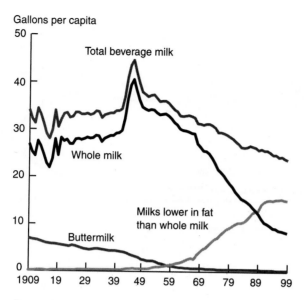

Gallons per capita

Figure 2-2
U.S. food consumption trends. (Reference 40)

Source: USDA's Economic Research Service.

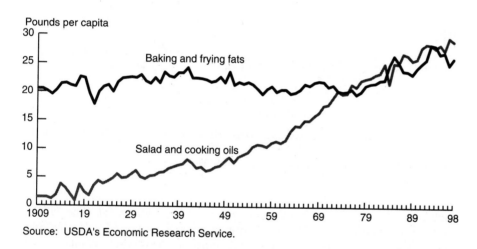

Pounds per capita

Source: USDA's Economic Research Service.

Fruit and vegetable consumption per capita was about 24 percent higher in 1997 than in 1970, with the greatest increase being since 1982. Use of flour and cereal products has increased considerably since 1970; however, Americans are still not eating the amounts of high-fiber foods, including whole-grain products, legumes, vegetables, and fruit, that are recommended in the dietary guidelines. Sugar and sweetener use has increased 28 percent since 1982, to 154 pounds of caloric sweeteners per person in 1997. This represents 53 teaspoons of added sugar per person per day. Since 1993 there has been a modest reduction in the consumption of added fats and oils [40, 41].

Food Consumption Surveys

Since the 1930s, the USDA has conducted periodic surveys of food consumption involving individual and household interviews and record keeping. These surveys constitute a check on the accuracy of food disappearance data and provide a picture of how much Americans are eating at home or away, and the

Figure 2-2
Continued

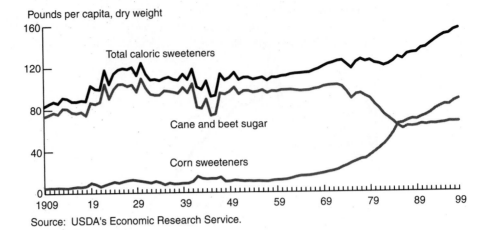

Source: USDA's Economic Research Service.

¹Boneless, trimmed weight. Excludes beef and pork organ meats.
Source: USDA's Economic Research Service.

degree to which they are meeting dietary recommendations [5]. The USDA conducts a nationwide survey—the Continuing Survey of Food Intakes by Individuals (CFII)—at periodic intervals. The most recent survey was taken from 1994 to 1996, during which 14,256 individuals were interviewed. Individual food intake for two nonconsecutive days was recorded [5,43].

Results from data collected in 1994–1996 indicate that Americans are eating more grain products. Since the late 1970's ready-to-eat cereal consumption increased by 60 percent and snacks such as popcorn, pretzels, and corn chips increased by 200 percent. The percentage of calories coming from fat decreased to 33 percent in 1994, from 40 percent in 1977 to 1978. Young children in 1994–1996 were consuming 16 percent less milk and 16 percent more soft drinks than children of about 20 years earlier. Since the 1970's our population has become increasingly overweight. One in three adults could be classified as overweight in 1994–1996, compared with about one in five in the late 1970's. The number of Americans eating breakfast has remained steady at about 85 percent [51].

Although our food habits may be quite firmly established, they are receptive to change with sufficiently compelling reasons for change. Diet and health concerns, as well as changing prices and increasing real disposable income, have probably contributed to changes seen in U.S. food consumption. Other factors influencing these changes are the plethora of new products on the market (especially convenience items), the aging population, expanded advertising campaigns, smaller households, more two-earner households, and an increasing proportion of ethnic minorities in the U.S. population [52].

CONSUMER FOOD WASTE

Trends toward increasing food prices, coupled with growing concerns about conservation of resources, have focused attention on food loss or waste. It is important to know how much food is generally being wasted by consumers to attack this problem sensibly and try to change wasteful practices [27].

What is food waste? Different definitions may be used. In a broad sense, however, any food that was once usable but has since been discarded and not eaten by humans may be considered waste. Food eaten by animals and birds that are household pets may be counted as waste if this food was originally prepared for human consumption.

Food loss may occur at different stages of the handling and preparation processes. As food is taken home from the market and transferred to cabinets, refrigerators, and freezers, it should be handled so as to minimize any potential losses. While food is in storage, even on a very temporary basis, waste may result from microbial spoilage, contamination by insects and rodents, and spilling as a result of broken or open containers. If food is held or stored too long, particularly with improper packaging or temperature control, it may be discarded simply because it is not fresh or has dried out.

Additional waste may occur during preparation as a result of discarding edible portions of the food before cooking, improper cooking procedures such as scorching or overcooking, preparing too much for the number of people to be served, and spoilage because of inappropriate holding of the food before service. Lack of utilization of leftovers also creates waste. Plate waste, or food left on plates by individual diners (Figure 2-3), accounts for a significant portion of total food loss.

Plate waste of edible food served in commercial establishments may also be substantial. In one hospital food service that used a cook-freeze production

Figure 2-3
Plate waste. (Courtesy of the U.S. Department of Agriculture)

system, plate waste for all food served averaged 21.3 percent [15]. In a study of a university dining hall serving 850 male and 490 female students who were on board plans, an average of 17 percent of the food items selected was wasted [37]. Considering the large number of students served, the total cost of food wasted was substantial.

There may be various reasons for food waste in institutional settings. For example, overall plate waste was reduced from 35 percent to 24 percent in a group of 6- to 8-year-old schoolchildren when they had recess before rather than after lunch [20]. The decrease in food waste was attributed to the fact that the students were under no pressure to hurry and finish eating in order to join their friends on the playground. In a continuing-care retirement community, there was less food waste when residents received family-style service or wait-staff service than when they were served trays [21]. A pleasant environment and appropriately sized servings should stimulate residents' appetites and influence the amount of food consumed.

A few studies have measured the amount of food waste in the home. One study of garbage discarded by 200 to 300 households in the United States suggested that 9 to 10 percent of food, by weight, was wasted in these homes [18]. Six percent, by weight, of food available for eating in 243 Oregon households was estimated to have been discarded [53]. Major reasons why the Oregon householders discarded foods were that they judged the food to be unsafe to eat, that the quality had deteriorated, that the food was left over, that the expiration or pull date on the package was past, or that the food was left on the plate (plate waste). Discarded food does have associated expenses; thus practices to avoid food waste are suggested from an economic perspective. The impact of food and packaging waste on the environment is another factor to consider [1].

SOME FACTORS INFLUENCING FOOD COSTS

At the least, modestly rising food prices are a reality in the United States (Figure 2-4), although U.S. food costs are among the lowest in the world. Lower food costs allow Americans to spend a smaller percentage of their incomes on food and more on other goods and services, or on savings. Of course, the total family income affects the proportion of this income that is spent for food. For example, in 1998, 8 percent of the income of affluent American

Figure 2-4
The percentage of increase in annual retail food prices is shown for several years. (Courtesy of the U.S. Department of Agriculture)

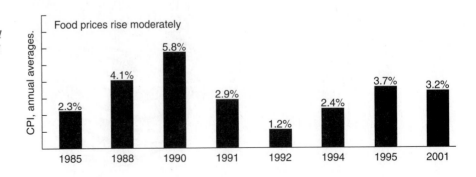

households went for food, whereas low-income households spent 48 percent of their income for food [4]. In addition to the general effects of inflation, some other factors affect the cost of food.

Crop Production

Food production is costly, yet farmers receive a relatively small percentage of the consumer food dollar. In 2000, the **farm-value share** of food purchased in grocery stores was 19 percent [14]. Substantial initial investments must be made by farmers in property and equipment before they can even begin to produce crops. More and more, farmers have become dependent on such items as fuel to operate their equipment, and fertilizers, herbicides, and insecticides that they must purchase to promote high crop yields. Recent years have brought substantially increased costs for both farm machinery and wages for farm workers. Today, farming is a highly technical enterprise requiring large capital investment and skilled management.

Poor weather conditions often reduce the size of crops of fruits, vegetables, and grains. The weather is not controllable, and efficient management of commodity production thus becomes quite difficult. When farmers experience crop shortages, prices rise.

farm-value share the proportion of the retail price of food that is received by the farmer

Trade Policies

The United States presently enjoys a competitive advantage for a number of products in world agricultural trade. Processed products are representing an increased share of exports as compared to bulk commodities (Figure 2-5) [45]. U.S. food and agricultural exports average nearly $61 billion per year [54]. Abundant natural resources and technological developments have contributed to this country becoming a net exporter of agricultural products. However, changing international economies, world demand for certain commodities, and

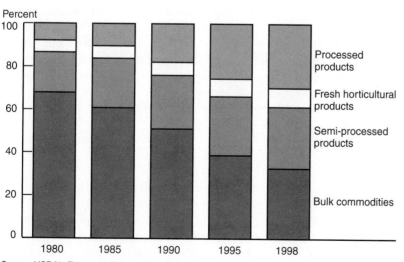

Source: USDA's Economic Research Service.

Figure 2-5

U.S. bulk commodities export share dropped about 30 percent during 1980–98 (Reference 45)

government policies concerning production or international sales can change trade advantages and affect prices. Ecology and food-safety regulations may also be controversial trade issues [19,45,50]. Sound policy decisions help control wide fluctuations in export sales.

Food Processing and Packaging

Much of the food on supermarket shelves has been processed to some degree. Even the trimming of retail meat cuts and the packaging of fresh vegetables are types of processing, though minimal, that increase the cost of the food items offered to the consumer. Examples of highly processed foods include fabricated breakfast cereals, meat substitutes produced from textured vegetable proteins, frozen ready-to-eat entrees of various descriptions, and packaged salads.

Food processing and food production are both costly. Large investments in equipment and facilities are essential. Labor costs are high. Additional costs in food processing include packaging materials and labeling to meet governmental regulations. Many new, expensive packaging materials have recently been developed (see Chapter 29), and as a result, packaging costs are sometimes substantial in proportion to the cost of the food itself.

Technological developments have made possible many new food products scarcely dreamed of a century ago that are marketed domestically and internationally. Most new products are extensions of existing lines, offering new flavors, sizes, packages, and so on. Because of changing demographics, many ethnic-style foods are being introduced. For example, Americans now use more salsa than catsup.

The research and development necessary to produce new food products are costly. Once new foods are developed, they require extensive promotional campaigns and test-marketing procedures. Typically, only about one-third of all new products are successful [22]. Losses to the manufacturer due to a new product's lack of success in the marketplace are reflected in increased prices at the consumer level.

convenience foods foods that are partially or completely prepared by the food processor, with little or no additional food preparation required of the consumer

An increasing number of today's foods have built-in "maid service," with partial or complete preparation having been accomplished before the food is purchased. These so-called **convenience foods** must include the costs of preparation in their prices. In foodservice operations, informed decisions must be made regarding the cost advantages of buying prepared and partially prepared food products versus paying labor costs to completely prepare the foods on the premises. However, in today's labor market, produce foods such as cleaned, ready-to-eat broccoli and peeled carrots may be more economical to purchase than to prepare on premise. There will be more discussion about convenience foods later in this chapter.

Marketing

The USDA calculates marketing costs for food purchased by consumers in the United States, including food purchased both in retail markets and in foodservice establishments. These marketing expenses include the cost of food processing, packaging, transportation, advertising, energy use, and other costs incurred in bringing food from the farmer to the consumer (Figure 2-6). In 2000, marketing expenses accounted for 81 percent of the cost of a food product [14].

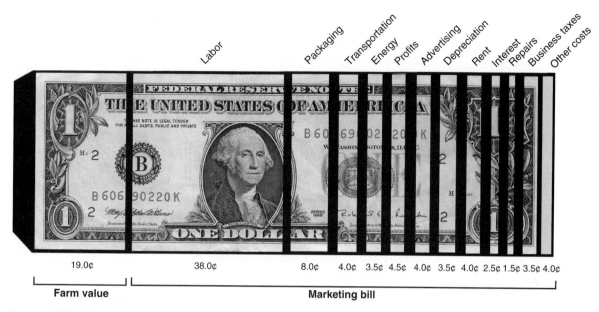

Labor — Packaging — Transportation — Energy — Profits — Advertising — Depreciation — Rent — Interest — Repairs — Business taxes — Other costs

| 19.0¢ | 38.0¢ | 8.0¢ | 4.0¢ | 3.5¢ | 4.5¢ | 4.0¢ | 3.5¢ | 4.0¢ | 2.5¢ | 1.5¢ | 3.5¢ | 4.0¢ |

Farm value — **Marketing bill**

Source: USDA's Economic Research Service.

Figure 2-6

81 percent of every dollar spent on food goes to pay marketing costs. (Reference 14)

Types of Food Stores. There are a number of different types of stores through which food is marketed on a retail basis. For foodservice institutions, a variety of vendors supply different types of food products, generally on a wholesale basis. *Specialty stores,* such as bakeries and fish markets, offer only one type of food. *Food cooperatives,* or *co-ops,* are organized by groups of consumers to purchase food on a wholesale basis. *Farmers' markets* are open seasonally as outlets for local farm produce. *Convenience stores,* almost miniature supermarkets, carry a limited stock of merchandise that has high turnover. They are often part of a large chain of stores and usually remain open 24 hours a day. This type of store has become very popular in the United States in recent years. It usually offers fast service but somewhat higher prices. *Warehouse* or *discount markets* forgo some consumer services such as bagging of groceries. They generally buy in very large quantities and pass some of their cost savings on to the customer. Grocery sales in *wholesale clubs* have increased markedly in recent years. *Supercenters* are giant stores that include a wide range of merchandise from clothing to groceries. Wal-Mart, Kmart, Target and other major retailers are pursuing these stores as a way to corner the market on consumers seeking to purchase multiple products including food with one stop [9, 25]. Other means for consumers to obtain food include the Internet purchase of groceries and take-out foods.

Supermarkets, however, handle the largest volume of retail food sales in the United States. These stores stock thousands of food items and, usually, other merchandise including beauty aids, pharmaceutical supplies, kitchen tools, flowers, and plants. Foodservice offerings in supermarkets are increasing in number and complexity. Catering is offered by some. The concept of supermarkets as full-service centers is growing. They may include florist shops, bakeries, ethnic food take-out services, delicatessens, tortillerias, sushi bars, pharmacies, photo-finishing shops, and even branch banks and post offices. In addition, some stores offer cooking classes, home delivery, and valet parking [25]. Nevertheless, supermarket sales have flattened since 1990 as consumers spend more on meals outside the home [35]. A new term, home meal replacement, is being used to describe ready-made meals that can be taken home for eating. Supermarkets, in cooperation with food manufacturers, are expanding in this area of food merchandising. Currently, 80 percent of supermarkets sell ready-to-eat foods [25].

Prices are influenced by services offered. You should evaluate the various kinds of markets in terms of the services and benefits you desire and what you are willing to pay for them. The following items may be considered in this evaluation:

1. Quality and variety of merchandise carried
2. Layout and organization of the market
3. Pricing policies, such as specials, discounting, advertising, availability of in-store brands and **generic** or unbranded products, coupons, trading stamps, and games
4. Location of market
5. Sanitation and food safety
6. Customer services, such as bagging, carryout, and rapid service, and availability of printed information concerning nutrition and food.

generic a class of packaged food products that do not carry a specific brand name

Shopping Aids. Food manufacturers and retailers offer the consumer several conveniences to facilitate efficient shopping for food. These include unit pricing, open-date labeling, and nutrition labeling. Computerized checkout systems are the norm in supermarkets. Some of these aids involve additional labor and skill in producing and/or marketing food products and may thus increase the cost of food to the consumer.

Unit Pricing. The cost per pound or ounce for products sold by weight or the cost per quart, pint, or fluid ounce for products sold by volume is printed on a label, which is usually attached to the edge of the shelf where the products are displayed. This information allows the shopper to compare prices per unit for different sized packages of the same product. The most economical size to buy can thus be readily determined. Generally, the smaller package sizes and individual-size convenience items are more expensive per unit because of the basic package cost. Unit pricing is mandatory in some states, but voluntary in others.

Open-date Labeling. A date code is on each packaged food product for the customer to read and interpret. The date may appear in different forms on different packages. It may represent the last recommended day of retail sale, the end of the period of optimum quality, or the date of processing or final packaging. Open-date labeling provides some information for the shopper, but the conditions, particularly of temperature, under which the products are handled and stored greatly affect the quality.

Food Labeling.   The basic requirements for *all* food labels include net weight of contents, manufacturer's or distributor's name and address, and ingredient declaration. Regulations governing the labeling of most food products are prepared by the U.S. Food and Drug Administration (FDA), but the labeling of meat and poultry products is under the jurisdiction of the USDA. In the early 1970s, the FDA completed a major revision of labeling requirements which included regulations governing **nutrition labeling.** Under these regulations, nutrition labeling was voluntary, except when the products contained added nutrients or when nutrition claims were made.

In November 1990, President Bush signed into law the Nutrition Labeling and Education Act. Regulations to implement this legislation were issued by the FDA and finalized by the end of 1992. The USDA's Food Safety and Inspection Service established similar regulations for meat and poultry products. The federal agencies required compliance by August 8, 1994. By the end of May 1995, the FDA found that 80 percent of the domestic and imported products checked were in compliance with the regulations [32]. Three years after the regulations were enacted, a FDA Food Label and Package Survey (FLAPS) found that 97 percent of the products had nutritional labeling. Two out of five packaged products included a nutrient content claim; however, few products display health claims [7].

Nutrition labeling was designed to help consumers choose diets that are well balanced, health promoting, and at the lowest cost. Nutrition labeling mandates information in addition to the basic labeling requirements listed earlier. This additional information details the nutrient content of the packaged product.

Most foods are required to carry nutrition labels. Exemptions include food sold by small businesses; food sold in foodservice establishments; ready-to-eat foods prepared on site for later consumption; foods that contain insignificant amounts of nutrients, such as tea and spices; medical foods; and meat and poultry products produced or packaged at retail, such as sliced bologna. However, if a nutrition or health claim is made for any of these foods, they must have nutrition labeling.

Fresh fruits and vegetables and raw fish also do not require nutrition labeling. However, the FDA has a *voluntary* program in which nutrition information about these products is displayed at the point of purchase in retail food markets [39]. If the FDA, through future surveys, does not find that a substantial number of markets are supplying nutrient information, they will propose mandatory nutrition labeling for these foods.

Nutrition labeling is *mandatory* for most meat and poultry products except raw, single-ingredient items. Labeling of these exempted products is encouraged, however, either by package labeling or by presenting nutrition information at the point of purchase. Restaurants and other foodservice establishments may make certain health and nutrition claims for items on their menus. When they do so, they must explain how the food meets the FDA criteria for that claim and must have a reasonable basis for believing that the food meets the criteria. This information must be provided to the customer [31].

Required nutrition information is presented on a label, usually as percent of **daily values,** under the heading of Nutrition Facts, and, on a per-serving basis, includes calories, calories from fat, and grams of total fat, saturated fat, cholesterol, sodium, total carbohydrates, dietary fiber, sugars, and protein. (Serving sizes have been standardized by the FDA and the USDA.) Vitamin A, vitamin

nutrition labeling a special type of food labeling, in addition to basic requirements concerning net contents and manufacturer, that gives information about the nutrient and caloric content of the food on a per-serving basis

daily values nutrient standards used for labeling purposes; they include Daily Reference Values (DRVs) and Reference Daily Intakes (RDIs)

C, calcium, and iron are presented as percent of Daily Values based on a 2,000 calorie diet. Additional information on other nutrients is optional. Figure 2-7 gives an example of how the required information is presented.

Daily Values are dietary standards used for labeling purposes, and include two types. *Daily Reference Values (DRVs)* refer to fat, carbohydrates (including fiber), protein, cholesterol, sodium, and potassium. These are listed on the label for 2,000 and 2,500 calorie intakes. *Reference Daily Intakes (RDIs)* are for other nutrients. RDIs replace the U.S. recommended daily allowances (U.S. RDAs) that were previously used and are listed in Table 2-1.

The FDA has defined certain descriptive terms to be used on food labels. Some of these terms and their definitions are given in Table 2-2. Standardized definitions are established with the aim of decreasing consumer confusion when such terms as *high*, *low*, *reduced*, and *less* are used with food products.

Certain health claims are also allowed on labels. The following relationships between a nutrient or food and the risk of a disease have been approved for labeling purposes with some specific requirements governing their use [7].

Calcium and osteoporosis

Dietary fat and cancer

Dietary saturated fat and cholesterol and coronary heart disease

Fiber containing fruits, vegetables, and grain products and cancer

Fruits, vegetables, and grain products that contain fiber and risk of coronary heart disease

Fruit and vegetables and a reduced risk of cancer

Sodium and hypertension

Soluble fiber from whole oats and coronary heart disease

Sugar alcohol and dental caries

Folic acid and neural tube birth defects

nutrient content claim foods may be labeled to inform consumers about the calories, fat, saturated fat, cholesterol, sodium, sugar, or dietary fiber levels in the food. Claims such as "reduced calories," "low fat," "excellent source of fiber" are regulated and must meet government accepted definitions to be used.

health claim foods may be labeled to inform consumers of a relationship between the consumption of the food and health, for example, products containing fruits and vegetables and the reduced risk of cancer. These claims are regulated and must meet government accepted conditions to be used.

In 1997, the FDA granted food processors the right to claim that soluble fiber (beta-glucan) in oatmeal, oat bran, and other whole-oat formulations may reduce the risk of heart disease [23]. This narrow ruling represents the first time that a health claim has been made for a specific food.

Under the provisions of the Food and Drug Administration Modernization Act of 1997, **health** and **nutrient-content claims** may be approved by an alternative procedure to that originally outlined. Food companies may submit to the FDA a claim, based on an authoritative statement published by a scientific body of the U.S. government, at least 120 days *before* introducing the product into interstate commerce. The burden for disproving the claim then rests with the FDA.

Nutrition labeling gives consumers much more information about the foods they buy than they would have without this feature. For those on diets modified because of health reasons, nutrition labeling is especially useful. A study of consumers in Washington State found a strong association between reading labels and eating a lower fat diet. Most residents in this study reported using the "Nutrition Facts" from the food labels [36].

The cost to manufacturers for nutrition labeling may be appreciable because they are required to have accurate nutrient information from laboratory

Serving sizes are stated in both household and metric measures.

Nutrition Facts

Serving Size ½ cup (114g)
Servings Per Container 4

Amount Per Serving

Calories 90	Calories from Fat 30

	% Daily Value*
Total Fat 3g	5%
Saturated Fat 0g	0%
Cholesterol 0mg	0%
Sodium 300mg	13%
Total Carbohydrate 13g	4%
Dietary Fiber 3g	12%
Sugars 3g	
Protein 3g	

Vitamin A	80%	•	Vitamin C	60%
Calcium	4%	•	Iron	4%

* Percent Daily Values are based on a 2,000 calorie diet. Your daily values may be higher or lower depending on your calorie needs:

	Calories	2,000	2,500
Total Fat	Less than	65g	80g
Sat Fat	Less than	20g	25g
Cholesterol	Less than	300mg	300mg
Sodium	Less than	2,400mg	2,400mg
Total Carbohydrate		300g	375g
Fiber		25g	30g

Calories per gram:
Fat 9 • Carbohydrates 4 • Protein 4

Calories from fat are shown on the label to help consumers meet dietary guidelines that recommend people get no more than 30 percent of their calories from fat.

% Daily Value shows how a food fits into the overall daily diet.

The list of nutrients covers those most important to the health of today's consumers, most of whom need to worry about getting too much of certain items (fat, for example), rather than too few vitamins or minerals, as in the past.

Daily values are something new. Some are maximums, as with fat (65 grams or less); others are minimums, as with carbohydrates (300 grams or more). The daily values on the label are based on a daily diet of 2,000 and 2,500 calories. Individuals should adjust the values to fit their own calorie intake.

Figure 2-7

An example of the nutrition labeling panel that appears on almost all packaged foods. (Courtesy of the U.S. Food and Drug Administration)

Table 2-1
Reference Daily Intakes. (RDIs)

Nutrient	RDI Value
Vitamin A	5,000 IU
Vitamin C	60 mg
Thiamin (B_1)	1.5 mg
Riboflavin (B_2)	1.7 mg
Niacin	20 mg
Calcium	1,000 mg
Iron	18 mg
Vitamin D	400 IU
Vitamin E	30 IU
Vitamin B_6	2.0 mg
Folic acid	0.4 mg
Vitamin B_{12}	6 mcg
Phosphorus	1,000 mg
Iodine	150 mcg
Magnesium	400 mg
Zinc	15 mg
Copper	2 mg
Biotin	0.3 mg
Pantothenic acid	10 mg

analyses of samples of their food products. This expense ultimately affects the cost of food to the customer.

Computerized checkout systems. Computer-assisted electronic cash register systems are commonly used in supermarkets. The cost of the items in the customer's shopping cart is tabulated by using a laser optical scanner to read Universal Product Code (UPC) symbols, which are affixed to each food package. The scanner is connected to a computer that then retrieves the necessary information from its storage and prints the name and price of each item on a screen for the customer to see. It also prints this information on the sales receipt. The computer must be properly programmed at all times with current price information. The UPC symbol contains a series of dark lines and spaces of varying widths, as shown in Figure 2-8. The left half of the symbol identifies the manufacturer, and the right half identifies the product. Most of the items on supermarket shelves carry a UPC symbol.

Use of a computerized system allows pricing of items to be done on the display shelves only and not on each individual product. It also speeds up checkout time and reduces errors at the cash register. Additional advantages are a meaningful record of purchases for the customer and improved inventory control for the retailer. However, a disadvantage is not having cost information readily available on the item itself for later reference.

AVAILABILITY AND USE OF CONVENIENCE FOODS

Convenience foods may be defined as fully or partially prepared foods for which significant preparation time, culinary skills, or energy use have been transferred from the consumer's kitchen to the food processor and distributor. Most of the foods in a supermarket have had some preparation treatment.

Descriptor	Definition
Free	No amount or an amount that is of no physiological consequence based on serving size
Calorie-free	Less than 5 calories
Sodium-free	Less than 5 milligrams
Fat-free	Less than 0.5 gram of fat and no added fat
Cholesterol-free	Less than 2 milligrams
Sugar-free	Less than 0.5 gram
Low	Would allow frequent consumption of a food low in a nutrient without exceeding the dietary guidelines
Low-calorie	Less than 40 calories
Low-sodium	Less than 140 milligrams
Very low-sodium	Less than 35 milligrams
Low-fat	Less than 3 grams
Low in saturated fat	Less than 1 gram and less than 15% of calories from saturated fat
Low in cholesterol	20 milligrams or less with less than 2 grams of saturated fat
Reduced	Nutritionally altered product containing 25% less of a nutrient or 25% fewer calories than a reference food
Less	Contains 25% less of a nutrient or 25% fewer calories than a reference food
Light	33% fewer calories or 50% of the fat in a reference food; if 50% or more of the calories comes from fat, reduction must be 50% of the fat; or sodium content of a low-calorie, low-fat food has been reduced by 50%: thus the term "light in sodium" may be used; or describes such properties as texture and color, as "light brown sugar" or "light and fluffy"
High	20% or more of the Daily Value for a nutrient
Good source	Contains 10–19% of the Daily Value for a particular nutrient

Source: Reference 30.

* Per serving basis

Table 2-2
Nutrient Content Descriptors Used on Food Labels. *

However, the term *convenience food* commonly applies to a food that has undergone a comparatively large amount of processing or market services and may be served with a minimum of effort and skill. Other names for these types of foods are *service ready*, *prefabricated*, *ready prepared*, or *efficiency* foods.

Habits of cooking in an American kitchen are undergoing pronounced change. One survey indicated that 72 percent of consumers reported spending

0

12345 67890

Manufacturer
identification
number

Item code

Figure 2-8
Universal Product Code.

Healthy Eating

Nutraceuticals or Functional Foods—A lucrative and challenging market?

Although the word *nutraceuticals* is already an accepted dictionary term, meaning bioactive compounds (or chemicals) that have health benefits [28], only 10 percent of shoppers are familiar with this name [49]. They know nutraceuticals or functional foods (a term previously used) only as health-promoting foods. And they are aggressively pursuing a strategy to manage their health through food choices. The nutraceutical or functional food market is large—and expanding rapidly as consumers seek to ensure overall good health and lessen their risk of disease development. Thus, exciting opportunities await manufacturers and marketers of functional foods and beverages, ingredient manufacturers, and support services [49].

Nutraceuticals or functional foods include nutrients—such as vitamins C and E and beta-carotene—and foods fortified with nutrients—a few examples are fortified cereals, orange juice with added calcium, and low-fat milk fortified with *extra* calcium. They also include non-nutrients—such as lycopene—which Heinz Ketchup advertisements make the most of as they design their product "America's Favorite Source of Lycopene" [49]. Nutraceuticals are found in foods naturally—e.g., garlic, soy, broccoli, tomatoes, tea, almonds, oats—for those who prefer naturally nutritious foods to supplements or fortified foods—and these characteristics may be valuable advertising slogans in marketing. Functional beverages and snacks are also becoming popular, with nutrition bars being prominently displayed [26]. In any case, a great market awaits, targeting both genders, all ages and ethnic populations.

between 16 and 45 minutes preparing dinner during the work week. More than two-thirds of Americans say they struggle with cooking. Nearly 80 percent of households purchase pretrimmed and washed produce, and 86 percent buy convenience entrees. Sales of take-out suppers have more than doubled in the last 10 years [48].

Convenience foods help consumers to prepare dinner in a minimum amount of time. Convenience foods also help those who have limited preparation skills by providing high quality foods requiring minimal preparation. Although it could appear that a "homemade" item made from "scratch" is becoming an endangered species, many consumers are very sophisticated in their tastes and abilities. Home-cooked meals generally provide more nutritional value [29] and allow consumers to be creative in the development of their own special dishes.

The food industry is actively involved in the production of convenience foods. Many different processes are used in their preparation, including dehydrating the food to variable moisture levels by freeze-drying and other methods, compressing the food to decrease bulk, precooking and freezing, and using various flexible packaging materials or pouches that withstand both high and low temperatures. **Retort pouches** were developed as a new food technology in the 1960's to be used even at the temperatures well above boiling needed for canning low-acid meats and vegetables. Retort pouches have been successfully used in the production of military rations for a number of years. However, with the introduction of retort pouch tuna in 2000, more commercial uses are anticipated in the years ahead (Figure 2-9) [8].

retort pouch a flexible laminated package that withstands high-temperature processing in a commercial pressure canner called a retort

Figure 2-9

(a) Starkist provides consumers with convenient new retort packaging for tuna. (Courtesy of Starkist Seafood)

(b) Perfect for packed lunches or on-the-go snacks, Dole Fruit bowls are a shelf stable, travel-ready food. (Courtesy of Dole Foods Company Inc.)

(c) Yoplait has made yogurt readily accessible with its "no-spoon-necessary" packaging. (Courtesy of Yoplait USA, Inc.)

The production of convenience foods actually began many years ago with the development of canning. Several canned products are now well-established convenience foods. In the 21st century, canned foods have a "new look" with contoured cans and fruit packaged in multilayer barrier plastic cups with peel-able closures (Figure 2-9). Other "canned" foods are sold in glass containers for a more upscale product or polyester bottles for the convenience of a see-through non-breakable container [8].

Frozen foods were perfected by Clarence Birdseye in the 1920's [2]. Today, many frozen foods have entered the market through widespread product avail-ability, consumer desire for convenience, and the use of home freezers [11]. Also plentiful are dehydrated convenience items.

Some convenience foods are designed for the snack shelf, but the majority are for regular use in food preparation both in the home and in foodservice establishments. Among the convenience foods sold are a growing number of products that are reduced in fat and caloric content. Also popular are many ethnic dishes. The aging population, the focus on health and fitness, the increasing number of women in the workforce, and the increasing numbers of Hispanics and Asians in the population have fragmented the consumer market. There are many different groups whose needs must be met [16]. Food processors are producing a variety of convenience items to supply the needs of all. Cookbooks also reflect the convenience food market, with many convenience items included in recipes.

Both industry and the consumer benefit from storage and transportation savings. Dehydrated fruit and tomato juices, which can be shipped and stored without refrigeration and reconstituted with water before use, are examples of products that create great savings in transportation costs and storage space. Industry also has the advantage of knowing about and being able to obtain and use ingredients that are well suited to prolonged storage. Suitable packaging, including modified atmosphere packaging, aids in the retention of desirable qualities in the final product (Figure 2-10).

Space-age Convenience Foods

Travel into space brought special requirements with regard to food for the astronauts. The demanding specifications for weight, volume, and ease of preparation were met by convenience-type foods [6,34]. Because the astronauts have much work and experimentation to do in space, the time required to prepare and eat must be kept to a minimum. Foods must be stable to store at temperatures up to 100°F (38°C). Their packaging must be flexible and able to withstand extremes of pressure, humidity, temperature, and vibration that could cause breakage or cracking. Packages of food must also be convenient to handle (Figure 2-11 and Plate I).

Many changes have been made in space foods since space exploration began. Much had to be learned about how foods could be handled in a state of weightlessness. During the Mercury flights, it was learned that a person could

Figure 2-10
Dole ready-made salads in modified atmosphere-packaging. (Courtesy of U.S. Department of Agriculture)

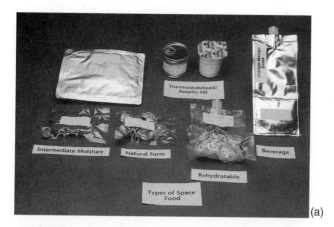

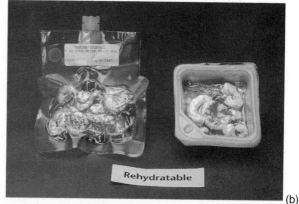

Figure 2-11
(a) Several types of foods and packaging are used in space. (Courtesy of NASA)
(b) Shrimp cocktail is ready to rehydrate as part of a space meal. (Courtesy of NASA)
(c) A typical meal tray in space. (Courtesy of NASA)
(d) This astronaut demonstrates one way to make sure the candy melts in your mouth and not in your hand. (Courtesy of NASA)

chew and swallow while weightless. Early space foods were either pureed so they could be forced into the mouth through tubes or compressed into compact, bite-sized pieces that were coated to avoid any loose crumbs that would float in zero gravity. During the *Apollo* flights, a spoon, rather than a tube, was used to eat moist foods and hot water was available for the first time to make the rehydration of foods easier [34].

During the Skylab program, space was available for a dining room with tables, and a refrigerator and freezer. Astronauts had knives and forks available to them and ate from a food tray with cavities to hold containers of food. Beverages were still sent as dry powders and were rehydrated by putting water through a one-way valve into a special container. The menu was much more extensive, with 72 food items featured.

A new era in the exploration of space began with the space shuttle. A galley has been designed on the shuttle for astronauts' foodservice needs. The galley has hot and cold water, an oven, and a small refrigeration unit, but no freezer. Food packaging has been simplified to some degree compared with that used for previous space ventures. The food includes (a) rehydratable foods such as macaroni and cheese; (b) thermostabilized foods in cans, plastic cups, or flexible retort packages such as puddings, fruits, and tuna; (c) intermediate moisture foods such as dried peaches; (d) natural form foods such as granola bars; and (e) irradiated meat. Condiments such as salt and pepper are packaged with liquid so that these seasonings can be used without floating into equipment on the shuttle. Many foods are dehydrated to reduce weight at takeoff and because water is produced onboard as a by-product of the spacecraft's fuel cells and thus is readily available in space [34].

Space station foods are frozen, refrigerated, or theromostabilized then heated to serving temperatures with an onboard microwave/forced air convection oven. Few dehydrated foods are used on the space station because the solar panels used to provide electricity do not produce water.

Food developed for space travel is researched at the Food Systems Engineering Facility (FSEF) at NASA Johnson Space Center. Food scientists, dietitians, and engineers analyze the foods for nutritional, sensory, and packaging quality. Before foods are used on space flights, FSEF personnel test the foods on the NASA Zero-Gravity KC-135 airplane [34].

Future space travel is likely to involve manned flights of longer duration, such as a 5-year mission to Mars. Establishing bases on the moon or Mars may also be considered. In planning for such events, the National Aeronautics and Space Administration (NASA) is cooperating with universities and the food industry in the research and development of controlled ecological life-support systems. Such a system includes biomass production, food processing, waste treatment, atmosphere regeneration, and water purification. You may well imagine the challenge to food scientists and engineers as they discover how to produce nutritious, safe, palatable foods from a limited amount of biomass materials, with serious constraints in space and facilities for food processing and preparation [17].

Military rations for battlefield foodservice have also undergone many changes over the years. During World War II, canned meats such as Spam were common. The basic combat ration used today is the Meal, Ready-to-Eat (MRE). MREs provide a full meal consisting of 9–10 components that provide about 1,300 kcal. The packaging consists of retort pouches, flexible packaging, in a meal bag (Figure 2-12). The MRE must be able to be dropped out of aircraft, withstand environmental extremes from −60°F to +120°F, shelf stable for three years at 80°F, resistant to wildlife, and taste good. MREs may be eaten cold, or if heated, heated by a variety of ways including with a flameless heating device provided in the meal bag. MREs have improved considerably since they were used during Operation Desert Storm in the Persian Gulf War of 1991. Product developers go into the field with soldiers to assess performance of the MREs and interview the soldiers. This approach has increased soldiers' satisfaction [33].

Cost of Convenience

How much does convenience cost? In making cost comparisons between various convenience foods and similar home-prepared products, some difficulties may be encountered. Although food labels list ingredients from the greatest amount to the least, the exact proportions of ingredients contained in convenience foods are not identified and, therefore, home-prepared products may not contain the same amounts of component ingredients. The eating quality of

(a)

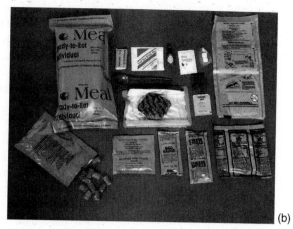
(b)

Figure 2-12
(a) Foods for the military must offer special conveniences as well as high quality. (Courtesy of U.S. Army Soldier Systems Center)
(b) Components of a Meal, Ready-to-Eat. (Courtesy of U.S. Army Soldier Systems Center)

the two products may also be very different. Nevertheless, some cost comparisons have been made with these limitations in mind. Consumers may often feel that convenience foods are more costly, as shown by the results of a survey regarding shopping habits. Fifty-six percent of the survey participants reported purchasing fewer convenience foods as a method of minimizing food bills [47].

Consumer Reports periodically evaluates convenience foods and compares them with similar homemade products. In a comparison of pancake mixes and frozen pancakes, frozen pancakes were reported to cost as much as 53 cents per serving and were generally tough and chewy. Standard mixes, which called for added eggs, oil, and milk, were of better quality and cost between 14 and 26 cents per serving, including the cost of the added ingredients [38].

Although many convenience products generally have a higher food cost than home-prepared products, when fuel and time costs are also considered, the total cost often may be similar or potentially less than the homemade counterpart.

Eating Quality

Today's convenience foods offer the consumer variety, high quality, interesting culinary flavors, dietary modifications, and convenience [44]. Consumers now seek convenience with few compromises in quality and the food industry has responded [24]. However, no convenience food can match your individual tastes perfectly; thus home cooking provides quality attributes that will continue to be difficult for the industry to match.

Nutritive Value

Nutritive value of convenience foods should be an important consideration in purchasing, but should be considered on the basis of individual items. In commercial products, the more expensive components, particularly meat, fish, and poultry, may be present in somewhat lower quantities than in home-prepared dishes.

The dehydration of potato products causes substantial loss of vitamin C, but instant potatoes are often fortified with this vitamin to make them more comparable to the fresh product. Many canned and dehydrated soups contain very small amounts of protein or other nutrients. Soups made at home vary greatly in the amount and type of ingredients used and thus in nutritional value, so comparisons with commercial soups are difficult to make. Extra ingredients may be added to purchased soups to make them more hearty and nutritious.

Saving Time and Effort

A major consideration for many in the purchase of convenience foods is the promise of reduced preparation time and effort, including fewer cleanup chores such as dishwashing. From annual supermarket sales figures it is obvious that households rely heavily on convenience foods. Some of them, such as frozen orange juice and gelatin or pudding mixes, have become so well established and widely used that they are probably not considered to be convenience foods in the same sense as frozen entrees. A relatively new trend might be called "speed scratch." In this circumstance, for example in the making of lasagna, you might use frozen or fresh prepared noodles and canned sauce as ingredients to reduce the preparation time for this dish.

There are both advantages and disadvantages to the use of convenience foods. Personal preferences vary from one household to another. We need to consider several factors when deciding whether to purchase convenience foods: time, equipment, and storage space available; comparative costs; aesthetic appeal; our ability to cook and the joy and pride that we, and others around us, may feel when we cook "from scratch"; and concerns regarding nutrition and health.

Preparing Your Own Basic Mixes

An incredible variety of mixes are numbered among the convenience foods found on supermarket shelves and many are also available to foodservice institutions. There are many dry flour mixes for preparing such items as cakes, cookies, gingerbread, brownies, piecrusts, muffins, cornbread, coffee cakes, biscuits, pancakes, and hot rolls. Seasoning mixes such as taco mix, meatloaf mix, and a variety of salad dressing mixes are widely used. Pudding mixes, canned fruit pie fillings, and many, many others are available.

Although commercial mixes are convenient and timesaving, do-it-yourself mixes may also provide convenience. You can save considerable time by making mixes, as compared with cooking from "scratch," because the basic ingredients for a large number of prepared items are mixed at one time. The time for preparing the mix may also be scheduled during less busy periods, thus making more effective use of time.

Eliason, Harward, and Westover [12,13] have published two cookbooks on how to make your own mixes. They have suggested that the convenience of cooking with mixes may be combined with the quality advantages of cooking "from scratch" when mixes are made.

BUYING FOOD

Because a substantial portion of all household budgets is used to buy food, wisdom in food purchasing will pay dividends. For the foodservice professional purchasing food, wise decisions are imperative for the financial success of the business operation. Decisions about household food budgets can also influence the health status of families, since leading causes of death and disease in the United States are diet related.

A study was made of primary food preparers in the United States who agreed or disagreed with the following: *I run my household on a strict food budget.* Those participants who reported using a strict food budget were more likely than others to be concerned whether the meals they served were nutritious [10]. However, several of the most commonly recommended planning and budgeting tools for food shoppers were not widely used by those on a strict budget. These strategies include (1) making a complete list before shopping, (2) stocking up when your brands are on sale, (3) comparison shopping, and (4) redeeming coupons. Many useful suggestions may be made for the food shopper. Here are a few general guidelines to follow:

1. Compare prices for specified quality items; use unit pricing; consider cost of packaging; watch advertised specials.

2. Buy only quantities that can be utilized well; do not overbuy in terms of storage facilities available.

3. Buy staples in quantity but store them properly.

4. Buy in-store brands or generic items when the quality is acceptable for a particular use.

5. Make reasonable substitutions when desired items are too expensive or unavailable.

6. Plan ahead and purchase on a regular basis; use specifications or a written list; avoid impulse buying.

7. Choose vendors or markets that generally have reasonable pricing.

CHAPTER SUMMARY

- Food economics is the wise use of all available resources to obtain food that is acceptable, enjoyable, and healthful to an optimal extent. The percent of the budget spent on food varies with the income level of the family. Food purchasing is a major responsibility because the choices made will have a significant impact on the resources available for other expenses.

- Food consumption in the United States is estimated by use of food disappearance data collected by the Economic Research Service of USDA and a nationwide Continuing Survey of Food Intakes by Individuals (CFII) that is conducted by USDA. Food disappearance data can be subject to errors from sampling, incomplete reporting, and the techniques used for estimation. The accuracy of the CFII data is influenced by the ability of those interviewed to completely describe their food intake for two days. Both of these methods of assessing what Americans eat have shown that the American diet has changed over time.

- Food is wasted in commercial foodservice operations and in households for a variety of reasons. Careful purchasing, planning, food preparation, and storing will reduce waste. Food waste can represent a considerable expense depending on the amount that is wasted. The environmental impact of waste also should be taken into consideration.

- Food costs generally increase over time. Crop production, trade policies, food processing, food packaging, and marketing all add to the cost of food.

- Food may be purchased on a retail basis through a variety of stores. Specialty stores, food cooperatives, farmers' markets, convenience stores, warehouse markets, and wholesale clubs offer consumers choices for food purchases. Supermarkets handle the largest volume of retail foods in the United States and over time have increased the variety of foods as well as other services offered. Supercenters are becoming more common. These stores offer a wide array of retail products, including clothing, along with food.

- There are a number of shopping aids available to assist consumers in making good food selections. Unit pricing simplifies the price comparison of products. Open-dating provides consumers with information to assess the freshness of the product.

- Information on food labels is regulated by the government. All food labels must include net weight of contents, manfacturer's or distributor's name and address, and ingredient declaration. In addition, the Nutrition Labeling and Education Act mandates the format and type of *nutrition* information that is to be included. Some foods are exempt from this requirement. Health claims on food labels also are regulated.

- Convenience foods help consumers prepare dinner in a minimum amount of time and enable the consumption of safe, palatable foods in space or during military exercises. The production of convenience foods began many years ago with the development of canning. Canned foods now come in many shapes and styles that include plastic cups with peelable closures. Frozen foods were perfected in the 1920's and have led to a wide variety of foods for the consumer to choose from. Dehydrated foods also are plentiful in the marketplace. Retort pouches were developed in the 1960's. Retort pouches have been used for miliary rations and space travel for many years and are now becoming more popular for retail foods.

- Consumers should evaluate the cost, quality, and nutritional content of convenience foods as compared to home made foods. The quality of convenience foods has increased considerably over the years. However, no convenience food can match your individual tastes perfectly; thus home cooking provides quality attributes that will continue to be difficult for industry to match.

KEY TERMS

farm-value share	daily values
convenience foods	nutrient content claim
generic	health claim
nutrition labeling	retort pouch

STUDY QUESTIONS

1. Explain the relationship among food choices, family income, and economics.
2. Describe two different methods that have been used by the USDA to obtain information on what and how much food is eaten in the United States.

Evaluate the advantages and inaccuracies that may be associated with each method.

3. (a) Describe several findings from food consumption surveys that give us information concerning the types and amounts of food being consumed in the United States. (b) What types of information collected from these surveys may be useful to professionals working in the areas of food and nutrition?

4. (a) What is *food waste* and how may food be wasted at the household level? (b) Identify multiple ways that food waste in commercial food services and in households may be reduced.

5. List at least six factors that are likely to influence food cost to the consumer and briefly explain how they exert their influence.

6. Describe what is meant by *unit pricing* and *open-date labeling* and explain their possible usefulness to the consumer.

7. What is required when a food product is given nutrition labeling and what is the purpose of this type of labeling?

8. Define the term *convenience foods* and give several examples.

9. Identify several challenges to developing foods for the military or the space program.

10. Explain how the widespread availability of convenience foods may affect food preparation techniques used in the home.

11. Convenience foods are sometimes compared with similar home-prepared products. Discuss how they generally compare in these factors: (a) Cost (both food cost alone and cost that includes energy use and preparer's time), (b) Eating quality, (c) Nutritive value, (d) Preparation time and effort.

12. Discuss advantages and disadvantages of making your own mixes at home.

13. Suggest several useful guidelines to follow when purchasing food.

REFERENCES

1. American Dietetic Association. (2001). Position of the American Dietetic Association: Dietetic professionals can implement practices to conserve natural resources and protect the environment. *Journal of the American Dietetic Association, 101,* 1221–1227.

2. American Frozen Food Institute. (n.d.). History of frozen food. Retrieved June 20, 2002, from www.affi.com/factstat-history.asp

3. Anonymous. (2001). Food spending by U.S. households grew steadily in the 1990's. *Family Economics and Nutrition Review, 13*(2), 68–69.

4. Blisard, N. (2000). Food spending by U.S. households grew steadily in the 1990's. *Food Review, 23*(3), 18–22.

5. Borrud, L., Enns, C. W., & Mickle, S. (1996). What we eat in America: USDA surveys food consumption changes. *Food Review, 19*(3), 14.

6. Bourland, C. T., Fohey, M. F., Rapp, R. M., & Sauer, R. L. (1982). Space shuttle food package development. *Food Technology, 36*(9), 38.

7. Brecher, S. J., Bender, M. M., Wilkening, V. L., McCabe, N. M., & Anderson, E. M. (2000). Status of nutrition labeling, health claims, and nutrient content claims for processed foods: 1997 food label and package survey. *Journal of the American Dietetic Association, 100,* 1056.

8. Brody, A. L. (2002). Food canning in the 21st century. *Food Technology, 56*(3), 75–78.

9. Davis, D. E., & Stewart, H. (2002). Changing consumer demands create opportunities for U.S. food system. *Food Review, 25*(1), 19–23.

10. Dinkins, J. M. (1997). Food preparers: Their food budgeting, cost-cutting, and meal planning practices. *Family Economics and Nutrition Review, 10*(2), 34.

11. Dyson, L. K. (2000). American cuisine in the 20th century. *Food Review, 23*(1), 2–7.

12. Eliason, K., Harward, N., & Westover, M. (1978). *Make-a-mix cookery*. Tucson, AZ: H. P. Books.

13. Eliason, K., Harward, N., & Westover, M. (1980). *More make-a-mix cookery*. Tucson, AZ: H. P. Books.

14. Elitzak, H. (2001). Food marketing costs at a glance. *Food Review, 24*(3), 47–48.

15. Frakes, E. M., Arjmandi, B. H., & Halling, J. F. (1986). Plate waste in a hospital cook-freeze production system. *Journal of the American Dietetic Association, 86*, 941.

16. Frank, G. C., Zive, M., Nelson, J., Broyles, S. L., & Nader, P. R. (1991). Fat and cholesterol avoidance among Mexican-American and Anglo preschool children and parents. *Journal of the American Dietetic Association, 91*, 954.

17. Fu, B., & Nelson, P. E. (1994). Conditions and constraints of food processing in space. *Food Technology, 48*(9), 113.

18. Gallo, A. E. (1980, Fall). Consumer food waste in the United States. *National Food Review* NFR-12, p. 13. Washington, DC: U.S. Department of Agriculture.

19. Garrett, E. S. (2002). The "shrouded threat" of foodborne parasites. *Food Technology, 56*(4), 20.

20. Getlinger, M. J., Laughlin, C. V. T., Bell, E., Akre, C., & Arjmandi, B. H. (1996). Food waste is reduced when elementary-school children have recess before lunch. *Journal of the American Dietetic Association, 96*, 906.

21. Hackes, B. L., Shanklin, C. W., Kim, T., & Su, A. Y. (1997). Tray service generates more food waste in dining areas of a continuing-care retirement community. *Journal of the American Dietetic Association, 97*, 879.

22. Harris, J. M. (2002). Food product introductions continue to decline in 2000. *Food Review, 25*(1), 24–27.

23. Hollingsworth, P. (1997). Mainstreaming healthy foods. *Food Technology, 51*(3), 55.

24. Hollingsworth, P. (2001). Convenience is key to adding value. *Food Technology, 55*(5), 20.

25. Hollingsworth, P. (2001). Supermarket trends. *Food Technology, 55*(3), 20.

26. Hollingsworth, P. (2002). Surveying the crowded (nutrition) bar scene. *Food Technology, 56*(6), 20.

27. Kantor, L. S., Lipton, K., Manchester, A., & Oliveira, V. (1997). Estimating and addressing America's food losses. *Food Review, 20*(1), 2.

28. Lachance, P.A. (2002). Nutraceuticals, for real. *Food Technology, 56*(1), 20.

29. Lin, B. H., Guthrie, J., & Frazao, E. (1999). Nutrient composition of food away from home. In: Frazao, E., ed. *America's Eating Habits: Changes and consequences*. Washington, DC: USDA, ERS, AIB-750.

30. Mermelstein, N. H. (1993). A new era in food labeling. *Food Technology, 47*(2), 81.

31. Mermelstein, N. H. (1993). Nutrition labeling in foodservice. *Food Technology, 47*(4), 65.

32. Mermelstein, N. H. (1995). A regulatory look back at 1995. *Food Technology, 49*(12), 44.

33. Mermelstein, N. H. (2001). Military and humanitarian rations. *Food Technology, 55*(11), 73–75.

34. National Aeronautics and Space Administration. (n.d.). NASA facts: Food for space flight. Retrieved June 12, 2002, from http://www.jsc.nasa.gov/pao/factsheets/nasapubs/food.html

35. Neff, J. (1996). Will home meal replacement replace packaged foods? *Food Processing, 57,*(11), 35.

36. Neuhouser, M. L., Kristal, A. R., & Patterson, R. E. (1999). Use of food nutrtition labels is associated with lower fat intake. *Journal of the American Dietetic Association, 99,* 45–50.

37. Norton, V. P., & Martin, C. (1991). Plate waste of selected food items in a university dining hall. *School Food Service Research Review, 15*(1), 37.

38. Pancakes. (1992). *Consumer Reports, 57,* 56.

39. Pennington, J. A. T., & Wilkening, V. L. (1992). Nutrition labeling of raw fruit, vegetables, and fish. *Journal of the American Dietetic Association, 92,* 1250.

40. Putnam, J. J. (2000). Major trends in U.S. food supply, 1909–99. *Food Review, 23*(1), 8–14.

41. Putnam, J. J., & Allshouse, J. E. (1999, April). Food consumption, prices, and expenditures, 1970–97. Food and Rural Economics Division, Economic Research Service, U.S. Department of Agriculture. Statistical Bulletin No. 965.

42. Putnam, J. J., & Duewer, L. A. (1995). U.S. per capita food consumption: Record-high meat and sugars in 1994. *Food Review, 18*(2), 2.

43. Putnam, J. J., Kantor, L. S., & Allshouse, J. (2000). Per capita food supply trends: Progress toward dietary guidelines. *Food Review, 23*(3), 2–14.

44. Pszczola, D. E. (2001). Convenience foods: They've come a long, long way. *Food Technology, 55*(9), 85–94.

45. Regmi, A., & Gehlhar, M. (2001). Consumer preferences and concerns shape global food trade. *Food Review, 24*(3), 2–8.

46. Regmi, A., & Pompelli, G. (2002). U.S. food sector linked to global consumers. *Food Review, 25*(1), 39–44.

47. Sloan, A. E. (1994). How food shoppers make decisions. *Food Technology, 48*(5), 34.

48. Sloan, A. E. (1997). What's cooking? *Food Technology, 51*(9), 32.

49. Sloan, A. E. (2000). The top ten functional food trends. *Food Technology,* 54(4) 33.

50. Unnevehr, L., Deaton, L., & Kramer, C. (1994). International trade agreement provides new framework for food-safety regulation. *Food Review, 17*(3), 2.

51. U.S. Department of Agriculture. Results from 1994–1996 continuing survey of food intakes by individuals. Retrieved June 18, 2002, from http://www.barc.usda.gov/ghnrc/foodsurvey/96result.html

52. U.S. per capita food consumption. (1997). *Family Economics and Nutrition Review, 10*(1), 38.

53. Van Garde, S. J., & Woodburn, M. J. (1987). Food discard practices of householders. *Journal of the American Dietetic Association, 87,* 322.

54. Waino, J., & Gibson, P. (2001). U.S. exports face high tariffs in some key markets. *Food Review, 24*(1), 29–38.

Food Safety

3

Food safety is everyone's responsibility. From the farmer to the processor, the packager, the wholesaler, the retailer, the foodservice operator, and the consumer, everyone should recognize potential health hazards related to food and know how to control them. Why is food safety so important? Foodborne microbes remain one of the most common causes of illness in the United States. Exactly how many people become sick each year from foodborne illness is not clear. Estimates suggest that 5,000 deaths, 76 million illnesses, and 325,000 hospitalizations in the United States are caused by foodborne illness [51]. Young children, pregnant women, elderly people, people with weakened immune systems, and people taking medications are at the highest risk for foodborne illness.

Although the federally operated Centers for Disease Control and Prevention (CDC) collect data on foodborne illness, they are well aware of the limitations of these data because only a fraction of the cases that occur are reported. A surveillance system began in 1996. This system collects data from nine sites including 37.8 million people (13 percent of the U.S. population). In 2001, the surveillance data provided documentation of 13,705 laboratory-diagnosed cases of foodborne diseases [76]. In addition to the human aspect of foodborne illness, the annual costs related to foodborne illness in the United States have been estimated to be in excess of 7 billion dollars [13, 20].

A Food Safety Council was established in 1998 by executive order of President Clinton. This Council, with representatives from the United States Department of Agriculture (USDA), the U.S. Food and Drug Administration (FDA), and the Environmental Protection Agency (EPA), developed a comprehensive strategic federal food safety plan to be used to set priorities, improve coordination and efficiency, and strengthen prevention and intervention strategies. Reports from this council recognize past successes in reducing the prevalence of foodborne illnesses and provide recommendations to make America's food supply even safer [64].

PREVENTING FOODBORNE ILLNESS

Foodborne illness is prevented through the multifaceted efforts of all who have a role in producing, processing, regulating, and preparing food. The concept of food safety from farm to table was emphasized in the 1997 report to the President prepared by the FDA, USDA, EPA, and CDC [25]. On the farm, good

food safety a judgment of the acceptability of the risk involved in eating a food; if risk is relatively low, a food substance may be considered safe

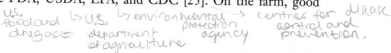

agricultural practices help to prevent or reduce contamination of produce foods [26] and promote healthy herds and flocks.

The food-processing industry utilizes a variety of measures to limit potential food hazards. It **pasteurizes**, **sterilizes**, uses specialized packaging, freezes, refrigerates, dehydrates, and applies approved antimicrobial preservatives to various food products. The government promotes food safety through oversight and monitoring by the U.S. Food and Drug Administration (FDA), U.S. Department of Agriculture (USDA), Environmental Protection Agency (EPA), and the Centers for Disease Control and Prevention (CDC). Local health departments inspect foodservice establishments to enforce safe food handling practices in the commercial sector. (Regulations are discussed further in Chapter 4.) All of these components help to ensure that the American food supply remains the safest and most wholesome in the world.

Consumers have important responsibilities for food safety through the selection, preparation, and proper storage of foods. Survey data have shown a decline in consumer knowledge about safe food handling [45]. Consumers in one study erroneously believed contaminated food could be identified by taste or smell and did not refrigerate hot foods quickly as recommended, but instead left foods to cool slowly at room temperature before refrigeration [52]. A multistate survey of consumer food handling practices found nearly 20 percent did not adequately wash hands or cutting boards after contact with raw meat or chicken [1]. A number of food handling errors were observed by researchers at Utah State University, who concluded that consumers report safer food handling practices on surveys than observations of actual food preparation reveals [5]. In general, many consumers do not appear to be acting on the messages concerning food safety that have been used for years by both government and industry groups by consuming undercooked eggs and other risky behaviors [73].

Several efforts have been made to increase the food safety knowledge of consumers. A public–private partnership was organized in 1997 to launch a food-safety consumer education campaign. A new Fight BAC cartoon character was developed (Figure 3-1) and an animated public service announcement distributed to television stations nationwide [20]. The Partnership for Food Safety Education continues to be active in the promotion of safe food handling practices. For the first time, the Dietary Guidelines include food safety as one of the recommendations and provide guidance on safe food handling practices [78]. A food safety campaign to promote the use of food thermometers was launched by the U.S. Department of Agriculture in Spring 2000 [28]. "Thermy" is a cartoon thermometer used in the food thermometer educational materials (Figure 3-2).

Hazard Analysis and Critical Control Points

One methodology designed to ensure food safety is the use of the Hazard Analysis and Critical Control Points (HACCP) system [44]. This preventive attempt in safety is built into the entire process of food manufacture. It is a quality control tool that focuses on critical factors directly affecting the **microbiology** of foods. HACCP operates on a set of basic procedures and involves the following steps:

1. Analyze **hazards** and assess **risks**.

---

pasteurize to treat with mild heat to destroy pathogens—but not all microorganisms—present in a food product

sterilize to destroy essentially all microorganisms

microbiology the branch of biology that deals with microorganisms

hazard a source of danger, long- or short-term, such as microbial food poisoning, cancer, birth defects, and so on

risk a measure of the probability and severity of harm to human health

FIGHT BAC!

CLEAN Wash hands and surfaces often.

SEPARATE Don't cross-contaminate.

CHILL Refrigerate promptly.

COOK Cook to proper temperatures.

Keep Food Safe From Bacteria™

Figure 3-1
An eye-catching Fight BAC™ *character is used to attract attention of the public in a campaign to teach consumers about food safety.* (Courtesy of the Partnership for Food Safety Education)

2. Identify **critical control points** in the process for each hazard where loss of control may result in an unacceptable health risk.

3. Establish preventive measures with critical limits for each control point.

4. Establish procedures to monitor the control points.

5. Establish corrective action to be taken if a deviation occurs at a critical control point.

6. Establish record-keeping procedures that document the hazard analysis so that the problems can be effectively traced.

7. Establish procedures for verifying the HACCP system.

critical control point any point in the process where loss of control may result in a health risk

The HACCP system is an important part of food processors' overall quality-assurance programs and helps to ensure the safety of their products. In 2001, the final rule requiring the adoption of HACCP systems by juice processors was announced by the FDA [81]. Five years earlier, in 1996, the USDA announced the final rule that requires the more than 6,200 slaughter and meat-processing plants that operate under federal inspection to adopt the HACCP system and to meet government standards for *Salmonella* microorganisms [20]. In addition, slaughter plants must test for generic *Escherichia coli* bacteria to verify that their control systems are preventing fecal contamination, the primary source of these organisms in the plant. The USDA is also requiring plants to adopt and follow

Figure 3-2
Thermy the cartoon thermometer promotes the use of thermometers in the home. (Courtesy of U.S. Department of Agriculture)

standard operating procedures
written instructions for performing a certain process; they must be followed exactly and a record kept of completion of the task

written **standard operating procedures** (SOPs) for sanitation as part of good manufacturing practices. These requirements were phased in over a period of 6 to 42 months [19]. Likewise, HACCP regulations for seafood manufacturers were implemented in 1997. These rulings are designed to reduce contamination of juice, meat, poultry, and seafood in the processing plant. After the product leaves the plant, it is the responsibility of the wholesaler, retailer, and consumer to properly handle, store, and cook the product in such a way as to ensure safety.

According to the CDC, in 1997, approximately 43 percent of the total reported foodborne illness outbreaks involved foodservice establishments, 22 percent occurred as a result of food consumed in the home, and 3 percent were from school, picnic, church, or camp food [60]. Many additional cases occurring in homes were probably not reported. It is thought that small outbreaks in homes comprise most of the foodborne illness cases in the United States [45]. Clearly, both food handlers and consumers have a tremendous responsibility to maintain proper control measures to prevent foodborne illness.

Well over 800,000 restaurants and many other foodservice establishments serve the American public [58]. Many of them use the HACCP system as part of their quality-assurance program [22, 71], which is highly recommended.

Workers in the foodservice industry, including those employed in fast-food and carryout restaurants, delicatessens, self-service food counters, mobile refreshment stands, family and gourmet restaurants, schools, hospitals, and other establishments, *must* be educated about potential food-safety hazards. The ServeSafe program developed by the Educational Foundation of the National Restaurant Association has been widely used by the industry to provide education and food safety certification [22]. Some states mandate that commercial foodservice operations have a food safety certified employee or manager on premise during all hours of operation. Education is vitally important so the sanitary procedures that ensure microbial quality and safety in the food served to the public are fully understood. The primary responsibility of foodservice managers and dietetic practitioners is to supply consumers with safe products that are as free as possible from pathogenic microorganisms and other health hazards [2, 3, 22].

The following safeguards are essential for safe foodservice: control time and temperature through appropriate heating and cooling of **high risk or potentially hazardous foods,** good personal hygiene, and prevention of contamination and **cross-contamination** in preparation and storage [22]. At each of these critical control points in production, a schedule for monitoring should be established and followed precisely. If monitoring reveals a potential hazard, then a clearly defined corrective action is to be taken and documented.

It may seem an insurmountable task to protect food from contamination, because pathogenic microorganisms are widespread in air, dust, soil, insects, and even in about half of the foodservice workers themselves. However, recognizing the potential risk of mishandling various foods, following proper programs for food and equipment sanitation, and using a little common sense can go a long way toward averting possible problems.

Proper Handling of Food

Data from the CDC concerning foodborne illness outbreaks during 1997 suggests that the leading contributing factor was improper holding temperatures for food. Poor personal hygiene, contaminated equipment, inadequate cooling, and food from an unsafe source followed as important factors [60]. Outbreaks of foodborne illness occur in homes, restaurants, schools, camps, picnics, and similar areas. In most cases, regardless of the location, the cause is linked to improper handling of food at the point of preparation.

National surveys have indicated a need for more consumer education concerning the proper handling of food [5, 29, 45, 73, 84]. Consumers' knowledge of food-safety issues in many cases appears to be limited. It has been suggested that the concept of HACCP should be extended to the consumer at home [8]. Safe handling instructions on egg cartons were required starting in 2001 and since 1994, the USDA has required safe handling instructions on packages of all raw or partially cooked meat and poultry products (Figure 3-3). Of consumers surveyed by the Food Marketing Institute in 1997, 45 percent reported that they have made some meat-handling changes as a result of the safe handling information on the package. The most common behavior change was washing surfaces and utensils after contact with meat [29].

The consumer education campaign of the Partnership for Food Safety Education focuses on four critical messages:

1. Wash hands and surfaces often.

high risk or potentially hazardous foods these foods support the rapid growth of microorganisms. Potentially hazardous foods are generally moist, high in protein, and have a neutral or slightly acidic pH. Examples include: milk and milk products, sliced melons, garlic and oil mixtures, poultry, meat, seafood, sprouts and raw seeds, baked or boiled potatoes, shell eggs, tofu, soy-protein foods, cooked rice, beans or other heat-treated plant foods

cross-contamination contamination of one substance by another; for example, cooked chicken is contaminated with *Salmonella* organisms when it is cut on the same board used for cutting raw chicken

Figure 3-3
The USDA requires safe handling instructions on packages of all raw or partially cooked meat and poultry products. (Courtesy of the American Meat Institute and the U.S. Department of Agriculture)

2. Don't cross-contaminate.
3. Cook to proper temperatures.
4. Refrigerate promptly.

Wash hands and surfaces. Following simple rules of sanitation such as washing hands before handling food, putting clean bandages on cuts and sores before working with food, and wearing plastic gloves can prevent numerous outbreaks of illness. Poor personal hygiene accounted for 37 percent of the known causes of foodborne illness in 1997 [60]. Although Americans may say they wash their hands, researchers observed handwashing practices of the general public in five metropolitan areas and found only 6 out of 10 washed their hands after using the restroom.

When working with food, handwashing is necessary before food preparation and multiple times during food preparation. Additionally, hands must be washed properly. Hands should be washed in hot running water, with soap, and scrubbed for at least 20 seconds with care taken to clean under the fingernails. Hands should be rinsed under clean running water, then dried with a single use towel [22]. Saying the "ABC's" is one way to see that hands are washed for the appropriate length of time. In a study where the food preparation practices of consumers were video-taped, researchers found the average length of handwashing was only 4.4 seconds and 34 percent of the handwashing attempts were without soap [5].

Surfaces in kitchens need to be cleaned thoroughly as well. Fight BAC recommends the use of paper towels. If cloth towels are used, they must be clean and not left damp for extended periods of time such as between meals. A damp dish towel contaminated with even small amounts of food soil is a perfect growing medium for bacteria which will cross-contaminate the surfaces later being "cleaned." In commercial foodservice operations, towels are either used clean from the laundry and if to be used again a short while later, then the towels are stored in a solution of a foodsafe chemical sanitizer.

All dishes and equipment used in food preparation should be carefully cleaned. Machine-washed dishes, both in the home and in commercial foodservice establishments, may have a very low if not almost nonexistent bacteria count because hot water and strong sanitizing agents are used in machine washing. In homes where infectious diseases exist, it is important to keep all dishes used by patients separate from other dishes until they are sanitized.

Don't cross-contaminate.   Cross-contamination can occur because of a dirty cloth, unclean surfaces, contaminated cutting boards, dirty hands, or poor storage techniques. In the Utah State University study, dirty hands accounted for 51 percent of the cross-contamination cases observed. Another key problem was the storage of raw meat on the middle or top shelf of the refrigerator that could drip into other foods such as lettuce or fruit that would be consumed without cooking [5]. Foods should be stored in the refrigerator so that ready-to-eat foods are placed above raw foods that may be contaminated with pathogenic bacteria (Figure 3-4).

Cook to proper temperatures.   Foods such as poultry, eggs, ground beef, pork, and seafood are cooked to specified temperature to enhance sensory qualities also to kill pathogenic organisms such as *Salmonella, E. coli, Listeria monocytogenes, Staphlococcus aureus, Trichinella spiralis, Anisakis simplex, Vibrio parahaemolyticus, Vibrio vulnificus* and others that may be present. Food cooking temperature guidelines provided from the U.S. Department of Agriculture as part of the "Thermy" consumer education materials are given in Table 3-1a. The temperatures, recommended for consumer use, include an additional margin of safety and thus are different than the temperature recommendations published in the FDA Food Code for use by foodservice operators (Table 3-1b) [22, 28].

More consumer education about food temperatures and the use of thermometers is needed. For example, ground beef that is cooked to less than the recommended temperature of 155–160°F (68–71°C) has been found to be brown throughout [48, 65]. Consequently, color alone as a measure of doneness is ineffective. Many consumers in the the Utah State University study undercooked chicken, meatloaf, or fish. Only 5 percent of the consumers in the Utah study used a thermometer, but many of the consumers who used a thermometer did not know the recommended temperatures [5].

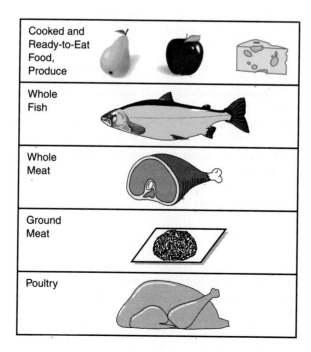

| Cooked and Ready-to-Eat Food, Produce |
| Whole Fish |
| Whole Meat |
| Ground Meat |
| Poultry |

Figure 3-4
Proper placement of food in the refrigerator helps to reduce chances of contracting a foodborne illness.

Table 3-1
(a) Cooking temperatures recommended by Thermy and the USDA.

TEMPERATURE RULES!

Food	°F
Ground Meat & Meat Mixtures	
Beef, Pork, Veal, Lamb	160
Turkey, Chicken	165
Fresh Beef, Veal, Lamb	
Medium Rare	145
Medium	160
Well Done	170
Poultry	
Chicken & Turkey, whole	180
Poultry breasts, roast	170
Poultry thighs, wings	180
Duck & Goose	180
Stuffing (cooked alone or in bird)	165
Fresh Pork	
Medium	160
Well Done	170
Ham	
Fresh (raw)	160
Pre-cooked (to reheat)	140
Eggs & Egg Dishes	
Eggs	Cook until yolk & white are firm
Egg dishes	160
Leftovers & Casseroles	165

(Courtesy of U.S. Department of Agriculture)

Table 3-1 *(cont.)*
(b) Cooking temperatures recommended in the 2001 FDA Food Code.

Product	Temperature
Poultry Stuffing, Stuffed Meat, and Dishes Combining Raw and Cooked Food (including soups and casseroles)	165°F (74°C) for 15 seconds
Ground Meats (beef, pork, or other meat or fish)	155°F (68°C) for 15 seconds
Injected Meats (including brined ham and flavor-injected roasts)	155°F (68°C) for 15 seconds
Pork, Beef, Veal, Lamb	Steaks/Chops: 145°F (63°C) for 15 seconds; Roasts: 145°F (63°C) for 4 minutes
Fish	145°F (63°C) for 15 seconds
Fresh Shell Eggs for Immediate Service	145°F (63°C) for 15 seconds
Any Potentially Hazardous Food Cooked in a Microwave Oven	165°F (74°C); let food stand for 2 minutes after cooking

Adapted from Reference 22.

Accurate temperature readings when using a thermometer depend on proper use and maintenence. A stem thermometer must be inserted up to the dimple on the stem (typically 2–3 inches) and sufficient time allowed for the temperature to register. When taking the temperature of a thin food such as a hamburger or chicken breast, the thermometer should be inserted from the side (Figure 3-5b). Thermocouples often are used in foodservice operations. Thermocouples record the temperature quickly and often require only one-fourth inch of food contact to provide an accurate reading; however, the cost is high so home use is not common. Most thermometers must be calibrated periodically to provide accurate measurements. Thermometers may be calibrated in ice water to 32°F (0°C) or in boiling water to 212°F (100°C) (Figure 3-5c).

Refrigerate promptly.   High risk, hazardous foods must be held hot or cold. Any temperature between 40° and 140°F (4.4° and 60°C), a **temperature danger zone,** permits growth of food-poisoning bacteria (Figure 3-6). Improper holding and inadequate cooling accounted for 76 percent of the reported foodborne illness outbreaks in 1997 [60]. More than one researcher has documented that a significant number of consumers leave perishable foods at room temperature to cool before refrigeration [5,52]. Bacteria grow most rapidly between 70°F (21°C) and 125°F (52°C), therefore keeping food at room temperatures is very hazardous.

Even when foods are placed under refrigeration quickly following a meal, the food may still not cool quickly. Foods should not be in the temperature danger zone for more than four hours, including the preparation, service, and cooling times. To accomplish rapid cooling, the hot foods should be put in cool, shallow containers (preferably less than two inches deep) and promptly placed

temperature danger zone a range of temperatures which allow rapid growth of bacteria and, in some cases, toxin production

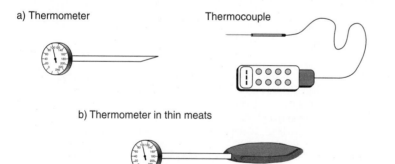

a) Thermometer   Thermocouple

b) Thermometer in thin meats

Figure 3-5
(a) Stem thermometer and thermocouple. (b) Proper use of thermometer in thin meats. (c) Method of thermometer calibration

c) Calibration of thermometer

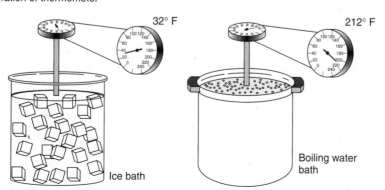

32° F   212° F

Ice bath   Boiling water bath

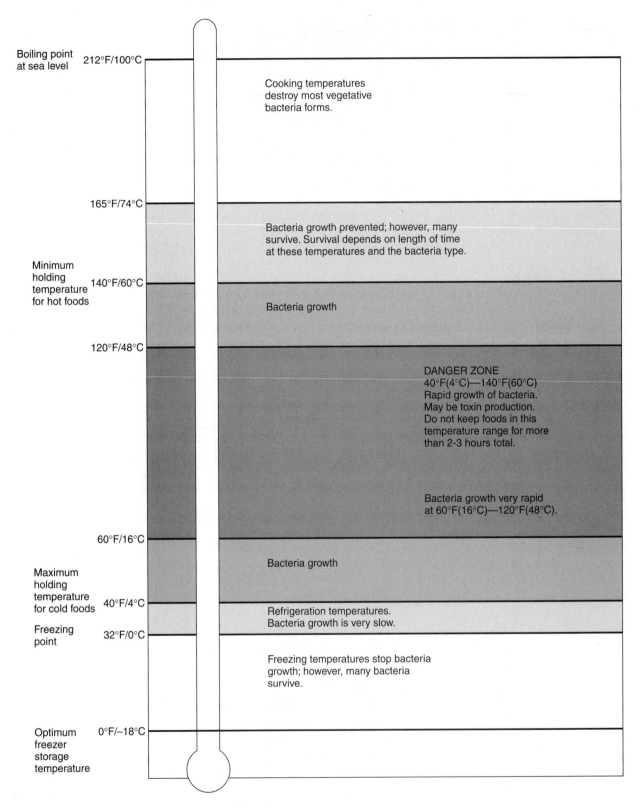

Figure 3-6
Effect of temperature on growth of bacteria.

under refrigeration. Large roasts of meat should be cut into smaller portions before refrigerating. Additionally, the refrigerator must be at or below 41°F (5°C). Many consumers may have the refrigerator temperature regulator set too high [5] and may not be aware of the actual temperature being maintained inside the box. Using refrigerator and freezer thermometers and checking them regularly will both enhance food quality and promote safe food storage.

Ionizing Radiation as a Food Safety Measure

The risk of foodborne illness may be reduced through the use of ionizing radiation by food processors. This method is also referred to as cold pasteurization because it is a method of destroying harmful bacteria in certain foods without complete sterilization, and the shelf life is also extended. The sources of radiation energy allowed for food processing include cobalt 60 and cesium 137 (which give off gamma rays), electron accelerators, and machine-generated X-rays [4]. Food thus irradiated does not become radioactive because the dosage of radiation permitted is low and controlled. One method, an electron-beam (e-beam) system, uses commercial electricity to accelerate electrons that kill harmful bacteria in frozen beef patties [54]. Food irradiation is regulated by the FDA and the USDA.

The improved microbiological quality of the food is a most important benefit from the use of ionization radiation. Consumers can prepare foods such as ground beef and chicken with greater confidence, if irradiated, because 99.9 percent of any *E. coli* 0157:H7 or *salmonella* would be destroyed [4] while maintaining sensory qualities of the food. Irradiated foods are labeled with the Radura, and the words "treated by irradiation" or "treated with radiation" (Figure 3-7). Consumers have been slow to purchase and use irradiated foods. Consumer education about this method of processing has been shown to increase consumer acceptance [50].

CHARACTERISTICS OF MICROORGANISMS

Because the most common food-related illnesses result from growth of and/or toxin production by certain microbes in foods, we will briefly review some of the basic characteristics of microorganisms. Then we will discuss the two general types of bacterial foodborne disease that are recognized: intoxications and infections. **Food intoxication** occurs when microorganisms have grown and produced a toxin in food, and the toxin-laden food is consumed. **Food infection** results when live microorganisms that can cause illness (called *pathogens*)

food intoxication illness produced by microbial toxin production in a food product that is consumed; the toxin produces the illness

food infection illness produced by the presence and growth of pathogenic microorganisms in the gastrointestinal tract; they are often, but not necessarily, present in large numbers

Figure 3-7
An irradiated food on the retail market should bear the international symbol along with either of the statements "treated with radiation" or "treated by irradiation."

are present, often in large numbers, in food that is eaten and they continue to grow in the gastrointestinal tract.

The microorganisms with which we are primarily concerned in food science include bacteria, molds, and yeasts. These tiny organisms perform some extremely useful functions in food preparation and processing. We should not always think of them in terms of the undesirable effects of food spoilage and illness. For example, the delightful flavors and characteristic textures of a variety of cheeses result from the activity of various bacteria or molds. Sauerkraut and pickles are made by using bacterial **fermentation.** Baker's yeast leavens bread and other baked products and contributes flavor. Those who enjoy Oriental foods with soy sauce are indebted to molds used in its manufacturing process. Various bacteria and molds are also used in industries that manufacture such things as citric acid and a great number of different enzymes.

Molds

Molds are multicellular, filamentous microbes that appear fuzzy or cottonlike when they grow on the surface of foods. The growth may be white, dark, or various colors, such as green or orange. Mold **spores,** by which molds can reproduce, are small, light, and resistant to drying. They easily spread through the air and can contaminate any food on which they settle.

Molds may grow readily on relatively dry foods such as bread or stored cereal grains because they require less moisture than most other microorganisms. They thrive at ordinary room temperatures but, given sufficient time, can also grow under cool conditions in refrigerators. Some molds can grow even at relatively high temperatures.

Yeasts

Yeasts are one-celled organisms that are often spherical in shape. They usually reproduce asexually through budding, during which new daughter cells are pinched off from the parent cell (Figure 3-8). Unlike molds, most yeasts grow best with a generous supply of moisture. They also grow in the presence of greater concentrations of sugar than do most bacteria. The growth of many yeasts is favored by an acidic reaction (**pH** 4.0 to 4.5), and they grow best in the presence of oxygen. Thus, yeasts thrive particularly in acidic fruit juices, where they can ferment the sugar, producing alcohol. The range of temperature for the growth of most yeasts is, in general, similar to that for molds, with the optimum around 77° to 86°F (25° to 30°C).

Bacteria

Tiny one-celled microbes smaller than either molds or yeasts, bacteria may be rod shaped (bacilli) or round (cocci). There are many different families of bacteria involved in food spoilage and food poisoning.

Generally, bacteria require more moisture than either molds or yeasts. They grow best where concentrations of sugar or salt are low and where the pH is about neutral (neither acid nor alkaline). Some bacteria love the cold; these are called psychrophilic and thrive at refrigerator temperatures. Others are heat loving (thermophilic) and may create particular hazards in cooked foods. Many others, however, are mesophilic, meaning that they do best at moderate temperatures. Bacteria also vary in their need for oxygen or air. Aerobic bacteria

fermentation the transformation of organic molecules into smaller ones by the action of microorganisms; for example, yeast ferments glucose to carbon dioxide and alcohol

spores an encapsulated, resistant form of a microorganism

pH expression of the degree of acidity on a scale of 1 to 14, 1 being most acid, 7 neutral, and 14 most alkaline

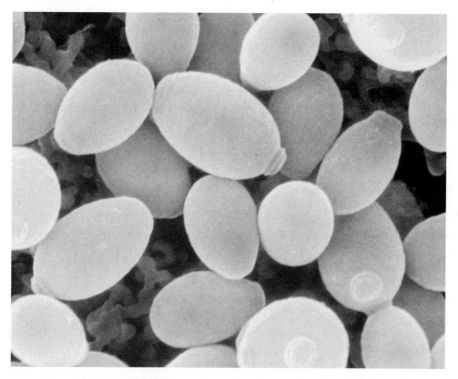

Figure 3-8
Photomicrograph of baker's yeast, Saccharomyces cerevisiae. *The yeast cell in the lower right-hand corner is in the process of reproducing by budding; a new daughter cell is being created.* (Courtesy of Universal Foods Corporation)

must have oxygen, anaerobic bacteria can grow only in the absence of oxygen, and facultative bacteria can grow either with or without free oxygen.

Some bacteria are able to form spores or endospores that have special protective coatings, making them highly resistant to destruction by heating. These spores are especially resistant in low-acid environments. Vegetables and meats are generally considered to be low-acid foods.

FOODBORNE INFECTIONS AND INTOXICATIONS

Data from CDC show a 23 percent drop in foodborne illnesses due to bacteria since 1996 [79]. Technological progress in food processing and distribution in recent years, including improved techniques for the chemical and bacteriological identification of injurious agents in food, public education, and the increased use of HACCP have helped to reduce the frequency of foodborne illness. Nevertheless, foodborne illness is still too common. It continues to create a great deal of unnecessary human misery.

The establishment of an early warning surveillance system in 1996, called FoodNet, has increased the monitoring capabilities of foodborne illness in the United States [20]. Although outbreaks of food-related illness in the United States and in other countries have often been inadequately reported or not reported at all, FoodNet has improved foodborne illness surveillance. The diagnosis of foodborne illness should be improved as well by the release, in 2001, of the publication "Diagnosis and Management of Foodborne Illnesses: A Primer for Physicians" [27]. This product was a joint effort of the American Medical Association, CDC, FDA, and USDA.

Improvement is still needed in collecting complete information about the incidence of foodborne illnesses and the identification of specific causes in order

Hot Topics

Probiotics—Friendly bacteria?

Remember the Nobel prize-winning Russian scientist Elie Metchnikoff who suggested in the early 1900s that the long healthy lives of Bulgarian peasants resulted from their regular consumption of Bulgarian milk—now known as yogurt? He claimed that live friendly bacteria, such as lactic acid bacteria, needed to be ingested regularly through fermented dairy products to minimize **putrefactive fermentations** in the intestine and promote general health of the body [74]. This concept now goes by the name of "probiotics" and has exciting market potential for food manufacturers in the United States. In Japan and Europe these products are already common.

Probiotic foods are those containing live microorganisms which, when consumed in sufficient numbers, actively enhance health by improving intestinal microbial balance [72]. There are many health claims for probiotics—including suppression of **pathogenic bacteria**, improvement in lactose metabolism, and anticarcinogenic activity—but definitive scientific studies are limited at present. An FDA Advisory Committee is considering the safety and potential health effects of probiotics in discussing **GRAS** status [17]. Safe use is founded on centuries of consumption of fermented foods.

There are challenges in formulating probiotic foods since bacteria often die during manufacturing, storage, and passage through the acid stomach. Organisms commonly used in regular yogurt manufacture do not survive in the gastrointestinal tract. Thus a trend is to add probiotic bacteria—*Lactobacillus acidolphilus*, *bifidobacteria*, and *Lactobacillus casei*—to the yogurt. A **microencapsulation** process has been suggested as a way to overcome the major hurdles of the GI tract [74].

putrefactive fermentations decomposition of organic matter by microorganisms, producing foul-smelling end products

pathogenic bacteria bacteria that can cause disease

GRAS generally regarded as safe—a status designated by the FDA for certain food ingredients

microencapsulation A coating is applied to very fine particles of a probiotic culture, which protects them until an appropriate time for their release in the GI tract.

to support future prevention efforts. Many different causative microbial agents of foodborne illness have been identified. In recent years, several new bacteria have been added to the list of microorganisms involved [45]. Many of these so-called *new* or *emerging* foodborne disease agents are well-known pathogens of domestic animals. What is new about them is the recognition that they can be transmitted to humans via food and may produce illness. When an outbreak of food poisoning occurs, a search should be made for the causative organisms.

Some pathogenic microbes may be carried by food even though they do not actually grow in the food. Others are able to grow in foods, increasing dramatically in numbers when held under certain conditions, particularly warm temperatures. In yet other cases, microbes grow and produce toxins that cause illness when consumed. The contamination of foods by pathogens may occur through food handlers, air, soil, water, flies, roaches, and rodents, and from animals or birds that produce milk or eggs or are used for meat. Food utensils used for eating, drinking, or food preparation may become contaminated when used by persons who are carrying potential disease-producing organisms. Examples of pathogens most often transmitted by food contaminated by infected persons who handle food are the hepatitis A virus, *Salmonella typhimurium*, and *Staphylococcus aureus*. Pathogens that are usually transmitted by contamination at the source of the food, in food processing, or by nonfoodborne routes are *Campylobacter jejuni*, enteropathogenic *Escherichia coli*, and *Yersinia enterocolitica*. However, even these pathogens may occasionally be transmitted by food handlers [59].

Common Food Infections

Salmonella. *Salmonella* bacteria are one of the leading causes of foodborne illness on a worldwide basis. The approximately 2,000 different strains of *Salmonella* are all capable of causing infection in humans. During recent years, *Salmonella enteritidis* has become a main cause of salmonellosis. The organisms, which appear under the microscope as short rods (Figure 3-9), usually enter the body orally in contaminated food or water and may produce a food-poisoning syndrome as they multiply in the intestinal tract. It has been assumed that large numbers of salmonellae growing in food are necessary to cause illness, but the investigation of several outbreaks has led to the conclusion that even small numbers can cause initiation of infection.

The primary signs and symptoms of **salmonellosis** are nausea, diarrhea, abdominal pain, and fever. These symptoms usually appear within 12 to 72 hours after the contaminated food has been eaten. In most cases, recovery occurs within 5 or 7 days; however, some individuals develop complications that persist for weeks or even months [14]. Approximately 40,000 cases of salmonellosis are reported each year in the United States [14]. Surveillance data from 1993–1997 revealed that *Salmonella* was responsible for the largest percentage of total food poisoning outbreaks, cases, and deaths. Furthermore, most of these outbreaks were attributed to eggs [59]. Death may sometimes occur with this disease, especially among the very young, the aged, and the infirm. The major factors involved in salmonellosis are summarized in Table 3-2.

salmonellosis illness produced by ingestion of *Salmonella* organisms

Salmonellae are found in many animals, both wild and domestic. Of particular concern is the presence of these organisms in eggs, poultry, and meat, because these appear to be the most important sources of human salmonellosis. At present, processing methods cannot ensure that raw meat, poultry, and eggs are free of salmonellae unless the food has been irradiated. However, the implementation of HACCP in plants processing high risk foods and testing by the Food Safety Inspection Service of the USDA have helped to reduce the prevalence of *Salmonella* [20].

There is a constant introduction of contaminated animal products into the food supply. Eggs became a greater concern for *Salmonella* in the early 80's when it was found that ovarian tissues of some hens are contaminated with *Salmonella enteritidis*. These hens produce eggs with contaminated yolks in the intact egg. Previously, consumers had been cautioned about the safety of cracked eggs; now even intact eggs can be risky. Precautions must therefore be taken to properly refrigerate eggs from the time they are laid. New governmen-

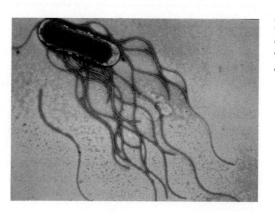

Figure 3-9
Salmonella is a rod-shaped bacterium with multiple flagellum. (Courtesy of U.S. Department of Agriculture)

Table 3-2
Food Infections and Intoxications

Disease/ Organism	Cause of Illness	Incubation Time	Nature of Illness	Foods Involved	Control Measures
Salmonellosis	Infection with *Salmonella* species	12–24 hours	Nausea, diarrhea, abdominal pain, fever, headache, chills, prostration	Meat, poultry, and egg products; milk products	Cook thoroughly; no cross-contamination; use sanitary practices
Staphylococcus poisoning	Toxin produced by certain strains of *Staphylococcus aureus*	1–6 hours	Severe vomiting, diarrhea, abdominal cramping	Custard- or cream-filled baked goods, ham, tongue, poultry, dressing, gravy, eggs, potato salad, cream sauces, sandwich fillings	Refrigerate foods; use sanitary practices
Botulism	Toxin produced by *Clostridium botulinum*	12–36 hours	Nausea, vomiting, diarrhea, fatigue, headache, dry mouth, double vision, muscle paralysis, respiratory failure	Low-acid canned foods, meats, sausage, fish	Properly can food following recommended procedures; cook foods properly
Clostridium perfringens poisoning	Toxin released in intestine	8–24 hours	Diarrhea, abdominal cramps, chills, headache	Meat, poultry, and other foods held for serving at warm but not hot temperatures	Cool foods rapidly after cooking; hold hot foods above 55°C (131°F)
Campylobacter jejuni	Infection, even with low numbers	1–7 days	Nausea, abdominal cramps, diarrhea, headache: varying in severity	Raw milk, eggs, poultry, raw beef, cake icing, water	Pasteurize milk; cook foods properly; prevent cross-contamination
Escherichia coli 0157:H7	Strain of enteropathogenic *E. coli*	2–4 days	Hemorrhagic colitis, possible hemolytic uremic syndrome	Ground beef, raw milk, chicken	Thoroughly cook meat; no cross-contamination
Yersiniosis	Infection with *Yersinia enterocolitica*	1–3 days	Enterocolitis, may mimic acute appendicitis	Raw milk, chocolate milk, water, pork, other raw meats	Pasteurize milk; cook foods properly; no cross-contamination; use sanitary practices
Listeriosis	Infection with *Listeria monocytogenes*	2 days–3 weeks	Meningitis, septicemia, miscarriage	Vegetables, milk, cheese, meat, seafood	Pasteurize milk; cook foods properly; no cross-contamination; use sanitary practices

Source: Reference 68.

tal regulations effective in 2001 require retail establishments to hold eggs at or below 45°F (7°C).

Chicken also has commonly been associated with *Salmonella*. It is not unusual to find that a significant percent of a particular lot of broiler chickens are carrying salmonellae. During slaughtering of poultry and meat, microorganisms may be spread from one carcass to another, widely distributing the original contamination. Therefore, close attention must be paid to operating procedures in poultry and meat processing plants in order to prevent or minimize cross-contamination. Turkeys and swine, as well as chicken, may be contaminated with salmonellae organisms. Techniques involving steam and/or various washes may be employed to aid in the control of spreading contamination.

The use of good food handling practices in foodservices and in the home can significantly reduce if not eliminate the risk of salmonellosis. Good personal hygiene and thorough hand washing are essential. Humans who have had salmonellosis may carry the infecting organisms in their digestive tracts for some time after the symptoms of the disease have disappeared and may contaminate foods that they handle improperly. Household pets (especially reptiles) can also carry salmonellae. Hands should be washed after handling pets and pets should not be fed from plates and utensils used by humans.

Care should be taken when storing and preparing foods most likely to harbor *Salmonella*. The specific foods most commonly involved in the development of salmonellosis are various kinds of meat and poultry products; eggs and foods made with eggs, such as cream or custard fillings; milk and milk products, such as ice cream, cream, and custard-filled confectionery; and fish and shellfish. The most vulnerable foods are those that are lightly cooked and subject to much handling, especially if they are unrefrigerated for long periods. Cantaloupe also has been implicated in outbreaks of salmonellosis. Cantaloupe must be washed carefully to remove any bacteria on the rind before cutting, then kept under refrigeration after cutting.

Most of the outbreaks of illness traced to this organism have been associated with eggs. The eggs involved typically were held at improper temperatures during preparation, allowing the microbe population to increase markedly. For example, in one case hundreds of eggs were cracked into large containers (pooled) and held for many hours at temperatures that permitted organisms to grow. The eggs were then either undercooked before being served or used uncooked in foods such as mousse. The pooling of eggs in commerical foodservice operations is no longer permited and thus pasteurized eggs are used for foods requiring large numbers of cracked eggs.

The consumer or foodservice worker cannot completely control contamination of animal products with salmonellae that occurs before the food is brought into the kitchen. However, selection of high quality foods that are properly refrigerated, along with proper cooking and careful handling practices after the products have been received, provides protection against illness. Salmonellae are sensitive to heat and are destroyed by normal conventional cooking of foods and pasteurization of milk.

Caution should be used when cooking certain foods by microwave. In one study, poultry cooked in a microwave oven to an internal temperature of 185°F (85°C) was not sufficiently heated to destroy *Salmonella* organisms in five of six contaminated birds. Because of uneven heating in microwave-cooked products, internal temperature cannot be used as an exclusive means of determining the safety of these products [49]. Salmonellae also survive for long periods in dried or frozen foods and in moist foods held at room temperature.

Milk should be pasteurized before drying, and eggs should be pasteurized before freezing or drying. Fresh meats, poultry, and eggs should be refrigerated at 35° to 40°F (2° to 4°C) or frozen and held at 0°F (−18°C). Poultry should be cooked to a minimum of 165°F (74°C) throughout. Higher temperatures generally are recommended for whole birds to ensure the entire bird has been cooked adequately. Eggs should be cooked; raw eggs should not be used in foods, such as ice cream, eggnog, and mayonnaise, that do not receive heat treatments sufficient to kill salmonellae. Pasteurized eggs are a good option to permit the safe preparation of products such as eggnog.

Cooked meat or poultry and leftovers should be tightly covered and stored immediately in the refrigerator or freezer. Perishable foods should be kept chilled when they are carried on a trip or a picnic. Cutting boards used for cutting up raw poultry or meat should be disinfected by washing with a dilute solution (1 tablespoon per quart) of sodium hypochlorite (household bleach) before being used for the cutting of other foods, such as the slicing of potatoes for salad, to prevent cross-contamination from an infected food to a noninfected one.

Eradication of salmonellae from animals seems unlikely. Therefore, the only truly effective way to reduce the incidence of salmonellosis is to educate foodservice workers and consumers about the proper handling of foods, particularly eggs, raw meat, and poultry.

At present, processing methods cannot ensure that raw meat, poultry, and eggs are free of salmonellae. However, in 1992, the USDA approved a new process designed to reduce the incidence of *Salmonella* during the processing of chicken [33]. Using specialized equipment installed in the processing line, a solution of trisodium phosphate is applied to the poultry carcasses. Little or no residue is left on the finished poultry. It has been suggested that this process removes a fat coating on the surface of the poultry, thus allowing bacteria to be more effectively washed from it. Also, the FDA has approved the irradiation of poultry to destroy *Salmonella* and to increase the shelf life of the product.

Campylobacter jejuni.   During the 1980s, *Campylobacter jejuni* ceased to be a pathogen encountered mainly in veterinary science and became a leading cause of acute bacterial **gastroenteritis** in humans in the United States. This occurrence came after the development of procedures for detecting the organism in stool specimens [24]. It is estimated that *C. jejuni* is the most common cause of diarrhea.

gastroenteritis inflammation of the gastrointestinal tract

Symptoms and signs of illness caused by *Campylobacter* infection include nausea, abdominal cramps, headache, diarrhea, and sometimes fever. If the diarrhea is severe, it may be bloody. Symptoms usually last 7 to 10 days but may last longer [24]. The infectious dose of *C. jejuni* can be quite low, with illness resulting from the ingestion of only a few hundred cells. Therefore, growth of the organism in foods held improperly is not necessary for food to serve as a vehicle for illness. Over 10,000 cases are reported to the CDC each year, in spite of limited surveillance [14].

Campylobacter is a relatively fragile organism, being sensitive to drying, normal atmospheric concentrations of oxygen, storage at room temperature, acidic conditions, and high heat. It cannot grow at temperatures below 86°F (30°C), grows slowly even under optimal conditions, and does not compete well with other bacteria. It grows at temperatures between 86° and 117°F (30° and 47°C) and is preserved by refrigeration, but it is readily destroyed by heat sufficient to cook foods. Therefore, *C. jejuni* is not likely to be a problem in properly cooked foods or in processed foods that have been pasteurized or dehydrated.

C. jejuni is often found in the intestinal tract of cattle, swine, sheep, chickens, and turkeys, where it is harmless. Therefore, the most likely sources of human infection are raw or inadequately cooked foods of animal origin, and foods that are contaminated after cooking through contact with *C. jejuni*-infected materials. Illness can be prevented by thorough cooking of poultry and meat, pasteurization of milk, and proper handling of foods both before and after preparation for service.

Raw meats and poultry become infected during processing when intestinal contents come into contact with meat surfaces. Reseach has shown that up to 88 percent of retail chickens carry *C. jejuni* [39]. Undercooked poultry and ground beef have been suspected in several outbreaks of illness. Raw milk and non-chlorinated water have been implicated in some infections. Between 1981 and 1990, 20 outbreaks of illness associated with the consumption of raw milk during youth activities occurred and were investigated by health departments in the 11 states involved. Among 1,013 persons who drank raw milk, 458 cases of *Campylobacter* infection developed [85]. This type of information should be useful in educating young people and school personnel about the dangers of drinking raw milk.

Escherichia coli. *Escherichia coli* is a normal inhabitant of the human intestinal tract and occurs in high numbers in fecal material. It was long considered to be harmless to human health, even though its presence in food or water indicated fecal contamination. In recent years, however, certain strains of *E. coli* have been identified as the causative factors in several food poisoning outbreaks in the United States and Canada (Figure 3-10). Each year in the United States, 73,000 cases of infection and 61 deaths are estimated to occur [14].

A subgroup of *E. coli* called **enteropathogenic** *E. coli* may produce foodborne illness. One particular strain of this subgroup, *E. coli* 0157:H7, is hardier than other strains, is more difficult to detect, and can be deadly [53]. It appears to be a relatively new pathogen that has acquired genetic changes, making it virulent [45]. The *E. coli* 0157:H7 organism causes **hemorrhagic colitis**, producing bloody diarrhea and severe abdominal pain. Most cases of a rare disease called *hemolytic uremic syndrome*, the leading cause of acute kidney failure in children, are caused by E. coli 0157:H7 [14]. Damage to the central nervous system can be another complication. As few as 10 organisms may result in illness; therefore the careful handling of foods that may be contaminated with *E. coli* 0157:H7 is essential (Figure 3-10).

An unfortunate example of this organism's deadly power received national attention in January 1993, when more than 700 people in the northwestern United States became seriously ill after eating hamburgers at a chain of fast-food restaurants. Four children subsequently died [20]. Investigations into the

enteropathogenic causing illness in the intestinal tract

hemorrhagic colitis bleeding and inflammation of the colon or large intestine

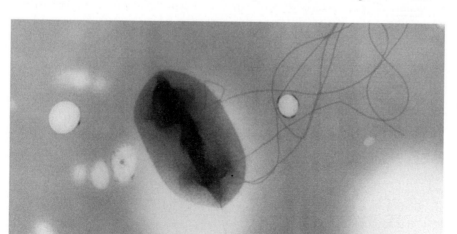

Figure 3-10
Transmission electron micrograph of E. coli. (Courtesy of The Centers for Disease Control and Prevention, Public Health Image Library, Peggy S. Hayes)

cause of the food poisoning outbreak revealed that the hamburgers were contaminated with *E. coli* and served undercooked. The hamburgers were cooked to a minimum internal temperature of 140°F (60°C), according to company policy and as recommended by the FDA. Company personnel were apparently unaware that the Washington State Health Department had set a minimum internal temperature requirement of 155°F (68°C). The FDA Food Code now requires that hamburgers in foodservice establishments be cooked to a minimum internal temperature of 155°F (68°C) [80] and USDA's Food Safety Inspection Service (FSIS) now tests raw ground beef for the pathogen [20]. In 1999, irradiation of meat products was approved by the FSIS as another method to assure the safety of meat products [55]. Consumers, however, have been slow to embrace irradiated foods, unless education about the irradiation process is provided [66].

Consumers should cook ground meat to an internal temperature of 160°F (71°C). Although consumers were initially encouraged to check the doneness of ground beef products by the color of the meat in the center of the meat [53], research has shown that ground beef may be light gray or brown when below the safe temperature of 160°F [48, 65]. Consequently, consumer education efforts are now directed at encouraging the use of thermometers.

Although *E. coli* 0157:H7 is generally associated with dairy cattle and their products—beef and milk—*E. coli* food poisoning has also been associated with water, unpasteurized apple cider and apple juice, and produce foods such as lettuce that have been cross-contaminated either in the field or in the kitchen. The FDA recommends that children, older adults, and people with weakened immune systems drink *only* pasteurized cider and juice. Fresh fruits and vegetables should be washed thoroughly before eating. *E. coli* 0157:H7 can survive freezer storage as well as refrigeration [53].

To avoid illness caused by *E. coli*, foods should be adequately cooked and postcooking contamination avoided through careful handwashing and cleaning of surfaces and equipment that have come in contact with raw meat. Food may be contaminated by contact with contaminated equipment, water, infected food handlers, or careless food handling or storage practices. Foodservice establishments, particularly, should carefully monitor adequacy of cooking, holding times, temperatures, and personal hygiene of food handlers. The USDA now requires that livestock slaughter operations and meat-processing plants operating under federal inspection use the HACCP system. The plants must also test for generic *E. coli* bacteria to verify that fecal contamination is not occurring. Processing methods such as steam pasteurization of the carcass, sprays and organic washes are helping to reduce contamination during processing [55].

Yersinia enterocolitica.   An infection caused by *Yersinia enterocolitica*, known as yersiniosis, may cause gastroenteritis. Pigs are the primary animal source of this organism [14]. Foods involved in outbreaks of yersiniosis have included chocolate milk, pasteurized milk, and tofu that was packed in unchlorinated spring water [24]. The precise manner by which the organism contaminated these foods was not determined, but in each case it was thought to be a lack of good sanitary practice. *Y. enterocolitica* can grow at refrigeration temperatures, but is sensitive to heat; therefore, to control illness from this cause, it is important to eliminate the organism from foods by pasteurization or cooking. Care should be taken to cook pork thoroughly, to avoid cross-contamination of processed, ready-to-eat foods with pork and porcine wastes, and to practice good hygiene and handwashing practices.

Listeria monocytogenes. The importance of *Listeria monocytogenes* as a causative agent in the development of foodborne illness has been recognized only in recent years. This organism is normally present in the environment and frequently contaminates many foods, being found most often in raw milk, soft ripened cheeses, ice cream, raw vegetables, fermented raw sausages, raw and cooked poultry, raw meat, and seafood products [24]. It may also be present in some vegetables. Soil is a common reservoir of *L. monocytogenes*, which may be carried in the intestinal tracts of a variety of animals, including humans. Home environments are often contaminated with *L. monocytogenes*.

Listeriosis was in the national spotlight in 1998, when 21 deaths and 80 illnesses were traced to a single plant producing deli meat and hot dogs [86]. Because *L. monocytogenes* is able to grow at refrigerator temperatures, there is concern for potential problems with the increasing number of refrigerated ready-to-eat foods, salads, and minimally processed foods that are being marketed [69]. Refrigerator storage temperatures must be carefully controlled because fluctuations in temperature are likely to affect the growth of this and other organisms. *L. monocytogenes* can grow well at temperatures as low as 32°F (0°C), but is sensitive to heat and is destroyed by pasteurization.

This organism can be responsible for a variety of health problems, including meningitis, **septicemia,** and miscarriage. Six of the 21 deaths in 1998 from contaminated hot dogs and deli meats were due to miscarriages or stillbirths. Pregnant women are about 20 times more likely than the general population to get listeriosis [14]. Therefore, pregnant women must thoroughly cook hot dogs, avoid soft cheeses such as feta, Brie, Camembert, blue-veined, and Mexican-style cheeses, and may be advised to avoid deli meats [6]. In addition to pregnant women, illness occurs principally in individuals whose immune system is compromised in some way by such conditions as cancer, cirrhosis, AIDS, or transplantation of organs. In these cases, the mortality rate is high. Healthy individuals are usually able to overcome the infection with considerably fewer problems. Most people do not appear to be susceptible to listeric infection even though many foods contain low levels of the organism.

septicemia the presence of pathogenic microorganisms in the blood

Since the late 1990's there have been a number of meat recalls, especially involving products such as sausages, hot dogs, and soft cheeses, because of *Listeria* contamination. *Listeria* grows well in the manufacturing environment that is usually cool and moist. Many methods to further reduce the possibilty of post cooking contamination of products in manufacturing are being researched. In 2000, the FSIS announced that the levels of sodium lactate and sodium diacetate could be increased in meat products to further control *Listeria* [55].

Other food infections. Microorganisms of the *Shigella* species may be carried by food and cause gastrointestinal symptoms, including diarrhea, vomiting, fever, and abdominal cramps. Relatively small numbers of the organisms can cause disease. The major cause of shigellosis is infected food handlers who are carrying the organism in their intestinal tracts and practice poor personal hygiene. Most outbreaks result from contamination of raw or previously cooked foods during preparation in the home or in foodservice establishments. One outbreak involving 29 airline passengers was found to be due to *Shigella sonnei*, with the food vehicle being submarine sandwiches. The sandwiches had been prepared in an in-flight kitchen at the

Minneapolis–St. Paul airport. An investigation indicated that the food was contaminated by one or more food handlers [59]. The best preventive measure is education of the food handler, with an emphasis on good personal hygiene.

Vibrio parahaemolyticus is associated with the consumption of raw or improperly cooked fish and shellfish [24]. Outbreaks in the United States have occurred during the warmer months of the year and have been reported along coastal areas. A outbreak in 1998 was associated with oysters and clams harvested from the Long Island Sound. In 1997, the largest reported outbreak in North America was associated with eating raw oysters harvested in waters off the west coast of the United States. The growth of *V. parahaemolyticus* is slowed or arrested at refrigeration temperatures. Most important with respect to human infections is prevention of their multiplication in uncooked seafoods and employment of hygienic handling procedures to avoid the recontamination of cooked foods. Consumption of raw seafoods should be avoided, particularly during the warmer months of the year when the *Vibrio* organisms tend to increase in numbers [22]. It is particularly important that the elderly and those whose immune systems are compromised because of cancer, HIV, renal disease, and so on be informed of the dangers associated with eating raw shellfish [67].

Common Food Intoxications

Staphylococcus food poisoning.   Certain strains of *Staphylococcus aureus* produce a potent toxin that is recognized as a common cause of food poisoning. It is called an *enterotoxin* because it produces gastroenteritis or inflammation of the lining of the stomach and intestines. The symptoms of staphylococcal poisoning—severe vomiting and diarrhea—appear between 1 and 6 hours after the food is consumed, and usually disappear a few hours later. Complete recovery normally takes 1 or 2 days. The mortality rate for this type of food poisoning is essentially zero, but it could be fatal in severely malnourished infants or in infirm adults [24]. *Staphylococcus* organisms are shown in Figure 3-11.

The food-poisoning strains of *S. aureus* are present in the nasal passages and throats, and on the hair and skin, of 50 percent or more of healthy people [24]. Boils and some wounds may also be infected with them. Food may be contaminated with these potentially dangerous organisms when transfer occurs from the nasal passage or a sore on the hands of the food handler to the food being prepared.

If foods contaminated with staphylococcal organisms cool very slowly or are held without refrigeration, these organisms grow and produce the toxin that

Figure 3-11
Scanning electron micrograph of Staphylococcus aureus. (Courtesy of The Centers for Disease Control and Prevention, Public Health Image Library, Jim Biddle and Janice Carr)

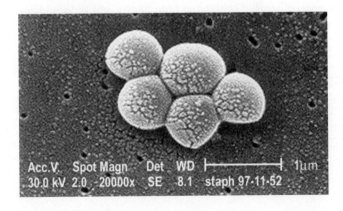

is responsible for illness. Because the toxin is preformed, the gastrointestinal symptoms occur relatively quickly. Once it has formed in the food, the staphylococcal toxin is not easily inactivated or destroyed. Because it is stable to heat and may withstand boiling for 20 to 60 minutes, it is important to prevent the formation of the toxin. Prevention is accomplished by the sanitary handling of food during preparation and by proper refrigeration of prepared foods.

Because staphylococci usually get into food by way of human handlers, contamination can be controlled by such simple rules as washing hands before preparing food and rewashing hands after using a handkerchief or tissue. Rubber or plastic gloves should be worn if cuts or sores are present on the hands, which not only keeps staphylococci from being transferred to the food from the cuts, but also prevents additional bacteria from getting into the sores.

A wide variety of foods may provide excellent media for the growth of staphylococcal bacteria. Cooked poultry, baked ham, tuna, egg products, potato salad, and custard- or cream-filled baked goods are often involved. These foods, in particular, should be refrigerated at 35° to 40°F (2° to 4°C). Failure to refrigerate foods that have been contaminated with the microorganisms, thus allowing the toxin to form, is the usual reason for an outbreak of the disease. The toxin does not necessarily affect the taste of the product and thus individuals consuming such foods are not aware that they are eating "spoiled" food.

In 1989, several outbreaks of staphylococcal food poisoning occurred in the United States as a result of people consuming canned mushrooms imported from the People's Republic of China [38]. More than 100 people became ill. Canned food is not usually associated with this type of poisoning because the staphylococcal organism is easily destroyed by heat, so a team of specialists went to China to investigate the cause. They concluded that the toxin had been produced during the period when the fresh mushrooms were packed in nonpermeable polyethylene bags as they were being shipped to the processing plant. Because the mushrooms used up the oxygen in the bags through respiration, the carbon dioxide level became elevated and inhibited the growth of competing microorganisms. The staphylococcal organisms thus grew and produced the heat-stable toxin that was not destroyed in the canning process. This situation emphasizes the importance of careful control at *all* phases of food production—processing, packaging, and delivery—to ensure safety in the final product.

An accurate figure for the number of cases of staphylococcal food poisoning in the United States is not available because so many cases are not reported. Usually, only outbreaks that involve large groups of people, such as those at conventions or company picnics, are reported. A large proportion of all cases of food poisoning are probably of this type, and many of us encounter this organism several times during our lives. Table 3-2 summarizes the major factors involved in staphylococcal food poisoning.

Clostridium perfringens. The symptoms associated with *Clostridium* food poisoning include severe abdominal cramps and pronounced diarrhea. Nausea and vomiting are rare. The symptoms appear 8 to 12 hours after eating the contaminated food and the illness lasts no more than 24 hours. It is usually not serious. Foods responsible include beef, chicken, turkey, stews, meat pies, and gravy that have been mishandled. These foods may have been cooled too slowly after cooking or kept several hours without refrigeration then reheated to less than the recommended 165°F (74°C). Because *C. perfringens* will grow at relatively warm temperatures, foods that have been kept on a serving line steam table at a temperature below 130°F (55°C) for an extended period are another common cause of illness. *C. perfringens* organisms multiply rapidly under these conditions of poor temperature control during cooling, heating, or hot holding.

The mechanism causing illness seems to involve the ingestion of large numbers of live vegetative cells of *C. perfringens*. These cells then form encapsulating spores in the intestinal tract and release an enterotoxin. The toxin produces the characteristic symptoms [24]. Thus, this microorganism exhibits characteristics of both a food infection and a food intoxication.

Clostridium botulinum.   Botulinum food poisoning is the most feared of all foodborne diseases. Between 1910 and 1919, the death rate of those contracting this disease was 70 percent. By the 1980s the rate had dropped to 9 percent. In 1993 it was less than 2 percent, probably the result of early diagnosis and improved treatment. However, recovery is still slow [83].

Botulism is a condition that results from the action of a potent toxin on the neurological system of the body, causing paralysis. The toxin is produced by the bacterium *C. botulinum*. Symptoms include nausea, vomiting, diarrhea, double vision, drooping eyelids, slurred speech, difficulty in swallowing, inability to talk, and finally, respiratory paralysis and death. Infants with botulism are lethargic, feed poorly, are constipated, have a weak cry and poor muscle tone [14]. The signs of disease usually appear about 18 to 36 hours after eating food that contains the active toxin [14].

C. botulinum is able to form spores (Figure 3-12) that are very resistant to destruction by heat in a low-acid environment. It is also *anaerobic*, meaning that it can grow and produce toxin only in the absence of free oxygen. The organism itself and its spores are not pathogenic or disease producing in adult humans, but the toxin that it produces in such foods as inadequately heated canned meats, low-acid vegetables, low-acid tomatoes, and some processed fish is one of the most potent known. Toxin production has also occurred in such foods as fresh mushrooms kept in tight plastic bags, baked potatoes wrapped in foil and left at room temperature for several days before being used to make potato salad, and seasoned cooked onions that were kept warm for extended periods of service. If fresh garlic cloves are placed in oil to season the oil, a danger of botulinum toxin production exists [22] because the oil creats an anaerobic environment favorable to *C. botulinum*. Garlic oil should be purchased from a source that has properly processed it and kept it refrigerated.

Spoiled foods containing the botulinum toxin may have off-odors and gas and appear to be soft and disintegrated. However, cases of botulism have been reported from eating foods that had little or no abnormal appearance or odor. Because of this problem and because the toxin can be inactivated by boiling temperatures, the USDA has recommended that home-canned low-acid foods (including low-acid tomatoes) that have not been processed using recommended procedures be boiled for 10 to 15 minutes before being tasted.

Although adults can apparently consume the *C. botulinum* cells themselves without ill effect, this may not be the case with infants up to about 12 months of age. Out of about 110 cases of botulism reported in the United States each year, 72 percent are infant botulism [14]. *C. botulinum* is apparently able to colonize, grow, and produce toxin in the colons of certain infants, causing typical signs of neurological distress. Possibly, because infants' intestinal bacteria are colonized after birth, *C. botulinum* organisms may grow before other bacteria that inhibit their growth have become well established. *C. botulinum* spores may be found in

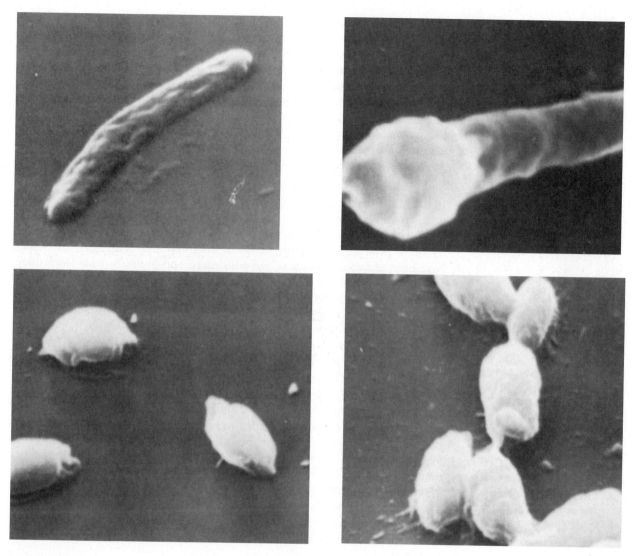

Figure 3-12

Scanning electron photomicrographs of (top left) a cell of Clostridium botulinum, *type A, prior to formation of a spore and (top right) another type A cell during actual sporulation. At the bottom are spores of type B (left) and type E (right).* (Courtesy of the U.S. Department of Health and Human Services, Food and Drug Administration. Kautter, D. A., and R. K. Lynt, Jr. 1971. Botulism, *FDA Papers,* 5 (9), p. 16.)

honey, which has been implicated in some cases of infant botulism. Consequently, infants up to one year of age should not be fed honey.

Home canned foods are the most common cause of the approximately 25 foodborne cases of botulism reported each year in the United States that do not involve infants. Botulism in commercially canned products is extremely rare and generally involves a damaged can. Inadequate processing of home-canned foods that are low in acid—particularly vegetables, low-acid varieties of tomatoes, and meats—creates the greatest problem with respect to botulism. If spores of this bacterium are present, boiling will not destroy them unless the solution is sufficiently acid or unless boiling is continued for 6 to 10 hours. Various strains of the organism vary in their temperature resistance, but low-acid foods are never safely processed unless they are heated at temperatures considerably above the boiling point of water, 212°F (100°C). It is recommended that temperatures no lower than 237° to 246°F (114° to 119°C) be used for low-acid vegetables. These temperatures can be achieved by processing in a pressure cooker at 10 to 15 pounds pressure. Low-acid foods should never be processed in a boiling water bath. Because the botulinum toxin is so deadly, procedures recommended by the USDA [77] or by established companies that manufacture home-canning equipment should always be carefully followed in the home canning of low-acid foods to guard against any possibility of toxins developing.

Mycotoxins

It was discovered in 1960 that toxins produced by molds growing on cereal grains were responsible for the deaths of thousands of young turkeys that were fed the grain. These toxins were called *aflatoxins*, because it was found that they had been produced by certain strains of the mold *Aspergillus flavus*. Aflatoxins have been detected in peanuts and cottonseed and in meals made from them. Other toxins produced by molds, including some species of *Penicillium* and *Fusarium*, have also been identified and are generally called **mycotoxins**. These toxins are capable of causing harm to both animals and humans [57]. A correlation exists between the incidence of liver cancer in humans in certain areas of Africa and Asia and dietary exposure to aflatoxins [62].

When adverse weather conditions, including both unusually wet spring and summer months and certain drought environments, occur during the growth of cereal crops, certain types of *Fusarium* molds may colonize on the plants and produce mycotoxins (Figure 3-13). Contamination of the harvested grains by the toxin is a problem because the toxins survive most processing methods. Fortunately, accumulation of mycotoxins on cereal crops is not a significant problem during normal growing seasons [9]. The FDA has established regulatory limits for aflatoxins on both human and animal food. Monitoring programs are important in controlling the levels of mycotoxins in foods [31].

Generally, foods that develop mold growth in the home should be discarded; however, solid cheeses may be trimmed of mold and the nonmoldy portion used if the cheese has been kept under refrigeration. Studies indicate that

mycotoxins toxins produced by molds

Figure 3-13
A healthy wheat head (left) and one with Fusarium *head blight disease (right).* (Courtesy of U.S. Department of Agriculture)

aflatoxins do not develop under refrigeration and that other toxins may be produced only in very small amounts or not at all [57]. In the holding or storing of foods, precautions should always be taken to minimize mold growth by such practices as adequate refrigeration and use of foods within a reasonable time.

Animal Parasites

The globalization of the world's food supply is causing exposure to parasites not previously common in a given geographical area. Consequently, the risk to American consumers of parasites has increased significantly. Only 13 species of parasistic animals were of concern in the United States in the 1990's. In 10 years that number has increased to over 100 species [61]. Current estimates suggest there are up to 2.5 million cases of illness annually in the United States due to food- and beverage-borne parasites [51].

In some parts of the world, infestation by such parasites as roundworms, flatworms, and certain species of **protozoa** may be common problems, and food or water may be carriers of these infecting agents. Protozoa include *Entamoeba histolytica*, the cause of amoebic dysentery, which is spread principally by fecal contamination of water, food, and diverse objects. Food handlers can spread this parasite. *Ascaris lumbricoides* is a roundworm or nematode that is spread fecally and is resistant to sewage treatment. It may survive for years in the soil and contaminate vegetables. *Trichinella spiralis*, another nematode, becomes encysted in meat and may be spread by this route. Certain tapeworms (flatworms) may also be encysted in meat, while other types may be acquired from the eating of raw or insufficiently cooked fish [61].

Anisakis simplex is a roundworm that can be found in especially cod, haddock, fluke, Pacific salmon, herring, flounder, monkfish, and fish used in sushi and sashimi. Fish must be cooked properly or if consumed raw, the fish must have been previously frozen. To protect against anisakiasis by freezing, the fish must be maintained at −4°F (−20°C) for 7 days. Marinades are not protective and therefore marinated fish must still be properly cooked or previously frozen [22].

In the United States, a protozoa, *Cyclospora cayetanensis*, became a focus of public attention in the summer of 1996 [47]. This organism was recovered in multiple, clustered cases of prolonged diarrhea in the United States and Canada. More than 1,400 cases appeared from the Rocky Mountains eastward and were associated with the eating of fresh raspberries. The implicated raspberries were grown in Guatemala, but the *Cyclospora* was not actually found on the fruit. None of the available standardized tests for protozoan contamination of raw products was specifically intended for use on raspberries, creating difficulties in analysis.

There is a continuing, though small, risk in the United States from the tiny roundworm, *Trichinella spiralis* (Figure 3-14). During the 1990's an annual average of fewer than 40 cases were reported [16]. Legislation controlling hog feed, the increased freezing of pork, and public understanding of the need to properly cook pork products have all promoted a reduction in cases.

Trichinella is now most often associated with the consumption of undercooked game meats such as bear, boar, and rabbit. When the meat from these animals is consumed before it has been sufficiently cooked to destroy the larvae in it, trichinosis results. The larvae are freed in the digestive tract after consumption of the meat and enter the small intestine, where they develop into mature worms. Their offspring (newborn larvae) migrate throughout the body via the circulatory system and invade striated muscles. Here they become en-

protozoa one-celled animals

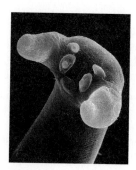

Figure 3-14
Scanning electron micrograph of a Trichinella spiralis *tail. This parasite harbors itself in capsules inside flesh and in large quantities can cause severe muscular problems.* (Courtesy of J. Ralph Lichtenfels)

cysted and may persist for years. In the first few weeks after ingestion of trichinae, symptoms include nausea, vomiting, diarrhea, sweating, and loss of appetite. Later, after the larvae reach muscles in the body, muscular pains, facial edema, and fever may occur. Several medications are available to treat trichinosis.

The USDA has recommended a procedure for processing cured pork products so that any trichinae present are destroyed. Therefore, these pork products should be free of trichinae. Poultry products that contain pork are subject to the same requirements concerning treatment for trichinae as are meat products containing pork. Thorough cooking of fresh pork to an internal temperature of at least 137°F (58°C) should ensure the destruction of any trichinae that might be present; however, a minimum of 145°F (63°C) is generally recommended for pork products. Cooking pork to an internal temperature of 160°–170°F (71–77°C), as recommended by the U.S. Department of Agriculture "Thermy" temperature chart, allows a margin of safety. Pork cuts that are less than 6 inches thick can be frozen for 20 days at 5°F (−15°C) to destroy any trichinae present. However, the freezing of game does not consistently protect against trichinosis; thus game meats must be thoroughly cooked regardless of freezing [16].

Precautions must be taken when cooking pork or game meats by microwaves to ensure that a final temperature sufficient to destroy any trichinae is achieved throughout the meat. Microwaves may heat unevenly. The microwave cooking of pork is discussed in Chapter 25.

Viruses

Viruses are now recognized as important causes of foodborne disease in the United States [46]. Essentially all foodborne viruses are transmitted to humans enterically, that is, by the fecal-oral route. They are shed in feces and infect by being ingested. Infection may come directly by person-to-person contact or indirectly via the vehicles of food and water. Infection often results from mishandling of food by infected persons.

hepatitis inflammation of the liver

mollusks a type of shellfish characterized by a soft unsegmented body enclosed in a shell of one or more pieces; examples are oysters and clams

jaundice a condition in which the skin and eyeballs become abnormally yellow due to the presence of bile pigments in the blood

The **hepatitis** A virus and the Norwalk-like gastroenteritis viruses are those most often foodborne. During 1988 to 1992, the hepatitis A virus was reported to be the fourth leading cause of foodborne illness and Norwalk-like viruses were the ninth leading cause [46]. Hepatitis A was known in the 1940's as a foodborne viral disease and was first associated with shellfish. **Mollusks,** such as clams and oysters, are especially prone to transmit viruses. When hepatitis symptoms occur, they often include fever, malaise, anorexia, nausea, and abdominal discomfort, followed in a few days by **jaundice.** After a few weeks the illness usually subsides, but may produce debility that lasts for months.

Gastroenteritis, characterized by vomiting and diarrhea, may be caused by Norwalk-like viruses that are shed in the feces. Although food is not the only means by which these viruses can be spread, it is a very effective one. Outbreaks have been traced both to ill persons and to food workers who had recovered from illness days earlier. Unlike infection with the hepatitis A virus, infection with the Norwalk virus does not confer immunity [59].

Viruses cannot multiply in foods, and can usually be inactivated by cooking. It is important to avoid contamination of ready-to-eat foods that will not be cooked. Sanitary personal hygiene habits among food handlers are extremely important in avoiding the spread of these viruses via food. The Norwalk virus is notable in that it has been spread through ice that was contaminated due to unsanitary water or the poor personnel hygiene of those who handled the ice.

Environmental Contaminants

Toxic substances may contaminate the environment in which people, plants, and animals live. These substances include both inorganic elements, such as arsenic, cadmium, mercury, and lead, and organic substances, such as various chemicals used in pesticides. When contaminants persist in the environment, they may accumulate along the food chain in amounts that are toxic to humans when various animals and plants are consumed.

Fish taken from water contaminated by the industrial use of mercury contain high levels of mercury, which may cause illness in humans if consumed in large amounts. Pregnant women, nursing women, and young children have been advised by the Food and Drug Administration to avoid shark, swordfish, king mackerel or tilefish because these fish may contain high levels of mercury [31]. The Environmental Protection Agency also provides water advisories to inform sport fisherman of the areas where fish may be contaminated [82].

Metals may enter foods from certain utensils. Galvanized containers are not suitable for foods because the zinc used for galvanizing is toxic. Cadmium and brass are also undesirable metals for use as food containers. Tin-coated cans are used in food processing, but only very small amounts of tin are generally found in most foods. Acid fruits and fruit juices packed in **lacquered tin-coated cans** and stored in the opened cans in the refrigerator were found to contain increased amounts of both tin and iron [37]. Food stored in opened tin-coated cans may also change in color or develop a metallic taste. Although these changes are undesirable, illness will not result from the canning materials currently used in the food-processing industry.

Small quantities of aluminum are dissolved from utensils in many cooking processes. This is apparently not harmful, but scientists are continuing to study the effects of aluminum in the diet. The element copper is nutritionally essential, yet certain salts of copper are toxic. Cooking green vegetables in copper containers to get a bright green color is no longer practiced because of the danger of toxicity. It has been reported that foods cooked in iron utensils, steel woks, and stainless steel cookware show increases in iron content [63]. Although the increase in iron is small, it is substantial enough to be considered in calculating dietary iron intake. Iron deficiency is widespread, although iron overload may be a problem in some cases.

Foods are packaged in various types of containers from which certain chemical molecules may migrate to the food contained inside. The FDA is responsible for approving food-grade packaging materials to ensure that the type and amount of material that may migrate into the food will not be harmful to the consumer.

lacquered cans cans with an inner lacquer or enamel coating; the coating is of variable composition and overlies the basic tin-coated steel, protecting certain canned foods from discoloration

Pesticide Residues

A 1993 survey by the Food Market Institute found that 79 percent of the participants viewed pesticide residues on foods as a serious health hazard [7]. Today's consumers are less concerned about pesticide residues as compared to other potential food safety issues [34]. Food scientists and an increasing number of consumers consider the predominant risk in the food supply to be microbiological, not chemical. Evidence from the scientific community and from governmental agencies generally supports the premise that the level of pesticides in the American food supply is quite low and represents a negligible health risk [21]. In 1999, the FDA tested a total of 9,438 samples of domestic and imported foods for pesticide residues. Fifty-nine percent of the domestically grown foods and 54 percent of the import samples (including foods from 92 countries) contained no pesticide residues [23]. Those samples with residues were within the limits set by the EPA. Research on pesticide residues will continue to ensure a safe food supply.

The Federal Fungicide, Rodenticide, and Insecticide Act is administered by the EPA, whereby it approves pesticides for specific uses and, after careful study, sets tolerances for residues on foods. These tolerances may be zero. Foods grown in other countries and imported into the United States are regulated under provisions of the law the same as foods grown domestically. The Food Quality Protection Act (FQPA) of 1996 enhances the regulatory roles of the governmental agencies responsible for pesticides. The law applies a uniform safety standard to pesticide residues in raw and processed foods. Pesticide residues in processed foods are no longer defined as food additives; therefore they are not subject to the Delaney Clause of the Federal Food, Drug, and Cosmetic Act. The FQPA applies a general rule to all pesticide residues on foods: that these residues are unsafe, and the foods containing them are adulterated, unless the residue is within the tolerance limit set, or a tolerance exemption is in effect. Tolerance limits are set at "safe" levels, defined as "a reasonable certainty that no harm will result from aggregate exposure to the pesticide chemical residue, including all anticipated dietary exposures and all other exposures for which there is reliable information." The EPA is also required to consider the risks from pesticide residues to infants and children, and the USDA must collect improved data on the consumption patterns of children [56]. The FDA regularly monitors pesticide residues on foods, including in its program the completion of a yearly Total Diet Study [23]. Representative foods that might be consumed by various age and sex groups are purchased from grocery stores across the United States and analyzed in FDA laboratories for pesticide residues, as well as for other contaminants and some nutrients. The 1999 Total Diet Study found the pesticide levels to be well below regulatory standards.

Pesticides are widely used in the intensified agriculture practiced today in the United States. They are intentionally added to agriculture crops, although they are not intended to become part of the consumed food. Pesticides may also get into foods accidentally as they move through soil, water, and air in the environment. Pesticides aid in preventing food destruction during growth and storage; however, they also constitute hazards when misused. For this reason, pesticides today are being increasingly used in combination with nonchemical control practices, including biological control methods and selective plant breeding. The Institute of Food Technologists encourages implementation of such procedures to further enhance the quality of the American food supply and to contribute to a more ecologically favorable agricultural production system [43].

In spite of much scientific evidence supporting the safety of our food supply, many in the public sector continue to be concerned about chemicals. Better communication is needed between persons who regulate risk and those who believe that risk is being imposed upon them. Some preliminary data on attitudes were gathered using focus groups of both consumers and food producers [7]. Four types of concerns about the use of pesticides were identified: adverse effects of residues on foods, worker or applicator safety, adverse environmental consequences, and the use of banned pesticides in foreign countries. An international committee on pesticides, as part of the **Codex Alimentarius Commission,** is also developing guidelines for use [70]. Efforts to develop better communication are continuing.

Codex Alimentarius Commission a group established by the United Nations in 1963 to set international food standards

Naturally Occurring Toxic Substances in Foods

Although the term *natural* is always associated with safety in the minds of some people, certain plants and animals may contain *natural* constituents that are toxic, thereby producing gastrointestinal disturbances or even death when they are consumed in sufficient quantities. Poisonous varieties of mushrooms, mistaken for edible kinds, are a well-known example of toxic plants. Oxalic acid is a constituent of plants such as spinach and beet greens. In large amounts, these may be responsible for oxalic acid poisoning in certain individuals. A very high content of oxalic acid is found in leaves of the rhubarb plant.

Solanine is a water-soluble toxin that may be present in potatoes and increases during sprouting or exposure to light. This toxin is found principally in the skin and in the green portion directly underneath the skin, which may be removed by paring. In recent years, potato-peel products have increased in popularity. A wide range in solanine content of both raw and cooked potato peels has been reported for 12 different varieties of potatoes [12]. The upper ranges in these analyses exceeded the upper safety limit of 20 milligrams per 100 grams of whole potato established for use in releasing new potato varieties. It has been recommended, therefore, that potato varieties with low solanine concentrations be chosen for use in the preparation of commercial peel products.

Toxins have been associated with seafood. Some tropical fish contain poisonous substances. Scombrotoxic fish poisoning can occur when fish such as tuna, mackerel, and bonito have begun to spoil, resulting in high histamine levels in the fish. Symptoms of scombroid poisoning include rash, diarrhea, flushing, sweating, headache, and vomiting. These symptoms occur within two minutes to two hours of consumption [15]. Consuming fish, such as barracuda, that is contaminated by microscopic sea plants (dinoflagellates) causes ciguatera poisoning. Paralytic shellfish poisoning is caused by another dinoflagellate that in high concentrations in the ocean causes "red tide." Shellfish such as mussels, cockles, clams, scallops, oysters, crabs, and lobsters typically from the colder coastal waters of the Pacific and New England states are most often affected. Symptoms of paralytic shellfish poisoning include numbness, tingling, and gastrointestinal upset that begins within one to three hours after eating the contaminated fish [15].

Many toxic substances are found in tiny amounts in plant foods as normal components. Plants may manufacture toxins to protect themselves from environmental predators. It has been suggested that we ingest thousands of times more "natural pesticides" than man-made pesticides. Vegetables of the cabbage family contain substances called **goitrogens** that can depress the activity of the thyroid gland. Legumes contain **protease** inhibitors that may interfere with the digestion of proteins. These inhibitors are destroyed by cooking. Substances called hemagglutinins, which cause **agglutination** of red blood cells, are found in soybeans, peanuts, kidney beans, and wax beans. Most of these substances are

goitrogen a substance that is capable of causing enlargement (goiter) of the thyroid gland in the neck area

protease an enzyme that breaks down or digests proteins

agglutination the sticking together, as with glue

food allergy an abnormal immune response to components in food (usually proteins). Symptoms can include gastrointestinal, cutaneous, and respiratory responses or other symptoms such as laryngeal edema, anaphylatic shock, or hypotension.

anaphylactic shock a multiple system reaction including the gastrointestinal tract, the skin, the respiratory tract, and the cardiovascular system that may be the result of a severe allergic reaction. Severe hypotension and cardiovascular or respiratory collapse can occur within minutes, resulting in death.

destroyed or inactivated in the human digestive tract. Seeds of the *Senecio* genus, which grow among and may contaminate the harvest of grains, contain substances that are toxic to the liver.

Many foods doubtless contain small amounts of naturally occurring substances that could cause toxicity if eaten in excess. However, the amounts of oxalic acid, solanine, and several other natural toxins in foods have not been shown to be toxic in the amounts usually eaten. These toxins, therefore, represent only minor hazards [18].

Food Allergies and Intolerances

Foods safe for the general population may be unsafe for selected individuals who are allergic to specified foods. True allergies are characterized by abnormal immune system response to naturally occurring proteins in foods [75]. **Food allergy** symptoms are varied and can include gastrointestinal, cutaneous, respiratory, or other symptoms. Some individuals experience **anaphylactic shock** that can result in death within minutes of consuming an offending food unless

---

Hot Topics

Genetic Engineering of Foods—A blessing or a curse?

During August 2001, hundreds of anti-biotechnology activists in France laid ruin to two major test sites for genetically modified (GM) corn owned by Monsanto Co. The activists claim that GM crops are the *unsafe* products of greedy multinational agribusiness [40]. And the majority of GM patents are held by American companies [35]. The food safety issue plays well with Europeans who are still anxious about mad cow and hoof-and-mouth scares. The European Union (EU) continues to work for restriction of GM products in the food supply, and other countries are following the trend.

But what are the *real* issues behind this food safety concern? The United States is the largest producer of GM grains, particularly soybeans and corn. Some U.S. officials claim that restrictive regulations are attempted to protect EU farmers from competition—global politics [40]? Perhaps along with some social and environmental politics?

GM crops produced through **recombinant DNA technology,** were originally developed to produce higher crop yields in marginal growth areas, that is, to help poor farmers in developing countries of the world. The United Nations Development Program has emphasized this point—higher production at less cost. All of the existing GM foods have undergone rigorous testing for safety and most scientific evidence supports claims that GM grains are safe. So what is the problem?

It has been suggested that we look to history for an explanation [41]. Remember Pasteur and the biotechnology of pasteurization? Pasteur applied his discovery that microorganisms were a cause of disease and decay to the pasteurization of wine. But it took many years to apply this technique to raw milk, which has been associated, over many years, with disease, illness, and death. Opponents of milk pasteurization gave all kinds of reasons why this biotechnology was harmful—reasons sounding familiar 100 years later. Opposition to new food technologies is not new. Perhaps we can learn from the past to bring opposition groups into the *developmental* process for technology instead of waiting for controversy to surround the *implementation* phase [41].

prompt medical attention is received. Each year, approximately 150 Americans die from a severe allergic reaction [30].

Prevalence of allergies in the United States population is estimated to be 2–2.5 percent of the population overall. Comparatively, children exhibit a higher rate of allergies, ranging from 5 to 8 percent [75]. Children will often grow out of their allergies, whereas adults tend to remain allergic throughout their lives.

The "Big Eight" causes of food allergy are wheat, crustacea such as shrimp and crabs, eggs, fish, peanuts, milk, tree nuts, and soybeans [75]. Individuals who experience the most severe symptoms must carefully avoid even traces of the food responsible for the allergic reaction. Understandable and accurate food labels are essential if allergic individuals are to avoid offending foods. Albumin or caseinate are often found on food labels to represent components of eggs and milk. The National Food Processors Association has developed a voluntary "code of practice" to assure that the most common allergens are labeled in plain language [30]. Good manufacturing practices to reduce cross-contamination of products during processing is another important strategy. Meanwhile, the Food and Drug Administration is studying potential enhancement of labeling regulations.

Food intolerances are different from allergies because food intolerances occur through nonimmunological means. Three categories of intolerances include **anaphylactoid reactions, metabolic food disorders,** and **idiosyncratic illnesses.** Sensitivity to strawberries is an example of an anaphylactoid reaction. Metabolic disorders include the intolerance of lactose or fava beans. Lactose intolerant individuals have an impaired ability to digest lactose, the principle sugar in milk. Sulfite induced asthma has been well documented and represents an idiosyncratic illness because the mechanism for this reaction is not understood [75].

Products of Biotechnology

The breeding of plants using cross-pollination has been a common, acceptable practice for many years in developing new plant varieties. However, along with increased understanding of deoxyribonucleic acid (DNA) and genetics, beginning during the 1950's, a technology was developed by which DNA material (that is, genes) could be taken from an unrelated plant, bacterium, or animal and inserted into the genetic material of the plant being modified. Thus, this new **biotechnology,** called **genetic engineering,** offered the ability to more efficiently introduce new and desirable traits [32].

Many plants have their own natural mechanisms for defense against pests. Plant breeders have been able to produce, with genetic engineering, plants that have increased resistance to pests in the field. Such techniques may also be used to improve the eating quality of a fruit or vegetable. In 1994, the "Flavr Savr" tomato was the first genetically altered food to be sold to U.S. consumers [32]. These tomatoes have increased resistance to softening so that they can be vine ripened, with consequent increased flavor. The safety of such products is regulated by the FDA and potentially negative consequences to the environment are scrutinized by the USDA.

The first food-processing aid produced by a genetically engineered microorganism was approved by the FDA in March 1990—the enzyme *rennin* or *chymosin*. Other enzymes, processing aids, and food ingredients are being devel-

recombinant DNA technology a technique whereby DNA (gene material) may be taken from a bacterium, plant, or animal and inserted into or recombined with the genetic material of another plant, such as corn, for the purpose of improving certain traits in that plant

food intolerances abnormal responses to food that do not involve the immune system

anaphylactoid reactions generally involves several systems, including the gastrointestinal tract, the skin, the respiratory tract, and the cardiovascular system. Death can occur within minutes of consuming an offending food

metabolic food disorders the result of inherited defects in the ability to metabolize some components of a food or from a genetically determined enhanced sensitivity due to an altered metabolic pattern. Lactose intolerance is an example of a metabolic food disorder

idiosyncratic illnesses illnesses attributed to food although the mechanism for the illness is unknown. Sulfite induced asthma is a documented idiosyncratic illness

biotechnology the use of biological systems and organisms to produce goods and services; may include biology, genetics, and biochemistry processes

genetic engineering the use of recombinant DNA or rDNA technology to genetically modify plants and microorganisms. Genetic engineering or modification allows for the efficient transfer of genetic material as compared to traditional cross-breeding, that may require multiple generations.

oped. A growth hormone (rbST) given to cows to increase milk production is derived through the use of new techniques in biotechnology. Implants of certain hormones to enhance growth and feed utilization in beef cattle have been used for many years.

Biotechnology provides an important tool for growth and progress in the area of food and agriculture. However, the entire area of biotechnology may cause safety concerns for some people. Most in the scientific community endorse the safety of genetic engineering stating that the risks are no different than the risks posed by traditional breeding methods [42]. Biotechnology has the potential to ensure safe, abundant, affordable, and highly nutritious foods [36]. Plants can be made resistant to insects and viruses, thus reducing crop losses and the use of chemical insecticides [10]. The public's concerns must therefore be addressed and satisfied by the scientific community. Consumers have been found to be more favorable toward biotechnology when educational information is provided about the risks and benefits [11].

CHAPTER SUMMARY

- Food safety is everyone's responsibility. From the farmer to the processor, the packager, the wholesaler, the retailer, and the consumer, everyone should recognize potential hazards related to food and know how to control them. Foodborne illness is estimated to be the cause of 76 million illnesses per year. Young children, pregnant women, the elderly, people with weakened immune systems, and those taking medication are at the highest risk for foodborne illness.

- The government promotes food safety through oversight and monitoring by the USDA, FDA, EPA, and CDC.

- Consumers have important responsibilities for food safety. Studies have found many consumers do not follow safe food handling practices. Fight-Bac, "Thermy" and the Dietary Guidelines provide safe food handling information for consumers.

- HACCP is a coordinated system composed of seven steps for ensuring the safety of a food product. HACCP is used in food processing and many foodservice operations. Through the assessment of risks and hazards, identification of critical control points, and establishment of preventive measures, corrective actions, record-keeping procedures, and system verification procedures, HACCP reduces the risk of foodborne illness.

- Improper holding temperatures, poor personal hygiene, contaminated equipment, inadequate cooling, and food from unsafe sources are the leading causes of foodborne illness. Four critical messages to reduce the incidence of foodborne illness include: Wash hands and surfaces often, don't cross-contaminate, cook to proper temperatures, and refrigerate promptly.

- Ionizing radiation may be used for some foods to reduce the risk of foodborne illness. Foods are irradiated with gamma rays or electron beams that destroy bacteria in food. Irradiated foods are regulated by the FDA and USDA and must be labeled with the Radura symbol.

- Food intoxication and food infection are two general types of bacterial foodborne diseases. *Salmonella, Campylobacter jejuni, Escherichia coli, Yersinia enterocolitica, Listeria monocytogenes, Shigella, and Vibrio parahaemolyticus, Staphlococcus aureas, Clostridium perfringens,* and *Clostridium botulinum* are bacteria that cause foodborne illness. Certain foods and food handling practices are associated with the growth of these microorganisms.

- Molds, yeasts, parasites, and viruses are additional types of organisms that may cause foodborne illness. The globalization of the food supply is creating the potential for the American public to be exposed to many more parasites than in the past. Some parasites such as *Anisaskis simplex* are found in fish in U.S. coastal waters. *Trichinella spiralis* is a parasite associated primarily with undercooked pork and game meats. Viruses are an important cause of foodborne illness in America and are commonly the result of poor personal hygiene on the part of food handlers or contaminated water.

- Toxic substances may contaminate the environment in which people, plants, and animals live. The FDA has advised pregnant women, nursing women, and young children to avoid some fish due to the potential levels of mercury that may contaminate the fish. Packaging and containers can be another source of food contamination. Based on standards set by the EPA, pesticides used on food crops are monitored by the FDA and USDA. Testing has shown pesticide residues to be low in the United States food supply.

- Foods safe for the general population may be unsafe for selected individuals who have food allergies or intolerances. The "Big Eight" causes of food allergy are wheat, crustacea such as shrimp and crabs, eggs, fish, peanuts, milk, tree nuts, and soybeans. Understandable and accurate food labels are essential so that allergic individuals can avoid offending foods.

- Biotechnology permits the development of new plants through more precise methods than cross-pollination. Genes may be inserted into a plant to provide resistance to pests, higher nutritional value, greater crop yields, or improved sensory qualities. Most in the scientific community endorse the safety of these biotechnology techniques.

KEY TERMS

food safety
pasteurize
sterilize
microbiology
hazard
risk
critical control point
standard operating procedures
high risk foods or potentially hazardous foods
cross-contamination
temperature danger zone
food intoxication
food infection
fermentation
spores
pH
putrefactive fermentations
pathogenic bacteria
GRAS

microencapsulation
salmonellosis
gastroenteritis
enteropathogenic
hemorrhagic colitis
septicemia
mycotoxins
protozoa
hepatitis
mollusks
jaundice
lacquered cans
Codex Alimentarius Commission
goitrogen
protease
agglutination
food allergy
anaphylactic shock
recombinant DNA technology
food intolerances

anaphylactoid reactions   biotechnology
metabolic food disorders   genetic engineering
idiosyncratic illnesses

STUDY QUESTIONS

1. Why is food safety so important and who is most at risk for foodborne illness?

2. Identify departments and agencies in the United States government who monitor and regulate the safety of food.

3. What is HACCP?
   a. What general steps are involved in its implementation?
   b. Discuss its role in helping to prevent foodborne illness.

4. List and discuss several precautions that should always be taken in preparing, cooking, and storing foods to ensure their safety for human consumption.

5. Identify the temperatures recommended by FightBac and the FDA for the safe end point cooking temperature for ground beef, chicken, and pork. Why are the temperature recommendations of FightBac and FDA different?

6. Explain how to use a stem thermometer properly. Include a description of how to calibrate thermometers and how to take the temperature of thin foods such as hamburgers.

7. Discuss the proper refrigeration of foods. (a) How should food be stored in the refrigerator to prevent cross-contamination? (b) Describe storage methods for foods so cooling is rapid.

8. Why is it extremely important that food handlers observe appropriate sanitary procedures when working with food? (a) Explain the process for washing hands thoroughly. (b) Identify multiple times before, during, and after food preparation that hands should be washed.

9. Compare the optimum conditions for growth of molds, yeasts, and bacteria in foods.

10. Explain the difference between *food infection* and *food intoxication*. Give examples of each.

11. For each type of food poisoning listed below, (a) indicate if it is an infection or an intoxication, (b) list the usual symptoms, (c) list the types of food most likely to be involved, and (d) suggest measures that should prevent the occurrence of an outbreak of illness.
   a. Salmonellosis
   b. *Campylobacter jejuni* poisoning
   c. *Escherichia coli* 0157:H7 poisoning
   d. Yersiniosis
   e. Listeriosis
   f. Staphylococcal poisoning
   g. *Clostridium perfringens* poisoning
   h. Botulism

12. Describe some other types of bacterial food poisoning.

13. What is *trichinosis*? How is it caused? How might it be prevented?

14. Describe examples of potential food-related problems that may result from:
- **a.** Mycotoxins
- **b.** Animal parasites
- **c.** Viruses
- **d.** Environmental contaminants
- **e.** Naturally occurring toxicants

15. What are food allergies and food intolerances? (a) Identify the "Big Eight" causes of food allergies. (b) Discuss the importance of food labels for those who are allergic to foods.

16. Describe the monitoring process for pesticides in the United States food supply.

17. What is meant by biotechnology? Give some examples of its use in improving the food supply.

REFERENCES

1. Altrekruse, S. F., Yang, S., Timbo, B. B., & Angulo, F. J. (1999). A multistate survey of consumer food-handling and food-consumption practices. *American Journal of Preventative Medicine, 16*(3), 216–221.

2. American Dietetic Association. (1997). Position of the American Dietetic Association on food and water safety. *Journal of the American Dietetic Association, 97,* 184–189.

3. American Dietetic Association. (1997). Position of the American Dietetic Association on management of health care food and nutrition services. *Journal of the American Dietetic Association, 97,* 1427–1430.

4. American Dietetic Association. (2000). Position of the American Dietetic Association: Food irradiation. *Journal of the American Dietetic Association, 100,* 246–253.

5. Anderson, J. B., Shuster, T. A, Gee, E., Hansen, K., & Mendenhall, V. T. (2000). A camera's view of consumer food handling and preparation practices. Final report prepared for the U.S. Food and Drug Administration. North Logan, UT: Spectrum Consulting.

6. Association of Women's Health, Obstetric, and Neonatal Nurses, International Food Information Council, U.S. Department of Agriculture, and U.S. Department of Health and Human Services. (2001, September). Listeriosis and pregnancy: What is your risk? Brochure retrieved May 22, 2002, from www.fsis.usda.gov/OA/pubs/lm_tearsheet.htm

7. Auld, G. W., Kendall, P. A., & Chipman, H. (1994). Consumer and producer perceptions and concerns regarding pesticide use. *Food Technology, 48*(3), 100.

8. Beard, T. D. (1991). HACCP and the home: The need for consumer education. *Food Technology, 45*(6), 123.

9. Bennett, G. A., & Richard, J. L. (1996). Influence of processing on *Fusarium* mycotoxins in contaminated grains. *Food Technology, 50*(5), 235.

10. Blackburn, G. L. (2001). Feeding 9 billion people—A job for food technologists. *Food Technology, 55*(6), 106.

11. Bruhn, C., & Mason, A. (2002). Community leader response to educational information about biotechnology. *Journal of Food Science, 67,* 399–403.

12. Bushway, R. J., Bureau, J. L., & McGann, D. F. (1983). Alpha-chaconine and alpha-solanine content of potato peels and potato-peel products. *Journal of Food Science, 48,* 84.

13. Buzby, J. C., & Roberts, T. (1996). ERS updates U.S. foodborne disease costs for seven pathogens. *Food Review, 19*(3), 20.

14. Centers for Disease Control and Prevention, Division of Bacterial and Mycotic Diseases. (2001). Disease information. Retrieved June 26, 2002, from http://www.cdc.gov/ncidod/dbmd/diseaseinfo/

15. Centers for Disease Control and Prevention, Division of Bacteria and Mycotic Diseases. (2002). Disease information: Marine toxins. Retrieved June 26, 2002, from http://www.cdc.gov/ncidod/dbmd/diseaseinfo/marinetoxins_g.htm

16. Centers for Disease Control and Prevention, Division of Parasitic Diseases. (1999). Fact sheet: Trichinosis. Retrieved June 26, 2002, from http://www.cdc.gov/ncidod/dpd/parasites/trichinosis/factsht_trichinosis.htm

17. Clemens, R. A. (2001). Friendly bacteria—a functional food? *Food Technology*, 55(1), 27.

18. Crocco, S. (1981). Potato sprouts and greening potatoes: Potential toxic reaction. *Journal of the American Medical Association*, 245, 625.

19. Cross, H. R. (1996). HACCP: Pivotal change for the meat industry. *Food Technology*, 50(8), 236.

20. Crutchfield, S. R. & Roberts, T. (2000). Food safety efforts accelerate in the 1990's. *Food Review*, 23(3), 44–49.

21. Dunaif, G. E., & Krysinski, E. P. (1992). Managing the pesticide challenge: A food processor's model. *Food Technology*, 46(3), 72.

22. Educational Foundation of the National Restaurant Association. (2002). *ServSafe Coursebook*, 2nd ed. Chicago, IL: National Restaurant Association.

23. Food and Drug Administration, Center for Food Safety and Applied Nutrition. (2000, April). FDA pesticide program residue monitoring, 1993–1999. Retrieved June 23, 2001 from http://www.cfsan.fda.gov/~dms/pesrpts.html

24. Food and Drug Administration, Center for Food Safety and Applied Nutrition. (n.d.). Bad Bug Book. Retrieved June 25, 2002, from http://www.cfsan.fda.gov/~mow/intro.html

25. Food and Drug Administration, U.S. Department of Agriculture, U.S. Environmental Protection Agency, and Centers for Disease Control and Prevention. (1997). Food safety from farm to table: A national food safety initiative, Report to the President. Retrieved June 24, 2002 from http://vm.cfsan.fda.gov/~dms/fsreport.html

26. Food and Drug Administration, U.S. Department of Agriculture, and Centers for Disease Control and Prevention. (1998). Guidance for industry: Guide to minimize microbial food safety hazards for fresh fruits and vegetables. Retrieved June 24, 2002, from http://www.cfsan.fda.gov/~dms/prodguid.html

27. Food Safety and Inspection Service, U.S. Department of Agriculture. (2000). For physicians: A foodborne illness primer. *The Food Safety Educator*, 5 (3), 1. Retrieved June 25, 2002, from http://www.fsis.usda.gov/OA/educator/educator5-3.htm

28. Food Safety and Inspection Service, U.S. Department of Agriculture. (2000, May). USDA launches food safety education campaign to encourage use of food thermometers in meat, poultry, and egg products. Retrieved June 24, 2002, from http://www.fsis.usda.gov/OA/thermy/newsfeature.htm

29. Food safety perspectives. (1997). *Food & Nutrition News*, 69(1),1. National Cattlemen's Beef Association.

30. Formanek, R. (2001). Food allergies: When food becomes the enemy. *FDA Consumer*, 35(4).

31. Formanek, R. (2001). Highlights of FDA food safety efforts: Fruit juice, mercury in fish. *FDA Consumer*, 3(2).

32. Formanek, R. (2001). Proposed rules issued for bioengineered foods. *FDA Consumer*, 35(2).

33. Giese, J. (1993). *Salmonella* reduction process receives approval. *Food Technology*, 47(1), 110.

34. Giese, J. (2000). Pesticide analysis. *Food Technology, 54*(12), 64–65.

35. Gilmore, R. (2000). GMOs: Progress at a cost. *Food Technology,* 54(6), 146.

36. Greger, J. L. (2000). Biotechnology: Mobilizing dietitians to be a resource. *Journal of the American Dietetic Association, 100,* 1306–1308.

37. Greger, J. L., & Baier, M. (1981). Tin and iron content of canned and bottled foods. *Journal of Food Science, 46,* 1751.

38. Hardt-English, P., York, G., Stier, R., & Cocotas, P. (1990). Staphylococcal food poisoning outbreaks caused by canned mushrooms from China. *Food Technology, 44*(12), 76.

39. Hingley, A. (1999). Campylobacter: Low-profile bug is food poisoning leader. *FDA Consumer, 33*(5).

40. Hollingsworth, P. (2001). GMO safety: A Trojan horse. *Food Technology,* 55(10), 20.

41. Hotchkiss, J. H. (2001). Pasteur and biotechnology: Lessons from the past. *Food Technology,* 55(9), 146.

42. Institute of Food Technologists' Expert Report on Biotechnology and Foods. (2000). Human food safety evaluation of rDNA biotechnology-derived foods. *Food Technology, 54*(9), 53–61.

43. Institute of Food Technologists' Expert Panel on Food Safety and Nutrition. (1990). Organically grown foods. *Food Technology, 44*(6), 26.

44. Institute of Food Technologists' Expert Panel on Food Safety and Nutrition. (1992). Government regulation of food safety: Interaction of scientific and societal forces. *Food Technology, 46*(1), 73.

45. Institute of Food Technologists' Expert Panel on Food Safety and Nutrition. (1995). Foodborne illness: Role of home food handling practices. *Food Technology, 49*(4), 119.

46. Institute of Food Technologists' Expert Panel on Food Safety and Nutrition. (1997). Virus transmission via food. *Food Technology, 51*(4), 71.

47. Jackson, G. J. (1997). *Cyclospora*—Still another new foodborne pathogen. *Food Technology, 51*(1), 120.

48. Killinger, K. M., Hunt, M. C., Campbell, R. E., & Kropf, D. H. (2000). Factors affecting premature browning during cooking of store-purchased ground beef. *Journal of Food Science, 65,* 585–587.

49. Lindsay, R. E., Krissinger, W. A., & Fields, B. F. (1986). Microwave vs. conventional oven cooking of chicken: Relationship of internal temperature to surface contamination by *Salmonella typhimurium. Journal of the American Dietetic Association, 86,* 373.

50. Lusk, J. L., Fox, J. A., & McIlvain, C. L. (1999). Consumer acceptance of irradiated meat. *Food Technology, 53*(3), 56–59.

51. Mead, P. S., Slutsker, L., Dietz, V., McCaig, L. F., Bressee, J. S., Shapiro, C., Griffen, P. M., & Tauxe, R.V. (1999). Food-related illness and death in the United States. *Emerging Infectious Diseases, 5,* 607–625.

52. Meer, R. R. & Misner, S. L. (2000). Food safety knowledge and behavior of expanded food and nutrition education program participants in Arizona. *Journal of Food Protection, 63,* 1725–1731.

53. Mermelstein, N. H. (1993). Controlling *E. coli* 0157:H7 in meat. *Food Technology, 47*(4), 90.

54. Mermelstein, N. H. (2000). E-beam irradiated beef reaches the market, papaya and gamma-irradiated beef to follow. *Food Technology, 54*(7), 88–92.

55. Mermelstein, N. H. (2001). Sanitizing meat. *Food Technology, 55*(3), 64–68.

56. Mintzer, E. S., & Osteen, C. (1997). New uniform standards for pesticide residues in food. *Food Review, 20*(1), 18.

57. Mycotoxins and food safety. (1986). *Food Technology, 40*(5), 59.

58. National Restaurant Association. (2002). 2002 Restaurant Industry Pocket Handbook. Washington, DC: National Restaurant Association.

59. Ollinger-Snyder, P., & Matthews, M. E. (1996). Food safety: Review and implications for dietitians and dietetic technicians. *Journal of the American Dietetic Association, 96,* 163.

60. Olsen, S. J., MacKinon, L. C., Goulding, J. S., Bean, N. H., & Slutsker, L. (2000). Surveillance for foodborne disease outbreaks—United States 1993–1997. *Morbidity and Mortality Weekly Report, 49*(SS01): 1–51.

61. Orlandi, P. A., Chu, D. M. Y., Bier, J. W., & Jackson, G. J. (2001). Scientific status summary: Parasites and the food supply. *Food Technology, 56*(4), 72–81.

62. Park, D. L. (1993). Controlling aflatoxin in food and feed. *Food Technology, 47*(10), 92.

63. Park, J., & Brittin, H. C. (1997). Increased iron content of food due to stainless steel cookware. *Journal of the American Dietetic Association, 97,* 659.

64. President's Council on Food Safety. (2001, January). Food safety strategic plan. Retrieved June 24, 2002, from http://www.foodsafety.gov/~fsg/cstrpl-4.html

65. Ralston, K., Starke, Y., Brent, P., & Riggins, T. (2000). Awareness of risks changing how hamburgers are cooked. *Food Review, 23*(2), 44–50.

66. Resurreccion, A. V. A., & Galvez, F. C. F. (1999). Will consumers buy irradiated beef? *Food Technology, 53*(3), 52–55.

67. Ross, E. E., Guyer, L., Varnes, J., & Rodrick, G. (1994). *Vibrio vulnificus* and molluscan shellfish: The necessity of education for high-risk individuals. *Journal of the American Dietetic Association, 94,* 312.

68. Ryser, E. T., & Marth, E. H. (1989). "New" foodborne pathogens of public health significance. *Journal of the American Dietetic Association,* 89, 948.

69. Saguy, I. (1992). Simulated growth of *Listeria monocytogenes* in refrigerated foods stored at variable temperatures. *Food Technology, 46*(3), 69.

70. Sandusky, C. B. (1996). Developments of the Codex Committee on pesticide residues. *Food Technology, 50*(7), 20.

71. Setiabuhdi, M., Theis, M., & Norback, J. (1997). Integrating hazard analysis and critical control point (HACCP) and sanitation for verifiable food safety. *Journal of the American Dietetic Association, 97,* 889.

72. Shah, N. P. (2001). Functional foods from probiotics and prebiotics. *Food Technology,* 55(11), 46.

73. Shiferaw, B., Yang, S., Cieslak, P., Vugia, D., Marcus, R., Koehler, J., Deneen, V., & Angulo, F. (2000). Prevalence of high-risk food consumption and food handling practices among adults: A multistate survey, 1996–1997. *Journal of Food Protection, 63,* 1538–1543.

74. Siuta-Cruce, P. & Goulet, J. (2001). Improving probiotic survival rates. *Food Technology,* 55(10), 36.

75. Taylor, S. L., & Hefle, S. L. (2001). Food allergies and other sensitivities. *Food Technology,* 55(9), 68–83.

76. U.S. Center for Disease Control and Prevention. (2002). Preliminary FoodNet data on the incidence of foodborne illnesses—selected sites, United States, 2001. *Morbity and Mortality Weekly Reports, 51*(15), 325–329. Retrieved May 7, 2002, from http://www.cdc.gov/mmwr/preview/mmwrhtml/mm5115a3.htm

77. U.S. Department of Agriculture. (1994). *Complete guide to home canning.* Agriculture Information Bulletin No. 539. Washington, DC: U.S. Government Printing Office.

78. U.S. Department of Agriculture and U.S. Department of Health and Human Services. (2000). *Nutrition and your health: Dietary guidelines for Americans, 5th edition.* Home and Garden Bulletin No. 232.

79. U.S. Department of Health and Human Services. (2002, April). Foodborne illnesses post dramatic six-year decline. *HHS News.* Retrieved June 24, 2002, from http://www.hhs.gov/news/press/2002pres/20020418a.html

80. U.S. Department of Health and Human Services, Public Health Service, and Food and Drug Administration. (2001). 2001 Food Code. Retrieved June 24, 2002, from http://www.cfsan.fda.gov/~dms/foodcode.html

81. U.S. Department of Health and Human Services, Food and Drug Administration. (2001). FDA publishes final rule to increase safety of fruit and vegetable juices. Retrieved June 24, 2002, from http://www.cfsan.fda.gov/~lrd/hhsjuic4.html

82. U.S. Environmental Protection Agency. (2001, June). Fact sheet: Mercury update: Impact on fish advisories. EPA 823-F-01-011.

83. Vangelova, L. (1995). Botulinum toxin. *FDA Consumer, 29*(10),16.

84. Williamson, D. M., Gravani, R. B., & Lawless, H. T. (1992). Correlating food safety knowledge with home food-preparation practices. *Food Technology, 46*(5),94.

85. Wood, R. C., MacDonald, K. L., & Osterholm, M. T. (1992). *Campylobacter* enteritis outbreaks associated with drinking raw milk during youth activities: A 10-year review of outbreaks in the United States. *Journal of the American Medical Association, 268,* 3228.

86. Young, A., Taylor, J., & Fix, J. L. (1999, August). A killer in our food. *Detroit Free Press.* Retrieved May 22, 2002, from http://www.freepress.com/outbreak/

Food Regulations and Standards

4

 Supermarket shelves hold thousands of different food items from which we may choose when shopping. As we make our selections, we all like to feel confident that we are getting our money's worth. But how can we be assured that we are receiving the quality and safety for which we are paying?

Most food processors and manufacturers work hard to establish and maintain reputations for good quality and safety in their products. They want to keep customers coming back again and again. The government also plays a role, through legislation and regulation, in ensuring quality and safety in the foods we purchase. Government intervention in this area is not new. History is filled with examples of concern about, and resulting regulation of, food adulteration [11]. From the dietary laws of Moses to Roman statutes to early English laws enacted by Parliament, regulation of food safety has been regarded as an important function of government. Knowledge of English laws concerning food was brought to America by the early settlers and similar legislation was later enacted in state laws. Since passage of the first Pure Food and Drug Act of 1906, the role of the federal government has expanded in this area. Various federal agencies now have responsibilities to regulate the food supply, including the setting of standards, control of adulteration and misbranding, promotion of **good manufacturing practices (GMPs),** approval of **food additives, inspection,** and **grading.** By promulgating regulations and setting standards, the government is attempting to implement the constitutional mandate to "promote the general welfare."

good manufacturing practices recommended rules for maintaining sanitation, safety, and quality assurance to be followed in a food processing plant

food additive a substance, other than usual ingredients, that is added to a food product for a specific purpose, for example, flavoring, preserving, stabilizing, thickening

inspection the examining of food products or processes carefully and critically in order to assure proper sanitary practices, labeling, and/or safety for the consumer

grading the examining of food products and classifying them according to quality, such as Grade A, B, or C, based on defined standards

FOOD AND DRUG ADMINISTRATION

The U.S. Food and Drug Administration (FDA) is housed in the U.S. Department of Health and Human Services (HHS) and includes the Center for Food Safety and Applied Nutrition, with responsibility for much of the policy and enforcement having to do with human food [15]. The Federal Food, Drug, and Cosmetic Act of 1938 and its several amendments are administered by the FDA, which regulates all food except red meats, poultry, and eggs. These are the responsibility of the U.S. Department of Agriculture (USDA).

Much activity in the FDA is also devoted to enforcement of the Fair Packaging and Labeling Act and the 1990 Nutrition Labeling and Education Act (discussed in Chapter 2). Sanitation in food-processing plants, foodservice sanitation, and interstate travel facilities also comes under the jurisdiction of the

FDA. The FDA regulates seafood safety and requires seafood processors to adopt the Hazard Analysis Critical Control Points (HACCP) program to further ensure the safety of the nation's seafood [40]. This program focuses on prevention of product contamination rather than on detection of contaminated products [43]. The FDA published the final rule requiring juice processors to implement HACCP in 2001 [34]. The FDA recommends that other food-processing plants also use the HACCP system. (HACCP is discussed in Chapter 3).

Under the Federal Food, Drug, and Cosmetic Act, the FDA sets three kinds of mandatory standards for products being shipped across state lines: standards of identity, standards of minimum quality, and standards of fill of container. By law, anyone may participate in the rule-making process by commenting in writing on the FDA proposals [7] and sending these comments directly to the FDA. When the FDA plans to issue a new regulation or revise an existing one, it places an announcement of such in the *Federal Register,* which also provides background on the issue and gives the address for submitting written comments by a specified deadline. The *Federal Register* is available in many public libraries and colleges and on the Internet. Public input is carefully considered by the FDA.

Federal Register provides citizens with official text of federal laws, presidential documents, administrative regulations and notices. Also included are descriptions of federal organizations, programs and activities. The *Federal Register* may be accessed on the Internet from http://www.archives.gov/federal_register

Standards of Identity

The basic purpose for setting standards of identity for food products is to "promote honesty and fair dealing in the interest of consumers." Standards of identity define what a food product must be or must contain if it is to be legally labeled and sold by its common or usual name. The standard also lists optional ingredients that may be used but are not required. For example, the standard of identity for mayonnaise specifies the ingredients it must contain—oil, egg, and an acid component—and requires that at least 65 percent oil be included in the finished dressing. Prior to the establishment of standards of identity, consumers could not be assured that a product, such as mayonnaise or ice cream, was composed of the generally expected ingredients.

Standards of identity have been established for a large number of food products, including bakery and cereal products, cacao products, canned fruits and vegetables, fruit butters and preserves, fish and shellfish, eggs and egg products, margarine, nut products, dressings for foods, cheeses and cheese products, milk and cream, frozen desserts, macaroni and noodle products, and tomato products. Only after many public hearings and much discussion were the standards set. Both food industry representatives and consumers had opportunities for input.

Many of the standards of identity for food were established in the early years following passage of the Federal Food, Drug and Cosmetic Act in 1938. The FDA has promulgated few new standards of identity since 1970. In 1998, the standards of identity for several enriched grain products were amended to require fortification with folic acid [35]. However, to permit the use of new approved food additives, such as emulsifiers, thickeners, and so on, without amending existing standards each time, the FDA has increased the flexibility of many standards. It has done so by modifying the requirement to specifically list certain processing aids so that *any* "safe and suitable" functional ingredient is permitted [10].

Some of the standards of identity include high amounts of nutrients, such as fat, that consumers would want to avoid. Prior to the 1990 Nutrition Labeling and Education Act, reduced fat foods that did not meet the standards of identity were labeled as *imitation* or with completely different names such as ice milk instead of ice cream. FDA has defined *imitation* solely in terms of nutritional inferiority—it must be labeled "imitation" only if it is not nutritionally equal to the food that it is imitating or replacing. The FDA emphasized that a new food product, rather than being called "imitation," should have its own descriptive name.

With the new regulations in the 1990 Nutrition Labeling and Education Act, reduced fat versions of foods such as sour cream, mayonnaise, and ice cream may still be called by their respective names even if the traditional standard of identity has not been met. To maintain the standard name, these reduced fat versions must (a) be labeled "low fat" or "light" as appropriate, (b) not be nutritionally inferior (Vitamin A must be added to reduced fat products to replace the Vitamin A lost when the fat was removed), (c) perform like the standard product, and (d) contain a significant amount of any mandatory ingredients [29, 38].

FDA revoked the standards of identity for many fat-reduced milk and other dairy products in 1996 so that milk labeling could become consistent with the existing labeling requirements for other products with nutrient content claims such as "fat free," "low-fat," and others [16]. As a result of this change milk previously labeled as skim is now labeled nonfat milk.

Although prior to 1993, foods with a standard of identity were not required to list ingredients, standardized foods now must list ingredients on the label [25]. Essentially, all foods, including those with a standard of identity, are subject to nutrition labeling under the 1990 Nutrition Labeling and Education Act.

Standards of Minimum Quality

Standards of minimum quality have been set for several canned fruits and vegetables, specifying minimum requirements for such characteristics as tenderness, color, and freedom from defects. If a food does not meet the minimum standard, it must be labeled "below standard in quality; good food—not high grade." Other words may be substituted for the second part of the statement to show in what respect the product is substandard, such as "below standard in quality; excessively broken." The consumer seldom sees a product with a substandard label at retail stores. Standards of minimum quality, as well as other grade standards, are indications of quality characteristics and are not concerned specifically with safety. Both lower- and higher-grade products are safe to eat.

Standards of Fill of Container

Standards of fill of container state, for certain processed foods, how full a food container must be. These standards aim to avoid deception by preventing the selling of air or water in place of food. They are needed especially for products that are made up of a number of pieces packed in a liquid, such as various canned vegetables, or for products, such as nuts and ready-to-eat cereals, that shake down after filling.

Sanitation Requirements

One basic purpose of the Federal Food, Drug, and Cosmetic Act is the protection of the public from articles that may be deleterious, that are unclean or decomposed, or that have been exposed to unsanitary conditions which may contaminate the article with filth or render it injurious to health. The law requires that foods be protected from contamination at all stages of production and that they be produced in sanitary facilities. Foods may not be distributed if they contain repulsive or offensive matter considered to be filth, whether or not it poses actual physical danger to an individual. Filth includes rodent hair and excreta, insects or insect parts and excreta, maggots, larvae, pollution from the excrement of humans and animals, or other materials that, because of their repulsiveness, would not be eaten knowingly.

The Federal Food, Drug, and Cosmetic Act declared any food prepared, packed, or held under unsanitary conditions to be adulterated. Therefore, the FDA has produced directives called *current good manufacturing practices (GMPs)*. These directives establish regulations regarding many facets of the food-manufacturing process, including requirements for cleanliness; education, training, and supervision of workers; design and ease of cleaning and maintenance of buildings, facilities, and equipment; and adequate record keeping to ensure quality control.

Labeling

The FDA shares with the Federal Trade Commission (FTC) the responsibility for enforcing fair packaging and labeling laws. The USDA is also involved for some foods.

If a food is packaged, the following must appear on the label:

1. Name and address of the manufacturer, packer, or distributor
2. Accurate statement of the net amount of food in the package—weight, measure, or count
3. Common or usual name of the product (i.e., peaches, and the form, i.e., sliced, whole, or chopped)
4. Ingredients listed by their common names in order of their predominance by weight
5. Nutrition information, with few exceptions, as mandated by the 1990 Nutrition Labeling and Education Act (discussed in Chapter 2)

certified colors synthetic colors tested on a batch-by-batch basis and certified by the FDA as having met set standards

protein hydrolysate the resulting mixture when a protein is broken down or hydrolyzed, by an enzyme or other means, to smaller units called peptides and amino acids

caseinate a protein salt derived from milk

Food additives are required to be listed as ingredients. Spices and flavors may be simply mentioned as such, without each specific item being named. The presence of any artificial colors or flavors must be indicated as such. **Certified colors,** such as FD&C Yellow No. 5, commonly known as tartrazine, must be listed by name. The original source of **protein hydrolysates** must be stated. **Caseinate** must be identified as a milk derivative in foods that claim to be nondairy, such as coffee whiteners. Beverages that are claimed to contain juice must have the total percentage of juice identified on the label [19]. Unpasteurized, packaged fruit juices also must include a warning label informing consumers of the risk of unpasteurized juice [4]. However, this labeling requirement will be phased out as processors implement HACCP according to the new rule published in 2001.

Food Additives

The roles of food additives have become more prominent in recent years as the production of processed foods has increased. Several issues concerning food safety have been raised by consumer groups. The popular press and television news programs have paid particular attention to such alleged hazards in the U.S. food supply as animal drug residues in meat and poultry and pesticide residues on fruit crops. Scientific issues that previously were discussed only in journals and other scholarly publications today often make headlines, with the scientific terminology translated into the vernacular. If such information is effectively reported from a sound scientific basis, it provides the advantage of educating consumers so that they can make informed choices. However, if it is not explained well or misrepresented in any way, it may create special challenges for food professionals both in industry and governmental regulatory agencies in adequately educating the public [26]. It is very important that accurate information reach the public and that scientifically unjustified concern and fear not be created.

Definition.   What is a food additive? Under a broad definition, it is any substance that becomes part of a food product either when it is added *intentionally* or when it *incidentally* becomes part of the food. Examples of incidental additives are substances that may migrate from the packaging material into a food. The amount of additive involved in these cases is extremely small, but is nevertheless regulated [34].

The legal definition of *food additive* extends only to those substances that must receive special approval from the FDA after they have been thoroughly tested for safety and before they can be used in food. In addition to these specially tested and approved additives, the FDA maintains an official list of other substances added to foods that are "generally recognized as safe" (GRAS) for human consumption by experts in the field. Although GRAS substances do not require the detailed clearance for safety that is specified for legally defined food additives, they are evaluated and reevaluated for safety by the FDA on a case-by-case basis. Ongoing industry assessment of GRAS substances also occurs. A Flavor and Extract Manufacturers' Association's Expert Panel completed a comprehensive assessment of the GRAS flavoring substances in 1985, with the completion of a second assessment anticipated during 2005 [22]. Occasionally, substances may be removed from the GRAS list as more sophisticated analytical tools and methodologies for evaluation of safety are developed. It should be emphasized that there is an ongoing process of reassessment and evaluation by the FDA on all issues of food safety, including additives.

Justifiable uses.   An additive is intentionally used for one or more of the following general purposes.

1. To maintain or improve nutritional quality. Vitamins and minerals are used to fortify some foods when these nutrients may have been lost in processing or when they might be otherwise lacking in the usual diet.

2. To enhance the keeping quality with consequent reduction in food waste. Freshness may be maintained by the use of additives to retard spoilage, preserve natural color and flavor, and retard the development of rancid odors in fats.

3. To enhance the attractiveness of foods. Many additives will make food look and taste better. Natural and synthetic flavoring agents, colors, and flavor enhancers serve this purpose.

4. To provide essential aids in processing or preparation. A large variety of additives are used to give body and texture to foods as stabilizers or thickeners,

to distribute water-soluble and fat-soluble particles evenly together as emulsifiers, to control the acidity or alkalinity, to retain moisture as humectants, to leaven or make rise many baked products, to prevent caking or lumping, and to perform other functions.

Legislation. The Federal Food, Drug, and Cosmetic Act governs the use of additives in food entering interstate commerce. The FDA recalls products found to be adulterated. However, state and local governments are responsible for regulations concerning the safety and quality of foods produced and sold within a state.

Federal legislation of foods began in a serious way in 1906 with the passage of the Pure Food and Drugs Act and the Meat Inspection Act [46]. The USDA initially administered both of these pieces of legislation. The chief chemist of the USDA was Harvey Wiley. Dr. Wiley was an early pioneer involved in the struggle for adequate laws to protect the public's food supply (Figure 4-1). During the late 1800s and early 1900s he tried various tactics, including feeding measured amounts of chemical preservatives to 12 young volunteers in a so-called "poison squad" experiment, to increase understanding of food additive safety and highlight food safety concerns. These volunteers were fed borax, sali-

(a)

(b)

Figure 4-1
(a) Members of the "Poison Squad" dine together consuming wholesome meals containing potentially harmful substances. This Scientific investigation, conducted by Dr. Harvey W. Wiley, dramatized the need for pure food legislation. (Courtesy of FDA)
(b) William R. Carter was hired as the chef for the Poison Squad experiments. He later earned a degree in pharmaceutical chemistry and worked in FDA laboratories for 43 years. (Courtesy of FDA)

cylic, sulphurous, and benzoic acids, and formaldehyde, over a five-year period
to assess if these chemicals were injurious to health [13]. The "poison squad"
experiment gained the attention of citizens and helped to convince Congress
and the President of the need for pure food legislation. Finally, in 1906, the first
Pure Food and Drug Act was passed. It was a beginning.

Although the first legislation on foods was implemented by the USDA, it
was later decided that, for products not of animal origin, the emphasis should
be less on agriculture and more on health. Thus, in 1940, the FDA was transferred out of the USDA into the Federal Security Agency. In 1953, FDA was
moved again to the Department of Health, Education, and Welfare, which became the Department of Health and Human Services in 1979 [30, 46].

The original 1906 pure foods act was completely revised in 1938 and re-
named the Federal Food, Drug, and Cosmetic Act. Among other things, the
1938 law required truthful labeling of additives. Several amendments to the
Federal Food, Drug, and Cosmetic Act have been passed to strengthen the law
and keep up with changes in food technology and medical science.

Pesticide amendments. The Miller Pesticide Amendment of 1954 was
passed to establish a procedure for setting safe levels or tolerances for pesticide
residues on fresh fruits, vegetables, and other raw agricultural commodities.
Growers were using many new pesticides to produce more and better crops,
and some of these chemicals left a residue on the food even at harvest. The
safety of these incidental residues had to be determined and regulations set.

The Food Quality Protection Act was signed into law in 1996. This act
amended the Federal Food, Drug, and Cosmetic Act and the Federal Insecticide, Fungicide, and Rodenticide Act to (a) include a new pesticide safety standard, (b) resolve inconsistencies in the regulation of pesticide residues on raw
and processed commodities, (c) provide special protection for children and infants, and (d) require periodic re-evaluation of pesticides [6]. The safety standard for pesticides is currently defined as "a reasonable certainty that no harm
will result from aggregate exposure to the pesticide chemical residue, including
all anticipated dietary exposures and all other exposures for which there is reliable information." Tolerance limits for all pesticide residues, whether carcinogens or not, are set by the EPA at "safe" levels. The maximum allowable levels
for pesticide residues are established after careful consideration of the risks and
benefits for all consumers, with special attention to children. These tolerances
are monitored and enforced by the FDA and the USDA [6]. The FDA monitoring of pesticides is discussed further in Chapter 3.

Prior to the 1996 Food Quality Protection Act, when a pesticide residue
was found to concentrate in a processed food to levels higher than those found
on the original agricultural product before processing, the EPA was required to
treat the residue as a food additive. For example, when grapes are dried and become raisins, any pesticide residue present on the fresh grapes may be concentrated. As food additives, these pesticide residues were subject to the Delaney
clause in the Food Additives Amendment that was passed in 1958. The Delaney
clause is discussed later in this section. It requires zero tolerance for any cancer-
causing residues in food. Thus, under the law, pesticide residues on raw and
processed commodities had to be treated differently, causing confusion. The
1996 legislation provides for a single, health-based standard for all pesticides in
foods. Pesticide residues on processed foods no longer come under the *legal* definition of food additive and are not subject to the Delaney clause.

Food Additives Amendment.   The 1958 Food Additives Amendment was designed to protect the public by requiring approval of new additives *before* they can be used in foods. The responsibility for proving the safety of additives rests with the manufacturer, who must file a petition with the FDA showing the results of extensive tests for safety. The FDA must approve the additive as safe before it can be marketed. The FDA also prescribes the types of foods in which the additive can be used and specifies labeling directions. Additives in meat and poultry products are under the jurisdiction of the USDA.

The food additive approval system in the United States had become slow and laborious. Between 1970 and 1998, only six new direct human food additives that could not be regarded as GRAS were approved [11]. The approvals for olestra, a fat substitute, and for sucralose, an artificial or alternative sweetener occurred in 1996 and 1998, respectively. The petitions requesting approval for olestra and sucralose were each filed in 1987. However, the FDA Modernization Act of 1997 reformed the regulation process [37] and in 1998 additional funds were provided to support the review of food and color additives [39]. In 2001, as of September, 13 final rules for the use of additives were recorded in the Federal Register [41].

Color Additives Amendment.   All coloring substances added to foods are regulated under the Color Additives Amendment, passed in 1960. Rules regarding color additives were made stronger under this amendment, and previously approved certified colors were retested. A batch certification of any coal-tar colors is required of the FDA. Every color additive, of any kind, must be approved by the FDA before use [11].

Delaney clause and safety.   Included in the Food Additives Amendment is a special clause carrying the name of Congressman James J. Delaney, who was chairman of the congressional committee that investigated, for two years, the use of chemicals in foods. Their report was issued in 1952. A similar clause is contained in the Color Additives Amendment. The Delaney clause provides "that no additive shall be deemed to be safe if it is found to induce cancer when ingested by man or animal, or if it is found, after tests which are appropriate for the evaluation of the safety of food additives, to induce cancer in man or animals" [44].

The Delaney clause has created much discussion and disagreement in the years since the legislation was passed. Science, in relation to the study of cancer and carcinogenesis (cancer development), has changed, and the causes and nature of cancer have become better understood. Many people believe that an absolute prohibition of carcinogens under the Delaney clause is unnecessarily restrictive. No distinction is made between cancer in humans or experimental animals, nor is there a specification on the amount of the substance to be consumed in testing. If the maximum tolerated dose of the substance to the test animals causes an increase in cancer incidence over that in the control group, the substance cannot be used as a food additive, regardless of its level of potency [46]. As an alternative to strict enforcement, the FDA could estimate the risk that might result from exposure of humans to chemicals that show a carcinogenic effect in animals. In this assessment, the FDA could conclude that in some cases the estimated risk to the public is insignificant, if it exists at all. This policy would apply a negligible risk standard to decisions concerning the approval of food additives. Some scientists have suggested that the debate about the Delaney clause should be viewed as a statutory issue, having to do only with the fine points of the law, rather than a true food-safety issue, since the health benefits provided by a strict interpretation of the clause would appear to be trivial [44].

Actually, there is no way in which the *absolute* safety of a food additive, either a legally defined or GRAS substance, can be guaranteed. Clearance through the FDA should ensure that the risk of adverse effects is minimal. However, benefits from the use of additives must also be considered—improved shelf life for many foods and reduced distribution costs, increased aesthetic qualities and convenience, and improved nutritional value. It has been suggested that there are three interacting components of risk issues—science, politics, and social communication (to the public) of the chemical food risks. Each component is complex and subject to limitations, subjectivity, and a reliance on value judgments [45]. Society must continue to work on the problem of developing appropriate policies concerning food chemical risks.

Food biotechnology. The FDA has developed a food biotechnology policy for foods derived from genetically modified plants. This policy is science-based and reflects the FDA's understanding that changes in food composition can be accomplished using new genetic engineering techniques. In many cases, the changes in plants involve familiar substances—proteins, carbohydrates, and fats—that raise no new safety questions. However, if substances that have no history of safe use in foods are produced, they will be subject to the same careful testing and approval used to ensure the safety of all food additives [14]. The first substance produced by genetic engineering to be approved by the FDA was an enzyme, *chymosin* or *rennin*, used in cheesemaking. This approval was given in 1990. The first genetically engineered vegetable approved was a tomato that ripens on the vine without undue softening, thus increasing its natural flavor while allowing normal shipping procedures. New rules for bioengineered foods are under discussion that include a premarket notification system [5] and appropriate labeling of both products that have and do not have genetically engineered components [12]. Biotechnology is discussed further in Chapter 3.

Irradiation. Through the legislation on food additives, the regulatory responsibility for irradiated foods was given to the FDA, although the USDA also has some involvement in the process [31]. Food irradiation is a recognized method for reducing postharvest food losses and ensuring hygienic quality [17]. Approval has been granted for the production and marketing of several irradiated food products, including fresh or frozen meats and poultry. However, commercial applications of food irradiation are still limited and consumers are not well informed about its advantages. Nevertheless, it is likely that an increasing number of irradiated foods will become available in the marketplace in the near future. See Chapter 3 for more information on irradiation and the role in food safety.

Additives used. Each approved additive must serve a useful purpose. It cannot be placed in food to conceal damage or spoilage or to deceive the consumer. There are many different, specific functions of food additives, but most may be grouped into classes based on similar function. Some of the more important classes or types of additives follow. Examples of each class are given in Table 4-1.

Table 4-1
Some Additives in Use for Various Types of Foods

Type or Class	Additive	Food in Which Used
Nutrients	Thiamin Niacin Riboflavin Iron Vitamin C	Flour, breads, and cereals in enrichment process Fruit juices, fruit drinks, and dehydrated potatoes
Antioxidants	Butylated hydroxyanisole (BHA) Butylated hydroxytoluene (BHT) Tertiary butylated hydroxyquinone (TBHQ) Ascorbic acid (vitamin C)	Animal fats such as lard, ready-to-eat cereals, crackers, and potato chips to retard rancidity Frozen peaches and apples to prevent browning
Antimicrobial agents	Propionates Benzoates	Bread to retard molding and development of "rope" Carbonated beverages, fruit drinks, and margarine
Coloring agents	β-carotene Certified colors: Citrus Red No. 2, Red No. 3, Green No. 3, and Yellow No. 6 Annato	Margarine, butter, and cheese Limited to use on skins of oranges Candies, cereals, soft drinks, and bakery goods Cheese
Flavoring agents	Benzaldehyde Vanilla Monosodium glutamate (MSG)	Almond flavoring Ice cream, baked goods, and candies Soups and Chinese foods as a flavor enhancer
Emulsifiers	Mono- and diglycerides Lecithin	Margarines and shortenings Bakery products, chocolate, and frozen desserts
Stabilizers and thickeners	Alginates Carrageenan Pectin Modified starches	Ice cream Evaporated milk, sour cream, and cheese foods Fruit jellies, confections, and sherbets Puddings and pie fillings
Sequestrants	Ethylenediamine tetraacetic acid (EDTA)	Wine and cider
Humectants	Glycerine Sorbitol	Marshmallows, flaked coconut, and cake icings
Anticaking agents	Calcium silicate Magnesium carbonate	Table salt, powdered sugar, and baking powder
Bleaching and maturing agents	Chlorine Chlorine dioxide Benzoyl peroxide (bleaches only)	Cake flour All-purpose flour All-purpose flour
Acids, alkalies, and buffers	Citric acid and its salts Acetic acid Sodium bicarbonate Sodium hydroxide	Soft drinks Processed cheese Baking powders Dutch processed cocoa, pretzels (glazing)
Alternative sweeteners	Aspartame Sucralose Acesulfame-K	Lemonade and cocoa mixes, ready-to-eat cereals, and many other foods Carbonated beverages, baked goods, confections, frozen desserts, and many other foods Dry beverage mixes and chewing gum
Fat replacers	Sucrose polyester (as olestra) Microparticulated protein (as Simplesse®)[†] Hydrocolloids such as gums and starch derivatives[†]	Snack Foods Ice cream, sour cream, salad dressing, and margarine Salad dressings, frozen desserts, beverage mixes, and many other foods
Bulking agents	Polydextrose	Baked goods, confections, puddings, and other foods

[†]GRAS substances

Nutrient supplements. Vitamins and minerals are often added to processed foods either to restore or to improve their nutritive value. Examples include the enrichment of bread and cereals, the addition of iodine to salt, and the fortification of milk with vitamin D. Some vitamins—for example, vitamins C and E—also play functional roles such as acting as **antioxidants.**

Preservatives. Antioxidants are a group of preservatives. Fatty foods are particularly susceptible to spoilage as **rancidity** develops with unpleasant off-odors. Some antioxidants retard the development of rancidity. Another type of antioxidant may prevent **enzymatic oxidative browning** in fresh fruits and vegetables. Vitamin C is an effective antioxidant in this regard.

Antimicrobial agents are another group of preservatives. These additives prevent or inhibit spoilage caused by such microorganisms as molds and bacteria. The effectiveness of such preservation methods as refrigeration may be enhanced by the judicious use of certain antimicrobial agents.

Coloring agents. Proper use of color makes foods more visually appealing and corrects natural variations and irregularities. Artificial colors must be certified to meet specifications set by the FDA on a batch-by-batch basis. Some natural pigments, such as **carotenoids,** are available for use in foods, although they are generally less stable than artificial colors.

Flavoring materials. A wide variety of substances are used to improve the flavor of processed foods. These include natural extractives and **essential oils** as well as synthetic or artificial flavorings. Flavor enhancers are also used. Flavorings, which include herbs and spices, comprise the largest group of intentional additives.

Emulsifiers. **Emulsifiers** are substances widely used to mix fat and water-soluble substances uniformly together in the making and stabilizing of **emulsions**. They are also used to stabilize foams and suspensions.

Stabilizers and thickeners. Texture and body are important characteristics of many foods. A variety of stabilizers and thickeners are used to achieve desired smoothness and consistency, including many vegetable gums, such as carrageenan, and a number of starch products.

Sequestrants. **Sequestrants** are used to bind (chelate) small amounts of metals, such as iron and copper, that may have undesirable effects on flavor or appearance.

Humectants and anticaking agents. **Humectants** are used to retain moisture and keep certain foods soft. Some humectants are added to finely powdered or crystalline foods to prevent caking as moisture is absorbed.

Bleaching and maturing agents. The baking properties of wheat flours are improved by the addition of certain oxidizing agents (**maturing agents**). Many of these also have a bleaching effect.

Acids, alkalis, and buffers. Acidity or alkalinity is very important in many processed foods. Acids, alkalis, and **buffers** are used to adjust and control the pH. The alkaline salt—sodium bicarbonate or baking soda—is also used to produce carbon dioxide gas to leaven baked products.

antioxidant a substance that can stop an oxidation reaction

rancidity a special type of spoilage in fats that involves oxidation of unsaturated fatty acids

enzymatic oxidative browning the browning of cut surfaces of certain fruits and vegetables catalyzed by enzymes in the presence of oxygen

antimicrobial agents substances that prevent or inhibit the growth of microorganisms

carotenoids yellow-orange-red, fat-soluble pigments found in some plant materials such as fruits and vegetables

essential oils concentrated flavoring oils extracted from food substances, such as oil of orange or oil of peppermint

emulsifier a substance that acts as a bridge between two immiscible liquids and allows the formation of an emulsion

emulsion the dispersion of one substance within another with which it ordinarily does not mix (is immiscible)

sequestrant a substance that binds or isolates other substances; for example, some molecules can tie up trace amounts of minerals that may have unwanted effects in a food product

humectant a substance that retains moisture

maturing agent a substance that brings about some oxidative changes in white flour and improves its baking properties

buffer a substance that resists change in acidity or alkalinity

Alternative sweeteners. A sweet tooth has apparently always been part of the human anatomy. The harvesting of honey and sugar cane has a long history. Substitutes for the taste of caloric sweeteners, including sucrose (table sugar), honey, and corn syrups, have been developed; however, only in the past century. Four alternative sweeteners have approval from the FDA: saccharin, aspartame, sucralose, and acesulfame-K [8]. Because of increased health and nutrition concerns, the market for reduced-calorie foods has expanded greatly in recent years, thus increasing the demand for new alternative sweeteners.

Fat replacers. Professional groups' and public health agencies' current stress on the important relationship between high fat intake and the risks of developing coronary heart disease and some cancers has generated much interest in low-fat substitutes for many traditional high-fat food products. Many consumers are changing their high-fat consumption habits. The food industry is thus motivated to develop substances that can replace fat but leave flavor and texture unchanged or minimally changed. Some of the approved fat replacers are GRAS (generally regarded as safe), whereas others require special approval by the FDA as food additives.

Carbohydrate-based fat replacers include cellulose, various gums such as xanthan gum and carrageenan, dextrins, and modified starches. Microparticulated protein, whose trade name is Simplesse®, is a protein-based fat replacer produced from whey protein or milk and egg protein. Some emulsifiers can also replace part of the fat in a food product [3].

Sucrose polyesters (olestra) are nonabsorbable and thus noncaloric fat replacers. They may be used in cooking oils and shortenings, commercial frying, and snack foods [3]. Olestra was approved by the FDA in 1996 for use in snacks. Because it may affect gastrointestinal function in some people and absorption of some fat-soluble vitamins, products containing olestra are required to be fortified with vitamins A, D, E, and K and be labeled with the statement, "This product contains Olestra."

Bulking agents. Polydextrose contains only 1 calorie per gram and helps to add texture and body when fat and sugar are reduced in some food products. Some of the modified starches also add body and texture to low-fat products. When used to provide texture and body in reduced-fat or reduced-sugar food products, these substances are called *bulking agents.*

DEPARTMENT OF AGRICULTURE

The USDA is involved with food processing and marketing in several different ways. Under the auspices of the Food Safety and Inspection Service, the USDA inspects meat and poultry products for wholesomeness and truthful labeling, administering the Federal Meat Inspection Act and the Poultry Products Inspection Act (see Figure 4-2).

Beginning in 1997, the Food Safety and Inspection Service of the USDA modernized its inspection service for meat and poultry [1]. All meat and poultry slaughter and processing plants must have a Hazard Analysis and Critical Control Points (HACCP) plan; they must develop written sanitation standard operating procedures (SOPs) to show how they meet daily sanitation requirements; and they must test for generic *E. coli* to verify that the process is under control with respect to preventing and removing fecal contamination. The Food Safety

(a)

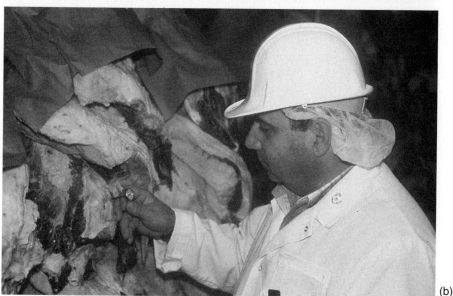

(b)

Figure 4-2
(a) U.S. Department of Agriculture meat inspectors, under regulation of the Federal Meat Inspection Act, examine cattle before slaughter and beef carcasses (b) for wholesomeness and freedom from disease. (Courtesy of U.S. Department of Agriculture)

and Inspection Service will test for *Salmonella* on raw meat and poultry products to verify that pathogen reduction standards are being met for this organism.

The Agricultural Marketing Service is responsible for administering the Egg Products Inspection Act, which requires inspection of all plants that process liquid, dried, or frozen egg products. It also offers grading services for meat, poultry, fruits, vegetables, eggs, and dairy products.

Official certification that a particular food product meets a predetermined standard of quality is available through grading services. These services are generally voluntarily requested but are sometimes required on a local level or for a particular industry program. They are performed by USDA inspectors but paid for by the manufacturer requesting the service. Grading may be done for meat, poultry, eggs, dairy products, some fish, nuts, rice, and fresh fruits and vegetables. The grading of each of these products is discussed in more detail in other chapters. Only a general discussion of grading and inspection is given here.

Grade standards were originally established to aid in wholesale food trading, but many consumer grades have become useful. These consumer grades apply to small units of food that are usually sold in a retail market. The quality of the food at the time it was graded is indicated by the grade on the package, but no allowance is made for changes in quality that may occur during the handling and

grade a symbol, such as Grade A or No. 1, that indicates that the food product carrying this label has met specified predetermined standards

Hot Topics

A Single Food Safety Agency—Is this the answer?

At the beginning of the year 2002 there were at least 12 different federal agencies and 35 different federal laws governing food safety [18, 20]. Although a number of these organizations—including the Bureau of Alcohol, Tobacco, and Firearms—are only peripherally involved in assuring food safety, several agencies play key roles that call for close coordination and collaboration with others. The FDA and the USDA are primary among these. The need for close working relationships among agencies became even more apparent when terrorism struck the United States on September 11, 2001. What is the answer to this problem?

Senator Dick Durbin, chair of a Senate Governmental Affairs Oversight Subcommittee, has offered legislation that would consolidate all federal food safety responsibilities into a single, independent agency. He proposes this single agency as an answer to the present problems of duplication, overlap, turf wars, and lack of resources to assure that the U.S. food supply remains the safest in the world [20]. The system clearly needs fixing in order to safeguard against tragedy resulting from any acts of bioterrorism or agroterrorism. However, a panel of experts testifying on Capitol Hill advanced a variety of opinions on the subject of "a single agency."

Most agreed on two principles—first, that the United States now has the safest food supply in the world and second, that there are problems to be fixed in order to maintain that position. The agricultural and food industries are vulnerable to both deliberate and accidental disturbances. The current food safety regulatory system is a patchwork structure that has developed over many decades and is fragmented in organization and legal configuration. Efforts at collaboration among agencies are evident in such partnerships as **FoodNet**, **PulseNet**, and **FORC-G.** But are they enough?

In the short term, such collaboration efforts, and others, should probably continue. In the long term, some "experts" suggest that a single agency is definitely desirable. Others realize the tremendous costs associated with setting up a new government agency and suggest a second option would be to consolidate food safety activites in an existing department [20]. But Joe Regenstein, of Cornell University, is against a single food safety agency [24]. If we could start all over again from scratch, he says, he would probably favor it. But from our present state, which has resulted from historical accidents and political expediency, he does not see a clear path to the end of the journey toward a single agency. The current system is working. It is not perfect, but Regenstein believes that the proposed cure is worse than what is wrong with the present system. What do you think?

FoodNet the Foodborne Disease Active Surveillance Network, a project with FDA, USDA, the Centers for Disease Control and Prevention (CDC), and nine states.

PulseNet a national network of public health laboratories to "fingerprint" bacteria that may be foodborne, a project with FDA, USDA, CDC, and all 50 states

storage involved in the marketing process. At any rate, graded foods offer a choice of quality and enable us to pick the one that is most suitable for the intended use.

Grade standards are defined to cover the entire range of quality of a food product. Some products are more variable in quality than other products and therefore may require more grades. For example, there are eight grades for beef but only three for chicken. Most federal grades for consumers are preceded by the abbreviation *U.S.* and are enclosed in a shield-shaped mark (Figure 4-3).

Because the grade standards for various products were developed at different times, the naming systems vary. For instance, the top-quality grade for cantaloupes is U.S. Fancy; for beets, it is U.S. No. 1; for carrots, it is U.S. Grade A; and for celery, it is U.S. Extra No. 1. U.S. Grades A, B, and C are used on poultry and on canned fruits and vegetables. To help achieve a more uniform grad-

Figure 4-3
Shield-shaped marks used by the U.S. Department of Agriculture in grading food products. (Courtesy of the U.S. Department of Agriculture)

ing system, the USDA has issued a policy statement that when future standards for fresh fruits, vegetables, and nuts are issued, revised, or amended, only the classifications U.S. Fancy and Grades 1, 2, and 3 may be used.

Even though a product may have been officially graded, the law still does not require that a designation of grade appear on the label. If the grade shield is used on a food product, however, the food must have been officially graded.

Foods are inspected for grade determination, or it might be said that they are "inspected for grade." However, the term *inspection* has different meanings when applied to various commodities. The USDA administers a mandatory inspection program for meat and poultry that is sold in interstate commerce and in those states that do not have an inspection program of their own that is equal to the federal program. This inspection is for wholesomeness (safety) and proper labeling; it is not for grading. The meat and poultry must be from healthy animals or birds, be processed under strict sanitary conditions using good manufacturing practices and an HACCP system, be tested for the presence of some microorganisms, and be truthfully labeled. All meat and poultry must be inspected before it can be graded. The inspection determines wholesomeness; the grading determines quality.

Food grading aids foodservice managers as they write **specifications** for the purchasing of various food products. The required quality of the product being ordered can be easily specified by grade, since the grade standards are known to both purchasers and vendors. Food grading is also an aid available to retail shoppers to help them more effectively meet their needs and desires. However, many consumers are not knowledgeable about specific details of the grading systems and may need more education to clarify differences between inspection and grading.

National standards for the production and marketing of **organic foods** were authorized by a special title under the 1990 Farm Bill [2]. Under these standards, growers cannot use most conventional pesticides; petroleum-based fertilizers or sewage sludge-based fertilizers; bioengineering; or ionizing radiation [33]. A National Organic Standards Board proposes allowable and prohibited substances. These proposals are reviewed and submitted for public comment, resulting in a national list of exemptions and prohibitions. The board may also make recommendations concerning residue testing in the foods and allowable tolerance levels. The USDA established a certification program for organic production or processing.

Starting in 2002, USDA labeling rules for organic foods were implemented. Certified foods labeled as "100 percent organic," or "95 percent organic" may include the USDA Organic seal (Figure 4-4). Foods containing 70–95 percent organic ingredients may be labeled "made with organic ingredients." Products with less than 70 percent organic ingredients may not include

FORC-G Foodborne Outbreak Response Coordinating Group, a project with USDA, FDA, and the Environmental Protection Agency (EPA)

specifications a written description of the food or product that is desired. This written description must be thorough so that misunderstandings of the item wanted are unlikely.

organic foods foods grown and/or produced under conditions that replenish and maintain soil fertility, use only nationally approved materials in their production, and have verifiable records of the production system

Figure 4-4
Government certified organic symbol that can be placed on foods only after they meet government guidelines. (Courtesy of U.S. Department of Agriculture)

organic claims on the front of the package, but may list specific organically produced ingredients on the side panel. Products may still be labeled as free-range, hormone free, and natural. However, "natural" and "organic" are not interchangeable terms; only "organic" foods have been certified by USDA [21, 33]. These labeling standards will help consumers to decide whether they want to pay a premium price for these products. With annual sales of over $5 million, the organic food industry has become an important component of the U.S. food system [21].

ENVIRONMENTAL PROTECTION AGENCY

The Environmental Protection Agency (EPA) protects the public health through the oversight of environmental risks from pesticides. It administers the 1947 Federal Insecticide, Fungicide, and Rodenticide Act that was amended by the 1996 Food Quality Protection Act. The EPA establishes maximum legally permissible levels for pesticide residues in food. Genetically engineered foods also may fall under EPA oversight if the alteration includes a component that functions as a natural pesticide.

CENTERS FOR DISEASE CONTROL AND PREVENTION

The Centers for Disease Control and Prevention (CDC) promotes health by preventing and controlling disease. CDC collaborates with FDA and USDA in the Foodborne Disease Active Surveillance Network (FOODNET) system to measure the incidence and sources of bacterial foodborne diseases. CDC manages the PulseNet system that is another collaborative effort with FDA and

accredited certifiers individuals or groups who have met all of the requirements of the Organic Foods Protection Act, including personnel training, document retention, and conflict-of-interest restrictions, are recognized by the USDA, and can certify that foods are "organic" in the legal sense

standardized legal meaning a legal definition of a term, recognized by the U.S. Food and Drug Administration

Hot Topics

Organic Foods—Exploding sales

Sales of organic foods are growing at an explosive rate of 24% per year and, according to Elizabeth Sloan [27,28], the future market potential is awesome. Why the explosion? There is a growing mainstream desire for clean, pure, and "close-to-nature" foods, being reinforced by concern for healthful eating and fear over food safety. Food marketing surveys indicate that many shoppers want to avoid artificial preservatives and additives and are attracted to organic foods as part of their effort to maintain health. However, the question of whether or not organic foods are actually more nutritious than conventionally grown foods has yet to be definitely answered [32].

Also contributing to the increased sales was implementation of a National Organic Program in October 2002. Since passage of the Organic Foods Protection Act of 1990, which mandated an organic foods cetification program, the USDA has been working with related groups to develop this program [21]. Organic foods are certified by **accredited certifiers** and labeling regulations are in place. Consumers benefit because there is a **standard legal meaning** to the word "organic" [32], whereas there is no legal definition for the term "natural", as applied to foods. Organic produce and other foods must be produced without conventional pesticides and petroleum-based fertilizers. Organic meat, poultry, eggs, and dairy products must come from animals that have received no antibiotics or growth hormones. Consumers are protected from false and misleading labels.

Food growers and processors also benefit from the National Organic Program because certification means uniformity of standards and consistency in labeling. Major food marketers with knowledge, initiative, and proven distribution systems face exciting possibilities and challenges as the exploding organic food markets, both domestic and international, are satisfied.

Figure 4-5
These sample cereal boxes show the four organic labeling categories. From left: 100 percent organic ingredients, 95–100 percent organic ingredients, at least 70 percent organic ingredients, less than 70 percent organic ingredients. (Courtesy of U.S. Department of Agriculture)

USDA. PulseNet helps to control foodborne outbreaks through a national laboratory and computer database. Through this database, distinctive DNA "fingerprint" patterns for microorganisms may be identified, thereby permitting the tracing of foodborne illnesses that may be linked by one common food. Early identification of the source of foodborne illness helps the FDA and USDA to prevent further illnesses from the same food.

FEDERAL TRADE COMMISSION

The Federal Trade Commission (FTC) is an independent law enforcement agency charged with promoting free and fair competition in the marketplace. One major activity of the FTC is ensuring that fair and honest competition is allowed in the marketing of food products. The FTC attempts to protect the consumer from false or misleading advertising and misbranding, and shares with the FDA responsibility for enforcing labeling laws.

OTHER FEDERAL AGENCIES

The U.S. Department of Commerce's National Oceanic and Atmospheric Administration (NOAA) oversees the management of fisheries in the United States. The Seafood Inspection Program of NOAA operates under the 1946 Agricultural Marketing Act. The voluntary inspection service provides product grading, establishment sanitation inspection, product lot inspection, process and product inspection, laboratory analysis, training, and consultation. FDA oversees the mandatory HACCP regulations for seafood processors. However, the NOAA Seafood Inspection Program provides additional services for processors.

The Bureau of Alcohol, Tobacco, and Firearms in the Department of the Treasury regulates most alcholic beverages. The qualifications and operations of distilleries, wineries, and breweries are controlled. New products coming into the market are tested to ensure that alcoholic ingredients are within legal limits. Labels are examined to see that legal requirements have been met.

STATE AND LOCAL AGENCIES

The legislation and regulations previously discussed in this chapter are federal, and they apply only in interstate commerce. Within each state and within cities are many laws and regulations dealing with food processing, quality, and marketing. Each state has its own unique problems and attempts to solve them in individual ways, but federal laws and regulations are often used as models. States are usually organized with their own departments of agriculture and health and their own food and drug commissions. Assurance of sanitation, milk quality, inspection of meat and poultry, and protection of vegetable crops are some of the activities conducted by state organizations.

State and local governments provide for the inspection of foodservice establishments to protect the public who eat in restaurants, cafeterias, and other places where foodservice is offered. This service is usually the responsibility of state, county, and city health departments, which assess cleanliness and sanitary practices. In many cases, those working with food served to the public are required to obtain food-handling permits, sometimes involving both a physical examination and educational certification.

INTERNATIONAL STANDARDS

In our rapidly shrinking world, international trade in food is accelerating. The U.S. food industry plays a major role in international food marketing and the world demand for processed foods continues to rise [9]. In addition, an ever-growing number of food products made outside the United States are appearing on our supermarket shelves, probably because consumers' attitudes toward eating are changing. Most consumers today are more open and eager to try new foods and new **cuisines.** They are buying more specialty products and becoming familiar with imported items.

cuisine a style of cooking or manner of preparing food

Increased international trade in foods has created an even greater need for international standards to safeguard the consumer's health and ensure fair food-trade practices. The Codex Alimentarius Commission was established by a joint effort of the United Nations' Food and Agriculture Organization (FAO) and the World Health Organization (WHO) in 1963 to meet this need. Any nation that is a member of the FAO or the WHO may become a member of the commission. The international standards are quite comprehensive and include a description of the product; composition requirements; additives that may be allowed, if any; sanitary handling practices; fill of container, weight, and measure or count of units; labeling provisions; and methods of analysis and sampling necessary to determine that the standard is being met [42].

After the commission develops a recommended international standard, it sends it to the member nations for consideration of adoption. Individual members may adopt the standard for themselves. The World Trade Organization (WTO) accepts Codex food standards, guidelines, and recommendations as representing international consensus in this area [23].

CHAPTER SUMMARY

- The government, through legislation and regulation, plays a role in ensuring quality and safety in the foods we purchase. The FDA and USDA together are the primary agencies that oversee the food we consume.

- The FDA is housed in the U.S. Department of Health and Human Services. All food except red meat, poultry, and eggs are regulated by the FDA.

- Under the Federal Food, Drug, and Cosmetic Act, the FDA sets three kinds of mandatory standards for products being shipped across state lines: standards of identity, standards of minimum quality, and standards of fill of container. The 1990 Nutrition Labeling and Education Act made new provisions for the labeling of standard foods using qualifiers such as "low fat" or "light."

- The FDA shares with the FTC the responsibility for enforcing fair packaging and labeling laws. USDA is also involved for some foods. Several requirements are specified for food labels pertaining to the product name, ingredients, nutrition labeling and amount in package.

- As a general definition, a food additive is any substance that becomes part of a food product either when it is added intentionally or when it incidentally becomes part of the food, such as can occur with migration from packaging. Food additives, as legally defined, must be thoroughly tested and receive approval for use in food. The "generally recognized as safe" (GRAS) list includes substances that do not require detailed clearance before use in foods; however, ongoing reassessment of these substances is done by FDA and industry.

- The 1958 Food Additives Amendment and 1960 Color Additives Amendment strengthened the regulation of additives. The Delaney Clause in the Food Additives Amendment that specifies that no additives that are found to cause cancer in man or animals when present in the diet in any amount can be approved for use in foods. This clause has been debated over the years as the science, in relation to the study of carcinogenesis and cancer risk, has changed.

- Additives must serve a useful purpose in foods to be approved. Additives may be used as nutrient supplements; preservatives; antimicrobial agents; coloring agents; flavoring materials; emulsifiers; stabilizers and thickeners; humectants and anticaking agents; bleaching and maturing agents; acids, alkakis, and buffers; alternative sweeteners; fat replacers; and bulking agents.

- The Miller Pesticide Amendment of 1954 and the Food Quality Protection Act of 1996 include standards for the use of pesticides in food and food products. The FDA monitors and enforces the EPA-established pesticide tolerance levels.

- FDA has developed policies for foods derived from genetically modified plants. Both FDA and USDA have regulatory responsibility for irradiated foods.

- The Department of Agriculture (USDA) is involved with food processing and marketing in several different ways. Under the auspices of the Food Safety and Inspection Service, the USDA inspects meat and poultry products for wholesomeness and truthful labeling. The Agricultural Marketing Service is responsible for administering the Egg Products Inspection Act.

- USDA provides grading services for a variety of products. The grade standards inform the consumer of the product quality.

- National standards for the production and marketing of organic foods were authorized by a special title under the 1990 Farm Bill. Starting in 2002, USDA labeling rules enable consumers to know how much of the product contains organic ingredients.

- Additional agencies with involvement in the quality, wholesomeness, or marketing of our food supply include the Environmental Protection Agency, Centers for Disease Control and Prevention, Federal Trade Commission, U.S. Department of Commerce's National Oceanic and Atmospheric Administration, Bureau of Alcohol, Tobacco, and Firearms, and state and local agencies. The Codex Alimentarius Commission works to develop international standards.

KEY TERMS

good manufacturing practices
food additive
inspection
grading
Federal Register
certified colors
protein hydrolysate

caseinate
antioxidant
rancidity
enzymatic oxidative browning
antimicrobial agents
carotenoids
essential oils

emulsifier
emulsion
sequestrant
humectant
maturing agent
buffer
grade
FoodNet

PulseNet
FORC-G
specifications
organic foods
accredited certifiers
standardized legal meaning
cuisine

STUDY QUESTIONS

1. Which agencies of the federal government are particularly involved in setting standards and regulations for food? How is each involved? Discuss this.

2. What are the distinguishing characteristics of each of the following standards?
   a. Standards of identity
   b. Standards of fill of container
   c. Standards of minimum quality
   d. U.S. grade standards

3. What sanitary requirements for food processors are included in the Federal Food, Drug, and Cosmetic Act? Why does the FDA outline current good manufacturing practices (GMPs) for food processors?

4. Respond to the following:
   a. Define *food additives* in a general sense.
   b. What is the legal definition of *food additives?*
   c. What are GRAS substances?
   d. Give examples of intentional and incidental food additives.

5. Describe four justifiable uses for food additives.

6. Discuss implications for foods resulting from each of the following federal laws or amendments:
   a. 1906 Pure Food and Drug Act
   b. 1938 Federal Food, Drug, and Cosmetic Act
   c. 1954 Miller Pesticide Amendment
   d. 1958 Food Additives Amendment
   e. 1960 Color Additives Amendment
   f. 1996 Food Quality Protection Act

7. What is the Delaney clause, and why is it important to both the food processor and the consumer?

8. How can a consumer know that a food additive is safe? Discuss this.

9. List at least 10 different types or groups of food additives and give examples of specific additives for each group. Also, indicate the foods in which these additives are generally used.

10. List the four pieces of information that are required to be listed on food package labels.

11. What are *organic foods?* How can consumers know that they are truly getting organic food after they pay for it?

12. How is grading of food products useful to the wholesaler, the retailer, and the consumer? Discuss this.

13. Describe differences between *inspection* and *grading* of meat and poultry as applied to USDA regulations.

14. What is the Codex Alimentarius Commission, and what functions does it perform?

REFERENCES

1. Buzby, J. C., & Crutchfield, S. R. (1997). USDA modernizes meat and poultry inspection. *Food Review, 20*(1), 14.

2. Dunn, J. A. (1995). Organic foods find opportunity in the natural food industry. *Food Review, 18*(3), 7.

3. *Fat replacers.* (1992). Calorie Control Council, Suite 500-G, 5775 Peachtree-Dunwoody Road, Atlanta, GA 30342.

4. Formanek, R. (2001). Highlights of FDA food safety efforts: Fruit juice, mercury in fish. *FDA Consumer, 35*(1).

5. Formanek, R. (2001). Proposed rules issued for bioengineered foods. *FDA Consumer, 35*(2).

6. Giese, J. (2000). Pesticide analysis. *Food Technology, 54*(12), 64-65.

7. Henkel, J. (1996). How to comment on proposals and submit petitions. *FDA Consumer, 30*(3), 6.

8. Henkel, J. (1999). Sugar substitutes: Americans opt for sweetness and lite. *FDA Consumer, 33*(6).

9. Hollingsworth, P. (1994). Global opportunities. *Food Technology, 48:* 65(3).

10. Hutt, P. B. (1989). Regulating the misbranding of food. *Food Technology, 43*(9), 288.

11. Hutt, P. B. (1996). Approval of food additives in the United States: A bankrupt system. *Food Technology, 50*(3), 118.

12. Institute of Food Technologists' Expert Report on Biotechnology and Foods. (2000). Labeling of rDNA biotechnology-derived foods. *Food Technology, 54*(9), 62-74.

13. Janssen, W. F. (1981). The story of the laws behind the labels. *FDA Consumer, 15*(5). Retrieved June 23, 2002 from http://vm/cfsan/fda.gov/~lrd/history1.html

14. Kessler, D. A. (1992). Reinvigorating the Food and Drug Administration. *Food Technology, 46*(8), 20.

15. Kurtzweil, P. (1997). Center for food safety and applied nutrition. *FDA Consumer, 31*(3), 27.

16. Kurtzweil, P. (1998). Skimming the milk label. *FDA Consumer, 35*(1).

17. Loaharanu, P. (1994). Status and prospects of food irradiation. *Food Technology, 48*(5), 124.

18. Looney, J. W., Crandall, P. G., & Poole, A. K. (2001). The matrix of food safety regulations. *Food Technology, 55*(4), 60-76.

19. Mermelstein, N. H. (1993). A new era in food labeling. *Food Technology, 47*(2), 81.

20. Mermelstein, N. H. (2001). Terrorism spurs renewed call for single food safety agency. *Food Technology, 55*(11), 32.

21. Montecalvo, J. (2001). The national organic program: An opportunity for industry. *Food Technology, 55*(6), 26.

22. Newberne, P., Smith, R. L., Doull, J., Feron, V. J., Goodman, J. I., Munro, I. C., Portoghese, P. S., Waddell, W. J., Wagner, B. M., Weil, C. S, Adams, T. B., and Hallagan, J. B. (2000). GRAS flavoring substances, 19. *Food Technology, 54*(6), 66-84.

23. Newsome, R. (1997). Codex, international trade, and science. *Food Technology, 51*(9), 28.

24. Regenstein, J. (2002). A single food safety agency is not the answer. *Food Technology, 56*(3), 104.

25. Segal, M. (1993, May). Ingredient labeling: What's in a food? *FDA Consumer, Special edition.* Retrieved July 2, 2002 from http://www.fda.gov/fdac/special/foodlabel/ingred.html

26. Shank, F. R. (1992). Science in the marketplace. *Food Technology, 46*(2), 78.

27. Sloan, A. E. (2001). Clean foods. *Food Technology, 55*(2), 18.

28. Sloan, A. E. (2002). The natural and organic foods marketplace. *Food Technology, 56*(1), 27.

29. Stehlin, D. (1993). A little "lite" reading. *FDA Consumer—Special edition.* Retrieved July 3, 2002, from http://fda.gov/fdac/special/foodlabel/lite.html

30. Swann, J. P. (2001). History of the FDA. Retrieved June 23, 2002, from http://www.fda.gov/oc/history/historyoffda/default/htm

31. The American Dietetic Association. (1996). Position of the American Dietetic Association: Food irradiation. *Journal of the American Dietetic Association, 96,* 69.

32. Turner, R. E. (2002). Organic standards. *Food Technology, 56*(6), 24.

33. U.S. Department of Agriculture. (n.d.). Organic food standards and labels: The facts. Retrieved July 5, 2002, from http://www.ams.usda.gov/nop/consumerbrochure.htm

34. U.S. Department of Health and Human Services. (2001, January). FDA publishes final rule to increase safety of fruit and vegetable juices. Retrieved June 23, 2002 from http://www.cfsan.gov/~lrd/hhsjuic4.html

35. U.S. Department of Health and Human Services, Food and Drug Administration. (1996, March). Food standards: Amendment of standards of identify for enriched grain products to require addition of folic acid. *Federal Register, 61*(44), 8781-8797. Retrieved July 2, 2002 from http://www.cfsan.fda.gov/~lrd/fr96305b.html

36. U.S. Department of Health and Human Services, Food and Drug Administration. (2002, May). Food additives: Food contact substance notification system. *Federal Register, 67*(98), 35724-35731. Retrieved July 5, 2002, from http://www.cfsan.fda.gov/~lrd/fr020521.html

37. U.S. Food and Drug Administration. (1997, November). The FDA Modernization Act of 1997. *FDA Backgrounder.* Retrieved July 5, 2002, from http://www.fda.gov/opacom/backgrounders/modact.htm

38. U.S. Food and Drug Administration. (1999, May). The food label. *FDA Backgrounder.* Retrieved July 2, 2002, from http://www.cfsan.fda.gov/~dms/fdnewlab.html

39. U.S. Food and Drug Administration. (2000, October). "Dear Colleague" letter on improvements to the food and color additive petition review process. Retrieved July 5, 2002, from http://www.cfsan/fda.gov/~dms/opa-stak.html

40. U.S. Food and Drug Administration. (2001, February). FDA's seafood HACCP program: Mid-course correction. Retrieved June 23, 2002, from http://www.cfsan.fda.gov/~comm/shaccpl.html

41. U.S. Food and Drug Administration. (2001, September). Federal register rules issued by the Office of Food Additive Safety: Year 2001. Retrieved July 5, 2002, from http://www.cfsan.fda.gov/~dms/opa-appr.html

42. U.S. Food Safety Inspection Service. (1999). Backgrounder: Codex alimentarius. Retrieved July 6, 2002, from http://www.fsis.usda.gov/OA/backgrounder/codex.htm

43. Williams, R., & Zorn, D. J. (1994). New inspection program for the nation's seafood. *Food Review, 17*(2), 32.

44. Winter, C. K. (1993). Pesticide residues and the Delaney clause. *Food Technology*, *47*(7), 81.

45. Winter, C. K. (1997). Assessing, managing, and communicating chemical food risks. *Food Technology*, *51*(5), 85.

46. Wodicka, V. O. (1996). Regulation of food: Where have we been? *Food Technology*, *50*(3), 106.

5

Back to Basics

Correct proportions of ingredients are vital to success in the preparation of many food products. These proportions are best achieved when the measuring or weighing of each individual ingredient in a recipe is done accurately and consistently. Likewise, the use of standardized recipes and the proper use of selected tools and equipment will enable the preparation of many delicious and attractive foods. The development of good knife skills is important to protect your safety while at the same time allowing the efficient use of your time.

WEIGHTS AND MEASURES

In the United States, recipes generally call for volume measurements, particularly in home cooking. Tablespoons, cups, pints, and gallons are the units commonly used. In some foodservice operations and in other countries, however, ingredients may be more commonly weighed than measured. When using U.S. standard weights and measures, eight fluid ounces equals one cup and there are 32 fluid ounces in a quart (see Appendix A). However, it is important to realize that dry ingredients do not have the same **density** as liquids. For example, in U.S. standard weights, one cup of white flour equals only four ounces, whereas one cup of leaf tarragon is only one ounce [6]. Thus, if the recipe calls for weights, these units cannot be changed into measures, or vice versa, unless the appropriate conversion factor is known.

Weighing is generally more accurate than measuring. Consequently, weights are often used in quantity cookery, especially in baking, because the need for accuracy is especially critical in baked goods. Some ingredients, such as flour, may pack down in the container [5], thereby resulting in inconsistent, and thus inaccurate, measurements. Weight and volume relationships also vary with certain chopped foods, such as onions, depending on the fineness and uniformity of chopping before measuring. Because of these differences in density, the use of standardized measuring techniques and equipment is particularly important.

density mass or weight per unit of volume

The Metric System

During the French Revolution, France's lawmakers asked their scientists to develop a system of measurement based on science rather than custom. The result was the metric system, which has since been adopted by most of the nations of the world. The metric system is a decimal system based on multiples of 10. The basic unit of length is the meter, which is slightly longer than a yard. When the meter is divided by ten, it produces 10 decimeters; a decimeter divided by ten produces 10 centimeters; and a centimeter divided by ten results in 10 millimeters. In other words, 1 meter equals 1,000 millimeters or 100 centimeters or 10 decimeters. The same prefixes are combined with the basic unit of **mass** or weight (gram) and the basic unit of volume or capacity (liter) to indicate designated amounts. Prefixes and symbols for mass, volume, and length are shown in Table 5-1. Other units and symbols associated with the metric system are given in Table 5-2.

The United States is one of the very few nations in the world that has not fully converted to metric. In this day of rapid transport and instantaneous communication, the global marketplace predominates [7]. The United States will undoubtedly benefit by fully changing over to the metric system since its participation in international trade is increasing daily. The United States' existing infrastructure based on the U.S customary weights and measures has slowed the change to metric in the domestic market. However, a number of international trade partners require the use of metric in trade transactions.

Conversion to Metric

A change in the United States from the U.S. customary system of weights and measures to the metric system was recommended and became public policy with passage by the U.S. Congress of the Metric Conversion Act of 1975. The change to metric was to be voluntary; however, the conversion process moved slowly and in 1988 an amendment to the 1967 Fair Packaging and Labeling Act

mass the tendency of an object to remain at rest if it is stationary or to continue in motion if it is already moving; mass can be determined by measuring the force with which an object is attracted to the earth, i.e., by measuring its weight

Table 5-1
The Metric System—Prefixes and Symbols

	Prefix	Mass	Symbol	Volume	Symbol	Length	Symbol
0.000001	micro-	microgram	µg	microliter	µL	micrometer	µm
0.001	milli-	milligram	mg	milliliter	mL	millimeter	mm
0.01	centi-	centigram	cg	centiliter	cL	centimeter	cm
0.1	deci-	decigram	dg	deciliter	dL	decimeter	dm
1.0		gram	g	liter	L	meter	m
10	deka-	dekagram	dag	dekaliter	daL	dekameter	dam
100	hecto-	hectogram	hg	hectoliter	hL	hectometer	hm
1000	kilo-	kilogram	kg	kiloliter	kL	kilometer	km

Table 5-2
Some Metric Units and Symbols.

	Unit	Symbol
Energy	Joule	J
Temperature	Degree Celsius	°C
Pressure	Pascal	Pa
Frequency	Hertz	Hz
Power	Watt	W

required that manufacturers show both U.S. customary and metric designations on most consumer products. Some metric containers, such as 1-liter soft drink bottles, are being used, but most food packages are labeled with the U.S. customary weight first and then the metric weight. Legislation has been passed as recently as 1996 regarding the use of metric in the United States and progress, although gradual, is evident.

As indicated, food manufacturers list the net contents of a package in both U.S. customary and metric units. For example, the label on a 1.5 quart bottle of fruit juice may read "48 fl. oz. (11/2 qts.) 1.42 L." This type of conversion to the metric system is called *soft conversion*.

Hard conversion to the metric system involves actually designing containers and packages to hold a certain number of metric units of food. For example, many soft drinks are now being marketed in 1, 2, or 3 liter bottles. U.S. customary measures are listed *after* the metric measure on these labels. More containers will be designed in this manner as the conversion from U.S. customary to metric becomes more widespread.

Hard and soft conversion to the metric system is occurring with food-measuring equipment and food containers. Most standard liquid measuring cups are stamped with both metric and U.S. customary quantity indicators. In a 1-cup measure, the graduations are usually marked at 1/4, 1/3, 1/2, 2/3, and 3/4 cup. The metric scale is usually marked at 250, 200, 150, 100, and 50 milliliters. One cup or 8 fluid ounces of liquid converts precisely to 236.59 milliliters and 1/2 cup converts to 118.29 milliliters, neither of which fits exactly the markings for milliliters on the cup. Separately designed metric measures use hard conversion; they are standardized at 250 milliliters, approximately equal to 1 cup; 125 milliliters, approximately equal to 1/2 cup; and 50 milliliters, approximately equal to 1/4 cup. Measuring spoons are available to measure 1, 2, 5, 15, and 25 milliliters.

Some adjustment is necessary in converting recipes made with U.S. customary measures to metric measurements to make the converted recipe practical. For example, as indicated, 1 cup will convert to 237 milliliters; however, a metric measure will not be available for exactly this quantity—it will be more practical to use the 250 milliliter measure. Depending on the recipe, these small differences could affect the final product. Therefore, standardization of each converted recipe is necessary.

The use of the metric system affects Americans in all types of jobs and as consumers in the marketplace. If the conversion to metric in the United States is to be successful, foodservice managers and workers will need to convert recipes to metric units for measuring and/or weighing, obtain metric measuring and weighing equipment, and purchase quantities in metric units. Measuring rather than weighing will probably continue to be used in home food preparation, but the foodservice worker may use a combination of scales and volume-measuring devices when preparing metric recipes.

Although the change to metric offers some challenges, a strong benefit will be greater ease when adjusting recipes to smaller or larger sizes. Compared to the U.S. customary units, the conversions currently necessary from ounces to pounds, tablespoons to cups, cups to gallons, and so forth will no longer be necessary because the metric system is based on multiples of ten. Information about conversion between U.S. customary units and metric units is found in Appendix A. Conversion formulas and charts for changing Fahrenheit and Celsius temperatures are given in Appendix B.

Measuring Equipment

Standard U.S. customary measures are available in various sizes. Gallon measures (4 quart or 16 cup capacity), 1/2 gallon or 2 quart measures, and quart measures are commonly used in quantity food preparation. The glass measuring cup of 1/2 pint or 8 fluid ounce capacity is usually used in home food preparation (Figure 5-1). Metric measures are available in various equivalents of 1 liter and 500 and 250 milliliter capacities.

For more accurate measurement of dry or solid ingredients, it is best to use dry-measuring containers that are to be filled and leveled at the top. Fractional cups and 1 and 2 cup measures are available (Figure 5-1). Metric cups for dry measure are also available.

Measuring spoons are commonly available in sets that measure 1 tablespoon, 1 teaspoon, 1/2 teaspoon, and 1/4 teaspoon. One tablespoon measures 1/16 cup; there are 16 tablespoons in 1 cup. Three teaspoons are equal to 1 tablespoon. Metric measuring spoons are available in 1 milliliter, 2 milliliters, 5 milliliters, and 15 milliliters.

The American Home Economics Association (currently named the American Association of Family and Consumer Sciences) and the American Standards Association (now called the American National Standards Institute) published a set of standards and tolerances for household measuring utensils in 1963 [2]. These standards allow for a deviation of 5 percent from the precise measure indicated on the measuring utensil. Not all measuring utensils on the market meet the tolerance of 5 percent, however. The teaspoons and tablespoons that are part of flatware or silverware sets should not be trusted as accurate measurements.

A scale or balance can be used to weigh foods (Figure 5-2). To be accurate, the scale must be of good quality. Such scales are usually relatively expensive.

Figure 5-1

Household measuring utensils can be labeled with metric or U.S. customary units. Dry measuring cups should be used for dry ingredients such as flour or sugar. Liquid measuring cups are best for liquids such as milk, water, or vegetable oil. (Courtesy of World Kitchens, makers of Pyrex®.)

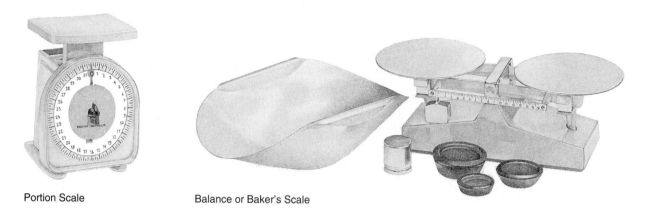

Portion Scale   Balance or Baker's Scale

Figure 5-2
Two types of scales, portion and balance, used to accurately weigh ingredients.

Weighing is often more practical than measuring, in terms of time and convenience, when large quantities are involved. Weighing also is generally more accurate than measuring volumes, particularly for foods that tend to pack down as do flours and chopped ingredients. However, scales are not usually available in U.S. homes and homesized recipes are typically printed with measures.

Measurement of Staple Foods

Even though accurate measuring equipment is available, measuring problems may still exist, for either metric or U.S. customary measures. Inaccuracies may occur through the manner in which the equipment is used. Most recipes allow small deviations in the amounts of ingredients used, which result from differences in measuring techniques, and acceptable products are still produced. However, the quality of some products, such as shortened cakes, for example, may be adversely affected by different methods of measuring the flour [3]. Accurate and consistent measurement of ingredients is important in producing uniform products of high quality time after time [1]. Some common measurements and symbols used in food preparation are found in Appendix A.

Flour. White wheat flour is a difficult ingredient to measure consistently because it is composed of tiny particles of different sizes that tend to pack [3]. For this reason, it is generally recommended that white flour be sifted once before measuring. Graham or whole wheat flours are usually not sifted before they are measured because the bran particles may be sifted out. Finely milled whole wheat flour may be sifted, however. Instantized flour, which contains agglomerated particles of quite uniform size, does not require sifting before being measured.

To measure sifted or unsifted flour, spoon tablespoons of the flour lightly into a dry-measure cup until the cup is heaping full. Do not pack the flour by shaking the cup while filling or hitting it with the spoon. Then level the top of the filled cup with the straight edge of a spatula (Figure 5-3). Quantities of less than 1 cup should be measured in the smaller fractional cups.

Figure 5-3
A recommended procedure for measuring white flour.

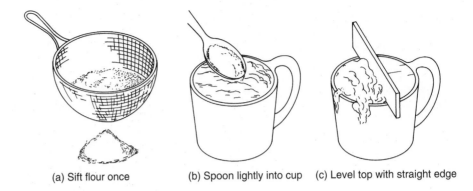

(a) Sift flour once   (b) Spoon lightly into cup   (c) Level top with straight edge

When measuring with a tablespoon or teaspoon, the spoon should be heaped full by dipping into the flour and then leveled with the straight edge of a spatula. Fractional spoons should be used to measure half and quarter spoonfuls. If these are not available, half spoonfuls may be measured by using a straight edge to divide the flour in half lengthwise and scrape out half. Quarter spoonfuls may be measured by dividing a half spoonful crosswise into two portions as nearly equal as possible and scraping out half.

The mass or weight of equal measures of white and whole wheat flour are not the same. One cup of whole-wheat flour weighs approximately 132 grams (4.4 ounces) whereas 1 cup of white flour weighs approximately 115 grams (3.8 ounces). Also, there is a difference between the mass of sifted and unsifted white flour, because unsifted flour is generally more tightly packed. If unsifted white flour is substituted for sifted flour in a recipe previously standardized with the use of sifted flour, the amount of flour may be adjusted by removing 2 level tablespoons from each cup of unsifted flour measured [5]. This adjustment should give satisfactory results in baking of homesize quantities.

Solid fats. Solid fats should be removed from the refrigerator long enough before they are measured so that they will be **plastic.** Very hard fats are difficult to measure accurately except in the case of sticks of butter or margarine that have measurements marked on the wrapper. In this case they may be cut, as marked, with a sharp knife. To measure plastic fats, press the fat into the cup with a spatula or knife so that air spaces are forced out. Then level the cup or fractional cup with a straight edge. For measurements up to 1/4 cup, level tablespoons may be used.

As an alternative, a water displacement method may be used if the water that clings to the fat does not affect the product. Pour cold water into a liquid-measure cup up to the measure that will equal 1 cup when added to the amount of fat to be measured. Then add enough fat to bring the water up to 1 cup when the fat is completely submerged in the water. Finally, drain off the water.

Sugar. Sifting is not necessary before measuring sugar unless the sugar becomes lumpy. Simply spoon granulated sugar into a dry-measure cup and level the top with the straight edge of a spatula.

For brown sugar, any lumps should first be rolled out before the sugar is pressed into the cup firmly enough that it holds its shape when turned out of the cup. Measured in this way, 1 cup of brown sugar is approximately equal in mass to 1 cup of granulated sugar.

plastic able to be molded into various shapes without shattering as a force is applied; plastic fats can be mixed or creamed

For the measurement of confectioners' or powdered sugar, sifting is followed by spooning of the sugar into a cup, as for flour. One cup of confectioners' sugar is slightly heavier than 1/2 cup of granulated sugar. About 1 3/4 cups of confectioners' sugar is equal in mass to 1 cup of granulated sugar.

Syrups.   To measure syrups or molasses, place the cup or fractional cup on a flat surface and fill completely. Because it is thick, the liquid may tend to round up higher than level full. It should be cut off level with the straight edge of a spatula. Measure spoonfuls by pouring syrup into the spoon and cutting off level with the straight edge of a spatula. To keep the syrup from sticking to the measuring cup or spoon, the empty measuring utensil may be lightly sprayed with a nonstick vegetable spray, provided that minute amounts of fat will not compromise the recipe.

Liquids.   For the measurement of liquids, a cup that extends above the largest measure mark should be used to increase ease and accuracy of measurement. The cup should have a lip for pouring. Only liquids are measured accurately in liquid measuring cups; these cups should not be used for measuring dry ingredients. Place the cup on a flat surface and fill to the desired measure mark.

The eye should be at the level of the measure mark when reading the contents. In clear liquids, a **meniscus** can be seen at the upper surface as a curved concave line. The eye should read the lowest point of this meniscus (Figure 5-4).

meniscus the curved upper surface of a column of liquid

RECIPES

A recipe lists the ingredients and the procedure for preparing a food product. Recipes may be found from a variety of sources such as cookbooks, friends and family, or the Internet. You also may develop your own special dishes over time through experimentation in the kitchen. The study of food science will provide a foundation of knowledge on the ingredient functions that will enable you to

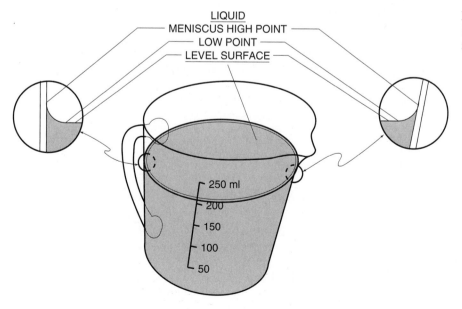

Figure 5-4
When measuring clear liquids, read the meniscus at the lowest point.

successfully adjust recipe ingredients to suit your particular tastes or nutritional preferences.

Recipe Styles

To be effective, the recipe must be written simply and clearly so that it is easily understood. Four general styles of written recipes [1], with a description and an example of each style, are discussed next.

Standard style.   Ingredients are listed first, in the order in which they will be used, followed by the method of combining ingredients in either step or paragraph form. For example:

> 1 cup sifted all-purpose flour
>
> 2 Tbsp granulated sugar
>
> 1 tsp baking powder
>
> 1/4 tsp salt
>
> 1/4 cup shortening (at room temperature)

(And so on.)

1. Preheat oven to 350°F (177°C).
2. Sift dry ingredients together into mixing bowl.
3. Add shortening.

(And so on.)

Action style.   The narrative describing the action or method is combined with the listing of ingredients in order of the steps involved in the procedure. For example:

Measure and sift together in a mixing bowl:

> 1 cup sifted flour
>
> 2 Tbsp sugar
>
> 1 tsp baking powder
>
> 1/4 tsp salt

Add:

1/4 cup shortening

(And so on.)

Descriptive style.   Each ingredient, followed by the modification for that ingredient, is listed in one column. The amount of each ingredient is listed in a separate column, and each step in the procedure is listed in a third parallel column. For example:

Flour, all-purpose, sifted	1 cup	Sift dry ingredients together in mixing bowl.

Sugar, granulated	2 Tbsp	
Baking powder	1 tsp	
Salt	1/4 tsp	
Shortening	1/4 cup	Add to dry ingredients.
	(And so on.)	

Narrative style. The amounts of ingredients and the method are combined in narrative. This may be difficult to follow unless the recipe is short or has few ingredients. For example:

> Sift all-purpose flour once. Measure 1 cup sifted flour, 2 Tbsp granulated sugar, 1 tsp baking powder, and 1/4 tsp salt. Sift all dry ingredients together in a mixing bowl. Add 1/4 cup shortening. (And so on.)

This last style is more easily used for a recipe with few ingredients. For example:

> Thaw 2 pounds of frozen fish fillets. Cut into serving-size pieces. Place on broiler rack. Brush with melted butter or margarine. (And so on.)

Standardization

A recipe is considered standardized only after it has been tried and evaluated for quality, and any necessary adaptations or adjustments have been made. Equipment, types of ingredients available, and skill of the person preparing the recipe differ from one situation to another. Therefore, each recipe must be adapted and standardized for use in a particular situation. Once a recipe has been standardized for a particular setting, it is useful in making out market orders, calculating food costs or nutritional content. Recipes that are standardized for inclusion in cookbooks generally use the methods for measuring ingredients outlined earlier in this chapter. Recipes with eggs are generally standardized using large eggs.

Recipes standardized for foodservice operations should include food safety critical control points as part of the directions. For example, a recipe for chicken may state the chicken should be cooked to a minimum of 165°F (74°C) as a critical control point. Also, mixer bowl, steam-jacketed kettle, and baking pan sizes and serving sizes need to be indicated for each quantity recipe tested.

Recipe yields may need to be adjusted to meet individual situations. Probably the most accurate method for yield adjustment, particularly when large volumes are involved, is called the *percentage method*. In this case, the weight of the total ingredients in the recipe is determined. Then the percentage of each ingredient in the recipe is calculated by dividing the individual ingredient weight by the total weight of ingredients in the recipe. Recipe increases and decreases can then be made by multiplying the percentage of each ingredient by the total weight desired to yield the number of servings to be prepared [6].

In enlarging home-size recipes for quantity use, it is well to first prepare the recipe and evaluate the result to be sure that it produces an acceptable product. Then the recipe may be adjusted for a larger or smaller yield by using the *factor method*. To increase the yield of a recipe using the factor method, first determine the desired number of portions. Then divide the desired number of portions by the current recipe yield to get a factor to be used to increase or decrease the recipe yield. For example if a recipe yields 8 servings and 32 servings are desired, then divide 32 by 8 to get 4 as the factor. Multiply each ingredient weight or measure by the factor you have calculated. In the example given, each ingredient quantity will be multiplied by the factor of 4. Many restaurants and home cooks increase or decrease recipe yields by the factor method. However, when the recipe yield is changed by a large factor, inaccuracies can occur and result in a product failure.

SMALL EQUIPMENT AND TOOLS

Knives are one of the most important tools used in the preparation of food. Understanding the best knife for each task and the development of good knife skills will enable you to prepare high quality foods, efficiently and safely. In addition to the measuring cups and scales previously discussed, whisks, spatulas, scoops, ladles, and multiple other tools each have an important purpose in food preparation.

Knives

A knife should be balanced and made from high quality materials for both the blade and the handle. The parts of the knife are shown in Figure 5-5. A full tang and bolster result in a well-balanced and durable knife. Handles may be made from wood or molded polypropylene. However, regardless of the material, the handle should be comfortable in the hand and easily cleanable.

Knife blades are generally made from carbon steel, stainless steel, or high carbon stainless steel. Carbon steel is an alloy of carbon and iron that sharpens easily. However, carbon steel blades also corrode and discolor easily. Stainless steel blades do not corrode or discolor, but these blades are difficult to sharpen. High carbon stainless steel blades share advantages of carbon steel and stainless steel by sharpening easily and not corroding [4].

A sharp knife is easier to use and reduces fatigue and, more important, the risk of injury. Sharp knives will cut through food products more easily, thereby reducing the risk of dangerous slips. Knives should be sharpened regularly as the edge becomes dull. A sharpening stone or whetstone is used to place an edge on a dull blade (Figure 5-6). To use a stone, the blade is pressed evenly against the stone at a 20-degree angle as if slicing the stone. This step is repeated on both sides of the blade until sharp. Generally, the stone is lubricated with water or mineral oil when sharpening knives. Vegetable oil is not recommended because it will become gummy. The final step in sharpening is to hone the blade with a steel. A steel is a long, thin, cylindrical metal tool that hones and straightens the blade immediately after sharpening and between occasions of sharpening (Figure 5-6). As with the sharpening process, a 20-degree angle is maintained. Although there are other methods of sharpening knives, the use of a stone and steel, with practice, will provide the highest quality edge and maintain the life of the blade.

Figure 5-5
The parts of a chef's or French knife.

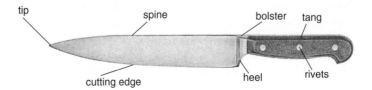

tip   spine   bolster   tang

cutting edge   heel   rivets

(a) Three-Sided Sharpening or Whetstone

(b) Steel

Figure 5-6
(a) A whetstone is used to sharpen knives. (b) A steel is used to straighten the knife blade between sharpenings.

A variety of knives are available, each with a specific purpose. In foodservices, a number of different knives are used because using the proper knife for a given task is safer and more efficient. The same is true in the home. In addition, to using the proper knife for the task, a cutting board is a must to protect you, your work surface, and your knife. Cutting on surfaces other than cutting boards will dull your knife and holding foods in your hands will increase the risk of cuts.

A chef or French knife is used for chopping, slicing, and mincing vegetables such as onions or meats such as diced ham or turkey. This knife should be held with the thumb and index finger gripping the blade. The other three fingers hold the handle (Figure 5-7). This method of gripping the knife provides added stability and control. Although in foodservices, 10–14 inch blades are common, a 6–8 inch knife may be best in home-use. Also, those with a small hand may find a smaller chef knife easier to handle.

When cutting foods, the product should be held with all the fingers, including the thumb, curled back. The blade of the chef knife is guided by the flat surface of the fingers between the first and second knuckles (Figure 5-8). With the finger tips tucked back, cuts are much less likely than when the food is held with the fingertips pointed outward. Initially, gripping the chef knife and food as described may feel awkward. However, with added practice these positions will become natural and will permit the rapid and safe dicing, mincing, and chopping of foods.

Several other kinds of knives are used for specific tasks (Figure 5-9). The utility knife is an all-purpose knife that may be used for cutting fruits and vegetables or carving poultry. A paring knife is usually 2-4 inches in length and is used

Figure 5-7
The most common grip: Hold the handle with three fingers while gripping the blade between the thumb and index finger.

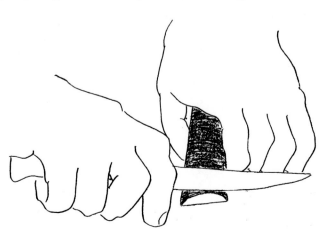

Figure 5-8
The proper cutting method shown with fingers and thumb curled back with blade of the chef knife guided against the knuckles.

Figure 5-9

Knife varieties: (a) French or chef's knife, an all-purpose knife for chopping, slicing, and mincing. (b) Utility knife used for cutting fruits, vegetables, and poultry. (c) Rigid boning knife, is useful for separating meat from bone. (d) Paring knife is short for detailed work such as fruit or vegetable work. (e) Cleavers are used for chopping through bones. (f) Slicer is primarily used for cutting cooked meats. (g) Serrated slicer used for cutting bread or pastry. (h) Butcher's knife is used to prepare raw meats. (i) Oyster and clam knives effectively open oyster and clam shells.

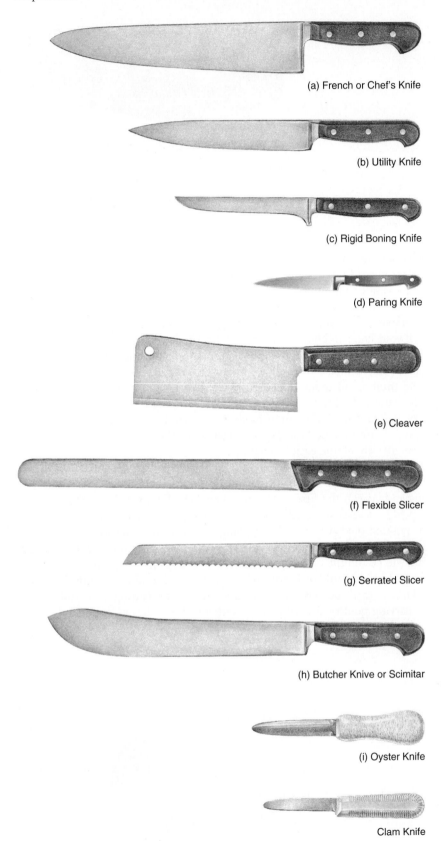

(a) French or Chef's Knife

(b) Utility Knife

(c) Rigid Boning Knife

(d) Paring Knife

(e) Cleaver

(f) Flexible Slicer

(g) Serrated Slicer

(h) Butcher Knive or Scimitar

(i) Oyster Knife

Clam Knife

for very detailed work. Although used by some for many tasks in the kitchen, it is not the best choice for most products that are to be sliced, chopped, or diced. The French knife is more efficient for these types of jobs. A slicer is used for carving cooked meat, whereas a serrated knife is typically used for slicing bread or pastry products. The butcher knife is usually used to cut raw meats [4].

Hand Tools

Many hand tools are used in the kitchen to stir, whip, flip, peel, or grasp foods. Spoons may be solid, perforated, or slotted. Perforated spoons have round holes in them to drain away liquid from small foods such as peas whereas slotted spoons have large slots to drain liquid from larger, more coarse foods. Whisks can be used to whip eggs, egg whites, or heavy cream by hand. Although whisks may be used to mix some bakery products, they may not be the best choice for delicate products that need to be mixed lightly. A number of common hand tools are shown in Figure 5-10.

Portioning and Measuring Tools

Scales and measuring cups were discussed earlier; however, there are other tools that may be used to measure or portion foods. Ladles come in ounce sizes and may be used to measure liquids in the kitchen or for portioning food when served (Figure 5-11). Portion scoops or dishers are sized by a number that corresponds to the number of level scoops per quart [4]. For example, a number 12 scoop is equivalent to 1/3 cup because there are 12 portions of 1/3 cup per quart. Scoops not only measure the amount of food, but are the most efficient way to portion cookies onto a cookie tray or muffins into muffin tins for baking.

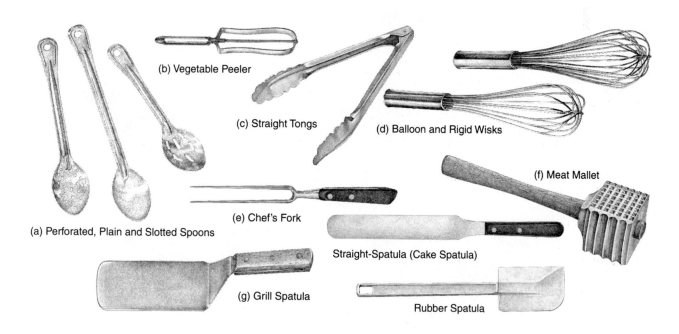

Figure 5-10
Variety of hand tools: (a) Perforated, plain, and slotted spoon. (b) Vegetable peeler. (c) Tongs. (d) Balloon and rigid whisks. (e) Chef's fork. (f) Meat mallet. (g) Grill, rubber, and straight or cake spatulas.

(b) Portion Scoop

(a) Ladles

Figure 5-11
(a) Two ladle sizes used for portioning liquids. (b) Portion scoops are used for dishing cookie dough onto cookie sheets or ice cream into a dish.

Thermometers are an essential item to have in the kitchen. Thermometers are used to measure the endpoint cooking temperatures and to monitor proper refrigeration, and freezer temperatures, thereby promoting food safety (see Chapter 3). Food preparation can be better controlled by measuring the temperature of the oven, of oils when deep fat frying, and of the point at which a candy mixture should be removed from the heat (see Chapter 11).

Other Small Equipment

When draining liquid from large quantities of food a colander, strainer, china cap, or chinois all have specific intended purposes (Figure 5-12). For example, both a colander and a china cap usually are constructed of metal bodies whereas chinois and strainers are composed of fine mesh screens. The piece of equipment you choose will depend on the type of product that you are preparing.

Foods may be mixed using different hand tools depending on whether the product is to be stirred, folded, or whipped. Likewise, mixers have different attachments such as flat paddles, whips, or dough hooks and each performs the mixing function in a specified way (Figure 5-13). The science behind food preparation will provide you with understanding as to why a flat paddle is more appropriate for muffins than a whip, even though a whip is necessary for making angel food cake. Food processors, food choppers, and food blenders are additional pieces of small equipment that can make food preparation quicker and easier.

As you develop skill in food preparation and an understanding of food science, knowing the most appropriate knife, tool, or piece of equipment will come naturally. There are many more pieces of equipment available for use in the home and commercially that have not been discussed in this chapter. You are encouraged to learn how to use equipment to the best advantage to prepare high quality food. In some cases you may find that some functions are best done

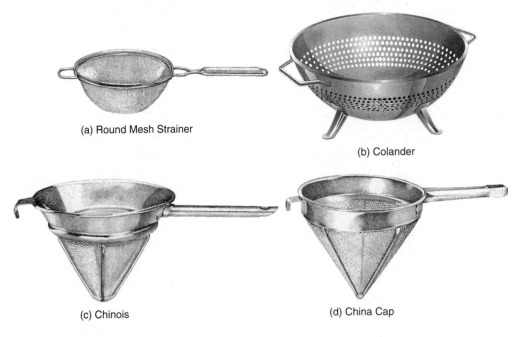

(a) Round Mesh Strainer

(b) Colander

(c) Chinois

(d) China Cap

Figure 5-12
(a) Round mesh strainer. (b) Colander. (c) Chinois. (d) China cap.

Figure 5-13
Mixer and three attachments: the flat paddle, the whip, and the dough hook.

Flat Paddle

Whip

Dough Hook

20-Quart Mixer and Attachments

by hand even though the use of a mixer or processor would complete the task quicker. Safe and efficient work in a kitchen includes knowing how to use small tools and equipment.

CHAPTER SUMMARY

- The correct proportion of ingredients is vital to success in the preparation of many food products. In the United States, recipes generally call for volume measurements, particularly in home cooking.

- Weighing is generally more accurate than measuring, particularly for ingredients such as flour that may pack down in the container. Likewise, the weight and volume relations vary with certain chopped foods, such as onions, depending on the fineness and uniformity of chopping before measuring. Consequently, weights are often used in quantity cookery because of the greater accuracy provided.

- Dry ingredients do not have the same density as liquids. Therefore, one cup (250 milliliters) of water, flour, sugar, chopped onions, and so forth will not have the same weight. If a recipe provides weights for the ingredients, these units of measure cannot be changed into measures or vice versa unless the appropriate conversion factors are known.

- The metric system is a decimal system based on multiples of 10. French scientists developed this system of measurement during the French Revolution. Most of the nations in the world have adopted the metric system. A change in the United States from the U.S. customary system of weights and measures to the metric system was recommended and became public policy with passage by the U.S. Congress of the Metric Conversion Act of 1975. To promote the use of metric, a 1988 amendment to the 1967 Fair Packaging and Labeling Act required that manufacturers show both U.S. customary and metric designations on most consumer products.

- Recipe ingredients are measured with the use of dry-measuring cups, liquid-measuring cups, and measuring spoons or weighed with scales. Dry measuring cups are best used for dry ingredients because these measuring cups are filled to the top with an ingredient such as flour or sugar then leveled off with a straight spatula. Liquid measuring cups allow for space above the liquid to be measured, thereby preventing spills. Dry ingredients may not be properly leveled in a liquid measuring container and any attempts to level the ingredient would result in packing, thereby decreasing the accuracy of the measurement. A set of standards and tolerances for U.S. household measuring utensils was established in 1963.

- Recipes list the ingredients and describe the procedure for preparing food products. To be effective, a recipe must be written simply and clearly so that it is easily understood. The four general styles of written recipes include: standard, action, descriptive, and narrative.

- A recipe is standardized only after it has been tried and evaluated for quality, and any necessary adaptations or adjustments have been made. Recipes standardized for quantity foodservice operations should include food safety critical control points.

- Recipe yields may be adjusted to meet individual situations. The percentage method of yield adjustment is most accurate, especially for large quantity food production. The factor method is commonly used in the home and smaller foodservice operations; however, this method may not provide consistently high quality products if large adjustments in yield are made.

- Knives and cutting boards are among the most important tools used in the preparation of foods. French or chef, utility, paring, butcher, and other knives are designed for specific tasks. The French knife is best for cutting or dicing a wide array of foods. Developing good knife skills includes knowing which knife to use for the job and the proper method of grasping the knife and holding the foods.

- Knives should be well balanced and made from high quality materials. High carbon stainless steel blades both sharpen easily and resist corrosion. A sharp knife is safer and easier to use than a dull one. Knives should be sharpened on a whetstone and honed on a steel to maintain a sharp edge.

- Many hand tools are used in the kitchen to stir, whip, peel, or grasp foods. Thermometers are an essential item to have in the kitchen. The safety and quality of food can be controlled by the measurement of cooking and storage temperatures. Safe and efficient work in the kitchen includes knowing how to use small tools and equipment.

KEY TERMS

density	plastic
mass	meniscus

STUDY QUESTIONS

1. Discuss why accurate measurements are important in the preparation of quality food products.
2. **a.** What is the metric system of measurement and where did it originate?
   b. Why is it important for the United States to convert from the U.S. customary to the metric system?

   c. Name the basic metric units for length, volume or capacity, and weight or mass. What is indicated by the prefixes *deci-*, *centi-*, *milli-*, and *micro-*?

   d. What is meant by *soft conversion* and *hard conversion* to the metric system?

3. What type of measuring cups should be used to measure liquids? What type should be used to measure dry ingredients? Explain.

4. How many tablespoons are there in 1 cup? How many teaspoons are there in 1 tablespoon? How many cups in a quart or in a gallon?

5. If a recipe calls for the *weight* for a dry ingredient and you want to *measure* the ingredient instead, can you convert the weight of any dry ingredient to a measure using the conversion of 1 cup is equal to 8 fluid ounces? Explain.

6. Describe appropriate procedures for measuring flour, liquid, solid fat, sugar, and syrups.

7. What is a standardized recipe? What advantages are there to the use of standardized recipes?

8. Identify two methods of recipe yield adjustment and explain how they are used. Which method is most accurate when large changes in yield are to be calculated?

9. Describe several styles of written recipes and discuss the advantages of each.

10. What are the advantages and disadvantages of the three materials commonly used for knife blades?

11. Explain how to sharpen a knife and describe the tools that are used.

12. Explain how to grasp a knife and to hold food when cutting or slicing.

13. Identify the purpose for which each of the following knives is best used: French/chef, utility, paring, slicer, serrated, and butcher.

14. Identify the purpose for each of the tools described in the text.

REFERENCES

1. American Association of Family and Consumer Sciences. (2001). *Food: A handbook of terminology, purchasing, and preparation* (10th ed.). Alexandria, VA: American Association of Family and Consumer Sciences.

2. American Standards Association. (1963). *American standard dimensions, tolerances, and terminology for home cooking and baking utensils*. New York: American Standards Association, Inc.

3. Arlin, M. L., Nielsen, M. M., & Hall, F. T. (1964). The effect of different methods of flour measurement on the quality of plain two-egg cakes. *Journal of Home Economics, 56*, 399.

4. Labensky, S. R. & Hause, A. M. (2003). *On Cooking: A textbook of culinary fundamentals* (3rd ed.). NJ: Prentice Hall.

5. Matthews, R. H., & Batcher, O. M. (1963). Sifted versus unsifted flour. *Journal of Home Economics, 55*, 123.

6. Molt, M. (2001). *Food for Fifty* (11th ed.). NJ: Prentice Hall.

7. Randal, J. (1994). Going metric: American foods and drugs measure up. *FDA Consumer, 28*: 23(7).

Heat Transfer in Cooking

6

Heat is a form of energy that results from the rapid movement or vibration of **molecules** within a substance. This movement of molecules is called *kinetic energy*. With the use of a thermometer, we can measure the average intensity of the heat resulting from the molecular movement within a substance. We record it as *temperature*.

As the molecules move, they constantly collide with other molecules in the same substance or with molecules of another substance with which they come into contact; and, as molecules collide, their speed of movement may be changed. Rapidly moving molecules striking slower-moving molecules transfer some of their energy to the slower-moving ones. Thus, heat energy is transferred from a warmer substance to a cooler one.

Cooking results when heat is transferred to or produced in a food and is distributed from one part of the food throughout the whole. Heating or cooking produces many changes in foods that, when the cooking is properly done, increase their palatability and appetite appeal.

molecule the smallest particle of a substance that can exist separately and still preserve its characteristic properties. For example, a molecule of water (H_2O) still exhibits the chemical and physical properties of water. Molecules are composed of atoms bonded together. If the atoms are alike (as in oxygen formation, O_2) the resulting molecule is called a compound.

EFFECTS OF COOKING FOOD

There are several important reasons for cooking food. Probably the major one is to make certain foods edible and increase their palatability. Some basic staple foods, such as dry legumes and whole grains, are not in an edible form when they are harvested. These products must be **rehydrated** and softened so that the raw starch is made more palatable and digestible. A remarkable transformation occurs when flour mixtures are baked or cooked, with many new flavor and color changes contributing to their increased palatability and appeal. Meat, poultry, and seafood may be consumed raw in some instances and particularly within certain cultures. However, in terms of food safety, this is not a recommended practice. Proper cooking destroys *most* **pathogenic microorganisms** that may be present in these raw products (see Chapter 3). Thus, cooking improves their sanitary quality. Actually, these foods are generally more aesthetically pleasing, palatable, and acceptable when they have been cooked.

Cooking improves the sanitary quality of other foods as well. The extent of destruction of microorganisms in food is dependent on time and temperature relationships. For example, the threat posed by potentially pathogenic microorganisms in milk is eliminated by **pasteurization,** a relatively mild heat process with carefully controlled times and temperatures.

rehydrate to add water to replace that lost during drying

pathogenic microorganisms microbes capable of causing disease

pasteurization a mild heat treatment that destroys microorganisms that may cause disease but does not destroy all microorganisms in the product

Digestibility and nutritive value may, in some cases, be increased by cooking. Starch in cooked grain products and legumes becomes more readily available to digestive enzymes than that in compact raw **starch granules.** Some antidigestive factors in dry beans and peas are also destroyed by heating. Of course, cooking may bring about decreases in nutritive value as well. For instance, some loss of vitamins and minerals occurs when vegetables and meats are cooked. By avoiding overcooking and improper cooking methods, we can minimize these losses.

The keeping quality or shelf life of some foods is extended by cooking. For example, very perishable fresh peaches or other fruits keep somewhat longer if cooked. When cooked and canned, they keep for a considerably longer period.

Finally, let us not forget that food is to be enjoyed. Cooking foods makes possible the creation of many new delectable dishes, greatly increasing variety and interest in dining.

Flavor, **texture,** and color of foods are affected in various ways by the cooking process. Some new flavors are formed by heating, as meats are browned, breads are baked, and caramels are cooked, for example. Flavor may also be lost or undesirable flavors may be produced by cooking, as is the case when vegetables are overcooked or toast is burned.

Texture is often softened by cooking—the fiber of vegetables becomes limp and the connective tissue of meat is tenderized. Some foods, however, become crisp on cooking (e.g., bacon, potato chips, and other fried foods). Eggs, both whites and yolks, become more firm on heating. The entire character of a texture may be changed by cooking. Note the great difference in texture between a cake batter and the finished cake or between bread dough and the baked loaf. A starch-thickened pudding or sauce also undergoes a remarkable change in texture after sufficient heating.

Color changes occur during cooking as well. Bright green vegetables turn dull and drab when they are overcooked or cooked with acid, whereas a short **blanching** period may actually enhance the color of fresh green peas. Rich brown gravy is made from drippings that have browned during the roasting of meat. Light brown crusts on baked goods enhance their eye appeal and improve flavor and texture characteristics. The effects on food of cooking are truly diverse and, in many cases, highly desirable.

HEAT INVOLVED IN CHANGE OF STATE

A substance may exist as a solid, a liquid, or a gas. When it changes from a solid to a liquid or from a liquid to a gas, we say that a *change of state* occurs. The physical state of the matter—solid, liquid, or gas—has changed. Energy is involved in this change of state. Let us use water as an example, because water is commonly employed as a medium for applying heat in food preparation.

The solid form of water is ice. In a chunk of ice, the water molecules have formed an ordered crystalline pattern and are held in a fixed arrangement in relation to each other. In a solid such as ice, the molecules may vibrate in place but do not move around freely.

When heat is applied to ice, the water molecules vibrate more rapidly and push against each other. When sufficient heat has been applied, the ice melts and becomes liquid water. In a liquid, the molecules have broken away from each other and are free to move about; however, they remain together and take the shape of the container in which they are placed.

starch granules Starch molecules are organized into tight little bundles, called granules, as they are stored in the seeds or roots of plants; the granules, with characteristic shapes and sizes, can be seen under the microscope.

texture the arrangement of the particles or constituent parts of a material that gives it its characteristic structure

blanch to heat for a few minutes by immersing in boiling water, surrounding with steam, or applying microwaves

Liquid water may form water vapor, which is a gas. The molecules in a gas are widely separated and move freely in space. When liquid water stands in an open container, some of its molecules vaporize, or become gas, even at room temperature. These gaseous molecules hovering over the surface of liquid water create a pressure called *vapor pressure*. As heat is gradually applied to liquid water, more gaseous molecules form, thus increasing the vapor pressure. When the vapor pressure is increased to a point just greater than the atmospheric pressure, bubbles that are formed in the liquid will begin to break at the surface and boiling ensues. This process equalizes the vapor pressure and the atmospheric pressure. The water vapor coming from hot or boiling water is called steam.

At sea level, the temperature at which water boils is 212°F (100°C). Water boils at lower temperatures at higher elevations because the atmospheric pressure is lower at higher elevations. As a consequence, food must be cooked longer in mountainous regions in the world because it is the temperature and not the boiling action that influences cooking time. In contrast, vapor pressure builds up in a pressure cooker to levels greater than the atmospheric pressure, thereby increasing the boiling point of water to above 212°F (100°C). Thus, foods cook faster in a pressure cooker.

Heat Capacity of Water

Liquid water has a relatively large capacity to absorb heat. In fact, it is used as a standard for measuring the heat capacities of other substances. Water has been assigned a heat capacity of 1.00, called its *specific heat*, which indicates that 1 **calorie** is required to increase the temperature of 1 gram of water 1 degree Celsius. Thus, to take 100 grams of water (about 2/5 cup) from 0°C (32°F) to boiling at 100°C (212°F), 10,000 calories of heat or energy (1 calorie per gram per degree = 1 calorie × 100 grams × 100 degrees = 10,000 calories) are required. (These are *small* calories; 1,000 of these equal 1 kilocalorie, which is the unit used in nutrition.)

calorie a unit of heat measurement; in this chapter, we are referring to the small calorie used in chemistry; the kilocalorie (1 kilocalorie is equal to 1000 small calories) is used in nutrition

Latent Heat

A special kind of heat or energy is used to bring about the change from one physical state to another, for example, from solid ice to liquid water. This heat or energy is called *latent heat*, which is required to change the physical state without changing the temperature as measured by a thermometer. Heat measured by use of a thermometer is called *sensible heat*.

In the case of water, the latent heat involved is 80 calories for each gram of ice that changes to liquid water. This energy is *absorbed* by the melting ice and is used to break up the ordered molecules of water in the ice structure. Actually, the same amount of energy—80 calories per gram—was *released* from the liquid water as it froze and formed solid ice crystals. This heat that is absorbed during a change from solid to liquid state and released during a change from liquid to solid state is called *latent heat of fusion* or *solidification*. We take advantage of the latent heat of fusion when we freeze ice cream using an ice and salt mixture. As the ice melts, the heat necessary for bringing about this change of state is taken from the ice cream mixture to be frozen, thus making it colder, since *cold* is really the absence of heat. Pure water freezes to ice at 32°F (0°C), and ice melts at this same temperature. A salt solution freezes at a lower temperature. Addition of salt to ice causes more rapid melting of the ice as equilibrium in vapor

Figure 6-1
Two thermometer scales are used in measuring temperature, the Fahrenheit and the Celsius.

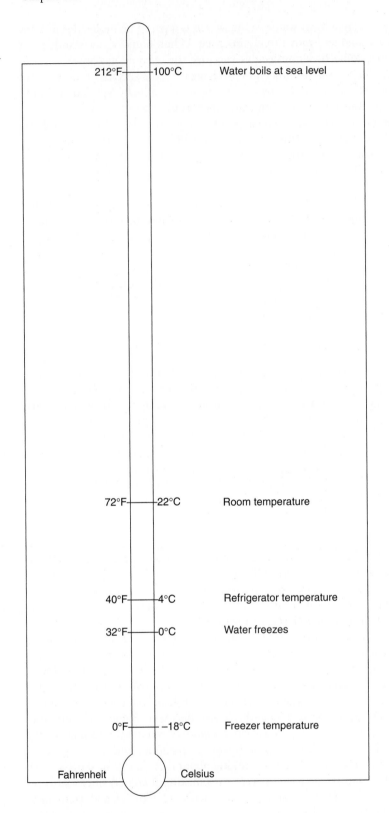

pressure is established for the mixture, thus enabling the freezing of ice cream in home style ice cream makers (see Chapter 12).

Latent heat is also involved when liquid water changes to a gas in the form of water vapor or steam. When liquid water changes to steam, latent heat is absorbed. In this case, it is called *latent heat of vaporization*. For each gram of water vaporized at the boiling point, 540 calories are absorbed, but the temperature of the newly formed steam is the same as that of the boiling water, 212°F (100°C). The energy of latent heat is necessary to bring about the wide separation of water molecules from each other as they form a gas. In the reverse process—the condensation of steam to liquid water—the same amount of energy is given off as the *latent heat of condensation*. We take advantage of this released heat when we steam foods. As steam touches the cooler surface of the food, it condenses to liquid and releases the 540 calories per gram of water condensed. This energy is absorbed by the food, thus actually aiding in the cooking process. It is this same energy absorption that accounts for the severity of steam burns when our skin comes in contact with steam.

THERMOMETER SCALES

Thermometers are used to measure sensible heat—that which can be felt by the senses. Two thermometer scales may be used to indicate the temperature of a substance. The Fahrenheit scale (F) is commonly used in the United States in connection with the U.S. customary system of weights and measures. With conversion to the metric system, the Celsius (or Centigrade) scale (C) will be used. It is presently used in scientific research, and commonly used in most other nations of the world.

Using the Fahrenheit scale, water at sea level freezes at 32° and boils at 212°. On the Celsius scale, water freezes at 0° and boils at 100°. The usual room temperature of 72°F is 22° on the Celsius scale (Figure 6-1). As long as the two scales are in use, it may be necessary to convert from one to the other. Formulas that can be used for the conversion, and a partial conversion chart, are found in Appendix B. Conversion tables may also be found in the *Food: A Handbook* and *Food for Fifty* [1, 3].

TYPES OF HEAT TRANSFER

Conventional cooking methods transfer heat energy from its source to the food by means of conduction, convection currents, and radiation (Figure 6-2). In most cooking methods, more than one means of heat transfer is involved. Some cooktops may be specially designed to cook by magnetic induction (discussed later in the chapter).

Conduction

In the case of conduction, heat is transmitted from one molecule or particle to the next one in direct contact with it. Heat moves from the heated coil of an electric unit, the touching flame of a gas unit, or other heat source to the saucepan placed on it and from the saucepan to the first layer of food, water, or fat in contact with the bottom and sides of the pan. Then heat is conducted throughout the mass of the food in the pan the same way, particle by particle (Figure 6-3). Using a pan with a flat bottom that comes in close contact with the heat source conserves heat and utilizes it most efficiently.

Figure 6-2
Arrows indicate heat patterns during conduction, convection, and radiation.

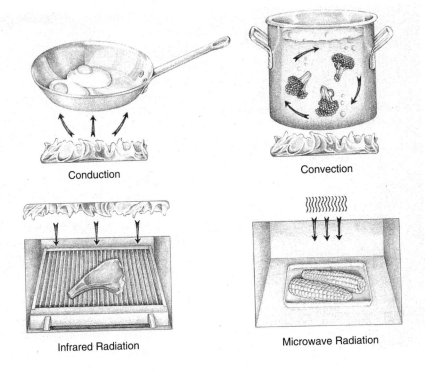

Conduction   Convection

Infrared Radiation   Microwave Radiation

Heat source

Figure 6-3
Conduction. Heat is transferred from an electric heating unit or from a gas flame that touches the bottom of the pan, through the pan, to the layer of the food that is next to the pan, and then throughout the food mass.

Fat can be heated to much higher temperatures than water; thus it is possible to bring more heat into the pan during the frying process. Water boils at 212°F (100°C), but it is common to fry foods at about 375°F (190°C).

Materials used in the construction of cooking utensils vary in their ability to conduct heat efficiently. Metals that are good conductors include copper, aluminum, and iron. Pans are commonly made of either cast aluminum or aluminum formed from sheets (Figure 6-4). Cast-iron skillets and dutch ovens are heavy cooking utensils that distribute and hold heat well. Stainless steel is an alloy of iron with a small percentage of carbon and other metals, such as chromium and nickel. It is a very durable, easily cleaned metal, but it does not conduct heat uniformly. Because so many of its other properties are desirable for cooking utensils, however, it is often combined in various ways with other metals to improve heating efficiency and eliminate "hot spots." For example, the heating base of a stainless steel pan may be clad with copper or aluminum, or a core of iron or other high-conductivity metal may be placed between the sheets of stainless steel used to form the pan. Cooking utensils used in the home are also made of heat-resistant glass, ceramic materials, and metal coated with a porcelain type substance. Nonstick finishes such as Teflon™ may also be applied to the inner surfaces of pans and skillets.

Ideally, pans should be sturdy and warp resistant even with extended use. It is important that the bottom of the pan maintain contact on a flat heating surface for efficient heat conduction. The durability of a metal is determined to a great extent by its thickness, which is measured by its *gauge*. Gauge may be defined as the number of metal sheets of this particular thickness required to equal 1 inch. For example, ten sheets of 10-gauge stainless steel or aluminum would equal a thickness of 1 inch; in other words, each sheet is 1/10 inch thick.

Figure 6-4
Various styles of cookware allow for a variety of preparation methods.

Ten-gauge metal will produce a sturdy pan. Pans should be cared for in a manner that will prevent warping, such as never placing hot pans or skillets immediately in cold water.

Convection Currents

An aid to heating by conduction for liquid and gaseous substances is convection. When gases and liquids are heated, they become lighter or less dense and tend to rise. The colder portions of these gases and liquids are more dense or heavier and move to the bottom. The lighter air rises and cooler, heavier air moves to the bottom, thus setting up circular convection currents as illustrated in (Figure 6-5.)

Convection currents move the molecules around in their enclosed space and tend to distribute the heat uniformly throughout. Examples of the usefulness of these currents include cooking in a saucepan or other container with food particles dispersed in water (as is done with soups and stews), deep-fat frying, and baking in an oven. When foods are cooked in water, convection currents move the heated water molecules up and around the larger particles of food, transferring heat to the surfaces of the food. This heat can then be transferred into the particles by the process of conduction. In deep-fat frying, the molecules of fat are moved upward and around the surfaces of the foods being fried in them. During cooking on a gas surface burner, radiant heat is also transferred to the outside surface of the pan by convection.

Figure 6-5

When liquids and gases are heated they become lighter (less dense) and rise, whereas cooler molecules of the liquid or gas move to the bottom of a container or closed compartment. These movements create convection currents that aid in distributing heat throughout the liquid or gas.

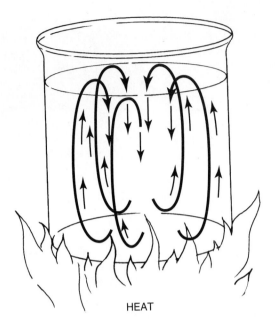

HEAT

In conventional-oven baking, heated gas molecules of air rise from the energy source in the bottom and move around the surfaces of the baking containers. This movement particularly aids in the browning of the tops of baked products and other foods. Placement of containers in the oven is important to take full advantage of convection currents in cooking and browning. When it is necessary to use two racks, the pans should be staggered so that one is not directly underneath the other (see Figure 6-6).

Figure 6-6

Convection currents move heated air around cake surfaces to aid in baking and browning.

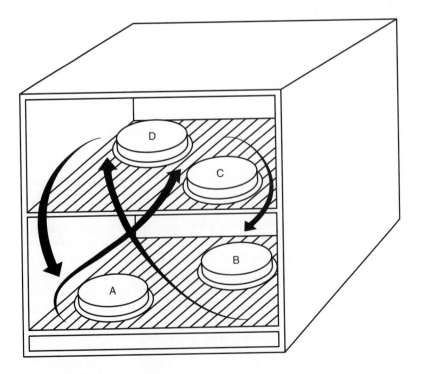

A convection oven employs a mechanical fan that increases air movement in the oven during baking, thus increasing the efficiency of heat transfer and decreasing cooking time. Convection ovens are common in foodservices and are becoming popular in the home. When using a convection oven, the baking time and temperature should be reduced to avoid overcooking. A temperature reduction of about 25°F (10°F) is suggested.

Radiation

Energy can be transmitted as waves or rays that vibrate at high frequency and travel very rapidly through space. An example of radiant energy is sunlight, which travels at the rate of 186,000 miles per second. Radiant waves go directly from their source to the material they touch without any assistance in the transfer of energy from the air molecules in between.

When radiant waves or rays reach the exterior parts of a food mass, energy is absorbed on the surface of the food and produces heat by increasing the vibration of the molecules in the food. Because the waves cannot penetrate below the surface, the interior is heated by conduction as the surface energy is transferred from one molecule to the next until it reaches the center of the food mass. Therefore, a combination of radiation and conduction is responsible for the heating of food in some cooking processes.

The broiling, barbecuing, and toasting of foods utilize radiant energy for cooking. The glowing coals of a fire, the red-hot coils of an electric heating unit, and the burning of a gas flame give off waves of radiant energy that travel from their source in a straight line to the surface of food that is placed in close proximity.

Radiant energy is an important factor in oven baking. The waves of energy reach the exposed surface of the food and the outer surface of the utensil that holds the food. The utensil absorbs the energy and becomes hot. Heat is then transferred by conduction from the utensil to the food that is in it. The characteristics of the utensil being used affect the amount of energy absorbed by it from the radiant waves. Dull, dark, rough surfaces absorb radiant energy readily, whereas bright, shiny, smooth surfaces tend to reflect the waves and absorb less energy, thus slowing the cooking and browning. Sometimes shiny aluminum bakeware is desirable, for example, to produce a light crust on layer cakes and cookies. Ovenproof glass dishes generally transmit radiant waves. Therefore, when glass bakeware is used, the oven temperature should be about 25°F (14°C) less than that used with aluminum bakeware.

Air molecules in the oven absorb some of the radiant energy coming from the heating unit and become less dense or lighter. The lighter air rises and is replaced by colder, heavier air, thus setting up convection currents. These convection currents help to distribute the heat uniformly throughout the interior oven space, although they are separate from the radiant waves. The radiant energy continues to travel from its source in a straight line, with some fanning out as the distance from the source increases.

Infrared radiation is heat or energy from a slightly different wavelength. Infrared heat may be produced by high-energy lamps. These are sometimes used to keep food warm on a serving line. Infrared radiation has been used to dry fruits and vegetables and for heat blanching.

Although microwave cooking utilizes a form of radiant energy, microwaves are different from other radiant waves used in cooking food. In all cases, they are high-frequency electromagnetic waves, but microwaves have longer wavelengths and are somewhat lower in frequency than visible-light and infrared waves in the electromagnetic spectrum (see Figure 7-4). Microwaves cook food differently from the way radiant waves cook. Microwave cooking is discussed in Chapter 7.

Induction Heating

induction coil a coiled apparatus made up of two coupled circuits; interruptions in the direct current in one circuit produce an alternating current of high electrical potential in the other

ferrous iron-containing

Induction cooking utilizes a high-frequency **induction coil** that is placed just beneath the cooktop surface. The cooktop is made of a smooth, ceramic material (Figure 6-7). A magnetic current is generated by the coil, and **ferrous** metal cooking utensils placed on the cooktop are heated with magnetic friction. The cooking surface itself remains cool. Only the cooking utensil gets hot. The hot utensil rapidly transmits heat to the food.

Flat cooking utensils made of cast iron, magnetic stainless steel, or enamel over steel are required for use on induction cooktops; utensils made of nonferrous materials cannot be heated. Heating by induction is rapid, and numerous power settings are available. Another advantage of the induction cooktop is the ease of cleaning. Because there is no exposed heating unit and the surface does not get hot, spills do not burn onto the unit.

MEDIA FOR HEAT TRANSFER

Media for transferring heat to food include air, water, steam, and fat. Combinations of these media may be employed.

Air

Roasting, baking, broiling, and cooking on an outdoor grill are methods that employ heated air as the cooking medium. These are generally considered to be dry-heat cookery methods, because the surface of the food comes into contact with dry air; however, in the interior of most foods, water participates in the transfer of heat. Also, where part of the product is in direct contact with a pan or cookie sheet, the heat from the air is conducted through the pan to the food. In convection ovens, a blower circulates the heated air and the food heats more rapidly. When the surface of a food is dehydrated, temperatures higher than the boiling point of water may be attained, aiding in browning.

stew to simmer in a small to moderate quantity of liquid

braise to cook meat or poultry slowly in a small amount of liquid or in steam in a covered utensil

poach to cook in a hot liquid, carefully handling the food to retain its form

Water

Simmering, boiling, **stewing, braising,** and **poaching** are methods that use water as the primary cooking medium. For obvious reasons, these are called *moist-heat* cookery methods. When water is the cooking medium, the highest

Figure 6-7
Induction cooktops generate a magnetic current to heat cast iron or magnetic stainless steel cookware.

Induction Cooktop

temperature attainable is that of boiling, 212°F (100°C) at sea level. Simmering and poaching use temperatures just below boiling. At altitudes higher than sea level, the boiling point of water is decreased 1°C (1.8°F) for each 900 feet of elevation.

Water is a better conductor of heat than air; therefore, foods cooked in water cook faster. Heat is transferred or conducted directly from the hot water to the food with which it comes into contact. Convection currents are also set up in hot water and help to distribute heat uniformly throughout the food mass.

Steam

Steaming is also a moist-heat method of cooking. Foods are steamed when they are placed on a rack above boiling water in a covered container that holds in the steam. Steaming also occurs when a food that contains water is closely wrapped and baked in the oven, such as a baked potato or a cut of meat wrapped in aluminum foil or placed in a cooking bag. Cooking a covered casserole in the oven involves cooking with steam, because the steam produced when the liquid boils is contained in the dish.

Heat is transferred from the steam to the surface of the food it touches. The food is often cooler than the steam, so the steam condenses on the surface, releasing the latent heat absorbed when the steam was formed from boiling water. This process aids in cooking and as discussed previously, explains why a steam burn is likely to be more severe than one caused by boiling water.

In a pressure canner, steam is the cooking medium; however, because the close containment of the steam within the canner raises the vapor pressure, the boiling point of the water producing the steam is increased (Figure 6-8). Therefore, the temperature of cooking within the pressure canner is elevated above the boiling point of water at atmospheric pressure and cooking is much more

Figure 6-8
A pressure canner is necessary to obtain tempertures higher than 212°F (100°C). (Courtesy of National Presto Industries, Inc.)

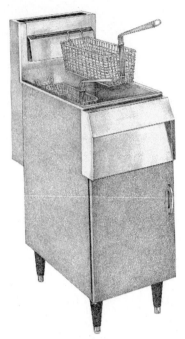

Deep-Fat Fryer

Figure 6-9
Deep-fat fryers are equipped with wire baskets so fried foods can be raised and lowered to achieve adequate frying time.

rapid. In a pressure saucepan, an adjustable gauge on the pan regulates the pressure and thus the temperature by releasing some steam during the cooking process. Canning is discussed further in Chapter 30.

Fat

Fat is the cooking medium in sautéing, panfrying, and deep-fat frying. To *sauté* means to cook quickly in a very small amount of fat at a high temperature. Some sautéed foods may be lightly dusted with flour. Stir-frying is similar to sautéing, but it is commonly done in a wok (Figure 6-4). Panfrying is cooking in a small amount of fat that comes about one-third to one half of the way up the food to be cooked. Thus, more fat is used in panfrying as compared to sautéing. Pan-frying also is at a more moderate temperature and the foods are frequently coated in breading [2]. Cooking a food immersed in fat at a controlled temperature is deep-fat frying (Figure 6-9). In all these methods of cooking, heat is transferred by conduction from the energy source through the pan to the fat. Convection currents are set up in the heated fat and aid in distributing the heat. The heated fat then conducts heat to the food it touches.

Fat can be heated to a much higher temperature than the boiling point of water. Because some fat also is absorbed by the food, the flavor is changed to a considerable degree. Frying is discussed in more detail in Chapter 10.

CHAPTER SUMMARY

- Heat is a form of energy that results from the rapid movement or vibration of molecules within a substance. A thermometer is used to measure the average intensity of sensible heat. Two thermometer scales are commonly employed, the Fahrenheit and the Celsius or Centigrade scales.

- Food is cooked so as to make it edible, increase palatability, increase digestibility, reduce or eliminate pathogenic microorganisms, improve keeping quality, and enhance enjoyment. In some cases, such as with dry beans and peas, the nutritive value is increased by cooking. Cooking changes textures, colors and flavors.

- Heat is involved in the change of a substance from a solid to a liquid, then to a gas. Ice is the solid form of water, whereas steam is the gas form. Latent heat is required to change the physical state of a substance, such as water, from a solid (ice) to a gas (steam). Latent heat does not result in a change of temperature; thus boiling water is at 212°F (100°C), as is steam. The amount of energy needed to change ice to water without a change in temperature is 80 calories. When liquid water changes to steam, 540 calories are needed. These calories are small calories: 1000 calories equal 1 kilocalorie. The unit used in nutrition, although often called "calories," is kilocalories.

- In conventional cooking, heat is transferred from the energy source to the food by conduction, convection, and/or radiation. More than one type of heat transfer is typical when cooking.

- Materials used in the construction of cooking utensils vary in their ability to conduct heat efficiently. Copper, aluminum, and iron are excellent conductors. Although stainless steel is a high quality material that resists stain-ing and corrosion, it is not one of the best conductors. Thus, stainless steel pans often are copper clad or have a high-conductivity metal placed be-tween the sheets of stainless steel used to form the pan.

- Induction cooking utilizes a high-frequency induction coil that is placed just beneath the cooking surface. The coil generates a magnetic current that heats ferrous metal cooking utensils placed on the cooking surface. Non-ferrous cooking utensils will not heat up on induction cooktop sur-faces.

- Air, water, steam, and fat are media for the transfer of heat. Roasting, bak-ing, broiling, and cooking on an outdoor grill are methods that employ heated air as the major cooking medium. These are called dry-heat cook-ing methods. Simmering, boiling, stewing, braising, and poaching are cooking methods that use water as the primary cooking medium. These are called moist-heat cooking methods. Steam is also a moist-heat cooking method. Fat is the cooking medium in sautéing, pan-frying, and deep-fat frying.

KEY TERMS

molecule
rehydrate
pathogenic microorganisms
pasteurization
starch granules
texture
blanch

calorie
induction coil
ferrous
stew
braise
poach

STUDY QUESTIONS

1. List and explain five reasons for cooking food.
2. Give examples of changes in flavor, texture, and color of foods that may occur during cooking.
3. **a.** Define and compare *latent heat* and *sensible heat.*
   b. How much energy is involved in the latent heat of fusion for water? The latent heat of vaporization at boiling?
   c. What is *vapor pressure* and how is it related to the boiling point of water?
   d. What is meant by the *specific heat* of water?
4. Compare the Fahrenheit and Celsius thermometer scales.
5. Describe how heat is transferred in food preparation by (a) conduction, (b) radiation, (c) convection currents, and (d) induction heating.
6. **a.** Name four different media commonly used for transferring heat to food and give examples of several cooking methods that use each medium.
   b. What types of heat transfer are generally used in each method that you cited in question (a)?

REFERENCES

1. American Association of Family and Consumer Sciences. (2001). *Food: A handbook of terminology, purchasing, and preparation.* (10th ed.). Alexandria, VA: American Association of Family and Consumer Sciences.

2. Labensky, S. R., & Hause, A. M. (2003). *On Cooking: A textbook for culinary fundamentals* (3rd ed.). NJ: Prentice Hall.

3. Molt, M. (2001). *Food for Fifty* (11th ed.). NJ: Prentice Hall.

Microwave Cooking

7

Microwave heating stemmed from the development of radar during World War II. It was then recognized that radar antennas generated heat and that this principle might be useful in heating food. The first microwave oven (called the Radarange) became available for foodservice establishments in 1947 and the first one for consumer use was introduced in 1955. These early manufactured models were large, heavy, specially wired, and very expensive with pricetags around $1,300. Microwave ovens are now used in more than 90 percent of U.S. households [2]. The microwave oven of today is very different from the pioneer models; it is convenient, attractive, easy to use, and available in varying sizes, wattages, and prices (Figure 7-1).

Microwave ovens have had a tremendous impact on food preparation practices. In fact, an expert panel meeting in 1989 called the microwave oven one of the 10 most significant innovations in food science and technology during the previous 50 years [13]. The commercial foodservice microwave market was developed first, but it has since been extended to include convenience stores, lounges, taverns, snack bars, and restaurants of all sizes [7]. The consumer microwave oven market developed later, after advances in technology made it possible to produce reliable ovens at an affordable cost.

Microwaves are useful in food processing. The most commercially successful industrial applications include the tempering of frozen meat, poultry, and fish to condition them for such operations as grinding, blending, and patty forming; and precooking of bacon in meat-processing plants for use in foodservice establishments. Microwaves are also used in pasta drying and potato chip processing [13].

The widespread use of microwave ovens in homes and foodservice establishments has created a challenge for food processors. Foods that can be reheated or prepared in microwave ovens are in demand. These foods must reproduce the appearance, texture, and flavor of foods prepared by conventional-oven cooking. Thus, conventional recipes may need to be reformulated [1]. Directions for *both* microwave and conventional heating and/or cooking are found on the packages of convenience foods that require heat processing before consumption.

Because of the widespread use of microwave ovens in food preparation and processing, it is important for students of food science to understand the principles of microwave cookery. Although the cooking of vegetables, meats, eggs, and some starch and flour mixtures by microwaves is discussed in the various

Chapter Seven

Figure 7-1
Microwave ovens are a common appliance in today's kitchens. (Courtesy of World Kitchens, makers of CorningWare®.)

chapters about these foods, general principles of microwave cookery are addressed in this chapter.

FOOD-RELATED USES OF MICROWAVES

Microwave heating of food is useful in households, institutional foodservice, and also in the food industry for processing.

Home

Microwaves ovens are used most frequently in the home to boil water, heat frozen foods, defrost frozen foods, or make popcorn [10]. Consumers have not been quick to embrace cooking entire meals in the microwave, even though there are a number of microwave cookbooks that provide recipes and guidance for those interested in cooking applications. Instead, consumers often use the microwave for speed and convenience (Figure 7-2). Younger members of the household also use microwave ovens. Some parents may be more comfortable allowing their older children to heat a snack in the microwave rather than in an oven. The interior of microwave ovens, as well as generally the food container, stay cool when heating a food item, and thus may be perceived as safer.

Microwave popcorn became very popular with consumers in the 1980's due to the development of susceptor technology in popcorn packaging [3]. **Heat susceptors** may consist of metallized paperboard, which strongly absorbs energy and becomes very hot. The metal itself does not absorb the microwave energy but it readily absorbs the heat produced by the other materials in the packaging. Thus, the use of susceptors allowed the popcorn to become hot enough to pop. Likewise, susceptors are used for microwavable pizza, sandwiches and other products where the concentration of heat is useful to promote browning or crispness.

Manufacturers are continuing to develop new microwavable foods that respond to consumers' desires for speed and convenience. Frozen juice can now be taken from the freezer and reconstituted in only 1–2 minutes when packaged in plastic microwavable cans [10]. A variety of other products including soups, rice and pasta entrees, pizzas, and sandwiches are being developed with packaging specifically designed for effective microwave heating [3,16]. These newly

heat susceptors materials that intensify localized heating in microwavable packaged food products

Figure 7-2
A snack like nachos can be conveniently prepared in the microwave. (Courtesy of World Kitchens, makers of CorningWare®.)

developed products provide a much higher level of quality for the consumer as compared to the microwavable foods of a decade earlier.

Foodservice

Heavy-duty commercial microwave units are often installed in foodservice establishments. These units have high-output capabilities and are designed to withstand rough treatment. They are currently used primarily for reheating. For example, hospital foodservices may use microwaves as part of a system in which individual plates of chilled menu items are reheated, one meal at a time, just prior to service to the patient [19].

Microwave tunnel ovens may be used in foodservices for continuous microwave heating of cooked, portioned foods [7]. However, primary cooking currently consumes a relatively small proportion of total use time for microwaves in foodservice. When cooking in quantity, microwave ovens do not result in a time saving unless the microwave tunnel oven is used. Consequently, there is the potential for expansion in the use of microwave cooking in foodservice application, particularly in the area of primary cooking, if the food quantity and equipment are not limiting factors.

Food Industry

The **tempering** of meat, precooking of bacon, and sausage cooking represent the largest uses of microwave processing by the food industry [14]. Microwave processing equipment is used to temper 4 billion pounds of food each year. As the foods are tempered, they are brought to a temperature just below the freezing point of water, where they are not frozen but are still firm. Conventional thawing of these foods may take several days, whereas microwave tempering

tempering holding a substance at a specified temperature to give it the desired consistency; frozen foods may be tempered by holding them just below 32°F (0°C)

can be completed within minutes, with less drip loss and reduced microbial growth [8].

The precooking of bacon is another major use of microwave technology by food processors. In bacon processing, 80,000 slices may be precooked per hour in microwave processing equipment [14]. Currently, nearly all of the bacon processed for foodservice use is precooked in microwave ovens and 10 percent of the bacon used in the home has been similarly precooked.

Microwave equipment can be custom designed and tailored to the needs of a particular food product, process, or package [8]. Conveyer belts are often used to move products through a microwave field, resulting in more uniformity in the distribution of energy throughout the food products (Figure 7-3). Mathematical modeling is an advance in microwave processing that uses software to model microwave heating patterns [14].

A combination of microwave and conventional heating can be used for drying pasta, saving both time and energy as compared with conventional drying. Microwave drying may also be used for fruit juice concentrates, herbs, bread crumbs, potato chips, and snack foods [8]. High-intensity microwaves may be combined with external heat sources, such as hot-air or infrared energy, to cook products quickly while simultaneously producing a browned surface. Often high yields, superior quality, and more rapid processing result [14].

Fresh pasta, bread, granola, yogurt, meat products, and prepared meals can be **pasteurized** using microwave energy. **Sterilization** can be achieved with microwaves using overpressure conditions to produce temperatures of 230° to 266°F (110° to 130°C) when proper packaging materials are used. The **proofing** of yeast-leavened products can also be accomplished in a short time with the use of microwaves. Microwaves may be used for baking bread, pizza,

pasteurization the process of heating a food to 140°–180°F (60°–82°C) to destroy pathogenic organisms of public health significance

sterilization the process of heating a material sufficiently to destroy essentially all microorganisms

proofing the last rising of yeast-leavened dough after it is shaped and placed in a baking pan

Figure 7-3
A microwave pasteurization unit with a continuous conveyer passing through a microwave field. (Reprinted from *Food Technology*, 46, (9), p. 121, 1992. Copyright © by Institute of Food Technologists)

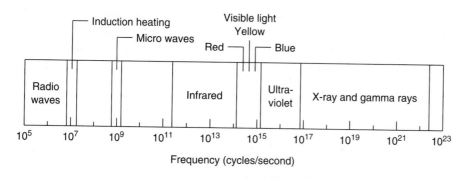

cake, and pastry products, often in combination with conventional baking methods [8].

ACTION OF MICROWAVES IN HEATING

Microwaves are high-frequency electromagnetic waves of radiant energy. They can be described as radio waves of very short wavelength, falling between television and infrared frequencies on the electromagnetic spectrum (see Figure 7-4). In comparing wavelengths, radio waves are measured in kilometers, television frequencies in meters, microwaves in centimeters, and infrared waves in microns [7]. Microwaves are generated in a vacuum tube called a *magnetron*, which converts alternating electric current from a household circuit into electromagnetic energy radiation. Microwaves radiate outward from their original source and can be absorbed, transmitted, or reflected. In most microwave ovens, a stirrer blade in the top of the oven helps to distribute the waves (Figure 7-5). In other ovens, foods are rotated by turntables as a means of uniformly distributing energy.

The short, straight microwaves are reflected by metals. The metal walls of a microwave oven reflect and thus contain the microwaves within the oven cavity. Microwaves reach the food that is to be cooked both directly from the magnetron unit and indirectly by reflection from the metal walls.

The Federal Communications Commission has assigned certain frequencies for microwave cooking to avoid interference with communication systems that operate in closely associated frequencies. These assigned frequencies are

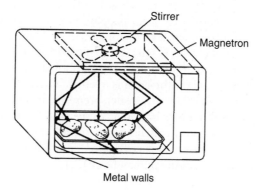

Figure 7-5
Microwaves are produced by a magnetron, from which they enter the oven. A stirrer deflects the microwaves and distributes them to various parts of the oven. They are reflected back from the metal walls of the oven. The food in the oven absorbs the microwave energy, and heat is created in the food as a result of the friction produced between the rapidly moving molecules.

915 and 2,450 megahertz (million cycles per second). The higher the frequency, the shorter the wavelength and the more shallow the depth of penetration of the waves into the food being cooked. At a frequency of 2,450 megahertz, the wavelength is approximately 4.8 inches, whereas at a frequency of 915 megahertz, the wavelength is about 13.5 inches. The shorter wavelengths produce more uniform heating and better results for small items being cooked. Thus, although microwave cooking can be satisfactorily accomplished at either frequency, only the 2,450 megahertz frequency is used in the microwave ovens being manufactured today for commercial foodservice and home use [7].

Some manufacturers have combined a conventional electric oven with a microwave oven in the same compartment, whereas others have provided conventional electric ovens as part of a cooking center. A microwave–convection oven combination is also available.

Variable cooking power outputs are made possible in a microwave oven by varying the design of the magnetron tube. Microwave ovens for consumer use usually have an output capability of 600 to 700 watts, whereas commercial units often have a higher wattage. The design assumption for the heavy-duty units is that they will be used hundreds of times per day. Microwave ovens with lower power—400 to 500 watts—are also available for home use. These units cost less than those with higher wattages and although they heat more slowly than the units with higher wattages, they have sold well in the United States, representing 35 to 50 percent of total microwave oven sales [7].

High-speed cooking can be slowed in most microwave ovens presently being manufactured, allowing cooking on various medium and low speeds. The reduced-power settings actually give full power intermittently, with on-off cycling, which reduces localized overheating and helps to protect sensitive foods. Variable settings have increased the adaptability of the oven for many different products.

Automatic features also add to the greater efficiency of today's microwave ovens. For example, some ovens automatically determine the cooking time and power level when the weight of a roast of meat or poultry is entered into the program. Some sensor programs can automatically determine doneness and then turn off the oven, or, alternatively, the product can be cooked and then held warm for a period. In addition, defrost cycles are often automatic.

Since 1971, the U.S. Food and Drug Administration (FDA) has regulated the manufacture of microwave ovens in terms of performance standards and design safety. A radiation safety standard enforced by the FDA limits the amount of microwaves that can leak from an oven throughout its lifetime [22]. The limit is 5 milliwatts of microwave radiation per square centimeter at a distance of 5 centimeters (2 inches) from the oven surfaces. This amount is far below the level known to harm people, and the exposure decreases as one moves away from the oven. For example, the exposure to microwave radiation at 20 inches from the oven is only one-hundredth of the level at 2 inches. Microwave ovens also are required to have two interlocking systems to prevent the production of microwaves if the latch is opened. The FDA tests microwave ovens in commercial establishments, dealer premises, manufacturing plants, FDA labs, and in a limited number of homes to see that the standard for allowable leakage is met. The standard is believed to protect the public from radiation hazards. Nevertheless, research is conducted on an ongoing basis to assess the impact of microwaves on the human body [22].

How Microwaves Work

Microwaves, in themselves, are not hot and do not heat directly. They contain energy that is absorbed by the food in the oven as the microwaves strike and penetrate the food. As the microwaves enter the product, they interact with electrically **polarized molecules,** sometimes called dipolar molecules, in the food. These dipolar molecules include water, proteins, and some carbohydrates. They act like tiny magnets and align themselves in the microwave electromagnetic field. The field alternates millions of times each second, causing the polarized molecules in the food to rapidly rotate due to forces of attraction and repulsion between the oppositely charged regions of the field. Heat is produced by the friction that is created between the rapidly moving molecules, thereby cooking the food. Positive and negative ions of dissolved salts in the food, including table salt or sodium chloride (NaCl), also migrate toward oppositely charged regions of the electric field and generate additional heat by their movement [8]. Both microwave heating and the radiant heating used in conventional broiling and baking produce heat in the food by increasing the motion of the molecules as energy is absorbed.

> **polarized molecules** molecules that have both (+) and negative (−) charges on them, creating two poles

Microwaves generally penetrate about 1 to 2 inches into the food, the depth varying with the frequency of the microwaves and the composition of the food. Further distribution of the heat, particularly toward the center of a relatively large mass of food, occurs by conduction, as it does in conventional heating. Microwaves do not, as is sometimes supposed, cook from "the inside out." Microwave cooking is faster, however, because microwaves penetrate farther into food than the infrared radiant waves used in conventional cooking and, therefore, deposit more energy at greater depths in the food.

Because the air inside microwave ovens is cool, the surface of the food does not become hot enough to develop a brown, dry, and crusty surface as do the surfaces of conventionally baked products. The lack of browning of foods in a microwave oven has implications for the taste of the food as well as the appearance.

The composition of a food affects the rapidity of heating. Fats and sugars have low **specific heats** compared with water; therefore, foods high in fat or sugar heat more rapidly than foods high in water. Foods with less **density** also heat more rapidly than high-density foods when similar weights of these products are heated. Dense foods limit the depth of penetration of the microwaves. For example, a dense brownie batter heats more slowly than a light, porous cake.

> **specific heat** the number of calories needed to raise the temperature of 1 gram of a given substance 1 degree C; the specific heat of water has been set at 1.0 and other substances are related to this figure; fats and sugars have lower specific heats, thus requiring less heat than does water to raise their temperature an equal number of degrees
>
> **density** weight per unit of volume

ADVANTAGES OF MICROWAVE COOKING

One of the great advantages of using a microwave oven is the speed with which cooking can be accomplished—two to 10 times faster than conventional methods. The actual time required for cooking depends on the volume and type of food being cooked. Microwave ovens are not generally designed for quantity cookery, and the time of cooking must be lengthened as the quantity of food to be cooked is increased. One potato, for example, cooks in 4 to 6 minutes in a microwave oven, whereas four potatoes require 16 to 19 minutes to cook.

In microwave cooking, the oven walls and surrounding air do not become hot. Only the food is heated. During warm seasons of the year, cooking methods that do not contribute to the warmth in the home are advantageous. Furthermore, the container holding the food will only become hot if the cooking period is sufficiently long. Therefore, the chance of receiving burns from hot containers may be lessened as compared to conventional baked products.

Microwave cooking has special advantages in reheating precooked foods, both individually packaged and packaged in meals, and in thawing frozen foods. The microwave oven not only reheats precooked foods more rapidly than conventional methods, but also avoids a reheated or warmed-over flavor [5]. Microwave oven owners often use these ovens for heating convenience meat items and casseroles, in preference to using conventional heating appliances.

Microwaves are also popular for the cooking of vegetables. A minimum amount of water is needed to cook vegetables in the microwave oven, thus conserving soluble nutrients. Additionally, researchers have found that microwave blanching of vegetables as compared to blanching in water resulted in less nutrient loss [17].

The microwave oven has a real advantage in the saving of energy when compared with conventional ovens, particularly for cooking up to about six servings at one time. In cooking pork sausage links, the microwave oven had the lowest energy requirement, followed by the convection oven, with the still-air oven requiring the most energy [12]. Additional savings of energy from microwave use comes from the lesser amount of dishwashing that is generally required. Containers used for microwave cooking are usually suitable for serving as well.

In the food-processing industry, the gap between the cost of conventional and microwave equipment is apparently closing. A number of applications lend themselves to the use of microwaves, and environmental concerns may make the saving of energy desirable. In addition to energy savings, advantages of microwave cooking may come from speed of operation, precise process control, and faster start-up and shutdown times [8].

LIMITATIONS OF MICROWAVE COOKING

Lack of surface browning is a disadvantage of microwave cooking for some foods, particularly baked products. A loaf of bread, for example, without a crisp, golden-brown crust does not have the same appeal as one that possesses this characteristic. Foods that require cooking for a relatively long time, such as a roast of meat, may develop some browning, but most food items would be greatly overcooked before browning would occur.

The lack of browning of microwave-cooked products is due to the cool air temperature inside the microwave oven, and to the cooling effects of moisture evaporation at the surface of foods cooked with microwaves; the temperature inside the microwave-cooked food is actually higher than it is at the surface [6].

To overcome to some degree the problems created by the lack of browning in microwave cooking, a special browning dish can be used to sear chops, meat patties, steaks, and similar products. A special coating on the bottom of the dish absorbs the microwave energy and becomes very hot (450° to 550°F or 232° to 289°C). The dish is preheated according to the manufacturer's directions, the food is added, and cooking is continued according to the recipe being used.

Special disposable packaging that uses heat susceptors is often beneficial for cooking such products as microwave pizza, french-fried potatoes, and some filled pastry products in which crispness and browned surfaces are desirable characteristics. Microwave-interactive containers have increased the options for microwave cooking, but the need exists for careful analysis of degradation products that might result from their use and adulterate the foods with which they come in contact. Components that may migrate from packaging materials to food are considered to be indirect food additives and thus require approval as food additives by the FDA. As new packaging materials are developed, careful consideration must be given to possible interactions with microwave energy.

Foods that need long cooking periods at simmering temperatures to tenderize or to rehydrate are not as satisfactorily prepared in a microwave oven as they are in conventional ovens. Some flavors do not have an opportunity to develop well in the short cooking periods of microwave ovens.

It is relatively easy to overcook foods in the microwave oven, because heating is rapid. Caution must be exercised to avoid the dehydrating effects that may result from only a few seconds, in some cases, of overheating. Safety also is a concern when some products such as liquids are overheated. Superheated water has been reported to FDA [22]. Superheated water is water that has been heated past its boiling temperature without appearing to boil. This is most likely to occur in a very clean cup. When superheating has occurred, a slight movement such as picking up the cup or adding instant coffee may result in an eruption of boiling water that may cause a severe burn.

Unevenness of heating is a major disadvantage in the use of the microwave oven. This lack of uniformity in heat distribution raises some questions about the microbiological safety of certain foods heated with microwaves; sensory characteristics may also be affected. In the heating of meals made of ground meat patties, sauce, mashed potatoes, and carrots, it was reported that cold and hot spots were present near each other. The high-low temperature difference could be greater than 30°C (54°F) at spots within a few centimeters of each other [18]. When individual portions of meat loaf (beef), mashed potatoes, and green beans were heated in a microwave oven during one study that simulated procedures used in cook-chill foodservice systems, a wide range (up to 83°F [46°C]) of endpoint temperatures was observed [6]. It has also been reported that the usual procedures followed in cooking chicken by microwaves may not destroy all of the **Salmonella** organisms that may be present [11]. Concern has been expressed in regard to the destruction of **Trichinella spiralis** in pork prepared in the microwave oven (discussed in more detail in Chapter 25). It is important to ensure the safety of these foods by checking the final temperature in several locations within the product with a meat thermometer or the oven's temperature probe. It has been recommended that meats cooked by microwaves be heated 25°F (14°C) higher than those attained with conventional heating. Thus, ground beef should reach a temperature of at least 180°F (82°C), poultry at least 190°F (88°C), and pork 170°F (77°C).

The voltage being fed to the microwave oven must be consistent at all times that the oven is operating to ensure quality control in the cooking process. The voltage may vary, however, particularly in metropolitan areas during peak periods of electricity use. Software programs are being designed to indicate to the oven when it is operating on less current and allow it to adjust appropriately [20].

It is a challenge to the food processor to develop microwavable food products that reproduce the appearance, texture, and flavor of foods prepared by conventional-oven cooking. The use of **hydrocolloids,** such as xanthan gum, carrageenan, and **microcrystalline cellulose,** which have high water-binding

Salmonella a bacterium that may cause food poisoning

Trichinella spiralis a tiny parasite that may be present in some fresh pork and, if not destroyed by cooking, causes a disease called *trichinosis*

hydrocolloids colloidal materials, such as vegetable gums, that bind water and have thickening and/or gelling properties

microcrystalline cellulose a purified nonfibrous form of cellulose (a complex carbohydrate) that is physically broken into very tiny particles

capabilities, may help to stabilize many microwavable products and prevent dry spots due to uneven heating and loss of moisture [4]. Stale bread is freshened with heating by conventional methods, but bread reheated in a microwave oven becomes tougher. The addition of certain emulsifiers, and increased water content (by use of fiber), decreased the toughness of microwave-reheated bread [15]. Custom-made flavors may also help to overcome the problems with flavor that can occur when cooking times are shortened.

PACKAGING MATERIALS AND COOKING UTENSILS

The commercial packaging of microwavable foods serves several functions. It protects the product in storage and distribution, controls the heating of the product, may function as a serving dish, and helps to sell the product [7]. Manufacturers are continuing to develop new packaging that allows the effective heating of foods and thereby enhances quality [3].

When cooking with a microwave in the home, plastic, ceramic, and glass containers that are labeled as microwave safe must be used [21]. Generally, materials that are transparent to microwaves should be utilized; the waves pass through these materials, as light passes through a window, and heat the food inside the container. Metal containers, or glass containers with a metal glaze, rim, or trim are not acceptable for microwave use.

Heat-resistant or ovenproof glass utensils can be used in both conventional and microwave ovens. This type of container can also be used for freezing foods and can be taken from freezer to oven without danger of breakage. Unglazed glass-ceramic dishes are highly recommended for microwave use. These products are sold under the trade name CorningWare™. Ceramic products, which include pottery, earthenware, fine china, and porcelain, vary somewhat in microwave absorption characteristics, but in general, they all are satisfactory for use in the microwave oven. Some ceramic dishes, however, may become too hot to handle before the contents have reached their serving temperature [7]. Use of such dishes should be avoided in microwave cooking.

Utensils with metal trim or screws in lids or handles and dinnerware with gold or silver trim should not be used because arcing is likely to occur, producing sparks. Ceramic mugs or cups with glued-on handles should be avoided, because the handles may come unglued. Some utensils that are acceptable for use in the microwave oven are shown in Figure 7-6.

If it is uncertain that a container is microwave-oven safe, it should be tested by placing it in the oven with a heat-resistant glass cup containing 1 cup of water and running the oven on high power for 1 minute. If the dish remains cool, it is suitable for microwaving. If it becomes hot, it has absorbed some microwave energy and should not be used.

Paper products, such as white, microwave-safe paper towels, can be placed either under or over a food in the microwave oven to absorb moisture and splatters during cooking. Paper products that have been dyed are generally not recommended as the dye may migrate into the food during cooking. Some paper dishes are made from formed or pressed paperboard and coated with a highly heat-resistant polyester resin. Others are molded from pulp and coated with polyester. These containers are usable in both microwave and conventional ovens [7]. Brown paper bags or newspapers should not be used in the microwave [21] because of the inks and other chemicals that may have been used in the manufacture of these items.

(a)

(b)

Figure 7-6
Several kinds of dishes may be used in the microwave.
(a) This casserole dish may be used with a microwave safe cover.
(b) A variety of glass dishes are appropriate for microwave cooking.
(c) This casserole dish comes with a microwave plastic pop-top lid that will vent steam. (Courtesy of World Kitchens, makers of CorningWare® and Pyrex®.)

(c)

Microwave plastics are designed especially for microwave cooking. Microwave-safe plastic films and cooking bags hold in steam and speed cooking, but slits must be made in the bags or film to prevent pressure buildup. Many conventional plastics are unacceptable, because although plastics are transparent to microwaves, some are sensitive to heat from the food and melt or distort when used to cook foods that reach high temperatures. Foam trays, plastic wraps, and one-time use plastic containers such as margarine tubs are not stable to microwave heating and therefore should not be used [21].

Plastic wraps and thin plastic storage bags should not be allowed to touch foods during microwaving. Consequently, frozen foods, such as meat or poultry, should be removed from store wrap prior to microwave defrosting. Some plasticizers, used in flexible packaging films, may migrate into the food during microwaving, depending on cooking time, the temperature achieved, and the extent of contact of the plastic film with the food being heated. Levels of migration have been found to be highest when direct contact occurs between the film and foods with a high fat content [9]. Efforts are being made to produce plastic packaging materials from which plasticizers do not migrate. With many new packaging materials being developed for microwavable foods, it is important to follow the instructions on the label so that overheating will not occur.

GENERAL COOKING SUGGESTIONS

Browning

Large pieces of food, such as meat roasts, brown during cooking in a microwave oven because cooking time is relatively long, but smaller quantities of food cooked for short periods need to be browned by some means other than the use of microwave energy. Small cuts of meat may be broiled conventionally after microwave cooking to develop browned color and flavor. Bacon is easily cooked in a microwave oven, however, and does brown. The fat on the surface of the bacon aids in browning. The optimum time for cooking should not be extended to increase the likelihood of browning. Foods dry out very rapidly with only slight overcooking when using microwaves.

Creative use of dark-colored toppings, sauces, crumbs, and spices can compensate for lack of browning in many dishes. Melted cheese and gravies also may be used to improve the appearance of casseroles and meat dishes.

Some formulated products are available for use in coating the surfaces of meats to encourage browning. Their major ingredient may be salt, which, when applied to a wetted surface, increases the electrical conductivity of the surface. Electrical conductors absorb microwave energy avidly and produce higher temperatures on the surface [7].

Stirring and Turning

Power is unevenly distributed in the microwave oven; therefore, foods need to be turned around, turned over, stirred, or relocated in the oven at various times during cooking. Multiple items such as individual potatoes, pieces of fish, and custard cups should be placed in a circle. Some microwave ovens are equipped with a turntable whose rotation automatically distributes power more evenly; turntables can also be purchased separately. Although metal is generally not acceptable for use in a microwave oven, small strips of aluminum foil may be used in many brands of microwave ovens to shield thin or sensitive parts of the food. The foil should not be allowed to touch the inside of the oven [1].

Standing Time

A food continues to cook for several minutes after it is removed from the microwave oven. This fact should be taken into account when cooking time is determined to avoid overcooking. During this standing time, heat continues to be conducted from hotter parts of the food mass to cooler ones and the internal temperature of the food may increase. Allowance should be made for longer standing time for foods of large volume and density, such as meat roasts. Wrapping individual potatoes in foil *after* they have been cooked in the microwave oven and allowing them to stand for several minutes will complete the cooking process with limited danger of overcooking.

Defrosting

One benefit of a microwave oven is the ease of defrosting. Most ovens have a defrost setting with a low- to medium-power input. The oven cycles on and off, and during the off periods, the heat produced in the food is distributed or equalized throughout.

As defrosting proceeds, some attention to the product improves the outcome. Ground meat, stew meat, whole poultry, or whole fish should be turned. As soon as possible during the defrosting process, small pieces of meat, poultry, or fish should be broken apart and separated in the oven while defrosting is completed. Meat and poultry should be cooked *immediately* after defrosting.

Combining Microwave and Conventional Cooking

Many foods can be prepared most efficiently if they are cooked partly by microwaves and partly by conventional methods. Bread can be toasted conventionally and then combined with sandwich fillings prepared by microwaves. Cheese placed on top of a sandwich is easily melted in the microwave oven. A casserole can be cooked in the microwave oven, then a crumb topping placed on it, and the topping finished by broiling in a conventional oven. Chicken can be browned on a grill after it is cooked in a microwave oven. Sauces for pasta can be cooked in the microwave while the pasta is prepared conventionally. Since microwave energy does not increase the water-absorption rate of the starch granules in most cereal products, microwave cooking does not generally save time for such foods.

The microwave oven can increase efficiency in food preparation in other ways. For example, syrup for pancakes can be warmed by microwaving while it is in the serving pitcher. Sprinkling a few teaspoons of water over raisins, covering tightly, and microwaving 30 to 60 seconds will plump the raisins. Baking chocolate can be melted in its paper wrapper in the microwave oven, and butter or margarine is also easily melted. Brown sugar can be softened by placing an apple slice in the bag, closing tightly, and microwaving 15 seconds or until lumps soften.

Heating Meals

Factors affecting the heating in microwave ovens include, in addition to the oven itself, the packaging and the food. Because different foods have different **dielectric** (and thermal) **properties**, uneven heating may occur in meals with several different components. Temperatures near the edges of a plate or tray of

dielectric properties permit the passage of the lines of force of an electrostatic field but do not conduct the current; nonconducting

food tend to be higher than in the center; the edge of the food seems to act as an antenna in the microwave field, absorbing energy. In the heating of a meal consisting of ground meat patties, sauce, mashed potato, and carrots, it was reported that the arrangement of the foods on the tray had the most pronounced effect on heating rates and final temperatures. The best heating effect was achieved when mashed potato was piled up along the sides of the tray. The saltiness of the food did not notably affect the heating uniformity [18].

Microwave ovens are widely used, in both homes and institutions, to reheat fully cooked, plated meals. Individual meal items should be chosen and grouped so that they are as compatible as possible in terms of heating rate and uniformity of heating. Dense meal items, including baked potatoes, mounded mashed potatoes, lasagna more than 1/2 inch thick, cabbage rolls, stuffed peppers, and thickly sliced meat or fish, heat relatively slowly. Therefore, such foods should be thinly portioned. Examples of meal items that heat more rapidly and easily are piped, mashed potatoes or mashed potatoes with the center pressed down and a butter pat placed in the depression; thinly sliced meats, centered on the plate with gravy over them; and thinly portioned fish without sauce. Denser items should be placed toward the outside of the plate. Subdivided vegetables or loose rice and pasta may be placed in the center.

CHAPTER SUMMARY

- Microwave ovens are used most frequently in the home to boil water, heat frozen foods, defrost frozen foods, or make popcorn. Consumers have not been quick to embrace cooking entire meals in the microwave. Manufacturers are continuing to develop new microwavable foods that respond to consumers' desires for speed and convenience.

- Foodservices may use microwave ovens to reheat chilled or frozen foods generally for individual meals. Microwave ovens used in foodservice are heavy-duty units designed to withstand rough treatment and frequent use.

- The food industry uses specialized microwave equipment to temper meat, precook bacon, and cook sausage. Four billion pounds of food are tempered in microwave ovens by the food industry each year. There is a variety of other ways that the food industry uses microwave ovens in the processing of food.

- Microwaves are high-frequency electromagnetic waves of radiant energy. They may be described as radio waves of very short wavelength, falling between television and infrared frequencies on the electromagnetic spectrum. Microwaves are reflected by metals and thus are contained within the oven cavity.

- Microwaves work by interacting with electrically polarized molecules in food such as water, proteins, and some carbohydrates. The polarized molecules in the food rapidly rotate, resulting in the production of heat due to friction. Microwaves penetrate 1–2 inches into the food, but do not cook from "the inside out," as has been suggested by some. The interior of foods, cooked in a microwave, is heated by conduction.

- The FDA has regulated the manufacture of microwave ovens since 1971. A radiation safety standard enforced by the FDA limits the amount of microwaves that can leak from an oven throughout its lifetime.

- Cooking in microwave ovens offers several advantages. Microwave cooking of foods is very fast, although the speed varies with the quantity, density, and composition of the food. Microwave oven walls remain cool and therefore do not heat up the kitchen and the energy usage is generally less than that required for cooking similar products conventionally. Some foods such as vegetables retain more nutrients when cooked by microwave rather than in medium to large amounts of water.

- Limitations of cooking in a microwave oven include: foods generally do not brown; foods that need long cooking periods at simmering temperatures to tenderize or rehydrate are not as satisfactorily prepared by microwave; heating is uneven and can pose food safety concerns unless temperatures are carefully and appropriately monitored; burns can occur due to superheated liquids; and microwave safe cooking utensils must be used.

- When cooking with a microwave oven, plastics, ceramic, and glass containers that are labeled as microwave safe must be used. Paper products such as white, microwave safe paper towels are acceptable, but newspaper or brown paper bags should not be used. One-time-use plastic containers and foam containers or trays should not be used because they may melt or release undesirable chemicals. Some plasticizers, used in flexible packaging films, may migrate into the food during microwaving and thus, these plastics should not be in contact with foods being heated in a microwave oven.

- The use of specific cooking suggestions for the browning, stirring, standing, and defrosting of foods will enhance success when cooking in a microwave oven.

KEY TERMS

heat susceptors	density
tempering	*Salmonella*
pasteurization	*Trichinella spiralis*
sterilization	hydrocolloids
proofing	microcrystalline cellulose
polarized molecules	dielectric properties
specific heat	

STUDY QUESTIONS

1. What are microwaves and how do they produce heat when they are absorbed by food?

2. Discuss several advantages and several limitations to the use of microwave equipment in home cooking, institutional foodservice, and industrial food processing.

3. What types of containers should be used to hold food during cooking in the microwave oven and why?

4. Why should foods be stirred or turned at intervals during cooking in a microwave oven? Of what value is standing time after cooking? Explain.

5. What precautions should be taken when reheating fully cooked, plated meals in a microwave oven and why?

6. Why are *on* and *off* cycles used for defrosting in a microwave oven?

7. Give several suggestions for using the microwave oven in combination with conventional methods of cooking.

REFERENCES

1. American Association of Family and Consumer Sciences. (2001). *Food: A handbook of terminology, purchasing, and preparation.* (10th ed.). Alexandria, VA: American Association of Family and Consumer Sciences.

2. Bowers, D. E. (2000). Cooking trends echo changing roles of women. *Food Review, 23*(1), 23–29.

3. Brody, A. L. (2001). The return of microwavable foods. *Food Technology, 55*(3), 69–70.

4. Carroll, L. E. (1989). Hydrocolloid functions to improve stability of microwavable foods. *Food Technology, 43*(6), 96.

5. Cipra, J. S., & Bowers, J. A. (1971). Flavor of microwave- and conventionally-reheated turkey. *Poultry Science, 50,* 703.

6. Dahl, C. A., & Matthews, M. E. (1980). Effect of microwave heating in cook/chill foodservice systems. *Journal of the American Dietetic Association, 77,* 289.

7. Decareau, R. V. (1992). *Microwave foods: New product development.* Trumbull, CT: Food & Nutrition Press, Inc.

8. Giese, J. H. (1992). Advances in microwave food processing. *Food Technology, 46*(9), 118.

9. Institute of Food Technologies' Expert Panel on Food Safety and Nutrition. (1989). Microwave food processing. *Food Technology, 43*(1), 117.

10. Katz, F. (1999). Microwave packaging addresses speed, clarity, and ease of use. *Food Technology, 53*(7), 106–107.

11. Lindsay, R. E., Krissinger, W. A., & Fields, B. F. (1986). Microwave vs. conventional oven cooking of chicken: Relationship of internal temperature to surface contamination by *Salmonella typhimurium. Journal of the American Dietetic Association, 86,* 373.

12. Mandigo, R. W., & Janssen, T. J. (1982). Energy-efficient cooking systems for muscle foods. *Food Technology, 36*(4), 128.

13. Mermelstein, N. H. (1997). How food technology covered microwaves over the years. *Food Technology, 51*(5), 82.

14. Mermelstein, N. H. (1999). Microwave processing of food. *Food Technology, 53*(7), 114–116.

15. Miller, R. A., & Hoseney, R. C. (1997). Method to measure microwave-induced toughness of bread. *Journal of Food Science, 62,* 1202.

16. Pszczola, D. E. (2001). Convenience foods: They've come a long, long way. *Food Technology, 55*(9), 85–94.

17. Ramesh, M. N., Tevini, D., & Wolf, W. (2002). Microwave blanching of vegetables. *Journal of Food Science, 67*(1), 390–398.

18. Ryynanen, S., & Ohlsson, T. (1996). Microwave heating uniformity of ready meals as affected by placement, composition, and geometry. *Journal of Food Science, 61,* 620.

19. Spears, M. (2000). *Foodservice organizations: A managerial and systems approach.* NJ: Prentice Hall.

20. Toops, D. (1998). Microwave science's Bob Thompson. New technology zaps microwave inconsistencies. *Food Processing, 59*(1), 45.

21. USDA Food Safety and Inspection Service, FDA Center for Food Safety and Applied Nutrition. (2000, November). Food safety facts: Cooking safely in the microwave. Retrieved July 24, 2002, from http://www.foodsafety.gov/~fsg/fs-mwave.html

22. U.S. Food and Drug Administration, Center for Devices and Radiological Health. (2000, March). Microwave oven radiation. Retrieved July 24, 2002, from http://www.fda.gov/cdrh/consumer/microwave.html

Seasoning and Flavoring Materials

8

Our senses determine the pleasure of our experiences with food. We may eat to maintain life; but this becomes a difficult task without the enjoyment that comes from the blending of various sensations into what one might call a marvelous flavor bouquet. A steaming bowl of clam chowder, for example, may entice us to taste it because of its attractive appearance or perhaps because of its delicious aroma. Once we taste it, we relish its *flavor*—that complex combination of taste, aroma, and mouthfeel that is characteristic of that particular dish. We, therefore, enjoy this experience of eating and want to repeat it.

Can you imagine a food without flavor? Actually, flavor is probably the number one reason why consumers purchase food. Over 90 percent of shoppers surveyed in 1993 ranked taste as an important factor in food selection. Taste was cited as a purchase factor even more frequently than nutrition, price, and product safety [7]. In 2001, restaurants responded to consumer interest in flavor by making menu mentions of seasonings 72 percent more often than previously [32]. Overall, spice consumption in the United States has nearly doubled since 1980 [23], reflecting our change in taste preferences over the past two decades.

The natural flavors of many foods—fresh, ripe strawberries, for example—are enticing in themselves, but the judicious use of seasonings and flavoring materials can greatly enhance the natural flavors of many foods, either alone or combined in a recipe. Flavorful food is always the ultimate goal of the cook. Attainment of this goal requires the proper use of seasonings and flavorings.

Seasonings, in general, are substances that enhance the flavor of a food or combination of foods. Basic seasonings—salt and pepper—are added to improve the flavor of foods without being specifically perceived or detected as themselves. They may bring out hidden flavors. Some seasonings, called flavor enhancers, act somewhat differently. A flavor enhancer does not itself bring flavor to a dish. Instead it acts to heighten the diner's perception of flavor, probably by affecting the taste buds in some way. Examples of flavor enhancers include monosodium glutamate and some other substances called **5'-ribonucleotides.**

Flavorings are substances that are added for their own distinctive flavors, such as extracts of lemon or peppermint oil. Still other substances called flavor builders may be added at the beginning of cooking to blend with and enhance other flavors in the dish, producing a total flavor bouquet in which individual flavors are not generally distinguished. Most dried herbs and spices are used to build flavor.

5'-ribonucleotides compounds similar to the RNA found in all body cells; certain ones have been shown to act as flavor enhancers

171

BASIC SEASONINGS

Salt

Salt is one of the oldest commodities known to man. It has played a major role in history. For example, Roman soldiers were sometimes paid in salt and our word *salary* comes from the Latin word *sal*, meaning "salt" [22]. Salt is one of the most widely used seasonings and is also found naturally in some foods. It is a **crystalline** substance with the chemical name sodium chloride (NaCl); it may be obtained from salt beds or from solar evaporation of saline waters from the oceans, and is purified before being marketed for food use. Sometimes an anti-caking agent is added to it, and it may be **iodized** for nutritional purposes. Kosher salt, also known as coarse or pickling salt, is used in Jewish recipes. It may also be used when a clear product is desired, because it does not contain magnesium carbonate, that may cloud some items. Sea salt is obtained by evaporating seawater. Sea salt has a more complex flavor because unlike salt from other sources it has additional mineral salts such as magnesium, calcium, and potassium [14].

The optimal amount of salt depends on the food product being prepared and the preferences of the persons who will consume the food. A certain amount of caution is necessary, however, to avoid overuse. A large amount of salt in food is undesirable from both a health and flavor standpoint. Because of the possible relationship between a high sodium intake and hypertension (high blood pressure), at least for some people, governmental and professional organizations have encouraged Americans to reduce their intakes of salt. The fifth edition of *Nutrition and your health: Dietary guidelines for Americans*, like the previous editions, includes dietary guidance on salt and sodium [34]. However, since more than half of the salt consumed by Americans comes from commercially processed foods, advice on choosing these convenience foods in addition to low salt preparation of foods is needed [15].

One study found that dietitians and/or foodservice managers can produce quantity food recipes that are reduced in sodium and acceptable to customers [18]. The recipes tested included two dessert items, nine entrées, six vegetables, four starch items, six salads, and one bread item. Only six of the 28 recipes with no added salt were rated significantly less acceptable than the control recipes in which salt was added.

The desirable level of saltiness varies depending on the food product. In one study, the simpler the food item (i.e., one containing few ingredients), the greater the perceived saltiness at similar sodium concentrations [1]. Acceptability of potato chips, tortilla chips, whole wheat bread, and oatmeal bread, all prepared commercially, was not affected by sodium level, even with a 15- to 20-fold difference. Perceived saltiness increased without a significant change in acceptability. These studies suggest that considerable reduction in sodium levels can be made in some foods and recipes without affecting acceptability.

For most cooked dishes, salt and other seasonings should be added in small increments, with a tasting after each addition, until the most desirable taste is achieved. Many recipes specify the amount of salt as "to taste" or "tt" which means salt is added just until the taste of salt is perceptible. In foods that are cooked to concentrate, such as tomato juice cooked to paste, salt should be added at the end of the cooking period. Generally in liquids, salt should be added at the end of the cooking period.

Some interesting flavor profiles for various soups prepared both with and without the addition of salt have been reported [9]. Salt enhanced the sweetness

---

crystalline the aggregation of molecules of a substance in a set, ordered pattern, forming individual crystals

iodized salt table salt to which small amounts of a stabilized iodide compound have been added to increase dietary iodine and prevent goiter (enlargement of the thyroid gland); its use is encouraged particularly in areas where the soil is deficient in iodine

and the saltiness of soups and decreased bitterness. It also affected the mouth-feel of the soup, giving the impression of increased thickness and fullness, as if the product were less watery and thin. The addition of salt produced an overall flavor balance that was more "rounded out" and "fuller." Figure 8-1 compares the flavor profile for tomato soup to which salt was added with those for soup to which dill seed or onion powder was added.

The usual amount of salt consumed varies from one population to another and from one individual to another. The food industry is making serious attempts to reduce the level of sodium in processed foods, offering consumers a variety of low-sodium and lightly salted products, such as lower salt bacon, unsalted peanuts and potato chips, and canned vegetables without added salt. As the reduction of dietary sodium becomes desirable or necessary, the judicious use of herbs and spices, and fresh lemon juice, may make foods acceptable with little or no added salt.

Pepper

Pepper was the first Oriental spice to arrive in Europe and today remains one of the most widely used spices in the world. The "hot spices," which include black and white pepper, red pepper, and mustard seed, represent 41 percent of U.S. spice usage [2]. Pepper is cultivated in the tropics, with 86 percent of the pepper imported into the United States coming from India, Indonesia, and Brazil [23].

Not all pepper is the same. Black pepper is the dried unripe berry of a climbing vine. During drying, the green berry becomes dark brown or black.

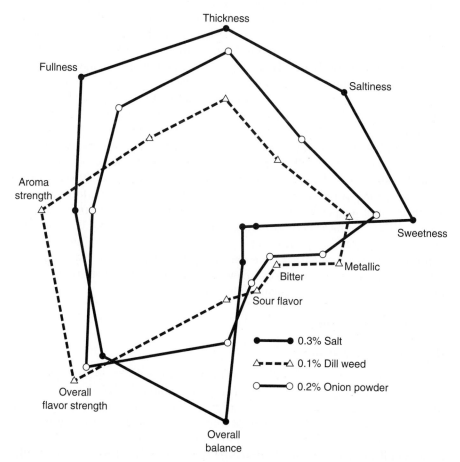

Figure 8-1
Aroma and flavor profiles for tomato soup with (1) 0.3 percent salt, (2) 0.1 percent dill weed, or (3) 0.2 percent onion powder. The farther away a point is placed from the center point, the more pronounced is the attribute. (Reprinted from Gillette, M. Flavor effects of sodium chloride. *Food Technology*, 39 (6), p. 47, 1985. Copyright © by Institute of Food Technologists)

White pepper is the kernel of the ripe red berry that has had the skin removed to reveal the white interior [19, 14]. Red pepper comes from plants of the genus *Capsicum*, and although hot, it is not botanically related to *Piper nigrum*, that produces the berries for black and white pepper. Red peppers also have their own distinctive flavor.

Black table-ground pepper is used as a seasoning only in dark-colored foods; it spoils the appearance of light-colored foods. Light peppers, white and red, are used in both light and dark menu items. Ground white pepper is good for all-around seasoning. It blends well, both in appearance and in flavor, in white dishes, and it has the necessary strength to season dark dishes. White pepper is generally hotter than black, thus, very little white pepper is usually needed [19].

"Hot" peppers originated in the New World and were taken back to Europe by Christopher Columbus. Hot peppers, commonly called chilies (or chiles), are basic to many **cuisines** of the world and are increasing in popularity in the United States (Plate II). The worldwide capsicum crop exceeds 7.7 billion pounds annually and represents a greater tonnage than pepper [22]. In the United States, ethnic trends, including an interest in Caribbean, Mexican, and South American dishes, is promoting the consumption of "hotter" dishes. Worldwide, the cuisines of India, Asia, Africa, and many other countries utilize the hot flavors of capsicums in their dishes to convey distinctive flavors.

Chilies are from the capsicum genus that encompasses over 300 varieties of plants varying in hotness, color, and flavor [23, 4]. Some of the commonly used peppers include the *sweet green pepper, habañero* or *scotch bonnet, jalapeño, chipotle, poblano, ancho, anaheim, and paprika.* Sweet green peppers unlike many other chilies are not hot, but are nevertheless flavorful. The habañero or scotch bonnet is generally considered to be the hottest chili in the world at 100,000 to 300,000 **Scoville Heat Units.** Jalapeños are hot to medium-hot and are used in many Mexican dishes. The chipotle is a smoke-dried jalapeño with a deep smoky flavor. The ancho chili is a dried poblano chili; both types are mild to medium-hot. Paprika is the powder of a mild sweet chili and is frequently valued in cooking for the rich, red color it adds to a dish [16].

Although we commonly think of heat in reference to our sensory reaction to peppers, the effect is really not thermal but rather a chemically induced irritation that stimulates the endings of the trigeminal nerve—quite different from the sense of taste or the sense of touch. The chemical responsible for this stimulation in black pepper is called *piperine*, and the active agent in red pepper is *capsaicin*. The chemical composition of capsaicin ($C_{18}H_{27}O_3N$) is similar to piperine ($C_{17}H_{19}O_3N$) [4]. However, capsaicin is about 100 times more potent than piperine. Even when handling chili peppers, "burning" of the hands can occur if latex gloves are not used. Likewise, care should be taken to not touch the face or eyes when working with chili peppers.

FLAVOR ENHANCERS

Monosodium Glutamate

Monosodium glutamate (MSG) is a crystalline material that looks something like salt. Chemically, it is the sodium salt of an amino acid called *glutamic acid.* Glutamic acid occurs naturally in a variety of foods, including tomatoes and mushrooms, and also is a component of some protein molecules present in such foods as meat, fish, poultry, legumes, and cereal grains. In past years, MSG was often manufactured from wheat gluten or corn protein, but today it is usually

"hot" peppers peppers that contain a substance known as capsaicin, which gives them the highly pungent characteristic called "hot." This substance also stimulates the flow of saliva. "Hotter" peppers contain more capsaicin, concentrated mainly in the thin tissues or veins where the seeds are attached to the spongy central portion.

cuisine a style of cooking or manner of preparing food

Scoville Heat Units a measurement of chili pungency that was developed through taste testing of a trained sensory panel. High performance liquid chromatography is now used to measure a chili's "heat."

made in a **fermentation** process that starts with molasses or some other carbohydrate food material.

The history of MSG as a flavor enhancer is long and interesting. Many hundreds of years ago, Oriental cooks used a dried seaweed called *sea tangle* to make a stock. Dishes prepared from foods cooked in this stock had a remarkably full and rich flavor. Much later, in 1908, a Japanese professor in Tokyo discovered that it was the glutamate in the seaweed that was responsible for flavor enhancement. The Japanese began producing glutamate almost immediately, and about 30 years later it was manufactured in North America [12].

MSG is generally considered to be a flavor enhancer or intensifier, bringing out the flavors of other foods. The distinctive taste that MSG and the 5'-nucleotides produce, particularly in meat, fish, and poultry products, has been called *umami*. This word is derived from the Japanese word meaning "delicious" or "savory." The umami taste appears to be distinct from the four classical tastes: sweet, sour, salty, and bitter. It has been suggested that MSG, and possibly the 5'-nucleotides, interact with a flavor molecule through receptors on the taste buds of the tongue, strengthening and enhancing the effect of the flavor molecule [17]. At the levels ordinarily used in cooking, MSG does not have a taste of its own; however, when used in sufficiently large amounts, it may add its own flavor. It has the greatest flavor effect in low-acid foods such as vegetables, meats, poultry, and fish. It does not improve the taste of high-acid foods, including fruits and fruit juices; neither does it enhance the flavor of milk products or sweet doughs. Approximately 1/2 teaspoon for each pound of meat or four to six servings of vegetables is generally recommended for use.

Controversy exists over the safety of the widespread use of MSG in foods. Extensive study of its effects on a variety of animal species, however, has led to the conclusion that, in the amounts commonly used, it presents no public health hazard [12, 6]. A comprehensive report was prepared for the Food and Drug Administration (FDA) by the Life Sciences Research Office of the Federation of American Societies for Experimental Biology (FASEB) in 1995 which concluded that MSG is safe for the general population at levels normally consumed [11]. Some persons, however, respond to large doses (3 grams or more) of MSG with temporary adverse reactions; some persons with asthma are sensitive to amounts of 1.5 to 2.5 grams of glutamate consumed without food. These sensitivities are called "MSG symptom complex" in the FASEB report, rather than using the old term "Chinese restaurant syndrome" [13]. The broad array of temporary reactions to MSG may include tingling and burning sensations in the head and neck and a feeling of pressure in the upper part of the body. Elimination of MSG from the diet may be necessary in certain sensitive individuals [28]. The FDA requires that MSG be listed as an ingredient when it is added to foods. Consideration is also being given to requiring label declaration of the free glutamate content of foods that contain significant amounts of this substance. This requirement would allow consumers to make informed decisions in choosing to eat certain foods. Although MSG is commonly used in many manufactured foods, processed foods marketed primarily for babies and small children do *not* include this flavor substance as an ingredient.

fermentation the breakdown of more complex molecules to simpler ones by the action of microorganisms

5'-Ribonucleotides

A group of compounds called 5'-ribonucleotides are present naturally in some foods, such as beef, chicken, fish, and mushrooms. They may act as flavor enhancers and, in combination with MSG, create the umami taste. Their action with MSG has been called synergistic. Synergism refers to cooperative action among two or more substances so that the total effect of the mixture is greater than the sum of the individual effects. Even a very small amount of the ribonucleotides increases the flavor-enhancing properties of MSG [12].

In crystalline form, the ribonucleotides are available to the food processor for use in flavoring various snack foods and other dishes. Commercially they are usually prepared from yeast extracts or **yeast autolysates.** These flavor enhancers are widely used in Japan, and various combinations of the ribonucleotides, such as a 50:50 ratio of **disodium 5'-inosinate to disodium 5'-guanylate,** have been marketed by Japanese companies for several years. The inosinate and guanylate compounds appear to have the strongest flavor effects of all the ribonucleotides. It is claimed that they unlock natural taste characteristics and suppress harsh flavor [22].

SPICES AND HERBS

History

Utilized since antiquity, spices have always been treasured for their ability to flavor foods, but they were valued also for many nonfood purposes—as ingredients of incense, perfumes, cosmetics, embalming preservatives, and medicines. After the first century A.D., spices were increasingly utilized to improve the bland qualities of many foods. The ancient Greeks seasoned their foods with spices, using, for example, caraway and poppy seeds in bread, fennel seed in vinegar sauces, and mint in meat sauces. Spices became valuable commodities imported from India, China, and Southeast Asia, with the Arabians controlling the spice trade for many years [8].

The desire for and quest for tropical spices was instrumental in provoking trade wars and in encouraging exploration. Marco Polo went to the Far East in search of spices and precious stones, and Columbus was searching for a new trade route when he discovered America. Spices were so important, costly, and scarce, even being accepted as currency in the late 13th century, that wars were fought over them. The United States is now the world's largest importer of spices and herbs, which come mainly from the Orient, the Mediterranean area, and Central and South America. The spice market in the United States is growing as consumers demand more seasoning in their foods. By the end of 2003 consumption of spices in the United States is anticipated to be 1.4 billion pounds [23].

Classification and Use

The term *spice* is used to describe a wide variety of dried, **aromatic** vegetable products that are used in building the flavors of prepared foods. The American Spice Trade Association describes spice as "any dried plant used primarily for seasoning purposes." This definition is broad enough to include herbs [23]. However, others distinguish true spices from herbs as parts of aromatic plants, such as bark, roots, buds, flowers, fruits, and seeds, which are grown in the tropics [14, 19]. Allspice, anise, cardamom, cayenne pepper, cinnamon, cloves, cumin, ginger, mace, nutmeg, paprika, and turmeric are all spices. Some spices are sweet, some are spicy sweet, and some are "hot."

The term *herb* usually refers to leaves and stems of soft-stemmed plants that grow in temperate climates; however, some woody-stemmed plants also produce culinary herbs, such as sage. Bay leaves come from an evergreen tree,

yeast autolysate the preparation of yeast in which the cells have been destroyed; contains many flavorful substances

disodium 5'-inosinate and disodium 5'-guanylate two of the 5'-ribonucleotides that appear to have the greatest strength as flavor enhancers

aromatic having an aroma or fragrance; an ingredient added to enhance the natural aromas of food. Most herbs and spices, along with some vegetables, are aromatic.

the laurel [14]. Other herbs include basil, marjoram, mint, oregano, rosemary, savory, tarragon, and thyme.

Seeds used in cooking may sometimes be classified separately, because they come from plants cultivated in both tropical and temperate regions. Caraway, celery, sesame, and dill seeds are examples.

Mixtures of several true spices, herbs, seeds, and/or dehydrated vegetables are marketed as spice blends for use in food preparation. Chili powder, for example, is a blend of ground chili pepper (usually about 85 percent by weight) and some combination of cumin, garlic powder, and oregano. Other spices may also be present. Examples of other blends are curry powder, garam masala, poultry seasoning, pickling spice, Italian seasoning blend, and celery or garlic salt. Garam masala is a blend used in Indian cooking that often contains peppercorns, cardamom, cinnamon, cloves, coriander, nutmeg, turmeric, bay leaves, and fennel seeds [14]. Food processors can have custom blends created for them by spice suppliers. In addition, spice blends are being marketed to consumers to reflect new culinary trends including Latin American, Pacific Rim, North African, Middle Eastern, and Indian cuisines [24].

In practical use it is difficult to separate spices and herbs. They are both generally used as flavor builders in the cooking process so that their separate flavors merge indistinguishably with the total flavor as it develops. Some herbs and spices, however, have very distinctive flavors and, when used in quantities large enough to taste, become major flavors for prepared foods rather than blending into the total flavor. These special flavored spices and herbs include basil, with a warm sweet flavor that blends well with tomato dishes; oregano, with a strong bittersweet taste commonly associated with spaghetti sauce; tarragon and anise, with a licoricelike flavor; and sage, with a pungent, fragrant flavor that permeates many stuffings for poultry or meat.

Spices are available as whole or ground. Spice extractives are also available to food processors. They include essential oils, which are the volatile, distilled fraction of spices; and spice oleoresins, which are extracted from spices by solvents and include both volatile and nonvolatile components [8]. Ground spices allow for more uniform distribution and more rapid release of flavor than whole spices and thus are often added near the end of cooking, as opposed to whole spices that are introduced earlier.

A mixture of herbs (usually fresh) in a cheesecloth bag, or *bouquet garni*, can be cooked with some prepared dishes; the bag is removed before serving. A bouquet garni commonly consists of parsley stems, celery, thyme, leeks, and carrots [14], although some recipes may call for slightly different ingredients. A sachet, also known as a *sachet d'épices*, likewise is a bundle of spices tied in cheesecloth (Figure 8-2). A sachet consists of peppercorns, bay leaves, parsley stems, thyme, cloves, and possibly garlic, depending on the recipe. The description and use for several herbs and spices are given in Table 8-1. As you use herbs and spices, your ability to identify each by its particular aroma, color, and appearance will increase.

Storage

The storage life of spices depends not only on the storage conditions, but also on the age, type, and source of the spice. Whole spices retain flavor strength quite well, although quality gradually decreases during long storage. The flavor of ground spices and herbs is lost much more readily because of their greatly increased surface area.

Multicultural Cuisine

Explore Ethnic Flavors—Excite your tastebuds!

During the last decade, awareness and trial of ethnic cuisines has increased dramatically in the United States. The last time you "ate out," what type of meal did you have? Italian, Mexican, and Cantonese foods have, of course, become part of our everyday lives. But now, with increased immigration, more emphasis on a healthful diet, and many globe-trotting American citizens, we are expanding our food horizons to include flavors from India, Thailand, Vietnam, the Caribbean, Korea, Japan, the Mediterranean region, and Latin America. The popularity of such cuisines is growing, too. And choices of Chinese food include Mandarin, Szechuan, and Hunan, as well as the more tradition Cantonese [30, 31].

If we are to join in the enjoyment of these emerging cuisines, we need to become well acquainted with the spices and herbs, as well as exotic vegetables and fruits, that give them their distinctive characteristics. Indian cookery uses a wide array of spices—some recipes calling for 20 or more different ones. The American palate will need time to get used to some of these flavor profiles, but it is worth the trying. Favorite Indian spices include curry, cardamom, cumin, coriander, and black pepper.

Chili is the star of Caribbean cookery, with a variety of hot pepper sauces, either red (with tomatoes) or golden (with turmeric). The native spice, annatto, has a more delicate flavor. Curry powders are also common. And a flavoring called *cassareep* is made from the juice of the cassava root that is boiled with sugar, cinnamon, and cloves until thick [19].

Asian flavors are popular in America. Soy, sesame, teriyaki, ginger, and garlic have all become mainstream. And flavorful vegetables such as *ong choy* (water spinach), *gai lan* (Chinese broccoli), and *dau mui* (snow pea shoots) range from spicy to bitter as they contribute to the flavor bouquet [29].

We could go on and on—there are so many enticing foods and flavors. But you will want to explore for yourself. Happy eating!

Spices, herbs, and seasoning blends should be stored in a cool, dry place in airtight containers. Light-sensitive materials such as paprika, parsley, chives, and other green herbs should be protected against direct exposure to sunlight and fluorescent lights [8]. Under favorable conditions they should keep their aroma and flavor for several months. Storage may be extended by refrigerating or freezing in airtight containers if the space is available. In general, if the color,

Figure 8-2
This bouquet garni includes leeks, celery, fresh thyme, and carrots. The sachet includes peppercorns, bay leaves, parsley stems, thyme, cloves, and garlic.

aroma, and flavor of a spice have changed over the course of storage, it should be replaced.

Because ground spices release their flavor immediately when added to prepared dishes, they should usually be added near the end of the cooking period. Whole spices are added at the beginning of long cooking periods so that their full flavor can be extracted. They may be tied in a cheesecloth bag so that they can be easily removed. Crumbling whole herbs just before use helps to release their flavor. The flavor of seeds may be enhanced by toasting.

Quality

Spices come from every part of the world. They are grown and harvested on many small farms; some are even found growing wild. Quality is therefore difficult to control. Cleanliness, insect and rodent infestation, and microbiological quality are important concerns.

To control microorganisms and insect infestation in ground spices and other processed natural seasoning materials, the FDA allows treatment with ethylene oxide. Tolerances are set for remaining residues of this material on ground spices. Ionizing radiation is also allowed by the FDA for microbial reduction on culinary herbs, seeds, spices, and vegetable substances used as seasonings [8].

Fresh Herbs

Many herbs can be successfully grown in backyard or windowbox gardens. In the summer, you can gather them fresh and use them to enhance the flavors of grilled meats and fish, fresh garden vegetables, and even some desserts and beverages. In the fall, you can dry or freeze them to be used all winter, or you can move the windowbox garden indoors. A few examples of useful herbs to grow include mint, tarragon, many different varieties of basil, rosemary, chives, oregano, parsley, and cilantro (Figure 8-3).

Fresh herbs are used in a variety of ways. In cooked recipes, the amount of fresh minced herb used is approximately twice that called for with the dried product. Placing a few sprigs of fresh tarragon in a bottle of red wine vinegar and setting the bottle aside in a warm place for a month will produce tarragon vinegar for use in salad dressings. Fresh basil has a special affinity for tomato dishes; for example, it gives spaghetti sauce a delightful flavor. Any stuffing recipe for poultry is enhanced by a combination of such fresh herbs as sage, thyme, and oregano.

Fresh marjoram, oregano, cilantro, chives, and other herbs make a pleasant-flavored garnish for salads, tomato slices, and freshly cooked vegetables. Minced fresh herbs add delicious flavor to stir-fried or broiled garden vegetables, for example, snow peas sautéed with snipped fresh tarragon and spearmint in a small amount of oil, or broiled zucchini brushed with oil containing minced marjoram and topped with grated Parmesan cheese. Many combinations are possible with a little experimentation.

Edible Flowers

The growing of edible flowers has become a thriving business for some business entrepreneurs. In selecting flowers, be sure that they have been grown to be eaten and have not been subjected to various insecticide sprays. Also, you

Table 8-1
Characteristics and Uses of Some Spices and Herbs

Spice/Herb	Description	Flavor Characteristics	Applications
Allspice	Dried berry of tree grown in West Indies and Latin America	Resembles mixture of nutmeg, cloves, cinnamon, and pepper	Pickling, meats, fish, cakes, soups, vegetables, chili sauce
Anise seed	Dried greenish-brown seed of annual herb of the parsley family	Strong licoricelike flavor and odor	Beverages, baked goods, confections, lunch meats, soups
Basil	Leaves and tender stems from annual herb of the mint family	Pungently aromatic, sweet, spicy flavor	Tomato paste, tomato sauce, vegetables, pizza, chicken dishes, salad dressing
Bay leaves	Leaves of evergreen member of the laurel family	Aromatic, bitter, spicy, pungent flavor	Bouillons, meats, fish, barbecue sauces, soups, vegetables
Capsicum, red pepper	Dried pod of member of nightshade family	Intensely pungent, biting, hot, sharp taste	Chili powder blends, meat seasonings, condiments, soups, beverages, baked goods
Caraway seed	Fruit of biennial herb of the parsley family; long curved seeds tapered at one end	Warm, biting, acrid but pleasant, slightly minty, medicinal flavor	Rye breads, baked goods, cheese, goulash, vegetables
Cardamom	Seeds from the fruits of a perennial herb of the ginger family	Sweet, pungent, highly aromatic, camphoraceous flavor	Baked goods, Indian curry dishes, lunch meats, pickles
Chervil	Leaves of an annual of the parsley family	Highly aromatic; resembles mixture of anise, parsley, caraway, and tarragon	Instant soups, fish dishes, condiments, baked goods
Chives	Leaves of a perennial of the onion family	Delicate onion flavor	Soups, salad dressings, dips
Cinnamon	Dried inner bark of an evergreen tree of the laurel family	Warm, spicy, aromatic, pungent flavor	Confections, ice cream, cakes, pies, cookies, beverages, soup bases, processed meats
Cloves	Dried flower buds from evergreen of the myrtle family	Warm, spicy, astringent, fruity, slightly bitter flavor	Pickling, beverages, baked goods, confections, spiced fruits, processed meats, pudding mixes
Cumin seed	Dried ripe fruits of an annual herb of the parsley family	Aromatic, warm, heavy, spicy, bitter flavor	Chili powder, chili con carne, curry powder, salad dressings
Ginger	Rhizome (underground stem) of perennial tropical plant	Aromatic, biting, fragrant, pungent, warm, camphoraceous flavor	Baked goods, beverages, gingerbread, cookies, sauces, condiments, processed meats

should be aware that all flowers are not edible. Some, like lily of the valley and daffodils, are poisonous. Rose petals, nasturtiums, Johnny-jump-ups, and pinks are good for eating.

Some suggestions for using edible flowers include nasturtium blossoms stuffed with crab meat, with each blossom affixed to a small cracker with a tiny amount of cream cheese mixture. These make a colorful dish when served on a bed of deep-green nasturtium leaves. Or edible flowers make an eye-catching and tasty addition to tossed greens. Nasturtium blossoms have a peppery taste and thus are very good in dishes such as salads where the flavor will be complementary (Figure 8-4).

Flowers make a beautiful addition to many desserts. The top of an iced white cake can be sprinkled with coconut and calendula petals before the icing has set. Roses, in particular, are sweet and therefore very pleasing with desserts. Edible flowers, such as roses, violets, and others can be sugared by

Table 8-1

Continued

Spice/Herb	Description	Flavor Characteristics	Applications
Marjoram	Leaves and floral parts of a perennial of the mint family	Warm, aromatic, sweet-minty, slightly bitter flavor	Gravies, soups, stews, poultry, fish, processed meats
Nutmeg	Seed of a fruit of the evergreen nutmeg tree	Sweet, warm, pungent; highly spicy flavor	Sauces, custards, puddings, baked goods, dehydrated soups mixes, processed meats
Oregano	Leaves of a perennial of the mint family	Strong, pungent, aromatic, bitter flavor	Tomato dishes, pizza, meats, omelets, soups, vegetables
Parsley	Leaves of a biennial	Grassy, herbaceous, bitter flavor	Chicken and tomato soup bases, lasagna, salad dressings, potato chips
Rosemary	Narrow leaves of small evergreen shrub of mint family	Sweet, fresh, spicy, peppery	Soups, stews, vegetables, beverages, baked goods
Saffron	Dried stigmas of crocuslike flower of iris family; bright yellow; very expensive	Earthy, bitter, fatty, herbaceous flavor	Baked goods, rice dishes
Sage	Leaves of a perennial semi-shrub of the mint family	Fragrant, warm, astringent, camphoraceous flavor	Sausages, poultry seasonings, fish, meat loaf, condiments
Savory	Leaves of an annual of the mint family	Spicy, peppery taste	Meats, fish sauces, chicken, eggs, dry soup mixes, baked goods
Sesame seed	Seeds of an annual herb	Nutty flavor	Breads, rolls, crackers, cakes, salad dressings, confections
Tarragon	Flowering tops and leaves of a perennial herb	Minty aniselike flavor	Salad dressings, vegetables, meats, fish, soup bases, condiments
Thyme	Leaves and flowering tops of a shrublike perennial of the mint family	Biting, sharp, spicy, herbaceous, pungent	Fish, meat, poultry, vegetables, fresh tomatoes, poultry stuffing, canned soups
Turmeric	Rhizomes of tropical perennial herb	Mild, peppery, mustardlike, pungent taste	Curry powders, mustards, condiments

Source: References 5 and 27.

dipping them in gum Arabic (edible gum), then dusting them in granulated sugar, and placing them on waxed paper to dry [19]. Slightly beaten eggs whites may be used in place of the edible gum; however, if egg whites are used, it is best to use reconstituted powdered egg whites since they have been pasteurized. Sugared flowers can be used to garnish rose petal sorbet or other desserts.

FLAVOR EXTRACTS

Extracts and essential oils from aromatic plants, dissolved in alcohol, are often used to flavor baked products, puddings, sauces, and confections. These include extracts of vanilla [19, 26], lemon, orange, and almond, and oils such as peppermint and wintergreen. Only small amounts of these flavorful materials are required, but they add their own distinctive flavors to the final products. The extraction solvent is often alcohol and, thus, very volatile. Consequently, the flavorings should be stored in tightly closed containers and kept in a cool place. In puddings and other products cooked on surface units, the flavorings should

Rosemary

Tarragon

Thyme

Parsley

Chives

Dill

Cilantro

Figure 8-3
Herbs such as cilantro, dill, rosemary, thyme, chives, parsley, and tarragon can be used fresh or dried to add flavor or color to recipes.

be added at the end of the cooking period. In baked products, they should be added to the fat during preparation to reduce volatilization.

Many different flavor extracts are produced from botanical materials for use in the food-processing industry. These extracts may be in solid, paste, or liquid form. The food industry continues to develop new flavors to meet the demands of consumers and food processors who are seeking bolder flavors [25].

Some flavoring materials are added to processed foods in **encapsulated** forms [21]. Flavors are encapsulated for a number of reasons: The process helps to retain flavor in food products during storage, protects the flavor from unde-

encapsulate to enclose in a capsule; flavoring materials may be combined with substances such as gum acacia or modified starch to provide an encapsulation matrix and then spray-dried

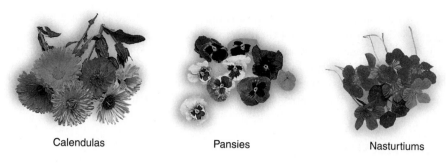

Calendulas   Pansies   Nasturtiums

Figure 8-4
Calendulas, pansies, and nasturtiums are just a few of the edible flower varieties that can be used to liven up any salad or dish.

sirable interactions with the food, minimizes oxidation, and allows the controlled release of flavors.

Vegetable gums, or hydrocolloids, are often used in the industrial preparation of food. Many of these substances modify the perception of flavor, taste, and aroma. Flavors may be suppressed in systems thickened with hydrocolloids. Perceived sweetness is decreased, as is the sour (acid) taste. Aroma intensities may also be decreased. These and other effects should be considered when formulating new food products [10]. Flavorists may work as part of the research and development team when new food products are being developed. They can create flavors that work best with the ingredients, storage requirements, and manufacturing processes in yielding the desired end product [20]. Natural vegetable essences have been produced from such items as onions, celery, and cilantro [33]. Applications for these essences include dips, salad dressings, soup bases, and prepared foods.

VEGETABLES AND FRUITS AS FLAVORINGS

We season and flavor foods not only with basic seasonings, herbs, and spices, but also by the ingredients we choose to include. Onions, garlic, tomatoes, mushrooms and many other vegetables have pronounced flavors that influence the final taste of the product [19]. Many soup and sauce recipes use a *mirepoix* to flavor the dish. A standard mirepoix is a mixture of diced vegetables including 50 percent onions, 25 percent carrots, and 25 percent celery [14].

Fruits also are used in some dishes for the distinctive flavor they can provide. Citrus fruits in particular are aromatic and flavorful. Lemons, limes, and oranges contribute to the flavor of many dishes including baked products, entrees, vegetables, or sweet desserts.

ALCOHOL

Wines, liqueurs, and distilled spirits can be used in preparing main dishes, sauces, and desserts, creating new and interesting flavors. It has generally been assumed that, because of its low boiling point, the alcohol is evaporated from the foods during cooking; however, a study of six alcohol-containing recipes found that from 4 to 85 percent of the alcohol was retained in the food [3]. For a pot roast that was heated over 2 hours the retention was 4 to 6 percent. For a sauce to which Grand Marnier was added when the sauce was boiling, the alcohol retention was 83 to 85 percent. Flamed cherries jubilee retained 77 to 78 percent of the alcohol. The presence of alcohol in significant amounts affects the energy value of a food because alcohol contributes approximately 7 kilocalories per gram.

CHAPTER SUMMARY

- The natural flavors of many foods are enticing in themselves, but the judicious use of seasonings and flavoring materials can greatly enhance the natural flavors of foods.

- Seasonings, in general, are substances that enhance the flavor of the food or combination of foods without being specifically perceived or detected as themselves.

- Flavor enhancers act differently by heightening the perception of flavors. Examples of flavor enhancers include monosodium glutamate (MSG) and some other substances called 5'-ribonucleotides. Although there have been reported adverse affects from the consumption of MSG, it is considered to be safe.

- Flavorings are substances added for their own distinctive flavors, such as extracts of lemon. Most spices and herbs are used to build flavor. Flavor builders blend with and enhance other flavors in the dish, producing a total flavor bouquet.

- Salt is a crystalline substance with the chemical name sodium chloride (NaCl). There are many varieties of salt that may be used in cooking. Salt also is found naturally in some foods.

- Black pepper and white pepper are produced from the berry of a climbing vine. White pepper is most appropriate for dishes in which black pepper would be unattractive.

- Hot peppers are botanically different than black and white pepper. Hot peppers, commonly called chilies, are from plants of the genus *Capsicum*. There are many varieties of hot peppers that differ in hotness, color, and flavor.

- Spice may be defined broadly to include herbs or may be defined more specifically as parts of aromatic plants, such as bark, roots, buds, flowers, fruits, and seeds. Herbs may be described as the leaves and stems of soft-stemmed plants. When substituting fresh herbs for dried herbs in a recipe, approximately twice the amount of fresh herbs should be used. Spices, herbs, and seasoning blends should be stored in a cool, dry and dark place in airtight containers to extend storage life.

- Edible flowers may be used for flavor and color in many dishes. Not all flowers are edible; therefore when using flowers, be sure that the flower is an edible variety and that it has not been contaminated with insecticide sprays.

- Flavor extracts and essential oils from aromatic plants, dissolved in alcohol, are often used to flavor baked products, puddings, sauces, and confections.

- Ingredients such as onions, garlic, tomatoes, mushrooms, and citrus fruits also flavor foods. Wines, liqueurs, and distilled spirits can be used in preparing main dishes, sauces, and desserts, creating new and interesting flavors.

KEY TERMS

5'-ribonucleotides
crystalline
iodized
"hot" peppers
cuisine
Scoville Heat Units

yeast autolysate
disodium 5'-inosinate and disodium
   5'-guanylate
aromatic
fermentation
encapsulate

STUDY QUESTIONS

1. Distinguish among seasonings, flavorings, and flavor builders.

2. Describe the basic effects or roles of salt and pepper when properly used in cooking.

3. What is a flavor enhancer? Give examples.

4. What is MSG? How was it discovered? With which types of food is it most effectively used?

5. What is meant by the *umami* taste? Discuss.

6. In a strict classification, what are *spices* and what are *herbs?*
   a. Give examples of each.
   b. Describe their basic roles in cooking.
   c. Give suggestions for proper storage.
   d. Suggest uses for fresh herbs.

7. Identify and discuss ingredients other than spices, herbs, and basic seasonings that add flavor in recipes.

REFERENCES

1. Adams, S. O., Maller, O., & Cardello, A. V. (1995). Consumer acceptance of foods lower in sodium. *Journal of the American Dietetic Association, 95,* 447.

2. American Spice Trade Association. (n.d.). ASTA frequently asked questions. Retrieved August 17, 2002, from http://astaspice.org/main_faqs.htm

3. Augustin, J., Augustin, E., Cutrufelli, R. L., Hagen, S. R., & Teitzel, C. (1992). Alcohol retention in food preparation. *Journal of the American Dietetic Association, 92,* 486.

4. Bosland, P. W. (1996). Capsicums: Innovative uses of an ancient crop. In J. Janick (ed.), *Progress in new crops* (pp. 479–487). Arlington, VA: ASHS Press.

5. Dziezak, J. D. (1989). Spices. *Food Technology, 43*(1), 102.

6. Geha, R. S., Beiser, A., Clement, R., Patterson, R., Greenberger, P. A., Grammer, L. C., Ditto, A. M., Harris, K. E., Shaughnessy, M. A., Yarnold, P. R., Corren, J., & Saxon, A. (2000). Supplement–Review of alleged reaction to monosodium glutamate and outcome of a multicenter double-blind placebo-controlled study. *Journal of Nutrition, 130,* 1058S–1062S.

7. Giese, J. (1994). Modern alchemy: Use of flavors in food. *Food Technology, 48*(2), 106.

8. Giese, J. (1994). Spices and seasoning blends: A taste for all seasons. *Food Technology, 48*(4), 88.

9. Gillette, M. (1985). Flavor effects of sodium chloride. *Food Technology, 39*(6), 47.

10. Godshall, M. A. (1988). The role of carbohydrates in flavor development. *Food Technology, 42*(11), 71.

11. Institute of Food Technologists. (1995). Monosodium glutamate. *Food Technology, 49*(10), 28.

12. Institute of Food Technologists' Expert Panel on Food Safety and Nutrition. (1987). Monosodium glutamate (MSG). *Food Technology, 41,*(5), 143.

13. Kerr, G. R., Wu-Lee, M., El-Lozy, M., McGandy, R., & Stare, F. J. (1979). Prevalence of the "Chinese restaurant syndrome." *Journal of the American Dietetic Association, 75,* 29.

14. Labensky, S. R., & Hause, A. M. (2003). *On cooking: A textbook of culinary fundamentals* (3rd ed.). NJ: Prentice Hall.

15. Loria, C. M., Obarzanek, E., & Ernst, N. D. (2001). Supplement—Choose and prepare foods with less salt: Dietary advice for all Americans. *Journal of Nutrition, 131,* 536S–551S.

16. McCormick. (n.d.). Hot, hot, hot, stuff! Retrieved August 2, 2002, from http://www.mccormick.com/content.cfm?ID=9079

17. Nagodawithana, T. (1994). Flavor enhancers: Their probable mode of action. *Food Technology, 48*(4), 79.

18. Norton, V. P., & Noble, J. M. (1991). Acceptance of quantity recipes with zero added salt by a military population. *Journal of the American Dietetic Association, 91,* 312.

19. Ortiz, E. L. (1992). *The encyclopedia of herbs, spices, and flavorings: A cook's compendium.* New York: DK Publishing, Inc.

20. Pollock, C. (1994). Flavor development in the 1990s. *Food Technology, 48*(2), 141.

21. Popplewell, L. M., Black, J. M., Norris, L. M., & Porzio, M. (1995). Encapsulation system for flavors and colors. *Food Technology, 49*(5), 76.

22. Pszczola, D. E. (1997). Salty developments in food. *Food Technology, 51*(10), 79.

23. Pszczola, D. E. (2001). 2001: A spice odyssey. *Food Technology, 55*(1), 36–44.

24. Pszczola, D. E. (2001). Suppliers' night 2000 proves to be a spicy affair. *Food Technology, 55*(1), 68–73.

25. Pszczola, D. E. (2002). Exploring novel flavor and health concepts on the west coast front. *Food Technology, 56*(5), 34–90.

26. Riley, K. A., & and Kleyn, D. H. (1989). Fundamental principles of vanilla/vanilla extract processing and methods of detecting adulteration in vanilla extracts. *Food Technology, 43*(10), 64.

27. Rosengarten, F., Jr. (1969). *The book of spices.* Wynnewood, PA: Livingston Publishing Company.

28. Shovic, A., Bart, R. D., & Stalcup, A. M. (1997). 'We think your son has Lennox-Gastaut syndrome'—A case study of monosodium glutamate's possible effect on a child. *Journal of the American Dietetic Association, 97,* 793.

29. Sloan, A. E. (2001). Eastern influence. *Food Technology, 55*(3), 18.

30. Sloan, A. E. (2001). Ethnic foods in the decade ahead. *Food Technology, 55*(10), 18.

31. Sloan, A. E. (2001). More on ethnic foods: Move over BBQ, Cajun, and Caesar. *Food Technology, 55*(11), 18.

32. Sloan, A. E. (2002). A flavored forecast–2002. *Food Technology, 56*(1), 16.

33. Staff. (1995). Groups cooperate to produce natural vegetable essences. *Food Technology, 49*(5), 92.

34. U.S. Department of Agriculture and U.S. Department of Health and Human Services. (2000). *Nutrition and your health: Dietary guidelines for Americans, 5th edition.* Home and Garden Bulletin No. 232.

Food Composition

Foods contain different chemical molecules that are put together in a variety of ways. It is obvious, simply by looking, that some food products are not homogeneous. From casual observation of a sliced tomato, for example, you may note skin, seeds, and soft tissues, each with a different structural appearance. Even foods that appear to be homogeneous, such as cheddar cheese, are composed of an ultrastructure that may be seen by examining a sample of the food under a microscope. Even with the aid of the finest microscope, however, some molecules and structures still cannot be seen. Foods are very complex materials.

Determination of the amount of each chemical component in a food, called its chemical composition, may be made in the laboratory. Water, carbohydrates, fats, and proteins are the chemical substances found in largest amounts in foods. Enzymes are special types of proteins found in small amounts in unprocessed plant and animal tissues. Minerals, vitamins, acids, and many flavor substances, and pigments that give color, are also present in foods in minute amounts.

Comprehensive tables of food composition have been produced by compiling the results of numerous analyses of food samples done in laboratories. The Agricultural Research Service (ARS) in the U.S. Department of Agriculture (USDA) provides a database that reports nutrients in over 6,000 foods. This database, called the *Nutrient Database for Standard Reference, Release 15 (SR15)*, is available on CD-ROM or from the USDA Web page [16]. The Nutrient Database for Standard Reference replaced the print version known as USDA Handbook No. 8.

In addition to knowing the quantity of each chemical component present in foods, we need some knowledge of the characteristics and properties of the major constituents. Changes may occur in these components as a food is processed and prepared. For example, water is removed in large quantities from fruits, vegetables, and meats when they are dehydrated. Fat melts and is found in the drippings when meat is roasted. Oil and water or vinegar separate from each other when the **emulsion** in mayonnaise is broken. Addition of fresh pineapple to a gelatin mixture prevents setting of the gelatin, because the gelatin, which is a protein, is broken down into **peptides** or **amino acids** by an enzyme in the pineapple.

In this chapter, we briefly describe some chemical characteristics of the major components of foods. This information is useful for those who have not previously studied chemistry and increases understanding of the nature of foods as discussed in other chapters of this text.

emulsion the dispersion of one liquid in another liquid with which it usually does not mix (is immiscible), such as oil and water

peptide a variable number of amino acids joined together

amino acids small molecules, each having both an organic acid group ($-COOH$) and an amino acid group ($-NH_2$), that are the building units for protein molecules

WATER

All foods, even those that appear to be quite dry, contain at least some water. Amounts present range from as low as 1 or 2 percent to as high as 98 percent, although most foods contain intermediate amounts. Table 9-1 gives the water content of selected foods. Examples of foods that are high in water are raw vegetables and juicy fruits. Fresh greens contain about 96 percent water, and watermelon has about 93 percent. Crackers, an example of a low-moisture food, usually contain only 2 to 4 percent water.

Much of the water in plant and animal tissues is held inside the cells (intracellular). In many cases it is held within the cells as a hydrate, which means that it does not flow from the cells when the tissues are cut or torn. For example, by visual observation, lean broiled beefsteak does not appear to contain about 60 percent water, and a sliced stalk of celery does not appear to be 94 percent water. The ability of a food to hold water in this way is called its *water-holding capacity*. Although much of the water in plant and animal tissues is held as a

Table 9-1
Water Content of Selected Foods

Food	Water Content %
Lettuce, iceberg, raw	96
Celery, raw	95
Broccoli, cooked	90
Carrots, raw	88
Milk, whole	88
Orange juice	88
Oatmeal, cooked	85
Apples, raw	84
Creamed cottage cheese	79
Eggs, raw, whole	75
Bananas	74
Chicken breast, cooked	65
Ice cream	61
Beef roast, lean, cooked	57
Pork, ham, cooked	53
Pizza, cheese, baked	46
Potatoes, french-fried	38
Cheddar cheese	37
Bread, whole wheat	38
Bread, white	37
Cake, white layer	24
Butter	16
Raisins	15
Brownies	10
Cookies, chocolate chip	4
Popcorn, popped, plain	4
Cornflakes	3
Peanuts, roasted in oil	2

Source: Reference 10.

hydrate, it is still available. That is, it may be removed by pressure and it retains the properties of pure water—it can be frozen or act as a **solvent** to dissolve other molecules. It may be called *free water.*

Some of the water in foods, however, is held in an extremely tightly bound form called **bound water.** Bound water actually becomes part of the structure of large molecules such as proteins and **complex carbohydrates,** has reduced mobility, and does not have the same properties as free water—it does not readily freeze or boil and cannot easily be pressed from the tissue. Some water is bound by the interaction with **ions** and small molecules.

The more water that is bound in a food, the less the activity of the water. Water activity (a_w) is defined as the ratio of the **vapor pressure** of water in a food (p) at a specified temperature to the vapor pressure of pure water (p_o) at the same temperature, that is, p/p_o. The presence of **nonvolatile** substances in a food, such as sugars and salts, lowers the vapor pressure of the water present. Therefore, the water activity value of a food will be less than 1.0.

The perishability of a food is related to its water content, the food being generally more perishable with higher water content. This relationship occurs because microorganisms require water for their growth. However, an even closer relationship exists between the water activity and perishability. Water activity can be reduced by drying a food. In this case, some water is removed by vaporization, thus causing the substances that are dissolved in the water remaining in the food to become more concentrated and the vapor pressure, therefore, to be lowered. Water activity can also be reduced by freezing, because water is removed from the system when it forms ice. The addition of sugar or salt lowers the water activity of a food because some water is bound by these substances; that water is then unavailable for use by microorganisms. Intermediate-moisture foods normally have water activity between 0.7 and 0.9 and are not susceptible to microbial growth, although they are soft enough to eat without rehydration. Fresh meats, fruits, and vegetables have usual water activity values of 0.95 to 0.99 and are very susceptible to spoilage.

Uses of Water in Food Preparation

Water plays several important roles in food preparation, affecting both the sensory characteristics of food [9] and the processes by which heat is transferred and foods are cooked.

Water has been called a *universal solvent,* indicating that it can dissolve many different substances. It acts as a solvent or a dispersing medium for most of the chemical substances in foods. For example, many of the flavor molecules in beverages such as coffee and tea are dissolved in water; sugars are dissolved in fruit juices and in syrups; and starch granules may first be dispersed in cold water and then, as they are heated, absorb large amounts of water to produce a thickened mixture, as a pudding or sauce. A negative aspect of water when it is used in cooking is that it may leach out and dissolve some important nutrients, particularly vitamins and minerals, found in vegetables. If the cooking water is not consumed, then some major nutrient losses occur.

In cooking, water is an important medium for applying heat. It may be used for this purpose both in its liquid form as hot or boiling water and in its vapor form as steam. When water boils, the forces of attraction between water molecules are overcome and the water molecules become gaseous. They leave the container in bubbles of steam. At sea level, the temperature of boiling water is

solvent a liquid in which other substances may be dissolved

bound water water that is held so tightly by another molecule (usually a large molecule such as a protein) that it no longer has the properties of free water

complex carbohydrates carbohydrates made up of many small sugar units joined together, for example, starch and cellulose

ion an electrically charged (+ or −) atom or group of atoms

vapor pressure the pressure produced over the surface of a liquid as a result of the change of some of the liquid molecules into a gaseous state and their escape from the body of the liquid

nonvolatile not able to vaporize or form a gas at ordinary temperatures

latent heat the heat or energy required to change the state of a substance, that is, from liquid to gas, without changing the temperature of the substance

212°F (100°C). Making water boil rapidly does not increase this temperature. Steam that is not under pressure has the same temperature as boiling water. However, a certain amount of energy, called **latent heat** or *heat of vaporization*, is necessary to change the state of water from its liquid form to its vapor form as steam. This heat is absorbed by the steam but does not register on a thermometer. When steam condenses on a cooler surface and returns to its liquid form, the latent heat is released and helps to cook the food. For example, steamed vegetables are cooked both by the heat of the steam itself and also by the release of latent energy from the steam as it condenses on the surface of the vegetables and changes back to its liquid water form.

freezing mixtures mixtures of crushed ice and salt that become very cold, below the freezing point of plain water, because of the rapid melting of the ice by the salt and the attempt of the system to reach equilibrium; freezing mixtures are used to freeze ice creams in ice cream freezers

Water is involved in the preparation of **freezing mixtures** that may be used to freeze ice creams and other frozen desserts, particularly those made at home. When crushed ice (water in its solid form) is mixed with salt, the salt dissolving on the surface of the ice increases the melting rate. As ice changes from its solid form to liquid (water), heat is absorbed. This energy is called *latent heat of fusion*. The same amount of heat is given off when water freezes to ice. Water freezes at 32°F (0°C).

Water also performs an important function as a cleansing agent both for food itself and for utensils and equipment used in the preparation and serving of food. It removes soil particles and many microorganisms as well. Cleaning agents, such as soaps and detergents, increase the cleaning capacity of water.

Water promotes chemical changes in certain cases. Some mineral salts become ionized in solution—they break apart, and each part develops either a positive (+) or a negative (−) charge. For example, common table salt is known chemically as sodium chloride or $NaCl$. When this salt is placed in water, it dissolves and ionizes as follows:

$$NaCl \rightarrow Na^+ \, Cl^-$$

Ionization often causes other chemical reactions to occur. As long as baking powder remains dry, for example, no chemical reactions take place; however, when it dissolves in water, some of the chemicals that it contains ionize and then react with each other to produce new chemical substances. Among these products is carbon dioxide (CO_2) gas, which rises in tiny bubbles and makes a baked product light or leavened.

Water also affects the reactions of acids and bases (or alkalies). The chemical phenomenon that characterizes an acid substance is the ionization of a hydrogen atom, producing a positively charged hydrogen ion (H^+). This hydrogen ion, among other things, stimulates our taste buds to give us the impression of sourness. The ion that is characteristic of bases or alkalies is a negatively charged hydroxyl ion (OH^-).

The degree of acidity or alkalinity affects the characteristics of many foods and food mixtures during preparation. The color of fruit juices and of vegetables during cooking, and the color of chocolate in baked products, is affected by the acidity. To simplify the quantification of degrees of acidity, the pH scale was developed. This scale runs from 1 as the most acidic to 14 as the most alkaline. A pH of 7, in the middle, indicates an essentially neutral solution (neither acidic nor basic).

Pure water that has an equal number of hydrogen (H^+) and hydroxyl (OH^-) ions has a pH of 7. Tap water, however, usually has small amounts of other ions that affect its acidity or alkalinity, thus changing the pH from 7. For example, the harder the tap water, the more calcium and magnesium ions it contains.

Food	pH
Limes	2.0
Lemons	2.2
Vinegar	2.9
Strawberries	3.4
Pears	3.9
Tomatoes	4.2
Buttermilk	4.5
Bananas	4.6
Carrots	5.0
Bread	5.4
Meat, ripened	5.8
Tuna	6.0
Potatoes	6.1
Corn	6.3
Egg yolk	6.4
Milk	6.6
Egg white	7.0–9.0

Table 9-2
pH of Selected Foods

Source: Reference 6.

The presence of these ions increases the alkalinity of hard water, so its pH is above 7. This alkaline or basic pH will affect the color of some vegetables cooked in the water. The pH values of selected foods are given in Table 9-2.

Water has an active part in a special type of chemical reaction called *hydrolysis,* which refers to the breaking of a linkage between units of a larger or more complex molecule to yield smaller molecules. If a complex molecule is completely hydrolyzed, all of the linkages between the small building blocks that comprise the larger molecule are broken. In this process, a water molecule actually becomes part of the end product. For example, starch is a complex carbohydrate molecule made up of hundreds of small glucose (a simple sugar) molecules. When starch is hydrolyzed, the chemical linkages between the glucose units are broken. For each linkage that is broken, one molecule of water enters into the reaction and becomes part of the glucose molecules, as shown:

Part of a starch molecule   (Two linkages broken)   glucose   glucose

The Nature of Water

Water is a small molecule containing two hydrogen atoms and one oxygen atom (H_2O) bonded strongly together by what are called **covalent bonds.** It is interesting to note, however, that water does not behave in the same manner as most other molecules of similar size with regard to such characteristics as boiling point, freezing point, and vapor pressure. Water is a unique molecule, fortu-

covalent bond a strong chemical bond that joins two atoms together

Figure 9-1
The water molecule is called a dipolar
molecule *because part of it is positively charged and another part is
negatively charged.*

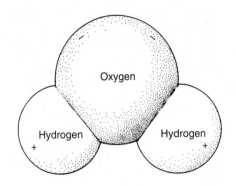

nately for all of us living on Planet Earth, who depend so much on water for
our very existence.

Water is unique chiefly because of its **polar** nature [2]. Although the hydrogen and oxygen atoms of water are joined by strong covalent bonds, the positive
and negative charges are not evenly distributed over the whole molecule. Figure
9-1 is a representation of a water molecule with a negative (−) charge on the
oxygen side and positive (+) charges on the hydrogen sides. The water molecule
has positive and negative poles and thus is *dipolar.* Because opposite charges attract each other, the negative part of one water molecule is attracted to the positive part of another water molecule, causing these molecules to cluster
together, as demonstrated in Figure 9-2. The attraction between the negatively
charged oxygen and the positively charged hydrogen is a type of bonding in itself, although much weaker than covalent bonding. This special bond is called a
hydrogen bond (see Figure 9-3).

polar having two opposite
natures, such as both positive and
negative charges

Figure 9-2
*Water molecules cluster together be-
cause the positive charge on one molecule is attracted to the negative
charge on another molecule, forming
a weak bond.*

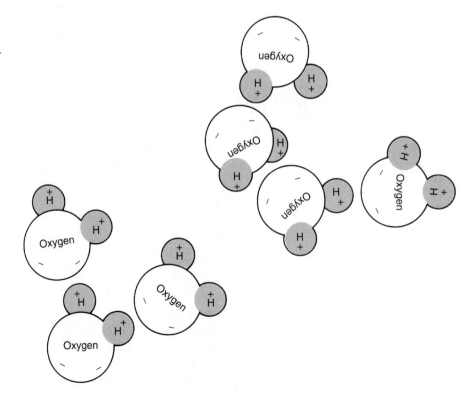

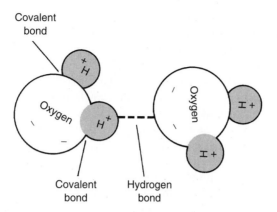

Figure 9-3
A hydrogen bond forms as water molecules are attracted to each other.

Because water molecules have such a special attraction for their fellow molecules, considerable energy is necessary to separate them from each other. This fact is apparent when water is boiled and its state is changed from the liquid to the gaseous molecules of steam or water vapor. The boiling point of water (212°F [100°C] at sea level) is quite high, considering the small size of this molecule.

The *vapor pressure*, which is the pressure produced by those water molecules that have already become vapor and are close to the surface of the liquid water even at room temperature (see Figure 9-4), is comparatively low. Therefore, because water does not readily change to a gaseous state, a considerable amount of heat must be applied to the water to overcome the special attraction of the molecules for each other and raise the vapor pressure before the water will boil. The amount of heat or energy required to change water from the liquid state to a gaseous state (called latent heat of vaporization) at its boiling point is 540 calories (0.54 **kilocalories**) for each gram of water that is changed to steam. The temperature of the steam itself is the same as the temperature of the boiling water. The boiling point of water is discussed in more detail in connection with boiling sugar solutions in Chapter 11.

kilocalorie one kilocalorie is equal to 1000 small calories; the small calorie is used in chemistry, whereas the kilocalorie is used in nutrition

Water Hardness

Water is generally classified as being soft or hard to various degrees. What is it that makes water hard? Basically, it is the presence of various mineral salts.

The two general types of hard water are temporary and permanent. *Temporarily hard water* contains calcium, magnesium, and iron bicarbonates that precipitate as insoluble carbonates when the water is boiled. These mineral de-

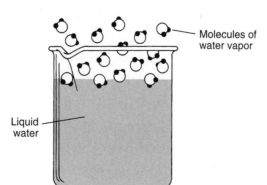

Molecules of water vapor

Liquid water

Figure 9-4
Vapor pressure is the pressure produced over the surface of a liquid, such as water, as a result of the escape of some of the liquid molecules into the vapor or gaseous state. This process causes water to gradually disappear or evaporate from an open container even at room temperature.

posits may accumulate as *scale* in hot water heaters and kettles used over a long period primarily for boiling water. *Permanently hard water* contains calcium, magnesium, and iron sulfates that do not precipitate on boiling. They form insoluble salts with soap and decrease its cleaning capacity.

The mineral salts of hard water may affect food preparation in various ways. Calcium retards the rehydration and softening of dried beans and peas during soaking and cooking. Hard water is often fairly alkaline and may thus affect the color of some of the pigments in cooked vegetables. Iced tea may be cloudy because some compounds in the tea (polyphenols) precipitate with the calcium and magnesium salts in hard water. Water that is naturally soft contains very few mineral salts.

Hard water may be softened by several different processes. In one method, water-softening agents, such as washing soda and polyphosphates, may be added to water to precipitate the calcium and magnesium salts. Another method uses an ion-exchange process in which calcium and magnesium ions are exchanged for sodium ions. A resinous material may be contained in a water-softening tank through which the hard water flows. Sodium ions held by the resin are exchanged for calcium and magnesium in the hard water until the resin has exhausted its sodium supply. At this point, the resin may be recharged with sodium by flushing it with a strong salt solution. Water softened in this manner is, of course, higher in sodium than it was originally.

CARBOHYDRATES

What comes to mind when you hear the word *carbohydrate?* You may think of sugars and starch, and perhaps fiber. Sugars are *simple carbohydrates*, consisting of either one basic sugar unit or a few of these small units linked together. Starch and fiber belong to the class of *complex carbohydrates*, because they may have thousands of basic sugar units linked together to form very large molecules. Thus, carbohydrates are either sugars or more complex substances, such as starch, which are formed by the combination of many sugars.

Carbon (C), hydrogen (H), and oxygen (O) are the elements that comprise carbohydrates. The ratios of these elements to each other form a pattern: One molecule of water (H_2O), containing the hydrogen and oxygen, is present for each atom of carbon. *Hydrated carbon* is suggested by the ratio $[C_x(H_2O)_y]$ and from this the name *carbohydrate* has been derived.

Carbohydrates are formed in green plants through *photosynthesis*, by which process energy from the sun is harnessed to convert carbon dioxide (CO_2) from the atmosphere and water (H_2O) from the soil into the simple sugar, glucose ($C_6H_{12}O_6$). Oxygen (O_2) is given off by the plant during this photosynthetic process. Thus begins the cycle of nature on which animal life depends.

High carbohydrate foods, including various cereal grains, legumes, and starchy roots or tubers, are staples in the diets of millions of people throughout the world. Foods classified as largely carbohydrate include the following:

Sugars	Jellies and jams
Syrups	Flours
Molasses	Dried fruits
Honey	Legumes
Candies	Cereal products

Chemical Classification

Carbohydrates are classified according to the number of basic sugar units that are linked together. They may thus be grouped in the following way.

Monosaccharides: simple sugars with one basic unit

Disaccharides: simple sugars with two basic units

Oligosaccharides: intermediate-size molecules containing approximately 10 or fewer basic units

Polysaccharides: complex carbohydrates with many basic units (up to thousands)

Monosaccharides. The simplest sugar carbohydrates are monosaccharides. *Saccharide* refers to their sweetness and *mono* to the fact that they are a single unit. Those with which we are most concerned in food preparation contain six carbon atoms and are thus called **hexoses,** although some five-carbon sugars, called **pentoses,** are important components of certain fibers and **vegetable gums.**

Three important hexose monosaccharides are glucose, fructose, and galactose. Another name for glucose is *dextrose,* and fructose is sometimes called *levulose.* Each sugar has the same number of elements, $C_6H_{12}O_6$, but slight differences in position of the chemical groups produce differences in properties, including sweetness and solubility. Chemical structures for these sugars are shown in Figure 9-5, and some sources are given in Table 9-3. Sugars are discussed in more detail in Chapter 11.

Glucose. The most widely distributed monosaccharide in foods is glucose, which is present in at least small amounts in all fruits and vegetables. The sugar that circulates in the bloodstream is also glucose. A number of complex carbohydrates, including starch, have glucose as their basic sugar unit. Glucose is a major component of corn syrup, which is produced by the breakdown or hydrolysis of the complex starch molecule. Crystalline glucose and corn syrup are widely used in bakery products and other manufactured foods. Glucose is present in honey with relatively large amounts of fructose.

Fructose. Probably the sweetest of all the common sugars is fructose. It contributes much of the sweetness to honey and is found in many fruits, sometimes being called fruit sugar. Because it is very soluble, fructose is not easily crystallized.

Technology has made possible the production of a high-fructose corn syrup by employing a special enzyme, called *glucose isomerase,* to change glucose to fructose. This syrup is widely used in processed foods, particularly soft drinks.

Galactose. Although galactose is generally not found free in natural foods, it is one of the two building blocks of milk sugar (lactose). Some galactose is formed from the breakdown or **hydrolysis** of lactose when fermented milk products, such as yogurt, are made. Galactose is also present in some oligosaccharides, such as raffinose, and a derivative of galactose (galacturonic acid) is the basic unit of pectic substances. Galactose is a basic building block of many vegetable gums, which are complex carbohydrates.

hexose a simple sugar or monosaccharide with six carbon atoms

pentose a simple sugar or monosaccharide with five carbon atoms

vegetable gums polysaccharide substances that are derived from plants, including seaweed and various shrubs or trees, have the ability to hold water, and often act as thickeners, stabilizers, or gelling agents in various food products; for example, algin, carrageenan, and gum arabic

hydrolysis the breaking of a chemical linkage between basic units of a more complex molecule to yield smaller molecules; water participates in the reaction and becomes part of the end products

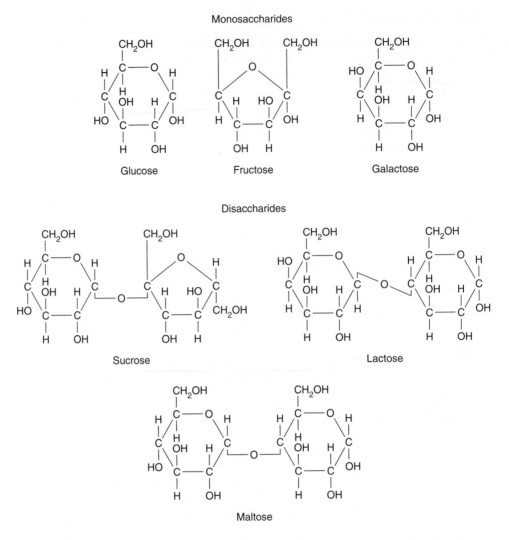

Figure 9-5
Chemical structures for monosaccharides and disaccharides of importance in food preparation.

Disaccharides. Monosaccharides are the building blocks of disaccharides, which consist of two monosaccharides linked together. Disaccharides of particular interest in the study of foods are sucrose, lactose, and maltose. Their chemical structures are shown in Figure 9-5, and some sources are listed in Table 9-3.

Sucrose. Sucrose is table sugar and is widely used in crystalline form for food preparation. It is usually extracted from sugar cane or the sugar beet. Sucrose is composed of one molecule of glucose and one of fructose. These two monosaccharides are linked through their most reactive chemical groups, the aldehyde group ($HC{=}O$) of glucose and the ketone group ($C{=}O$) of fructose.

When sucrose is hydrolyzed, the linkage between glucose and fructose is broken and a molecule of water is added in the reaction. The resulting mixture,

Table 9-3
Sugars, Their Sources, and Products of Hydrolysis

Sugar	Common Sources	Products of Hydrolysis
Monosaccharides, $C_6H_{12}O_6$		
Glucose or dextrose	Fruit and plant juices. Often present with other sugars. Honey. Formed by hydrolysis of sucrose, lactose, and maltose.	
Fructose or levulose	Fruit and plant juices. Often present with other sugars. Honey. Formed by hydrolysis of sucrose.	
Galactose	Does not occur free in nature. Formed by hydrolysis of lactose or galactans.	
Disaccharides, $C_{12}H_{22}O_{11}$		
Sucrose	Present with other sugars in many fruits and vegetables. Sugar cane and sugar beets are rich sources. Maple sugar and syrup. Used in many processed foods.	One molecule each of glucose and fructose. A mixture of equal amounts of glucose and fructose is called *invert sugar*.
Lactose	Milk and whey.	One molecule each of glucose and galactose.
Maltose	Malted or germinated grains. Corn syrup. Formed by hydrolysis of starch.	One molecule yields two molecules of glucose.
Oligosaccharides		
Raffinose (a trisaccharide)	The seed coats of legumes, nuts, and dried beans.	One molecule each of galactose, glucose, and fructose.
Stachyose (a tetrasaccharide)	Legumes, nuts, seeds, and dried beans.	One molecule of raffinose plus galactose.

containing equal molecular amounts of glucose and fructose, is sometimes called *invert sugar* and is important in controlling sugar crystallization during the process of making crystalline candies (see Chapter 11). Sucrose may be hydrolyzed by an enzyme called *sucrase* or *invertase*.

Lactose. Lactose, commonly called milk sugar, is found naturally only in milk and milk products. The two monosaccharides that comprise lactose are glucose and galactose. Whey, produced during cheese making, is a rich source of lactose and is sometimes used in processed or manufactured foods.

Maltose. Two molecules of glucose link to form maltose. Maltose is one of the products of hydrolysis when the complex carbohydrate starch is broken down. Therefore, it is present in germinating or sprouting grains, where starch hydrolysis provides energy for the grain growth. It is also an important component of corn syrups, which are made by breaking down corn starch.

Oligosaccharides. The term *oligosaccharide* may be used to refer to carbohydrate molecules containing 10 or fewer monosaccharide units. (*Oligo* is a Greek word meaning "few.") This category includes the trisaccharide (three sugar units) raffinose and the tetrasaccharide (four sugar units) stachyose. These carbohydrates are not digested by humans and may be broken down by bacteria in the intestinal tract, resulting in some gas formation. They are present in dried beans.

In Japan, oligosaccharides are added to several foods, including soft drinks and cereals, to act as **prebiotics** by stimulating the metabolism of indigenous bifidobacteria in the colon [15]. Growth of bifidobacteria apparently suppresses the activity of putrefactive bacteria.

prebiotics non-digestible foods that beneficially affect the host by selectively stimulating the growth and/or activity of one or more bacteria in the colon.

Polysaccharides.   Polysaccharides are complex carbohydrates containing monosaccharide units numbering from about 40 to thousands. These basic units are
linked in various ways. Linkages may produce long, straight chains in some
cases and branched-type molecules in other instances.

Starch and Dextrins.   Starch is the basic storage carbohydrate of plants and
is therefore found in abundance in seeds, roots, and tubers. Hundreds or even
thousands of glucose molecules join to make a starch molecule. Basically, there
are two kinds of starch molecules, sometimes called *fractions of starch.* One is a
long chain or linear type of molecule called *amylose.* The other is a highly
branched, bushy type of molecule referred to as *amylopectin.* Most natural
starches are mixtures of these two fractions, each contributing its own properties in relation to thickening and gelling. Illustrations for the chemical structures of amylose and amylopectin are shown in Figure 9-6.

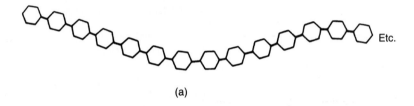

(a)

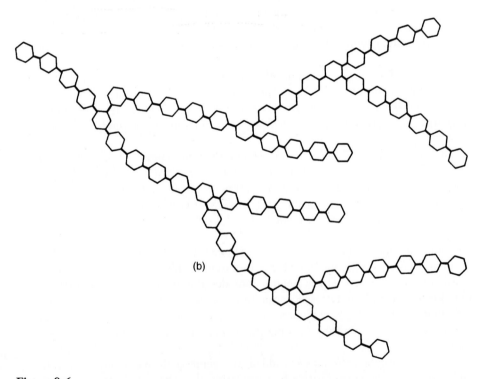

(b)

Figure 9-6
Portions of starch molecules, of which there are two types: (a) amylose, the linear fraction, and
(b) amylopectin, the branched fraction. Each small unit represents one molecule of glucose.

As starch molecules are produced in a growing plant, they are placed in a tightly organized formation called a *granule*. **Starch granules** are large enough to be seen under an ordinary microscope. When starch granules are heated in water, they swell tremendously in a process called *gelatinization*. The swollen starch granules are responsible for the thickening that occurs when starchy puddings and sauces are cooked. Starch and gelatinization are discussed in more detail in Chapter 13.

Dextrins are produced when starch molecules are partially broken down by enzymes, acid, or dry heat. We might think of dextrins as large chunks of broken starch molecules. They are formed from starch when corn syrup is made, when bread is toasted, and when flour is browned. They have less thickening power than starch.

Glycogen.   Glycogen, a polysaccharide, is sometimes called *animal starch* because it is found in animal tissues. It is similar in structure to the amylopectin or branched fraction of starch. When completely hydrolyzed, it yields only glucose. The liver stores glycogen on a short-term basis until it is hydrolyzed to help maintain a normal blood sugar level. The muscles also temporarily store glycogen.

Plant Fiber Components.   The term *dietary fiber* refers to the remnants of plant cells that are resistant to hydrolysis or breakdown by human digestive enzymes. Fiber is sometimes called *roughage* or *bulk* and is a complex mixture composed primarily of *cellulose*, *hemicelluloses*, *beta-glucans*, *pectins*, and *gums*, which are all polysaccharides. The fact that oligosaccharides are indigestible by human digestive juices may qualify them to be called low-molecular weight, water-soluble dietary fibers. A noncarbohydrate molecule called **lignin** also is part of the fiber complex, particularly in woody portions of vegetables. The Food and Nutrition Board at the National Academy of Sciences has proposed new definitions "Dietary Fiber" and "Added Fiber" that distinguish between intact fiber in plants and fiber that has been isolated and added to foods [1, 5].

The fiber components are found primarily in or around the cell walls of plants. Many of them play important structural roles, whereas some, including various gums, are nonstructural. The importance of fiber in our diets for the prevention or control of several chronic disorders, including colon cancer, cardiovascular disease, and diabetes has been recognized by the health and scientific communities [1, 12]. The outer bran layers of cereal grains, legumes, nuts, and seeds, as well as fruits and vegetables, contain relatively large amounts of dietary fiber, many of whose components have the capacity to absorb water and swell.

Cellulose.   Cellulose has thousands of glucose units linked together, as does the linear fraction of starch; however, the glucose molecules in cellulose are linked in a different way than the glucose units in starch, and form long, strong fibers. The linkage of glucose molecules in cellulose is not subject to hydrolysis or breakdown by human digestive enzymes. Therefore, unlike starch, which is digestible, cellulose is indigestible. The cell walls of plant tissues contain cellulose in tiny fibrils, helping to give structure to these tissues.

Cellulose may be chemically modified to make it more soluble and able to form gels. Examples of modified cellulose include methylcellulose and car-

starch granule a particle formed in the plant seed or root when starch is stored; composed of millions of starch molecules laid down in a very organized pattern; the shape of the granule is typical for each species

lignin a woody, fibrous, noncarbohydrate material produced in mature plants; component of the fiber complex

boxymethyl cellulose, which are used to thicken, stabilize, gel, and provide bulk in various processed foods [4].

Hemicelluloses.   Also found in plant cell walls are hemicelluloses. These are a heterogeneous group of polysaccharides that contain a variety of different monosaccharide building blocks. In many cases these molecules have branching side chains. Hemicelluloses, along with cellulose, play important structural roles in plants. Xylose and arabinose, which are pentoses (monosaccharides with five carbon atoms), are common components of hemicelluloses.

Beta-glucans.   Beta-glucans are polysaccharides made up of glucose building blocks that are linked together differently from the glucose components of cellulose. Beta-glucan molecules are less linear than cellulose molecules and more soluble in water. Oats and barley are rich sources of beta-glucans [1, 11]. Foods high in beta-glucans are authorized by the FDA to be labeled with a health claim stating the food may reduce the risk of heart disease.

Pectic Substances.   Pectic substances are polysaccharides found in the spaces between plant cells and in the cell walls, and aid in cementing plant cells together. **Galacturonic acid,** a derivative of the sugar galactose, is the basic building block of pectic substances. The largest of the pectic molecules, sometimes called the parent, is *protopectin.* It is present in largest amounts in unripe fruit and is hydrolyzed by enzymes in the tissues to the less complex *pectinic acid,* also called *pectin,* as the fruit ripens. *Pectic acid* is produced from pectin by additional hydrolysis of special chemical groups on the molecule called **methyl esters.** Pectin is the substance responsible for forming gels in various jams, jellies, and preserves; it also occurs naturally in many fruits.

Vegetable Gums.   The term *vegetable gum* or *gum* describes a wide variety of water-soluble polysaccharides that have the ability to act as thickeners or gelling agents in food products [3]. They are a major part of a group of food-processing aids called **hydrocolloids.** Gums are long-chain **polymers** of monosaccharides; various hexose and pentose sugars and their derivatives are the basic building blocks. When they are dissolved or dispersed in water, they have a thickening or texture-building effect, creating *body* and improving mouthfeel in a variety of food products [13, 14]. They also make it more difficult for dispersed materials to separate. In other words, they *stabilize* suspensions (solids dispersed in water). Thus, gums may help to retain water, reduce evaporation rates, modify ice crystal formation, and produce other desired changes in the consistency and flow characteristics of various foods. The preparation of low-calorie and reduced-fat foods often requires the ingenious use of hydrocolloids; for example, gums can thicken and stabilize low-calorie salad dressings made with reduced amounts of oil or with none at all. The U.S. Food and Drug Administration (FDA) regulates gums, classifying them as either food additives or GRAS (generally regarded as safe) substances [4]. Vegetable gums include the following:

galacturonic acid a chemical molecule very similar to the sugar galactose and containing an organic acid (carboxyl) group in its chemical structure

methyl ester of galacturonic acid Ester is the chemical word used to describe the linkage between an organic acid group (−COOH) and an alcohol group (−OH); in this case, the alcohol is methanol (which contains only one carbon atom) and the acid is galacturonic acid.

hydrocolloids large molecules, such as those that make up vegetable gums, that form colloidal dispersions, hold water, and often serve as thickeners and stabilizers in processed foods

polymer a giant molecule formed from smaller molecules that are chemically linked together

Source	Examples
Extracts from seaweed	Agar
	Alginates
	Carrageenan

Seed gums	Guar gum
	Locust bean gum
Plant exudates	Gum arabic
	Gum tragacanth
	Gum karaya
Chemically modified materials	Methyl cellulose
	Sodium carboxymethyl cellulose
Fermentation products	Xanthan gum
	Gellan gum

plant exudates materials that ooze out of certain plants; some that ooze from certain tree trunks and branches are gums

Browning

Chemical reactions that cause browning of foods often occur during preparation and storage. In some cases this color is desirable, but in other cases it is not. It is important to be able to control browning so that it can be inhibited or encouraged as needed. Some browning reactions are **catalyzed** by enzymes. Those involved in the browning of fresh fruits and vegetables are discussed in Chapter 20. Other browning results from nonenzymatic reactions, some of which involve carbohydrates.

catalyze to make a reaction occur at a more rapid rate by the addition of a substance, called a catalyst, which itself undergoes no permanent chemical change

When sugars are heated to temperatures above their melting points, they undergo a series of chemical reactions that begin with dehydration and end with polymerization, which produces brown compounds. This process is called **caramelization.** If this operation is not too extensive, a desirable caramel flavor and a light brown color result. As heating is continued, however, many bitter compounds are produced and the color becomes very dark.

caramelization the process by which a brown colored and characteristically flavored substance is produced when dry sugar is heated to very high temperatures

Another type of browning is produced by the *Maillard reaction.* This reaction also involves a carbohydrate—a sugar—in its initial step. The **carbonyl group** of a sugar combines with the **amino group** of an amino acid or protein with the removal of a molecule of water. After this, a series of chemical reactions occurs, including fragmentation and then polymerization, with the eventual formation of brown pigments. The specific compounds involved and the conditions of temperature, pH, moisture, and so on, under which the reaction occurs, all affect the final flavor and color, which may be desirable or not desirable. The browning of a loaf of bread during baking is due mainly to the Maillard reaction. The flavor and color, in this case, are desirable; however, the browning and off-flavor that may develop when nonfat dry milk solids are stored for a long time are not.

carbonyl group a ketone ($C=O$)

or an aldehyde ($HC=O$) group

amino group a chemical group ($-NH_2$) characteristic of all amino acids

LIPIDS OR FATS

The term *lipids* is used to describe a broad group of substances with similar properties or characteristics of insolubility in water and a greasy feel. The lipid classification includes at least three major groups with which we are particularly concerned in the study of food and nutrition: neutral fats known as triacylglycerols or triglycerides, phospholipids, and sterols.

Triglycerides (Triacylglycerols)

Approximately 90 to 95 percent of the fatty substances in foods fall into the triglyceride group. Thus, when we talk of fats in food, we are actually talking about triglycerides or triacylglycerols. For our discussions in this text, we use the older term *triglyceride*, rather than *triacylglycerol*; both refer to the same kind of chemical molecule.

Triglycerides are made up of three *fatty acids* combined with one molecule of an alcohol called *glycerol*. Glycerol has three carbon atoms and three hydroxyl groups ($-OH$). Fatty acids are commonly composed of linked chains of carbon atoms, with an organic acid group ($-\overset{\overset{\displaystyle O}{\|}}{C}-OH$) on the end of the chain. The fatty acids are joined to the glycerol molecule by what is called an *ester linkage*, as shown in the following, where *R* represents the chain of carbon atoms.

glycerol   3 fatty acids   triglyceride

Fatty Acids. Most fatty acids in foods are not free fatty acids but rather are combined in triglycerides. Different fatty acids may be joined with the glycerol in the same triglyceride molecule. Fatty acids vary in two important ways—they differ in the length of the chain of carbon atoms and in the number of hydrogen atoms that are attached to the carbons.

The carbon chain in fatty acids may be as short as four carbons or as long as 24 or more carbons. Generally, however, the fatty acids in foods have an even number of carbons. Names of some common fatty acids and the lengths of their carbon chains are listed in Table 9-4.

A carbon atom has four bonds with which it joins to other atoms. Within a carbon chain, two of the bonds join with adjacent carbon atoms. Each of the remaining two bonds on a carbon atom may bond with a hydrogen atom. Some fatty acids have all of the hydrogen atoms with which the carbon atoms can bond. There are no *double bonds* between carbon atoms, which might be broken to allow bonding with more hydrogens. These types of fatty acids are called *saturated*. Other fatty acids contain double bonds between some carbon atoms and are *unsaturated* in terms of the amount of hydrogen they contain. Examples of saturated fatty acids are butyric acid, which is present in butter, and stearic acid, which is a major component of beef fat. Palmitic acid, a saturated fatty acid with 16 carbon atoms, is widely distributed in meat fats, vegetable oils, and cocoa butter.

Oleic acid contains one double bond. It is thus a *monounsaturated* fatty acid. Linoleic, linolenic, and arachidonic acids contain two, three, and four double bonds, respectively. Fatty acids with more than one double bond are often called *polyunsaturated*. Polyunsaturated fatty acids that have a double bond between the third and fourth carbon atoms from the left (as you look at the fol-

(butyric acid; 4 carbon atoms)

(stearic acid; 18 carbon atoms)

(palmitic acid; 16 carbon atoms)
Saturated Fatty Acids

lowing chemical structures) are called omega-3 (ω-3) polyunsaturated fatty acids. Some ω-3 fatty acids appear to be of importance in body metabolism related to the prevention of coronary heart disease. Fish, particularly fatty fish, contains ω-3 fatty acids.

The body is not able to make linoleic acid with its two double bonds. Linoleic acid is therefore considered to be an essential fatty acid for both

Fatty Acid Common Name	Systematic Name	Number of Carbon Atoms
Saturated		
Butyric	Butanoic	4
Caproic	Hexanoic	6
Caprylic	Octanoic	8
Capric	Decanoic	10
Lauric	Dodecanoic	12
Myristic	Tetradecanoic	14
Palmitic	Hexadecanoic	16
Stearic	Octadecanoic	18
Arachidic	Eicosanoic	20
Monounsaturated		
Palmitoleic	Hexadecenoic	16
Oleic	Cis-Octadecenoic	18
Polyunsaturated		
Linoleic	Octadecadienoic	18
Linolenic	Octadecatrienoic	18
Arachidonic	Eicosatetraenoic	20

Table 9-4
Fatty Acids Found in Foods

$$H{-}\underset{\underset{\text{H}}{|}}{\overset{\overset{\text{H}}{|}}{C}}{-}\underset{\underset{\text{H}}{|}}{\overset{\overset{\text{H}}{|}}{C}}{-}\underset{\underset{\text{H}}{|}}{\overset{\overset{\text{H}}{|}}{C}}{-}\underset{\underset{\text{H}}{|}}{\overset{\overset{\text{H}}{|}}{C}}{-}\underset{\underset{\text{H}}{|}}{\overset{\overset{\text{H}}{|}}{C}}{-}\underset{\underset{\text{H}}{|}}{\overset{\overset{\text{H}}{|}}{C}}{-}\underset{\underset{\text{H}}{|}}{\overset{\overset{\text{H}}{|}}{C}}{-}\underset{|}{\overset{\overset{\text{H}}{|}}{C}}{-}\overset{\overset{\text{H}}{|}}{C}{=}\overset{\overset{\text{H}}{|}}{C}{-}\underset{\underset{\text{H}}{|}}{\overset{\overset{\text{H}}{|}}{C}}{-}\underset{\underset{\text{H}}{|}}{\overset{\overset{\text{H}}{|}}{C}}{-}\underset{\underset{\text{H}}{|}}{\overset{\overset{\text{H}}{|}}{C}}{-}\underset{\underset{\text{H}}{|}}{\overset{\overset{\text{H}}{|}}{C}}{-}\underset{\underset{\text{H}}{|}}{\overset{\overset{\text{H}}{|}}{C}}{-}\underset{\underset{\text{H}}{|}}{\overset{\overset{\text{H}}{|}}{C}}{-}\underset{\underset{\text{H}}{|}}{\overset{\overset{\text{H}}{|}}{C}}{-}COOH$$

(oleic acid; 18 carbon atoms)

(linoleic acid; 18 carbon atoms)
Unsaturated Fatty Acids

infants and adults, because it must be obtained in the diet. Skin lesions and poor growth have been reported in infants receiving a diet limited in fat, and these symptoms disappeared after a source of linoleic acid was added to the diet. It has been suggested by the Food and Nutrition Board of the National Research Council–National Academy of Sciences that a linoleic acid intake equivalent to 2 percent of the total dietary kilocalories for adults and 3 percent for infants is probably satisfactory to avoid any deficiency. The average American diet apparently meets this recommendation.

Good food sources of linoleic acid include seed oils from corn, cottonseeds, and soybeans (50 to 53 percent linoleic acid) and special margarines and peanut oil (20 to 30 percent). Corn oil contains more than six times as much linoleic acid as olive oil, and chicken fat contains up to 10 times as much as the fat of **ruminant animals** such as cattle. The fat from an avocado is about 10 percent linoleate.

ruminant animal an animal with multiple stomachs, one of which is called a *rumen*, where bacterial action occurs on the food that has been eaten; the animal—for example, a cow—"chews its cud" (material regurgitated and chewed a second time)

Cis-trans configuration. The shape of a fatty acid is changed by the presence of a double bond, because the double bond limits the rotation of the carbon atom at this point. The particular molecular shape produced by a double bond is dependent on the configuration of the bond. It may be either cis or trans. A cis configuration has the hydrogen atoms on the same side of the double bond, as illustrated here.

In a trans configuration, the hydrogen atoms are on opposite sides of the double bond, as shown here.

Because it is part of a triglyceride molecule, the fatty acid's shape affects the melting point of the triglyceride. An unsaturated fatty acid with a trans configuration has a higher melting point than the same size molecule with a cis configuration, because the bending of the chain in the cis fatty acid does not allow the triglyceride molecules to pack as closely together when they crystallize in a solid state. Thus, less energy is required to separate them when they melt; therefore they melt at a lower temperature.

Types of Triglyceride Molecules.   A triglyceride molecule may be formed with three of the same kind of fatty acids, for example, three palmitic acid molecules. In this case the triglyceride would be called a *simple* triglyceride and could be named tripalmitin. More commonly, however, triglycerides in foods are *mixed*, that is, they contain different fatty acids, either all three different or two alike and one different.

Phospholipids

Phospholipids are present in foods in relatively small amounts but play some important roles, chiefly as **emulsifying agents.** Lecithin is a phospholipid that is used as a food additive in various processed foods, including margarines. Phospholipids are present in buttermilk, resulting from the churning of cream. Certain baked products made with dried buttermilk may benefit from the emulsifying action of the phospholipids present. Egg yolk is a good source of phospholipids.

> **emulsifying agent** a substance that allows an emulsion to form because it has some characteristics of each of the two immiscible liquids and forms a bridge between them

Structurally, phospholipids are much like triglycerides. They contain glycerol attached through an ester linkage to two fatty acids; however, they differ from triglycerides in that instead of a third fatty acid, there is a phosphoric acid group joined to the glycerol. A **nitrogen base,** such as choline, is also linked with the phosphoric acid.

> **nitrogen base** a molecule with a nitrogen-containing chemical group that makes the molecule alkaline

$$
\begin{array}{l}
\quad\ \ \overset{\displaystyle H}{\underset{\displaystyle |}{\ }}\qquad\qquad \overset{\displaystyle O}{\underset{\displaystyle \|}{\ }} \\
H-C-O-C-R_1 \quad \text{(fatty acid No. 1)}\\
\quad\ \ | \qquad\qquad\ \ \overset{\displaystyle O}{\underset{\displaystyle \|}{\ }}\\
H-C-O-C-R_2 \quad \text{(fatty acid No. 2)}\\
\quad\ \ |\\
H-C-O-\text{phosphoric acid + nitrogen base}\\
\quad\ \ |\\
\quad\ \ H
\end{array}
$$

In a mixture, the fatty acid portions of the phospholipid molecules are attracted to other fat substances, whereas the phosphoric acid–nitrogen base portion is attracted to polar molecules such as water or vinegar. Thus, the phospholipid may act as a bridge between fat and water and allow them to be mixed in an emulsion. The phospholipid functions as an emulsifying agent.

Sterols

Cholesterol is probably the most widely known sterol and is found only in animal foods—meat, fish, poultry, egg yolks, and milk fat. Cholesterol is an essential component in the cells of the body, but too high a level of cholesterol in the bloodstream is one factor associated with an increased incidence of coronary heart disease. Vitamin D is also a sterol.

Plants do not manufacture cholesterol, but plant oils do contain some other sterols, generally called *phytosterols*. These sterols, however, are not well absorbed from the human digestive tract and actually interfere with the absorption of cholesterol. In 2000, the FDA authorized a health claim identifying the role of plant sterols or plant sterol esters in lowering the risk of heart disease [8, 7, 11]. Vegetable oil spreads high in plant sterols are available in grocery stores, but are not yet popular with consumers. The chemical structures of sterols are complex and quite different from those of the triglycerides.

Fats in Food Preparation

Several important roles are filled by fats in food preparation. They act as primary tenderizing agents in baked products. For example, contrast the marked tenderness of a croissant, which contains a high proportion of fat, with the chewiness of a bagel, which is made with very little fat.

Oils are major components of salad dressings and mayonnaise. Fats may be heated to high temperatures and act as a medium of heat transfer in the frying of foods. High-fat products such as butter and margarine are used as table spreads. Several flavor compounds are fat soluble and are carried in the fat component of many food products. The properties and processing of fats are discussed in Chapter 10.

Foods high in fat include the following (see also Table 10-1 in Chapter 10):

Butter	Deep-fat fried foods
Cream	Chocolate
Lard	Cheese
Oils	Nuts
Margarine	Fat meats
Hydrogenated shortening	

PROTEINS

Proteins are large, complex molecules found in every living cell. The name *protein* is derived from the Greek word *proteos*, meaning "of prime importance" or "to take the first place." Thus, all foods that were once living animal or plant tissues, including meats, vegetables, and cereal grains, contain some protein. Protein is an essential nutrient for human life and growth. In food preparation, proteins play important functional roles, for example, binding water, forming **gels,** thickening, producing **foams,** and aiding browning. In addition, enzymes, which are special kinds of protein molecules, catalyze many reactions that affect the characteristics of prepared foods.

gel forms when the material can be molded; that is, it holds its shape when turned out of a container

foam the dispersion of a gas in a liquid, such as a beaten egg-white mixture

peptide linkage linkage between two amino acids that connects the amino group of one and the acid (carboxyl) group of the other

Structure of Proteins

Proteins are unique because, in addition to the elements carbon, hydrogen, and oxygen, they also contain nitrogen. Often, sulfur is present as well, and some proteins contain phosphorus or iron. Proteins are large molecules made up of hundreds or thousands of small building blocks called *amino acids*, which are joined in a special chemical linkage called a **peptide linkage.** These linkages produce long chains that are said to constitute the *primary structure* of proteins.

Figure 9-7
Representation of an alpha helix.

The *secondary structure* of proteins results from the springlike coiling of the long peptide chains (see Figure 9-7). The characteristic coil is called an *alpha helix*, and special bonds, called **hydrogen bonds,** help to hold the coils in place.

The secondary coils of peptide chains may fold back on themselves, usually in an irregular pattern, to form more compact structures. This folding, which is characteristic for each particular protein, produces what is called the *tertiary structure* of a protein molecule. The long chains of amino acids, when coiled and folded, often produce a globular shape for the protein. A still higher level of organization, called the *quaternary structure*, may result when some globular proteins combine with others, and each forms subunits in a more complex whole. The structure of many protein molecules is indeed intricate, but the final shape of the protein is often of critical importance to its function in a living cell or in food preparation.

hydrogen bond the relatively weak chemical bond that forms between a hydrogen atom and another atom with a slight negative charge, such as an oxygen or a nitrogen atom; each atom in this case is already covalently bonded to other atoms in the molecule of which it is part

Amino Acids. About 22 different amino acids are used as building blocks for proteins. Each of these amino acids has two chemical groups that are the same for all of the amino acids—an amino group (H_2N-) and a carboxyl or acid group.

$$\begin{array}{c} O \\ \parallel \\ -C-OH \end{array}$$

The remainder of the molecule differs specifically for each amino acid. A general formula for amino acids is written as follows, with the R representing a side chain of variable structure.

$$\begin{array}{c} O \\ \parallel \\ C-OH \\ | \\ H_2N-C-H \\ | \\ R \end{array}$$

The side chains or R groups give a protein its particular characteristics. Some R groups have short carbon chains, some contain sulfur, some have additional amino or acid groups, and some have a cyclic structure. The side chain structures are shown in Table 9-5.

The peptide linkage is between the amino group of one amino acid and the acid or carboxyl group of another. Protein molecules are formed as hundreds of these linkages are made. The following hypothetical protein molecule shows several amino acids joined together by peptide linkages.

$$H_2N-\underset{\underset{C_6H_5}{\overset{|}{\underset{|}{CH_2}}}}{CH}-CO-NH-\underset{\overset{|}{CH_3}}{CH}-CO-NH-\underset{\underset{NH_2}{\overset{|}{\underset{|}{(CH_2)_4}}}}{CH}-CO-(NH-\underset{\overset{|}{R}}{CH}-CO)_n-NH-\underset{\underset{OH}{\overset{|}{\underset{|}{CH_2}}}}{CH}-COOH$$

phenylalanine   alanine   lysine   serine

Table 9-5
Side Chain (R) Groups for Selected Amino Acids

Amino Acid	Structure for Side Chain (R) Group
Glycine	—H
Alanine	—CH₃
Valine	—CH< (CH₃, CH₃)
Leucine	—CH₂—CH< (CH₃, CH₃)
Isoleucine	—CH(CH₃)—CH₂—CH₃
Serine	—CH₂—OH
Threonine	—CH—OH, CH₃

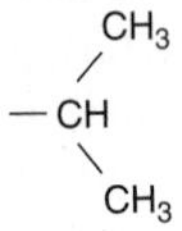

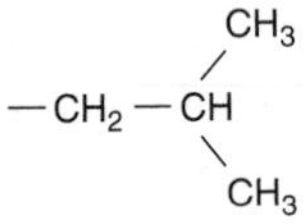

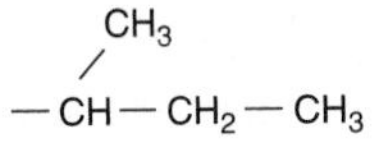

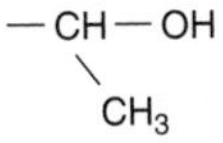

Sulfur-Containing

Cystine	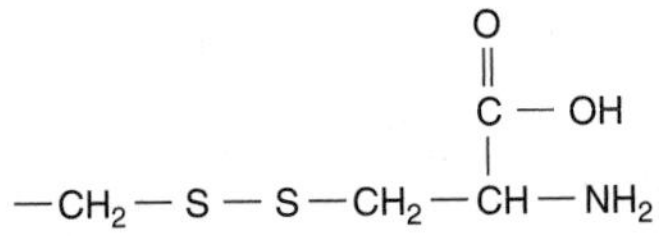 —CH₂—S—S—CH₂—CH(NH₂)—C(=O)—OH
Cysteine	—CH₂—SH
Methionine	—CH₂—CH₂—S—CH₃

Acidic

Aspartic acid	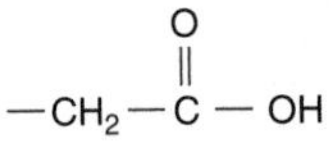 —CH₂—C(=O)—OH
Glutamic acid	—CH₂—CH₂—C(=O)—OH

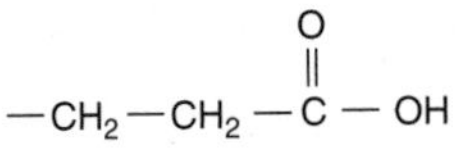

Protein Quality

Nine amino acids are considered nutritionally essential for tissue maintenance in the adult human, in the sense that the diet must furnish them in suitable amounts. These essential amino acids are isoleucine, leucine, lysine, methionine, phenylalanine, threonine, tryptophan, valine, and histidine. Histidine has been shown to be essential in the diet of adults and infants. The other amino acids, considered nonessential, may be synthesized in the body if nitrogen sources are available.

The balance of essential amino acids in a protein determines the biological value of that protein. Proteins of high biological value contain adequate amounts of the essential amino acids to promote the normal growth of animals and are sometimes called *complete proteins*, whereas proteins of low biological value do not. Because the amino acid requirement for growth is more rigid than

Table 9-5
Continued

Basic

Lysine	$-CH_2-CH_2-CH_2-CH_2-NH_2$
Arginine	$-CH_2-CH_2-CH_2-NH-C-NH_2$ with $\parallel NH$
Histidine	$-CH_2-C{=}CH$ ring with N, NH, CH

Aromatic

Phenylalanine	$-CH_2-C$ attached to benzene ring
Tyrosine	$-CH_2-C$ attached to benzene ring with $C-OH$
Tryptophan	$-CH_2-C$ attached to indole ring structure

that for the maintenance of tissues, some proteins that are inadequate for growth may function satisfactorily for maintenance or repair of body tissues. Specific examples of proteins of high biological value are those found in milk, cheese, eggs, meat, poultry, and seafood.

Vegetable sources of protein are often lacking to some degree in one or more of the essential amino acids and have a lower score for biological value. In addition, the total amount of protein in relation to the total calories found in certain vegetable products, such as cereal grains, is low. An exception among plant protein foods is the soybean, which contains a relatively large amount of high-quality protein. Some protein foods of relatively low biological value may be combined with other protein sources that complement them, one supplying more of an essential amino acid(s) than the other is able.

Cereals or legumes are more valuable in the diet if they are combined with even a small amount of protein from an animal source, such as milk, cheese, egg, meat, fish, poultry, or with soy protein, which furnishes amino acids that cereals and most legumes lack. Cereals and legumes also complement each other to improve protein quality. For example, a peanut butter sandwich contains a better quality protein mixture than the bread or peanut butter eaten separately. Table 9-6 lists the common names of several food proteins, their sources, and their general biological value.

Food Sources

Protein is present in many foods, but in varying amounts. Because it is an essential substance for living cells, one would expect to find it in both plant and animal tissues. Foods that are relatively high in protein (20 to 30 percent) include

Table 9-6

Sources and Qualitative Values of Some Common Proteins

Protein	Source	Biological Value
Casein	Milk or cheese	High
Lactalbumin	Milk or cheese	High
Ovovitellin	Egg yolk	High
Ovalbumin	Egg white	High
Myosin	Lean meat	High
Gelatin	Formed by hydrolysis from certain animal tissues	Low
Gliadin	Wheat	Low
Glutenin	Wheat	High
Hordein	Barley	Low
Prolamin	Rye	Low
Glutelin	Corn	High
Zein	Corn	Low
Glycinin	Soybean	High
Legumelin	Soybean	Low
Legumin	Peas and beans	Low
Phaseolin	Navy beans	Low
Excelsin	Brazil nut	High

meats, fish, poultry, eggs, cheese, nuts, and dry legumes. Even after dry legumes are rehydrated and cooked, they make an excellent contribution to dietary protein requirements. Although milk contains only about 4 percent protein, it is an excellent source of good-quality protein because of the amounts usually consumed on a regular basis. Cereal grains contain lesser amounts of protein; however, in the quantities of cereal grains that are often eaten, they make an important contribution to protein needs.

Properties and Reactions

Buffering.   Amino groups act as bases or alkalies, whereas carboxyl groups act as acids. As both of these groups are present on the same amino acid or protein structure, amino acids and proteins may act as either acids or bases, and are said to be *amphoteric*. This characteristic is important for many aspects of food preparation when the degree of acidity or alkalinity affects the quality of a food product. Proteins may combine with either acid or base within a limited range and resist any change in acidity. Because of this characteristic, they are called **buffers.**

buffer a substance that resists changes in pH

Denaturation and Coagulation.   The large complex protein molecules may undergo changes in their structures when they are subjected to the various conditions commonly encountered in food processing and preparation. If the protein molecule unfolds to some degree yet still retains all of the peptide linkages between the amino acids that comprise the molecule, it is said to be *denatured*. The process of *denaturation* is illustrated in Figure 9-8. Some of the properties of the protein change when it is denatured. For example, it usually becomes less soluble. If it is an enzyme, it loses its ability to function as such. The extent of denaturation may be either limited or extensive. If the conditions causing de-

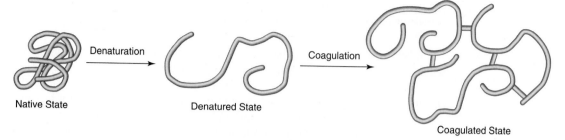

Figure 9-8

Denaturation of a protein involves unfolding of the molecule. The denatured molecules may bond together again to form a coagulated mass.

naturation persist, additional changes may occur in the protein. The unfolded parts of the molecule recombine in different ways to produce a new molecular shape, and protein molecules may bond together to form a continuous network. The term *coagulation* has been used to describe some of the later stages of protein denaturation in which denatured protein molecules bind together and produce a gel or a solid mass. The coagulation of egg white upon being heated is an example of this process.

Applying heat in the cooking of food produces denaturation and/or coagulation of proteins. An example is the roasting of meat, which denatures the meat proteins. Proteins may also be denatured by mechanical beating. For example, when egg whites are whipped to produce a foam, denaturation and coagulation of the egg white proteins occur. Changing the degree of acidity, changing the concentration of mineral salts, and freezing may also cause denaturation.

Enzymes. Enzymes are protein molecules with a special function. Produced by living cells, they act as *catalysts* to change the rate of a chemical reaction without actually being used up in the reaction itself. Enzymes catalyze a wide range of reactions in living matter, from the digestion of foods in the digestive tract of animals to most of the complex processes occurring in plant and animal metabolism. Enzymes in plant and animal tissues do not stop functioning when the animal is slaughtered or the plant tissue is harvested. Thus, we must deal with enzymatic activity when we handle foods from these sources. Enzymes and enzymatic action in foods are mentioned frequently throughout the text.

Nomenclature. Names of enzymes often include the substrate or substance on which they act, joined with an *-ase* ending. For example, *lactase* is an enzyme that works on lactose to bring about its hydrolysis, and *maltase* catalyzes the hydrolysis of maltose to yield glucose. Sometimes an enzyme is named for the product that results from its action. Sucrase, for example, is sometimes called *invertase* instead, because its action to hydrolyze sucrose produces an equimolecular mixture of glucose and fructose, which is commonly called *invert sugar.* In other cases, the name describes the reaction catalyzed; **oxidase,** for example, is the name of an enzyme involved in an **oxidation reaction.** Still other names, such as *papain* and *bromelin,* do not provide any information about the substrate, end products, or reaction.

A systematic nomenclature program that attempts to describe both the substrate and the type of reaction has been established; however, the names are

oxidase an enzyme that catalyzes an oxidation reaction

oxidation reactions chemical reactions in which oxygen is added or hydrogen is removed or electrons are lost

often cumbersome and difficult to use on a practical basis. Numerical codes are sometimes used, but they, too, are difficult to use.

Mechanism of action.   It has been suggested that enzymes function somewhat like a lock and key. They first combine with the substrate on which they will act, forming an intermediate compound sometimes referred to as the *enzyme-substrate (E-S)* complex. This complex formation undoubtedly involves a specific catalytic site on the enzyme. When the reaction is complete, the enzyme separates from the product and is free to react with another molecule of substrate. This process may be depicted as

$$\text{enzyme (E)} + \text{substrate (S)} \rightarrow \text{E-S} \rightarrow \text{E} + \text{product (P)}$$

Some types of enzymes.   Enzymes may be classified into groups according to the type of reaction they catalyze. For example, some enzymes catalyze hydrolysis reactions (*hydrolytic enzymes*) and some catalyze oxidation and **reduction reactions.** Hydrolysis is a chemical reaction that involves the breaking or cleaving of a chemical bond within a molecule. Water plays an essential role in this reaction, and the hydrogen and oxygen atoms of water are added to the two new molecules formed. Within the classification of hydrolytic enzymes, some are designated *proteases*, or *proteinases*, because they hydrolyze or digest proteins; *lipases* hydrolyze fats; and *amylases* act on starch. *Sucrase* breaks down sucrose into two simpler sugars. Some enzymes that catalyze oxidation-reduction reactions are commonly called oxidases or **dehydrogenases.**

reduction reactions chemical reactions in which there is a gain in hydrogen or in electrons

dehydrogenase an enzyme that catalyzes a chemical reaction in which hydrogen is removed, similar to an oxidation reaction

Some hydrolytic enzymes occur in plant tissues and have importance in food preparation. For example, the enzyme bromelin, which occurs in pineapple, is a protease and causes gelatin (a protein) to liquefy when fresh or frozen uncooked pineapple is added to gelatin. It is necessary to inactivate (denature) bromelin by heating the pineapple before adding it to a gelatin mixture if the gelatin is to set. Bromelin has been used as a meat tenderizer because of its proteolytic action. Papain, which is obtained from the papaya plant, also acts on proteins to hydrolyze them. It forms the basis of some tenderizing compounds applied to less tender meats. Enzymes used as meat tenderizers do not penetrate very far into the meat and may tenderize only on the surface. Certain oxidases in plant tissues are involved in the darkening of cut or bruised surfaces of many fresh fruits and vegetables. *Chymosin, or rennin,* is an enzyme that brings about the clotting of milk and is used in the manufacture of cheese.

Enzyme activity.   Each enzyme acts most effectively under optimal conditions. Temperature, degree of acidity or pH, amount of substrate, and amount of enzyme are all important. In general, the rate or speed of an enzymatic reaction increases as the temperature increases until a critical level is reached, at which point denaturation or coagulation of the enzyme by heat stops the activity. At its optimum temperature enzymatic activity is greatest, and denaturation does not occur. For example, the optimum temperature for the activity of papain is 140° to 160°F (60° to 70°C). When it is used as a meat tenderizer, it does not begin to hydrolyze meat proteins to any significant extent until this temperature range is reached during the cooking process. The enzyme is then inactivated as the temperature rises above 160°F (70°C).

Each enzyme also has an optimal pH. Often, this pH range is quite narrow, outside of which activity does not occur. For example, chymosin (rennin) clots

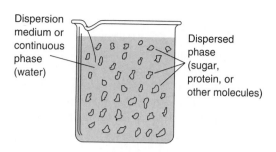

Dispersion medium or continuous phase (water)

Dispersed phase (sugar, protein, or other molecules)

Figure 9-9
A dispersion system.

milk most effectively when the pH is about 5.8. Clotting does not occur if the pH is strongly alkaline.

The rate of an enzymatic reaction increases with increasing substrate up to a certain point and then remains constant. The rate of an enzymatic reaction also increases with increasing amounts of enzyme. Enzyme activity in foods may thus be at least partially controlled by controlling the conditions under which the food is held or handled.

SOLUTIONS AND DISPERSIONS

Foods are usually mixtures of the various chemical substances that we have discussed—sugars, starch, fiber, fats, proteins, minerals, vitamins, water—and also air. To complicate things still further, some of these substances may be in different states—solid, liquid, or gas. Substances combined with other substances are often called *dispersion systems*. One (or possibly more) substance called the *dispersed phase* is scattered or subdivided throughout another continuous substance called the *dispersion medium* (Figure 9-9). For example, table sugar or sucrose may be dispersed in water; the individual molecules of sucrose are the dispersed phase and the water surrounding each of the sucrose molecules is the dispersion medium or continuous phase.

Dispersion systems may be classified on the basis of the state of matter in each phase. According to this classification, a food system may have a gas dispersed in a liquid (air in whipped egg white [a foam]), a liquid dispersed in a liquid (oil dispersed in vinegar to make mayonnaise [an emulsion]), or a solid dispersed in a liquid (proteins such as **casein** dispersed in milk or **ovalbumin** dispersed in egg white).

Another classification of dispersion systems is according to the size of the dispersed particles (see Table 9-7). In this classification, the tiniest molecules or particles dispersed in a liquid are said to form true solutions. Particles of intermediate size, although still very small, form colloidal dispersions. Comparatively large particles, such as corn starch granules dispersed in cold water, form suspensions. In line with this classification, small molecules or ions such as sugars, salts, and vitamins are usually found in true solutions; larger molecules such as proteins, pectic substances, cellulose, hemicelluloses, and cooked starch are

casein a major protein found in milk

ovalbumin a major protein found in egg white

System	Particle Size
True solutions	Less than 1 nm[a] in diameter
Colloidal dispersions	1 nm to 0.1 or 0.2 μm[b] in diameter
Suspensions	Greater than 0.2 μm in diameter

Table 9-7
Particle Size in Various Types of Dispersion Systems

[a] A nanometer (nm) is one thousandth of a micrometer.

[b] A micrometer (μm) is one millionth of a meter.

usually colloidally dispersed; and clumps of molecules such as fat globules and uncooked starch granules are usually suspended and readily separate from the dispersion medium on standing. In true **solutions,** the dispersed phase is called the **solute** and the dispersion medium is referred to as the **solvent.** In food systems, water is the most common solvent or dispersion medium; however, in a few cases, such as those of butter and margarine, fat is the dispersion medium and small droplets of water form the dispersed phase.

Characteristics of Solutions

Solutions are common phenomena with respect to food systems. Sugars are in water solutions in fruits, fruit juices, and vegetables. In fact, in all foods containing sugars or salts and water, a solution is formed.

The solutes in solutions are always tiny molecules or ions. These minute particles are in constant **kinetic motion,** but are evenly distributed throughout the solvent; therefore, the mixture is homogeneous. Because solutions are very stable, they remain unchanged indefinitely unless water evaporates and the solute becomes so concentrated that it **crystallizes** out of solution. The solute is so finely dispersed that it passes through most membranes and filters and cannot be seen under a microscope. True solutions do not usually have the capacity to form gels.

Characteristics of Colloidal Dispersions

The colloidal state is intermediate between a true solution and a coarse suspension, with dispersed particles that are either large molecules, such as proteins or pectin, or clumps of smaller molecules, such as minute globules of fat containing small bunches of triglyceride molecules. Because colloidal particles are larger than those in true solution, they do not have as much kinetic energy and do not move as rapidly in the dispersion medium. Therefore, they are not as homogeneous and not as stable. They do, however, remain dispersed under usual conditions of food preparation and storage.

Three major factors are responsible for the stabilization of colloidal dispersions. (1) The colloidal particles are moved back and forth by the smaller, faster moving water molecules of the dispersion medium in what is called *Brownian movement.* (2) There are similar net electric charges on the dispersed particles—either all positive or all negative—and like charges repel each other, keeping the colloidal particles separated. (3) The colloidal particles often bind water closely around them (called water of hydration), forming a somewhat protective shell.

A unique characteristic of many colloidal systems is the ability to form gels, which are more or less rigid systems. A colloidal dispersion in a liquid, pourable condition is called a *sol,* thus distinguishing it from a true solution in which the dispersed particles are smaller. The sol, under proper conditions of temperature, pH, and concentration, may be transformed from a pourable mixture into a gel. It has been suggested that during gel formation, the relatively large colloidal particles loosely join to form a continuous network, sometimes called a brush-heap structure, trapping the liquid dispersion medium in its meshes. Figure 9-10 suggests how this might happen. Gel formation in foods may involve proteins, such as egg and gelatin gels, or carbohydrates, such as pectin jams or jellies and starch-thickened pies or puddings.

Foams, characterized as a gas dispersed in a liquid substance, are considered to be colloidal systems. Emulsions are also colloidal dispersions, where one liquid is finely dispersed throughout a second liquid with which the first liquid

solution the resulting mixture of a solute dissolved in a solvent

solute a dissolved or dispersed substance

solvent the liquid in which another substance is dissolved

kinetic motion the very rapid vibration and movement of tiny molecules or ions dispersed in true solution

crystallize to form crystals, each of which consists of an orderly array of molecules in a pattern characteristic of that particular substance

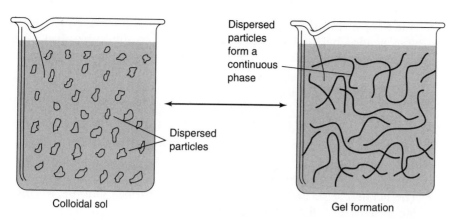

Colloidal sol

Gel formation

Dispersed particles form a continuous phase

Dispersed particles

Figure 9-10
A representation of gel formation. This is sometimes called sol-gel transformation *and is typical of colloidal dispersions.*

is generally considered to be immiscible or insoluble. The formation of a stable emulsion requires a third agent, called an emulsifying agent. Certain proteins and phospholipids often act as emulsifying agents in food products.

Characteristics of Suspensions

Suspensions are generally very unstable. The dispersed particles are composed of large groups of molecules, and the force of gravity tends to cause separation of the particles from the dispersion medium. The particles are large enough to be seen under an ordinary microscope. Examples of suspensions in food preparation include French dressings without added emulsifying agents. When the mixture is shaken, the oil becomes dispersed in the vinegar; however, the two phases separate immediately on standing. When corn starch and cold water are mixed together in the preparation of a starch-thickened pudding, the starch granules are suspended in the water; however, on standing only a short time, they settle to the bottom of the container. Tiny crystals of sugar in a crystalline candy such as chocolate fudge also represent an example of a suspension. In this case, the system is more stable; however, larger crystals may form and the candy may become "sugary" if it stands too long in a dry atmosphere where moisture is evaporated from the product.

CHAPTER SUMMARY

- Foods contain different chemical molecules that are put together in a variety of ways. Determination of the chemical composition of a food may be made in the laboratory. Water, carbohydrates, fats, and proteins are the chemical substances found in the largest amounts in foods.

- All foods contain at least some water. Much of the water in plant and animal tissues is held inside the cells. Water in foods may be free water or bound water.

- Water activity is the ratio of the vapor pressure of water in a food at a specified temperature to the vapor pressure of pure water at the same temperature. Foods with a high water activity level are more perishable than foods with a low water activity level because microorganisms need water for growth. The addition of salt or sugar lowers the water activity level of a food.

- Water plays several important roles in food preparation. It serves as a solvent, a medium for applying heat, and a cleansing agent. Water promotes chemical changes in some cases.

- Water is a small molecule containing two hydrogen atoms and one oxygen atom bonded by covalent bonds. Water functions differently than other molecules of similar size. Water is unique chiefly because of its polar nature.

- Water may be soft or hard. Water that is hard has various mineral salts that may affect food preparation.

- Carbohydrates are either sugars or more complex substances such as starch. Carbon, hydrogen, and oxygen are the elements that comprise carbohydrates. Carbohydrates are classified as monosaccharides, disaccharides, oligosaccharides, or polysaccharides according to the number of basic sugar units that are linked together.

- The simplest sugar carbohydrates are monosaccharides. Glucose, fructose, and galactose are all monosaccharides.

- Sucrose, lactose, and maltose are disaccharides. Disaccharides consist of two monosacccharides linked together.

- Polysaccharides are complex carbohydrates containing 40 to thousands of monosaccharide units. Starch, dextrins, glycogen, plant fiber, cellulose, hemicelluloses, beta-glucans, pectic substances, and vegetable gums are polysaccharides.

- Starch molecules are in a tightly organized formation called a granule. When starch granules are heated in water, they swell in a process called gelatinization.

- Dietary fiber refers to the remnants of plant cells that are resistant to hydrolysis or breakdown by human digestive enzymes. Fiber has been recognized as important in our diets to prevent or control several chronic disorders.

- Some nonenzymatic browning reactions in foods involve carbohydrates. Sugar caramelizes when heated to temperatures above its melting point, resulting in a caramel flavor and a light brown color. The Maillard reaction is another type of browning that can be desirable or undesirable.

- Lipids are a broad group of substances with similar properties or characteristics of insolubility in water and a greasy feel. The lipid classification includes three major groups of importance in food preparation: triglycerides, phospholipids, and sterols.

- Approximately 90–95 percent of the fatty substances in foods are triglycerides. Triglycerides are made up of three fatty acids combined with one molecule of an alcohol called glycerol.

- Saturated fatty acids have all of the hydrogen atoms with which the carbon atoms can bond. There are no double bonds between carbon atoms that could be broken to allow bonding of more hydrogens.

- Unsaturated fatty acids contain double bonds between some carbon atoms and thus are unsaturated in terms of the amount of hydrogen they contain. Monounsaturated fatty acids contain one double bond. Fatty acids with more than one double bond are called polyunsaturated.

- The shape of a fatty acid is changed by the presence of a double bond. A cis configuration has the hydrogen atoms on the same side of the double bond. In a trans configuration, the hydrogen atoms are on the opposite sides of the double bond.

- Phospholipids, although present in relatively small amounts in foods, are important in food preparation, chiefly as emulsifying agents. Lecithin is an example of a phospholipid.

- Cholesterol is probably the most widely known sterol and is found only in animal foods. Plants do not manufacture cholesterol, but plant oils do contain some other sterols, generally called phytosterols.

- Fats have several important roles in food preparation. Fats are tenderizing agents and serve as a medium of heat transfer in the frying of foods.

- Proteins are large, complex molecules found in every living cell. In food preparation, proteins play important functional roles, for example, binding water, forming gels, thickening, producing foams, and aiding in browning.

- Proteins are unique because, in addition to the elements carbon, hydrogen, and oxygen, they also contain nitrogen. Proteins are large molecules made up of hundreds or thousands of small building blocks called amino acids.

- About 22 different amino acids are used as building blocks for proteins. Nine amino acids are considered nutritionally essential for adult humans. Nonessential amino acids may be synthesized in the body.

- Proteins function as buffers to resist a change in acidity. This characteristic is important in the preparation of some foods.

- Applying heat in the cooking of food produces denaturation and/or coagulation of proteins. Proteins also may be denatured by mechanical beating, as is done when egg whites are whipped.

- A protein molecule is said to be denatured when the molecule unfolds to a degree yet retains the peptide linkages. Coagulation is a term used to describe the later stages of protein denaturation in which the denatured protein molecules bind together and produce a gel or solid mass.

- Enzymes, a special kind of protein molecule, catalyzes many reactions that affect the characteristics of prepared foods. Bromelin and chymosin (rennin) are examples of enzymes.

- Foods are usually mixtures of various chemical substances. These substances may be in different states—solid, liquid, or gas. Substances combined with other substances are often called dispersion systems.

- Dispersion systems may be classified on the basis of the state of the matter in each phase. Dispersion systems may also be classified according to the size of the dispersed molecules as true solutions, colloidal dispersions, or suspensions.

KEY TERMS

emulsion
peptide
amino acids
solvent
bound water
complex carbohydrates
ion
vapor pressure
nonvolatile
latent heat
freezing mixtures
covalent bond

polar
kilocalorie
hexose
pentose
vegetable gums
hydrolysis
prebiotics
starch granule
lignin
galacturonic acid
methyl ester of galacturonic acid
hydrocolloids

polymer
plant exudates
catalyze
caramelization
carbonyl group
amino group
ruminant animal
emulsifying agent
nitrogen base
gel
foam
peptide linkage
hydrogen bond

buffer
oxidase
oxidation reactions
reduction reactions
dehydrogenase
casein
ovalbumin
solution
solute
solvent
kinetic motion
crystallize

STUDY QUESTIONS

1. The chemical composition of food can be determined in the laboratory. List the major components and the minor components that are present in foods.

2. Give examples of foods that are high, intermediate, and limited in water content. Explain what is meant by *water activity*.

3. Describe four or five important functions of water in food preparation.

4. What is the pH scale and what does it indicate? Place several common foods on the scale.

5. Describe some unique characteristics of the water molecule.

6. a. Name two types of hard water and the types of mineral salts contained in each.
   b. Describe two methods of softening permanently hard water.

7. a. What are carbohydrates? Simple carbohydrates? Complex carbohydrates?
   b. In the following list of carbohydrates, indicate which are monosaccharides, which are disaccharides, and which are polysaccharides?

   (1) Starch   (6) Fructose (levulose)
   (2) Glucose (dextrose)   (7) Galactose
   (3) Lactose   (8) Dextrins
   (4) Cellulose   (9) Glycogen
   (5) Maltose   (10) Sucrose

   c. Identify the monosaccharide building blocks for each disaccharide and polysaccharide listed in question b.
   d. What are oligosaccharides? Give examples.
   e. Give several examples of vegetable gums and describe some of their uses in food processing.
   f. Name two fractions of starch and describe the major differences in their chemical structures.
   g. List at least four chemical components of dietary fiber. Indicate which are carbohydrates.

8. **a.** Describe in words the chemical structure of a triglyceride.
   b. Distinguish among saturated, unsaturated, and polyunsaturated fatty acids.
   c. For each of the following fatty acids, indicate if it is saturated, monoun-saturated, or polyunsaturated.
      1. Palmitic acid
      2. Linoleic acid
      3. Butyric acid
      4. Stearic acid
      5. Oleic acid
   d. Distinguish between cis and trans fatty acids.
   e. What is a simple triglyceride? A mixed triglyceride?
   f. In the following list of foods, check those that are rich sources of fat.

Whipped cream	Lard	Pork spareribs
Spinach	Walnuts	Potato chips
Pinto beans	Cheddar cheese	Shortening
Corn tortillas	Chocolate	White bread
Margarine	Corn oil	Apples

   g. How do phospholipids differ from triglycerides in chemical structure? What useful role do phospholipids play in food preparation?
   h. List several food sources of cholesterol.

9. **a.** What chemical groups characterize amino acids?
   b. How are amino acids joined to make proteins?
   c. What is meant by the side chains or R groups of a protein? Explain why proteins may act as buffers in foods.
   d. What is an essential amino acid and how many amino acids are so designated for adult humans?
   e. From the following list of amino acids, identify those that are nutritionally essential.

Methionine	Threonine	Glutamic acid
Phenylalanine	Isoleucine	Cystine
Tryptophan	Glycine	Leucine
Serine	Alanine	Valine
Lysine	Tyrosine	Histidine

   f. Explain the meaning of *biological value* in relation to proteins. Why do some protein foods, such as eggs and milk, have high biological value while others, such as kidney beans and wheat flour, have lower biological value?
   g. Explain how proteins can supplement each other to improve the net nutritional value.
   h. Name several food sources that are relatively high in protein.
   i. Describe, in general, the primary, secondary, tertiary, and quaternary structure of proteins.

10. **a.** Describe what probably happens when a protein is denatured. List at least four treatments, likely to be applied to foods, that can cause protein denaturation.

      b. Explain what probably happens when proteins are coagulated and describe some examples of coagulation in foods.

11. a. What is a catalyst? What are enzymes and how do they act as catalysts?
      b. Suggest a general mechanism of action for enzymes.
      c. Give examples of hydrolytic enzymes.
      d. Explain why enzymes are important in food processing and preparation.

12. a. Describe what is meant by the terms *dispersion system*, *dispersed phase*, *dispersion medium*, *solution*, *solute*, and *solvent*.
      b. Give examples from foods of types of dispersion systems classified according to the state of matter in each phase.
      c. Describe three types of dispersion systems classified on the basis of size of dispersed particles.
      d. Describe what probably happens during a sol–gel transformation in a food product. What types of dispersion systems are likely to show this phenomenon?

REFERENCES

1. American Dietetic Association. (2002). Position of the American Dietetic Association: Health implications of dietary fiber. *Journal of the American Dietetic Association, 102*, 993–1000.

2. Buswell, A. M., & Rodebush, W. H. (1956). Water. *Scientific American, 194*(4), 2.

3. Carr, J. M. (1993). Hydrocolloids and stabilizers. *Food Technology, 47*(10), 100.

4. Dziezak, J. D. (1991). A focus on gums. *Food Technology, 45*(3), 116.

5. Gordon, D. T. (2002). Intestinal health through dietary fiber, prebiotics, and probiotics. *Food Technology, 56*(4), 23.

6. *Handbook of Food Preparation* (9th ed). Washington, DC: American Home Economics Association, 1993.

7. Hicks, K. B., & Moreau, R.A. (2001). Phytosterols and phytostanols: Functional food cholesterol busters. *Food Technology, 55*(1), 63–67.

8. Hollingsworth, P. (2001). Margarine: The over-the-top functional food. *Food Technology, 55*(1), 59–62.

9. Katz, E. E., & Labuza, T. P. (1981). Effect of water activity on the sensory crispness and mechanical deformation of snack food products. *Journal of Food Science, 46*, 403.

10. *Nutritive value of foods.* (1991). Home and Garden Bulletin No. 72. Washington, DC: U.S. Department of Agriculture.

11. Ohr, L. M. (2002). Circulating heart smart news. *Food Technology, 56*(6), 109–115.

12. Papazian, R. (1998, September). Bulking up fiber's healthful reputation. *FDA Consumer.* Retrieved August 27, 2002, from http://www.cfsan.fda.gov/~dms/fdafiber.html

13. Pszczola, D. E. (1999). Starches and gums move beyond fat replacement. *Food Technology, 53*(8), 74–80.

14. Sanderson, G. R. (1996). Gums and their use in food systems. *Food Technology, 50:* 81(3).

15. Shah, N. P. (2001). Functional foods from probiotics and prebiotics. *Food Technology, 55*(11), 46.

16. U.S. Department of Agriculture, Agricultural Research Service. (2002). USDA nutrient database for standard reference, release 15. Retrieved August 20, 2002, from http://www.nal.usda.gov/fnic/foodcomp

Fats, Frying, and Emulsions

10

Fat is present naturally in many foods; it may comprise an important part of their gross chemical composition. The fat present naturally is often referred to as **invisible fat.** Examples of foods containing appreciable quantities of invisible fat include meat, poultry, fish, dairy products, eggs, nuts, and seeds. Sometimes labeled as **visible fats** are shortening, lard, salad and cooking oils, margarine, and butter. Many of these products contain essentially 100 percent fat. The so-called visible fats are often incorporated by the food-processing or foodservice industries into baked products, such as cakes and cookies, into fried foods, such as french-fried potatoes and doughnuts, and into other manufactured foods. If one does not have a clear understanding of food composition and food preparation practices, the fat in these prepared foods may also be invisible.

Classification of **lipids,** including **triglycerides** (triacylglycerols), **fatty acids, phospholipids,** and **sterols,** is discussed in Chapter 9. In food preparation, we are concerned mostly with only one of these groups, the triglycerides, as these comprise the major part of the fat naturally found in foods as well as the more purified fats.

Fats play a variety of roles in both food preparation and nutrition. They give flavor and a mouthfeel that is associated with moistness, thus contributing greatly to palatability and eating pleasure [13]. Some fats, such as butter and bacon fat, are used specifically to add flavor. As an ingredient in baked products, fats "shorten" strands of the protein **gluten** and thereby tenderize it. Some fats also contribute to the aeration of batters and doughs. Their capacity to be heated to high temperatures makes them an excellent medium for the transfer of heat to foods in the process of frying. Fats are major components of salad dressings, in which they usually constitute one phase of an **emulsion.** One type of fat—the phospholipid, lecithin—may act as the **emulsifying agent,** or emulsifier. In addition, fats are a concentrated source of energy for the body.

FAT CONSUMPTION AND NUTRITIVE VALUE

Concern about fat has become one of the nation's primary nutrition issues. During the past decade, the American Heart Association, the surgeon general, and other health organizations have called for a reduction in total dietary fat to 30 percent of kilocalories [11]. They have also recommended that no more than 10 percent of total kilocalories come from saturated fats. Relationships among

invisible fat fat that occurs naturally in food products such as meats, dairy products, nuts, and seeds

visible fat refined fats and oils used in food preparation, including edible oils, margarine, butter, lard, and shortenings

lipids a broad group of fatlike substances with similar properties

triglycerides a type of lipid consisting chemically of one molecule of glycerol combined with three fatty acids

fatty acid a chemical molecule consisting of carbon and hydrogen atoms bonded in a chainlike structure; combined through its acid group (−COOH) with the alcohol glycerol to form triglycerides

phospholipid a type of lipid characterized chemically by glycerol combined with two fatty acids, phosphoric acid, and a nitrogen-containing base, for example, lecithin

sterol a type of lipid with a complex chemical structure, for example, cholesterol

gluten a protein found in wheat that gives structure to baked products

emulsion the dispersion of one liquid within another with which it usually is immiscible (does not mix)

emulsifying agent a substance that is attracted to both of the immiscible liquids and helps mix them together to form an emulsion

saturated fat intake, high blood cholesterol levels, and coronary heart disease have been reported. Total dietary fat has also been associated with some types of cancer and other health problems [24].

The food industry has responded to the interest in dietary fat reduction by producing a wide variety of foods in no-fat/low-fat forms. Although consumers have purchased many of these items, concern about fat among the public appears to have peaked and the percentage of consumers buying reduced- or low-fat products is decreasing somewhat [45]. The fast-food industry continues to grow and takeout foods are popular. Nevertheless, Americans will apparently continue to respond to lowfat alternatives to traditional food if they taste good [29].

The consumption of food in the United States is measured through food disappearance data and a nationwide food consumption survey (see Chapter 2). The food disappearance data generally provides higher estimates since this data does not fully account for food that may spoil or be otherwise wasted and thus not consumed. According to food disappearance data, the U.S. food supply in 1999 contained 164 grams of fat per person per day [21]. This figure is about 8 percent higher than the 151 grams available in 1970. Using disappearance data, 40 percent of the calories available in the food supply are from fat.

Types of fats available in the food supply have changed over time as well. Saturated fats dropped slightly from 1970 to 1999, whereas both monounsaturated and polyunsaturated fats have increased. Polyunsaturated fats have increased by nearly one-third since 1970 [21].

The nationwide food consumption survey is based on interview and survey data. The 1994–1996 survey included a sample of more than 10,000 people living in the United States. Results from the 1994–1996 nationwide food consumption survey revealed that fat accounted for 33 percent of the calories consumed by the American public [49]. This compares with 40 percent in 1977 to 1978 (Figure 10-1). The percentage of kilocalories from saturated fat was 11 percent [8, 49]. The 33 percent for total fat is still above the recommended level

Figure 10-1

The percentage of kilocalories from fat consumed by Americans decreased from 40 percent in 1977–78 to 33 percent in 1994–1996 (Source: Reference 8, 21)

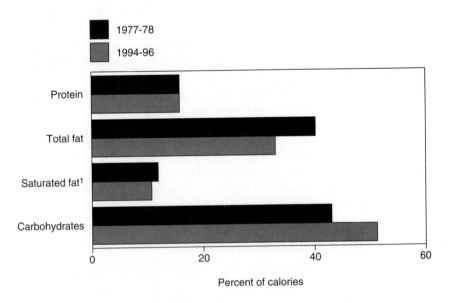

Note: [1]Earlier time-period data on saturated fat are for 1989-91; data not available in 1977-78.
Source: USDA, Agricultural Research Service, Nationwide Food Consumption Surveys.

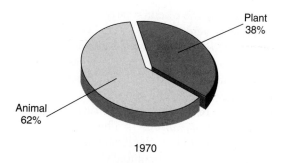

Plant
38%

Animal
62%

1970

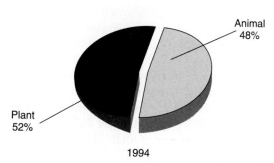

Animal
48%

Plant
52%

1994

Figure 10-2
Animal sources of fat in the U.S. diet have declined relative to plant sources. (Courtesy of the U.S. Department of Agriculture)

of 30 percent. The food consumption survey also found that kind of fat used has changed over time. Animal sources comprised 48 percent of the total fat consumption in 1994, compared with 62 percent in 1970 (Figure 10-2).

Fats are valuable in the diet as concentrated energy sources. On a weight basis, pure fat supplies more than two times the kilocalories of pure carbohydrate or protein. Table 10-1 gives the approximate weight and measure of various fats and fat-rich foods required to furnish 100 kilocalories. The percent of fat in each food is also indicated.

Food	Fat Content (%)	Weight (g)	Approximate Measure (Tbsp)
Butter	80	13	1
Margarine	80	13	1
Hydrogenated fat	100	11	1
Lard	100	11	1
Salad oil	100	11	1
Bacon fat	100	11	1
Peanut butter	46	16	1
Cream, light	20	50	3
Cream, whipping	35	33	2, or about double the volume if whipped
Cream, sour	25	48	4
Cheese, cheddar	32	24	1" cube
Egg, scrambled	11	61	1 egg
Ground beef, regular, broiled	21	35	1 ounce
Doughnut, yeast	21	26	1/2 doughnut

Table 10-1
Approximate Amounts of Various Fat and Fat-Rich Foods Required to Furnish 100 Kilocalories

linoleic acid a polyunsaturated fatty acid with 18 carbon atoms and two double bonds

omega-6 polyunsaturated fatty acids (PUFA) polyunsaturated fatty acids that have the first double bond on the sixth carbon atom from the methyl ($-CH_3$) end of the carbon chain

omega-3 fatty acids polyunsaturated fatty acids that have the first double bond on the third carbon atom from the methyl ($-CH_3$) end of the carbon chain

Fats provide essential fatty acids. **Linoleic acid, an omega-6 polyunsaturated fatty acid (PUFA),** is an essential nutrient. The role of the more highly unsaturated **omega-3 fatty acids** in body metabolism continues to be investigated. Omega-3 PUFAs have been associated with a decreased risk of developing coronary heart disease and hypertension [14, 47]. The most important of these fatty acids would appear to be *eicosapentaenoic acid (EPA)*. Fish is an excellent source of this lipid, from which the body can make the hormonelike compound *prostaglandin* [27]. This particular prostaglandin reduces the blood clotting rate and thus the likelihood of a clot blocking the coronary arteries.

Fats carry the fat-soluble vitamins. The average vitamin A content of butter is approximately 15,000 international units (IUs) or 3,000 retinol equivalents (REs) per pound, and margarines are fortified with a similar amount of this vitamin. Refined vegetable oils and hydrogenated shortenings contain little or no vitamin A, but vegetable oils are good sources of vitamin E.

Nutrition labeling requirements for packaged foods include the number of calories from fat, and grams of total fat, saturated fat, and cholesterol. Food products labeled "low fat" must contain less than 3 grams per serving, whereas those labeled "low in saturated fat" must have less than 1 gram per serving and less than 15 percent of total calories from saturated fat. This label information should be useful to anyone seriously attempting to follow recommendations for a low-fat intake.

PROPERTIES OF FATS

The chemical structure of triglycerides and their component fatty acids is discussed in Chapter 9.

melting point the temperature at which a solid fat becomes a liquid oil

saturated fatty acid a fatty acid with no double bonds between carbon atoms; it holds all of the hydrogen that can be attached to the carbon atoms

unsaturated fatty acid a general term used to refer to any fatty acid with one or more double bonds between carbon atoms; capable of binding more hydrogen at these points of unsaturation

polyunsaturated fatty acid a fatty acid with two or more double bonds between carbon atoms, for example, linoleic acid with two double bonds

P/S ratio the ratio of polyunsaturated to saturated fatty acids in a food, also sometimes calculated for a total diet; for example, a diet sometimes prescribed for certain individuals with high blood lipids may have a P/S ratio of 3/1 or 3

Solubility

Fats are insoluble in water and therefore do not mix readily with water-based food systems. They also have a greasy feel. In the laboratory they are soluble in a group of organic solvents that include chloroform, ether, and petroleum ether.

Melting Point

In common usage, fats that have a relatively high **melting point** and are solid at room temperature are called *fats*, whereas those that have lower melting points and are liquid at room temperature are called *oils*.

The melting point of a fat is greatly influenced by the types of fatty acids it contains. The chemical structures of some common fatty acids, both **saturated** and **unsaturated,** are described in Chapter 9. When fats contain a relatively high proportion of saturated fatty acids, such as palmitic and stearic acids, they have relatively high melting points and are usually solid at room temperature. However, when fats contain a relatively high proportion of unsaturated fatty acids, such as the monounsaturated oleic acid and the polyunsaturated linoleic acid, they have relatively low melting points and are oils at room temperature. The melting point of a fat, therefore, decreases with an increase in the number of double bonds in the fatty acids making up the triglyceride molecules. Fatty substances that have a relatively high content of **polyunsaturated fatty acids,** or a high ratio of polyunsaturated fatty acids to saturated fatty acids **(P/S ratio),** are commonly called *polyunsaturated oils* or *fats*. Examples of such products are corn, soybean, cottonseed, and safflower oils, and many soft margarines.

The *trans* form of a fatty acid has a higher melting point than its *cis* form, likely due to the shapes of the molecules. The cis form is more bent and thus less able to pack tightly together with other molecules. Tightly packed triglyceride molecules require more heat or energy to move them apart, thus increasing the melting temperature.

In addition to the degree of unsaturation and the cis or trans form, another effect on melting point results from the length of the carbon chains in the fatty acid molecules of the triglycerides. As the number of carbon atoms in the fatty acids increases, thus making longer-chain fatty acids, the melting point increases. For example, butyric acid with four carbon atoms melts at a lower temperature than stearic acid with 18 carbon atoms. Both of these fatty acids are saturated. Butter contains a relatively large proportion of short-chain fatty acids, many of them saturated, and melts at a lower temperature than beef fat or hydrogenated shortenings, which contain more long-chain fatty acids.

All food fats are mixtures of triglycerides, although each contains different kinds of triglyceride molecules. Thus, fats usually do not have a sharp melting point, but rather melt over a range of temperatures. An exception is the fat in chocolate. Because many of its triglyceride molecules are alike in chemical structure, having similar component fatty acids, chocolate melts over a fairly narrow temperature range that is close to body temperature, thus releasing in the mouth, as it is eaten, its delightful flavor bouquet and smooth mouthfeel.

Plasticity

Most fats that appear to be solid at room temperature actually contain both solid fat crystals and liquid oil. The liquid part is held in a network of small crystals. Because of this unique combination of liquid and solid, the fat can be molded or pressed into various shapes without breaking, as would a brittle substance. The fat is said to exhibit **plasticity**. The type and size of the crystals in a plastic fat influence the performance of the fat in baked products and pastry. Plastic fats can be creamed, that is, mixed with the incorporation of air.

plasticity the ability to be molded or shaped; in plastic fats, both solid crystals and liquid oil are present

Flavor

Some fats that are used for seasoning, at the table, and in salad dressings possess distinctive and pleasing flavors. These include butter, bacon fat, olive oil, sesame seed oil, and margarines. Margarines have a certain amount of butterlike flavor because in their manufacture, the fat is churned with cultured milk or whey and additional flavoring substances are often added.

In choosing fats for flavor purposes, the cost may also have to be considered. Corn, soybean, and cottonseed oils are commonly used to make satisfactory salad dressings, but lack the flavor of the more expensive olive oil. Similarly, butter may be an expensive fat for use in cakes. Other fats, such as hydrogenated shortenings, make cakes of excellent texture and volume but obviously lack the flavor of butter.

The ability of fats to take up or dissolve certain aromatic flavor substances is frequently used in food preparation. Onions, celery, peppers, and similar flavorful foods are cooked in fat to produce a savory fat that can be incorporated into food mixtures. Aromatic fruit and other flavors are also dissolved by fat.

PROCESSING AND REFINING OF FATS

Fats and oils commonly used in food preparation are separated from various materials and refined. Many oils come from seeds or fruits, lard comes from pork tissue, and butter comes from cream. Further processing produces fats such as margarines and hydrogenated shortenings.

Hydrogenation

The process of hydrogenation changes liquid oils into more solid plastic shortenings and increases their stability to oxidative changes and heat. Oxidation results in undesirable **rancid** flavors and odors. Fluid shortenings that can be poured or pumped, and thereby meet certain requirements for use in food-processing or foodservice operations, are also prepared by partial hydrogenation. The final crystallization process differs, however, from that used for regular shortenings.

Hydrogenation occurs in a reactor, where hydrogen gas is bubbled through the liquid oil in the presence of a nickel catalyst, which speeds the reaction. In the process of hydrogenation, some of the double bonds between the carbon atoms of the fatty acid portion of the triglyceride molecule are broken and hydrogen is added. This chemical change makes the fatty acids more saturated. The melting point of the fat is thereby increased. With sufficient hydrogenation it becomes a solid at room temperature. Careful control of temperature and pressure in the hydrogenation process allows the food processor to achieve the desired end result—the proper degree of plasticity. The fat can then be creamed and blended with other ingredients, if desired [36].

The hydrogenation process can be easily stopped at any point. A completely hydrogenated oil would be very hard and brittle. Plastic shortenings are hydrogenated only enough to obtain the desired consistency and stability. Often, products that have received different degrees of hydrogenation are combined to produce the desired effect [36].

In the United States, soybean oil is the major oil hydrogenated to produce shortenings. Smaller amounts of cottonseed and palm oils are often included with soybean oil to obtain the desired characteristics in the finished shortening. Hydrogenation greatly improves the stability of soybean oil and therefore its resistance to the development of undesirable flavors, sometimes called *flavor reversion* (discussed later in the chapter), to which soybean oil is particularly susceptible.

In a partially hydrogenated fat, changes occur in some of the remaining double bonds. For example, a bond may move along the fatty acid molecule to a different position not normally found in nature. The double bond may also change from the usual configuration, **cis** to **trans.** Although some trans fatty acids occur naturally in foods such as butter, approximately 90 percent of trans fatty acids in the American diet are found in partially hydrogenated vegetable oil (margarines and shortenings) [52]. The exact percentage of trans fatty acids in margarines varies widely, depending on the method of hydrogenation and processing of the product. A typical range is perhaps 15 to 35 percent of the total fat.

Trans fatty acids are not metabolized in the body as are cis fatty acids. Research has shown a positive, linear link between trans fatty acid intake and the elevation of plasma cholesterol [19, 31]. The food label has been shown to influence consumers' fat intake [40]. Therefore, to assist consumers in choosing

rancidity the deterioration of fats, usually by an oxidation process, resulting in objectionable flavors and odors

cis hydrogen atoms are on the same side of the double bond

$$\begin{array}{cc} H & H \\ | & | \\ (-C & = C -) \end{array}$$

trans hydrogen atoms are on opposite sides of the double bond

$$\begin{array}{c} H \\ | \\ (-C = C -) \\ | \\ H \end{array}$$

foods with a lower trans fatty acid content, the FDA has proposed new rules for the nutrient labeling, nutrient content claims, and health claims of foods that contain trans fatty acids or are trans fatty acid free [50]. Manufacturers have responded to these findings by developing lower trans fatty acid shortenings [42].

Winterization

Some cooking oils become cloudy when stored in the refrigerator, because some of the triglyceride molecules in the oil have higher melting points than other molecules in the mixture and crystallize or become solid at the low refrigerator temperature.

In the manufacture of oils intended to be used primarily for making salad dressings, a winterizing process is applied. In this process, the temperature of the oil is lowered to a point at which the higher-melting triglycerides crystallize. Then the oil is filtered to remove these crystals. The remaining oil, referred to as *salad oil*, has a lower melting point and does not crystallize at refrigerator temperatures [36].

Churning Cream

Butter is the fat of cream that is separated more or less completely from the other milk constituents by agitation or churning. The mechanical rupture of the protein film that surrounds each of the fat globules in cream allows the globules to coalesce. Butter formation is an example of the breaking of an oil-in-water emulsion by agitation. The resulting emulsion that forms in butter itself is a water-in-oil emulsion, with about 18 percent water being dispersed in about 80 percent fat and a small amount of protein acting as the **emulsifier.** Buttermilk remains after butter is churned from cream.

Butter is made from either sweet or sour cream, with butter from sour cream having a more pronounced flavor. The cream may be allowed to sour naturally or a pure culture of lactic acid bacteria may be added to pasteurized sweet cream. The latter method yields butter of better flavor and keeping quality, as it excludes many undesirable types of microorganisms that may cause off-flavor. Pasteurization also destroys any pathogenic bacteria present. Ripening of the cream after pasteurization by the addition of acid-forming bacteria permits acid fermentation to occur.

After churning separates the butterfat from the other constituents, the mass is washed, salted, and worked to remove excess water or buttermilk and to distribute added salt. Some sweet-cream butter is marketed unsalted as sweet butter. Salted butter is preferred by most Americans; sweet butter is used extensively in Europe and by European-trained chefs.

If coloring matter is used, it is added to the cream before churning. The season of the year and the demands of various markets for butter of different degrees of color affect the use of coloring matter. Butter produced when cows are on green feed is naturally more pigmented than butter produced when green feed is not consumed. Carotene is the coloring agent commonly used.

The USDA has set grade standards for butter. Experienced government graders check the quality and the keeping ability of the butter when assigning a grade [1]. Grades for butter include U.S. Grade AA and U.S. Grade A. U.S. Grade AA butter must have a smooth, creamy texture, delicate sweet flavor, and be made from high-quality fresh, sweet cream. U.S. Grade A butter rates close

emulsifier an emulsifying agent; a substance adsorbed at the interface between two immiscible liquids that aids in the formation and stabilization of an emulsion

to the top grade, however may not be as smooth and spreadable as Grade AA. Butter must have at least 80 percent milkfat by federal law.

Butter flavor is complex, resulting as it does from the combination of many flavor compounds. A substance called *diacetyl*, formed from bacterial action, is an important flavor component of butter. Butter is highly valued by many for its flavor.

Margarine

Oleomargarine was first developed in 1869 by a French chemist, Mège-Mouries, in response to the offer of a prize by Napoleon III for a palatable, nutritious, and economical alternate for butter. Beef fat was the chief constituent of the original margarine. Since that time, many changes have occurred in the composition and processing of margarine.

Over the years, the use of butter as a table spread has decreased, while margarine consumption has markedly increased. The lower cost of margarine has undoubtedly been a major factor in this shift. Other reasons for using margarines are its improved quality and uniformity, and a desire to decrease the cholesterol content of the diet. Although margarines do contain trans fatty acids, margarine is considered to be a better choice than butter if concerned about heart disease since butter contains saturated fats and cholesterol [51].

Margarine is made from one or more optional fat ingredients churned with cultured pasteurized skim milk or whey. It is a water-in-fat emulsion and must contain not less than 80 percent fat according to the **standard of identity** for margarine established by the FDA. Most regular margarines contain about 80 percent fat.

standard of identity a standard set by the U.S. Food and Drug Administration to specifically describe a food; to be labeled as such, a food must meet these specifications

Soybean and cottonseed oils, refined and partially hydrogenated to the desired consistency, are extensively used to produce margarines. Liquid oils may be blended with partially hydrogenated oils in such a way that the total polyunsaturated fatty acid content is higher than in ordinary margarines. If the first ingredient listed on the label is oil, rather than partially hydrogenated oil, the polyunsaturated fatty acid content of the margarine is likely to be relatively high. Soft margarines with particularly high percentages of polyunsaturated fatty acids may be sold in plastic tubs.

Other ingredients permitted in margarine by the federal standard of identity are vitamins A and D for nutritive purposes; diacetyl as a flavor constituent; lecithin, monoglycerides, and/or diglycerides of fat-forming fatty acids as emulsifying agents; artificial color; salt; citric acid or certain citrates; and sodium benzoate, benzoic acid, or sorbic acid as a preservative to the extent of 0.1 percent.

In addition to regular margarine and margarine with a particularly high content of polyunsaturated fat, a variety of other margarine products are available. For example, you can purchase sweet unsalted margarine that is made with no milk products if you are concerned about sodium and/or milk in your diet. A whipped margarine containing an inert gas to increase the volume and decrease the density is available, with six sticks to the pound instead of four. The caloric value of whipped margarine is similar to that of regular margarine, but less whipped margarine is likely to be used because of its fluffy nature. Blends of margarine and butter are also available.

Reduced-calorie margarines contain a lesser amount of fat, a greater amount of water, and a stronger emulsifying system than regular margarines; thus, they do not meet the standard of identity established for margarine. These products however may be labeled with a nutrient content claim such as "low-fat" margarine providing the labeling requirements for "low-fat" have been met and the product is not nutritionally inferior to margarine. The amount of oil and/or hydrogenated oil contained in these reduced-calorie products varies between roughly 45 and 75 percent. The modified margarines are labeled in accordance with the rules established by the 1990 Nutrition Education and Labeling Act (see Chapter 2). If health claims are made for relationships between fat and cancer or between fat and cholesterol and coronary heart disease, the claims must meet the specifications outlined by the FDA.

In 1999, plant stanol and sterol ester (also called phytostanols and phytosterols) based margarines were introduced in the United States [30]. Stanol and sterol esters have been found to lower cholesterol levels up to 14 percent in adults [28]. In 2000, the FDA issued a rule allowing a health claim on stanol and sterol ester containing products for reducing the risk of coronary heart disease providing the foods are low in saturated fat and cholesterol. However, some concern has been expressed about the impact of these products on the absorption of beta-carotene, lycopene, and vitamin E.

LDL cholesterol cholesterol that is combined with low density lipoproteins in the blood; sometimes called the "bad cholesterol," in contrast to the "good cholesterol" combined with blood high density lipoproteins

GRAS the list of food additives that are "generally recognized as safe" by a panel of experts; this list is maintained and periodically reevaluated by the FDA

Hot Topics

Plant Sterol Esters—Natural phytonutrients

It has been known for several decades that plant sterols can reduce blood cholesterol levels. They have been used to some extent as supplements and as drugs to lower cholesterol levels in hypercholesterolemic patients and appear to inhibit the uptake of dietary cholesterol from the intestine. But to be useful to a larger group of people, these substances needed to be formulated as ingredients in familiar food products. This was difficult because of their insolubility, but it has now been done. In 1999, two margarines containing plant sterol esters were put on the market with brand names of Benecol™ and Take Control™ [30].

What are plant sterols, or phytosterols as they are commonly called? They are chemical cousins of cholesterol but are produced in plants, rather than in animals, where they stabilize cell membranes. Phystanols are a related group of compounds that are chemically staturated, having two more hydrogen atoms in their ring structures. Because of their insolubility, it was not possible to add these compounds to commonly used food products until it was discovered

that, when they were combined with fatty acids as esters, they could be readily incorporated into fatty foods [28]. The result, as we have said, is margarine with cholesterol-fighting potential.

Phytosterols and phyostanols are safe enough to be classified as **GRAS** and are highly effective in relatively small amounts. Two servings a day of the special margarines can reduce **LDL cholesterol** by about 10 percent. And in fall 2000, the FDA approved a health claim that "plant sterols esters and plant stanols esters may reduce the risk of coronary heart disease by lowering blood cholesterol levels" [30].

Phytosterols may be derived from the vegetable oil refining process. Phytostanols are often produced from "tall oil," a phytosterol-rich by-product from the pulping of pine and other trees [28]. These substances are then purified and esterified with food-grade fatty acids. With the availability of these products, an entirely new line of heart-healthy foods may be marketed. The consumer will ultimately make the decision as to whether or not they are successful.

Lard

Lard is one of the oldest culinary fats; however, the lack of uniformity in the production of lard, as well as its flavor and some of its physical properties, such as grainy texture, resulted in a reduction in the use of lard by many Americans as other shortenings became available. In 1999, the per capita annual availability of lard in the food supply was 6 pounds as compared to 13 pounds in 1909 [5]. Lard is still the preferred fat in Mexican cuisine, especially for such dishes as refried beans.

Because lard is the fat rendered from the fatty tissues of the hog, the supply of lard depends on the number and size of hogs slaughtered. With the trend toward producing leaner pork meats, the supply of lard has decreased somewhat [36].

Rendering involves subdividing the fatty tissue into small particles and heating. The melted fat then separates from the connective tissue and other cell residues. The quality of lard depends on such factors as the part of the body from which the fat is obtained, the feed used for fattening the animal, and the rendering process. Leaf fat, which lines the abdominal cavity, is used to make the better qualities of lard.

Lard is susceptible to spoilage by the development of rancidity. **Antioxidants** are added to lard in processing to increase its shelf life. Some lard samples have relatively low smoking temperatures and have not been commonly used for frying; however, lards with high **smoke points** can be produced. One desirable property of lard is its excellent shortening power.

Technology has provided methods for improving the quality, uniformity, and functional properties of lard. Improved rendering methods have been developed; one involves the division of the fatty tissues into fine particles, after which flash heating is applied for 15 seconds. The product is then pulverized and centrifuged. This method gives a high yield and a bland and stable product at minimum cost.

A chemical modification, called *interesterification*, can be applied to lard to improve its plasticity and creaming qualities. Interesterification involves treating the fat with a catalyst at a controlled temperature, which produces a movement of some of the fatty acids to other triglyceride molecules in the mixture. This creates a more random distribution of fatty acids on the triglyceride molecules. The degree of unsaturation is not changed, but the way the fat crystallizes does affect its creaming properties and improves its performance in such baked products as shortened cakes. Some of this lard may be combined with hydrogenated vegetable fat in combination shortening or margarine. Antioxidants are added to shortenings containing lard to improve their keeping quality.

Hydrogenated Shortening

The process for hydrogenation of vegetable oils (described earlier in this chapter) was discovered more than 95 years ago and has since developed into one of the major chemical processes in the fat and oil industry. The fats produced are neutral in flavor, have a high enough smoke point to make them useful for frying, and have good shortening power.

In making hydrogenated shortenings, it is important to develop the best possible crystal structure to produce a shortening that is smooth in appearance and firm in consistency. To accomplish this, the chilling of the fat must be carefully controlled. The melted fat is chilled rapidly in a large heat exchanger that vigorously agitates the fat while removing heat from it. An inert gas is also

---

antioxidants a substance that retards or stops the development of oxidative rancidity; added to fatty foods in very small amounts

smoke point the temperature at which smoke comes continuously from the surface of a fat heated under standardized conditions

whipped into the crystallizing fat. After packaging, the shortening is then tempered—held for 24 to 72 hours at about 85°F (30°C) to further ensure proper crystal growth [36]. The desired crystals are small, long, and needlelike when examined under the microscope. In the production of fluid shortenings, the fat is agitated during tempering to form a larger crystal that contributes to its fluidity.

Hydrogenated shortenings often have emulsifiers, such as **monoglycerides** and **diglycerides,** added to them. The addition of emulsifiers to fats used in cakes makes possible the addition of higher proportions of sugar and liquid to fat, as is desired for some cake formulas. The presence of mono- and diglycerides in hydrogenated shortening, however, decreases the smoke point of the fat, thus making it somewhat less valuable for frying purposes. Special shortenings are used in commercial food-processing and foodservice establishments for frying and for cake making. General-purpose shortenings are also available; these are commonly sold on the retail market.

monoglyceride glycerol combined with only one fatty acid

diglyceride glycerol combined with two fatty acids

Refined Oils

Refined vegetable oils that are marketed for consumption in the United States include soybean, cottonseed, sunflower, peanut, olive, corn, canola, and safflower oils. Tropical oils such as coconut, palm, and palm-kernel oils are also used by food processors in many foods. Liquid oils may be categorized as cooking oils or salad oils. Cooking oils are used in frying operations, whereas salad oils are clear oils that have been "winterized." The salad oils are used in mayonnaise and salad dressings and are marketed as bottled oils [24].

Vegetable oils are removed from oil-containing seed fruits or nuts by various pressing processes, by solvent extraction, and by a combination of these [14]. A seed cake that is relatively high in protein remains after fat extraction and is often used for animal feed. After extraction, the crude oils are refined. The first step is usually to react the oil with an alkaline material to remove the free fatty acids that are not attached to a glycerol molecule. Free fatty acids in excess can detract from the oil's flavor and decrease its effectiveness when used for frying. The unwanted products of this reaction are then removed by centrifuging and washing, with a final drying process, which is then followed by bleaching and deodorizing to remove color pigments and further purify the oil [36]. *RBD* refers to an oil that has been refined, bleached, and deodorized.

Soybean oil is one of the dominant edible oils in the United States. Until the early 1940s, it was not used in this country chiefly because of its susceptibility to oxidation and development of off-flavors described as being "grassy" and "painty." These off-flavors, or flavor reversion (discussed later in this chapter), appear to be related to the content of linolenic acid. Partially hydrogenated soybean oil has improved stability and is a major component of vegetable shortenings and margarines [16]. Also, low-linolenic acid soybean oil, with higher stability toward oxidation, has been developed using conventional plant-breeding methods [17].

Cottonseed oil was America's first vegetable oil, developed over a century ago as a by-product of the cotton industry. With lower cotton production, the supply of cottonseed oil has decreased. Much of the cottonseed oil used in the United States is consumed as a salad or cooking oil or is formulated into shortenings that are used in baking and frying. It has a neutral flavor that does not mask the flavor of other products [16].

The most expensive of the edible oils is olive oil, also one of the most ancient oils. It has always been prized for its flavor, particularly by those who have lived in the Mediterranean area, where olive oil is the major cooking and salad oil. The popularity of olive oil in the United States has grown as consumers embrace world cuisines and seek to use oils with perceived health benefits. Olive oil contains a high percentage (approximately 92 percent) of the monounsaturated fatty acid oleic. It is also more stable to oxidation than most oils because of its low content of linoleic acid, a polyunsaturated fatty acid.

Good grades of olive oil are those that have not been refined, deodorized, or otherwise processed. The terms *extra virgin, virgin, and pure* indicate the acidity level and amount of processing. *Virgin olive oil* applies only to oil obtained from the first pressing of the olives without further processing. *Extra virgin olive oil* is a top grade of virgin olive oil because of its low acidity level. The term *pure* can be used for blends of virgin and refined oils that have been processed from the pulp remaining after the first pressing of the olives. Pure olive oil is less expensive and less flavorful as compared to extra virgin and virgin olive oils [35].

Canola is the name given to cultivars of rapeseed that are low in erucic acid, an unsaturated fatty acid suspected of being physiologically harmful. Canola oil is a highly stable oil that is high in unsaturated fat (94 percent), 58 percent of which is the monounsaturated fatty acid, oleic [16]. This oil has increased in popularity during the 1990's because of its health advantages over other oils. Canola oil, as compared to other oils, is relatively new on the market, but it is being used in salad dressings, margarines, shortenings, and fats produced for commercial frying operations.

Coconut oil is solid at room temperature because it contains a high proportion of saturated fatty acids, about 92 percent. Many of these are short-chain fatty acids, particularly lauric acid. Coconut oil has a sharp melting point, similar to the fat found in chocolate, and is therefore useful in confections and cookie fillings.

Palm-kernel oil is much like coconut oil. Palm oil, which is extracted from the fruit rather than the kernel of the palm tree, is different [6]. Although half of the fatty acids in palm oil are saturated, it contains few short-chain fatty acids. It is semisolid at room temperature and has a long shelf life. Palm oil has been used in margarine and shortening and thus has appeared on the labels of a number of processed foods. However, the use of palm and coconut oils has declined in recent years, since products that use these oils have higher saturated fat levels as compared to products made with other oils.

Sunflower oil has good flavor stability and is growing in popularity. The oil with the highest polyunsaturated fatty acid content is safflower oil, with 78 percent linoleic acid. Safflower oil, however, is more expensive than many other oils and lacks flavor stability [36]. Peanut oil, on the other hand, has excellent oxidative stability. It is preferred by some snack food manufacturers because of its flavor [16]. Corn oil has a naturally sweet taste and is used primarily in margarines. It is a relatively stable source of polyunsaturated fatty acids because of its low linolenic acid content [24].

Biotechnology or genetic engineering techniques are being combined with traditional plant breeding to enhance vegetable oil quality. Plant breeding has the potential of modifying fatty acid composition and of either increasing or decreasing saturated fatty acid content in the plant oils [37]. High-oleic acid oils, including modified soybean, safflower, and canola, are being developed through plant breeding. Advantages of these oils include increased stability to oxidation (without hydrogenation and the consequent increase in trans fatty acids) and nutritional effects of a low saturated fat in the diet [4, 33].

A solid shortening produced by the blending of a vegetable oil with a meat or milk fat from which cholesterol has been removed is being marketed as Appetize®. This product is recommended for a variety of frying and baking applications and would appear to have positive effects on blood lipids [26]. A number of other lipids are being developed by researchers. Some have been designed to have nutritional benefits, whereas others have increased functionality and oxidative stability [42].

DETERIORATION OF FAT AND ITS CONTROL

A special type of chemical spoilage that commonly occurs in fats and fatty foods is rancidity. It may develop on storage, particularly if the fats are highly unsaturated and the environmental conditions are appropriate for initiating the reaction. The chemical changes that result in rancidity are chiefly of two types: hydrolytic and oxidative.

Hydrolytic Rancidity

Hydrolysis involves breaking chemical bonds and, in the process, adding the elements of water—hydrogen and oxygen. When triglycerides are hydrolyzed, they yield free fatty acids and glycerol. This reaction may be catalyzed by the enzyme *lipase*. Release of free fatty acids does not produce undesirable odors and flavors in fats unless they are short-chain fatty acids, such as **butyric acid** and **caproic acid.** These fatty acids predominate in butter. They are volatile and largely responsible for the unpleasant odor and flavor of rancid butter. They may render butter inedible even when present in low concentrations. Long-chain free fatty acids, such as stearic, palmitic, and oleic acids, do not usually produce a disagreeable flavor unless other changes, such as oxidation, also occur.

Oxidative Rancidity

The characteristic unpleasant odor of fats in which oxidative rancidity has developed is difficult to describe but widely recognized. Oxidative rancidity may be caused by the action of an enzyme called *lipoxygenase*, which is present in some foods. However, rancidity most often results from a strictly chemical reaction that is self-perpetuating, called a *chain reaction*. Primarily it is the unsaturated fatty acid portions of triglycerides that are susceptible to oxidative changes. Highly hydrogenated fats and natural fats composed largely of saturated fatty acids are relatively resistant to this type of chemical change, but all natural fats contain some unsaturated fatty acids.

The chemical oxidation of fat is initiated when a hydrogen atom (H) is lost from a carbon which is located next to a double bond in the fatty acid chain. This loss leaves the carbon atom as a *free radical*, which is a highly reactive chemical group. This free radical reacts with a molecule of oxygen from the environment to produce a *peroxide free radical*, which is still quite reactive. To propogate the chain reaction, the peroxide free radical pulls a hydrogen atom from an adjacent fatty acid chain, thus leaving a free radical on the carbon atom of the adjacent fatty acid. This free radical reacts with oxygen and continues the chain reaction [23].

Hydroperoxides themselves do not appear to have unpleasant rancid odors and flavors, but these molecules readily break into pieces, producing smaller volatile substances that give the characteristic odors of rancid fat. Because the

hydrolysis a chemical reaction in which a linkage between subunits of a large molecule is broken; a molecule of water enters the reaction and becomes part of the end products

butyric acid a saturated fatty acid with four carbon atoms that is found in relatively large amounts in butter

caproic acid a saturated fatty acid with six carbon atoms; as a free fatty acid, it has an unpleasant odor

$$[-C-\underset{|}{\overset{H}{C}}-C=C-C-]\xrightarrow{-H}[-C-\underset{\cdot}{\overset{H}{C}}-C=C-C-]\xrightarrow{+O_2}[-C-\underset{|}{\overset{H}{C}}-C=C-C-]$$

  fat   fat free radical   peroxide free
                                                                   radical

$$[-C-\underset{|}{\overset{H}{C}}-C=C-C-]+[-C-\underset{|}{\overset{H}{C}}-C=C-C-]\longrightarrow[-C-\underset{|}{\overset{H}{C}}-C=C-C-]+[-C-\underset{\cdot}{\overset{H}{C}}-C=C-C-]$$

  peroxide free   another fat   hydroperoxide   fat free radical
  radical   to continue
                             chain reaction

reaction is a chain reaction, once a fat develops a slight rancid odor, the production of more pronounced rancidity occurs rapidly. This type of rancidity is responsible for most of the spoilage of fats and fatty foods. It may also be a problem in dry foods containing only small quantities of fat, such as prepared cereals. When rancidity develops in fatty foods, the fat-soluble vitamins A and E that are present may also be oxidized.

Flavor Reversion.   A special type of oxidative deterioration, *flavor reversion*, involves a change in edible fats characterized by the development, in the refined material, of an objectionable flavor prior to the onset of true rancidity. Reversion may develop during exposure of the fat to ultraviolet or visible light or heat. A small amount of oxygen seems to be necessary for the reaction, which is catalyzed by the presence of small amounts of metals such as iron and copper.

The kinds of off-flavors that develop during reversion vary with the particular fat and with the conditions that cause the change. Reverted soybean oil has been described as "painty," "beany," "haylike," "grassy," and, in the final stages, "fishy."

No fat is entirely free from the tendency to develop flavor reversion, but some oils, such as corn and cottonseed oils, are quite resistant to this type of deterioration. Soybean oil is highly susceptible to flavor reversion, which could cause problems in food processing because soybean oil is so widely used in the preparation of edible fats. Soybean oil is known to contain traces of iron and copper, which may act as **pro-oxidants.** The flavor of soybean oil is stabilized by the use of metal inactivators or sequestrants, which tie up the trace amounts of iron and copper that are present.

The chief precursors of the reversion flavor in oils are thought to be the triglycerides containing **linolenic acid,** although linoleic acid is probably also

pro-oxidant a substance that encourages the development of oxidative rancidity

linolenic acid a polyunsaturated fatty acid with 18 carbon atoms and three double bonds between carbon atoms; omega-3 fatty acid

involved to some degree [46]. The fats that are most susceptible to reversion contain linolenic acid in larger amounts than the relatively stable fats. Selective hydrogenation of soybean oil to decrease the amount of linolenic acid aids in preventing flavor reversion. Plant breeding and genetic engineering are developing oils that are lower in linolenic acid content [33].

Antioxidants and the Prevention of Rancidity. Fats can be protected to some degree against the rapid development of rancidity by controlling the conditions of storage. Storage at refrigerator temperature with the exclusion of light, moisture, and air aid in rancidity prevention. Because only certain rays of light catalyze the oxidation of fats, the use of colored glass containers that absorb the active rays protects fats against spoilage. Certain shades of green in bottles and wrappers and yellow transparent cellulose have been found to be effective in retarding rancidity in fats and fatty foods such as bacon. Vacuum packaging also helps to retard the development of rancidity by excluding oxygen. Products such as peanut butter and hydrogenated shortening are used from a package or container, so it is well to compact the material remaining in the container and smooth off the surfaces or repackage it in a smaller container to reduce the amount of air that comes in contact with the product.

Antioxidants have been used in the United States since 1947 to stabilize fats and control the development of rancidity [15]. Several compounds with antioxidant activity, including the nutrients vitamin C and beta carotene, are naturally present in certain foods. Vitamin E (tocopherols), present in seeds and in the oil extracted from seeds, is an effective antioxidant that protects edible vegetable oils [44].

Antioxidants generally appear to act as oxygen interceptors in the oxidative process that produces rancidity, providing a hydrogen atom to satisfy the peroxide free radical. Thus, the chain reaction that perpetuates the process is broken or terminated, until another hydrogen atom is lost from a fatty acid chain and the chain reaction begins again. Antioxidants, therefore, greatly increase the shelf life of fats and fatty food. Once the antioxidant itself is used up, having no more hydrogens to contribute, however, the oxidative process may continue.

The addition of antioxidants to fats and fatty foods to retard the development of rancidity has become an important commercial practice. For example, lard, used as an ingredient in many food products, has no natural antioxidants of its own and must be protected from the development of rancidity by the use of antioxidants. Four synthetic antioxidants approved as food additives by the FDA are butylated hydroxyanisole (BHA), butylated hydroxytoluene (BHT), tertiary butyl hydroquinone (TBHQ), and propyl gallate. These four substances have found widespread use in food processing [12, 43]. Some substances, such as citric acid, may be used with antioxidants in foods as *synergists*. A synergist increases the effectiveness of an antioxidant, but is not as effective an agent when used alone. Metals such as iron and copper that may be present in trace amounts in foods act as pro-oxidants in encouraging the development of oxidative rancidity. Some synergists may be effective because of their ability to bind or **chelate** the metals and prevent them from catalyzing the oxidation process. Chelating agents are sometimes called *sequestering agents*.

The protection of fats against spoilage is important not only for more or less purified fats, but also for many other foods containing fat, such as processed meats, whole-grain and dry-prepared cereal products, nuts, fat-rich biscuits and crackers, potato chips, and flour mixes.

chelate to attach or bind a substance and hold it tightly so it does not react as usual; for example, to bind iron and copper atoms and hold them so they cannot act as pro-oxidants

FRYING

The two methods of frying are panfrying, in which a shallow layer of fat is used (Figure 10-3), and deep-fat frying, in which the food is submerged in heated fat (Figure 10-4).

Panfrying

Panfrying is used to cook such foods as hamburgers, chicken, fish fillets, bacon, potatoes, eggplant, and eggs. It is difficult in panfrying to know the exact temperature of heating because of the shallow depth of the fat, which is usually less than 1/2 inch; however, smoking of the fat is a definite indication that decomposition is occurring and should never be permitted. Moderate temperatures are generally used. The frypan should be seasoned before its first use by pouring a small amount of shortening into the warm frypan and rubbing the pan surface with a cloth to produce a mirrorlike finish. Once the pan is seasoned, it is best to wipe it clean after each use but not wash it [20]. If washing with soapy water is necessary to properly clean the pan, then the pan will need to be reseasoned.

Panfrying is often done using butter, margarine, or shortening. However, butter has a lower smoke point and both butter and margarine contain water which can cause spattering. In foodservice operations, a specialty griddle shortening is generally used. For frying, the skillet should be merely coated with fat, not filled with an excessive amount.

Deep-fat Frying

The deep-fat frying process is of interest to several different groups, including suppliers of oils, ingredients, and equipment; processors of deep-fat fried foods and their quality control laboratories; and foodservice outlets. Deep-fat frying has become common in many foodservice establishments (Figure 10-4). People generally enjoy these foods, and having them prepared by restaurant employees eliminates some problems that are encountered when they prepare them in their own kitchens. These include handling hot frying fat with the dangers of spilling and burning, filtering the used fat, and storing the remaining fat when frying is done only infrequently. For foodservice operations, deep-fat frying is fast and economical in terms of energy and labor costs. Specialty frying fats and frying equipment have made possible the production of quality fried foods [36]. Nevertheless, foodservice frying requires higher stability in the frying fat than any other edible-oil application. The turnover of the fat is usually less than in the food-processing industry and the fat is often abused by the variety of products being fried. Low linolenic acid oils and high oleic acid oils give increased

Figure 10-3
Panfrying breaded veal cutlets produces tender, juicy cutlet with a golden brown and crisp coating. Stir-frying asparagus and mushrooms in a wok or sauté pan uses only a small amount of oil and results in a flavorful dish.

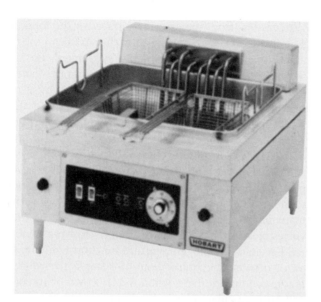

Figure 10-4
Deep-fat frying is common practice at many foodservice establishments. A small counter fryer holds 28 pounds of shortening. This large fryer can hold 50 pounds of shortening and produce 110 pounds, or about 440 servings of French fries per hour. (Courtesy of Hobart Corporation)

stability to heat and oxygen exposure when compared with a number of other frying fats [17]. The popularity of fried foods continues in spite of public concern about dietary fat and caloric intake.

In deep-fat frying, there is a direct transfer of heat from the hot fat to the cold food that continues until the food is cooked. Water present in the food to be fried plays some important roles in heat transfer and the frying process [4].

Water is lost from the exterior surfaces of the food as it is converted to steam. The steam carries off energy from the surface of the food and prevents charring or burning. While water is being evaporated, the temperature of the food is only about 212°F (100°C). Water then migrates from the central portion of the food outward to the edges to replace that lost by evaporation. Finally, the interior of the food is cooked. Sufficient heat must be transferred to gelatinize starch and coagulate proteins that may be present in the food.

When cold food is first placed in the fryer, the temperature of the frying fat decreases. A thermostatic control on the fryer then signals for the production of additional heat energy to bring the temperature back to the desired frying temperature. If an automatic fryer is not used, a thermometer should be employed to monitor the temperature and protect against overheating. A test for approximate temperatures that has some value, in case no thermometer is available, involves measuring the time required to brown a 1-inch cube of bread in the hot fat. Fats of a suitable temperature for thoroughly frying some raw foods, as well as for browning, require about 60 seconds to brown a cube of bread. Fats that are hot enough to fry cooked foods brown or to cook some raw, watery foods will brown a cube of bread in about 40 seconds. Table 10-2 provides a range of temperatures that can be used for deep-fat frying.

Changes in Heated Fats and Interaction with Food

When fats are heated to extremely high temperatures, certain chemical and physical changes occur. For example, overheated fats begin to give off smoke. As discussed, the smoke point of a fat is defined as the temperature at which smoke is continuously emitted from the surface of the fat, and this point is measured under standardized conditions as a specific temperature. Present in the smoke that comes from overheated fats is the substance *acrolein*. Acrolein results from the dehydration of glycerol. It is highly irritating to the eyes and throat.

$$\begin{array}{ccc}
CH_2OH & CH_2 & \\
| & || & \\
CHOH \xrightarrow{\text{heat}} & CH & + 2H_2O \\
| & | & \\
CH_2OH & C=O & \\
& | & \\
& H & \\
\\
\text{glycerol} & \text{acrolein} & \text{water}
\end{array}$$

The glycerol from which acrolein is produced comes from the hydrolysis of some of the triglyceride molecules of the fat to their component parts, free fatty acids and glycerol. The production of free fatty acids during frying contributes to a decrease in the smoke point. Frying large amounts of high-moisture foods tends to increase the rate of development of free fatty acids. Suspended matter, such as flour or batter particles, also lowers the smoke point. In addition, the greater the surface of the fat exposed to air, the more rapidly the smoke point is lowered.

Heated oils and their degradation products interact with the food being fried. Some materials are leached from the food into the frying fat and some of the fat itself is gradually broken down or degraded. Oxygen from the air may

Type of Product	Temperature of Fat	Approximate Time to Brown a 1-inch Cube of Bread in Hot Fat (sec)
Doughnuts		
Fish		
Fritters	350°–375°F (175°–190°C)	60
Oysters, scallops, and soft-shelled crabs		
Croquettes		
Eggplant	375°F (190°C)	40
Onions		
Cauliflower		
French-fried potatoes	385°–395°F (195°–200°C)	20

Table 10-2
Temperature Ranges for Deep-Fat Frying

react with the fat in the fryer at the oil-air interface, thus creating many different chemical compounds in the frying fat in addition to the basic triglyceride molecules that originally made up the fat. Some of the chemicals produced are surfactants—molecules that interact at the air-oil or oil-food interfaces and lower the surface or interfacial tension. A surfactant theory of frying suggests that the lowered **surface tension** allows oxygen to be drawn in, producing some oxidized compounds that aid in heat transfer. Also, the contact time between the hot oil and the aqueous food surfaces is increased and more heat is transferred to cook the food. If surfactant levels become too high, however, degradation of the fat is enhanced, **polymers** are formed, increased viscosity results from the gum formation, and foaming is excessive. Oil that foams should be replaced or inferior products will be prepared. The optimum level of surfactants in the frying fat results in a quality fried product that is golden brown in color, crisp with rigid surfaces, and has delicious odors, fully cooked centers, and optimal oil absorption [7].

As frying fat is used, darkening occurs. As the fat darkens, the foods fried in it darken more rapidly and may be uneven in color. Color is one of the indicators used commercially to determine when the oil should be replaced. The ingredients in the product being fried influence the color changes of the frying fat. Potatoes form little color in the frying fat, whereas chicken causes considerably more darkening. The composition of the breading mixture also affects darkening. The presence of egg yolk in a batter or dough causes greatly increased darkening of the fat with continued use.

It is important to control frying temperatures and to use proper procedures to avoid undesirable chemical changes in the fat. Scientific literature contains many studies concerning the safety of heated fats and oils [8]. Some of these studies involved fats that were excessively abused and therefore did not simulate ordinary conditions of frying. Fats can apparently be seriously damaged when heated to extreme temperatures over long periods, particularly when heated in the laboratory without frying. However, under reasonably well-controlled conditions of actual frying, adverse effects are generally not apparent [3], and the fried products become unacceptable from a sensory standpoint before the fat appears to be damaged excessively [8]. The fats in baked products appear to change very little under ordinary conditions of baking [41].

surface tension tension produced at the surface of a substance due to the attraction of the molecules of this substance for each other; they are more attracted to themselves than to the interfacing substance, such as oil at the surface where it contacts air

polymers very large molecules produced by linking small molecules together, sometimes forming a gummy material

Fat Turnover

Turnover indicates the amount of fat in the frying kettle that is replaced by fresh fat in a given period. Because fat is absorbed by the foods that are fried, the amount of fat in the kettle continuously decreases as frying proceeds, unless fresh fat is added periodically. In the processing of such foods as potato chips, which is done on a continuous basis, the frying fat may be turned over completely (100 percent) in only one day of frying; however, in foodservice operations, frying is usually intermittent and the rate of fat turnover may average only about 20 to 35 percent each day. When turnover is slow, it is necessary to periodically discard all of the fat in the deep fat fryer and start again with fresh fat. To avoid the excessive costs resulting from the disposal of large amounts of used frying fat, it is best to use the smallest amount of fat possible in relation to the amount of food to be fried [36]. However, if the fryer is overloaded with too much food in relation to the quantity of frying fat, the temperature drop at the beginning of frying is quite significant and a relatively long time is required to regain the proper temperature for frying. In this case, the food may become greasy and lack a characteristic crispy texture.

Fat Absorption

From the standpoint of palatability, ease or rapidity of digestion, and contribution to total daily fat intake, it is desirable to hold fat absorption by fried food to a minimum. Among the factors that affect the amount of fat absorbed are (1) the character and composition of the food, (2) the condition of the frying fat, including the level of surfactants present, (3) the amount of surface exposed to the fat, and (4) the length of time of heating. An optimum level of surfactants in the frying fat produces optimal fat absorption. With excessive amounts of surfactants, more oil is drawn into the food.

The temperature of the fat indirectly affects the amount of fat absorbed during frying, because foods cooked at a lower temperature must be cooked for a longer period to achieve the desired amount of brownness. In general, the longer the food remains in the fat, the greater the absorption. However, some foods, such as breaded chicken breasts, must be cooked at lower temperatures to permit the product to reach appropriate internal temperatures before the exterior is excessively brown. Fat absorption also is greater when a greater amount of surface area is exposed to the fat.

The proportions and types of ingredients in doughnuts and fritters and various manipulative procedures affect fat absorption. Doughnuts containing a high percentage of sugar and fat absorb more fat while frying than doughnuts containing lesser amounts of sugar and/or fat. Doughnuts containing more lecithin (a phospholipid) have been reported to absorb more fat than doughnuts with lesser amounts of lecithin [39]. The addition of egg to a fritter-type batter that contains no additional shortening significantly increases fat absorption. Egg yolk contains phospholipids.

Doughnuts made from soft wheat flours and from soft doughs absorb more fat than doughnuts made from strong flours and from stiff doughs. The development of gluten by the extensive manipulation of the dough decreases fat absorption as compared with doughs in which gluten has not been developed. Rough dough surfaces caused by cracks or undermanipulation, or by allowing the dough to stick to the board, increase the surface area and therefore increase fat absorption.

A pectin coating for french-fried potatoes and some breaded items such as fish and chicken reduces the amount of fat absorbed by these products. The total calorie content of the fried items is, therefore, reduced.

The type of fat does not appear to significantly affect the amount of fat absorbed during frying. Under identical conditions of time, temperature, and type of food being fried, various fats commonly used for frying appear to be absorbed in similar amounts.

Choosing the Frying Fat

Several factors may be considered in choosing a frying medium. First, it should be a fat that, during use, develops flavor that enhances the quality and acceptability of the fried product. It has been reported, for example, that the volatile materials produced by hydrogenated soybean oils were less favorably judged on the basis of flavor and odor than those from hydrogenated corn, cottonseed, or peanut oil [32]. The flavor should also be stable enough that it remains appetizing throughout the shelf life of the product. Antioxidants having effects that carry through after heating may be added to frying fats to lengthen the shelf life of the fried product. Minute amounts of methyl silicone are often added to fats during processing to help retard foaming and deterioration during frying.

A certain amount of hydrogenation of the frying oil is needed to provide good flavor stability and to increase the frying life of the fat before too much degradation occurs. Partially hydrogenated fluid shortening can be poured and is therefore easier to handle in foodservice operations than solid shortening. Shortenings that are specially formulated for frying are available for foodservice use. Oils with increased stability toward heating are being developed by plant breeding and genetic engineering. They may be characterized as high oleic and low linolenic acid oils.

Many fast-food businesses have switched from using a mixture of animal **tallow** and vegetable fat for frying to all-vegetable shortenings [25]. Tallow is an ingredient used in some frying oils because of the desirable flavor it provides to foods such as french fries. Fewer restaurants are using oils with tallow because of negative public opinion by customers who are vegetarian or expect their foods to be prepared in more healthful monounsaturated or polyunsaturated oils. In 2002, one fast food restaurant announced another change in their frying oil, this time to reduce the trans fatty acids. This new frying oil formulation, developed with Cargill, Inc., reduces trans fatty acids by about 48 percent, saturated fat content by 16 percent, while increasing polyunsaturated fats by 167 percent as compared to the previous frying oil.

A canola-based frying fat is sometimes used in foodservice operations because of its superior heat stability [9]. Canola oil contains a relatively low proportion of saturated fatty acids and a high percentage of monounsaturates, particularly oleic acid, which appeals to some consumers from a nutritional standpoint.

The resistance of a fat to smoking at high temperatures is also important in choosing a frying medium. The smoke point of a fat is partly a result of its natural composition and partly a result of the processing it has received. Most oils on the consumer market are highly refined and deodorized, and they have relatively high smoke points, usually above 442°F (228°C). They can be used for frying in the home kitchen but do not have the stability needed for most foodservice operations.

tallow is fat extracted from sheep or cattle. Tallow is highly saturated and is desirable for some purposes because of its meaty flavor.

Hydrogenated shortenings without added emulsifiers may smoke within the range 430° to 450°F (220° to 232°C); however, most shortenings sold on the retail market are for general-purpose use and contain added mono- and diglycerides as emulsifiers. This composition makes them particularly suitable for making shortened cakes but less desirable for frying, because the addition of these emulsifiers lowers the smoke point. In this case, the first smoke given off is not from the breakdown of the fat itself but from the emulsifier. It is an interesting fact that on continued heating, as the emulsifier is decomposed, the smoke point may rise somewhat.

Other desirable factors to look for in choosing a fat are light color, resistance to foaming and gum formation, uniformity in quality, stability for long-term use, and ease of use, considering both form and packaging.

Care of Frying Fat

To maintain high quality in fried foods, it is important to regularly monitor the frying fat. A fat that is fabricated for frying may be used for a considerable period if the turnover with fresh fat is fairly high and if the fat is cared for properly. The maintenance of proper frying temperatures and avoidance of overheating are important considerations in caring for fat. The thermostats on fryers should be checked regularly.

In the beginning, efficient frying equipment should be selected. In foodservice operations, the frying fat should be filtered at least daily. It is necessary to remove charred batter and breading or other materials that have accumulated in the frying fat, as these can ruin the appearance of the fried product, contribute bitter flavor, lower the smoke point, and darken the fat [32]. The tiny crumbs that flake off products during frying are sometimes called *fines* and must be removed regularly to preserve the integrity of the frying fat. Various filtration systems are available, including screens, cartridges, and paper filters with and without filter aids. Some filters are built into the frying equipment; portable filters are also available. When using pressure fryers, which were developed primarily for the frying of poultry, filtering of fat should be done more frequently. Frying under pressure when steam is retained places an extra burden on the frying shortening [36]. Frying equipment and hoods over the equipment must be kept clean and in proper working order.

After fat has been used for home frying, all foreign matter should be strained from the fat. The fat should then be stored in a cold place out of contact with light and air.

polar materials chemical molecules that have electric charges (positive or negative) and tend to be soluble in water

Commercial kits are available for measuring **polar materials** in the frying fat [32]. These materials reflect the total level of degradation products that have resulted from the frying process. This is considered by many to be a reasonable indicator of the overall quality of the fat and can be useful in any frying operation.

BUYING FATS

It is important in purchasing fats to consider their specific uses in food preparation and to select fats in accordance with needs and budget. Fats are often tailored for specific uses in foodservice operations, such as deep-fat frying, panfrying or griddling, and cake making. Separate fats are generally purchased for each of the specific needs.

Most consumers probably do not need to keep more than three or four different household fats on hand. Butter, because of its flavor, is sometimes preferred for table use, as well as for use in some baked products and for the seasoning of certain foods. Margarine serves a similar purpose, usually at a somewhat lower cost, although the different brands of margarine vary widely in price. A blend of butter and margarine is also available. Margarines, particularly those types that are high in polyunsaturated fatty acids, may be chosen over butter for health reasons. However, margarines may contain varying levels of trans fatty acids, which may be a concern for health reasons. Some flavorful drippings, such as bacon fat, are also used for flavoring.

Most households require some shortening, but one general-purpose shortening can be used satisfactorily for both shortening and frying purposes. However, for health reasons, monounsaturated or polyunsaturated oils may be preferable when frying to reduce the level of trans fatty acids consumed. Lard is preferred by some for use in pastry or biscuits; usually, modified methods of mixing are required to produce desirable results in shortened cakes. Lard is commonly added to refried beans in the preparation of Mexican food, primarily because of its flavor, and may be preferred for the making of flour tortillas. To satisfy those customers seeking a traditional flavor as well as those who want to avoid lard, prepared refried beans may be purchased with or without lard. The use of fats for shortening is considered in Chapter 15.

COOKING LOW FAT

Consumers have been bombarded with messages concerning the detrimental health effects of high-fat diets and are encouraged to lower their fat intakes. Why do we like fat? It tastes good. Diets rich in fat tend to be more flavorful and heighten the pleasures of eating.

We can, however, lower the fat to some degree and still have delicious food. Acceptable muffins, yellow cake, and drop cookies can be prepared using less fat than typically is used [20]. Using questionnaires of restaurant patrons to evaluate acceptability of lower-fat menu items, it was found that customer satisfaction was actually higher for the lower-fat items than for the regular menu items [18]. This finding indicates that many consumers are interested in the availability of nutritious menu items and will choose them. If they do not taste good, however, they will not choose them repeatedly.

Many ideas for cooking low in fat have been suggested. These include choosing lean cuts of meat that are trimmed well of fat, using nonstick pots and pans that require less fat for cooking, using roasting or broiling methods instead of sautéing and frying, stir-frying with a small amount of vegetable oil cooking spray, and seasoning with a variety of herbs [34]. Favorite recipes can be modified to be lower in fat, for example, making lasagna with less meat or with vegetables and using less or low-fat cheese. Egg whites can be substituted for whole egg in some baked recipes and cocoa for chocolate, thus reducing the fat. Several cookbooks are available with emphasis on low-fat cooking. By adjusting ingredients and cooking methods we can eat for health while maintaining taste and enjoyment.

FAT REPLACERS

Food processors are using a wide variety of ingredients to replace or partially replace fat in food products. The American Dietetic Association has issued a position paper on fat replacers [38]. The organization states that the fat content of foods may be safely reduced or replaced using approved processing methods and constituents. The statement emphasizes, however, that individuals who choose such foods should do so within the context of a diet consistent with the Dietary Guidelines for Americans.

Unless the fat replacer is generally regarded as safe (GRAS), it must be approved by the Food and Drug Administration (FDA) as a food additive. The last fat replacer additive to be approved was olestra, in 1996. This approval process is usually long and tedious. For example, the manufacturers of olestra petitioned the FDA in 1987 for use of this substance as a calorie-free replacement for fats in shortenings and oils. This petition contained more than 150,000 pages and included results of more than 150 safety studies, several chronic feeding studies, and clinical studies performed by a noted medical school. In 1990, the petition was amended to limit the use of olestra to 100 percent replacement for conventional fats in the preparation of savory snacks, such as potato chips. Finally on January 24, 1996, after 9 years, the FDA announced the approval of olestra for savory snacks [10].

Fat plays several roles in various food products. Although many of its functions are related to texture, it is very difficult, if not impossible, to find a fat substitute that will perform well in all food products [48]. Several different fat replacers are presently in use and are sometimes employed in combinations. Generally, fat replacers can be classified into two groups—fat substitutes and fat mimetics or imitators. Fat substitutes are macromolecules that chemically and physically resemble triglycerides and can replace fat in foods. They are often referred to as fat-based fat replacers. Fat substitutes are usually stable at cooking and frying temperatures [2].

Fat mimetics are substances that imitate sensory properties of triglycerides but cannot replace fat on a weight-to-weight basis. These products are often called protein-based or carbohydrate-based fat replacers. Many are modified common ingredients, such as starch and cellulose, and act to bind a substantial amount of water [2].

Fat-based Replacements

ester a chemical combination of an alcohol (−OH) with an organic acid (−COOH)

Chemically, olestra consists of six to eight long-chain fatty acids combined as **esters** with sucrose to produce compounds called *sucrose fatty acid polyesters*. Olestra, or Olean®, is neither digested nor absorbed from the human digestive tract, and is therefore noncaloric; yet olestra has characteristics similar to triglycerides when used in food preparation. It is heat stable and can be used in frying. Because olestra is not absorbed from the intestinal tract, it has the potential to cause gastrointestinal symptoms, such as cramping. Therefore, the FDA requires a label on foods containing olestra that states: "This product contains olestra. Olestra may cause abdominal cramping and loose stools. Olestra inhibits the absorption of some vitamins and other nutrients. Vitamins A, D, E, and K have been added."

Several structured triglycerides have been developed as fat substitutes that have fewer kilocalories per gram than the usual triglycerides. One of these is salatrim (Benefat). Salatrim consists of a family of structured triglycerides containing at least one short-chain fatty acid (two, three, or four carbon atoms long) and at least one long-chain fatty acid (predominantly stearic acid with eighteen carbon atoms) esterified with the glycerol molecule, and yields 5 kilocalories per gram when metabolized in the body. Salatrim is used in confectionery products, baked goods, and some dairy foods [2].

The use of emulsifier systems that will "stretch" the function of the fat makes possible some fat reduction in many fat-containing products. For example, the addition of mono- and diglycerides as emulsifiers to cake shortenings allows a reduction in the fat content without sacrifice to quality. Emulsifier systems can be designed to function well in many low-fat products, but other ingredients must also be used in conjunction with the emulsifier system to help replace the fat that is lost. Included in the emulsifier group are fatty acid esters of sucrose that are similar to olestra but contain only one, two, or three fatty acid esters instead of the six to eight esterified in olestra. Lecithin is another emulsifier that can help in fat replacement in many food products.

Carbohydrate-based Replacements

Many of the reduced-fat products introduced into the market in recent years have contained carbohydrate-based fat replacers. These include derivatives of cellulose, maltodextrins, gums, modified starches, pectin, and polydextrose. Ingredient developers have produced several products marketed under specific brand names, using, in many cases, a combination of ingredients [16].

Carbohydrates such as starches, cellulose, and gums have a long history of use in the food industry. They often function as thickeners and stabilizers. When used to replace fat, they add form and structure, hold water as hydrophilic agents, and act as emulsifiers when a small amount of fat is used. They may produce a mouthfeel that is similar to that created by fat, but they do not taste exactly like fat. Stickiness and other textural problems may result if large amounts are used. A combination of gums, cellulose, and/or modified starches can be used to produce a fat replacement system.

Maltodextrins are nonsweet carbohydrates made from partially hydrolyzed starch. They can partly or totally replace fat in a variety of products, including margarine, frozen desserts, and salad dressings. They are classified as GRAS by the FDA and have the same caloric value as starch [16].

Polydextrose is a "designed" ingredient, prepared from a mixture of dextrose (glucose), **sorbitol,** and citric acid. It has multiple functions, which include acting as a bulking agent, a texturizer, and a **humectant,** and it may be used to replace sugar or fat. Polydextrose contains only 1 kilocalorie per gram, in comparison with 4 kilocalories provided by sugars and starch. It is approved by the FDA for use in such products as frozen dairy desserts, baked goods, confections, puddings, and salad dressings [22].

sorbitol a sugar alcohol similar to glucose in chemical structure

humectant a substance that can absorb moisture readily

Oatrim is produced by partial enzymatic hydrolysis of the starch-containing portion of the bran obtained from whole oat and/or corn flour. It contains 5 percent beta-glucan, a soluble plant fiber. A research group of the USDA developed Oatrim® and is also developing Z-trim, an indigestible, insoluble fiber for blending with Oatrim [2].

Protein-based Replacements

Several fat replacers come from protein sources, including egg, milk, whey, soy, gelatin, and wheat gluten. Some are microparticulated to form microscopic, coagulated round, deformable particles that give a mouthfeel and texture similar to fat. Others are treated in ways to modify their functional properties, such as water-holding capacity and emulsifying characteristics. These substances are generally not heat stable but are used in dairy products, salad dressings, frozen desserts, and margarines [2].

One microparticulated-protein fat replacer is Simplesse®, which has received approval by the FDA as a GRAS substance. It is produced by reshaping, into tiny round particles, proteins from milk and egg. These particles are so small that they are perceived as fluid. Microparticulated protein has a caloric value of 4 kcal/gram on a dry basis, compared with 9 kcal/gram for the fat it replaces. A hydrated gel form provides 1 kcal per gram. It cannot be used for frying but can be used in frozen desserts, yogurt, cheese spreads, cream cheese, and sour cream. It should also be suitable for use in baked products [2].

EMULSIONS

The term *emulsion* is applied to a system consisting of one liquid dispersed in another liquid with which it is **immiscible.** A third substance, an emulsifying agent or emulsifier, is necessary to stabilize the system and keep one liquid dispersed in the other on a permanent basis (see Figure 10-5).

immiscible describing substances that cannot be mixed or blended

Emulsions in Foods

Emulsions are found naturally in many foods, such as milk, cream, and egg yolk. In all such foods the fat is divided into small particles or globules and dispersed throughout the watery portion of the food. The **homogenization of whole milk** further divides the naturally emulsified fat into particles that are so fine they tend to remain in suspension and do not rise to the surface on standing, as does the fat in nonhomogenized milk.

homogenization of whole milk a process in which whole milk is forced, under pressure, through very small openings, dividing the fat globules into very tiny particles

Many food products are emulsions that have been formed during processing or preparation. The manufacture of emulsions is a highly energetic and dynamic process. Work is necessary to divide the fat into tiny globules or droplets. These newly formed globules must be rapidly protected against coalescence by the **adsorption** of an emulsifier at their surface. Shaking, beating, stirring, whipping, and high-pressure homogenization are some methods used to form an emulsion of one immiscible liquid dispersed in another.

adsorption the collection of a substance on the surface of a particle or globule without being taken in and incorporated into the globule

From food preparation, examples of emulsions are mayonnaise and other salad dressings, sauces, gravies, puddings, cream soups, shortened cake batters, and other flour mixtures in which the fat is dispersed. Other emulsions are produced in the commercial processing of foods such as peanut butter, margarine, sausages, and frankfurters. The dispersing medium may be water, milk, dilute vinegar, lemon or other fruit juice, or some similar liquid. The dispersed substance may be any of the commonly used food fats and oils. Some emulsions, such as margarine, have fat as the dispersing medium and water as the dispersed substance. Even though the fat is not always a liquid at ordinary temperatures of holding, the food system is still called an emulsion.

A variety of substances act as emulsifying agents and stabilizers in manufactured food systems, including the isolated milk protein casein, whey proteins

Figure 10-5
An emulsion consists of one substance dispersed in another substance with which it is immiscible. An emulsifying agent surrounds each dispersed particle. This diagram represents an oil-in-water emulsion; the oil droplets, surrounded by an emulsifying agent, are dispersed in water.

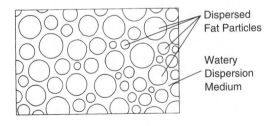

Dispersed
Fat Particles

Watery
Dispersion
Medium

and concentrated whey products, isolated soy proteins, oilseed protein concentrates, gelatin, lecithin, cellulose derivatives, fine dry powders such as ground spices, various vegetable gums, and starch pastes. Several emulsifiers are present in some batters. For example, shortened cake batter may contain egg lipoproteins, casein from milk, gluten and starch from flour, and mono- and diglycerides that have been added to the shortening.

Temporary Emulsions

If oil and water alone are shaken together, an emulsion is formed, but on standing, the oil particles reunite and separate from the water. Emulsions of this kind are called *temporary emulsions*. They must be used immediately or, if made in quantity and stored, they must be reshaken or beaten before each use. Simple French and Italian dressings are examples of this type of emulsion.

Permanent Emulsions

Permanent emulsions, which can be held or stored without separation of the two immiscible liquids, require an emulsifying agent or emulsifier to form a protecting or stabilizing film around the dispersed droplets and prevent them from reuniting. The term *stabilizer* is also used to describe the emulsifier or the substance that assists the emulsifier in some food products. An example of a permanent emulsion is mayonnaise. Actually, any food containing fat that is distributed throughout and does not appear on the surface as a separate layer is a permanent emulsion.

The two general types of emulsions are an oil-in-water emulsion and a water-in-oil emulsion. Oil-in-water emulsions are more common in foods, but butter and margarine are examples of water-in-oil emulsions. The type of emulsion formed depends to a considerable extent on the nature of the emulsifier.

How does an emulsifier act to form an emulsion? Emulsifiers have a special type of chemical nature: They are **amphiphilic** molecules. Part of the emulsifier molecule is attracted to or soluble in water (hydrophilic), whereas another part of the same molecule is soluble in fat (lipophilic). Thus, the emulsifier molecule may be oriented at the interface of the two immiscible liquids with its hydrophilic group in the watery phase and its lipophilic group in the fat or oil phase. One of these amphiphilic groups is a little stronger than the other and causes one phase to form droplets that are dispersed in the other continuous phase, with the emulsifier between them as it surrounds droplets of the dispersed phase. Figure 10-6 suggests how an emulsifier might orient itself at an oil-water interface to form an emulsion.

amphiphilic liking or being attracted to both water and fat

If the emulsifier is more attracted to the water, or more water soluble, it promotes the dispersion of oil in water. If the emulsifier is more attracted to the oil, or more oil soluble, it tends to produce a water-in-oil emulsion. A photomicrograph of the fat-in-water emulsion of milk, both before and after homogenization, is shown in Figure 23-3 (Chapter 23). Breaking of emulsions or separation of the two phases may occur under certain conditions. In some cases, the emulsion can re-form.

SALAD DRESSINGS

Classification

Definitions and standards of identity for mayonnaise, French dressing, and salad dressing have been published by the FDA. If products are labeled and sold under these names they must meet the standards of identity unless the product

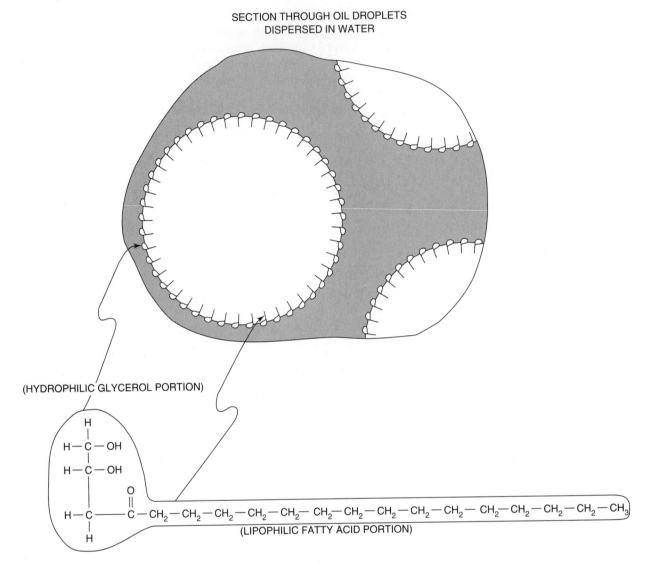

Figure 10-6
An emulsifier stabilizes an emulsion by virtue of its chemical structure. In a simplified presentation, this structure includes one part that is attracted to water and another part that is attracted to fat. The attraction of one of the groups is somewhat stronger than the other. For example, a monoglyceride molecule is shown with the fatty acid portion being attracted to the oil and the glycerol portion attracted to the water, forming a filmlike layer around the oil droplets and keeping them dispersed in the continuous watery phase.

is labeled with a nutrient claim such as "reduced fat." These modified products must not be nutritionally inferior and must function like the standard product. Thus, although the standard of identify for mayonnaise states that it must contain not less than 65 percent by weight of edible vegetable oil and an egg yolk–containing ingredient, reduced fat products are available such as "light" mayonnaise. French dressing must contain not less than 35 percent by weight of edible vegetable oil. Salad dressing must contain not less than 30 percent by weight of edible vegetable oil and also may contain a cooked starchy paste and an egg yolk–containing ingredient. All of these dressings may be labeled with a nutrient claim and contain less fat than specified by the standard of identity.

Figure 10-7
A basic vinaigrette dressing adds flavor to this tomato, greens, and asparagus salad with fresh mozzarella cheese.

All three dressings contain an acidifying ingredient. Many variations of these three basic dressings are created by using different, optional ingredients. Thus, a wide variety of dressings are available commercially, for example, Thousand Island, blue cheese, bacon and tomato, creamy cucumber, Italian, ranch, and taco dressings. Citrus flavors in dressings have gained popularity in recent years [44]. Exciting new flavors in salad dressings may encourage healthful eating, bringing into the daily diet more vegetables, salads, and nutritious sandwich fillings (Figure 10-7).

A mixture of seasonings and emulsifiers or stabilizers are included in dry salad dressing mixes. These are usually added to sour cream or to milk and mayonnaise to make a creamy dressing or to vinegar and oil to make a French-type dressing.

Dressings for salads made in home kitchens are not, of course, governed by standards of identity. Many of these dressings are simple combinations of ingredients and are difficult to classify. In fruit dressings, fruit juices replace vinegar and

Healthy Eating

Salad Dressings—A way to more flavor and nutrition

Have you noticed the tremendous variety of choices now offered for salad dressings, both on the grocer's shelf and on the restaurant menu? How do you react to names such as Parmesan Basil Italian, Bacon Ranch, Honey French, Mango, Roasted Garlic Ranch, Sweet 'n Spicy French, Orange Vinaigrette, or Ruby Red Ginger [44]? Now imagine these dressings poured over a large bowl of cold, fresh, salad greens, tomatoes, cucumbers, broccoli flowerets, celery, carrots, onions—you finish the list. Or on a plate of fresh fruits sprinkled with nuts. Irresistible?

Salad dressings were made for salads, of course. But their utility does not stop there. They are being promoted for a variety of other uses, as well—for marinades on meat, poultry, or seafood, toppings for vegetables, including baked potatoes, as a base for dips, and to enhance sandwich fillings. Pszczola [44] reminisces about eating hero sandwiches topped with salad dressing—like "eating a giant salad between two slices of bread." Salad dressings may also play an important role in the development of more enticing veggie burgers. In addition, they may be carriers of specially designed fats and oils that are heart-healthy. Don't forget the important role of salad dressings in the diet as they combine flavorfully with a whole host of other nutritious foods!

other liquids. Sour cream, sometimes with added ingredients such as crumbled cheese, can be added to vegetable or fruit salads. Mixtures of vinegar or lemon juice and seasonings, with or without small amounts of fat-containing ingredients, are sometimes used as low- or reduced-calorie dressings. Dry salad seasoning mixes can also be prepared in home kitchens. Cost and flavor comparisons might well be made between commercial dressings and those prepared from scratch.

Salad Dressing

Salad dressing is the emulsified semisolid food prepared from edible vegetable oil, an acidifying ingredient, egg yolk or whole egg, and a cooked or partly cooked starchy paste prepared with a food starch or flour. Water may be added in the preparation of the starchy paste. Optional seasonings and emulsifying agents may also be used. Salad dressing must contain not less than 30 percent by weight of edible vegetable oil and not less than 4 percent by weight of liquid egg yolks or their equivalent unless a legally defined nutrient claim has been made. All of this is specified in the standard of identity for salad dressing.

Many different dressings for salads can be made in both home and foodservice operations. Some of these are cooked dressings and may be of the custard type, in which all thickening is accomplished with egg yolk or whole egg. More frequently, a starchy agent is used to aid in thickening because there is less tendency for curdling to occur when cream or milk is used as the liquid. Some cooked dressings made with milk or cream are of a consistency suitable for immediate use, but the dressing may be made thicker than desirable and highly seasoned to permit dilution without impairment of flavor.

French Dressing.   According to its standard of identity, French dressing is the separable liquid food or the emulsified viscous fluid food prepared from edible vegetable oil (oil content not less than 35 percent by weight), specified acidifying agents, and optional seasonings. Reduced fat or calorie dressings may still be called French dressing with the appropriate nutrient claim. If it is emulsified, certain gums, pectin, or other emulsifiers, including egg or egg yolk, may be used to the extent of 0.75 percent by weight of the finished dressing. Large amounts of paprika and other powdered seasonings also help to keep the oil and acid emulsified. In unemulsified French dressing, a temporary emulsion is formed as the dressing is shaken or beaten. Oil and acid ingredients separate soon after mixing, but can be shaken or mixed each time the dressing is used.

The usual proportions for French dressing are 3/4 cup salad oil for each 1/3 cup vinegar or lemon juice. Various seasonings can be used.

Reduced-fat Dressings.   Reduced-fat salad dressings and mayonnaise are sold on the retail market and are prominently labeled as such. The caloric content of reduced-calorie dressings depends on how much oil is used. Those that contain essentially no fat in the finished dressing contain 6 to 14 kilocalories per tablespoon. Others, with up to 3 grams of fat per tablespoon of finished dressing, provide 30 to 40 kilocalories per tablespoon. A comparable full-fat salad dressing contains 60 to 80 kilocalories per tablespoon.

A mixture of emulsifying agents and stabilizers, including xanthan gum, alginate, cellulose gum, locust bean gum, and modified starch, is used to produce an emulsion and to substitute for the fat that is being eliminated. These stabilizers are hydrophilic and hold relatively large amounts of water, giving body or thickness to the product.

The 1990 Nutrition Education and Labeling Act requires that a product labeled as fat free have less than 0.5 gram of fat per serving and no added fat. A product labeled as low fat must contain less than 3 grams of fat per serving. A product labeled as light must contain 33 percent fewer calories or 50 percent of the fat in a reference food. If 50 percent or more of the calories in the product come from fat, the reduction must be 50 percent of the fat.

No-oil low-calorie dry dressing mixes are also available. The dry mix is added to water and vinegar, producing a product with about 6 kilocalories per tablespoon. Some reduced-calorie dry mixes require the addition of milk and mayonnaise. These produce creamy dressings with about 35 kilocalories per tablespoon. The dry mixes contain stabilizers and emulsifiers, plus various herbs and other flavoring materials.

Mayonnaise

According to its standard of identity, mayonnaise or mayonnaise dressing is the emulsified semisolid food prepared from edible vegetable oil, vinegar and/or lemon juice or citric acid, egg yolk or whole egg, and one or more optional ingredients, such as salt, mustard, paprika, a sweetening agent, and monosodium glutamate. If there is no qualified health claim, then the edible oil content of mayonnaise must be not less than 65 percent by weight and is emulsified or finely divided in the vinegar or lemon juice. In mayonnaise, oil is dispersed in vinegar or lemon juice. Certain components of egg or egg yolk (apparently lipoproteins) act as the emulsifying agent, coating the dispersed particles of oil to keep them dispersed on a permanent basis.

Mayonnaise can be made in the home kitchen (Figure 10-8). The factors that affect the formation of mayonnaise, its stability, and the ease of preparation are similar wherever the product is made. However, recipes with raw egg yolks should be modified through the use of a pasterized egg yolk to reduce the use of food borne illness. For food safety reasons, in addition to the time involved in the preparation of mayonaise, few make this product from scratch.

Factors Affecting Mayonnaise Preparation. Cold oil is more difficult to break up into small globules than warm, less viscous oil. Thus, the start of emulsification is delayed by chilling, but after the emulsion is formed, chilling thickens and stabilizes the product.

Figure 10-8
Mayonnaise may be made in the home. The use of pasteurized eggs is recommended. 1) whip egg yolks until frothy, 2) drizzle the oil slowly into the yolks while mixing to allow the emulsion to form, 3) the finished mayonnaise

Egg yolk is the chief emulsifying ingredient in mayonnaise. Freezing egg yolks, particularly without an additive such as salt or sugar, changes their physical properties so that on thawing they are highly viscous. A larger quantity of frozen yolk than of fresh yolk is required for making mayonnaise. Salt, mustard, paprika, and pepper are used mainly for flavor, but both the salt and the powdery seasoning ingredients help to stabilize the emulsion as well.

Mayonnaise usually contains about 3/4 to 1 cup of oil per egg yolk and 2 tablespoons of acid ingredient. Stable mayonnaise can be mixed by various methods:

1. All of the acid and seasonings can be added to the egg yolk before any additions of oil.
2. Acid can be added at various intervals during the mixing.
3. Acid can be added alternately with the oil.
4. Acid can be added after a large percentage of the oil is added to the egg yolk.

The first additions of oil must be small to allow a stable emulsion to form. After the first two or three additions of oil, the volume that is added at one time may be increased to a variable extent, depending on the temperature of the ingredients, the rate of beating, and other factors, but in any case it should be less than the volume of emulsion that is already formed.

Breaking and Re-forming an Emulsion. If oil particles coalesce, the emulsion breaks and the oil separates from the watery portion of the dressing. When this occurs while the emulsion is forming, the cause is incomplete preliminary emulsification, too rapid an addition of oil, too high a ratio of oil to emulsifier (or another wrong proportion), or an inefficient method of agitation.

Prepared emulsified mayonnaise may separate during storage. Freezing may damage or rupture the film of emulsifying agents and allow the dispersed oil to coalesce, resulting in a broken emulsion. Mayonnaise stored at too high a temperature may separate because of differences in the rate of expansion of warm water and oil. Mayonnaise stored in an open container may lose sufficient moisture from the surface by evaporation to damage the emulsion. Excessive jarring or agitation, particularly during shipping and handling, can cause separation, but this occurrence is uncommon.

A broken mayonnaise emulsion may be re-formed by starting with a new egg yolk, or with a tablespoon of water or vinegar, and adding the separated mayonnaise to it gradually. Thorough beating after each addition of separated mayonnaise is important. If separation occurs in the preparation of mayonnaise before all the oil is added, the remainder of the original oil may be added only after reemulsification has been achieved as described.

Variations. Additions can be made to mayonnaise to vary the flavor and consistency. Chopped foods, such as vegetables, olives, pickles, hard-cooked eggs, and nuts, may be added with discretion. Chili sauce, sour cream, and whipped cream can also enhance flavor and consistency for certain uses.

CHAPTER SUMMARY

- Fat is present in many foods and plays a variety of roles in food preparation and nutrition. Fat present naturally is often referred to as invisible fat, whereas fats that are added to foods are called visible fats.

- A reduction in dietary fat intake to 30 percent of kilocalories has been recommended. The food industry has responded by producing lower fat products. According to the 1994–1996 nationwide food consumption survey, fat accounts for 33 percent of the calories consumed by Americans. The types of fat have changed as well. Both monounsaturated and polyunsaturated fat consumption has increased, with a slight drop in saturated fat consumption.

- Fats do provide essential fatty acids and carry the fat-soluble vitamins and therefore are an important part of the diet.

- Fats are insoluble in water, are solid or liquid, may be plastic, and may have distinctive flavors. Oils that are solid at room temperature are called fats, whereas those that have lower melting points are liquid at room temperature and are called oils. Highly saturated fats are generally solid at room temperature. The melting point is influenced by a variety of other factors, including the degree of saturation and whether the fatty acids are in the cis or trans form. Longer-chain fatty acids also melt at a higher temperature. Fats demonstrate plasticity because of a unique combination of liquid and solid crystals that allows the fat to be molded or pressed into various shapes.

- Hydrogenation is a process whereby some of the double bonds between the carbon atoms of the fatty acid portion of the triglyceride molecule are broken and hydrogen is added. Oils such as soybean oil become solid shortenings due to hydrogenation.

- Approximately 90 percent of the trans fatty acids in the American diet are found in partially hydrogenated oil. Research has shown a positive, linear link between trans fatty acid intake and elevation of plasma cholesterol. Thus, manufacturers are seeking to develop new fats with lower levels of trans fatty acids and the FDA has proposed the nutrient label includes information about trans fatty acid content of foods.

- Winterized oils have been processed to remove the triglyceride molecules that crystallize or become cloudy under refrigeration. These oils are commonly called salad oils.

- Butter is the fat of cream that is separated from the other milk constituents by agitation or churning. Butter is a water-in-oil emulsion. USDA has set grade standards for butter that take into consideration both the quality and keeping ability of the butter.

- Soybean and cottonseed oils, refined and partially hydrogenation to the desired consistency, are extensively used to produce margarines. The standard of identity for margarine established by the FDA states the product must contain not less than 80 percent fat. However, there are a variety of types of margarine available in the marketplace that may be called margarine with appropriate labeling.

- Lard is one of the oldest culinary fats. Although lard is not used as widely today, it is still preferred by some for pie crusts and biscuits due to its shortening ability and for the flavor it provides in Mexican cuisine.

- A variety of refined oils are used by Americans. These include in part: soybean, cotton seed, olive, sesame, sunflower, safflower, canola, corn, and peanut oils.

- Fat may deteriorate in flavor due to rancidity. The chemical changes that result in rancidity are chiefly of two types: hydrolytic and oxidative. Hydrolysis involves breaking chemical bonds and releasing free fatty acids from the glycerol molecule. Oxidated rancidity may be caused by the action of an enzyme called lipoxygenase but most often results from a strictly chemical reaction that is self-perpetuating, called a chain reaction. A special type of oxidative deterioration, flavor reversion, involves a change in edible fats charactized by the development of an objectional flavor prior to the onset of true rancidity. Fats can be protected against rancidity to some degree by controlling the storage conditions and by using antioxidants.

- Pan frying and deep fat frying are two methods of cooking that utilize fat as the cooking medium. Pan frying uses a shallow depth of fat (usually 1/2 inch), whereas foods are submerged in hot fat when deep fat frying. Fats selected for deep fat frying must be highly stable, have a high smoke point, and have a neutral or desirable flavor. Fats that become excessively dark, foam, or smoke at normal temperatures for deep fat frying should be discarded. Fats that are well maintained by routine straining and filtering will last longer. Several factors influence the amount of fat absorbed by foods when cooked by deep fat frying.

- The amount of fat can be reduced when cooking through the careful selection of low fat foods, cooking methods, and recipes. Favorite recipes can be modified to reduce the amount of fat.

- Food processors are using a variety of ingredients to replace or partially replace fat in food products. Fat replacers must be generally recognized as safe (GRAS) or must be approved by the FDA as food additives. Fat replacements may be fat-based, carbohydrate-based, or protein-based.

- Emulsions are found naturally in many foods or may be formed during processing or preparation. The term emulsion is applied to a system consisting of one liquid dispersed in another liquid with which it is immiscible. Temporary emulsions separate on standing, whereas permanent emulsions can be held or stored without separation of the two immiscible liquids.

- There are many types of salad dressings that can be purchased commercially or made in the home. Mayonnaise is an example of a permanent emulsion. Mayonnaise, French dressing, and salad dressing all must meet standards of identity to be labeled with these names. If a legally defined nutrient claim is made and other requirements have been met, a salad dressing that has a reduced fat content may be labeled with the standard dressing name—for example, "light" mayonnaise.

KEY TERMS

invisible fat
visible fat
lipids
triglycerides
fatty acid
phospholipid
sterol
gluten
emulsion
emulsifying agent
linoleic acid

omega-6 polyunsaturated fatty acids (PUFA)
omega-3 fatty acids
melting point
saturated fatty acid
unsaturated fatty acid
polyunsaturated fatty acid
P/S ratio
plasticity
rancidity
cis

trans	linolenic acid
emulsifier	chelate
standard of identity	surface tension
LDL cholesterol	polymers
GRAS	tallow
antioxidant	polar materials
smoke point	ester
monoglyceride	sorbitol
diglyceride	humectant
hydrolysis	immiscible
butyric acid	homogenization of whole milk
caproic acid	adsorption
pro-oxidant	amphiphilic

STUDY QUESTIONS

1. For what general purposes are fats used in food preparation? Name at least four uses.

2. Explain two chemical reasons why fats vary in their melting points so that some are liquid at room temperature, whereas others are solid.

3. Most fats used in food preparation are separated from other tissues and refined or processed. Briefly describe how each fat listed below is produced. Also indicate for which of the general uses listed in question 1 each fat may be appropriate.
   a. Butter
   b. Margarine
   c. Lard
   d. Hydrogenated shortening
   e. Oil
   f. High oleic, low linolenic acid oil

4. a. Explain what happens when oils are hydrogenated and when they are winterized.
   b. What purposes do these processes serve in the production of food fats?
   c. What is a *plastic* fat? Give examples.

5. a. What is *rancidity?*
   b. Distinguish between hydrolytic rancidity and oxidative rancidity.
   c. Explain what probably happens when a fat is oxidized and becomes rancid.
   d. List several factors that may contribute to the development of rancidity. How can these be controlled?
   e. How does an antioxidant retard the development of rancidity?
   f. Name several antioxidants that may be added to or are present in fatty foods.

6. a. What is *panfrying?* What is *deep-fat frying?*
   b. Explain the importance of using a proper temperature in frying foods. What do smoke point and acrolein have to do with a proper temperature for frying?
   c. Discuss factors to consider when choosing a frying fat.
   d. Give suggestions for the appropriate care of used frying fat.
   e. What is meant by fat *turnover?* Why is it important in frying?

   f. Discuss several factors that may influence the amount of fat absorbed during frying.

7. Discuss several factors to consider in deciding which fats to purchase.

8. Give several suggestions for cooking lower-fat, yet delicious, foods.

9. a. What types of substances are being used or tested for use as fat replacers in food products? Discuss.
   b. Give examples of carbohydrate-based, protein-based, and fat-based fat replacers.

10. a. What is an *emulsion?* What is necessary to produce a permanent emulsion?
   b. Give several examples of emulsions in natural foods and of emulsions in prepared or processed foods.
   c. Describe the difference between an oil-in-water emulsion and a water-in-oil emulsion.
   d. How does an emulsifier act to stabilize an emulsion?

11. a. Standards of identity have been published for which three types of dressings for salads?
   b. What percentage of oil is specified for each type?
   c. Which governmental agency is responsible for these standards?

12. a. Describe mayonnaise and list its major ingredients.
   b. Discuss several factors that may affect the formation of a stable emulsion in the making of mayonnaise.
   c. Describe what happens when an emulsion breaks. How can a broken mayonnaise emulsion be re-formed?

13. Describe French dressing and list its major ingredients.

14. Explain how salad dressing generally differs from mayonnaise.

REFERENCES

1. Agriculture Marketing Service, U.S. Department of Agriculture. (1995, February). *How to buy dairy products.* Home and Garden Bulletin 201.

2. Akoh, C. C. (1998.) Fat replacers. *Food Technology, 52*(3), 47.

3. Alexander, J. C., Chanin, B. E., & Moran, E. T. (1983). Nutritional effects of fresh, laboratory heated, and pressure deep-fry fats. *Journal of Food Science, 48,* 1289.

4. Bennett, B. (1987). Oil's well. *Food Processing, 58*(9), 39.

5. Bente, L., & Gerrior, S. A. (2002). Selected food and nutrient highlights of the 20th century: U.S. food supply series. *Family Economics and Nutrition Review, 14*(1), 43–51.

6. Berger, K. (1986). Palm oil products. *Food Technology, 40*(9), 72.

7. Blumenthal, M. M. (1991). A new look at the chemistry and physics of deep-fat frying. *Food Technology, 45*(2), 68.

8. Borrud, L., Enns, C. W., & Mickle, S. (1996). What we eat in America: USDA surveys food consumption changes. *Food Review, 19*(3), 14.

9. Carr, R. A. (1991). Development of deep-frying fats. *Food Technology, 45*(2), 95.

10. Clydesdale, F. M. (1997). Olestra: The approval process in letter and spirit. *Food Technology, 51*(2), 104.

11. Crutchfield, S. R., & Weimer, J. (2000). Nutrition policy in the 1990's. *Food Review, 23*(3), 38–43.

12. Dorko, C. (1994). Antioxidants used in foods. *Food Technology*, *48*(4), 33.

13. Drewnowski, A. (1997). Why do we like fat? *Journal of the American Dietetic Association*, *97*, S58.

14. Dunford, N. T. (2001). Health benefits and processing of lipid-based nutritionals. *Food Technology*, *55*(1), 38–44.

15. Dziezak, J. D. (1986). Preservatives: Antioxidants. *Food Technology*, *40*(9), 94.

16. Dziezak, J. D. (1989). Fats, oils, and fat substitutes. *Food Technology*, *43*(7), 66.

17. Erickson, M. D., & Frey, N. (1994). Property-enhanced oils in food applications. *Food Technology*, *48*(11), 63.

18. Fitzpatrick, M. P., Chapman, G. E., & Barr, S. J. (1997). Lower-fat menu items in restaurants satisfy customers. *Journal of the American Dietetic Association*, *97*, 510.

19. Food and Nutrition Board, Institute of Medicine. (2002). Letter report on dietary reference intakes for *trans* fatty acids. Retrieved August 30, 2002, from www.iom.edu/fnb

20. Fulton, L., & Hogbin, M. (1993). Eating quality of muffins, cakes, and cookies prepared with reduced fat and sugar. *Journal of the American Dietetic Association*, *93*, 1313.

21. Gerrior, S., & Bente, L. (2001). Food supply nutrients and dietary guidance, 1970–1999. *Food Review*, *24*(3), 39–46.

22. Giese, J. H. (1993). Alternative sweeteners and bulking agents. *Food Technology*, *47*(1), 114.

23. Giese, J. (1996). Antioxidants: Tools for preventing lipid oxidation. *Food Technology*, *50*(11), 73.

24. Giese, J. (1996). Fats, oils, and fat replacers. *Food Technology*, *50*(4), 78.

25. Haumann, B. F. (1987). Fast food trends in frying fat usage. *Journal of the American Oil Chemists' Society*, *64*, 789.

26. Hayes, K. C. (1996). Designing a cholesterol-removed fat blend for frying and baking. *Food Technology*, *50*(4), 92.

27. Hearn, T. L., Sgoutas, S. A., Hearn, J. A., & Sgoutas, D. S. (1987). Polyunsaturated fatty acids and fat in fish flesh for selecting species for health benefits. *Journal of Food Science*, *52*: 1209.

28. Hicks, K. B. & Moreau, R. A. (2001). Phytosterols and phytostanols: Functional food cholesterol busters. *Food Technology*, *55*(1), 63–67.

29. Hollingsworth, P. (1997). Jack Sprat revisited: Fat and the American consumer. *Food Technology*, *51*(1), 28.

30. Hollingsworth, P. (2001). Margarine: The over-the-top functional food. *Food Technology*, *55*(1), 59–62.

31. Institute of Food Science and Technology. (1999, June). Position statement: *Trans* fatty acids (TFA). Retrieved September 7, 2002, from http://www.ifst.org/hottop9.htm

32. Jacobson, G. A. (1991). Quality control in deep-fat frying operations. *Food Technology*, *45*(2), 72.

33. Katz, F. (1997). The move towards genetically improved oils. *Food Technology*, *51*(11), 66.

34. Kostas, G. (1997). Low-fat and delicious: Can we break the taste barrier? *Journal of the American Dietetic Association*, *97*, S88.

35. Labensky, S. R. & Hause, A. M. (2003). *On cooking: A textbook of culinary fundamentals*. Upper Saddle River, NJ: Prentice Hall.

36. Lawson, H. W. (1985). *Standards for fats and oils*. Westport, CT: Avi Publishing.

37. Liu, K., & Brown, E. A. (1996). Enhancing vegetable oil quality through plant breeding and genetic engineering. *Food Technology*, *50*(11), 67.

38. Mattes, R. D. (1998). Position of the American Dietetic Association: Fat replacers. *Journal of the American Dietetic Association, 98,* 463.

39. McComber, D., & Miller, E. M. (1976). Differences in total lipid and fatty acid composition of doughnuts as influenced by lecithin, leavening agent, and use of frying fat. *Cereal Chemistry, 53,* 101.

40. Neuhouser, M. L., Kristal, A. R., & Patterson, R. E. (1999). Use of food nutrient labels is associated with lower fat intake. *Journal of the American Dietetic Association, 99,* 45–50.

41. Phillips, J. A., & Vail, G. E. (1967). Effect of heat on fatty acids. *Journal of the American Dietetic Association, 50,* 116.

42. Pszczola, D. E. (2000). Putting fat back into foods. *Food Technology, 54*(12), 58–63.

43. Pszczola, D. E. (2001). Antioxidants: From preserving food quality to quality of life. *Food Technology, 55*(6), 51–59.

44. Pszczola, D. E. (2001). Salad days? Not for these dressings. *Food Technology, 55*(4), 78–86.

45. Sloan, A. E. (1997). Fats and oils slip and slide. *Food Technology, 51,*(1), 30.

46. Smouse, T. H. (1979). Review of soybean oil reversion flavor. *Journal of the American Oil Chemists' Society, 56,* 747A.

47. Staff report. (2001). Combining nutrients for health benefits. *Food Technology, 55*(2), 42–47.

48. Szczesniak, A. S. (1990). Texture: Is it still an overlooked food attribute? *Food Technology, 44*(9), 86.

49. U.S. Department of Agriculture. (n.d.). Results from 1994–1996 continuing survey of food intakes by individuals. Retrieved June 18, 2002, from http://barc.usda.gov/ghnrc/foodsurvey/96result.html

50. U.S. Department of Health and Human Services. (1999, November). FDA proposes new rules for *trans* fatty acids in nutrition labeling, nutrient content claims, and health claims. Retrieved August 27, 2002, from http://www.cfsan.fda.gov~lrd/hhtfacid.html

51. U.S. Food and Drug Administration, Center for Food Safety and Applied Nutrition. (1999, November). Questions and answers on trans fat proposed rule. Retrieved July 2, 2002, from http://vm.cfsan.fda.gov/~dms/qatrans.html

52. Wardlaw, G. M. & Kessel, M. W. (2002). *Perspectives in nutrition* (5th ed.). New York: McGraw-Hill.

Sweeteners and Sugar Cookery

11

Sweeteners have been used for food since prehistoric times, probably beginning with the discovery of honey. From drawings in Egyptian tombs we learn that, as early as 2600 B.C., beekeeping was practiced for honey production. It is doubtful, however, that the honey was available to anyone but the rich and powerful. Today, some type of sweetener is found in most people's diets.

Commonly used sweeteners are generally extracted from plant sources and refined. The term "sugar" usually refers to crystallized sucrose (table sugar). In addition, sweeteners include other concentrated sources of sugar such as corn syrups, maple syrup, molasses, and honey. Artificial or alternate sweeteners produce sweetness but are usually noncaloric substances.

TRENDS IN SWEETENER CONSUMPTION

From so-called **disappearance data,** published by the U.S. Department of Agriculture (USDA), it is apparent that the consumption of sugar and sweeteners in the United States has increased since 1909. Disappearance rates of sugar, however, are only indicators of *availability*. Sugar can "disappear" in a number of ways without being consumed in the human diet. For example, some sugar is used in pet foods and in fermentation processes such as breadmaking and distilling, and some is wasted. Dietary survey data give much lower levels of consumption [5]. (See Chapter 2 for more information about food consumption and disappearance data).

Disappearance data suggest however, that Americans consumed 75 percent more caloric sweeteners in 1997 than in 1909 [36]. Between 1982 and 1997, the per capita consumption of sweeteners, as measured by disappearance data, increased 28 percent. The type of sweeteners used has changed as well [35]. Corn sweeteners increased from 16 percent of the total caloric sweeteners available in 1970 to 56 percent in 1997. During this same time period sucrose's (table sugar's) share of total caloric sweeteners dropped from 83 percent to 43 percent (Figure 11-1). High-fructose corn syrup and aspartame has largely replaced sugar in soft drinks. Beverage manufacturers reduced the use of sucrose from 19 pounds to 1 pound per capita between 1980 and 1997 [36].

The source of sweeteners in the American diet also has changed over the years. In 1909, two-thirds of the available sugar was purchased for use in the home. Currently, over three-quarters of refined and processed sweeteners are

disappearance data the amount of food going into the national supply, calculated from beginning inventories, annual production, imports, and exports

Figure 11-1
The amount of added sugars has nearly doubled between 1909 and 1998. (Courtesy of U.S. Department of Agriculture, Economic Research Service)

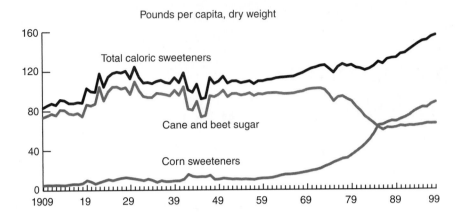

used by the food and beverage industries in the manufacture of products that are then purchased by consumers. The rise in sweetener consumption since the mid 1980's corresponds with the 47 percent increase in annual per capita consumption of carbonated soft drinks [36]. Data from the 1994–1996 Continuing Survey of Food Intakes by Individuals also suggests that regular (nondiet) soft drinks are an important source of added sweeteners in the American diet. Sugars and sweets are second in importance to regular soft drinks [18]. The consumption of candy reached a high of 25 pounds per person in 1997 [36].

NUTRITIVE VALUE

Sugar provides only energy for the body; the dry product is essentially 100 percent carbohydrate. Therefore, foods that contain relatively large amounts of sugar generally have low nutrient density. Increasing the consumption of sugar-rich foods may contribute to an unbalanced diet by proportionately decreasing the consumption of protein, minerals, and vitamins. In addition, disguising many natural food flavors by adding excessive amounts of sugar to foods results in a loss of variety and appreciation for individual food flavors. The Dietary Guidelines for Americans recommend that only moderate amounts of sugars be consumed. Molasses, which contains the natural ash of the plant juices from which it is made, furnishes some nutrients other than carbohydrates, such as a small amount of calcium and iron; however, the less refined sugars and syrups, including honey, are still essentially energy foods and, on the whole, cannot be relied on to furnish other nutrients in significant amounts.

A position paper of the American Dietetic Association points out that, on the basis of present research evidence, dietary sugars are not an independent risk factor for any particular disease, nor do they appear to be responsible for behavioral changes. Sugars can contribute, along with other fermentable carbohydrates, to acid production in the mouth, which promotes dental cavities [1]. Sugars have their proper place in food preparation, providing variety and satisfying the apparently inborn desire for sweet taste. However, the total caloric need, as well as the requirements for protein, vitamins, and minerals, must be carefully considered when adding sugar-rich foods to the diet.

PROPERTIES OF SUGARS

The chemical classification of sugars as **monosaccharides** and **disaccharides,** and a description of some of the common sugars, is provided in Chapter 9.

Solubility

In the natural state of foods, sugars are in **solution. Crystallization** of sugar occurs from a sufficiently concentrated sugar solution, and use is made of this fact in the commercial production of sugar from sugar cane and beets.

    The common sugars vary in their solubilities. Sucrose is the most soluble of the disaccharides, and lactose is the least soluble. Fructose is the most soluble of the monosaccharides and is more soluble than sucrose. At room temperature, the relative solubilities in water of the common sugars are fructose (most soluble), followed by sucrose, glucose, maltose, and lactose. The solubility of all sugars in water is increased by heating. At 68°F (20°C), 203.9 grams of sucrose may be dissolved by 100 grams of water, whereas at 158°F (70°C) and 212°F (100°C), 320.5 grams and 487.2 grams of sucrose, respectively, may be dissolved by the same amount of water.

    When small amounts of sugar are added to water and the mixture is stirred, the sugar dissolves and the solution appears to be transparent. We call this solution *unsaturated* because it will dissolve more sugar if it is added. The solution becomes *saturated* when it is dissolving all of the sugar that can be dissolved at that particular temperature. The only way that you can know if a solution is truly saturated is by adding sufficient solute (the dispersed substance, which is sugar in this case) so that some remains undissolved in the bottom of the container and is in contact with the solution.

    A solution is *supersaturated* when it holds more solute than is usually soluble at a particular temperature. To produce a supersaturated sugar solution, more sugar than can dissolve at room temperature is added to water and the mixture is heated to the boiling temperature, at which point all of the sugar dissolves. As this solution is carefully cooled to room temperature without being disturbed, the solution gradually becomes saturated and then supersaturated.

    Only by careful cooling and the avoidance of factors that promote crystallization can a solution be held in the supersaturated state. Because supersaturation is such an unstable state, crystallization eventually occurs and all excess solute beyond saturation is precipitated or crystallized. Some substances require more time to crystallize from a supersaturated solution than others, unless agitation or seeding (adding a few already formed crystals) starts the process of crystallization. The sugars that are the most soluble, such as fructose, are the most difficult to crystallize; those that are the least soluble, such as lactose, crystallize readily. In the making of candies, close attention is given to the solubility and ease of crystallization of sugars.

Melting Point and Decomposition by Heat

With the application of sufficient dry heat, sugars melt or change to a liquid state. Heating beyond the melting point brings about several decomposition changes. As sucrose melts at about 320°F (160°C), a clear liquid forms that gradually changes to a brown color with continued heating. At about 338°F (170°C), caramelization occurs with the development of a characteristic caramel flavor along with the brown color. Caramelization is one type of browning, called *nonenzymatic browning* because it does not involve enzymes. It is a com-

monosaccharide a simple sugar with a single basic unit

disaccharide two monosaccharides linked together

solution ions or small molecules, called the *solute*, dispersed in a liquid, called the *solvent*

crystallization the formation of crystals from the solidification of dispersed elements in a precise, orderly structure

polymerization the formation of large molecules by combining smaller chemical units

plex chemical reaction, involving the removal of water and eventual **polymerization,** and is not very well understood. Caramel has a pungent taste, is often bitter, is much less sweet than the original sugar from which it is produced, is noncrystalline, and is soluble in water. Both the extent and rate of the caramelization reaction are influenced by the type of sugar being heated. Galactose and glucose caramelize at about the same temperature as sucrose, but fructose caramelizes at 230°F (110°C) and maltose caramelizes at about 356°F (180°C).

Granulated sugar, when heated dry in a heavy pan, caramelizes. When hot liquid is added, the caramelized sugar dissolves and can be used to flavor puddings, ice creams, frostings, and sauces. Caramel is also produced during the cooking of such foods as peanut brittle and caramel candy.

Absorption of Moisture

That sugars absorb moisture is clearly shown in many ways. Crystalline sugars become caked and lumpy unless they are stored in dry places. Baked flour mixtures that are rich in sugar take up moisture when surrounded by a moist atmosphere in tightly closed containers. Because of this tendency to absorb moisture from the atmosphere, sugars are said to be *hygroscopic*. Fructose is more hygroscopic than the other sugars commonly found in food. Therefore, higher moisture absorption occurs in products containing fructose, such as cakes or cookies made with honey, molasses, or crystalline fructose. These baked products remain moist noticeably longer than similar products made with sucrose. Exactly how the water is associated with sugars in food systems has not been clearly defined. At least in systems in which the sugar is dissolved, the water surrounding the sugar molecule does not appear to be tightly bound. It is still mobile [11].

Fermentation

fermentation the transformation of organic molecules into smaller ones by the action of microorganisms; enzymes produced by the microbes catalyze each of the many steps in the process

Most sugars, except lactose, may be fermented by yeasts to produce carbon dioxide gas and alcohol. **Fermentation** is an important reaction in the making of bread and other baked products; the carbon dioxide leavens the product and the alcohol is volatilized during baking. The spoilage of canned or cooked products containing sugar may occur by fermentation.

Acid Hydrolysis

The disaccharides are hydrolyzed by weak acids to produce their component monosaccharides. Sucrose is easily hydrolyzed by acid, but maltose and lactose are slowly acted on. The end products of sucrose hydrolysis are a mixture of glucose and fructose. This mixture is commonly called *invert sugar*. The monosaccharides are not appreciably affected by acids.

cream of tartar the acid salt of tartaric acid; a weak acid substance commonly added to fondant to produce variable amounts of invert sugar from the hydrolysis of sucrose

The extent of acid hydrolysis in a sugar solution is variable, depending on whether the solution is heated, the kind and concentration of acid used, and the rate and length of heating. Application of heat accelerates the reaction, and long, slow heating tends to bring about more hydrolysis than rapid heating for a shorter period. The higher the acidity, the greater the rate and extent of decomposition. Hydrolysis may occur incidentally, as in the cooking of acid fruits and sugar, or it may be brought about purposely as a means of improving the textures or consistencies of certain sugar products, such as fondant, for which it is often produced by the addition of **cream of tartar,** an acid salt.

Enzyme Hydrolysis

Enzymes also hydrolyze disaccharides. The enzyme *sucrase*, also called *invertase*, is used in the candy industry to hydrolyze some of the sucrose in cream fondant to fructose and glucose. This process produces soft, semifluid centers in chocolates. The enzyme is commonly added to the fondant layer around the fruit in chocolate-coated cherries. It must be added after the sugar solution is boiled and cooled so that the enzyme is not destroyed. The addition is usually made during beating or when the fondant is molded for dipping. The fondant must be dipped in chocolate shortly after the enzyme is added, and chocolate coatings must completely cover the fondant to prevent leakage as the enzyme acts on the sucrose. Because the enzyme acts best in an acid medium, the fondant is acidified.

Decomposition by Alkalies

The decomposition of sugars by alkalies also has significance in sugar cookery. Alkaline waters used in boiling sugar solutions may bring about some decomposition of sugars. The monosaccharides, which are only slightly affected by weak acids, are markedly affected by alkalies. Both glucose and fructose are changed into many decomposition products both by standing and by being heated in alkaline solutions. The stronger the alkali solution, the more pronounced are the effects on sugars. Sucrose, one of the disaccharides, is the least affected by alkalies, but the invert sugar formed by the hydrolysis of sucrose is readily decomposed. The decomposition products of glucose and fructose are brownish, and, when the process is extensive, the flavor may be strong and bitter.

Fondant made with glucose or corn syrup is usually less white than fondant made with cream of tartar, at least partly because the fondant mixture is more alkaline without the addition of cream of tartar and because some decomposition of monosaccharides may occur. When hard water, which is alkaline, is used, the effect is more pronounced.

Other examples of cooked products may be cited to illustrate the color and flavor changes resulting from the decomposition of glucose and fructose: Baked beans are more brown in color and have a more caramelized flavor if they are made with glucose- or fructose-containing sweeteners, such as corn syrup, rather than table sugar; and cakes and cookies made from honey and baking soda invariably have a darkened color and strong flavor. These are complex food products, and browning may occur not only as a result of sugar decomposition by alkali but also because of the Maillard browning reaction. This reaction begins with the interaction of sugars and amino groups from proteins.

Sweetness

The flavor of purified sugars is described as being sweet. We humans love sweetness, as do virtually all mammals since history began, with honey, dates, and figs providing early sources of sweetness [3]. The degree of sweetness that we perceive is affected by several factors, including genetic variation among individuals as well as concentration of the sweetener, temperature, viscosity, pH, and the presence of other substances with the sweetener [29]. It is therefore sometimes difficult to make consistent and reproducible comparisons of sweetness among the various sweeteners, including the common sugars.

In general, it appears that, of the sugars, lactose is the least sweet, followed by maltose, galactose, glucose, and sucrose, with fructose being the most sweet;

however, these orders of sweetness do not hold at all temperatures or in all products. For example, fructose was reported to give a sweeter lemonade than sucrose when added in equal weights; but sugar cookies, white cake, and vanilla pudding were sweeter when made with sucrose as compared with fructose [19]. A maximum sweetness from fructose is most likely to be achieved when it is used with slightly acid, cold foods and beverages.

CRYSTALLINE FORMS OF SUGAR

Crystals will form in a concentrated, supersaturated sugar solution. In the process of crystallization, molecules that are dispersed in a liquid solution pack closely together in a precise, organized, set pattern to form a solid substance. The tiny crystals, which have a characteristic shape for each substance crystallized, may sometimes be gathered into clusters of crystals.

The size of the crystals formed depends on a number of factors, including concentration, temperature, agitation, and the presence of other substances that interfere with crystal formation. The factors are carefully controlled both in the crystallization of commercial sugars and in the making of candies.

Granulated Sugar

Granulated sugar or crystalline sucrose, called *table sugar*, plays a variety of roles in food systems. To the food scientist, sucrose is much more than a sweetener. For example, it affects the texture of many baked products, it improves the body and texture of ice creams, it is fermented by yeast to produce carbon dioxide gas which leavens breads, and it preserves jams and jellies by retarding the growth of microorganisms.

Table sugar is produced commercially from both sugar beets and sugar cane. The product, refined sucrose, is chemically the same from both sources. In the production of table sugar, the plant materials are crushed or sliced, and the high sugar content is extracted. The juice is filtered, clarified, and evaporated under a vacuum to form a concentrated sugar syrup, from which the sugar is crystallized. In the processing of cane sugar, an intermediate product with 2 to 3 percent impurities is *raw sugar*. Raw sugar is sent to refineries for further treatment through a series of steps involving dissolving, purifying, and recrystallizing to produce granulated sugar. The crude raw sugar is not suitable for human consumption.

Beet sugar production is done in one continuous stage, without a raw sugar intermediate. A by-product of the manufacture of sugar from beets is sugar beet fiber. It is available in varying particle sizes to food processors who desire to increase the fiber content of certain manufactured foods.

Many grades and granulations of refined sugar are available. Fine granulated sugar with uniform grain size is the principal granulated sugar for consumer use. Other classes, each more finely granulated than the preceding one, are extra-fine granulated, berry or fruit, coating, and superfine sugars. Coarse sugars with larger crystal size are available, mostly for industrial use. Large grain sugars are crystallized from the purest sugar solutions and are ideal for boiled syrups and boiled icings when clear, stable solutions are required. Sanding sugar is a coarsely granulated sugar used either in boiled syrups or as a topping for pies, turnovers, and cookies. Manufacturers' grade is a coarse grain sugar but with crystals of a smaller size than sanding sugar. Loaf sugars are prepared by the pressing of wet sucrose crystals into a cake. When it is hard, the cake is cut into cube or tablet form, which is commonly designated *lump sugar*.

Other Crystalline Sugars

A white crystalline form of glucose, 75 to 80 percent as sweet as sucrose, is produced by the complete hydrolysis of corn starch. It can be obtained in various particle sizes, including powdered and pulverized, but is used chiefly in the food industry. The crystals sometimes found in honey are mostly glucose; the fructose remains in the syrup.

Crystalline fructose that is more than 99 percent pure is available but, like crystalline glucose, is used mainly by food processors. When used in combination with sucrose, the sweetness is greater than when an equal amount of either sugar is used alone, thus allowing less sugar to be used. Compared with sucrose, fructose produces more rapid development of viscosity and increased gel strength in starch-thickened pies and puddings [39]. Crystalline lactose, which is about one-sixth as sweet as sucrose, and maltose are also available for special uses.

Maltodextrins, which are derived from corn starch, are available as dry products and as concentrated solutions. The starch in maltodextrins is less completely hydrolyzed to glucose than corn syrup solids, and therefore, they are less sweet and have a very bland flavor. They also contribute chewiness, binding properties, and viscosity to candy [15].

Powdered Sugars

Powdered sugars are machine ground or pulverized from the granulated sucrose obtained from sugar cane or sugar beets. They usually contain small amounts of corn starch to control caking. The letter X is used to designate degree of fineness, such as XXXX, 6X, 10X, or 12X, which is the most fine.

Brown Sugars

Brown sugar is obtained from cane sugar during the late stages of refining. It is composed of clumps of sucrose crystals coated with a film of molasses. Molasses is a by-product of the sugar production process; it is the liquid remaining after most of the sugar crystals have been separated from it. Some invert sugar, which is an equal molecular mixture of fructose and glucose, is present in molasses and thus in brown sugar. A small amount of ash, an organic acid, and flavoring substances are also present in brown sugar, contributing to the characteristic pleasant caramel flavor and light yellow to dark brown color. The lighter the color, the higher the stage of purification and the less pronounced the flavor. Brown sugar is available in a free-flowing form for use in pre-mixes and also in a liquid form for use in continuous-process systems [15]. A one-half measure of the liquid is roughly equivalent to one measure of the crystalline product.

Cocrystallized Sucrose

An interesting process known as *cocrystallization* can be applied to the crystallization of sucrose, resulting in several novel functions for this product in the food industry. In the cocrystallization process, spontaneous crystallization of a purified supersaturated sugar solution is accomplished by rapid agitation, resulting in the production of aggregates of microsized crystals as cooling proceeds. The aggregates have a spongelike appearance, with void spaces and an increased surface area (Figure 11-2). In the presence of a second ingredient, an infinite dispersion of this ingredient occurs over the entire surface area of the sucrose aggregate. This cocrystallization process may be defined as one whereby a second ingredient is incorporated in or plated onto a microsized sucrose crystal by spontaneous crystallization [2]; there is no settling out of the second ingredient. The resulting sugar product is homogeneous and readily

(a)

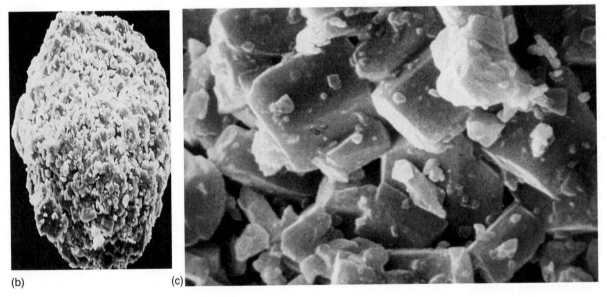

(b)   (c)

Figure 11-2

A new generation of sucrose products can be made by cocrystallization.

(a) Ordinary sugar crystals at 35× magnification.

(b) Cocrystallized sugar aggregates of microsized sucrose crystals at 175× magnification.

(c) Surface structure of cocrystallized sugar aggregates at 1,750× magnification.

(Reprinted from Food Technology 47(1), p. 147, 1993. Copyright© by Institute of Food Technologists. Photographs courtesy of Ahmed Awad, PhD, Domino Sugar Corporation.)

dispersed in food ingredients. The second ingredient may be flavorings such as honey, fruit juice, maple, peanut butter, chocolate, and alternate sweetener–sugar combinations. The incorporation of mixtures of ingredients into a crystallized sugar matrix is also used to make instant-type products with improved functions in gelling, aeration, and emulsification, such as pudding mixes, gelatin dessert mixes, flavored drink mixes, and icing mixes.

SYRUPS, MOLASSES, AND HONEY

Corn Syrups

Regular corn syrups contain about 75 percent carbohydrate and 25 percent water; however, the proportions of the various sugars present in the carbohydrate portion may vary greatly, depending on the manufacturing process and the proposed use of the product. In Europe, a similar syrup is called *glucose syrup* because it is produced from starches other than corn [15].

Corn syrup has traditionally been produced in the United States by using acid and high temperatures to hydrolyze corn starch. The carbohydrate of the resulting product is composed of 10 to 36 percent glucose and 9 to 20 percent maltose, the remainder consisting of higher sugars and **dextrins** [25]. With the additional use of selected enzymes, a corn syrup that contains a much higher proportion of glucose and/or maltose may be prepared. The use of **glucoamylase** yields more glucose, whereas the use of **β-amylase** yields more maltose. High-glucose syrups have lower viscosity and higher sweetening power.

The extent of conversion of starch to glucose is described by the term *dextrose equivalent (DE)*, which is defined as the percent of **reducing sugar** calculated as dextrose (glucose) on a dry-weight basis. Dextrose or glucose thus has a DE of 100. Corn syrups are available with different sugar compositions having DEs of 20 to 95 [15].

Dried corn syrups or corn syrup solids are produced by the spray or vacuum drying of refined corn syrup. The dried product is useful in such foods as dry beverage mixes, instant breakfast mixes, cereal bars, and sauce mixes.

High-fructose Corn Syrup. A high-glucose corn syrup is used as the basis for production of a high-fructose corn syrup (HFCS) by use of the enzyme **glucose isomerase**. This enzyme catalyzes the chemical reaction that changes about half of the glucose in the mixture to fructose. HFCS containing about 42 percent of the carbohydrate as fructose was produced in the early 1970's. Syrups containing up to 90 percent fructose have since been prepared by a fractionation process that removes much of the glucose from a 42 percent HFCS. To produce a syrup of 55 percent fructose content, a stream of 90 percent fructose syrup is blended into a stream of 42 percent fructose syrup [31]. The primary feature of HFCS is sweetness.

HFCSs are widely used in the manufacture of soft drinks. They are also used in a variety of other products, including prepared cereals, chocolate products, icings, canned and frozen fruits, frozen desserts, confections, and sauces [13].

Molasses and Sorghum

Molasses is the residue that remains after sucrose crystals have been removed from the concentrated juices of sugar cane. It contains not more than 25 percent water and not more than 5 percent mineral ash. The sugar, which may be

dextrins polysaccharides, somewhat smaller in size than starch, resulting from the partial hydrolysis of starch

glucoamylase an enzyme that hydrolyzes starch by breaking off one glucose unit at a time, thus producing glucose immediately

β-amylase an enzyme that hydrolyzes starch by breaking off two glucose units at a time, thus producing maltose

reducing sugar a sugar with a free aldehyde or ketone group that has the ability to chemically "reduce" other chemical compounds and thus become oxidized itself; glucose, fructose, maltose, and lactose, but not sucrose, are reducing sugars

glucose isomerase an enzyme that changes glucose to fructose

present in amounts up to 70 percent, is a mixture of sucrose, glucose, and fructose, but is chiefly sucrose.

Molasses differs in sugar and mineral content depending on the stage of the crystallization process from which it is derived. After the first crystallization of sucrose, the molasses is high in sugar and light in color. After the final process, a dark and bitter product with a relatively high mineral content, called *blackstrap molasses*, remains. Most molasses sold on the market is a blend of different types. Sorghum is made from cane sorghum and is similar to molasses in appearance. Its total sugar content is about 65 to 70 percent.

Maple Syrup

Maple sugaring has been an early-spring tradition in some parts of the United States ever since Native Americans first discovered that sap from the maple tree cooked over an open fire produced a sweet syrup. Vermont is particularly well known for its delicious pure maple syrup.

Maple syrup is probably the most highly prized of all syrups used for culinary and table purposes. It is made by evaporation of the sap of the sugar maple to a concentration containing no more than 35 percent water. The special flavor that gives maple syrup its economic importance is not in the sap as it comes from the tree. It is developed in the processing or cooking down of the sap into syrup. Organic acids present in the sap enter into this flavor-developing process. It has been found that evaporating the sap at low temperatures through distillation or freeze-drying results in a syrup that is practically flavorless and colorless. Approximately 40 gallons of sap are necessary to yield a single gallon of maple syrup.

Honey

Honey is flower nectar that is collected, modified, and concentrated by the domesticated European honeybee. Honey contains about 17 percent water and 82.5 percent carbohydrate, with small amounts of minerals, vitamins, and enzymes. The carbohydrate portion of honey includes fructose (38 percent), glucose (31 percent), maltose (7 percent), and sucrose (2 percent). As specified by the U.S. Food and Drug Administration (FDA), honey may not contain more than 8 percent sucrose; a higher percentage is taken as an indication of adulteration. The addition of any other sugar substances—such as HFCS—to honey is also considered to be adulteration.

The flavor of honeys differs according to the characteristic flavoring compounds present in the nectar of different flowers. Over half of the honey produced in this country is mild-flavored sweet clover, clover, or alfalfa honey (Figure 11-3). Honeys also come from orange and other citrus blossoms, wild sage, cultivated buckwheat, and the tulip tree. Much of the honey on the market is a blend of different floral types. The color of honey may vary from white to dark amber. The color of fresh honey is related to its mineral content and is characteristic of its floral source. Grades of honey are independent of color, but darker colored honey generally has a stronger flavor than the white or light-colored product.

Honey is stored in the comb by bees and in that form is marketed as comb honey. If the comb is uncapped and centrifuged, the honey is extracted. Extracted honey may optionally be pasteurized by a mild heat treatment to destroy yeasts and to delay crystallization. Honey may then be strained to remove wax

Figure 11-3
Honey can be added to many foods for flavor. Here it is used to sweeten a biscuit. (Courtesy of U.S. Department of Agriculture)

particles and foreign matter. It may also be filtered to remove pollen, air bubbles, and other fine particles. Controlled crystallization produces a product called *crystallized honey*. A process has also been developed for producing dried honey. This product has a color and flavor that are quite close to those of the original honey. It is granular in form, is free flowing, and has a long shelf life. Whipped honey may have part of the fructose removed, leaving a higher proportion of glucose, which crystallizes to some degree. A thickened mixture results.

The USDA has set standards for grades of honey, including comb honey and extracted honey (filtered and strained; liquid and crystallized). The grades are based on moisture content, minimum total solids, flavor, aroma, clarity, and absence of defects.

Honey is a supersaturated solution and, with storage, glucose tends to crystallize out of solution, producing granulation. Granulation is reversed by heating.

Table 11-1 lists some sugar and syrup substitutions that can be made in food preparation. Adjustment must be made for the liquid present in syrups.

ALTERNATIVE SWEETENERS

Although sugar has been used to sweeten foods for many decades, concerns about caloric excess in the diet and tooth decay, particularly in the Western world, have sparked a desire for alternatives. The food industry has responded with a variety of reduced-sugar products. To produce acceptable products with little or no sugar, high-intensity sweeteners and/or low-calorie bulking agents must be used.

The American Dietetic Association has taken the position that there is an appropriate use for nonnutritive, as well as nutritive, sweeteners when they are consumed in moderation and within the context of a diet consistent with the Dietary Guidelines for Americans [1]. It is interesting to note, however, that the use of alternate sweeteners does not necessarily decrease the amount of sugar in the diet. A study of college students in the 1990's revealed a higher incidence of use of high-intensity sweeteners than was reported in 1980, with 61 percent of the women and 31 percent of the men surveyed using alternative sweeteners regularly [10]. No evidence indicated that this use was associated with a biologically significant reduction in sugar intake, however.

Sweeteners may be classified into two groups: bulk sweeteners that provide calories (sometimes called *nutritive sweeteners*) and alternative sweeteners that have a sweet taste but are essentially noncaloric (sometimes called *nonnutritive sweeteners*) [17]. The alternative sweeteners are often called *high-intensity sweeteners* because they are more potent than bulk sweeteners and therefore can be used in much smaller quantities to achieve a similar degree of sweetness.

Alternative sweeteners currently approved for use in the United States include saccharin, aspartame, acesulfame-K, sucralose, and neotame. Neotame and sucralose are the two most recently approved alternative sweetners. The FDA approved neotame in 2002 and sucralose in April 1998. Although cyclamates were considered **GRAS** by the FDA at one time and are currently approved for use in 50 countries, they are now banned from use in the United

GRAS food additives that are "generally recognized as safe" by a panel of experts; this list is maintained and periodically reevaluated by the FDA

1 cup brown sugar = 1/2 cup liquid brown sugar
1 cup honey = 1 1/4 cup sugar + 1/4 cup liquid
1 cup corn syrup = 1 cup sugar + 1/4 cup liquid

Table 11-1
Substitution among Sugar and Syrup Products

Healthy Eating

Formulated foods for diabetics

Sedentary life styles and an abundance of food are contributing to the growing plague of obesity in the United States—along with one of its side effects, the increased risk for developing diabetes. About 5.9% of the U.S. population has been diagnosed with some form of diabetes—Type 2 being the most common—and diabetes is the seventh leading cause of death in the U.S. [24].

The food industry is becoming a scapegoat for obesity, with class-action lawsuits being filed against such fast food chains as McDonalds for making customers overweight and putting them at risk for illness. Whatever happened to free choice and self discipline? But there is a positive side to this situation. The growing concern about diabetes has created a new market segment for specialized foods and the industry is designing new products to serve this group. Playing important roles in these developments are high intensity or alternative sweeteners [24].

Foods designed for diabetics are different from the usual low-sugar, low-fat foods found on the market and are not to be used for weight reduction. They attempt to provide a balance of nutrients for diabetics that work with drugs to control blood glucose levels more effectively. As examples, Mead Johnson Nutritionals has developed a *Choice DM*® line of ready-to-use beverages and nutrition bars and Ross Products Division of Abbott Laboratories markets the *Glucerna*® line of similar products. Both the beverages and the bars provide a balance of carbohydrate, fat, and protein with added vitamins and minerals and use alternative sweeteners such as aspartame and sucralose. The bars contain a special starch that is resistant to digestion, giving a lower glycemic response—that is, the blood glucose level does not rise as rapidly or as high after the bar is eaten. These products give diabetics greater choice in managing their daily diets. And research continues in an effort to improve these "designer" foods [27].

States [28]. A petition to approve cyclamates as food additives was submitted in 1982 [17]. A petition for alitame, a potential new alternative sweetener, was also filed with the FDA in 1986 and action is pending.

No one alternative sweetener is best for every food product [28]. Therefore, sweeteners are chosen for the applications for which they will be best suited. Combinations of different alternative sweeteners, called *sweetener blends*, offer promise for improved taste and stability and can overcome the limitations of the individual sweeteners [42, 28].

Saccharin

Saccharin was first synthesized in 1879, when it was accidentally discovered that it has a sweet taste. It has been used in the United States since 1901 for both food and nonfood purposes. Intensely sweet, 300 to 500 times as sweet as sucrose, it is stable in a wide variety of products under extreme processing conditions [23]. It can be synthesized with relatively few impurities and is inexpensive. One major disadvantage of saccharin is its perceived bitter aftertaste, particularly at higher concentrations; however, when used in combination with other nonnutritive sweeteners such as aspartame or cyclamate, sweetness is enhanced and bitterness decreased somewhat.

Saccharin (sold under the trade name Sweet 'n Low) has been the only approved nonnutritive sweetener used in the United States during certain periods.

Some concern about its safety, however, has been expressed since it was first used. Because an increase in bladder tumors in laboratory rats was found to be associated with the ingestion of high levels of dietary saccharin, the FDA proposed banning this GRAS substance in 1977. Strong public protest influenced the U.S. Congress to impose a moratorium against any action to ban saccharin, in part due to the highly controversial methodology of the laboratory rat study. The moratorium was extended periodically to allow continued use of saccharin as further research clarified saccharin's role in the **carcinogenic** process [12]. However, the Congress ruled, as a compromise measure, that a warning statement had to be placed on labels of foods containing saccharin. This label reads: "Use of this product may be hazardous to your health. This product contains saccharin, which has been determined to cause cancer in laboratory animals" [20]. Saccharin has since been found to be a carcinogen only in rats and only if administered over two generations. **Epidemiological** studies in humans have not shown the risk of developing bladder cancer to be increased with exposure to saccharin.

> **carcinogen** a cancer-causing substance

In December 1991, the FDA officially withdrew the proposed federal ban on saccharin, indicating that "the safety of saccharin is no longer of concern and that these 1977 proposals have become outdated" [4]. Nevertheless, in 1997, a National Toxicology Program panel, which reports to the National Institute of Environmental Health Sciences, recommended that saccharin remain listed in its report on carcinogens, where it had been placed in 1981 [22]. In 2000, the label requirement was rescinded when saccharin was removed from the U.S. Department of Health and Human Service's list of cancer-causing substances [23].

> **epidemiology** the study of causes and control of diseases prevalent in human population groups

Aspartame

Aspartame is made by joining two amino acids—aspartic acid and phenylalanine—and adding methyl alcohol to form a methyl **ester** (see Figure 11-4). Aspartame is a white, odorless, crystalline powder that has a clean, sugarlike taste and a sweetness potency 180 to 200 times that of sucrose [24]. No bitter aftertaste is associated with aspartame. The registered trade name for aspartame as a food ingredient is NutraSweet®. Equal® is a tabletop low-calorie sweetener containing NutraSweet®. Another tabletop sweetener is Spoonful®, which consists of aspartame and maltodextrin. It is designed to measure like sugar [17]. Aspartame can be utilized as an energy source in the body; however, it is used in such small amounts that its caloric value is insignificant.

> **ester** a special chemical linkage involving an alcohol and an organic acid

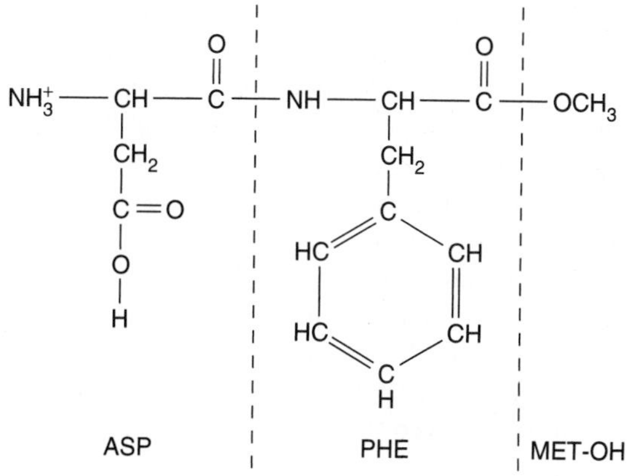

Figure 11-4
Chemical structure of aspartame. ASP, aspartic acid; PHE, phenylalanine; MET-OH, methyl alcohol.

In 1981, aspartame was approved by the FDA for use in several foods. It is now approved for use in many countries and has applications in more than 3,000 products throughout the world, including carbonated soft drinks, refrigerated flavored milk beverages, yogurt products, cold cereals, powdered soft drinks, chewing gum, instant coffee and tea, dry pudding mixes and gelatins, ready-to-serve gelatin desserts, refrigerated or frozen drinks with and without juice, frozen novelties on a stick, breath mints, and ready-to-drink tea beverages and concentrates. In 1996 the FDA approved the use of aspartame as a general-purpose sweetener.

Because aspartame is not stable to heat but changes chemically and loses sweetness, it has not been useful in such foods as baked layer cakes [21]. Its instability to heating can be corrected, however, by encapsulating a core of granulated aspartame with a water-resistant coating of polymer and/or a layer of fat. After the outer layer melts, the core layer slowly hydrates, releasing the aspartame in the final stages of baking. The use of low-calorie bulking agents with aspartame is also necessary to produce the effects on volume and texture that sugar provides in many baked products.

Rigorous testing has been done to ensure the safety of aspartame [28, 23]. Although some have questioned the wisdom of its use, particularly in soft drinks kept at high temperatures, research from several sources has documented the safety of aspartame use by healthy adults and children, and by individuals with diabetes. Aspartame-containing foods should not, however, be used by individuals with **phenylketonuria (PKU)**, because phenylalanine is released during its metabolism.

phenylketonuria (PKU) a genetic disease characterized by an inborn error in the body's ability to metabolize the amino acid phenylalanine

The stability of aspartame in fruit preparations used for yogurt has been assessed [16]. About 60 percent of the original aspartame remained after 6 months of storage. It was estimated that the shelf life for the fruit preparations was 1.5 months when stored at 70°F (21°C). Enhancement of fruitiness has been reported in aspartame-sweetened, fruit-flavored systems at low flavor levels [43].

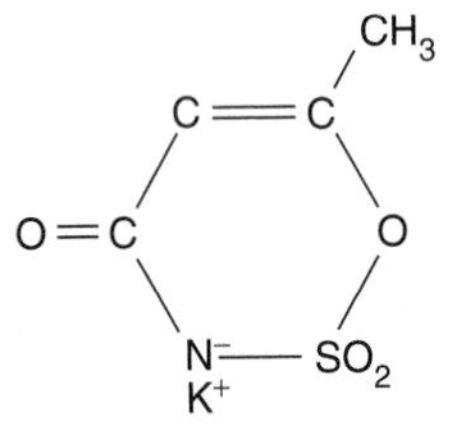

Figure 11-5
Chemical structure of acesulfame-K.

Acesulfame-K

Acesulfame is a synthetic derivative of acetoacetic acid. It is apparently not metabolized in the body and is excreted unchanged. This sweetener is characterized by a rapid onset of sweetness. It has little undesirable aftertaste, although at high concentrations it does exhibit lingering bitter and metallic flavor attributes [23]. Acesulfame-K, the potassium salt of acesulfame (see Figure 11-5), is up to 200 times sweeter than a 3 percent sucrose solution [14].

Acesulfame-K was inadvertently discovered by a German chemist in 1967. In 1988, the FDA approved this compound as a food additive. It is used in a variety of products and is marketed under the brand name Sunette® [23]. In mixtures of acesulfame-K and aspartame (1 : 1 by weight) there is a strong **synergistic** enhancement of sweetness. Blends were found to be 300 times sweeter than sucrose solutions, whereas individually they were only 100 times sweeter [17].

synergism an interaction in which the effect of the mixture is greater than the effect of the sum of component parts

Acesulfame-K is heat stable. It does not decompose under simulated pasteurization or baking conditions [28]. It thus has potential for use in cooked and baked products. Baked custard made with half sucrose and half acesulfame-K was equally as acceptable to a taste panel as custard made with sucrose alone or with fructose, even though the crust was less smooth and tender [41].

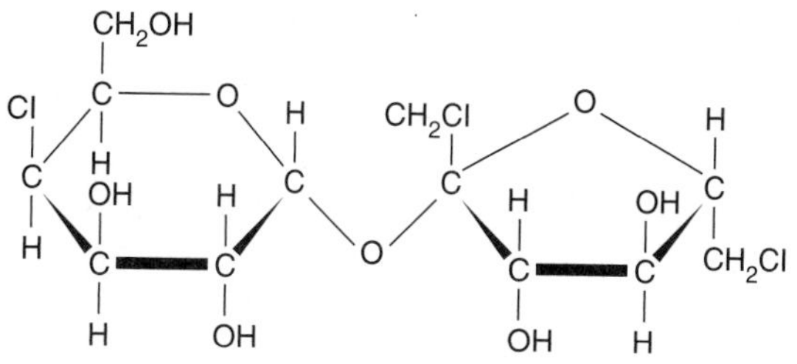

Figure 11-6
Chemical structure of sucralose.

Structure of sucralose

Sucralose

Sucralose is a white, crystalline solid produced by the selective addition of chlorine atoms to sucrose (Figure 11-6). It is 600 times sweeter than sugar, tastes very much like sucrose, and has no bitter aftertaste [28]. It is highly soluble in water and is stable under extreme pH conditions and at high temperatures; therefore, it can be used in **retort** applications, hot-filled and carbonated beverages, and baked goods. Sucralose does not interact with any other food components. Because absorption of sucralose is limited and the small amount that is absorbed is not metabolized, it imparts no caloric value to foods [22,33].

In April 1998, sucralose was approved by the FDA for use in several food and beverage categories. This sweetener was developed by a British firm and licensed for U.S. distribution. As a tabletop sweetener it is marketed in packets, tablets, and granular form under the Splenda® brand. Sucralose has been marketed for some time in several other countries, including Canada and Mexico, as a component of a diverse range of food products.

retort a commercial pressure canner

Neotame

In July 2002, the FDA approved neotame for use in foods (Figure 11-7). Neotame is 7,000–13,000 times sweeter than sucrose [28]. Thus, it is more potent than any of the other alternative sweeteners currently approved in the United States [30]. It functions as a low calorie sweetener and a flavor enhancer. Neotame has a clean sweet taste that is "sugar-like" without undesirable taste characteristics. It has been shown to enhance some flavors like mint and to suppress other flavors such as bitterness and the "beany" flavors in some soy products.

The stability of neotame has some similarities to aspartame, although neotame is more stable in neutral pH conditions and can be used successfully in dairy foods and baked products. French scientists Claude Nofre and Jean-Marie Tinti, in work with the NutraSweet Company, developed this alternative sweetener [30]. Neotame can be made by the reaction of aspartame with 3,3-dimethylbutyraldehyde. However, unlike aspartame, neotame does not metabolize to phenylalanine, and thus no special labeling is needed for those with phenylketonuria (PKU). Neotame has been found safe for the general population, including children, pregnant women, and people with diabetes [30].

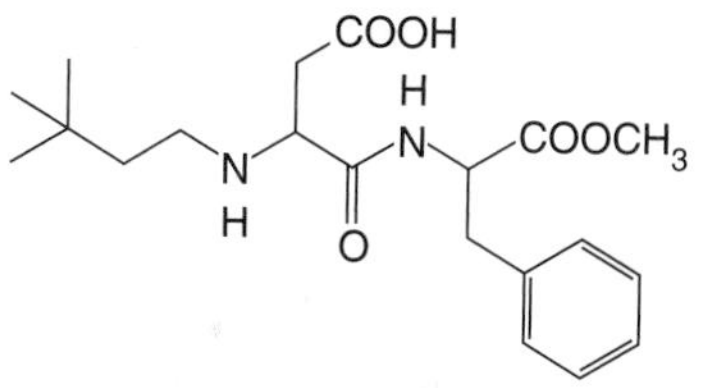

Figure 11-7
Structure of neotame. (Adapted from Reference [30])

Cyclamates

Cyclamates are currently not approved for use in the United States. In 1970, cyclamates were removed from the GRAS list and their use banned because of some questions about their possible carcinogenicity. A chronic toxicity study implicated sodium cyclamate as a possible bladder carcinogen in rats. Since

1970, several additional safety studies have been done on cyclamates and they have not been able to confirm the original findings of bladder cancer. A petition for their approval as a food additive was again filed with the FDA in 1982 and is still pending. Several other nations have approved the use of cyclamates [23].

Cyclamates are 30 times sweeter than sucrose, taste much like sugar, and are heat stable. The sweetness has a slow onset and then persists for a period of time. Cyclamate was discovered in 1937 and was used in the United States for a number of years. In 1958, with the passage of the Food Additives Amendment, cyclamates were classified as GRAS substances until their ban.

Other Alternative Sweeteners

peptide a chemical molecule composed of amino acids linked together

Other high-intensity sweeteners hold promise for future regulatory approval in the United States. Alitame is a **peptide** that is 2,000 times sweeter than a 10 percent solution of sucrose. It may be metabolized in the body, but would give minimal caloric value, because only a small amount of sweetener would be required to match the sweetness of sucrose. Alitame is highly soluble and has good stability under a variety of manufacturing conditions, although an off-taste may occur in warm acidic solutions. It may be used in combination with other low-calorie sweeteners. Alitame is already in use in several other countries, including Mexico [22].

Thaumatin is a small protein extracted by physical methods from the berry of a West African plant—sometimes called the miraculous fruit. It is listed in the *Guinness Book of World Records* as the sweetest substance known—2,000 to 2,500 times sweeter than an 8 to 10 percent solution of sucrose. Although it is metabolized in the body and yields 4 kilocalories per gram, its low usage levels make it basically noncaloric. Since it is a natural product, it is listed as GRAS in the United States. A United Kingdom company produces and markets thaumatin under the trade name Talin®. This protein interacts with taste receptors on the tongue to mask unpleasant tastes, such as metallic and bitter flavors. It also acts as a flavor enhancer in a similar fashion to monosodium glutamate and the 5′-nucleotides. It functions synergistically with other high-intensity sweeteners, allowing reduced levels of these substances [40].

SUGAR ALCOHOLS (POLYOLS)

polyol a sugar alcohol

Low calorie sweeteners lack the bulk needed for many food products. Sugar alcohols are therefore used with low calorie sweeteners to improve bulk, mouth-feel, and texture [28]. Eight **polyols** (erythritol, mannitol, isomalt, lactitol, maltitol, xylitol, sorbitol, and hydrogenated starch hydrolysates) are approved for use in the United States. Foods sweetened with polyols may be labeled with "sugar free" or "does not promote tooth decay" claims; however, these foods may not meet the requirements of a "reduced calorie food." Reduced calorie foods must contain 25 percent less calories than the full calorie product. Those who are following a diabetic or weight reduction diet should be aware of the caloric value of sugar alcohols [26]. The following caloric values are permitted by the FDA in the labeling of polyols: 0.2 kcal/gram for erythritol, 1.6 for mannitol, 2.0 for isomalt and lactitol, 2.1 for maltitol, 2.4 for xylitol, 2.6 for sorbitol, and 3.0 for hydrogenated starch hydrolysates [28].

Erythritol is a monosaccharide polyol that is naturally present in a number of fruits and vegetables. It is produced by the hydrolysis and fermentation of starch and purified by crystallization. Like other sugar alcohols, erythritol does not promote tooth decay or sudden increases in blood glucose. Unlike other sugar alcohols, however, it does not cause undesirable laxative side effects. It is about 70 percent as sweet as sucrose, has only 0.2 kilocalories per gram, and, when used with other high-intensity sweeteners, may round off the flavor. The FDA, in 1997, accepted for filing a GRAS affirmation petition [22,33]. Acceptance of this petition by the FDA allows manufacturers to produce and sell erythritol-containing foods in the United States. Erythritol is suitable for a variety of food products including chewing gum, candies, bakery products, beverages, and others.

Mannitol is used in food and pharmaceutical products. Mannitol is about 65 percent as sweet as sucrose [15]. It is often used as a dusting powder for chewing gum to prevent the gum from sticking with the wrapper. In medications, it effectively masks the bitter tastes of vitamins, minerals, and other ingredients. If the daily consumption of a particular food may exceed 20 grams of mannitol, the FDA requires the statement "excess consumption may have a laxative effect" on the label [28].

Isomalt is 0.45–0.6 times as sweet as sugar and can replace sugar in many products, often with minimal modifications in the formula [28]. Unlike most polyols, it does not produce a cooling effect. Lactitol is 0.4 times as sweet as sucrose. It is produced by hydrogenation of the milk sugar lactose [6]. A low calorie sweetener may need to be used in combination with lactitol to achieve the desired level of sweetness in some products [28]. Maltitol is made by hydrogenation of maltose [37]. It has a sweetness level that is 0.8 times that of sucrose. Like isomalt, malititol does not produce a cooling effect. Maltitol can be used as a fat replacer in some products in addition to its use as a sweetener.

Xylitol is used primarily in confections such as chewing gums, candies, chocolates, and gum drops. Xylitol is as sweet as sugar and has a significant cooling effect that enhances mint flavors. It has the advantage of being associated with the significantly reduced formation of new caries [28]. Sugar alcohols, such as xylitol, are **noncariogenic** because they are not fermented by bacteria [15]. Xylitol appears to be the best nutritive sweetener with respect to caries prevention.

noncariogenic not contributing to the development of caries in teeth

Sorbitol has been used for half a century in processed foods [28]. It is 0.6 times as sweet as sucrose and exhibits a cool, pleasant taste. Sorbitol is used in many food products for its sweetening ability, moisture stabilizing, and texture properties. Similar to the requirement for mannitol, the FDA requires that if the consumption of a food might exceed 50 grams of sorbitol, then the product must be labeled to inform consumers of the potential laxative effect.

Hydrogenated starch hydrolysates describes the broad group of polyols that contain hydrogenated oligo- and polysaccharides in addition to polyols such as sorbitol, mannitol, or maltitol. However, if the polyol mixture contains more than 50 percent sorbitol, for example, then it would be called sorbitol syrup [28]. Hydrogenated starch hydrolysates are 40–50 percent as sweet as sugar, and like the other polyols discussed, they are used as bulk sweeteners, bulking agents, and humectants, along with other functional roles.

BULKING AGENTS

Although many consumers today are looking for foods that are low in calories or "light," they still want them to be good tasting. Often, good-tasting food is synonymous with sweet food. Although it is relatively easy, with the approved nonnutritive sweeteners, to make a low-calorie product sweet, it is more challenging to match the other functions provided by sugar in the formulation [14]. One method is to use a bulking and bodying agent—something that is low in calories but provides volume, texture, and a thickened consistency. Bulking agents are also called *macronutrient substitutes*.

Polydextrose is a bulking agent that has been shown to be safe through extensive testing. It is an approved food additive used—often with an artificial sweetener—in such products as frozen desserts, puddings, baked goods, frostings, and candies. Polydextrose contributes 1 kilocalorie per gram, only one-fourth of the calories that sucrose or other sugars provide. Therefore, when used with aspartame and/or saccharin, it can reduce the caloric content of an item by 50 percent or more [14]. The materials used in the production of polydextrose are an 89 : 10 : 1 mixture of dextrose, sorbitol, and citric acid. One polydextrose product is marketed under the brand name Litesse™ [17].

Other bulking agents include cellulose and maltodextrins. Maltodextrins consist of glucose units with a dextrose equivalent (DE) of less than 20, and contribute 4 kilocalories per gram. Some fat-free products in which bulking agents may be used, such as fat-free cookies and granola bars, contain concentrated fruit juices and dried fruits as substitutes for added sugar.

Cookie dough intended to be frozen and then baked at the point of purchase was developed using acesulfame-K as the sweetener, with polydextrose, powdered cellulose, or soy fiber used as a bulking agent [7]. In one taste test, cookies made with polydextrose received the highest ratings by college students with a mean rating of 4.4 on a seven-point **hedonic scale.** Cookies made with cellulose were rated 3.3, and those with soy fiber 2.8. In another study involving the formulation of crisp oatmeal cookies, it was found that polydextrose was a suitable replacement for at least one-fourth of the shortening and a portion of sugar [8]. Both the bulking agent and the alternative sweetener should be chosen carefully to produce cookies with optimum hedonic scores.

hedonic scale a rating scale indicating the degree of liking, usually involving a range from 1 for "dislike extremely" to 7 for "like extremely"

SUGAR COOKERY

Sucrose, or table sugar, is the mainstay of the enormous worldwide chocolate and sugar confectionery industry. This industry has seen steady growth in the United States, at about 3 percent per year from 1980 through 2001.

In the preparation of concentrated sugar products, such as candies and frostings, many of the chemical and physical properties of sugar are of particular importance. The foundation for cooked frosting and candies is a boiled sugar solution. Some properties of solutions, therefore, are discussed here.

Boiling Points and Solutions

Boiling Pure Liquids. The boiling point of a liquid may be defined as the temperature at which the **vapor pressure** of the liquid is equal to the atmospheric pressure resting on its surface. At the boiling point, the vapor pressure of the liquid pushes against the atmospheric pressure to the extent that bubbles of vapor break and are released. Once boiling occurs, the temperature of the boiling liquid does not increase; an equilibrium is established.

vapor pressure the pressure produced over the surface of a liquid as a result of a change in some of the molecules from a liquid to a vapor or gaseous state

The boiling point of a liquid varies with altitude, because atmospheric pressure is lower at high altitudes and higher at low altitudes. The boiling point of water at sea level, where atmospheric pressure is about 15 pounds per square inch or barometric pressure is 760 millimeters of mercury, is taken as a standard. At sea level, water boils at 212°F (100°C). At higher altitudes, water boils below this temperature. For each 960 feet above sea level the boiling point of water drops 1°C (1.8°F). In mountainous areas, the low boiling point of water seriously interferes with many cooking operations, and thus methods and formulas usually require modification for use at high altitudes.

The boiling point of water may be lowered artificially by creating a partial vacuum, which is accomplished by withdrawing part of the air and steam above a boiling liquid, and thus lowering the air and steam pressure. Similarly, the boiling point may be elevated by an increase in air or steam pressure. The pressure cooker, which is a tightly closed utensil, increases pressure by preventing the vapor above the liquid from escaping. The pressure of the accumulated steam is thus added to that of the atmosphere above the liquid.

Boiling Solutions. Anything that decreases the vapor pressure of a liquid increases its boiling point. Substances in true solution, such as sugar or salt, that do not become volatile or gaseous at the boiling point of water will decrease the vapor pressure of the water in which they are dissolved, because these molecules displace water molecules on the surface of the liquid. The boiling point is thus increased because it takes more heat to raise the lowered vapor pressure to the point where it is equal to atmospheric pressure (Figure 11-8). When dissolved substances ionize in solution, as does salt, they decrease the vapor pressure and, therefore, raise the boiling point of the water to an even greater degree. The extent is dependent on the number of particles or ions formed. The larger the number of particles of solute in the solution, the more the vapor pressure is lowered and the higher the temperature of boiling.

Boiling sugar solutions do not reach a constant boiling point as does water alone. As water evaporates and the remaining solution thus becomes more con-

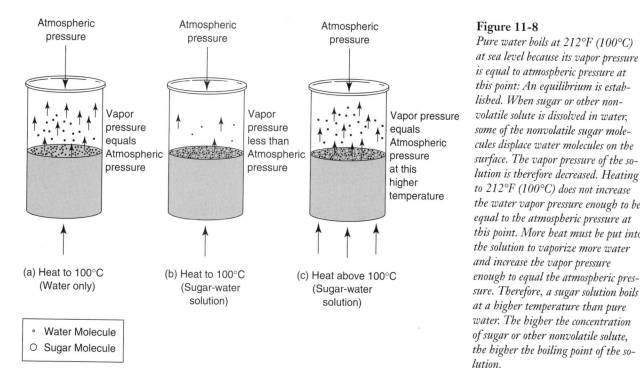

(a) Heat to 100°C
    (Water only)

(b) Heat to 100°C
    (Sugar-water solution)

(c) Heat above 100°C
    (Sugar-water solution)

∘ Water Molecule
○ Sugar Molecule

Figure 11-8
Pure water boils at 212°F (100°C) at sea level because its vapor pressure is equal to atmospheric pressure at this point: An equilibrium is established. When sugar or other non-volatile solute is dissolved in water, some of the nonvolatile sugar molecules displace water molecules on the surface. The vapor pressure of the solution is therefore decreased. Heating to 212°F (100°C) does not increase the water vapor pressure enough to be equal to the atmospheric pressure at this point. More heat must be put into the solution to vaporize more water and increase the vapor pressure enough to equal the atmospheric pressure. Therefore, a sugar solution boils at a higher temperature than pure water. The higher the concentration of sugar or other nonvolatile solute, the higher the boiling point of the solution.

centrated, the boiling temperature increases. This process continues until all the water is evaporated or the solubility of the sugar is exceeded. The boiling points of some pure sucrose solutions of various concentrations are given in Table 11-2. These figures are for sucrose solutions alone and do not apply to mixed sugar solutions such as sucrose solutions containing corn syrup, glucose, or molasses, which are more commonly used in making candy than pure sucrose solutions. Candy mixtures are, however, predominantly sucrose.

Calibrating and Reading the Thermometer. The first step in candy making is to calibrate the thermometer by taking the temperature of boiling water. If the thermometer does not show the proper temperature for the altitude, an adjustment is made by adding or subtracting, as appropriate, the difference in degrees between the expected and observed temperatures.

In taking the temperature of boiling sugar solutions, the bulb of the thermometer should be completely immersed in the solution but should not touch the bottom of the pan. In reading the scale, the eye should be on a level with the top of the mercury column.

Inversion of Sucrose

The hydrolysis of some sucrose to produce equal amounts of glucose and fructose, a mixture called *invert sugar*, helps control sugar crystallization in candy making. Thus, it deserves some special consideration in our discussion.

Because a mixture of invert sugar and sucrose is more soluble than a sucrose solution alone, and thus less easily crystallized, the mixture allows the process of crystallization to be more easily controlled than when invert sugar is not present. Desirably small sugar crystals can therefore be produced in crystalline candies such as fondant and fudge. Although a small amount of invert sugar is formed by the long, slow heating of a plain sucrose solution, the reaction is accelerated by the presence of a weak acid. Cream of tartar, an acid salt, is probably the preferable acid to use in most candy making, because its composition is fairly uniform and measurements are usually quite accurate. In addition, fondant made with cream of tartar is snowy white.

The amount of inversion that occurs when sucrose is heated with water and acid varies greatly and is difficult to control. The rate of heating, the length of heating, and the quantity of cream of tartar used all affect the amount of invert sugar formed. If too much acid is used, or if the period of heating is too long, too much inversion occurs, with the result that the fondant is extremely soft or fails to crystallize at all. It has been found that the presence of 43 percent invert sugar prevents crystallization completely.

Usually, about 1/4 teaspoon of cream of tartar is used with 2 cups of sugar in making fondant. It has been reported [44] that in fondant cooked to 239°F

Table 11-2
The Boiling Points of Sucrose Solutions of Various Concentrations at Sea Level

Percent Sucrose	10	20	30	40	50	60	70	80	90.8
Boiling Point									
°F	212.7	213.1	213.8	214.7	215.6	217.4	223.7	233.6	266.0
°C	100.4	110.6	101.0	101.5	102.0	103.0	106.5	112.0	130.0

Source: Browne's *Handbook of Sugar Analysis.* Reprinted by permission of John Wiley & Sons, Inc.

(115°C) in 20 minutes, approximately 1/8 teaspoon cream of tartar with 1 cup (200 grams) sugar produced about 11 percent invert sugar in the finished fondant.

Glucose, fructose, or invert sugar may be added directly to sucrose solutions in candy making rather than producing invert sugar during cooking by the addition of cream of tartar. Direct addition of these substances makes control of their quantity easier than trying to regulate the amount of invert sugar produced by sucrose hydrolysis. Corn syrup, which contains a high proportion of glucose, is sometimes used instead of cream of tartar in fondant mixtures. The glucose in the sucrose solution has an effect similar to that of invert sugar in increasing the solubility of the sucrose and allowing better control of the crystallization process so that small sugar crystals are produced in the final product.

CLASSIFICATION OF CANDIES

Either *crystalline* or *noncrystalline* candies may be produced from boiled sugar solutions. Crystalline candies are generally soft. If properly made, they are so smooth and creamy that the tiny sugar crystals that comprise their microscopic structure cannot be felt on the tongue. The principal crystalline candies are fondant, fudge, and panocha. Divinity, with added egg white, is also a crystalline candy.

Noncrystalline candies are sometimes called *amorphous*, which means "without form." In their preparation, by use of various ingredients and techniques, crystallization of sugar is prevented. Noncrystalline candies may be chewy, such as caramels, or hard, such as butterscotch, toffees, and brittles.

Crystalline Candies

Fondant. Fondant is the soft, smooth candy that results from the cooking of a sucrose solution to a certain range of temperatures, after which the solution is cooled and beaten until crystallization occurs. A simple sucrose and water solution sometimes makes good fondant; however, more satisfactory results are generally obtained by the addition of acid to accelerate inversion or by the direct addition of invert sugar, glucose, or corn syrup to aid in keeping crystals small. Use of milk or cream (as the liquid) increases the creamy character of fondant.

Essential steps in the making of fondant include (1) complete solution of the crystalline sugar, (2) concentration of the solution to the desirable stage, and (3) prevention of crystallization until conditions are favorable for the formation of fine crystals.

Solution. Complete solution of sugar is accomplished by adding sufficient liquid to dissolve the amount of sugar used, stirring, and covering the pan at the beginning of cooking to allow steam to dissolve any crystals that may remain on the sides of the pan. Instead of covering the pan, the sides of the pan may be washed with a small piece of moistened paper towel or cheesecloth wrapped around a fork (see Figure 11-9).

Undissolved crystals may cause seeding while the solution is cooling and start crystallization before it is desirable. The pan cannot remain covered throughout the cooking period, however, because evaporation must occur to bring about the necessary concentration within a reasonable time period. Stirring the solution during cooking does not start crystallization, but stirring and vigorous boiling may splash syrup on the sides of the pan above the level of the

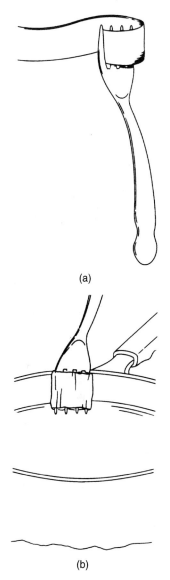

(a)

(b)

Figure 11-9

Complete solution of sugar. Wipe all sugar crystals from the sides of the pan as the candy mixture begins to boil. (a) Roll a small strip of moistened paper towel or cheesecloth around the tines of the fork. (b) Dip the covered fork in and out of a cup of clean water as the sides of the pan are wiped free of sugar crystals. The extra water on the wrapped fork goes into the boiling sugar solution.

liquid. Here it may dry, crystallize, drop into the cooling syrup, and start premature crystallization. The spoon used for stirring may also introduce dried crystals unless it is well rinsed between stirrings. It is best to wash the crystals from the sides of the pan again during the boiling period if more crystals form after the initial washing.

Concentration. Table 11-3 gives the temperatures and tests of doneness for candies of various types. As may be seen, the temperature range for the final cooking of fondant mixtures at sea level is 234° to 240°F (112° to 115°C). The lower temperature gives a very soft fondant, and the upper temperature gives a firmer, drier fondant for easier molding. A temperature of 234°F (112°C) may be a little low except for fondants for special uses (remelting) or for fondants containing corn syrup. When corn syrup is used in candy, definite stages of firmness are reached at slightly lower temperatures than when it is not used. For general use, 235° to 237°F (113° to 114°C) are the most satisfactory temperatures for fondants. The higher the temperature, the lower the water content and consequently the drier the fondant. When the humidity is high, higher temperatures are desirable, because more water is absorbed by fondant in damp weather. At altitudes above sea level, the final boiling temperatures should be lowered to the extent that the boiling point of water is decreased below 212°F (100°C).

Testing the doneness of candy mixtures by measuring the temperature of the boiling solution is a method of estimating the concentration of sugar in the mixture. The final concentration of sugar is related, in general, to the consistency of the candy when it is completely prepared—the more concentrated the sugar solution, the firmer the consistency of the finished candy. Another method of measuring doneness in candy making is to drop a small portion of the boiling syrup into very cold water, allow the syrup to cool, and evaluate its

Table 11-3
Temperatures and Tests for Syrup and Candies

Product	Final Temperature of Syrup at Sea Level*		Test of Doneness	Description of Test
	°F	°C		
Syrup	230–234	110–112	Thread	Syrup spins a 2 in. thread when dropped from fork or spoon.
Fondant	234–240	112–115	Soft ball	Syrup, when dropped into very cold water, forms a soft ball that flattens on removal from water.
Fudge				
Panocha				
Caramels	244–248	118–120	Firm ball	Syrup, when dropped into very cold water, forms a firm ball that does not flatten on removal from water.
Divinity	250–256	121–130	Hard ball	Syrup, when dropped into very cold water, forms a ball that is hard enough to hold its shape, yet plastic.
Marshmallows				
Popcorn balls				
Butterscotch	270–290	132–143	Soft crack	Syrup, when dropped into very cold water, separates into threads that are hard but not brittle.
Taffies				
Brittle	300–310	149–154	Hard crack	Syrup, when dropped into very cold water, separates into threads that are hard and brittle.
Glacé				
Barley sugar	320	160	Clear liquid	The sugar liquifies.
Caramel	338	170	Brown liquid	The liquid becomes brown.

*For each increase of 500 feet in elevation, cook the syrup to a temperature 1°F lower than the temperature called for at sea level. If readings are taken in Celsius, for each 960 feet of elevation, cook the syrup to a temperature 1°C lower than that called for at sea level.

(a)   (b)   (c)

Figure 11-10

The concentration of sugar syrups is best measured with a candy thermometer. Spooning a few drops of the syrup into very cold water will provide another measure of concentration as shown by the soft, hard, and hard crack stages in these pictures. (a) Soft ball stage; (b) Hard ball stage; (c) Hard crack stage.

consistency. The results of the cold water tests of doneness are compared with the temperatures of cooking in Table 11-3 and are shown in Figure 11-10.

The desired rate of cooking fondant mixtures depends partly on the proportions of ingredients used. Faster boiling is necessary if a high proportion of water is used to avoid too long a cooking period and consequently too great inversion in acid solutions. Violent boiling is usually to be avoided because of the larger amount of syrup that is splashed on the sides of the pan.

When the syrup is boiled to the desired degree of doneness, it may be poured onto a smooth flat surface, such as a marble-topped counter, on which it can later be beaten. Alternatively, it may be cooled in the pan in which it was cooked. In this case, the cooling period is considerably extended. As the hot syrup cools, it becomes saturated and then supersaturated because it is holding in solution more solute (sugar) than is normally soluble at the lower temperatures. As discussed, this condition is unstable so the product must be handled carefully to avoid premature crystallization. The syrup should be poured quickly, taking care not to scrape the pan. Scraping, prolonged dripping from the pan, or jostling of the poured syrup usually start crystallization. Uneven cooling may start crystallization in those portions of the syrup that first become supersaturated. If a thermometer is placed in the syrup to determine when the syrup is ready for beating, it should be read without its being moved in the syrup.

Crystallization.   An important aim in making crystalline candies is to produce a very smooth texture. For this to be achieved, many fine crystals, rather than few large crystals, must be formed. For small-crystal structure, conditions must be conducive to the formation, within the supersaturated solution, of many nuclei or small clumps of molecules. These act as centers around which crystal formation may begin. Some substances readily crystallize from a water solution with only a slight degree of supersaturation. With other substances, such as sugar, there must usually be a high degree of supersaturation before formation of nuclei and crystallization start.

The presence of substances that interfere with crystallization of sucrose in fondant and other candies is desirable, but at an optimum level. Glucose, corn syrup, or invert sugar, either added directly or formed by acid hydrolysis, affect crystallization because they make the sugar solution more soluble and, therefore, decrease the ease of crystal formation. Other substances, including fats from milk, cream, butter, margarine, and chocolate, and proteins from milk and egg white, do not themselves crystallize. They physically interfere with the process of sugar crystallization, retarding the growth of crystals. All of these interfering substances aid in fine crystal formation and smooth texture in crystalline candies.

The temperature at which crystallization occurs affects the size of crystals, primarily because it affects the rate of crystallization. In general, the higher the temperature at which crystallization occurs, the faster the rate of crystallization and the more difficult it is to keep the crystals separated, resulting in larger crystals. Cooling the mixture to about 104°F (40°C) before starting to beat it favors the formation of more nuclei and finer crystals. The viscosity of the solution is also greater at lower temperatures. High viscosity is a further aid in the production of fine crystals because it retards crystallization. Figure 11-11 shows the sizes of crystals formed in fondant beaten at different temperatures. The syrup could be cooled to so low a temperature that beating is impossible. Too low a temperature may also hinder the formation of many nuclei.

Agitation or stirring favors the formation of finer crystals than are produced spontaneously. Therefore, it is important to stir a crystalline candy, not only until crystallization starts, but until it is complete. As crystallization proceeds, the candy stiffens and becomes moldable. It can be kneaded in your hands (see Figure 11-12). It is important to work rapidly to prevent hardening and crumbling of the fondant before kneading is started. It is usually possible to see when the fondant is about to set in a more stiff mass. Its shiny appearance becomes dulled, and it seems to soften temporarily. The softening is the result of the heat of crystallization being given off as the crystals form.

Ripening.   As crystalline candy stands after crystallization is complete, it becomes somewhat more moist and smooth and kneads more easily, because some of the very small crystals dissolve in the syrup. Changes that occur during the initial period of storage are called *ripening*. Adsorbed substances that interfere with crystallization aid in retarding the growth of crystals during storage.

Proportions for Fondant

With Cream of Tartar	With Corn Syrup
2 cups (400 g) granulated sugar	2 cups (400 g) granulated sugar
1/4 tsp cream of tartar	1 to 1 1/2 Tbsp (21 to 39 g) syrup
1 cup (237 mL) water	1 cup (237 mL) water

Fudge.   The principles of making fudge do not differ from those of making fondant. Usually the butter or margarine, the fat of chocolate, and the milk proteins and fat furnish the substances that interfere with crystallization. Acid is sometimes used, and corn syrup may be used. If brown sugar replaces part or all of the white sugar, some invert sugar is introduced into the mixture. Also, a small amount of acid in the brown sugar helps invert sucrose. Therefore, brown sugar fudge (panocha) crystallizes less rapidly than white sugar fudge. When

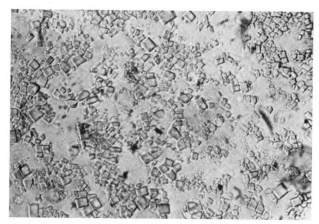

Crystals from fondant made with sugar, water, and cream of tartar, boiled to 239°F (115°C) and cooled to 104°F (40°C) before beating.

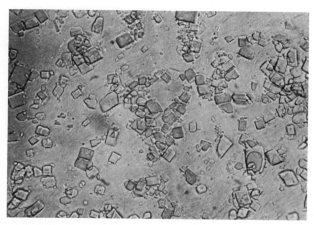

Crystals from fondant made with sugar and water with 7 percent glucose added, boiled to 239°F (115°C), and cooled to 104°F (40°C) before beating.

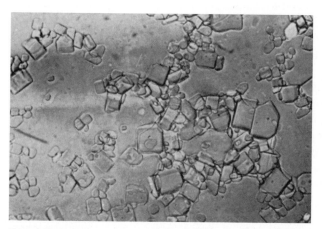

Crystals from fondant made with sugar and water only, boiled to 239°F (115°C) and cooled to 104°C) before beating.

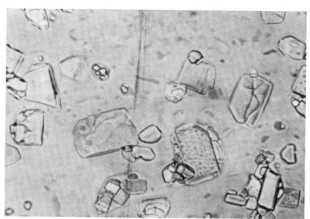

Crystals from fondant made with sugar and water only, boiled to 239°F (115°C) and beaten immediately.

Figure 11-11
Comparison of sugar crystal size with various methods of making fondant. (Courtesy of Dr. Sybil Woodruff and the *Journal of Physical Chemistry*)

crystallization is almost complete, the initially glossy fudge becomes dull, and the whole mass softens slightly, as it does for fondant (Figures 11-13 and 11-14). The fudge should be poured from the pan before it hardens.

Noncrystalline Candies

Sugar does not crystallize in noncrystalline candies. The crystallization is prevented by (1) cooking to very high temperatures so that the finished product hardens quickly or solidifies before the crystals have a chance to form, (2) adding such large amounts of interfering substances that the crystals cannot form, or (3) combining these methods.

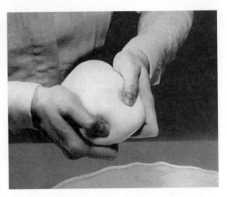

Figure 11-12
Fondant is manipulated with a spatula after it has cooled to 104°F (40°C). Some form of agitation is needed until crystallization is complete. The fondant is then quickly formed into a ball and kneaded until smooth. (Courtesy of General Foods, Inc.)

Maillard reaction the carbonyl group of a sugar combines with the amino group of a protein, initiating a series of chemical reactions which result in a brown color and change in flavor

Brittles. Brittles are cooked to temperatures that are high enough to produce a hard, brittle candy that solidifies before it has a chance to crystallize. The brown color and characteristic flavor of brittles result from nonenzymatic browning reactions, probably both the **Maillard** type and the caramelization of sugar. The development of caramel also helps to prevent crystallization of sugar in the brittles because it is noncrystalline.

Some brittles are made merely by melting and caramelizing sucrose. Soda is sometimes a constituent of brittles and is added after cooking is completed. It neutralizes acid decomposition products and forms carbon dioxide gas, which gives the candy a porous texture. The flavor is also made milder and less bitter by the use of soda. The degree of bitterness in a brittle depends on the extent of decomposition of the sugar. Brittles include butterscotch, nut brittles, and toffee.

Fudge that has been beaten too long and has hardened in the pan.

Fudge beaten to the correct stage for pouring into a dish to harden.

Figure 11-13
Fudge should be beaten to the correct consistency before it is poured out to harden. (Courtesy of Best Foods)

Figure 11-14
Blonde and chocolate fudge.
(Courtesy of Best Foods)

Chocolate fudge is made by adding unsweetened chocolate to the basic ingredients before starting to cook.

Caramels. Caramels are firm, noncrystalline candies containing large amounts of interfering substances. They are cooked to temperatures between those for crystalline candies and hard brittle candies. The added substances that interfere with crystallization are usually butter or margarine and viscous corn syrup or molasses, which contain glucose, fructose, or invert sugar. Corn syrup also contains dextrins, which do not crystallize. Acid hydrolysis may be used to produce invert sugar, but more inversion is necessary for caramels than for fondant. Fats and proteins in milk or cream also aid in preventing crystallization. The final cooking temperature varies with the kind and proportion of ingredients. The brown color of caramels results chiefly from the Maillard reaction. The color and flavor of caramels develop better with long, slow heating than with rapid cooking. The characteristic flavor of plain caramels may be modified somewhat by the addition of chocolate or molasses.

Taffy. Taffy can be made from a simple sucrose syrup with the addition of cream of tartar, vinegar, or lemon juice to invert part of the sucrose and prevent crystallization. Flavoring extracts may be added when the solution has cooled sufficiently for pulling. Glucose, corn syrup, or molasses can be used instead of acid. Taffies are harder than caramels and therefore require higher cooking temperatures.

Fondant Confections

Fondant has many possible uses. It may be made into bonbons, which are fondant centers dipped in melted fondant, or into fondant loaves, which have fruit and nut mixtures added. Centers for chocolates are commonly made from fondant. Fondant patties are made from melted fondant that is flavored and colored as desired. Candy cookbooks suggest many specific combinations of fondant with other ingredients.

Fondant Dipping. Fondant centers are prepared ahead of time from fondant of a suitable texture for molding. The molded centers are allowed to stand on waxed paper until firm and slightly hardened on the outside. The fondant for melting may be of softer consistency than that used for molding.

Only a small quantity—about 1 cup—of fondant should be melted at one time. In a container of appropriate size, this quantity provides sufficient depth to coat the centers easily yet not enough to become too coarse and granular before it can be used.

The fondant is best melted over hot water. While melting, the solid fondant is broken up or turned frequently but with a minimum amount of stirring. Formation of coarse crystals by the stirring of a hot solution is as important here as in the making of the original fondant. While the fondant is melting, food colors in liquid or paste form may be applied on the point of a toothpick. Care should be taken to avoid adding too much color. Food flavors, if they are in the form of oils, must be added with equal care to avoid too strong a flavor. Extracts are more dilute.

After the fondant is melted, colored, and flavored, it must be cooled slightly to such a consistency that it clings to the molded fondant during dipping. The molded pieces of fondant are quickly dipped into the melted fondant and are then placed on waxed paper in a cool environment to set. The following colors and flavors are often used together:

Color	Flavor
Red	Oil of cinnamon or cloves
Green	Oil of lime
White	Oil of peppermint
Pink	Oil of wintergreen
Yellow	Oil of lemon
Orange	Oil of orange

Fondant Patties.   Fondant patties are also made from melted fondant. After the melted fondant is colored and flavored, it is dropped on waxed paper from a teaspoon—1/2 to 1 teaspoon may be used, according to the size of patty desired. Speed is necessary to dip and pour the fondant before it begins to harden. If the melted fondant becomes too stiff to flow into a smooth patty, it should be remelted or a very small amount of hot water should be added to it.

Chocolate Dipping

The chocolate used for ordinary culinary purposes is not generally suitable for dipping candies. Dipping chocolate should be of fine quality and contain sufficient cocoa butter to promote hardening with a smooth, glossy finish.

Centers to be coated with chocolate should be prepared several hours before dipping so that they are firm enough to handle easily. An exception is fondant centers to which invertase enzyme has been added; this type of fondant becomes softer the longer it stands.

Successful chocolate dipping depends largely on the use of a suitable chocolate; the control of temperatures and avoidance of a humid atmosphere; and thorough stirring or hand manipulation of the chocolate while it is melting and cooling, and, so far as possible, while dipping. Manipulation of the chocolate ensures uniform blending of the cocoa butter with the other chocolate constituents and produces a more even coating.

Temperatures and Techniques. Room temperature and humidity are well controlled in commercial chocolate dipping rooms. The temperature should be 60° to 70°F (15° to 20°C). A clear, cool day of low relative humidity is desirable. Drafts should be avoided, as uneven cooling affects the gloss and color of chocolates.

Even melting of the chocolate is facilitated by grating, shaving, or fine chopping. The chocolate should be melted over hot (not boiling) water; higher temperatures may allow the cocoa butter to separate out. While the chocolate is melting, it should be stirred continuously. Stirring prevents uneven heating and overheating and maintains a uniform blend. Water should not be allowed to get into the melting chocolate, as it can cause the chocolate to become lumpy.

After the chocolate has melted, it should be taken to a temperature of about 120°F (49°C) for tempering. It should then be continuously stirred while being cooled to about 85°F (29°C). At this point the chocolate is ready for dipping. The range of temperatures at which chocolates can be satisfactorily dipped is narrow; hence rapid dipping is necessary. Fondant centers may be dropped into the chocolate, coated, and lifted out with a wire chocolate dipper or a two-tined fork. The coated chocolate is inverted on waxed paper. Another method of dipping chocolates is to pour the melted chocolate onto a marble-topped surface and stir it with the hand. Fondant centers may be rolled in the melted chocolate; the surplus chocolate is removed by tapping the fingers lightly on the marble surface, and then the coated chocolate is dropped quickly onto waxed paper (see Figure 11-15).

Defects of Dipped Chocolates. The chief defects of dipped chocolates are gray or streaked surfaces, a broad base on the dipped chocolate, or sticky spots on the surface. Gray surfaces are caused by unfavorable room temperatures, incorrect temperatures during melting and handling the chocolate, direct drafts, excessive humidity, insufficient stirring of the chocolate, and not rapid enough cooling of the chocolate. The surface of a defective chocolate appears dull and gray because the fat of the chocolate has not crystallized in a stable form.

Chocolate is mixed until it reaches the correct temperature for dipping.

A fondant center is rolled in the chocolate and then placed on waxed paper in a cool room. The chocolate should set up or harden immediately.

Figure 11-15
Chocolate dipping. (Photographs by Roger P. Smith and Ava Winterton)

A broad base on the dipped chocolate results from dipping at too high temperatures or from failure to remove excess chocolate after dipping. Sticky spots result from leakage of the centers because of incomplete coating with chocolate. These spots are particularly likely to occur in chocolates made from fondants that liquefy on standing.

THE CONFECTIONERY INDUSTRY

The confectionery business has experienced a healthy growth rate in recent years [38]. Increased sales have occurred in both the nonchocolate and chocolate sectors.

A variety of ingredients are available to the commercial confectioner to help improve texture, prevent defects, add gloss, enhance flavor release, and aid processing in the manufacture of candies. These include quick-setting starch to reduce drying time for jelly gum candies, encapsulated flavors and colors for customized products, blends of acidulants to improve taste properties of hard candies, lecithin products to act as emulsifiers in caramels and toffees, and polishing and sealing systems for chocolate-based products. Sugar-free and low-fat confections are being developed in increasing quantities. Various hydrocolloids, such as pectins, starches, gelatin, and gums, are playing important roles as textural or stabilizing agents in the manufacture of many confectionery products, including lower-fat and calorie-reduced items [9, 32].

inulin a white polysacchride found in the roots of some plants, which yield fructose when hydrolyzed

oligofructose an oligosaccharide; a carbohydrate molecule made up of a small number of fructose molecules linked together

---

Healthy Eating

Confections—Indulging or health-promoting?

Donald Pszczola [34] attended the 2002 All Candy Expo in Chicago and found himself in a new world of candies and confectionary ingredients, including a product called Atomic Fizzzion. Pressurized carbon dioxide is injected into this candy in its molten form, trapping small gas bubbles inside which, as the candy dissolves in the mouth, produce tiny explosions.

The liking for "sweets" appears to be universal. And some of us find particular reassurance in the enjoyment of chocolate confections when things are not going so well in our lives. Consumers are apparently purchasing more snack-size chocolate bars and bite-size chocolate candies and are also showing preference for higher-quality, gourmet chocolates [34]. Pure indulgence?

Well, potential health benefits of chocolate continue to be studied, including its content of antioxidants and the ability of dark chocolate to raise HDL cholesterol (the good kind) levels in the blood. With a wide variety of confectionery ingredients being developed, candies are increasingly being promoted for their health properties as well as for their gastronomic enjoyment. Examples of "functional confections" may include candies with added cholesterol-lowering phytosterols and phytostanols, chocolate with increased levels of antioxidants, and vitamin and mineral fortified confections. Using dietary fibers, **inulin** and **oligofructose,** unique candies can be produced that are lower in sugar and contribute desirable dietary fiber to the diet. With such ingredients as soy protein, special oils, antioxidant and other nutrients, alternative sweeteners, and exotic flavorings, the possibilities for health-promoting confections that also indulge our appetites seem almost limitless. Enjoy! Chocolate can be part of a healthy eating plan if based on balance, variation, and moderation [34].

PLATE I

Food in space. (Courtesy of National Aeronautics and Space Administration (NASA))

NASA astronauts gather around to decide what's for dinner.

A typical space station meal tray with utensils anchored to the tray.

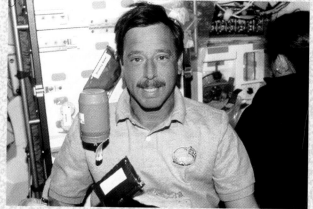

An ordinary PB&J sandwich made on a flour tortilla in a not-so-ordinary way.

Astronauts catching their food adds a whole new meaning to meals on the go.

PLATE II

Seasonings and flavorings.

Yellow onions are used in many dishes to add flavor. (Courtesy of U.S. Department of Agriculture)

Peppers not only add flavor but color as well. This group of peppers represents many colors as well as "degrees of heat." (Courtesy of U.S. Department of Agriculture)

PLATE III

Soup.

Rice and vegetables combined with chicken, cheese, and crispy tortillas makes a different and delicious soup. (Courtesy of Riceland U.S.A)

Black beans are mixed with peppers and topped with rice to create a hearty soup. (Courtesy of Riceland U.S.A)

Grains and Pasta.

This dish is made with couscous and accented with various vegetables. (Courtesy of Land O'Lakes)

Breaded and baked ravioli is a non-traditional way to serve pasta and makes a great appetizer. (Courtesy of Land O'Lakes)

PLATE IV

Grains and pasta.

These tomatoes are filled with rice and seasonings then baked producing an interesting way to eat your grains and veggies. (Courtesy of the USA Rice Federation)

Bulgur, a grain, can be combined with fruit to make a tasty breakfast dish. (Courtesy of Dole Food Company Inc.)

Herbs and bowtie pasta are tossed to create this Mediterranean style pasta salad. (Courtesy of Dole Food Company Inc.)

Pasta can be combined with almost any type of food. Here a primavera is created using vegetables and surimi. (Courtesy of Alaska Seafood Marketing Inst.)

PLATE V

Quick breads.

These waffles are topped with berries and whipped cream for a dessert-like breakfast treat. (Courtesy of Land O'Lakes)

Muffins and scones such as these make great tea time snacks. (Courtesy of Land O'Lakes)

Sandwiches.

A cheeseburger can be garnished with cheese. (Courtesy of Cattlemen's Beef Board through the National Cattlemen's Beef Association.)

This sandwich made with cucumbers, cheese, tomatoes, lettuce, and dill cream cheese spread puts a new twist on lunch ideas. (Courtesy of Land O'Lakes)

This Hawaiian inspired sandwich features grilled chicken topped with pineapple rings. (Courtesy of Dole Food Company Inc.)

PLATE VI

Baking yeast breads can be a rewarding and creative experience. (Courtesy of Fleischmann's Yeast)

Breadsticks, white loaf bread, and seeded braid loaf

French bread, Italian bread, and Russian black bread displayed with fruit

Pecan caramel rolls

PLATE VII

Yeast breads.

These hearth breads are blended with various spices prior to baking. (Courtesy of Wheat Foods Council.)

Wheat before milling into flour. (Courtesy of Wheat Foods Council.)

A collection of bread types ranging from pretzels to bread sticks and loaves to pitas. (Courtesy of Wheat Foods Council.)

PLATE VIII

Cookies and desserts.

Cookies fresh out of the oven are always a family favorite. (Courtesy of Land O'Lakes)

Cookie bars, chocolate chip pie, and fudge can fulfill any chocolate lovers craving. (Courtesy of Nestlé.)

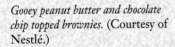
Gooey peanut butter and chocolate chip topped brownies. (Courtesy of Nestlé.)

PLATE IX

Quiche, pie, and tarts.

A New England chicken and corn quiche. (Courtesy of Land O'Lakes)

A dessert tart composed of fresh fruit, cream cheese, and a tart shell. (Courtesy of American Dairy Association)

An all-American classic—the apple pie. (Courtesy of the U.S. Department of Agriculture)

PLATE X

Varieties of apples. (Courtesy of Washington Apple Commission)

Red Delicious

Golden Delicious

Rome

Granny Smith

Winesap

Gala

Fuji

Criterion

Other fruits. (Courtesy of Washington State Fruit Commission; cherries courtesy of Northwest Cherry Growers)

Early Red Haven peaches

Red Gold nectarines

Empire plums

Lambert cherries

PLATE XI

Fresh fruits—pears. (1-5: Courtesy of Pear Bureau Northwest; 6: Courtesy of U.S. Department of Agriculture)

Bartlett

Red Bartlett

Anjou

Comice

Bosc

Pears growing on the tree

PLATE XII

Fresh fruits.

Strawberry shortcake, one of the many delicious desserts that can be made using fresh fruit. (Courtesy of U.S. Department of Agriculture)

Freshly picked blackberries, strawberries, and blueberries. (Courtesy of U.S. Department of Agriculture)

Cherries, grapefruit sections, and melon slices make an attractive fruit salad. (Courtesy of Northwest Cherry Growers)

Nectarine slices may be served with cheese for dessert. (Courtesy of Washington State Fruit Commission)

PLATE XIII

Specialty fruits.

Hawaiian papayas. (Courtesy of Agriculture Research Service, U.S. Department of Agriculture, photo by Scott Bauer.)

Carambolas, also called star fruit. (Courtesy of Agriculture Research Service, U.S. Department of Agriculture, photo by Scott Bauer.)

(Lower left) Asian pear, prickly pears, feijoas, fig (in front); (Right) passion fruit, tamarinds, tamarillos, carumbola (star fruit); (Upper left) atemoya (black seeds), cherimoya. (Courtesy of the United Fresh Fruit and Vegetable Association).

PLATE XIV

Potatoes and vegetables.

Cucumber, garlic, carrots, and green onions. (Courtesy of the U.S. Department of Agriculture)

(Lower left) tomatillos, chayote (cut); (Upper right to lower right) cilantro, radicchio, arugula; (Upper left to lower right) enoki mushrooms, shiitake mushrooms, oyster mushrooms. (Courtesy of the United Fresh Fruit and Vegetable Association)

(Left to right outside colander) russet, round white, round red, long white, russet, yellow; (Inside colander) two round red and round white. (Courtesy of The National Potato Promotion Board)

PLATE XV

Salads can add variety to menus.

Greens can be combined with non-traditional items, such as mango, to create an exotic salad. (Courtesy of Land O'Lakes)

A salad can be a simple, yet attractive vegetable and dip tray. (Courtesy of American Egg Board)

Spinach adds green color to orange and grapefruit sections, red onion wedges, and sliced avocado, the mixture tossed with lemon sesame dressing. (Courtesy of Sunkist Growers)

Broccoli florets, red sweet bell pepper, and orange slices are served with a mustard-dill salad dressing. (Courtesy of Sunkist Growers)

PLATE XVI

Several varieties of cheese.

(Clockwise from lower left) butter, cheese powder in scoop, flavored butter in dark crock, cheese powder in two tan crocks, milk, Cottage Cheese in Wisconsin crock, Cheddar wheel, cold pack in tan crock, Gouda, Brie with strawberry garnish, Manteche, Italian-style Gorgonzola, large Cheddar wheel, and shredded mild Cheddar. (©1998, Courtesy of Wisconsin Milk Marketing Board)

Camembert cheese, bread, peaches, and wine make a delicious combination. (Courtesy of American Dairy Association)

Swiss, Colby and Jack marble, cheddar, pepper jack, and a parmesan cheese wedge pictured with bread and sesame sticks. (Courtesy of American Dairy Association)

CHAPTER SUMMARY

- From disappearance data, published by the U.S. Department of Agriculture, it is apparent that the consumption of refined (cane and beet) sugar in the United States has increased since 1909.

- Sugar provides only energy for the body. Therefore, foods that contain relatively large amounts of sugar generally have low nutrient density.

- In the natural state of foods, sugars are in solution. The crystallization of sugar occurs from a sufficiently concentrated sugar solution. Common sugars vary in their solubilities. At room temperature, the relative solubilites in water of the common sugars are fructose (most soluble), followed by sucrose, glucose, maltose, and lactose. Solutions may be unsaturated, saturated, or supersaturated depending on the amount of sugar that is dissolved in the solution.

- With the application of sufficient dry heat, sugars melt or change to a liquid state. Granulated sugar, when heated dry in a heavy pan, caramelizes. Caramelization is one type of browning called *nonenzymatic browning*.

- Sugars absorb water as shown in many ways. Crystalline sugars become caked and lumpy when stored in moist environments and baked flour mixtures that are rich in sugar will take up moisture. Sugars are said to be hygroscopic because of the tendency to absorb moisture from the atmosphere. Fructose is more hygroscopic than the other sugars commonly found in food.

- Most sugars, except lactose, may be fermented by yeasts to produce carbon dioxide gas and alcohol. Fermentation is an important reaction in the making of bread and other baked products.

- The disaccharides are hydrolyzed by weak acids to produce their component monosaccharides. The end products of sucrose hydrolysis are a mixture of glucose and fructose, commonly called invert sugar. Hydrolysis may occur incidentally, or may be brought about purposely by the addition of an acid such as cream of tartar. Invert sugar is desirable in some sugar products, such as fondant, to improve the texture or consistency of the product.

- Enzymes also hydrolyze disaccharides. The enzyme sucrase, also called invertase, is used in the candy industry to hydrolyze some of the sucrose in cream fondant to fructose and glucose. Chocolate-coated cherries with a soft, semifluid center are an example of this reaction.

- The decomposition of sugars by alkalies also has significance in sugar cookery. The decomposition products of glucose and fructose are brownish and may be strong and bitter if the process of decomposition was extensive. Baked beans, fondant, cakes, and cookies may be browner and stronger in flavor as a result of alkaline decomposition of the sugars in these foods.

- The flavor of purified sugars is described as being sweet. The degree of sweetness that we perceive is affected by several factors, including genetic variation among individuals as well as the concentration of the sweetener, temperature, viscosity, pH, and the presence of other substances with the sweetener. In general, lactose is the least sweet, followed by maltose, galactose, glucose, and sucrose, with fructose being the most sweet.

- Crystals will form in a concentrated, supersaturated sugar solution. Table sugar is crystalline sucrose. It plays a variety of roles in food systems by affecting the texture of many baked goods, improving the body and texture of ice cream, being fermented by yeast to leaven breads, and preserving jams and jellies by retarding the growth of microorganisms. Table sugar is produced commercially from both sugar beets and sugar cane.

- Other forms of crystalline sugar include crystalline glucose, fructose, lactose, maltose, and maltodextrins. These forms often are used by the food industry.

- Other kinds of sugar include powdered and brown sugars. Powdered sugar is machine ground or pulverized from granulated sucrose. Brown sugar is obtained from cane sugar during the late stages of refining and is composed of clumps of sucrose crystals coated with a film of molasses.

- Corn syrups, high-fructose corn syrup, molasses, maple syrup, and honey each offer unique properties and flavors that are useful in food preparation.

- Sweeteners may be classified into two groups: nutritive sweeteners and nonnutritive sweeteners. Nonnutritive sweeteners (alternative sweeteners) are often called high-intensity sweeteners. Alternative sweeteners currently approved for use in the United State include saccharin, aspartame, acesulfame-K, sucralose, and neotame. Cyclamates are currently not approved for use in the United States. A petition for reapproval of this alternative sweetener has been filed with the FDA. No one alternative sweetener is best for every food product; therefore, sweeteners are chosen for the applications for which they will be best suited.

- High-intensity sweeteners lack the bulk needed for many food products. Sugar alcohols (polyols) are therefore used with low calorie sweeteners to improve bulk, mouthfeel, and texture. Eight polyols (erythritol, mannitol, isomalt, lactitol, maltitol, xylitol, sorbitol, and hydrogenated starch hydrolysates) are approved for use in the United States. Foods sweetened with polyols may be labeled with "sugar free" or "does not promote tooth decay" claims; however, these foods may not meet the requirements of a "reduced calorie food."

- Polydextrose, cellulose, and maltodextrins are bulking agents that may be used in low calorie foods. Bulking agents provide volume, texture, and a thickened consistency in products using nonnutritive sweeteners.

- In the preparation of candies and frostings, many of the chemical and physical properties of sugar are of particular importance. The foundation for cooked frostings and candies is a boiled sugar solution, thus the properties of solutions must be understood. Boiling sugar solutions do not reach a constant boiling point as does water alone because as the water evaporates, the solution becomes more concentrated, resulting in an increase in the boiling temperature.

- Invert sugar is important in candy making because a mixture of invert sugar and sucrose allows the process of crystallization to be more easily controlled. Thus, desirably small sugar crystals can be produced in crystalline candies such as fudge and fondant.

- Crystalline candies include fondant, fudge, panocha, and divinity with added egg white. An important aim in the preparation of crystalline candies is to produce a very fine texture. Agitation or stirring once the candy is at the desired temperature favors the formation of finer crystals.

- Noncrystalline candies include brittles, caramels, and taffy. Sugar does not crystallize in noncrystalline candies. The crystallization is prevented by (1) cooking to a very high temperature, (2) adding large amounts of interfering substances that prevent crystal formation, and (3) a combination of these methods.

KEY TERMS

disappearance data
monosaccharide
disaccharide
solution
crystallization
polymerization
fermentation
cream of tartar
dextrins
glucoamylase
β-amylase
reducing sugar
glucose isomerase
GRAS

carcinogen
epidemiology
ester
phenylketonuria
synergism
retort
peptide
polyol
noncariogenic
hedonic scale
vapor pressure
Maillard reaction
inulin
oligofructose

STUDY QUESTIONS

1. Sugars have many properties that are of importance in the preparation of candies and other sugar-containing foods.
   a. List the common sugars in order of their solubilities in water at room temperature and describe how the solubility of sugars is affected by temperature.
   b. Describe a saturated and a supersaturated solution and explain the significance of a supersaturated solution in making crystalline candies.
   c. What happens when sugar is heated in a dry state above its melting point? Why is this reaction important in food preparation?
   d. What is meant by *hygroscopic?* Which is the most hygroscopic sugar?
   e. Name the two monosaccharides that result from the hydrolysis of sucrose. What catalysts may cause sucrose hydrolysis? Describe examples of the importance of this reaction in food preparation, particularly in candy making.
   f. Describe examples from food preparation of the effect of sugar decomposition by alkali.
   g. Compare the common sugars for relative sweetness and discuss several factors that affect these comparisons. Under what conditions is fructose likely to taste most sweet?
2. Various types of sugars and syrups are available on the market. Describe the major characteristics of each of the following:
   a. Granulated sugar (sucrose)
   b. Powdered sugar
   c. Brown sugar

     d. Corn syrup

     e. High-fructose corn syrup

     f. Molasses

     g. Honey

     h. Maple syrup

3. Discuss trends in sweetener consumption in the United States in recent years.

4. List some sugar alcohols and describe their possible uses in foods.

5. **a.** Give several examples of nonnutritive, high-intensity, or alternative sweeteners.

     b. What is the present legal status of saccharin in the United States? Discuss.

     c. What is the chemical nature of aspartame? Of acesulfame-K? Of sucralose? Of neotame?

     d. Discuss some advantages and limitations to the use of alternative sweeteners in manufactured foods.

     e. Give examples of bulking agents and describe their role in the production of reduced-sugar foods.

6. **a.** What is the effect of sugar on the boiling point of water? Explain.

     b. Describe what happens as one continues to boil a sugar solution.

7. **a.** Name two major classifications for candies and describe the general characteristics of each type.

     b. Classify caramels, toffee, fondant, taffy, butterscotch, fudge, brittles, and panocha into the appropriate groups described in question a.

8. Describe the basic steps involved in the preparation of crystalline candies such as fondant and fudge. Explain what is happening in each step and how crystallization is controlled.

9. Describe the basic steps involved in the preparation of brittles and caramels. Explain how crystallization is prevented in each case.

10. Suggest several uses for basic fondant.

11. Describe and explain several precautions that must be observed for successful dipping of chocolates.

REFERENCES

1. American Dietetic Association. (1998). Position of the American Dietetic Association: Use of nutritive and nonnutritive sweeteners. *Journal of the American Dietetic Association, 98,* 580.

2. Awad, A., & Chen, A. C. (1993). A new generation of sucrose products made by cocrystallization. *Food Technology, 47*(1), 146.

3. Bartoshuk, L. M. (1991). Sweetness: History, preference, and genetic variability. *Food Technology, 45*(11), 108.

4. Bell, J. (1993). High intensity sweeteners—A regulatory update. *Food Technology 47*(11), 136.

5. Black, R. M. (1993). Sucrose in health and nutrition—Facts and myths. *Food Technology, 47*(1), 130.

6. Blankers, I. (1995). Properties and applications of lactitol. *Food Technology, 49*(1), 66.

7. Bullock, L. M., Handel, A. P., Segall, S., & Wasserman, P. A. (1992). Replacement of simple sugars in cookie dough. *Food Technology, 46*(1), 82.

8. Campbell, L. A., Ketelsen, S. M., & Antenucci, R. N. (1994). Formulating oatmeal cookies with calorie-sparing ingredients. *Food Technology, 48*(5), 98.

9. Carr, J. M., Sufferling, K., & Poppe, J. (1995). Hydrocolloids and their use in the confectionery industry. *Food Technology, 49*(7), 41.

10. Chen, L. A., & Parham, E. S. (1991). College students' use of high-intensity sweeteners is not consistently associated with sugar consumption. *Journal of the American Dietetic Association, 91*, 686.

11. Chinachoti, P. (1993). Water mobility and its relation to functionality of sucrose-containing food systems. *Food Technology, 47*(1),134.

12. Cohen, S. M. (1986). Saccharin: Past, present, and future. *Journal of the American Dietetic Association, 86*, 929.

13. Coulston, A. M. & Johnson, R. K. (2002). Sugar and sugars: Myths and realities. *Journal of the American Dietetic Association, 102*, 351–353.

14. Dziezak, J. D. (1986). Sweeteners and product development. *Food Technology, 40*(1), 112.

15. Dziezak, J. D. (1989). Ingredients for sweet success. *Food Technology, 43*(10), 94.

16. Fellows, J. W., Chang, S. W., & Shazer, W. H. (1991). Stability of aspartame in fruit preparations used in yogurt. *Journal of Food Science, 56*, 689.

17. Giese, J. H. (1993). Alternative sweeteners and bulking agents. *Food Technology, 47*(1), 114.

18. Guthrie, J. F., & Morton, J. F. (2002). Food sources of added sweeteners in the diets of Americans. *Journal of the American Dietetic Association, 100*, 43–51.

19. Hardy, S. L., Brennand, C. P., & Wyse, B. W. (1979). Fructose: Comparison with sucrose as sweetener in four products. *Journal of the American Dietetic Association, 74*, 41.

20. Henkel, J. (1999). Sugar substitutes: Americans opt for sweetness and lite. *FDA Consumer, 33*(6).

21. Hess, D. A., & Setser, C. S. (1986). Comparison of aspartame- and fructose-sweetened layer cakes: Importance of panels of users for evaluation of alternative sweeteners. *Journal of the American Dietetic Association, 86*, 919.

22. Hoch, G. J. (1997). Sweet anticipation. *Food Processing, 58*(12), 45.

23. Hollingsworth, P. (2002). Artificial sweeteners face sweet 'n sour consumer market. *Food Technology, 56*(7), 24–27.

24. Hollingsworth, P. (2002). Developing and marketing foods for diabetics. *Food Technology, 56*(10), 38.

25. Koivistoinen, P., & Hyvönen, L. (1980). *Carbohydrate sweeteners in foods and nutrition*. New York: Academic Press.

26. McNutt, K. (2000). What clients need to know about sugar replacers. *Journal of the American Dietetic Association, 100*, 466–469.

27. Mermelstein, N. H. (2002). Formulating foods for diabetics. *Food Technology, 56*(10), 42.

28. Nabors, L. O. (2002). Sweet choices: Sugar replacements for food and beverages. *Food Technology, 56*(7), 28–34, 45.

29. Noble, A. C., Matysiak, N. L., & Bonnans, S. (1991). Factors affecting the time-intensity parameters of sweetness. *Food Technology, 45*(11), 121.

30. Prakash, I., Corliss, G., Ponakala, R., & Ishikawa, G. (2002). Neotame: The next-generation sweetener. *Food Technology, 56*(7), 36–40, 45.

31. Pszczola, D. E. (1987). American fructose unveils new technologies in HFCS plant. *Food Technology, 41* (10), 50.

32. Pszczola, D. E. (1997). Ingredient developments for confections. *Food Technology, 51*(9), 70.

33. Pszczola, D. E. (1999). Sweet beginnings to a new year. *Food Technology, 53*(1), 70.

34. Pszczola, D. E. (2002). Confectionery ingredients bridge indulgence with health. *Food Technology, 56*(9), 64.

35. Putnam, J. J. (2000). Major trends in the U.S. food supply, 1909–1999. *Food Review, 23*(1), 8–14.

36. Putnam, J. J., & Allshouse, J. E. (1999, April). Food consumption, prices, and expenditures, 1970–97. Food and Rural Economics Division, Economic Research Service, U.S. Department of Agriculture. Statistical Bulletin No. 965.

37. Rapaille, A., Gonze, M., & Van der Schueren, F. (1995). Formulating sugar-free chocolate products with maltitol. *Food Technology, 49*(7), 51.

38. Sloan, A. E. (1997). How sweet it is. *Food Technology, 51*(3), 26.

39. Staff. (1987). Crystalline fructose: A breakthrough in corn sweetener process technology. *Food Technology, 41*(1), 66.

40. Staff. (1996). Thaumatin—The sweetest substance known to man has a wide range of food applications. *Food Technology, 50*(1), 74.

41. Thielen, T. F., & McComber, D. R. (1993). Effect of alternative sweeteners on egg-thickened mixtures. *Journal of the American Dietetic Association, 93*, 814.

42. Verdi, R. J., & Hood, L. L. (1993). Advantages of alternative sweetener blends. *Food Technology, 47*(6), 94.

43. Wiseman, J. J., & McDaniel, M. R. (1991). Modification of fruit flavors by aspartame and sucrose. *Journal of Food Science, 56*, 1668.

44. Woodruff, S., & Van Gilder, H. (1931). Photomicrographic studies of sucrose crystals. *Journal of Physical Chemistry, 35*, 1355.

Frozen Desserts

12

Frozen desserts are among the most popular desserts in the United States, especially during the warm months of the year, when something cold and sweet is particularly inviting. However, they are served and enjoyed year round. Americans enjoy over 23 quarts of ice cream per person per year [7]. Old favorites among frozen desserts include ice cream, sherbet, and fruit ices. Frozen yogurt has also become popular. Between 1980 and 1994, frozen yogurt consumption increased 1,000 percent—from 0.3 to 3.3 pounds per person per year [15]. However, super-premium ice cream enjoyed the highest rate of growth among all ice cream segments in 1998, up nearly 13 percent [7]. Frozen desserts are often sold in bulk, and many are also sold as novelty items.

A great variety of novelty frozen dessert items are now marketed. These include frozen pudding on a stick, frozen cheesecake, chocolate-covered ice cream bars with caramel and nut centers, small chocolate-covered ice cream bonbons, and many different fruit-flavored bars, both creamy and noncreamy. Another frozen dessert product is *sorbet*, which contains fruit puree with sweeteners and stabilizers (Figure 12-1). Like fruit ice, sorbet contains no fat. Tofutti is the name of a nondairy frozen dessert that resembles ice cream in appearance, texture, and flavor. It contains tofu or soybean curd with sweeteners, stabilizers, and a fat component such as corn oil. A "light" tofutti is also marketed, containing no fat and less than half the kilocalories of regular tofutti. Other nondairy frozen desserts are produced with a number of different plant protein sources, including pea protein isolate [3].

Reduced-calorie, low-fat, or no added sugar frozen desserts are among the "light" dairy products that consumers apparently want and the food industry is attempting to supply. In the mid-1990's, sales of low-fat ice cream increased by 50 percent [8]. Low-fat and nonfat frozen yogurts are offered, plus many other modified-fat frozen desserts with ice cream–like characteristics. Lower-fat ice creams represent the third largest segment of the subzero frozen dessert market [11]. Even a super-premium brand of low-fat ice cream has been developed. Ingredients for both fat and sugar replacement are available to the food industry for the development of reduced-calorie frozen desserts. One fat replacer that has been used in frozen desserts resembling ice cream is a microparticulated protein with the trade name Simplesse®. It is produced in a patented process using heat and shear to form spheroidal particles so tiny that they are below the perceptual threshold of the tongue, creating the rich, creamy mouthfeel charac-

Figure 12-1
This lemon sorbet makes for a wonderfully refreshing dessert.

teristic of fats [5]. Reduced-calorie frozen desserts often make use of high-intensity or alternative sweeteners such as aspartame.

COMMERCIAL ICE CREAM PROCESSING

Phytochemicals chemical substances found in plants, a number of which may be of benefit to human health; examples include several antioxidants and antimicrobials compounds

Most ice cream used in this country is commercially manufactured, although some ice cream is still prepared at home. Electrically operated ice cream freezers are available for home use. These include equipment for operation inside a home freezer and traditional ice cream makers that utilize crushed ice and rock salt. Commercial ice creams differ from products made at home. They generally contain more emulsifiers and stabilizers and have a greater increase in vol-

---

Hot Topics

The changing Olde Ice Cream Shoppe

Did you know that U.S. production of ice cream and related frozen desserts amounts to more than 1.6 billion gallons annually? This means about 23 quarts per person and makes this country the world leader in the consumption of these products [14]. The manufacture of ice cream and other frozen desserts is exploding with varieties of flavors, forms, and combination ingredients. Nevertheless, according to the International Ice Cream Association, vanilla is still the most popular ice cream flavor, at 29 percent.

In addition to creating delectable objects to tempt the palate, manufacturers are looking for ways to improve the health-promoting properties of their products. Donald Pszczola, after attending a symposium on "The Changing Landscape of Ice Cream" at the 2002 annual meeting of the Institute of Food Technologists, has described more than 30 new ingredients that create exciting possibilities for frozen dessert innovation. These include new stabilizer/emulsifier systems that can produce an indulgent frozen dessert with no added sugar; customized systems of vegetable gums that can be tested in a new pilot plant; flaxseed as a partial replacer for milkfat; a rice-based mix designed to produce a creamy dessert that is free of lactose and cholesterol; soluble rice bran to increase fiber content of ice cream shakes; soy powder without a "beany" taste; fruit and vegetable extracts with standardized levels of **phytochemicals**; and flavors with floral profiles designed to appeal especially to women. What will be next in ice creams?

ume when they are frozen. The increase in volume during freezing that results from the beating of air into the mixture is called *overrun*.

In the making of commercial ice creams and other frozen desserts, mixes are first prepared. The ingredients are assembled, weighed or metered, and mixed. The mix is then **pasteurized** to destroy pathogenic organisms. Pasteurization also aids in the blending of ingredients, makes a more uniform product, and improves flavor and keeping quality. The mix is **homogenized** by forcing the liquid through a small orifice under conditions of temperature and pressure suitable to finely divide the fat globules, which are reduced to about one-tenth of their usual size. The texture and palatability of ice cream are improved by homogenization. The homogenized mix is cooled and usually aged for a few hours before freezing. During this time, the fat globules solidify, and the viscosity increases [13].

During agitation or stirring of the ice cream mix as it is frozen, some of the fat globules **agglomerate** into a form similar to a bunch of grapes. If this agglomeration process is too extensive, however, with extended freezing time and agitation, actual churning may take place and clumps of butter will result. Commercial ice cream manufacturers add emulsifiers, such as monoglycerides and diglycerides, to the ice cream mix. These help to control the degree of agglomeration and thus decrease freezing time, improve whipping quality, and produce a dry ice cream with a fine, stiff texture that melts slowly and uniformly [1]. Various stabilizers, including a number of vegetable gums such as alginate and carrageenan, also aid in fine ice-crystal formation. All of these additives contribute to a smooth texture in frozen desserts.

The commercial freezing process usually involves two stages. (1) The mix is rapidly frozen so that small ice crystals are quickly formed while agitation incorporates air into the mixture. (2) When the ice cream is partially frozen to a certain consistency, it is drawn from the freezer into packages and quickly transferred to cold storage rooms. Here the freezing and hardening process is completed without agitation. Processing procedures in commercial ice cream manufacturing are fully mechanized. Many phases of the process are automatically controlled [13].

Soft-serve ice cream and frozen yogurt are popular items in many fast-food and buffet-type foodservice establishments. These products are similar in composition to their harder frozen counterparts, but they are served directly from the ice cream maker and therefore do not undergo the hardening process. Additional stabilizers or emulsifiers may be used in soft-serve ice cream, yogurt, and reduced fat ice cream products. State regulations vary regarding the sale of soft-serve products.

Even though commercial and homemade ice creams differ considerably in quality characteristics, the basic principles involved in their preparation are similar. Although few people prepare ice cream at home, a better understanding of the various factors that influence the quality of ice creams may still be profitable. Also useful in making wise purchasing decisions is a recognition of the standards of identity and composition for frozen desserts.

pasteurize to subject to a mild heat treatment that destroys vegetative bacteria but does not completely destroy microorganisms

homogenize to subdivide particles, usually fat globules, into very small, uniform-sized pieces

agglomerate to gather into a cluster, mass, or ball

"LIGHT" FROZEN DESSERTS

Prior to the the passage of the 1990 Nutrition Labeling and Education Act, reduced fat ice creams were labeled "ice milk." Starting in 1994, reduced-fat, low-fat, light, and fat-free ice creams were sold in place of ice milk [12]. Reduced-fat ice cream contains 25 percent less fat than the original product. A "light" product has been defined by the U.S. Food and Drug Administration (FDA) as one containing either 33 percent fewer calories or 50 percent of the fat in a reference food, and, if 50 percent or more of the calories come from fat, the reduction must be 50 percent of the fat. Low-fat ice cream contains 3 grams or less of fat per serving and fat-free ice cream contains less than 0.5 grams of fat. (See Chapter 2 for more information about the Nutrition Labeling and Education Act.)

Major changes in the composition of frozen desserts are necessary to achieve reduced calories and/or fat and to attain "light" status. It is a complex process to produce acceptable frozen desserts with useful reductions in sugar and fat. Fat contributes greatly to the flavor and richness that consumers have come to expect in frozen desserts that are similar to ice cream. The smooth mouthfeel of fat may be only partially replaced by the addition of low-calorie texturizers such as vegetable gums and cellulose derivatives. However, a variety of fat substitutes and fat-replacement technologies are available to produce a product of desirable texture. Maintaining flavor quality may be even more difficult. Fat serves as a reservoir of flavor as it interacts with many flavor components. Thus, flavor is slowly released in the mouth, resulting in a pleasant aftertaste. Flavor challenges are increased as fat is decreased in a creamy frozen dessert [6].

In frozen desserts, sugar has important functions beyond its sweetening power. For example, the freezing point of the mixture is markedly increased when sugar is replaced by a high-intensity sweetener such as aspartame. This exchange increases the amount of water frozen at any given temperature below the freezing point of the mixture and thus affects the texture and body of the frozen dessert [13]. It also affects the overrun of the finished product, which modifies its usual characteristics.

So-called **bulking agents** have been used to replace some of the nonsweetening functions of sugar in frozen desserts, including **polydextrose, maltodextrins,** and **sorbitol.** However, some disadvantages of one or more of these ingredients include the development of off-flavors and the possible development of gastrointestinal distress. In addition, some bulking agents have the same caloric value as sucrose [9]. (Bulking agents and polyols are discussed further in Chapter 11.)

Another adjustment sometimes made in light frozen desserts is an increase in the nonfat milk solids. This increase is normally limited, however, because of the insolubility of lactose, which may produce a sandy texture. If the enzyme lactase is added to the mix before processing, lactose is hydrolyzed to glucose and galactose. These products are more soluble and sweeter than lactose and allow an acceptable light product to be made with increased milk solids [10].

As fat replacers in frozen desserts, a maltodextrin product and a microparticulated protein product were compared with ice milk containing 4.8 percent fat [16]. Schmidt et al. reported that, overall, the protein-based fat replacer resulted in a product containing 2.1 percent fat that had quality characteristics more similar to the ice milk containing 4.8 percent fat than did the carbohydrate-based fat replacer. Microparticulated proteins, one marketed as Simplesse®, appear to be relatively successful fat replacers in frozen desserts. Fantesk™, another fat replacer that is composed of a starch-lipid composite, was tested in soft-serve ice cream and found to produce a product similar to standard commercial products [2].

bulking agent a substance used in relatively small amounts to affect the texture and body of some manufactured foods made without sugar or with reduced amounts; it compensates to some degree for the nonsweetening effects of sugar in a food product

polydextrose a bulking agent made from an 89 : 10 : 1 mixture of glucose, sorbitol, and citric acid; in body metabolism it yields one kilocalorie per gram

maltodextrins a mixture of small molecules resulting from starch hydrolysis, having a dextrose equivalent (DE) of less than 20

sorbitol a sugar alcohol similar to glucose in chemical structure but with an alcohol group ($-C-OH$) replacing the aldehyde group ($H-C=O$) of glucose

Understanding the role of ingredients available for the production of acceptable light frozen desserts is essential. Consumer demand for light frozen desserts, and for a variety of other light food products, is high. With continued research and development, more low-fat, high quality products will be created to satisfy consumers' appetite for these products.

TYPES OF FROZEN DESSERTS

The classification of frozen desserts, particularly those made in home kitchens, is somewhat difficult because of the large variety of recipes and combinations of ingredients used. Commercial frozen desserts, however, are subject to state regulations, and to federal regulations if they enter interstate commerce. These regulations were specifically designed to control the milkfat content.

The three main types of frozen desserts are ice creams, sherbets, and water ices [4]. Some ice creams contain enough egg yolk solids to be considered a custard-type ice cream. Several ice creams also contain bulky flavoring ingredients such as fruits, nuts, chocolate syrup, cookie pieces, and peanut butter mixtures. Table 12-1 summarizes the distinguishing characteristics of and regulatory limitations for the basic types of frozen desserts.

Commercial ice creams made according to traditional formulations contain milkfat, milk solids, sweeteners, flavorings, and small amounts of emulsifiers and stabilizers. The emulsifiers and stabilizers permitted under federal ice cream standards include monoglycerides and diglycerides, polysorbates, sucrose–fatty acid esters, lecithin, gelatin, sodium carboxymethylcellulose, agar,

Table 12-1

Classification of Frozen Desserts

Type	Distinguishing Characteristics	Regulatory Limitations
Plain ice cream	Medium to high in milkfat and milk-solids-not-fat. With or without small amounts of egg products. Without visible particles of flavoring materials. With the total volume of color and flavor less than 5 percent of the volume of the unfrozen ice cream mix.	Not more than 0.5 percent edible stabilizer. Not less than 10 percent milkfat. Not less than 20 percent total milk solids.
Frozen custard (Also called French ice cream or New York ice cream.)	High in egg yolk solids, cooked to a custard before freezing. Medium to high in milkfat and milk-solids-not-fat. With or without fruits, nuts, bakery products, candy, or similar materials.	Not more than 0.5 percent edible stabilizer. Not less than 1.4 percent egg solids for plain and 1.12 percent for bulky flavors. Not less than 10 percent milkfat. Not less than 20 percent total milk solids.
Composite ice cream or bulky flavors	Medium to high in milkfat and milk-solids-not-fat. With or without small amounts of egg products. With the total volume of color and flavor material more than 5 percent of the volume of the unfrozen ice cream mix, or with visible particles of flavoring materials.	Not more than 0.5 percent edible stabilizer. Not less than 8 percent milkfat. Not less than 16 percent total milk solids.
Sherbet	Low in milk-solids-not-fat. Tart flavor.	Not less than 0.35 percent acidity. Not less than 1 percent nor more than 2 percent milkfat. Not less than 2 percent nor more than 5 percent total milk solids.
Ice	No milk solids. Tart flavor.	
Imitation ice cream	Proper labeling required. Mellorine types have milkfat replaced by another fat (not less than 6 percent fat). Parevine types contain no dairy ingredients.	

Source: Reference 13.

algin, carrageenan, gum acacia, and several other vegetable gums. Whey can comprise part of the nonfat milk solids in ice cream.

Commercial water ices are water-sugar syrups combined with fruits, fruit juices, or other flavoring materials; a small amount of gelatin, vegetable gum, or other stabilizer is added to produce body and a smooth texture. Commercial sherbets have ingredients similar to those of water ices except that they contain a certain amount of a dairy product, such as milk or cream.

Mellorine is similar to ice cream except that the milkfat has been replaced with a nondairy substance such as a vegetable fat. Mellorine is less expensive to produce than ice cream and generally sells for less. *Parevine* contains no dairy products but has characteristics similar to those of ice cream and mellorine.

A frappé is a dessert that is frozen to a mush. A high percentage of salt is used in the freezing mixture to produce a coarse granular texture.

Mousse is sweetened and flavored whipped cream. It may contain a small amount of gelatin and is usually frozen without stirring. Biscuit is similar to mousse but is frozen in individual forms.

NUTRITIVE VALUE

The higher the percentage of milk constituents in frozen desserts, the more important is the contribution of protein, minerals, and vitamins. Desserts with a high butterfat content are obviously of higher caloric value and higher vitamin A content than those with a low percentage of fat. However, Vitamin A may be added to reduced fat products so that the Vitamin A content is the same as the reference product. Frozen desserts, to taste desirably sweet, must have a higher sugar content than most other types of desserts because of the dulling effect of cold temperatures on taste sensations. Fruit ices and sherbets, because of their acidity, also require a fairly high sugar content. Vitamins are probably unaffected by freezing.

CHARACTERISTICS OF FROZEN DESSERTS

Frozen desserts are generally complex food systems. They are foams with air cells dispersed in a continuous liquid phase that contains ice crystals, emulsified fat globules, proteins, sugars, salts, and stabilizers. For a high-quality ice cream product, desirable characteristics are a smooth, creamy, somewhat dry and stiff texture with tiny ice crystals, enough body so that the product melts slowly and uniformly, and a sweet, fresh characteristic flavor.

Crystal Formation

All types of frozen desserts are crystalline products in which water is crystallized as ice. The aim in preparation is generally to obtain fine crystals and produce a smooth mouthfeel; however, some differences in crystal size and creamy texture are apparent among products, depending on the fat content and the use of stabilizers. For example, fruit ices containing no fat usually have a more crystalline texture than high-fat, creamy ice creams. Many of the same general factors that tend to produce fine crystals in crystalline candies, in which the crystals are sugar, also produce fine ice crystals in frozen desserts. Both fat and nonfat solids such as proteins interfere mechanically with crystal formation and growth. Many stabilizers, including vegetable gums, are hydrocolloids that bind large amounts of water, increase viscosity, and interfere with crystallization.

Overrun

Overrun is the amount of ice cream obtained above the amount of mix frozen. Overrun may be calculated by volume or by weight using one of the following formulas.

Percent overrun = (volume of ice cream made − volume ice cream mix) / (volume of mix used) × 100

Percent overrun = (weight of gallon of mix − weight of gallon of ice cream) / (weight of gallon of ice cream) × 100

Ice cream, being a partly frozen foam, typically contains 40 to 50 percent air by volume [1]. Thus, during freezing, the volume of the ice cream mix increases by 70 to 100 percent. Homemade ice creams usually have no more than 30 to 40 percent overrun. The higher percentage of overrun in commercial ice creams in comparison with homemade products results from a better control of freezing conditions, such as the rate of freezing and the stage of hardness at which the freezing is discontinued. Homogenization increases the viscosity of the mix, which favors retention of air.

Too little overrun produces a heavy, compact, coarse-textured frozen dessert, which is more expensive per serving, whereas too great an overrun results in a frothy, foamy product. Better ice creams are often sold by weight, and federal standards require weight of 4.5 pounds per gallon, thereby controlling the amount of overrun. Sherbet must weigh not less than 6 pounds per gallon [19].

Body

The term *body* as used in connection with frozen desserts implies firmness or resistance to rapid melting. Homemade ice creams usually have less body than commercial ice creams because stabilizers used in the commercial products often add body. Homemade ice creams generally melt faster in the mouth and give the impression of being lighter desserts, although they may actually be richer mixtures than many commercial ice creams.

Texture

Texture refers to the fineness of particles, smoothness, and lightness or porosity. The size and distribution of ice crystals is a major factor influencing the texture of frozen desserts. Substances that interfere with large-crystal formation, such as fat and certain stabilizers, help to produce a fine, smooth texture in frozen desserts. Preference tests show that consumers generally like smooth, fine-grained ice cream.

PREPARATION OF FROZEN DESSERTS

Commercial ice cream mixes are pasteurized and homogenized. The latter process finely divides the fat particles, thus producing a more homogeneous and smooth mixture. When homemade ice cream is prepared from pasteurized products, the mixture does not require pasteurization, although heating in a double boiler for 15 to 20 minutes at 145°F (63°C) blends ingredients thoroughly and may be an extra precaution from a health standpoint. After it is heated, the mixture should be cooled quickly to 55°F (13°C) or below. A smoother ice cream and improved flavor result from aging or holding the mix for 3 or 4 hours at refrigerator temperature before freezing.

If gelatin is used in a frozen dessert, it may be mixed with the sugar and added to the liquid when the latter has reached a temperature of 109°F (43°C). The entire mixture is then heated further. If egg yolks are used, they may be mixed with the sugar to form a smooth paste, which is then mixed with the liquid and heated to 165°F (74°C) to kill any salmonellae that may be present. Unpasteurized raw eggs should not be used in ice cream because of the possible danger of *Salmonella* infection in the eggs. Flavoring and coloring are added just before freezing.

Both sweetened and unsweetened fruit are used in ice creams, but sweetened fruit gives the better flavor. Two pounds of strawberries require about 1 pound of sugar for good flavor. Other fruits may require different amounts of sugar, depending on the acidity of the fruit. To avoid hard particles of frozen fruits in ice cream, the fruit should be finely crushed or run through a strainer.

Effect of Ingredients on Quality Characteristics

Milkfat.   An optimum amount of milkfat gives desirable flavor to ice cream and also improves body and texture, resulting in a firm, smooth product. The amount of milkfat influences the viscosity of the mix and affects the incorporation of air. A moderate viscosity is desirable, as both a highly viscous mixture and a thin, nonviscous one resist the incorporation of air. The air cells are desirably small and the texture is smooth in a mixture with optimum viscosity.

Homemade ice creams with a high milkfat content may have a tendency to churn, producing agglomerated particles of butter. The homogenization of commercial ice cream mixes helps to avoid this problem. Commercial ice creams usually contain 10 to 14 percent milkfat.

Nonfat Milk Solids.   Homemade ice creams usually are not reinforced with milk solids, although some may be added. Unless they are reinforced, homemade ice creams probably contain not more than 6 percent milk serum solids as compared with an average of about 9 or 10 percent in commercial ice creams. A relatively high percentage of milk solids reduces the free water content of ice cream and thus improves its texture by encouraging finer ice crystal formation. Commercial ice creams can be reinforced with milk solids by the use of evaporated skim milk or nonfat dry milk.

Too high a percentage of nonfat milk solids gives a sandy ice cream as a result of the crystallization of lactose at the low temperature of holding. About 11 percent nonfat milk solids is close to the upper limit for prevention of a sandy product, unless the enzyme *lactase* is added to hydrolyze the lactose. In this case, a higher level of nonfat milk solids can be used without the development of sandiness. Too low a percentage of nonfat milk solids encourages high overrun, which creates fluffiness and poor body.

Sweeteners.   Sweeteners, of course, affect flavor. Consumers generally seem to prefer a fairly sweet ice cream (one containing about 14 or 15 percent sugar). Sugar also lowers the freezing point and affects the amount of water frozen at the usual holding and serving temperatures for ice cream. If too much sugar is added, the freezing point is lowered excessively and freezing is retarded. If too little sugar is used, the freezing point is high enough that much of the water is frozen, adversely affecting the texture of the ice cream [17]. Although table sugar is the usual sweetener in homemade frozen desserts, various sweeteners are used in commercial products. These include corn syrups and high-fructose corn syrups

(HFCSs), as well as sugar. The use of corn sweeteners is increasing. A comparatively large amount of HFCS, which produces a lower freezing point, has been reported to contribute to the development of iciness on storage of ice cream [20].

Stabilizers and Emulsifiers.   Several different **stabilizers** and **emulsifiers** are used in commercial frozen desserts in amounts up to 0.5 percent. The emulsifiers affect the fat-globule structure and the agglomeration of these globules during freezing, which contributes to improved whipping quality and texture. Stabilizers interfere somewhat with ice crystal formation, helping to keep the crystals small; they also give body to the mixture [18]. Some of the water in frozen desserts is bound by the stabilizers, thus inhibiting ice crystal growth, particularly during distribution and storage [20].

stabilizer a water-holding substance, such as a vegetable gum, that interferes with ice crystal formation and contributes to a smooth texture in frozen desserts

emulsifier a substance that aids in producing a fine division of fat globules; in ice cream, it also stabilizes the dispersion of air in the foam structure

The Freezing Process

Freezing Points of Liquids.   Pure liquids have characteristic freezing points at constant pressure. The freezing point is the temperature at which the vapor pressures of the pure liquid and its pure solid substance are equal and the liquid and solid forms remain in equilibrium. The melting point and freezing point are identical. Because a liquid can be supercooled to a temperature below its freezing point before freezing occurs, it is not altogether accurate to describe the freezing point as the temperature at which the liquid changes to a solid.

Water freezes at 32°F (0°C) at a pressure of 760 millimeters of mercury. After freezing, the temperature of ice may be lowered below 32°F (0°C). If the temperature of the surroundings is lower than 32°F (0°C), then the ice and the air eventually reach the lower temperature. Water expands during freezing to occupy more space than it did in the liquid form. The swelling or increased volume of frozen desserts results partly from the expansion of watery mixtures on freezing; however, the incorporation of air as the mixture is agitated during freezing is the major reason for the increase in volume.

Substances dissolved in a liquid to form a true **solution** cause the freezing point of the solution to be lower than the freezing point of the pure liquid. A sugar solution, which is the basis for frozen desserts, has a lower freezing point than pure water. The higher the concentration of the solution, the lower the freezing point. Ices and sherbets that contain acid fruit juices have a higher percentage of sugar than ice creams, and therefore freeze at a lower temperature.

solution a mixture resulting from the dispersion of small molecules or ions (called the *solute*) in a liquid such as water (called the *solvent*)

Freezing Mixtures.   The freezing mixture used in an ordinary ice cream freezer consists of crushed ice and a salt. The salt is usually coarse sodium chloride (NaCl), called *rock salt*. The greater the proportion of salt to ice in the mixture, the lower the temperature of the mixture. This proportion holds true until no more salt will dissolve in the water coming from the melting ice, that is, until a **saturated solution** of salt is produced. The lowest temperature possible in a brine from a salt and ice mixture is about −6° to −8°F (−21° to −22°C). Few dessert mixes require a temperature lower than 14° to 18°F (−8° to −10°C) to freeze.

saturated solution a solution containing all of the solute that it can dissolve at that temperature

When ice and salt are mixed, the surface of the ice is usually moist and dissolves some of the salt. The vapor pressure of the concentrated salt solution that is formed on the surface of the ice is lower than that of the ice itself. In an attempt by the system to establish equilibrium, more ice melts. More salt then dissolves, and the process is repeated.

As ice melts, it absorbs heat, and the rapid melting of ice that occurs when salt is added to it increases the rate of heat absorption. Some heat is also absorbed as the salt dissolves in the film of water on the ice surface. The heat that is absorbed in both of these processes is taken from the brine, from the air, or from the mixture to be frozen. Because cold is actually the absence of heat, as heat is removed, the temperatures of the brine and mixture to be frozen are lowered. When the mixture to be frozen reaches its freezing point, ice crystals begin to form and precipitate out.

The removal of some water from the ice cream mix (as ice) causes the remaining unfrozen mixture to become more concentrated, with a freezing temperature lower than that of the original dessert mixture. Thus, as freezing proceeds, the freezing temperature is gradually lowered, just as the evaporation of water that occurs in the boiling of a sugar solution produces a gradual increase in the boiling temperature of the mixture.

When freezing is accompanied by stirring, a proportion of salt to ice that is efficient for home freezing is about one part coarse salt to six parts crushed ice by weight. This amount is equivalent to about one to twelve by measure. For faster freezing, a proportion of about one part salt to eight parts ice, by measure, is also satisfactory. The higher the percentage of salt, the shorter the time required for freezing; however, if freezing is too rapid, not enough time is available to keep the ice crystals separated and small while stirring, and the crystals of ice formed may be large enough to produce a granular texture.

If desserts are frozen without stirring, that is, packed in the freezing mixture, the proportion of salt to ice is about one to two by measure. Mixtures frozen without stirring require a longer time and a colder temperature to freeze than stirred mixtures. Removing heat from the center of the mass may be difficult in unstirred frozen desserts, because they are high in fat and have air beaten into the heavy cream that is normally used as the basis of the mixture. Both cold fat and air are poor conductors of heat.

The fineness of the division of salt and ice is also a factor influencing the rate of freezing in the preparation of frozen desserts. Finely crushed ice has more surface exposed to the action of salt than coarsely chopped ice; hence, the finer ice melts faster. Fine salt dissolves more rapidly, but because of its lumping and collecting in the bottom of the freezer, it is less desirable to use than coarse salt.

Ice Cream Freezers

Construction.　　Figure 12-2 illustrates the structure of an ice cream freezer. The outer container of the freezer is usually made of a material that conducts heat poorly, such as wood or plastic foam, which minimizes the absorption of heat from the air. The goal is to have the melting ice absorb heat from the mixture to be frozen.

The container that holds the ice cream mix inside the outer container is metal, which conducts heat readily and permits the rapid absorption of heat from the ice cream mix. A paddle or dasher inside the metal can agitates the ice cream mixture as the freezer is turned, thus incorporating air. The dasher scrapes the mixture from the side walls, permitting a new layer of mixture to come in contact with the can. Agitation also tends to form many nuclei on which ice crystals may form, which favors small crystal formation.

Rate of Turning the Freezer.　　Slow agitation of the ice cream mixture is desirable at the beginning of the freezing period until the temperature of the freezing mixture is lowered below the critical churning temperature. At 40°F (5°C)

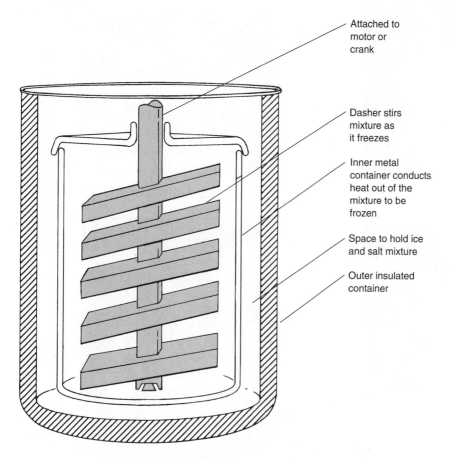

Attached to
motor or
crank

Dasher stirs
mixture as
it freezes

Inner metal
container conducts
heat out of the
mixture to be
frozen

Space to hold ice
and salt mixture

Outer insulated
container

Figure 12-2
Structure of an ice cream freezer.

or above, agitation tends to cause the formation of clumps of butterfat, resulting in a buttery ice cream or in actual butter.

Rapid agitation after the mixture is chilled not only incorporates much air
but also favors the formation of many nuclei and fine ice crystals. It is difficult
to produce fine crystals in ice creams that are frozen without stirring, because
relatively few nuclei for ice crystal formation are present and thus large crystal
growth can occur.

In quick-freezing procedures that are practiced commercially, many nuclei
and small crystals are formed because of the extremely low temperatures used.
The shortness of the time of freezing prevents the growth of crystals.

Packing the Freezer.   The mixture to be frozen should occupy only about
two-thirds of the capacity of the inner metal can to allow for overrun or swell
during freezing (Figure 12-3). After the paddle or dasher is adjusted, the space
between the inner can and the outer container is best filled about half-full with
crushed ice before any salt is added to prevent the salt from collecting in the
bottom of the freezer. The remainder of the ice and salt needed to fill the
freezer may be added alternately. It is also possible to mix the crushed ice and
salt together before adding it to the freezer, but then the first cooling effect obtained when the salt is added to the ice is lost.

The brine that forms as the ice begins to melt is not drained off. When the
mixture is frozen, the crank turns with difficulty. The lid may be removed, the

(1) The ice cream mixture is placed in the freezing canister and the dasher is in place.

(2) The freezer is closed; crushed ice and rock salt are added.

(3) Brothers can help each other in turning the freezer as they eagerly await the final result.

(4) The freezing is completed and the cover carefully lifted.

(5) The dasher is removed from the freezing canister.

(6) Anticipation is finally at an end and the boys can spoon out the delicious frozen ice cream.

Figure 12-3

Freezing ice cream at home can be a family activity.

dasher taken out, and the ice cream pressed down solidly in the can. The hole in the inner metal can top is corked to prevent the salty freezing mixture from getting into the can, and the excess brine is drained off.

If the frozen dessert is to be used soon, the freezer may be packed with a freezing mixture containing a percentage of salt higher than that used for freezing. The hardening of the dessert to a consistency desirable for serving is thus accomplished more rapidly. If the ice cream is to stand for a longer time before serving, the same mixture used for freezing may also be used for packing the frozen dessert.

Freezing without Stirring. The freezing compartment of a refrigerator provides a temperature low enough for freezing and for holding frozen mixtures. Without stirring, however, the rate of freezing is retarded and ice crystals tend to be larger than when stirring occurs.

Mixtures that can be frozen most successfully without stirring are those rich in fat, such as whipped cream products, or mixtures containing gelatin, cooked egg custard, evaporated milk, or a cooked starch base. These substances interfere with the formation of large ice crystals. Because these mixtures are not stirred to incorporate air, air must be beaten into cream or evaporated milk prior to freezing. Partially frozen mixtures may be removed from the freezing trays and beaten once or twice during the freezing period. Air cells tend to interfere with coarse-crystal formation.

Egg Custard. Custards thickened with egg yolk or whole egg are sometimes used in ice creams. (Raw eggs should not be used in frozen desserts because of the possible presence of *Salmonella* even in unbroken eggs.) The cooked custard must be well chilled before it is combined with whipped cream. Three-fourths cup of custard is the maximum amount to combine with a cup of whipping cream.

Time Required for Freezing. The time required for freezing refrigerator desserts depends on the quantity being frozen, the composition of the mixture, and the temperature. About 4 to 6 hours may be needed, and the cold control is best set on the lowest temperature. When the mixture is frozen without stirring, freezing as quickly as possible aids in the production of many small ice crystals. Faster freezing occurs if the mixture is stirred occasionally in the tray to permit unfrozen portions to come in contact with the tray.

CHAPTER SUMMARY

- A great variety of frozen desserts are marketed. Ice cream, reduced fat ice cream, sherbet, fruit ices, sorbet, tofutti, and a number of novelty frozen desserts are available.

- Commercial ice creams generally contain more emulsifiers and stabilizers than ice cream prepared at home. Commercial ice creams also have a greater overrun compared to home products. In commercial ice cream production, the mix is prepared, then pasteurized, homogenized, and cooled for a few hours prior to freezing. The ice cream mix is agitated during the freezing process to incorporate air into the mixture and to keep the ice crystal size small. When the ice cream is partially frozen, it is packaged and transferred into freezer storage to complete the hardening of the ice cream. Each step in this process is important in the production of a high quality product.

- Soft-serve ice creams and yogurts are served in many restaurant operations. These products are similar to their harder frozen counterparts, but they are served directly from the ice cream maker and therefore do not undergo the hardening process.

- Prior to the passage of the 1990 Nutrition Labeling and Education Act, reduced fat ice creams were labeled "ice milk." Starting in 1994, reduced-fat, low-fat, light, and fat-free ice creams became available. Manufacturers must meet specific fat or calorie guidelines to label their ice cream product with one of these nutrient claims.

- Major changes in the composition of frozen desserts are necessary to reduce calories or fat and still have a high quality product. Fat contributes to the flavor and richness in frozen desserts that are intended to be similar to ice cream. The smooth mouthfeel of fat may be partially replaced by the addition vegetable gums and cellulose derivatives. Likewise, sugar has several important functions in frozen desserts that contribute to the texture and body of the frozen dessert.

- Nonfat milk solids may be added to reduced fat or reduced calorie ice creams; however, because lactose is less soluble than other sugars, high levels of nonfat milk solids can result in an undesirable "sandy" product.

- Commercial ice cream ingredients and characteristics are regulated. Ice cream, frozen custard, sherbet, and mellorine must contain the level of milkfat, milk solids, and other ingredients as specified to be labeled with these product names. Reduced fat, low-fat, and "light" ice creams must meet the labeling and content requirements set forth in the 1990 Nutrition Labeling and Education Act.

- Frozen desserts are complex food systems. They are foams with air cells dispersed in a continuous liquid phase that contains ice crystals, emulsified fat globules, proteins, sugars, salts, and stabilizers. All types of frozen desserts are crystalline products in which water is crystallized as ice. The aim in preparation is generally to obtain fine crystals and produce a smooth mouthfeel.

- Overrun is the amount of ice cream obtained above the amount of mix frozen. Ice cream, being a partially frozen foam, typically contains 40–50 percent air by volume. Thus, during freezing, the volume of the ice cream mix increases by 70–100 percent. Both too little and too much overrun have a negative impact on the quality of the product.

- The term body, as used in connection with frozen desserts, implies firmness or resistence to rapid melting. Texture refers to the fineness of particles, smoothness, and lightness or porosity. The size and distribution of ice crystals is a major factor influencing the texture of frozen desserts.

- Milkfat, nonfat milk solids, sweeteners, stabilizers, and emulsifiers have an impact on the quality characteristics of frozen desserts. An optimum amount of milkfat gives desirable flavor to ice cream and also improves body and texture, resulting in a firm, smooth product. A relatively high percentage of milk solids (9–10 percent in commercial ice creams) reduces the free water content of ice cream and thus improves its texture by encouraging finer ice crystal formation. Too high a percent of nonfat milk solids results in a "sandy" texture.

- Sweeteners affect flavor and lower the freezing point of the mix. If too little sugar is used, the freezing point is high enough that much of the water is frozen, adversely affecting the texture of the ice cream. Emulsifiers contribute to improved whipping quality and texture. Stabilizers interfere somewhat with ice crystal formation, helping to keep the crystals small; they also give body to the mixture.

- The freezing point is the temperature at which the vapor pressures of the pure liquid and its pure solid substance are equal and the liquid and solid forms remain in equilibrium. Substances dissolved in a liquid to form a true solution cause the freezing point of the solution to be lower than the freezing point of a pure liquid.

- The freezing mixture used in an ordinary ice cream freezer consists of crushed ice and salt. As ice melts, it absorbs heat, and the rapid melting of ice that occurs when salt is added to it increases the rate of heat absorption. The paddle or dasher inside the metal container holding the ice cream mix scrapes the mixture from the side walls, permitting a new layer of mixture to be frozen.

- Mixtures that can be frozen successfully without stirring are those rich in fat, such as whipped cream products, or mixtures containing gelatin, cooked egg custard, evaporated milk, or a cooked starch base. These substances interfere with the formation of large ice crystals.

KEY TERMS

pasteurize
homogenize
agglomerate
bulking agent
polydextrose
maltodextrins

sorbitol
stabilizer
emulsifier
solution
saturated solution
phytochemicals

STUDY QUESTIONS

1. Describe the major characteristics of a well-prepared frozen dessert such as ice cream or sherbet.

2. Describe identifying characteristics of each of the following:
   a. Sherbet
   b. Water ice
   c. Ice cream
   d. Mousse
   e. Sorbet
   f. Tofutti
   g. Frozen yogurt
   h. Mellorine
   i. Parevine

3. What is the effect of each of the following on the flavor, texture, and/or body of a frozen ice cream?
   a. Milkfat
   b. Nonfat milk solids
   c. Sweeteners
   d. Stabilizers
   e. Overrun

4. Discuss some of the problems often involved in the formulation of acceptable "light" frozen desserts. What are some possible solutions to these problems?

5. Explain how a mixture of ice and salt is able to act as a freezing mixture to freeze frozen desserts.

6. Describe an appropriate procedure for preparing homemade ice cream in an ice cream freezer. Explain what happens at each step.

7. What procedures should be used when freezing a frozen dessert without stirring, and why?

REFERENCES

1. Buck, J. S., Walker, C. E., & Pierce, M. M. (1986). Evaluation of sucrose esters in ice cream. *Journal of Food Science, 51,* 489.

2. Byer, J. (2002). Effect of a starch-lipid fat replacer on the rheology of soft-serve ice cream. *Journal of Food Science, 67,* 2177–2182.

3. Chan, A. S. M., Pereira, R. R., Henderson, H. M., & Blank, G. (1992). A nondairy frozen dessert utilizing pea protein isolate and hydrogenated canola oil. *Food Technology, 46*(1), 88.

4. Code of Federal Regulations. Definitions and Standards under the Federal Food, Drug, and Cosmetic Act: Frozen Desserts. Title 21, Part 20.

5. Dzieczak, J. D. (1989). Fats, oils, and fat substitutes. *Food Technology, 43*(7), 66.

6. Hatchwell, L. C. (1994). Overcoming flavor challenges in low-fat frozen desserts. *Food Technology, 48*(2), 98.

7. Hollingsworth, P. (1999). Self-indulgence trends. *Food Technology, 53*(7), 64–67.

8. Katz, F. (1999). Fran's indulgences. *Food Technology, 53*(7), 48–53.

9. Keller, S. E., Fellows, J. W., Nash, T. C., & Shazer, W. H. (1991). Application of bulk-free process in aspartame-sweetened frozen dessert. *Food Technology, 45*(6), 100.

10. Keller, S. E., Fellows, J. W., Nash, T. C., & Shazer, W. H. (1991). Formulation of aspartame-sweetened frozen dairy dessert without bulking agents. *Food Technology, 45*(2), 102.

11. Kevin, K. (1997). Frozen delights. *Food Processing, 58*(2), 36.

12. Kurtzweil, P. (1998). Skimming the milk label: Fat-reduced milk products join the food labeling fold. *FDA Consumer, 32*(1).

13. Marshall, R. T., & Arbuckle, W. S. (1996). *Ice Cream* (5th ed.). New York: Chapman & Hall.

14. Pszczola, D. E. (2002). 31 ingredient developments for frozen desserts. *Food Technology, 56*(10), 46.

15. Putnam, J. J., & Duewer, L. A. (1995). U.S. per capita food consumption: Record-high meat and sugars in 1994. *Food Review, 18*(2), 2.

16. Schmidt, K., Lundy, A., Reynolds, J., & Yee, L. N. (1993). Carbohydrate or protein-based fat mimicker effects on ice milk properties. *Journal of Food Science, 58,* 761.

17. Tharp, B. W., & Gottemoller, T. V. (1990). Light frozen dairy desserts: Effect of compositional changes on processing and sensory characteristics. *Food Technology, 44*(10), 86.

18. Thomas, E. L. (1981). Structure and properties of ice cream emulsions. *Food Technology, 35*(1), 41.

19. U.S. Food and Drug Administration. (2002, April 1). Code of Federal Regulations, Title 21, Part 135.3—Frozen Desserts. Washington, DC: U.S. Government Printing Office, 358–366.

20. Wittinger, S. A., & Smith, D. E. (1986). Effect of sweeteners and stabilizers on selected sensory attributes and shelf life of ice cream. *Journal of Food Science, 51,* 1463.

Starch

Starch is one of the most abundant substances found in nature. A storage form of carbohydrate in plants, starch is located in roots, seeds, fruits, and stems. During **germination** of a seed, this stored **polysaccharide** molecule undergoes enzymatic **hydrolysis** to yield **glucose,** which then supplies energy for the germination and early stages of plant growth.

The human digestive system produces enzymes, called **amylases,** that break down or hydrolyze this nutritive polysaccharide, starch, yielding the disaccharide **maltose.** Maltose is then hydrolyzed to glucose, which is absorbed and metabolized by body cells, providing energy.

Starch is available to the food industry, and also to the consumer, as a purified material. In this form, it belongs to a group of substances called **hydrocolloids,** a group that also includes **pectin** and a number of gums, sometimes called **vegetable gums.** Hydrocolloids are **colloidal** substances. They are water loving and absorb relatively large amounts of water. In manufactured foods, they are often used as stabilizers, texturizers, thickeners, and binders.

SOURCES OF STARCH

The parts of plants that serve most prominently for the storage of starch are seeds, roots, and **tubers.** Thus, the most common sources of food starch are cereal grains, including corn, wheat, rice, grain sorghum, and oats; legumes; and roots or tubers, including potato, sweet potato, arrowroot, and the tropical cassava plant (marketed as tapioca). Sago comes from the pith or core of the tropical sago palm.

Corn is grown in temperate to warm climates with half of the world's production in the United States. Wheat is grown primarily in North America, Europe, and Russia. Approximately 90 percent of the world's rice supply is produced in southern and southeastern Asia, whereas about 70 percent of the world's potato supply is grown in the cool, moist climate of Europe and Russia.

Purified starch may be separated from grains and tubers by a process called *wet milling.* This procedure employs various techniques of grinding, screening, and centrifuging to separate the starch from fiber, oil, and protein. Natural

germination the sprouting of a seed

polysaccharide a complex carbohydrate made up of many simple sugar (monosaccharide) units linked together; in the case of starch, the simple sugars are all glucose

hydrolysis a chemical reaction in which a molecular linkage is broken and a molecule of water is utilized

glucose a monosaccharide or simple sugar that is the basic building unit for starch

amylase an enzyme that hydrolyzes starch to produce dextrins, maltose, and glucose

maltose a double sugar or disaccharide made up of two glucose units

hydrocolloid a substance with particles of colloidal size that is greatly attracted to water and absorbs it readily

pectin a gel-forming polysaccharide found in plant tissues

vegetable gums polysaccharide substances that are derived from plants, including seaweed and various shrubs or trees, have the ability to hold water, and often act as thickeners, stabilizers, or gelling agents in various food products

colloidal a state of subdivision of dispersed particles; intermediate between very small particles in true solution and large particles in suspension

tuber an enlarged underground stem, for example, the potato

modified starches natural or native starches that have been treated chemically to create some specific change in chemical structure, such as linking parts of the molecules together or adding some new chemical groups to the molecules; the chemical changes create new physical properties that improve the performance of the starches in food preparation

gel a colloidal dispersion that shows some rigidity and will, when unmolded, keep the shape of the container in which it had been placed

starches are often chemically modified (**modified starches**) to enhance those properties that are desirable for specific applications in food manufacturing. Through crossbreeding and genetic research, native starches with properties similar to the chemically modified ones may be developed.

COMPOSITION AND STRUCTURE

The Starch Molecule

Starch is a polysaccharide made up of hundreds or even thousands of glucose molecules joined together. The molecules of starch are of two general types, called *fractions*: amylose and amylopectin.

Amylose is a long chainlike molecule, sometimes called the *linear fraction*, and is produced by linking together 500 to 2,000 glucose molecules. A representation of the amylose molecule is shown in Figure 13-1. The amylose fraction of starch contributes gelling characteristics to cooked and cooled starch mixtures. A **gel** is rigid to a certain degree and holds a shape when molded.

Amylopectin has a highly branched, bushy type of structure, very different from the long, stringlike molecule of amylose. In both amylose and amylopectin, however, the basic building unit is glucose. Figure 13-2 represents the chemical nature of amylopectin, with many short chains of glucose units branching from each other, much like the trunk and branches of a tree. Cohesion or thickening properties are contributed by amylopectin when a starch mixture is cooked in the presence of water, but this fraction does not produce a gel.

Most natural starches are mixtures of the two fractions. Corn, wheat, rice, potato, and tapioca starches contain 24 to 16 percent amylose, with the remainder being amylopectin. The root starches of tapioca and potato are lower in amylose content than the cereal starches of corn, wheat, and rice. Certain strains of corn, rice, grain sorghum, and barley have been developed that are practically devoid of amylose. These are called *waxy* varieties because of the waxy appearance of the kernel when it is cut. They contain only the amylopectin fraction of starch and are nongelling because of the lack of amylose. Through genetic manipulation, high-amylose starches have also been produced. For example, a high-amylose corn, called *amylomaize*, has starch that contains approximately 70 percent amylose. High-amylose starches have a unique ability to form films and to bind other ingredients.

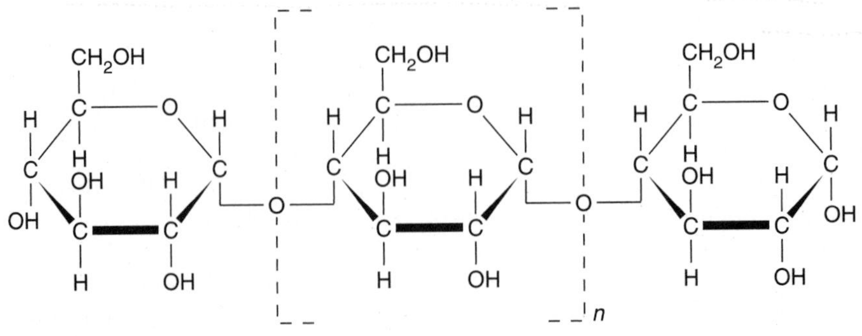

Figure 13-1
Amylose is a linear molecule with hundreds of glucose units linked together. A portion of the molecule is represented here. The glucose units are joined between the No. 1 carbon atom of one glucose molecule and the No. 4 carbon atom of the next one. The n may represent hundreds of similarly linked glucose molecules. See also Figure 9-6.

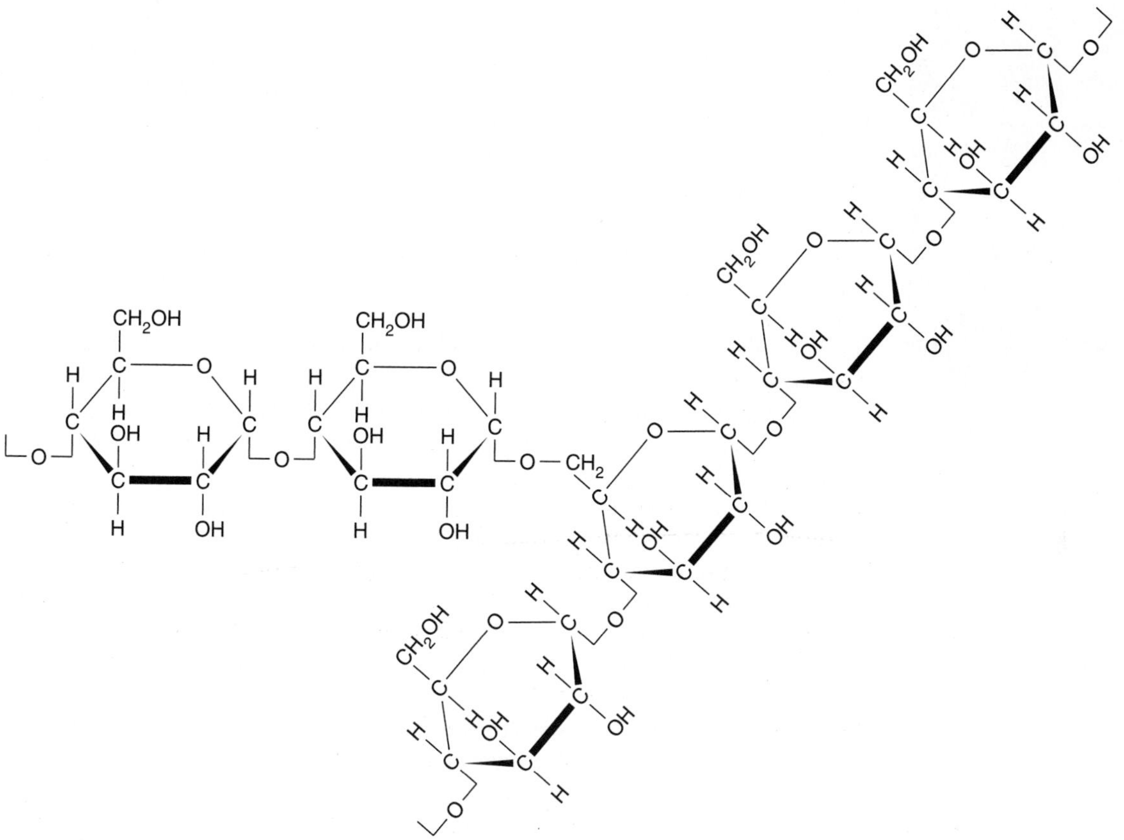

Figure 13-2

Amylopectin is a bushy, treelike molecule with many short branches of glucose units linked together. A portion of the molecule is represented here. The glucose units in the chains are joined between the No. 1 and the No. 4 carbon atoms. However, at the points of branching, the linkage is between the No. 1 carbon atom of one glucose unit and the No. 6 carbon atom of the other. See also Figure 9-6.

The Starch Granule

In the storage areas of plants, notably the seeds and roots, molecules of starch are deposited in tiny, organized units called *granules*. Amylose and amylopectin molecules are placed together in tightly packed stratified layers formed around a central spot in the granule called the *hilum*. The starch molecules are systematically structured in the granule to form crystalline-like patterns. If the starch granules, in a water suspension, are observed microscopically under **polarized light,** the highly oriented structure causes the light to be rotated so that a Maltese cross pattern on each granule is observed (Figure 13-3). This phenomenon is called **birefringence.** The pattern disappears when the starch mixture is heated and the structure disrupted. The sizes and shapes of granules differ among starches from various sources, but all starch granules are microscopic in size. Figure 13-4 shows photomicrographs of starch granules from various sources.

polarized light light that vibrates in one plane

birefringence the ability of a substance to refract light in two directions; this produces a dark cross on each starch granule when viewed with a polarizing microscope

Figure 13-3
Potato starch seen under polarized light shows birefringent crosses resulting from the highly organized nature of the granules (magnified 700×).
(Courtesy of Eileen Maywald, Corn Products Company)

Modified Starches

Starches from different sources behave differently in food preparation because of their varying compositions and ratios of amylose to amylopectin fractions. These differences should be considered when choosing a starch for a particular use, such as thickening a fruit pie filling or preparing a gravy or sauce. However, the natural or native starches may still have limitations when they are employed in food processing and manufacturing. Deliberate chemical modification of natural starches is often needed in the food-processing industry to achieve a desired texture and flavor in a finished product that must undergo high temperatures, high shear, low pH, or freeze-thaw cycles during its production [9]. Starch modification may be said to tailor functional characteristics to desired applications.

The U.S. Food and Drug Administration (FDA) has published regulations governing the modification of natural food starches, providing guidelines concerning the types and amounts of modifiers allowed, the residuals permitted, if any, and the combinations that are acceptable [8]. Within these guidelines, starch manufacturers work to develop new and innovative starch derivatives. The most common modifications of starch utilized by the food industry involve hydrolysis, cross-linking, and substitution [3]. Combinations of these treatments may also be applied in modifying natural starches. A wide variety of specialty starches is therefore available to the food processor with new types of starches continuing to be developed [12,13,14,11]. Some manufacturers are turning to starches to replace gelatin in their products to satisfy vegetarian customers [12]. Specialty starches provide the viscosity, texture, mouthfeel, and other desired properties for many types of foods, from creamy sauces to crispy snacks.

Chemical Processes Involved. Hydrolysis of starch may be accomplished by mixing starch with water and an acid to produce a random breaking of linkage points along the molecular chain. Most of the starch still remains in the form of granules and is dried after the acid treatment. This modified starch is known as *thin-boiling* or *acid-thinned starch*. It produces a paste with low viscosity when it is boiled and it hydrates at a lower temperature than the unmodified starch, but it still retains its gelling properties. Acid-thinned starch is often used in the confectionery industry [8].

Cross-linking is produced by the use of reagents that have two or more reactive groups. These groups react with starch molecules at selected points and create a cross bond between two chains of the starch molecule. Reagents include phosphorus oxychloride and adipic acid. Pronounced changes in starch characteristics result from cross-linking, including lower viscosity, increased temperature for hydration, increased stability in acid conditions, increased resistance to shear or stirring, and increased tolerance to heat. Food processors, therefore, have greater flexibility and control when they use cross-linked modified starches in manufactured foods [8]. Cross-linking may be thought of as welding molecular starch chains together at various spots or locations, thus limiting the swelling of the granules. Starches modified by cross-linking are valuable for foods that are heated for extended periods of time or are subjected to exceptionally high shear (e.g., spaghetti sauces and certain pie fillings).

Starches may be modified by *substituting* certain monofunctional chemicals (those having only one reactive group, such as acetate) on the hydroxyl groups (−OH) of the starch molecule at random points, which decreases the tendency

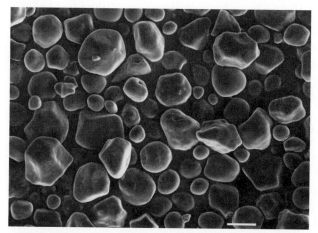

Corn starch

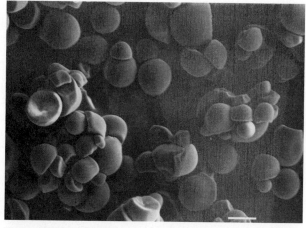

Tapioca starch

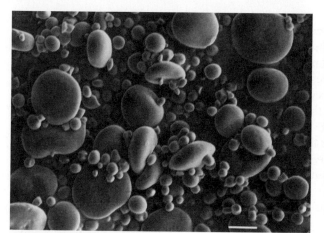

Wheat starch

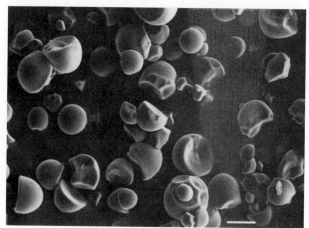

Arrowroot starch

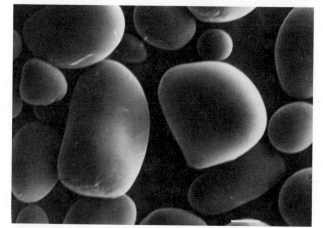

Potato starch

Figure 13-4

Starch granules from different plant sources have characteristic shapes. Granule size ranges from small to large within each plant source. The bar at the bottom of each photograph represents 10 μ m (micrometers). (Photographs courtesy of Dr. James Be-Miller, Whistler Center for Carbohydrate Research, Purdue University)

of bonding between molecular chains of the starch and increases the stability of the starch-thickened product as it is frozen and then thawed. Substitution also improves clarity and reduces *syneresis*, which is a weeping of liquid from the cooked starch mixture upon standing [8].

An example of the improved properties that result from modification of starches is found in lightly modified **waxy maize** starch. The natural starch is nongelling because it contains no amylose fraction, only amylopectin. In this regard, it should make a good thickening agent for fruit pies, providing a soft, thickened but not rigid mixture; however, it is quite stringy in texture, which is an undesirable characteristic for fruit pies. When it is chemically treated to produce cross-linking, the resulting starch retains its nongelling properties but loses the stringy characteristic. It is also much more stable to heating and freezing and makes an ideal thickening agent for many of the frozen fruit pies that are marketed. Modified starches are tailor made for specific uses in many convenience foods.

Instant Starches

Starch processors produce, for use by the food industry, starches that hydrate or absorb water in cold liquid systems. The two types of instant starches are precooked or pregelatinized starch, and so-called cold water swelling starch. The pregelatinized starch is cooked and dried, and in the process is degraded into granule fragments. In the preparation of cold water swelling starch, the starch granules remain intact. Thus, foods prepared with cold water swelling starch generally have better stability, appearance, and clarity, as well as a smoother texture, than foods prepared with pregelatinized starch [8,16]. In both cases, however, the starches hydrate and produce thickened mixtures when cold liquid is added.

Instant starches are utilized in instant dry-mix puddings, gravies, and sauces. They are also useful in the preparation of many microwavable prepared foods. Improved instant starches are important tools for food technologists to use in meeting the demands of today's changing marketplace.

Improved Native Starches

Many techniques and strategies are available today to help develop new varieties of starch-producing plants that have increased crop yield and improved resistance to pests. It is also important to breed plants that will produce natural starch with the desired functional properties, without the necessity of chemical modification during processing. This area of research is sometimes called genetic engineering (genetic engineering is discussed further in Chapter 3). To produce a plant, such as corn, potato, or tapioca, that forms starch with a particular function during its use in food processing, the scientist must know what genes in that plant produce the starch structure and composition that gives the desired function. Although this field presents many challenges for researchers, they are making progress. Strict government constraints on the amount and type of chemicals used to modify starches have encouraged starch producers to seek out hybrid plants that offer desired functional properties as native starches without chemical treatment [5,18]. A line of functional native starches that claims to give better texture with enhanced taste qualities when compared with traditional modified starches is now on the market, produced by a patented technology [10,11].

waxy maize a waxy variety of corn; the starch of this variety contains only the amylopectin fraction

Starch-based Fat Replacers

Many consumers want foods that are lower in fat content but, at the same time, are rich, creamy, flavorful, and satisfying. To meet this demand, the food industry has developed a variety of low-calorie, starch-based materials to replace fat in processed foods. These types of products are sometimes called *fat mimetics*. Carbohydrate fat replacers are usually modified starch hydrolysates, although several products are modified by substitution [19,12].

It has been suggested that the fat-replacing properties of starch-based materials result from an association of water with the structure of the carbohydrate particle. The carbohydrate strongly binds and orients water in such a way as to provide a sensation in the mouth that is similar to that produced by fat. Of course, formulating low-fat foods requires complete reformulation of traditional products. All attributes of the traditional food, such as flavor, sweetness, saltiness, acidity, texture, viscosity, mouthfeel, and appearance, must be considered and ingredient adjustments made to ensure that the desired characteristics continue to be present in the reformulated result [19].

HYDROLYSIS OF STARCH

Because glucose is the basic building block for starch molecules, complete hydrolysis of starch produces glucose. Intermediate steps in the breakdown first yield large chunks of starch molecules called **dextrins,** which are still large enough to be classified as polysaccharides; then sugars called **oligosaccharides,** which contain several glucose units; and finally maltose, a **disaccharide** with two **monosaccharide** units, which yields only glucose. Starch hydrolysis may be brought about or catalyzed by the action of enzymes called *amylases*. Acid may also act as a **catalyst** in the breakdown.

EFFECT OF HEAT ON STARCH

Dry Heat

When dry heat is applied to starch or starchy foods, the starch becomes more soluble in comparison with unheated starch and has reduced thickening power when it is made into a cooked paste. Some of the starch molecules are broken down to dextrins in a process that is sometimes called *dextrinization*. Color and flavor changes also take place when starch-containing foods are subjected to high temperatures with dry heat. A nonenzymatic browning occurs, and a toasted flavor, which may turn to a burned flavor if the process is continued, develops. Brown gravy or an **espagnole sauce** is usually relatively thin in consistency if the dry flour is browned or a **brown roux** is produced in the process of making the gravy without making adjustments to compensate for the decreased thickening ability of the roux. A larger proportion of flour to liquid, or more brown roux than is normally used, is necessary to obtain a thick gravy. Or, alternatively, some white flour may be used with the browned flour. Brown roux has a "peanut" flavor component as a result of browning. Dry-heat dextrins, known as *pyrodextrins*, are formed in the crust of baked flour mixtures, on toast, on fried starchy or starch-coated foods, and on various ready-to-eat cereals.

dextrins polysaccharides composed of many glucose units, produced at the beginning stages of starch hydrolysis; they are somewhat smaller than starch molecules

oligosaccharide the general term for sugars composed of a few—often between three and ten—simple sugars or monosaccharides

disaccharide a sugar composed of two simple sugars or monosaccharides

monosaccharide a simple sugar unit, such as glucose

catalyst a substance that changes the rate of a chemical reaction without being used up in the reaction; enzymes are catalysts

espagnole sauce pronounced ess-span-yol, this is a classic brown sauce composed of brown stock, brown roux, mirepoix (diced onions, carrots, celery), and tomato purée.

brown roux equal parts, by weight, of flour and fat that are cooked together until a dark color and nutty aroma develops. A brown roux enhances the color and flavor of sauces and gravies.

Moist Heat

The starch granule is generally insoluble in cold water. A nonviscous suspension of starch is formed when raw starch is mixed with cold water and, on standing, the granules gradually settle to the bottom of the container. After this starch and water suspension is heated, a colloidal dispersion of starch in water is produced. The resulting thickened mixture is called a *starch paste.*

When starch is heated in water, a number of changes gradually occur over a temperature range that is characteristic for a particular starch. The starch granules absorb water and swell and the dispersion increases in **viscosity** or thickness until a peak viscosity is reached. The dispersion also increases in **translucency** to a maximum as heating continues [7]. Starch granules vary in size and do not swell at the same rate. Large granules swell first. Potato starch granules, generally larger than those of other starches, begin to swell at a lower temperature than corn starch or tapioca. In any case, swelling is usually complete at a temperature of 190° to 194°F (88° to 92°C).

As starch is heated in water, the set molecular order within each starch granule is disrupted as water is absorbed. This gradual process is called **gelatinization.** Irreversible changes that occur during gelatinization include the swelling of granules, the melting of small crystallite areas within the granule, the loss of birefringence (the crosses seen when granules are viewed under polarized light), and the solubilization of some of the starch molecules [1]. Figure 13-5 shows various stages in the heating of starch in water.

When the heating of the starch–water mixture continues after gelatinization, some further granular swelling occurs, as well as movement of more molecular components from the granule into the surrounding medium, and eventually total disruption of the granules. This process is called *pasting.* Gelatinization and pasting are generally described as sequential processes [1].

Continued heating under controlled conditions after gelatinization is complete results in decreased thickness. Boiling or cooking starchy sauces and puddings in the home for longer periods usually does not produce thinner mixtures, however, because the loss of moisture by evaporation is usually not controlled. The loss of moisture, which increases concentration of the starch, results in increased thickness and counterbalances the first process.

Most starch-based products prepared by the food industry are subjected to additional treatments after cooking is completed. These may include pumping, stirring, cooling, aging, drying, and packaging, all of which may cause additional changes that fragment the swollen starch granules [17].

Some cooked starch pastes are opaque or cloudy, but others are more clear in appearance. In general, the pastes made with cereal starches, such as those of corn and wheat, are cloudy in appearance, whereas those made from root starches, such as potato and tapioca, are more clear.

To obtain uniformity in the cooking of starch pastes, certain conditions must be standardized and controlled. These include temperature of heating, time of heating, intensity of agitation or stirring (shear), acidity (**pH**) of the mixture, and addition of other ingredients.

Temperature and Time of Heating. Starch pastes may be prepared most quickly by bringing them to a boiling temperature over direct heat, constantly stirring as they thicken, and simmering them for approximately 1 minute. Longer cooking to improve the flavor is not necessary; however, if a starch mix-

viscosity resistance to flow; increase in thickness or consistency

translucency partial transparency

gelatinization the sum of changes that occur in the first stages of heating starch granules in a moist environment; includes swelling of granules as water is absorbed and disruption of the organized granule structure

pH a scale of 1 to 14 indicating the degree of acidity or alkalinity, 1 being most acid, 7 neutral, and 14 most alkaline

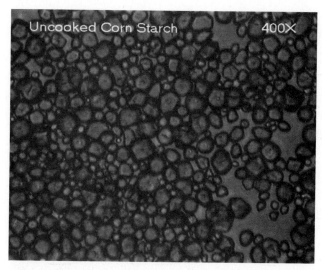

Unheated corn starch granules

Figure 13-5

Photographs showing the change in corn starch granules (magnified 400×) as heating in water (causing gelatinization) proceeds. The slides were stained with iodine. (Courtesy of Angela Macias, National Starch and Chemical Company)

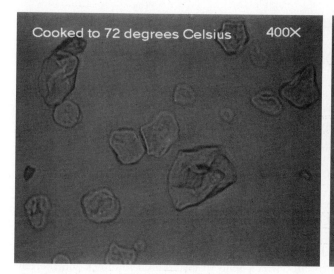

Corn starch granules heated in water to 162°F (72°C).

Corn starch granules heated in water to 195°F (90°C).

ture is not fully cooked, then a **raw starch flavor** and a less smooth or silky mouthfeel will be evident. Under carefully controlled conditions, starch pastes that are heated rapidly are somewhat thicker than similar pastes heated slowly [6]. More concentrated dispersions of starch show higher viscosity at lower temperatures than less concentrated mixtures because of the larger number of granules that can swell in the early stages of gelatinization. Each type of starch gelatinizes over a characteristic temperature range, although this range may be affected by starch concentration.

Agitation or Stirring. Stirring while cooking starch mixtures is desirable in the early stages to obtain a smooth product of uniform consistency. If agitation is too intense or is continued too long, however, it accelerates the rupturing of

raw starch flavor an undercooked starch in a sauce, gravy, or soup will reduce the flavor of the other ingredients and will provide a flat flavor. You can learn to identify this flavor by tasting a product shortly after the starch has been added, then by tasting it again as cooking proceeds. A fully cooked product should have no raw starch flavor.

the starch granules, decreases viscosity, and may give a slick, pasty mouthfeel. Stirring should therefore be minimized.

Acidity (pH).   A high degree of acidity appears to cause some fragmentation of starch granules and hydrolysis of some of the starch molecules, thus decreasing the thickening power of the starch granules [4]. In cooked starch mixtures containing fruit juices or vinegar, such as fruit pie fillings and salad dressings, the acidity may be high enough (pH below 4) to cause some thinning. Specially prepared modified starches resistant to acid breakdown are used in commercial food processing when this may be a problem. When a high concentration of sugar is also present in a starch paste, the sugar may help to decrease the effect of acid, because sugar limits the swelling of starch granules, and the starch molecules are therefore not as available for hydrolysis by acid. Proportions of ingredients in recipes for acid-starch products, such as lemon pie filling, have been adjusted to compensate for the usual effects of acid and sugar so that a desirable consistency results. Acid juices, such as lemon juice, can also be added after the starchy paste has been cooked, thus limiting the acid's contact with starch molecules.

Addition of Other Ingredients.   Various ingredients are used with starch in the preparation of food. Some of these ingredients have a pronounced effect on gelatinization and on the gel strength of the cooled starch mixture. Sugar raises the temperature at which a starch mixture gelatinizes [2,15]. The use of a relatively large amount of sugar delays the swelling of the starch granules and thus decreases the thickness of the paste, at least partially, by competing with the starch for water. If not enough water is available for the starch granules, they cannot swell sufficiently. In a recipe calling for a large amount of sugar, only part of the sugar need be added before cooking. After the starch mixture has been cooked, the remainder of the sugar can be added with much less effect on viscosity.

High concentrations of sucrose (table sugar) are more effective in delaying swelling or gelatinization than are equal concentrations of monosaccharides such as glucose and fructose. At a concentration of 20 percent or more, all sugars and syrups cause a decided decrease in the gel strength of starch pastes. The presence of fats and proteins, which tend to coat starch granules and thereby delay hydration, also lowers the rate of viscosity development.

GEL FORMATION AND RETROGRADATION

As a starch-thickened mixture is cooled without stirring after gelatinization is complete, additional changes ensue. These changes may include gel formation and also a process called **retrogradation.** Gel formation generally occurs first, followed by retrogradation.

Many starch molecules are disrupted during the process of gelatinization as the starch granules swell. Some of the molecules of amylose, the linear starch fraction, leach out from the granule. Two or more of these chains may form a juncture point, creating a new bond, which gradually leads to more bonds and more extensively ordered regions. Bonding with the amylose molecules begins immediately after cooking. Amylopectin, the branched fraction, usually remains inside the swollen granule where it more slowly forms new bonds between branches in a process of recrystallization [17]. Bonds formed between the

retrogradation the process in which starch molecules, particularly the amylose fraction, re-associate or bond together in an ordered structure after disruption by gelatinization; ultimately, a crystalline order appears

branches of the bushy amylopectin molecules are weak and have little practical effect on the rigidity of the starch paste; however, bonds between the long-chain amylose molecules are relatively strong and form readily. This bonding produces a three-dimensional structure that results in the development of a gel, with the amylose molecules forming a network that holds water in its meshes. The rigidity of the starch mixture is increased.

Gel formation or *gelation* is different from gelatinization. Gelation takes place on cooling of the starch paste after the starch granules have been gelatinized. Gel formation in cooked starch pastes is a gradual process that continues over a several-hour period as the paste cools. Waxy varieties of starch without amylose do not form gels. Starches containing relatively large amounts of amylose, such as corn starch, form firmer gels than starches with a somewhat lower concentration of amylose, such as tapioca.

As starch-thickened mixtures continue to stand after gel formation is complete, the process of retrogradation may continue to produce changes as additional bonds are formed between the straight-chain amylose molecules. The amylose molecules associate more closely together. Some of these molecules aggregate in a particular area in an organized, crystalline manner. As the amylose molecules pull together more tightly, the gel network shrinks, and water is pushed out of the gel. This process of weeping, called *syneresis*, results from the increased molecular association as the starch mixture ages. Ultimately an ordered crystalline structure develops [1]. Gel formation and retrogradation are illustrated in Figure 13-6.

Nongelling modified waxy starches are effectively used for products that are frozen or items such as a stir-fry sauce or gravy that is to be cooled and reheated for later use. A wheat flour or corn starch sauce or gravy is difficult to reheat into a smooth sauce after cooling due to gel formation.

STARCH COOKERY

Combining Starch with Hot Liquids

A potential problem in starch cookery results from the tendency of dry starch particles to clump or form lumps. Before hot liquids are combined with starch, the particles of starch must be separated to bring about a uniform dispersion of well-hydrated starch granules. This process can be accomplished by dispersing the dry starch with melted fat, by blending it with sugar, or by mixing it with cold water to form a **slurry** before adding it to hot liquid.

slurry a thin mixture of water and a fine insoluble material such as flour

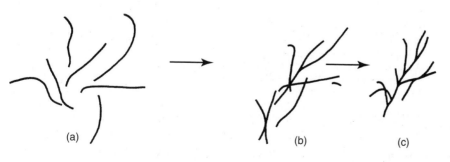

(a)　　　　(b)　　　　(c)

Figure 13-6
A diagram representing gel formation and further retrogradation of a starch dispersion: (a) solution, (b) gel, (c) retrograded. (From Elizabeth Osman, "Starch and Other Polysaccharides." (In Food Theory and Applications. Pauline C. Paul and Helen H. Palmer, editors. Copyright© 1972, John Wiley & Sons, Inc. Reprinted by permission of John Wiley & Sons, Inc.)

White Sauces

A white sauce is a starch-thickened sauce made from fat, flour, liquid, and seasonings. When the liquid is milk, the basic sauce is called *béchamel* (bay'-sha-mel *or* besh'-a-mel). When the liquid is a light stock of veal, chicken, or fish, the sauce is called a *velouté* (vayl'-oo-tay'). White sauces are used in the preparation of a variety of dishes, including creamed eggs, fish, and vegetables; cheese sauce; cream soups; soufflés; croquettes; and certain casserole mixtures. The finished sauce should be smooth and satiny and free of lumps. The consistency depends on the amount of starchy agent used. Table 13-1 gives proportions for white sauces of various consistencies along with suggested uses.

With the current emphasis on reducing our fat intake, we Americans may well look for ways to modify recipes toward this end. The making of white sauces is the perfect opportunity to begin reducing fat intake. Only enough fat to separate the starch granules is actually needed. Thus, for the thicker white sauces particularly, the amount of fat that has traditionally been recommended may be reduced without affecting the quality of the finished sauce.

Ingredients for a white sauce may be mixed in different ways as long as a smooth, creamy product results. Most commonly, the fat is melted and the flour and salt are then stirred into it to help separate the starch granules so that lumping is less likely when the hot liquid is added. The fat-flour mixture, called a **roux,** is cooked until bubbly. Milk or other liquid is then added with constant stirring, and the sauce is brought to boiling over direct heat. A double boiler may also be used, but cooking is then slower.

roux a thickening agent made by heating a blend of fat and flour

In an alternative method for preparing white sauce, the flour or starch is mixed with some of the cold liquid to form a slurry (it should be the consistency of thick cream). The remainder of the liquid is then added, and the mixture is cooked over direct heat until it boils. At this time the fat and seasonings are added (if butter is the fat, the volatile flavor may be better retained with this method). Because **instantized flour** has less of a tendency to form lumps when mixed with liquid than noninstantized flour, it may be more successful in the making of white sauce. Although the slurry method is useful for many products, it may not provide as rich a flavor and generally will be less stable in a soup or sauce than when these products are prepared with a roux. However, a sauce will be more clear and glossy when cornstarch is used instead of flour and so some dishes such as stir fry vegetables are best prepared with the slurry method. If corn starch is substituted for flour in making a white sauce, only half as much corn starch should be used as compared to the original amount of flour.

instantized flour wheat flour that has been moistened and redried in such a way that many tiny particles of flour agglomerate to form larger, more uniform particles; does not pack down easily and pours more like salt

Table 13-1
Proportions of Ingredients and Uses for White Sauce

Sauce	Fat*	Flour	Liquid	Salt	Pepper	Uses
Thin	1 ½ tsp (7 g)	1 Tbsp (7 g)	1 c (237 mL)	¼ tsp (1.5 g)	fg	Cream soups
Medium	1 Tbsp (14 g)	2 Tbsp (14 g)	1 c	¼ tsp	fg	Creamed vegetables and meats; casseroles
Thick	1 ½ Tbsp (21 g)	3 Tbsp (21 g)	1 c	¼ tsp	fg	Soufflés
Very thick	2 Tbsp (28 g)	4 Tbsp (28 g)	1 c	¼ tsp	fg	Croquettes

*Amounts may be adjusted, if desired. A roux should be the consistency of wet sand.

Cream Soups

Cream soups may vary in consistency, but their usual thickness corresponds to that of thin white sauce. One tablespoon of flour is used for each cup of liquid, which may be part milk and part vegetable cooking water or meat broth and finely diced vegetables. Combined vegetable waters sometimes produce a soup of better flavor than the water from a single vegetable. A mirepoix, composed of diced onions, carrots, and celery is used in a number of soups because of the flavor provided. If starchy vegetables are used for pulp, such as is done in some purée or cream soups, then the flour must be reduced to about one-half the usual amount. The fat must then also be reduced, or, lacking enough flour to hold it in suspension, it will float on top of the soup. Some flour is desirable for starchy soups, such as potato or dried bean soup, to hold the pulp in suspension. In preparing a cream soup, a medium white sauce can be made from milk, fat, flour, and seasonings. An amount of vegetable juice and pulp equal to the milk used is then heated and added to the sauce, thus diluting the mixture to the consistency of thin white sauce.

If acid juices, such as tomato, are used, the acid is added gradually to the white sauce at serving time to minimize the tendency to curdle. Baking soda is not a necessary ingredient in cream of tomato soup, and its use is not recommended because it may increase the alkalinity of the soup so much that vitamin C and some of the B vitamins are essentially destroyed by **oxidation.** The use

oxidation a chemical reaction that involves the addition of oxygen

Multicultural Cuisine

Soups—Less traditional and more diverse?

The image of soup is expanding! We may relate chicken soup to the comforting of a loved one who is ill—and this may still be an important role. But many different varieties of soup, some with exotic flavors and textures, can take us on culinary journeys across the globe.

Food technologists are assisting in the expansion by developing ingredients that capture Asian, French, Caribbean, and Italian cooking and can serve as key components in formulating soups. For example, coconut is used as both a flavor and a fat base in many Eastern and tropical cuisines, much the same as Western cuisines use butter, cream, or cheese. Interest in Indian and Thai cuisines is growing in the United States and Kraft Food has produced a dehydrated coconut, refined to a very fine particle size, that can be used in soups that are typical of these cuisines [13]. Soups also adapt well to the growing demand for vegetar-

ian products and are excellent vehicles for "hot" ingredients such as chilies, which are valued in many cultures.

Modified starches can aid in developing many food products, including soups and sauces such as instant cream-style soups, creamy jalapeño sauces, and microwavable spaghetti sauces, where high viscosity, smooth texture, and stability are desired. The bland or nonmasking flavor profiles of these starches allow more exotic flavors to come through in the finished recipe.

Soup is not just a first course or a side dish these days, either. It can also be the featured entrée, standing by itself. And a variety of vegetables and savory flavor combinations may also add to both nutritional quality and esthetic enjoyment. Many traditional soups can be upscaled for greater diversity in exploring other cuisines (plate III). Soup can truly be both a comfort and an indulgence [13].

Figure 13-7
This New England clam chowder has an attractive appearance and has been properly prepared so that the sauce is smooth and creamy.

Figure 13-8
Meringue is placed on this chocolate cream pie.

temper or tempering gradual warming of beaten eggs before adding to a hot liquid. If a recipe states to temper the eggs, then when the mixture (usually milk and starch) is thoroughly hot, pour one-fourth or more of the hot mixture slowly into the beaten eggs while mixing. Complete the process by pouring this hot mixture containing eggs into the pan and finish cooking.

of soda may also seriously mar flavor if an excess is used. Making a tomato sauce from the tomato juice, fat, and flour (roux) instead of making a white sauce is preferred by some cooks and is a common practice in the production of canned tomato soup. The hot tomato sauce should be added to the hot milk just at serving time to minimize curdling. Fresh, recently opened milk will be more stable in resisting curdling and whole or reduced fat milk generally shows less tendency to curdle than nonfat (skim) milk. Although a curdled cream soup is edible, it is aesthetically undesirable (Figure 13-7).

Starch-thickened Desserts

Corn starch pudding is probably the most common starch-thickened dessert. Although similar desserts are made from other cereal sources, including wheat flour alone or combined with tapioca or sago, puddings made with corn starch are often considered to have a smoother mouthfeel and less "pasty" texture than those made with flour. The consistency of starchy puddings varies according to personal preference. If a pudding stiff enough to form a mold is desired, it will have better flavor and texture if it is made as soft as possible while still holding its form when unmolded. Many prefer pudding to have a relatively soft consistency, in which case it must be spooned into individual dishes. Tapioca and sago puddings, particularly, are usually more acceptable when they are relatively soft.

The preparation of puddings and pie fillings often combines starch and egg cookery to produce a creamy mixture (Figure 13-8). The product is thickened with starch before the egg is added, because starch tolerates higher temperatures than egg. The pudding is first prepared in the same manner as a corn starch pudding containing no egg. After starch gelatinization is complete, a small amount of the hot starchy mixture may be added to the egg. This dilutes or **tempers** the egg so that it does not coagulate in lumps when it is added to the bulk of the hot mixture (Figure 13-9). Alternatively, a small amount of cold milk may be withheld in the beginning of the preparation and mixed with the egg to dilute it. This milk-egg mixture is then added all at once, with stirring, to the hot starchy pudding mixture, producing a smooth, creamy product.

Starchy puddings containing egg should be cooked sufficiently after the addition of the egg to coagulate the egg proteins. If this is not done, the pudding may become thin on standing. If a fairly large amount of egg is used, then the temperature of the pudding after the egg is added should not reach boiling, because this may result in curdling of the egg with a consequent grainy texture of the pudding.

Numerous additions or substitutions may be made to the basic formula for corn starch pudding to vary the flavor. These additions include chocolate or cocoa, caramelized sugar, shredded coconut, nuts, maple syrup, or diced fruits. Recipe books should be consulted for specific directions in preparing the variations.

Basic Formula for Corn Starch Pudding

2 to 3 Tbsp (16 to 24 g) corn starch	2 cup (474 mL) milk
1/4 cup (50 g) sugar	1 tsp vanilla
1/8 tsp salt	1 egg or 2 egg yolks (optional)

Mix sugar, salt, and starch. Add 1/2 cup of cold milk gradually to form a smooth mixture. Heat remaining milk in a saucepan and add the starch-sugar mixture

Figure 13-9
(a) Hot liquid is slowly poured into eggs while beating so as to warm the eggs gradually. (b) The egg and hot liquid are returned to the range to finish cooking.

(in which the starch particles have been separated by the sugar and then the cold milk) to the hot milk with constant stirring. Cook the mixture over direct heat, stirring constantly, until the mixture boils; continue simmering for 1 minute. Remove from heat and add vanilla. Chill. If egg is used in the pudding, add a small amount of the hot boiled mixture to the slightly beaten egg; then add this to the hot mixture in the saucepan. Cook over moderate heat for 3 or 4 minutes to a minimum of 165°F (74°C). After cooking is completed, add vanilla. Chill.

Microwave Cooking of Starch Mixtures

The microwave oven is a quick and convenient tool in the preparation of relatively small quantities of starch-thickened sauces and puddings. For example, a smooth, creamy chocolate pudding to serve only one or two persons may be prepared in just a few minutes. First, semisweet baking chocolate is heated in milk in a 2-cup measure with the microwave oven on high for 1 to 2 minutes until the mixture is hot. A blend of dry corn starch and sugar is then added to the hot chocolate milk, and the mixture is heated on high for 1/2 to 1 minute, stirring after each 30 seconds. Vanilla, butterscotch, and other types of starch-thickened puddings are prepared in a similar manner. Microwaved sauces and puddings need less stirring than conventionally cooked sauces and puddings, because there is no tendency for the material on the bottom of the container to scorch as in range-top cooking.

It is just as easy to prepare small amounts of a basic white sauce in the microwave oven. First, butter or margarine is melted by heating on high for 1/2 to 1 minute to make approximately 1 cup of sauce. The flour and seasonings are then added, and milk is blended into the fat-flour mixture. Microwaving 6 to 8 minutes then produces a smooth, creamy white sauce. The mixture is stirred at approximately 1-minute intervals during the cooking.

Gravies can be prepared using the microwave oven by first blending broth with flour and meat drippings. Then this mixture is heated in the microwave oven on high, with occasional stirring, until thickened.

Microwave cooking is not always efficient for large amounts of starch-thickened foods. If three or more cups of white sauce are to be prepared, for example, the microwave oven is not necessarily a timesaver. When large amounts of raw cereal are to be cooked, little time will be saved by using the microwave oven, because larger volumes of water must be heated and there must be sufficient time for gelatinization of the starch. An individual serving of cereal such as oatmeal, however, can be cooked in a few minutes in the microwave oven. One type of starch-based food that is not cooked properly in any amount by microwaves is conventional pastas.

Manufacturers of foods designed specifically for reheating or cooking in the microwave oven need to choose carefully the type of starch they use. The rate of heating in the microwave oven is accelerated compared with that achieved by conventional methods, and the heat distribution throughout the food is generally more variable, so traditional starches are not always appropriate. There may be insufficient time for proper hydration of the starch granules. Specially modified starches can, however, be designed to hydrate at a lower temperature. Instant starches of the cold water swelling type may also be effectively used in the production of microwavable foods.

CHAPTER SUMMARY

- The parts of plants that serve most prominently for the storage of starch are seeds, roots, and tubers. Thus, the most common sources of food starch are cereal grains, including corn, wheat, rice, grain, sorghum, and oats; legumes; and roots or tubers, including potato, sweet potato, arrowroot, and the tropical cassava plant. Purified starch may be separated from grains and tubers by a process called wet milling.

- Starch is a polysaccharide made up of hundreds or even thousands of glucose molecules joined together. The molecules of starch are of two general types, called fractions: amylose and amylopectin. The amylose fraction of starch contributes gelling characteristics to cooked and cooled starch mixtures. Amylopectin contributes to cohesion or thickening properties of a starch mixture. Most natural starches are a mixture of the two fractions. Starches from different sources behave differently in food preparation because of their varying compositions and ratio of amylose to amylopectin fractions.

- Molecules of starch are deposited in tiny, organized units called granules in the storage areas of plants, notably seeds and roots.

- Natural or native starches may be modified to achieve a desired texture or flavor in a finished product that must undergo high temperature, high shear, low pH, or freeze-thaw cycles in its production. The most common modifications of starch utilized by the food industry involve hydrolysis, cross-linking, and substitution.

- Hydrolysis of starch may be accomplished by mixing starch with water and an acid to produce a random breaking of linkage points along the molecular chain. Cross-linking is produced by the use of reagents that have two or more reactive groups that react with the starch molecule and create cross bonds. Starches may be modified by substituting certain monofunctional chemicals on the hydroxyl groups of the starch molecule at random points.

- Instant starches hydrate or absorb water in cold liquid systems. The two types of instant starches are precooked or pregelatinized starch, and so-called cold water swelling starch.

- Starch-based materials may be used in some food products to replace fat while maintaining the desirable rich and creamy characteristics associated with a high-fat food.

- When dry heat is applied to starch or starchy foods, the starch becomes more soluble in comparison with unheated starch and has reduced thickening power when it is made into a cooked paste. Some of the starch molecules are broken down to dextrins. Color and flavor changes also take place when starch-containing foods are subjected to high temperatures.

- The starch granule is generally insoluble in cold water. After a starch and water suspension is heated, a colloidal dispersion of starch in water is produced, eventually becoming a starch paste. As starch is heated in water, the starch granules absorb water and swell. Gelatinization and pasting are the terms used to describe the gradual change in the starch granules when heated in water.

- Starch pastes may be prepared most quickly by bringing the mixture to a boil over direct heat, while constantly stirring, then simmering approximately 1 minute. A starch mixture that has not been fully cooked will have a raw starch flavor and a less smooth or silky mouthfeel.

- Although stirring is desirable while cooking a starch mixture, excessive agitation will accelerate the rupturing of the starch granules, decrease viscosity, and may give a slick, pasty mouthfeel.

- A high degree of acidity appears to cause some fragmentation of starch granules and hydrolysis of some of the starch molecules, thus decreasing the thickening power of the granules.

- As a starch-thickened mixture is cooled without stirring, gel formation and a process called retrogradation may occur. Gel formation or gelation is different from gelatinization. Waxy varieties of starch, without amylose, do not form gels.

- Retrogradation produces changes after gel formation as additional bonds are formed between the straight-chain amylose molecules. As the amylose molecules associate more closely together, the gel network shrinks, and water is pushed out of the gel. Syneresis results from this increased molecular association as the starch mixture ages.

- Dry starch particles may clump or form lumps unless the dry starch is dispersed with melted fat, blended with sugar, or mixed with cold water. A roux is the name used in cooking to describe melted fat and a starch such as flour that are cooked together. A slurry is a mixture of starch and a cold liquid.

- In the preparation of starch-thickened desserts, the starch is first mixed with sugar. Generally the starch and liquid mixture is cooked together before the addition of the eggs. To prevent curdling, eggs should be tempered before adding to the hot starch mixture to complete cooking.

- Starch mixtures may be prepared in the microwave, providing relatively small quantities of starch-thickened sauces and puddings are to be made.

KEY TERMS

germination
polysaccharide
hydrolysis
glucose

amylase
maltose
hydrocolloid
pectin

vegetable gums   espagnole sauce
colloidal   brown roux
tuber   viscosity
modified starches   translucency
gel   gelatinization
polarized light   pH
birefringence   raw starch flavor
waxy maize   retrogradation
dextrins   slurry
oligosaccharide   roux
disaccharide   instantized flour
monosaccharide   oxidation
catalyst   temper or tempering

STUDY QUESTIONS

1. Starch is a storage form of carbohydrate deposited as granules in plant cells.
   a. Describe the appearance of starch granules when viewed under a microscope; how do their size and shape differ from one plant source to another?
   b. Name the two fractions of starch and explain how they differ in structure.
   c. Explain why some natural starches are chemically modified and give examples of the types of chemical modification most commonly used.
   d. How can native starches be improved for desirable uses in food processing, lessening the need for chemically modified starches?
   e. What products are produced as starch is hydrolyzed, and what may catalyze this process?

2. a. Describe what happens when dry starches are heated. What is this process called?
   b. Why is gravy made from browned flour usually thinner than gravy made from the same amount of unbrowned flour? Explain.
   c. Describe what happens when starch granules are heated in water. What is this process called?
   d. Distinguish between the process described in question c and *pasting* of starch.
   e. Describe the general effect of each of the following on the thickness of a cooked starch mixture: (1) rate of heating, (2) excessive stirring, and (3) addition of sugar.

3. Many starch-thickened mixtures become stiff or rigid on cooling.
   a. What is this process called and what happens in the starch mixture to bring it about?
   b. How does the amount of amylose in the starch affect the rigidity and why?
   c. What is meant by *retrogradation* of a starch paste?
   d. What is *syneresis* and why may it occur in cooked starch mixtures?
   e. Which of the common starches forms the stiffest and which the softest pudding when used in equal amounts? Explain.

4. Distinguish between *gelatinization* and *gelation* of starch mixtures.

5. Describe three ways to keep powdery starches from lumping when they are added to hot liquid. Explain what is happening in each case.

6. Describe appropriate methods for preparing each of the following items and explain why these methods should be successful.
   a. White sauce
   b. Cream of vegetable soup
   c. Cream of tomato soup
   d. Corn starch pudding
   e. Corn starch pudding with egg

7. What two types of instant starch are available to the food processor and how do these differ from each other? Give examples of products in which the consumer may expect to find instant starches used.

8. Suggest appropriate procedures for preparing puddings and white sauces in the microwave oven.

REFERENCES

1. Atwell, W. A., Hood, L. F., Lineback, D. R., Varriano-Marston, E., & Zobel, H. F. (1988). The terminology and methodology associated with basic starch phenomena. *Cereal Foods World, 33,* 306.

2. Bean, M. M., & Yamazaki, W. T. (1978). Wheat starch gelatinization in sugar solutions. I. Sucrose: Microscopy and viscosity effects. *Cereal Chemistry, 55,* 936.

3. Filer, L. J. (1988). Modified food starch: An update. *Journal of the American Dietetic Association, 88,* 342.

4. Hansuld, M. K., & Briant, A. M. (1954). The effect of citric acid on selected edible starches and flours. *Food Research 19,* 581.

5. Hoch, G. J. (1997). The starch search. *Food Processing, 58*(5), 60.

6. Holmes, Z. A., & Soeldner, A. (1981). Effect of heating rate and freezing and reheating of corn and wheat starch–water dispersions. *Journal of the American Dietetic Association, 78,* 352.

7. Holmes, Z. A., & Soeldner, A. (1981). Macrostructure of selected raw starches and selected heated starch dispersions. *Journal of the American Dietetic Association, 78,* 153.

8. Luallen, T. E. (1985). Starch as a functional ingredient. *Food Technology, 39*(1), 59.

9. Luallen, T. E. (1994). The use of starches in frozen food formulation. *Food Technology, 48*(5), 39.

10. Messenger, B. (1997). Going native. *Food Processing, 58*(1), 48.

11. Pszczola, D. E. (1996). Native starches offer functionality comparable to modified starches. *Food Technology, 50*(12), 75.

12. Pszczola, D. E. (1999). Starches and gums move beyond fat replacement. *Food Technology, 53*(8), 74–80.

13. Pszczola, D. E. (2000). Less traditional soups and sauces would meet Warhol's approval. *Food Technology, 54*(3), 74–90.

14. Pszczola, D. E. (2002). Exploring novel flavor and health concepts on the West Coast front. *Food Technology, 56*(5), 34–90.

15. Spies, R. D., & Hoseney, R. C. (1982). Effect of sugars on starch gelatinization. *Cereal Chemistry, 59,* 128.

16. Staff. (1988). Introducing new line of cold water–swelling starches. *Food Technology, 42*(6), 160.

17. Waniska, R. D., & Gomez, M. H. (1992). Dispersion behavior of starch. *Food Technology, 46*(6), 110.

18. Wiesenborn, D. P., Orr, P. H., Casper, H. H., & Tacke, B. K. (1994). Potato starch paste behavior as related to some physical/chemical properties. *Journal of Food Science, 59*, 644.

19. Yackel, W. C., & Cox, C. (1992). Application of starch-based fat replacers. *Food Technology, 46*(6), 146.

Pasta and Cereal Grains

14

Cereal grains are seeds of the grass family. The word *cereal* is derived from *Ceres*, the Roman goddess of grain. Wheat, corn (maize), rice, oats, rye, barley, and millet are the most important cereals used for human food. Grain sorghum is used chiefly for animal feed, but starch is extracted from it for commercial food use. Triticale is a grain produced by cross-breeding wheat and rye. Although it is not a seed of the grass family, buckwheat is often classified with the cereal grains because buckwheat flour has properties and uses similar to those of cereal flours. A rediscovered cereal-like plant is amaranth, which produces an abundance of tiny seeds (Figure 14-1). About 1,000 of these seeds weigh approximately 1 gram. Amaranth is one of those rare plants whose leaves are eaten as a vegetable, and the seeds are used as cereals [38].

CONSUMPTION

Cereal is not limited to breakfast foods—it applies to a large group of foods made from grains, including flours, meals, breads, and alimentary pastes or pasta. The ease with which grains can be produced and stored, together with the relatively low cost and nutritional contribution of many cereal foods, particularly whole grain products, has resulted in the widespread use of grain commodities throughout the world. Actually, cereal grains are the principal crops that have made the continuation of humankind possible. They are the staple in the diets of most population groups.

On the basis of **disappearance data,** per capita use of flour and cereal products in the United States, after falling dramatically from the levels of the first half of the century, has increased over the past 25 years, rising to 200 pounds annually in 1999 [1](see Table 14-1). Wheat is the major grain eaten in the United States, with wheat products representing 75 percent of total grain consumption in 1997 [27, 28]. However, rice, corn, and oat products are gaining favor and have increased their share of total grain consumption since 1980 (see Figure 14-2). Several marketplace trends indicate that the grain business will be good or very good for years to come [34].

In spite of the information gained from the use of disappearance data for the available food supply, surveys of *actual* food intake by representative samples in the United States suggest that Americans are falling far short of consuming the amounts of grain products recommended by the Food Guide Pyramid.

disappearance data data about food that "disappears" into the nation's food distribution system; quantities calculated from inventories and from food produced and imported minus food exports

331

Figure 14-1
Amaranth seeds are very tiny, which is emphasized by showing them alongside small wheat kernels (on the left). The dime in the picture helps you to judge sizes by comparison. (Photograph by Chris Meister)

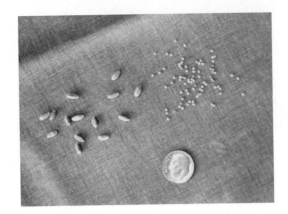

Participants in the U.S. Department of Agriculture's 1994–1996 Continuing Survey of Food Intake by Individuals consumed an average of 6.7 servings of grain products per day. Only 8 percent consumed the recommended three servings of whole-grain foods—such as brown rice, rolled oats, and whole wheat products—per day [6]. The average consumption of whole grains was one or fewer servings per day [11]. However, the consumption of grain-based products has increased since the late 1970's. The consumption of ready-to-eat cereal has increased by 60 percent and the consumption of snacks such as crackers, popcorn, pretzels, and corn chips has increased 200 percent [12].

STRUCTURE AND COMPOSITION

All whole grains have a similar structure: outer bran coats, a germ, and a starchy endosperm portion, as shown in Figure 14-3. Cereal products vary in composition depending on which part or parts of the grain are used.

Bran

The chaffy coat that covers the kernel during growth is eliminated when grains are harvested. The outer layers of the kernel proper, which are called the *bran*, constitute about 5 percent of the kernel. The bran has a high content of fiber and mineral ash. Milled bran may also contain some germ. The *aleurone* layer comprises the square cells located just under the bran layers of the kernel (see Figure 15-1). These cells are rich in protein, phosphorus, and thiamin, and also contain some fat. The aleurone layer comprises approximately 8 percent of the

Table 14-1
Annual Per Capita Grain Consumption in the United States

Years	Flour and Cereal Products (lbs)
1910-1915	287
1945-1949	204
1970-1974	135
1980-1984	148
1989	175
1990	185
1994	199
1999	200

Source: References 1, 23, 29.

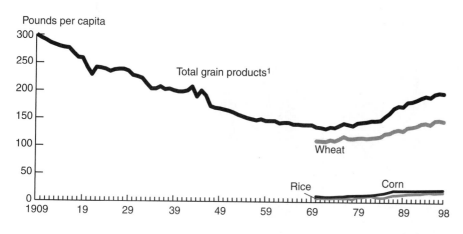

Figure 14-2
Since 1909 total grain consumption has declined; however, consumption has increased since the 1970s. Total also includes oat, barley, and rye products not shown separately. (Source: USDA's Economic Research Service.)

phytochemicals chemical substances that have a health benefit and are found in plant foods

phytoestrogens substances found in plant foods, such as soybeans, that have an estrogen-like effect on the body when consumed in the diet.

Healthy Eating

Whole-grain foods—How many servings today?

How many servings of whole-grain foods have you eaten today? If you are an average consumer in the United States, the answer to this question is *"less than one."* Many professional groups concerned with public health nutrition recommend that we eat at least six grain servings each day and that at least half of these be whole grains. "Three are key" is a suggested motto when it comes to whole grains.

Joanne Slavin and David Kritchevsky, of the University of Minnesota and Wistar Institute of Anatomy and Biology, respectively, recently outlined some basic reasons why whole grains are so important to our health [33]. We know that whole grains provide dietary fiber, vitamins, and minerals. We can get these from other foods. But whole grains also provide **phytochemicals** that function as nutrients, antioxidants, and **phytoestrogens.** And whole-grain consumption reduces the risk of certain cancers, stroke, diabetes, and cardiovascular disease.

The researchers point out that the whole is greater than that sum of the parts. The total protectiveness of whole-grain intake against heart disease appears to be greater than the sum of the protection seen with the parts—vitamins, minerals, soluble fiber, etc. that are found in whole grains. Consumers need to get this message and act on it by making significant changes in their diets.

The food industry can also help by overcoming barriers to whole-grain consumption—including flavor characteristics, price, informative labeling, and convenience. In 1999, the FDA approved a health claim for whole grains; "Diets rich in whole grains and other plant foods that are low in total fat, saturated fat, and cholesterol may reduce the risk of heart disease and some cancer." To qualify for this claim, the food must contain at least 51 percent whole-grain ingredients. Food manufacturers need to find ways to produce healthful whole-grain products that meet the taste test of consumers. Science supports the importance of this effort. So, how many servings of whole grains will you eat tomorrow?

Figure 14-3
Several common grains have similar structures. They are used to make a variety of breakfast cereals.
(Courtesy of Cereal Institute, Inc.)

GRAINS FOR BREAKFAST CEREALS

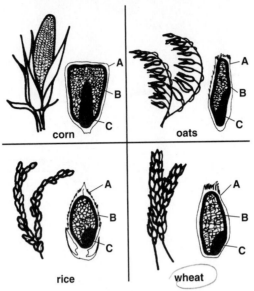

corn   oats

rice   wheat

A BRAN consists of several thin outer layers of the grain kernel and is its protective coat.

B ENDOSPERM is the stored food supply for the new plant which develops as the kernel germinates. It comprises about 85% of the kernel.

C EMBRYO or GERM is the miniature plant which enlarges and develops after the kernel germinates.

whole kernel. In the milling of white flour, the aleurone layer is removed with the bran.

Endosperm

The *endosperm* is the large central portion of the kernel and constitutes about 83 percent of the grain. It contains most of the starch (Figure 14-4) and most of the protein of the kernel, but very little mineral matter or fiber and only a trace of fat. The vitamin content of the endosperm is generally low. Milled white flour comes entirely from the endosperm.

Germ or Embryo

The *germ* is a small structure at the lower end of the kernel from which sprouting begins and the new plant grows. It usually comprises only 2 to 3 percent of the whole kernel. It is rich in fat, protein, ash, and vitamins. When the kernel is broken, as it is in certain processing procedures, the fat is exposed to oxygen in the air. This greatly reduces the storage life of the grain because the fat may become rancid. The broken or milled grain is also more susceptible to infestation by insects.

NUTRITIVE VALUE AND ENRICHMENT

Cereal grains are important dietary components for several nutritional reasons. They provide the world population with a majority of its food calories and about half of its protein. For the emphasis on dietary fat reduction and in-

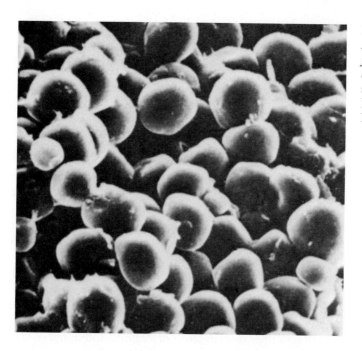

Figure 14-4
A scanning electron micrograph of the fractured surface of the endosperm of corn showing the corn starch granules. (Courtesy of the Northern Regional Research Center, U.S. Department of Agriculture)

creased complex carbohydrate intake (starch and fiber), cereal grains are "made to order." They are excellent sources of starch, the nutritive polysaccharide, and indigestible fiber. They are low in fat and supply a number of valuable vitamins and minerals.

The proteins of cereal grains are generally of relatively low biological value; however, when cereals are used with other protein-containing foods that supply the amino acids lacking in cereals, the nutritive value of the cereal protein is greatly improved. Various cereals and legumes supplement each other with respect to essential amino acid content so that the quality of the protein actually eaten is considerably increased. In a vegetarian diet, the lack of the essential amino acid lysine in cereal grains is complemented by the sufficiency of lysine in legumes, including soybeans. The presence of the amino acid methionine in cereal grains makes up for its lack in legumes.

The nutritive value of cereal products varies with the part of the grain that is used and the method of processing. The endosperm, which is the part used in refined flours and cereals such as farina, contains chiefly starch and protein. Therefore, refined cereals and flours furnish little more than these two nutrients unless they are enriched with some of the vitamins and minerals lost in milling. It is, then, to our benefit to use whole-grain products that are higher in a number of micronutrients [6].

Enriched and **fortified** flour, according to a legal definition, is white flour to which specified B vitamins (thiamin, riboflavin, and niacin) and iron have been added. In 1996, the U.S. Food and Drug Administration (FDA) mandated the addition of folic acid, in an attempt to help prevent birth defects due to a deficiency of this vitamin [17]. Optional enrichment ingredients include calcium and vitamin D. Enriched bread may be made from enriched flour, or the bread may be enriched by the addition of an enrichment wafer during mixing. The standards for enriched white flour published by the FDA are listed in Table 14-2. Enrichment is required for refined cereal products that enter interstate

enriched enriched foods have had nutrients added so that the food meets the specified legal minimum or maximum levels of nutrients normally found in the food before processing. For example: flour and grain products are enriched to replace the nutrients lost when the bran and germ were removed to produce white flour.

fortified fortified foods have had ingredients, not normally found in the food, added so as improve nutritional content. For example: orange juice is fortified with calcium because calcium is a nutrient not found in oranges.

	Thiamin	Riboflavin	Niacin	Iron	Folic acid
Whole wheat flour	2.49	0.54	19.7	15.0	
Enriched white flour	2.0–2.5	1.2–1.5	16–20	13.0–16.5	0.43–1.4
Enriched bread, rolls, or buns	1.1–1.8	0.7–1.6	10–15	8.0–12.5	0.43–1.4

*One pound of flour is usually equivalent to 1 1/2 pounds of bread.

commerce. Many states have also passed laws requiring that various refined cereal products and flours sold within their boundaries be enriched.

Enrichment of white flour does not make it nutritionally equivalent to whole-grain flour since only a few of the nutrients lost in milling are replaced by the enrichment process. Whole-grain products are particularly valuable as dietary sources of iron, phosphorus, thiamin, and vitamin B_6, as well as fiber. In fact, they are an excellent source of fiber, which is lacking in the diets of many Americans [35]. Many breakfast cereals are highly fortified with vitamins and minerals, well beyond the usual enrichment standards. One study found that ready-to-eat cereals consumed by 10-year-old children made an important contribution to their diets in terms of vitamins and minerals [21].

COMMON CEREAL GRAINS

Wheat

Wheat is one of the most widely cultivated plants on earth. Every month of the year, a crop of wheat is maturing at some place in the world. This plant has been cultivated since very early times and has grown to several thousand different varieties. Plant breeders have created wheat varieties with high yields and with strong disease resistance.

Wheat is commonly milled into flour. Varieties of wheat used for flour are often classified in terms of their "hardness" or "softness." Hard wheats are higher in protein content than soft wheats and usually have greater baking strength in that they result in a loaf of bread of large volume and fine texture. Soft wheats are therefore commonly used to make pastries, cookies, crackers, and other products where a high protein content is undesirable [8]. Wheat flour is uniquely suitable for bread making because it contains proteins that develop strong, elastic properties in dough. No other common cereal grain equals wheat in bread-making qualities. Classes of wheat, milling, and flour are discussed in more detail in Chapter 15.

Durum wheat is a very hard, non–bread-making wheat of high protein content. It is grown chiefly for use in making macaroni and other pasta. Nearly 73 percent of the durum wheat produced in the United States is grown in North Dakota [20].

Bulgur is wheat that is parboiled and then dried. A small amount of the outer bran layers is removed, and the wheat is then usually cracked. It is an ancient form of processing wheat, used in biblical times. Bulgar may be dried by solar or microwave methods without a significant effect on flavor, mouthfeel, or appearance [14]. Armenian restaurants commonly serve cooked bulgur in the form of pilaf and it may be found as an ingredient in vegetarian dishes. Additionally, bulgar may be present in recipes originating in Turkey, Greece, Cyprus, the Middle East, North Africa, and East Europe.

Wheat is also used for the production of wheat starch and, in large quantity, for the making of various types of breakfast cereals. A comparison of composition and nutritive value for various cereals is given in Appendix C.

Corn

Corn is a plant that is native to America. Early settlers in the New World were introduced to the uses of corn by Native Americans. The United States produced 43 percent of the world's corn in 2000 and is the leading exporter of corn [39]. Corn is a major food for the peoples of Mexico and Central America and is a staple ingredient in America's fastest growing ethnic cuisine—Mexican. The most popular items in Mexican restaurants—tacos, quesadillas, and fajitas—contain corn [34]. Corn is also quite popular in the southern United States, used as grits, hominy, and cornbread.

Corn used as a grain is called *dent* or *field* corn and is different than sweet corn that is consumed as a vegetable. Field corn is harvested in the fall when it is dry and the kernel has formed a dent. The corn kernel is versatile and can take a great variety of forms. When the corn kernel endosperm is freed of the bran and germ, hominy is produced (see Figure 14-5). The whole endosperm of hominy is broken into fairly small pieces to make hominy grits. Corn is also milled into cornmeal, a ground granular product made either without the germ and most of the bran, or with all of the kernel except the larger bran particles. Both white and yellow corn are used to make cornmeal. Refined cornmeal and hominy grits may be enriched. In the southern part of the United States, hominy grits are often served as a breakfast cereal.

The corn tortilla plays a central role in Mexican cuisine and the tortilla is becoming one of the fastest growing segments of the baking industry in the United States [36]. Either corn or flour tortillas make excellent "wraps" for a variety of food mixtures. Tortillas are traditionally made from corn that is **steeped** and cooked in alkali solution, washed to remove excess alkali, and

steep to soak

Figure 14-5
Hominy is the endosperm of the corn kernel, freed from bran and germ.
(Photograph by Chris Meister)

ground on a stone mill into a dough called *masa*. Masa is pressed into flat, circular shapes, which are then cooked on a hot griddle [16]. This traditional procedure for making tortillas, however, is being replaced by large-scale commercial operations in which corn is cooked and ground immediately with little or no steeping, and the tortillas are cooked in large, automated cookers.

Corn is an important component of many breakfast cereals. Additionally, corn flour is used in several commercial flour mixes. Corn oil, which contains a high proportion of polyunsaturated fatty acids, is extracted from the germ of the corn kernel. Corn syrups and glucose are produced by the hydrolysis of corn starch, which is the principal starch used in the United States for culinary purposes.

Corn is highly versatile, which is why American farmers annually devote millions of acres to its growth. It has thousands of uses, not only in foods, but in all kinds of consumer and industrial products. For example, corn is the source of the ethanol that is blended with gasoline for cleaner-burning fuel, and corn starch is used as a clay binder in ceramics, an adhesive in glues, and a bodying agent in dyes.

Rice

Considered as a world crop, rice is one of the most used of all cereal grains. It is the major food in the diets of many people living in Asia. In the last decade, Americans doubled their consumption of rice to more than 21 pounds per person [26]; in 1974, only 7 pounds of rice were consumed per person per year in the United States [23]. Six states now produce more than 90 percent of the rice consumed in America: Arkansas, California, Louisiana, Mississippi, Missouri, and Texas [32, 10]. The United States is the third largest exporter of rice on the world market; only Thailand and Vietnam export more rice.

More than 40,000 different varieties of rice are grown worldwide [26], although only about 20 are grown commercially in the United States. Rice is classified as long-, medium-, and short-grain varieties (Figure 14-6 and Figure 14-7). The food industry also recognizes a fourth category called *specialty rices*. These are distinguished by characteristics other than shape and size and include varieties such as jasmine, basmati, arborio, and sweet glutinous or waxy rice [10]. Some of these have fragrant aromas.

Long-grain varieties of rice have comparatively high **amylose** content and are light and fluffy when cooked. The cooked kernels tend to separate. The

amylose the long-chain or linear fraction of starch

Figure 14-6
Short-, medium-, and long-grain varieties of rice. (Courtesy of The Rice Council)

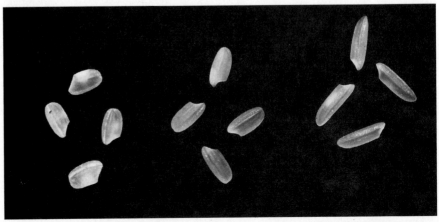

→ less amylose
→ absorb less water
→ kernels more clingy / sticky

→ less amylose

→ lots of amylose
→ light + fluffy
→ kernels seperate when cooked

Figure 14-7
This long-grain rice is grown in the United States. (Courtesy of U.S. Department of Agriculture Photo by Keith Weller)

medium- and short-grain varieties contain less amylose, absorb less water in cooking, and the kernels are more clingy or sticky when cooked. The preference for fluffy versus sticky rice depends on the culture of the consumer and the desired characteristics of the dish being prepared.

Specialty rices have become more popular in the United States as the interest in ethnic cuisines and new flavors has increased (Figure 14-8). Aromatic

Figure 14-8
An array of rice varieties are pictured (from top left, going clockwise) black japonica, aromatic red rice, basmati, brown, precooked, sweet, arborio, short, medium, long, parboiled, and jasmine. (Courtesy of USA Rice Federation)

Figure 14-9
A geneticist compares two kinds of low-phytate rice. (Courtesy U.S. Department of Agriculture Photo by Scott Bauer).

rices such as della, jasmine, and basmati have a flavor and aroma similar to roasted nuts or popcorn. Della and basmati are dry, separate, and fluffy when cooked, whereas jasmine tends to cling together [26]. Arborio is a medium-grain rice with a characteristic white dot in the center of the grain. Arborio is typically used in rissoto, a classic Italian dish, because it will absorb flavors and produce a creamy texture.

New rice varieties are being produced through genetic engineering. A product called golden rice with enhanced levels of vitamin A is under development. In areas of the world where vitamin A deficiency is common and rice is a staple in the diet, this rice could have a positive impact on health. Golden rice may be planted as early as 2003, pending approval [26]. Other researchers are working on a rice with lower levels of phytic acid (Figure 14-9). Phytic acid binds several minerals including iron, calcium, magnesium, and zinc. Since phytic acid is poorly digested, these minerals also become less available for use by our bodies when bound by phytic acid [9].

Wild rice is not true rice but rather the hulled and unmilled grain of a reed-like water plant. It is available only in limited quantity and is therefore usually relatively expensive. During the 1980's, methods were developed for cultivating wild rice. It is now grown in California, as well as in the Great Lakes region, where it was first discovered growing wild [10]. It is prized for its unusual nut-like flavor and uniquely long brown grains. Like many whole-grain cereals, it has relatively poor keeping quality, especially at warm temperatures.

Rice may be processed in several ways to produce brown rice, polished white rice, parboiled rice, precooked rice, or rice flour. Cultivated rice is available as white polished rice, which is basically the starchy endosperm of the rice grain. The bran coats and germ are rubbed off by an abrasive process. The polishing procedure also removes more than half of the minerals and most of the vitamins from the kernel. White rice may be enriched; often, a powdery material is applied to the surface of the grain. In this case, it is particularly important that the rice not be washed before cooking or rinsed after cooking to avoid loss of the enrichment nutrients. For brown rice, only the outer husk or chaffy coat is removed from the kernel. Brown rice is the least processed form, retaining the germ and most of the bran, which are rich in vitamins and minerals.

Parboiled or converted rice, which is always southern long grain, is soaked in water, drained, and then heated, typically by steaming, before it is dried and milled. In this process, nutrients that are normally lost during milling are retained in the rice kernel; thus, the nutritive value of milled rice is improved by parboiling [4]. The keeping quality of parboiled rice is also improved over that of the untreated grain. Although it takes more time to cook parboiled rice than regular milled white rice, the parboiled product disintegrates less during cooking, remains more separated, and retains its shape and texture longer during cooking. These characteristics are advantageous in foodservice systems that place food under heat lamps, and for manufacturers of canned soups and frozen dinners.

Precooked or instant rice is a long-grain rice that has been cooked, rinsed, and dried by a special process. It requires very little preparation. Precooked parboiled rice, because of better taste and texture, has replaced some sales of precooked regular milled rice in recent years [4].

Rice may be used to make rice flour, which has become a useful product in the manufacture of baked goods, pancake and waffle mixes, snack foods, and baby foods. It is made from grinding the grains that are broken during milling.

Rice flour is relatively resistant to syneresis in frozen/thawed foods and may replace modified starch in some applications. Rice flour has been shown in preliminary studies to reduce the absorption of oil by as much as 70 percent in donuts and 60 percent when used in a batter for fried chicken [26]. Therefore, rice flour may be used more in the future to produce lower fat deep-fried products. Rice flour also supplies a nonallergenic alternative to wheat flour products [22].

Rice bran is the outer brown layer that is removed during the milling of white rice. It deteriorates rapidly once it is separated from the rice kernel, because a **lipase** enzyme is exposed to the oil in the bran. The fat breaks down and an unacceptable musty taste rapidly develops. The bran may be treated, using dry-heat extrusion equipment, so that the enzyme is deactivated and the bran is stabilized [3]. Stabilized rice bran is currently being promoted as a major source of fiber for use in various manufactured foods.

lipase an enzyme that catalyzes the hydrolysis of triglycerides to yield glycerol and fatty acids

Oats

Oats are utilized in a rolled form as both old-fashioned and quick-cooking products. The husk clings very tightly to the oat kernel. When the grain is processed, the outer hull is removed, but most of the germ and bran remain with the endosperm. Rolled oats sold commercially, therefore, contain nearly the whole oat kernel. Because of the retention of most of the germ, rolled oats are higher in fat than most other cereals. They are also a good source of thiamin and other B vitamins and iron. Oat kernels with the outer hulls removed are called *groats*. Rolled oats are made by passing groats through rollers to form flakes. For quick-cooking rolled oats, the groats are cut into tiny particles that are then rolled into thin, small flakes. Regular or old-fashioned rolled oats are rolled without cutting.

Oatmeal has been a common breakfast cereal for many years, but has become even more popular with the publication of research indicating that oat bran is particularly effective in diets designed to lower elevated blood cholesterol levels. The use of oat fiber by the food industry thereafter increased greatly, as evidenced by a dramatic rise in the sale of oat bran by the Quaker Oats Company from 1 million pounds per year in 1986 to 2 million pounds per *month* by 1989 [30]. The benefit appears to come from oat bran's content of beta-glucan, a glucose polymer. Still, there are other cereal sources of beta-glucan, including barley, which is the subject of continuing nutrition research.

At the USDA Northern Regional Research Center, a process was developed for producing a granular or powdered material that contains an appreciable amount of beta-glucan from enzyme-treated oat bran or oat flour. This product is called *oatrim* and is being marketed commercially as a fat replacer.

Many prepared breakfast cereals contain oats. In addition, oats are used in the making of cookies, granola bars, baby foods, variety breads, candy, and snack items.

Rye

Rye is grown and used in the United States chiefly as a flour, but is also available as rye flakes and as a **pearled** grain. Although rye is a dark cereal grain, it actually has a mellow taste that may enhance the flavor of breads and cereals without overpowering them. Rye is used in the United States much less than wheat, but its use more nearly approaches wheat in baking quality than other

pearled a process that removes the outer hull, leaving a small, round, light "pearl" of grain

grains. In parts of Europe, rye is established as an important bread flour. Rye flour is available in three grades: light, medium, and dark.

Barley

Pearled barley is the chief form in which this grain is used at the present time in the United States. Pearling is a process that removes the outer hull of barley, leaving a small, round, white pearl of grain, the kind seen in some soups. Barley may become a valuable source of beta-glucan for the food industry. Some barley flour is available and may be used in breakfast cereals and baby foods. Sprouted barley is a source of malt, which is rich in the enzyme **amylase.** A commercially available source of barley for baking and cooking may be malted barley, which is a by-product of the beer-brewing industry. Although most of the beta-glucan is removed in the malting process, a concentrated oily substance called *tocotrienol* remains, and it appears to have blood cholesterol–lowering capabilities [30].

amylase an enzyme that catalyzes the hydrolysis of starch to yield dextrins and maltose

Triticale

Triticale is a hybrid plant produced by crossing wheat and rye. It combines desirable characteristics of each of the parent species. Generally, triticale has a higher protein content and better amino acid balance than wheat. It could be a valuable source of nutrients for many peoples of the world. Certain varieties of triticale have been shown to produce acceptable breads, snack crackers, and noodles [15, 31]. Although triticale is now used primarily for animal feed, it may find increasing use in the human diet as research on this grain continues [24].

Buckwheat

Buckwheat is not a seed of the grass family; it is the seed of an herbaceous plant. Because it contains a glutenous substance and is made into flour, it is commonly considered a grain product. Fine buckwheat flour has little of its thick fiber coating included. In that respect, it is similar to refined white flour. It is prized for its distinctive flavor and is commonly used in the making of griddle cakes. The volume of buckwheat flour sold in the United States is relatively small.

BREAKFAST CEREALS

Breakfast foods made from cereal grains vary widely in composition, depending on the kind of grain, the part of the grain used, the method of milling, and the method of processing. They may be uncooked, partially cooked, or completely cooked. Considerable amounts of sugars, syrups, molasses, or honey are added to some cereals. In certain products, heating dextrinizes part of the starch and produces toasted flavors.

Ready-to-Cook and Instant Cereals

Raw cereals that are cooked in both home and institutional kitchens include whole grains, cracked or crushed grains, granular products made from either the whole grain or the endosperm section of the kernel, and rolled or flaked whole grains. Finely cut flaked grains cook in a shorter time and hence are described as being *quick cooking*. Disodium phosphate is sometimes added to farina to make it quick cooking. It changes the pH of the cereal, becoming more alkaline, and thus causes more rapid absorption of water with faster cooking.

The starch in instant cereals, such as instant oatmeal, has been pregelatinized by prior cooking. Therefore, when boiling water is added and the mixture is simply stirred, the cereal is ready for consumption.

Ready-to-Eat Cereals

Basic processes used in the production of prepared cereals include shredding, puffing, granulating, flaking, and extruding (see Figure 14-10). Mixtures of cereals or cereal flours are often used. Ingredients commonly added to ready-to-eat cereals include sweetening agents, salt, flavorings, coloring agents, and antioxidants as preservatives. In most cases, the cereals are fortified to a comparatively high degree with minerals and vitamins, which are added at stages in the processing beyond which they are not subject to destruction by heat.

In the production of puffed cereals, the whole grain is cleaned and conditioned and put into a pressure chamber. The pressure in the chamber is raised to a high level and then suddenly released. The expansion of water vapor on release of the pressure puffs up the grains to several times their original size. The puffed product is dried by toasting, then cooled and packaged.

Flaked cereals are made by lightly rolling the grain between smooth rolls to fracture the outer layers of the cleaned and conditioned whole grain. This grain is then cooked, and various flavoring or sweetening substances are added so that they penetrate the rolled grain. The cooked product is dried, conditioned, flaked on heavy flaking rolls, toasted, cooled, and packaged.

In the preparation of granular breakfast cereals, a yeast-containing dough is made from a blend of flours. The dough is fermented and made into large loaves that are baked. The baked loaves are then broken up, dried, and ground to a standard fineness.

A white, starchy wheat is used for shredded cereals. The whole grain is cleaned and cooked with water so that it is soft and rubbery. The cooked grain is cooled, conditioned, and fed to shredders, which consist of a pair of metal rolls, one smooth and the other having circular grooves. The cereal emerges between the grooves as long parallel shreds. These shreds can be layered to form a thick mat. The mat is cut into the desired size, baked, dried, cooled, and packaged.

A number of fabricated products—snack foods and breakfast cereals—are extruded. In this process, the cereal-based material is made into a dough, which is fed into the extruder. Moisture content, time, temperature, and pressure are carefully controlled to achieve the desired result. A high-temperature, short-duration cooking period is used in many cases to produce expanded ready-to-eat cereals. Starch is gelatinized in the material as it moves through the extruder, and a colloidal gel is formed. When the product emerges from the nozzle of the extruder, the sudden drop in pressure permits the superheated water to form water vapor or steam. The mass then inflates with numerous tiny cells and is fixed in its expanded state [5].

Economics in Purchasing Cereals

Despite the large numbers of cereals on the market in the United States today, no federal standard of identity has been developed for breakfast cereals other than farina. The great variety available may cause some confusion in the buying and use of cereals, particularly since a great deal of advertising of these cereal products is done in the mass media, much of it aimed at young children.

GRAINS INTO BREAKFAST CEREALS

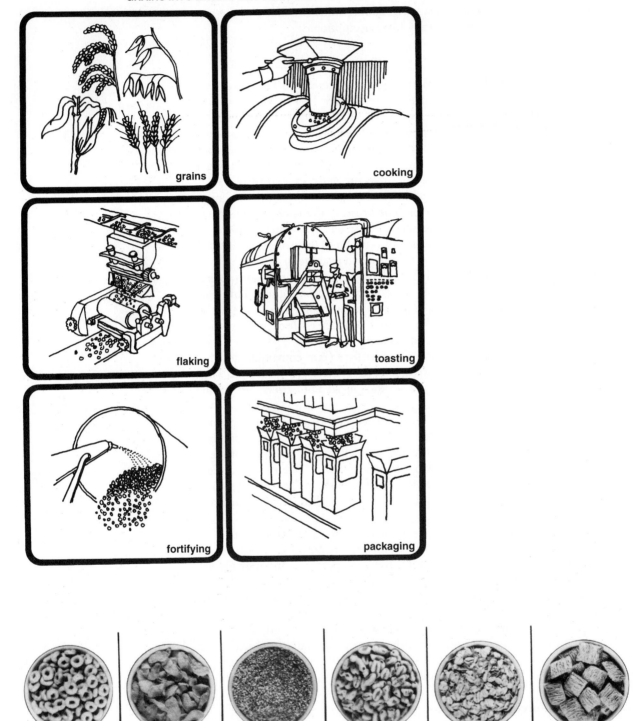

Figure 14-10
Major steps in the processing of grains into flaked cereals and types of prepared cereals. (Courtesy of Cereal Institute, Inc.)

Information on nutritive value and cost are essential aids to making wise purchases. Too much food money is sometimes spent for products that are no better nutritionally than many others that are available at a fraction of the cost. A large amount of sugar, up to 35 percent of the product by weight, is used in the production of some prepared cereals. Nutrition labeling provides useful information when making comparisons between products.

In general, the more processing done to a breakfast cereal and the more ingredients added, the higher the retail price. Packaging costs may also be high. Cereals cooked in the kitchen are usually much less costly than ready-to-eat cereals; however, ready-to-eat cereals are often popular with children and they are convenient. Those concerned about the highest nutritional return for their food dollar and those who are interested in high-fiber, low-sugar products would do well to choose the less processed cereals over the more convenient ready-to-eat cereals. Whole-grain cereals should be given preference because of their fiber content and generally higher nutrient density.

Cooking of Breakfast Cereals

The main purposes of cereal cookery are to improve palatability and digestibility. Historically, cereals may have first been consumed as whole grains with no preliminary preparation. Later, heat was applied in the parching of grains. Still later came the addition of water before the application of heat.

Cereal cookery is fundamentally starch cookery because starch is the predominant nutrient of cereals. Other factors involved are fiber, which is found chiefly in the exterior bran layers, and protein, which is a prominent constituent of the cereal endosperm. Until softened, or unless disintegrated mechanically, bran may interfere with the passage of water into the interior of the kernel and presumably may retard the swelling of starch. If cellulose is finely divided, its affinity for water is greatly increased. The temperatures necessary to cook starch are more than adequate for cooking the protein in the cereal.

Techniques for Combining Cereal and Water. If the cereal is in a finely divided form, such as with farina and cornmeal, it should be added to water in a way that avoids lumping so that a uniform gelatinous mass is formed on heating. All cereal particles should be equally exposed to water and heat. If lumps form, dry material remains inside a gelatinous external coating. The following two methods are commonly used to combine cereal with water. (Salt is usually added to the boiling water before the cereal is combined with it.)

1. Gradually pour the dry cereal into boiling water. Slight stirring may be required, but if the water does not cease boiling, stirring may be unnecessary.
2. Mix the cereal with cold water before adding it to the boiling water. The cold water tends to hold the particles apart.

Excessive stirring breaks up cereal particles so that they lose their identity. Even granulated cereals may be broken up to form a more gummy mass than would result from heating with the minimum amount of stirring.

Temperature and Time Periods. Cereals may be cooked entirely over direct heat using low to moderate temperatures, or they may be placed in a double boiler after the cereal has been added to the boiling water. Cooking times are somewhat less over direct heat than in a double boiler.

The principal factors that affect the time required for the cooking of cereals are the size of the particle, the amount of water used, the presence or absence of the bran, the temperature, and the method used. Finely granulated endosperm cereals, such as farina, cook in less time than whole or cracked cereals. Quick-cooking and precooked cereals, of course, can be prepared much faster than completely raw and untreated cereals.

Whole wheat is available in some areas and may be used as a breakfast cereal. If it is soaked before cooking, it cooks in less time than when it is cooked without soaking. In any case, 1 to 2 hours of cooking on a conventional surface unit is needed to soften the bran and completely gelatinize the starch granules. Soaking is best started in 2 cups of boiling water per cup of wheat. If the mixture is heated just to the boiling point after the grain is combined with the water, in a hot-soak method, undesirable fermentation is less likely to occur during a soaking period of several hours. The grain is cooked in the water in which it is soaked, more water being added as needed.

The cooked whole wheat may be stored in the refrigerator and reheated in the microwave oven for breakfast cereal as desired. It may also be used in casseroles and salads. When relatively small quantities are prepared, the microwave oven cooks cereals rapidly and satisfactorily with little or no stirring. The water may be first brought to boiling, the cereal added, and cooking completed on high power.

Proportions of Water to Cereal.   Proportions of water to cereal vary according to the type of cereal, the quantity cooked, the method of cooking, the length of cooking, and the consistency desired in the finished cereal. The majority of people appear to prefer a consistency that is fairly thick but not too thick to pour. The amount of water must be adequate to permit swelling of the starch granules. If the consistency is then too thin, further cooking may be necessary to evaporate the excess water.

Table 14-3 provides the common proportions used for various types of cereals. The amount of salt will vary according to taste.

COOKING OF RICE

White Rice

The challenge of rice cookery is to retain the form of the kernel while at the same time cooking the kernel until it is completely tender. It is usually suggested that rice be cooked with amounts of water that will be fully absorbed during cooking. Rice needs no more than about twice its volume of water. Regular rice increases to about three times its volume in cooking. One-half teaspoon of salt per cup of uncooked rice is usually used for seasoning. Enriched rice should not be rinsed before cooking because the enrichment mixture will be washed off.

Table 14-3

Approximate Proportions of Water to Cereal for Cooked Breakfast Foods

Type of Cereal	Water (cups)	Cereal (cups)
Rolled or flaked	2 or 2 1/2	1
Granular	4 or 5	1
Cracked grain	About 4	1
Whole grain	About 4 unless grain was soaked for several hours	1

When cooked by the boiling method, rice is added to 2.25 times its volume of boiling water, brought back to a boil, and then covered and finished over reduced heat. Cooking time is usually 15 to 20 minutes, although parboiled or converted rice takes a little longer. If rice is cooked in a double boiler, the volume of water may be reduced to 1 3/4 cups per 1 cup of rice. After the water is brought back to a boil over direct heat, the top of the double boiler is placed over boiling water and the covered rice is cooked for about 45 minutes, or until tender. Rice cookers have become popular and may be a convenient way to cook rice. In general, less liquid is needed to prepare rice in a rice cooker than when preparing it on top of the range.

For oven cooking, about the same amount of boiling water is needed as for the boiling method, because a longer time is required for cooking in a closed baking dish at 350°F—about 25–35 minutes for white rice or parboiled rice. Rice may be prepared in the microwave oven by covering in a microwave safe dish and cooking on high until boiling. Cooking should be completed on 50 percent power for 15–20 minutes, depending on the type of rice. Only a minimal amount of time is saved when preparing rice in the microwave because the rice kernel still must absorb water and soften during the cooking process.

Rice can be cooked in milk with the use of the double-boiler method. Cooking rice in chicken or beef broth can also give it a desirable flavor. Many ingredients such as herbs, spices, garlic, sautéed onions, or lemon zest can result in a delicious rice dish. A variety of hot and cold dishes may be made with rice as a basic ingredient (see Figure 14-11 and plate IV).

In some parts of the country where the water is hard, the minerals in the water can produce a grayish green or yellowish tint to the cooked rice. The addition of 1/4 teaspoon of cream of tartar or 1 teaspoon of lemon juice to 2 quarts of water will maintain the white color.

Figure 14-11
Rice tabbouleh is a cold salad that combines rice, cucumber, tomato, mint, olive oil, and spices, thereby creating an unconventional way to serve rice. (Courtesy of USA Rice Federation)

Brown Rice

Brown rice can be cooked by the same methods used to cook white rice, but it must be cooked about twice as long. Because of the longer cooking time, somewhat more water is needed to allow for evaporation—up to 2.5 times the volume of the rice. Brown rice can be soaked for an hour in water to soften the bran and to shorten the cooking period. It does not tend to become sticky with cooking.

Researchers are developing methods of processing brown rice to reduce the cooking time from 45 minutes to 15 minutes to encourage consumers to use brown rice. Brown rice is highly nutritious and higher in fiber than white rice; however, the longer cooking time discourages some from preparing it. Researchers have found that by "sandblasting" the rice grains with rice flour under 60–70 pounds of air pressure per inch that the rice bran develops water-absorbing holes that result in a faster preparation time [37]. Also available is precooked brown rice, which has a slightly different flavor profile than regular brown rice, but cooks quickly. Wild rice is usually cooked in salted water for about 20 to 25 minutes until tender.

Precooked or Instant Rice

Precooked rice can be prepared very quickly. Boiling water is added to the rice. The mixture is then brought back to a boil, removed from the source of heat, and allowed to stand closely covered until the rice swells.

Rice Pilaf

Browning rice in a small amount of hot fat before cooking it in water converts part of the starch to dextrins. Swelling will also be somewhat decreased. The rice develops an interesting color and flavor that make the method desirable to use as a basis for Spanish rice, as rice pilaf, or as a side dish. Chicken or beef broth rather than water is used as the cooking liquid for pilaf.

PASTA

Definition and History

The term *pasta* or *alimentary paste* is applied to macaroni products, which include spaghetti, vermicelli, noodles, shells, linguine, rotini, ziti, couscous, and many other shapes. There are more than 600 pasta shapes available world wide, with more being developed [25]. Spaghetti is a long, solid, round rod. Capellini, vermicelli, spaghettini, and fettuccini are variations of spaghetti, ranging from very fine to oversize in diameter. Linguine is flat. Rotini is spiral shaped. Shells come in many sizes, from large for stuffing to tiny for soup. Rigatoni are large, ridged, hollow tubes. In general, the delicate pasta shapes should be paired with a delicate sauce and sturdy pastas should be complemented with a robust, hearty sauce (see Figure 14-12).

The principal ingredient in the making of pasta is a flour coarsely ground from durum wheat called *semolina*. Durum wheat is a high-protein grain containing carotenoid pigments in higher concentration than is found in bread wheats, giving pasta its characteristic yellow or amber color. Macaroni products originated in the Orient centuries ago and were brought to Italy by Venetian traders and explorers in the Middle Ages. The Italians adopted pasta as their national dish. From Italy, the popularity of pasta spread throughout Europe. European immigrants to the United States introduced the process of making macaroni, spaghetti, and egg noodles to this country before the Civil War. For

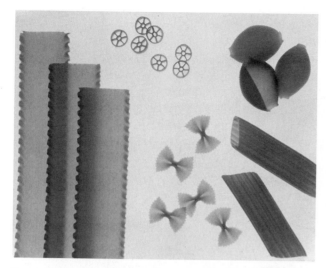

Lasagne, wagon wheels, bow ties, manicotti, and jumbo shells.

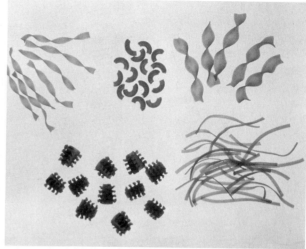

Egg noodles, elbows, and radiatore.

Fettuccine, linguine, spaghetti, thin spaghetti, and angel hair.

Penne, rotini, rigatoni, medium shells, and ziti.

Figure 14-12
Pasta comes in many shapes and sizes. (Courtesy of National Pasta Association)

many years these products were made in the home, although industrial production of pasta had developed in America by 1900. To supply durum wheat for pasta manufacture, the growing of this variety of wheat was introduced in the early 1900's to the farmers of the Dakotas and nearby states, where climatic conditions are well suited to its cultivation. This ensured an ample supply of durum wheat for American macaroni production (Figure 14-13).

Manufacture

In the commercial manufacture of pasta, measured amounts of flour and water are automatically fed into a mixer, which, under vacuum, thoroughly blends the ingredients into a dough. The dough then goes automatically into a single-screw continuous extruder and is extruded through a thick disk or *die* with

Figure 14-13
Several types of pasta are shown with their main ingredient—durum wheat. (Courtesy of Wheat Foods Council)

openings that produce the desired size and shape of pasta. As the dough is forced through the openings by tremendous pressure, these various shapes are formed. Cutting blades cut the strands to desired lengths [13]. The pasta is then automatically placed on drying trays. The drying process is carefully controlled to maintain the optimum temperature and humidity necessary to prevent the development of chips and cracks in the pasta. In recent years, high-temperature drying has speeded this process and improved the pasta products. The conventional drying process takes place at approximate temperatures of 140°F (60°C), but the high-temperature process uses temperatures above 212°F (100°C) [13]. Prior to the development of machines to carefully control the drying of pasta, it was hung on racks to dry in the sun [19].

Optional ingredients in macaroni products, according to the federal standards of identity, include eggs and various seasonings. In egg noodle products, whole eggs or egg yolks are added to the flour and water mixture to form a soft dough. The dough is run between rollers until it is of the desired thickness. The sheet of dough is automatically cut into ribbons of the desired width or into other shapes. The cut dough is then carefully dried.

Precooked pasta and quick-cooking noodles can be manufactured using twin-screw extruders [7]. The process involves a high-temperature–short-time extrusion following a preconditioning period that utilizes steam. The starch in the pasta is gelatinized before drying, so the precooked pasta can be reconstituted with boiling water in a very short time. Pregelatinized lasagna noodles, for example, are produced. During consumer preparation, the dry lasagna product can be layered directly with the sauce, cheese, and other ingredients, and then baked in less than half the time required in traditional preparation. The pasta will absorb about twice its weight in water. This precooked product can also be conveniently used in cooked prepared foods for both industrial and foodservice applications [13].

Durum flour is available in some areas for use in the home production of pasta. Pasta machines or pasta attachments to food processors are used to make the pasta.

High-protein macaroni products have been developed that contain 20 to 25 percent protein on a dry-weight basis. Soy and corn flour are often combined with wheat flour in the production of these protein-fortified, enriched macaroni-type products. Nonfat dry milk may also be used. The USDA has issued specifications for the use of these products as alternatives to meat in school foodservice.

Preparation of Pasta

Macaroni, spaghetti, and other pastas are cooked by adding the pasta to boiling water, which is usually salted. Approximately 2 to 3 quarts of boiling water are used for 8 ounces of pasta product. The more water used, the less likely it is that the pasta will stick together. Addition of a small amount of oil to the cooking water also may help to keep the pasta pieces separate. The pasta should be added gradually so that the water continues to boil rapidly.

Pasta generally increases 2 to 2.5 times its original volume on cooking. Pasta that is to be served without further preparation is cooked, uncovered, and occasionally stirred, until it is tender yet still firm to the bite. The standard for final cooking is called *al dente* (to the tooth). Because of the very high protein content of the flour used in the manufacture of pastas of good quality, their form is almost always retained on cooking. If cooking time is prolonged, however, the pasta will become soft, sticky, and may break up.

If the pasta is to be further baked or simmered with other ingredients, it should be cooked until almost tender. Cooking is completed after the pasta is combined with the other ingredients.

When the boiling process is complete, the pasta should be drained thoroughly in a colander or strainer. It is usually suggested that enriched pasta not be rinsed in water after cooking, because this process increases the loss of vitamins and minerals. If cooked pasta must be held a while before serving, it may be placed over hot water in a strainer. Steam will keep the product hot and moist without further cooking. Stickiness is reduced by this procedure, as compared with overcooking.

Holding pasta for a length of time in a foodservice setting may cause problems. Spaghetti combined with meat sauce, for example, becomes soft and sticky when held hot for an extended time. Refrigerating the spaghetti before it is combined with the meat sauce, then reheating it by pouring boiling water over it shortly before serving, has been suggested as an alternative procedure [2]. Appropriate time and temperature controls must be used when reheating pasta to avoid the risk of foodborne illness.

Pasta can be designed especially for use in microwave ovens. Because most conventional pastas are too thick to be cooked properly and uniformly by microwaves and will not achieve the desired firm texture, special pasta can be produced with thinner walls and selected additional ingredients such as egg albumen [18]. The additional protein helps to form an insoluble network that traps starch granules and controls gelatinization more effectively [13].

Fresh or high-moisture pasta packaged in barrier trays under a modified atmosphere is being marketed successfully as a convenience food, along with companion sauces [13]. Because microbial safety is not ensured by the modified atmosphere packaging alone, care must be taken to keep the product refrigerated after it has been processed and packaged under carefully controlled conditions.

The variety of dishes that can be prepared with macaroni products is almost endless: soups, salads, main dishes, meat accompaniments, and even desserts can be prepared with pasta (plate III, IV). For example, pasta may be combined with flavorful roasted vegetables or with fruits in dishes such as pasta salad with

Multicultural Cuisine

Pasta—Reflecting global tastes?

Italians recognized a good thing when they adopted pasta as their national dish—after Venetian traders brought it to Italy during the Middle Ages. But pasta is a favorite dish for many other nationalities also. It has been reported that consumers in the United States eat pasta dishes more than once a week and children eat more pasta than any other age group in this country [25].

Pasta—which simply means "dough" or "paste"—adapts itself to the unique flavoring spices and sauces of a wide variety of cuisines. And recipes utilizing pasta have been formulated by the thousands. To examine some of these, we suggest that you visit the Web site of the National Pasta Association at www.ilovepasta.org. As you browse through the many delectable recipes and photographs offered here, your mouth may water in anticipation, but you will get a taste of many different cultures. Sicilian stuffed shells feature jumbo shells stuffed with yellow raisins, green olives, onion, and three kinds of cheese—ricotta, mozzarella, and parmesan—baked in tomato sauce. Bow ties with Asian chicken uses a marinade of soy sauce, honey, lime juice, and mustard for cubes of skinless chicken breast, before blending this mixture with the bow tie–shaped pasta.

A Japanese pasta uses spaghetti with thin strips of flank steak, soy sauce, peppers, carrots, and scallions. And Thai cuisine is represented in a recipe for linguine with spicy shrimp sauce. Ingredients in this dish include shrimp, red bell peppers, and scallions cooked in a mixture of sesame oil, chicken broth, red pepper flakes, jalapeño pepper, ground ginger, soy sauce, peanut butter, and white vinegar. And a curried pasta salad, to be served cold, may remind you of India.

Regional differences are represented in such recipes as Tex-Mex lasagna, which includes kidney beans and corn alongside chili seasoning and Monterey Jack cheese. And a spicy texas breakfast casserole, with egg noodles, sausage, eggs, cream of mushroom soup, diced tomatoes, and picante sauce should give even a Texan a good start for the day. There is also a pasta recipe with a Thanksgiving flavor that features radiatore with pumpkin sauce, turkey, and cranberries. How about that? And all these recipes—and more—are for trying. Enjoy your browsing!

---

pineapple-mint salsa [25]. Pasta also may be used in dishes with hot and spicy ingredients including peppers and cayenne. Fish and seafood pair nicely with pasta: Traditional Italian sauces are not the only way to serve pasta center of the plate.

CHAPTER SUMMARY

- Cereal grains are seeds of the grass family. Wheat, corn (maize), rice, oats, rye, barley, and millet are the most important cereals used for human food. Cereal refers to a large group of foods made from grains including flours, meals, breads, and alimentary pastes or pasta.

- All whole grains have a similar structure: outer bran coats, a germ, and a starchy endosperm portion. The bran has a high content of fiber and mineral ash. In the milling of white flour, the bran and aleurone layer is removed. Milled white flour comes entirely from the endosperm that contains most of the starch and protein of the kernel. The germ comprises only 2 to 3 percent of the whole kernel and is rich in fat, protein, ash, and vitamins.

- The nutritive value of cereal products varies with the part of the grain that is used and the method of processing. Enriched flour, according to legal definition, is white flour to which specified B vitamins and iron have been added.

- Wheat is commonly milled into flour. Hard wheats are higher in protein content than soft wheats and usually have greater baking strength. Durum wheat is a very hard wheat used for making macaroni and other pasta. Bulgur is a wheat that is parboiled and then dried.

- The corn kernel is versatile and can take a great variety of forms. Hominy is produced when the corn kernel endosperm is freed of the bran. Hominy grits are made from breaking the hominy into fairly small pieces. Corn is also milled into cornmeal.

- Rice is one of the most used of all cereal grains. More than 40,000 different varieties of rice are grown world wide. Long-grain varieties of rice are high in amylose and fluffy when cooked. The medium- and short-grain varieties are stickier when cooked, in large part due to the low amylose content. Aromatic rices have a flavor and aroma similar to roasted nuts or popcorn. New varieties of rice with nutritional benefits are being developed through genetic engineering.

- Wild rice is not true rice, but the hulled and unmilled grain of a reedlike water plant.

- Rice may be processed in several ways to produce brown, polished white rice, parboiled rice, precooked rice, or rice flour. White rice may be enriched, and if so, it should not be washed before cooking or rinsed after cooking to avoid loss of enriched nutrients. Parboiled or converted rice has a greater nutrient value than white rice and disintegrates less during cooking. However, converted rice takes more time to cook as compared to regular milled white rice.

- Oats are utilized in a rolled form as both old-fashioned and quick-cooking products. In the processing of oats, most of the germ and the bran remain with the endosperm. Therefore, rolled oats are higher in fat that most other cereals and are a good source of B-vitamins and iron. Oat kernels with the outer hulls removed are called groats.

- Rye is used in the United States chiefly as flour, but it is also available as rye flakes and as pearled grain. Rye flour is available in three grades: light, medium, and dark.

- Barley is used as pearled barley and as malted barley. Pearled barley is commonly used in soups and other dishes. Pearling is the process that removes the outer husk of barley. Malted barley is used for making beer and other beverages.

- Triticale is a hybrid plant produced by crossing wheat and rye. It may be used in breads, crackers, and noodles.

- Buckwheat is the seed of a herbaceous plant but is commonly considered a grain product because it can be made into flour. Buckwheat flour provides a distinctive flavor when used in making griddlecakes.

- A wide variety of breakfast cereals are made from grains. Raw cereals that are cooked in home and foodservice kitchens include: whole grains, cracked or crushed grains, granular products made from either the whole grain or the endosperm, and rolled or flaked whole grains.

- Ready-to-eat cereals are produced using processes that include: shredding, puffing, granulating, flaking, and extruding. Sweetening agents, salt, flavoring, coloring agents, antioxidants, vitamins, and minerals are ingredients commonly added to ready-to-eat cereals.

- The main purposes of cereal cookery are to improve palatability and digestibility. The principal factors that affect the time required for the cooking of cereals are the size of the particle, the amount of water used, the presence or absence of bran, the temperature, and the method used.

- The challenge of rice cookery is to retain the form of the kernel while at the same time cooking the kernel until it is completely tender. Rice generally needs no more than twice its volume of water. Regular rice increases to about three times its volume in cooking. Rice may be cooked on top of the range, in the oven, in a microwave oven, or in a rice cooker. The amount of water needed and the length of cooking time will vary with the method of cooking used. Brown rice takes about twice as long to cook as white rice.

- The principal ingredient in the making of pasta is semolina flour that is ground from durum wheat. Optional ingredients in macaroni products, according to the federal standards of identity, include eggs and various seasonings.

- Macaroni, spaghetti, and other pastas are cooked by adding the pasta to boiling water. Approximately 2 to 3 quarts of boiling water are used for 8 ounces of pasta. Pasta generally increases 2 to 2.5 times its original volume on cooking. The standard for the final cooking is called al dente.

KEY TERMS

disappearance data	steep
phytochemicals	amylose
phytoestrogens	lipase
enriched	pearled
fortified	amylase

STUDY QUESTIONS

1. Name the most important cereal grains used for food.
2. The structures of all grains are somewhat similar.
   a. Name three major parts of a grain and describe the general chemical composition of each part.
   b. What is the *aleurone* of a cereal grain? Describe its general composition and indicate where it usually goes during the milling of grain.
3. a. What is meant by *enrichment* of cereals and flours? What nutrients must be added to meet the standards of the federal government?
   b. Compare the general nutritional value of refined unenriched, enriched, and whole-grain cereal products.
4. Cereal grains are often processed in preparation for use. Indicate which grains are commonly used to make the following products and briefly describe the processes involved in preparing the grain.
   a. Uncooked breakfast cereals
   b. Prepared breakfast cereals
   c. Flour
   d. Meal
   e. Hominy

    f. Grits

    g. Pasta

5. What are the main purposes for cooking cereals?

6. Suggest appropriate methods for cooking each of the following cereal products and explain why these methods are appropriate.

    a. Granular cereals such as farina and cornmeal

    b. Rolled oats

    c. Rice

    d. Macaroni or spaghetti

7. Describe the general processes involved in the production of each of the following types of ready-to-eat cereal.

    a. Puffed

    b. Flaked

    c. Granulated

    d. Shredded

    e. Extruded

8. Discuss several factors to consider when purchasing cereals.

REFERENCES

1. Bente, L., & Gerrior, S. A. (2002). Selected food and nutrient highlights of the 20th century: U.S. food supply series. *Family Economics and Nutrition Review, 14*(1), 43–51.

2. Brown, N. E., & Bernard, A. I. (1988). Sensory and instrumental assessments of spaghetti and meat sauce subjected to three holding treatments. *Journal of the American Dietetic Association, 88,* 1587.

3. Carroll, L. E. (1990). Functional properties and applications of stabilized rice bran in bakery products. *Food Technology, 44*(4), 74.

4. Childs, N. (1993). Americans are eating more rice. *Food Review, 16:* 19(2).

5. Chinnaswamy, R., & Hanna, M. A. (1987). Nozzle dimension effects on the expansion of extrusion cooked corn starch. *Journal of Food Science, 52,* 1746.

6. Cleveland, L. E., Moshfegh, A. J., Albertson, A. M., & Goldman, J. D. (2000). Dietary intake of whole grains. *Journal of the American College of Nutrition, 19*(3), 331S–338S.

7. Cole, M. E., Johnson, D. E., Cole, R. W., & Stone, M. B. (1991). Color of pregelatinized pasta as influenced by wheat type and selected additives. *Journal of Food Science, 56,* 488.

8. Comis, D. (2002). Let them eat cake. *Agricultural Research Magazine, 50*(3).

9. Core, J. (2002). New rice could benefit malnourished populations. *Agricultural Research Magazine, 50*(9).

10. Dziezak, J. D. (1991). Romancing the kernel: A salute to rice varieties. *Food Technology, 45*(6), 74.

11. Food Surveys Research Group. (1999, February). Pyramid servings data: Results from USDA's 1994–96 Continuing Survey of Food Intakes by Individuals. Beltsville Human Nutrition Research Center, Agricultural Research Service, U.S. Department of Agriculture. Table Set 9. Retrieved October 12, 2002, from www.barc.usda.gov/bhnrc/foodsurvey/pdf/3yr_py.pdf

12. Food Surveys Research Group. (1998, August). Results from the 1994–1996 Continuing Survey of Food Intakes by Individuals. Retrieved June 18, 2002, from http://www.barc.usda.gov/bhnrc/foodsurvey/96result.html

13. Giese, J. H. (1992). Pasta: New twists on an old product. *Food Technology, 46*(2), 118.

14. Hayta, M. (2001). Bulgar quality as affected by drying methods. *Journal of Food Science, 67*, 2241–2244.

15. Kahn, C. B., & Penfield, M. P. (1983). Snack crackers containing whole-grain triticale flour: Crispness, taste, and acceptability. *Journal of Food Science, 48*, 266.

16. Khan, M. N., Des Rosiers, M. C., Rooney, L. W., Morgan, R. G., & Sweat, V. E. (1982). Corn tortillas: Evaluation of corn cooking procedures. *Cereal Chemistry, 59*, 279.

17. Kurtzweil, P. (1996). How folate can help prevent birth defects. *FDA Consumer, 30*(7),7.

18. Mermelstein, N. H. (2001). Processing pasta for ingredient use. *Food Technology, 55*(7), 72–75.

19. National Pasta Association. (2002). Industry statistics. Retrieved October 7, 2002, from http://www.ilovepasta.org

20. National Pasta Association. (2002). The inside story: How pasta is made. Retrieved October 7, 2002, from http://www.ilovepasta.org

21. Nicklas, T. A., Myers, L., & Berenson, G. S. (1994). Impact of ready-to-eat cereal consumption on total dietary intake of children: The Bogalusa Heart Study. *Journal of the American Dietetic Association, 94*, 316.

22. Parlin, S. (1997). Rice flour makes its mark. *Food Processing, 58*(10), 60.

23. Putnam, J. J. (1991). Food consumption, 1970–90. *Food Review, 14*(3), 2.

24. Pszczola, D. E. (1998). What's beyond the horizon? *Food Technology, 52*(9), 94.

25. Pszczola, D. E. (2000). A pasta for all paisans. *Food Technology, 54*(4), 84–92.

26. Pszczola, D. E. (2001). Rice: Not just for throwing. *Food Technology, 55*(2), 53–59.

27. Putnam, J. J. (2000). Major supply trends in U.S. food supply, 1909–1999. *Food Review, 23*(1), 8–14.

28. Putnam, J. J., & Allshouse, J. E. (1999, June). Food consumption, prices, and expenditures, 1970–1997. Food and Rural Economics Division, Economic Research Service, U.S. Department of Agriculture. Statistical Bulletin No. 965.

29. Putnam, J. J., & Duewer, L. A. (1995). U.S. per capita food consumption: Record-high meat and sugars in 1994. *Food Review, 18*(2), 2.

30. Raloff, J. (1991). Beyond oat bran. *Food Technology, 45*(8), 62.

31. Rao, D. R., Patel, G., & Nishimuta, J. F. (1980). Comparison of protein quality of corn, triticale, and wheat. *Nutrition Reports International, 21*, 923.

32. Riceland Foods, Inc. (1996). All about rice: U.S. production. Retrieved October 7, 2002, from http://www.riceland.com

33. Slavin, J. and Kritchevsky, D. (2002). Pass the whole-grain snack food, please. *Food Technology, 56*(5), 216.

34. Sloan, A. E. (1997). Grain: All it's cracked up to be. *Food Technology, 51*(7), 24.

35. Smallwood, D. M., & Blaylock, J. R. (1994). Fiber: Not enough of a good thing? *Food Review, 17*(1), 23.

36. Solganik, H. (1997). A toast to tortillas. *Food Processing, 58*(11), 64.

37. Suszkiw, J. (2002). Rice, Oh so nice. *Agricultural Research Magazine, 50*(5).

38. Teutonico, R. A., & Knorr, D. (1985). Amaranth: Composition, properties, and applications of a rediscovered food crop. *Food Technology, 39*(4), 49.

39. U.S. Grain Council. (n.d.). Barley, corn, and sorghum: World corn production and trade. Retrieved October 12, 2002, from http://www.grains.org/grains/corn.html

Batters and Doughs

15

Batters and doughs, sometimes called *flour mixtures,* include a large variety of baked products such as muffins, biscuits and other quick breads, pastry, shortened and unshortened cakes, cookies, and breads. The market for baked goods has been growing in recent years and many new products are being sold; however, the amount of "home baking" appears to be decreasing.

Producing the final result that is desired in a flour mixture is dependent on such factors as accuracy in measurements or weights (Chapter 5), skill in manipulation, control of oven or other temperatures, and knowledge about the kinds and proportions of ingredients used. A so-called standard product may vary somewhat from one group of people to another, depending on preferences; however, it is important that you learn what characteristics are generally preferred in various baked products and what proportions of ingredients and techniques of mixing might be used to achieve these characteristics.

In this chapter, we discuss basic ingredients and their usual effects in baked products, and some basic methods of mixing. This information should be useful in learning to produce any "standard" that you desire.

INGREDIENTS

The principal ingredients used in foundation formulas for doughs and batters are flour, liquid, fat, egg, sugar, leavening agent, and salt. Flavoring substances are added to some types of mixtures. Several additives may be used by commercial bakers and by producers of such manufactured food products as cookies, granola bars, pastries, and various packaged flour mixes. Fat replacers and alternative sweeteners are important ingredients in reduced-fat or reduced-calorie items.

Flour

The principal grain used in the United States for flour is wheat. White wheat flour is defined by the U.S. Food and Drug Administration (FDA) as a food made by the grinding and sifting of cleaned wheat (Figure 15-1). The flour is freed from the bran and germ of the wheat kernel to such an extent that specifications as to moisture, ash, and protein content are met. Because of its protein and starch content, flour provides structure and body in baked flour products.

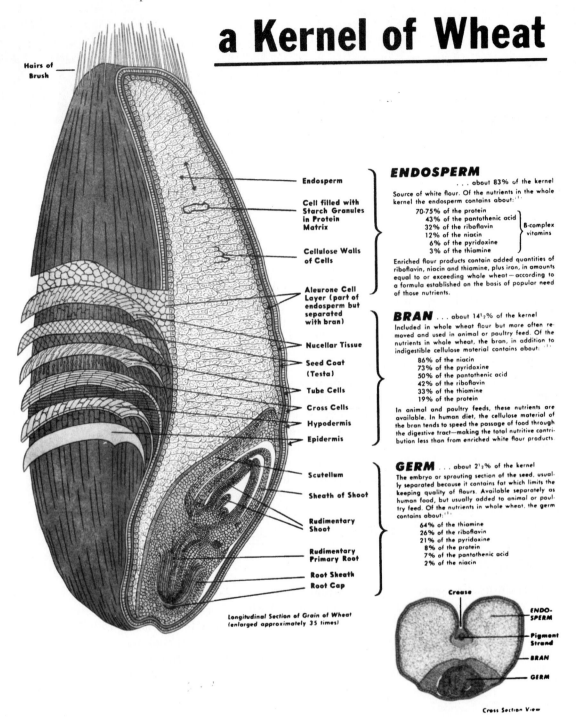

a Kernel of Wheat

Hairs of
Brush

Endosperm

Cell filled with
Starch Granules
in Protein
Matrix

Cellulose Walls
of Cells

Aleurone Cell
Layer (part of
endosperm but
separated
with bran)

Nucellar Tissue

Seed Coat
(Testa)

Tube Cells

Cross Cells

Hypodermis

Epidermis

Scutellum

Sheath of Shoot

Rudimentary
Shoot

Rudimentary
Primary Root

Root Sheath

Root Cap

Longitudinal Section of Grain of Wheat
(enlarged approximately 35 times)

ENDOSPERM

. . . about 83% of the kernel

Source of white flour. Of the nutrients in the whole
kernel the endosperm contains about: [1]

70-75% of the protein
43% of the pantothenic acid
32% of the riboflavin   B-complex
12% of the niacin   vitamins
6% of the pyridoxine
3% of the thiamine

Enriched flour products contain added quantities of
riboflavin, niacin and thiamine, plus iron, in amounts
equal to or exceeding whole wheat—according to
a formula established on the basis of popular need
of those nutrients.

BRAN . . . about 14½% of the kernel

Included in whole wheat flour but more often removed and used in animal or poultry feed. Of the
nutrients in whole wheat, the bran, in addition to
indigestible cellulose material contains about: [1]

86% of the niacin
73% of the pyridoxine
50% of the pantothenic acid
42% of the riboflavin
33% of the thiamine
19% of the protein

In animal and poultry feeds, these nutrients are
available. In human diet, the cellulose material of
the bran tends to speed the passage of food through
the digestive tract—making the total nutritive contribution less than from enriched white flour products.

GERM . . . about 2½% of the kernel

The embryo or sprouting section of the seed, usually separated because it contains fat which limits the
keeping quality of flours. Available separately as
human food, but usually added to animal or poultry feed. Of the nutrients in whole wheat, the germ
contains about: [1]

64% of the thiamine
26% of the riboflavin
21% of the pyridoxine
8% of the protein
7% of the pantothenic acid
2% of the niacin

Crease

ENDO-
SPERM

Pigment
Strand

BRAN

GERM

Cross Section View

Figure 15-1
The structure of a kernel of wheat. (Courtesy of the Wheat Flour Institute)

Classes of Wheat. Wheats may be classified on the basis of the time of planting or the growing season, the color of the kernel, and the hardness or softness of the kernel. Wheats that are planted in the spring and harvested in the fall are called *spring wheats*, whereas those that are planted in the fall and harvested the following summer are called *winter wheats*. Because these wheats remain in the ground all winter, they are grown in areas with relatively mild weather. Some wheat kernels have a reddish appearance and are called *red wheats*, whereas others are white. A hard wheat has a hard, vitreous kernel, whereas a soft wheat appears to be more powdery. Hard wheats are usually higher in protein than soft wheats, and the protein has more baking strength when flour from this wheat is made into dough. Therefore, flour from hard wheat is especially good for breadmaking. Spring wheats include hard red varieties, hard white and soft white varieties, and durum wheats, which are used for the production of macaroni products. Winter wheats may be hard, semihard, or soft. Hard winter wheats have a fairly strong quality of protein and are suitable for breadmaking purposes.

The geographical areas in which most of the hard spring wheats are produced are the north central part of the United States and western Canada. Hard winter wheats are grown mainly in the middle central states. Soft winter wheat is grown east of the Mississippi River and in the Pacific Northwest. Because climatic and soil conditions affect the composition of wheat, wide variations can be expected within these classes. Wheat also is discussed in Chapter 14.

Milling. The milling of white flour is a process that involves separating the endosperm from the bran and germ and subdividing it into a fine flour. Specific procedures in milling may vary from one mill to another, but the major steps are shown in the simplified chart in Figure 15-2. The wheat kernel is divided into three main parts approximately as follows: 83 percent endosperm, 14.5 percent bran layers (including the aleurone layer), and 2.5 percent germ [17]. The endosperm contains many starch granules embedded in a cell matrix that includes protein (Figure 15-3). When the parts of the wheat kernel are not separated and the whole kernel is ground, the flour resulting from this process is called *whole wheat, entire wheat*, or *graham* flour.

Many years ago, white flours were made by sifting wheat that had been ground in a stone mill. This method of separation yielded a flour that was generally less white and of poorer baking quality than the flour produced in today's mills, where the wheat passes through a series of rollers. The first sets of corrugated rolls crush the grain and detach the endosperm from the bran. The portion of the endosperm that is separated and pulverized is sifted after each crushing. The flours resulting from the first siftings are known as *break flours*, of which there are about five streams.

The small pieces of the inner portion of the kernel, which are granulated with difficulty, are known as *middlings*. After their separation from the bran, the middlings are fed through a series of smooth rolls that further reduce the size of the particles and produce fine flour. About six to eight streams of flour are obtained from the rolling and sifting of the purified middlings.

From the many streams of flour resulting from the roller process various grades and types of flours are formulated. The streams vary in their protein content. Break flours and those from the last reductions of the middlings are inferior to the other streams of flour for baking purposes.

Figure 15-2

Steps involved in the milling of flour.
(Courtesy of the Wheat Flour Institute)

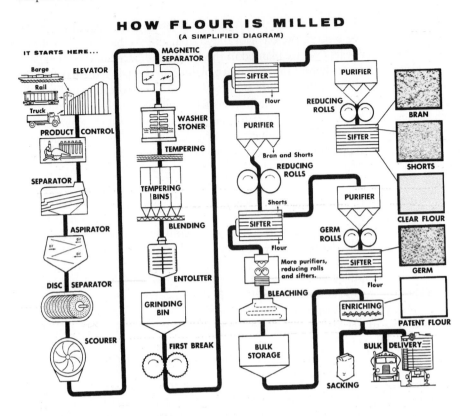

Because the endosperm represents approximately 83 percent of the total kernel, about that same amount of white flour should theoretically be obtained by milling. In actual practice, however, only 72 to 75 percent is separated as white flour. The separation of endosperm from bran and germ is neither a simple nor an extremely efficient process. The inner bran layers and the germ are tightly bound to the endosperm, and it is impossible to make a complete separation. The usual 72 to 75 percent extraction produces white flour containing essentially no bran and germ and exhibiting good baking properties. In times of national emergency, the usual percentage of extraction has been increased as a conservation measure. It has been suggested that the regular extraction rate of

Figure 15-3

A scanning electron micrograph (2,100 ×) of fractured wheat endosperm cells showing small and large starch granules embedded in the cell matrix. (Reprinted from Freeman, T. P., and D. R. Shelton. Microstructure of wheat starch: From kernel to bread. *Food Technology,* 45: 165(3), 1991. Copyright © by Institute of Food Technologists. Photograph supplied by Thomas P. Freeman.)

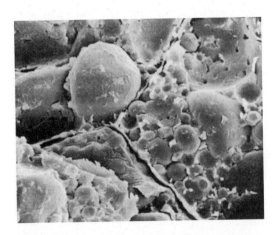

white flour could be increased up to 80 percent without sacrificing baking quality [24].

Milled white flour usually contains 65 to 70 percent starch and 8 to 13 percent protein. Another milling method based on separation of flour particles by air currents, called *air classification*, can be used to divide the resulting flour into various fractions with differing ratios of starch to protein. A change in composition affects the baking properties and, thus, potential uses of the flour. To meet specific requirements of bakers, flours varying in protein content from 5 to 20 percent can be produced by air classification.

Bleaching and Maturing.   Included in the final stages of white flour production are bleaching and maturing. Let us look at these two processes and discuss why they are important.

We begin with bleaching. Freshly milled, unbleached flour is yellowish in color, primarily because of the presence of **carotenoid pigments.** If this flour is held for a time, the yellow color becomes lighter. It is bleached because the yellow pigments gradually become **oxidized.**

Next, we discuss the maturing process. When freshly milled flour is used to bake bread, the result is a loaf of relatively low volume and coarse texture. A loaf with higher volume and finer texture can be made from the same flour after it has had an opportunity to mature or age. *Aging* involves simply holding or storing the flour for several weeks or months. During this time, not only does the flour lighten in color because the carotenoid pigments are being oxidized, but the baking quality also improves. Baking improvement, shown in higher volume and finer texture of bread, probably results from chemical changes that occur in the proteins of the flour. These complex chemical changes possibly involve oxidation of some type. *Maturing* of the flour is said to have taken place. Thus, although the aging of white flour brings about both bleaching and maturing, these two chemical processes are separate and distinct.

The addition of certain chemical substances to freshly milled flour produces effects similar to aging but in a much shorter period. This process saves the cost of storing the flour. The FDA permits the use of specified chemical substances, one being benzoyl peroxide, which is primarily a bleaching agent. Chlorine dioxide, chlorine, and acetone peroxides have both a bleaching and a maturing effect. Azodicarbonamide may be added to flour as a maturing agent but does not react until the flour is made into a dough. Flour that has been treated with any of these chemicals must be labeled "bleached." Both bleached and unbleached flours are available to the consumer on the retail market.

Grades of Flour.   The miller grades white flour on the basis of which streams of flour are combined. *Straight grade* theoretically should contain all the flour streams resulting from the milling process, but actually 2 to 3 percent of the poorest streams is withheld. Very little flour on the market is straight grade. *Patent* flours come from the more refined portion of the endosperm and can be made from any class of wheat. They are divided into *short patent*, which includes 60 to 80 percent of the total flour streams, *medium patent* with 80 to 90 percent, and *long patent* with 90 to 95 percent. Most patent flours on the market include about 85 percent of the straight flour. *Clear grade* is made from streams withheld in the making of patent flours. Clear-grade flours are used in some commercial flour products such as pancake mixes.

carotenoid pigments yellow-orange compounds produced by plant cells and found in various fruit, vegetable, and cereal grain tissues; for example, β-carotene

oxidation a chemical reaction in which oxygen is added or electrons are lost

inulin a complex carbohydrate (a polysaccharide) found in the roots of some plants that yields fructose when broken down or hydrolyzed

prebiotic substances such as certain nondigestible carbohydrates that promote the growth and redistribution of intestinal bacteria to create a healthy environment

pentosans complex carbohydrates (polysaccharides) that yield five-carbon sugars (pentoses) when hydrolyzed

Types of Wheat Flour. It is important to understand the differences in composition and characteristics of wheat flours in order to use them most effectively. Within certain limits, various types of flour may be interchanged in different recipes by altering the proportions of the nonflour constituents of the mixture. The composition and nutritive value of some wheat flours are given in Appendix C.

Whole wheat flour. Whole wheat flour may also be called *graham* flour or *entire wheat* flour. It contains essentially the entire wheat kernel and may be ground to different degrees of fineness. The keeping quality of whole wheat flour is lower than that of white flour, because it contains fat from the germ that may be oxidized on storage. It has been reported that up to a month's supply of flour ground from freshly harvested wheat in home grinders may be stored at room temperature before rancidity develops and sensory quality decreases [8]. Whole wheat flour is higher in fiber than white flour because it contains the bran.

Bread flour. Bread flour is a white flour made chiefly from hard wheat. It contains a relatively high percentage of protein that develops into a substance

---

Healthy Eating

Designer Fibers—Into the mainstream?

Health-conscious Americans are becoming even more aware of the health benefits of dietary fiber. They emphasize its positive role in preventing constipation, improving desirable weight loss, helping to prevent heart disease by lowering blood cholesterol levels, and helping to prevent cancer. Many say that they are trying to increase their fiber intake, but still have a way to go before meeting the Daily Value of 25 g/day recommended on the "Nutrition Facts" food labels [22]. At any rate, fiber is "in"; it is "trendy" in food and nutrition circles.

The old dietary fiber was defined as "the remnants of edible plant cells, polysaccharides, lignin, and associated substances resistant to digestion by the alimentary enzymes of humans" [7]. But this definition is being expanded to include, somewhere in the definition, new compounds, not necessarily derived from plant cell walls, that are important in creating positive physiological changes in the body. For instance, the carbohydrates **inulin** and fructooligosaccharides may act as **prebiotics** in stimulating growth of desirable bacteria, such as bifidobacteria, in the intestine. These prebiotics, which might be called designer fibers, are now being added to a wide range of food products in Europe and Japan, including cookies, pasta, brioche, nutrition bars, puddings, and breakfast drinks.

There is a flurry across the globe of new product activity that includes trends toward oat drinks, rye-based heart-friendly products, and heart disease–preventative cereals or nutrition bars as part of a new world of exciting product options [22]. One company has patented the technology for producing a stabilized rice bran extract. This process captures the nutrient-rich, water-soluble portion of rice bran (which includes soluble **pentosans**) in a spray-dried powder that is stable to oxidative changes. This designer product is being marketed as a dough conditioner and emulsifier combined to give bakery products with high moisture, longer shelf life, and improved consumer acceptance [18].

With a new image for dietary fiber and a worldwide market, food technologists are eager to produce new designer ingredients. Watch for them!

called *gluten* (described in more detail in the next section). Gluten contributes very strong, elastic properties when the flour is made into a dough. Bread flour has a slightly granular feel when touched and does not form a firm mass when pressed in the hand. It may be bleached or unbleached. Bread flour is used by commercial and foodservice bakers for yeast breads and is also available for use in the home kitchen. It produces breads of relatively high volume and fine texture with an elastic crumb.

All-purpose flour. A white flour, all-purpose flour is usually made from a blend of wheats to yield a protein content lower than that of bread flour. It contains enough protein that it can be used for making yeast bread and rolls under household conditions. Foodservice operations generally use a bread flour. All-purpose flour is used for making quick breads. The gluten that develops in doughs made from all-purpose flour is less strong and elastic than that produced in bread-flour doughs. All-purpose flour may be used for making pastry, cookies, and certain cakes. It usually has too high a protein content to make a delicate, fine-textured cake.

Pastry flour. A white flour, pastry flour is usually made from soft wheat and contains a lower percentage of protein than is found in all-purpose flour. Its chief use is for baking pastries and cookies, and it is used primarily in commercial baking.

Cake flour. Prepared from soft wheat, cake flour usually contains only the most highly refined streams of flour from the milling process and is a short patent grade of flour. The protein content of cake flour is very low in comparison with other types of flour. Cake flour is also highly bleached with chlorine [16]. So finely milled that it feels soft and satiny, rather than a granular texture, cake flour forms a firm mass when pressed in the hand. The high starch content and weak quality of gluten produced from cake flour make it desirable chiefly for the preparation of delicate and fine-textured cakes.

Instantized flour. Also called *instant, instant-blending,* or *quick-mixing* flour, instantized flour is a granular all-purpose flour that has been processed by moistening and then redrying to aggregate small particles into larger particles or agglomerates. The agglomerated particles are of relatively uniform size and do not pack; therefore, this flour does not require sifting before measuring. It flows freely without dust, is easily measured, and blends more readily with liquid than regular flour. Instantized flour is most useful when blended dry with a liquid, such as in the thickening of gravies and certain sauces. Some changes should be made in formulas and preparation procedures if this flour is substituted for regular flour in baked products.

Self-rising flour. Leavening agents and salt are added to self-rising flour in proportions desirable for baking. Monocalcium phosphate is the acid salt most commonly added in combination with sodium bicarbonate (baking soda) as leavening ingredients. Self-rising flours are popular for preparing quick breads, such as baking powder biscuits.

Gluten flour. Wheat flour is mixed with dried extracted gluten to form gluten flour. This flour has a protein content of about 41 percent compared with the 10 to 14 percent protein content of most wheat flour. The gluten is extracted by the gentle washing of a flour-and-water dough and is dried under mild conditions to minimize any effects on its viscoelastic properties. Gluten that retains its desirable baking qualities is sometimes called *vital wheat gluten*. Gluten flour is used by the baking industry to adjust the protein level in various doughs. Gluten may also be used in breakfast foods.

Enrichment of Flour. Enriched flour is white flour to which has been added specified B vitamins (thiamin, riboflavin, niacin, and folic acid) and iron. Vitamin D and calcium are optional additions. Many states have laws requiring enrichment of flour and cereals, which is mandatory for those flour and cereal products that enter interstate commerce. Enrichment is discussed in Chapter 14.

Gluten. Various proteins have been extracted from wheat. Some of these are the more soluble **albumins** and **globulins** that do not appear to play major roles in baking. Approximately 85 to 90 percent of the proteins of white flour are relatively insoluble. In early research, the insoluble wheat proteins were separated into two fractions called *gliadin* and *glutenin*. These fractions have since been subdivided further. When flour is moistened with water and thoroughly mixed or kneaded, the insoluble proteins form *gluten*, which is primarily responsible for the viscous and elastic characteristics and high loaf volume of wheat flour doughs [4,11].

Gluten can be extracted from a flour-and-water dough that has been vigorously kneaded by thorough washing of the dough with water to remove the starch (Figure 15-4). The moist gluten thus extracted has elastic and cohesive properties similar to those of chewing gum. When the gliadin and glutenin fractions are separated from each other, the gliadin fraction is found to be a syrupy substance that can bind the mass together. It has little or no resistance to extension and may be responsible for the viscous properties of the dough. The glutenin fraction exhibits toughness and rubberiness (Figure 15-5). It resists the extension of the dough and apparently contributes to elasticity.

The gliadin fraction may be divided into four subgroups of differing sizes. These molecules would seem to be single chain with compact globular shapes; they may be linked together by the formation of **disulfide bonds** ($-S-S-$) [9]. The glutenin fraction consists of a low-molecular-weight component and a high-molecular-weight component. High-molecular-weight glutenin molecules apparently have subunits bound together by disulfide bonds between the

albumins simple proteins that are soluble in water

globulins simple proteins that are soluble in dilute salt solutions

disulfide bond a bond between two sulfur atoms, each of which is also joined to another chemical group; these bonds often tie protein chains together

Figure 15-4
Gluten can be extracted from a flour-and-water dough by washing it carefully with cold water to remove the starch. The amounts and characteristics of gluten from various flours can thus be compared. Pictured are samples of unbaked and baked gluten. (Left) Cake flour; (center) all-purpose flour; (right) bread flour. (Courtesy of the Wheat Flour Institute)

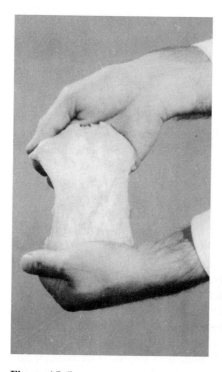

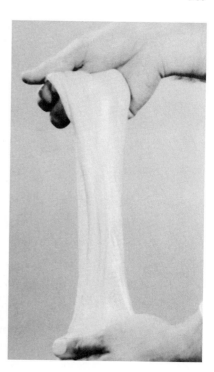

Figure 15-5
The different properties of the glutenin fraction (left), the gliadin fraction (center), and gluten (right). (Courtesy of *Baker's Digest* and R. J. Dimler)

peptide chains. Disulfide bonds may also be present within the subunits. The exact nature of the associations between subunits has not been clarified, although models have been proposed. Other types of bonds, such as hydrogen bonds, may also form intramolecular linkages.

During the mixing of a dough, the long strands of glutenin evidently are aligned in the direction of mixing and interact with gliadin molecules to form a strong elastic uniform film that envelops the starch granules in the mixture (Figure 15-6). An appropriate amount of water must be present to form a dough. Air and carbon dioxide gas bubbles incorporated in the dough produce a foam. Interactions probably also occur in the dough between gluten proteins

peptide chains amino acid molecules linked together through their amino and acid (carboxyl) groups to form chains of varying length (protein chains)

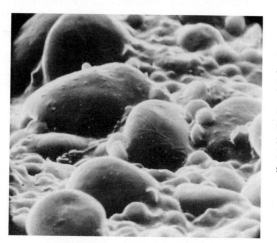

Figure 15-6
Scanning electron photomicrograph of a dough sample showing a developed gluten film covering starch granules of variable sizes. (Reprinted from Varriano-Marston, E. A comparison of dough preparation procedures for scanning electron microscopy. *Food Technology*, 31: 34(10), 1977. Copyright © by Institute of Food Technologists)

and lipids and other dough components as well [12]. Wheat-flour dough is a complex but interesting phenomenon.

To make possible a high volume and fine texture in yeast breads, gluten is developed to its maximum strength. In other baked products, such as shortened cakes, gluten development is retarded to yield a more tender product.

Other Wheat Products.   *Cracked wheat*, although not a flour, is used extensively in baking breads and quick breads. It should be soaked in double its volume of water for 24 hours before use. Cracked wheat may be combined in varying proportions with whole wheat or white flour. Rolled wheat is also used to make cookies and quick breads.

Wheat germ, which contains essentially all the fat from the wheat kernel, is available as yellowish tan flakes that may have been toasted. Raw wheat germ, containing up to 10 percent oil, begins to develop rancidity as soon as it is milled. It may be vacuum packed to control the oxidative changes that produce rancidity. A process that involves careful, controlled heating to inactivate the enzymes, *lipase* and *peroxidase*, which catalyze the oxidation of fat can produce a stabilized wheat germ with a 6-month shelf life. Stabilized wheat germ retains its vitamin and mineral content, including the antioxidant vitamin, vitamin E. Wheat germ is a good source of B vitamins and iron. It may be added to both yeast and quick breads. Commercial applications for the use of wheat germ include crackers, breakfast cereals, variety breads, and snacks. The vitamin potency of wheat germ is not appreciably decreased by baking in the yeast breads that contain it; however, the germ has been found to exert a deleterious effect on the baking quality of flour. For this reason, a relatively strong flour is best used with the wheat germ. The germ may be substituted to the extent of one-fifth to one-third of the flour.

Defatted wheat germ is also available. It is stable, and is a good source of protein, fiber, and certain vitamins and minerals.

Flours and Meals Other Than Wheat Flour.   Flours other than wheat are used in quick breads and yeast breads.

Rye flour.   The sifting of rye meal results in rye flour. It has some gluten-forming properties, but it contains chiefly gliadin with only small amounts of glutenin. Therefore, bread made from rye flour, although not necessarily soggy or heavy, is more compact and less elastic than bread made with wheat flour. Some white flour is often combined with rye flour in making bread to yield a lighter, more porous product than is possible with rye flour alone.

Cornmeal and corn flour.   Cornmeal, a granular product made from either white or yellow corn, is commonly used in several types of quick breads. Its chief protein, *zein*, has none of the properties of the gluten of wheat. If a crumbly product is to be avoided, cornmeal must be combined with some white flour, preferably all-purpose flour, to bind it. Corn flour has the same properties as cornmeal except that it is finer. It is used chiefly in commercial pancake mixes and prepared cereals.

Soy flour.   Made from soybeans, which are legumes, soy flour is high in protein, although the protein has none of the characteristics of gluten. Soy flour must be used with a strong or moderately strong wheat flour for good results in the baking of breads. An important advantage of using soy flour in baked products is the contribution it makes to the amount and quality of the protein. In baked items, soy flour also promotes moisture retention, improves crust color, and extends shelf life. Federal standards for commercial white breads permit the use of 3 percent soy flour as an optional ingredient.

Miscellaneous flours. *Buckwheat flour* does not have the same baking properties as wheat flour. The principal use of buckwheat is in pancakes and waffles. Some of the pancake batters are fermented to increase the flavor.

Triticale flour, made from the cereal that is a cross between wheat and rye, may be used to make yeast bread of satisfactory quality. Its flavor has been reported to be like that of a very mild rye bread [10].

Rice flour is fundamentally rice starch. *Potato flour* is used in some countries and, like rice flour, is chiefly starch.

Amaranth flour, made by grinding the tiny amaranth seed, is used in some areas of Latin America, Africa, and Asia. Amaranth is now being cultivated in limited amounts in the United States. Some interesting historical notes tell us that amaranth grain was a staple cereal during the Mayan and Aztec periods of Central America. On some ceremonial occasions, the seed was ground and shaped with human blood into figures representing gods or revered animals and eaten as part of religious rites. However, to eliminate the established worship rituals, amaranth cultivation was prohibited when Cortez conquered this area in 1519. This grain has therefore been dormant as a popular food crop until recent decades [21]. Amaranth flour has a high content of the amino acid lysine, which is limited in wheat flour. It may make a valuable nutritional contribution when combined in wheat breads, cookies, and other baked products [20].

Leavening Agents

To *leaven* means to "make light and porous." Most baked flour products today are leavened. This process is accomplished by incorporating or forming in the product a gas that expands during preparation and subsequent heating.

Major Leavening Gases. Three major leavening gases are air, steam or water vapor, and carbon dioxide. In some flour mixtures, one of these leavening gases predominates, whereas in other products, two or three of the gases play important roles.

Air is incorporated into flour mixtures by beating eggs, by folding and rolling dough, by creaming fat and sugar together, or by beating batters. In common practice, some air is incorporated into all flour mixtures.

Because all flour mixtures contain some water and are usually heated so that the water vaporizes, steam leavens all flour mixtures to a certain degree. Some products leavened almost entirely by steam are popovers, cream puffs, and éclairs (Figure 15-7). These mixtures have a high percentage of liquid, and baking is started at a high oven temperature, which rapidly causes steam to form. Because one volume of water increases to more than 1,600 volumes when converted into steam, it has tremendous leavening power. The water available for conversion to steam may be added as liquid or as a component of other ingredients, such as eggs. Egg whites contain enough water to furnish two to three times more expansion in baking angel food cakes than the air that was added by beating. Even stiff doughs, such as pie crust, are partially leavened by steam.

Figure 15-7
The rapid expansion of puff pastry leaves a large air hole in éclairs that may be filled with pastry cream.

fermentation the transformation of organic substances into smaller molecules by the action of microorganisms; yeast ferments glucose to yield carbon dioxide and alcohol

maltose a disaccharide or double sugar composed of two glucose units

amylase an enzyme that hydrolyzes starch to dextrins and maltose

maltase an enzyme that hydrolyzes maltose to glucose

Carbon dioxide may be produced in a flour mixture either by a biological process or by a purely chemical reaction.

Biological Production of Carbon Dioxide. Carbon dioxide is produced by the action of yeast and certain bacteria on sugar. This process is called **fermentation,** and carbon dioxide is a by-product of the overall reaction. Yeast ferments sugar to form ethyl alcohol and carbon dioxide. The alcohol is volatilized by the heat of baking. The fermentation is catalyzed by a mixture of many enzymes produced by the yeast cells. Sugar is usually added to yeast-flour mixtures to speed fermentation and the production of carbon dioxide gas. If no sugar is used, yeast can form gas slowly from the small amount of sugar that is present in flour. **Maltose** is also produced in flour from the action of **amylase** as it hydrolyzes starch. **Maltase,** an enzyme produced by yeast, then hydrolyzes the maltose to yield glucose, which is available for fermentation by the yeast. The use of yeast in leavening is discussed further in Chapter 17.

Certain bacteria may also produce leavening gas in flour mixtures. One type produces hydrogen and carbon dioxide gases in salt-rising bread. Although the organisms occur normally in the cornmeal used to make the sponge for salt-rising bread, they have, in addition, been isolated and put on the market as a starter for this type of bread. Sourdough bread also uses bacteria in producing leavening gas.

Chemical production of carbon dioxide. Sodium bicarbonate (baking soda) in a flour mixture gives off carbon dioxide (CO_2) gas when heated in accordance with the reaction

$$2NaHCO_3 \; + \; \text{heat} \; \rightarrow \; Na_2CO_3 \; + \; CO_2 \; + \; H_2O$$

| sodium bicarbonate | | sodium carbonate | carbon dioxide | water |

However, the sodium carbonate (Na_2CO_3) residue from this reaction has a disagreeable flavor and produces a yellow color in light-colored baked products. Brown spots may also occur in the cooked product if the soda is not finely powdered or is not uniformly distributed throughout the flour.

To avoid the problem of a bitter, soapy-flavored residue in the baked product, sodium bicarbonate is combined with various acids to release carbon dioxide gas. The flavor of the residue remaining after the gas is released is dependent on the particular acid involved in the reaction. The salts formed with many acids are not objectionable in flavor.

The following food substances contain acids and may be combined with soda in flour mixtures, where they release carbon dioxide gas.

1. Buttermilk or sour milk (containing lactic acid)
2. Molasses (containing a mixture of organic acids)
3. Brown sugar (which has a small amount of molasses coating the sugar crystals)
4. Honey
5. Citrus fruit juices (containing citric and other organic acids)
6. Applesauce and other fruits
7. Vinegar (containing acetic acid)

The optimum amount of soda to combine with an acid food in a recipe depends on the degree of acidity of that food. The acid-containing foods listed vary in acidity and yield variable results when combined with soda; however, the usual amount of soda to combine with 1 cup of buttermilk or fully soured milk is 1/2 teaspoon. Less soda is required for milk that is less sour. Because the pronounced flavor of molasses may mask any undesirable flavor resulting from an excess of soda, up to 1 teaspoon of soda is often recommended for use with 1 cup of molasses, but less may be used. The acidity of honey and of brown sugar is too low to allow their use in flour mixtures as the only source of acid to combine with soda.

Cream of tartar is an acid salt (potassium acid tartrate) and may be combined with soda to produce carbon dioxide gas when the mixture is moistened. The salt that is left as a residue in this reaction (sodium potassium tartrate) is not objectionable in flavor. The chemical reaction between cream of tartar and soda is

$$HKC_4H_4O_6 \;+\; NaHCO_3 \;\rightarrow\; NaKC_4H_4O_6 \;+\; CO_2 \;+\; H_2O$$

| cream of tartar | sodium bicarbonate | sodium potassium tartrate | carbon dioxide | water |

Baking powders were developed as one of the first convenience foods. They contain mixtures of dry acid or acid salts and baking soda. Starch is added to standardize the mixture and help stabilize the components so that they do not react prematurely. Baking powders have been classified into different groups or types depending on the acid constituent used; however, not all types are available to the consumer. The type of baking powder that is generally available for home use is called *SAS-phosphate* baking powder. It is a double-acting baking powder, which means that it reacts to release carbon dioxide gas at room temperature when the dry ingredients are moistened and reacts again when heat is applied in the process of baking. SAS-phosphate baking powder contains two acid substances. Each reacts with soda to release carbon dioxide gas at different times in the baking process. One acid is a phosphate, usually calcium acid phosphate. This acid salt reacts with soda at room temperature as soon as liquid is added to the dry ingredients. Thus, the batter or dough becomes somewhat light and porous during the mixing process. The other acid substance is sodium aluminum sulfate (SAS). It requires heat and moisture to complete its reaction with soda. Therefore, additional carbon dioxide gas is produced during baking.

The reactions of calcium acid phosphate and baking soda are complex and difficult to write. Many different salts are probably produced in this reaction and they may interact with each other.

$$CaH_4(PO_4)_2 \;+\; NaHCO_3 \;\rightarrow\; \text{insoluble calcium phosphate salts} \;+\; \text{soluble sodium phosphate salts} \;+\; CO_2 \;+\; H_2O$$

| calcium acid phosphate | sodium bicarbonate | | | carbon dioxide | water |

Sodium aluminum sulfate apparently reacts in two stages. The first reaction is with water and results in the production of sulfuric acid as heat is applied, after which the sulfuric acid reacts with soda to produce carbon dioxide gas, according to the following equations.

(1) $Na_2SO_4Al_2(SO_4)_3 \; + \; 6H_2O \; \xrightarrow{heat} \; Na_2SO_4 \; + \; 2Al(OH)_3 \; + \; H_2SO_4$

sodium aluminum sulfate   water   sodium sulfate   aluminum hydroxide   sulfuric acid

(2) $3H_2SO_4 \; + \; 6NaHCO_3 \; \rightarrow \; 6CO_2 \; + \; 6H_2O \; + \; 3Na_2SO_4$

sulfuric acid   sodium bicarbonate   carbon dioxide   water   sodium sulfate

Importantly, *all baking powders are composed of soda plus an acid ingredient*. The carbon dioxide gas (CO_2) comes from the soda. Different acid components may be used. The food industry has available to it a wide variety of baking powders, utilizing various acid components.

According to federal law, all types of baking powders must contain at least 12 percent available CO_2 gas. Those powders manufactured for home use generally contain 14 percent, and some powders for commercial use have 17 percent available gas. Baking powder containers should always be kept tightly covered to avoid the absorption of moisture that causes the acid and alkali constituents to react prematurely with the loss of some carbon dioxide.

All baking powders leave residues in the mixture in which they are used. The sodium sulfate (Na_2SO_4) residue from the SAS-phosphate baking powder has a somewhat bitter taste which may be objectionable to certain individuals. Some people are more sensitive than others to this bitter taste.

An optimum amount of baking powder is desirable for any baked product. If too much baking powder is used, the cell walls of the flour mixture are stretched beyond their limit, and they may break and collapse. If too little baking powder is present, insufficient expansion occurs, and a compact product results. Use of the minimum amount of SAS-phosphate baking powder that leavens satisfactorily is particularly desirable because of the bitter residue formed with this baking powder. Between 1 and 1 1/2 teaspoons of SAS-phosphate baking powder per cup of flour should be adequate for the leavening of most flour mixtures.

Methods of Adding Baking Powder and Soda. Dry chemical leavening agents, including baking powders, are usually sifted or mixed with the flour. They are not allowed to become wet, and thus begin to release their carbon dioxide gas, until the later stages of the mixing process, when the liquid ingredients are combined with the dry ingredients. It has sometimes been suggested that the soda be mixed with the sour milk or molasses called for in a recipe. This method is generally not recommended, however, because leavening gas is more readily lost in this case and it is important to retain as much gas as possible in the flour mixture. Nevertheless, because of the high viscosity of molasses, gas tends to be lost slowly from a mixture of soda and molasses.

It is expected that carbon dioxide gas will be more rapidly lost from a mixture of buttermilk and soda than from a batter made by mixing the soda with dry ingredients and then adding the buttermilk. However, students in laboratory classes have compared the volumes of chocolate cakes containing soda and buttermilk when the soda was either sifted with the dry ingredients or added directly to the buttermilk. They found that when the soda-buttermilk mixture is added immediately to the batter, the volumes of the finished cakes are quite similar. Allowing the soda-buttermilk mixture to stand before adding it to the batter results in a lower cake volume.

Substitutions of Chemical Leavening Agents. Buttermilk and soda may be substituted for sweet milk and baking powder and vice versa in many recipes for baked products. One-half teaspoon of soda and 1 cup of buttermilk or fully soured milk produce an amount of leavening gas almost equivalent to that produced by 2 teaspoons of SAS-phosphate baking powder. Other approximately equivalent substitutes include 1/2 teaspoon of baking soda plus 1 1/4 teaspoons cream of tartar and 1/2 teaspoon baking soda plus 1 cup molasses. Sweet milk can be made sour by taking 1 tablespoon of vinegar or lemon juice and adding enough sweet milk to make 1 cup, or by adding 1 3/4 teaspoons of cream of tartar to 1 cup of sweet milk. An example of making a substitution in a recipe follows:

Original Recipe

2 cups (230 g) flour   3 tsp (9.6 g) SAS-phosphate powder
1 cup (237 mL) sweet milk

Recipe with Substitution of Soda and Sour Milk

2 cups (230 g) flour   1/2 tsp (2 g) soda
1 cup (237 mL) buttermilk   1 tsp (3.2 g) SAS-phosphate powder

Fat

The major role of fat in flour mixtures is to tenderize or "shorten" the strands of gluten. This tenderizing effect is produced through formation of layers or masses that physically separate different strands of gluten and prevent them from coming together. To shorten effectively, a fat must have the capacity to coat or spread widely and to adhere well to flour particles.

It is difficult to make definite statements concerning the comparative shortening power of various fats because many factors have been shown to modify their effects. For example, the manner in which a fat is distributed in a mixture, the extent of distribution, the temperature of the fat and of the mixture, the presence or absence of **emulsifiers** in the mixture, the type of mixture, and the method and extent of mixing, as well as the method by which the fat itself has been processed, may have an effect on the shortening power of the fat.

Smoothness of the batter and desirable texture in some finished baked products, such as shortened cakes, are related to the emulsification of the fat in the batter. The presence of some **monoglycerides** and **diglycerides** in the fat increases the degree of emulsification of the fat, allowing it to be dispersed in small particles throughout the batter. The addition of emulsifiers to shortened cake batters has been shown to yield cakes of increased volume and finer texture than usually result without the use of emulsifiers.

The *plasticity* of a fat is related to its shortening power. In a **plastic fat,** some of the **triglyceride** molecules are present in a liquid form and some are crystallized in a solid form. The presence of both solid and liquid phases in the fat means that the fat can be molded or shaped rather than being fractured or broken when force is applied to it. Fats that are more plastic are more spread-

emulsifier a surface-active agent that acts as a bridge between two immiscible liquids and allows an emulsion to form

monoglyceride glycerol combined with one fatty acid; used as an emulsifier

diglyceride glycerol combined with two fatty acids; usually present with monoglycerides in an emulsifier mixture

plastic fat a fat that can be molded or shaped, such as hydrogenated shortening, margarine, or butter

triglyceride glycerol combined with three fatty acids; most food fats are triglycerides

polyunsaturated fats fats that contain a relatively high proportion of polyunsaturated fatty acids, which have two or more double bonds between carbon atoms; these fatty acids are shaped differently from saturated fatty acids because of the double bonds

saturated fatty acids fatty acids that contain no double bonds between carbon atoms and thus hold all of the hydrogen that can be attached to the carbons

able and, presumably, can spread over a greater surface area of flour particles than less plastic fats. The temperature of fat affects plasticity. At 64°F (18°C), butter is less plastic than at 72° to 83°F (22° to 28°C). At higher temperatures, butter tends to become very soft or to melt completely.

A shortometer measures the weight required to break a baked wafer. This instrument can test the shortening value of fats on pastry. The results of these tests have been somewhat variable but, in many cases, lards have been shown to have more shortening power than most hydrogenated fats, butter, and margarine. Oils that are high in **polyunsaturated fats** usually produce more tender pastries than lards. One explanation that has been offered is that these oils cover a larger surface area of flour particles per molecule of fat than fats containing a relatively high proportion of **saturated fatty acids.** The relationship between the degree of unsaturation and shortening power of fats, however, needs further clarification.

With other proportions and other conditions standardized, the higher the concentration of fat in a mixture, the greater the shortening power. This point deserves consideration in the substitution of one fat for another. Butter and margarines contain approximately 82 percent fat and about 16 percent water. Reduced-calorie spreads that are marketed as substitutes for margarine or butter contain even less fat. Lard, hydrogenated fats, and oils contain essentially 100 percent fat. Disregarding other factors that appear to affect the shortening power of fats, the mere substitution of an equal weight of a fat of higher fat concentration for one of lower concentration affects the tenderness of baked flour mixtures. Fats are discussed further in Chapters 9 and 10.

Fat in Leavening.   Plastic fats appear to play important roles in some flour mixtures in the trapping of air bubbles that later contribute to the texture of the finished product. This role of fat may be particularly important in the preparation of shortened cakes. It has been suggested that creaming fat and sugar crystals together and also vigorously beating fat-containing batters cause air cells to be entrapped in the mixture. Fats that incorporate air readily and allow it to be dispersed in small cells are said to have good creaming properties.

Fat Replacers.   Surveys of consumer attitudes regarding food have confirmed their concern about the fat content of food products [3]. Interest in reduced-fat baked goods has been high although recently it has moderated somewhat. Products such as no-fat and low-fat cookies, crackers, granola bars, and breakfast bars are being successfully marketed.

Substances used to replace fat in a flour mixture must mimic the effects of fat on the eating quality of the finished product [13]. This challenges the ingenuity of the food industry as new products are formulated. Cellulose, gums, maltodextrins, modified starches, and polydextrose are carbohydrate-based substances that are used as fat replacers. Dehydrated fruit products, such as banana flakes and prune paste, may be used in low- or no-fat bakery products to maintain a desirable texture. A microparticulated whey protein concentrate, Simplesse®, can be combined with selected emulsifiers for easy, effective use in low-fat baked products [23]. Specially designed emulsifier systems are also important components in fat-reduced products because they extend the effects of the fat [15]. However, without jeopardizing the quality of the finished item, the fat in many baked product formulas can be reduced, at least slightly. Fat replacers are discussed in Chapter 10.

Liquids

Liquids have various uses in flour mixtures. They hydrate the starch and gluten and dissolve certain constituents, such as sugar, salts, and baking powder. It is only when baking powders are wet that the evolution of carbon dioxide gas begins. The typical structure or framework of doughs and batters is not formed until the protein particles become hydrated. **Starch gelatinization** during baking requires moisture. Various liquids may be used in flour mixtures, including water, potato water, milk, fruit juices, and coffee. The water content of eggs is also a part of the total liquid.

starch gelatinization the swelling of starch granules when heated with water, often resulting in thickening

Eggs

Eggs may be used as a means of incorporating air into a batter, because egg proteins coagulate on beating and give some structure or rigidity to the cell walls surrounding the air bubbles. Egg whites can form a particularly stable foam. As they are beaten, the cell walls become increasingly thinner and more tender to an optimum point. Beaten egg whites can be carefully folded into a batter, retaining much of the air in the foam.

Egg yolks add flavor and color to flour mixtures. They also aid in forming emulsions of fat and water because of their content of **lipoproteins,** which are effective emulsifying agents. Because egg proteins coagulate on heating, the addition of eggs to flour mixtures increases the rigidity of the baked product.

lipoprotein a lipid or fatty substance combined with a protein; egg yolk contains lipoproteins that combine phospholipids with protein

Sugar and Other Sweeteners

Granulated sugar is used in many flour mixtures for sweetening purposes. It also contributes to the browning of outer surfaces of baked products. **Caramelization** occurs at high oven temperatures as the surface of the product becomes dry. In yeast mixtures, sugar is a readily available food for the yeast plant. Sugar has a tenderizing effect because it interferes with the development of gluten in a batter or dough by tying up water so that less water is available for the gluten and more manipulation is necessary to develop the gluten structure than when sugar is not present. The volume of many baked flour mixtures is increased by the addition of optimal amounts of sugar, because the gluten mass is tenderized and expands more easily under the pressure of leavening gases. Sugar may also help to achieve a fine, even texture in many baked products [14].

caramelization the development of brown color and caramel flavor as dry sugar is heated to a high temperature; chemical decomposition occurs in the sugar

The **coagulation** temperature of egg proteins is elevated by sugar. Sponge-type cakes contain relatively large amounts of egg as well as sugar. Sugar also increases the temperature at which starch gelatinizes, which is of particular importance in high-sugar products such as cakes of several types. Brown sugar imparts a distinctive flavor to baked foods and yields products that tend to remain moist longer than those made with granulated sugar. Measured lightly, brown sugar weighs less per cup than granulated sugar. It should be firmly packed in the cup during measurement or be substituted by weight for granulated sugar.

coagulation change in protein, after it has been denatured, that results in hardening or precipitation and is often accomplished by heating

Other sweeteners are sometimes used in baked products. Honey, molasses, and syrups in yeast breads provide distinctive flavors and a substrate for yeast fermentation. High-fructose corn syrup can replace up to 25 percent of the sugar in angel cake without greatly affecting quality characteristics [5]. Crystalline fructose has replaced sucrose (table sugar) in some cakes and cake mixes on the market.

High-intensity or alternate sweeteners, including saccharin, encapsulated aspartame, acesulfame-K, and sucralose, are stable under high temperatures and retain sweetness in baked products. Some of these products have a nonsweet aftertaste [19]. A bulking or bodying agent such as polydextrose must be added with high-intensity sweeteners to substitute for some of sugar's effects on texture. Compensation must also be made for the effect of sugar on the tenderness of the finished product. Again, the food industry faces challenges in formulating no-sugar baked products. Alternate sweeteners are discussed in Chapter 11.

CLASSIFICATION OF BATTERS AND DOUGHS

Flour mixtures vary in thickness depending largely on the proportion of flour to liquid. Based on thickness, flour mixtures are classified as batters or doughs.

Batters

Batters are classified as pour batters or drop batters, but considerable variation exists within each group; some pour batters are very thin, whereas others pour with difficulty. A pour batter contains 2/3 to 1 cup of liquid per cup of flour. A drop batter usually has 1/2 to 3/4 cup of liquid per cup of flour. In batters containing approximately 1 part liquid to 2 parts flour, gluten development readily occurs on mixing. Popovers and thin griddle-cake and shortened-cake batters are examples of pour batters. Some drop batters are stiff enough to require scraping from the spoon. Drop batters include muffins, many quick breads, and various kinds of cookies. A batter containing yeast is called a *sponge*.

Doughs

Doughs are thick enough to be handled or kneaded on a flat surface (Figure 15-8). Most doughs are rolled in the final stages of preparation, although yeast dough is not usually rolled except for the shaping of certain types of rolls. Doughs may be soft (just stiff enough to handle) or stiff. Soft doughs contain about 1/3 cup of liquid per cup of flour. A stiff dough may contain only 1/8 cup of liquid per cup of flour. Examples of soft-dough products include baking powder biscuits, rolled cookies, yeast bread, and rolls. Pie crust is an example of a stiff dough.

GENERAL METHODS FOR MIXING BATTERS AND DOUGHS

General objectives in the mixing of doughs and batters are uniform distribution of ingredients, minimum loss of the leavening agent, optimum blending to produce characteristic textures in various products, and optimum development of

Figure 15-8
Yeast bread dough is thick enough to be kneaded by hand.

gluten for the desired individual properties. Although many different methods are employed for the mixing of batters and doughs, three basic methods may be adapted for use with a variety of products.

Muffin Method

In the muffin method, dry ingredients are sifted together into the bowl used for mixing. The eggs are lightly beaten and the liquid and melted fat (or oil) are added to the eggs. The liquid ingredients are then blended with the dry ingredients, the amount of stirring depending on the mixture.

For thin mixtures, such as popovers, thin griddle cakes, and thin waffle mixtures, lumping can be prevented by adding the liquid ingredients gradually to the dry ingredients. Conversely, the overstirring of thicker batters, such as thick waffle mixtures and muffins, can be prevented by adding liquid ingredients all at once to the dry ingredients. Thicker batters are stirred only until the dry ingredients are dampened to avoid an undesirable development of gluten and a resulting decrease in tenderness (Figure 15-9).

Pastry or Biscuit Method

In the pastry or biscuit method, the dry ingredients are sifted together. Fat is cut in or blended with the dry ingredients, and liquid is then added to the fat-flour mixture. The "cutting in" of the fat, instead of thorough blending, results in a more flaky product which is desirable in both biscuits and pie crusts. Although this method is used mainly for pastry and biscuits, it is also appropriate for other flour mixtures. The techniques of handling the dough after the addition of liquid differ for pastry and biscuits. Biscuits are generally mixed more thoroughly than pie crusts and are lightly kneaded before they are rolled out and cut into the desired shapes.

Conventional Method

Although cakes are mixed by more than one method, the conventional cake method, or simply the conventional method, is usually understood to mean the conventional way in which fat and sugar are creamed together, beaten eggs are added, and dry and liquid ingredients are alternately blended with the fat-sugar-

Figure 15-9
The muffin method of mixing is used to prepare waffles such as this one.

egg mixture. This method may also be used for making cookies, various quick breads, and other flour products. Yeast bread, cream puffs, and sponge-type cake are mixed by special methods applicable only to these products. Whatever the method, the optimum amount of manipulation varies with the type of product, with the character and proportion of the ingredients used, and with the temperature of the ingredients.

STRUCTURE OF BATTERS AND DOUGHS

The structure that develops in batters and doughs varies according to the kind and proportion of ingredients used; however, in all mixtures, except those of high liquid content, the gluten particles, on becoming hydrated, tend to adhere and form a continuous mass that spreads out into a network. Some components of the mixture, such as salts and sugar, are partially or completely dissolved in the liquid. The starch granules from the flour tend to be embedded in the gluten network (see Figure 15-6). Other components act as emulsifying agents by separating or dividing the fat in the mixture into particles of varying fineness. The temperature and the physical and chemical state of the ingredients partially determine the degree of dispersion of the emulsion. Melted fats or oils may behave differently from solid fats in certain doughs and batters.

The texture of the finished product depends largely on the structure obtained in the mixing of the dough or batter. Texture is a combination of such characteristics as the distribution of cells, the thickness of cell walls, the character of the crumb (elastic, crumbly, velvety, or harsh), and the grain (the size of the cells). Optimum texture cannot be expected to be the same for all products, because of the variation in the kinds and amounts of constituents used. Typical textures for different baked products are discussed with those products in later chapters. Variations from typical textures and possible causes for variation are also discussed.

When all the factors that affect texture are considered, it is not surprising that products made from the same formula may differ with several bakings. Although a certain degree of control of materials, manipulation, and temperatures is possible, it is difficult in practical baking in the kitchen to always control all factors that play a part in determining the quality of the end products obtained. In industrial operations and in many foodservice establishments, controls are sufficiently precise and reproducible that the same quality product is guaranteed each time. Quality assurance programs are geared to achieve just that.

DRY FLOUR MIXES

A wide variety of flour-based mixes are marketed. Excellent directions to the consumer in the use of these prepared mixes tend to ensure uniform, good-quality finished products. In addition to flour, they may contain leavening, salt, fat (sometimes powdered shortening), nonfat dry milk, dried eggs, sugar, and flavoring ingredients, such as dried extracts, cocoa, ginger, and dried molasses, depending on the type of mixture. Some mixes are yeast mixtures for making fermented bread or rolls.

Numerous additives are used and have contributed to the success of commercial flour mixes. These include various emulsifiers, modified starches, caseinate, gums, cellulose, and whipping aids. A combination of added substances is often necessary in the production of reduced-fat or reduced-calorie mixes.

Mixes are convenient timesavers, and they often cost no more (and some-times even less) than a similar product prepared in the kitchen. Costs must be determined on an individual basis and are sometimes difficult to compare be-cause of differences in ingredients and yields. (The cost of convenience foods is discussed in Chapter 2.)

A number of mixes may be used in foodservice operations. The savings in labor cost and an evaluation of quality are important considerations in making decisions regarding the use of dry flour mixes in quantity foodservice.

Various flour mixes can also be made in the home kitchen, saving time by measuring and mixing at least some of the ingredients at one time. However, because the techniques used in the production of commercial mixes are not available for home use, homemade mixes do not have as long a shelf life. They should be adequately packaged and stored at cool temperatures. Commercial mixes usually contain a leavening acid that dissolves slowly, such as anhydrous monocalcium phosphate or sodium acid pyrophosphate, to prevent the prema-ture reaction of the baking powder during storage. Also, off-flavors do not readily develop in the mixes with these acids.

BAKING AT HIGH ALTITUDES

Some balancing of ingredients and variation of baking temperature may be nec-essary at high altitudes. Because the atmospheric pressure is less, the leavening gases in baked products meet less resistance and are apt to overexpand, espe-cially during the early part of baking. This overexpansion may stretch the cells to the extent that they break and collapse, producing a coarse texture and de-creased volume.

Corrections in recipes that are standardized for use at sea level may involve decreasing the leavening agent or strengthening the cell walls by decreasing the sugar or adding more flour. Increased liquid may also be added because of greater loss by evaporation. Oven temperatures may be increased. However, definite rules cannot be strictly applied in all recipe adjustments because of the varying proportions of ingredients in recipes. Each recipe needs to be tested in-dividually. Agricultural experiment stations in the western United States have studied the effects of altitudes up to 10,000 feet on baked products and have de-veloped appropriate adjustments and recipes [2,6].

Altitude corrections are not necessary for pastry and cream puffs. Yeast products may require shorter, and possibly more frequent, rising periods. Muffins and biscuits can usually be made at higher altitudes with little change in recipes, although a small decrease in baking powder may be desirable above

Adjustment	3,000 Feet	5,000 Feet	7,000 Feet
Reduce baking powder			
For each teaspoon, decrease:	1/8 tsp	1/8–1/4 tsp	1/4 tsp
Reduce sugar			
For each cup, decrease:	0–1 Tbsp	2–3 Tbsp	4–5 Tbsp
Increase liquid			
For each cup, add:	1–2 Tbsp	2–4 Tbsp	3–4 Tbsp

Table 15-1
Adjustments for Shortened Cakes

Source: Reference 1.

5,000 feet. Because cakes have a very delicate structure, they are more affected by altitude than most other baked products. The amount of sugar may be decreased and the amount of flour increased in angel food and sponge cakes as altitude increases. Suggested adjustments for shortened cakes are given in Table 15-1. Oven temperatures may be increased 15° to 25°F (8° to 14°C) to set the batter structure before cells can expand too much. Baking times may then be decreased.

CHAPTER SUMMARY

- Batters and doughs, sometimes called flour mixtures, include a large variety of baked products such as muffins, biscuits and other quick breads, pastry, shortened and unshortened cakes, cookies, and breads. The principal ingredients used for doughs and batters are flour, liquid, fat, egg, sugar, leavening agent, and salt.

- Wheat is the principal grain used in the United States for flour. Because of its protein and starch content, flour provides structure and body in baked flour products. Wheats may be classified on the basis of the time of planting or the growing season, the color of the kernel, and the hardness or softness of the kernel. Hard wheats are usually higher in protein than soft wheats, and the protein has more baking strength when flour from this wheat is made into dough.

- The milling of white flour is a process that involves separating the endosperm from the bran and germ and subdividing it into a fine flour. Milled white flour usually contains 65 to 70 percent starch and 8 to 13 percent protein.

- Various grades and types of flours are formulated from the many streams of flours resulting from the milling process. Break flours and those from the last reduction of the middlings are inferior to the other streams of flour for baking purposes. Air classification may be used to divide the flour, produced by milling, into various fractions with differing ratios of starch to protein.

- Included in the final stages of white flour production are bleaching and maturing. Flours may be "bleached" by the addition of approved chemicals or may lighten in color due to the oxidation of the carotenoic pigments after extended holding. Flour is aged by holding the flour for several weeks or months. This matured flour produces breads with higher volumes and finer textures.

- The miller grades of flour include straight grade, patent flours—short patent, medium patent, long patent—and clear grade. These grades are determined on the basis of which streams of flour are combined.

- Several types of wheat flour are available that function effectively for specialized baking or cooking purposes. These include: whole wheat, bread, all-purpose, pastry, cake, instantized, self-rising, and gluten flour. Other wheat products include cracked wheat and wheat germ.

- Flours and meals may be made from other grains. Rye, cornmeal, corn, soy, buckwheat, triticale, rice, potato, and amaranth flour may be used to make a variety of products. Because several of these flours contain little or no gluten, wheat flour is often used with flours from other grains so that high quality baked goods may be produced.

- To leaven means to "make light and porous." Three major leavening gases are air, steam or water vapor, and carbon dioxide. One or more of these leavening gases may be used in flour mixtures.

- Carbon dioxide may be produced in flour mixtures either by biological processes or by a purely chemical reaction. Carbon dioxide is produced by the action of yeast and certain bacteria on sugar in a process called fermentation. Sodium bicarbonate (baking soda) in a flour mixture gives off carbon dioxide gas when heated with water. To avoid the disagreeable flavor of this reaction, sodium bicarbonate is combined with various acids, such as buttermilk, vinegar, citrus juices and others, to release the carbon dioxide gas.

- Baking powders are mixtures of dry acid or acid salts and baking soda. The type of baking powder that is generally available for home use is called SAS-phospate baking powder. It is a double-acting baking powder, which means that it releases carbon dioxide gas when the dry ingredients are moistened *and* when heat is applied in the process of baking.

- Baking soda may be substituted for baking powder in a recipe if the correct proportion of an acid ingredient, such as cream of tartar or buttermilk, is added to the recipe.

- The major role of fat in flour mixtures is to tenderize or "shorten" the strands of gluten. To shorten effectively, a fat must have the capacity to coat or spread widely and to adhere well to flour particles. The presence of emulsifiers in fat, such as monoglycerides and diglycerides, allows it to be dispersed in small particles throughout the batter. The plasticity of a fat also is related to its shortening power.

- When substituting fats in recipes, the amount of fat in butter versus oils or hydrogenated fats should be considered. Butter and margarines contain approximately 82 percent fat as compared to 100 percent fat in oils or hydrogenated fats. Thus, the product that contains a higher percentage of fat will have a greater shortening power.

- Plastic fats appear to play important roles in some flour mixtures, such as shortened cakes, in the trapping of air bubbles during creaming that later contributes to the texture of the finished product.

- Liquids hydrate the starch and gluten and dissolve certain constituents, such as sugar, salts, and baking powder. Starch gelatinization during baking requres moisture.

- Eggs may be used as a means of incorporating air into the batter and add flavor and color to flour mixtures. Eggs also aid in forming emulsions of fat and water because of the content of lipoproteins. Because egg proteins coagulate on heating, the addition of eggs to flour mixtures increases the rigidity of the baked product.

- Granulated sugar sweetens, contributes to browning, provides food for yeast, tenderizes, and increases the volume of baked goods. Sugar also may help to achieve a fine, even texture in many baked products.

- Brown sugar and other sweeteners such as honey, molasses, and syrups add distinctive flavors and characteristics in baked products.

- Flour mixtures are classified as batters or doughs. Batters may be thin and pour readily or may be stiffer and are called drop batters. Doughs are thick enough to be handled or kneaded on a flat surface.

- The general objectives in the mixing of doughs and batters are uniform distribution of ingredients, minimum loss of the leavening agent, optimum blending to produce characteristic textures in various products, and optimum development of gluten for the desired individual properties. Three basic methods of mixing are used for a variety of products: muffin method, pastry or biscuit method, and conventional method.

- Some balancing of ingredients and variation in baking temperature may be necessary at high altitudes.

KEY TERMS

carotenoid pigments
oxidation
inulin
prebiotics
pentosans
albumins
globulins
disulfide bond
peptide chains
fermentation
maltose
amylase

maltase
emulsifier
monoglyceride
diglyceride
plastic fat
triglyceride
polyunsaturated fats
saturated fatty acids
starch gelatinization
lipoprotein
caramelization
coagulation

STUDY QUESTIONS

1. a. What is meant by the *milling* of flour?
   b. How is white flour produced?
   c. How is whole wheat or graham flour produced?
   d. How do hard and soft wheat flours generally differ in characteristics and composition?
   e. Name three grades of white flour and indicate which is usually found on the retail market.

2. For each of the following types of flour, describe general characteristics and uses in food preparation.
   a. Bread flour
   b. All-purpose flour
   c. Pastry flour
   d. Cake flour
   e. Instantized flour
   f. Self-rising flour

3. About 85 percent of the proteins in white wheat flour are relatively insoluble and play an important role in developing the structure of baked products.
   a. Name the two wheat flour protein fractions that develop into gluten with moistening and mixing or kneading.
   b. Describe the characteristics of wheat gluten and discuss its role in the preparation of baked flour mixtures.

4. a. What is meant by the term *leaven?*
   b. Name three leavening gases that are commonly present in baked products.

   c. Describe several ways in which air may be incorporated into a batter or dough during preparation.

   d. Explain why steam is such an effective leavening gas and name two products that are leavened primarily by steam.

5. Carbon dioxide (CO_2) gas may be produced by biological and by chemical means.

   a. Describe how CO_2 may be produced biologically in baked products.

   b. Describe examples of the chemical production of CO_2 in flour mixtures.

6. Although CO_2 will be released when soda is heated in a moist environment, explain why it cannot satisfactorily be used for leavening in baked products without an accompanying acid.

7. Baking powders always contain at least two active ingredients. Name them. Which one is responsible for the production of CO_2?

8. Name several acid foods that are commonly used with soda in baked products.

9. Generally, the only type of baking powder available to the consumer is SAS-phosphate baking powder.

   a. Explain why this baking powder is called "double-acting."

   b. Name the active ingredients in this baking powder.

   c. Explain how the active ingredients participate in the production of CO_2 gas.

10. a. How much soda is normally used with 1 cup of buttermilk in a baked product?

   b. How much SAS-phosphate baking powder is normally used per 1 cup of flour to leaven a baked product?

11. Briefly describe the general role of each of the following ingredients in baked flour mixtures.

   a. Fat

   b. Flour

   c. Liquids

   d. Eggs

   e. Sugar

12. Why is it a challenge to produce acceptable baked products that are reduced in fat, sugar, and/or calories? Explain.

13. What are batters? Doughs? Give examples of each.

14. Describe each of the following general methods of mixing batters and doughs and give examples of baked products commonly prepared by each method.

   a. Muffin method

   b. Pastry or biscuit method

   c. Conventional method

15. a. Why do some adjustments need to be made in baked products when they are prepared at high altitudes? Briefly discuss this.

   b. Suggest appropriate adjustments for shortened cakes that are baked at high altitudes when using recipes standardized at sea level.

REFERENCES

1. American Association of Family and Consumer Sciences. (2001). *Food: A handbook of terminology, purchasing, and preparation* (10th ed.). Alexandria, VA.

2. Boyd, M. S., & Schoonover, M. C. (1965). *Baking at high altitude.* University of Wyoming Agricultural Experiment Station Bulletin No. 427. Laramie: University of Wyoming.

3. Bruhn, C. M., Cotter, A., Diaz-Knauf, K., Sutherlin, J., West, E., Wightman, N., Williamson, E., & Yaffee, M. (1992). Consumer attitudes and market potential for foods using fat substitutes. *Food Technology, 46*(4), 81.

4. Butaki, R. C., & Dronzek, B. (1979). Comparison of gluten properties of four wheat varieties. *Cereal Chemistry, 56*, 159.

5. Coleman, P. E., & Harbers, C. A. Z. (1983). High fructose corn syrup: Replacement for sucrose in angel cake. *Journal of Food Science, 48*, 452.

6. Dyar, E., & Cassel, E. (1958). *Mile-high cakes: Recipes for high altitudes.* Colorado Agricultural Experiment Station Bulletin No. 404-A. Fort Collins, CO.

7. Gordon, D.T. (1999). What is dietary fiber? *Food Technology, 53*(6), 242.

8. Hansen, L., & Rose, M. S. (1996). Sensory acceptability is inversely related to development of fat rancidity in bread made from stored flour. *Journal of the American Dietetic Association, 96*, 792.

9. Il, B., Daun, H., & Gilbert, S. G. (1991). Water sorption of gliadin. *Journal of Food Science, 56*, 510.

10. Lorenz, K. (1972). Food uses of triticale. *Food Technology, 26*(11), 66.

11. Ma, C., Oomah, B. D., & Holme, J. (1986). Effect of deamidation and succinylation on some physicochemical and baking properties of gluten. *Journal of Food Science, 51*, 99.

12. Mani, K., Tragardh, C., Eliasson, A. C., & Lindahl, L. (1992). Water content, water soluble fraction, and mixing affect fundamental rheological properties of wheat flour doughs. *Journal of Food Science, 57*, 1198.

13. Mattes, R. D. (1998). Position of the American Dietetic Association: Fat replacers. *Journal of the American Dietetic Association, 98*, 463.

14. Myhre, D. V. (1970). The function of carbohydrates in baking. *Baker's Digest, 44*(3), 32.

15. Nabors, L. O. (1992). Fat replacers: Options for controlling fat and calories in the diet. *Food and Nutrition News, 64*(1), 5.

16. Ngo, W., Hoseney, R. C., & Moore, W. R. (1985). Dynamic rheological properties of cake batters made from chlorine-treated and untreated flours. *Journal of Food Science, 50*, 1338.

17. Pomeranz, Y., & MacMasters, M. M. (1968). Structure and composition of the wheat kernel. *Baker's Digest, 42*(4), 24.

18. Psczcola, D. E. (2002). Adding to the family of rice bran extracts. *Food Technology, 56*(1), 66.

19. Redlinger, P. A., & Setser, C. S. (1987). Sensory quality of selected sweeteners: Unbaked and baked flour doughs. *Journal of Food Science, 52*, 1391.

20. Sanchez-Marroquin, A., Domingo, M. V., Maya, S., & Saldana, C. (1985). Amaranth flour blends and fractions for baking applications. *Journal of Food Science, 50*, 789.

21. Saunders, R. M., & Becker, R. (1984). Amaranthus: A potential food and feed resource. In Y. Pomeranz (ed.), *Advances in cereal science and technology* (Vol. VI). St. Paul, MN: American Association of Cereal Chemists, Inc.

22. Sloan, A. E. (2001). Dietary fiber moves back into the mainstream. *Food Technology, 55*(7), 18.

23. Staff. (1994). Blends reduce fat in bakery products. *Food Technology, 48*(6), 168.

24. Watson, C. A., Shuey, W. C., Crawford, R. D., & Gumbmann, M. R. (1977). Physical dough, baking, and nutritional qualities of straight-grade and extended-extraction flours. *Cereal Chemistry, 54*, 657.

Quick Breads

16

 Traditionally, quick breads have included a variety of products that can be prepared without the rising or proofing time required by yeast breads. Quick breads are often served warm. Examples of quick breads are popovers, pancakes or griddle cakes, waffles, muffins, biscuits, scones, coffee cakes, and loaf breads made with baking powder as a leavening ingredient. Cream puffs and éclairs may also be classified with quick breads.

Quick bread ideas and recipes are borrowed from many different ethnic groups. There are Swedish pancakes and pancake balls, Finnish oven pancakes, and German potato pancakes. In many parts of Mexico, flour tortillas are made in the home from a basic flour dough that usually contains baking powder; the dough is rolled into flat circles before being baked on a hot griddle. Sesame turnovers come from Greece; they are made of a pastrylike dough containing a small amount of baking powder and are filled with ground nuts and seeds. The variety of quick breads with ethnic origins is almost limitless.

Table 16-1 provides proportions of ingredients for some basic quick breads. Ingredients are balanced to produce the type of product desired. Structural ingredients, such as flour and egg, are balanced against tenderizing ingredients, primarily sugar and fat, so that the product will have form or structure yet be appropriately tender. The consistency of the batter or dough is generally determined by the ratio of flour to liquid ingredients.

POPOVERS

Ingredients

Popovers contain a relatively high proportion of liquid, usually milk, and are leavened chiefly by the steam produced in a hot oven in the early stages of baking. They are usually mixed by the muffin method, as described in Chapter 15. Although either pastry or all-purpose flour may be used for making popovers, the crusts are usually more rigid when all-purpose flour is used. Because of the high percentage of moisture in the batter, the gluten particles, on becoming hydrated, tend to float in the liquid. Because the gluten particles do not adhere to each other sufficiently to form a continuous mass, the batter may be stirred much or little without appreciably affecting the finished product. The batter should be smooth and free from lumps. With so small an amount of flour, the liquid is best added gradually at first until the lumps are stirred out.

Table 16-1
Proportions of Ingredients for Quick Breads

Product	Flour	Liquid	Eggs	Fat	Sugar	Salt	Baking Powder	Soda
Popovers	1 c	1 c	2–3	0–1 Tbsp		¼–½ tsp		
Cream puffs	1 c	1 c	4	½ c		¼ tsp		
Muffins	1 c	½ c	½–1	1–2 Tbsp	1–2 Tbsp	½ tsp	1½–2 tsp	
Waffles	1 c	⅔ c	1–2	3 Tbsp	1 tsp	½ tsp	1–2 tsp	
Pancakes								
Sweet milk	1 c	⅔ c	1	1 Tbsp	1 tsp	¼–½ tsp	1–2 tsp	
Thick buttermilk	1 c	1 c	1	1–2 Tbsp		¼–½ tsp	¼–½ tsp (optional)	½ tsp
Thick sour cream	1 c	1 c	1			¼–½ tsp	¼–½ tsp (optional)	½ tsp
Biscuits	1 c	Rolled, ⅓ c Dropped, ⅓–⅜ c		2–3 Tbsp		½ tsp	1½–2 tsp	
Scones	1 c	⅓ c cream	1	2–3 Tbsp	1 Tbsp	⅛ tsp	2 tsp	

Egg is an essential constituent of popovers and gives them structure. The floating gluten particles do not form a mass of sufficient continuity to expand under the pressure of the steam formed during baking. With no egg, the popover is heavy and has a very small volume; with two eggs per cup of flour, enough extensible and coagulable material is furnished to form rigid walls. If the eggs are small or if pastry flour is used, three eggs per cup of flour provide more desirable results than two eggs. Fat serves little purpose in popovers. It tends to float on top of the thin batter, and thus chiefly affects the top crust. If as much as 1 tablespoon of fat is used, the top crust may have a flaky appearance.

Characteristics

Popovers are high rising and usually have irregular shapes. They are hollow, with thick crusty walls (Figure 16-1). Because of the high percentage of liquid in the mixture, the interior is moist but not similar to raw dough. Crusts should not be so brown that their flavor is impaired.

Baking

Muffin pans (preferably deep ones) or heat-resistant glass cups can be used for baking popovers. They are greased to keep the popovers from sticking. When iron pans are used, baking may be speeded up if the pans are prewarmed, because iron requires more time to become hot than tin or aluminum. Because steam is the chief leavening agent in popovers, a hot oven temperature (450°F or 232°C) is required to form steam quickly. After 15 minutes at 450°F (232°C), the oven is reduced to 375°F (191°C) for the remainder of the baking time, about 45 minutes. If popovers are baked for the whole time at a hot temperature, the crusts may become too brown in the time required to form rigid walls that do not collapse on removal from the oven. Popovers should be pricked with a fork to allow steam to escape upon removal from the oven to avoid a soggy interior. If a crisper popover is desired, then turn off the oven and return the pricked popovers to the oven for several minutes.

Figure 16-1
Well-made popovers have a large volume and a moist, hollow interior. (Photograph by Roger P. Smith)

Browning in popovers is apparently produced primarily by the **Maillard reaction.** The amount of milk sugar or lactose in the mixture is probably sufficient for this reaction to occur. **Dextrinization** of starch in the flour may also contribute to browning.

Maillard reaction the carbonyl group of sugar combines with the amino group of a protein, initiating a series of chemical reactions which result in a brown color and change in flavor.

Causes of Failure

Probably the chief cause of failure in making popovers is insufficient baking. Popovers are not necessarily done when they are brown and may collapse on removal from the oven if the egg proteins are not adequately coagulated. Popovers will not rise to a sufficient volume unless they are baked in a hot oven for the first part of baking so that steam can quickly be generated. An inadequate amount of egg in the formula may also result in decreased volume.

dextrinization the process in which starch molecules are broken down into dextrins. Dextrins are polysaccharides composed of many glucose units, but are smaller than starch molecules.

CREAM PUFFS AND ÉCLAIRS

Ingredients and Mixing

Cream puffs and éclairs contain the same proportion of liquid to flour as popovers and are also leavened primarily by steam, but they are made with eight times as much fat. Cream puffs and éclairs are therefore considerably more tender than popovers. A large proportion of egg is used in cream puffs to emulsify the high percentage of fat.

The method of mixing the cream puff batter, also called pâte à choux, is unique to this product. The fat is melted in hot water, and the flour is added all at once with vigorous stirring. Heating is continued until the batter is smooth and forms a stiff ball. **Gelatinization** of the starch occurs during this cooking process. The mixture is then cooled slightly, and the eggs are added (either one unbeaten egg at a time, or one-third of the beaten eggs at one time). Thorough beating is necessary after each addition of egg. The eggs contain lipoproteins that act as emulsifying agents to divide the fat into small particles throughout the mixture. At this stage, the batter is smooth, stiff, and glossy. The egg also

gelatinization the sum of changes that occur in the first stages of heating starch granules in a moist environment; includes swelling of granules as water is absorbed and disruption of the organized granules' structure plays a role in obtaining a large volume. Egg proteins aid in the stretching process during the first stages of baking and are later coagulated by heat to contribute to the rigid structure of the final product. Even though the cream puff batter is stiff, it can be beaten without danger of toughening the puffs. The high percentage of fat and water in relation to flour interferes with the development of gluten and prevents it from forming a tenacious mass.

Characteristics

Puffs are usually irregular on the top surface, although the surface may vary depending on the consistency of the batter before baking. The walls are rigid but tender because of the high fat content. The center of the puff is hollow and moist. Some of the moist interior strands may be removed, if desired, and the puff dried out in the oven. The crust should have a light golden-brown color (Figure 16-2). The hollow center of cream puffs is usually filled. A wide variety of mixtures can be used as fillings, including chicken, tuna, and other types of salads, custards and starch-thickened puddings, flavored and sweetened whipped cream mixtures, and ice cream and other frozen desserts. Smaller puffs are generally used for hors d'oeuvres and larger ones for desserts.

Baking

The cream puff batter is dropped in mounds onto an ungreased baking sheet, allowing some room between mounds for expansion during baking. Eclairs are piped with a pastry bag into an oblong shape (Figure 16-3). A high oven temperature of 450°F (232°C) is necessary to form steam quickly and bring about the puffing or expansion of the batter. The high temperature may be maintained throughout the baking period, providing that overbrowning does not occur. The baking time is decreased to about 30 to 35 minutes if a high temperature is used continuously. If 450°F (232°C) is used for 15 minutes, followed by about 375°F (191°C) for the remainder of the baking time, about 45 minutes of total baking time will be required. The puffs should feel rigid and should not collapse on removal from the oven. They are not necessarily done when they are brown.

Figure 16-2
Cream puffs. (Photograph by Roger P. Smith)

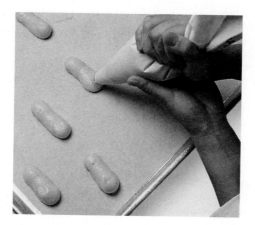

Figure 16-3
A pastry bag is being used to pipe the éclair batter into oblong shapes on a cookie tray prior to baking.

Causes of Failure

As in the making of popovers, one possible cause of failure in making cream puffs is insufficient baking. If the walls of the puffs are not rigid, they will collapse on removal from the oven.

Another possible cause of failure is the excessive evaporation of moisture during the cooking of the paste, which alters the proportions of the ingredients and makes formation of a stable emulsion unlikely. Excessive evaporation may be caused by boiling the water and fat too long before adding the flour, and by overcooking the flour-fat-water mixture. When the emulsion is destabilized, the fat tends to separate from the mixture. The batter appears oily and separated instead of shiny and viscous, and the fat oozes from the puffs during baking. Inaccurate measurements may so increase the percentage of fat in the mixture that the results are similar to those obtained by overcooking. Failure may also result from insufficient beating so that the mixture is not smooth, stiff, and glossy.

PANCAKES

Ingredients

Pancakes, sometimes called griddle cakes, are more variable both in the proportion of flour to liquid and in the characteristics of the finished product than most flour mixtures. The cooked cakes may be thin and moist or thick and porous according to the proportions of ingredients used (Figure 16-4). Crepes are thin, tender pancakes that contain a high proportion of egg. Crepes are discussed in Chapter 24.

Pancake mixtures contain flour, liquid, a leavening agent, and salt. Egg is normally used but may be omitted. Cakes are more tender if they contain fat, but it is possible to omit fat. Sugar may be used as an aid in browning, because of its **caramelization,** and may slightly modify the flavor.

If thick buttermilk or sour cream is used in the cakes, the proportion of flour to liquid may be about one to one. In sweetmilk cakes, 1 1/3, 1 1/2, or 1 3/4 cups of flour may be used per cup of liquid, depending on the type of flour and on the desired thickness of the cake. Because the cream contains fat, shortening can be omitted in cakes made with cream.

Pancakes are leavened by carbon dioxide gas produced either from baking powder or from a sour milk and soda combination. Overstirred pancakes may

caramelization the process by which a brown colored and characteristically flavored substance is produced when dry sugar is heated to a very high temperature

Figure 16-4
Pancakes or griddle cakes can be made thin and moist (left) or thick and porous (right). (Photograph by Chris Meister)

be soggy because of a loss of carbon dioxide during stirring and may show some tunnel formation. Thin batters tend to lose more carbon dioxide gas on standing than thicker batters. More baking powder may be required if batters are to stand for some time than if they are baked immediately.

Pancakes are usually mixed by the muffin method described in Chapter 15. The stiffer the batter, the less the batter should be stirred, to avoid toughening the cakes by developing the gluten. Pancake batters, like muffins batters, are slightly lumpy, rather than completely smooth when mixed properly.

Cooking

Seasoned griddles can be used without being greased, particularly if the batter contains 2 or more tablespoons of fat per cup of liquid used. Specially coated, non-stick cooking surfaces are normally used without being greased.

Much of the success in making pancakes depends on the temperature of the griddle. If the griddle is appreciably below the appropriate temperature, the pancakes cook so slowly that they lose leavening gas. They do not expand sufficiently to produce light, porous cakes. They also do not brown desirably. Browning in pancakes is primarily the result of the Maillard reaction. Too hot a griddle may burn the cakes before they are sufficiently done. Even if the griddle is not hot enough to cause burning, it may produce uneven browning and a compact texture from too rapid cooking. The temperature of the griddle can be tested by cooking a few drops of batter.

A uniformly heated griddle is essential for the griddle cakes to brown evenly. Large griddles over small flames may be practically cold in the outer areas. As cakes cook on a griddle of a desirable temperature, bubbles of gas expand and some of them break at the surface. When the edges of the pancakes appear slightly dry, they should be turned. If the entire surface becomes dry, the cakes will not brown evenly on the second side after turning. After being turned, the cakes rise noticeably and become slightly higher in the center. They do not form peaks, however, unless the mixture is very stiff or was greatly overstirred. Pancakes are done when they are browned on the second side. Although pancakes may sometimes be turned a second time provided that they are almost done when turned, more desirable cakes usually result from one turning.

WAFFLES

Ingredients and Mixing

Waffle mixtures are similar to pancakes except that they contain more egg and more fat (plate V). They are leavened by carbon dioxide gas, usually from baking powder, although yeast may sometimes be used. Because tenderness and crispness are desirable characteristics in waffles, a flour of relatively low gluten content and weak gluten quality is a good choice for making them (see Chapter 15 for a discussion on types of flours). By using a sufficient amount of fat and by avoiding overstirring, however, a stronger flour can be successfully used. In general, a stronger flour tends to yield a less tender, more breadlike waffle.

The proportion of flour may vary from 1 1/3 to 1 3/4 cups per cup of liquid. If optimum stirring is used with each consistency of batter and if all batters are baked under equally good conditions, there seems to be little difference in the waffles obtained. Thinner batters lose their leavening gas more quickly and it is more difficult, without loss of air, to blend beaten egg whites with batters of thin consistency; but ease of pouring is a point in favor of somewhat thinner batters.

Some waffle mixtures that are to be used as dessert or as shortcake are richer in fat than the proportions suggested in Table 16-1. They often contain sugar and may contain cocoa or molasses. Such mixtures require longer, slower baking than batters with no sugar, to be crisp and done without scorching. Caramelization of the sugar contributes to browning.

Waffles of excellent quality usually result when the batter is mixed by a modified muffin method that involves separating the eggs and adding the beaten egg whites last. However, the whole beaten egg may be used successfully in the muffin method for mixing waffles. Refer to Chapter 15 for further discussion on the muffin method of mixing.

Baking

A waffle baker (iron) is preheated before the batter is poured on the grids. An automatic heat control with an indicator usually shows when the appliance is ready. The batter may stick to the grids if they are either too hot or insufficiently heated. It is also likely to stick if there is not enough fat in the batter. Waffle grids should be greased, at least for the first waffle, even if they have a nonstick finish. Manufacturer's directions should be followed in preconditioning and using new waffle bakers.

Very thin batters made with 1 cup of flour per cup of liquid are too thin to fill the waffle iron sufficiently to bake the waffle crisp and brown on both sides. Crispness depends partly on the depth of batter that the waffle baker holds. A thicker waffle has a tendency to be less crisp than a thin waffle.

MUFFINS

Ingredients

Muffins usually contain flour, leavening, salt, sugar, fat, egg, and liquid. Sugar may be omitted and muffins may be made without egg, but better flavor and texture result from including both ingredients. Fat may be reduced to 1 tablespoon per cup of flour and still make reasonably acceptable muffins if sugar is present at a moderate level [1]. In commercial baking, modified waxy starches, substituted for flour at a 2 percent level, have been reported to enhance the eating quality of low-fat fresh-baked muffins. These starches could also be used in muffin mixes [2]. Composite flour blends may be used to extend wheat flour supplies or to enhance nutritional qualities. For example, wheat flour formulations containing peanut, sorghum, cassava, or cowpea flours at levels of 12 to 33 percent have been reported to produce acceptable muffins [3]. There were no significant differences observed between the formulations tested and the control muffins made with 100 percent wheat flour for 22 of 31 sensory, physical, and compositional characteristics.

Muffins are leavened by carbon dioxide gas, usually produced from baking powder. Muffins that contain an acidic ingredient, such as buttermilk or mashed bananas, typically use baking soda or a combination of baking soda and baking powder. Structure is provided by the flour components, starch and some gluten, and by egg proteins as they coagulate on heating.

Characteristics

A well-made muffin is uniform in texture, but the grain is usually not very fine and the cell walls are of medium thickness. The surface is lightly browned, has a somewhat pebbly appearance, and is rounded but not peaked. The crumb of the muffin is slightly moist, light, and tender. The muffin breaks easily without crumbling. The flavor is, of course, characteristic of the particular ingredients used, but is usually slightly sweet and pleasant tasting. Figure 16-5 shows well-made muffins.

Mixing

Muffins are generally mixed by the muffin method. The fat, if it is solid, is melted and combined with the liquid ingredients, including egg, which are then added, all at once, to the dry ingredients. The ratio of flour to liquid in a muffin mixture is approximately two to one.

The amount of stirring is more important for muffins than for most mixtures blended by the muffin method. The gluten forms most readily when a 2 : 1 ratio of flour to liquid is used and is easily overdeveloped with too much stirring.

In an overstirred muffin, peaks and tunnels tend to form. When a muffin batter is stirred only enough to blend the liquid and dry ingredients, dampening

Figure 16-5
These berry muffins have a rounded, pebbly crust and tender crumb.

A properly mixed muffin batter results when dry ingredients are just moistened. The batter appears pebbly, not smooth.

In an overmixed muffin batter, the gluten has partially developed and the batter appears to be smooth and cohesive.

dry flour lumps carefully, the batter appears lumpy and drops sharply from the spoon (Figure 16-6). With continued stirring, the batter becomes smooth and tends to string from the spoon (Figure 16-6). An elastic gluten mass begins to form. Moderately overstirred muffins tend to increase slightly in volume, but further stirring results in a decrease in volume. Carbon dioxide gas is probably lost with excessive stirring. A crust then forms on the overmixed muffin during baking, before additional carbon dioxide gas is produced by the heat of the oven. As the gas is produced it is forced through the softer center of the muffin and contributes to tunnel formation.

The effects of overmixing a muffin batter can be clearly seen in Figure 16-7. A more compact texture, rather than an open grain, is associated with peaks or knobs and tunnels in the overmanipulated muffin. With extreme overmixing, sogginess may occur and, owing to the loss of much carbon dioxide gas, few tunnels may form.

Muffins containing relatively large amounts of fat may be mixed by the conventional method. Such muffins are more cakelike in texture. They are sweeter and more tender than plain muffins. Because sugar and fat interfere with the development of gluten in the batter, the effects of increased mixing are less pronounced than in a plain muffin, and tunnel formation is less likely [5].

Variations

A wide variety of muffins can be made by modifying the ingredients. For example, cornmeal, bran, or whole wheat flour can be substituted for part of the white flour. Nuts, dates, blueberries, apples, other fruits, or bits of crisp bacon may be added to the batter while it is being mixed. Maple syrup muffins are made by substituting maple syrup for half of the milk in the recipe. Preparation of orange-honey muffins calls for placing 1 teaspoon of honey and a thin slice of fresh orange in the bottom of each baking cup before adding the muffin batter. Or, 1 teaspoon of jelly can be placed in a half-filled muffin cup and then the remainder of the batter added, resulting in a "surprise" muffin.

Bran and cornmeal muffins can tolerate more manipulation without undesirable results than muffins made entirely of all-purpose wheat flour. Bran

Figure 16-7
*External and internal characteristics
of muffins made from batters mixed
for varying lengths of time.*

Dry ingredients were just dampened.

Additional stirring was done. Some tunnels are beginning to form.

Muffins were overstirred. Tunnels and peaks are apparent.

interferes with the development of gluten, and cornmeal does not contain gluten proteins. In the making of bran muffins, flavor may be improved by first soaking or hydrating the bran in the liquid before combining it with the other ingredients. The substitution of wheat or corn bran for up to 25 percent of the weight of the flour still allows for an acceptable muffin while increasing the fiber content to a considerable degree [6].

Baking

Pans should be prepared before the muffins are mixed. The batter becomes full of gas bubbles and rises perceptibly if allowed to stand in the mixing bowl while the pans are being prepared. Cutting into the batter later to fill muffin pans permits gas to escape and decreases the volume of the finished muffins. The bottoms of the pans should be greased, but the greasing of the side walls is optional. The muffin structure may receive some support from clinging to ungreased sides of the muffin pan as the batter rises in baking; however, muffins may be removed from the pans more easily when the sides are greased.

An oven temperature of 400°F (204°C) is satisfactory for baking muffins in about 20 to 25 minutes. A product leavened by carbon dioxide gas must be allowed to rise before crust formation occurs. For that reason, a very hot oven must be avoided. A temperature slightly under 400°F (204°C) is satisfactory if sufficient time is allowed for baking. Browning appears to be chiefly the result of the Maillard reaction, but the caramelization of sugar may also contribute to browning. Muffins baked at too low of a temperature may not develop a pleasing brown crust without being overbaked.

NUT BREADS, COFFEECAKES, AND FRIED QUICK BREADS

Nut breads and coffeecakes, like muffins, contain flour, leavening, salt, sugar, fat, egg, and liquid. Nut breads are often characterized by the inclusion of ingredients such as bananas, pumpkin, apples, carrots, zucchini, and nuts that provide flavor and moistness. Nut breads may be baked in small or standard-sized loaf pans. A small crack down the center of the loaf is common and is not considered to be defect. Because of their larger size, nut breads are typically baked at a lower temperature (350°F / 177°C) as compared to muffins so as to not develop too dark of a crust.

Coffeecakes are similar to muffins, but are made in cake or pie pans. Many coffeecakes are distinguished by fruit, nut, or crumb toppings, which provide flavor, texture, and a decorative appearance. Although many coffeecakes are classified as quick breads because baking powder is the leavening agent, some coffeecakes are made from yeast bread dough.

Cake donuts, hush puppies, and fritters are similar to other quick breads. However, these quick breads are deep fat fried rather than baked. Cake donut dough may be refrigerated and then rolled out before cutting into a donut shape that is fried in hot fat. Both hush puppies and fritters are batters that can be dropped by spoonfuls or with small dishers or scoops into the hot fat. Hush puppies typically contain cornmeal, whereas, fritters may contain small pieces of fruit such as apple, or a spicy ingredient such as jalapênos.

BISCUITS

Ingredients

Biscuits usually contain flour, fat, milk, baking powder, and salt. Soda and buttermilk, either the fresh cultured product or dried churned buttermilk, may be used instead of sweet milk and baking powder for the leavening of biscuits. Dried churned buttermilk contains phospholipids that act as emulsifiers and aid in the fine distribution of fat in baked products. Cultured buttermilk is usually made from fluid skim or low-fat milk, so it does not have the same composition as churned buttermilk.

Characteristics

Rolled baking powder biscuits may be compact and flaky or light and fluffy, depending on how much they are kneaded and how thin the dough is rolled before baking. A well-made biscuit usually has a fairly uniform shape, an evenly browned and tender crust, a tender crumb of creamy color, and good flavor (Figure 16-8). Flakiness is a desirable characteristic of biscuits that have been rolled. Easily separated sheets of dough can be seen when a flaky biscuit is broken open.

Dropped biscuits have slightly more liquid in the recipe and are not kneaded as a soft dough. They are dropped by spoonfuls onto a cookie sheet for baking. The resulting biscuit is usually irregular in shape and slightly coarse in texture, but tender with a crisp crust.

Mixing

Biscuits are mixed by the biscuit or pastry method, which involves cutting a solid fat into the flour, baking powder, and salt mixture before adding milk and stirring. The dough for rolled biscuits should be a soft, rather than a stiff, dry dough (Figure 16-9). Biscuit dough that is patted or rolled with no preliminary kneading yields biscuits that are very tender and have crisp crusts; however, they are coarse in texture, are small in volume, and have slightly rough surfaces. Kneading lightly, using 10 to 30 strokes (depending on the amount of stirring used to mix the dough), produces a biscuit of fine texture that displays evidence of layering when broken open. It also rises to a larger volume than an unkneaded biscuit (Figure 16-8). The top crust is smoother and the general external appearance is better in slightly kneaded biscuits than in unkneaded ones. Kneading past the optimum amount produces a compact, toughened biscuit.

The flakiness of a biscuit results from the distribution of fat particles coated with dough. The fat melts on baking and leaves spaces between the sheets of dough.

For variation in the preparation of biscuits, cooked bacon chips, grated cheese, chopped chives, or other herbs may be added to the flour mixture before the liquid (Figure 16-10). Grated orange rind may also be added to the flour mixture, and a sugar cube soaked in orange juice can be placed on top of the biscuit before baking.

Figure 16-8
The proper amount of kneading improves the volume and quality of baking powder biscuits. The biscuit on the left was prepared from unkneaded dough; the one on the right was made from dough kneaded 15 times before rolling and cutting. (Photograph by Chris Meister)

Figure 16-9
*(a) Sifting the dry ingredients to-
gether; (b) cutting in the fat can be
done by hand as shown here or with
the use of a pastry cutter; (c) kneading the dough; (d) cutting the biscuits.*

(a)

(b)

(c)

(d)

Baking

The baking sheet requires greasing for dropped biscuits but not for rolled ones. Rolled biscuits can be placed on the baking sheet about 1 or 1 1/2 inches apart if crusty biscuits are desired. Otherwise, no space need be allowed between biscuits. A hot oven of 425° to 450°F (218° to 232°C) for 8 to 10 minutes is satisfactory for baking biscuits. The hot oven produces steam that aids in separating sheets of dough as the fat melts. Biscuits may stand for at least an hour before baking without loss of quality.

SCONES

Scones, although similar to biscuits, are much richer (plate V). Scones usually contain eggs, butter, and half-and-half or cream [4]. The biscuit method of mixing is used when making many scones and like biscuits, scones are rolled out and baked on an ungreased cookie sheet.

CHAPTER SUMMARY

- Quick breads include a variety of products that can be prepared without the rising or proofing time required by yeast breads. Common leavening agents in quick breads are baking powder, baking soda with an acidic ingredient in the recipe, or steam.

- Popovers contain a high percentage of moisture. Steam produced in a hot oven is the chief leavening agent in popovers. Popovers are usually mixed

Figure 16-10
These rosemary biscuits can be served alone or with a simple spread. (Courtesy of Land O'Lakes)

by the muffin method and are characterized by a hollow center and thick, crusty walls.

- Cream puffs and éclairs contain the same proportions of liquid to flour as popovers and are also leavened primarily by steam, but they are made with eight times as much fat. Cream puffs and éclairs are therefore considerably more tender than popovers. The method of mixing cream puff batter is unique. Fat is melted in hot water, and then the flour is added all at once with vigorous stirring. Heating continues until the batter is smooth and forms a stiff ball. After cooling slightly, the eggs are beaten into the mixture one at a time. The batter should be smooth, stiff, and glossy.

- Like popovers, cream puffs and éclairs have a brown exterior with a large hollow center. Cream puffs and éclairs are filled with a variety of mixtures.

- Pancakes may be thin and moist or thick and porous depending upon the proportions of ingredients used. Pancakes are leavened by carbon dioxide gas produced either from baking powder or from a sour milk and soda combination. Overstirred pancakes may be soggy because of loss of carbon dioxide during stirring and may show tunnel formation due to the overdevelopment of gluten. The temperature of the griddle is important to success in the making of pancakes.

- Waffle mixtures are similar to pancakes except they contain more egg and more fat. Waffles of excellent quality usually result when the batter is mixed by a modified muffin method that involves separating the eggs and folding in the beaten eggs whites last. Waffles are cooked in a preheated waffle iron that has been lightly greased before the first waffle is cooked.

- A well-made muffin is uniform in texture, but the grain is usually not very fine and the cell walls are of medium thickness. The surface is lightly browned, has a somewhat pebbly appearance, and is rounded but not peaked. The crumb of the muffin is slightly moist, light, and tender. Muffins are generally mixed by the muffin method. The quality of muffins will suffer if the batter is overstirred. In overstirred muffins, peaks and tunnels tend to form. Properly mixed muffin batter will appear lumpy and will drip sharply from the spoon.

- Nut breads and coffeecakes are similar to muffins, but nut breads are baked at a lower temperature for a longer time in loaf pans and coffeecakes are baked in cake or pie pans. Cake donuts, hush puppies, and fritters are similar to other quick breads but are cooked by deep-fat frying.

- A well-made biscuit usually has a fairly uniform shape, an evenly browned and tender crust, a tender crumb of creamy color, and a good flavor. Flakiness is a desirable characteristic of biscuits that have been rolled. Biscuits are mixed by the biscuit or pastry methods, which involves cutting a solid fat into the flour, baking powder, and salt mixture before adding milk and stirring. Kneading the dough lightly, before rolling out and cutting into shapes, produces a biscuit of fine texture that displays evidence of layering when broken open.

- Scones are similar to biscuits but are richer. Scones usually contain eggs, butter, and half-and-half or cream.

KEY TERMS

Maillard reaction
dextrinization

gelatinization
caramelization

STUDY QUESTIONS

1. For each of the following products, describe (1) the usual ingredients, (2) the usual method of mixing, and (3) any special precautions to be observed in their preparation or potential problems to be avoided.
   a. Popovers
   b. Cream puffs
   c. Pancakes
   d. Waffles
   e. Muffins
   f. Biscuits

2. What characterizes a quick bread?

3. Compare and contrast the following:
   a. Cream puffs, eclairs, and popovers
   b. Pancakes and waffles
   c. Muffins, coffeecake, and nut breads

    d. Cake donuts, hush puppies, and fritters

    e. Biscuits and scones

REFERENCES

1. Fulton, L., & Hogbin, M. (1993). Eating quality of muffins, cake, and cookies prepared with reduced fat and sugar. *Journal of the American Dietetic Association*, 93, 1313.

2. Hippleheuser, A. L., Landberg, L. A., & Turnak, F. L. (1995). A system approach to formulating a low-fat muffin. *Food Technology*, 49: 92(3).

3. Holt, S. D., McWatters, K. H., & Resurreccion, A. V. A. (1992). Validation of predicted baking performance of muffins containing mixtures of wheat, cowpea, peanut, sorghum, and cassava flours. *Journal of Food Science*, 57, 470.

4. Labensky, S. R., & Hause, A. M. (2003). *On cooking: A textbook of culinary fundamentals*. (3rd ed.). NJ: Prentice Hall.

5. Matthews, R. H., Kirkpatrick, M. E., & Dawson, E. H. (1965). Performance of fats in muffins. *Journal of the American Dietetic Association*, 47, 201.

6. Polizzotto, L. M., Tinsley, A. M., Weber, C. W., & Berry, J. W. (1983). Dietary fibers in muffins. *Journal of Food Science*, 48, 111.

Yeast Breads

17

Disappearance data from the U.S. Department of Agriculture (USDA) indicate that consumption of wheat flour increased to 150 pounds per person in 1997, reflecting a 35 percent increase from 1970 [25]. Surveys of actual consumption by the USDA suggest that the increased use of cereals and snacks accounted for much of the increase in consumption of total grain products. From 1970 to 1996, ready-to-eat cereal consumption increased by 60 percent and snacks such as crackers, popcorn, pretzels, and corn chips increased by 200 percent [34]. However, yeast breads are an important component of American's grain intake, representing nearly three out of the 6.7 daily servings of grain consumed on the average in 1994–1996. Furthermore, yeast breads and breakfast cereal provided nearly one-third of the whole grain servings consumed [5].

Many new bakery products have been introduced into U.S. markets, and items such as bagels, pita bread, and focaccia, which were once considered to be strictly specialty items, are now enjoying great popularity. In any supermarket with an in-store bakery, one is likely to find a wide variety of breads and rolls, including such breads as honey wheat, crushed wheat, branola, oatnut, 12-grain, 7-grain, sour dough, dark rye, light rye, pumpernickel rye, light oatmeal, light stone-ground wheat, and Roman meal, as well as the usual white, whole wheat, and French breads. In addition, five or six different kinds of English muffins and four or five different types of bagels may be offered.

Foodservice outlets, from fast-food units to upscale restaurants, are selling large quantities of sandwiches, all of which have as a major component breads, buns, or rolls. A loaf of bread hollowed out to form a bowl and utilized to serve soup has been featured in a variety of foodservice operations, including a fast-food restaurant [23]. The use of "wraps," including tortillas filled with a variety of ingredients (plates XVIII and XIX), are rising in popularity, and a number of innovative ingredients for the bakery have become available for use in baked items such as bagels and pizza.

The making of bread has become a huge industry. Most Americans buy bread rather than make it at home. From many sources we hear that traditional home cooking is losing out to fast foods and convenience foods in our busy and changing society. We should all hope that home cooking does not become a lost art, however. It has been suggested that the rewards of cooking extend beyond the benefits of providing healthful foods for the body. Cooking may also nourish the spirit, providing quality companionship with family and friends as both preparation and eating are shared. The making of bread at home can be a particularly rewarding experience if you take the time to develop a certain amount of skill. Hot homemade bread can make any ordinary meal a special one and automatic bread machines make this easy. Bread is not only a delicious menu component, but also provides an economical and healthful source of calories.

Well-made baker's bread is of uniform quality but its moisture content is generally high, especially for white bread; often it is extremely compressible. A good-quality homemade bread is often conceded to be superior in flavor and in eating quality, particularly when it is very fresh. Because of differences in ingredients available to the consumer and the commercial baker, however, homemade bread tends to stale more rapidly than the commercial product.

Multicultural Cuisine

Evolution of the sandwich

It was an Englishman, John Montague, the fourth Earl of Sandwich, who in 1762 satisfied his hunger in a hurry by ordering two slices of meat between two pieces of bread. Thus was born the sandwich, of which about 45 billion are now being consumed each year in America. Lord Sandwich truly started something—and a very good thing at that.

The basis of a sandwich is bread. And bread is an important component of almost every cuisine around the world. Everybody loves bread—flat breads such as foccacia from Italy and tortillas from Mexico or chapatti from India, French baguettes and croissants, Jewish bagels, peasant breads of Eastern Europe, and many more. Bread—a great foundation for a vast variety of fillings—meats, fish, eggs, cheeses, tofu, vegetables, savory herbs, sauces, and condiments. The sandwich has been rejuvenated recently with a rise in the production of fresh-baked artisan and ethnic breads, promising a continuation of this food as an American favorite. And sandwiches are a great way to deliver nutritional benefits—healthy vegetables and protein foods, along with whole grains [29].

While the peanut butter and jelly sandwich remains a favorite of American students (even now a pre-made individually wrapped reproduction with a 30 day shelf-life is being marketed) and will always find a soft spot in their hearts as they look back on childhood, the possible variety for sandwiches is limitless. We will mention just a few examples.

Greek salad heroes—mushrooms, cucumbers, olives, oregano, garlic, tomato, vinegar, feta cheese on a big bun. Crescent roll dough wrapped around wieners and cheddar cheese, or chicken tenders and Swiss cheese, and baked. Rye bread with honey mustard, sliced turkey, Gouda cheese, and thin tart apple slices—buttered on the outside of the sandwich bread and grilled on both sides. Onion and Gorgonzola cheese stuffed in foccacia dough before baking. Pita bread stuffed with a mixture of crumbled tofu, shredded carrots, diced onions, sunflower seeds, turmeric, curry powder, mayonnaise, and mustard. Barbequed crab, olives, cheese, and tomato sauce spread on English muffins and broiled. Mashed avocados, chopped red onions, cilantro, garlic, and jalapeño wrapped in a warmed tortilla and fastened with a toothpick. The possible variety is limited only by your imagination.

Has the sandwich evolved since 1762? Certainly it has, and promises to continue to do so in the foreseeable future. Viva the sandwich!

Figure 17-1
Bread of relatively high volume and fine texture can be made using all-purpose flour.

CHARACTERISTICS OF YEAST BREADS

The texture of good-quality bread is fine, the cell walls thin, and the grain uniform (Figure 17-1). Cells tend to be slightly elongated rather than round, although the shape of the cell varies. The crumb is elastic and thoroughly baked so that it does not form a gummy ball when pressed between the fingers. The fresh crumb should spring back quickly when touched with the finger.

A well-shaped loaf of bread has a rounded top and is free from rough, ragged cracks on the sides. The **shred** on the sides of the loaf where the dough rises is smooth and even. Careful and uniform shaping of the loaf and placing the shaped dough in the center of the baking pan contribute to the production of a well-shaped baked loaf of bread. However, abnormalities in shape have numerous causes in addition to problems created by the way the dough is shaped. Such factors as the stiffness of the dough, the strength of the gluten, the extent of **fermentation** and **proofing,** the baking temperature, and the position in the oven may all affect the shape of the loaf as well as its volume and texture. Bread of good quality is light, having a large volume in relation to the weight of the loaf.

If a loaf has been allowed to proof too long before being placed in the oven, the cells overexpand and collapse somewhat. The result is a loaf of bread that is flat or sunken on top and has overhanging eaves on the sides, somewhat like a mushroom shape. The texture of such a loaf is coarse, with an open grain and crumbly character (Figure 17-2). If a loaf has not proofed long enough before

shred the area on the sides of a loaf of bread, just above the pan, where the dough rises in the oven before the crust is formed; a desirable shred is even and unbroken

fermentation the transformation of organic substances, such as simple sugars, into smaller molecules by the action of microorganisms

proofing the last rising of bread dough after it is molded into a loaf and placed in the baking pan

Figure 17-2
A loaf of bread that has proofed too long in the pan before being baked. The texture is open and coarse, and "eaves" are seen on the sides of the loaf.

Figure 17-3
A loaf of bread that did not rise sufficiently in the pan before being baked. A ragged crack appears on the end and side where the dough rose unevenly during the process of baking. The volume is relatively low and the texture rather coarse.

being placed in the oven, it may have wide cracks on the sides after baking, because the crust structure will have set before sufficient expansion of the loaf has occurred. The texture may be somewhat compact and coarse (Figure 17-3).

INGREDIENTS

The essential ingredients for yeast-leavened dough are flour, liquid, yeast, and salt. Other constituents, mainly sugar and fat, affect texture and flavor. Additives are also used commercially in the baking of bread and rolls. These include oxidants and vital wheat gluten, which strengthen the dough and assist in the retention of leavening gas [11].

Yeast

metabolic having to do with any of the chemical changes that occur in living cells

precursor a forerunner or predecessor such as a molecule that later develops into a flavor molecule

For thousands of years yeast has been the leavening agent for baking bread, although it has been produced industrially for only about 150 years [32]. It is a microscopic one-celled plant (shown in Figure 17-4) that undergoes **metabolic** activity in dough, affecting the functional properties of the dough and the quality of the bread. Among the metabolites are amino acids, which are necessary for the activity of the yeast and also serve as important sources of bread flavor **precursors** [6]. The yeast produces carbon dioxide gas, which makes the dough light, or leavened. Carbon dioxide results from the breaking down of simple sugars in a series of chemical reactions collectively called fermentation. Many enzymes, produced by the yeast cells, are responsible for these metabolic processes, which yield ethyl alcohol and various additional flavoring substances, as well as carbon dioxide.

The species of yeast that is used in making bread, often called baker's yeast, is *Saccharomyces cerevisiae*. Strains of this microorganism are carefully selected, grown, and sometimes cross-bred to produce a final product with desirable characteristics for baking. (Changes during fermentation of yeast dough are discussed later in this chapter.)

Types of Yeast.   Baker's yeast is marketed as *compressed yeast, active dry yeast,* and *instant quick-rising active dry yeast.* Compressed yeast is produced from a blend of wet yeast cells and emulsifiers that is extruded and then cut into a block form in a variety of sizes. It is perishable and must be kept refrigerated. When held at

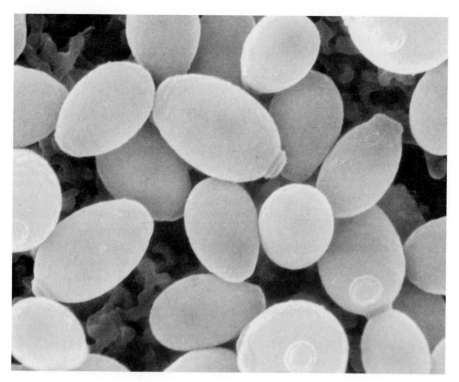

Figure 17-4
Photomicrograph of baker's yeast, Saccharomyces cerevisiae. *The yeast cell in the lower right-hand corner is in the process of reproducing by budding; a new daughter cell is being created.* (Courtesy of Universal Foods Corporation)

room temperature for more than several hours, this yeast loses leavening activity. A fresh sample of compressed yeast is creamy white in color, is moist but not slimy, crumbles easily, and has a distinctive odor. When stale, the yeast becomes brownish and may develop a strong unpleasant odor. Because compressed yeast undergoes minimal processing, it is the most consistent in quality of all the baker's yeasts. Compressed yeast is used in the baking trade; however, very little is to be found on the retail market [7].

Compressed yeast must be softened in lukewarm liquid at approximately 85°F (29°C) so that it will blend with other dough ingredients. It may be softened either in a small amount of water or in the total amount of liquid used in the dough. Because compressed yeast contains added moisture and conditioners not found in active dry yeast, the dry yeast cannot be substituted interchangeably on a weight basis. The weight of active dry yeast used should be approximately 60 percent of the weight of compressed yeast.

Active dry yeast is prepared from a yeast strain selected for its ability to retain activity when it is dried. The moist yeast is extruded into fine, cylindrical strands that are dried over a 6-hour period at 75° to 110°F (25° to 45°C) under a continuous process. For consumer use, the large dense granules are usually ground and packaged, with the exclusion of oxygen, in glass jars, metal cans, or foil pouches. Active dry yeast has much better storage stability than compressed yeast. It may be stored for up to a year when packaged properly [7]. Packages of dry yeast are usually dated, after which time optimal activity is not guaranteed. The conditions that contribute to loss of viability in the yeast are mainly air, moisture, and warm temperatures.

Before it can be added to a dough mix, active dry yeast must be rehydrated 5 to 10 minutes in water at 110° to 115°F (43° to 46°C), to allow proper reconstitution of the yeast without a loss of cell contents. The temperature of rehydration is critical. Water above 130°F (54°C) kills the yeast plants; cool water can shock the yeast, causing some of the cell contents to be leached out and resulting in a "slackened" dough that flows in the pan when proofed [7].

The development of instant quick-rising active dry yeast was made possible because of advances in genetics and drying technology [32]. A specially selected strain of *Saccharomyces cerevisiae* is used, and drying is done in special equipment that allows very rapid dehydration. No loss of optimal activity occurs in the drying process. The instant yeast consists of cylindrical and porous, rod-shaped particles that are very fine and light, with a large surface area. They therefore rehydrate very rapidly. In fact, they rehydrate so rapidly that they can be mixed with the dry ingredients of a dough and need not be softened separately in liquid [7]. Doughs containing instant active dry yeast rise substantially faster than doughs containing the same amount of regular active dry yeast (Figure 17-5). Quick-rising active dry yeast works well in automatic bread-making machines. When yeast is added to the pan of an automatic bread-making machine, it should be placed in or near the flour. It should not come into contact with liquid or salt, especially when the timer is being used to delay the mixing and baking of the bread.

The same properties of instant quick-rising active dry yeast that are responsible for its ease of rehydration also contribute to its high instability in air. It is packaged in a vacuum or in the presence of nitrogen gas with oxygen excluded to preserve its activity. After 4-oz jars are opened, the unused portion of the yeast should be protected by resealing the jar and storing it in the refrigerator [32].

sponge the mixture of liquid, yeast, sugar, and part of the flour to make a thin batter that is held at a lukewarm temperature to allow yeast activity for a period before the remaining ingredients are added to form a dough

Starters. A *starter* is some of the **sponge** from a previous baking saved for future use (to replace yeast). It has sugar added as food for the yeast plant and should be used frequently (once or twice a week) to keep the yeast cells alive and to prevent undesirable flavor changes. Sourdough starters were highly valued in early history, as the starter provided the only available source of yeast for making breads. Today, artisanal bakers prize their starters, because of the distinctive flavor of the breads produced by the bakery as a result of their unique starter.

Sourdough starters apparently get their gaseous action and flavor components from fermentation by bacteria. Certain types of flour probably supplied the desired bacteria. Similar bacteria are present in yogurt. Flour and water are

Figure 17-5
Bread dough containing quick-rising yeast (left) rises substantially faster than dough containing the same amount of regular active dry yeast (right). Both doughs proofed for 15 minutes at 100°F (38°C).
(Reprinted from Trivedi, N. B., E. J. Cooper, and B. L. Bruinsma. Development and applications of quick-rising yeast. *Food Technology,* 38 (6), p. 51, 1984. Copyright © by Institute of Food Technologists.)

the only two required ingredients for a sourdough starter. In a basic starter such as this, yeast from the air will grow in the mixture [37]. Alternatively, sourdough starter may be prepared by first mixing 1 cup of warm nonfat or low-fat milk with 3 tablespoons of plain yogurt, covering the jar tightly, and letting the mixture stand in a warm place for 18 to 24 hours. Once a clot is formed, 1 cup of flour is added and this covered mixture is kept in a warm place for 2 to 5 days. The pleasantly sour-smelling starter is tightly covered and refrigerated until used in making bread [4]. A variety of recipes may use the sourdough starter; the remaining starter can be replenished by adding 1 cup warm milk and 1 cup flour to each cup of starter that remains, covering, and letting the mixture stand in a warm place until it is bubbly and sour smelling. Starter must be used and replenished frequently to avoid spoilage. Starters also may be made from a mixture of 1 cup flour, 1 cup warm water, 1 package of dry yeast, and 1 tablespoon of sugar.

Liquid yeast usually is made from potato water, sugar, and yeast. Like sourdough starter, it must be used frequently. Both starter and liquid yeast are more uncertain sources of gas-forming organisms than compressed or dry yeast. Their chief advantages are convenience and economy in families in which bread is baked frequently or where markets are not easily accessible for the purchase of yeast; however, a sourdough starter is often used because of its flavor.

Amount of Yeast to Use. The amount of yeast to be used may be altered within limits according to the amount of time to be used for the bread-making process. Small amounts of yeast, such as 1/4 to 1/3 cake or package per 1 cup liquid, are satisfactory when the yeast is given enough time to activate. With small amounts of yeast, a sponge method of mixing permits more rapid growth of yeast. Excess yeast causes an undesirable odor and flavor in bread. Coarse texture, gray color of crust and crumb, and loaves of distorted shapes may also result from a great excess of yeast and too rapid fermentation. Bread can be made in about 2 1/2 hours using 1 cake or package of yeast per 1 to 1 1/4 cups of liquid. The use of quick-rise active dry yeast can shorten the rising time even further. For ordinary use, however, the smallest amount of yeast that will serve the purpose is desirable.

The carbon dioxide gas produced during yeast fermentation causes the bread dough to expand or rise. Ethyl alcohol is volatilized during baking. By-products of the fermentation reaction also include many flavor substances. Organic acids, amino acids, and other substances produced during fermentation participate in complex reactions that result in characteristic bread flavor.

Flour

Wheat flour is unique in that it has the components necessary to produce bread of high volume and fine texture with a cohesive, elastic crumb, because the flour provides the proteins that, when hydrated and mixed, produce gluten. Gluten is responsible for extensibility and elasticity in the dough. (Gluten is discussed in Chapter 15.) After the gluten structure has been expanded by gas cells, heat coagulates the gluten proteins and sets the structure. Because of the weakening effect of fermentation on gluten, the flour best adapted to the making of bread is one of strong gluten quality, such as bread flour. A weak gluten becomes so highly dispersed that a bread of poor volume and quality is likely to result. If soft wheat flours are used for bread, variations in proportions, method, and technique are necessary to obtain a good product.

potassium bromate an oxidizing substance often added to bread dough to strengthen the gluten of strong or high-protein flour

A high-protein bread flour is used in commercial bread making. Bread flour is also available in retail markets for use in home kitchens. It usually has a dough conditioner such as ascorbic acid or **potassium bromate** added to it. Although bread flour is the most desirable for bread making, acceptable bread can also be prepared using all-purpose flour.

The baking performance of flour is measured in the lab by food scientists. The relationship between laboratory tests and flour performance in production is complex, and two lots of flour with the same lab analysis rating may bake quite differently in a commercial operation. Among the factors that can contribute to a change in flour performance are genetics of the developed wheat varieties and changes in milling practices (See Chapter 15 for more on wheat and milling). The average level of protein in the wheat crop has declined over the years [11]. Bakers today more routinely than in the past use additives to strengthen the desirable characteristics of the dough.

Approximately 3/4 pound or 3 cups of flour are required to make a pound loaf of bread. The amount depends chiefly on the hydration capacity of the flour proteins. Strong flours with a high protein content have a higher **hydration capacity** than flours of lower protein content, and the quantity of high-protein flours required is slightly smaller. Thus, the amount of liquid used in making bread varies with the hydration capacity of the gluten-forming proteins in the flour. For good bread flours, about 60 to 65 percent of the weight of the flour as liquid gives a dough of the best consistency. In terms of measurements, 65 percent of the weight of the flour is approximately 1 cup of water for a 1 pound loaf.

hydration capacity the ability of a substance, such as flour, to absorb water

Weak flours have a low imbibition capacity and therefore require a lower percentage of moisture. If milk is used instead of water, a slightly higher proportion is needed because of the 12 to 14 percent of milk solids present. The amount of flour required in bread making also may vary with the level of humidity in the environment. Thus it is common to make small adjustments in the amount of flour in a bread recipe so as to achieve a soft, but not sticky dough.

Liquid

Liquid is essential in bread dough to hydrate flour proteins and contribute to the development of gluten. In addition, it is essential for the partial gelatinization of starch, which makes an important contribution to bread structure [12]. Other components are also dissolved or dispersed in the liquid. The liquid used in making bread may be milk, water, potato water, or whey. Eggs also may serve as part of the liquid in bread dough. If the liquid is milk, it should be scalded. Heating destroys certain enzymes and changes some proteins so that an undesirable softening of the dough does not occur during fermentation. Dry milk used by commercial bakers has been heat treated.

The type of liquid used will affect the characteristics of the dough. Water only is used in lean doughs when a crisp crust is desirable. The addition of milk and egg results in a richer, more tender bread. Eggs also add color. A small quantity of mashed potato may be added to bread dough. Potato water and cooked potato introduce gelatinized starch into the mixture, which favors fermentation and also enhances the keeping quality and flavor of the baked bread. Milk and whey increase the nutritive value of bread to some extent.

Beyond the amount of liquid required to achieve maximum loaf volume, additional absorption of water produces a less tenacious or more tender gluten, and results in decreased loaf volume. Too small a proportion of moisture may not provide enough water for optimal gluten development and may result in decreased loaf volume of the finished bread.

Sugar

Although it is not an indispensable ingredient in a bread formula, sugar plays several roles in bread making. It increases the rate of fermentation by providing readily available food for yeast so that the bread rises in a shorter period. If larger amounts of sugar are used, however, as in sweet rolls, the action of the yeast is somewhat repressed, and the fermentation and proofing periods must be longer. Flavor (primarily sweetness), texture, and browning are also affected by the use of sugar, although the browning of bread is primarily the result of the **Maillard reaction.** Sugar in bread dough comes from three sources: that present in the flour, that produced by the action of enzymes hydrolyzing starch, and that added as an ingredient [21].

Maillard reaction the carbonyl group of sugar combines with the amino group of a protein, initiating a series of chemical reactions which result in a brown color and change in flavor

For loaf breads, 2 teaspoons to 1 1/2 tablespoons of sugar per 1 pound loaf are common amounts used. Doughs for rolls usually contain slightly more sugar—about 2 to 4 tablespoons per cup of liquid used. Some recipes use honey, corn syrup, brown sugar or molasses instead of granulated sugar because of the flavor and colors that these forms of sugar may supply.

Fat

Fat is used in commercial bread making to facilitate the handling of the dough, to increase the keeping quality of the bread, and to improve loaf volume and texture [20]. The tenderness of the bread is also increased. Liquid oils do not perform the same functions that allow an increase in volume as solid shortenings; however, commercial bakers can combine various conditioners and softeners with liquid oil and produce a bread of acceptable quality [10].

For loaf breads, 1 to 1 1/2 tablespoons of fat per 1 pound loaf are sufficient to improve tenderness, flavor, and keeping quality. Two to 4 tablespoons or more per cup of liquid may be used in roll dough for increased tenderness.

Salt

Salt is added to bread dough for flavor, but it also has other effects. Salt retards yeast fermentation and therefore increases the time required for bread dough to rise. Salt has a firming effect on gluten structure. Bread made without salt is often crumbly in texture and may easily become overlight.

The amount of salt usually considered to produce good flavor in bread is approximately 1 teaspoon per 1 pound loaf. An excess of salt should be avoided from the standpoint of both texture and flavor. It would appear, however, that the usual level of salt might be reduced in bread without sacrificing quality or acceptability. In one study, a panel of 40 untrained judges found both white and wheat breads acceptable when salt was reduced by 50 percent of the normal level [39].

MIXING AND HANDLING

Two basic methods of mixing yeast bread are the straight-dough method and the sponge method. The batter method may also be used for some breads.

Straight-dough Method

In the mixing of yeast bread by the straight-dough method, the liquid is generally warmed with the sugar, salt, and softened fat. If scalded milk is used, it must be cooled to the proper temperature before yeast is added. Yeast may be softened in a small amount of warm water and added to the liquid mixture, or it may be softened in the total liquid. The temperature of the liquid used for softening should be appropriate for the type of yeast used. Instant quick-rising active dry yeast does not need to be softened in liquid and may be stirred with part of the flour.

About one-third of the flour is then blended with the liquid ingredients and vigorously mixed. Beating the batter blends ingredients uniformly, starts the development of gluten, and incorporates air cells. The remainder of the flour is added gradually to form a dough that is then transferred to a floured board for kneading. The dough is kneaded (see "Kneading" later in the chapter) until it has a smooth, satiny outside surface.

The kneaded dough is next placed in a clean mixing bowl and allowed to rise until it is at least doubled in bulk, after which it is lightly punched down (Figure 17-6). It may then either be allowed to rise a second time or be molded into loaves or rolls. If special bread mixers are available, the entire mixing process can be done by machine.

The number of times the dough should be allowed to rise in the fermentation period varies with the strength of the flour. Doughs made from strong gluten flours may be allowed to rise more times than doughs made from flours with lower protein content before the dough is placed in the pans. Weak glutens tend to become too highly dispersed with too long a fermentation period. More thorough mixing of the bread alters the quality of the gluten so that a shorter fermentation time gives as good a volume and quality of loaf as may be obtained by a shorter preliminary mixing and a longer fermentation period (more risings). Satisfactory bread can be made at home with only one rising period, if either all-purpose flour or bread flour is used.

When rapid-rising yeast is used, it is possible to let the dough rest for about 10 minutes after kneading in lieu of a rising period. The dough is then molded and placed in a pan to proof before baking.

Figure 17-6
(a) The dough before rising; (b) Punching down the risen dough.

(a)

(b)

Sponge Method

In the sponge method, a sponge consisting of liquid, sugar, yeast, and part of the flour is mixed as in the straight-dough method. When the mixture has stood until it is light and full of gas bubbles, it is then made into a dough by the addition of slightly cooled melted fat, salt, and the remainder of the flour. The dough is kneaded and allowed to rise until it is at least double its original volume, after which it is molded and placed in baking pans.

Batter Method

Breads may be made from batters that contain less flour than doughs. The straight-dough method is modified to eliminate the kneading and shaping steps. The batters are allowed to rise at least once in the bowl and/or in the baking pan. These unkneaded breads usually have a more open grain and uneven surface than kneaded breads and lack the elasticity of the crumb; however, they require less preparation time.

Automatic Bread Machines

Machines are available that will accomplish the total bread-making process automatically for one loaf of bread. Since these machines first came on the market about a decade ago they have been improved and have decreased in cost. New models have more adjustable controls and can make larger and conventionally shaped loaves. Some can be used to also make quick breads and cakes. With the convenience of these machines, you may, if you desire, plan to return home and find fragrant odors of baking bread permeating your kitchen.

In using bread machines, the ingredients are placed in the pan and the timing cycle is set according to the manufacturer's instructions. At the scheduled time, the loaf of bread will be mixed, proofed, and baked. To make specialty breads, you may process in the machine on the dough cycle, then remove the dough, shape, and bake in a conventional oven. Rapid-rise yeast is well suited for use in bread machines.

Kneading

Kneading of bread dough is essential for the development of strong elastic gluten strands from flour of relatively high protein content. Skillful handling of the dough ball is necessary at the beginning of kneading. The mass may rather easily be collected into a ball of dough that, with proper handling, tends to remain smooth on the outer surface in contact with the board. All wrinkles and cracks are best kept on the side in contact with the hands to minimize the tendency for the dough to stick to the board. Wet spots on the outside surface may require frequent coating with flour until the dough becomes elastic enough to knead easily. The kneading movement is a rhythmical one in which the fingers are used to pull the mass over into position for kneading and the lower part of the hand is used for applying pressure to the dough. Forcing the fingers into the dough or using too heavy a pressure tends to keep the mass of dough sticky and difficult to handle (see Figures 17-7 and 17-8).

Kneading should be thorough. Properly kneaded dough should be smooth, elastic, and have evidence of small air pockets or blisters under the surface of the dough. It is unlikely that bread dough will be overkneaded by hand. Various mixers are available with motors powerful enough to mix bread dough completely,

Figure 17-7
Dough development. (left) Dough barely mixed; (center) dough partially developed; (right) dough developed. (Courtesy of the Wheat Flour Institute)

thus eliminating the necessity of kneading by hand. The manufacturers' directions should be followed in the use of these mixers. Special attachments called dough hooks are commonly used in both commercial and commercial-style home mixers. The dough should cling to the dough hook in one ball as mixing progresses. If the dough is too soft to form a ball, additional flour should be added. After fermentation has been completed, doughs should be handled lightly to avoid pressing together the thin filaments of gluten that are formed.

When kneading bread by machine, the dough can overheat due to friction during the mixing and kneading process. This effect can be observed when making large quantities of bread in foodservice or when using a food processor in the home setting. This undesirable rise in dough temperature can be controlled by a formula that calculates the desired temperature of liquid by taking into account the friction heat generated by the equipment, flour temperature, and room temperature [17]. Recipes provided by home food processors generally recommend a specific water temperature, which is cooler than used in traditional hand mixed recipes, so as to control the dough temperature.

Whether kneading by hand or by machine, care must be used during kneading to avoid the incorporation of excess flour into the mixture, which results in too stiff a dough. With the development of a good hand kneading technique, it is surprising how little flour need be used on a board for the handling of any kind of dough. Later handling can be done with practically no flour because of the increased extensibility of the dough after fermentation.

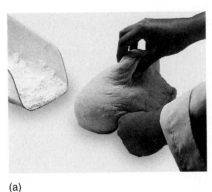

(a)

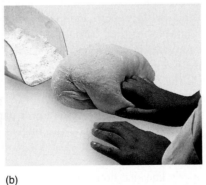

(b)

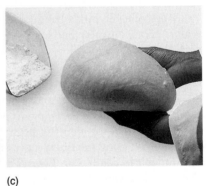

(c)

Figure 17-8
To knead bread: (a) bring the edge of the dough toward you; (b) push the dough away from you with your fist or the heel of your hand; (c) turn the dough one-quarter of a turn and repeat the process until the dough is elastic and smooth.

During the kneading process, the swollen particles of the protein fractions, *gliadin* and *glutenin,* adhere to each other and become aligned in the long elastic strands of gluten. Starch granules from the flour are entrapped in the developing gluten. The development of gluten during kneading is important to provide structure and strength for the dough and the finished loaf of bread. The starch also plays an important role in bread structure.

FERMENTATION AND PROOFING

Fermentation occurs primarily during the rising periods in the preparation of yeast breads. It is catalyzed largely by a variety of enzymes produced in the yeast cells and is a complex process. However, additional enzyme action also occurs in bread dough. A starch-splitting enzyme called *amylase* is present in the flour and may be added in commercial bread making. This enzyme catalyzes the hydrolysis of starch to dextrins and maltose. Gelatinized starch is more easily broken down by amylase than uncooked starch, so mixing some cooked potato in the dough favors amylase action. There may also be some action of proteases in bread dough. These enzymes hydrolyze proteins to peptides and amino acids. If the proteases are too active, they may hydrolyze too much of the protein and produce harmful effects, such as poor texture and decreased volume. Slight action of protease may be beneficial.

Acidity increases in bread dough during fermentation. The increase in acidity is attributed largely to the carbon dioxide, but organic acids, chiefly acetic and lactic, are also formed. Advantageous effects of a certain degree of increased acidity are the promotion of fermentation and amylase activity and the holding in check of some unwanted organisms.

The changes in gluten quality during fermentation are attributed partly to the increased acidity. Greater dispersion of the gluten with loss of elasticity and tenacity occurs as acidity increases. The action of proteases may possibly be a factor in the softening of the gluten, although this is not well understood. The stretching of the dough under the pressure of gas also appears to have a modifying effect on the gluten.

The optimum amount of fermentation varies with flours of different gluten strength and of different amylase activity. Bread must be baked before gluten strands become so thin and weak that they break, thus allowing carbon dioxide gas to escape. Overfermentation with excessive loss of gas results in poor **oven spring** and is likely to produce a loaf that is flat or sunken on top.

oven spring the rapid increase in volume in a loaf of bread during the first few minutes of baking

Overfermented bread has a coarse grain and thick cell walls. It may also have an unpleasant sour odor and flavor and a crust that does not brown well. The volume is small and the loaf is heavy and compact. Weak glutens are more easily overfermented than strong glutens, which not only tolerate but require more fermentation to yield bread of a good quality. Underfermentation produces bread that has thick cell walls and is heavy, small in volume, and less tender than bread that has fermented sufficiently to bring about a desirable dispersion of the gluten.

Fermentation can take place over a wide range of temperatures, but the best flavor is probably developed at 79° to 90°F (26° to 32°C). Cold inhibits yeast activity, and a temperature of about 130°F (55°C) destroys yeast plants. Warm temperatures may favor the growth of organisms that produce undesirable flavors in bread.

Dough that is exposed to air develops a crust or film that must later be discarded to avoid the formation of heavy streaks throughout the dough. To avoid crust formation, a proofing cabinet should be used. Proofing cabinets control

Figure 17-9
Placing three small dough balls into a muffin tin to make cloverleaf rolls. This is a simple yet attractive way to shape rolls.

the temperature and the humidity to provide ideal conditions for the fermentation and proofing of the dough. If one is not available, the bowl containing the dough may be placed in a pan of warm water and then covered with another pan of the same size. The vaporization of moisture from the surface of the water maintains a humidity that keeps the bread surface from drying out. Alternatively, the surface of the dough may be lightly greased and the bowl covered with a plastic wrap. Fermentation is usually continued until the dough has risen to 2 to 2 1/2 times its original volume.

After the dough has undergone fermentation and is molded into a loaf and placed in a baking pan, it is allowed to rise again (Figure 17-9). This final rising in the pan is called *proofing*. Proofing should be terminated when the loaf has approximately doubled in size and the dough does not spring back when it is lightly touched. In foodservice operations, proof boxes with temperature and humidity controls are used for both fermentation and proofing of bread dough.

Decorative Finishes

Before proofing, breads may be shaped into rolls or braided so as to create beautiful rolls and breads (Figure 17-10, 17-13) Additional decorative touches may be added immediately before baking that change the appearance of the bread. A glaze or a wash may be brushed onto the dough to attach seeds, oats, other toppings to the crust. A wash also may be used to create a shiny, crisp, or soft crust. A whole egg and water wash will promote a shiny crust, whereas a whole egg and milk wash will create a shiny, soft crust. Egg white and water is used when a shiny, firm crust is desired. Milk or cream will make the crust soft and a water wash will create a crisp crust [13].

Many breads are slashed to create an attractive design on the crust. Doughs are *slashed* by cutting lightly into the surface of the dough with a sharp knife just before baking. In addition to the decorative effect, hard crusted breads may be slashed to permit the escape of gases and allow additional rising during baking [13].

Figure 17-10
This panettone bread is braided to create a beautiful appearance. (Courtesy of Wheat Foods Council)

COMMERCIAL PROCESSES

Numerous technological advances have been applied in the baking industry. Many processes used in commercial bread making are, of course, very different from procedures used in the home kitchen. Some foodservice establishments bake their own bread; others may prepare only hot breads such as rolls, biscuits, and muffins. The equipment used for bread making in most foodservice kitchens is less automated than that usually found in large commercial bakeries.

Pure yeast cultures and standardized ingredients, including many chemical additives, are available to commercial bakers. Powerful mixers, fermentation rooms, dough dividers, and automatic proofing, baking, and wrapping systems are used. Through the 1940's, the predominant bread-making system in the United States was a sponge and dough system. Since then, several alternative methods have been developed, including a conventional straight-dough method, a continuous dough process, and a short-time bread-making system. Short-time doughs involve a single mixing step and little or no bulk fermentation of the dough before panning. Short-time breads are generally made with warmer doughs, more yeast, and higher levels of oxidants than are used in the preparation of conventional doughs [38]. High-speed mixing of doughs substitutes to some degree for the fermentation period. Addition of oxidizing and/or reducing agents also helps to develop the dough with less fermentation required. Shortening the fermentation period in commercial bread production results in large savings in time and labor costs.

Dough Conditioners

Dough conditioning formulations are commonly added to yeast doughs. They were once used sparingly or not at all but today are often used at their legal limits [11]. These include oxidizing agents that act on the gluten structure to produce a better-handling dough and a higher-quality bread. Gluten may be envisioned as a coiled protein that contains a number of disulfide bonds ($-S-S-$) linking parts of the molecule together to provide more strength and rigidity (see Figure 17-11) [31]. During mechanical mixing, many of these bonds are broken and the gluten becomes more expanded and relaxed so that it may be stretched by the leavening gases. The gluten is "developed" and becomes more extensible and elastic. To maintain this expanded structure, however, new linkages need to reform, strengthening the expanded gluten structure. This role is played by oxidizing dough conditioners. Many of the sulfhydryl groups ($-SH$) formed during dough development are oxidized back to disulfide linkages to lock the new structure in place. Finer texture, better volume, and a softer crumb result.

The U.S. Food and Drug Administration (FDA) has approved several oxidizing substances for use as dough conditioners, including potassium bromate, ascorbic acid, calcium iodate, azodicarbonamide, and calcium peroxide. Potassium bromate may be added to bread flour sold on the retail market. A number of emulsifiers such as lecithin, mono- and diglycerides, diacetyl tartaric esters of mono- and diglycerides, and sodium stearoyl lactylates may also be added to bread dough. Bread dough is a highly complex system, and emulsifiers interact with several components in the dough to achieve their effects on volume and crumb softness. In addition, yeast nutrients such as monocalcium phosphate and calcium sulfate are used in commercial bread making.

Figure 17-11
Gluten molecules. (Reprinted from Tieckelmann, R. E. and R. E. Steele. Higher-assay grade of calcium peroxide improves properties of dough. *Food Technology*, 45(1), p. 108, 1991. Copyright © by Institute of Food Technologists.)

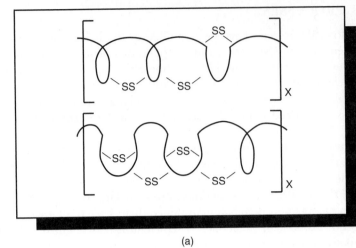

Proposed structure of gluten molecules.

(a)

Expanded and relaxed gluten molecules after mechanical mixing.

(b)

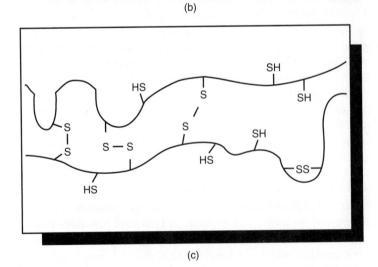

Formation of new linkages by chemical oxidation to strengthen the expanded gluten structure.

(c)

Addition of certain enzymes, including **amylases** and **proteases,** to flours or doughs can initiate improvements such as retardation of staling, enhancement of bread crust color, and softer crumb. Most of the enzymes that are commercially available for use in bakery processing come from fungi and bacteria [8].

New bakery ingredients continue to be developed. Whey protein ingredients have been found to improve the mixing of bread dough, while producing high quality breads with desirable characteristics [24]. Rice bran extracts offer functionality as both a dough conditioner and an emulsifier. Encapsulated flavorings offer advantages in flavor and bread quality. Savory Betrflakes™ is a lipid-based flavor delivery system that offers tomato-basil and cheddar-garlic flavors for breads such as foccacia [24]. The addition of garlic to wheat flour doughs has been shown to weaken the dough and result in an undesirable crumb and low volume; however, these negative effects are not present when the garlic has been encapsulated [16]. Encapsulated cinnamon, sold as Flavor-Shure™ Cinnamon, offers advantages in bread quality as well, since raw cinnamon added to bread dough will inhibit rise [24].

amylase an enzyme that breaks down or hydrolyzes starch

protease an enzyme that hydrolyzes protein

BAKING BREAD

Conventional Baking

As heat is applied to the bread during baking, gas production and expansion are greatly accelerated, which results in a sharp rising of the dough for the first few minutes of the baking period. As discussed, the rapid increase in loaf volume is called oven spring. The temperature of the interior of the loaf gradually rises until a temperature is reached that destroys yeast plants, inactivates enzymes, and stops fermentation. Alcohol is volatile and is almost completely driven off during the baking of bread. The maximum temperature of the interior of the loaf is approximately the boiling point of water, but as moisture evaporates from the exterior surface and crust formation occurs, the temperature of the crust becomes higher than that of the crumb. Gluten undergoes a gradual change in properties over a rather wide range of temperatures—122° to 175°F (50° to 80°C)—and finally becomes firm as it coagulates. Partial gelatinization of starch occurs during baking. Starch absorbs only about one-third of its weight of water at room temperature, but because it constitutes about four-fifths of flour, it is responsible for about half the total water absorption of flours when they are made into dough. As the gluten loses water during baking and the starch swells with the imbibition of additional water during heating, at least a partial gelatinization of the starch is made possible [14]. In fresh bread, the gluten holds less water and the starch holds more water than in the uncooked dough. The partially gelatinized starch contributes to bread structure as it is embedded within strands of coagulated gluten proteins.

The Maillard reaction appears to be chiefly responsible for the brown crust color in baked bread. The browning reaction probably also contributes to bread flavor. Browning of bread, as with other baked products, is influenced by the type of pan used. Pans with dark or dull finishes absorb heat more readily than bright shiny ones that reflect heat. Therefore, the surfaces of bread in contact with dull or dark pans brown more readily and uniformly.

Greasing the inside bottom of the pan aids in removing the baked bread from the pan. The greasing of side walls is optional, but a somewhat larger volume of loaf may result from allowing the dough to cling to the side walls while rising.

Baking temperatures and times vary according to the type of dough and size of mass to be baked. Whether a hot or moderate oven is used at the beginning depends on the extent of rising before the bread is placed in the oven. Bread that has risen approximately double its bulk should go into a hot oven (400° to 425°F or 204° to 218°C) to set the structure of the bread and prevent too much rising in the oven. Bread that has risen less than double its bulk may be allowed to continue rising in the oven by the use of a more moderate oven temperature (375° to 400°F or 191° to 204°C). The oven temperatures should be hot enough to avoid overfermentation in the oven before yeast destruction occurs. Too hot an oven, however, sets the bread before optimum oven spring occurs, thus reducing the final volume and affecting the texture.

One-pound loaves can bake for 35 minutes at 400°F (204°C). Alternatively, they can bake for about 15 minutes at 425°F (218°C) and for an additional 30 to 45 minutes at 375°F (191°C).

Microwave Baking

White bread is generally not acceptably cooked by microwaves because of the lack of crust formation; however, relatively dark breads, such as rye and whole wheat or oatmeal wheat, have been satisfactorily prepared in the microwave oven with little additional heating in a hot conventional oven. Medium (50 percent) power is generally used. Brown-and-serve rolls are successfully prepared in the microwave. They are browned in a hot conventional oven before being served.

Frozen Yeast Doughs

Frozen bread dough that is already shaped into a loaf is marketed at the retail level. The dough is thawed at room temperature and allowed to rise before baking. This convenience food allows one to have the aroma of freshly baked bread in the kitchen without the mixing and kneading processes. The most significant problem associated with the freezing of dough is how to maintain the viability and gassing power of frozen yeasts. The longer the active fermentation time undergone by yeast before freezing, the less stable the yeast is to freezing. Thus, the addition of yeast at the end of mixing, a reduction in proofing time, and an increase in yeast amount are possible aids in producing acceptable frozen doughs. The addition of extra wheat gluten and oxidants, as well as other additives, may also help to ensure yeast viability and baking strength. The possibility of using yeast strains other than *Saccharomyces cerevisiae* in frozen doughs has been suggested [3].

ROLLS

Rolls usually contain somewhat larger amounts of fat and sugar than are generally found in bread. Eggs may also be added, although satisfactory roll dough can be made without eggs. The eggs may be beaten lightly and added in the early stages of dough making. An egg adds about 3 tablespoons of liquid.

Rolls require 15 to 25 minutes of baking at 425°F (218°C). Pan rolls require a longer baking time than single rolls separated on a baking sheet or in muffin pans. A pan of rolls may require almost as much baking time as a pound loaf of bread.

Although any roll dough can be held in the refrigerator for 1 or 2 days before baking, refrigerator rolls are probably best made from a dough of slightly different proportions from plain rolls. For refrigerator rolls, only a moderate amount of yeast is used to avoid overfermentation, and slightly more than the usual amount of sugar is added to serve as food for the yeast during the approximately 1-week period that the dough may be held before baking. The rolls may contain egg. When the rolls are first mixed they are kneaded and allowed to undergo one fermentation, after which they are punched to release gas and stored closely covered at refrigerator temperature to be used as needed. If the dough rises appreciably during holding, it is punched from time to time to release gas. When it is needed, part of the dough is removed from the refrigerator, shaped into rolls, and allowed to rise in a warm room until the rolls double in bulk. This process may require 2 to 3 hours, depending on the temperature of the dough and the room. Rolls can be formed into a variety of shapes and sizes (Figure 17-12 and Color Plates VI and VII).

WHOLE-GRAIN AND VARIETY BREADS

Artisan breads, flat breads, hearth breads and other specialty breads have gained in popularity among American consumers [33, 29]. Restaurants and bakeries are featuring more of these products to satisfy the changing tastes of customers. Contrast in the flavor and texture of breads is made possible by the use of a variety of grains in various forms (Figure 17-13). Flours, meals, and flakes can all be used.

| Twist | Wreath | Twin Roll-Up | Posy |

| Mini Sub | Figure 8 | Clover Leaf | Lucky Clover |

| Pan Rolls | Coil | Crescent | Fan Tan |

Figure 17-12
Rolls can be formed into many different shapes. (Courtesy of Fleischmann's Yeast®)

Whole-grain flours contain essentially all the vitamins and minerals, as well as fiber, present in unmilled grain and thus offer nutritional advantages over highly milled flours. The importance of incorporating whole grain products into the diet on a regular basis has been emphasized [5, 30, 35]. Four slices of most variety breads furnish appreciable amounts of minerals and vitamins to help meet daily nutritional needs [26, 27].

Other nutritive ingredients may be added to breads to meet the needs of particular groups. For example, some researchers developed a bread formulation designed to supply the elderly with essential nutrients that are often deficient in their diets. Soy-based ingredients have been developed for use in bread products marketed for women [24]. With the use of whey, a nutritive yeast product, and low-fat cheese, an acceptable bread was formulated that increased the calcium, thiamin, and riboflavin content 1.2, 2.0, and 1.2 times, respectively, over that of the best-liked commercial bread [19].

Whole Wheat Bread

Whole wheat bread is prepared with whole wheat flour. If some white flour is used with the whole wheat flour in commercial bread making, the bread is labeled simply wheat bread. Wheat bread generally contains about 75 percent white flour and 25 percent whole wheat flour [36]. The procedure for mixing, fermenting, and baking whole wheat dough is similar to that described for white bread dough, although the kneading does not have to be as extensive. The small particles of bran in whole wheat flour interfere with the development of gluten. Even extensive kneading does not overcome this effect. The volume of the finished loaf of whole wheat bread is therefore usually somewhat less than that of white bread. If the whole wheat flour is very finely ground, however, the volume of the bread made from this flour may approach that of white bread.

High-fiber Breads

With an emphasis on the need for increased fiber in the diets of most Americans, the baking industry has developed ways of adding extra bran to breads without sacrificing quality [28]. Vital wheat gluten and certain conditioners can be used to counteract the deleterious effects of up to 15 parts of bran per 85 parts of flour. Bran flakes or prepared bran cereals may be used at home as added ingredients in wheat bread or rolls to provide additional fiber.

A survey of breads marketed in one local area suggests that there are considerable differences in the amounts of dietary fiber found in specialty breads and breads labeled "wheat bread." The fiber content ranged from 0.5 gram to about 2.0 grams per slice. Whole wheat bread contains about 1.5 grams of dietary fiber per slice [18].

Use of Flours Other Than Wheat

Some wheat flour is needed in all yeast breads to provide gluten for bread structure and lightness. Flours milled from grains other than wheat may be combined with wheat flour to give varied and flavorful baked products. Of all the grains, rye flour comes closest to wheat in terms of gluten-forming properties, but rye flour alone does not make a light loaf of bread. Rye yeast bread generally contains some wheat flour. Approximately equal portions of rye and wheat flour yield good results. Pumperknickel bread is composed of dark rye flour and molasses.

The germ of wheat or other grains is a good source of protein, vitamins, and minerals, but it also contains a **reducing substance** that has a detrimental effect on bread volume. Heat treatment inactivates this substance. A gentle heat treatment may also be used to inactivate enzymes (lipase and peroxidase) that cause rancidity in raw wheat germ, thus producing stabilized wheat germ. Heat-treated wheat germ may be added to bread in amounts of up to 15 percent of the weight of the flour with no deleterious effect on bread volume.

Soy flour increases the protein content of breads and has been used commercially to make high-protein breads. Additives are commonly used by commercial bakers to overcome the adverse effects of soy flour on the absorption, mixing, and fermentation of dough. However, bread containing about 1/3 cup of soy flour to 5 cups of all-purpose flour can be satisfactorily made at home. This bread can be made higher in protein by the use of extra nonfat dry milk solids.

Other grains that may be used in bread making, in combination with wheat flour, include oatmeal, cornmeal, barley flakes, and buckwheat flour. Molasses and honey are often used as the source of sugar in whole-grain breads to contribute flavors that blend well with whole-grain products. The relatively coarse textures and dark colors of some specialty breads lend variety to meals.

reducing substance a molecule that has an effect opposite that of an oxidizing agent; hydrogen or electrons are gained in a reaction involving a reducing substance

Other Specialty Breads

Artisan breads are old world–style breads that are sturdy and chewy. These breads are generally prepared with a starter. French baguettes are prepared from a lean dough, which is a dough that contains only water, yeast, bread flour, and salt. A crisp, chewy crust with a tender interior is produced when

Figure 17-14
These French baguettes have a golden, crisp crust.

steam is produced in the oven from a pan of hot water or a specially designed oven capable of injecting steam (Figure 17-14). In contrast, brioche is a tender bread made from a very rich dough containing butter and eggs. Challah, a traditional Jewish bread, is another rich bread that contains eggs as well as honey.

Flat breads are traditional in many parts of the world. Pita bread, from the Middle East, is a flat bread with a large pocket produced by steam. Stuffing the pocket with sandwich fillings can make delicious sandwiches. Other flat breads that do not contain a pocket but may be called pita bread are used for Greek gyros. Like pocket pita bread, the variety of sandwiches that can be made with this flat bread is only limited by your imagination. Ingredients of your choosing may be placed on this flat bread, gently folded, and enjoyed. Focaccia is an Italian flat bread that has gained popularity in America in recent years. It is distinguished by the use of olive oil and savory toppings such as fresh rosemary, Parmesan cheese, and cracked black pepper. Focaccia may be eaten alone or as a sandwich bread (Figure 17-15). A muffuletta sandwich, a New Orleans–style hero sandwich, is often made using focaccia bread.

Bagels are a donut-shaped yeast bread that have been prepared from a yeast dough that is proofed, then molded and boiled. Following boiling the bagel is dried and baked until brown in an oven. Traditional bagels, which are dense and chewy, are made from lean formulas with a low proportion of yeast. A higher proportion of sugar and yeast will result in a lighter bagel [1].

Pizza dough is generally made from a lean yeast dough which is allowed to rise for about 30 minutes before rolling into rounds. Cornmeal may be used on the bottom of the pizza pan for a distinctive texture and appearance. Pizza dough also may be used for calzones. Calzones are an Italian-American dish composed of pizza dough folded like a turnover with fillings such as an Italian tomato sauce, ricotta cheese, pepperoni or spinach and then baked.

Figure 17-15
Foccacia, a bread made with seasonings, adds flavor to any sandwich.
(Courtesy of Wheat Foods Council)

STALING OF BREAD

Staling refers to all the changes that occur in bread after baking. These include increasing firmness of the crumb, decreasing capacity of the crumb to absorb moisture, loss of flavor, crumbly texture, and development of a leathery crust. Changes in crystallinity that can be detected in the laboratory in the starchy portion of bread have led to the conclusion that starch is mainly responsible for staling. It is apparently the **amylopectin** fraction of starch that is most involved in staling, as it undergoes a type of retrogradation. Retrogradation of **amylose** also occurs, but primarily during baking and initial cooling. However, the firming of bread, associated with staling, can be slowed if moisture loss is controlled, such as is done through the formulation and packaging of *meal, ready-to-eat* (MRE) breads [9]. Thus, bread has been shown to firm due to factors in addition to amylopectin recrystallization.

Monoglycerides seem to form a complex with amylose molecules, decreasing retrogradation, and to exert a softening effect on the crumb. Some interaction between starch and gluten has also been suggested in explaining staling [15]. Fat in the bread formula helps to retard staling, while emulsifiers added by commercial bakers have a similar effect, as do certain amylase enzymes.

If stale bread is reheated to 122° to 140°F (50° to 60°C) or above, the staling is reversed and the bread regains many of the characteristics of fresh bread. The soluble fraction of the starch that decreased during staling is increased. The process can be reversed several times until the bread has lost too much moisture. In the practical application of this freshening process, moisture may even be supplied if rolls are covered with a slightly dampened cloth or paper toweling during heating. Freezing also seems to reverse the staling process. Freezing combined with heating to thaw the frozen product brings about considerable freshening of stale bread products. This process can be quickly accomplished in a microwave oven; however, microwave energy produces some toughening in bread and caution must be exercised to avoid the dehydrating effect of microwaving too long. Bread stales more rapidly when it is held at refrigerator temperatures than when it is stored at room temperature.

amylopectin a fraction of starch with a highly branched and bushy type of molecular structure

amylose a fraction of starch in which the molecules are generally long chains of glucose linked together

Spoilage of Bread

Bread spoils most commonly by molding. Any mold spores in the dough are destroyed in baking, so mold growth on baked bread comes from contamination of the loaf after baking. Conditions favorable to mold growth are moisture and warm temperatures. Commercially, sodium or calcium propionate is added to the bread dough as an antimolding additive and is quite effective. In warm, humid weather, however, even bread containing this additive is likely to mold if it is held for more than a few days at room temperature. Refrigeration retards mold growth but also speeds the staling process. Bread should be frozen if it is not to be used within a few days.

Rope is a bacterial contamination that can originate in the flour bin or in the various constituents used to make the bread. The spores of this bacterium are not destroyed in baking, and within a few days the interior of the loaf becomes sticky and may be pulled into "ropes" of a syrupy material. The odor of the loaf becomes foul and somewhat like the aroma of overripe melons. Bread is inedible when rope has developed extensively. The cure consists mainly of eliminating the source of the bacteria, although acidifying dough to a pH of 4.5 or lower will prevent rope development. Sour milk or buttermilk may be substituted for one-fourth to one-half of the total liquid, or approximately 1 tablespoon of distilled vinegar per quart of liquid may be added. This addition does not change the flavor of the bread. Calcium or sodium propionate that is added to bread to retard molding is also effective in preventing rope.

Bread may be packaged in a plastic film under a modified atmosphere, which in most cases is carbon dioxide alone or in combination with nitrogen gas. This method limits the loss of moisture and microbial growth to extend the shelf life of the bread. The carbon dioxide also has an anti-staling effect, possibly due to a change in the ability of amylopectin to bind water in the bread [2]. Shelf-stable meal, ready-to-eat (MRE) bread is preserved by controlling water activity, pH, oxygen content, and initial microbial load [22].

CHAPTER SUMMARY

- A wide variety of yeast breads can be prepared in the home or purchased from bakeries and stores. Bagels, pita bread, focaccia, and many different kinds of artisan breads, which were once considered to be strictly specialty items, are now enjoying great popularity.

- The texture of good-quality bread is fine, the cell walls thin, and the grain uniform. The crumb is elastic, but does not form a gummy ball when pressed between the fingers. The fresh crumb should spring back quickly when touched with the finger.

- A well-shaped loaf of bread has a rounded top and is free from rough, ragged cracks on the sides. A loaf of bread that is flat or sunken on top and has overhanging eaves on the sides has been proofed too long. A loaf that has not proofed long enough may have wide cracks on the sides after baking.

- The essential ingredients for yeast-leavened dough are flour, liquid, yeast, and salt. Yeast is a microscopic one-celled plant. Enzymes produced by the yeast cells are responsible for metabolic processes which yield ethyl alcohol and various additional flavoring substances, as well as carbon dioxide to leaven the bread.

- Three types of baker's yeast commonly marketed are compressed yeast, active dry yeast, and instant quick-rising active dry yeast. Active dry yeast must be rehydrated in warm water (110° to 115°F/43° to 46°C). Water above 130°F (54°C) kills yeast plants; cool water can shock the yeast, causing some of the cell contents to be leached out and resulting in "slackened" dough. Generally one package of yeast per 1 to 1 1/4 cups of liquid is satisfactory. Excess yeast can cause an undesirable odor and flavor as well as other quality defects.

- A starter is some of the sponge from a previous baking saved for future use that is used in place of yeast. Sourdough starters may be made from flour and water or from milk, yogurt, and flour. Some sourdough starters use packaged yeast. Starters must be used and replenished frequently to avoid spoilage.

- Wheat flour has the components necessary to produce bread of high volume and fine texture with a cohesive, elastic crumb. The flour best adapted to the making of bread is one of strong gluten quality, such as bread flour. The amount of flour needed to make bread dough will vary with the type of flour used, type of liquid, and level of humidity present in the surrounding environment.

- Liquid is essential in bread dough to hydrate flour proteins and contribute to the development of gluten. In addition, it is essential for the partial gelatinization of starch, which contributes to bread structure. Milk, water, potato water, or whey may be used for making bread. Milk should be scalded, and then adequately cooled before mixing with yeast. Heating of milk destroys certain enzymes and changes some proteins so that an undesirable softening of the dough during fermentation is avoided. The type of liquid used will affect the characteristics of the dough.

- Sugar is not an essential ingredient in bread formulas; however, it plays several important roles. Sugar in bread dough comes from three sources: that present in the flour, that produced by the action of enzymes hydrolyzing starch, and that added as an ingredient. Sugar provides food for the yeast, thus increasing the rate of fermentation. However, high levels of sugar, as present in some sweet rolls, repress yeast activity. Flavor, texture, and browning are also affected by the use of sugar.

- Fat is used in bread making to facilitate the handling of the dough, to increase the keeping quality of the bread, and to improve loaf volume and texture.

- Salt is added to the bread dough for flavor; however, salt retards yeast fermentation and has a firming effect on gluten structure. Bread made without salt is often crumbly in texture and may easily become overlight. Excess salt impairs flavor and texture.

- Two basic methods of mixing yeast bread are the straight-dough method and the sponge method. The batter method may also be used for some kinds of bread. Batter breads are not kneaded and thus usually have a more open grain and uneven surface as compared to breads prepared with the straight-dough and sponge methods.

- Automatic bread machines mix, proof, and bake bread, thus accomplishing the total bread-making process with the exception of the measurement of ingredients.

- Kneading of dough is essential for the development of strong elastic gluten strands. During the kneading process, the swollen particles of the protein fractions, gliadin and glutenin, adhere to each other and become aligned in the long elastic strands of gluten. Kneading should be thorough and result in a smooth, elastic ball of dough with air pockets visible under the surface. Care must be used during kneading to avoid the incorporation of excess flour into the mixture.

- Fermentation occurs primarily during the rising periods in the preparation of yeast breads. During fermentation enzyme action occurs, acidity increases, gluten quality changes, and carbon dioxide is produced. Overfermented bread has a coarse grain and thick cell walls. An unpleasant sour odor and flavor, as well as a crust that does not brown well, also may be present. Underfermented bread has thick cell walls, is heavy, small in volume, and is less tender.

- After the dough has undergone fermentation and is molded into the desired shape and placed in a baking pan, it is allowed to rise again. This final rising is called proofing. The bread is ready to be baked when the loaf has approximately doubled in size and the dough does not spring back when it is lightly touched.

- Decorative finishes such as slashing, braiding, or the use of a wash or glaze will add to the appearance of bread. The type of wash selected will have an influence on the color, texture, and shine of the crust.

- In commercial bread baking, different mixing procedures and ingredients may be used as compared to bread baking in the home. Dough conditioners, emulsifiers, yeast nutrients, enzymes, encapsulated flavorings, and other ingredients may be used by the baking industry to produce high quality bread products.

- During conventional baking several changes to the bread dough occur. Gas production and expansion greatly increase, resulting in oven spring. The temperature of the bread rises so that the yeast plants are destroyed, enzymes are deactivated, alcohol is driven off, and moisture evaporates. The gluten changes over a range of temperatures until it becomes firm and coagulates. Partial gelatinization of starch occurs during baking. Bread browns chiefly due to the Maillard reaction.

- White bread is generally not acceptable cooked by microwaves because of the lack of crust formation. However, some dark breads have been made in the microwave with additional heating in a hot conventional oven.

- Frozen bread dough is marketed at the retail level. The dough is thawed at room temperature and allowed to rise before baking. Some modifications in the preparation of bread dough to be frozen are necessary to maintain the viability and gassing power of frozen yeasts.

- Rolls generally contain somewhat higher amounts of fat and sugar than are generally found in loaf breads.

- Artisan breads, flat breads, hearth breads, and other specialty bread have gained popularity among American consumers. Whole-grain breads are prepared with whole wheat flour. The small particles of bran in whole wheat interfere with the development of gluten. Therefore, the volume of a finished loaf of whole wheat bread is generally less than that of white bread. Wheat bread, as compared to whole wheat bread, generally contains 75 percent white flour and 25 percent whole wheat flour.

- Flour from other grains may be combined with wheat flour to give varied and flavorful products. Rye flour comes closest to wheat in terms of gluten-forming properties; however, rye yeast breads generally contain some wheat flour so as to produce a light loaf. Soy, oatmeal, cornmeal, barley flakes, and buckwheat are additional grains that may be used in bread making.

- Artisan breads are old world–style breads that are sturdy and chewy. Flat breads are traditional in many parts of the world and have become popular in American. Bagels and pizza dough are additional ways in which yeast dough is used to make products other than breads and rolls.

- Staling refers to all the changes that occur in bread after baking. Increasing firmness, decreasing capacity of the crumb to absorb moisture, loss of flavor, crumbly texture, and the development of a leathery crust are common signs of staling. Stale bread may be reheated to reverse staling. Bread stales more rapidly when stored under refrigeration; room temperature or frozen storage are preferred.

- Bread spoils most commonly by molding. Moisture and warm temperatures are favorable conditions for mold growth. Rope is a bacterial contamination that can originate in the flour bin or the various constituents used to make bread. Bread is inedible when rope has developed.

KEY TERMS

shred
fermentation
proofing
metabolic
precursor
sponge
potassium bromate
hydration capacity

Maillard reaction
oven spring
amylase
protease
reducing substance
amylopectin
amylose

STUDY QUESTIONS

1. Describe desirable characteristics of yeast bread.
2. Explain the role played by each of the following ingredients in the making of yeast bread.
   a. Yeast
   b. Flour
   c. Liquid
   d. Sugar
   e. Fat
   f. Salt
   g. Dough conditioners
3. Compare the similarities and differences among compressed yeast, active dry yeast, and instant quick-rising dry active yeast as they are used for the preparation of yeast breads.
4. Compare bread flour and all-purpose flour in terms of mixing, handling, and expected outcome in the making of yeast bread.
5. What steps are involved in mixing yeast bread by the straight-dough method? The sponge method? The batter method?
6. Explain why kneading is such an important step in the preparation of yeast bread at home.
7. What is meant by *fermentation* of yeast dough and by *proofing?* What occurs during these processes?
8. What are the purposes for *slashing* bread prior to baking?
9. Why may a *wash* be used prior to baking?
10. a. Describe changes that occur during the baking of yeast bread.
    b. What is meant by *oven spring?*

    c. Why is it important to bake bread at precisely the right time after proofing in the pan?

11. How do ingredients and their proportions generally differ between rolls and bread?

12. What is the difference between wheat and whole wheat bread?

13. Identify characteristics of some of the specialty breads available.

14. a. What changes occur as bread stales?
    b. Which component of bread appears to be responsible for staling?
    c. How can somewhat stale bread be refreshened?

15. a. Give suggestions as to how to store bread appropriately.
    b. What is *rope* in bread, and how can it be controlled?

REFERENCES

1. American Institute of Baking. (n.d.). Bagels: Frequently asked questions. Retrieved November 5, 2002, from http://techserv.aibonline.org

2. Avital, Y., Mannheim, C. H., & Miltz, J. (1990). Effect of carbon dioxide atmosphere on staling and water relations in bread. *Journal of Food Science, 55,* 413.

3. Baguena, R., Soriano, M. D., Martinez-Anaya, M. A., & Benedito de Barber, C. (1991). Viability and performance of pure yeast strains in frozen wheat dough. *Journal of Food Science, 56,* 1690.

4. Baker, A., & Goldman, B. (1998, March). Our daily bread: Easier than you think. *Sunset Magazine,* 96.

5. Cleveland, L. E., Moshfegh, A. J., Albertson, A. M., & Goldman, J. D. (2000). Dietary intake of whole grains. *Journal of the American College of Nutrition, 19*(3), 331S–338S.

6. Collar, C., Mascaros, A. F., & Benedito de Barber, C. (1992). Amino acid metabolism by yeasts and lactic acid bacteria during bread dough fermentation. *Journal of Food Science, 57,* 1423.

7. Dziezak, J. D. (ed.). (1987). Yeasts and yeast derivatives: Definitions, characteristics, and processing. *Food Technology, 41*(2), 104.

8. Dziezak, J. D. (1991). Enzymes: Catalysts for food processes. *Food Technology, 45*(1), 78.

9. Hallberg, L. M., & Chinachoti, P. (2002). A fresh perspective on staling: The significance of starch recrystallization on the firming of bread. *Journal of Food Science, 67,* 1092–1096.

10. Hartnett, D. I., & Thalheimer, W. G. (1979). Use of oil in baked products—Part I: Background and bread. *Journal of the American Oil Chemists' Society, 56,* 944.

11. Harwood, J. (1991). U.S. flour milling on the rise. *Food Review, 14*(2), 34.

12. Hoseney, R. C., Lineback, D. R., & Seib, P. A. (1978). Role of starch in baked foods. *Baker's Digest, 52*(4), 11.

13. Labensky, S. R., & Hause, A. M. (2003). *On Cooking: A textbook of culinary fundamentals.* (3rd ed.). NJ: Prentice Hall.

14. Marston, P. E., & Wannan, T. L. (1976). Bread baking. *Baker's Digest, 50*(4), 24.

15. Martin, M. L., Zeleznak, K. J., & Hoseney, R. C. (1991). A mechanism of bread firming. I. Role of starch swelling. *Cereal Chemistry, 68,* 498.

16. Miller, R. A., Hoseney, R. C., Graf, E., & Soper, J. (1997). Garlic effects on dough properties. *Journal of Food Science, 62,* 1198–1201.

17. Molt, M. (2001). *Food for Fifty.* (11th ed.). NJ: Prentice Hall.

18. Patrow, C. J., & Marlett, J. A. (1986). Variability in the dietary fiber content of wheat and mixed-grain commercial breads. *Journal of the American Dietetic Association*, *86*, 794.

19. Payton, S. B., Baldwin, R. E., & Krause, G. F. (1988). Bread formulation designed for the elderly using response surface methodology. *Journal of Food Science*, *53*, 302.

20. Pomeranz, Y. (1980). Molecular approach to breadmaking—An update and new perspectives. *Baker's Digest*, *54*(1), 26.

21. Pomeranz, Y., & Finney, K. F. (1975). Sugars in breadmaking. *Baker's Digest*, *49*(1), 20.

22. Powers, E. M., & Berkowitz, D. (1990). Efficacy of an oxygen scavenger to modify the atmosphere and prevent mold growth on meal, ready-to-eat pouched bread. *Journal of Food Protection*, *53*, 767.

23. Pszczola, D. E. (1998). Ringing in the New Year with innovative bakery ingredients. *Food Technology*, *52:* 70(1).

24. Pszczola, D. E. (2002). Bakery ingredients: Past, present, and future directions. *Food Technology*, *56*(1), 56–72.

25. Putnam, J. J., & Allshouse, J. E. (1999). Food consumption, prices, and expenditures, 1970–1997. Food and Rural Economics Division, Economic Research Service, U.S. Department of Agriculture. Statistical Bulletin No. 965.

26. Ranhotra, G., Gelroth, J., Novak, F., & Matthews, R. (1985). B vitamins in selected variety breads commercially produced in major U.S. cities. *Journal of Food Science*, *50*, 1174.

27. Ranhotra, G., Gelroth, J., Novak, F., & Matthews, R. (1985). Minerals in selected variety breads commercially produced in four major U.S. cities. *Journal of Food Science*, *50*, 365.

28. Shogren, M. D., Pomeranz, Y., & Finney, K. F. (1981). Counteracting the deleterious effects of fiber in bread making. *Cereal Chemistry*, *58*, 142.

29. Sloan, A. E. (1999). The upper crust. *Food Technology*, *53*(10), 26.

30. Sloan, A. E. (2001). Dietary fiber moves back into the mainstream. *Food Technology*, *55*(7), 18.

31. Tieckelmann, R. E., & Steele, R. E. (1991). Higher-assay grade of calcium peroxide improves properties of dough. *Food Technology*, *45*(1), 106.

32. Trivedi, N. B., Cooper, E. J., & Bruinsma, B. L. (1984). Development and applications of quick-rising yeast. *Food Technology*, *38*(6), 51.

33. Unrein, J. (2002). U.S. customers get serious about artisan bread. *Milling and Baking News*, *81*(10), 28–91.

34. U.S. Department of Agriculture, Food Surveys Research Group. (1998). Results from the 1994–1996 continuing survey of food intakes by individuals. Retrieved June 18, 2002, from http://www.barc.usda.gov/gnhrc/foodsurvey/96result/html

35. U.S. Department of Agriculture and U.S. Department of Health and Human Services. (2000). *Nutrition and your health: Dietary guidelines for Americans, 5th edition.* Home and Garden Bulletin No. 232.

36. Wheat Foods Council. (n.d.). Commercial breads. Retrieved November 5, 2002, from http://www.wheatfoods.org/grain_combread.html

37. Wheat Foods Council. (n.d.). Sourdough. Retrieved November 5, 2002, from http://www.wheatfoods.org/grain_info/sour/html

38. Wu, J. Y., Maningat, J. I., Ponte, Jr., J. G., & Hoseney, R. C. (1988). Short-time breadmaking systems. Effect of formulation, additives, temperature, and flour quality. *Journal of Food Science*, *53*, 535.

39. Wyatt, C. J. (1983). Acceptability of reduced sodium in breads, cottage cheese, and pickles. *Journal of Food Science*, *48*, 1300.

Cakes and Cookies

18

 Although a wide variety of formulations are included in the class of baked products called *cakes*, these recipes can usually be classified into two major groups: shortened cakes or cakes containing fat, and unshortened cakes or cakes with no fat. A third category might be added—the chiffon cake, which has characteristics of both shortened and unshortened cakes. A chiffon cake usually contains a larger proportion of egg than a shortened cake, a proportion similar to that found in unshortened cakes. It does contain fat in the form of oil.

Cookies differ in several ways from cakes. Fine texture and velvety crumb are less prominent characteristics of cookies than of cakes, and often, less skill is required to prepare them. Special skills are required to make certain types of cookies, such as rolled cookies or meringue-type cookies; the inexperienced person may find the preparation of these products quite challenging.

Among the fat-reduced bakery items that are appearing on the market are a variety of reduced-fat, low-fat, or no-fat cakes, cake mixes, and cookies. These items are similar to shortened cakes and cookies in general characteristics, but have been formulated using various fat replacing systems.

SHORTENED CAKES

Types and Characteristics

Shortened cakes are of two types: pound cake and standard shortened cake. The pound cake, as commonly prepared, has no added leavening agent except for the air incorporated in the creaming of the fat and sugar and in the beaten eggs. Steam has been found to be responsible for about half the expansion during baking, provided that the air cells are retained. Theoretically, the moisture evaporates into the air cells and the vapor expands during baking. In commercial pound cakes, improved textures have resulted from the addition of a small amount of baking powder.

The standard shortened cake is leavened chiefly by carbon dioxide gas from baking powder or from soda and buttermilk. Air incorporated into the plastic fat or into the beaten eggs or egg whites also aids in leavening the mixture.

The textures of the two types of shortened cakes are different. Pound cakes have a close grain and are somewhat compact in character, yet they are very tender (Figure 18-1). They should not be heavy or soggy, but they lack the soft, light, velvety crumb of a well-made shortened cake. A good standard shortened cake

has a fine grain, cells of uniform size, thin cell walls, and a crumb that is elastic rather than crumbly. Crusts should be thin and tender. Top crusts should be smooth or slightly pebbly and have top surfaces that are only slightly rounded.

Proportions of ingredients vary widely for ordinary shortened cakes. Mixtures may be classified as lean or rich depending largely on the relationship of fat and sugar (the tenderizing ingredients) to the ingredients that give structure (flour and egg). One has only to study recipe books and experiment a little with the many proportions given for cakes to realize that numerous variations are possible. Maximum and minimum quantities doubtless exist for most of the essential ingredients for cake, but all are yet to be known. Specific ingredients can be increased or decreased within certain limits without producing undesirable results.

Change in proportion often requires change in manipulation. The optimum amount of stirring that produces the best results from one set of proportions or a definite quantity of mixture usually cannot be applied to another set of proportions or a smaller or larger quantity of mixture.

Ingredients

Usual ingredients in a standard shortened cake include sugar, fat, egg, liquid, a leavening agent, salt, and flour. A proper balance between the tenderizing effects of sugar and fat and the firming or structural effects of flour and egg is particularly important in shortened cakes [19].

Sugar. Sugar adds sweetness to a shortened cake, but it also has an important effect on texture and volume. It interferes with gluten development from the flour and has a weakening effect on the structure of the cake. Sugar probably affects gluten development because it attracts and holds water that would otherwise be absorbed by the gluten proteins. Only when the proteins of flour become sufficiently hydrated to adhere to each other is gluten produced. Gelatinized starch is an important part of the structure of a cake. Sugar delays gelatinization of the starch, raises the temperature at which the starch gelatinizes, and causes a decrease in the viscosity of the batter in the early stages of baking [15].

It has been suggested that the resistance to movement of a cake batter during baking, referred to as *cohesive forces*, influences the development of the structure of the finished cake. Various ingredients affect these cohesive forces in different ways. Added in increasing amounts up to an optimum quantity, sugar decreases the cohesive forces and allows the batter to move more freely. The volume of the cake therefore increases [24]. As sugar is increased in a formula, stirring must also be increased to develop the gluten sufficiently to overcome the weakening effects of excess sugar. Without increased stirring, an increase in the percentage of sugar in a cake causes the cake to fall and to have a coarse texture and thick cell walls. Both crust and crumb are gummy. The crust may appear rough, sugary, and too brown (Figure 18-2).

Sucrose or table sugar is that which is most commonly used in cakes; however, successful layer cakes can be made with glucose or fructose substituted for sucrose if the sugar/water ratio in the batter is adjusted to achieve a desirable starch gelatinization temperature [3]. The temperature at which starch gelatinizes in cake batters appears to be an important factor in determining cake volume and contour. More fructose and glucose than sucrose are required in the formula to attain the same starch gelatinization temperature. Cakes made with fructose also tend to be darker because the browning (Maillard) reaction is more pronounced.

High-fructose corn syrup has become an important alternative sweetener in place of sucrose for such products as beverages and soups, and the use of this sweetener in baked products has been tested. Acceptable cakes have been made with 50 and 75 percent of the sucrose replaced with high-fructose corn syrup using all-purpose flour in the recipe [20]. Although the cakes with the corn syrup were more brown and of somewhat lower volume, the adverse effects on sensory quality were slight. Kinds of sweeteners are discussed further in Chapter 11.

Egg. The optimum amount of egg in a given cake mixture produces finer cells, thinner cell walls, and usually larger volume than are obtained with a lower or

Figure 18-2
A cake containing too much sugar may fall in the center and have a coarse, gummy texture.

higher percentage of egg. Although the way the eggs are added may modify the effects, an excess of egg gives a rubbery, tough crumb. When beaten egg whites are added last, the effects of increased egg are less noticeable. The cohesive forces in a baking cake batter are increased as egg white is added in increasing amounts [24].

Fat. Increasing the fat in a shortened cake increases tenderness. Fat weakens structure and tends to decrease volume when added beyond the optimum amount. Cohesive forces decrease with increasing amounts of fat [24].

In substituting a shortening containing 100 percent fat for butter or margarine (which contain approximately 80 percent fat) in a formula that has a fairly high fat content, it is best to use only 80 percent as much fat (types of fat are discussed in greater detail in Chapter 10). Fat of good creaming quality yields a cake of better texture than soft or liquid fats unless the methods of mixing are altered. In comparing various fats, butter has been reported to make cakes that scored highest for tenderness and velvetlike texture, whereas hydrogenated shortening produced cakes with the highest rating for evenness of grain [19]. Decreasing by half the amount of oil added to a commercial yellow cake mix batter did not appreciably change the appearance, moistness, flavor, or overall acceptability of the baked cake [4]. Thus, this method achieved a reduction in calories and fat content with no decrease in quality (Figure 18-3).

In addition to tenderizing, plastic fats aid in incorporating air into the batter. Most hydrogenated fats contain some inert gas as they are marketed. Creaming fat and sugar together adds additional air bubbles to the fat. It has been suggested that the air bubbles incorporated into fat during creaming act as a base for the distribution of leavening gas (carbon dioxide, particularly) during mixing and baking. Some research with microscopic studies on freeze-dried cake batters showed that the air bubbles were not necessarily incorporated into the fat but were distributed throughout the watery phase of the batter [25]. The

Figure 18-3
Vanilla and butter extract add delicious, rich flavors to this cake prepared with a low fat formula.
(Courtesy of McCormick & Co., Inc.)

fat probably still plays an important role, however, in the trapping of air bubbles in a batter mixture.

Interest in reduced-fat and reduced-calorie foods has led to the development of fat replacers for cakes [32]. One such product is a dry, free-flowing powder, which can be incorporated into both cake mixes and batters, that contains a mixture of emulsifiers, pregelatinized modified starch, and guar gum, with nonfat dry milk as a carrier. The replacer allows air to be entrapped in the batter, similar to the way in which shortening entraps air.

An instantized modified high-amylose starch has been developed specifically for use in reduced-fat bakery products. It is designed to aid in the aeration of the batter, which in turn increases batter viscosity and entraps air during the baking process, resulting in a fine texture. The shelf life is also extended. All of the fat or oil in a cake can be replaced by one of the systems containing modified starches, gums, emulsifiers, and stabilizers. Acceptable ratings have come from the sensory evaluation of many of the resulting cakes. No-fat cake mixes are available for use in foodservice establishments. Light cake mixes containing reduced amounts of shortening, with gums, modified starch, and emulsifiers to compensate for the decreased fat, are sold on the retail market. Fat may be reduced by up to 50 percent and calories by about 20 percent.

It has been reported that the shortening in yellow cakes made in the home kitchen may be reduced by half without substantially changing the acceptability, as evaluated by a trained sensory panel [12]. This allows typical recipes to be adjusted in order to decrease fat consumption to some degree.

Emulsifiers. Emulsifying agents in cake batter cause the fat to be distributed more finely throughout the mixture and allow the cake formula to carry more sugar than flour. Shortenings that contain small amounts of emulsifiers are sometimes called *high-ratio* shortenings because of the higher ratio of sugar to flour that is possible with their addition. When optimum amounts of an emulsifier are used, the cohesive forces in the cake batter are decreased, the batter moves or flows more readily because the viscosity is decreased during the early part of the baking period before the structure sets, and the volume of the finished cake is increased [15]. The emulsifier may interact with the starch as it gelatinizes. A fine and even texture in the finished cake is the result (Figure 18-4).

Emulsifiers are commonly added to shortenings that are to be used for making cakes. Hydrogenated shortenings on the retail market often contain small amounts (about 3 percent) of mono- and diglycerides. Polysorbate 60 (about 1 percent) is also frequently used in commercial emulsified shortenings.

Figure 18-4
The volume and quality of a shortened cake improve when an emulsifier is used. (Courtesy of *Food Engineering* and C.D. Pratt, Atlas Powder Company. Photograph by R. T. Vanderbilt Company)

A larger variety of emulsifiers are available to commercial bakers [9]. In food-service operations, prepared baking mixes containing emulsified shortening are used to a considerable extent [17].

Leavening Agents.   Cakes may be leavened by baking powder, baking soda, air entrapped in creamed shortening or beaten egg whites, and steam. Too little baking powder in a cake produces a compact, heavy product. Increasing the baking powder increases cake volume until the optimum quantity is reached. Beyond that, volume decreases and the cake falls. A coarse texture and a harsh, gummy crumb may also result from an excess of baking powder. Cakes made using SAS-phosphate powder may be disagreeably bitter if large amounts are used. Less baking powder is needed to produce the best volume and texture when more air is incorporated into the cake by means of a creamed fat-sugar mixture or beaten egg whites.

Baking soda is used in cakes that have an acidic ingredient such as sour milk, buttermilk, or fruit juice. Although cocoa generally does not provide enough acid to allow the use of only baking soda, some chocolate cake recipes will use both baking soda and baking powder as leavening agents.

Flour.   Too little flour has the same effect on a cake as an excess of fat or sugar. The structure is weak, the texture is coarse, and the cake may fall. Excess flour, on the other hand, produces a compact, dry cake in which tunnels form readily. Tunnels, however, may form in a cake of good proportions if the mixture is overmanipulated or is baked at too high a temperature.

Flour contributes structure to shortened cakes. Cakes made with all-purpose flour are generally lower in volume and have a coarser texture than similar cakes made with cake flour because all-purpose flour has a higher protein content than cake flour. If only all-purpose flour is available, 1 cup of all-purpose flour minus 2 tablespoons can be used in place of one cup of cake flour [1]. Others suggest replacing the 2 tablespoons of flour removed from the cup of all-purpose flour with 2 tablespoons of cornstarch and then substituting this flour-starch blend for cake flour. Types of flour are discussed further in Chapter 15.

In the making of cakes with cake flour, the gelatinized starch is probably more important to structure than the small amount of gluten developed. The gelatinization of the starch helps to convert a fluid phase into a solid, porous structure.

Cake flour used in making high-ratio cakes, containing more sugar than flour, are treated with chlorine gas to produce high-quality cakes [22]. Chlorine not only bleaches pigments in the flour, but it also oxidizes some of the proteins, destroys the normal gluten-developing properties of the flour, and interacts with the starch. Apparently some of the lipids in the flour are also affected [13]. Because cake batter is a complex system, the chlorine-treated flour undoubtedly reacts with other formula components to produce the texture and volume of the final product [22].

Cakes have been successfully prepared without chlorine treated flour when the flour has first been heat-treated and the formula is adjusted to include xanthan gum. These cakes were found to have slightly greater volumes and a crumb grain that was essentially equivalent to the control cake prepared with chlorinated flour [31]. Other researchers found that nonchlorine-treated flour could be used to produce white layer cakes with better quality characteristics as compared to the control cakes prepared with chlorine-treated flour. The formula of the nonchlorine-treated flour cakes was modified to include starch, soya lecithin, and xanthan gum, in addition to an increase in the concentration of dried egg albumen [8].

Liquid.   The liquid ingredient in cakes dissolves the sugar and salt and makes possible the reaction of baking powder or baking soda. Liquid disperses the fat and flour particles and hydrates the starch and protein in the flour, allowing both starch gelatinization and gluten development. Some steam is produced from the liquid, which helps to leaven the cake. Various liquids may be used, including milk, water, and fruit juices. A moist cake of low volume results with excess liquid.

Chocolate Cakes.   Because of the starch content of cocoa and chocolate, a smaller percentage of flour than that used in a yellow cake produces a more desirable chocolate cake. With the same proportions of flour, fat, and sugar that are used in plain shortened cakes, chocolate cake batters tend to be undesirably stiff and the cakes are dry, with a tendency to crack on top. Chocolate cake recipes usually contain relatively high percentages of sugar or fat or both, however, and the proportion of flour may approach that usually used in other shortened cakes. Cocoa has a greater thickening effect than chocolate because the percentage of starch in cocoa is about 11 percent as compared with 8 percent in chocolate. From the standpoint of flavor, color, and thickening effect, best results are usually obtained by using about two-thirds, by weight, as much cocoa as chocolate in a recipe. This amounts to about 3 to 3 1/2 tablespoons of cocoa as a substitute for 1 ounce of chocolate.

The acidity of chocolate is not sufficiently high to necessitate the use of soda unless buttermilk is used in the cake mixture. The color of chocolate cakes gradually changes from cinnamon brown to a mahogany red as the acidity decreases and the alkalinity increases. Devil's food cakes, which are characteristically mahogany red, contain enough soda to produce an alkaline pH in the batter. The characteristic chocolate flavor is changed with increasing amounts of soda.

Proportions of Ingredients.   Salt is used in cakes for flavor, and only small amounts are needed. A satisfactory plain standard cake has, by measure, one-third as much fat as sugar, two-thirds as much milk as sugar, and about three times as much flour as liquid, as in the following example of a cake formula. Formula adjustments for high altitude baking are discussed in Chapter 15.

Sugar 1 1/2 cups	Eggs 2
Fat 1/2 cup	Salt 1/2 tsp
Milk 1 cup	Baking powder 3 tsp
Cake flour 3 cups	Flavoring 1 tsp

In foodservice, recipes designed for household use are often adjusted for quantity production. Various methods may be used for making this adjustment, including multiplying the weight of each ingredient by a certain factor or calculating recipe percentages [21]. In the factor method, a factor is determined by dividing the desired yield by the yield of the current recipe. These calculations can be done quickly on a computer, and such software programs are available.

The way that a particular computer program calculates the recipes is important. Five German chocolate cakes, in quantities serving 60 people, were prepared with formulations that were generated from a household recipe. Several different computer programs were utilized to perform the calculations for the same home-size recipe and the prepared cakes then evaluated for quality characteristics [16]. Because significant differences were found among the cakes, foodservice managers were encouraged to assess the accuracy of calculations provided by the computer program and to test product quality for each adjusted recipe to be sure that the new recipe would produce the same product as the original recipe. The five computer programs used for this study gave somewhat different ingredient quantities and these differences appeared to affect quality. The percentage method of recipe calculation will provide the most consistent and accurate measurements when adjusting recipes [21].

Mixing

A variety of methods can be used to combine the ingredients in shortened cakes. Four commonly used methods are described here.

Conventional Method. The conventional method consists of creaming a plastic fat (Figure 18-5), adding the sugar gradually to the fat with continued creaming, adding the egg or egg yolks to the fat-sugar mixture, and beating until the mixture is well blended and very light. The dry ingredients are sifted together and added alternately with the milk in about four portions. The egg whites may be beaten separately until stiff but not dry, and quickly folded into the batter at the end of mixing to avoid excessive loss of gas.

Flavoring extract may be added to the creamed mixture, to the milk, or when the dry and liquid ingredients are being added. The conventional method of mixing is more time consuming than the other methods described here. It should produce a fine-textured cake and may be conveniently used for mixing cakes by hand.

Conventional Sponge Method. The conventional sponge method is used with lean cake mixtures, in which the amount of fat is not sufficient to produce a light creamed mass when all the sugar is added to the fat. To avoid the dry, crumbly character of the fat-sugar mixture, about half of the sugar is reserved to be beaten with the eggs until this mixture is very stiff. The rest of the sugar is creamed with the shortening. The liquid and dry ingredients are added alternately to the sugar-fat mixture. The beaten egg-sugar mixture is then folded into the batter at the end of mixing. Note, however, that a surprisingly large amount of sugar can be creamed with a small or moderate amount of fat if the fat is at the most favorable temperature for creaming, 75° to 85°F (24° to 29°C), and if the addition of sugar is gradual. A good cake can be made from oil by the use of the conventional sponge method.

Muffin Method. In the muffin method, the eggs, milk, and melted fat are mixed together and added all at once to the sifted dry ingredients. This method is simple and rapid and is particularly useful for lean formulas when the cake is to be eaten while still warm.

Quick-mix Method. The quick-mix method is known by several other names, including the *single-stage, one-bowl,* or *one-mix* method. It requires a change in the proportions of ingredients from those that are satisfactory for the conventional method of mixing. Higher proportions of sugar and liquid are used with the quick-mix method, and the shortening should contain an emulsifying agent. All the ingredients, particularly the fat, should be at room temperature so that the ingredients can be readily dispersed. Use of this method is difficult when

Figure 18-5
Creamed butter and sugar are shown in this mixer bowl.

mixing by hand. An electric mixer is desirable; however, commercial cake mixes, which are designed for the one-bowl method of mixing, may be mixed by hand if the number of mixing strokes, rather than time, is used as the measure. The quick-mix method used with an appropriate formula yields a fine-grained, tender, moist cake of good volume that remains fresh for a relatively long period.

The mixing of the batter can be completed in two stages. At Stage I, sift all dry ingredients into the bowl used for mixing. Add all fat, *part* of the liquid, and flavoring or add all fat, liquid, and flavoring. Beat for a specified time. At Stage II, add unbeaten eggs or egg whites and the remaining liquid if part of the liquid was withheld in the first stage, then beat for a specified time.

In some recipes, the baking powder may be omitted from the first stage and stirred in quickly (all by itself) between the two stages. For uniformity of blending, both the sides and the bottom of the bowl should be scraped frequently during mixing.

Effects of Under- and Overmanipulation. The amount of mixing needed to produce the best cake texture varies with the proportions of ingredients and the quantity of batter. The temperature of the ingredients is also a factor, as is the quantity of baking powder and the time at which the baking powder is added.

The thoroughness of creaming the fat-sugar mixture affects the extent of subsequent mixing. Thorough creaming makes possible a wider range in the amount of mixing that will produce a good texture. A good creamed mixture is light and spongy but has enough body to prevent an oily, pasty, or frothy mass. When eggs are added to the creamed fat and sugar, the mass becomes softer but should retain enough air to remain light. When the fat-sugar mixture separates into large flecks or curds on the addition of eggs, the resulting cake usually has a coarser texture than a cake produced from an uncurdled batter. A more stable emulsion may result from adding eggs gradually to the fat-sugar mixture. The use of a shortening containing an emulsifier, such as mono- and diglycerides, also aids in forming a stable emulsion.

Mixing a cake batter barely enough to dampen the dry ingredients may yield a cake of good volume, but the texture is coarse and the cell walls are thick. The optimum amount of stirring produces a cake of optimum volume, uniform texture, small cells, and thin cell walls. Stirring beyond the optimum amount tends to produce a compact cake of smaller volume. The texture may be fine, but tunnels are likely to be formed. When cakes are greatly overstirred, they become heavy or soggy. Cakes stirred close to the optimum amount tend to be slightly rounded on top. As stirring is increased, peaks tend to form and the side walls of the cake are not as high as those in cakes stirred the optimum amount. If cakes are cut or broken where the peaks occur, long tunnels will be found. Certain rich mixtures may show a concave surface if they are understirred.

The fact that cake mixtures contain more sugar and fat than most other flour mixtures decreases the tendency for toughness to result from stirring. Gluten development is retarded by sugar and fat. But more than the optimum amount of stirring may appreciably toughen cakes, especially those made from lean mixtures and from flours of stronger gluten quality.

Preparation of Pans

If the baking pans are prepared before the cake batter is mixed, the batter can then be transferred to them immediately after mixing. Allowing the batter to stand in the mixing bowl more than 15 to 20 minutes before placing it in the baking pans is undesirable, as transfer of the batter at this point may have adverse effects on the volume and texture of the baked product.

Pans may be greased on the sides and bottoms, or the sides may be left dry (Figure 18-6). If the sides of the pan are not greased, the cake volume may be somewhat greater because the cake structure is supported by clinging to the sides. Flouring the greased bottom of the pan aids in removing the cake from the pan, but the flour coating should be light. An alternative procedure is to cut a piece of paper, waxed or unwaxed, to fit the bottom of the pan. After the paper is in place in the greased pan, it is greased on the top surface, which will come in contact with the cake.

Baking

Baking Temperatures.   The oven temperatures commonly used for baking shortened cakes range from 350° to 375°F (177° to 191°C). The optimal temperature may vary with the cake formula. Some data indicate that plain cakes increase in volume and in total cake scores (including such characteristics as texture, tenderness, velvetiness, and eating quality) up to 365°F (185°C) but decrease at 385°F (196°C). Chocolate cakes, which have often been baked at lower temperatures than other shortened cakes on the theory that chocolate scorches easily, also show increased volume and total cake scores when baked at higher temperatures—loaf cakes at 385° to 400°F (196° to 204°C) and layer cakes at 400°F (204°C). High temperatures are sometimes not recommended because of excessive browning and humping of the top. The browning of cakes is apparently the result of both the Maillard reaction and the caramelization of sugar.

The better results obtained with higher temperatures would seem to indicate that a more rapid coagulation of cake batter in relation to the rate of gas formation and gas expansion prevents the collapse of cells. Such collapse results in coarse grain and thick cell walls in the baked cake.

If dark, dull pans are used, the cake will brown more readily and uniformly than when bright, shiny pans are used. The shiny pans tend to reflect heat, whereas the dull pans absorb it more easily.

Use of commercial air **impingement ovens** for the baking of white layer cakes reduced the baking time by almost half when compared with baking in a

impingement oven sometimes called a conveyor oven. Food is placed on a conveyor belt which carries the food through the oven. Impingement ovens may be used to bake cakes, but are more frequently used for baking pizza.

Figure 18-6
Grease the bottom and sides of the pan and dust with flour before beginning to mix the cake.

conventional oven. The quality of the cakes was similar in both cases. Concern for energy conservation motivates efforts to improve oven technology [18].

Cooling the Cake before Removal from the Pan. It is recommended that cakes not be removed from the pan until the interior reaches a temperature of about 140°F (60°C). At this point, they have usually become firm enough to handle without damage to the structure of the cake. Allowing the baked cake to stand about 10 minutes before removal from the pan is usually sufficient for this temperature to be reached (Figure 18-7).

Microwave Baking. Flour mixtures do not form a brown crust when cooked by microwaves. Because cakes are usually frosted, the lack of crust formation is of less importance from the standpoint of appearance for cakes than for some other baked products. However, the flavor associated with browning is not developed. A browning unit in the microwave oven may aid in browning the top surface of the cake. Waxed paper laid over the surface of cake batters before cooking gives them a smooth surface.

When double layers of cakes were baked in a combination microwave/convection oven using 10 percent microwave power, they were rated equal or near equal to similar cakes baked in a conventional oven [29]. The microwave/convection-baked cakes were rated slightly lower than the conventional cakes for crust color, moistness, and total sensory score when only single layers were baked.

Many cake mixes are satisfactorily cooked in a microwave oven. Rich, moist mixes with pudding added are excellent for microwaving. Because microwaved cakes rise higher than conventionally baked cakes, the pans should be filled no more than one-third to one-half full. The method of starting the cake at 50 percent power and finishing it at high power results in a more even top than cooking on high for the entire period. The top of a microwaved cake may be slightly moist when done, but the moisture will evaporate during standing time out of the oven. Numerous cake mixes designed especially for the microwave oven are marketed and special pans for use in the microwave oven are packaged with the cake mixes (Figure 18-8).

UNSHORTENED CAKES

Unshortened cakes are of two types: white angel food, which is made from egg whites, and yellow sponge, which is made from the whole egg.

Angel Food Cake

Some may consider angelfood cake the ultimate fat-free cake. Angel food cakes are often made using commercial mixes in which the egg white foam is stabilized by the addition of a whipping aid; however, good-quality cakes can also be made at home using fresh egg whites. Without the incorporation and retention of air, proper expansion and a typical texture do not develop in the baking of unshortened cakes. Air accounts for approximately half of the leavening in angel food cakes, but steam also plays an important role in the leavening of this product. Steam that is formed from the vaporization of the water of egg white brings about two or three times the expansion in baking angel food cake as is accounted for by the expansion of air.

Characteristics. A desirable angel food cake is porous or spongy, is of large volume, and has thin cell walls (Figure 18-9). Tenderness and moistness are also

Pour the batter into prepared pans. The batter should be divided evenly between the layer pans.

Place the pans on the middle rack at least 1 inch from the sides of the oven. The pans should not touch.

After minimum baking time, touch the center lightly. If no imprint remains, the cake is done. Or insert a wooden pick in center; if it comes out clean, the cake is done.

Allow cakes to cool 10 minutes on wire racks before removing them from the pans. If cakes are left in the pans too long, they will steam and become soggy.

The finished cake has a moist, velvety crumb and good volume.

Figure 18-7
(Courtesy of Kitchens of Betty Crocker, General Mills, Inc.)

(a)

Figure 18-8
(a) Special pans must be used to bake cakes in microwave ovens. These plastic pans are used to bake cake and brownie mixes engineered especially for the microwave oven. The layer cake at the top of the picture was baked in the round pan at the left. The frosted cake in the center may be baked and served in the same pan. The round pan at the right was used to bake a bundt cake. (Photograph by Chris Meister)

(b)

(b) Many kinds of pans are available for baking. The glass bowls, custard cups, and measuring cup are microwave safe. Glass bread and brownie pans can also be used for conventional oven cooking. (Courtesy of World Kitchens Inc., makers of Pyrex®)

important characteristics. The size of the cells varies, but the grain is generally more open and less fine than that of good-quality shortened cakes.

Ingredients. The ratio of sugar to flour in the following cake formula is appropriate for tenderness yet not high enough to cause the collapse of the cake.

Egg whites 1 cup	Cream of tartar 1 tsp
Sugar 1 1/4 cup	Salt 1/4 tsp
Cake flour 1 cup	Flavoring 1 tsp

Egg whites. Egg whites incorporate air as they are beaten to form a foam. Important in stabilizing the foam is the coagulation of egg proteins by the mechanical forces of beating (see Chapter 24 for a discussion of beating eggs). Fresh eggs are preferable to older eggs for making angel food cakes because the fresh whites are thicker and produce a more stable foam. Good-quality angel

food cakes may be prepared using frozen or dried egg whites [11]. In addition to the important role of egg white proteins in foam formation and stabilization, some proteins in egg white are coagulated by heat and give structure to the baked cake.

Flour. Cake flour, because of its low percentage of protein, its weak quality of gluten, and its fine granulation, produces a more tender, delicate angel food cake than flour of stronger gluten quality. Flour increases the strength of the cake crumb and contributes to the structure. As the amount of sugar is increased, the flour also, within certain limits, must be increased to provide a satisfactory ratio of sugar to flour so that sufficient structure is maintained in the cake.

Sugar. Sugar has a stabilizing effect on the egg white foam and allows more beating without overcoagulation of the egg white proteins. Sugar also sweetens the cake and aids in browning. The higher the percentage of sugar in the formulation, the greater the tendency toward development of a sugary crust. Sugar interferes with gluten development and therefore tends to produce a more tender and fragile cake when used in increasing amounts. Sugar elevates the coagulation temperature of egg proteins and, if used in excess, may retard coagulation to such an extent that the cake collapses. In addition, the temperature for starch gelatinization is increased by sugar, and that structure of the cake for which gelatinized starch is responsible is affected by increasing amounts of sugar.

A fine granulated sugar is normally used in making angel food cakes; however, 25 percent of the sugar may be replaced by high-fructose corn syrup with little effect on the physical or sensory characteristics of the cake [7].

Cream of tartar. Cream of tartar is an important constituent of angel food cake because of its beneficial effect on color, volume, and tenderness. The anthoxanthin pigments of flour are yellowish in an alkaline medium but are white in an acid or neutral medium. The Maillard or browning reaction between sugars and proteins also is less likely to occur in an acid than an alkaline medium. Therefore, the addition of cream of tartar (an acid salt) produces a cake that is more white than yellow or tan. Cream of tartar, as an acid substance, also stabilizes the egg white foam to allow heat to penetrate and bring about coagulation without collapse of the foam. Large air cells and thick cell walls (coarse grain) are the effects of an unstable foam that has partially collapsed. Cream of tartar prevents extreme shrinkage of the cake during the last part of the baking period and during the cooling period. Cream of tartar also produces a more tender cake. The optimal proportion is about 1 teaspoon per 1 cup of egg whites.

Mixing. The whites can be beaten with an electric mixer, a rotary beater, or a wire whisk. The whisk usually produces a somewhat larger volume of cake, but the cells are also larger. Egg whites should not be overbeaten, as this contributes to dryness and a lack of extensibility in the film surrounding the air bubbles. The air cells break and collapse, which results in a cake of low volume, thick cell walls, and coarse texture. The whites should be stiff but the peaks and tails that form should bend over slightly, instead of standing rigid and upright.

Egg whites beat more easily to a foam of large volume when they are at room temperature than when they are beaten at a lower temperature. Therefore, eggs to be used in angel food cake should be removed from the refrigerator some time before they are to be beaten. Cream of tartar is added to the egg whites, and they are beaten until a foam begins to form. Sugar may be beaten into the whites as they are being whipped, or it may be folded in after the egg whites are completely beaten. In the first case, the sugar is added gradually as for meringue, starting after the cream of tartar is added. Beating the sugar into the whites is known as the *meringue method* and is preferable if an electric mixer is used. Beating some sugar into the egg white foam seems to have a greater stabilizing effect on the cake than folding all the sugar in with the flour. Regardless of the method used for adding sugar, about 2 tablespoons of sugar at a time are sifted over the surface of the egg whites. Adding either sugar or flour in too-large portions results in the loss of air and often in the uneven blending of the sugar or flour.

After the sugar is added, the flour is gently folded into the mixture. If an electric mixer is being used, it should be turned down to the lowest speed setting. Part of the sugar may be reserved to be mixed with the flour. The flour mixed with some sugar unquestionably folds into the mixture more easily, but usually a better cake is obtained when as much of the sugar as possible is added to the egg white foam before the addition of any flour. Thorough mixing of the sugar with the egg white produces a mixture into which the flour blends easily.

The number of strokes needed by different individuals for folding the flour varies. Thorough blending is necessary, but overmanipulation results in a loss of air and in decreased tenderness.

The flavoring extract may be added after the whites are partially beaten. Adding the extract at this stage allows it to become thoroughly distributed without the necessity for overmanipulation later. In no case is it desirable to add extract at the end of mixing because the extract is either incompletely blended with the batter or extra manipulation is needed to blend it uniformly. Alternatively, extract may be added while sugar or flour is being folded into the mixture. The salt may be added toward the end of the beating of the foam and before the addition of flour, because salt may have a slight destabilizing effect on the egg white foam if it is added earlier.

Preparation of Pans. Pans are not greased for either type of sponge cake. It is desirable to have the mixture cling to the sides of the pan until it is coagulated by the heat of the oven. After baking, the pan is inverted and allowed to stand until the cake is thoroughly cooled. This gives the delicate cake structure a chance to set with the least amount of strain placed on it.

Baking Temperatures.   Baking at 350°F (177°C) has been found to result in a more tender and moist angel food cake of larger volume and thinner cell walls than baking at lower temperatures [2]. A wide range of oven temperatures would appear to be satisfactory, however, if the minimum time required to bake the cake is used. Longer baking tends to toughen the cake whatever the temperature, but greater toughening occurs with longer baking at higher temperatures.

Angel food cakes made from commercial mixes and baked at 350° and 375°F (177° and 191°C) scored higher in all quality characteristics than those baked at 400° and 425°F (204° and 218°C) [10]. Compact layers formed as a result of partial collapse of the structure after the cakes baked at 400° and 425°F (204° and 218°C) were removed from the oven. It has been suggested that, for angel food cakes made from commercial mixes, baking initially at 375°F (191°C) and then lowering the temperature to 350°F (177°C), 325°F (163°C), and finally 300°F (149°C) at 10-minute intervals yields tender baked cakes of very high volume. When the baking cake begins to shrink, it may be tested with a toothpick or cake tester. If moist or sticky crumbs cling to the tester, the cake must be baked longer.

Sponge Cake

Ingredients.   The usual ingredients and proportions for yellow sponge cake are as follows.

Eggs 6	Water 2 Tbsp
Sugar 1 cup	Lemon juice 1 Tbsp
Cake flour 1 cup	Grated lemon rind 1 Tbsp
Salt 1/4 tsp (lightly measured)	

Mixing.   Yellow sponge cakes can be made by either separated or whole egg methods. In the whole egg method, the eggs are beaten until they are foamy. The water, lemon juice, and lemon rind are then added, and the mixture is beaten until it is as stiff as possible. (This mixture can be made very stiff.) The sugar is added gradually and beaten into the mixture. The flour and salt are mixed together and then sifted over the surface, about 2 tablespoons at a time, and folded into the egg mixture until all is well blended.

This method is desirable when preparing a very small recipe. It produces a cake no better than that produced by a method in which egg whites and yolks are separated, but it is difficult to beat one or two separated egg yolks as thoroughly as they should be beaten for best results.

In one separated egg method, the egg yolks are partially beaten. The sugar, salt, water, lemon juice, and lemon rind are added, and the whole mass is beaten until very stiff. The flour is folded lightly into the mixture, after which the stiffly beaten egg whites are folded in [5]. Alternatively, the stiffly beaten mixture of yolks, sugar, water, lemon juice and rind, and salt is combined with the beaten egg whites before the flour is folded into the mixture.

In a meringue method, the sugar is boiled with about three-fourths the volume of water to 244°F (118°C). It is then poured gradually over the beaten egg whites with constant stirring until a stiff meringue is formed. The egg yolks, lemon juice, lemon rind, and salt are beaten together until very stiff. The yolk mixture is folded into the whites, and the flour is then gradually folded in.

Certain types of emulsifiers may be used by commercial bakers of sponge cakes. These allow the use of a simplified one-stage mixing procedure and result in a lighter cake of uniform grain, greater tenderness, and longer shelf life.

Baking. Baking temperatures for sponge cakes are similar to those used for angel food cakes. Sponge cakes are toughened by overbaking.

COOKIES

Classification

Cookies are of six basic types. (1) *Rolled cookies*, when baked, may form either a crisp or a soft cookie depending on the proportions of the ingredients and the degree of doneness. (2) *Dropped cookies* are made from a stiff batter that may be dropped or scraped from the spoon. (3) *Bar cookies*, a cake-type mixture, are baked in a thin sheet and later cut into bars or squares. (4) *Pressed cookies* are made from an extra-rich stiff dough that is pressed through a cookie press into various shapes. (5) *Molded cookies* are made from a stiff dough that is shaped into balls, bars, or crescents and sometimes flattened before baking. (6) So-called *icebox* or *refrigerator cookies* are made from a mixture so rich in fat that the dough is difficult if not impossible to roll; it is chilled in the refrigerator to harden the fat and is then sliced from the roll or mold and baked (Figure 18-10 and Color Plate VIII).

Ingredients

Formulas for cookies are at least as varied as those for cakes. In general, the same ingredients that produce good cakes also produce good cookies. Cake flour is not generally used for cookies because few cookies have a soft, velvety crumb or the texture of good sponge or shortened cakes. All-purpose flour is satisfactory for most cookies; however, pastry flour may be used in some foodservice operations.

Crisp cookies are usually made from a mixture that is rich in fat or sugar or both. Many rolled cookie recipes call for little or no liquid. Because high volume is not desired in rolled cookies, the mixtures contain little or no leavening agent other than air incorporated into the creamed fat-sugar mixture.

Cookies are a major snack item in many countries of the world. Particularly in countries where wheat flour is imported but other flours are abundant, a composite flour may be used in the making of cookies. Cookies prepared from formulas containing 50 : 45 : 5 or 50 : 40 : 10 parts of wheat flour, rice flour, and defatted soy flour were found to be acceptable by both trained and consumer panels in Brazil [14]. These cookies were baked in a microwave oven as an alternative method for preventing nutrient degradation from extensive browning.

Cookie aroma is unique. Some of the volatile flavor compounds of cookies are formed during processing. For example, nonenzymatic (Maillard) browning reactions produce flavor compounds in the baking of cookies. Some of these sweet aroma compounds have been characterized [23], but a wide range of aromatic compounds are added to cookies during preparation, making the study of the final flavor profile more difficult. Extraction methods have been developed for the analysis of cookie aroma [26].

Texture is an important attribute in determining the acceptability of a cookie—some cookies being crisp whereas others are soft and chewy (Figure 18-11). Shortening has an important impact on the final texture. Various ingredients may be used to produce fat-reduced and/or calorie-reduced cookies with desirable texture characteristics. One suitable replacement for at least one-fourth

Figure 18-10
Several types of cookies are illustrated in this photograph. Beginning at the bottom center of the tray with the rolled bear cookies and proceeding clockwise, there are two kinds of bar cookies, drop cookies, pressed spritz cookies, Bavarian refrigerator cookies, and molded crescent cookies.
(Photograph by Chris Meister)

Drop Cookies are dropped onto the Cookie Sheet. Rolled out Cookies are cut into decorative shapes and placed carefully on the pan. (Courtesy of World Kitchens Inc., makers of Baker's Secret®)

(a)

Figure 18-11
(a) Many types of bar cookies can be prepared. Frosted cake-like bars, tender blonde brownies, and rich, fudge brownies are all tasty desserts.

(b)

(b) Drop cookie dough may be baked on a cookie sheet for individually sized crisp cookies, in a pan and cut into squares, or into a round pie pan and decorated for a special treat.
(Courtesy of Nestlé USA)

of the shortening, and for a portion of the sugar, in crisp oatmeal cookies has been reported to be Litesse™, which is a form of **polydextrose** [6]. Cellulose gums and mixtures of emulsifiers are also used in low- or reduced-fat cookies.

    The acceptability of cookies prepared with fat substitutes has been reported in the literature. In one study, oatmeal, peanut butter, and chocolate chip cookies were prepared with applesauce or prune puree to reduce the fat content [30]. The reduced-fat peanut butter cookies were the most difficult to prepare with acceptable quality attributes. Flavor acceptability in all of the cookies was impaired somewhat when fruit purees were used. However, the sensory panel did

polydextrose a condensation polymer of dextrose with minor amounts of sorbitol and citric acid; it contains only 1 kilocalorie per gram find the reduced-fat oatmeal and chocolate chip cookies to be acceptable. The use of pureed white beans as a fat substitute in oatmeal chocolate chip cookies also was found to prepare an acceptable cookie [27]. The cookies became less acceptable when the amount of beans was increased.

Mixing and Handling

The conventional method is used for mixing most cookies, but beaten egg whites are seldom added last. Cookies of the sponge type are made by sponge cake methods.

Doughs for rolled cookies are usually soft, but allow handling and rolling. Stiffer doughs and those rehandled and rerolled give dry, compact cookies. Many cookie mixtures must be chilled to facilitate rolling. Rolling only a portion of the dough at one time prevents continued rerolling. All trimmings can then be collected at the end for rerolling. Rolling between sheets of heavy waxed paper is sometimes done, but the usual method is to roll the dough on a floured board. Care must be used to avoid incorporating much extra flour into the dough while rolling it and to avoid having the cookie covered with excess flour when it is ready for baking. If excess flour is on the surface of the cut cookie dough, it will remain on the cookie after baking and mar the external appearance and flavor. A pastry cloth and stockinet-covered rolling pin may also be used for rolling cookies.

The thickness of rolled dough ready for cutting is usually 1/8 or 3/16 inch. If the dough is to be used for cutouts, especially large ones, it is good to roll it to a 1/4 inch thickness (Figure 18-12). In the removal of cut cookies from the board to the baking sheet, the use of the side, rather than the end, of a spatula usually avoids marring the shape of the cookie. Sticky cookie dough and dough that is rolled tightly to the board are difficult to remove by any method.

Dropped cookie mixtures vary in consistency depending on the finished product desired. Some mixtures are meant to be spread into a round, flat cookie of about 3/8 to 1/2 inch thickness after baking. Such mixtures produce softer cookies than the average rolled dough. Other dropped cookies are meant to hold their form. Judgment and experience with the recipe are necessary if too

Figure 18-12
These decorated gingerbread cookies are an example of a rolled and cutout cookie. Decorations add the final touch. (Courtesy of World Kitchens Inc., makers of Baker's Secret®)

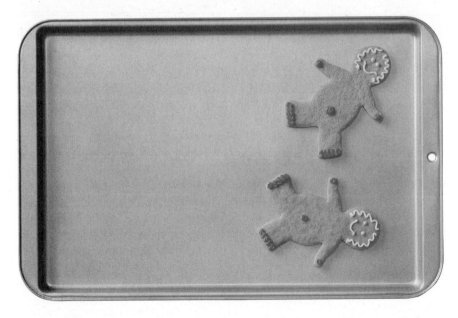

stiff or too soft a mixture is to be avoided. A mixture that is stiff enough to hold its form almost completely while baking usually produces a dry, breadlike cookie that may crack on top while baking. A cookie that only partially holds its shape during baking is usually of a more desirable texture and eating quality and has a better appearance. The type of mixture partially determines how stiff it can be without producing undesirable results. A mixture very rich in fat can be stiffer than a leaner mixture. Practically all mixtures will be stiff enough to require scraping rather than dropping from the spoon if they are expected to hold their form fairly well. Flour of strong gluten quality tends to produce a dry, breadlike drop cookie, particularly if the mixture is very stiff before baking.

Baking

Baking sheets rather than cake pans are more efficient for baking most cookies, because there are no high side walls to interfere with the circulation of heat. Cookies baked in pans with high sides may cook until they are done, but their

---

Healthy Eating

Sugar or sucralose? Tips for baking

Athough people with diabetes may include small amounts of sugar in their diets, they still have to include this sugar in a total allowance of carbohydrate for the day. Thus a diabetics's diet may be extremely *unbalanced* if a high-sugar—and usually also high-fat—dessert is consumed frequently. Sugar substitutes or alternative sweeteners come to the rescue to provide sweetness without carbohydrate or calories, making it easier to enjoy more frequently some of the foods they used to love.

Sugar substitutes have been used for many years, beginning with saccharin. (Alternative sweeteners are discussed in Chapter 11.) One of these products, approved by the FDA in 1998, is sucralose. Sucralose is a chlorinated derivative of sugar (sucrose) but is 600 times sweeter and is not absorbed and metabolized in the body. Also important, it does not have an aftertaste, as do some of the other sugar substitutes. In addition, it withstands prolonged heat treatment and can therefore be used in baking. Sucralose is now being marketed in granular form for easy measuring under the brand name of Splenda®. In this product, sucralose is blended with maltodextrin so that, for sweetness, 1 teaspoon or 1 cup of Splenda® is equivalent to 1 teaspoon or 1 cup of sugar. We should probably mention, however, that Splenda® is considerably more expensive than sugar.

As you know, sugar in baking does much more than sweeten. Sugar tenderizes, contributes to browning, aids in moisture retention, gives structure, and adds volume to a baked product. Thus it is obvious that some adjustments for sucralose substitution must be made. Therefore, several tips may be useful as you begin to experiment in baking with Splenda®.

Proportions of other ingredients can be adjusted to make up for differences in the total volume of a recipe. The addition of small amounts of honey, molasses, cocoa, or other dark ingredients can help achieve browning and increase moistness. Addition of nonfat dry milk powder and baking soda may help in adapting a cake recipe to the use of Splenda® instead of sugar. Check your baked goods sweetened with Splenda® for doneness a little earlier than for the sugar sweetened product because they bake more quickly. The Splenda® sweetened products will last longer if stored in a refrigerator. Splenda® granular may be successfully incorporated into a recipe by (1) combining it thoroughly with other dry ingredients, (2) dissolving it in the liquid, or (3) creaming it with fat in the recipe [28].

Many recipes for cakes, cookies, and pies using Splenda® are available on the Internet [28]. You may enjoy experimenting with this product.

tops may be only slightly browned, or not at all. Bar cookies are usually baked in pans with sides, however. Baking sheets require no greasing for rolled or refrigerator cookies, which are rich in fat, but do require greasing for dropped cookies or cookie bars. Cookie dough should be put on cool cookie sheets, since the dough will melt and spread if it is placed on a hot pan. You may want to bake a test cookie first to be sure that the consistency of the dough is just right. If the cookie is too flat, additional flour may be added to the dough. Rolled cookies spread little in baking, so little space is needed between them. Icebox cookies spread somewhat more, and dropped cookies must have space to spread.

The methods used to test for doneness of cakes are generally not effective for most cookies. Cookies should be lightly brown and may still appear to be slightly moist when ready to be removed from the oven. Cookies will be affected by carryover baking and therefore will continue to "bake" after removal from the oven. Failure to take into account this carryover cooking will result in cookies that are very crisp or hard after cooling. Fudge brownies and some other bar cookies can be especially difficult to assess. These bar cookies, unlike cakes, should be slightly moist when removed from the oven.

Several cookie doughs ready for baking are marketed in the refrigerated state. The dough is spooned or molded into balls and baked. One company markets cookie dough in the form of little balls or pieces that are frozen and packaged, which allows the option of baking part of the package, if desired. Ready-to-bake brownies are also available, as either frozen or refrigerated doughs, for both microwaving and conventional baking.

Some restaurants with buffet-type service bake cookies on a continuous basis for customer consumption. The dough is previously prepared but baked where customers can see the process and smell the aroma.

CHAPTER SUMMARY

- Cakes are generally classified into two major groups: shortened cakes or cakes containing fat, and unshortened cakes or cakes with no fat. Chiffon cakes could be considered a third category. Cookies are different from cakes in texture and formula.

- Shortened cakes are of two types: pound cake and standard shortened cake. The pound cake generally has no leavening agent except for air incorporated in the creaming of the fat and sugar and in the beaten eggs. Pound cakes have a close grain and are somewhat compact, yet they are very tender.

- Standard shortened cakes are leavened chiefly by carbon dioxide gas from baking powder or soda and milk. A good standard shortened cake has a fine grain, cells of uniform size, thin cell walls, and a crumb that is elastic rather than crumbly. Crusts should be thin and tender.

- Usual ingredients in a standard shortened cake include sugar, fat, egg, liquid, a leavening agent, salt, and flour.

- Sugar adds sweetness to a shortened cake, but it also has an important effect on texture and volume. Sugar interfers with gluten development from the flour, delays the gelatinization of starch, and decreases the cohesive forces in the cake batter. Excess sugar in a cake formula may result in a fallen cake with a coarse texture and a gummy crust and crumb. Although sucrose is most commonly used in cakes, other kinds of sugar may be used.

- The optimum amount of egg in a given mixture produces finer cells, thinner cell walls, and usually a larger volume than are obtained with a lower or higher percentage of egg. Excess eggs in a recipe give a rubbery, tough crumb.

- Fat weakens structure and tends to decrease volume when added beyond the optimum amount. Butter is reported to make cakes that are tender and velvetlike, whereas hydrogenated shortening produces cakes with even grain. In addition to tenderizing, plastic fats aid in incorporating air into the batter as a result of creaming the fat and sugar together. When substituting shortening for butter, the different percent of fat in these two products should be taken into account. Fat replacers have been successfully used in shortened cakes.

- Emulsifying agents in cake batter cause the fat to be distributed more finely throughout the mixture and allow the cake formula to carry more sugar than flour. Shortenings that contain small amounts of emulsifiers are sometimes called high-ratio shortenings.

- Cakes may be leavened by baking powder, baking soda, air entrapped in creamed shortening or beaten egg whites, and steam.

- Flour contributes structure to shortened cakes. Too little flour has the same effect as too much fat or sugar. Excess flour produces a compact, dry cake in which tunnels form readily. Cake flour produces high quality cakes. Cakes made with all-purpose flour are generally lower in volume and have a coarser texture than cakes made with cake flour.

- Liquid performs a variety of functions in cake. Liquid dissolves dry ingredients, allows the reaction of baking powder or soda, disperses ingredients, hydrates starch and protein, and when heated produces steam. Excess liquid in a cake formula results in a moist, low volume cake.

- A smaller percentage of flour is used in chocolate cakes because of the starch content of the cocoa and chocolate. The color of chocolate cakes will vary as the level of acidity or alkalinity changes.

- Four common methods of mixing cakes are the conventional method, conventional sponge method, muffin method, and quick-mix method.

- The amount of mixing needed for a high quality cake varies with the ingredient proportions and the batter quantity. Undermixed cakes may yield a cake of good volume, but the texture is coarse and the cell walls thick. Overmixing tends to produce a compact cake of smaller volume. Although the texture may be fine, overmixed cakes may have tunnels or become heavy or soggy.

- Pans should be prepared by greasing, or greasing and flouring before the batter is mixed. Cake batters that are allowed to stand in the bowl may result in cakes with less than an optimum volume and texture.

- The oven temperatures commonly used for baking shortened cakes range from 350° to 375°F (177° to 191°C). If dark, dull pans are used the cake will brown more readily than if bright, shiny pans are used. Cakes should not be removed from the pan until cooled to about 140°F (60°C) so that the cake is firm enough to handle. Cakes may be satisfactorily baked in the microwave; however, a brown crust will not be formed.

- Unshortened cakes are of two types: white angel food, which is made from egg whites, and yellow sponge, which is made from whole egg.

- A desirable angel food cake is porous, springy, tender, moist, of large volume, and has thin cell walls. Air accounts for approximately half of the leavening in angel food cakes, but steam also plays a role. Egg whites incorporate air as they are beaten to form a foam. Flour increases the strength of the cake crumb and contributes to structure. Cake flour produces a more tender, delicate angel food cake as compared to flours with stronger gluten quality. Sugar has a stabilizing effect on the egg white foam, sweetens the cake, and aids in browning. Cream of tartar is an important ingredient in angel food cakes because of its beneficial effect on color, volume, and tenderness.

- Yellow sponge cakes may be made by either separated or whole egg methods.
- Pans are not greased for angel food or yellow sponge cakes. Baking at 350°F (177°C) has been found to produce a tender cake with a large volume and thin cell walls. After baking, the pan is inverted and allowed to stand until the cake is thoroughly cooled. Both angel food and sponge cakes will toughen if overbaked.
- Cookies are of six basic types: (1) rolled, (2) dropped, (3) bar cookies, (4) pressed cookies, (5) molded cookies, and (6) icebox or refrigerator cookies. Formulas for cookies, like cake formulas, are varied.
- Crisp cookies are usually made from a mixture that is rich in fat or sugar, or both. Shortening also has an important impact on the final texture. Acceptable cookies may be prepared using fat substitutes, although in general the quality of cookies containing fat is perceived more favorably.
- The conventional method is used for mixing most cookies. The consistency of the cookie dough will vary with the type of cookie being prepared.
- Cookies should be lightly browned and may still appear to be slightly moist when ready to be removed from the oven. Cookies will be affected by carry-over baking and therefore will continue to "bake" after removal from the oven

KEY TERMS

impingement oven   polydextrose

STUDY QUESTIONS

1. Shortened cakes are of two types. Name them and describe distinguishing characteristics of each.
2. Describe the usual role and the effect of an excessive amount of each of the following ingredients in the production of a shortened cake.
   a. Sugar
   b. Egg
   c. Fat
   d. Baking powder
   e. Liquid
   f. Flour
3. What role is played by an emulsifier in a shortened cake batter, and what effect does it have on the finished product?
4. Briefly describe each of the following methods for mixing a shortened cake and explain advantages or disadvantages of each method.
   a. Conventional
   b. Conventional sponge
   c. Muffin
   d. Quick-mix
5. Describe the effects of under- and overmixing a shortened cake batter. What factors affect the desirable amount of mixing to be done?

6. Why is it important to prepare the pans for a shortened cake batter before the batter is mixed? Explain.

7. Suggest an appropriate temperature for baking a shortened cake and explain why this temperature is recommended.

8. Why should a shortened cake be allowed to stand for about 10 minutes after baking before removal from the pan?

9. a. Name and describe characteristics of two types of unshortened cakes.
   b. What is a *chiffon cake?*

10. Describe the usual role of each of the following ingredients in angel food cake.
   a. Egg whites
   b. Sugar
   c. Cream of tartar
   d. Flour

11. a. Describe appropriate methods for mixing angel food and sponge cakes.
   b. Point out precautions that should be taken in the mixing of unshortened cakes to ensure finished cakes of good quality.

12. Suggest appropriate baking temperatures for angel food and sponge cakes.

13. How should angel food and sponge cakes be cooled after baking and why?

14. a. Describe six basic types of cookies.
   b. Suggest some precautions that are necessary in the preparation of rolled cookies of good quality.
   c. What types of baking pans are generally recommended for cookies and why?

REFERENCES

1. American Association of Family and Consumer Science. (2001). *Food: A handbook of terminology, purchasing, & preparation* (10th ed.). Alexandria, VA: American Association of Family and Consumer Sciences.

2. Barmore, M. A. (1936). *The influence of various factors including altitude in the production of angel food cake.* Colorado State University Experiment Station Technical Bulletin No. 15.

3. Bean, M. M., Yamazaki, W. T., & Donelson, D. H. (1978). Wheat starch gelatinization in sugar solutions. II. Fructose, glucose, and sucrose: Cake performance. *Cereal Chemistry, 55,* 945.

4. Berglund, P. T., & Hertsgaard, D. M. (1986). Use of vegetable oils at reduced levels in cake, pie crust, cookies, and muffins. *Journal of Food Science, 51,* 640.

5. Briant, A. M., & Willman, A. R. (1956). Whole-egg sponge cakes. *Journal of Home Economics, 48,* 420.

6. Campbell, L. A., Ketelsen, S. M., & Antenucci, R. N. (1994). Formulating oatmeal cookies with calorie-sparing ingredients. *Food Technology, 48*(5), 98.

7. Coleman, P. E., & Harbers, C. A. Z. (1983). High fructose corn syrup: Replacement for sucrose in angel cake. *Journal of Food Science, 48,* 452.

8. Donelson, J. R., Gaines, C. S., & Finney, P. L. (2000). Baking formula innovation to eliminate chlorine treatment of cake flour. *Cereal Chemistry, 77*(1), 53–57.

9. Ebeler, S. E., Breyer, L. M., & Walker, C. E. (1986). White layer cake batter emulsion characteristics: Effects of sucrose ester emulsifiers. *Journal of Food Science, 51,* 1276.

10. Elgidaily, D. A., Funk, K., & Zabik, M. E. (1969). Baking temperature and quality of angel cakes. *Journal of the American Dietetic Association, 54,* 401.

11. Franks, O. J., Zabik, M. E., & Funk, K. (1969). Angel cakes using frozen, foam-spray-dried, freeze-dried, and spray-dried albumen. *Cereal Chemistry, 46,* 349.

12. Fulton, L., & Hogbin, M. (1993). Eating quality of muffins, cake, and cookies prepared with reduced fat and sugar. *Journal of the American Dietetic Association, 93,* 1313.

13. Gaines, C. S., & Donelson, J. R. (1982). Contribution of chlorinated flour fractions to cake crumb stickiness. *Cereal Chemistry, 59,* 378.

14. Gonzales-Galan, A., Wang, S. H., Sgarbieri, V. C., & Moraes, M. A. C. (1991). Sensory and nutritional properties of cookies based on wheat-rice-soybean flours baked in a microwave oven. *Journal of Food Science, 56,* 1699.

15. Kim, C. S., & Walker, C. E. (1992). Changes in starch pasting properties due to sugars and emulsifiers as determined by viscosity measurement. *Journal of Food Science, 57,* 1009.

16. Lawless, S. T., Gregoire, M. B., Canter, D. D., & Setser, C. S. (1991). Comparison of cakes produced from computer-generated recipes. *School Food Service Research Review, 15*(1), 23.

17. Lawson, W. (1985). *Standards for fats and oils.* Westport, Conn.: Avi Publishing Company, Inc.

18. Li, A., & Walker, C. E. (1996). Cake baking in conventional, impingement and hybrid ovens. *Journal of Food Science, 61,* 188.

19. Matthews, R. H., & Dawson, E. H. (1966). Performance of fats in white cake. *Cereal Chemistry, 43,* 538.

20. McCullough, M. A. P., Johnson, J. M., & Phillips, J. A. (1986). High fructose corn syrup replacement for sucrose in shortened cakes. *Journal of Food Science, 51,* 536.

21. Molt, M. (2001). *Food for Fifty* (11th ed.). Upper Saddle River, NJ: Prentice Hall.

22. Ngo, W., Hoseney, R. C., & Moore, W. R. (1985). Dynamic rheological properties of cake batters made from chlorine-treated and untreated flours. *Journal of Food Science, 50,* 1338.

23. Nishibori, S., & Kawakishi, S. (1990). Effects of dough materials on flavor formation in baked cookies. *Journal of Food Science, 55,* 409.

24. Paton, D., Larocque, G. M., & Holme, J. (1981). Development of cake structure: Influence of ingredients on the measurement of cohesive force during baking. *Cereal Chemistry, 58,* 527.

25. Pohl, P. H., Mackey, A. C., & Cornelia, B. L. (1968). Freeze-drying cake batter for microscopic study. *Journal of Food Science, 33,* 318.

26. Prost, C., Lee, C. Y., Giampaoli, P., & Richard, H. (1993). Extraction of cookie aroma compounds from aqueous and dough model system. *Journal of Food Science, 58,* 586.

27. Rankin, L. L., & Bingham, M. (2000). Acceptability of oatmeal chocolate chip cookies prepared using pureed white beans as a fat ingredient substitute. *Journal of American Dietetic Association, 100,* 831–833.

28. Splenda. (n.d.). Cooking and baking tips. Retrieved December 2, 2002, from www.splenda.com

29. Stinson, C. T. (1986). A quality comparison of devil's food and yellow cakes baked in a microwave/convection versus a conventional oven. *Journal of Food Science, 51,* 1578.

30. Swanson, R. B. & Musayac, L. J. (1999). Acceptability of fruit purees in peanut butter, oatmeal, and chocolate-chip reduced-fat cookies. *Journal of the American Dietetic Association, 99,* 343–345.

31. Thomasson, C. A., Miller, R. A., and Hoseney, R. C. (1995). Replacement of chlorine treatment for cake flour. *Cereal Chemistry, 72*(6), 616–620.

32. Waring, S. (1988). Shortening replacement in cakes. *Food Technology, 42*(3), 114.

Pastry

19

 Pastries are products made from doughs containing moderate to large amounts of fat and mixed in such a way as to produce flakiness. Note the following three examples.

1. Plain pastry or pie crust is used to make all types of tarts, turnovers, and dessert pies, including single- and double-crust fruit pies (Figure 19-1); custard-type pies baked in the shell; and soft starch-thickened cream pies and gelatin-based chiffon pies in which the fillings are added after the pie shells are baked. (Plate IX)

2. Plain pastry is also used as a carrier of high-protein foods to be served as a main dish: various types of meat, poultry, and fish pies with single or double crusts; patty shells to hold chicken à la king and similar types of creamed mixtures; and quiches, which are pies that can be made with a variety of ingredients, such as bacon, ham, Swiss cheese, mushrooms, onions, and other vegetables, baked in a custard-type filling (Figure 19-2).

3. Puff pastry—flaky layers of light, buttery dough—is used to make crisp, sugar-glazed and cream-filled French pastry or flaky sweet rolls called *Danish pastry* (Figure 19-3). Puff pastry is made by rolling chilled butter in a well-kneaded flour-and-water dough, then folding and rerolling several times to make many thin layers of dough separated by thin layers of butter. During baking, the butter melts and permeates the dough.

This chapter focuses on the making of plain pastry.

CHARACTERISTICS OF PLAIN PASTRY

Good-quality pastry is tender but does not easily break when served. It is flaky, with a blistered surface, is slightly crisp, evenly and lightly browned, and pleasantly flavored.

Flakiness

Flakiness is described as thin layers of baked dough separated by open spaces (Figure 19-4). Some factors that have been found to affect flakiness are (1) the character of the fat used (solid versus melted or liquid fat), (2) the consistency of solid fat, (3) the type of flour used, (4) the proportion of water, (5) the degree of

Figure 19-1

A lattice-top fruit pie. (Courtesy of Sun-Maid Growers of California)

mixing, (6) the method of mixing, and (7) the number of times the dough is rolled.

Flakiness is thought to result from a process in which small particles of fat are coated with moistened flour or dough and then flattened into thin layers when the dough mixture is rolled out. On baking, the fat melts, is absorbed by the surrounding dough, and leaves empty spaces between thin layers of the baked dough.

Solid fats yield a flaky crust more easily than melted or liquid fats; however, flaky pastry can be produced with melted fats or oils. Liquid fats generally tend to blend more completely with flour. They may yield a very tender and crumbly crust when used in the same proportion as solid fats.

Figure 19-2

A quiche that contains fresh sliced mushrooms, sliced green onions, and shredded Swiss cheese. The custard base is made with eggs and light cream or milk. (Courtesy of the American Egg Board)

Firm fats that remain in layers when they are rolled yield a flakier crust
than soft fats. The method used in making puff pastry, in which the fat is reserved to be rolled between the layers of dough, increases flakiness. Merely
rerolling increases flakiness, but unless the percentage of fat in the mixture is
high, rerolling may also develop the gluten sufficiently to increase toughness.
Rerolling as a means of increasing flakiness is valuable chiefly for puff pastry.

A regular pastry flour may yield a very flaky crust, but flakiness increases with
the strength of gluten. Toughness may also increase with the use of a stronger
flour unless additional fat is used and greater care is taken in manipulation.

Tenderness

Because tenderness is one of the most desirable characteristics of good pastry, it
requires at least as much consideration as flakiness; yet some of the factors that
produce flakiness tend to decrease tenderness and vice versa. Tenderness is at a

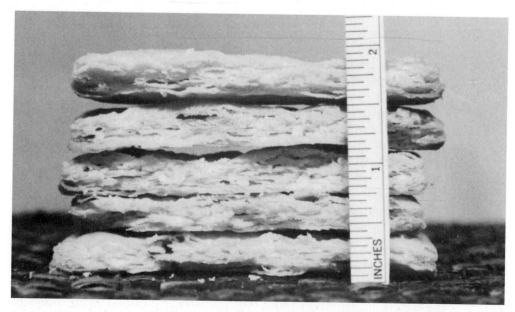

Figure 19-4
A very flaky pastry can be made with lard as the fat.

maximum when the fat spreads over the flour particles, interferes with the hydration of gluten proteins in the flour, and thus decreases the formation of gluten strands. If the fat blends too thoroughly with the dough, the crust is too tender to handle and tends to be crumbly. Adjustments in both ingredients and techniques of mixing and handling must be made so that both flakiness and tenderness are achieved in the baked pastry.

INGREDIENTS IN PLAIN PASTRY

Plain pastry contains only a few ingredients—flour, fat, salt, and water. Either pastry or all-purpose flour can be used; pastry flour requires less fat for optimum tenderness and is used primarily by commercial bakers. Because of the larger amount of gluten formed with all-purpose flour, about 1/3 cup of fat per cup of flour may be needed to produce a tender crust. This proportion is also dependent on the kind of fat used and the skill of the handler.

The amount of water required for plain pastry varies with the hydration capacity of the flour, the amount and type of fat, the temperature of the ingredients, and the individual technique of handling. An excessive amount of water added in the making of pastry dough allows the hydration and development of more gluten than is desirable for optimum tenderness. Toughness of pastry is therefore increased by too much water in the dough. Too little water produces a dry dough that is crumbly and difficult to handle. The amount of liquid should be sufficient to barely form a dough; the dough should not be wet and sticky [7].

Fat is responsible for the tenderness of pastry because it spreads over the particles of flour and retards their hydration. Fats vary in their tenderizing properties [6]. Liquid oils spread more than plastic fats and usually have greater tenderizing power. Reduction of the level of soybean or safflower oil in pie crust results in a product that compares favorably in quality characteristics with pie crust made with a standard level of shortening [1]. Softer plastic fats spread more readily than harder fats. Butter and margarine contain only about 80 percent fat and therefore have less tenderizing power than 100 percent fats such as lard and hydrogenated shortening when substituted on a weight basis. A cup of lard weighs more than a cup of hydrogenated shortening because the shortening has been precreamed and contains an inert gas to make it lighter. In addition to the role of fat in tenderizing, plastic fats, in particular, play an important part in the development of flakiness in pastry.

Plain pastry is leavened primarily by steam, which is produced by baking in a hot oven. Leavening in plain pastry is not extensive, however.

Very hard fat, direct from the refrigerator, and iced water are not necessary in the making of pastry. The fat should be cold enough to be firm rather than pasty or oily, but plastic enough to be measured accurately and to cut into the flour. In warm weather, some chilling of fat may be necessary. Likewise, some chilling of water may be required, but both water and fat at room temperature can produce good results.

TECHNIQUES OF MIXING

Fat can be cut into the flour with a pastry blender or with a knife or spatula. It can even be lightly blended with the fingers (Figure 19-5). Electric mixers or food processors can also be used both to mix the fat with the flour and to mix the liquid with the fat-flour mixture in the final stages of dough preparation.

Figure 19-5
Fat may be cut into the flour with a pastry cutter, knife, or by hand as shown here.

However, care must be taken to avoid overmixing. A reasonably uniform blending of fat with flour produces a more uniformly tender crust. Fat particles may vary in size. Cutting of the fat into particles the size of peas is generally suggested. Those who favor a relatively coarse division of fat in the flour-salt mixture do so on the theory that flakiness is increased by the rolling of larger fat masses into thin layers.

Unless sufficient water is added, the baked crust will be too tender and crumbly; however, too much water toughens the pastry. Gluten forms to a greater than desirable extent when water is used in excessive amounts [4].

Several methods of mixing pastry, other than the traditional pastry method shown in Figure 19-6, have been suggested. A satisfactory pastry product can be obtained by using any one of these methods. A modified method of mixing pastry has been developed in which 1/4 cup of a 2 cup portion of flour is reserved to be mixed with liquid to form a paste. After the fat and the remainder of the flour have been combined as described, the paste is added all at once and blended with the fat-flour mixture.

In the hot water method of mixing pastry, solid fats can be melted by stirring them into boiling water; this mixture is then stirred into the flour and salt. If oil is used as the fat, it can be shaken with water and added in a similar manner. Alternatively, the oil can be sprinkled over the flour-salt mixture followed by stirring to disperse the oil. The water can then be added as in the traditional method. Pastry made by the hot water and oil methods may be somewhat less flaky than pastry made by the traditional method.

Pastry can also be made by a modified puff pastry method: About 2 tablespoons of the fat-flour mixture are removed before the liquid is added. After the pastry has been rolled out, this fat-flour mixture is sprinkled over the dough. The dough is rolled up like a jelly roll and cut into two pieces. One piece is placed on top of the other, and they are then rerolled for the pie pan. This method tends to increase flakiness in pastry.

ROLLING PASTRY

Pastry can be rolled as soon as it has been mixed, but allowing the dough to stand for a few minutes increases the extensibility or elasticity of the dough, making it easier to handle and to roll. When the work area is warm, refrigeration of the dough before rolling can help maintain flakiness. For ordinary pie crust, the dough is rolled to about 1/8 inch thickness. Enough flour is required for the board to keep the crust from sticking, but the minimum amount should

1. After the flour and salt are measured and mixed together in the bowl, the shortening is cut in with a pastry blender.

2. Sprinkle the water, a tablespoon at a time, over the flour-fat mixture.

6. Divide dough approximately in half; round up larger part on a lightly floured cloth-covered board.

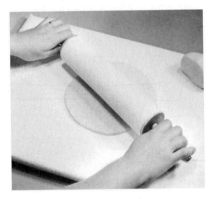

7. Roll out not quite 1/8 inch thick.

be used to avoid toughening the pastry. Occasional lifting of the crust while rolling also tends to prevent sticking. The dough can be rolled on a canvas-covered board, into which a small amount of flour has been rubbed, or between two layers of waxed paper. Crusts that are rolled very thin become too brown when baked as pie shells and break in handling or in serving. If they are used for fruit pies, they may break during baking and allow juices to flow out.

Crusts are rolled into a circular shape. The dough for a lower crust or a pie shell should be about 1 to 2 inches greater in diameter than the top of the pan, which allows for variable pan depth (Figure 19-6). To avoid excessive rolling of dough, which toughens the pastry, each crust is rolled separately. For future use, the rolled pastry can be frozen before baking [2], or the baked shells can be frozen.

Although pie shells tend to shrink somewhat in baking, excessive shrinkage can be prevented if the dough is not stretched when it is fitted into the pan. Preparing enough dough to make a rim or a frilled edge is also an advantage if shrinking occurs. Overdevelopment of the gluten by rerolling may result in greater shrinkage during baking than occurs when gluten is not developed to an appreciable extent.

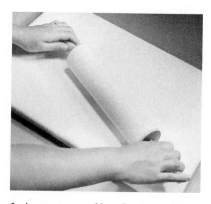

3. Mix lightly with a fork until all the flour is moistened.

4. Gather the dough together with your fingers and press into a ball.

5. A canvas-covered board and a stockinet-covered rolling pin prevent the pastry from sticking while being rolled out.

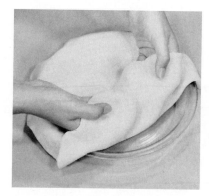

8. Keep the pastry circular and roll it about 1 to 2 inches larger than the pie pan.

9. Fold the pastry in half. Quickly transfer to a pie pan and unfold.

10. Fit the pastry carefully down into the pan. Avoid trapping air underneath the dough. Trim off the overhanging edges. Place the filling in the pastry-lined pan. Roll out the other part of the dough for the top crust.

The formation of large blisters in pastry shells during baking can be prevented by forcing air from under the dough while fitting the dough into the pan and by pricking the dough adequately with a fork before baking. Crusts in which fillings are to be cooked are never pricked.

Top crusts for fruit pies are less likely to break under the pressure of steam if small openings are made near the center for the escape of steam. Large gashes should be avoided because they are unattractive and permit the loss of juices. Making the air vents into the decoration results in an attractive pie (Figure 19-7). Top crusts adhere more closely to lower crusts if the latter are moistened with water before the crusts are pressed together.

BAKING

Plain pastry that is baked prior to the addition of the filling is baked at a hot oven temperature (425°F to 450°F or 218° to 232°C). This heat allows rapid production of steam, which separates the layers of dough formed as the fat

Maillard reaction the carbonyl group of sugar combines with the amino group of a protein, initiating a series of chemical reactions which result in a brown color and change in flavor.

particles melt. Baking is continued until the surface is delicately browned, which probably occurs chiefly as a result of the **Maillard reaction.**

Baking temperatures are adjusted according to the type of filling in pastry shells. The filling must be adequately cooked before the crust becomes too brown. Soaking of bottom crusts by fruit and custard fillings sometimes creates problems in baking.

Preventing Soaked Crusts

Many methods have been suggested and tried for preventing soaked crust in fruit, custard, and pumpkin pies. Some methods—partially baking the crust, coating the crust with raw egg white, or heating the crust until the egg white is coagulated—have no value. A partially baked crust becomes more soaked than one that is not baked. It also tends to be heavy or soggy. Raw egg white, being soluble in water, blends with the filling, thus offering no protection against the soaking of the crust.

So how can the crusts be protected? For fruit pies, you can coat the upper surface of the lower crust with melted butter, use a hot oven temperature for the first 15 minutes of baking, and thicken the filling before placing it in the pastry-lined pan. Thickening the filling gives you the added advantage of knowing the precise consistency of the juice before the pie is baked.

For custard and pumpkin pies, the problem of soaked crusts is even more difficult to solve. The lower baking temperatures required for egg mixtures prolong the baking time and permit increased soaking before the pie is done. A method that has been suggested to improve the crusts of custard pies is chilling the pastry for 1 hour before adding the filling, and using a high oven temperature (450°F or 232°C) for the first 10 minutes of baking. Increasing the percentage of egg in the mixture (three eggs per pint of milk) lowers the coagulation temperature of the egg proteins and increases the ease of coagulation for the mixture. Scalding the milk used for the filling also shortens coagulation time. A coagulated custard does not penetrate the crust as readily as an uncooked mixture. An overcooked custard may exude sufficient water to produce a wet crust.

Using a Microwave Oven

Microwaved pastry is tender, flaky, and puffy, but it does not brown. A few drops of yellow food coloring can be added to the dough, or the pastry can be brushed with egg yolk before microwaving. A one-crust pastry shell is cooked on high power for about 6 or 7 minutes, the dish being rotated one half turn after 3 minutes. Alternatively, the pastry shell can be baked in a conventional oven and the filling cooked in a microwave oven. Commercial pie filling mixes are easily prepared by mixing the packet contents with milk and cooking on a high-power setting for 2 to 3 minutes with periodic stirring.

The bottom crust of a two-crust pie can be cooked by microwave on a medium setting for 5 to 6 minutes, the uncooked filling added, the top crust put in place, and the pie cooked again. The pie should be turned midway in the cooking period. If a broiling unit is not available for browning, the pie can be finished by baking for 10 to 15 minutes in a hot conventional oven. Meringues can be cooked by microwaves but must be browned in a conventional heating unit.

Prepared Pie Crust

Homemade pie crusts can be frozen baked or unbaked for later use. Alternatively, partially prepared pie crust is available on the market in several forms. Ready-to-bake pie crust in aluminum pie pans is sold as a frozen product. Instructions generally suggest that the dough be thawed before baking. If the product is to be used in the preparation of a fruit pie, however, it should be filled with the fruit and put in to bake without being thawed. Rolled sheets of pie crust, enclosed in plastic sheets and folded, are sold as refrigerated dough. They should be allowed to warm to the degree that they are pliable before being unfolded and placed in a pie pan for baking. Pie crust is also marketed as a dry mix that needs only the addition of water to form a dough that can be rolled and placed in pie pans.

OTHER TYPES OF PASTRY AND CRUSTS

Crumb, Cookie, and Sweet Tart Crusts

The bottom crust on pies as well as some other desserts such as cheesecakes may be made from crumbs. Graham cracker crumbs are frequently used; sugar cookies, chocolate sandwich cookies, gingersnaps, and other cookies may be

Hot Topics

Acrylamide—A carcinogen in foods?

A major media news release from a research group in Sweden in July 2002 alerted the whole world to the presence of a potential carcinogen formed in some starchy foods cooked at high temperatures. The whole world seemed to listen—nobody wants to think that the food they are eating is cancer-causing.

The substance in question—acrylamide—is a colorless, crystalline chemical structure that is classified by the U.S. Environmental Protection Agency as a medium hazard and probable carcinogen. It is used in the manufacture of plastics and in a water purification process. Acrylamide is known to cause cancer in laboratory animals but no studies on its relationship to cancer in humans have been done. Its possible role in this regard cannot even be predicted at present. When investigated in rats, its carcinogenic potential appeared to be similar to that of aromatic hydrocarbons formed in meats when they are fried or grilled [3]. The question is—At what level of intake is there a risk to humans? And how much acrylamide is present in foods? The foods analyzed included staples such as bread, French fries, and processed cereals.

The Swedish findings brought an immediate response from several governmental agencies concerned with food. A U.N. World Health Organization/Food and Agriculture Organization consultation, which included representatives of the U.S. Food and Drug Administration (FDA), met in June 2002 and reported that the average intake of acrylamide by consumers appears to be below levels which produce nerve damage but that its presence in food is a major concern because of its carcinogenic potential. The FDA issued a statement assuring the public that it is carefully analyzing the research findings in this area and will make this analysis an integral part of its ongoing assessment of the scope and significance of the presence of acrylamide in foods. Until further information and research is available, a change in usual dietary habits because of the Swedish study is not recommended [3]. The world has indeed been alerted, however, and we will all watch closely for further developments, particularly for those involving our favorite breads and baked cereal products.

crumbed and used (Figure 19-8). The typical ratio of ingredients in crumb crusts is one part melted butter, two parts sugar, and four parts crumbs [5]. When cookies are used instead of graham cracker crumbs, the amount of sugar may need to be decreased.

The preparation of crumb crusts is generally quick and easy. The crumbs, sugar, and melted butter are blended. If the mixture is too dry to stick together,

Figure 19-8

This cream cheese pumpkin dessert has a tasty gingersnap crumb crust. (Courtesy of McCormick & Co. Inc.)

additional melted butter may be slowly added until the desired consistency is achieved. Then the crumbs are pressed into the bottom of the pan to a depth between 1/8 and 1/4 inch. This crust may be refrigerated and then filled after the butter has firmed or baked in an oven preheated to 350°F (177°C) for about 10 minutes or until lightly browned and then filled. Baked crusts will be firmer and will provide a stronger crust.

Tart crusts may be made from a sweet dough that usually contains egg yolk [5]. The fat is blended in thoroughly in a mixing procedure similar to making cookies as opposed to the mixing procedure for standard pie pastry. These sweet dough crusts generally are not flaky like other pie crusts, but have the advantage of being crisp and sturdy. These characteristics are desirable for tarts, which are usually made in a shallow, straight-sided pan (Figure 19-9).

Puff Pastry and Phyllo Dough

Puff pastry is a rich dough that separates into many light, crisp layers when baked. Steam is the leavening agent in this dough and the rolling into the dough of a sheet of butter results in the flaky layers that are charateristic of puff pastry. Making puff pastry from scratch requires care and patience, as the chilled dough must be rolled multiple times to create the layers from the butter that has been folded and rolled into the dough. Alternatively, puff pasty is available frozen for use in creating a number of desserts and other dishes.

Phyllo dough is a paper thin pastry that is bland in flavor. It is used in Mediterranean, Middle Eastern, and Central Asian dishes [5]. Phyllo dough is generally purchased frozen because of the time and skill required to make this dough. Sheets of phyllo dough may be layered into custard cups to prepare phyllo cups that can be filled with a custard or cheese filling and topped with fruit. Phyllo dough also is used for the classic Greek dessert called baklava. Frozen phyllo dough should be thawed slowly in the refrigerator because attempts to thaw phyllo dough quickly create difficulties in separating and handling the sheets. While working with phyllo dough it should be covered with plastic wrap to prevent it from drying out. Many recipes will call for the dough to be lifted one sheet at a time and placed in the pan and brushed with butter before adding another sheet and repeating the process.

Figure 19-9
This sweet dough tart shell has been filled with a pastry cream and topped with carefully arranged fruit. A fruit glaze will finish this beautiful dessert.

CHAPTER SUMMARY

- Pastries are products made from doughs containing moderate to large amounts of fats and mixed in such a way as to produce flakiness. Pie crust, puff pastry, and phyllo dough are examples.

- Good-quality pastry is tender but does not easily break when served. It is flaky with a blistered surface, is slightly crisp, evenly and lightly browned, and pleasantly flavored.

- Factors that affect flakiness are the type and consistency of fat, type of flour, proportion of water, degree of mixing, method of mixing, and number of times the dough is rolled.

- Tenderness is at a maximum when the fat spreads over the flour particles. However, some of the factors that encourage flakiness tend to decrease tenderness. Thus, mixing and handling techniques must be used to achieve a balance in flakiness and tenderness.

- Plain pastry contains flour, fat, salt, and water. Plain pastry is leavened primarily by steam produced in a hot oven.

- A standard technique for mixing pie crust includes the following steps: (1) cut fat into the flour until about the size of peas; (2) sprinkle the water a tablespoon at a time over the fat-flour mixture and mix lightly; (3) gather the dough into a ball and refrigerate; (4) roll the dough out on a lightly floured surface or a canvas-covered board to about 1/8 inch thick into a circular shape about 1–2 inches larger than the pie plate; (5) gently fold the pastry in half or quarters, then lift into the pie plate and unfold; and (6) fit the pastry into the pie pan without trapping air or stretching the crust.

- Top crusts on pies should have steam vents created through small slashes or decorative patterns.

- Plain pastry may be baked before filling or after filling, depending on the type of pie being prepared. Crusts filled with fruit fillings before baking may be protected from soaking by coating the upper surface of the lower crust with melted butter, using a hot oven for the first 15 minutes, and by thickening the filling before before baking. Custard pies are more difficult to prevent from soaking, but some methods have been suggested.

- Microwave pastry is tender, flaky, and puffy, but does not brown.

- Crumb crusts may be prepared using the following ratio of ingredients: one part butter, two parts sugar, and four parts crumbs. These crusts may be used with or without baking, although a baked crust will generally be firmer.

- Puff pastry is a rich dough that separates into many light, crisp layers when baked. These doughs may be prepared from scratch or purchased frozen and ready to bake. Phyllo dough is typically purchased frozen due to the skill and time required to make this paper-thin dough.

KEY TERM

Maillard reaction

STUDY QUESTIONS

1. Describe desirable characteristics of good-quality pastry.

2. Describe the role of each of the following ingredients in the preparation of good-quality pastry.
   a. Flour
   b. Fat
   c. Water

3. a. Suggest an appropriate ratio of fat to flour for making pastry.
   b. Explain how the type of fat and the type of flour used might affect these proportions.

4. a. Describe several procedures for mixing pastry.
   b. What techniques of mixing are likely to produce the most flaky pastry and why?

5. Describe a satisfactory procedure for making pastry with oil. How does this pastry compare with one made using a solid fat?

6. What is the effect of each of the following on tenderness of pastry?
   a. Type of fat used
   b. Type of flour used
   c. Technique of mixing and handling

7. Suggest an appropriate temperature for baking plain pastry and explain why this temperature may be recommended.

8. How might one prevent or minimize the soaking of bottom crusts of custard and fruit pies during baking?

9. What is puff pastry? Phyllo dough?

REFERENCES

1. Berglund, P. T., & Hertsgaard, D. M. (1986). Use of vegetable oils at reduced levels in cake, pie crust, cookies, and muffins. *Journal of Food Science, 51*, 640.

2. Briant, A. M., & Snow, P. R. (1957). Freezer storage of pie shells. *Journal of the American Dietetic Association, 33*, 796.

3. Giese, J. (2002). Acrylamide in foods. *Food Technology, 56*(10), 71.

4. Hirahara, S., & Simpson, J. I. (1961). Microscopic appearance of gluten in pastry dough and its relation to the tenderness of baked pastry. *Journal of Home Economics, 53*, 681.

5. Labensky, S. R., & Hause, A. M. (2003). *On Cooking* (3rd ed.). Upper Saddle River, NJ: Prentice Hall.

6. Matthews, R. H., & Dawson, E. H. (1963). Performance of fats and oils in pastry and biscuits. *Cereal Chemistry, 40*, 291.

7. Miller, B. S., & Trimbo, H. B. (1970). Factors affecting the quality of pie dough and pie crust. *Baker's Digest, 44*(1), 46.

Vegetables and Vegetable Preparation

20

 What exactly is a vegetable? We can define vegetables broadly as plants or parts of plants that are used as food. However, so broad a definition includes fruits, nuts, and cereals, which, although of vegetable origin, are not commonly classified as vegetables. The term *vegetable* has through usage come to apply in a more narrow sense to those plants or parts of plants that are served either raw or cooked as part of the main course of a meal. Sweet corn and rice are two examples of cereals that, through usage, are sometimes given the place of vegetables on the table.

Regardless of how we define vegetables, we value them for their unique contributions to color, flavor, and texture in our menus. In addition, they rank importantly in the Food Guide Pyramid [72] because of their nutritional merit, particularly in regard to their content of vitamins, minerals, and fiber.

Various parts of plants are used as vegetables. One grouping by plant part is shown in Table 20-1. Technically, some vegetables might be placed under more than one heading.

COMPOSITION AND NUTRITIVE VALUE

The composition, and thus the nutritional value, of the parts of a plant are influenced to a large extent by their functions in the life of the plant. For example, the leaf is an actively working or metabolizing part of a plant and does not generally store energy nutrients. It is therefore low in energy value but high in many vitamins that function in its metabolic processes. The root and seed act more as storage depots for starch and protein.

Vegetables as a group may be depended on to contribute indigestible fiber, minerals, and vitamins to the diet. Potatoes and sweet potatoes supply starch and sugars, and many dried legumes are high in both starch and protein. The protein of most vegetables, with the exception of soybeans, is of lower biological value than that of most animal foods such as meat and milk.

Most fresh vegetables furnish about 25 kilocalories for an average serving, but some leaves and stems, such as lettuce and celery, are even lower in caloric value. Some roots, such as carrots and beets, and seeds, such as peas, furnish 35 to 50 kilocalories per average serving. These differences in caloric value are due basically to differences in composition. The leaves are high in water content and low in carbohydrate and protein, and, therefore, low in calories. The roots contain a little less water and a little more sugar, whereas the seeds store starch

Table 20-1

Parts of Plants Commonly Used as Vegetables

Leaves	Seeds	Roots	Tubers	Bulbs	Flowers	Fruits	Stems and Shoots
Beet greens	Beans, Dry	Beet	Ginger root	Chives	Artichoke	Cucumber	Anise (fennel)
Bok choy	Corn (a seed	Carrot	Potato (Irish)	Garlic	(French	Eggplant	Asparagus
(Chinese	of the grass	Celeriac	Sunchoke	Leek	or Globe)	Okra	Celery (a leaf
chard)	family fre-	(Celery	(Jerusalem	Onion	Broccoli	Pepper	stem)
Brussels	quently	root)	artichoke)	Shallot	Cauliflower	Pumpkin	Kohlrabi
sprouts	served as a	Jicama				Snap beans	
Cabbage	vegetable)	Parsnip				Squash	
Chard	Lentils	Radish				Sweet corn	
Chinese	Peas	Rutabaga				(on the	
cabbage		Salsify				cob)	
Collards		Sweet				Tomato	
Dandelion		potato					
greens		Turnip					
Endive							
Escarole							
Kale							
Lettuce							
Mustard							
greens							
Parsley							
Romaine							
Spinach							
Turnip greens							
Watercress							

and are therefore higher in carbohydrate and lower in water, particularly as they mature. Vegetables are low in fat.

Encouraging vegetable and fruit consumption is a major emphasis of the Dietary Guidelines for Americans, which recommends that we choose a diet with plenty of vegetables, fruits, and grain products [78]. "Plenty" means at least three servings of vegetables and two servings of fruits daily for adults. How much is a serving? Table 20-2 gives the amounts of vegetables and fruits recommended by the National Cancer Institute as a serving [34].

Americans are generally concerned about health and are learning to appreciate the important relationship of nutrition to the prevention of disease. Scientific evidence has been presented for a protective effect of greater vegetable and fruit consumption against cancer, particularly that of the stomach, esophagus, lung, pancreas, and colon. Benefits against heart disease, stroke, and other

Table 20-2

What Is a Serving Size for Vegetables and Fruits?

The National Cancer Institute recommends:

1/2 cup raw non-leafy or cooked vegetables

1 cup raw leafy vegetables (such as lettuce)

1/2 cup cooked beans or peas (such as lentils, pinto beans, and kidney beans)

1 medium fruit or 1/2 cup of small or cut-up fruit

3/4 cup (180 milliliters) of 100 percent fruit juice

1/4 cup dried fruit

Source: Reference 34.

chronic diseases have also been postulated [81, 14, 66]. The health-protective benefits of plant foods appear to come from their content of certain nonnutritive substances commonly called **phytochemicals,** in addition to the nutrients present [85]. Vegetables that appear to be most protective against cancer are those of the onion and cabbage families, carrots, green vegetables, tomatoes, and raw vegetables generally. Tomato products, particularly cooked tomato sauce and canned tomatoes, provide a red pigment called *lycopene* that apparently acts as an antioxidant in providing health benefits [8].

Food supply data showed an increase in the consumption of vegetables in the United States from 279 pounds per person in 1975 to 302 pounds per person in 1999 [5]. However, consumption is concentrated among a small number of vegetables. In 1999, iceberg lettuce, frozen potatoes, fresh potatoes, potato chips, and canned tomatoes accounted for 52 percent of total vegetable servings [57]. The consumption of dark-green leafy vegetables and deep-yellow vegetables is well below recommendations, whereas the starchy vegetable consumption, especially potatoes, is above recommendations. Both public and private organizations are instituting programs aimed at consumers to make them more aware of the importance, as well as the enjoyment, of including more fruits and vegetables in their diets. Tips on purchasing, menu planning, and preparation of vegetables should encourage increased use [58].

Vegetables and fruits probably do more than any other group of foods to add appetizing texture, color, and flavor to daily meals. The composition and nutritive value of selected vegetables are given in Appendix C.

phytochemicals biochemical substances, other than vitamins, of plant origin that appear to have a positive effect on health; they include phenolic compounds, terpenoids, pigments, and other antioxidants

Fiber Components

Cellulose, a long-chain **polymer** of glucose, is the main structural component of plant cell walls. Other structural compounds include hemicelluloses and pectins. All these substances are complex carbohydrates called **polysaccharides** and, because they are not broken down or hydrolyzed by enzymes in the human digestive tract, comprise a major part of dietary fiber [31]. Pectins are found not only in the cell walls but also between the cells, where they act as a cementing substance to bind cells together. Pectic substances include protopectin, the insoluble "parent" molecule, pectinic acid or pectin, and pectic acid. Beta-glucans, which are also fiber components, are glucose polymers with linkages somewhat different from cellulose that make them more soluble in water. They appear to increase cholesterol excretion from the bowel, thus aiding in the prevention of heart disease [2]. A complex noncarbohydrate molecule, lignin, is present in woody parts of plants. Various gums and mucilages are also found in plants as fiber components, but they are nonstructural polysaccharides.

Heating can cause pectic substances to be broken down, which is one factor that affects the ease with which cooked plant tissues disintegrate. Acids and alkalies affect the structure of fruits and vegetables when they are boiled. Acids make the structure more firm, whereas alkalies tend to disintegrate the fibrous components, particularly the hemicelluloses.

Some fresh vegetables, depending partly on the way they are trimmed for marketing, may have a relatively high percentage of refuse or waste parts that are thrown away. In quantity food preparation, recipes will note if the ingredient weight or measure has been provided for *edible portion* (EP) or *as purchased* (AP). Edible portion is the amount of the product remaining after cleaning, and as purchased is the amount prior to peeling and cleaning. Whether at home or

polymer a large molecule formed by linking together many smaller molecules of a similar kind

polysaccharides complex carbohydrates containing many simple sugar units linked together

in a professional kitchen, an understanding of the amount of waste generated when cleaning vegetables is important because it will affect the quantity of food available for consumption after preparation as well as the cost of the food consumed. Table 20-3 shows the percentage of refuse from some vegetables.

Leaf Vegetables

Many different types of greens are available for the consumer to purchase or grow in a garden. Although iceberg lettuce is one of the most widely consumed greens, consumers are increasingly choosing romaine, leaf, and other specialty greens such as radicchio, arugula, and red oak. The per capita consumption of romaine and leaf lettuce increased by 69 percent between 1989 and 1997 [56]. Table 20-1 provides a list of many kinds of leaf vegetables.

Table 20-3
Refuse from Vegetables

Vegetable	Source of Refuse	Refuse (%)
Artichokes	Stem & edible parts of flowers	60
Asparagus	Butt ends	47
Beans, snap	Ends, strings, trimmings	12
Beets, without tops	Parings	33
Broccoli	Leaves, tough stalks, trimmings	39
Brussel sprouts	Outer leaves	10
Cabbage	Outer leaves, core	20
Carrots, raw	Crown, tops, scrapings	11
Cauliflower, raw	Leaf stalks, core, and trimmings	61
Celery	Root and trimmings	11
Chard, Swiss, raw	Tough stem ends, damaged leaves	8
Corn, sweet, raw	Husk, silk, trimmings	35
	Cob	29
Cucumber, pared*	Parings, ends	27
Eggplant, raw	Ends, parings, and trimmings	19
Garlic, raw	Knob and skin	13
Ginger Root	Scrapings	7
Lettuce, iceberg	Core	5
Lettuce, Romaine	Core	6
Potatoes	Parings, trimmings	19
Boiled, cooked in skin	Skin and eyes	9
Baked, fresh only	Skin and adhering flesh	23
Shallots, raw	Skins	12
Spinach, raw	Leaves, stems, & roots	28
Squash, summer	Ends	5
Squash, winter, all others, raw	Seeds, rind, and stem	29
Sweet potato, raw	Parings and trimmings	28
Turnip greens, raw	Root, crown, tough stems, and Discarded leaves	30
Tomato	Core and stem ends	9

*Refuse will be less when the vegetable is not pared or scraped.
Source: [77]

Leaf vegetables may be generally characterized as being high in water and low in carbohydrate and calories, with only small amounts of protein and little or no fat (Figure 20-1). These vegetables' chief nutritive contribution is providing vitamins and minerals, and they are particularly important sources of iron, vitamin A value, riboflavin, folate, and vitamin C. The greener the leaf, the higher its vitamin A value. Green leaves are also one of the better vegetable sources of calcium, but most of the calcium in spinach, chard, and beet greens is combined with **oxalic acid** in the plant and is not available for absorption from the digestive tract.

oxalic acid an organic acid that forms an insoluble salt with calcium

Vegetable-Fruits

Tomatoes, cucumbers, peppers, squash, and several other vegetables are classified as **vegetable-fruits** because although typically served as vegetables, these foods are botanically classified as fruits. Tomatoes may be consumed raw or cooked and are used by food processors for catsup, tomato sauces, tomato soup, tomato paste, and tomato juice. Cucumbers are often used in salads or may be made into pickles. There are many varieties of squash from which to choose including zucchini, yellow squash, spaghetti squash and others. Peppers can be mild or hot and used in many different kinds of foods. See Chapter 8 for a discussion of the types of peppers.

Most of the commonly eaten vegetable-fruits (Figure 20-2 and Table 20-1) are relatively high in water content (92 to 94 percent), with small amounts of carbohydrate. Because they do not taste sweet and are generally prepared in combination with other vegetables, many people do not think of them as fruits. Botanically, however, they are fruits because they each develop from a flower. Winter squash is an exception to the usually high water content of this group; it contains only about 85 percent water and 12 percent carbohydrate in the raw state, comparable in carbohydrate content with many of the sweet, fleshy fruits. Cucumbers are particularly low in carbohydrate content and high in water content—about 97 percent.

vegetable-fruit botanically, a fruit is the ovary and surrounding tissues, including the seeds, of a plant; a vegetable-fruit is the fruit part of a plant that is not sweet and is usually served with the main course of a meal, for example, squash, cucumbers, and tomatoes

Tomatoes and green peppers are vegetable-fruits that are important sources of vitamin C. Pumpkin and yellow squash, tomatoes, and green peppers contain **carotenoid** pigments, some of which are **precursors** of vitamin A. Although green and red peppers, string beans, and okra can be classified as vegetable-fruits, they are also seed pods.

carotenoids yellow-orange, fat soluble pigments

precursors a substance that "comes before"; a precursor of vitamin A is a substance out of which the body cells can make vitamin A

Flowers and Stems

Flowers and stems (Figure 20-3 and Table 20-1) are, in general, high in water and low in carbohydrates. Broccoli has been shown to be a particularly nutritious green vegetable in terms of its vitamin and mineral content and also as a source of phytochemicals. It is one of the richest vegetable sources of vitamin C; even the stems contain this vitamin so, when possible, they should be pared and used. Broccoli also provides vitamin A value and contributes some riboflavin, calcium, and iron. Cauliflower and kohlrabi are good sources of vitamin C, and green asparagus has vitamin A value.

Roots, Bulbs, and Tubers

Root vegetables include beets, carrots, turnips, rutabagas, and parsnips (Table 20-1). Examples of bulbs, which are enlargements above the roots, are onions, leeks, and shallots (Figure 20-4). The shallot is composed of several cloves

Figure 20-1
Leaf vegetables. (Courtesy of
Burpee Seeds)

Swiss chard

Chinese Cabbage

Spinach

Brussels sprouts

Cabbage

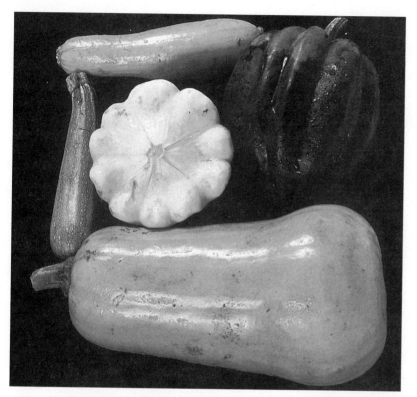

Squash. Clockwise from top: zucchini, yellow, acorn, and spaghetti. Patty pan in center.

Okra

Eggplant

Figure 20-2
Vegetable-fruits. (Squash courtesy of U.S. Department of Agriculture; okra courtesy of Burpee Seeds; and eggplant courtesy of Western Growers Association)

Kohlrabi

Celery

Cauliflower

Broccoli

Figure 20-3
Flowers and stems used as vegetables. (Courtesy of Burpee Seeds)

Left to right—turnips, beets, rutabaga; parsnips

Left, leeks; right, green onions

Figure 20-4
Roots and bulbs used as vegetables. (Courtesy of United Fresh Fruit and Vegetable Association)

covered by a thin skin, as is garlic, which is also a bulb vegetable. The potato is an example of a **tuber,** which is an enlarged underground stem. Bulb, root, and tuber vegetables are generally higher in carbohydrate and lower in water content than leaves, stems, and flowers. Most of the carbohydrate in potatoes is in the form of starch. Sweet potatoes also contain a fairly large amount of starch but have more sugar than white potatoes. Potatoes (Color Plate XIV) are significant sources of vitamin C, whereas the yellow carotenoids in sweet potatoes contribute vitamin A value. Potatoes are discussed in greater detail later in the chapter.

> **tuber** a short, thickened, fleshy part of an underground stem, such as a potato; new plants develop from the buds or eyes

There are two basic types of sweet potatoes. One has a somewhat dry, mealy, pale flesh; the other has a soft, moist, orange flesh. The moist type is known as the *yam;* however, the true yam is the root of a tropical vine that is not grown in the United States.

Seeds

Legumes are seeds of the Leguminosae family and include many varieties of beans, peas, soybeans, and lentils (Figure 20-5). They are used in both the green or fresh state and in the mature or dried state, in which the water content is very low and the starch content high. There is more protein in dried legumes than in any other vegetable group. Although the biological quality of the protein in most of the legumes, with the exception of soybeans, is substantially less than that of meat, fish, and poultry, legumes can make a valuable contribution to the body's protein requirement. Legumes can be used as alternates for meat in meal planning and play an important role in vegetarian diets.

> **legume** any of a large family of plants characterized by true pods enclosing seeds; dried beans and peas

Although it is a cereal product, corn is commonly used as a vegetable in the United States. It is relatively high in carbohydrate, chiefly in the form of starch.

The technique of sprouting soybean and mung bean seeds was developed by the Chinese centuries ago. Sprouts from many different seeds have become popular as vegetables and are particular favorites at fresh salad bars. The sprouts of some seeds provide significant sources of vitamin C, thiamin, riboflavin, and several minerals [21]. However, due to food safety concerns, current recommendations from the Food and Drug Administration (FDA) suggest

Figure 20-5
Seed vegetables. (Courtesy of
Burpee Seeds; lima beans, courtesy of the U.S. Department of
Agriculture; pinto beans, soybeans, and lentils, photograph
by Chris Meister)

Sweet corn

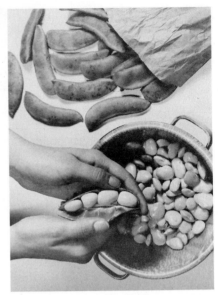

Lima beans

Green peas

Pinto beans (far right), soybeans (bottom),
and lentils (left)

that raw bean sprouts, including alfalfa sprouts, should be avoided, especially by
individuals at high risk for food-borne illness.

BIOTECHNOLOGY AND VEGETABLE PRODUCTION

For centuries humans have exploited the genetic diversity of living systems for
improvement of the food supply. Traditional **biotechnology** works with plant
and animal breeding and mutation for the selection of desired characteristics. A
new biotechnology, often called genetic engineering, produces genetic modification at the molecular level by transferring foreign DNA into the genetic ap-

biotechnology technology based
on biology

paratus of the plant. These newer genetic techniques provide a set of tools for improving the variety and efficiency of food production in less time and with more precision and control than with traditional methods [30, 86].

How does genetic engineering work for vegetable crops? It allows genetic information, even a single genetic trait, to be taken from one living organism and transferred to another. A gene may be taken from a bacterium and transferred to a plant. For example, some bacteria make insecticidal proteins; this capability can be given to plants to confer natural resistance to pests and thus decrease dependence on insecticides. Several varieties of corn and potato that have such insect resistance are sold commercially and a variety of squash with resistance to plant viruses is also available. The development and testing of genetically modified plants is closely monitored by the U.S. Department of Agriculture (USDA), the Food and Drug Administration (FDA), the Environmental Protection Agency (EPA), and most state governments. The goal of these agencies is to ensure the safety of any product that is used or consumed and also to protect the environment [86]. See Chapter 3 for additional information about biotechnology and food safety.

Molecular biotechnology has produced the Flavr Savr™ tomato. This vegetable has improved flavor and extended shelf life. Softening of tomatoes is associated with the presence of an enzyme that degrades or breaks down pectin. The activity of this enzyme has been greatly reduced by gene manipulation. Therefore, the tomato ripens on the vine where optimum flavor is produced. It also has extended shelf life in the market and home. Color, flavor, and shelf life all affect consumer selection and consumption of vegetables. Improvement in these characteristics should help to increase the vegetable and fruit intake of U.S. consumers.

Genetic engineering is being used to develop temperature-tolerant plants that can survive in warmer or cooler climates than those climates they can naturally tolerate. One major advantage thereby produced is the ability to control frost damage, which presently causes billions of dollars annually in crop losses worldwide. Nutritive value may also be improved through biotechnology. For example, more carotenoids may be bred into carrots and more vitamin C into peppers. An increase in phytochemicals that possess disease-preventive properties in such vegetables as garlic, cabbage, and tomatoes may be genetically produced as research in this area continues. Exciting possibilities lie ahead in the field of biotechnology.

SELECTION

Vegetables selected for purchase should be firm, crisp, and bright in color. In surveys of consumers, a high percentage of respondents have indicated that freshness, appearance, condition, and also taste are important selection criteria [32]. Size, shape, gloss, color, and absence of defects are considered. Vegetables may be highest in quality and lowest in price when they are in season in nearby production areas. Because of efficient transportation and marketing procedures, however, a wide variety of vegetables of generally good quality is available in local markets throughout the year. Prices vary, of course, depending on growing conditions, supply, demand, and the distance the produce must be shipped.

It is unwise to purchase greater quantities of fresh vegetables than you can properly store and utilize without waste. In making selections, you should distinguish between defects that affect appearance only and those that affect edible

Table 20-4
Selection of Fresh Vegetables

Vegetable	Quality Characteristics to Look for when Selecting
Artichoke, globe	Plump and compact; heavy in relation to size; green, fresh-looking scales
Asparagus	Closed, compact tips; smooth, round spears, mostly green; stalks tender almost as far down as the green extends
Bean, snap	Young, tender beans; pods firm and crisp
Beet	Firm, round, deep red color; smooth surface
Broccoli	Firm, compact clusters of small flower buds with none opened to show yellow flower; dark green; stems not too thick or tough
Brussels sprouts	Tight outer leaves; bright green color and firm body
Cabbage	Firm heads, heavy for size; outer leaves good color for variety, fresh, and free from serious blemishes
Carrot	Well formed, smooth, firm, and bright colored
Cauliflower	White to creamy, compact, solid, and clean curd; good green color in jacket leaves
Celery	Crisp, stalk with solid, rigid feel and fresh leaflets
Cucumber	Good green color; firm over entire length; well shaped but not too large
Eggplant	Firm, heavy, smooth, uniformly dark purple
Greens (chard, spinach, kale)	Fresh, young, tender leaves that are free from blemishes; good green color
Lettuce, iceberg	Large, round, solid heads with crisp medium green outer leaves
leaf	Fresh, unwilted leaves; bright color; somewhat soft texture in many varieties
Okra	Tender pods under 4½ inches long; bright green
Onion, globe	Firm, dry, with small necks; papery outer scales
green	Fresh, crisp, green tops; white portions 2-3 inches up from root
Pepper	Glossy sheen, firm and crisp, dark green
Potato	Well shaped, reasonably smooth, firm; free from blemishes, sun burn, and decay; no signs of sprouting
Radish	Medium size, plump, round, firm, good red color
Squash, summer	Firm, fresh-appearing, well formed, glossy skin
winter	Hard, tough rind; heavy for its size; free from cuts, sunken spots, or mold
Sweet potato	Well shaped, firm, smooth skins uniformly colored; free from signs of decay
Tomato	Well formed, smooth, well ripened; reasonably free from blemishes

quality. Fruits and vegetables should not be handled unnecessarily during selection. Some quality characteristics to look for in specific vegetables are provided in Table 20-4.

USDA Grades

In the wholesale market, most fresh vegetables and fruits are sold on the basis of USDA grades. These grades specify such characteristics as size, shape, color, texture, general appearance, uniformity, maturity, and freedom from defects. A common language is thus provided for wholesale trading and aids in establishing prices based on quality.

Grading is provided by the USDA upon request and a fee is charged to the producer or distributor. Grade labeling is not required by law, however, so most retail stores do not have a large quantity of grade-marked produce available. Generally, potatoes, carrots, and onions are the only fresh vegetables labeled for the consumer with a grade name. Sometimes, consumer fruit packages are marked with a grade; however, this is usually limited to citrus fruits and apples.

The USDA uniform grade terms for all fresh fruits and vegetables are: U.S. Fancy, U.S. No. 1, U.S. No. 2, and U.S. No. 3. U.S. Fancy is premium quality and only a few vegetables or fruits are packed in this grade. U.S. No. 1 is the grade most often found. Vegetables with this grade will be tender, fresh-appearing, have good color, and be relatively free from decay and bruises [75]. Some packers use their own grades. Because fresh vegetables are perishable, the quality may change between the time of grading and the time of purchase. This severely limits the usefulness of consumer grades on fresh fruits and vegetables. Extensive use of prepackaging may help to overcome this problem and make the use of consumer grades for fresh produce more practical. (See Chapter 4 for a general discussion of grading.)

USDA grades of quality have been established for many canned and frozen vegetables and fruits, based on color, uniformity of size, shape, tenderness or degree of ripeness, and freedom from blemishes. The label may designate U.S. Grade A or Fancy, U.S. Grade B or Choice, and U.S. Grade C or Standard [74, 73].

Availability of graded products allows the buyer to select the quality that will be most satisfactory for the intended use (Figure 20-6). Lower grades of fruits and vegetables are still good and wholesome although they are less perfect than Grade A in color, uniformity, and texture. When a product has been officially graded under continuous inspection by a USDA inspector, it may carry the official grade name and the statement "Packed under continuous inspection

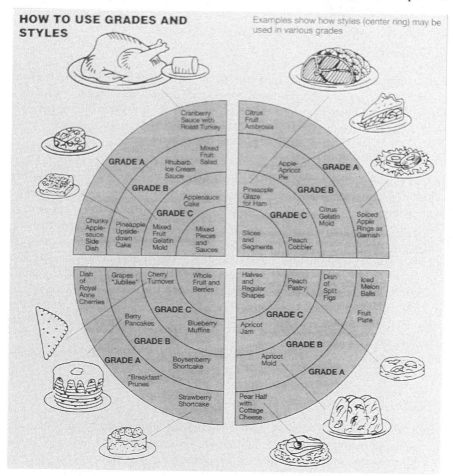

Figure 20-6
This circular diagram provides the proper uses for the different grades of certain foods. (Courtesy of U.S. Department of Agriculture)

of the U.S. Department of Agriculture" (Figure 20-7). The grade name and the statement may also appear within a shield-shaped outline.

Most canned and frozen vegetables and fruits are packed according to grade, whether or not that fact is indicated on the label, and are generally priced according to their quality. Most products marketed are at least Grade B quality, which is quite good. As with fresh produce, the use of the USDA grades is voluntary and is paid for by the packer. The specific brand name of a frozen or canned vegetable or fruit may be an indication of quality, since the packers set their own standards.

Federal regulations require that certain information appear on the label of canned and frozen fruits and vegetables:

1. Common or usual name
2. Form or style, such as whole, slices, or halves, unless the product is visible through the package
3. Variety or color for some products
4. List of syrups, sugar, or liquid in which the product is packed
5. Total contents (net weight); net weight includes the weight of the fruit or vegetable and the liquid
6. Additional ingredients, such as spices, flavoring, coloring, or sweeteners if used
7. Any special type of treatment
8. Packer's or distributor's name and place of business
9. Nutrition labeling

Labels may give other useful information about canned and frozen vegetables and fruits such as size and maturity, cooking directions, and recipes or serving ideas. If the label provides the number of servings per container then the size of the serving must be given in common measures such as ounces or cups.

Variety in Vegetables

In selecting vegetables, it is wise to remember that a liking for vegetables, as for other foods, is largely a matter of cultivation of habits and attitudes. A wider selection and variety in the preparation of vegetables can brighten menus and, at the same time, bring nutritional dividends. New and sometimes strangely unfamiliar vegetables and fruits are appearing with increasing frequency on grocers' shelves. Mostly tropical and often native to Asia, Latin America, and the Caribbean, these exotic products include winged beans from the Philippines, tamarillos (tart, egg-shaped tree tomatoes) from New Zealand, chayote (a green, soft, watery, squashlike vegetable known in Louisiana as *mirliton*), plantains (something like green bananas) from Central America, and jicama (knobby, earth-colored root) from Mexico. Some of these vegetables are becoming common in the United States as have ginger root, bean sprouts, shallots, tomatillos, and cilantro not so long ago.

STORAGE

Fresh vegetables and fruits are perishable, having limited shelf life. They are composed of living, respiring tissue that is also **senescing** and dying [32]. Although tomatoes will ripen after harvest, developing satisfactory color and fla-

senescence the state of growing old or aging

(a)

(b)

(c)

Figure 20-7

Food products displaying the official USDA certified symbols: (a) USDA shield for products packed under continuous inspection; (b) dates; (c) raisins. (Courtesy of U.S. Department of Agriculture)

vor, most other vegetables show little or no improvement in quality upon holding. However, most packing and handling systems move fresh produce from farm to consumer expeditiously with minimum deterioration of quality.

Most fresh immature vegetables retain their top quality for only a few days, even under ideal conditions of temperature and humidity for storage. Leafy vegetables are particularly perishable. All fresh vegetables of high water content, if they are allowed to stand long after harvesting without low-temperature and high-humidity controls, wilt and toughen through loss of moisture, or loss of *turgor* [35]. The flavor is also impaired, mainly because of enzyme actions in the tissues. Mature vegetables, particularly roots, tubers, and bulbs, deteriorate less in storage than immature ones.

respiration a metabolic process by which cells consume oxygen and give off carbon dioxide; continues after harvest

The short storage life of many vegetables is due to their rapid **respiration** or metabolism. A thin coating of a vegetable-oil **emulsion** on snap beans and other fresh vegetables has been found to decrease the respiration process [63]. When stored at 40°F (4°C), the waxed beans were generally in better condition than the unwaxed beans. Using this procedure to extend storage life and maintain product quality is common in the marketing of fresh vegetables, such as cucumbers and tomatoes, and many fruits. In practice, the vegetable or fruit is first washed thoroughly and rinsed, which removes the natural protective wax coating along with dust and dirt. The man-made edible wax is then applied to restore nature's own coating and extend the shelf life of the product.

emulsion the dispersion of one liquid in another with which it is usually immiscible, for example, oil in water

controlled atmosphere storage the monitoring and control of content of gases in the storage warehouse atmosphere; a low oxygen content slows down plant respiration and delays senescence (aging)

Lettuce may be stored in a **controlled atmosphere** to extend its shelf life [62]. In an atmosphere containing 2.5 percent carbon dioxide and 2.5 percent oxygen, lettuce heads can be stored up to 75 days. The controlled atmosphere combined with polyethylene packaging reduces the rate of respiration in the lettuce tissues (see Chapter 21 for a discussion of controlled atmosphere storage of fruits).

The superior quality of vegetables stored under refrigeration is well known. It is interesting to note that such treatment generally is also useful in conserving vitamin content. Vegetables vary, however, in the extent of change in vitamin C content, even when kept under refrigeration. In one study [18], fresh broccoli did not lose vitamin C when stored up to 7 days, whereas green beans lost as much as 88 percent when stored for 6 days at 36°F (2°C) and 95 to 100 percent relative humidity.

Most fresh green vegetables, such as lettuce and celery, can be kept fresh and crisp in kitchen storage by placing them in covered containers or plastic bags in the refrigerator. If they are washed before storing, they should be drained thoroughly because too much moisture can increase the possibility of spoilage or decay. Seeds, such as peas and limas, remain fresh longer when left in the pods. Tubers and bulbs that are to be held temporarily may be stored in a cool place without refrigeration.

If tomatoes are picked before being fully ripened, the quality and vitamin value will be better if the tomatoes are ripened at room temperature or a little below (59° to 75°F or 15° to 24°C) and kept in a lighted place unwrapped. Although the refrigeration of ripe tomatoes has been commonly recommended, researchers found that a trained sensory panel rated the flavor and aroma of tomatoes significantly lower when stored under refrigeration for two days [44]. These researchers concluded that the storage of ripe tomatoes under refrigeration could be an important contributing factor to consumer complaints about tomato flavor.

VEGETABLE PREPARATION

Emphasis on the important nutritional contributions of vegetables, along with the greater availability of vegetables year-round and the introduction into the U.S. market of new and interesting vegetables, has given impetus to the study of vegetable preparation. The nutrients that vegetables contain should be conserved as completely as possible. Such factors as changes in color, flavor, texture, and general appearance during preparation also require careful consideration to ensure that both raw and cooked vegetables retain their attractive and appetizing characteristics until they are served.

The vegetables that are generally eaten raw are those of high water and low starch content. Many such vegetables are tender and crisp and have distinctive pleasant flavors.

Color

Much of the appeal of vegetables and fruits is due to their bright colors, which result from the presence of various pigments in the plant tissues. Under appropriate temperatures for postharvest storage, green vegetables have been reported to undergo little change in color over a 12-day period [23]. Other vegetables also retain color well when stored properly. One challenge of cooking vegetables is to retain these bright colors, because heat and the various conditions of preparation may produce pigment changes that make them dull and less attractive.

Depending on the predominant colors, vegetables and fruits can be classified into four groups: green, yellow-orange, red-blue, and white. The yellow-orange and red-blue pigments predominate in fruits. Specific groups of plant pigments are responsible for these colors. The chlorophylls are green pigments; the carotenoids are yellow and orange (and some are pink or red); the anthocyanins are red, purple, and blue; the betalains are purplish red (although some are yellow); and the anthoxanthins are creamy white to colorless. Anthocyanins and anthoxanthins have many similarities in chemical structure. They are called **flavonoid pigments.**

flavonoid pigments a group of plant pigments with similar chemical structures; they include both anthoxanthins, which are white, and anthocyanins, which are red-blue

Chlorophyll. Chlorophyll plays an important role in photosynthesis, in which the plant uses the energy of the sun's rays with gases from the air to synthesize carbohydrates. Chlorophyll is concentrated in the green leaves, where it is present in tiny bodies called *chloroplasts.* It is mostly insoluble in water. When chlorophyll comes in contact with acids, which may be liberated during the cooking of vegetables, it chemically changes to a compound called *pheophytin,* which is a dull olive green. This effect also can be observed when preparing a fresh green bean or broccoli salad that is marinated in an acidic vinaigrette. Limiting the length of time the vegetables are marinated will reduce the tendency for the green colors to become dull.

In canned green vegetables, which have been subjected to prolonged periods of heating at high temperatures, essentially all of the chlorophyll is degraded to pheophytin and pyropheophytin, which appear to be responsible for the olive green to olive brown color that is characteristic of many canned green vegetables. Pyropheophytin is apparently the major degradation product of chlorophyll in canned vegetables [61]. The bright green to dull color change is obvious when you compare a newly cooked fresh vegetable such as garden peas with canned peas. Removing the cover from the pan during the first few minutes of boiling should allow some volatile acids to escape, decreasing the likelihood of their affecting the chlorophyll adversely. However, heating is not as even or as complete in an uncovered pan and the total cooking time may be slightly extended.

The hues of green vegetables progress from green-yellow toward yellow as cooking time increases beyond the just tender stage. Green beans, broccoli, brussels sprouts, cabbage, and other green vegetables show considerable change in color with 5 minutes of overcooking in boiling water and with even 1 minute of overcooking in a pressure saucepan. It is important, therefore, to cook vegetables for the minimum amount of time necessary to tenderize. The length of holding time for vegetables should also be minimized. Green vegetables that are held on a steam table before serving often show pronounced loss of chlorophyll and color [68].

When a small amount of baking soda (an alkaline substance) is added to green vegetables during cooking, it changes the chlorophyll to a bright green, more water-soluble pigment called *chlorophyllin*. However, the use of baking soda in cooking vegetables is not recommended, because it is difficult to avoid adding too much and the flavor, texture, and vitamin content of the vegetables may be adversely affected. Thiamin and vitamin C are particularly susceptible to destruction when baking soda is added during cooking. Texture may be undesirably soft because soda has a disintegrating effect on the hemicelluloses. When proper methods for cooking green vegetables are employed, the addition of soda serves no purpose.

An intensified green color that occurs at the beginning of cooking is explained in part by the removal of air from the tissues when the green vegetable is dropped into boiling water. This removal of air permits greater visibility of the underlying chlorophyll. The bright green color of frozen green vegetables results from brief blanching in boiling water or steam. Part of the plant acids are probably eliminated during the blanching period.

Carotenoids.   Carotenoids, like chlorophyll, are insoluble in water. They are present, along with chlorophyll, in the chloroplasts of green leaves. In the autumn, when the chlorophyll disappears, the yellow color can usually be seen. Carotenoids constitute a group of similar pigments, some of which are called *carotenes*. Three of the carotene pigments—α, β, and γ carotene—are found in relatively large amounts in carrots. Other carotenoids, which contain some oxygen in addition to carbon and hydrogen, are called *xanthophylls*. Cryptoxanthin is a xanthophyll that is found in many yellow vegetables. The red pigment of tomatoes, named lycopene, is a carotenoid. Lycopene is also found in watermelon and pink grapefruit and is believed to be an antioxidant that when consumed in the diet correlates with a reduced incidence of cancer and possibly heart attacks [4].

Some of the carotenoid pigments—including α, β, and γ carotene and cryptoxanthin—may be changed into vitamin A in the body and, therefore, contribute substantially to the vitamin A value of the diet. Carotenoid pigments may lose some of their yellow color when exposed to air because they are susceptible to **oxidation.** This reaction may occur in vegetables such as carrots when they are dehydrated.

The carotenoid pigments are quite stable during ordinary cooking procedures. The presence of alkali has little effect on the color. With longer heating,

oxidation a chemical reaction in which oxygen is added; addition of oxygen to carotenoid pigments lightens the color

especially with overcooking, the pigments may undergo some chemical change by a process called **isomerization** in the presence of acid, so that the orange color becomes somewhat more yellow.

Anthocyanins. The flavonoid pigments are water soluble and found in the cell sap. The pigments in the anthocyanin group of flavonoids are usually red in an acid medium and change to blues and purples as the pH becomes more alkaline.

Not all anthocyanins as they occur in the plant behave in the same way with changes of acidity and alkalinity, perhaps as the result of the presence of other pigments or of substances that modify the reactions. Red cabbage is easily changed in color, and it is difficult to retain its typical color while cooking it. The German custom of cooking red cabbage with an apple and adding a small amount of vinegar when it is ready to be served aids in retaining the desirable red color.

When it is cut with a nonstainless steel knife, red cabbage reveals another property of anthocyanins—their ability to combine with metals to form salts of various colors. The use of **lacquered tin** for canning red fruits and vegetables prevents the bluish red or violet that results from the combination of anthocyanin pigment with tin or iron. The salts of iron combined with anthocyanins are more blue than those formed with tin.

Betalains. The pigments in the root tissue of red beets are not chemically similar to those of anthocyanins; they contain nitrogen and are called *betalains* [83]. Some of these pigments are purplish red, whereas others are yellow. Beets lose much pigment and become pale when they are pared and sliced before cooking, because the pigments are very soluble in water and leach from the tissues. If beets are not peeled and one or two inches of the stem is left intact, they may be cooked in boiling water without loss of pigment and color. After cooking, they can be peeled.

Anthoxanthins. The anthoxanthin pigments change from white or colorless to yellowish as the **pH** increases from acidic to alkaline ranges. These pigments are widely distributed in plants and often occur with anthocyanins. They may combine with some metals, such as iron, to form a dark complex. Some combinations with aluminum produce a bright yellow. The anthoxanthin pigments are generally quite stable to heating. If the cooking water is alkaline, however, the pigments may appear yellow. If heating is excessive or prolonged, the pigments also darken. Table 20-5 summarizes the effect of various factors on the color of plant pigments.

Enzymatic Oxidative Browning. Some raw fruits, such as bananas, apples, and peaches, and some pared vegetables, including potatoes and sweet potatoes, darken or discolor on exposure to air. The darkening results from the oxidation of **phenolic compounds** in the fruit when oxygen from the air is available; the reaction is catalyzed by oxidizing enzymes, called **oxidases**, present in the plant tissue (see Chapter 9 for a discussion of enzymes). Unattractive, brown pigments are the end products of this enzymatic oxidative reaction.

It is, of course, desirable to prevent or control enzymatic darkening because it is aesthetically unappealing both in food freshly prepared for consumption and in susceptible products held prior to freezing, drying, or canning. Lemon juice, which is high in acid and evidently interferes with enzyme activity, can be

isomerization a molecular change resulting in a molecule containing the same elements in the same proportions but having a slightly different structure and, hence, different properties; in carotenoids, heat causes a change in the position of the double bonds between carbon atoms

lacquered tin an enamel coating on the inside of tin cans

pH a scale of 1 to 14, with 1 most acid, 14 most alkaline, and 7 neutral

phenolic compounds organic compounds that include in their chemical structure an unsaturated ring with −OH groups on it; these compounds are easily oxidized, producing a brownish discoloration

oxidase an enzyme that catalyzes an oxidation reaction

Table 20-5

Solubility in Water and Effect of Various Factors on the Color of Plant Pigments

Name of Pigment	Color	Solubility in Water	Effect of Acid	Effect of Alkali	Effect of Prolonged Heating	Effect of Metal Ions
Chlorophylls	Green	Slightly	Changes to olive green (pheophytin)	Intensifies green (chlorophyllin)	Olive green (pheophytin and pyro-pheophytin)	
Carotenoids	Yellow and orange; some red or pink	Slightly	Less intense color	Little effect	Color may be less intense*	
Anthocyanins	Red, purple, and blue	Very soluble	Red	Purple or blue	Little effect	Violet or blue with tin or iron
Betalains	Purplish red; some yellow	Very soluble	Little effect	Little effect	Pale if pigment bleeds from tissues	
Anthoxanthins	White or colorless	Very soluble	White	Yellow	Darkens if excessive	Dark with iron; bright yellow with aluminum

*Heating *usually* produces little effect.

sulfhydryl compound a chemical substance that contains an −SH group

antioxidant a substance that stops unwanted oxidations

used to coat fruit surfaces to reduce discoloration. Pineapple juice accomplishes the same purpose, although it is less acid than lemon juice. Pineapple juice contains a **sulfhydryl compound** that seems to act as an **antioxidant** in retarding browning. Added vitamin C, either alone or as part of several available commercial products, also aids in reducing discoloration because of its ability to act as an antioxidant. Commercially, sulfur dioxide is sometimes used to inhibit enzyme activity before fruits are dehydrated.

Sulfites are able to control browning on peeled raw potatoes and other fresh fruits and vegetables. They also have been used for other purposes, such as preventing "black spot" on shrimp and lobster and conditioning doughs. However, some people are sulfite sensitive. The FDA estimates that this sensitivity involves one of a hundred persons in the general population and 5 percent of those with asthma. In 1982, in response to numerous consumer reports, the FDA contracted with the Federation of American Societies for Experimental Biology (FASEB) to examine the link between sulfites and reported health problems. The FASEB, in 1985, concluded that, although sulfites are safe for most people, they pose a hazard of unpredictable severity to asthmatics and others who are sensitive to them. In 1986, therefore, the FDA prohibited the use of sulfites to maintain color and crispness on vegetables and fruits meant to be eaten raw, such as those served in salad bars. They also required that the presence of sulfites be disclosed on labels of packaged food. The FDA attempted to rule that sulfiting agents not be allowed on fresh, raw potatoes intended to be cooked and served unpackaged and unlabeled to consumers as, for example, french fries. However, this ruling was not upheld in a court battle in which the fresh potato industry prevailed on procedural grounds. Consumers at risk need to read labels and check carefully, especially when eating away from home [52]. Vitamin C derivatives and citric acid can replace sulfites in retarding undesirable enzymatic browning in fresh fruits and vegetables.

Flavor

Wide variation occurs in the flavor of vegetables—some are mild and others, such as asparagus and parsnips, have relatively strong, distinctive flavors. The sugar content is high enough to produce a definite sweet taste in carrots and sweet potatoes, whereas the flavor of spinach includes a slightly bitter component. Onions, garlic, broccoli, and cabbage have distinctive aromas. Vegetables of the cabbage and onion families are sometimes described as strong flavored, but not necessarily in the raw state.

The natural flavors that make each vegetable distinctive probably result from mixtures of many compounds, most of them present in tiny amounts. These compounds include **aldehydes, alcohols, ketones, organic acids, esters,** and sulfur-containing compounds. The flavoring compounds in several vegetables and fruits have been and are being studied extensively with the use of precision analytical equipment to find out more about the complex mixtures of substances that contribute to their individual flavors. Vegetables, with some exceptions, are relatively bland in flavor—different from the tart, fragrant flavor of fruits.

Cabbage Flavors. Vegetables of the cabbage or mustard family, called Cruciferae, include cabbage, cauliflower, broccoli, brussels sprouts, kale, kohlrabi, mustard, rutabaga, and turnips. These vegetables are relatively mild when raw, but may develop strong flavors or odors when improperly cooked because of extensive decomposition of certain sulfur compounds.

Chemical substances in vegetables of the cabbage family include *thioglucosides*—compounds which contain a sugar molecule with a sulfur-containing portion. *Sinigrin* is the thioglucoside found in cabbage, and when cabbage tissues are damaged by cutting or shredding, an enzyme (a thioglucosidase called myrosinase) breaks down the sinigrin to produce a mustard oil, chemically called *allyl isothiocyanate.* This compound gives a sharp, pungent flavor that is typical of shredded raw cabbage. An amino acid, S-methyl-L-cysteine sulfoxide, is also present in raw cabbage and several other members of the cabbage family. From this compound, on cooking, comes dimethyl disulfide, which contributes to the characteristic and desirable flavor of the cooked vegetable, along with a number of other volatile compounds [40].

In overcooked vegetables of the cabbage family, hydrogen sulfide and other volatile sulfur compounds may produce a strong, pungent, sulfurous flavor and odor. Vegetable acids may aid in the decomposition. Leaving the lid off for the first part of cooking, to allow some volatile acids to escape, may help to control these changes; however, it is more important to cook the vegetables for the shortest time possible, until just tender to a fork, before substantial decomposition of sulfur compounds occurs.

Vegetables of the cabbage family have a milder flavor when cooked in an open pan with enough water to almost cover them than when they are cooked in a tightly covered pan, a steamer, or a pressure saucepan. A large amount of water dilutes the natural flavors of the vegetables, usually to a substantial degree. The desirability of a milder flavor or stronger natural flavor is a matter of personal preference. The absence of many volatile flavor substances from dehydrated cabbage has been reported [41], which may explain why the dehydrated product is a poor substitute for freshly cooked cabbage in terms of eating quality.

Onion Flavors. The onion family includes onions, leeks, garlic, and chives (Plates II and XIV). These vegetables are usually strong flavored in the raw state, but tend to lose some of their strong flavors when cooked in water. Raw

aldehydes chemical compounds characterized by a

$$-\overset{\displaystyle O}{\overset{\displaystyle \|}{C}}-H$$

group

alcohols chemical compounds characterized by an $-OH$ group

ketones chemical compounds characterized by a

$$-\overset{\displaystyle O}{\overset{\displaystyle \|}{C}}-$$

group

organic acids generally weak acids characterized by a carboxyl

$$-\overset{\displaystyle O}{\overset{\displaystyle \|}{C}}-OH$$

group

ester a chemical linkage joining an organic acid and an alcohol group, with the removal of one molecule of water

vegetables of the onion family contain derivatives of the sulfur-containing amino acid, cysteine. These compounds are acted on by enzymes in the tissues when the vegetables are peeled or cut to produce volatile sulfur compounds that irritate the eyes and cause tearing or produce biting sensations on the tongue.

The sharp flavor of onions is reduced on cooking. The flavor of onions can be mild when cooked in a large amount of water with the lid of the pan loose or off, or the flavor can be sweeter and more concentrated when cooked in a small amount of water with the lid on. Personal preference may determine the cooking method. Onions generally tend to increase in sweetness on cooking.

Preliminary Preparation

Most vegetables grow near or in the ground. They may therefore be contaminated by various microorganisms present in the soil. For example, spores of *Clostridium perfringens* or *Clostridium botulinum* may be present in dirt that clings to some vegetables. Additional microbial contamination can occur from the many contacts incident to marketing. Raw vegetables may also be contaminated with pesticide residues unless they are organically grown. In organically grown produce, insects and rodents can inoculate plants in the field with microorganisms that can present a health hazard. In addition, molds can infect vegetables and fruits and produce mycotoxins [32]. Thorough washing in water that is safe for drinking is therefore essential; a stiff brush may also aid in cleansing. When sixty-one people in Connecticut, New York, and Illinois were found to be infected with the same strain of *E. coli* O157:H7, the source of the infection was traced to a California farm that produced precut, packaged lettuce. Inspectors found numerous sanitary violations at the farm, including the housing of farm animals near the processing facility and the use of unfiltered water for washing the produce in a shed with one wall open to the outdoors. A document was issued in 1998 by the FDA, recommending good agricultural and manufacturing practices to minimize food safety hazards common to growing, harvesting, packing, and transporting raw vegetables and fruits [79]. *If vegetables are to be consumed raw, extra care is needed in cleansing them.* Food safety is discussed further in Chapter 3.

All spoiled and discolored portions should be trimmed off. Pods, such as lima bean and pea pods, should be washed well before being shelled. Leafy vegetables should have all undesirable leaves and coarse stems removed. The usable leaves require several washings to cleanse. In washing, the vegetables should be lifted out of the wash water so that the heavier particles of dirt remain in the water. Alternatively, they may be washed under running water (Figure 20-8).

Figure 20-8
By filling a clean sink with cold water and stirring the greens, they can be efficiently washed.

Salad ingredients that are to be consumed raw should be stored under refrigeration, but some pathogenic microorganisms, such as *Listeria monocytogenes,* can grow at refrigerator temperatures. Avoidance of long storage times and strict adherence to sanitation are essential to avoid and control contamination on fresh vegetables.

Roots and tubers that are covered with skins may have their skins removed, depending on the method to be used in cooking and depending, in part, on the vegetable itself. Beets, for example, should not be peeled unless they are to be diced or sliced and cooked in a closely covered container with little or no water. The red coloring matter of beets is highly soluble in water and is best protected from loss by cooking the beets in the skin, with the roots and two or more inches of the tops left on.

When properly scrubbed with a brush, carrots can be cooked without paring or scraping. In some cases, however, the skins tend to make the vegetable appear darker. Carrots are delicious when cooked in their skins and scraped after cooking. When plunged into cold water after boiling, they are easily skinned and retain their sweetness and nutrients better than when they are scraped before cooking. If the method of preparation requires that carrots have the skin removed before cooking, they should be scraped or pared so as to remove as little tissue as possible with the peel, to retain more of the vitamins and minerals. Vegetables usually have a valuable layer of nutrients lying directly underneath the skin. Some roots and tubers, such as potatoes, have skins that are too thick to be removed by scraping. These also can be cooked in their skins and the skin may be consumed or peeled after cooking. If they must be pared before cooking, parings should be as thin as possible. The floating-blade type of peeler removes very thin layers.

Only the tips and tender stems of asparagus should be used. The woodiest parts of asparagus can be easily removed if the lower stems are snapped off with the fingers (Figure 20-9). The stems should break where the stalk is tender.

If the twigs and leaves of broccoli are tender, they may be used in addition to the flower buds. Woody stems are not easily softened by cooking and are usually inedible; however, large broccoli stems may be peeled and the tender center cores cooked. The outer leaves and heavy stalks of cauliflower and cabbage are usually discarded, although the process of prepackaging fresh vegetables often includes removal of the outer, less edible portions before the vegetables are placed in the retail market. When cooking heavier stalks with more tender portions of a vegetable, it is best to add the more tender parts to the stalks after a few minutes of cooking, so that the tender portions are not overcooked by the time the stalks are tender. Parsnips may have a woody core, which should be removed. See Figure 20-10 for the preparation of globe artichokes.

Some vegetables, such as peeled potatoes, that may be prepared in advance of being used or cooked, may discolor unless they are covered with water. As a general precaution against the loss of water-soluble nutrients, the soaking time should be kept to a minimum. Also, cabbage shredded with a sharp knife in advance of its use loses a negligible amount of vitamin C when it stands at room temperature for 1 hour in air or 3 hours in water. Using a sharp knife helps to avoid bruising and thereby decreases loss of the vitamin. These results with cabbage, however, do not justify indiscriminate and unnecessary cutting, shredding, and exposure of vegetables to air or soaking in water. In some vegetables, certain nutrients may occur in a form that is more stable or better protected against destruction than in other vegetables.

Asparagus can be washed under running water with the use of a small brush to remove soil.

Lower stems can be snapped off with the fingers to leave the tips and tender stems for cooking.

Figure 20-9
Preliminary preparation of vegetables. (Courtesy of Western Growers Association)

Some people have expressed concern about pesticide residues on vegetables and fruits as marketed. Government studies that have monitored actual pesticide residue levels in foods as prepared and consumed have shown no pesticide residues in more than half of the samples tested, and levels below the EPA tolerances in more than 99 percent of the samples tested [32]. Passage by Congress of the Food Quality Protection Act of 1996 reformed some of the past legislation regarding pesticide use in the United States, and will enable pesticide regulation to keep pace with scientific advancement [47]. A uniform safety standard has been set for raw and processed foods. Consumer access to information about possible dietary exposure to pesticides is mandated, and this information is to be distributed through grocery marketing channels.

Why Cook Vegetables?

Many vegetables are improved in palatability and more easily and completely digested when they are cooked. Some valuable vegetables, such as dried legumes, could not be masticated or digested in the raw state. The flavors of cooked vegetables are different from those of raw vegetables, adding variety to their use.

Figure 20-10
To prepare globe artichokes, (1) cut off the stem about 1 inch from the base, leaving a stub; (2) cut off about 1 inch of the top, cutting straight across with a knife; (3) pull off any heavy loose leaves around the bottom; (4) with scissors, clip off the thorny tip of each leaf; (5) drop into boiling, salted water. Season by adding a small clove of garlic, a thick slice of lemon, and 1 tablespoon of olive or other salad oil for each artichoke. Cover and boil until a leaf can be pulled easily from the stalk or until the stub can be easily pierced with a fork (20 to 45 minutes). Remove carefully from the water. Cut off the stub. (Courtesy of Western Growers Association)

Heating improves the utilization of protein from dried legumes, and some of the minerals and vitamins, particularly of soybeans, are more available after the beans are heated [36]. Cooking also causes **gelatinization of starch** and increases its digestibility. Microorganisms are destroyed by the heating process. Moreover, the bulk of leafy vegetables is greatly decreased, as they wilt during cooking.

gelatinization of starch the swelling of starch granules when heated in the presence of water

How Cooking Losses Occur

Cooking losses can occur (1) through the dissolving action of water or dilute salt solutions; (2) by chemical decomposition, which may be influenced by the alkalinity or acidity of the cooking medium; (3) by oxidation of specific molecules such as vitamins; (4) by the mechanical loss of solids into the cooking water; and (5) by volatilization. Mechanical losses of nutrients in vegetable cookery are the result of paring, rapid boiling (agitation), and overcooking. Loss of starch and other nutrients occurs from cut surfaces. Losses are greater when parings are thick and when overcooking results in marked disintegration.

The chief volatile loss is water, although volatilization of other substances may cause loss of flavor.

Changes During Cooking

Changes in Fiber Components.   There appears to be no great loss of **fiber** when vegetables are prepared by typical kitchen methods or commercial processing [88]. Cellulose is somewhat softened by cooking but appears to be mostly indigestible for humans. When calculated on a dry-weight basis, cellulose content seems to increase somewhat when vegetables are boiled, which may result from the liberation of cellulose from the cell walls, making it more available for analysis [25, 26, 43].

Sodium bicarbonate (baking soda) added to cooking water tends to cause the hemicelluloses to disintegrate, producing a soft texture in a short cooking period. Acid, on the other hand, prevents softening of vegetables. Neither of these substances should be added during the cooking of vegetables.

The pectic substances, which are part of the intercellular cementing material in plant tissues, may be **hydrolyzed** to a certain extent during cooking, resulting in some cell separation; however, the total pectin content appears to be well retained [88]. In the canning of many vegetables, the solubilization and hydrolysis of pectin apparently contribute to excessive softening. During prolonged cooking at approximately neutral pH, **de-esterification** and depolymerization (hydrolysis) occur [80].

Calcium salts, as calcium chloride, make vegetable tissues more firm, probably by forming insoluble calcium salts with pectic substances in the plant tissue. Commercially, traces of calcium are added during canning to help preserve the shape and firmness of tomatoes. The FDA allows calcium chloride to be added up to 0.07 percent. It can also be used to make melon rinds firm and brittle for pickling.

Vitamin Losses.   Generally there are two ways in which vitamins may be lost during cooking. Some of the vitamins may actually be destroyed by oxidation and some may be dissolved in the cooking water, although the latter applies only to the water-soluble vitamins (the B vitamins and vitamin C). Vitamin C is quite easily oxidized and hence tends to be better retained if conditions favoring oxidation can be eliminated. Some of the undesirable effects of covering the pan have been mentioned, but a covered pan hastens cooking and thus gives less time for either solution losses or inactivation of vitamins. A covered pan does not completely exclude air but reduces exposure to it.

The vitamin A value of vegetables is usually well retained during cooking. Thiamin is more unstable to heat than riboflavin and niacin, and it appears to be less stable when heated in a water medium than when heated in the dry state. The extent of destruction increases with rising temperature. Riboflavin and niacin are stable to heat even at temperatures above 212°F (100°C). The more alkaline the cooking water, the faster the rate of oxidation of several vitamins, particularly thiamin and vitamin C.

Some loss of vitamin C during the cooking of broccoli is inevitable regardless of the method used. Leaching of the vitamin into the cooking water rather than destruction by heat is the chief factor responsible for the loss. Except when excessive cooking liquid is used, broccoli cooked to satisfactory doneness retains 60 to 85 percent of the original vitamin C [69, 70].

fiber Dietary fiber is nondigestible carbohydrates (including cellulose, hemicelluloses, and pectin) and lignin (a noncarbohydrate material found particularly in woody parts of plants) that are intrinsic and intact in plants; functional fiber consists of isolated nondigestible carbohydrates that have beneficial physiological effects in humans; and total fiber is the sum of dietary fiber and functional fiber.

hydrolyze to break chemical linkages, by the addition of water, to yield smaller molecules

de-esterification the removal of the methyl ester groups from the galacturonic acid building blocks of the pectin molecule

Cooked vegetables lose significant amounts of vitamin C during even one day of refrigerator storage, and reheating causes additional loss [13]. A comparison was made of vitamin C and folate (a B vitamin) loss when a variety of vegetables were either cooked and then refrigerated for one day (cook/chill system) or cooked and held for different periods of time (cook/hot-hold system). Vegetables reheated after one day of chilled storage had greater losses of both vitamins than those held hot at 162°F (72°C) for 30 minutes. However, the cook/chill vegetables had better vitamin retention than those cooked and held hot for 2 hours [87]. Holding vegetables hot after cooking causes loss of flavor and nutritive value.

The foodservice industry is placing increased emphasis on the nutritional quality of meals it serves. For cooking vegetables in a foodservice operation, convection steaming has been found to retain vitamin C well. However, when broccoli and cauliflower were held an additional 30 minutes at 145°F (63°C) after cooking, considerable additional loss occurred. Although convection steaming of the fresh vegetables resulted in losses of only 6 to 12 percent of the vitamin C, the total loss after a 30-minute holding period was 36 to 45 percent [10]. Preservice holding of whipped potatoes in a simulated conventional foodservice system resulted in loss of 36.2 percent of the vitamin C present [65]. Care needs to be exercised during the entire foodservice cycle to ensure retention of nutritional value. Cooking in batches in food service is an important strategy that results in food with higher nutritional value as well as better sensory qualities because the texture and color are less likely to deteriorate if holding is kept to a minimum.

Other Changes. The water content of vegetables is altered during cooking. Water may be absorbed if the vegetable is cooked submerged in water or, to a lesser extent, in steam. Removal of water occurs during baking.

More flavor substances are extracted, and thereby lost, by cooking in a large amount of water versus a small amount of water. Sugars, acids, and some minerals that contribute to flavor are water soluble and easily extracted from the tissues.

The gelatinization of starch, described as the swelling of starch granules in the presence of moisture, occurs during the cooking of vegetables. This gelatinization may be partial or complete.

Specific Methods of Cooking Vegetables

Baking, frying, stir-frying or panning, steaming, cooking in steam under pressure, and microwave cooking are common methods of cooking vegetables. Broiling can also be utilized, for example, as with the broiling of fresh tomatoes.

The desire for variety is one factor that influences the choice of cooking method. Suitability of the method for the type of vegetable being cooked is a second factor. A third and important factor is the influence of the method on the retention of nutrients.

Some loss of food value probably occurs in most methods used in vegetable cookery. For this reason it is important to serve some vegetables in the raw state. Baking, steaming, panning, and cooking in the skins have been called *conservation methods* of cooking vegetables because they may retain food value more completely than other methods.

Baking and Grilling.   Baking or roasting of vegetables can be accomplished by the direct heat of the oven, or the vegetable can be pared, sliced, or diced and placed in a covered casserole. In the casserole, however, a moist atmosphere surrounds the vegetable as it cooks. All vegetables that contain a high enough water content to prevent drying and that have little surface exposed to the heat lend themselves well to baking. These include potatoes, sweet potatoes, winter squash, and onions. Vegetables are commonly baked in the skin. Corn on the cob may be shucked and wrapped in foil before baking; or, alternatively, the corn may be baked unshucked. In this case, the silk should first be removed and the ear soaked in water so that the shucks will not burn during the baking process.

Starchy vegetables, such as potatoes, dry out if overbaked or get soggy if the skin of the vegetable is not opened when baking is finished. Because the time required for baking is greater than for boiling, time and fuel must be considered when using this method. Moderately hot oven temperatures, which form steam quickly within the vegetable, give better texture to starchy vegetables than is obtainable at low temperatures. Prompt serving of baked vegetables as soon as they are done is recommended to maintain quality and lessen vitamin losses.

Vegetables may be grilled over hot charcoal to develop delicious vegetable dishes (Figure 20-11). Like baking, grilling is a dry heat cooking method and thus many of the same cookery principles apply to grilled vegetables. Corn may be prepared for cooking on the grill in the same way as it is prepared for baking. Other vegetables may be cut in pieces large enough to not drop through the grates, or placed on skewers that can be easily turned on the grill. Both baking or roasting and grilling result in flavorful vegetables in part due to carmelization. Also, flavors are not diluted in a waterless cooking medium.

Frying.   Panfrying (cooking to doneness in a small amount of hot fat) and deep-fat frying (cooking submerged in hot fat) are both methods of frying. Potatoes, onions, eggplant, and parsnips are probably more commonly cooked by this method than other vegetables; however, many others could be satisfactorily fried.

Onion rings, eggplant, and zucchini are often battered before being fried in deep fat (Figure 20-12). Carrots, green peppers, parsnips, and mushrooms should be parboiled before being covered with batter and fried in deep fat. There appears to be little loss of vitamins and minerals in the frying of vegetables. Table 20-6 gives approximate temperatures and time periods for the deep-fat frying of some vegetables and vegetable mixtures. Frying is discussed in more detail in Chapter 10.

Stir-frying, Panning, or Sautéing.   In panning, the vegetable is stirred briefly in a small amount of melted fat before the pan is covered. Some cookbooks may refer to this light cooking of the vegetables as "sweating." As the vegetables are cooked in the oil, then steamed in the moisture from the vegetables, a more intense and desirable flavor develops. The pieces of vegetable should be thin, to allow for rapid heat penetration and short cooking time. Overcooking should be avoided. When done, the vegetables should still be slightly firm or crisp. The short cooking time and the small amount of water used (usually only that which clings to the vegetable) aid in conserving vitamins and minerals.

Figure 20-11
(a) Pita bread topped with tomatoes, basil, and cheese can be grilled for a great appetizer.

(a)

(b) grilled garden kabobs are a summertime treat that adds excitement to eating your vegetables. (Courtesy of Land O'Lakes)

(b)

This method could be considered a modification of frying, as a small amount of fat is used in the pan; however, the vegetable is cooked mainly by steam produced from the vegetable's own moisture and held in with a tight-fitting cover. Finely shredded or diced roots, celery, sweet corn, french-cut green beans, and finely shredded cabbage are satisfactorily cooked by this method. We often associate stir-frying with Chinese cooking because many vegetables and mixtures are so prepared in that cuisine.

Vegetables may be sautéed as a preliminary cooking step in a recipe or as the cooking method for a side dish. The light browning of vegetables such as diced onions, carrots, or celery in a small amount of fat at a moderately high temperature enhances the flavor and appearance which is desirable when preparing soups and sauces with vegetable components. When sautéing a vegetable side dish, quick-cooking vegetables may be cooked from the raw state. Vegetables such as carrots may be blanched first and then sautéed to finish. When cooking vegetables with differing cooking times together, the vegetables that will take the longest to cook should be started earlier than the quick cook-

(a)

(b)

(c)

Figure 20-12
Onion rings may be made from scratch: (a) dredging the onion rings in flour; (b) dipping in batter; (c) frying.

ing vegetables. Vegetables may be sautéed and seasoned with a variety of herbs and sauces for a tasty vegetable dish.

Boiling. When vegetables are boiled, they are either partially or fully submerged in water, which means that soluble constituents are likely to be lost in the cooking water. Soluble substances in vegetables include water-soluble vitamins, relatively soluble mineral salts, organic acids, flavor substances, and sugars. Much less loss of soluble material occurs if vegetables are boiled in their

Table 20-6
Approximate Temperatures and Times for Frying Vegetables in Deep Fat

| Food | Temperature of Fat | | Time (min) |
	° F	° C	
Croquettes (cooked mixtures)	375–390	190–199	2–5
French-fried onions, potatoes, and cauliflower	385–395	196–202	6–8
Fritters	360–375	182–190	3–5

skins. For example, pared potatoes may lose up to nine times as many minerals and up to four times as much total dry matter as potatoes cooked in their skins.

Losses of water-soluble constituents vary with the time of cooking and the amount of surface exposed to the water. In general, the more surface exposed and the longer the cooking time, the greater the loss. Losses are also influenced by the amount of cooking water, with more losses occurring as the quantity of cooking water increases. If the vegetables are such that cooking can be done in little or no water, or if the cooking water is evaporated by the time the vegetable is done, little or no loss of soluble material may occur. Also, cooking waters should be utilized for soups, sauces, and gravies to save valuable nutrients that would otherwise be discarded. It is important to avoid overcooking by bringing vegetables to the just tender stage, as tested with a fork.

Studies [12, 24] have compared the losses of vitamin C incurred by cooking vegetables in various amounts of water with "waterless" methods using only the water that clings to the vegetables after washing. The percentage of retention in the cooked vegetable varies with each vegetable, but seems to be higher with the "waterless" method or with a small amount of water than with larger quantities of water.

To cover or not to cover boiling vegetables is a somewhat controversial matter. It is probably desirable to cover all vegetables whose flavor and/or color are not impaired by covering, because cooking occurs more rapidly and uniformly in a covered pan. The continuous exposure to air is avoided, although air is not totally excluded, and thus vitamins may be better conserved. The cover makes possible the use of a smaller volume of water. Some heavy, tightly covered saucepans may develop a small amount of pressure, also hastening cooking.

In general, it is the chlorophyll-containing vegetables and the high-sulfur vegetables whose color and flavor may be most adversely affected by covering, although there are exceptions. In an uncovered pan, some of the less desirable volatile sulfur compounds from high-sulfur vegetables can escape. However, enough water to cover the vegetable is necessary for more uniform heating in an uncovered pan, with a greater loss of soluble nutrients and other flavor compounds. Young, tender green peas may be sweeter and have more marked flavor when they are cooked covered; however, when compared with a like sample cooked in an open pan, particularly if more water is used, the color is likely to be superior in the latter. Thus, the choice to cover or not to cover may be made for different reasons.

From the standpoint of flavor, it is usually best to add salt to vegetables when they are put on to cook. The loss, if any, of nutrients as a result of the added salt is probably minimal. The Dietary Guidelines for Americans recommend that salt be used in moderation. Cooking fresh or frozen vegetables without salt and seasoning them with a variety of herbs is an excellent way to help achieve this goal.

In general terms, placing vegetables in just enough boiling water to prevent scorching, covering with a tight-fitting lid, and cooking until just tender constitute an appropriate method for boiling most vegetables to retain maximum flavor, sweetness and aromatic characteristics, and nutritive value.

Steaming and Pressure Cooking. Steaming consists of cooking in steam, with the vegetable suspended over boiling water in a perforated container (Figure 20-13). Although some tender young vegetables may cook quickly in steam,

Figure 20-13

These broccoli spears are placed in a perforated pan to be steamed in a commercial foodservice steamer. In the home, small perforated liners are used above boiling water in a sauce pan.

most vegetables cooked in an ordinary steamer take somewhat longer to cook than those that are boiled. The fact that the vegetable is not actually in water favors the retention of water-soluble constituents, but the longer time required to cook most vegetables tends toward a loss of color in many green vegetables.

Cooking in a pressure saucepan involves cooking in steam, but the steam is confined in the tightly closed pan and a high pressure is created. The cooking temperature rises as the steam pressure rises. At 15 pounds of pressure the temperature is 250°F (121°C). Small, lightweight pressure saucepans can conveniently be used to cook a variety of foods (Figure 20-14), especially roots, tubers, and legumes. With young, tender vegetables such as spinach, the pressure saucepan may easily result in overcooking, with accompanying loss of color and flavor. The fact that acids released from the vegetable are trapped in the pressure saucepan also contributes to a loss of green color.

Figure 20-14

A pressure saucepan may be used to cook a variety of foods. (Courtesy of National Presto Industries, Inc.)

Many models of pressure saucepans are adjustable for 5, 10, and 15 pounds of pressure, and, when the cooking period is completed, the temperature may be quickly reduced by placing the pan in cold water. These features aid in desirable results for various types of vegetables. One disadvantage is the difficulty of testing for doneness during the cooking period if various vegetables are being cooked that require a shorter or longer cooking time than the recommended average time.

Flavor, color, and vitamin C retention in vegetables cooked in a pressure saucepan, in sufficient boiling water to cover, and "waterless" methods have been compared [24]. Vegetables cooked in boiling water were generally more mild and green than those cooked by the other methods. Percentage retention of vitamin C was greatest in the pressure saucepan for the majority of vegetables. In cabbage, cauliflower, rutabagas, and turnips, vitamin C retention was somewhat greater with "waterless" cookery than with boiling water, but the reverse was true for broccoli and brussels sprouts. The investigators concluded that if the acceptability of cooking methods is based on a cooked vegetable that is mild, has good color, and retains vitamin C well, then no one method is completely satisfactory for all vegetables.

Table 20-7 shows the approximate times for cooking vegetables by several methods. It should be emphasized that all timetables used in cookery are approximate and are to be used merely as guides. In using a timetable, it is best to cook for the minimum time suggested and then test for doneness with a fork before continuing to cook. Variations in the maturity of samples of vegetables, the sizes of whole vegetables or cut pieces, the variety, the temperature of the vegetable when placed in the water as well as the temperature of the water itself, and the amount of water are known factors affecting the time required to cook the vegetable until tender. Some varieties cook in half the time required by other varieties of the same vegetable.

Microwave Cooking. Generally both fresh and frozen vegetables can be satisfactorily cooked in a microwave oven. Some vegetables have better color and/or flavor when cooked by microwaves, whereas others have higher-quality characteristics when boiled in a saucepan or cooked by other conventional methods [6, 67].

Potatoes may be cooked quickly in the microwave oven, making a convenient preparation method. Even though trained taste panels rated microwave-cooked potatoes lower in eating quality than conventionally baked ones, a group of 120 consumers tasting both products in a supermarket found no significant differences in their acceptability [7]. Another comparison of several varieties of potatoes cooked by microwaves and conventional baking resulted in somewhat higher taste panel scores for the conventionally baked vegetables in all cases [42]. Cooking potatoes in the microwave oven for a shorter period, removing them, and immediately wrapping them in aluminum foil for a standing time of 10 to 15 minutes allow cooking to be completed with improvement in texture and aroma. Potatoes hold their heat for up to 45 minutes when wrapped in foil. Greater retention of vitamin C has been reported in broccoli cooked by microwaves than in broccoli cooked by various conventional methods [9, 11]. In a comparison of steaming, microwave cooking, and boiling fresh and frozen broccoli, steaming generally produced the least loss of vitamins, while boiling caused the greatest. However, in a later study, frozen broccoli samples retained similar amounts of vitamin C and thiamin when steamed or cooked by microwaves [28].

Table 20-7
Approximate Cooking Time for Vegetables

Vegetable	Approximate Amount for 4 Servings	Preparation for Cooking	Approximate Amount of Water for Boiling	Amount of Water for Pressure Saucepan	Time (min)			
					Boiling	Steaming	Baking	Pressure Saucepan (15 lb of pressure)
Artichokes, French	2 lb	Whole	To cover	1 c	25–40			10
Jerusalem	1 lb	Whole, pared	Partially cover	1 c	20–30	35	30–60	15
Asparagus	1 lb	Woody ends broken off, scales removed	To cover butts	⅓ c	Tips, 5–10 Butts, 10–15	10–15		Tips, 1–1½ Large tips, 2
Beans young green or wax	¾ lb	Whole or broken, strings removed	About half the volume of beans	⅔ c	20–25	25–30		1½–3
Beans, fresh lima	2 lb in pod (2 c shelled)	Shelled	About 2 c	½ c	25–35	25–40		2–3 (5 lb pressure)
Beets, young	6 medium or 1½ lb	Whole, skin, root, and 2 in. of stem left on	To cover	¾ c	30–45	60–75		12, small 18, large
Beet greens	1–1½ lb	Whole leaf with tender stem and midrib	Partially cover	½ c	5–15			2
Broccoli	1 medium bunch (1½–2 lb)	Woody stems removed, coarse leaves removed, smaller stems pared and split to hasten cooking	To cover stems	⅓ c	Florets, 5–10 Stems, 10–15			1½–2
Brussels sprouts	¾–1 qt	Whole, outer leaves removed; larger compact heads may be partially split	Partially cover	½ c	10–15			1–2
Cabbage, new green	1 lb	Outer leaves and stalk removed; shredded.	Partially cover	½ c	6–9	9–10		1–1½
Mature, white	1 lb	Outer leaves and stalk removed; shredded	Partially cover	½ c	8–10	10–12		2–3
Red	1 lb	Outer leaves and stalk removed; shredded; cook with tart apple or add 2–3 Tbsp vinegar after cooking	Partially cover	½ c	15–20	25–30		3–4

Vegetable	Amount	Preparation	Cooking directions	Water				
Carrots, young	1 lb	Whole, skins on or scraped	Partially cover	⅓ c	20–25	25–30	35–45	4
		Scraped, cut into halves or quarters lengthwise or diced			10–15			2–3
Cauliflower	1½–2 lb	Outer leaves and stalks removed; separated into flowerets	Partially cover	½ c	8–10	10–15		1½
Celery	1 medium bunch	Whole flower	Partially cover	½ c	20–25	25–30		3–4
		Cut into ½- to ¾-in. pieces		⅓ c	15–20	25–30		2–3
Corn, young green	4 ears	On cob or cut off	½-in. depth in pan; add water if needed	½ c on cob	5–10	10–15		1–2
			Cover ears; partially cover cut corn	⅓ c off cob	5			2
Okra	1 lb	Sliced or whole	Partially cover	⅓ c	10–20	20–25		3 (sliced)
Onions	1 lb	Two outer layers removed	Cover or partially cover	½ c	Whole, 25–35, Quarters, 15–20		45–60	6–7
		Whole, cut into halves or quarters or slices						3
Parsnips	1 lb	Scraped or pared; cooked whole or cut in half lengthwise; woody core removed	Partially cover	½ c	15–25	30–35		2 (sliced)
								7 (whole)
Peas, green	2 lb in pod	Shelled	½- to 1-in. depth in pan; added as needed	½ c	10–15	15–20		2–2½ (5 lb pressure)
Potatoes, Irish	1–1½ lb	Whole, with or without skins	Barely cover	1 c	30–35	40	40–60	15
		Pared, cut lengthwise into halves or quarters	Partially cover	¾ c	20–30	30–35		8

(continued)

503

Table 20-7
Continued

| Vegetable | Approximate Amount for 4 Servings | Preparation for Cooking | Approximate Amount of Water for Boiling | Amount of Water for Pressure Saucepan | Time (min) | | | |
					Boiling	Steaming	Baking	Pressure Saucepan (15 lb of pressure)
Potatoes, sweet	1–1½ lb	Whole, with or without skins	Barely cover	1 c	30–35	35–40	30–50	8–10
		Pared, halved	Partially cover	½ c	20–30	30–35		6–8
Rutabaga	1¼ lb	Pared and diced	Partially cover	½ c	20–30			6
Spinach	1 lb	Coarse stems and roots removed	1 c per lb or more	½ c	3–6	5–10		1–1½
		Stems not removed			8–10	6–12		1–1½
Squash Hubbard	1½–2 lb	Pared; cut into 2 × 3-in. pieces	½- to 1-in. depth in pan	¾ c	20–25	30–35		6–8
		Cut into one-portion pieces; rind on					45–60	
summer	1½–2 lb	Pared and sliced	½- to 1-in. depth in pan	½ c	5–15	10–20	15–20	2
Tomatoes	1 lb	Whole	Little or none	¼ c	5–10	10	20–30 (whole stuffed)	1–2
Turnips	1 lb	Pared, sliced or diced	Partially cover	½ c	15–20	20–25		1½–4
Turnip greens	1–1½ lb		1–2 c		15–25			1–1½

Fresh spinach cooked by microwaves retained 47 percent of its vitamin C, whereas spinach boiled in a small amount of water retained 52 percent [33]. In many cases, vegetables may be cooked in a microwave oven without the addition of water, thus decreasing the nutrient loss through leaching.

Whole vegetables or pieces should be of uniform size for the microwave oven to allow more even cooking. Large pieces take longer to cook than small pieces, and microwaving time increases with the amount of food being cooked. Vegetables cooked in their skins should be pricked or cut to allow excess steam to escape. Tender portions of vegetables, such as the buds of asparagus and the florets of broccoli, should be arranged toward the center of the dish (Figure 20-15). Standing time outside the microwave oven should be considered in the cooking of large vegetables. If these vegetables are cooked until the center is tender, then the outer portions become mushy. Microwaving is a good method for cooking corn on the cob. Each cob of corn may be wrapped in waxed paper before microwaving. General principles of microwave cookery are discussed in Chapter 7.

Frozen Vegetables

Essentially, the cooking of frozen vegetables is no different from the cooking of fresh vegetables. With the exception of frozen green soybeans, which require almost as long to cook as fresh ones, the cooking time of frozen vegetables is about half that required for fresh vegetables because they have been blanched before freezing. Vegetables may be defrosted before cooking, or the frozen vegetable may be placed in boiling water. The vegetable cooks more uniformly and in slightly shorter time when defrosted, at least partially, before being cooked. It has been suggested that vegetables defrosted prior to cooking may rate higher in texture and flavor, because more water is taken up by the tissues when vegetables thaw slowly. Because vegetables tend to lose vitamin C more rapidly after defrosting and because many users of frozen foods are not aware of many of the changes that may occur in vegetables after defrosting, the producer generally recommends that most vegetables remain frozen until cooking is started.

Corn on the cob, however, should be defrosted before cooking because the time required for cooking the corn is not sufficient to defrost the cob. In preparation for freezing, corn on the cob requires a longer blanching time to destroy

Figure 20-15

Arrange tender portions of a vegetable toward the center of the dish when cooking in the microwave oven.

Asparagus Spears

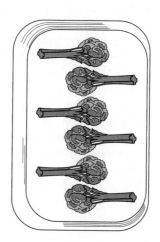

Broccoli

enzymes than cut corn. This longer blanching time cooks the corn more completely; thus, a short heating period is desirable in the final preparation after freezer storage.

Spinach and other leafy vegetables frozen in a solid block are better when partially defrosted before cooking to avoid overcooking the outer leaves before the block is defrosted. Using a fork to separate and redistribute the unthawed portions in the center midway during the cooking period is an aid in shortening cooking time and increasing the uniformity of cooking.

Canned Vegetables

Canned vegetables are already overcooked in the processing; hence, a relatively short reheating time is desirable to avoid further softening of the vegetables. A short heating period is safe for commercially canned foods; however, it is recommended that low acid home-canned vegetables be boiled for at least 10 minutes before tasting to destroy **botulinum toxin,** if present [1]. Boiling should be extended by one additional minute for each 1,000 foot increase in elevation. Commercially canned vegetables may be easily heated in the microwave oven or by conventional methods.

Retention of vitamins has been measured when canned vegetables were reheated in two ways: (1) concentrating the drained liquid, then heating the vegetable in the liquid and serving the small amount of concentrated liquid with the vegetable; (2) reheating vegetable and liquid together and discarding the liquid [27]. Vitamin C loss varied from 20 to 60 percent when the liquid was concentrated first; however, the loss was distinctly greater for the method in which the liquid was discarded. No thiamin or riboflavin was lost by oxidation in either method, but approximately 30 to 40 percent of these two vitamins was lost when the liquids were discarded. Obviously, other soluble nutrients are also lost when liquids are discarded. The flavor of many canned vegetables may be improved by concentrating and using the liquid in the can.

PARTIALLY PROCESSED VEGETABLES AND FRUITS

Fresh vegetables and fruits can be trimmed, peeled, cut, sliced, and so on for direct use by restaurants and other foodservice establishments without additional preparation. They offer freshlike quality plus convenience. These minimally processed vegetables and fruits are very perishable. In most cases they are more perishable than the unprocessed raw materials because the degradative changes related to senescence in the mature product are enhanced by the physical actions of cutting and slicing. Respiration by the cells increases in response to the injuries [84]. In any case, partially processed fruits and vegetables must be refrigerated and handled in a sanitary manner to ensure microbiological safety.

Food manufacturers are using a variety of technologies to produce minimally processed vegetables and fruits [60], including refrigeration, **modified-atmosphere packaging** in combination with refrigeration, and heat treatment in combination with **hermetic packaging** and refrigeration. Custom-tailored packaging films can help to slow the natural degradative changes due to cell respiration by controlling the oxygen, carbon dioxide, and moisture levels inside the package. The addition of vitamin C and calcium can help to maintain quality in some products while also enhancing nutritive value.

Methods of reducing spoilage in partially processed produce foods continue to be investigated. Fresh-cut iceberg lettuce treated with hydrogen perox-

---

botulinum toxin a very potent toxin produced by *Clostridium botulinum* bacteria; in a low-acid environment, the high temperatures achieved in a pressure canner are required for complete destruction of the spores of this microbe

modified-atmosphere packaging the enclosure of food products in gas-barrier materials in which the gaseous environment has been changed or modified in order to extend shelf life

hermetic packaging packaging that is airtight

ide and mild heat was found to maintain a higher level of sensory quality over 15 days of storage as compared to the control [46]. Consumers who participated in this study indicated they would be willing to purchase precut lettuce that had been treated with an antimicrobial solution. In another study, the effect of low-dose irradiation was compared to acidification, blanching, and chlorination as methods of maintaining the quality of diced celery. The irradiated samples were preferred in sensory tests and maintained color, texture, and aroma longer than the conventionally treated diced celery samples [53].

POTATOES

Potatoes are among the most important and economical of vegetables. Potatoes are consumed by 54 percent of Americans on a daily basis. In 1999, the per capita consumption of potatoes was 142 pounds [37]. Over the past several decades, the way in which potatoes are consumed has changed. Frozen potato use has increased and fresh potato consumption has declined (Figure 20-16). Frozen french-fry potatoes are consumed primarily away from home.

The white potato is a tuber of American origin, having been grown in northern Chile and Peru before the arrival of the Europeans. About half of the commerical crop of potatoes in the United States is grown in Idaho, Maine, California, and Washington [76].

Characteristics of Potato Varieties

Many varieties of potatoes are presently marketed. In the industry, potatoes are generally classified into five basic types: (1) round white, (2) russet Burbank (long russet group), (3) russet rural or round russet, (4) round red group, and (5) long white group. The skin of russet potatoes has a reddish brown, slightly

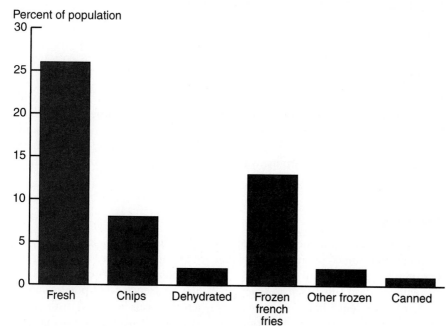

Source: USDA's CSFII 1994-96, 2-day dietary recall data.

Figure 20-16
Fresh potatoes and French fries are most likely to be consumed. (Courtesy of U.S. Department of Agriculture.)

mottled appearance. Several varieties of potatoes are pictured in Plate XIV. The Cobbler and Cherokee varieties are examples of the round white type; the Pontiac is a round red type; and White Rose is a long white type.

Mealiness and waxiness are qualities ascribed to cooked potatoes. A mealy potato separates easily into fluffy particles that feel dry. A type of potato exhibiting this quality to a marked degree is the russet Burbank, which is excellent for baking. On the other hand, a waxy potato is more compact and moist, or almost soggy, and does not separate easily into fluffy particles. Potato varieties that possess this characteristic are especially good for boiling and for salads and include Chippewa, Cobbler, Katahdin, Red Pontiac, and White Rose. Some varieties, such as Kennebec and Cherokee, are good all-purpose potatoes and function quite well in both boiling and baking.

Why some potatoes are mealy and others are waxy has not been completely clarified. The variety is an important influence on these cooking characteristics, but the soil in which they are grown, fertilizers, and climate may also have an effect. The content of starch in the potato may be related to its mealy or waxy tendencies. The starch granules swell markedly when potatoes are cooked, and water tends to be absorbed when they are boiled. It has been suggested that the swelling of starch causes the separation of plant cells that occurs in mealy potatoes.

density mass or weight per unit volume; potatoes with higher density or specific gravity are heavier for their size

It has been shown that potatoes with higher starch content are more dense. It has also been suggested that potatoes with a higher **density** tend to be more mealy. It is possible to test this characteristic by placing a potato in a brine solution of 1 cup salt to 11 cups water. If the potato floats, indicating a low solids content, it may be best for boiling; if it sinks, it may be a baker. However, not all researchers have found a correlation between specific gravity and textural characteristics of potatoes [45].

Mealy potatoes that are high in starch content tend to slough off their outer layers when boiled. Storage at temperatures between 50° to 70°F (10° and 21°C) seems to decrease the tendency of the potato to slough during cooking. Also, if the cooking water contains enough calcium salt to maintain or slightly increase the calcium content of the potato, sloughing can be partially controlled.

Grading

The U.S. quality standards for potatoes are revised as needed to keep up with changes in production and marketing. The top grade for potatoes is U.S. Extra No. 1, and the second grade is U.S. No. 1 [54]. The grade most commonly found on consumer packages is U.S. No. 1 [76]. Tolerances are set for defects, such as cuts, bruises, and sprouts, within each grade. Optional size designations may also be used by packers.

Processing

Large quantities of potatoes are processed in the United States into frozen, dehydrated, and canned potato products that are partially prepared for serving before they are brought into the kitchen. These products are part of the group of convenience foods discussed in Chapter 2. Frozen french-fried potatoes are a popular convenience item for consumers when they can be baked in the oven rather than finish-fried in the home. A surface-texturizing process that improves the quality of baked french-fried potatoes was developed at the USDA's

Western Regional Research Laboratory [51]. French fries may be fabricated from mashed potatoes or from raw potatoes [50].

Potatoes stored at refrigerator temperatures (below 40°F or 4.5°C) increase in sugar content because of changes in the metabolism of the plant tissue. Holding at room temperature for several days after refrigeration brings down the elevated sugar content. For the potato-chip processing industry, the sugar level is critical for the control of browning during frying.

Increasingly, foodservice operations and home consumers are using raw or precooked convenience potato products. For example, mashed potatoes may be purchased in a dehydrated form that is reconstituted with hot water or in a frozen state that only requires reheating. This trend began a number of years ago when the prepeeled potato processors recognized the need for a raw but more convenient potato in the restaurant and institutional foodservice market. After first offering only peeled and trimmed raw potatoes, they went on to provide many other convenient forms including diced, sliced, and french-fry strips. Some were preblanched or parfried. These products are primarily preserved by refrigeration or chilling [29].

Preparation

When harvested potatoes are exposed to light, a green pigmentation may develop on the surface. This greening has occurred even in retail stores, where the potatoes are exposed to artificial light. Unfortunately, greening is accompanied by the formation of solanine, a bitter alkaloid substance that is toxic if consumed in relatively large amounts [76]. Controlled atmosphere storage of potatoes may help to control greening [22]. Green potatoes should be avoided. If potatoes start to turn green before they are used, the green portions should be cut away during preliminary preparation.

Popular methods of preparing fresh potatoes include boiling and baking. Potatoes that are wrapped in aluminum foil before baking compare favorably in mealiness and flavor with those baked unwrapped [15], but baking time is somewhat increased for the foil-wrapped potatoes and the outside skin is softer. Microwave cooking of potatoes is discussed earlier in the chapter.

Some potatoes darken after cooking, the degree varying with the variety, the locality and/or soil where grown, the season, and differences in chemical composition. Discoloration is usually found at the stem end of the potato and apparently results from the formation of a dark complex of **ferric iron** and a polyphenol, probably chlorogenic acid. Addition of a small amount of cream of tartar (about 1 teaspoon per quart of water) to make the cooking environment more acidic appears to retard the development of after-cooking darkening in susceptible varieties.

ferric iron iron with a valence of 3^+ (Fe^{3+})

DRIED LEGUMES

Legumes have been the heart of many traditional cuisines for thousands of years [48]. Consumption in the United States has increased 19 percent between 1970 and 1999. In 1999, the per capita consumption of legumes was 8.6 pounds [57]. Many people are now recognizing the healthful benefits of a product that is rich in complex carbohydrate, dietary fiber, and protein, and is low in fat. Legumes are also relatively inexpensive as meat substitutes. They include dried beans, peas, and lentils in many different varieties, varying in color, shape, and size (see Figure 20-5). Table 20-8 lists some types of legumes. In the northeast-

Table 20-8
Some Varieties of Legumes

Type	Description and Use
Black beans	Sometimes called *black turtle-soup beans;* used in thick soups and in Oriental and Mediterranean dishes
Black-eyed peas	Also called *black-eyed beans* or *cowpeas;* small, oval-shaped, and creamy white with a black spot on one side; used primarily as a main-dish vegetable
Garbanzo beans	Also known as *chick peas;* nut flavored and commonly pickled in vinegar and oil for salads; may also be used as a main-dish vegetable
Great Northern beans	Larger than but similar to pea beans; used in soups, salads, casserole dishes, and baked beans
Kidney beans	Large, red, and kidney shaped; popular for chili con carne; used also in salads and many Mexican dishes
Lima beans	Broad, flat, and in different sizes; used as main-dish vegetable and in casseroles
Navy beans	Broad term that includes Great Northern, pea, flat small white, and small white beans
Pea beans	Small, oval, and white; hold shape even when cooked tender; used in baked beans, soups, and casseroles
Pinto beans	Beige and speckled; of the same species as kidney beans and red beans; used in salads, chili, and many Mexican dishes
Red and pink beans	Pink beans more delicate in flavor than red beans; both used in many Mexican dishes and chili
Dry split peas	Specially grown whole peas from which skin is removed and then pea broken in half; used mainly for split pea soup but combine well with many different foods
Lentils	Disk shaped and about the size of a pea; short cooking time (about 30 minutes); combine well with many different foods

ern United States, white beans for baking are the most popular. In the West, especially where there are Hispanic populations, pinto beans are preferred. Black-eyed peas, also known as cowpeas, are favored in the South. Black beans have gained in popularity in trendy restaurants.

Cooking

Legumes require cooking before eating. When they are cooked, proteins are made more available, starch is at least partially gelatinized [19], flavor is improved, and some potentially toxic substances are destroyed. A special problem in cooking is offered by the dry seeds—water lost in ripening and drying must be replaced by soaking and by heating. Because legumes are hard and the cellulose and other fiber components are well developed, the legumes must also be softened during the cooking process. The ease of softening depends somewhat on how readily the legumes absorb water.

Alkali in the form of baking soda has been used to hasten the softening of dried beans during cooking. Alkali increases water absorption, but there has been some question concerning the use of baking soda because of its destructive effect on the thiamin content of legumes. Another point of objection to the use of baking soda has been the possibility that the bean texture will become too soft.

It is generally not necessary or desirable to use baking soda. If it is used, however, the amount of soda needs to be carefully regulated (1/8 teaspoon per pint of water) to prevent deleterious effects insofar as the flavor and appearance of cooked beans are concerned. In these amounts, baking soda can serve as an aid in softening the seed coats if it is necessary to use hard water to cook the beans. Soft water is preferable for both soaking and cooking dry beans, because the calcium and magnesium salts in hard water may form insoluble salts with pectic substances in the cell walls and between cells in the bean tissue and inhibit proper hydration. There is more water absorbed and fewer hard beans remaining at the end of cooking when soft water rather than hard water is used.

The rate of hydration is faster in hot water than at room temperature or by the method of soaking all night in cold water [16]. Dry beans absorb as much water in 1 hour, when soaking is started by first boiling the beans for 2 minutes, as they do in 15 hours of soaking in cold water. If they are hot soaked, as generally recommended, the beans are cooked in the water used for soaking. Additional water is absorbed during the cooking process, making a gain in weight of 150 to 160 percent (about 4 cups of water per cup of dry beans for both soaking and cooking).

Legumes contain appreciable amounts of the oligosaccharides raffinose and stachyose, which are not digested by enzymes in the intestinal tract. It is assumed that the flatulence resulting from the ingestion of legumes results from the degradation of these carbohydrates by intestinal microorganisms. It has been suggested, as a result of one study on the carbohydrate content of various legumes after soaking and cooking, that the soaking and cooking water be discarded to maximize the removal of these gas-forming carbohydrates [82]. Flavor substances would then also be discarded, however.

One constraint limiting the utilization of dried beans is the length of preparation time required. The use of canned beans is convenient and saves time in preparation. A process involving a vacuum treatment in salt solutions before rinsing and drying has been developed to produce quick-cooking beans [59]. The resulting product cooks in less than 15 minutes. This process has not gained broad commercial application, however, partly because of the high energy cost [71]. Several precooked frozen and dehydrated bean products are available for the institutional market.

PLANT PROTEINS AND VEGETARIAN DIETS

According to a poll of approximately 2,000 men and women over 18 years of age, an estimated 1 percent of the U.S. population are vegetarians. Adoption of a vegetarian diet may be motivated by a variety of factors including ecological concerns, religious beliefs, economic considerations, and philosophical or ethical values [20]. The following general classifications of vegetarians have been outlined by the Institute of Food Technologists.

Semi-vegetarian: eats dairy products, eggs, chicken, and fish but no other animal flesh.

Pesco-vegetarian: eats dairy products, eggs, and fish but no other animal flesh.

Lacto-ovo-vegetarian: eats dairy products and eggs but no animal flesh.

Lacto-vegetarian: eats dairy products but no animal flesh or eggs.

Ovo-vegetarian: eats eggs but no dairy products or animal flesh.

Vegan: eats no animal products of any type.

It is the position of the American Dietetic Association that appropriately planned vegetarian diets are healthful, are nutritionally adequate, and provide health benefits in the prevention and treatment of certain diseases [3]. The lesser biological value of most plant proteins in comparison with animal products must be considered in choosing plant foods that will complement each other in essential amino acid content. For example, combining cereal grains that are low in the essential amino acid lysine but supply sufficient methionine

Hot Topics

Dry beans—Into the mainstream?

There is no question that people in the United States are eating more beans. Since bottoming out in the late 1970's and early 1980's, per capita consumption of dry edible beans has increased by one-third. You may ask, "Who eats beans?" This question has been addressed by the Economic Research Service of the USDA and they tell us that people in the southern and western states of the country account for 39 and 38 percent, respectively, of all bean consumption. People of Hispanic heritage represent 11 percent of the U.S. population but account for 33 percent of cooked dry bean consumption. California, Texas, and Florida have a high concentration of Hispanic population [39].

The USDA survey tells us that men consume more beans than women. As children grow up, they tend to develop a taste for Mexican-style food and therefore consume more beans. As a whole, cooked dry beans are favored by lower income households. The poor tend to consume more pinto and lima beans, while black and garbanzo beans might be termed the upscale members of the cooked dry bean community.

In a little different category of the many dry bean varieties available are soybeans. Production and use of soybeans as food began in China before the 11th century B.C. The Chinese and their neighbors consumed soybeans in traditional foods such as tofu, soy sauce, miso, soy sprouts, and green vegetable soybeans. However, this bean was not grown abundantly throughout the world until the 20th century [38].

Soy protein foods offer good alternatives to meat, poultry, and other animal-based products since soy has a complete protein profile. With greater emphasis on healthy diets, sales of soy products are increasing and soy is becoming "hot" [55]. The FDA has contributed to this trend by approving a health claim that "25 grams of soy protein a day, as part of a diet low in saturated fat and cholesterol, may reduce the risk of heart disease." No sooner had this regulation been issued, however, than questions arose about certain other components in soy products, particularly isoflavones, thus creating controversy.

The problem is that isoflavones, including genistein and daidzein, are phytoestrogens, a weak form of estrogen that could have a drug-like effect in the body, particularly in postmenopausal women. Research is far from conclusive but some studies suggest that high isoflavone levels might even increase rather than diminish the risk of breast cancer in some cases. There is still a lot of emerging data that is confusing and it is not clear exactly how soy acts.

So what should one do? Common sense and moderation are the best guides. Whole soy protein foods have benefits in promoting a healthy heart. Moderate soy consumption may be linked to a reduced risk of several illnesses, although soy by itself is not a magic food. But it is probably best at least for now to leave soy supplements—pills and powders containing high amounts of isoflavones—on the shelf.

with legumes that are lacking in methionine but supply adequate amounts of lysine yields a balanced protein. Vegetarian diets are generally high in dietary fiber and complex carbohydrate and low in fat, as recommended in the Dietary Guidelines for Americans, resulting in potential health benefits.

The food industry has responded to the interests of vegetarians in various ways. Meat analogs made from plant proteins are available as canned or frozen entrees; plant protein concentrates are produced from soy, wheat, peanut, glandless cottonseed, and other sources; tofu and wheat gluten are available; and more manufactured foods free of animal fats and milk proteins are being made. Some vegetarian dishes are shown in Color Plates XVIII and XIX.

Soybeans

Soybeans are a good source of protein of high biological value and have been used for centuries in various forms as a food staple by millions of people in China and Japan. Soybean products can play an important role in vegetarian diets. These beans were first grown in the United States in the 1920s, primarily because of their oil content. They still supply a large share of the vegetable oil used in this country. In the 1950s, processors began making protein products from soy: soy flour, soy protein concentrate, and isolated soy protein. Later, soy fiber was produced. Varied uses are made of these products in food manufacturing [64]; for example, soy lecithin is widely used in emulsifier systems for processed foods.

In past years, some uses of soybeans in the United States have been limited by their objectionable flavor and odor, sometimes characterized as being "painty" or "beany." Much research has gone into the study of this flavor problem, and several processes have been developed to control it. The off-flavor appears to be caused by the enzyme **lipoxygenase**, and it is now possible to inactivate the enzyme before it can catalyze the off-flavor.

lipoxygenase an enzyme that catalyzes the oxidation of unsaturated fatty acids

Soy Protein Products. Soy flour may be made from dehulled soybeans that contain the oil normally present in this product (about 18 percent); however, soy flour is more commonly prepared by grinding soy flakes from which soybean oil has been pressed. When soluble carbohydrates are extracted from defatted soy flour, *soy protein concentrate* is produced. It contains 70 percent or more protein. On further removal of nonprotein substances, *isolated soy proteins* remain, containing 90 percent or more protein. These several soy products are used for various purposes in food processing. Soy flour is shown in the large bowl in Figure 20-17.

Texture is given to soy and other high-protein products by special treatments. In one method, the protein isolate is spun into long fibers by a process

Figure 20-17
A variety of soy ingredients may be used in food preparation and processing. Top left to right, a glass of soy milk, a bowl of soy flour. Middle left to right, baked goods using soy flour; natto (fermented soybean paste). Bottom left to right, soy nuts; tofu. (Courtesy of United Soybean Board)

similar to the spinning of textile fibers. The wet protein mixture is forced through spinnerettes into a coagulating bath. The resulting fibers are gathered into bundles. Spun protein fibrils may be blended with other ingredients, often using egg albumen as a binding agent, and fabricated into many different foods. Some of these products simulate slices of beef or bacon.

Another method for producing texturized vegetable protein involves the process of *extrusion*. In this procedure, soy flour or protein concentrate is blended with water, flavors, colors, and possibly other additives. The mixture is then fed into a cooking extruder that works the material into a dough. As the dough flows within the channels of an extrusion screw and moves through the small openings of a die, the large protein molecules lose their original structure and form layered masses that cross-link with each other. These masses resist disruption on further heating or processing. The release of pressure as the protein mixture is extruded causes expansion, with tiny air pockets being uniformly dispersed throughout the mass. Texturized soy or vegetable protein (Figure 20-18) is available to the consumer and can be combined with other foods, such as ground beef. Consumer demand for the product has not yet been great. Extruded soy protein is used by food processors in such products as meat patties, tacos, chili, pizza, lasagna, stews, omelets, and stuffed peppers.

Before texturized soy products are combined with other foods, they are generally hydrated. Both seasoned and unseasoned forms are available. The USDA has written specifications for textured vegetable protein products that permit their use, on a voluntary basis, in school foodservice and other child-feeding programs. The vegetable protein mixtures are blended in specified amounts up to 30 percent with ground or diced meats in various menu items.

Figure 20-18
TVP (texture vegetable protein) can be processed from soybeans and comes in different colors and textures. (Courtesy of United Soybean Board)

Acceptable products can be prepared from whole soybeans, including canned soybeans with chicken or pork, vegetarian-style soybeans, and soybean soup [49]. Dry, whole soybeans are shown in Figure 20-19.

Soy milk is a common substitute for cow's milk in the United States and its sales have been increasing in recent years. This product is produced by grinding the softened soybeans and extracting the resulting liquid. Most of the bean's protein, oil, and other solids are present in the milk. To make the soymilk equivalent to cow's milk, it must be fortified with calcium. Commercially, the lipoxygenase enzyme is inactivated to avoid off-flavors. Soy milk in a glass is shown in Figures 20-17 and 20-20.

soy milk the liquid produced by cooking, mashing, and straining soybeans

Tofu (Figures 20-17 and 20-21), also known as soy cheese or bean curd, has a 2,000-year-old tradition as the protein staple for millions of people throughout the Orient. Now it is rising in popularity with Americans. Made by coagulating soy milk with a calcium or magnesium salt and then squeezing out the whey from the curd, tofu is a smooth-textured, bland-flavored, high-moisture product. It is available in different consistencies—silken, soft, firm, and extra firm. The soft, creamy textures blend well with other ingredients, whereas the firmer types can be cubed, sliced, deep fried, and baked. Many interesting dishes can be created with tofu (Figure 20-22). It can be **marinated** in a soy sauce and spice mixture to give it flavor; used to extend fish and chicken dishes; crumbled in salads; or blended with other ingredients in making salad dressing, dips, and puddings. It can also be used to make an attractive cheesecake (Color Plate XVIII).

marinated to soak in a prepared liquid for a time, in this case for seasoning purposes

Figure 20-20
Soy milk and cheese are common substitutes. (Courtesy of United Soybean Board)

Several fermented products are made with soybeans, including soy sauce, in which a soybean mash is inoculated with a culture of microorganisms and the mixture is fermented in a salt brine. Tempeh is an Indonesian food prepared by mold fermentation of cooked soybeans. Miso is a fermented soy paste used as a condiment.

Soybeans are a source of *phytoestrogens*, isoflavonoid compounds having weak estrogenic activity in the body. The physiological effects depend on the amount of soy products consumed, the age of the individual, and probably other factors. In October 1999 the FDA authorized a health claim regarding the association between soy protein and the reduced risk of coronary disease, to be used in food labeling. To qualify for this health claim, foods must contain at least 6.25 grams of intact soy protein per serving and also meet other criteria, such as being low in fat, cholesterol, and sodium. Tofu has been reported to contain considerably more isoflavones than a soy drink, but the soy-based formulas that were tested were found to be devoid of these compounds [17].

Figure 20-21
Tofu. (Courtesy of United Soybean Board)

(a)

(b)

(c)

(d)

Figure 20-22

Tofu may be used for a variety of tasty dishes:
(a) Tofu stirfry;
(b) this soup has a creamy base that uses soy instead of dairy products;
(c) this dairy-free pumpkin pie is low fat as well;
(d) this fiesta scramble may look like ordinary eggs, but in reality it is tofu seasoned with a hint of curry. (Courtesy of Morinaga Nutritional Foods, maker of Mori-Nu Tofu, www.morinu.com)

CHAPTER SUMMARY

- Vegetables can be defined broadly as plants or parts of plants that are used as foods. In common usage, vegetables are those plants or parts of plants that are served raw or cooked as part of the main course of a meal.

- At least three servings of vegetables per day and two servings of fruit per day are recommended. Vegetables provide vitamins, minerals, starch, protein, and fiber in the diet. Many vegetables are rich in phytochemicals that appear to have health protective benefits.

- Cellulose, a long-chain polymer of glucose, is the main structural component of plant cell walls. Other structural components include hemicelluloses and pectins. All of these substances are complex carbohydrates called polysaccharides. Pectins are found in the cell walls and between the cells. Pectic substances include protopectin, petinic acid or pectin, and pectic acid. Betaglucans are another fiber component. Lignin is present in the woody parts of plants.

- Vegetables may have a relatively high percentage of refuse or waste after trimming or peeling. Quantity recipes will express the amount of a vegetable in a weight or measure as either edible portion or as purchased.

- Leaf vegetables include a variety of greens. Iceberg lettuce is one of the most widely consumed greens. Leaf vegetables may be characterized as being high in water and low in carbohydrate and calories.

- Tomatoes, cucumbers, peppers, squash, and several other vegetables are classified as vegetable-fruits. Although these vegetables are botanically classified as fruits, they do not taste sweet and are generally prepared as vegetables.

- Broccoli and cauliflower are examples of flowers. Asparagus, celery, and kohlrabi are classified as stem vegetables.

- Root vegetables include beets, carrots, turnips, rutabagas, and parsnips. Onions, leeks, and shallots are vegetable examples of bulbs, which are enlargements above the roots. The potato is a tuber.

- Legumes are seeds and include many varieties of beans, peas, soybeans, and lentils. There is more protein in dried legumes than in any other vegetable group.

- Genetic engineering produces genetic modification at the molecular level. Genetic engineering allows genetic information to be taken from one living organism and transferred to another. This technology was used to produce the Flavr Savr™ tomato.

- Vegetables selected for purchase should be firm, crisp, and bright in color. In the wholesale market, fresh vegetables and fruits are sold on the basis of USDA grades. USDA grades are less commonly used in the retail market. The USDA uniform grades terms for all fruits and vegetables are U.S. Fancy, U.S. No. 1, U.S. No. 2, and U.S. No. 3.

- Fresh vegetables and fruits are perishable. They are composed of living respiring tissue that is also senescing and dying. All fresh vegetables of high water content will wilt and toughen through loss of moisture, or loss of turgor if stored for extended periods in unfavorable conditions.

- Lettuce may be stored in a controlled atmosphere to extend its shelf life. Many vegetables maintain quality for longer periods when stored under refrigeration.

- Preparation methods for vegetables should promote the retention of nutrients, while maintaining or developing a desirable color, flavor, texture, and general appearance.

- Vegetables and fruits can be classified into four groups on the basis of color: green, yellow-orange, red-blue, and white. The chlorophylls are green pigments; the carotenoids are primarily yellow and orange; the anthocynanins are red, purple, and blue; the betalains are generally purple-red; and the anthoxanthins are creamy white to colorless.

- In plant leaves, chlorophyll is present in tiny bodies called chloroplasts. When chlorophyll comes in contact with acids it chemically changes to a compound called pheophytin, which is a dull olive green. This change in color will be evident when green vegetables are marinated in an acidic vinaigrette or when green vegetables are canned and subjected to extended heating at high temperatures. Overcooked fresh green vegetables also will show this undesirable color shift.

- A small amount of baking soda will change the chorophyll to a bright green, more water-soluble pigment called chorophyllin. However, the use of baking soda is not recommended because of the potential for an adverse effect on the flavor, texture, and vitamin content of the vegetables.

- Carotenoids include the pigments *carotene*, found in carrots; *xanthophylls*, found in many yellow vegetables; and *lycopene*, found in tomatoes, pink grapefruit, and watermelon. Many carotenoid pigments may be changed to vitamin A in the body. These pigments are quite stable during ordinary cooking procedures.

- The anthocyanin group of flavonoid pigments is usually red in an acid medium and changes to blues and purples as the pH becomes more alkaline. Red cabbage is a vegetable containing anythocyanin pigments.

- Betalains are found in the root tissue of beets. These pigments are very soluble in water, thus peeling beets after cooking will help to retain color.

- Anthoxanthin pigments change from white to colorless to yellowish as the pH increases from acidic to alkaline ranges. Although these pigments are generally stable to heating, excessive or prolonged heating may cause darkening.

- Some raw fruits, such as bananas, apples, and peaches, and some pared vegetables including potatoes and sweet potatoes, will darken or discolor on exposure to air as a result of enzymatic oxidative reactions. Acids found in lemon juice or pineapple juice will interfere with the enzyme activity and prevent browning. Vitamin C reduces discoloration because of its ability to act as an antioxidant. Sulfites control browning and may be used in some food processing applications; however, some people are sulfite sensitive. Sulfites are not permitted for use on fresh fruits and vegetables to be used raw.

- The natural flavors that make each vegetable distinctive probably result from a mixture of many compounds including aldehydes, alcohols, ketones, organic acids, esters, and sulfur-containing compounds.

- Vegetables of the cabbage or mustard family, include cabbage, cauliflower, broccoli, brussels sprouts, kales, kohlrabi, mustard, rutabaga, and turnips. These vegetables are relatively mild when raw but when overcooked may result in strong, pungent, sulfurous flavor and odor.

- The onion family includes onions, leeks, garlic, and chives. These vegetables are usually strong flavored in the raw state, but tend to become more mild when cooked.

- Most vegetables grow near or in the ground. Therefore, contamination by microorganisms present in the soil is likely. Thorough washing of vegetables is necessary. Avoidance of long storage times and strict adherence to sanitation are essential to avoid and control contamination on fresh vegetables.

- The government monitors pesticide residues on vegetables and fruits.

- Vegetables are cooked to improve palatability, allow for easy and more complete digestion, and to destroy microorganisms. Some vegetables, such as dried legumes, would be difficult to consume if not cooked. Heating improves utilization of protein from dried legumes. Cooking also causes gelatinization of starch and increases digestibility.

- Cooking losses can occur through the dissolving action of water or dilute salt solutions, by chemical decomposition, by oxidation, by the mechanical loss of solids into the cooking water, and by volatilization.

- Fiber components appear to not be lost during cooking. Cellulose may be somewhat softened, but remains mostly indigestible for humans. Pectic substances may be hydrolyzed; however, the total pectin content is well retained. Calcium salts, as calcium chloride, make vegetable tissues more firm, probably by forming insoluble calcium salts with pectic substances.

- Vitamins may be lost two ways during cooking. Vitamins may be destroyed by oxidation or, if water soluble, the vitamins may be dissolved in the cooking water. The stability of vitamins varies by vitamin. Extended hot holding or chilling and reheating of vegetables results in increased vitamin losses.

- Vegetables may be cooked by baking, grilling, frying, stir-frying, panning, sautéing, boiling, steaming, pressure, and microwave. The cooking of frozen vegetables is similar to the cooking of fresh vegetables. Frozen vegetables, however, generally require less cooking time as compared to fresh vegetables because of being blanched prior to freezing. Canned vegetables should be reheated in a short period of time to avoid additional overcooking. However, low-acid home canned vegetables should be boiled for 10 minutes to destroy botulinum toxin, if present.

- Partially processed vegetables and fruits provide convenience for foodservice applications and home use. These minimally processed vegetables and fruits are very perishable and must be refrigerated and handled in a sanitary manner.

- Potatoes are generally classified into five basic types: (1) round white, (2) russet Burbank, (3) russet rural or round russet, (4) round red group, (5) long white group. The russet Burbank is an example of a mealy potato and is excellent for baking. Waxy potatoes, such as round white, round red, and long white, are best for boiling.

- Potatoes are generally not stored under refrigeration. The sugar content of potatoes increases when refrigerated. Holding at room temperature for several days after refrigeration brings down the elevated sugar content.

- A green pigment may develop on the surface of potatoes due to artificial or natural light. The greening is accompanied by the formation of solanine, a bitter alkaloid substance that is toxic when consumed in relatively large amounts. Green potatoes should be avoided. If some green areas are present, they should be cut away during preliminary preparation.

- Legumes include dried beans, peas, and lentils in many different varieties. Legumes are rich in complex carbohydrates, dietary fiber, and protein, and are low in fat. Legumes contain appreciable amounts of the oligosaccharides raffinose and stachyose, which are not digested by enzymes in the intestinal tract.

- Legumes require cooking before eating. Dried beans must be rehydrated by soaking in either hot water or cold water before cooking. Canned beans may be used to save time in preparation.

- Vegetarians may be classified as semi-vegetarian, pesco-vegetarian, lacto-ovo-vegetarian, lacto-vegetarian, ovo-vegetarian, or vegan. Vegetarian diets are healthful and nutritionally adequate. The food industry has responded to the interests of vegetarians through the development of plant protein foods.

- Soybeans are a good source of protein of high biological value and phyto-estrogens, which are isoflavonoid compounds having weak estrogenic activity in the body. Many types of products including soybean oil, soy milk and cheese, tofu, flour, soy lecithin, and texturized soy protein are available. Fermented products made from soy include soy sauce, tempeh, and miso.

KEY TERMS

phytochemicals
polymer
polysaccharides
oxalic acid
vegetable-fruit
tuber
carotenoids
precursors
legume
biotechnology
senescence
respiration
emulsion
controlled atmosphere storage
flavonoid pigments
oxidation
isomerization
lacquered tin
pH
phenolic compounds

oxidase
sulfhydryl compound
antioxidant
aldehydes
alcohols
ketones
organic acids
ester
gelatinization of starch
fiber
hydrolyze
de-esterification
botulinum toxin
modified-atmosphere packaging
hermetic packaging
density
ferric iron
lipoxygenase
soy milk
marinated

STUDY QUESTIONS

1. What are vegetables? (Define them.)

2. List eight classification groups of vegetables based on the parts of the plant that are used as food and give examples of vegetables in each category.

3. The composition and nutritive value of vegetables differ depending on the part of the plant used. Indicate which types of vegetables are generally
   a. high in water content
   b. high in starch
   c. high in protein

    d. high in fiber

    e. good sources of vitamins A and C

    f. low in kilocalories

4. **a.** List at least three plant polysaccharides that are components of dietary (indigestible) fiber.

   b. Name three pectic substances. What roles do these play in plant structure? Which pectic substance is important in making fruit jellies and jams?

5. The color of fruits and vegetables is due to their content of certain pigments.

   a. List five groups of plant pigments and describe the color for each group.

   b. How do the pigments and/or colors change in the presence of acid and alkali and with prolonged heating?

   c. Explain why it is important to preserve the natural colors of vegetables and fruits during cooking.

6. Flavor varies from one vegetable to another and many substances contribute to the characteristic flavors.

   a. List two different families of vegetables that are considered to be strong flavored and indicate what types of compounds are responsible for these flavors.

   b. Explain how cooking procedures may change these flavors.

7. **a.** Describe the usual characteristics of fresh vegetables of good quality.

   b. Suggest important factors to consider in purchasing fresh vegetables.

8. Both fresh and processed vegetables and fruits may be graded.

   a. What advantages result from the use of grades on fresh fruits and vegetables?

   b. What factor most limits the use of consumer grades for fresh fruits and vegetables?

   c. List three USDA grades that may be used on canned and frozen vegetables and fruits and discuss the value to the consumer of grading these products.

9. Suggest appropriate methods for storing various types of fresh vegetables to retain quality.

10. Describe some advances in biotechnology that can be used to improve some characteristics of vegetables and fruits. Give examples.

11. Why is it important to thoroughly cleanse fresh vegetables as a first step in their preparation?

12. Describe several ways in which losses may occur during the cooking of vegetables.

13. In the following list, check the items that describe what may happen when vegetables are cooked. Correct any incorrect statements.

   a. Starch swells and gelatinizes.

   b. Cellulose fibers harden.

   c. Volatile flavors are trapped inside the cells.

   d. Leafy vegetables become limp.

   e. Cellulose fibers soften slightly.

   f. Intercellular cement is hardened.

   g. Vitamins go off in the steam.

h. Some vitamins and minerals dissolve in the cooking water.
i. Texture becomes softer.
j. Some vitamins are lost by oxidation.
k. Some volatile flavors are lost.
l. Chlorophyll may be changed to anthocyanins.
m. Carotenes may become white.
n. Some volatile acids are released.
o. Pheophytin, an olive green pigment, may be produced from chlorophyll.
p. Proteins are coagulated.
q. Pectic substances are hydrolyzed or broken down.

14. Outline an appropriate procedure for boiling each of the following vegetables and explain why you would use the procedure in each case.
a. A green vegetable such as broccoli
b. Cabbage
c. Onions
d. Beets

15. Describe five appropriate methods for cooking vegetables in addition to boiling.

16. Describe an appropriate method for preparing frozen vegetables and canned vegetables.

17. Explain why frozen vegetables require less time for cooking than similar fresh vegetables.

18. a. Describe characteristics of mealy potatoes and waxy potatoes.
b. For what uses is each type of potato best suited and why?
c. Compare the probable characteristics of potatoes baked after wrapping in foil, those baked unwrapped, and those baked in a microwave oven.

19. Explain why the green pigmentation that sometimes develops on potatoes exposed to light should not be eaten.

20. a. Outline a satisfactory method for cooking dried beans and explain why this procedure would be appropriate.
b. List and describe several different legumes.

21. Describe various types of vegetarian diets.

22. a. What flavor problem has limited the use of soybeans in the United States in past years? How has it been solved?
b. Describe several soy products that are available for use in manufactured foods.
c. Describe two methods by which plant proteins may be texturized. Give examples of the use of these products in food processing and preparation.
d. What is *tofu* and how might it be used in food preparation?

REFERENCES

1. Alltrista Corporation. (2001). *Ball Blue Book: Guide to home canning, freezing, and dehydration.* Alltrista Corporation: Muncie, Indiana.

2. American Dietetic Association. (1997). Position of the American Dietetic Association: Health implications of dietary fiber. *Journal of the American Dietetic Association, 97*, 1157.

3. American Dietetic Association. (1997). Position of the American Dietetic Association: Vegetarian diets. *Journal of the American Dietetic Association, 97*, 1317.

4. Arnold, J. (2002). Watermelon packs a powerful lycopene punch. *Agricultural Research Magazine, 50*(6).

5. Bente, L. & Gerrior, S. A. (2002). Selected food and nutrient highlights of the 20th century: U.S. food supplies series. *Family Economics and Nutrition Review, 14*(1), 43–51.

6. Bowman, F., Page, E., Remmenga, E. E., & Trump, D. (1971). Microwave vs. conventional cooking of vegetables at high altitude. *Journal of the American Dietetic Association, 58*, 427.

7. Brittin, H. C., & Trevino, J. E. (1980). Acceptability of microwave and conventionally baked potatoes. *Journal of Food Science, 45*, 1425.

8. Broihier, K. (1997). Tomato tales. *Food Processing, 58*(8), 40.

9. Campbell, C. L., Lin, T. Y., & Proctor, B. E. (1958). Microwave vs. conventional cooking. I. Reduced and total ascorbic acid in vegetables. *Journal of the American Dietetic Association, 34*, 365.

10. Carlson, B. L., & Tabacchi, M. H. (1988). Loss of vitamin C in vegetables during the foodservice cycle. *Journal of the American Dietetic Association, 88*, 65.

11. Chapman, V. J., Putz, J. O., Gilpin, G. L., Sweeney, J. P., & Eisen, J. N. (1960). Electronic cooking of fresh and frozen broccoli. *Journal of Home Economics, 52*, 161.

12. Charles, V. R., & van Duyne, F. O. (1954). Palatability and retention of ascorbic acid of vegetables cooked in a tightly covered saucepan and in a "waterless" cooker. *Journal of Home Economics, 46*, 659.

13. Charles, V. R., & van Duyne, F. O. (1958). Effect of holding and reheating on the ascorbic acid content of cooked vegetables. *Journal of Home Economics, 50*, 159.

14. Craig, W. J. (1997). Phytochemicals: Guardians of our health. *Journal of the American Dietetic Association, 97*, S199.

15. Cunningham, H. H., & Zaehringer, M. V. (1972). Quality of baked potatoes as influenced by baking and holding methods. *American Potato Journal, 49*, 271.

16. Dawson, E. H., Lamb, J. C., Toepfer, E. W., & Warren, H. W. (1952). *Development of rapid methods of soaking and cooking dry beans.* Technical Bulletin No. 1051. Washington, DC: U.S. Department of Agriculture.

17. Dwyer, J. T., Goldin, B. R., Saul, N., Gualtieri, L., Barakat, S., & Adlercreutz, H. (1994). Tofu and soy drinks contain phytoestrogens. *Journal of the American Dietetic Association, 94*, 739.

18. Eheart, M. S., & Odland, D. (1972). Storage of fresh broccoli and green beans. *Journal of the American Dietetic Association, 60*, 402.

19. Elbert, E. M., & Witt, R. L. (1968). Gelatinization of starch in the common dry bean, *Phaseolus vulgaris. Journal of Home Economics, 60*, 186.

20. Farley, D. (1995). More people trying vegetarian diets. *FDA Consumer, 29*(8), 10.

21. Fordham, J. R., Wells, C. E., & Chen, L. H. (1975). Sprouting of seeds and nutrient composition of seeds and sprouts. *Journal of Food Science, 40*, 552.

22. Forsyth, F. R., & Eaves, C. A. (1968). Greening of potatoes: CA cure. *Food Technology, 22*, 48.

23. Gnanasekharan, V., Shewfelt, R. L., & Chinnan, M. S. (1992). Detection of color changes in green vegetables. *Journal of Food Science, 57*, 149.

24. Gordon, J., & Noble, I. (1964). "Waterless" vs. boiling water cooking of vegetables. *Journal of the American Dietetic Association, 44*, 378.

25. Herranz, J., Vidal-Valverde, C., & Rojas-Hidalgo, E. (1981). Cellulose, hemicellulose and lignin content of raw and cooked Spanish vegetables. *Journal of Food Science, 46*, 1927.

26. Herranz, J., Vidal-Valverde, C., & Rojas-Hidalgo, E. (1983). Cellulose, hemicellulose and lignin content of raw and cooked processed vegetables. *Journal of Food Science, 48,* 274.

27. Hinman, W. F., Brush, M. K., & Halliday, E. G. (1945). The nutritive value of canned foods. VII. Effect of small-scale preparation on the ascorbic acid, thiamine, and riboflavin content of commercially canned vegetables. *Journal of the American Dietetic Association, 21,* 7.

28. Hudson, D. E., Dalal, A. A., & Lachance, P. A. (1985). Retention of vitamins in fresh and frozen broccoli prepared by different cooking methods. *Journal of Food Quality, 8,* 45.

29. Huxsoll, C. C., & Bolin, H. R. (1989). Processing and distribution alternatives for minimally processed fruits and vegetables. *Food Technology, 43*(2), 124.

30. Institute of Food Technologists' Expert Report on Biotechnology and Foods. (2000). Human food safety evaluation of rDNA biotechnology-derived foods. *Food Technology, 54*(9), 53–61.

31. Institute of Food Technologists' Expert Panel on Food Safety and Nutrition. (1989). Dietary fiber. *Food Technology, 43*(10), 133.

32. Institute of Food Technologists' Expert Panel on Food Safety and Nutrition. (1990). Quality of fruits and vegetables. *Food Technology, 44*(6), 99.

33. Klein, B. P., Kuo, C. H. Y., & Boyd, G. (1981). Folacin and ascorbic acid retention in fresh raw, microwave, and conventionally cooked spinach. *Journal of Food Science, 46,* 640.

34. Kurtzweil, P. (1997). Fruits & vegetables. *FDA Consumer, 31*(2), 16.

35. Lazan, H., Ali, Z. M., Mohd, A., & Nahar, F. (1987). Water stress and quality during storage of tropical leafy vegetables. *Journal of Food Science, 52,* 1286.

36. Liener, I. (1979). Significance for humans of biologically active factors in soybeans and other food legumes. *Journal of the American Oil Chemists' Society, 56,* 121.

37. Lin, B. H., Lucier, G., Allshouse, J., & Kantor, L. S. (2001). Fast food growth boosts frozen potato consumption. *Food Review, 24*(1), 38–46.

38. Liu, K. (2000). Expanding soybean food utilization. *Food Technology, 54*(7), 46.

39. Lucier, G., Lin, B., Allshouse, J., & Kantor, L. S. (2000). Factors affecting dry bean consumption in the United States. Vegetable and Specialties Situation and Outlook Report/VGS-280. Retrieved November 25, 2002, from http://ers.usda.gov/briefing/drybeans/

40. MacLeod, A. J., & MacLeod, G. (1970). Effects of variations in cooking methods on the flavor volatiles of cabbage. *Journal of Food Science, 35,* 744.

41. MacLeod, A. J., & MacLeod, G. (1970). The flavor volatiles of dehydrated cabbage. *Journal of Food Science, 35,* 739.

42. Maga, J. A., & Twomey, J. A. (1977). Sensory comparison of four potato varieties baked conventionally and by microwaves. *Journal of Food Science, 42,* 541.

43. Matthee, V., & Appledorf, H. (1978). Effect of cooking on vegetable fiber. *Journal of Food Science, 43,* 1344.

44. Maul, F., Sargent, S. A., Sims, C. A., Baldwin, E. A., Balaban, M. O., & Huber, D. J. (2000). Tomato flavor and aroma quality as affected by storage temperature. *Journal of Food Science, 65,* 1228–1237.

45. McComber, D. R., Osman, E. M., & Lohnes, R. A. (1988). Factors related to potato mealiness. *Journal of Food Science, 53,* 1423.

46. McWatters, K. H., Chinnan, M. S., Walker, S. L., Doyle, M. P., & Lin, C. M. (2002). Consumer acceptance of fresh-cut iceberg lettuce treated with 2 percent hydrogen peroxide and mild heat. *Journal of Food Protection, 65,* 1221–1226.

47. Mintzer, E. S., & Osteen, C. (1997). New uniform standards for pesticide residues in food. *Food Review, 20*(1), 18.

48. Morrow, B. (1991). The rebirth of legumes. *Food Technology, 45*(9), 96.

49. Nelson, A. I., Wei, L. S., & Steinberg, M. P. (1971). Food products from whole soybeans. *Soybean Digest* (January).

50. Nonaka, M., Sayre, R. N., & Ng, K. C. (1978). Surface texturization of extruded and preformed potato products by a three-step, dry-steam-dry process. *Journal of Food Science, 43*, 904.

51. Nonaka, M., & Weaver, M. L. (1973). Texturizing process improves quality of baked French fried potatoes. *Food Technology, 27*(3), 50.

52. Papazian, R. (1996). Sulfites. *FDA Consumer, 30*(10), 10.

53. Prakash, A., Inthajak, P., Huibregtse, H., Caporaso, F., and Foley, D. M. (2000). Effects of low-dose irradiation and conventional treatments on shelf life and quality characteristics of diced celery. *Journal of Food Science, 65*, 1070–1075.

54. Produce Marketing Association. (1995). *The foodservice guide to fresh produce.* Newark, DE: Produce Marketing Association.

55. Pszczola, D. E. (2000). Soy: Why it's moving into the mainstream. *Food Technology, 54*(9), 76.

56. Putnam, J. J. & Allshouse, J. E. (1999, April). Food consumption, prices, and expenditures, 1970–97. Food and Rural Economics Division, Economic Research Service, U.S. Department of Agriculture. Statistical Bulletin No. 965.

57. Putnam, J., Kantor, L. S., & Allshouse, J. (2000). Per capita food supply trends: Progress toward dietary guideline. *Food Review, 23*(3), 2–14.

58. Reicks, M., Randall, J. L., & Haynes, B. J. (1994). Factors affecting consumption of fruits and vegetables by low-income families. *Journal of the American Dietetic Association, 94*, 1309.

59. Rockland, L. B., & Metzler, E. A. (1967). Quick-cooking lima and other dry beans. *Food Technology, 21*, 334.

60. Ronk, R. J., Carson, K. L., & Thompson, P. (1989). Processing, packaging, and regulation of minimally processed fruits and vegetables. *Food Technology, 43*(2), 136.

61. Schwartz, S. J., & Von Elbe, J. H. (1983). Kinetics of chlorophyll degradation to pyropheophytin in vegetables. *Journal of Food Science, 48*, 1303.

62. Singh, B., Yang, C. C., Salunkhe, D. K., & Rahman, A. R. (1972). Controlled atmosphere storage of lettuce. 1. Effects on quality and the respiration rate of lettuce heads. *Journal of Food Science, 37*, 48.

63. Singh, R. P., Buelow, R. H., & Lund, D. B. (1973). Storage behavior of artificially waxed green snap beans. *Journal of Food Science, 38*, 542.

64. Slavin, J. (1991). Nutritional benefits of soy protein and soy fiber. *Journal of the American Dietetic Association, 91*, 816.

65. Snyder, P. O., & Matthews, M. E. (1983). Percent retention of vitamin C in whipped potatoes after pre-service holding. *Journal of the American Dietetic Association, 83*, 454.

66. Steinmetz, K. A., & Potter, J. D. (1996). Vegetables, fruit, and cancer prevention: A review. *Journal of the American Dietetic Association, 96*, 1027.

67. Stone, M. B., & Young, C. M. (1985). Effects of cultivars, blanching techniques, and cooking methods on quality of frozen green beans as measured by physical and sensory attributes. *Journal of Food Quality, 7*, 255.

68. Sweeney, J. P. (1970). Improved chlorophyll retention in green beans held on a steam table. *Food Technology, 24*, 490.

69. Sweeney, J. P., Gilpin, G. L., Martin, M. E., & Dawson, E. H. (1960). Palatability and nutritive value of frozen broccoli. *Journal of the American Dietetic Association, 36*, 122.

70. Sweeney, J. P., Gilpin, G. L., Staley, M. G., & Martin, M. E. (1959). Effect of cooking methods on broccoli. I. Ascorbic acid and carotene. *Journal of the American Dietetic Association, 35*, 354.

71. Uebersax, M. A., Ruengsakulrach, S., & Occena, L. G. (1991). Strategies and procedures for processing dry beans. *Food Technology, 45:* 104(9).

72. U.S. Department of Agriculture. (1992, August). *The food guide pyramid.* Home and Garden Bulletin No. 252.

73. U.S. Department of Agriculture, Agricultural Marketing Service. (1994). *How to buy canned and frozen fruits.* Home and Garden Bulletin No. 261.

74. U.S. Department of Agriculture, Agricultural Marketing Service. (1994). *How to buy canned and frozen vegetables.* Home and Garden Bulletin No. 259.

75. U.S. Department of Agriculture, Agricultural Marketing Service. (1994). *How to buy fresh vegetables.* Home and Garden Bulletin No. 258.

76. U.S. Department of Agriculture, Agricultural Marketing Service. (1994). *How to buy potatoes.* Home and Garden Bulletin No. 262.

77. U.S. Department of Agriculture, Agricultural Research Service. (2002). *USDA National Nutrient Database for Standard Reference, Release 15.* Retrieved December 7, 2002, from the Nutrient Data Laboratory Home Page, http://www.nal.usda.gov/fnic/foodcomp

78. U.S. Department of Agriculture and U.S. Department of Health and Human Services. (2000). *Nutrition and your health: Dietary guidelines for Americans, 5th edition.* Home and Garden Bulletin No. 232.

79. U.S. Food and Drug Administration & Center for Food Safety and Applied Nutrition. (1998). Guidance for industry: Guide to minimize microbial food safety hazards for fresh fruit and vegetables. Retrieved November 30, 2002, from http://www.foodsafety.gov/~dms/prodguid.html

80. Van Buren, J. P., & Pitifer, L. A. (1992). Retarding vegetable softening by cold alkaline pectin de-esterification before cooking. *Journal of Food Science, 57*, 1022.

81. Van Duyn, M. A. S. & Pivonka, E. (2000). Overview of the health benefits of fruit and vegetable consumption for the dietetics professional: Selected literature. *Journal of the American Dietetic Association, 100*, 1511–1521.

82. Vidal-Valverde, C., Frias, J., & Valverde, S. (1993). Changes in the carbohydrate composition of legumes after soaking and cooking. *Journal of the American Dietetic Association, 93*, 547.

83. Von Elbe, J. H., Maing, I., & Amundson, C. H. (1974). Color stability of betanin. *Journal of Food Science, 39*, 334.

84. Watada, A. E., Abe, K., & Yamuchi, N. (1990). Physiological activities of partially processed fruits and vegetables. *Food Technology, 44*(5),116.

85. Wilkes, A. P. (1996). Phytochemical fighters. *Food Processing, 57*(11), 90.

86. Wilkinson, J. Q. (1997). Biotech plants: From lab bench to supermarket shelf. *Food Technology, 51*(12), 37.

87. Williams, P. G., Ross, H., & Miller, J. C. B. (1995). Ascorbic acid and 5-methyltetrahydrofolate losses in vegetables with cook/chill or cook/hot-hold foodservice systems. *Journal of Food Science, 60*, 541.

88. Zyren, J., Elkins, E. R., Dudek, J. A., & Hagen, R. E. (1983). Fiber contents of selected raw and processed vegetables, fruits and fruit juices as served. *Journal of Food Science, 48*, 600.

Fruits and Fruit Preparation

21

 What are fruits? To answer this question, we might begin by saying that all fruits are produced from flowers and are the ripened **ovaries** and adjacent tissues of plants. In this respect, from a botanical point of view, some foods used as vegetables, nuts, or grains are fruits of the plants from which they were harvested. However, the foods usually designated and used as fruits in food preparation have some common characteristics in addition to the botanical similarity—they are fleshy or pulpy, often juicy, and usually sweet, with fragrant, aromatic flavors.

ovary part of the seed-bearing organ of a flower; an enlarged hollow part containing ovules that develop into seeds

Thus, the definition of fruits according to botanical characteristics does not always agree with the classification of common usage. Several fleshy botanical fruits, including tomatoes and squash, are not sweet and are used as vegetables. Cereal grains, nuts, and legumes are dry (not fleshy) fruits and have been classified into separate groups for practical use. Rhubarb, which is not a fruit in the botanical sense, is often used as a fruit in meal preparation.

Fleshy fruits may be classified as simple, aggregate, or multiple, depending on the number of ovaries and flowers from which the fruit develops. Examples of simple fleshy fruits, which develop from a single ovary in one flower, are citrus fruits, such as oranges (Figure 21-1), grapefruit, lemons, and limes; drupes, such as apricots, cherries, peaches, and plums (Color Plates X and XII), in which a stone or pit encloses the seed; and pomes, such as apples and pears (Color Plates X and XI), which have a core. Examples of aggregate fruits, which develop from several ovaries in one flower, are raspberries, strawberries, and blackberries. Pineapple is an example of a multiple fruit that has developed from a cluster of several flowers.

COMPOSITION AND NUTRITIVE VALUE

Most fruits comprise an edible portion combined with some refuse. The refuse or waste may be as high as 33 to 39 percent in certain fruits, such as the banana and pineapple. The chief energy nutrient present is carbohydrate, which occurs mainly as sugars. Most fruits have only a trace of fat; two exceptions are coconut (35 percent) and avocado (17 percent). Only a very small amount of protein is found in fruits, and their water content averages about 85 percent. From a nutritional standpoint, fruits are valuable chiefly for their vitamin and mineral content and for their indigestible dietary fiber or bulk. Along with vegetables,

Figure 21-1
A cross section of an orange shows the various parts of the fruit. (Reprinted from Matthews, R. F., and R. J. Braddock. Recovery and applications of essential oils from oranges. *Food Technology*, 41 (1), p. 57. 1987. Copyright © by Institute of Food Technologists.)

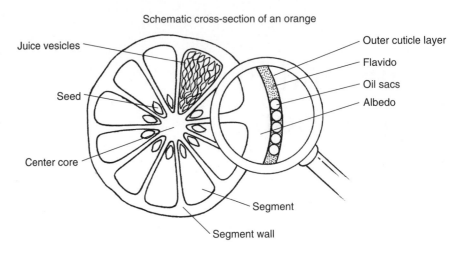

Schematic cross-section of an orange

Juice vesicles

Seed

Center core

Outer cuticle layer

Flavido

Oil sacs

Albedo

Segment

Segment wall

phytochemicals biochemical substances, other than vitamins, of plant origin that appear to have a positive effect on health; they include phenolic compounds, terpenoids, pigments, and other antioxidants.

succulent having juicy tissues; not dry

they appear to provide a protective effect against various types of cancer when consumed in recommended amounts [32, 40]. **Phytochemicals**, present in many fruits and vegetables, have been identified as being health protective [40]. Watermelon and tomatoes are both rich in lycopene, a phytochemical, that is a red pigment with antioxidant properties [2]. Usual serving sizes of fruits and vegetables are listed in Chapter 20, Table 20-2.

Whole fresh fruits are better sources of fiber than other forms. For example, a whole apple, with peel, has 2 grams of fiber. One-half cup of applesauce provides 0.65 gram of fiber, and 3/4 cup of apple juice supplies only 0.25 gram of fiber [30]. The caloric value of fruits, as served, is usually higher than that of **succulent** vegetables because of fruits' higher sugar content.

Certain fruits are especially valuable sources of vitamin C (Figure 21-2), whereas others contain only small amounts of this vitamin. The most dependable year-round source of vitamin C is probably citrus fruits. Tomatoes, although they contain only about half as much, are a significant source of vitamin C because of their wide use. In season, strawberries and cantaloupe make significant contributions. A generous serving of strawberries may easily provide the recommended daily allowance of vitamin C for an adult. So long as strawberries are not bruised or hulled, they retain vitamin C well. Slicing strawberries rather than crushing them in preparation for certain uses decreases loss of vitamin C.

When cantaloupe are at their optimum ripeness for fine flavor they have the greatest concentration of vitamin C, and the soft center flesh is richer in the vitamin than the harder, firmer flesh near the rind. Honeydew melons rate lower than cantaloupes, and watermelon is a comparatively poor source of vitamin C. The guava is extremely rich in vitamin C, containing an average of 242 milligrams per 100-gram portion of edible fruit. The kiwi is also an excellent source of this vitamin, containing 74.5 mg of vitamin C per serving, which is nearly equivalent to the amount of vitamin C found in an orange [37].

Yellow fruits contain carotenoid pigments that are precursors of vitamin A. Pink varieties of grapefruit have higher vitamin A value than white varieties. The B vitamins occur in relatively low concentration in fruits. Fruits vary widely in their vitamin content. Variety, growing climate and sunlight, and stage of maturity have been shown to be significant factors. In addition, handling practices, methods of processing, storage temperatures, and length of

(a)

(b)

storage of fruits may produce a decrease of as much as 50 percent in some vitamin values. The composition and vitamin content of some selected fruits and fruit juices are given in Appendix C.

Plants tend to concentrate calcium and iron in leaves and phosphorus in seeds. Fruits are therefore not generally considered excellent sources of these minerals. However, blackberries, raspberries, strawberries, dried apricots, prunes, dates, and figs may contribute appreciable amounts of iron to the diet. Of the fruits available year-round, only oranges, grapefruit, and figs are fair sources of calcium.

As with vegetables, fruit consumption is increasing, especially in the noncitrus category [29]. Between 1982 and 1997, fresh fruit consumption increased by 24 percent [27]. Processed fruit consumption increased by 4 percent during this time period. However, in spite of these increases, the per capita consumption of fruit falls short of the 2–4 fruit servings recommended per day by the U.S. Department of Agriculture, Food Guide Pyramid. Only 1.4 servings of fruit per capita were provided in the U.S. food supply in 1999 [28].

Overall, the increased availability of fruit is related to the greater variety of fruits in the food supply and the increase in juice consumption [3]. In the United States, juice is the number one form in which fruit is consumed [39]. During 1998–2000, 43 percent of the total fruit was consumed as juice, followed by 35 percent as fresh fruit. The variety of fresh fruit in the food supply is supported by the growth of imports. In 1999, 40 percent of the fresh fruit consumed in America was imported as compared to only 24 percent in the late 1970's [26]. Mexico is one of the largest suppliers of produce for American consumers, providing limes, melons, pineapples, mangoes, papayas, avocados, and strawberries.

Many kinds of fruit are now available year around. Winter fruit supplies had once been dominated by citrus fruits. With the development of improved transportation and storage, high-quality U.S.-produced fresh apples and pears are now available year-round. Tropical fruits, such as kiwi, pineapple, and mangoes are gaining in popularity and are available from both domestic and international sources. Fruits make excellent snacks, served fresh or processed. Applesauce and other canned fruits are being sold in snack-size containers. The availability of high-quality products, higher disposable personal income, the desire of many health-conscious Americans to improve their diets, and improved food distribution systems all contribute to the increase in fruit consumption [22].

COLOR

The pigments that give fruits their characteristic colors are the same as those in vegetables. In fruits, the predominant pigments are the yellow-orange carotenoids and the red-blue anthocyanins. Enzymatic oxidative discoloration is also similar for fruits and vegetables. Chapter 20 provides a discussion of these topics.

Mixing various colored fruit juices may sometimes produce surprising, often unattractive results. The tin or iron salts present in canned juices can explain some of the reactions that occur: The metals combine with the anthocyanin pigments to produce violet or blue-green colors. Pineapple juice contains a small amount of iron from the equipment used in its processing and, when added to red or purple fruit juices, changes their color to blue or intensifies the original blue color (Color Plate XXXII). Usually, acid in the form of lemon juice intensifies the red color of red or blue fruit juice mixtures. Orange

Healthy Eating

Fruits—"Feel good" foods?

A trend is developing in the fruit field! According to Elizabeth Sloan [31], Americans are in search of a "fruit fix." They hunt for fruit in the bottom of their yogurt and feel *less* guilty when they eat *fruit-covered* cheesecake. Many grocery shoppers say that they are increasing their consumption of fruits and vegetables, although as a nation we have yet to reach the recommended "5 servings a day." We are eating fresh fruits, fruit salads, canned fruits, and frozen fruits and buy more fresh-cut, ready-to-use fruits and vegetables. And fruit topped the list of desserts eaten at in-home suppers in the year 2000 at 23.3%, followed by frozen desserts and cake.

Health is one factor that is driving the fruit and vegetable trend. We hear much about reducing fat intake, lowering blood cholesterol, increasing fiber, and losing weight. And a number of fruits are promoted for their healthful content of antioxidants—particularly dried plums, raisins, blueberries, blackberries, raspberries, cherries and grapes [25].

But there are other factors besides health that are contributing to the trend. American interest in Far Eastern, Caribbean, and Island cuisines has created a requirement for lighter ingredients and sauces and for freshness in foods. Cooking and grilling with fruit is becoming popular and interest is increasing in many tropical fruit varieties. Fruits are great tools for chefs in foodservice as they create fruit chutneys, fruit-based salad dressings, and fruit 'n spice sauces. In the future, stir-frys and salads may highlight more fruits; meat and poultry dishes may be smothered in fruit sauces. In addition, there may be more fruit fondues, fruit sorbets, cobblers, and pies made with nontraditional fruit [31].

Indeed, Americans are looking for and finding their "fruit fixes." And food manufacturers have a great incentive to highlight the fruit content of their products as well as to create new and appealing fruit delights. Fruit is truly a potent sign and reminder of healthful, flavorful, and attractive food.

---

juice is best omitted from combinations of red or blue fruit juices because it often produces a brownish color when present in a fairly large quantity. Nevertheless, some very tasty and attractive juice blends, punches, and smoothies can be prepared (Figure 21-3).

The color of canned fruits containing anthocyanin pigments tends to deteriorate on storage whether the container is tin or glass. This deterioration is greater in the presence of light and warm temperatures. Canned or bottled shelf-stable cranberry juice cocktail is an example of a fruit product that will exhibit an unattractive reddish-brown color with extended storage.

FLAVOR

The flavor of each fruit is characteristic of that fruit. A ripe banana, for example, is readily identified by its odor and taste, which result from a specific complex combination of flavor components. The flavor of fruits, in general, may be described as tart, fragrant, and sweet, these characteristics blending together in a pleasant and refreshing flavor bouquet.

Aspartame, a high-intensity sweetener gaining widespread use, appears to enhance the fruitiness of natural fruit-flavored systems such as orange and

Figure 21-3
(a) Raspberry juice, raspberries, ba-
nanas, and vanilla yogurt blend to
make a beautiful and delicious fruit
smoothie.

(a)

(b) These fruit smoothies, composed of
bananas, strawberries, mangoes, and
cranberries, also make a wonderful
addition to any breakfast. (Courtesy
of Dole Food Company, Inc.)

(b)

strawberry. The addition of sucrose or table sugar does not produce a similar enhancement of fruit flavor [41].

Aromatic Compounds

Fruits owe their characteristic flavors largely to certain **aromatic compounds** that are present. Many of these compounds are **esters,** for example, methyl butyrate that is responsible for the typical odor and flavor of pineapple. Other compounds include aldehydes, such as benzaldehyde derivatives, and various alcohols, which have been found to be responsible for the floral and fruity part of the aroma of apricots [6]. In each fruit, many different compounds contribute to flavor; at least thirty-two different substances have been identified in the aroma of apricots, for example. In loquat fruit—a tropical or subtropical fruit with a flavor described as being mild, subacid, and applelike—researchers have identified eighty aroma substances. Benzaldehyde was a major aroma compound [13]. Some of the fruit flavor compounds can be synthesized in the laboratory, thus helping to improve the quality of artificial flavorings.

aromatic compounds compounds that have an aroma or odor

ester a type of chemical compound that results from combination of an organic acid ($-COOH$) with an alcohol ($-OH$)

Acids

Also contributing to flavor are **organic acids,** occurring in fruits in the free form or combined as **salts** or esters. Malic and citric acids are most commonly present, but tartaric acid is a prominent constituent of grapes. Although mixtures of acids may occur, one component usually predominates in each fruit. Fruits of the plum family and cranberries contain some benzoic acid that cannot be used by the body but is excreted as hippuric acid. Rhubarb contains variable amounts of oxalic acid, depending on the maturity of the plant. Oxalic acid usually combines with calcium in the plant to form insoluble calcium oxalate, which is not absorbed from the digestive tract. Fruits vary in acidity; some of this variation depends on variety and growing conditions. Scores for flavor have been positively correlated with pH in fruits such as peaches and raspberries [33].

organic acid an acid containing carbon atoms, for example, citric acid and acetic acid

salt a chemical compound derived from an acid by replacement of the hydrogen (H^+), wholly or in part, with a metal or an electrically positive ion, for example, sodium citrate

Essential Oils

Some fruits, as well as other plants, contain essential oils. Oil of lemon and oil of orange, well-known examples of such oils, occur in the leathery skin of the fruit (see Figure 21-1). They may be expressed and used as flavoring or as the basis of extracts, which are made by combining the oil with alcohol.

Other Components

Sugars, some mineral salts, and a group of **phenolic compounds** contribute to fruit flavor. Fruits cooked in metal containers may form some acid salts with the metals. Tin or iron salts in canned fruits may sometimes produce a metallic flavor, but these salts are not harmful. Phenolic compounds impart a bitter taste and produce an astringent or puckery feeling in the mouth. They appear to be present in the largest amount in immature fruits.

phenolic compound an organic compound that includes in its chemical structure an unsaturated ring with $-OH$ groups on it; polyphenols have more than one $-OH$ group

CHANGES DURING RIPENING

Distinct changes occur in fruits during ripening: (1) a decrease in green color and development of yellow-orange or red-blue colors, (2) a softening of the flesh, (3) the development of characteristic pleasant flavors, and (4) changes in soluble solids such as sugars and organic acids. The change in color is associated with both synthesis of new pigments and breakdown of the green pigment chlorophyll. Chlorophyll may mask yellow carotenoid pigments in the immature fruit. Anthocyanins are probably synthesized as ripening proceeds.

Involved in the softening of fruits are the pectic substances, the complex insoluble protopectin being degraded to pectin, which is also called *pectinic acid*. Gel-forming properties are characteristic of pectin, making it important in the preparation of jams and jellies. Further softening in ripening fruit produces pectic acid from pectin, with a consequent loss of gelling ability. The breakdown of pectic substances found between plant cells may cause separation of cells as part of the softening process. Many fruits soften faster when the temperature of the surrounding air is increased [5].

The development of a characteristic pleasant flavor in ripened fruit involves a decrease in acidity and an increase in sugar, along with the production of a complex mixture of volatile substances and essential oils. Thus, fruit that is not fully ripe may be tart and lack sweetness. In some fruits, such as bananas, the increase in sugar is accompanied by a decrease in starch; however, sugar content increases even in such fruits as peaches, which contain no appreciable amount of starch at any time. Some cell wall polysaccharides may decrease as the sugar content increases. In addition, the phenolic compounds, with their astringent properties, seem to decrease.

ethylene a small gaseous molecule (C_2H_4) produced by fruits and vegetables as an initiator of the ripening process

Fruits are living systems. Respiration occurs in the cells of the fruit as they carry on normal metabolic processes involving growth, maturation, and eventual ripening. **Ethylene** gas is a ripening hormone produced in small amounts by the cells after the fruit is mature. Without ethylene, the fruit does not ripen. Fruits that have been harvested well before ripening has started may be stored in an atmosphere that contains ethylene gas to speed the ripening process. Bananas are generally ripened in this way. This is the same concept that is being applied when fruit is placed in a closed bag to promote ripening. Because apples emit ethylene gas, an apple is sometimes placed in the bag with the fruit to be ripened. Ethylene gas, produced naturally by the fruit, builds up in the closed bag. Alternately, fruit that is fully ripe should not be stored in a closed bag or near apples, so as to reduce ethylene gas exposure. In general, there is no material difference in the gross composition (protein, fat, and carbohydrate) of fruits that ripen naturally and those that ripen by ethylene gas in a controlled atmosphere.

Ethylene production is stimulated when plant tissues are injured. Preparation of lightly processed fruits and vegetables for institutional use involves peeling, slicing, and cutting, which injure tissues and induce ethylene production. When these products are placed in sealed containers, the ethylene accumulates and accelerates undesirable changes in quality such as a decrease in firmness and loss of the pigment chlorophyll. It has been reported that when an absorbent for the ethylene gas (charcoal with palladium chloride) was placed in a small paper packet and enclosed in the package containing the processed fruit, the accumulation of ethylene was deterred, thereby preventing the softening of fruits such as kiwifruits and bananas [1].

Researchers also are exploring the use of an ethylene inhibiting chemical, 1-methylcyclopropene (MCP), to extend the shelf life of fruits and vegetables [7]. MCP is currently approved for use on flowers and plants; however, its use is not yet permited on foods. A petition is pending with the Environmental Protection Agency.

Ripeness and the method of ripening may influence the vitamin content of fruits. For example, the vitamin C content of bananas is greatest in fully ripe fruits, although the total amount present is relatively small. Vine-ripened tomatoes also have a higher vitamin C value than tomatoes picked green and ripened off the vine.

SELECTION OF FRESH FRUITS

An abundance of fresh fruits is available in U.S. markets year-round. In making selections, the consumer should look for signs of good quality, which are generally evident from the external appearance of the product. These signs include the proper stage of ripeness, good color, freedom from insect damage, and the absence of bruises, skin punctures, and decay. The grading of fruits, which may be useful to the consumer in making selections, is discussed with the grading of vegetables in Chapter 20. Quality may be better and prices lower when fruit is in season in nearby areas. In any case, when the fruit harvest is plentiful, the prices are lowest. Table 21-1 summarizes some points to consider in selecting various fruits.

Apples

Apples are among the most widely used fruits. They rank second in U.S. per capita fruit consumption behind bananas [26]. Apples are found locally in most parts of the United States in many varieties that differ in characteristics and seasonal availability. However, six states—Washington, Michigan, New York, California, Pennsylvania, and Virginia—account for more than 85 percent of the U.S. apple crop. Washington State is the leading producer of apples (Figure 21-4). Controlled atmosphere storage (discussed later in this chapter) has lengthened their seasons of availability. Of the more than 100 varieties of apples grown in the United States, only about a dozen are commonly marketed [24].

Apples have many culinary uses. They may be served fresh in salads (Figure 21-5) or as desserts and cooked in sauces, pies, and cobblers. Varieties differ in their suitability for being cooked or eaten fresh. Table 21-2 gives some suggestions for use, and Color Plate X pictures several different varieties of apples.

Avocados

The bland flavor and smooth texture of avocados blend well with many food combinations. Avocados are unique fruits in that they contain about 17 percent fat. Many varieties are grown in both California and Florida, and avocados are available all year [38]. They may be purchased slightly underripe and ripened at room temperature, preferably in a dark place. When ready for use they should yield to gentle pressure on the skin. Avocados should be refrigerated only after ripening. Figure 21-6 provides suggestions for avocado preparation.

Bananas

Banana plants grow in tropical areas and bananas of many different varieties are produced. As the plant blooms, a cluster of tiny blossoms emerges, each blossom producing one banana. The fruits grow together on a stem of about 300 bananas. After harvest, the stem is divided into hands, each of which contains 10 to 12 individual bananas. Bananas are picked green and ripen best after harvesting. As they ripen, the skin gradually turns yellow.

Table 21-1
Selection of Fresh Fruits

	Quality Characteristics to Look for during Selection
Fruit	
Apple	Firm, crisp, well colored; mature when picked; varieties vary widely in eating and cooking characteristics (see Table 21-2)
Apricot	Plump, firm, golden yellow; yield to gentle skin pressure when ripe
Avocado	Shape and size vary with variety; may have rough or smooth skin but no dark, sunken spots; yield to gentle skin pressure when ripened and ready for use
Banana	Shipped green and ripened as needed at 16° to 20°C (60° to 68°F); refrigerate only after ripened; firm, yellow, free from bruises
Blueberry	Dark blue, silvery bloom, plump, firm, uniform size
Cherry	Very delicate; handle carefully; fresh, firm, juicy, well matured, well colored
Citrus	Firm, well shaped, heavy for size, reasonably smooth-textured skin
Cranberry	Plump, firm, lustrous color
Grape	Well colored, plump, firmly attached to stem
Guava	Skin color green to yellow, depending on variety; flesh white to deep pink; round, firm but yielding to slight pressure when ripe
Kiwifruit	Chinese gooseberry renamed kiwifruit; light brown, furry, tender soft skin
Mango	Vary in size and shape; yellowish; firm, smooth skin; ripen at room temperature until yields to slight pressure; soft, aromatic flesh
Nectarine	Plump, rich color, slight softening along "seam," well matured
Papaya	Well shaped; well colored, at least half yellow and not green; smooth, unbruised
Peach	Fairly firm, yellow between red areas, plump, well shaped, "peachy" fragrance
Pear	Firm, well shaped, color appropriate for variety
Pineapple	Well shaped, heavy in relation to size; bright color, fragrant odor, slight separation of eyes
Plum	Fairly firm to slightly soft; good color for variety; smooth skin
Pomegranates	Unbroken, hard rind covering many seeds; varies in color from yellow to deep red; heavy for size; large sizes juicier; only seeds are edible
Strawberry	Full red color, bright luster, firm flesh, cap stem attached, dry, clean
Variety Fruits	
Atemoya	Small, green, rough skinned; creamy, soft, sweet pulp; large black seeds
Breadfruit	Oval or round, 2–15 pounds; yellowish-green rind with rough surface; white to yellow fibrous pulp; important food in South Sea Islands
Carambola (star fruit)	Waxy, yellow; five fluted sides; tart, sweet-sour flavor
Cherimoya (custard apple)	Almost heart shaped; uniform green when ripe; no mold or cracks at stem end; fresh pineapple-strawberry-banana flavor
Passion fruit (granadilla)	Size and shape of an egg; tough, purple skin; yellowish meat with many black seeds
Kumquat	Small, football shaped, yellow, firm; sweet skin and tart flesh
Loquat	Small, round or oval; pale yellow or orange; somewhat downy surface; thin skin; firm, mealy flesh
Persimmon	Bright orange; Hachiya variety slightly pointed and soft when ripe; Fuyu variety more firm when eaten (like an apple); smooth, rich taste
Plantain	Greenish looking bananas with rough skins and blemishes; frequently used as a vegetable; never eaten raw
Ugli fruit	About the size of a grapefruit; spherical; extremely rough peel, badly disfigured, with light green blemishes that turn orange when fruit is mature; very juicy with orangelike flavor

Source: Reference 35, 38.

Bananas rank second in world fruit production but are first in fruit sales in the United States. They are generally available year-round. The United States imports bananas primarily from Costa Rica, Guatemala, Ecuador, Colombia, and Honduras [26]. Until they are fully ripe, they should be kept at room temperature; they do not ripen normally if chilled. When the skin is green tipped, bananas are best for cooking—baking or broiling. Fully yellow bananas are good for eating or using in salads and desserts. Brown-speckled skins indicate very ripe fruit that is excellent for mashing and use in baked products. Skins with a gray appearance have been cold damaged and may not ripen properly.

Bananas have been used to reduce fat in baked products. A fat replacement system composed of banana flakes, cellulose gel, and cellulose gum is being de-

Table 21-2
Desirability of Apple Varieties for Different Uses

Variety	Flavor and Texture	Fresh and in Salads	Pies	Sauces	Baking	Freezing (Slices)	Main Season
Cortland	Mild, tender	Excellent	Excellent	Very good	Good	Very good	Oct. to Jan.
Red Delicious	Sweet, mellow	Excellent	Poor	Fair	Poor	Fair	Sept. to May
Golden Delicious	Sweet, semifirm	Excellent	Very good	Good	Very good	Very good	Sept. to Apr.
Gravenstein	Tart, crisp	Good	Good	Good	Good	Good	July to Sept.
R. I. Greening	Slightly tart, firm	Poor	Excellent	Excellent	Very good	Excellent	Oct. to Mar.
Jonathan	Tart, tender	Very good	Very good	Very good	Poor	Very good	Sept. to Jan.
McIntosh	Slightly tart, tender	Excellent	Excellent	Good	Fair	Good	Sept. to Apr.
Rome Beauty	Slightly tart, firm	Good	Very good	Very good	Excellent	Very good	Oct. to Apr.
Stayman	Tart, semifirm	Excellent	Good	Good	Good	Good	Oct. to Mar.
Winesap	Slightly tart, firm	Excellent	Good	Good	Good	Very good	Oct. to June
Yellow Transparent	Tart, soft	Poor	Excellent	Good	Poor	Poor	July to Aug.
York Imperial	Tart, firm	Fair	Good	Very good	Good	Good	Oct. to May

Source: Reference 35.

veloped. It can replace up to 100 percent of the fat in a baked product and up to 50 percent of the sugar. No banana flavor is perceptible [36].

Berries

Blueberries, strawberries (Color Plate XII), cranberries, raspberries, blackberries are some of the varieties of berries available in the marketplace. Blueberries are available from May through September. Large blueberries are cultivated varieties and the small berries are wild. High quality blueberries should be a dark blue color with a silvery bloom, which is a natural protective coating [38]. Blue-

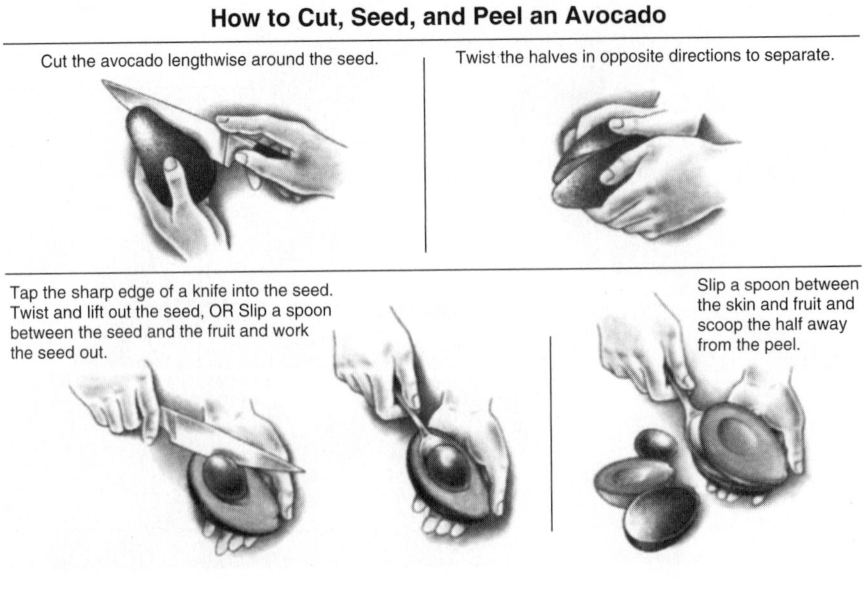

Figure 21-6
Preparation of avocado. (Courtesy of California Avocado Commission)

How to Cut, Seed, and Peel an Avocado

Cut the avocado lengthwise around the seed.

Twist the halves in opposite directions to separate.

Tap the sharp edge of a knife into the seed. Twist and lift out the seed, OR Slip a spoon between the seed and the fruit and work the seed out.

Slip a spoon between the skin and fruit and scoop the half away from the peel.

berries should be washed immediately before use, not before storage. Cranberries are marketed primarily from September through January and are a seasonal favorite in many homes over the fall and winter holidays.

Strawberries should have a full red color, firm flesh, and the cap stem attached [38]. Like other berries, strawberries should be washed just before use. Washed berries will mold rapidly during storage. Strawberries are most readily available in May and June, although with transportation from warmer U.S. climates and imports, strawberries can be purchased nearly throughout the year. Blackberries, raspberries, dewberries, and loganberries are similar to each other in structure. These berries should be plump and tender, but not mushy, when purchased.

Cherries

Cherries may be sweet or tart [24]. Tart cherries are generally used for cooking and baking. Sweet cherries include the dark red Bing and Lambert varieties and the yellowish Royal Anne (Color Plate X). Cherries do not ripen off the trees and decay rapidly. The marketing season, depending on the variety, is from May to August for domestic cherries.

Citrus Fruits

Oranges, lemons, grapefruit, limes, tangerines, kumquats, and tangelos (which are a cross between a tangerine and a grapefruit) are included in the citrus fruit classification. The chief producing areas of these fruits in the United States are Florida, California, Texas, and Arizona. Citrus fruits are a most valuable and reliable source of vitamin C in the diet and are also noted for the tart and appetizing flavor they contribute to fruit desserts and salads (Figure 21-7).

In addition to being graded, citrus fruits can be classified on the basis of size, depending on the quantity of fruit required to fill certain standard-size containers. Cartons holding 35 to 38 pounds are often used. Large oranges may be 56 count (fifty-six oranges per carton); medium oranges may be 88 count; and small oranges may be 113 or even 138 count. Large oranges are usually

Figure 21-7
Caramelized orange and grapefruit segments with raspberry sorbet make a tasty, light dessert. (Courtesy of © Sunkist Growers, Inc. All rights reserved.)

about 4 3/8 inches in diameter, medium ones about 3 1/2 inches, and small ones about 2 1/2 inches.

Except for making juice, large oranges are generally preferred by consumers over small ones. The most common criticisms of large oranges are excessive waste from thick skins and excessive expense. Large fruit is often classed as fancy fruit and its price may increase at a faster rate than the edible portion. For juice extraction, small sizes or ungraded stock may be most economical. Generally the juice from small oranges is higher in total solids, acid, and vitamin C than that of medium-size fruit and higher still than that of large fruit. In the purchase of citrus fruits, it should be noted that fruits that are relatively thin skinned, firm, and heavy in relation to size usually contain more juice than thicker-skinned and lighter-weight products. Russeting, which is a tan, brown, or blackish mottling or speckling on the skin of some Florida and Texas oranges and grapefruit, has no effect on eating quality.

Two principal market varieties of oranges are the Valencia and the navel. For juice extraction, the Valencia orange is often preferable, whereas for slicing or sectioning, the navel orange may be more satisfactory. The navel orange is distinguished by the formation of a navel at the apex or blossom end of the fruit. This formation appears to be a tiny orange within a larger one. The navel orange is available from California and Arizona from November until early May and has no seeds, less juice, and a thicker, somewhat more pebbled skin than the Valencia—a skin that is easily removed by hand, and segments that separate easily. The western Valencia is available from late April through October. Florida and Texas oranges are marketed from early October until late June and include several varieties, with the Valencias being marketed from late March through June. All Valencias have seeds, but the California Valencia has only a few. Most of the Florida Valencias have yellow skins, much juice, and light-colored juice and pulp. Valencia oranges have a tendency late in the season to turn from a bright orange to a greenish tinge, particularly around the stem end. This change in color affects only the outer skin. The oranges are matured and fully ripe inside. Some oranges are artificially colored to improve their external appearance.

Some varieties of grapefruit are classed as seedless, though they often contain a few seeds, and some as seeded. Some grapefruit varieties have white flesh, whereas others have pink or red flesh. Although Florida is the main producer of grapefruit, it is also supplied by Texas, California, and Arizona. Grapefruit is available all year but is most abundant from January through May.

Grapes

Grapes are the leading fruit crop in the world and the second in the United States. California produces 97 percent of the table grapes in the United States. Grapes also are grown in Arizona. Over half of all the grapes grown in the United States are used to make wine [30]. European types of grapes, which are firm fleshed and very sweet, include the Thompson seedless (an early green grape), the Tokay and Cardinal (early, bright red grapes), and the Emperor (late, deep red grape). American types of grapes have softer flesh and are very juicy. The blue-black Concord variety is commonly marketed and is unexcelled for juice and jelly making.

Grapes are picked ripe and thus do not ripen in storage. Like many other fresh fruits, grapes should not be washed until ready to use [24]. When selecting, look for grapes that are well colored, plump, and firmly attached to the stem [38]. Stems should be green and pliable.

Melons

Melons (Figure 21-8) are among the most difficult of fruits to select. No absolute guide for selection is available, but desirability is indicated by such qualities as ripeness, heaviness in relation to size, usually a characteristic aroma, characteristic color, and freedom from abnormal shape, decay, and disease. The ripeness of some melons, such as honeydew, crenshaw, casaba, and cantaloupe, is indicated by color and a slight yielding to thumb pressure on the bud end or on the surface. If the melon was mature when picked, it usually shows a round dent where the stem broke away from the melon.

Most cantaloupes are firm and not completely ripe when first displayed in markets. Holding them a few days at room temperature allows the completion of ripening. The color of uncut watermelons is probably the best key to ripeness. A yellowish underside, regardless of the green color of the rest of the melon, is a good sign. Other guides in selection might be a relatively smooth surface, a slight dullness to the rind, and ends of the melon that are filled out and rounded. In cut watermelons, desirable characteristics include firm, juicy flesh with a good red color, dark brown or black seeds, and no white streaks.

Foodborne outbreaks of salmonellosis have been traced to melons, the organisms probably having been introduced from the unwashed rind into the fruit during the cutting of the melons. The microbes will multiply on cut melon if temperatures are suitable for growth. Outbreaks of *E. coli* O157:H7 have been associated with cantaloupe from salad bars. The melon may have been innoculated with *E. coli* by cross-contamination from another product, such as beef, during kitchen preparation [12]. Thus, measures to prevent or reduce the risk of foodborne illness include: thorough washing of the melon before cutting, use of good personal hygiene and kitchen sanitation practices, and refrigeration of prepared melons. Food safety is discussed in Chapter 3.

Figure 21-8
A variety of melons include the cantaloupe (front and center), the casaba on the left; a cut honeydew behind the casaba; a cut crenshaw in the rear center; and a Santa Claus or Christmas melon in the upper right.
(Courtesy of the United Fresh Fruit and Vegetable Association)

Peaches and Nectarines

Both nectarines and peaches originated in Asia thousands of years ago. Although peaches and nectarines are similar, they each are distinct fruits (Color Plate X). Nectarines do not have the fuzzy coat of peaches, but will have a strong "peachy" fragrance even when only partially ripe. Nectarines and peaches may be freestone or clingstone. The flesh of freestone varieties will separate readily from the flesh and are used most commonly for eating fresh or freezing. The flesh clings to the pit of clingstone varieties. Clingstones are used primarily for canning [38].

An important factor in peach quality is the stage of maturity at harvest. Peaches will ripen off the tree. Once picked, they are immediately dipped in ice water to remove the field heat and stop the ripening process. Then they are stored at 34° to 40°F (1° to 5°C) to keep ripening at a minimum and retard decay. If peaches are picked too soon, they will never ripen after cold storage and they will lack flavor [23].

The best quality peaches have a good yellow undercover and yield slightly to finger pressure. The appearance of a peach does not always indicate the flavor, although our marketing system is such that appearance is of prime importance [23]. Peaches should be eaten at optimum ripeness. It may be necessary to keep them at room temperature in a paper bag until this stage is reached.

Plums

Many varieties of plums are available (Color Plate X). The peak season for domestic plums is June through September [24]. Plums are highly perishable, thus must be purchased and used at peak quality or spoilage will occur. Plums should range from firm to slightly soft when purchased.

Pears

The most popular type of pear is the Bartlett. Other varieties of pears, grown primarily in Washington, Oregon, and California, are Anjou, Bosc, Winter Nellis, and Comice (Color Plate XI) [38]. Pears are generally firm when purchased, but will soften at room temperature. Fully ripe pears will be sweet and juicy.

Pineapple

The pineapple plant bears its first fruit 18 to 22 months after planting. Each plant produces a single 4- to 5-pound fruit. The fruit is harvested when the appropriate stage of sweetness is reached. The optimum flavor is a balance between sweet and tart. The sweetest flavor and brightest yellow color are found at the base of the pineapple fruit.

A ripe pineapple has a rich fragrance. It springs back slightly when touched. Color may vary from green through brown to gold and is not an indication of ripeness. A hard pineapple should be kept at room temperature until it becomes fragrant and springy. Once ripe, it can be refrigerated.

Pineapple is a popular canned fruit. It may be processed as chunks, cubes, slices, or crushed. The preparation of pineapple in the home is shown in Figure 21-9.

(a) (b) (c)

Figure 21-9

Fresh pineapple may be quickly prepared. (a) slice off leaves and stem end then stand fruit upright and cut the peel off in vertical strips. (b) Cut the fruit in quarters then remove the woody core as shown. (c) Cut the flesh into wedges or chunks as desired. (Source: Reference 17)

Variety Fruits

Many uncommon fruits have appeared on the market throughout the United States in recent years. As consumers become more familiar with these fruits and learn to use them, their market share increases. *Kiwifruit* or Chinese gooseberries, grown in New Zealand and California, for example, has become a widely accepted fruit in a relatively short time. Californian kiwifruit are marketed from October through May. Although the furry skin is edible, most prefer to peel the skin to reveal the bright green flesh (Figure 21-10). Ripe kiwifruit should yield slightly to the touch.

Coconuts are familiar to American consumers as packaged flaked coconut. However, fresh coconuts may be preferred in some recipes due to their flavor. Fresh coconuts are prepared by puncturing the shell through one of the eyes with a ice pick or knife, then draining out the coconut milk. Next the shell is baked in a 350°F (177°C) oven for approximately 15 minutes and placed in the freezer until cool, but not frozen. This heating and cooling process will allow the flesh to separate easily from the shell. Any brown skin remaining on the coconut may be pared or peeled off. The coconut milk and the shredded coconut may be used in many dishes.

Mangoes have become popular with the interest in Caribbean and Mexican cuisines. Mangoes have a spicy, sweet flavor with an acidic note. These fruits are grown primarily in Florida, Mexico, Haiti, and Puerto Rico [24]. Ripe mangoes should have yellow, orange, or red skins. The preparation of mangoes is shown in Figure 21-11 [17].

Papayas are available year around, with supplies peaking in May through September (Color Plate XIII). A ripe papaya should yield to gentle pressure [24]. Papayas may be eaten raw or used for sauces, sorbets, pickles, or chutneys [17]. The seeds are edible, providing a peppery flavor with a crunch (Figure 21-12). Other exotic fruits include *passion fruit*, a small egg-shaped fruit with an intense and tart flavor that goes well in fruit punches and juices. The pulp can be used in desserts such as sherbets, ice creams, and parfaits. The *prickly pear* can be chilled, the spines and peel cut away, sliced, and served raw. The *cherimoya* can be chilled, cut in half, and eaten with a spoon. The *carambola*, or

Figure 21-10

Kiwifruit has a brown, fuzzy skin on the exterior and bright green flesh and small black seeds on the interior. (Source: Reference 17)

(a)   (b)   (c)

Figure 21-11
A mango can be pitted and cut by: (a) Cut along each side of the pit. (b) Cube each section by making crosswise cuts through the flesh, just to the skin. Press up on the skin side to expose the cubes. (c) Cut the cubes off for use in salads and other dishes. (Source: Reference 17)

star fruit, is recognized by the star shape of a slice. It is very tart, with a sweet-sour flavor, and is often cooked. Other variety fruits are listed in Table 21-1 and pictured in Color Plates XIII.

STORAGE OF FRESH FRUITS

Fruits are actively metabolizing tissues and, even after harvesting, continue to respire—to take in oxygen and give off carbon dioxide. Cold temperatures reduce the rate of metabolism and retard ripening but do not completely stop these processes. An additional aid in controlling metabolic changes and thus lengthening the possible storage period, or extending the shelf life, for certain fruits is an industrial process called *controlled atmosphere (CA) storage* [19].

In controlled atmosphere storage, the oxygen in the atmosphere is reduced below the usual 21 percent level to as low as 2 to 3 percent. This markedly lowers the rate of cell metabolism and aging in the fruit, delaying the changes that would normally occur and prolonging the storage life. For example, changes in pigments, decrease in acid, loss of sugars, and breakdown of pectic substances are retarded in apples stored at 38°F (4°C) in an atmosphere containing 5 percent carbon dioxide and 3 percent oxygen [15].

Figure 21-12
Papaya has golden to reddish-pink flesh with dark silver black seeds.
(Source: Reference 17)

Each stored fruit has a critical oxygen level, below which injury to the tissues occurs. Relatively high carbon dioxide levels are sometimes used with the low-oxygen atmosphere; however, the atmosphere is carefully monitored and excess carbon dioxide, produced by the fruit during respiration, is removed so that a desirable level of carbon dioxide is constantly maintained. Temperature and humidity are also carefully controlled. Apples that have been stored in controlled atmosphere are commonly marketed as CA apples. CA apples offer a level of freshness and quality not otherwise available in the spring and summer months.

Commercial generators and sensitive monitoring equipment make it possible to control the atmosphere, not only in airtight storage warehouses but in transportation vehicles. This process allows a higher quality to be maintained in fresh fruits and vegetables shipped over long distances. Not all products respond equally well to controlled atmosphere storage, however, and some may not be at all suited to this kind of treatment.

Another preservative technique closely related to controlled atmosphere storage is *modified-atmosphere packaging*. This technique involves a one-time modification of the air surrounding a product in a package. A semipermeable film used for packaging allows the natural process of respiration by the fresh or minimally processed fruit to reduce the oxygen and increase the carbon dioxide content of the atmosphere around the fruit. A low storage temperature must still be maintained, because changes in temperature may affect the gas concentrations in the package [34]. The initial microbial load on the fruit or vegetable should be as low as possible, as the modified atmosphere does not stop the growth of microorganisms [18]. Irradiation of fresh fruits, at controlled dosages, can delay senescence, reduce mold growth, and extend shelf life. It may be used in combination with modified atmosphere treatment.

Most fresh fruits are perishable and require refrigeration. Soft fruits such as berries keep better when spread out on a flat surface. Citrus fruits, except lemons, which keep best at a temperature of 55° to 58°F (13° to 15°C), should be refrigerated and covered to avoid drying out. Avocados and bananas are so injured by chilling that they discolor and lose the power of ripening even if they are later held at warmer temperatures. In fact, bananas are injured when held at temperatures lower than 55°F (13°C) *before* ripening. If these and other tropical fruits must be held for any time, then they should be ripened before being stored at colder temperatures. After ripening, avocados hold best at about 40°F (4°C).

FRUIT JUICES

Fruit juices are an important means of utilizing fresh fruits. The commercial fruit juice industry in the United States has had a spectacular rise since 1925, with fruit juice consumption in this country surpassing that of fruit processed in all other forms. Much of the increase in fruit juice production has been with citrus fruits. After the commercial introduction of frozen orange concentrate in 1945 and 1946, this product became the leader among processed fruits in terms of fresh-weight-equivalent consumed. A large share of the Florida orange crop is used to produce juice. By 1985, however, ready-to-drink juice, both reconstituted and not-from-concentrate, began to take over large shares of the juice market. The present trend is toward pasteurized, single-strength, not-from-concentrate orange juice [9]. Many consumers perceive this juice to be more wholesome, with better flavor than that of a reconstituted juice.

Sources of Vitamin C

Some edible material is lost when juices are extracted and the juice is strained, resulting in the total nutritive value of the whole fruit being somewhat higher than the juice coming from it. Regardless, little loss of vitamin C occurs during preparation and processing of citrus juices. The freezing and subsequent storage of orange juice at 0°F (−18°C) or below does not cause a significant loss of vitamin C, especially if aeration before freezing is avoided. Possibly because of their high acidity, citrus juices tend to retain vitamin C well.

Apple, cranberry, grape, pineapple, and prune juices and apricot nectar contain little vitamin C unless they are fortified with the added vitamin. Vitamin C is added to some juices, partly to increase the nutritive value and partly to improve their appearance, flavor, and stability during storage. The added vitamin C in noncitrus juices may be less stable than the vitamin naturally present in citrus juices. In opened containers stored in a refrigerator, the vitamin C in canned orange juice was found to be more stable, up to 16 days, than that in vitamin C–fortified canned apple juice [20]. Extra vitamin C and calcium are added to some orange juice.

Juice Processing

In preparing orange juice concentrate, the fruit is graded, washed, and sanitized before it enters the juice extractors. After leaving the extractors, the juice may go through a series of finishers, basically stainless steel screens, to remove the seeds and pulp. It is then concentrated [8]. Several different processes can be used to remove water from the juice, including evaporation under vacuum, use of osmosis or **reverse osmosis** through selective membranes, and partial freezing with separation of the resulting ice crystals. Evaporation is the most commonly used procedure, with thermally accelerated short-time evaporators being widely used in the juice-processing industry. With this equipment, evaporation can be accomplished in 6 to 8 minutes [8].

reverse osmosis a process of "dewatering" whereby ions and small molecules do not pass through a membrane but water does pass through

The concentrated juices are blended to produce the highest uniform quality. Concentrated orange aroma or essence solutions that are lost in the evaporation process may be recovered and returned to the concentrated juice to maintain fresh flavor [14]. The chilled concentrate is quick-frozen. Frozen concentrated juices should be kept at 0°F (−18°C) or below, both in market channels and in the kitchen, to retard losses of nutritive value, flavor, and other quality characteristics.

Membrane technology has made it possible to process fruit juices with fewer stages, less energy cost, and greater retention of flavor and aroma components [16]. This technology includes **microfiltration** and **ultrafiltration**, as well as reverse osmosis [10].

microfiltration a membrane process that filters out or separates particles of very small size (0.02–2.0 microns), including starch, emulsified oils, and bacteria

ultrafiltration a membrane process that filters out or separates particles of extremely small size (0.002–0.2 microns), including proteins, gums, glucose, and pigments

aseptic free from disease-producing microorganisms

After single-strength juice is extracted, it is chilled and tested for quality before being pasteurized in a heat exchanger. It is then rapidly chilled at about 35°F (1.7°C) before packaging. The package may be lined with a special material that prevents loss of volatile flavor substances in the packaging [9]. Some processors may use **aseptic** bulk storage in the marketing of chilled, pasteurized, single-strength orange and grapefruit juices. These juices require careful handling and storage to prevent microbial spoilage, because they rely primarily on cold temperatures and asepsis (keeping out harmful microorganisms) for preventing spoilage [21].

Noncitrus juices may be sold as concentrates. One major advantage of fruit juice concentrates is that the volume is greatly reduced and shipping and handling costs are less. Concentrated juices and fruit purees may be dehydrated by roller or drum drying, spray drying, or foam mat drying. Although some flavor loss occurs in drying, the final product is acceptable.

Cloud or haze, which is a desirable characteristic of citrus juices, is a complex mixture of cellular organelles, color bodies, oil droplets, flavonoids, and cell wall fragments which include pectic substances, cellulose, and hemicelluloses. Pectic substances play an important role in stabilizing the cloudy appearance; they also contribute a characteristic body or consistency. Present in cell walls and between cells, pectic substances are released into the juice when extracted. In citrus juices this cloud may be stabilized by flash-heating to a temperature higher than usual pasteurization temperatures to destroy **pectin esterase** enzymes that destabilize the cloud by allowing calcium ions to link deesterified pectin molecules into aggregates which settle out. Apple and grape juices, however, are preferred as clear. Pectin-degrading enzymes (**pectinases**) may be added to these juices to aid in the processing. The treated juice is less viscous and can be easily filtered. This process is called *clarification*. The color and flavor of the clarified juices are also stabilized. To increase yield, while still maintaining or improving the quality and stability of the final juice product, enzyme preparations that contain **cellulase and hemicellulase** activity, as well as pectinase, may be used. These additional enzymes act on the fruit tissue to macerate and further liquefy in order to extract more soluble solids [11]. Additionally, haze formation in apple juice may be commonly the result of a protein/tannin haze [4].

Pasteurization of juices is important for microbiological safety, as illustrated by the outbreak of *E. coli* O157:H7 illness in 1996 that was linked to the consumption of unpasteurized apple juice. See Chapter 3 for more information on food safety. Fruit drinks are also aseptically packaged, but in individual paperboard containers. This convenience has led to growth in fruit drink consumption [22].

pectin esterase an enzyme that catalyzes the hydrolysis of a methyl ester group from the large pectin molecule, producing pectic acid; pectic acid tends to form insoluble salts with such ions as calcium (Ca^{2+}); these insoluble salts cause the cloud in orange juice to become destabilized and settle

pectinase an enzyme that hydrolyzes the linkages that hold the small building blocks of galacturonic acid together in the pectic substances, producing smaller molecules

cellulase and hemicellulase enzymes that hydrolyze cellulose and hemicellulose, respectively

DRIED FRUITS

When fruits are preserved by drying, the water content is reduced to less than 30 percent. In some fruits, such as dates, figs, raisins, pears, and peaches, the water content may be only 15 to 18 percent when fruits come from the drying yards and dehydrators. As marketed, these fruits usually contain 28 percent or more moisture; therefore, they may be partially rehydrated before being packaged for the consumer. Dried fruits with 28 to 30 percent water are examples of intermediate-moisture foods that are plastic, easily chewed, and do not produce a sensation of dryness in the mouth, but are microbiologically stable.

In **vacuum-drying**, the water content is reduced to very low levels, about 2.5 to 5 percent. Fruits dried by this method are usually stored in sealed containers to retain the low moisture levels.

Carbohydrate, caloric, and mineral values of dried fruits are higher by weight than those of the corresponding fresh fruits because of the removal of water. Also, the flavor is more concentrated than that of fresh fruit.

vacuum-drying drying a product in a vacuum chamber in which water vaporizes at a lower temperature than at atmospheric pressure

The vitamin content of fruits is changed in drying depending on the methods of drying and sulfuring. Some fruits, such as apricots and peaches, are subjected to the fumes of sulfur dioxide gas or are dipped in a sulfite solution to prevent darkening of color and to kill insects. Sulfuring aids in the preservation of vitamin A and vitamin C, but adversely affects thiamin.

Methods and Storage

The term *dried* is commonly applied to all fruits in which the water content has been reduced to a low level. Sun-drying methods use the sun as a source of heat. Dehydration can also be accomplished by artificial heat under well-controlled conditions of humidity, temperature, and circulation of air. The sanitary practices involved in dehydration with artificial heat and the preservation of such physical properties as color, texture, and flavor in cooked dehydrated fruits as compared with cooked sun-dried fruits may represent possible advantages for this method.

Vacuum-drying results in fruit with very low moisture levels, although relatively low temperatures are used in the process. Under vacuum, water evaporates at a lower temperature. These fruits usually have excellent eating quality and they rehydrate quickly and easily. Fruits may also be **freeze-dried.**

Because dried fruits are greatly reduced in water content and consequently have increased sugar content, they are resistant to microbial spoilage. Light-colored fruits that have been exposed to sulfur dioxide to prevent darkening also become more insect resistant as a result of the sulfur treatment. Dried fruits should be stored in tightly closed plastic, glass, or metal containers to protect against insect infestation.

freeze-drying a drying process that involves first freezing the product and then placing it in a vacuum chamber; the ice sublimes (goes from solid to vapor phase without going through the liquid phase); the dried food is more flavorful and fresher in appearance because it does not become hot in the drying process

Prunes

Prunes are varieties of plums that can be dried without fermenting while still containing the pits. Two main varieties are the French plum, grown chiefly in California and France, and the Italian plum, grown chiefly in Oregon. These fruits are blue or purple on the outside, with greenish yellow to amber flesh. They have a high sugar content, so they produce a sweet-flavored prune when dried.

Before drying, plums are dipped in lye to puncture the skin and make it thinner, thus permitting rapid drying and improving the texture of the skin. Careful washing removes the lye before further processing. Some packaged prunes have been sterilized and packed hot in a package lined with aluminum foil. The residual heat in the pits seems to be sufficient to sterilize the package and also to tenderize the prune fiber to some extent, thus giving the prune its quick-cooking quality.

Prunes are classified according to size, that is, the approximate number to the pound. It is generally conceded that large prunes of the same variety and quality as small prunes have no better flavor than the small fruit. Large fruit may be preferred for dessert purposes, but it must be remembered that price usually increases with size at a faster rate than the amount of the edible portion. For the making of pulp, small and medium sizes are more economical.

The laxative value of prunes is the result of their fiber content and of a water-soluble extractive, *diphenylisatin*, that stimulates intestinal activity. Prune juice also contains the active laxative agent.

CANNED FRUITS

Canned fruit is essentially cooked fruit that has been sealed and processed for keeping and, as such, represents a widely used convenience food. Flavors and textures are somewhat altered by cooking or canning and vitamin values may be slightly reduced. The vitamins and minerals that go into solution are conserved because juices are usually eaten with the fruit.

Canned fruits lose nutrients and flavor less readily when stored at relatively low temperatures. If stored for prolonged periods above 72°F (22°C), they deteriorate in quality at a relatively rapid rate.

More "light" canned fruit products are being marketed in response to increasing concerns about health and nutrition. These fruits contain less sugar than the traditional canned products, often because they are packed in their juice with no sugar added. The grading of commercially canned fruits is discussed in Chapter 20 and home canning is explained in Chapter 30.

FROZEN FRUITS

The fruits that are most commonly frozen are cherries (both sour and sweet), strawberries (both sliced in sugar and whole), boysenberries, loganberries, red and black raspberries, blueberries, and sliced peaches. Frozen mixed fruits, rhubarb, plums, black mission figs, cranberries, pineapple, apple slices, and some varieties of melon are also available in some markets. Most frozen fruits are not heated during processing but are often frozen in a sugar syrup. Commercially, small whole fruits may be frozen quickly in liquid nitrogen. No sugar or syrup need be added in this process.

Frozen apples, cherries, and some other fruits used for pies should be partially defrosted to facilitate their use and to drain some of the juice. Otherwise, they are used in the same manner as fresh fruit. If the fruit has been frozen with some sugar or syrup, allowance must be made in adding sugar to prepared products. Rhubarb should be cooked without defrosting. Blueberries and other fruits frozen dry can be used either frozen or thawed in cooked dishes.

Frozen fruits should be moved quickly in market channels with proper precautions for maintaining cold temperatures. They should also be moved quickly from the market to the kitchen freezer to avoid partial thawing and consequent loss of quality on refreezing. For best quality retention, frozen fruits need to be stored at a temperature of 0°F (−18°C) or lower.

All frozen fruits to be used raw should be barely defrosted. If all the crystals have thawed, the fruit tends to become flabby, particularly when using berries or peaches in shortcake, which is often warm when served. The warm shortcake may complete the defrosting. Some frozen fruits, such as peaches and apples, tend to turn brown during frozen storage and after thawing. Use of vitamin C in the syrup aids in the retention of natural color by preventing oxidation.

PREPARATION

Most fresh fruits are generally considered to be at their best in the raw, ripened state and are thus served without cooking when possible. Fresh fruits should always be washed to remove dust, soil, some spray residues, and some microorganisms. See Chapters 3 and 4 for more information on food safety and food regulation. If fruits that brown easily, such as bananas and apples, are to be peeled and cut, they should be dipped in or covered with lemon juice, pineapple juice, or solutions of vitamin C mixtures so that discoloration does not readily occur. The acids and/or antioxidants in these solutions retard the enzyme activity and/or tie up oxygen to prevent brown compounds from forming. Placing the fruit in a sugar syrup or even immersing it in water retards browning to some degree by excluding air. Enzymatic oxidative browning is discussed in Chapter 20.

Citrus fruits are generally peeled, sectioned, sliced, or wedged. When peeling oranges it is desirable to remove as much of the white membrane between the peel and the fruit as possible because this membrane is bitter and may be tough. The peel may be removed with a knife (Figure 21-13) or alternatively, oranges may be placed in boiling water briefly and then peeled by hand. This method is best if several oranges are to be peeled because the oranges will peel more easily and quickly when heated.

Some recipes call for orange or lemon zest. Zest is the colored portion of the rind, excluding the white part of the rind. Zest may be prepared using a tool that cuts thin strips of the rind or by using a fine grater.

For some fruits, including green apples and rhubarb, cooking is sometimes desirable or necessary because they are more palatable and digestible when cooked. Cooking is also one way to add variety as fruits are included in daily menus. Overripe fruits may be further preserved by cooking.

Effect of Cooking Medium

The softening and breakage of pieces of fruit or vegetable during cooking is influenced by the cooking medium. If it is desirable to have fruits retain their shape, they may be cooked in a sugar syrup. If sauce is the expected end product, cooking in water hastens disintegration of the tissues.

The reason for these differences lies with the imbalance between sugar concentrations inside the fruit and in the cooking liquid. In uncooked fruit tissue, the cell walls act as *semipermeable membranes*, allowing passage only of water. If there is a difference in sugar concentration within and outside the cells, such as when sugar is sprinkled on fresh strawberries, water exits the cells in an attempt to dilute the concentrated sugar solution that has formed on the surface of the fruit: thus, juice forms when strawberries are left to stand with sugar. The reverse occurs, that is, water enters fruit cells, when fruit is placed in plain water, because the concentration of sugar within the cells is greater than in the water outside the fruit. This movement of water through a semipermeable membrane is *osmosis*.

diffusion the movement of a substance from an area of higher concentration to an area of lower concentration.

As fruit is heated, however, the permeability of the cell walls changes to allow not only the passage of water but also the movement of sugar and other small molecules. Simple **diffusion** then occurs as sugar and water move into or out of tissues. Therefore, in fruit slices cooked in a sugar syrup more concentrated than the 12 to 15 percent sugar solution found naturally in most fruits, sugar moves into the cells and water moves out into the cooking liquid in an attempt to equalize the sugar concentration throughout (Figure 21-14). Because fruits shrink slightly, they appear shiny and translucent and the tissue is firm. A desirable proportion of water to sugar for most fruits is about two to one by measure. When the shape of the fruit pieces is to be retained, the fruit should not be stirred during cooking.

Conversely, when fruit is cooked in water alone, sugar moves from the more concentrated solution within the cells to the plain surrounding water, and

To section citrus fruits, pare deeply enough to remove the membrane that covers the pulp.

Cut toward the center along the membrane and remove the section.

For a basketball method of peeling, first slice off the stem end of the orange. Without cutting into the meat, score the peel with a knife. Pull the peel away with the fingers, leaving the white inner skin that clings to the fruit.

Figure 21-13
Methods of preparing citrus fruit for serving. (Courtesy of Sunkist Growers, Inc.)

Figure 21-14
Cooking of fruit. (a) Apple slices cooked in a sugar solution will retain their shape. Sugar (S) moves into the fruit cells, and some water (H₂O) comes out into the surrounding sugar solution in an attempt to dilute it. (b) Apple slices cooked in plain water tend to break up more as water moves into the cells, expanding them.

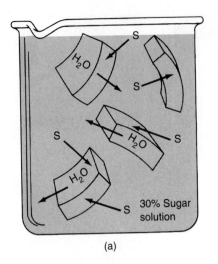

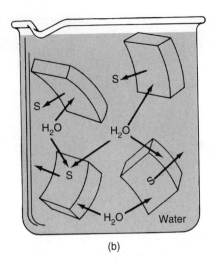

(a)   (b)

some water moves back into the tissues (Figure 21-14). Fruits that are to be cooked to a smooth pulp are stewed in water until they attain the desired softness, after which sugar is added. These fruits may be stirred during cooking. The same principles described earlier apply to vegetables cooked in water containing sugar versus plain water. The sugar content of most vegetables, however, is low, and they are usually enjoyed without sweetening.

Contrary to these general principles, some varieties of fruits do not cook to a smooth pulp in any circumstance, and not every variety holds its shape well when cooked in syrup. The final product obtained is therefore partly a matter of choice of variety.

Cooking proceeds most evenly when the pan is covered during cooking. The heat source should be regulated so that the liquid in the pan simmers or boils slowly.

Rhubarb is easily overcooked. Using a small amount of water and careful, slow cooking, only until the pieces are tender and partially broken, produces a desirable sauce from rhubarb. Apples sliced for cooking may sometimes include the skin, for added color, flavor, and nutritive value. After cooking, the fruit may be quickly run through a strainer or food mill to increase the smoothness of the pulp if applesauce is being prepared.

Excess sugar in fruit sauces mars the delicate flavor of many fruits. The desirable amount is often difficult to determine, especially when fruits are made into pies and other products, in which the amount of sugar may not be added gradually until the desired amount is determined. The same variety of apple or other fruits varies in acidity from season to season and at different times during the storage period.

Cooking Dried Fruits

Some of the water that has been removed from fruit in the drying process is returned by soaking. Cooking after soaking softens the tissues. Soaking in hot water for a short time results in good water absorption. The dried fruit, covered with water, may be brought to a boil, immediately covered and removed from the heat source, and then left to stand for 20 to 30 minutes (no longer than 1 hour). After soaking, the fruit is simmered until the desired degree of softness is achieved. Some commercially available dried fruits are tenderized and have a higher moisture content. They require little or no soaking and a short cooking period.

The higher sugar content of dried fruits makes the use of much sugar for sweetening undesirable. The small amount of sugar that is sometimes used is added at the end of the cooking period. The degree of acidity of the fruit determines the amount of sugar to be used. For example, dried apricots, being much more tart, require more sugar than prunes.

Baking

Some fruits lend themselves well to baking. The aim is to have the fruit hold its form but be cooked until tender throughout. Apples and pears are often baked in their skins (cores removed) to hold in the steam that forms within the fruit and cooks the interior. Pared slices or sections may be baked in a covered casserole (350° to 400°F [177° to 204°C] oven temperature). Bananas are sometimes baked, although in general they are preferred raw. Rhubarb can also be baked and will keep its shape.

Glazing

A rangetop method known as *glazing* can be satisfactorily used to cook apples. The apples are cored as for baking, and a slit is cut in the skin all around the apple at right angles to or parallel to the core. The apples are then placed in a saucepan with 1/4 cup of water and 1/8 cup of sugar for each apple in the pan. They are covered and cooked over low heat. The apples are turned once while cooking and are cooked until tender. The cover is removed for the last minute before the apples are done.

Broiling

Bananas, grapefruit halves, and pineapple slices are some of the fruits that can be satisfactorily broiled. To modify the bland flavor of cooked bananas, lemon juice or broiled bacon may be added.

Sautéing

Apples, bananas, and pineapple slices may be prepared by sautéing, or cooking quickly in a small amount of fat. A flavorful fat such as butter is preferred.

CHAPTER SUMMARY

- Using a botanical definition, fruits are produced from flowers and are the ripened ovaries and adjacent tissue of plants. In common usage, fruits are fleshy or pulpy, often juicy, usually sweet, with fragrant, aromatic flavors.

- Fleshy fruits may be classified as simple, aggregate, or multiple. Simple fruits include citrus fruits, drupes, and pomes. Drupes are fruits such as peaches in which a stone or pit encloses the seed. Pomes include apples and pears that have a core. Strawberries and other berries are examples of aggregate fruits. Pineapple is a multiple fruit.

- Fruits comprise an edible portion combined with some refuse. The chief energy nutrient is carbohydrate, which occurs primarily as sugars. Fruits are valuable in the diet due to their vitamin, mineral, phytochemicals, and fiber content. Vitamin C and vitamin A are prevalent in many fruits.

- Fruit consumption is increasing but is still below the recommended levels. In the United States, juice is the number one form in which fruit is consumed. Many kinds of fruits are now available year around due to the improvement in transportation, storage, and increase in imports.

- The pigments that give fruits their characteristic color are the same as those in vegetables. The yellow-orange carotenoids and the red-blue anthocyanins predominate. The interaction of pigments should be considered when mixing fruit juices, as either pleasing or unattractive color changes may occur. Anthocyanin pigments tend to deteriorate on storage whether the container is tin or glass.

- The flavor of fruits may be described as tart, fragrant, and sweet. Fruits owe their characteristic flavors largely to aromatic compounds. Other components contributing to fruit flavor include aldehydes, various alcohols, organic acids, essential oils, sugars, mineral salts, and phenolic compounds. Malic, citric, and tartaric acids are common. Oxalic acid is found in rhubarb.

- Distinct changes occur in fruits during ripening: (1) a decrease in green color and development of yellow-orange or red-blue colors, (2) a softening of the flesh, (3) the development of characteristic pleasant flavors, and (4) changes in soluble solids such as sugars and organic acids. Color changes as new pigments are synthesized and chlorophyll is broken down. During the softening of fruit, protopectin is degraded to pectin (pectinic acid), then with further softening to pectic acid. Pleasant flavors in fruit are developed as the acidity decreases and sugar increases.

- Fruits are living systems. Respiration occurs in the cells of the fruit as they carry on normal metabolic processes. Ethylene gas is a ripening hormone produced in small amounts by the cells after the fruit is mature. Fruits, such as bananas that are harvested before ripening, are stored in an atmosphere that contains ethylene gas to speed the ripening process. Some fruits such as apples emit ethylene gas and thus can promote ripening of other fruits stored nearby.

- High quality fruit should have the proper stage of ripeness, good color, freedom from insect damage, and the absence of bruises, skin punctures, and decay.

- Apples are a widely used fruit that is grown in most parts of the United States. Some varieties of apples are best for eating out of hand and others are excellent for baking.

- Avocados, unlike most other fruits, contain about 17 percent fat. Avocados should be refrigerated only after ripening.

- Bananas are first in fruit sales in the United States. Bananas do not ripen normally if chilled. A banana with a gray skin has been cold damaged.

- Many different kinds of berries are available in the marketplace. Berries should be washed just before use. Berries will mold and spoil more rapidly if washed before storage.

- Cherries may be sweet or tart. Tart cherries are generally used for cooking and baking.

- Citrus fruits include oranges, lemons, grapefruit, limes, tangerines, kumquats, and tangelos. Citrus fruits are an important source of vitamin C in the diet.

- Grapes may be consumed as table grapes or made into wine. Table grapes may be of the European types that include Thompson seedless grapes, or the American types that include the Concord variety.

- Many kinds of melons are available, including honeydew, crenshaw, casaba, cantaloupe, and watermelon. Melons are among the most difficult fruits to select; however a characteristic aroma and color with heaviness in relation to size are positive indicators. Good food handling practices, including washing of melons before cutting, should be followed when preparing melons.

- Peaches and nectarines are similar, yet are distinct fruits. The pit of free-stone varieties will separate readily from the flesh as compared to cling-stones that "cling" to the pit.

- The peak season for domestic plums is June through September. Plums should be slightly soft when ripe.

- The most popular type of pear is the Bartlett, although many varieties are available. Pears are generally firm when purchased, but will soften at room temperature.

- A ripe pineapple has a rich fragrance and springs back slightly when touched.

- Many other fruits are available in the marketplace. Kiwifruit, fresh coconut, mangoes, papayas, passion fruit, prickly pear, cherimoya, and carambola are fruits that some consumers may consider to be exotic.

- Fruits continue to respire after harvesting. Cold temperatures slow the rate of metabolism to extend shelf life. Controlled atmosphere storage is commonly used with apples and permits the sale of high quality apples in the spring and summer months. In controlled atmosphere storage, the oxygen in the atmosphere is reduced, thereby lowering the rate of cell metabolism and aging in the fruit.

- Modified atmosphere packaging and irradiation are additional methods that may be used with some fruits to extend shelf life.

- Fruit juices are an important means of utilizing fresh fruits. Fruit juices may be processed as a frozen fruit juice concentrate or a single-strength juice. Aseptic packaging may be used for juices. Cloud or haze is an undesirable characteristic in some juices such as apple juice and a process called clarification is used to reduce or eliminate the haze. Pasteurization of juices is important for microbiological safety.

- When fruits are preserved by drying, the water content is reduced to less than 30 percent. In some fruits the water content may be only 15–18 percent. Vacuum dried fruits may have a water content of 2.5–5 percent. Fruits may be dried by sun-drying or by artificial heat in controlled conditions of humidity, temperature, and circulation of air. Prunes are dried plums that have a laxative effect due to diphenylisatin.

- Canned fruit is cooked fruit that has been sealed and processed for keeping. Some fruits such as cherries and berries are commonly frozen. Frozen fruits to be used raw should be barely defrosted when served so the fruit will not become excessively soft prior to use.

- When preparing fruits, fresh fruits should be thoroughly washed and peeled, sliced, or trimmed as needed. Some fruits such as apples and bananas will brown readily and should be dipped in lemon juice, pineapple juice, or a solution of vitamin C.

- Some fruit may be cooked. To maintain the shape of a fruit, cook in a sugar syrup. If a sauce is the desired product, then cook the fruit in water to hasten the disintegration of the tissues. These different effects are the result of the imbalance between the sugar concentration inside the fruit and in the cooking medium.
- Dried fruits may be soaked in water to rehydrate prior to cooking. The higher sugar content of dried fruits makes the use of much sugar for sweetening undesirable.
- Other methods of cooking fruits include baking, glazing, broiling and sautéing.

KEY TERMS

ovary
phytochemicals
succulent
aromatic compounds
ester
organic acid
salt
phenolic compound
ethylene
reverse osmosis

microfiltration
ultrafiltration
aseptic
pectin esterase
pectinase
cellulase and hemicellulase
vacuum-drying
freeze-drying
diffusion

STUDY QUESTIONS

1. What is a *fruit?* Also define a *pome* and a *drupe.* Give examples of each.
2. **a.** What is the usual percentage of water found in fruits? What is the usual percentage of carbohydrate? What type of carbohydrate usually predominates in ripe fruits?
   b. List and be able to recognize fruits that are good sources of vitamin C.
3. Describe common characteristics of fruit flavor. List four types of chemical substances that contribute to the flavor of fruits.
4. **a.** What pigments are often present in fruits?
   b. Explain why pigment content should be considered when mixing various fruit juices to make a fruit drink.
5. Describe the major changes that occur during the ripening of fruit.
6. **a.** Describe the usual characteristics of fruits of good quality and suggest appropriate storage conditions to maintain quality.
   b. What factors are generally monitored during controlled atmosphere storage of fruits and vegetables? Why is this type of storage effective for some fruits?
   c. Explain what is involved in modified atmosphere packaging.
7. **a.** Describe the major steps in the production of orange juice concentrate.
   b. What contributes to the stability of the hazy cloud characteristic of orange juice? To what treatment may the juice be subjected during processing to maintain cloud formation? Explain why this treatment is effective.

    c. What special processing that involves enzyme action may be used to produce a sparkling clear fruit juice? Describe and explain.

8. Why are some fruits treated with sulfur before drying? Describe some effects of this process on nutritive value.

9. a. Compare the general effects of cooking fruits in water and in sugar syrups. Explain what is happening in each case.

    b. Suggest an appropriate procedure for cooking dried fruits and explain why you would recommend this procedure.

    c. Describe several additional methods for cooking fruits.

REFERENCES

1. Abe, K., & Watada, A. E. (1991). Ethylene absorbent to maintain quality of lightly processed fruits and vegetables. *Journal of Food Science, 56*, 1589.

2. Arnold, J. (2002). Watermelon packs a powerful lycopene punch. *Agricultural Research Magazine, 50*(6).

3. Bente, L. & Gerrior, S. A. (2002). Selected food and nutrient highlights of the 20th century: U.S. food supply series. *Family Economics and Nutrition Review, 14*(1), 43–51.

4. Beveridge, T. (1999). Electron microscopic characterization of haze in apple juice. *Food Technology, 53*(1), 44–48.

5. Bourne, M. C. (1982). Effect of temperature on firmness of raw fruits and vegetables. *Journal of Food Science, 47*, 440.

6. Chairote, G., Rodriguez, F., & Crouzet, J. (1981). Characterization of additional volatile flavor components of apricot. *Journal of Food Science, 46*, 1898.

7. Clark, J. P. (2002). Extending the shelf life of fruits and vegetables. *Food Technology, 56*(4), 98–100, 105.

8. Cook, R. (1983). Quality of citrus juices as related to composition and processing practices. *Food Technology, 37*(6), 68.

9. Demetrakakes, P. (1996). Unconcentrated effort. *Food Processing, 57*(11), 77.

10. Dziezak, J. D. (1990). Membrane separation technology offers processors unlimited potential. *Food Technology, 44*(9), 108.

11. Faigh, J. G. (1995). Enzyme formulations for optimizing juice yields. *Food Technology, 49*(9), 79.

12. Fain, A. R., Jr. (1994). A review of the microbiological safety of fresh salads. *Scope, 9*(3), 1 (Silliker Laboratories).

13. Frohlich, O., & Schreier, P. (1990). Volatile constituents of loquat (*Eriobotrya japonica* Lindl.) fruit. *Journal of Food Science, 55*, 176.

14. Guadagni, D. G., Bomben, J. L., & Mannheim, H. C. (1970). Storage stability of frozen orange juice concentrate made with aroma solution of cutback juice. *Food Technology, 24*, 1012.

15. Knee, M. (1971). Ripening of apples during storage. III. Changes in chemical composition of Golden Delicious apples during the climacteric and under conditions simulating commercial storage practice. *Journal of the Science of Food and Agriculture, 22*, 371.

16. Koseoglu, S. S., Lawhon, J. T., & Lusas, E. W. (1990). Use of membranes in citrus juice processing. *Food Technology, 44*(12), 90.

17. Labensky, S. R. & Hause, A. M. (2003). *On cooking, A textbook of culinary fundamentals* (3rd ed.). Upper Saddle River, New Jersey: Prentice Hall.

18. Labuza, T. P. (1996). An introduction to active packaging for foods. *Food Technology, 50*(4), 68.

19. Lidster, P. D., Lightfoot, H. J., & McRae, K. B. (1983). Production and regeneration of principal volatiles in apples stored in modified atmospheres and air. *Journal of Food Science, 48,* 400.

20. Noel, G. L., & Robberstad, M. T. (1963). Stability of vitamin C in canned apple juice and orange juice under refrigerated conditions. *Food Technology, 17,* 947.

21. Parish, M. E. (1991). Microbiological concerns in citrus juice processing. *Food Technology, 45*(4), 128.

22. Pearl, R. C. (1990). Trends in consumption and processing of fruits and vegetables in the United States. *Food Technology, 44*(2), 102.

23. Pratt, S. (1992). The "peachfuzz" plot. *Food Technology, 46*(8), 46.

24. Produce Marketing Association. (1995). *The foodservice guide to fresh produce.* Newark, DE: Produce Marketing Association.

25. Pszczola, D. E. (2001). Antioxidants: From preserving food quality to quality of life. *Food Technology, 55*(6), 51.

26. Putnam, J. J. & Allshouse, J. (2001). Imports' share of U.S. diet rises in late 1990's. *Food Review, 24*(3), 15–22.

27. Putnam, J. J. & Allshouse, J. E. (1999). Food consumption, prices, and expenditures, 1970–1997. Food and Rural Economics Division, Economic Research Service, U.S. Department of Agriculture. Statistical Bulletin No. 965.

28. Putnam, J., Kantor, L. S., & Allshouse, J. (2000). Per capita food supply trends: Progress toward dietary guidelines. *Food Review, 23*(3), 2–14.

29. Research Summary. (1997). U.S. per capita food consumption. *Family Economics and Nutrition Review, 10*(1), 38.

30. Segal, M. (1988). Fruit. U.S. Department of Health and Human Services Pub. No. (FDA) 88–2226. Rockville, MD.

31. Sloan, A. E. (2001). Fruit frenzy. *Food Technology, 55*(12), 14.

32. Steinmetz, K. A., & Potter, J. D. (1996). Vegetables, fruit, and cancer prevention: A review. *Journal of the American Dietetic Association, 96,* 1027.

33. Sweeney, J. P., Chapman, V. J., & Hepner, P. A. (1970). Sugar, acid, and flavor in fresh fruits. *Journal of the American Dietetic Association, 57,* 432.

34. Talasila, P. C., Chau, K. V., & Brecht, J. K. (1995). Design of rigid modified atmosphere packages for fresh fruits and vegetables. *Journal of Food Science, 60,* 758.

35. *The buying guide for fresh fruits, vegetables, herbs, and nuts* (8th ed.). (1986). Shepherdstown, WV: Blue Goose Growers, Inc.

36. Toops, D. (1997). Going bananas. *Food Processing, 58*(8), 51.

37. U.S. Department of Agriculture. (2002). Agricultural Research Service. (2002). *USDA National Nutrient Database for Standard Reference, Release 15.* Retrieved December 7, 2002, from the Nutrient Data Laboratory Home Page, http://www.nal.usda.gov/fnic/foodcomp

38. U.S. Department of Agriculture, Agricultural Marketing Service. (1994). *How to buy fresh fruits.* Home and Garden Bulletin No. 260.

39. U.S. Department of Agriculture, Economic Research Service. (2002, September). Briefing room: Fruit and tree nuts: Background. Retrieved December 16, 2002, from http://ers.usda.giv/briefing/fruitand treenuts/background.htm

40. Van Duyn, M. A. S. & Pivonka, E. (2000). Overview of the health benefits of fruit and vegetable consumption for the dietetics professional: Selected literature. *Journal of the American Dietetic Association, 100,* 1511–1521.

41. Wiseman, J. J., & McDaniel, M. R. (1991). Modification of fruit flavors by aspartame and sucrose. *Journal of Food Science, 56,* 1668.

Salads and Gelatin

22

SALADS

At one time the term *salad* may have applied only to green leaves or to stalks that were eaten raw (Figure 22-1). Although today we often refer to green leafy vegetables, such as lettuce, endive, and romaine, as *salad greens*, the term has a much broader meaning. It includes mixtures of meat, fish, poultry, cheese, nuts, seeds, and eggs, as well as all kinds of vegetables and fruits. Often, salads are made with raw or uncooked foods, but they are certainly not limited to these items. A salad may be composed entirely of cooked or canned products, or mixtures of raw and cooked items may be used. Congealed salads containing a variety of ingredients are popular menu items. A dressing is usually served either mixed with or accompanying the salad. The dressing may be rich and elaborate, or it may be as simple as lemon juice.

The salad is not a modern preparation. Green leaves were used by the ancient Romans. Other nationalities from the fifteenth century onward favored the use of flavorful herbs and raw vegetables. The introduction of salads into England was apparently made by Catherine of Aragon, one of the wives of Henry VIII and a daughter of Ferdinand and Isabella of Spain. The origin of present-day meat and fish salads was probably the salmagundi of England, used for many years as a supper dish. This meat dish made use of numerous garnishes that are used today, such as hard-cooked eggs, pickles, beets, and anchovies.

The influence of southern France is apparent in the use of French dressing for salads. The original dressing was made of olive oil and was seasoned to perfection. Spain has made the pepper a popular salad vegetable, and the Mediterranean countries introduced garlic flavor. The original German potato salad has many present-day variations.

The salad is an appealing form in which to use fresh fruits and vegetables, the increased intake of which is recommended in the Dietary Guidelines for Americans [9]. The element of crispness, which most salads introduce, provides an opportunity for greater variation in texture for many menus. Tartness and appetizing, fresh flavors are also easily added to the meal in the form of salads.

Uses of Salads

The salad may be served at numerous points in a meal. It often accompanies the main course, but is sometimes served as a separate course, either between the main course and the dessert or before the main course. Some salads, especially

Figure 22-1
This salad of sweet and bitter greens with balsamic mustard vinaigrette is simple yet flavorful. The greens in this salad include watercress, romaine, and bibb lettuce.

those with fruit and nuts that are dressed with a rich or somewhat sweet dressing, are appropriately served for dessert. For luncheon or supper, the salad may be the main course, with the remainder of the menu being built around it (Figure 22-2).

The type of salad served depends on its use or position in the meal. The dinner salad is usually a light, crisp, tart accompaniment to the meat or other entree. Heavier, high-calorie salads, such as macaroni and tuna fish or meat and potato, are not appropriately included in a meal already composed of filling, high-protein foods. Instead, meat, poultry, fish, egg, cheese, and potato salads

Figure 22-2
A pasta, black bean, and chicken salad with cheese cubes, summer squash, and green peppers is a delicious summer entrée. (Courtesy of Land O' Lakes, Inc.)

that are combined with some crisp vegetables and relishes are suitable for use as a main course. Some small fish salads of high flavor, such as crab, shrimp, lobster, and anchovy, may serve as an appetizer, similar to cocktails and canapés made of these fish. Usually the amount of fish used is not large, and it is combined with crisp, flavorful foods.

Potato salad may be an accompaniment to cold meats on a supper platter. Used in this way, the starchy potato functions as it does in the dinner menu. Potato salad is sometimes served hot, as was the original German potato salad.

The fruit salad is particularly suitable as an appetizer or dessert. If kept tart and not too large, it may also be appropriately used as an accompaniment in the dinner menu. A fruit salad can be a popular choice for refreshments at an afternoon or evening party. When a fruit salad is used as dessert, it may be served with a cheese plate and crisp crackers or a sweet creamy yogurt dressing.

Nutritive Value

With the emphasis on "5-a-day" servings of fruits and vegetables, salads can make an impressive contribution to the accomplishment of this goal (Figure 22-3). Usually there is a wide variety of produce from which to choose. The majority of salads prepared from fresh fruits and vegetables are comparatively low in kilocalories (not including the dressing, of course), but are important sources of minerals, vitamins, and fiber. They also may be an excellent source of so-called **phytochemicals** or "neutraceuticals," which are thought to contribute to a decrease in degenerative diseases such as heart disease and cancer [11]. The green leafy vegetable salads are especially valuable for iron, vitamin A, vitamin C, and beta carotene.

Starchy salads, such as potato, are higher in kilocalories than salads made with fruits and succulent vegetables. Meat, fish, egg, and cheese salads furnish chiefly protein, although some crisp vegetables often form a part of such mixtures.

The final caloric value of salads, as consumed, is greatly influenced by the type and quantity of dressing used. The amount of fat, usually contained in the salad oil or cream, is the major factor influencing the caloric content of dressings. Cooked dressings, particularly those made with water or milk, have a lower caloric value than mayonnaise and French dressings. French and a variety of commercial salad dressings average 60 to 80 kilocalories per tablespoon. Mayonnaise contains about 100 kilocalories per tablespoon. There are, however, many reduced-fat dressings on the market. Special fat-free dressings may furnish as little as 6 kilocalories per tablespoon. See Chapter 10 for more information about salad dressings.

Salad Ingredients and Their Preparation

Salad Plants. The best-known salad plant is lettuce, of which there are several types. Iceberg lettuce is a crisphead type and is the most popular of the salad greens. Butterhead types have soft, pliable leaves and a delicate, buttery flavor. They include the Bibb and Big Boston or butterhead varieties. Another type of lettuce, romaine, or Cos, is characterized by leaves that appear coarse yet are actually tender, sweet, and tasty. They are more flavorful than iceberg lettuce. Leaf lettuce, including both green and red varieties, is a still different type, with leaves loosely branching from the stalk.

Endive, escarole, and chicory are often used as salad greens; however, there is some confusion concerning the use of these three terms in various parts of

Figure 22-3
This 5-a-day logo promotes consumption of fruits and vegetables. (Courtesy of Produce for Better Health Foundation, www. 5aday.com)

phytochemicals biochemical substances, other than vitamins, of plant origin that appear to have a positive effect on health; they include phenolic compounds, terpenoids, pigments, and other antioxidants

the country. Curly endive grows in a head with narrow, ragged-edged leaves that curl at the ends. A broader leaf variety of endive that does not curl at the tips is usually marketed as escarole. Witloof chicory, commonly known as French endive, is a tightly folded plant that grows upright in a thin, elongated stalk. It is usually white. Watercress and Chinese cabbage or celery cabbage are also highly acceptable as salad plants. Figure 22-4 shows some of the common salad greens.

Any crisp, tender, young leaves, such as spinach, sorrel, mustard, and dandelion, may be used as salad plants. Shredded cabbage may make up the entire salad, as in cole slaw; it may serve as a foundation or bed for other salad ingredients; or it may be part of a vegetable salad mixture. Other, very flavorful ingredients include tomatoes, cucumbers, radishes, red and green peppers, green onions, and celery. Many of these vegetables are particularly valuable for their crisp textures. Foods with very pronounced flavor, such as pineapple, should be used sparingly in mixtures to avoid masking more delicate flavors.

Cooked beets have a desirable texture and flavor for some types of salads; however, because of the soluble red pigment present, they may mar the color of other salad ingredients. If used carefully and kept separate from other ingredients, beets are valuable additions.

Raw turnip is another interesting ingredient for salads. It can be used in thin slices (often allowed to curl in cold water), sticks, or fine shreds. Raw carrots can be used similarly. Small pieces of raw cauliflower and broccoli florets are also desirable salad components.

Edible flowers may be used as salad ingredients or as garnishes. For example, nasturtium blossoms can be filled with a seafood stuffing and served on a bed of dark green leaves. See Chapter 8 for more information about edible flowers.

Preparation of Salad Ingredients.   For maximum retention of freshness and nutritive value, many salad ingredients should be prepared shortly before the salad is to be made and served. Some vegetables such as green leaves and celery, however, will be crisp and fresh if they are washed, closely wrapped, and chilled in the refrigerator for several hours. Certain other salad ingredients, for example, sections of citrus fruits, can be prepared well in advance. If salad materials are kept ready in the refrigerator, salad preparation becomes a simple, easy procedure. Unless salads are purposely served hot, such as German potato salad and wilted lettuce, all materials should be cold.

Although not as commonly associated with food poisoning as some other foods, fruits and vegetables can harbor disease-causing bacteria. Sanitary food-handling practices are important in salad preparation. Potential sources of pathogenic bacteria in fresh salads include ingredients (particularly raw products), food handlers, and the processing environment. *Listeria monocytogenes* has been found on a significant number of fresh vegetables and prepackaged salads. This organism is of special concern because it can grow at refrigeration temperatures. Enterotoxigenic *E. coli* on green salads were found to be the causative agent of illness in two reported outbreaks [2].

Some tips for safe handling of salad ingredients include the following. Wash hands with warm water and soap for at least 20 seconds before and after handling food, especially fresh whole fruits and vegetables, as well as raw meat, poultry, and fish. Rinse raw produce in warm water. Use a small scrub brush to

Figure 22-4
Many different kinds of greens are available: (a) Boston, (b) iceberg, (c) leaf, (d) red oak leaf, (e) romaine, (f) radicchio, (g) dandelion, (h) spinach.

remove surface dirt, if necessary. Wash cutting boards with a solution of 1 tea-spoon (5 milliliters) of chlorine bleach in 1 quart (about 1 liter) of hot water. Al-ways wash boards after cutting raw meat, poultry, or seafood before cutting fruits and vegetables to prevent cross-contamination. Store cut, peeled, or broken-apart fruits and vegetables (including melon balls) at or below 40°F (4°C). Check that any juices or cider you buy are pasteurized. When buying from a salad bar, avoid fruits and vegetables that look brownish, slimy, or dried out. These are signs that the product has been held at an improper temperature [5]. See Chapter 3 for more on food safety.

When preparing salad plants, all inedible portions should be removed. Although some soluble nutrients may be leached out when the vegetables are allowed to stand too long in water, they need to take in some water through cut stems or cores to become crisp. The water that clings to leaves and stems after washing helps to develop crispness, provided that enough time is al-lowed for chilling in the refrigerator. Salad plants can be wrapped in plastic material or stored in a tightly closed hydrator. All excess water should be re-moved from the vegetables before storage to decrease the likelihood of spoilage. Careful drying before use prevents the bruising of leaves. Although the butterhead types of lettuce do not become crisp, their tender leaves and

Hot Topics

Are fresh fruits and vegetables safe?

Eating fruits and vegetables is associated with a healthy lifestyle. So, what hazards could possibly be connected to these favored food products? Actually, there are several points in the production of fruits and vegetables at which contamination could occur. For example, produce can become contaminated with pathogens directly through manure used as fertilizer. And the microbiological quality of irrigation water may need to be studied. Then, postharvest operations, such as packing, present potential risks for contamination related to water quality and manufacturing practices [4].

The President of the United States is concerned about food safety, and issued a directive on this subject in October 1997 which sparked a number of documents and reports from several federal agencies. Included in this activity, the Institute of Food Technologists has contracted with the FDA to study the microbial hazards on fresh and fresh-cut produce. Thus the power of food science and technology can be brought to bear on federal decisions and regulations concerning food safety.

That fresh-cut produce is becoming more popular is evident when you visit your local supermarket. All sorts of pre-cut and pre-packaged fruits, vegetables, and various salad or stir-fry combinations are displayed. And with the newer emphasis on healthful eating, fresh-cut produce has an important niche in the market. But the process of cutting up fruits and vegetables removes the protective skin of this produce and increases the surface area available for contamination. Also, the living tissues become more excited when cut and begin to respire more rapidly, decreasing the period of their peak quality. Modified atmosphere packaging (MAP) helps to control these changes, but must be done properly in order to avoid creating an atmosphere conducive to undesirable microbial growth.

Various washing and sanitizing processes are used in the packing of fresh vegetables and fruits, and newer technologies are being studied. Methods to remove pathogens include physical removal, chlorine dioxide, acidified sodium chlorite, acidic compounds, and ozone. Use of irradiation is another possibility [1]. And Good Manufacturing Practices (GMPs) and HACCP programs continue to be the primary pathogen control strategy [4].

In the meantime, wash your produce with water and use a produce brush to remove dirt and residues from the surfaces and crevices of the produce. Vegetable washes, usually made from baking soda and citric acid, may help in removing soil, wax, and pesticides, but it is important to rinse produce well after using these. Then enjoy your produce.

delicate flavors make them valuable salad ingredients. The softer texture of this type of lettuce provides an attractive contrast when combined with crisp salad plants.

Cutting out the core or stem from a head of iceberg lettuce speeds the absorption of water and simplifies separation of the leaves from the head. Firmly striking the core of a head of lettuce on a hard surface loosens the core for easy removal.

Sections of citrus fruits used in salads are usually left whole, but many fruits are cut into bite-sized pieces (Figure 22-5). Canned pineapple, peach, and pear can be cut easily with a fork and may be left whole.

Vegetables are left whole or are diced, shredded, sliced, or sectioned, depending on the type of vegetable (Figure 22-6). When vegetables are used in rel-

ish or crudité trays, some vegetables such as fresh green beans should be lightly blanched then chilled. Other vegetables such as carrots are served raw in sticks or sliced thinly and placed in ice water to curl. As carrots are very firm, they are best used as tiny sticks, thin slices, or shredded, depending on the type of salad. Tiny beets can be left whole; cauliflower and broccoli can be used in separate florets. Tomatoes are often peeled and left whole or cut into wedges or slices. Cucumbers are sliced or diced depending on the type of salad. Celery is usually diced but may be cut into sections that are prepared to form celery curls or cut into shreds. Although green beans in a combination salad are usually cut into short lengths, they may be left whole. Asparagus tips can also be used. Peppers are often cut into rings, but may be coarsely chopped or slivered for some purposes. Potatoes used for salad should be of a variety that holds its form when diced. Mealy potatoes tend to form a starchy mass when made into salad. It is important in most cases that salad ingredients not be finely minced, as soft foods that are too finely cut tend to form a paste when mixed with salad dressings.

Vegetables are often cut finer for molded gelatin salads than for other salads. Cabbage, regardless of how it is used, is more attractive and becomes better seasoned if it is finely shredded. Coarse shreds of cabbage are difficult to chew, particularly if the variety of cabbage is one that does not become crisp easily.

Meats and chicken used in salads are usually diced, but fish is most often coarsely flaked with a fork. Small shellfish, such as shrimp, may be left whole or diced. Canned salmon and tuna fish are difficult to prepare in a way that retains the form of pieces, although tuna is more firm than salmon. Fish canned with a considerable amount of oil can be washed off with hot water before being chilled. Thus, water-packed fish is preferable, or alternately, the oil may become part of the dressing.

Salad bars are a popular self-service feature in many restaurants. A wide variety of salad ingredients are presented separately, and the client chooses from

Figure 22-6
Fresh vegetables, sometimes called crudités, can be beautifully displayed as a salad or as an accompaniment for a salad. (a) Radish roses, green peppers, celery curls, carrot curls, cauliflower, and carrot sticks. (Courtesy of Western Growers Association)

(a)

(b) Carrots, broccoli, sugar snap peas, cucumbers, zucchini, mushrooms, and cherry tomatoes are artfully arranged with a dip. (Courtesy of the American Egg Board)

(b)

the assortment, according to personal taste. Various dressings are also offered separately.

Marinating.   Meat, fish, starchy vegetables, and whole firm pieces of more succulent vegetables may be improved by *marinating,* which is the process of coating foods lightly with a dressing or oil (a *marinade*) and letting the mixture stand in the refrigerator for an hour or more before being made into a salad. The major purpose of marinating most salads is to improve the flavor. Many flavorful marinades can be prepared using specialty oils, vinegars, wines, fruit juices, herbs, and spices.

Some pasta salads are marinated overnight in the refrigerator and due to the absorption of marinade it is important to cook the pasta only until "tender to the bite" or the pasta will be too soft. Leafy vegetables generally cannot be marinated, because they wilt. Also, the color of the vegetables in the salad should be considered. For example, a fresh green bean or broccoli salad will not maintain a bright green color if marinated in an acidic marinade for more than a few hours (see Chapter 20). Excess marinade is drained off when the salad is prepared.

Preparing the Salad

Arrangement and Garnishing.   Whether elaborate or simple, salads should be attractively arranged (Figures 22-6 and 22-7). Whole stuffed tomatoes, halves of peaches or pears, slices of pineapple, and gelatin molds necessarily take on a more fixed appearance than combination salads made from cut pieces. Color can be added by mixing a colorful ingredient in the main body of the salad or by adding a bed of greens and a garnish. The use of contrasting colors and shapes is especially effective. However, some colors may not combine attractively—for example, the clear red **lycopene** pigment of tomato and the purplish red pigment of beets.

lycopene a reddish, fat-soluble pigment of the carotenoid type

Garnishes are not used solely as decorations, but are also edible constituents that form part of the salad. Ripe or stuffed green olives, radishes, and small cheese-stuffed celery stalks often have the effect of garnishes when placed on lettuce beside the salad proper. Sprigs of watercress or parsley, which introduce a darker green color and an interesting leaf design, add appeal to many vegetable

(a)   (b)

Figure 22-7
*(a) This Salade Niçoise was prepared by carefully arranging tomato wedges, sliced cucumbers, green beans, wedged hard cooked eggs, quartered new potatoes, blanched green peppers, artichoke hearts, and fresh grilled tuna over a colorful bed of greens.
(b) An attractively arranged mix of baby greens and tomatoes creates a light and juicy summer salad.*

salads. Strips of pimiento or a bit of paprika add a touch of color, but too much paprika may be unattractive. Overgarnishing should be avoided. Color Plates XII and XV illustrate several different types of salads and their arrangements.

Dressing the Salad.   A wide variety of salad dressings is available. Most salad dressings are examples of **emulsions,** either temporary or permanent, and are discussed in Chapter 10.

emulsion the dispersion of one liquid within another with which it is immiscible, such as oil and water

Certain types of salad, including potato, macaroni, meat, chicken, and fish, and some fruit salads, are improved by being left to stand in the refrigerator for a time with the dressing. These salads are often mixed with the dressing and chilled for several hours before serving. Shredded cabbage may be improved by brief contact with the dressing. For most other leafy salads, however, the texture, appearance, and flavor are better if the dressing is added when the salad is served. The dressing may coat all the salad ingredients, as when the dressing is applied to a large amount of salad in a bowl either at the table or immediately before serving. The ingredients are tossed with a serving spoon and fork until they are well coated with dressing. Light mixing is necessary to retain the characteristic form of each of the salad plants in the mixture. Alternatively, a small amount of dressing may be applied to individual servings before the salad is placed on the table, or the dressing may be passed for individuals to serve themselves.

The hot summer months and the popularity of picnics combine to encourage the holding of meat and starchy salads with mayonnaise or creamy salad dressings for extended periods without chilling. Any salad composed of high protein, neutral pH, and high moisture foods will spoil readily if temperature abused. Furthermore, the cutting, dicing, arranging of salads must be done in a way to minimize cross-contamination from hands, cutting boards, kitchen sinks or other sources. Thus, salads have caused outbreaks of food poisoning when held too long without adequate refrigeration, which is why it is particularly important that they be refrigerated or iced in a cooler during the standing time to prevent the growth of any undesirable microorganisms (see Chapter 3). Although mayonnaise has historically been implicated in the outbreak of foodborne illness in some salads, commercial mayonnaise, which is acidic, is not the culprit—rather it is the lack of care in preparation and temperature control that is to blame.

GELATIN AND GELS

A gel is a special kind of structure that might be described as something between a solid and a liquid. Gels occur in a variety of food products, including most starch-thickened puddings and pie fillings, egg custards, fruit jellies, and gelatin molds used either as salads or as desserts. Starch-thickened mixtures and egg custards are treated in other chapters; gelatin is discussed in this chapter. First, however, let us discuss certain characteristics common to all gels.

Gel Structure and Characteristics

polymers molecules of relatively high molecular weight that are composed of many small molecules acting as building blocks

Gels are composed mainly of fluid but they behave much like rigid solids. These interesting characteristics appear to be the result of their special type of structure. Gels contain long, thin chainlike molecules, called **polymers,** that are joined or cross-linked at random spots to produce a three-dimensional structure something like a pile of dry brush (Figure 22-8).

amylose a straight-chain fraction of starch

Examples of polymers that form gels are (1) the **amylose** fraction of starch with its long chain of glucose molecules linked together; (2) the large protein

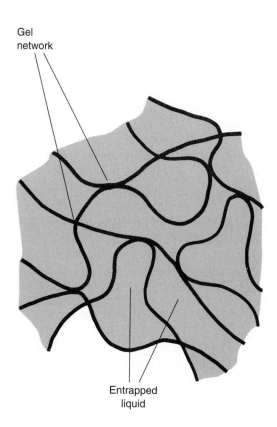

Gel network

Entrapped liquid

Figure 22-8
When a gel is formed, a network of long, thin molecules traps liquid in its meshes.

molecules of egg, which are composed of long chains of **amino acids;** (3) the linear protein molecules of gelatin; and (4) the **pectin** molecules, which are long chains of **galacturonic acid** and its **methyl esters.** Pectin is responsible for the setting of fruit jellies and jams.

The polymer network that is responsible for gel formation is immersed in a liquid medium to which it is attracted. In a sense, it traps the liquid in its chainlike network. The liquid and the polymer network then work together—the liquid keeps the polymer network from collapsing into a compact mass, and the network keeps the liquid from flowing away.

Gels are sometimes described as mixtures that hold the shape of the container after they are removed from it; however, gels vary from being soft to fairly rigid [6]. Most food gels are relatively soft but are resilient or elastic.

Environmental conditions affect the characteristics of many gels. Some gels shrink or swell with changes in temperature. Many food gels liquefy or melt over a relatively narrow temperature range. The melting and solidifying constitute a reversible process in such gels as gelatin mixtures. Gels may also be affected by pH, becoming softer with greater acidity. Some gels exhibit **syneresis.** This may occur in overcooked egg mixtures and in some starch and gelatin gels stored in the refrigerator for a few days.

Manufacture of Gelatin

Gelatin is obtained by the hydrolysis of **collagen,** which is found in the connective tissues of animals. The chief sources of commercial gelatin are animal hides, skins, and bones. The most significant raw material source for edible

amino acids small organic molecules, containing both an amino group and an acid group, that constitute the basic building blocks of proteins

pectin a complex carbohydrate (polysaccharide) composed of galacturonic acid subunits, partially esterified with methyl alcohol and capable of forming a gel

galacturonic acid a derivative of the sugar galactose, with an organic acid group

methyl ester the chemical combination of methyl alcohol with an organic acid, such as galacturonic acid

syneresis the oozing of liquid from a rigid gel; sometimes called *weeping*

collagen a fibrous type of protein molecule found in the connective tissue of animals; produces gelatin when it is partially hydrolyzed

gelatin in North America is porkskin [3]. The conversion of collagen to gelatin is, in fact, a fundamental part of the cookery of less tender cuts of meat. As cooked meat cools, the formation of a gel from the gelatin produced in the meat juices is often visible.

The industrial manufacture of gelatin comprises three basic stages: (1) the raw material is treated so as to separate the collagen from the other components present; (2) the purified collagen is converted into gelatin; and (3) the gelatin is purified, refined, and recovered in dry form [12]. The conditions of manufacture for edible gelatin that include an acid and a lime treatment, followed by washing and sterilization, ensure a product of high sanitary quality (Figure 22-9) [3]. The dry form in which gelatin is marketed also favors a low bacterial count. When gelatin is hydrated, however, and used to make a gel, the moist product is a favorable medium for bacterial growth and should be refrigerated as are other perishable foods.

Some concern has been expressed about the safety of gelatin as a result of bovine spongiform encephalopathy (BSE), which is sometimes called "mad cow disease." BSE is a progressive neurological disorder of cattle that was first found in Great Britain in the late 1980's. Epidemiological and laboratory evidence have suggested a causal relationship between a variant form of Creutzfeldt-Jacob disease (CJD) in Great Britain and BSE [7]. To date, BSE has not been detected in the United States. Surveilance and systems to protect U.S. cattle from this disease continue to be strengthened [8]. Guidance has been provided to the industry regarding the sourcing and processing of gelatin to reduce potential risks of BSE [10].

Gelatin is marketed in both granular and pulverized forms. Fine division of the gelatin allows it to be dispersed more easily in hot water. Gelatin mixes, which include sugar, acid, coloring, and flavoring substances, usually contain pulverized gelatin. A good quality of plain gelatin should be as nearly flavorless and odorless as possible.

Uses

Edible gelatin, which has met specified standards of quality, is used to form a basic gel structure. This structure may carry fruits, vegetables, cheese, meats, whipped cream, nuts, and other appropriate foods as various salads and desserts are prepared (Figure 22-10). It may also act as a foam stabilizer in whipped products and as a thickener in some puddings and pies. It is used in the making of certain candies, such as marshmallows, and in some frozen desserts in which it acts to control crystal size.

Gelatin is a highly efficient gelling agent. As little as 1 to 3 parts of gelatin in 97 to 99 parts of water produces a moldable gel.

Nutritive Value

Gelatin is a protein food derived from animal sources, yet it is a protein of low biologic value. It lacks several essential amino acids, particularly tryptophan. Regardless of the quality of protein, the amount of gelatin required to form a gel is so small (1 tablespoon per pint of liquid) that its nutritive contribution is insignificant. One tablespoon of granulated gelatin furnishes about 30 kilocalories and 9 grams of protein.

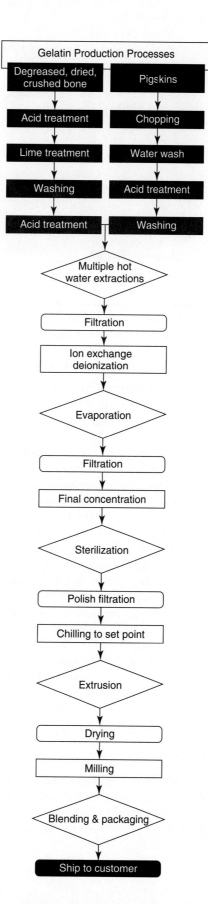

Figure 22-9
Gelatin production process. (Adapted from Gelatin Manufacturers Institute of America, reference 3)

Some gelatin desserts and salads may provide the means by which significant amounts of fresh fruits and vegetables are incorporated into the diet, but it is the added foods rather than the gelatin that are nutritionally valuable.

Hydration, Swelling, and Dispersion

Dry gelatin hydrates and swells when soaked in cold water. The water molecules are attracted to the gelatin molecules and form a water shell around them. This aids in later dispersion of the gelatin in hot water.

The ease, rapidity, and extent of swelling depend on several factors. If the gelatin is finely granulated or pulverized, more surface is exposed to the water. Consequently, the rate of swelling is increased. Directions on packages of most gelatin mixes suggest omission of the soaking in cold water and addition of boiling water directly to the pulverized gelatin, which has previously been mixed with sugar or nonnutritive sweeteners and flavorings.

The degree of acidity or alkalinity, the kinds of salts present, and the presence of sugar all influence the swelling of gelatin. Sugar and certain salts inhibit swelling, whereas other salts accelerate it. Because the fruit acids and sugar used for flavor are usually not added until the unflavored gelatin has swelled and been dispersed, they do not affect these processes.

When the temperature of soaked gelatin is elevated to 95°F (35°C) or higher, the gelatin molecules separate or disperse. Some hot liquid can be added to the hydrated gelatin to disperse it, after which the remaining liquid can be added cold; or the hydrated gelatin can be suspended over hot water until dispersion takes place, after which all remaining liquid can be added cold. Boiling all the remaining liquid before adding it is unnecessary and undesirable for two reasons: More time is required to cool the mixture, and some volatile flavor substances are lost with high temperatures.

Gelation

Gelation means gel formation or the stiffening of a gelatin dispersion. Gelation does not occur at a fixed or clearly defined point, but rather is a gradual process. It evidently involves the joining or linking of gelatin molecules in various places to form the three-dimensional "brush-heap" structure that is typical of gels (see Figure 22-8).

Effect of Temperature.   Different samples of gelatin set at different temperatures, but all require cooling below the temperature of dispersion, which is 95°F (35°C). Gelatins that require a low temperature to solidify tend to liquefy readily when brought back to room temperature. Gelatin dispersions that have set quickly because they were subjected immediately to very low temperatures also melt more readily at room temperature than similar gelatin mixtures that set at somewhat higher temperatures.

It is possible, because of rapid cooling, for a gelatin dispersion to remain liquid at temperatures that would ordinarily be low enough for gelation. Because of time schedules, it is sometimes necessary to chill gelatin dispersions rapidly and to hold them at low temperatures for quick setting. Sometimes, ice cubes are added as part of the cold water to speed the setting process. If more time is allowed, however, gelation occurs at a higher temperature. It also occurs more quickly at a cold temperature if the gelatin dispersion stands at room temperature for a time before being chilled. Temperatures required for the solidification of a gelatin dispersion vary from less than 50°F (10°C) to approximately 58° to 60°F (14° to 16°C).

Concentration.   The concentration of gelatin affects not only the firmness of the gel but also the rate of setting. The higher the concentration, the firmer the gel and the faster the rate of setting.

The usual percentage of gelatin in a gelatin mold of good texture is about 1.5 or 2 percent, depending on the ingredients used in the mixture. One tablespoon (7 grams) of unflavored gelatin per 2 cups of liquid gives a gelatin concentration of about 1.5 percent. Beating the gelatin dispersion to a **foam** or sponge increases the volume sufficiently to decrease the firmness of the gel. A higher concentration of gelatin is thus required to produce a firm texture in whipped products. Very weak dispersions of gelatin, such as those used in ice creams, eventually set if given a long time and a low temperature. If excess gelatin is used in ice cream, gumminess increases with longer storage.

Gels become stiffer with longer standing. Unless a relatively high concentration of gelatin is used, it is usually desirable to allow gelatin mixtures to stand several hours or overnight at a low temperature to develop optimum stiffness.

foam the dispersion of a gas in a liquid

Degree of Acidity.   The fruit juices and vinegar that are frequently added to the gelatin mixtures used for desserts and salads increase the acidity of the dispersions. Too high a concentration of acid can prevent gelation or cause the formation of a soft gel, even when a fairly high concentration of gelatin is present.

Lemon juice and vinegar have a more pronounced effect on gelation than tomato juice and some other fruit juices of lower acidity. Two tablespoons of lemon juice as part of 1 cup of liquid is usually enough for good flavor unless the dispersion is to be beaten to a foam. In this case, the flavor is diluted. This dispersion forms a more tender gel than one made without acid and yet is usually satisfactorily stiff even when no extra gelatin is added.

Chopped vegetables or diced fruits added to a gelatin mixture mechanically break up the gel and may prevent its setting into a sufficiently firm mass. If, in addition, enough acid is added to give good flavor, the resulting gel may be too weak to be molded. Use of a somewhat higher concentration of gelatin may be necessary in such circumstances. The time required for acid gelatin dispersions to set is greater than that required for neutral ones.

Effect of Salts. Gel strength is increased when milk is used as a liquid in gelatin mixtures, probably as a result of the salts present in milk. Even hard water that contains minerals produces a firmer gel than distilled water.

Addition of Sugar. Sugar weakens a gelatin gel and retards the rate of setting. Usual recipes for gelatin mixtures have been adjusted so that the weakening effect of sugar is counterbalanced by the firming effect of increased gelatin concentration.

proteinase an enzyme that hydrolyzes protein to smaller fragments, eventually producing amino acids

Effect of Enzymes. The bromelain enzyme in fresh pineapple is a **proteinase** that hydrolyzes protein. Some other tropical fruits, including kiwifruit and papaya, also contain proteinases. If these enzymes are not destroyed by heat before the fruit is added to a gelatin dispersion, they will break down gelatin molecules so that they cannot form a gel. Because the heat of processing has destroyed the enzyme in canned pineapple pieces or juice, these products can be satisfactorily used in gelatin mixtures. Freezing does not affect the activity of the enzyme, however, and thus frozen pineapple cannot be used in a gelatin gel.

Gelatin Salads and Desserts

Fruit, Vegetable, Meat, and Fish Jellies. Before fruits, vegetables, or other solid food materials are added to a gelatin mixture, they should be thoroughly drained of juices. The juices of fruits and some vegetables may be added as part of the liquid required to disperse the gelatin. Gelatin mixtures should stand until they are thickened and just ready to form a gel before solid food materials are added to them. If the gelatin mixture is too liquid, the added pieces will float. Waiting until the mixture is thickened allows the added materials to be dispersed more evenly throughout the mixture.

Aspics. Aspic is usually a beef-flavored gelatin mixture, although fish and poultry flavors may also be used. Tomato aspic salad is made with unflavored gelatin and seasoned tomato juice. Chopped celery may be added to a tomato aspic salad. As a variation of this salad, avocado slices can be placed in the salad mold before the tomato aspic mixture is poured over them, or the aspic can be layered with a cottage cheese and sour cream mixture to which unflavored gelatin has been added. Aspic is often used to make fancy canapés that may be part of buffet platters (Figure 22-11).

Foams and Sponges. A gelatin dispersion can be beaten to form a foam. It increases two or three times its original volume, depending largely on the stage at which the dispersion is beaten. If beating is not started until the gelatin begins to set, the volume obtained is small, and finely broken bits of solidified gelatin are evident throughout the mass. The best stage for beating is when the dispersion is about the consistency of whipping cream or thin egg whites. The gelatin mixture is elastic and stretches to surround the air bubbles. Beating is continued until the mass is very stiff, to avoid the formation of a clear layer in the bottom of the mold. However, it may be necessary to stop and chill the beaten mixture again in the middle of beating. Just the friction of continued beating can warm the mixture enough to thin it. On standing, the gelatin sets and stabilizes the foam. An increase in gelatin, sugar, and flavoring is required if the gelatin dispersion is to be beaten to a foam because the increased volume of a foam dilutes these ingredients.

PLATE XVII

Egg dishes.

Frittatas are open faced omelets with hearty fillings cooked into the egg mixture. This frittata is filled with O'Brien potatoes and cheese. (Courtesy of the American Egg Board)

Eggs baked in a rice nest and topped with cheese is an interesting way to serve eggs at dinner. (Courtesy of the American Egg Board)

A potluck classic—Deviled Eggs. (Courtesy of the American Egg Board)

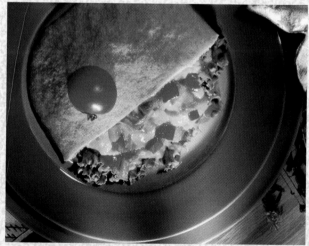

This vegetable scramble pocket is composed of eggs scrambled with carrots, onions, and red and green sweet peppers. The eggs are spooned into a pita pocket and dressed with honey mustard to finish this dish. (Courtesy of the American Egg Board.)

PLATE XVIII

Vegetarian dishes may be very creative and tasty.

Lemon tofu cheesecake combines silken tofu with some low-fat cream cheese. (Courtesy of the United Soybean Board)

Colorful spinach and red bell pepper contrast with dark ripe olives and Jack cheese in rolled flour tortillas spread with reduced-fat cream cheese, making rolled sandwiches. (Courtesy of the California Olive Industry)

Corn-olive cakes are cooked on a lightly oiled griddle and served with salsa. (Courtesy of the California Olive Industry)

Greek-style pizza may be prepared using foccacia bread topped with sour cream, tomatoes, fresh spinach, artichoke hearts, pepperoncini peppers, Greek kalamata olives, and feta cheese. (Courtesy of Land O'Lakes.)

PLATE XIX

Vegetarian dishes.

Meatless vegetarian burgers include fresh mushrooms, olives, onions, and Moz-zarella cheese combined with rolled oats and brown rice, bound together with egg whites. (Courtesy of the California Olive Industry)

Jeweled cheese burritos include pinto beans, shredded carrots, red bell peppers, ripe olives, chilies, and Jack cheese in a flour tortilla wrap. (Courtesy of the California Olive Industry)

Tortillas make a delicious covering for these veggie wraps that include bean sprouts, shredded cabbage, and a seasoned rice, textured vegetable protein, and diced firm tofu mixture with hoisin sauce. (Courtesy of the United Soybean Board)

An egg-less salad sandwich is made using tofu. Fooled you didn't it! (Courtesy of Morinaga Nutritional Foods, maker of Mori-Nu Tofu, www.morinu.com)

PLATE XX

Cuts of beef. (Courtesy of the National Live Stock and Meat Board)

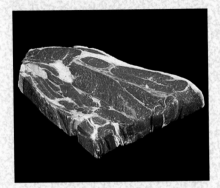

Beef chuck, seven-bone steak

Beef plate, skirt steak boneless (inner diaphragm muscle)

Beef flank steak

Beef loin, tenderloin steak

Beef loin, top sirloin steak boneless

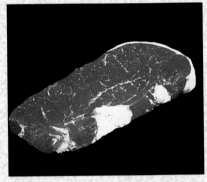

Beef round, top round steak

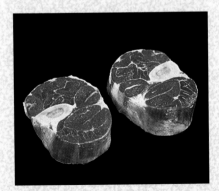

Beef shank, cross cuts

Beef round, eye round roast

Swiss steak piperade uses beef round steak with tomatoes, bell peppers, and seasonings and is served on a bed of cooked farfalle (bowtie) pasta.

PLATE XXI

Cuts of beefsteak. (Courtesy of the National Live Stock and Meat Board)

Beef rib steak

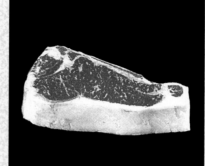

Beef loin, top loin steak

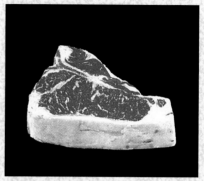

Beef loin, T-bone steak

Beef loin, porterhouse steak

Beef loin, flat-bone sirloin steak

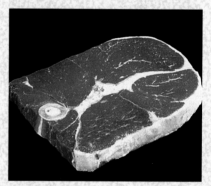

Beef round steak

Beef chuck, arm steak

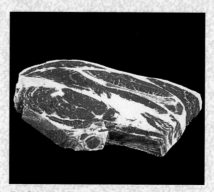

Beef chuck, blade steak

T-bone steaks, flavored with a pesto composed of parsley, garlic, and olive oil, are grilled with red and green peppers. (Courtesy of Cattlemen's Beef Board through the National Cattlemen's Beef Association.)

PLATE XXII

Cuts of beef. (Courtesy of the National Live Stock and Meat Board)

Beef chuck, top blade pot roast

Beef chuck, shoulder pot roast boneless

Beef chuck, under-blade pot roast (bottom portion of blade)

Beef chuck, short ribs

Beef brisket boneless

Beef for stew

Beef rib roast, small end

Beef rib eye roast

Beef round, rump roast

Beef, round, rump roast boneless

Beef round, tip roast

Beef round, heel of round

PLATE XXIII

Cooked beef.

Tropical grilled flank steak is served with fresh fruit salsa, which contains green apple, mango, papaya, pineapple, green and red bell peppers, and cilantro. (Courtesy of National Live Stock and Meat Board.)

Beef, pepper, and mushroom kabobs use beef top sirloin steak. A mixture of oil, lemon juice, mustard, honey, oregano, and pepper coats each kabob before broiling. (Courtesy of National Live Stock and Meat Board.)

Spicy grilled short ribs are marinated in barbecue sauce, lemon juice, minced jalapeno peppers, and green onion for several hours before cooking. (Courtesy of National Live Stock and Meat Board.)

Stir-fried beef gyros in pita pockets are prepared with seasoned beef round tip steaks, pita bread, tomatoes, and cucumber ranch dressing. (Courtesy of Cattlemen's Beef Board through the National Cattlemen's Beef Association.)

PLATE XXIV

Veal.

Veal loin chops

Veal cutlets (thin, boneless leg slices)

Veal shoulder, arm steak

Veal leg, round steak

Veal Breast with olive-mushroom filling is prepared by spreading the filling over the veal breast then rolling, tying, and cooking in a Marsala wine sauce. (Courtesy of Cattlemen's Beef Board through the National Cattlemen's Beef Association.)

Fruit 'n pecan stuffed veal crown roast is an eye-catching entree. The ribs are stuffed with dried apricots and prunes, celery, onion, toasted pecans, and cooked brown rice. (Courtesy of the National Live Stock and Meat Board.)

PLATE XXV

Cuts of lamb. (Courtesy of the National Live Stock and Meat Board)

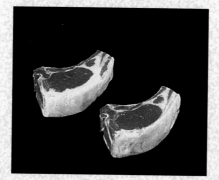

Lamb rib chops

Lamb shoulder, arm chops

Lamb loin chops

Lamb leg, French-style roast

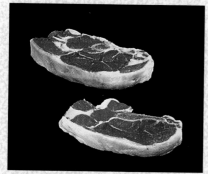

Lamb leg, sirloin chops

Lamb leg, American-style roast

This sautéed lamb loin with stuffed rösti potatoes, cherry confit, and fresh asparagus, has been beautifully presented.

PLATE XXVI

Cuts of pork. (Courtesy of the National Live Stock and Meat Board)

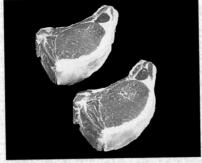

Pork loin, rib chops

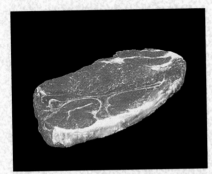

Pork shoulder, blade steak

Pork loin chops

Pork spare ribs

Pork loin, tenderloin whole

Pork loin, sirloin roast

Smoked ham, shank portion

Smoked ham, rump portion

Pork shoulder, arm picnic

Pork shoulder, arm roast

PLATE XXVII

Pork. (Courtesy of The National Pork Board)

A spiral cut ham seasoned with a hot pepper jelly can be prepared quickly.

Boneless pork chops prepared with red and yellow peppers is a tender and tasty dish.

Many different kinds of sauces may be used to create delicious spareribs.

This pork loin roast was prepared with an Italian dressing mix, cumin, and oregano. Fall vegetables are served on the side.

PLATE XXVIII

Poultry.

Turkey sausage vegetable kabobs and plum barbeque chicken can be served for a tasty summer time meal. (Courtesy of Land O'Lakes.)

Chicken breasts may be crusted with herbs for a unique flavor. (Courtesy of the National Chicken Council and U.S. Poultry and Egg Association.)

Roast chicken with fall vegetables. (Courtesy of the National Chicken Council and U.S. Poultry and Egg Association.)

Breaded and baked chicken served with corn on the cob. (Courtesy of the National Chicken Council and U.S. Poultry and Egg Association.)

PLATE XXIX

Poultry.

Bone-in chicken breast glazed and served with fresh fruit. (Courtesy of Dole Food Company, Inc.)

Chicken tenders seasoned with cilantro and served with red beans and rice. (Courtesy of Land O' Lakes.)

Thinly sliced chicken breast or chicken tenders may be used in the preparation of Hunan chicken. (Courtesy of the National Chicken Council and U.S. Poultry and Egg Association.)

Skinless chicken thighs marinated and grilled are served with green beans and walnuts. (Courtesy of the National Chicken Council and U.S. Poultry and Egg Association.)

PLATE XXX

Seafood. (Courtesy of the Florida Department of Agriculture and Consumer Services, Bureau of Seafood and Aquaculture)

Clams

Oysters

Spiny lobster

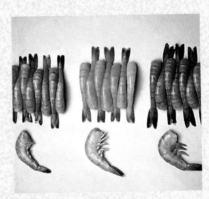

Brown, white, and pink shrimp

Fresh fish—bright scales and firm to the touch

This dish called shrimp tortilla towers is an unique way to present shrimp.

PLATE XXXI

Seafood.

Smoked Spanish mackerel. (Courtesy of the Florida Department of Agriculture and Consumer Services Bureau of Seafood and Aquaculture.)

Stuffed pompano fillets. (Courtesy of the Florida Department of Agriculture and Consumer Services Bureau of Seafood and Aquaculture.)

Sweet 'n sour shrimp. (Courtesy of the Florida Department of Agriculture and Consumer Services Bureau of Seafood and Aquaculture.)

A cobb salad prepared with surimi, hard-boiled eggs, bleu cheese, red peppers, avocado, bacon, and a bed of greens. (Courtesy of Alaska Seafood Marketing Institute.)

Basil broiled fish served with roasted vegetables. (Courtesy of Florida Department of Agriculture and Consumer Services, Bureau of Seafood and Aquaculture.)

PLATE XXXII

Beverages. (Courtesy of Dole Food Company, Inc.)

Blueberries, pineapple, bananas, and milk are blended to create this tropical blueberry smoothie.

A refreshing fruit bowl summer punch is prepared with bananas, frozen yogurt, raspberries, and lemon-lime soda.

A distinctly fall beverage is created with pineapple juice, cinnamon, figs, prunes, raisins, and vanilla extract.

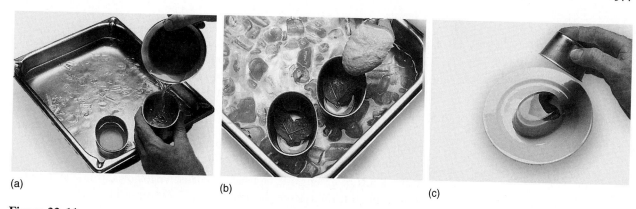

(a) (b) (c)

Figure 22-11
(a) Cool liquid aspic jelly is poured into the mold. (b) Mold is garnished with vegetable leaves, then filled with a cold mousse. (c) After refrigeration, the mold is dipped in warm water then inverted onto a plate.

To form a sponge, whipped egg white is beaten into the mixture after the syrupy gelatin mixture is beaten until it is thick and foamy. The sponge can be poured into molds and should be refrigerated until it solidifies. There is a danger of salmonellae organisms being present in raw egg white. For safety, the egg whites should be pasteurized. Frozen or refrigerated pasteurized eggs may be purchased. As another option, pasteurized egg white powder can be purchased. This ingredient is used in boxed angel food cake mixes. The dried pasteurized egg white may be more readily available at the retail level, although both dried and frozen or refrigerated pasteurized egg products are available in the commercial environment.

Bavarian and Spanish Creams. Gelatin mixtures that have stood long enough to be thickened and syrupy may have fruit pulp added and whipped cream folded into them to make Bavarian creams. Charlottes are similar to Bavarian creams but may contain a large proportion of whipped cream and are usually molded with lady fingers. Whipped evaporated or dried milks are sometimes substituted for whipped cream in gelatin desserts.

Fillings for chiffon pies have gelatin as a basic foam stabilizer. In the preparation of most chiffon fillings, a cooked custard mixture containing egg yolk and sugar is thickened with gelatin. Whipped egg whites (pasteurized) and possibly whipped cream are folded into the mixture. The gelatin sets and stabilizes the egg and/or cream foam.

Spanish cream is a soft custard made with egg yolks that is set with gelatin. The egg whites are beaten to a stiff foam and folded into the mixture after it is partially set. A danger of salmonellae organisms is also present in the making of chiffon pie and Spanish cream if raw egg white, rather than pasteurized egg white, is used. These products should not be made unless pasteurized egg whites are available.

Unmolding the Gel. To unmold a gelatin gel, the mold containing the gel should be dipped for a few moments in lukewarm (not hot) water. One side of the gel should then be carefully loosened with a knife to allow air to come between the gel and the mold. The gel should slide easily from the mold. The mold can be very lightly oiled before the gelatin mixture is placed in it to facilitate removal of the gel.

CHAPTER SUMMARY

- Salads include a wide array of dishes, including mixtures of meat, fish, poultry, cheese, nuts, seeds, and eggs, as well as all kinds of vegetables and fruits. Salads may be served before the main course, as the main course, or as a dessert. The type of salad served depends on its use or position in the meal.

- Salads can contribute to the goal of consuming more fruits and vegetables. The majority of salads prepared from fresh fruits and vegetables are comparatively low in kilocalories. The final caloric value of salads, however, is influenced by the caloric value of the dressing.

- Many kinds of greens can be used in salads. Vegetables, fruits, and edible flowers provide interesting flavors, colors, and textures in salads.

- Most salads should be prepared shortly before the salad is to be served. Sanitary food-handling practices are important in salad preparation to reduce the risk of foodborne illness.

- When preparing salad plants, all inedible portions should be removed. Washing vegetables is important to clean and to allow water to be taken in through the core or stems. Storage of the vegetables in the refrigerator after washing will provide an opportunity for the vegetables to crisp.

- Canned salmon and tuna fish are generally drained before use in a salad.

- Some salad ingredients may be marinated to improve flavor. The length of time salad ingredients are marinated varies with the type of ingredient. Excess marinade is drained off during final preparation of the salad.

- Salads should be attractively arranged. Contrasting colors and shapes are effective. Garnishes provide decoration, but also are edible constituents that form part of the salad.

- Many types of salad dressings are available. Dressing may be placed on some salads, such as a potato salad, well in advance. Other dressings are added just before service or are provided on the table for individuals to serve themselves.

- Salads should be properly refrigerated and maintained cold to prevent foodborne illness. Special attention to the temperature control of salads at summer picnics should be taken. Any salad composed of high protein, neutral pH, and high-moisture foods will spoil readily if temperature abused.

- A gel is a special kind of structure that might be described as something between a solid and a liquid. Gels occur in a variety of food products, including most starch-thickened puddings and pie fillings, eggs custards, fruit jellies, and gelatin molds.

- Gels are composed of mainly fluid but they behave much like rigid solids. Gels contain long, thin chainlike molecules, called polymers, that are joined or cross-linked at random spots to produce a three-dimensional structure something like a pile of dry brush. Although gels are sometimes described as mixtures that hold the shape of the container after they are removed from it, gels may vary from being soft to fairly rigid.

- Gelatin is obtained by the hydrolysis of collagen, which is found in the connective tissues of animals. The chief sources of commercial gelatin are animal hides, skins, and bones. The industrial manufacture of gelatin comprises three basic stages: (1) separation of collagen from other components, (2) conversion of collagen into gelatin, and (3) purification, refinement, and recovery into a dry form. Guidance has been provided to the industry regarding the sourcing and processing of gelatin to reduce potential risks of BSE.

- Gelatin is a highly efficient gelling agent. It may be used in various salads and desserts, as a foam stabilizer, thickener, or to control crystal size in some candies.

- Gelatin is a protein food derived from animal sources, yet it is a protein of low biological value. It lacks several essential amino acids, particularly tryptophan.

- Temperature, concentration, degree of acidity, and presence of salts, sugar, and enzymes influence the strength of the gelatin gel.

- When preparing gelatins with canned fruits, the juice should be drained and then used as part of the measured liquid. Generally solid ingredients should be added to a gelatin mixture after the gelatin has partially set or the ingredients will float rather than being evenly dispersed.

- Aspics are usually a beef-flavored gelatin mixture, although fish, poultry and tomato aspics may also be prepared.

- A gelatin dispersion can be beaten to form a foam. It will increase two to three times its original volume. Bavarian creams include fruit pulp and whipped cream. Spanish creams are prepared with a soft egg custard, whipped eggs whites and gelatin.

KEY TERMS

phytochemicals	galacturonic acid
lycopene	methyl ester
emulsion	syneresis
polymers	collagen
amylose	foam
amino acids	proteinase
pectin	

STUDY QUESTIONS

1. **a.** Describe four or five ways in which salads may be used in a meal.
   b. Describe ten or twelve different salads and suggest appropriate uses for them in a menu.

2. **a.** Describe and be able to identify several leafy plants that can be appropriately used as salad greens.
   b. Suggest a satisfactory way to prepare these greens for use in salads and explain why this procedure is effective.

3. Marinating may be appropriate for what types of salads? Explain why.

4. Give several appropriate suggestions for arranging salads as they are served.

5. Gels of various types have common characteristics.
   a. Give several examples of food products that are gels.
   b. Describe the theoretical structure of a gel.
   c. What is *syneresis?*

6. What is *gelatin?* What is its source commercially?

7. In what forms is gelatin usually sold on the market?

8. How should unflavored gelatin be treated—and why—as it is used in the preparation of gelatin gels?

9. Describe what probably happens as gelatin forms a gel.

10. What is the effect of each of the following on the gelation of gelatin gels?
    a. Temperature
    b. Concentration of gelatin
    c. Addition of acid
    d. Addition of sugar
    e. Addition of raw pineapple

11. Describe major characteristics of each of the following gelatin mixtures.
    a. Aspics
    b. Foams
    c. Sponges
    d. Bavarian creams
    e. Spanish creams

REFERENCES

1. Clark, J. P. (2002). Extending the shelf life of fruits and vegetables. *Food Technology*, *56*(4), 98.

2. Fain, A. R., Jr. (1994). A review of the microbiological safety of fresh salads. *Scope*, *9*(3),1 (Silliker Laboratories).

3. Gelatin Manufacturers Institute of America. (2001). How we make gelatin. Retrieved December 21, 2002, from http://www.gelatin-gmia.com/html/rawmaterials.html

4. Oria, M. (2001). Report addresses safety of fruit and vegetables. *Food Technology*, *55*(11), 22.

5. Staff. (1997). Safe handling of fruits and vegetables. *FDA Consumer*, *31*(2), 19.

6. Tanaka, T. (1981). Gels. *Scientific American*, *244*(1), 124.

7. U.S. Centers for Disease Control. (2001). Questions and answers regarding Bovine Spongiform Encephalopathy (BSE) and Creutzfeldt-Jacob Disease (CJD). Retrieved December 20, 2002, from http://www.cdc.gov/ncidod/diseases/cjd/bse_cjd_qu.htm

8. U.S. Department of Agriculture. (2002, February). News release: Administration continues to strengthen BSE protection systems. Retrieved December 20, 2002, from http://www.usda.gov/news/releases/2002/02/0070.htm

9. U.S. Department of Agriculture and U.S. Department of Health and Human Services. (2000). *Nutrition and your health: Dietary guidelines for Americans*, 5th edition. Home and Garden Bulletin No. 232.

10. U.S. Food and Drug Administration. (1997, December). Guidance for industry: The sourcing and processing of gelatin to reduce the potential risk posed by bovine spongiform encephalopathy (BSE) in FDA-regulated products for human use. Retrieved December 20, 2002, from http://www.fda.gov/opacom/morechoices/industry/guidance/gelguide.htm

11. Van Duyn, M. A. S. & Pivonka, E. (2000). Overview of the health benefits of fruit and vegetable consumption for the dietetics professional: Selected literature. *Journal of the American Dietetic Association*, *100*, 1511–1521.

12. Ward, A. G., & Courts, A. (eds.). (1977). *The science and technology of gelatin*. New York: Academic Press.

Milk and Milk Products* **23**

 Milk is the one food for which there seems to be no adequate substitute. It constitutes almost the entire diet for the young of all mammals. Each species produces milk that is especially adapted to the growth of its own young, but milk from one species may be used as food for others. Since animals were domesticated centuries ago, the milk from various species such as cow, buffalo, goat, and camel has been used in the diets of people throughout the world. Only cow's milk is of commercial importance in the United States, although small amounts of goat's milk are sold.

The dairy industry has traditionally operated under a philosophy of minimal modification of milk as it is preserved and handled in market channels. Relatively simple processes and physical separations have been used in the manufacture of various dairy products, preserving their natural properties to a large extent. At the same time, however, extensive research has been carried out worldwide on the composition and properties of milk and its products [25]. Because of this research and our considerable knowledge about the nature of milk and its components, many of the isolated components of milk, including its fat, protein, and sugar, are used as ingredients in nondairy foods. There they perform important functions. In addition, changes in labeling regulations for some milk products will allow more flexibility to milk processors in developing items with greater consumer appeal, for example, low- or no-fat milks with creamier texture and improved mouthfeel [27].

CONSUMPTION TRENDS

Annual consumption of milk and milk products, according to U.S. Department of Agriculture (USDA) food disappearance data, has increased from 279 pounds per person in 1975 to 502 pounds per person in 1999 [1]. Whole milk consumption has declined from a record high level of 344 pounds (43 gallons) per person in 1945 to 72 pounds (9 gallons) in 1999 (Figure 23-1) [1, 44]. Use of lowfat and nonfat (skim) milk has increased from 60 pounds (7.5 gallons) per person in 1975 to 131 pounds (16.4 gallons) in 1999. Cheese consumption increased eightfold between 1909 and 1999. In 1909, 4 pounds of cheese were consumed annually per capita, increasing to 19 pounds per capita in 1975, and to 32 pounds per capita in 1999. Pizza sales, ethnic foods, and new manufactured foods, such as frozen products and boxed dry mixes, contributed to this increase in cheese consumption. [8]

Milk products in the title of this chapter refers to those other than butter and ice cream.

Figure 23-1
American's consumption of milk has changed since the early 1900's. (Courtesy of U.S. Department of Agriculture, Reference 44)

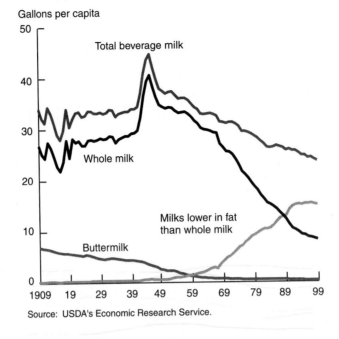

Gallons per capita

Total beverage milk

Whole milk

Milks lower in fat than whole milk

Buttermilk

Source: USDA's Economic Research Service.

COMPOSITION AND PROPERTIES OF MILK

An average percentage composition of whole cow's milk is water, 88; protein, 3.3; fat, 3.3; carbohydrate, 4.7; and ash, 0.7. The quantitative composition of milk varies somewhat in response to several physiological and environmental factors. The breed of the cow, the time of the milking, the feed consumed, the environmental temperature, the season, and the age and health of the cow are all factors that can affect the composition of milk [30] (see Figure 23-2).

The most variable component of milk is the fat, followed by protein. Carbohydrate and ash or mineral content vary only slightly. Different breeds of cattle may produce milk that varies from 3.5 to 5.0 percent fat. The fat content of pooled market milk is adjusted to a desired level by the dairy processor. Standards for minimum fat content differ somewhat in various states. The composition of some common milk products is given in Appendix C.

A new technology for milk production was approved by the U.S. Food and Drug Administration (FDA) in 1993. A naturally occurring protein hormone in cattle called bovine somatotropin, or bST, influences body maintenance and milk production. This hormone can be artificially synthesized (rbST) through use of genetic engineering and, given to cows, increases milk production by about 10 percent. The FDA has evaluated extensive research on rbST and found milk and meat from treated animals to be safe for human consumption [3]. A recent review of rbST affirmed the safety of this protein hormone [59].

Protein

About 80 percent of the protein in milk is *casein*. Most of the remainder is classified as *whey protein*, made up principally of *lactalbumin* and *lactoglobulin*. Very small amounts of other proteins are also present in milk. Casein, lactalbumin, and lactoglobulin are not single proteins, but rather are complexes of many closely related protein molecules [39]. For example, there is not just one casein molecule but several, including alpha$_{s1}$-, alpha$_{s2}$-, beta-, and kappa-casein.

Figure 23-2
A Holstein dairy cow poses for a photograph. (Courtesy of U.S. National Resources Conservation Service; photo by Bob Nichols)

Kappa-casein plays an important role in stabilizing the tiny casein particles or micelles in a **colloidal** dispersion. Colloidal calcium phosphate helps to link the casein molecules into tiny **micelles,** which are apparently responsible for the whiteness of milk. Proteins are discussed further in Chapter 9.

Casein is classified as a phosphoprotein because of the phosphoric acid that is contained in its molecular structure. At the normal acidity of fresh milk (about pH 6.6) casein is largely combined, through the phosphoric acid part of its structure, with calcium, as calcium caseinate. It is dispersed in the watery portion of milk, called *milk serum.* With the addition of sufficient acid to lower the pH to about 4.6, casein precipitates as a curd. A similar precipitation or co-agulation of casein may also be brought about by the addition of an enzyme substance called *rennet,* the main component of which is a **protease** called *chymosin.* Rennet, or other milk-clotting enzymes and bacterial cultures that produce lactic acid, is used to coagulate the casein of milk in the making of cheese. We thus have curds (primarily coagulated casein, with entrapped fat globules if whole milk is used) and whey (mainly the whey proteins lactalbumin and lactoglobulin and the sugar lactose, dispersed in most of the water of milk). Although the whey proteins are not precipitated by acid or rennet, they can be coagulated by heat. They seem to be chiefly responsible for the precipitate that usually forms on the bottom and sides of a container in which milk is heated.

By a procedure involving **ultrafiltration** and other processing techniques, whey protein concentrate (WPC) is produced from the whey, which is a by-product of cheesemaking. WPC may be made to contain about 35, 50, or 80

colloidal usually refers to the state of subdivision of dispersed particles; intermediate between very small particles in true solution and large particles in suspension

micelles a colloidal particle

protease an enzyme that acts on proteins to hydrolyze them

ultrafiltration filtration through an extremely fine filter

percent protein. Further processing may produce whey protein isolate (WPI), which contains greater than 90 percent protein. These whey products, in dried form, may be used in a wide range of food applications, including the formulation of high protein beverages that are popular with athletes, and used in bakery products, prepared mixes, soups, confectionery, and margarines [14, 20]. On heating, dispersions of WPC can act as gelling agents. Beta-lactoglobulin accounts for about 50 percent of total whey proteins and is apparently the principal gelling protein in whey [32, 34].

Surplus skim milk is a readily available source of isolated casein and caseinate products. A considerable quantity of caseinates is imported into the United States from New Zealand, Australia, and the European Economic Community. Caseinates are used in such products as imitation cheese, coffee whiteners, dessert toppings, and bakery items.

Fat

The fat in milk (milk fat or butterfat) is a complex lipid. It exists in whole milk as tiny droplets dispersed in the milk serum (watery portion); thus, milk is an **emulsion.** The fat globules vary in size; most are minute yet easily visible under the microscope (see Figure 23-3). To keep the fat globules dispersed in an emulsified form, they are surrounded by a thin film or membrane called the *milk fat globule membrane.* This membrane is composed of a lipid-protein complex and a small amount of carbohydrate [22]. The lipid portion includes **phospholipids, triglycerides,** and **sterols.** Refer to chapter 9 for a more extensive discussion on lipids in foods.

Milk fat as a whole is composed primarily of triglycerides. In addition to the small amount of phospholipids present, milk fat also contains some sterols—chiefly cholesterol. The triglycerides are characterized by the presence of many short-chain, **saturated fatty acids,** such as butyric and caproic acids. These are partly responsible for the relatively low melting point and, therefore, the soft-solid consistency of butter. When butter spoils as a result of **hydrolysis**

emulsion the dispersion of one liquid in another with which it is usually immiscible

phospholipid a type of fat or lipid molecule that contains phosphoric acid and a nitrogen-containing base along with two fatty acids and a glycerol molecule, all linked together chemically

triglyceride a neutral fat molecule made up of three fatty acids joined to one glycerol molecule through a special chemical linkage called an *ester*

sterol a type of fat or lipid molecule with a complex chemical structure, for example, cholesterol

saturated fatty acid a fatty acid with no double bonds between its carbon atoms

hydrolysis a chemical reaction in which a molecular linkage is broken and a molecule of water is utilized

Figure 23-3
Homogenization of milk decreases the size of the dispersed fat particles, as shown in this photomicrograph of evaporated milk. (Courtesy of the Evaporated Milk Association)

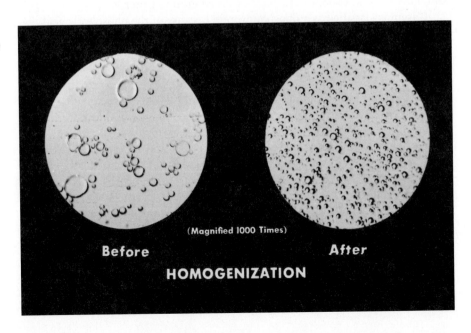

of triglyceride molecules, the disagreeable odor and flavor are due primarily to the release of free butyric and caproic acids from the triglyceride molecules.

Some fat globules in freshly drawn milk are loosely grouped in small clusters. Then, as whole, nonhomogenized milk stands, the fat globules tend to form larger and larger clusters. Because fat is less dense than the watery portion of milk, the fat clusters rise to the surface as cream. The size of the dispersed fat globules in milk is decreased by the process of homogenization. The dispersion is therefore more stable, and the fat no longer rises to the surface on standing. No cream line is formed. Homogenization is discussed later in the chapter.

Fat-soluble vitamins A, D, E, and K are carried in the fat globules. Some yellow fat-soluble carotenoid pigments are also found with the fat and give color to heavy cream and butter.

A decline in milk fat consumption has created a surplus of milk fat in the United States. Some of this surplus may be utilized by fractionation or separation of milk fat components into groups with different chemical and physical properties, so that they can be utilized in new food-processing applications [2, 9]. One method of fractionating milk fat involves crystallization, which separates the triglycerides by melting points. Another technology for milk fat fractionation is *supercritical fluid extraction (SFE)*. SFE relies on the enhanced ability of a gas to act as a solvent when heated above its **critical temperature,** and is also compressed so that its **density** increases and approaches that of a liquid. Carbon dioxide is the preferred gas in the food industry because it is nontoxic, noncorrosive, nonflammable, low in cost, and readily available. The cholesterol content of milk fat can also be reduced by supercritical fluid processing, as well as by steam-stripping and the use of enzymes [50].

critical temperature the temperature above which a gas can exist only as a gas, regardless of the pressure, because the motion of the molecules is so violent

density mass per unit of volume

Carbohydrate

The chief carbohydrate of milk, lactose or milk sugar, is a disaccharide. On hydrolysis, it yields the monosaccharides glucose and galactose (see Chapter 9 for the chemical structures of disaccharides and monosaccharides). Lactose is the least sweet and also the least soluble of the common sugars. Because of its low solubility, it may crystallize out and give some food products a sandy texture when present in too large an amount. For example, when too much nonfat dry milk, which is high in lactose, is added to ice cream, the less soluble sugar may produce sandiness at the low temperature required for freezing. Lactose separated from milk finds many uses in the food industry. It may be an ingredient in such products as cooked sausages and hams, confections, and infant formulas.

The enzyme *lactase*, normally produced in the small intestine, breaks down lactose into its two component simple sugars. In some people, however, this enzyme is present in insufficient quantity for them to handle more than a very small amount of milk sugar without discomfort. Because lactose is not digested in people who have an enzyme deficiency, it remains in the intestine and is broken down by microorganisms, producing gas, cramping, and diarrhea. A deficiency of lactase, producing a lactose intolerance, seems to develop quite frequently, even in early childhood, among certain populations, particularly non-Caucasian peoples. People with lactose intolerance may be able to tolerate small amounts of some fermented milk products, such as yogurt and buttermilk, if much of the lactose in these products has been broken down to glucose and galactose. Aged cheese may also be tolerated.

Since lactase has become available commercially, the dairy industry has produced fluid milks, both whole and reduced fat, treated with this enzyme so that the lactose content of the milks is reduced, typically by 70 percent [17, 39]. These milks are sweeter tasting because the lactose has been broken down to the sweeter sugars—glucose and galactose. Lactase is also available for home use in liquid and tablet or capsule form. The lactase can be consumed directly or added to regular milk.

Color

The white appearance of milk is due to the reflection of light by the colloidally dispersed casein micelles and by the calcium phosphate salts. Two yellowish pigments contribute to the color of milk—carotenes and riboflavin. The fat-soluble carotenes are found in the milk fat; the riboflavin is water soluble. Depending on the concentration of carotenes, the intensity of color in milk varies. The concentration of carotenes, in turn, depends on the amount of pigment in the feed of the cow and on her ability to change it to the colorless vitamin A molecule. A greenish yellow fluorescent color, particularly noticeable in liquid whey, is due to the presence of riboflavin.

Flavor

The flavor of milk is bland and slightly sweet because of its lactose content. A major flavor sensation of milk is thought to be its particular mouthfeel, which results from the emulsion of milk fat, as well as from the colloidal structure of the proteins and some of the calcium phosphate.

The slight aroma of fresh milk is produced by several low-molecular-weight compounds, such as acetone, acetaldehyde, dimethyl sulfide, methyl ketones, short-chain fatty acids, and lactones. Some of the volatile compounds contributing to the flavor of milk are unique to the fatty portion of milk.

Heat processing may affect the flavor of milk, the change in flavor being dependent on the time and temperature of heating. The effect on flavor of heating to pasteurize milk, including the use of ultrahigh temperatures for very short periods, is minimal and tends to disappear during storage. Ultrahigh-temperature sterilized milk tastes very much like conventionally pasteurized milk, although some people may notice a slightly cooked flavor [39].

The off-flavors that sometimes occur in milk may result from the feed consumed by the cow, the action of bacteria, chemical changes in the milk, or the absorption of foreign flavors after the milk is drawn. One chemical off-flavor is called *oxidized* flavor [51]. This flavor can result from the oxidation of phospholipids in the milk. Because traces of copper accelerate the development of oxidized flavor, copper-containing equipment is not used in dairies. An off-flavor may also be produced when milk is exposed to light. This off-flavor, which develops rapidly, involves both milk protein and riboflavin. The amount of riboflavin in milk decreases as the off-flavor develops. Waxed cartons and opaque plastic containers help to protect milk from light, thus reducing riboflavin loss and the development of off-flavors.

Acidity

Fresh milk has a pH of about 6.6, which is close to the neutral pH of 7. As milk stands exposed to air, its acidity decreases slightly because of the loss of carbon dioxide. Raw milk, which normally contains some lactic acid–producing bacteria, gradually increases in acidity on storage. Eventually, this process results in sour milk when enough lactic acid has been produced from lactose by bacteria in the milk. Pasteurized milk, however, does not generally become sour because the lactic acid bacteria are destroyed during the heating process. Spoilage of pasteurized milk is usually due to the action of putrefactive bacteria that break down proteins in the milk, resulting in a very bitter, unpleasant flavor.

Nutritive Value

Milk is much more than a beverage. Its caloric value and its content of high-quality protein are significant. It is also a rich source of minerals, particularly calcium (Figure 23-4), and the lactose in milk aids in the absorption of calcium and other minerals from the intestine. Most other foods commonly used in the United States cannot be favorably compared with milk and milk products as good dietary sources of calcium. Without milk or milk products in the diet, very careful planning must be done to meet the recommended dietary allowance for this mineral. Milk is a good source of phosphorus and several other minerals, but is a poor source of iron [42]. Young children may become anemic if they remain on an unsupplemented milk diet too long.

All vitamins known to be essential in human nutrition are present in milk to some extent. The vitamin A value varies with the diet of the cow. When fat is removed in the making of skim milk, vitamin A and other fat-soluble vitamins are lost with the cream; however, both vitamins A and D are usually added to skim and low-fat milks, and whole milk is commonly fortified with vitamin D.

Thiamin occurs in only fair concentration in milk, but is relatively constant in amount. Riboflavin is present in a higher concentration in milk than the other B vitamins, and its stability to heat makes milk a dependable source of this vitamin. Riboflavin is very unstable to ultraviolet light, which means that milk exposed to light may lose large amounts of this vitamin. Because approximately 38 percent of the riboflavin in the American diet comes from milk and dairy products, it is important to protect the riboflavin in milk. The retention of riboflavin in skim milk placed in blow-molded polyethylene containers and held in a lighted chamber for 5 days has been reported to average 58 percent at the top of the containers compared with 92 percent at the bottom of the containers [41]. Waxed cardboard cartons are protective. The use of a film overwrap for light-permeable milk containers may be helpful in preserving riboflavin while

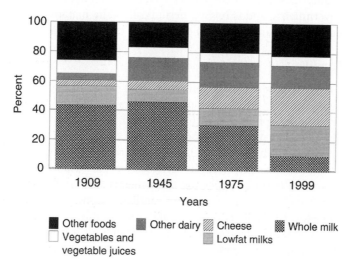

Figure 23-4
Sources of calcium in U.S. food supply for selected years. (Courtesy of Family Economics and Nutrition Review.)

milk is in market channels. Some milk in opaque light-blocking bottles is being marketed [4].

Milk is a good source of the amino acid tryptophan, which is a precursor or provitamin for niacin. Thus, the niacin value of milk is high. Only a small amount of vitamin C is present in raw milk, and approximately 25 percent is destroyed during pasteurization [48]. Milk is therefore not a dependable source of vitamin C, but it is added to some market milk [4].

SANITATION AND MILK QUALITY

Milk is among the most perishable of all foods because it is an excellent medium for the growth of bacteria. Some of these bacteria are harmless, but some may be pathogenic to humans. Quality milk is that which has been produced, processed, and distributed under rigid sanitary conditions so that it has a relatively low bacterial count, is free from disease-producing organisms, has good flavor and appearance, and is of high nutritive value and satisfactory keeping quality. Various controls and treatments for milk have been instituted to ensure quality in this product. The responsibility for a safe milk supply does not rest solely with the dairy industry, however. Public health officials and the consumer share in this responsibility.

The Grade A Pasteurized Milk Ordinance is a set of recommendations made by the U.S. Public Health Service—Food and Drug Administration (FDA). This ordinance describes the steps necessary to protect the milk supply. It outlines sanitary practices, which include the following:

> Inspection and sanitary control of farms and milk plants
>
> Examination and testing of herds
>
> Employee instruction on good manufacturing practices
>
> Proper pasteurization and processing
>
> Laboratory examination of milk
>
> Monitoring for chemical, physical, and microbial adulterants

Formulated as a guide to states and other jurisdictions responsible for milk quality, this ordinance has been voluntarily adopted by many state and local governments, and is revised periodically. The majority of people in the United States live in areas where the guidelines of this ordinance are in effect.

Grading

Sanitary codes generally determine the grading of milk. Grades and their meanings may vary according to local regulations unless the pasteurized milk ordinance has been adopted, in which case standards are uniform. Most rigid control is placed on the production and processing of Grade A market milk, the grade supplied to consumers as fluid milk. The Grade A Pasteurized Milk Ordinance recommends that state health or agriculture departments have programs to regularly monitor the milk supply for the presence of unintentional microconstituents, which include pesticide residues, antibiotics, and radioactivity. In addition, the FDA regularly conducts surveys and other monitoring activities [39].

The USDA has set quality grade standards for nonfat dry milk and also for butter and some cheeses. In addition, a Quality Approved rating is available for

Figure 23-5
USDA shields indicate quality in dairy products. (Courtesy of the U.S. Department of Agriculture)

U.S. Extra Grade is the grade name for instant nonfat dry milk of high quality.

The Quality Approved shield may be used on cottage cheese or other cheeses for which no official U.S. grade standards exist, if the products have been inspected for quality under the USDA's grading and inspection program.

certain products (Figure 23-5). If a manufacturer uses the USDA grade or Quality Approved shield on product labels, the plant must operate under the continuous inspection of USDA agents. The grades for regular nonfat dry milk are U.S. Extra and U.S. Standard. For the instantized product, the grade is U.S. Extra. Grading is a voluntary, fee-for-service program.

Pasteurization

Low bacterial count and high standards of production do not always ensure a milk supply that is free from pathogenic organisms. Even under the best sanitary practices, disease-producing organisms may enter raw milk accidentally from environmental and human sources. Therefore, milk is pasteurized as an additional safeguard for the consumer. Pasteurization is required by law for all Grade A fluid milk and milk products that enter interstate commerce for retail sale [57]. The pasteurization process involves heating raw milk in properly approved and operated equipment at a sufficiently high temperature for a specified length of time to destroy pathogenic bacteria [39]. It generally destroys 95 to 99 percent of nonpathogenic bacteria as well. Although milk is not completely sterilized by pasteurization, its keeping quality is greatly increased over that of raw milk.

Individual states may authorize the intrastate distribution of raw milk, generally with rigid specifications. Health authorities do not advocate its consumption, however, as a number of outbreaks of foodborne illness have resulted from the consumption of raw milk. Home pasteurization or boiling of any milk purchased raw is recommended by public health authorities [39].

Various time and temperature relationships can be used in pasteurization. Milk can be heated to at least 145°F (63°C) and held at this temperature for 30 minutes, which is the low-temperature longer-time (LTLT) process. A high-temperature short-time (HTST) process that consists of heating milk to at least 162°F (72°C) for 15 seconds is also commonly used. In addition, higher heat, shorter time combinations may be applied.

An ultrapasteurization process involves heating milk to 280°F (138°C) for 2 or more seconds. This product has a longer shelf life than milk pasteurized by other methods. After pasteurization, the milk is cooled rapidly to 45°F (7°C) or lower.

Ultrahigh-temperature processing at 280° to 302°F (138° to 150°C) for 2 to 6 seconds sterilizes the milk. When in **aseptic packaging** in presterilized containers, this milk may be kept on the shelf without refrigeration for at least 3 months. After it is opened, however, it must be refrigerated.

Various tests can be applied to ascertain the thoroughness of milk pasteurization. For example, measurements can be made of any activity of the enzyme alkaline phosphatase, which is naturally present in milk. If this enzyme is completely inactivated, the milk has been heated sufficiently to destroy any pathogenic microorganisms that might be present. It is also imperative that no raw milk be mixed accidentally with properly pasteurized milk.

The temperatures and times for pasteurization are not sufficient to significantly alter the milk constituents or properties. Whey proteins are denatured only slightly, minerals are not appreciably precipitated, and vitamin destruction is generally minimal. Changes in curd characteristics that occur as a result of pasteurization tend toward the production of a finer curd when milk is digested.

Care of Milk

Fundamentals in the care of fluid milk, whether by producer or consumer, are cleanliness, cold temperature, and the prevention of contamination by keeping the milk covered. So perishable a food as milk should be stored at 41° (5°C) or below immediately after purchase [35]. Proper containers should be used to protect the milk from exposure to light, which may produce an oxidized off-flavor. The milk container should always be kept closed during storage to prevent the absorption of other food odors and should be returned to the refrigerator immediately after use to prevent warming, which encourages bacterial growth. Milk that has been poured out but not used should never be returned to the original container, because it may contaminate the rest of the milk. Milk that has been properly refrigerated should remain fresh for approximately five days [57].

Nonfat dry milk should be stored in moisture-proof packages at a temperature no higher than ordinary room temperature. Dry milk takes up moisture and becomes lumpy and stale when exposed to air during storage. Because of the fat content, whole dry milk is not as stable to storage as the nonfat product. Unopened cans of evaporated milk can be stored at room temperature. Once the can is opened, however, it must be treated as fluid milk and refrigerated. When cans of evaporated milk are stored for several months, they should be turned over periodically to retard the settling out of milk solids.

MILK PROCESSING

Homogenization

The tendency of the fat globules in whole fluid milk to rise and form a cream line is changed by homogenization. In this process, fat globules are divided into such small particles that they are dispersed permanently in a very fine emulsion throughout the milk serum (see Figure 23-3). Most of the milk marketed in the United States is homogenized.

Homogenization consists of pumping milk or cream under pressures of 2,000 to 2,500 pounds per square inch through tiny openings in a machine

aseptic packaging a process that involves sterilizing the product and the package separately, filling the package without recontaminating the product, and sealing

called a *homogenizer.* A film of adsorbed protein or lipoprotein immediately surrounds each of the new globules, acting as an **emulsifier,** and prevents them from reuniting. It is estimated that about one-fourth of the protein of milk is adsorbed on the finely dispersed fat particles of homogenized milk. The increased dispersion of fat imparts richer flavor and increased viscosity to the milk. Homogenization causes the milk proteins to be somewhat more readily coagulated by heat or acid than the nonhomogenized product. Therefore, care must be taken to avoid curdling in the use of homogenized milk in food preparation.

The greatly increased surface exposed in the highly dispersed fat of homogenized milk increases the tendency toward the development of **rancidity.** Pasteurization before homogenization retards the development of rancidity, because it inactivates the enzymes that could otherwise attack the more highly dispersed fat.

emulsifier a substance that is active at the interface between two immiscible liquids, being attracted somewhat to each liquid; it acts as a bridge between them, allowing an emulsion to form

rancidity a special type of spoilage in fats that begins with the addition of oxygen to unsaturated fatty acids

Fortification

Fortification is the addition of certain nutrients to milk as a means of improving the nutritional value. The principal form of fortification is the addition of about 400 international units (IUs) of vitamin D per quart. In view of the relationship between vitamin D and calcium and phosphorus absorption and utilization in the body, and because milk is an outstanding source of these minerals, milk is generally regarded as a logical food to fortify with vitamin D. Upon exposure to light, a slight loss of vitamin D from fortified milk has been reported [46].

According to the standards of identity for milk, the addition of vitamin D is optional, whereas fortification of skim and low-fat milks with vitamin A is mandatory because vitamin A is present only in the fatty portion of milk. It is particularly important that nonfat dry milk sent to other countries be fortified with vitamin A. Many children in the world do not receive adequate amounts of vitamin A from other sources. Deficiencies are all too common.

TYPES OF MILK PRODUCTS

Milk is marketed in several different forms to appeal to the varied tastes and desires of the consuming public. Packaging of milk in individual milk "chugs" has promoted milk as a grab and go beverage (Figure 23-6). Development of new milk products has been motivated by the desire to improve keeping quality, to facilitate distribution and storage, to make maximum use of by-products, and to utilize surpluses [39]. Cost variations among different forms of milk depend on such factors as supply and demand, production and processing costs, and governmental policies.

Figure 23-6
Milk chugs create a convenient way to have milk on the go. A fat-free milk chug is shown here. (Courtesy of Reiter Dairy)

Federal standards of identity have been set for a number of milk products that enter interstate commerce. These standards define the composition, the kind and quantity of optional ingredients permitted, and the labeling requirements. The 1990 federal labeling legislation requires that virtually all packaged foods bear nutrition labeling. State and local agencies are encouraged to adopt the federal standards to enhance uniformity.

Fluid Milk

Fresh fluid milk is commonly labeled according to its content of milk fat. Beginning January 1, 1998, the labeling of fat-reduced milk followed the same requirements that the FDA established several years ago for the labeling of most other foods that are reduced in fat. Therefore, milk containing 2 percent fat is labeled "reduced fat" or "less fat" rather than "low fat." One percent milk is labeled "low fat" or "little fat." Skim milk may be labeled "skim," "fat free," "zero fat," or "no fat" milk. The regulations were also changed to give dairy processors more freedom to devise new formulations, for example, "light" milk with at least 50 percent less fat than whole milk and reformulated milks with reduced fat content but increased creaminess [27, 36]. The names for milk and fat content are summarized in Table 23-1.

Whole Milk. The term *milk* usually refers to whole milk. According to federal standards, whole milk packaged for beverage use must contain not less than 3.25 percent milk fat and not less than 8.25 percent milk-solids-not-fat, which are mostly protein and lactose. Other standards, however, allow the milk fat minimum in whole milk to vary from 3.0 to 3.8 percent. At milk-processing plants, the milk from different suppliers is standardized to one fat level by removing or adding milk fat as necessary.

Whole milk may be canned and is available in this form chiefly for use on ships or for export. It is heated sufficiently to sterilize and then is put into sterilized cans. It can be stored at room temperature until it is opened.

Fat-reduced Milks. Milks may be modified in fat content as listed in Table 23-1. The nutrients that lower-fat milk products provide, other than fat, must be at least equal to full-fat milk before vitamins A and D are added. The word *skim* is allowed in the labeling of no-fat milk because consumers realize that skim milk means no fat. *Skim* or *nonfat milk* is milk from which as much fat has been removed as is technologically possible. The fat content is less than 0.5 percent. All these milks contain at least 8.25 percent milk-solids-not-fat. Additional ingredients, such as Oatrim soluble oat fiber and nonfat milk solids, may be added to skim milk to increase the viscosity, white color, and creaminess. Skim milk so treated tastes more like milk with 2 percent fat content. Additional calcium and protein may also be added to improve the nutritive value [37]. Addition of vitamin A to low-fat and skim milk is required for milk shipped in interstate commerce. The addition of vitamin D is optional.

Ultrahigh-temperature Processed Milk. Ultrahigh-temperature (UHT) processed milk is heated at temperatures higher than those used for pasteurization—280° to 302°F (138° to 150°C) for 2 to 6 seconds. Then under sterile conditions, it is packaged into presterilized containers, which are aseptically sealed so that spoilage organisms cannot enter. Hydrogen peroxide may be used

Table 23-1
Names for Milk

Old Name	New Name	Total Fat per 240 mL or 1 cup	Kilocalories per 240 mL or 1 cup
Milk	Milk	8.0 grams	150
Low-fat 2 percent milk	Reduced-fat or less-fat milk	4.7 grams	122
Low-fat 1 percent milk	Low-fat milk	2.6 grams	102
Skim milk	Fat-free, skim, zero-fat, no-fat, or nonfat milk	less than 0.5 grams	80

Source: Reference 27.

to sterilize the milk packaging materials. UHT milk can be stored unrefrigerated for at least 3 months, thus representing a considerable savings of energy usually expended for the refrigeration process. After the milk is opened it must be refrigerated, however.

Immediately after processing, UHT milk has a "cooked" and "sulfury" flavor, apparently resulting from the heat denaturation of the whey protein β-lactoglobulin. This undesirable flavor dissipates as the milk is stored until a maximum flavor potential is reached. Thereafter, as storage continues, off-flavors described as "flat," "lacking freshness," "sweet," and "unclean" may gradually develop. After prolonged storage (up to 1 year), such flavors as "chalky," "coconut," "rancid," "musty," and "oxidized" may develop [12]. Off-flavors generally are due to chemical and enzymatic activity in the milk and are less pronounced when the milk is held at temperatures lower than ordinary room temperature. The addition of flavorings to the milk masks off-flavors. Low-temperature-inactivation treatments of milk after UHT processing can reduce off-flavors by destroying enzymes responsible for the changes [13]. UHT milk produced in the United States tastes very much like conventionally pasteurized milk [39].

Concentrated Fluid Milk

Evaporated Milk. In the production of evaporated milk, about 60 percent of the water is removed in a vacuum pan at 122° to 131°F (50° to 55°C). A forewarming period of 10 to 20 minutes at 203°F (95°C) is usually effective in preventing coagulation of the protein casein during sterilization. The heat sterilization process occurs after the product is homogenized and canned. In another process, the concentrated milk may be heated in a continuous system at ultrahigh temperatures and then canned aseptically. This product is less viscous, whiter, and tastes more like pasteurized milk than evaporated milk processed by the traditional method. Evaporated milk is fortified with 400 IUs of vitamin D per quart.

Federal standards require that evaporated milk contain not less than 7.5 percent milk fat and not less than 25 percent total milk solids. Evaporated skim milk must contain not less than 20 percent milk solids. In this case, both vitamins A and D must be added. Sterilized, canned evaporated milk should keep indefinitely without microbiologic spoilage; however, other changes affect its quality. On long standing, the homogenized fat particles tend to coalesce, thus breaking the emulsion. The solids begin to settle, and the product may thicken and form clots. To retard these changes, stored cans of evaporated and condensed milk should be turned every few weeks. The vegetable gum carrageenan is often added to evaporated milk as a stabilizer.

Sweetened Condensed Milk. To prepare sweetened condensed milk, about 15 percent sugar is added to whole or skim milk, which is then concentrated to about one-third of its former volume. Because the 42 percent sugar content of the finished product acts as a preservative, the milk is not sterilized after canning. Federal standards require 28 percent total milk solids. Whole sweetened condensed milk must contain 8 percent milk fat, whereas the skim milk product must have not more than 0.5 percent fat.

Browning of condensed milk and evaporated milk is probably of the **Maillard reaction** type and occurs during both sterilization and storage. The rate of browning is greater at room temperature and with longer storage time.

Maillard reaction a browning reaction in foods involving many complex chemical changes; in the first stages, a sugar and an amino acid or protein interact

Dry Milk

Nonfat dry milk powder is usually made from fresh pasteurized skim milk by removing about two-thirds of the water under vacuum and then spraying this concentrated milk into a chamber of hot filtered air. This process produces a fine powder of very low moisture content, about 3 percent. Nonfat dry milk may also be produced by spraying a jet of hot air into concentrated skim milk (foam spray-drying).

Regular nonfat dry milk reconstitutes in warm water with agitation. Instant nonfat dry milk disperses readily in cold water. To make the instant product, regular nonfat dry milk is remoistened with steam to induce agglomeration of small particles into larger, porous particles that are creamy white and free flowing. The lactose may be in a more soluble form, particularly on the outside of the particles. Vitamins A and D may be added to nonfat dry milk.

Whole milk or low-fat milk can also be dried. The presence of fat in these products reduces their shelf life, as the fat is subject to oxidation. Packaging under vacuum or with an inert gas increases stability.

Another dried dairy product is buttermilk, which has a rather wide use in commercial flour mixes. It is also available in the retail market. Dried churned buttermilk is an excellent ingredient for use in baked products, because it contains phospholipids that function as emulsifiers.

Dried whey and whey protein concentrate (WPC) also have the potential for use in a variety of manufactured foods. WPC can be used as a partial replacer or as a supplement for whole egg or egg white in many baked products [6]. The fortification of bread and pasta with WPC can be an economical way to increase nutritional value [47].

When dried milk is reconstituted, the powder is added to water and then shaken or stirred. For use in flour mixtures and some other products, the dry milk can be mixed with dry ingredients and the water added later. The quantity of instant milk powder needed to make 1 quart of fluid milk is usually 1 1/3 cups.

Cultured Milk Products

fermentation the process in which complex organic compounds are broken down to smaller molecules by the action of enzymes produced by microorganisms

Cultured or **fermented** milks are one of the oldest preserved foods, having been used for centuries. Several hundred different cultured milk products are consumed worldwide [26].

In their preparation, appropriate bacterial cultures are added to the fluid milk. The bacteria ferment lactose to produce lactic acid. A pH between 4.1 and 4.9 is common, and discourages the growth of undesirable microorganisms. Acids, such as lactic and citric, may also be added directly to milk, either with or without the addition of microbial cultures. The development of acidity is responsible for several physical and chemical properties that make the fermented products unique. Each bacterial culture produces its own characteristic flavor components. Some protein hydrolysis occurs, apparently contributing to a softer, more easily digested curd.

Health and nutritional benefits have been claimed for various fermented dairy products. *Lactobacillus acidophilus, Lactobacillus reuteri,* and bifidobacteria are normal inhabitants of the intestinal tract, contributing to increased acidity and deterrence of undesirable microbial growth. The addition of safe and suitable microbial organisms to milk products is allowed by the Pasteurized Milk Ordinance. Additional research is necessary to provide sufficient proof for the FDA to approve label claims for nutritional benefits of fermented milk products

[18, 21, 54]. At this time, however, evidence is strong for the ability of two **probiotics,** *Steptococcus thermophilus* and *Lactobacillus bulgaricus,* that are used in making yogurt, to digest lactose in the intestinal lumen. Thus, this may be the health claim that may be accepted by regulatory agencies [5].

Evidence suggesting the positive health benefits of probiotics in the diet and the market for cultured dairy foods is growing [40, 16, 24]. Annual per capita consumption of yogurt increased sixfold from 1970 to 1997. In 1997, 9.5 half-pint servings of yogurt were consumed per capita [45].

Yogurt. Whole, low-fat, and skim milks and even cream can be used to make yogurt. Often, nonfat dry milk solids are added. The nutrient composition of yogurt reflects the nutrient composition of the milk used in its production; however, there does appear to be a considerable increase in folic acid concentration during the fermentation process. Additional calcium is also found in yogurt when milk solids are added [49].

In the production of yogurt, a mixed culture of *Lactobacillus bulgaricus* and *Streptococcus thermophilus* is usually added to the pasteurized milk premix. *Lactobacillus acidophilus* or other strains may also be added to the culture, which is then incubated at 108° to 115°F (42° to 46°C) until the desired flavor, acidity, and consistency are attained. A sharp, tangy flavor is characteristic of yogurt. Two general types of yogurt are manufactured: The set style has a firm gel; stirred yogurt has a semiliquid consistency. Yogurt is often marketed with sweetened fruit added, producing a sundae-type product. The fruit may be placed on the bottom of the container, or it may be blended throughout the product. Sweetened fruit yogurt is sometimes served as a dessert. Frozen yogurt and frozen yogurt bars containing sugar, stabilizers, and flavorings have also become popular dessert items. They are particularly enjoyed in the hot summer months.

After yogurt has reached the desired flavor and consistency, further bacterial activity is retarded by chilling. The microorganisms are still alive, however, and contain the enzyme *lactase*, which may aid in lactose digestion in people who are lactose intolerant. The lactose content of yogurt is reduced during fermentation, as some lactose is hydrolyzed to the monosaccharides glucose and galactose. When the yogurt premix is enriched with nonfat milk solids, however, the initial level of lactose is actually higher than that of ordinary milk: 6 to 8 percent as compared with 5 percent in milk. During fermentation, the lactose level of yogurt typically falls to about 4 percent [49]. Some yogurt may be heat-treated to destroy the bacterial culture after fermentation is completed, thus extending its shelf life but eliminating any health benefits that might result from these live microorganisms.

Buttermilk. The term *buttermilk* was originally used to describe the liquid remaining after cream is churned to produce butter. This liquid is still used for the production of dried buttermilk, a baking ingredient. Today, however, fluid buttermilk is a cultured milk. Cultured buttermilk is usually made from pasteurized low-fat or skim milk, with nonfat dry milk solids added. It can also be made from fluid whole milk or reconstituted nonfat dry milk. If it is made from low-fat or whole milk, it really should be called cultured milk or cultured low-fat milk rather than buttermilk.

In the process of manufacturing, a culture of *Streptococcus lactis* is added to the milk to produce the acid and flavor components. The product is incubated

probiotic live microorganism food ingredients that enhance human health by improving intestinal microbial balance

at 68° to 70°F (20° to 22°C) until the acidity is 0.8 to 0.9 percent (pH 4.6), expressed as lactic acid [39]. Butter granules or flakes, salt, and a small amount of citric acid may be added to enhance the flavor.

Acidophilus Milks. Low-fat or skim milk may be cultured with *Lactobacillus acidophilus* and incubated at 100°F (38°C) until a soft curd forms. This formulation is then called *acidophilus-cultured milk*. It has an acidic flavor. In another process, a concentrated culture of *L. acidophilus* is grown and then added to pasteurized milk. This product is not acidic in taste, and its consistency is similar to that of fluid milk. Acidophilus milk introduces acidophilus bacteria into the intestine, where they are thought to help maintain a proper balance of microorganisms.

Filled and Imitation Milks

Filled Milk. Filled milk is a substitute milk that can be made by combining a fat other than milk fat with water, nonfat milk solids, an emulsifier, color, and flavoring. The mixture is heated, under agitation, and then homogenized. The resulting product appears to be very much like milk [7]. Cheese and cultured milk products may be produced from filled milk. In this process are created dairylike products that do not contain butterfat or cholesterol. In the past, coconut oil has been the main source of fat in filled milk because of its desirable flavor, even though it is a highly saturated fat. Partially hydrogenated soybean, corn, and cottonseed oils containing approximately 30 percent linoleic acid have also been developed for use in filled milk.

Imitation Milk. Imitation milk resembles milk, but usually contains no milk products per se. Such ingredients as water, corn syrup solids, sugar, vegetable fats, and a source of protein are most often used in imitation milk. Derivatives of milk, such as casein, casein salts, and other milk proteins, may be used as the protein source; soy proteins may also be used. Some imitation milk contains whey products. The vegetable fat is often coconut oil.

Both filled and imitation milks are subject to variable state regulations, but they are not as yet governed by the same rigid sanitation and composition requirements as pasteurized Grade A milk and milk products. Filled and imitation milks are subject to the 1990 federal labeling legislation, under which a substitute food must be nutritionally equivalent to its standardized counterpart except that calories and/or fat may be reduced.

People who must eliminate milk from their diet, possibly because of its lactose content, may use lactose-free imitation milks to advantage; however, it is extremely difficult to make a product that matches real milk in nutritional composition. Persons for whom imitation and substitute dairy products comprise a major portion of the diet may find it difficult to obtain adequate amounts of all nutrients required for good health.

A nonfat dry milk replacer has been designed for use in dry cocoa mixes that are blended with water to make hot chocolate. A whey product is an important ingredient in this replacer.

Some dairy processors use a special seal on their products to emphasize that their dairy products are real, not imitation. Figure 23-7 shows this seal, which consists of the word *REAL* enclosed in a symbolic drop of milk.

Figure 23-7
Sometimes dairy processors put on their packaged products a special symbol which contains the word REAL. *This emphasizes that these products are not imitation.*

Milk in Food Preparation

Milk and milk products are used to make a wide variety of dishes including salads, soups, entrees, side dishes, desserts, and beverages. When used in cooking, the prevention of curdling is desired. High temperatures, extended hot holding or cooking, and acidic or salty ingredients can all contribute to curdling. In addition, higher fat milk products, such as cream or whole milk, are more stable than low fat or nonfat milk and thus are less likely to separate.

Heating milk to temperature and time combinations more extensive than those used in pasteurization brings about some changes. The changes increase in number and degree with rising temperature and time of heating. The tendency for milk to curdle is diminished by the use of low or moderate temperatures. You may already have observed less curdling of the milk on scalloped potatoes cooked in a low or moderate oven than when a higher temperature is used.

The general effect of heat, acid, enzymes, phenolic compounds, salt, and freezing on milk during usual food preparation practices is considered in this section. Preparation of white sauces and cream soups, using heated milk, is discussed in Chapter 13, and preparation of hot chocolate containing milk is covered in Chapter 28.

Effects of Heat

Protein Coagulation. On heating, the whey proteins lactalbumin and lactoglobulin become insoluble or **precipitate**. Lactalbumin begins to **coagulate** at a temperature of 150°F (66°C). The amount of coagulum increases with rising temperature and time of heating. The coagulum that forms appears as small particles rather than a firm mass and collects on the bottom of the pan in which the milk is heated. This collection of particles, of course, contributes to the characteristic scorching of heated milk. You can stir the milk while it heats to lessen the amount of precipitate on the bottom, but some scorching may still occur, particularly if a large quantity of milk is heated at one time. One way to prevent scorching is to heat milk over hot water in a double boiler rather than with direct heat.

The protein found in the largest amount in milk, casein, does not coagulate at the usual temperatures and times used in food preparation. Although some of its properties may change slightly, it coagulates only when heated to very high temperatures or for a long period at the boiling point. In fact, as long as 12 hours may be required for casein to coagulate when heated at a temperature of 212°F (100°C).

Heating periods that produce casein coagulation are shorter when the concentration of casein is increased above that in regular fluid milk. For example, in the sterilization of canned evaporated milk, it is necessary to take certain measures to prevent coagulation of the casein. One such measure is to prewarm the milk prior to its sterilization.

The coagulation of milk proteins by heat is accelerated by an increase in acidity. It is also influenced by the kinds and concentrations of salts present. The salts in such foods as ham hocks and vegetables are partly responsible for coagulation of casein when these products are cooked in milk.

Mineral Changes. The dispersion of calcium phosphate in milk is decreased by heating, and a small part of it is precipitated. Some of the calcium phosphate

precipitate to become insoluble and separate out of a solution or dispersion

coagulate to form a clot, a semi-solid mass, or a gel, after initial denaturation of a protein

collects on the bottom of the pan with coagulated whey proteins, and some is probably entangled in the scum on the top surface of the milk.

Surface Film Formation. The formation of a film or scum on the surface of heated milk is often troublesome, and it is responsible for milk's boiling over the sides of the pan. A certain amount of pressure develops under the film, which forces the film upward, and the milk flows over the sides of the pan. A slight film may form at relatively low temperatures, but this may be prevented by a cover on the pan, by dilution of the milk, or by the presence of fat floating on the surface. As the temperature is increased, a tough scum forms that is insoluble and can be removed from the surface. As soon as it is removed, however, another film forms.

Sometimes, to break up the film, the heated milk is beaten with a rotary-type egg beater. This procedure has limited usefulness because of the continuous formation of fresh film; however, foam formation at the surface appears to aid in preventing a really tenacious scum from forming.

The composition of the film on heated milk is variable. It may contain coagulated protein, with some precipitated salts and fat globules entangled in the mesh of coagulated matter.

Coalescence of Fat Globules. The layer of fat that may form on milk that has been boiled results from the breaking of the films of protein that surround the fat globules in the unheated milk. The breaking of films of emulsifying agents permits the coalescence of fat globules.

Browning. When certain sugars and proteins are heated together, browning occurs. This particular nonenzymatic browning is of the Maillard type. Concentrated milk products such as evaporated milk contain substantial amounts of both protein and the sugar lactose and develop some brown color on heating. This reaction may also occur in dried milk stored for long periods. Heating sweetened condensed milk in a can which has been placed in a pan of water for several hours results in a brown-colored product of thickened consistency and sweet caramel flavor. This "pudding" is sometimes used as a dessert.

Acid Coagulation

Although the protein casein is hardly susceptible to coagulation by heating, it is highly sensitive to precipitation on the addition of acid. The acid may be added as such, or it may be produced by bacteria as they ferment milk sugar. The acid curdling of milk is a desirable reaction in the making of such products as cultured buttermilk, yogurt, sour cream, and some cheeses. Prevention of casein coagulation or curdling is fundamental to the success of such products as cream of tomato soup. Fruit-milk mixtures may also curdle, as you may have noticed when putting cream on fresh fruits or making fruit-milk beverages or sherbets (Figure 23-8).

What happens when acid is added to milk? The pH, which normally is about 6.6, begins to fall. When it reaches about 4.6, the colloidally dispersed casein particles become unstable. They adhere and form a coagulum or curd. This probably occurs because the usual negative charge on the casein particles, which causes them to repel each other and remain apart, is neutralized by the acidic hydrogen ion (H^+). A considerable amount of calcium is also released from the casein molecules to the liquid whey. The calcium was bonded through the

phosphoric acid groups of casein. The curd then traps the whey in its meshes. The whey, which contains the whey proteins, most of the lactose, and many minerals, is released when the curd is cut or stirred and heated. These processes occur in the manufacture of cheese.

Raw milk ordinarily contains bacteria that ferment lactose and produce lactic acid, thus "souring" the milk and producing a curd. A clean, acidic taste is characteristic. Pasteurized milk does not sour in this way. The heat of pasteurization destroys most of the lactic acid bacteria responsible for the souring process. Instead, pasteurized milk spoils by the action of putrefactive bacteria, which break down the proteins in milk.

Enzyme Coagulation

A number of enzymes from plant, animal, and microbial sources are capable of clotting milk. Chymosin or rennin is such an enzyme. It is found in the stomachs of young animals, and its function is to clot milk prior to the action of other protein-digesting enzymes. The name *chymosin* is derived from the Greek word *chyme*, meaning "gastric liquid," and is used in the recommended international enzyme nomenclature [55]. The crude chymosin enzyme is called *rennet*. Rennet has been used for many years in the preparation of most varieties of cheeses. When the sources of rennet became limited, several other nonrennin milk-clotting enzymes were used as rennet substitutes [10]. The FDA has affirmed that use of the chymosin preparation derived by fermentation from the genetically modified *Aspergillus* mold is GRAS (generally regarded as safe). This was one of the first genetically engineered food products to be approved.

Because rennet is an enzyme preparation, it requires specific conditions of temperature and acidity for its action. The optimum temperature is 104° to 108°F (40° to 42°C). Refrigerator temperatures retard its action. No action occurs below 50°F (10°C) or above 149°F (65°C). Rennet acts best in a faintly acid medium, and action does not occur in an alkaline environment.

When casein is precipitated by the action of rennet, the calcium is not released to the whey but remains attached to the casein. Therefore, cheese made with rennet is a much better source of calcium than cheese made by acid precipitation alone. Cottage cheese is often made by acid precipitation. Table C-4 in Appendix C shows that cottage cheese is considerably lower in calcium than Cheddar cheese.

The action of the enzyme bromelin from raw or frozen pineapple in preventing the gelation of gelatin is well known. The enzyme digests proteins and hence changes the gelatin to smaller compounds that do not form a gel. The enzyme bromelin also clots milk but later digests the clot. Other enzymes in fruits are probably responsible for some of the curdling action that occurs when milk or cream and certain fruits are combined. All fruits contain some organic acids, but not always in sufficient concentration to cause the curdling of milk. Destroying the enzymes before combining fruit with milk will, of course, prevent curdling caused by enzyme action.

Coagulation by Phenolic Compounds

Some phenolic-type compounds are present in fruits and vegetables. In fruits, these compounds are found chiefly in the green stages and are present in a greater amount in some varieties than in others. Seeds and stems may contain significant amounts of phenolic substances. Among vegetables, the roots, pods, some seeds, and woody stems are likely to contain more **phenolic compounds** than other parts of the plant, although distribution is general throughout the plant. Curdling of milk may occur if phenolic-containing foods, such as potatoes, are cooked in the milk; however, the time and temperature of heating also influence curdling. In addition, the low levels of organic acids present in potatoes contribute to curdling.

phenolic compounds organic compounds that include in their chemical structure an unsaturated ring with −OH groups on it

Coagulation by Salts

The cause of curdling in foods cooked in milk is likely to be a combination of factors. The salts present in the milk, in the food combined with the milk, or added sodium chloride may influence coagulation of the casein. Of the meats commonly cooked in milk, ham usually causes more coagulation than chicken, veal, or pork, although these may vary in their effect. The high sodium chloride content of ham may be responsible for the excessive curdling that occurs when ham is cooked in milk. Processed shrimp also can contain sodium levels that may cause curdling in a milk-based dish.

Freezing

When milk or cream is frozen at a relatively slow rate, the film of protein that acts as an emulsifying agent around the fat globules is weakened or ruptured. As a result, the fat globules tend to coalesce. The oily masses that float on top of hot coffee when cream that has been frozen is added to it demonstrate the cohesion of fat particles that results from freezing. The dispersion of protein and calcium phosphate is also disturbed by freezing. Both constituents tend to settle out on thawing and standing, thus reducing the whiteness of milk. The effects of freezing are not harmful and do not affect food value.

CREAM

Types of Cream Products

Cream is the high-fat, liquid product that is separated from whole milk. Cream adds richness and body to foods that are prepared with it and when whipped, provides a creamy, yet airy delicacy. According to federal standards of identity, cream must contain not less than 18 percent milk fat.

Several liquid cream products are marketed, including light or coffee cream containing 18 to 30 percent milk fat, light whipping cream with 30 to 36 percent milk fat, and heavy cream or heavy whipping cream with not less than 36 percent milk fat [39]. If cream is to be whipped, a minimum of 30 percent milk fat is necessary. Half-and-half is a mixture of milk and cream containing not less than 10.5 percent milk fat but less than 18 percent. This product is commonly used in place of light cream or coffee cream.

The thickness of cream is related to its fat content; it is generally thicker at higher fat levels. Other factors also affect thickness. Cream at room temperature is thinner than cream at refrigerator temperature because chilling makes the fat globules firmer, thereby increasing the **viscosity** of the cream. When chilled to a temperature of 41°F (5°C) and held at that temperature for 24 to 48 hours, cream gradually increases in thickness.

Commercial sour cream is a cultured or an acidified light cream. A culture of *Streptococcus lactis* organisms is added to cream, and the product is held at 72°F (22°C) until the acidity, calculated as lactic acid, is at least 0.5 percent [39]. Nonfat milk solids and stabilizing vegetable gums such as carrageenan may be added to sour cream, which can also be produced from half-and-half. If manufacturers use food-grade acid instead of bacteria to make sour cream the product must be labeled as "acidified sour cream" [57].

Dried cream, to be used reconstituted to liquid form, is available. An instant dry creamed milk made from modified skim milk (calcium reduced), light cream, and lactose has also been manufactured. When it is sprinkled on the surface of a beverage, it disperses quickly.

Cream containing sugar, stabilizers, and flavoring is sold in pressurized containers. When a valve is pressed, a whipped-cream product is emitted as a result of the action of propellant gases.

Many nondairy products for whipped toppings, coffee whiteners, sour cream–type mixtures, and snack dip bases have been developed and marketed. Initially, these were promoted as low-cost substitutes for the more expensive natural dairy products. Many of them, particularly whipped toppings and coffee whiteners, have been accepted on their own merits rather than as substitutes and have taken over much of the market. One advantage of whipped toppings is their stability. Whipped toppings will tolerate overmixing to a greater degree than real whipped cream and will maintain quality during storage for a longer period of time.

Nondairy whipped toppings often contain sugar, hydrogenated vegetable oil, sodium caseinate, and emulsifiers. They are available in a dry form, which is

viscosity resistance to flow; thickness or consistency

added to cold milk before whipping, and also in whipped form as a frozen product. The foam is stable and requires only defrosting before use. Nondairy products resembling whipped cream that contain water, vegetable fat, sugar, sodium caseinate, emulsifiers, and vegetable gums are also available in pressurized cans. These products must be refrigerated. Nondairy coffee whiteners are widely used in hot beverages. They usually contain corn syrup solids, vegetable fat, a source of protein such as sodium caseinate or soy protein, emulsifiers, and salts.

Although nondairy whipped toppings, coffee whiteners and other products are termed "nondairy," these products often contain casein or whey. Thus, those who are allergic to dairy products often must avoid these nondairy foods as well.

Whipping of Cream

A foam is a dispersion of a gas in a liquid. If the foam is stable, there must also be present a stabilizing agent to keep the gas dispersed. Certain conditions are necessary for the foam to form in the first place. A foaming agent must be dispersed in the liquid to lower the **surface tension** of the liquid, and thus allow the liquid to surround the gas bubbles. The stabilizing agent can then act to keep the gas bubbles separated.

In the whipping of cream, a foam is formed. The liquid is the water in the cream, the gas is air that is beaten in, and the foaming agent that lowers the surface tension of the water is protein that is dispersed in the cream. During whipping, air bubbles are incorporated and surrounded by a thin liquid film that contains protein. The foam cells are stabilized by coalesced fat globules. The globules apparently coalesce because much of the milkfat globule membrane surrounding them and keeping them separated has been removed in the whipping process [29]. At the cold temperature of the whipping cream, the fat globules are solid. Because whipping is the first stage of churning cream, the emulsion breaks and butter is formed if whipping is continued too long.

Air bubbles in whipped cream must be surrounded by protein films. Because so much of the protein of *homogenized* cream is used to surround the increased number of fat globules, little protein remains to surround the air bubbles formed in whipping. Therefore, whipping cream is usually not homogenized. Several factors affect the whipping properties of cream.

Temperature and Viscosity.   Cream held at a cold temperature (45°F or 7°C or below) whips better than cream held at warmer temperatures. Above 50°F (10°C), agitation of cream increases the dispersion of the fat instead of decreasing it. The beater and bowl that are used, and the cream, should be chilled. In the whipping of cream, the aim is to increase *clumping* of fat particles, and at low temperatures, agitation results in clumping. Lower temperatures increase viscosity, which increases the whipping properties of cream. Higher fat content also increases viscosity and furnishes more fat globules for clumping. Because viscosity increases with aging, the whipping property improves with the aging of cream.

Fat Content.   A fat content of 30 percent is about the minimum for cream that will whip with ease and produce a stiff product. Increasing the fat up to 40 percent improves the whipping quality of cream, because more solid fat particles are thus available to stabilize the foam.

surface tension tension created over the surface of a liquid because of the greater attraction of the liquid molecules for each other than for the gaseous molecules in the air above the liquid

Amount of Cream Whipped. In whipping large amounts of cream, it is better to do successive whippings of amounts tailored to the size of the whipper used, rather than to whip a large amount at one time. If a very small amount of cream is to be whipped, a small deep bowl should be used so that the beaters can adequately agitate the cream.

Effect of Other Substances. Increased acidity up to the concentration required to produce a sour taste (0.3 percent) has no effect on whipping quality. The addition of sugar decreases both volume and stiffness and increases the time required to whip cream if it is added before whipping. If sugar is to be added, it is best added after the cream is stiff or just prior to serving. If sugar is added just before serving, powdered sugar should be used, because granulated sugar needs more time to dissolve (Figure 23-9).

Whipping of Other Milk Products

Evaporated Milk. When evaporated milk is chilled to the ice crystal stage, it will whip to about three times its original volume. This ability to whip is evidently the result of the higher concentration of milk solids in evaporated milk than in fresh whole milk. The protein in the milk acts as a foaming agent and also aids in stabilizing. This foam, however, is not stable on standing. The addition of acid, such as a small amount of lemon juice (about 1 tablespoon per cup of undiluted milk), helps to stabilize the protein and makes a more lasting foam.

Nonfat Dry Milk. A light and airy whipped product may be produced by the whipping of nonfat dry milk. Equal measures of dry milk and very cold water are normally used, with the dry milk being sprinkled over the surface of the water before whipping. This foam is highly unstable but its stability may be increased somewhat by adding small amounts of an acid substance such as lemon juice before whipping.

Light Dairy Products

Under the FDA definition of *light,* a product must contain 33 percent fewer calories than or 50 percent of the fat in a reference food (if 50 percent or more of the calories come from fat, reduction must be 50 percent of the fat). *Light in sodium* may be used to describe a product when the sodium content of a low-calorie, low-fat food has been reduced by 50 percent.

Figure 23-9
This crème Chantilly was made by first whipping heavy chilled cream until thickened. Powdered sugar and vanilla were added and the mixture was whipped until of the consistency shown here. (Source: Reference 28)

aspartame a high-intensity sweetener with the trade name Nutrasweet™

A variety of light foods are being successfully marketed. Consumers use them for various reasons related to health. Dairy products are among the most popular light foods, and the dairy industry is responding to the opportunity to develop many of these formulated foods. The reduced- and low-fat milks have been well accepted for several years, of course. Light yogurts are available with no fat using **aspartame** as a sweetener. Frozen desserts may use microparticulated protein or hydrocolloids as fat replacers to qualify as light substitute ice creams. Also on the market are light versions of cheese that are reduced in fat, cholesterol, sodium, or combinations of these [23].

One of the major problems associated with light dairy products is taste. Panelists who rated high- and low-fat processed American cheese and vanilla ice cream liked the high-fat products better [30]. Despite receiving label information with the samples, panelists still liked the high-fat ice cream more than the low-fat product. When the panelists knew the fat content of the cheese, however, they tended to like the high-fat product somewhat less and the low-fat cheese somewhat more. The most important determinant of liking in this study was the fat level, regardless of the panelists' level of concern about fat-containing products.

New products are constantly being developed. An example is yogurtessee, a no-fat, no-cholesterol fat substitute made from a lightly cultured skim milk that is concentrated, acidified, and stabilized. This dairy-based product may be used in baked goods, sauces, salad dressings, and cheese spreads to produce light products [15].

CHEESE

Americans are consuming record high levels of cheese. In 1909, four pounds of cheese were consumed per capita annually as compared to 32 pounds per capita in 1999 [1]. Americans simply seem to enjoy the taste of cheese and are increasingly choosing foods such as cheeseburgers, nachos, and an array of Mexican and Italian foods that feature cheese [53]. Cheese may be enjoyed as part of a cheese, fruit, and cracker board or as a component of a recipe (Figure 23-10 and Color Plates XII and XVI).

Cheese is a concentrated dairy food defined as the fresh or matured product obtained by draining the whey (the moisture or serum of the original milk) after coagulation of casein, the major milk protein. Casein is coagulated by acid produced by added microbial cultures and/or by coagulating enzymes, resulting in curd formation. Rennet is the crude coagulating enzyme obtained from the stomach of calves. The purified enzyme from rennet, chymosin, may also be produced by genetic engineering. Milk can be acidified by adding suitable organic acids [38]. The curd may receive further treatment by heat or pressure or by the action of the microbial culture on holding. In the United States, almost all cheese is manufactured from the whole, partly skimmed, or skimmed milk of cows. The pigment carotene is added to give cheese a yellow color when it is desirable.

Most of the cheese consumed in the United States is made commercially. Some consumers, however, may make cottage cheese at home; the USDA has published a bulletin giving instructions on how to make this product [31].

The quality of the milk used in cheesemaking is extremely important and rigidly controlled. Most cheese is made from pasteurized or heat-treated milk. Pasteurization is not a substitute for sanitation but rather an additional safeguard [39].

Multicultural Cuisine

It's a small world!

The use of dairy products for food apparently predates history. Who knows when the first human discovered that milk soured by friendly bacteria was good to eat? Or when was it recognized that the flavors and textures of certain cheese-type products contaminated by molds were not only palatable but delicious?

As new foods were discovered or developed, they tended to remain the favorites of certain cultures and characterized their usual food intake or cuisine. But with falling trade barriers around the globe, and with worldwide travel becoming commonplace, ethnic foods are showing strong market growth in many countries. And dairy products are well positioned in this expansion.

Natural yogurt is one of the world's first and oldest health foods. It was appreciated in Europe and Asia long before it was introduced into the American market in the 1940's. Since then, however, many changes have been brought about in that first full-fat, simply fermented, unflavored yogurt—low-fat, milder fermentations, heavily flavored with fruit or caramel, sweetened, gelled, spoonable, liquefied, drinkable, and so on. Now the "big" thing is—probiotics! [16].

Probiotics are live microbial food ingredients that have a beneficial effect on the GI tract.

These microbes include members from the genera *Lactobacillus* and *Bifidobacterium*. New strains are under development on both sides of the Atlantic. The trick is to deliver a live culture that remains active in the lower intestinal tract. Various food manufacturers are competing in products and claims. Many consumers in Europe and Asia are already convinced of the value of probiotic dairy products and U.S. marketers are fast educating their clients in this country. In Europe, a Swiss muesli breakfast yogurt drink with added fruit, wheat flakes, and rolled oats, along with B vitamins, in a grab-and-go bottle is being marketed under the name of *Toni* [52]. With rapid cultural exchange, such delectables may soon be American favorites, too.

Americans also have a great appetite for cheese in many forms. The growing popularity of ethnic foods, especially Mexican and Italian, is reflected in the increased U.S. consumption of cheeses such as Monterey jack, Provolone, and Gorgonzola [53]. New flavors and international cheese varieties can add zest to the American cuisine. And an *added* benefit of all these exciting dairy products is a needed increase in calcium intake for the average American.

The manufacture of most cheeses follows similar steps. These include (1) promoting curd formation with acid produced by lactic acid–producing bacteria (a starter culture) and/or a coagulating enzyme; (2) cutting the curd into small pieces to allow the whey to escape; (3) heating the curd to contract the curd particles and hasten the expulsion of whey; (4) draining, knitting or stretching, salting, and pressing the curd; and (5) curing or ripening [38]. Some cheeses, including cottage cheese, cream cheese, and mozzarella, are not ripened.

Ripening

Ripening refers to the changes in physical and chemical properties, such as aroma, flavor, texture, and composition, that take place between the time of precipitation of the curd and the time when the cheese develops the desired characteristics for its type. Some changes that occur are the formation by bacteria of lactic acid from the lactose; the digestion of the protein by enzymes into end products, including peptides and amino acids; the development and pene-

Figure 23-10
Cheddar cheese in the pastry and the apple filling of these cheddar apple tarts with apricot-mint glaze creates a warm snack or dessert. (Courtesy of the American Dairy Association)

tration of molds in mold-ripened cheese; the gas formation by certain types of microorganisms used; and the development of characteristic flavor and aroma substances, including those developed from the decomposition of fat by lipase enzymes.

The flavor of ripened cheese results from a blending of the decomposition and hydrolysis products formed from the milk components. The hydrolysis of protein eventually results in free water-soluble amino acids that give the cheese a softer, more pliable texture, as well as improved flavor. The fat of some cheese is hydrolyzed by enzymes, liberating fatty acids. Most of the small amount of lactose that is present in cheese is converted to other compounds. Lactic acid is formed. A characteristic flavor is developed in each particular type of cheese.

The changes that occur in cheese during ripening not only affect flavor and texture but also improve the cooking quality. The increased dispersibility of the protein of ripened cheese contributes to the ease of blending cheese with other food ingredients, particularly for such products as cheese sauce.

Various types of organisms produce distinctive flavors, aromas, and textures in cheeses. The *Penicillium roqueforti* or *Penicillium glaucum* types of molds are responsible for the mottled blue-green appearance of blue, Roquefort, Gorgonzola, and Stilton cheeses. The curd is inoculated with pure cultures of the mold, which penetrate during the curing process.

Camembert cheese is inoculated with two molds: *Oidium lactis*, which covers the cheese in the first stages of ripening, and *Penicillium camemberti*, which grows later. The enzymes produced by the molds penetrate and soften the cheese. Organic acids used as food by the molds gradually disappear, providing a more favorable medium for putrefactive bacteria. The cheese is usually placed in small molds, with the curing agents on the outside surface. They gradually penetrate throughout the cheese during the holding period. Damp caves are used to ripen some types of cheese that depend on mold action for the development of flavor.

Swiss cheese owes its large holes to special gas-forming organisms. These organisms grow and produce carbon dioxide gas during the early stage of ripening, while the cheese is soft and elastic. Limburger cheese owes its characteristic odor to the development of putrefactive bacteria, which are allowed to act over a considerable period. Ordinary Cheddar cheese varies widely in flavor and texture, depending on the organisms that predominate and the length of time of ripening. *Lactobacilli* and *Streptococcus lactis* organisms play major roles in the ripening of good Cheddar cheese. The presence of salt delays bacterial growth, and therefore alters the rate of ripening.

Mild cheeses, such as brick and Monterey jack, are allowed to ripen for a shorter period than strong cheeses, such as Parmesan. Blue cheese is usually aged 3 to 4 months but may be aged up to 9 months for more pronounced flavor.

Grades

USDA grade standards U.S. Grade AA and U.S. Grade A have been developed for Swiss, Cheddar, Colby, and Monterey cheese. Cheese bearing these grades must be produced in a USDA-inspected and approved plant under sanitary conditions. Graders evaluate the flavor and texture of the cheese. Some cheese and cheese products not covered by a U.S. grade standard may be inspected and bear a USDA Quality Approved inspection shield on the label. This shield indicates that the cheese has been manufactured in a plant meeting USDA sanitary specifications and is a cheese of good quality [56].

Composition and Nutritive Value

Cheese is a highly concentrated food; 1 pound of cheese may contain the protein and fat of 1 gallon of milk. The protein is of high biologic value, and the fat is largely saturated. Vitamin A is carried in the fat. The addition of salt for flavor, as well as the concentration of the milk that naturally contains sodium, makes cheese a high-sodium food.

The composition of cheese varies widely with the fraction of milk used and the amount of moisture retained. When cheese is made from whole milk, the fat remains with the curd when the whey is drained off. Much of the milk sugar, the soluble salts, and the water-soluble vitamins are drained off in the whey, although even in hard cheeses the whey is never entirely removed. Whey cheeses and concentrated whey added to cheese spreads or cheese foods save some of these valuable nutrients.

Cheese made by rennet coagulation is an excellent source of calcium and phosphorus, whereas that coagulated by acid alone contains less calcium. The reason for this difference in calcium content is that the lower pH or greater acidity produced by adding acid causes the release of more calcium ions (Ca^{2+}) from the phosphate groups that are part of the casein molecule. Much of this released calcium goes into the whey and is not retained in the curd. Cheeses of the Cheddar type, made chiefly by rennet coagulation of the milk, may retain up to 80 percent of the original milk calcium. Soft cheeses made by acid precipitation, such as cottage cheese, may retain not more than one-fourth to one-half of the milk calcium.

American Cheddar cheese averages, roughly, one-third water, one-third fat, and one-fourth protein. It also contains about 4 percent ash and less than 1 percent carbohydrate, including lactic acid. Cheeses made from low-fat or skim milk are lower in fat content than cheeses made from whole milk. Cheese containing vegetable oil instead of milk fat is also available for those who want to decrease their intake of animal fat.

The moisture content of soft cheese varies from 40 to 75 percent, whereas hard cheeses tend to contain a more nearly uniform amount of water—from 30 to 40 percent. High moisture content is a factor in the perishability of cheese, those with a large amount of moisture being more perishable.

Types of Cheese Products

The groupings of cheeses may be determined by two factors: the amount of moisture in the finished cheese and the kind and extent of ripening. Based on moisture content, cheese may be classified as soft, semihard, or hard. Based on the kind and extent of ripening, cheese may be classified as unripened, mold ripened, or bacteria ripened. Ripened cheese may be strong and sharp or mild.

More than 2,000 names have been given to cheeses with somewhat different characteristics, but there are only about ten distinct types of natural cheese. Table 23-2 describes the characteristics of some popular varieties of natural cheeses; some of these are shown in Figure 23-11 and Color Plate XVI.

Cold-pack Cheese. Cold-pack or club cheese is made by grinding and mixing together one or more varieties of cheese without the aid of heat. Acid, water, salt, coloring, and spices may be added, but the final moisture content must not exceed that permitted for the variety of natural cheese from which it was prepared. The cheese is packaged in jars or in moisture-proof packages in retail-size units. Cold-pack cheese food is prepared in the same manner as cold-pack cheese, but it may contain other ingredients such as cream, milk, skim milk, nonfat dry milk, or whey. It may also contain pimientos, fruits, vegetables, or meats, and sweetening agents such as sugar and corn syrup.

Process Cheese. A significant part of the cheese produced in the United States today is made into pasteurized process cheese and related products. Process cheese is made by grinding and mixing together different samples of natural cheese with the aid of heat and an emulsifying agent. A selected blend of cheese or portions of the same variety selected at different stages of ripeness are used, and the product is pasteurized before packaging. The cheese is ground and heated, and sufficient water is added to replace that lost by evaporation. To aid in producing a uniform blend that melts without separation of fat, an emulsifying agent, such as disodium phosphate or sodium citrate, is added to the ground cheese before heating.

After the cheese is melted, it is run into molds. These are sometimes jars or glasses, but are often cardboard boxes lined with metal foil; the wrapper may be of a transparent plastic material. As the cheese hardens, it clings closely to the jar or foil, thus preventing molds from attacking the surface. Pasteurization of the cheese destroys bacteria and enzymes, thus stopping all ripening. Process cheese is also sold in individual slices and can be purchased with individual slices separately wrapped.

The quality and flavor of process cheese depend on the quality and flavor of the cheese used to make it. Several varieties of cheese are made into pasteurized process cheeses, including Cheddar, Swiss, and brick cheese. Convenience, ease

Table 23-2

Characteristics of Some Popular Varieties of Natural Cheeses

Kind or Name (place of origin)	Kind of Milk Used in Manufacture	Ripening or Curing Time	Flavor	Body and Texture	Color	Retail Packaging	Use
Soft, Unripened Varieties							
Cottage, plain or creamed (unknown)	Cow's milk skimmed; plain curd, or plain curd with cream added	Unripened	Mild, acid	Soft, curd particles of varying size	White to creamy white	Cup-shaped containers, tumblers, dishes	Salads, with fruits, vegetables, sandwiches, dips, cheese cake
Cream, plain (United States)	Cream from cow's milk	Unripened	Mild, acid	Soft and smooth	White	3- to 8-oz. packages	Salads, dips, sandwiches, snacks, cheese cake, desserts
Neufchatel (Nü-shä-tĕl′) (France)	Cow's milk	Unripened	Mild, acid	Soft, smooth, similar to cream cheese but lower in milkfat	White	4- to 8-oz. packages	Salads, dips, sandwiches, snacks, cheese cake, desserts
Ricotta (rĭc ŏ′-ta) (Italy)	Cow's milk, whole or partly skimmed, or whey from cow's milk with whole or skim milk added; in Italy, whey from sheep's milk	Unripened	Sweet, nutlike	Soft, moist or dry	White	Pint and quart paper and plastic containers, 3-lb metal cans	Appetizers, salads, snacks, lasagna, ravioli, noodles and other cooked dishes, grating, desserts
Firm, Unripened Varieties							
Gjetost* (Yĕt′ŏst) (Norway)	Whey from goat's milk or a mixture of whey from goat's and cow's milk	Unripened	Sweetish, caramel	Firm, buttery consistency	Golden brown	Cubical and rectangular	Snacks, desserts, served with dark breads, crackers, biscuits, or muffins
Mysost (mü sŏst) also called Primost (prē′m-ŏst) (Norway)	Whey from cow's milk	Unripened	Sweetish, caramel	Firm, buttery consistency	Light brown	Cubical, cylindrical, pie-shaped wedges	Snacks, desserts, served with dark breads
Mozzarella (mŏ-tsa-rel′la) (Italy)	Whole or partly skimmed cow's milk; in Italy, originally made from buffalo's milk	Unripened	Delicate, mild	Slightly firm, plastic	Creamy white	Small round or braided form, shredded, sliced	Snacks; toasted sandwiches; cheeseburgers; cooking, as in meat loaf; or topping for lasagna, pizza, and casseroles

(continued)

Soft, Ripened Varieties

Kind or Name (place of origin)	Kind of Milk Used in Manufacture	Ripening or Curing Time	Flavor	Body and Texture	Color	Retail Packaging	Use
Brie (brē) (France)	Cow's milk	4–8 weeks	Mild to pungent	Soft, smooth when ripened	Creamy yellow interior; edible thin brown and white crust	Circular, pie-shaped wedges	Appetizers, sandwiches, snacks, good with crackers and fruit, dessert
Camembert (kăm′ĕm-bâr) (France)	Cow's milk	4–8 weeks	Mild to pungent	Soft, smooth, very soft when fully ripened	Creamy yellow interior; edible thin white or gray-white crust	Small circular cakes and pie-shaped portions	Appetizers, sandwiches, snacks, good with crackers and fruit such as pears and apples, dessert
Limburger (Belgium)	Cow's milk	4–8 weeks	Highly pungent, very strong	Soft, smooth when ripened; usually contains small irregular openings	Creamy white interior; reddish-yellow surface	Cubical, rectangular	Appetizers, snacks, good with crackers, rye, or other dark breads, dessert
Bel Paese[†] (bĕl pä-ā′-ze) (Italy)	Cow's milk	6–8 weeks	Mild to moderately robust	Soft to medium firm, creamy	Creamy yellow interior; slightly gray or brownish surface sometimes covered with yellow wax coating	Small wheels, wedges, segments	Appetizers, good with crackers, snacks, sandwiches, dessert
Brick (United States)	Cow's milk	2–4 months	Mild to moderately sharp	Semisoft to medium firm; elastic, numerous small mechanical openings	Creamy yellow	Loaf, brick, slices, cut portions	Appetizers, sandwiches, snacks, dessert
Muenster (mün′stĕr) (Germany)	Cow's milk	1–8 weeks	Mild to mellow	Semisoft; numerous small mechanical openings; contains more moisture than brick	Creamy white interior; yellow-tan surface	Circular cake, blocks, wedges, segments, slices	Appetizers, snacks, served with raw fruit, dessert

Name	Kind of Milk	Ripening Time	Flavor	Body and Texture	Color	Shape	Uses
Port du Salut (por dü sälü') (France)	Cow's milk	6–8 weeks	Mellow to robust	Semisoft, smooth, buttery; small openings	Creamy yellow	Wheels and wedges	Appetizers, snacks, served with raw fruit, dessert

Firm, Ripened Varieties

Name	Kind of Milk	Ripening Time	Flavor	Body and Texture	Color	Shape	Uses
Cheddar (England)	Cow's milk	1–12 months or longer	Mild to very sharp	Firm, smooth; some mechanical openings	White to medium-yellow-orange	Circular, cylindrical loaf, pie-shaped wedges, oblongs, slices, cubes, shredded, grated	Appetizers, sandwiches, sauces, on vegetables, in hot dishes, toasted sandwiches, grating, cheeseburgers, dessert
Colby (United States)	Cow's milk	1–3 months	Mild to mellow	Softer and more open than Cheddar	White to medium-yellow-orange	Cylindrical, pie-shaped wedges	Sandwiches, snacks, cheeseburgers
Caciocavallo (kä'chō-kä-val'lō) (Italy)	Cow's milk; in Italy, cow's milk or mixtures of sheep's, goat's, and cow's milk	3–12 months	Piquant, similar to Provolone but not smoked	Firm, lower in milkfat and moisture than Provolone	Light or white interior; clay or tan surface	Spindle- or tenpin-shaped, bound with cord, cut pieces	Snacks, sandwiches, cooking, dessert; suitable for grating after prolonged curing
Edam (ē' dăm) (Netherlands)	Cow's milk, partly skimmed	2–3 months	Mellow, nutlike	Semisoft to firm; smooth; small irregularly shaped or round holes; lower milkfat than Gouda	Creamy yellow or medium yellow-orange interior; surface coated with red wax	Cannon ball-shaped loaf, cut pieces, oblongs	Appetizers, snacks, salads, sandwiches, seafood sauces, dessert
Gouda (gou'-dä) (Netherlands)	Cow's milk, whole or partly skimmed	2–6 months	Mellow, nutlike	Semisoft to firm; smooth; small irregularly shaped or round holes; higher milkfat than Edam	Creamy yellow or medium yellow-orange interior; may or may not have red wax coating	Ball shaped with flattened top and bottom	Appetizers, snacks, salads, sandwiches, seafood sauces, dessert
Provolone (prō-vō-lō-nē), also smaller sizes and shapes called Provolette and Provoloncini (Italy)	Cow's milk	2–12 months	Mellow to sharp, smoky, salty	Firm, smooth	Light creamy interior; light brown or golden yellow surface	Pear shaped, sausage and salami shaped, wedges, slices	Appetizers, sandwiches, snacks, soufflé, macaroni and spaghetti dishes, pizza, suitable for grating when fully cured and dried

(continued)

611

Kind or Name (place of origin)	Kind of Milk Used in Manufacture	Ripening or Curing Time	Flavor	Body and Texture	Color	Retail Packaging	Use
Swiss, also called Emmentaler (Switzerland)	Cow's milk	3–9 months	Sweet, nutlike	Firm, smooth, with large round eyes	Light yellow	Segments, pieces, slices	Sandwiches, snacks, sauces, fondue, cheeseburgers
Parmesan (pär'-mĕ-zän') also called Reggiano (Italy)	Partly skimmed cow's milk	14 months to 2 years	Sharp, piquant	Very hard, granular; lower moisture and milkfat than Romano	Creamy white	Cylindrical, wedges, shredded, grated	Grated for seasoning in soups, vegetables, spaghetti, ravioli, breads, popcorn, used extensively in pizza and lasagna
Romano (rō-mā'-nō), also called Sardo Romano and Pecorino Romano (Italy)	Cow's milk; in Italy, sheep's milk (Italian law)	5–12 months	Sharp, piquant	Very hard granular	Yellowish-white interior, greenish-black surface	Round with flat ends, wedges, shredded, grated	Seasoning in soups, casserole dishes, ravioli, sauces, breads, suitable for grating when cured for about 1 year
Sap Sago* (săp'-să-gō) (Switzerland)	Skimmed cow's milk	5 months or longer	Sharp, pungent, cloverlike	Very hard	Light green by addition of dried, powdered clover leaves	Conical, shakers	Grated to flavor soups, meats, macaroni, spaghetti, hot vegetables; mixed with butter, makes a good spread on crackers or bread

Blue-vein Mold Ripened Varieties

Name (Origin)	Made from	Ripening time	Flavor	Texture	Color	Shapes	Uses
Blue, spelled Bleu on imported cheese (France)	Cow's milk	2–6 months	Tangy, peppery	Semisoft, pasty, sometimes crumbly	White interior, marbled or streaked with blue veins of mold	Cylindrical, wedges, oblongs, squares, cut portions	Appetizers, salads, dips, salad dressing, sandwich spreads, good with crackers, dessert
Gorgonzola (gôr-gŏn-zō´-lä) (Italy)	Cow's milk; in Italy, cow's milk or goat's milk or mixtures of these	3–12 months	Tangy, peppery	Semisoft, pasty, sometimes crumbly, lower moisture than Blue	Creamy white interior, mottled or streaked with blue-green veins of mold; clay-colored surface	Cylindrical, wedges, oblongs	Appetizers, snacks, salads, dips, sandwich spreads, good with crackers, dessert
Roquefort* (rōk´-fêrt) or (rōk-fôr´) (France)	Sheep's milk	2–5 months or longer	Sharp, slightly peppery	Semisoft, pasty, sometimes crumbly	White or creamy white interior, marbled or streaked with blue veins of mold	Cylindrical wedges	Appetizers, snacks, salads, dips, sandwich spreads, good with crackers, dessert
Stilton* (England)	Cow's milk	2–6 months	Piquant, milder than Gorgonzola or Roquefort	Semisoft, flaky; slightly more crumbly than Blue	Creamy white interior; marbled or streaked with blue-green veins of mold	Circular, wedges, oblongs	Appetizers, snacks, salads, dessert

*Imported only.

†Italian trademark—licensed for manufacture in United States; also imported.

Source: Reference 19.

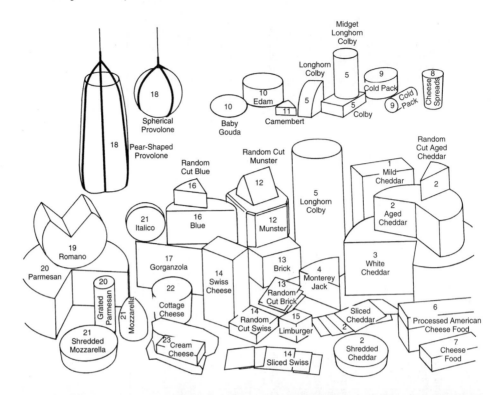

Figure 23-11
Many kinds of cheese are available. To identify the cheeses shown here, see the accompanying labeled drawing. (Courtesy of the American Dairy Association)

of blending in cooked dishes, and the protection offered by the package against spoilage are factors influencing the consumer's choice to use process cheese. The blend of cheeses is chosen to retain as far as possible the characteristic flavor of the type of cheese used; however, the flavor of the process cheese is seldom, if ever, equal to that of the original product. The characteristic differences in texture of the original cheeses tend to be lost, as the texture of process cheese is more or less uniform and soft. The moisture content of process cheese may not exceed 40 percent.

Low-fat (about 8 percent) pasteurized process cheese products in individual slices are also available on the market. These products contain skim milk cheese, water, emulsifier salts, flavorings, and a preservative (sorbic acid).

Process Cheese Foods and Spreads. Pasteurized process cheese food is produced in a manner similar to process cheese except that it contains less cheese. Cream, milk, skim milk, nonfat milk solids or whey, and sometimes other foods, such as pimientos, may be added to it. Cheese food is more mild in flavor, melts more quickly, and has a softer texture than process cheese because of its higher moisture content.

Pasteurized process cheese spread generally has a higher moisture and lower milk fat content than process cheese food. A stabilizer is added to prevent separation of ingredients. It is also generally more spreadable than process cheese food.

Low-Fat Cheese. Fat-free, "part skim," and low-fat cheeses are available. Low-fat milk is used to make many low-fat cheeses. Reduced fat cheeses are generally perceived to be less desirable than full-fat cheeses from a sensory perspective. Researchers have found that reduced fat cheeses have a texture that was more hard, waxy, chewy, and springy as compared to full-fat cheeses [11]. In addition, reduced fat cheeses may be less sticky, cohesive, meltable, and smooth.

Researchers are exploring methods of producing higher quality low-fat cheeses. One process involves the removal of fat from a full-fat cheddar cheese through centrifugation. A high quality cheddar cheese with about 16 percent fat, as compared to 34 percent fat in full-fat cheese, can be produced using this method [43]. The choice of culture also appears to be important in the production of a flavorful and functional low-fat cheese.

Cheese Storage

Soft and unripened cheeses have limited keeping quality and require refrigeration. The shelf life of cottage cheese may be extended two or three times the usual period by adding carbon dioxide gas and packaging the product in high-barrier material [33]. All cheese is best kept cold. To prevent the surfaces from drying out, the cheese should be well wrapped in plastic wrap or metal foil or kept in the original container if it is one that protects the cheese. In the refrigerator, strong cheeses that are not tightly wrapped may contaminate other foods that readily absorb odors.

Molds are used to make some kinds of cheeses and thus will be found on the exterior or interior of Roquefort, blue, Gorgonzola, Stilton, Brie, and Camembert. Molds used to produce cheese are safe to eat. Wild molds, that are not part of the manufacturing process, are undesirable when growing on the surface of cheeses. Wild molds may be safely cut off of hard cheeses such as Cheddar [58]. However, if soft or shredded cheeses mold, the cheese will need to be discarded because the mold cannot be completely removed.

Freezing is not recommended for most cheeses because, on thawing, they tend to be mealy and crumbly; however, some varieties of cheese can be frozen satisfactorily in small pieces (1 pound or less, not more than 1 inch thick). These varieties include brick, Cheddar, Edam, Gouda, Muenster, Port du Salut, Swiss, Provolone, Mozzarella, and Camembert. When frozen cheese is to be thawed, it may be taken from the freezer and placed in the refrigerator for a minimum of 10 days before using it. This so-called *slow thawing* helps to avoid the detrimental effects of freezing and aids in preserving the original flavor, body, and texture.

Cheese usually exhibits its most distinctive flavor when served at room temperature. An exception is cottage cheese, which should be served cold. The amount of cheese to be used should be removed from the refrigerator about 30 minutes prior to serving [38].

Cheese in Cooked Foods

Cheese adds flavor, color, and texture to a variety of cooked foods. Many casserole mixtures use cheese, either as a basic component or as a topping. And what would pizza be without cheese? In addition, a cheese tray combined with fresh fruits and/or vegetable relishes makes an easy snack or a colorful dessert (see Figure 23-12).

A hard cheese, such as Cheddar, softens and then melts when it is heated at low to moderate temperatures. Further heating results in the separation of fat and the development of a tough, rubbery curd, which will form long strings when manipulated with a spoon. If the cheese has been heated to the latter stage, it will tend to harden on cooling. Finely dividing the cheese by grating or grinding before combining it with other ingredients facilitates melting without overheating. Cheese sauces should be cooked in a double boiler or over low heat with continuous stirring. Well-ripened cheese and process cheese blend

Figure 23-12
Cheese and fruit can be served as either a snack or a dessert. These natural cheeses make a wonderful selection when mixed with grapes, pears, apples, or guava. (Reference 28)

(a)

(b)

(c)

Figure 23-13

(a) These bagels are topped with spinach, Swiss, and provolone cheese. (Courtesy of the American Dairy Association)

(b) Cheese soufflé is an egg dish prepared with whipped egg whites, a white sauce and cheese. (Courtesy of Kraft Foods)

(c) Apples and pears are topped with Monterey jack and cheddar cheeses then baked with a sugared crumb mixture to create a pleasing dish served with cinnamon-sugared flour tortillas. (Courtesy of the American Dairy Association)

better in heated mixtures than mild (less aged) natural cheese and are less likely to produce stringiness.

Welsh rabbit is a thickened cheese sauce with seasonings. It may also contain egg, and is usually served over toast. Cheese soufflé is a combination of white sauce and eggs, with grated cheese to give it flavor (Figure 23-13). The white sauce used as a basis may vary in consistency or in amount, but soufflés made with a thick sauce base are usually easier for the inexperienced person to make and tend to shrink less after baking. The baking dish containing the soufflé should be placed in a pan of water during baking to avoid overcooking. Several examples of the use of cheese in cooked foods are illustrated in Figure 23-13.

CHAPTER SUMMARY

- The annual per capita consumption of milk and milk products has increased. However, the types of dairy products most frequently consumed in America have changed considerably since the early 1900's. Cheese consumption increased eightfold between 1909 and 1999.

- Milk is composed of water, carbohydrate, protein, fat, and ash. The composition of milk varies in response to physiological and environmental factors. The most variable component of milk is the fat, followed by protein.

- Bovine somatotropin, or rbST, has been found safe by the FDA. This hormone, when given to cows, increases milk production by 10 percent.

- About 80 percent of the protein in milk is casein. Whey proteins account for much of the remaining protein in milk. Whey protein is a by-product of cheesemaking and may be processed to produce whey protein concentrate and whey protein isolate for use in other products.

- The fat in milk is a complex lipid that is dispersed in milk serum; thus, milk is an emulsion. Milk fat is composed primarily of triglycerides. A small amount of phospholipids and some sterols—chiefly cholesterol—also are present. The triglycerides are characterized by many short-chain, saturated fatty acids.

- The chief carbohydrate in milk is lactose. On hydrolysis, it yields the monosaccharides glucose and galactose. Lactose is the least sweet and least soluble of the common sugars. It may crystallize out and give some foods a sandy texture when present in too large an amount. Some individuals may have a deficiency of lactase, thereby producing a lactose intolerance manifested by gas, cramping, and diarrhea.

- The white appearance of milk is due to the reflection of light by colloidally dispersed casein micelles and calcium phosphate salts. Carotenes and riboflavin are two yellowish pigments that also contribute color to milk.

- The flavor of milk is bland and slightly sweet with a mild aroma. The mouthfeel of milk is thought to influence the sensation of flavor. Heat processing may affect the flavor of milk. Off-flavors may develop from the feed consumed by the cow, the action of bacteria, chemical changes in milk, or the absorption of foreign flavors after the milk is drawn. Off flavors also may be produced when milk is exposed to light.

- Fresh milk has a nearly neutral pH. Raw milk gradually increases in acidity on storage because of lactic-acid producing bacteria.

- Milk provides a rich source of calcium in the diet and is a dependable source of ribloflavin, vitamin A, vitamin D, and protein. Milk should be protected from light to retain the riboflavin which is unstable in ultraviolet light.

- Milk is a perishable food. The Grade A Pasteurized Milk Ordinance describes the steps necessary to protect the milk supply. Sanitary codes generally determine the grading of milk. If a manufacturer of dairy products uses the USDA grade or Quality Approved shield on product labels, the plant must operate under continuous inspection of USDA agents.

- Pasteurization is required by law for all Grade A fluid milk and milk products that enter interstate commerce for retail sale. The pasteurization process involves heating raw milk to a sufficiently high temperature for a specified length of time to destroy pathogenic bacteria.

- Fluid milk should be stored at 41°F (5°C) or below immediately after purchase. The milk container should be closed to prevent absorption of other food odors and protected from light. Nonfat dry milk should be stored in moisture-proof packages at a temperature no higher than ordinary room temperature.

- Homogenization consists of pumping milk or cream under pressure through tiny openings to increase the dispersion of fat and therby prevent the cream from separating upon standing.

- Milk is commonly fortified with vitamin D and vitamin A. The fortification with vitamin D is optional, but vitamin A fortification is required in low-fat and non-fat milks.

- Milk is marketed as fluid milk (whole, fat-reduced, ultra-high temperature processed), concentrated fluid milk (evaporated and sweetened condensed), dry milk, cultured milk products (yogurt, buttermilk, acidophilus), and filled or imitation milks. Each of these milk and milk products have specific characteristics.

- Heat, acid, enzymes, phenolic compounds, salt, and freezing have an effect on milk and milk products.

- On heating, whey proteins precipitate and contribute to the scorching of heated milk. A small part of calcium phosphate also precipitates with heat. A surface film forms when milk is heated which may contain coagulated protein, precipitated salts, and fat globules. Boiled milk may have a layer of fat form on the surface as the result of breaking the films of protein surrounding the fat globules. Browning is another reaction that can occur as sugars and proteins are heated together.

- Although the protein casein is hardly susceptible to coagulation by heating, it is highly sensitive to precipitation on the addition of acid. This acid curdling is desirable when making products such as cultured buttermilk, yogurt, sour cream, and some cheeses.

- A number of enzymes from plant, animal, and microbial sources are capable of clotting milk. Chymosin or rennin is such an enzyme. The crude chymosin enzyme is called rennet. The enzyme bromelin also clots milk but later digests the clot.

- Phenolic compounds, found in plants, may cause curdling of milk when cooked. Sodium chloride may influence coagulation of casein.

- Fat globules tend to coalesce when milk or cream has been frozen. The dispersion of protein and calcium phosphate also is disturbed by freezing.

- Cream is a high-fat, liquid product that is separated from whole milk. Several liquid cream products are marketed, including light or coffee cream, light whipping cream, heavy cream, or heavy whipping cream. Commercial sour cream is a cultured or an acidified light cream. Dried cream, which is generally reconstituted, is available as well.

- Many nondairy products for whipped toppings, coffee whiteners, sour cream-type mixtures, and snack dip bases are marketed. Although these products are termed "nondairy," these products often contain casein or whey.

- In the whipping of cream, a foam is formed. Cream held at a cold temperature whips better than cream that is warm. Higher fat content also increases viscosity. A fat content of 30 percent is the minimum for cream that will whip with ease and produce a stiff product. Sugar should be added after the cream is stiff or just prior to serving. Sugar will decrease volume and stiffness in addition to increasing the time required to whip the cream.

- Evaporated milk will whip to three times its original volume if chilled to the ice cystal stage. Equal measures of dry milk and very cold water may be whipped into an unstable foam.

- Dairy products containing fewer calories, less fat, and/or sodium are available. To be labeled *light*, a product must meet the FDA definitions.

- Cheese is a concentrated dairy food defined as the fresh or matured product obtained by draining the whey after coagulation of casein.

- The manufacture of different cheeses follows similar steps: (1) promoting curd formation with a starter culture and/or a coagulating enzyme; (2) cutting the curd into small pieces to allow the whey to drain; (3) heating the curd; (4) draining, knitting or stretching, salting, and pressing the curd; and (5) curing or ripening.

- Ripening refers to the changes in physical and chemical properties, such as aroma, flavor, texture, and composition, that take place between the time of precipitation of the curd and the time when the cheese develops the desired characteristics of its type. The changes that occur in cheese during ripening affect flavor, texture, and improve cooking quality.

- Various types of organisms produce distinctive flavors, aromas, and textures in cheeses. The mottled green appearance of some cheeses is due to the type of mold used. Swiss cheese owes its large holes to special gas-forming organisms.

- USDA grade standards have been developed for some varieties of cheese.

- Cheese may be classified by the amount of moisture (soft, semihard, or hard) and the kind and extent of ripening (unripened, mold ripened, or bacteria ripened).

- Cold pack or club cheese is made by grinding and mixing together one or more varieties of cheese without the aid of heat. Process cheese is made by grinding and mixing together different samples of natural cheese with the aid of heat and an emulsifying agent. Pasteurized process cheese food is produced in a manner similar to process cheese except that it contains less cheese.

- Soft and unripened cheeses have limited keeping quality. All cheese is best kept cold. However, the flavor of many cheeses is generally the best when served at room temperature. Freezing is generally not recommended; however, some cheeses may be satisfactorily frozen.

- When cooking with cheese, finely dividing the cheese by grating will facilitate melting without overheating. Overheating results in the separation of the fat and the development of a tough, rubbery curd.

KEY TERMS

colloidal	aseptic packaging
micelles	emulsifier
protease	rancidity
ultrafiltration	Maillard reaction
emulsion	fermentation
phospholipid	probiotic
triglyceride	precipitate
sterol	coagulate
saturated fatty acid	phenolic compounds
hydrolysis	viscosity
critical temperature	surface tension
density	aspartame

STUDY QUESTIONS

1. Describe present trends in the consumption of dairy products in the United States.

2. What is the average percentage composition of whole cow's milk?

3. Name the following items:
   a. Protein found in milk in largest amount
   b. Two major whey proteins
   c. Major carbohydrate of milk
   d. Two minerals for which milk is considered to be a particularly good source
   e. Vitamin for which milk is a good source that is easily destroyed when milk is exposed to sunlight

4. Explain why milk is classified as an emulsion. Describe how the fat in milk is dispersed.

5. How do opaque containers help to protect milk against the development of off-flavor? Explain.

6. Describe the purpose, process, and resulting product when milk is
   a. Pasteurized
   b. Homogenized
   c. Fortified

7. Briefly describe the major characteristics of each of the following processed milk products.
   a. Whole fluid milk
   b. Skim milk
   c. Reduced-fat milk

    d. Low-fat milk

    e. Ultrahigh-temperature processed milk

    f. Evaporated milk

    g. Sweetened condensed milk

    h. Nonfat dry milk, regular, and instant

    i. Dried buttermilk (churned)

    j. Buttermilk (cultured)

    k. Filled milk

    l. Yogurt

8. a. Explain why it is so important that milk be handled properly, both in processing and in the kitchen.

    b. What does the USDA Quality Approved shield mean when it is placed on certain dairy products?

    c. What is the Grade A Pasteurized Milk Ordinance?

9. a. What causes milk to scorch when it is heated over direct heat?

    b. Which milk proteins coagulate quite easily with heating? Which do not?

10. Suggest ways to prevent or control the formation of a film or scum on the surface of heated milk.

11. a. Which milk protein coagulates easily with the addition of acid?

    b. Give examples illustrating when the acid coagulation of milk is desirable and when it is undesirable.

12. a. What is *rennet* and what does it do to milk?

    b. What role does rennet play in cheesemaking?

    c. What is *chymosin?* List two sources.

13. a. Describe what happens when cream is whipped.

    b. What conditions should be controlled, and why, if cream is to whip properly?

    c. Suggest effective procedures for whipping evaporated milk and nonfat dry milk.

14. Describe the general steps usually followed in the manufacture of cheese.

15. a. What is meant by *ripening* cheese?

    b. Describe general changes that may occur during the ripening process.

16. Give examples of each of the following types of cheese.

    a. Soft, unripened

    b. Firm, unripened

    c. Soft, ripened

    d. Semisoft, ripened

    e. Firm, ripened

    f. Very hard, ripened

    g. Blue-vein mold-ripened

17. Describe the major characteristics of the following.

    a. Cold-pack cheese

    b. Process cheese

    c. Process cheese food

    d. Process cheese spread

18. a. Describe what happens when cheese is heated too long or at too high a temperature.

b. Suggest an appropriate way for preparing a cheese sauce and explain why this method should be effective.

19. Seek information about an unfamiliar cheese; see www.ilovecheese.com

REFERENCES

1. Bente, L. & Gerrior, S. A. (2002). Selected food and nutrient highlights of the 20th century: U.S. food supply series. *Food Review, 14*(1), 43–51.

2. Bhaskar, A. R., Rizvi, S. S. H., & Sherbon, J. W. (1993). Anhydrous milkfat fractionation with continuous countercurrent supercritical carbon dioxide. *Journal of Food Science, 58*, 748.

3. Blayney, D. P. (1994). Milk and biotechnology: Maintaining safe, adequate milk supplies. *Food Review, 17*(2), 27.

4. Broihier, K. (1998). Milking it. *Food Processing, 61*(3), 53.

5. Clemens, R. A. (2001). Friendly bacteria: A functional food? *Food Technology, 55*(1), 27.

6. Cocup, R. O. & Sanderson, W. B. (1987). Functionality of dairy ingredients in bakery products. *Food Technology, 41*(10), 86.

7. Council on Foods and Nutrition. (1969). Substitutes for whole milk. *Journal of the American Medical Association, 208*, 58.

8. Enns, C. W., Goldman, J. D., & Cook, A. (1997). Trends in food and nutrient intakes by adults: NFCS 1977–78, CSFII 1989–91, and CSFII 1994–95. *Family Economics and Nutrition Review, 10*(4), 2.

9. German, J. B., & Dillard, C. J. (1998). Fractionated milk fat: Composition, structure, and functional properties. *Food Technology, 52*(2), 33.

10. Gupta, C. B., & Eskin, N. A. M. (1977). Potential use of vegetable rennet in the production of cheese. *Food Technology, 31*(5), 62.

11. Gwartney, E. A., Foegeding, E. A., & Larick, D. K. (2002). The texture of commercial full-fat and reduced-fat cheese. *Journal of Food Science, 67*, 812–816.

12. Hansen, A. P. (1987). Effect of ultrahigh-temperature processing and storage on dairy food flavor. *Food Technology, 41*(9), 112.

13. Hill, A. R. (1988). Quality of ultrahigh-temperature processed milk. *Food Technology, 42*(9), 92.

14. Hoch, G. J. (1997). Whey to go. *Food Processing, 58*(3), 51.

15. Hoch, G. J. (1997). Yogurt "cheese" goes commercial. *Food Processing, 58*(2), 58.

16. Hollingsworth, P. (2001). Culture wars. *Food Technology, 55*(3), 43–46.

17. Holsinger, V. H., & Kligerman, A. E. (1991). Applications of lactase in dairy foods and other foods containing lactose. *Food Technology, 45*(1), 92.

18. Hoover, D. G. (1993). Bifidobacteria: Activity and potential benefits. *Food Technology, 47*(6), 120.

19. *How to buy cheese.* (1974). Home and Garden Bulletin No. 193. Washington, D.C.: U.S. Department of Agriculture.

20. Huffman, L. M. (1996). Processing whey protein for use as a food ingredient. *Food Technology, 50*(2), 49.

21. Hughes, D. B., & Hoover, D. G. (1991). Bifidobacteria: Their potential for use in American dairy products. *Food Technology, 45*(4), 74.

22. Kanno, C., Shimomura, Y., & Takano, E. (1991). Physicochemical properties of milkfat emulsions stabilized with bovine milkfat globule membrane. *Journal of Food Science, 56*, 1219.

23. Kantor, M. A. (1990). Light dairy products: The need and the consequences. *Food Technology, 44*(10), 81.

24. Katz, F. (2001). Active cultures add function to yogurt and others foods. *Food Technology, 55*(3), 46–49.

25. Kirkpatrick, K. J., & Fenwick, R. M. (1987). Manufacture and general properties of dairy ingredients. *Food Technology, 41*(10), 58.

26. Kroger, M., Kurmann, J. A., & Rasic, J. L. (1989). Fermented milks—Past, present, and future. *Food Technology, 43*(1), 92.

27. Kurtzweil, P. (1998). Skimming the milk label. *FDA Consumer, 32*(1), 22.

28. Labensky, S. R. & Hause, A. M. (2003). *On cooking: A textbook of culinary fundamentals* (3rd ed.). New Jersey: Prentice Hall.

29. Lee, S. Y., & Morr, C. V. (1993). Fixation staining methods for examining microstructure in whipped cream by electron microscopy. *Journal of Food Science, 58*, 124.

30. Light, A., Heymann, H., & Holt, D. L. (1992). Hedonic responses to dairy products: Effects of fat levels, label information, and risk perception. *Food Technology, 46*(7), 54.

31. *Making cottage cheese at home.* (1975). Home and Garden Bulletin No. 129. Washington, DC: U.S. Department of Agriculture.

32. Mangino, M. E. (1992). Gelation of whey protein concentrates. *Food Technology, 46*(1), 114.

33. Mermelstein, N. H. (1997). Extending dairy product shelf life with carbon dioxide. *Food Technology, 51*(12), 72.

34. Mulvihill, D. M., & Kinsella, J. E. (1987). Gelation characteristics of whey proteins and beta-lactoglobulin. *Food Technology, 41*(9), 102.

35. National Restaurant Association Educational Foundation. (2002). *ServSafe Coursebook* (2nd ed.). Chicago, IL: National Restaurant Association Educational Foundation.

36. Neff, J. (1997). Fattening up a new dairy niche. *Food Processing, 58*(1), 45.

37. Neff, J. (1997). Skim milk rises to top. *Food Processing, 58*(4), 31.

38. *Newer knowledge of cheese.* (1992). Rosemont, IL: National Dairy Council.

39. *Newer knowledge of milk.* (1993). Rosemont, IL: National Dairy Council.

40. Ohr, L. M. (2002). Improving the gut feeling. *Food Technology, 56*(10), 67–70.

41. Palanuk, S. L., Warthesen, J. J., & Smith, D. E. (1988). Effect of agitation, sampling location, and protective films on light-induced riboflavin loss in skim milk. *Journal of Food Science, 53*, 436.

42. Pennington, J. A. T., Wilson, E. B., Young, B. E., Johnson, R. D., & Vanderveen, J. E. (1987). Mineral content of market samples of fluid whole milk. *Journal of the American Dietetic Association, 87*, 1036.

43. Pszczola, D. E. (2001). Say cheese with new ingredient developments. *Food Technology, 55*(12), 56–66.

44. Putnam, J. J. (2000). Major trends in U.S. food supply, 1909–1999. *Food Review, 23*(1), 8–14.

45. Putnam, J. J. & Allshouse, J. E. (1999). Food consumption, prices, and expenditures, 1970–1997. Food and Rural Economics Division, Economic Research Service, U.S. Department of Agriculture. Statistical Bulletin No. 965.

46. Renken, S. A., & Warthesen, J. J. (1993). Vitamin D stability in milk. *Journal of Food Science, 58*, 552.

47. Renz-Schauen, A., & Renner, E. (1987). Fortification of nondairy foods with dairy ingredients. *Food Technology, 41*(10), 122.

48. Rolls, B. A., & Porter, J. W. G. (1973). Some effects of processing and storage on the nutritive value of milk and milk products. *Proceedings of the Nutrition Society, 32,* 9.

49. Savaiano, D. A., & Levitt, M. D. (1984). Nutritional and therapeutic aspects of fermented dairy products. *Contemporary Nutrition* (General Mills Nutrition Department), 9 (6).

50. Schroder, B. G., & Baer, R. J. (1990). Utilization of cholesterol-reduced milkfat in fluid milks. *Food Technology, 44*(11), 145.

51. Shipe, W. F., Bassette, R., Deane, D. D., Dunkley, W. L., Hammond, E. G., Harper, W. J., Kleyn, D. H., Morgan, M. E., Nelson, J. H., & Scanlan, R. A. (1978). Off-flavors of milk: Nomenclature, standards, and bibliography. *Journal of Dairy Science, 61,* 855.

52. Sloan, E. A. (2002). Got milk? Get cultured. *Food Technology, 56*(2), 16.

53. Sloan, E. A. (2000). Say cheese! *Food Technology, 54*(6), 18–19.

54. Speck, M. L., Dobrogosz, W. J., & Casas, I. A. (1993). *Lactobacillus reuteri* in food supplementation. *Food Technology, 47*(7), 90.

55. Staff. (1989). Rennet containing 100% chymosin increases cheese quality and yield. *Food Technology, 43*(6), 84.

56. U.S. Department of Agriculture. (1995). *How to buy cheeses.* Home and Garden Bulletin No. 193.

57. U.S. Department of Agriculture. (1995). *How to buy dairy products.* Home and Garden Bulletin No. 255.

58. U.S. Department of Agriculture. (2002, April). Molds on food: Are they dangerous? Retrieved August 20, 2002, from http://www.fsis.usda.gov/OA/pubs/molds.htm

59. U.S. Food and Drug Administration, Center for Veterinary Medicine. (1999, February). Report on the Food and Drug Administration's Review of the safety of recombinant bovine somatotropin. Retrieved December 22, 2002, from http://www.fda.gov/cvm/index/bst/rbrptfnl.htm

Eggs and Egg Cookery

24

 Although the eggs of all birds may be eaten, the egg of the chicken is used more often than any other. This discussion, therefore, pertains to chicken eggs unless otherwise specified.

The natural function of the egg is to provide for the development of the chick. Its whole structure and composition are designed to fulfill this natural purpose. Partly because the egg is associated with the beginning of "life," much symbolism has been attached to it, taking a variety of forms in different cultures over the centuries. In Christian communities, for example, the egg has special significance at Easter time, to the particular delight of children as they enjoy this symbol in many different forms.

In the preparation of food, the egg functions in several different roles, apparently unrelated to its original purpose of providing for the chick. It is used to make **emulsions** because it contains emulsifying agents of proven effectiveness. It also contains foaming agents that allow it to be advantageous in the production of food **foams,** including meringues and angel food cakes. The ability of the proteins of the egg to **coagulate** on heating allows it to perform a variety of functions, which include forming gels such as baked custards, coating breaded meats and fish, and **clarifying** some liquids such as broth and coffee. Egg yolk also provides color. Plain eggs—cooked in the shell, scrambled, and fried—also provide eating enjoyment. The egg gives all this to food preparation besides providing a package of essential nutrients that enrich the diet.

emulsion the dispersion of one liquid within another with which it is usually immiscible

foam the dispersion of a gas in a liquid

coagulate to produce a firm mass or gel by denaturation of protein molecules followed by formation of new crosslinks

clarify to make clear a cloudy liquid such as heated soup stock by adding raw egg white and/or egg shell; as the proteins coagulate, they trap tiny particles from the liquid that can then be strained out

COMPOSITION AND NUTRITIVE VALUE

Whole egg contains about 75 percent water, 12 percent protein, 10 percent fat, 1 percent carbohydrate, and 1 percent minerals. The white and the yolk are very different from each other in composition, however, as can be seen by an examination of Table 24-1. Essentially all the fat of the egg is found in the yolk; the white contains a larger percentage of water. Making up about 11 percent of the total weight of the egg is the shell, which is composed of approximately 95 percent calcium carbonate in crystal form [28].

Although the ratio of white to yolk varies in individual eggs, the white is usually about two-thirds by weight of the total edible portion and the yolk is approximately one-third. In general, the yolk has higher nutrient density than the white, containing more minerals and vitamins relative to its weight.

Table 24-1
Chemical Composition of Egg without Shell

	Amount	Weight (g)	Water (%)	Energy (kcal)	Protein (g)	Fat (g)	Iron (mg)	Vitamin A (RE)	Thiamin (mg)	Riboflavin (mg)
Whole egg, large	1	50	75	72	6	5	0.7	95	0.03	0.25
Egg white	1	33	88	15	4	0	trace	0	trace	0.15
Egg yolk	1	17	49	60	3	5	0.6	97	0.03	0.11

Source: Nutritive Value of Foods. Home and Garden Bulletin No. 72. Washington, DC: U.S. Department of Agriculture, 1991.

In 1967, Americans were eating about 320 eggs per person per year. As concerns about fat and cholesterol in the diet increased, however, the high cholesterol content of egg yolk made it a target. Egg consumption fell to 237 per person in 1996 [27]. More recent research indicates that dietary cholesterol has less effect on serum cholesterol than previously thought and eggs are getting better press. Eggs have several nutritional and economic advantages, including being a significant source of several vitamins. In 2001, 252 eggs were consumed per person [1].

Proteins

protein efficiency ratio a measure of protein quality assessed by determining the extent of weight gain in experimental animals when fed the test item

Egg proteins are of excellent nutritional quality, having the highest **protein efficiency ratio (PER)** of any of the common foods. The major protein in egg white is *ovalbumin*, a protein that is easily denatured by heat. Other egg white proteins are *ovotransferrin, ovomucoid, ovomucin,* and *lysozyme*. Ovomucin, although present in a comparatively small amount, has a large effect on the consistency of thick egg white. It is a very large molecule with a filamentous or fiberlike nature.

lipoproteins proteins combined with lipid or fatty material such as phospholipids

The major proteins in egg yolk are **lipoproteins,** which include *lipovitellin* and *lipovitellinin*. The lipoproteins are responsible for the excellent emulsifying properties of egg yolk when used in such products as mayonnaise. The preparation of mayonnaise is discussed in Chapter 10.

Lipids

atherogenic capable of contributing to the development of atherosclerosis (fatty deposits in the walls of the arteries)

The fatty materials in egg yolk, making up about one-third of the weight of fresh yolk, include triglycerides, phospholipids, and cholesterol. One large egg yolk contains about 215 milligrams of cholesterol; the egg white has no cholesterol. Because of the high level of cholesterol in the yolk, the egg has been considered to be an **atherogenic** food. That concept is now changing. The fatty acid composition of egg yolk may be altered by changing the hen's diet. For example, an increased level of omega-3 fatty acids has been reported to result from the addition of small amounts of menhaden fish oil or special mixtures to the laying hen's diet [35]. Eggs have been introduced into consumer markets that have 195 milligrams of cholesterol per egg, 25 percent less saturated fat, and three times the amount of omega-3 fatty acids as a result of a patented feed program (Figure 24-1) [29]. Cholesterol and triglycerides have been extracted from egg yolk by supercritical carbon dioxide extraction, resulting in a dry product containing protein and phospholipids. This product has potential for use in baked products, egg noodles, ice cream, mayonnaise, scrambled eggs, and sauces [4].

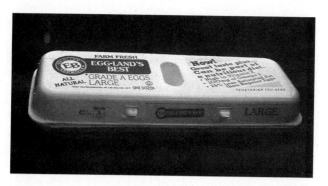

Figure 24-1
These grade A large eggs marketed by Eggland are high in vitamin E and omega-3 fatty acids and have 25 percent less saturated fat than regular eggs. (Courtesy of U.S. Department of Agriculture)

Pigments

Because certain yellow carotenoid pigments can be converted into vitamin A in the body, the question has been raised as to whether more highly colored egg yolks are a better source of vitamin A than pale yolks. The predominant yellow pigment of egg yolk is a xanthophyll, which is not changed to vitamin A in the body. Usually, however, deep-colored yolks are high in vitamin A content because the same rations that produce color in the yolks also contain more provitamin A, which the hen is able to convert into vitamin A and deposit in the yolk. Hens that do not have access to green or yellow feed and that produce pale yolks may be given vitamin A–supplemented rations. Then the pale yolks are high in vitamin A. The vitamin A content of egg yolk, therefore, cannot be predicted solely on the basis of the depth of the yellow color. In practice, egg producers usually feed chickens either sufficient green vegetation or xanthophyll pigments to yield a yolk of medium color intensity.

STRUCTURE

The egg shell is porous and allows exchange of gases and loss of moisture from the egg. It is brown or white, depending on the breed of the hen. The color of the shell has no effect on the flavor or quality of the contents. An air cell formed at the large end of the egg is produced on cooling by the separation of two thin, fibrous protein membranes that are present between the shell and the egg white (Figure 24-2).

THE PARTS OF AN EGG

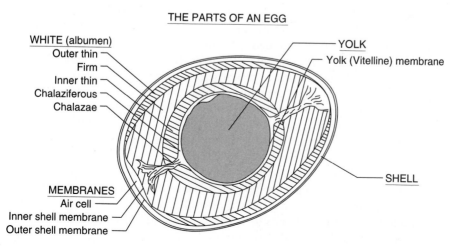

WHITE (albumen)
Outer thin
Firm
Inner thin
Chalaziferous
Chalazae

YOLK
Yolk (Vitelline) membrane

SHELL

MEMBRANES
Air cell
Inner shell membrane
Outer shell membrane

Figure 24-2
The parts of an egg.

In the past, it has been suggested that the protective dull waxy coat on the outside of the egg, referred to as the *cuticle* or the *bloom*, should not be washed off. When it is washed, the porous shell may then more easily permit bacteria, molds, and undesirable flavors or odors to enter the egg. There may also be a greater evaporation of moisture unless preventive measures are taken. However, dirt or soil on shells is probably the most prominent cause of the bacterial invasion of eggs. In commercial practice, therefore, dirty eggs are washed. The eggs are usually washed in automatic washers using alkaline cleaning compounds. After washing, the eggs may be rinsed with a sanitizing agent. If eggs are washed properly, the undesirable effects of washing are kept at a minimum [16]. To replace the natural bloom, the eggs are lightly oiled before packaging [2].

Egg white consists of thin and thick portions. The proportions of thin and thick white vary widely in different eggs and change during storage under varying conditions. It has been estimated that about 20 to 25 percent of the total white of fresh eggs (1 to 5 days old) is thin white. Thick white is characterized by a higher content of the protein ovomucin than is found in thin white.

Immediately adjacent to the *vitelline membrane*—the thin membrane that surrounds the egg yolk—is a *chalaziferous* or inner layer of firm white. This chalaziferous layer gives strength to the vitelline membrane and extends into the *chalazae*. The chalazae appear as two small bits of thickened white, one on each end of the yolk, and anchor the yolk in the center of the egg. Chalazae appear to have almost the same molecular structure as ovomucin [15].

The yolk is composed of tiny spheres of various sizes and shapes, closely packed in the vitelline membrane. Protein granules and oil droplets exist within the spheres [26]. Marketed eggs are usually infertile and the germinal disc on the surface of the yolk does not develop. No difference in nutritive value is noted between infertile and fertilized eggs, but fertile eggs may tend to deteriorate more rapidly.

EGG QUALITY

Characteristics of Fresh and Deteriorated Eggs

A very fresh egg, when broken onto a flat plate, stands up in rounded form due, to a considerable extent, to the viscosity of the thick portion of the egg white. As eggs deteriorate, the proportion of thin white increases, whereas that of thick white decreases. This thinning of the thick white appears to involve some changes in the filamentous protein ovomucin. Lysozyme may also be involved.

The yolk takes up water from the white, and the yolk membrane stretches. When broken out, the deteriorated egg flattens and tends to spread over a level surface. If stretched excessively by movement of water into the yolk, the yolk membrane is weakened and may break when the egg is removed from the shell. Separation of the yolk from the white is thus rendered difficult or impossible. The chalazae start to disintegrate and no longer hold the yolk in the center of the egg, and the yolk moves freely. As an egg ages, especially in a warm, dry atmosphere, moisture escapes through the shell. The air cell, which is very small in a fresh egg, increases in size.

The yolks of fresh eggs are slightly acid (usual pH 6.0 to 6.2), whereas the whites are alkaline (usual pH 7.6 to 7.9). A loss of carbon dioxide from the egg in storage results in increased alkalinity of both white and yolk. The white may eventually reach a pH of 9.0 to 9.7. This increase in pH or alkalinity of eggs during storage may be slowed to an appreciable degree by coating the egg shells with a thin layer of oil on the day the eggs are laid. It has been suggested that damage to some egg white proteins by a very alkaline pH results in angel food cakes of decreased volume [23].

The flavor and odor of fresh eggs are affected by the feed, the individuality of the hen, and storage. During storage, off-flavors may be produced in eggs by the invasion of microorganisms or by the absorption of flavors from the environment. One study of the **headspace** over scrambled eggs reported the presence of thirty-eight volatile substances, including alcohols, aldehydes, ketones, esters, benzene derivatives, and sulfur-containing compounds [22]. A comparison with the volatile compounds of polystyrene packaging materials, commonly used in egg cartons, suggested that some migration of volatile compounds from the packaging into the eggs may have occurred during storage. Further studies of cooked egg flavors will be interesting and useful.

headspace the volume above a liquid or solid in a container

Most eggs reach the stores only a few days after being laid and thus exhibit the characteristics of fresh eggs. Consumers can gauge the freshness of eggs by the pack or expiration date on the egg carton. The "pack date" must be displayed on eggs cartons using the USDA grade shield [32]. The pack date is generally provided using the *Julian date*, which is a three-digit code representing the day of the year; thus, January 1 is 001 and December 31 is 365. Eggs also generally have a "sell-by" or "exp" (expiration date) on the carton. Properly refrigerated eggs should maintain good quality for 3–5 weeks after purchase [32] or 4–5 weeks after the Julian date [2]. USDA grades are discussed later in the chapter.

Measuring Quality

Candling is the method used to determine the interior quality of eggs that go into trade channels. Hand candling, shown in Figure 24-3, is used little in present commercial grading operations, having been replaced by automated equipment and mass scanning devices. Candling may still be used for spot checking, however, and is useful for teaching and demonstrating quality determination. When candling by hand, the egg is held to an opening, behind which is a source

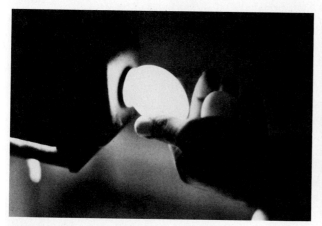

Eggs are held to a bright light during hand candling.

Mass scanning devices speed the candling process.

Figure 24-3
Candling is used to determine the interior quality of eggs. (Courtesy of the U.S. Department of Agriculture)

of strong light. As the light passes through the egg, it shows the quality of the shell, the size of the air cell, the position and mobility of the yolk, blood spots, molds, and a developing embryo, if one is present. As eggs deteriorate and the chalazae weaken, the yolk tends to settle toward the shell rather than remain suspended in the firm white. In such circumstances the yolk is more fully visible when the egg is candled. Dark yolks also cast a more distinct shadow than light yolks. USDA grades for eggs are based on their candled appearance. In Grade AA eggs, the air cell is about 1/8 inch in depth and the diameter of a dime [2].

Although candling is the best method available for rating unbroken eggs, it may not always be reliable in indicating the quality of the egg when it is opened. Some tests done on the broken-out egg include measurement of the height of the thick white in relation to the weight of the egg (Haugh unit), and measurement of the height of the yolk in relation to the width of the yolk (yolk index). Figure 24-4 shows the operation of an instrument for measuring Haugh units in a broken-out egg.

Grading

The classification of individual eggs according to established standards constitutes grading for quality. The egg grade standards widely used throughout the United States have been formulated by the U.S. Department of Agriculture; these are summarized in Table 24-2.

In grading, the candled appearance of the egg shell, air cell, white, and yolk are considered. According to the results of the candling inspection, the eggs are

Figure 24-4
A micrometer is used to evaluate the quality of an egg that has been removed from the shell. This is done by measuring the height of the thick white. This instrument gives a direct reading in Haugh units. (Courtesy of the U.S. Department of Agriculture)

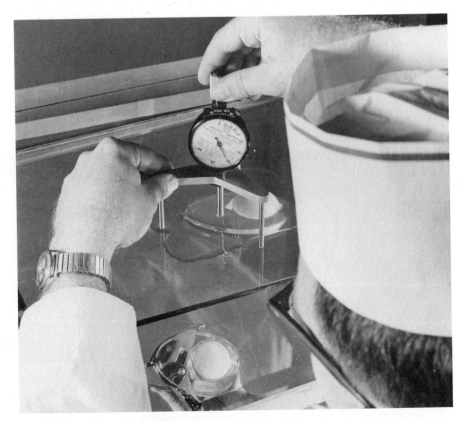

Table 24-2

Summary of U.S. Standards for Quality of Individual Shell Eggs

| Quality Factor | Specifications for Each Quality Factor | | |
	AA Quality	A Quality	B Quality
Shell	Clean	Clean	Clean to slightly stained
	Unbroken	Unbroken	Unbroken
	Practically normal	Practically normal	Somewhat abnormal
Air Cell	⅛ in. or less in depth	3/16 in. or less in depth	Over 3/16 in. in depth
	Unlimited movement and free or bubbly	Unlimited movement and free or bubbly	Unlimited movement and free or bubbly
White	Thick	Clear	Clear
	Firm	Reasonably firm	Somewhat watery
			Small blood and meat spots may be present
Yolk	Outline slightly defined	Outline fairly well defined	Outline plainly visible
	Practically free from defects	Practically free from defects	Enlarged and flattened
			Clearly visible germ development but no blood

Source: References 8, 31.

assigned one of three consumer grades: U.S. Grade AA, U.S. Grade A, or U.S. Grade B. These grades are illustrated by photographs of broken-out eggs in Figure 24-5, and the grade marks are shown in Figure 24-6.

Grades AA and A have a large proportion of thick white that stands up around a firm, high yolk. These eggs are especially good for frying and poaching, when appearance is important. Grade B eggs, which have thinner whites and spread out more, are good for general baking and cooking. Grade B eggs are generally not found in retail stores. The nutritional value for all grades is similar.

Eggs must be properly handled at all times, because egg quality is relatively unstable. The interior quality of the egg deteriorates from the time it is laid until it is consumed. Figure 24-7 indicates how egg quality decreases with the time of holding. With proper care, however, this decline in quality can be minimized.

USDA grading services are available for individuals, firms, and agencies that request them on a fee-for-service basis. Cooperative agreements may be made between the USDA and parties within each state to supply official graders and services. The Egg Products Inspection Act of 1970 assures the consumer that only wholesome, unadulterated, and truthfully labeled egg products are marketed. Among the provisions of this act is the requirement that frozen and dried egg products be pasteurized so that they are free from any contamination by *Salmonella* microorganisms [32].

Sizing

Separate from the process of grading, eggs are sorted for size into six weight classes, as shown in Figure 24-8. This separation is on the basis of weighing individual eggs. The commercial weighing and packaging of eggs may be auto-

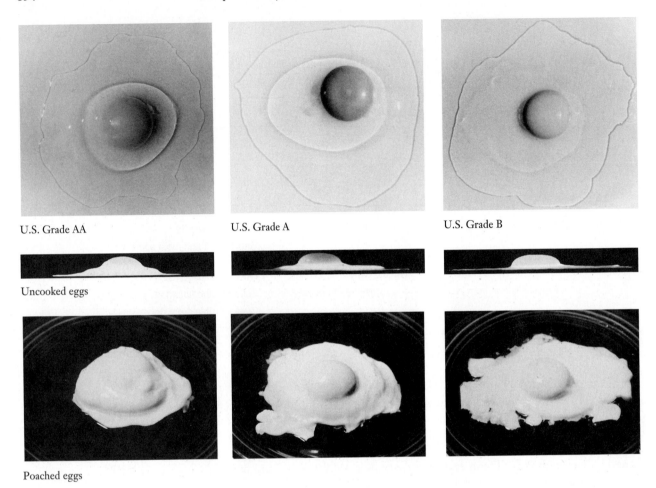

U.S. Grade AA

U.S. Grade A

U.S. Grade B

Uncooked eggs

Poached eggs

Figure 24-5
Characteristics of egg quality, with the yolk standing highest on the thick white of the U.S. Grade AA eggs, are evident in broken-out eggs and in poached eggs. (Courtesy of the U.S. Department of Agriculture)

mated, as illustrated in Figure 24-9. Within each grade are several sizes usually available on supermarket shelves.

Size relative to cost per dozen is an important factor to consider when buying eggs. Most eggs are marketed in cartons, on which the minimum weight per dozen, in ounces, is usually listed. This weight can be divided into the price per dozen to determine the cost per ounce of egg. The cost per ounce of each of the sizes of eggs can then be compared to determine which is the best buy.

Another point to consider in buying eggs is the use for which they are purchased. There is no one best size to buy. Large eggs may be preferred for table use, but for cooking purposes price in relation to size may be a more important consideration.

Recipes calling for a specific number of eggs are usually formulated on the basis of the large size. Actually, measuring or weighing eggs in recipes gives much more uniform results. If jumbo and extra large or small and peewee-size eggs are used in a recipe, some adjustment should be made, reducing or increasing the number of eggs by one-fourth to one-third for the jumbo and extra large or for the small and peewee sizes, respectively. If several eggs are used in a recipe, the potential for error becomes great.

Safety and Handling

The U.S. Food and Drug Administration (FDA) and the U.S. Department of Agriculture's Food Safety and Inspection Service (FSIS) share federal responsibility for egg safety [5]. About 1 out of 20,000 eggs produced is contaminated with *Salmonella enteritidis*. With 47 billion shell eggs consumed annually, this translates into about 2.3 million eggs that are positive for *Salmonella enteritidis* [24]. Eggs are estimated to be the cause of 230,000 cases of foodborne illness per year [5]. A 1999 Egg Safety Action Plan developed by the FDA and FSIS seeks to reduce and eventually eliminate eggs as a source of *Salmonella enteritidis*. An interim goal is to reduce illnesses by 50 percent by 2005. To achieve this reduction, producers, processors, foodservice operators, and consumers all will need to do their part.

Since the mid-1980's, *Salmonella enteritidis* has been a frequently implicated species of the genus *Salmonella* in human illness cases reported to the Centers for Disease Control and Prevention. Unbroken shell eggs may contain salmonellae bacteria because *Salmonella enteritidis* may infect the reproductive system of laying hens, which then results in the contamination of the egg in advance of shell formation. These eggs are laid already contaminated with the organism inside the intact shell. Eggs also may become infected from pathogens carried in fecal and dirt contamination on the shell exterior and then move through the shell pores to the inner parts of the eggs [32]. Washing of eggs during processing and a light oil coating to seal the shell reduces this risk. Raw or undercooked eggs and foods containing them have been implicated in about 80 percent of those *S. enteritidis* outbreaks in which a food source was identified [20].

In 2000, the FDA finalized regulations to require safe food handling instructions on cartons and new refrigeration requirements [34]. Starting in September 2001, cartons of untreated shell eggs are required to have the following statement: "Safe Handling Instructions: To prevent illness from bacteria: keep eggs refrigerated, cook eggs until yolks are firm, and cook foods containing eggs thoroughly." The refrigeration requirements took effect in June 2001 and specify that untreated shell eggs sold at stores, roadside stands and so forth must be held and displayed at or below 45°F (7°C) [33].

If salmonellae are present in an egg, the numbers would likely be small at the time of laying and would probably not create a problem if the product were eaten immediately. The real problems occur with the mishandling of the egg at any place along the production line from the hen to the consumer. At warm temperatures, microorganisms can increase rapidly, which is why eggs should always be properly refrigerated.

A cryogenic system of cooling eggs has been developed to quickly cool eggs from the "just-laid" temperature of 110°F (43°C) down to 45°F (7°C) in 80–90 seconds [24]. Eggs are conveyed into a cooling tunnel in which liquid CO_2 is piped, creating a vapor/snow mixture that rapidly chills the eggs. Eggs can take as long as 7–14 days to cool from 110°F (43°C) to 45°F (7°C) under normal processing and packaging conditions. Quickly cooled eggs are fresher and microbial testing has shown lower levels of *Salmonella enteritidis*.

Additional methods of processing shell eggs to increase food safety have been developed. Shell eggs may be pasteurized by using a hot-water immersion

AA

A

B

Figure 24-6
Three grade marks for eggs graded under federal and state supervision. The marks show both grade and size. (Courtesy of the U.S. Department of Agriculture)

Figure 24-7
*The graded quality of eggs declines
with the time of holding.* (Courtesy
of the U.S. Department of Agriculture)

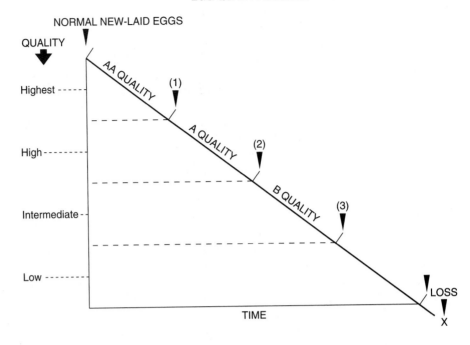

EGG QUALITY DECLINE

Figure 24-8
*When purchasing eggs, you should be
aware of both size (an indication of
quantity) and grade (an indication of
quality). There are six sizes shown.
The weights shown in the illustrations
represent ounces per dozen eggs.*
(Source: Reference 19)

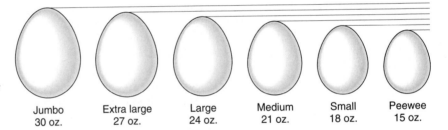

| Jumbo | Extra large | Large | Medium | Small | Peewee |
| 30 oz. | 27 oz. | 24 oz. | 21 oz. | 18 oz. | 15 oz. |

Figure 24-9
*Eggs are handled and weighed by au-
tomatic in-line scales. Eggs of different sizes are weighed and ejected from
the line at different points.*
(Courtesy of the U.S. Department
of Agriculture)

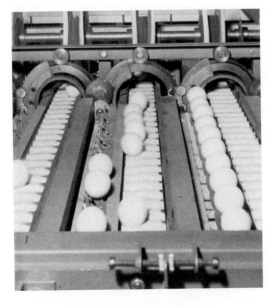

Hot Topics

Focusing on eggs!

Federal and state governments, the scientific community, and the egg industry are all focusing on eggs—and egg products. Why? Because they want to protect the health of the American people, and eggs—even unbroken, fresh, clean shell eggs—may contain *Salmonella enteritidis* bacteria that can cause foodborne illness. No matter how hard we try to control these tiny organisms, *Salmonella* and other pathogens keep causing major outbreaks. For example, in May 2001 an outbreak occurred in Minneapolis involving raw eggs used in the preparation of Hollandaise sauce for eggs Benedict served at a buffet in a major hotel. At least 46 of those attending the buffet were ill, along with a chef, 8 hotel engineers, and at least 2 waiters [39].

Many government agencies are involved in the regulation—surveillance, inspection, investigation, and enforcement—of our food supply, from farm to table. At the federal level we have the Animal and Plant Health Inspection Service (APHIS) monitoring the incidence of *Salmonella enteritidis* in flocks of laying hens. The Agricultural Research Service (ARS) conducts research to study the habits of *Salmonella*, while the National Agricultural Statistics Service (NASS) analyzes the economic impact on the egg-producing industry. Now the Food Safety and Inspection Service (FSIS) works together with the Food and Drug Administration (FDA) to strengthen regulations with the goal of finally solving the problem of *Salmonella enteritidis* in eggs. The FSIS is also responsible for educating the consumer about the safe handling of eggs. And we should not forget the Agricultural Marketing Service (AMS) that administers the egg-quality grading program.

The federal agencies involved in food safety are numerous indeed. Therefore, in 1998 the President established a Council on Food Safety, with representatives from each of these agencies, to coordinate and *focus* activities in this area.

In addition, state agriculture departments and state and local health departments monitor compliance with U.S. standards as eggs are packed, transported, and sold in retail markets. A recent rule requires that, at all times, shell eggs packed for consumers be stored and transported under refrigeration not to exceed 45°F and must be labeled to state that refrigeration is required.

Even with all of this vigilant surveillance, however, *you* must focus on safe egg handling and cooking methods. Follow the safe handling instructions now required on all raw, unpasteurized shell eggs sold in retail markets—"To prevent illness from bacteria: Keeps eggs refrigerated, cook eggs until yolks are firm, and cook foods containing eggs thoroughly." Then enjoy your favorite egg recipes.

---

process that controls time and temperature to result in a **5-log reduction** in *Salmonella* [25]. A high-moisture hot air method of pasteurization also is being studied. Both of these methods maintain the desirable characteristics of shell eggs, including the whippability of the white. In 2000, the FDA approved use of ionizing radiation on eggs in the shell to reduce *Salmonella*. Although irradiation is effective, the white may become slightly opaque and lose some of the whipping ability [25]. A few tips on egg and egg product safety follow [32, 33].

Purchasing. Buy eggs at retail from refrigerated cases only; for foodservice, use only eggs delivered under refrigeration. Buy clean eggs with uncracked shells.

Storage. Refrigerate eggs immediately, in cartons or cases, at 45°F (7°C) or slightly below. Do not wash eggs unless they are to be used immediately. Use

5-log reduction represents a reduction in organisms by a factor of 100,000 fold. This reduction represents a risk of less than 1 in 100,000. This reduction is accepted as making a product safe to eat when the pathogenic organism is one, such as *Salmonella*, that requires a large number of microorganisms to cause illness.

shell eggs within 3 to 5 weeks. Leftover egg dishes should be stored in small enough containers so cooling down to 41°F (4°C) is rapid.

Handling.   Wash hands, utensils, equipment and work surfaces before or after contact with eggs. Do not keep eggs out of the refrigerator for more than two hours. Cooked eggs for a picnic should be packed in a cooler with enough ice to keep cool.

Preparation.   Do not eat raw eggs, including foods such as milkshakes, Caesar salad, ice cream, or eggnog made from recipes in which the raw egg ingredients are not cooked. Foods such as ice cream and eggnog should be prepared from a cooked base heated to 160°F (71°C). Prepare other foods such as Caesar salad with pasteurized or irradiated eggs.

Cook eggs slowly over moderate heat. Cook at least until the whites are completely coagulated and the yolks are firm. Scrambled eggs should not be runny. Especially those at risk, such as infants, pregnant women, the elderly, or the ill, should avoid eating soft-cooked or runny eggs. However, pasteurized shell eggs or egg products are safe for these individuals. In foodservice, only pasteurized eggs must be used in dishes such as scrambled eggs where a large number of eggs would be pooled. When serving high-risk populations, the use of only pasteurized egg products is recommended.

Casseroles and other dishes containing eggs should be cooked to 160°F (71°C) and checked by thermometer. Divinity candy and 7-minute frosting are safe when prepared by combining hot sugar syrup with the beaten egg whites. Meringue topped pies are safe when meringue is placed on a hot filling and baked at 350°F (177°C) for 15 minutes. Cooked eggs and egg-rich foods, such as custards, puddings, and pumpkin pie, should be served immediately after cooking or refrigerated at once for use within 3 to 4 days.

PRESERVATION AND PROCESSING

Commercial Cold Storage

In the past, some eggs produced in the United States were placed in commercial cold storage during periods of higher production. Eggs were stored at 29° to 32°F (−1.5° to 0°C), which is just above their freezing point. Only eggs of original high quality were stored. These eggs remained in desirable condition when the storage room was well controlled as to humidity (85 to 90 percent), circulation of air, and freedom from objectionable odors. A controlled atmosphere of carbon dioxide or ozone was advantageous in maintaining quality. Eggs stored under these conditions could be maintained at Grade A quality for as long as six months. However, extended commercial cold storage is rarely used today since modern breeding and flock management have virtually eliminated seasonal differences in production [1].

Processed Egg Products

Egg breaking, separation, and pasteurization in preparation for freezing or drying are usually done by egg-processing plants. After washing and candling, the eggs go to egg-breaking machines. Completely automated equipment processes the eggs, removing them from filler flats, washing and sanitizing the outside shells, and breaking and separating the eggs into white, yolks, and mixture of white and yolk. The liquid egg product is then filtered and chilled before further processing. Scrupulous cleanliness must be maintained throughout the process and contamination from the introduction of unwholesome eggs into the whole egg mass must be avoided. All egg products are monitored for pathogenic organisms, and tests for salmonellae are made regularly by the egg products industry and the USDA. Only products negative for salmonellae organisms can be sold.

Pasteurized. Pasteurization is required by the federal government for all processed eggs whether frozen, dried, or liquid to ensure freedom from pathogenic microorganisms. However, eggs must be pasteurized in such a way that while bacteria are destroyed, the functional properties (whipping and baking performances) are not damaged [17].

The USDA regulates the minimum temperature and holding time for the pasteurization of egg products. The pasteurization of liquid whole egg involves heat treatment at 140°F (60°C) for not less than 3 1/2 minutes. Whole egg blends must be heated to a slightly higher temperature. Egg white proteins cannot tolerate the temperatures usually used to pasteurize whole eggs; they become denatured, with consequent decreases in foaming power. Increasing the acidity of the egg whites before pasteurization seems to protect the proteins from damage by heat. The pasteurization of egg whites without the addition of chemicals is done at 134°F (57°C) for 3 1/2 minutes or 132°F for 6.2 minutes. Plain egg yolks are pasteurized at 140°F (60°C) for 6.2 minutes or 142°F for 3.5 minutes. The pasteurization temperatures for egg yolks with sugar or with salt added are slightly different [6].

Frozen. The functional properties of raw egg whites are not altered by freezing and thawing. However, frozen egg yolks become viscous and gummy on thawing unless they are mixed with sugar, salt, or syrup before freezing (see Chapter 30 for directions on freezing eggs at home). It has been suggested that the freezing process destabilizes the surface of the tiny lipid-protein particles (lipoproteins) in egg yolk. The fragments that are liberated then aggregate on thawing to form a mesh-type structure or gel [18]. Whole mixed eggs are often frozen without added salt or sugar; however, because of the presence of the yolk, they probably retain their culinary qualities better when a stabilizer is added. Cooked egg white is not stable to freezing and thawing. The gel structure of the coagulated protein is damaged by ice crystal formation. **Syneresis** occurs on thawing.

syneresis separation or "weeping" of liquid from a gel

Egg-processing firms design and produce several specialty egg products, many of which are frozen. Hard-cooked, chopped and peeled eggs are used for salad bars. Frozen or refrigerated hard-cooked egg rolls or *long eggs* offer the advantage of providing consistently sized sliced eggs for salad garnishes. To make these long eggs, albumen is cooked around a center core of egg yolk that may be approximately 10 inches in length, thus the name. Frozen, precooked products such as egg patties, fried eggs, crepes, omelets, French toast, quiche, and egg breakfast sandwiches also are available in grocery stores and for foodservice use.

Dried. Drying is a satisfactory method for preserving eggs, either whole or as separated yolks or whites. Spray-dried egg whites and egg yolks have long shelf lives, and are used in many food product formulations. To retain their func-

Maillard reaction a special type of browning reaction involving a combination of proteins and sugars as a first step; it may occur in relatively dry foods in long storage as well as in foods heated to high temperatures

tional properties, good color, and flavor, and to help control the **Maillard reaction** during storage, dried whites require treatment to remove the last traces of glucose. Dried eggs keep best if the initial moisture content is low and if they are kept in a tightly sealed container. Low storage temperatures are also important in maintaining the quality of the dried products.

Dried eggs can be reconstituted before use, or they can be sifted with dry ingredients and extra liquid can be added later to the recipe. General directions for use are to sift prior to measuring and to place lightly in a measuring cup or spoon before leveling off the top with a spatula or straight edge. For reconstitution, dried egg should be sprinkled over the surface of lukewarm water, stirred to moisten, and then beaten until smooth. Reconstituted dried whites are beaten very stiff for most if not all uses. Dried egg whites are commonly found in angel food cake mixes.

Liquid. Liquid eggs, broken out of the shell, are available to foodservice operators and food processors, as whole eggs, egg whites, egg yolks, or blended egg products such as scrambled egg mix. When these eggs are pasteurized, any *Salmonella* or other pathogenic organisms that may be present are destroyed, but the product is not sterile. Some microorganisms capable of causing postpasteurization spoilage are still present. Consequently, the shelf life of pasteurized, refrigerated liquid eggs is limited. Shelf lives of 12 days at 36°F (2°C) and 5 days at 48°F (9°C) have been reported. An ultrapasteurization process, with heating at temperatures up to 154°F (68°C) and subsequent aseptic packaging, has been developed for homogenized liquid whole eggs [10]. These products must be refrigerated but have an extended shelf life of 6 to 7 weeks.

Liquid refrigerated egg products offer advantages for use in foodservice operations and food-processing facilities. They may be easily poured, the need for thawing is eliminated, functional properties and quality are maintained, there is no need to dispose of egg shells, and they are pasteurized. Furthermore, quantity foodservice operations would not be able to serve menu items such as scrambled eggs without the use of pasteurized egg products because food safety regulations prohibit the pooling of shell eggs in quantity.

EGGS IN FOOD PREPARATION

Few ingredients in food preparation are as useful in so many different ways as eggs. Used alone or in combination with other foods, eggs may become the major protein dish for a meal. Their color, **viscosity**, emulsifying ability, and coagulability, as well as flavor, make it possible for them to play a variety of roles in cookery processes.

viscosity resistance to flow as indicated in a thickened consistency

The presence in the yolk of lipoproteins makes the egg yolk especially valuable as an emulsifying agent. (Eggs as emulsifiers are discussed in Chapter 10.) The **surface activity** of the proteins of egg white, in particular, also makes the egg useful in the production of films that hold air and thus create a foam. The leavening of a variety of food mixtures results from this characteristic. An egg white foam used in certain candies also improves the texture by controlling crystallization of sugar.

surface activity the lowering of the surface tension of a liquid because of agents that tend to concentrate at the surface

The ability of egg proteins to coagulate when heated, resulting in thickening or **gel** formation, contributes much to the characteristic properties of such dishes as custards, puddings, and various sauces. Coagulation of egg protein, along with the viscosity of the uncooked egg, is the basis for the use of egg as a

gel a colloidal dispersion that shows some rigidity or moldability

binding agent and as a coating to hold crumbs together for crust formation on breaded foods. Rigidity of cell walls and of crusts in numerous doughs and batters is increased by coagulation of egg.

Use of the egg as a clarifying agent is also dependent on the coagulation of egg proteins. In addition, most dishes to which eggs are added are improved in color and flavor by their inclusion in the mixture.

Heat Coagulation of Egg Proteins

Both egg white and yolk proteins coagulate when heated and, as previously noted, can therefore be used for thickening or gel formation. Upon heating, the egg proteins are **denatured** and then gradually aggregate to form a three-dimensional gel network. The network is stabilized by cross-bonds that include **disulfide linkages** and hydrogen bonding [21].

denaturation the unfolding of protein chains to produce a more random arrangement

disulfide linkages bonding through two sulfur atoms $(-S-S-)$

Egg functions best as a thickener when it is beaten only enough to blend the egg mass smoothly. Beating to the extent of incorporating a considerable amount of air results in the floating of egg foam on the surface of the mixture to be thickened. The following factors affect the heat coagulation of egg proteins.

Concentration and Part of Egg Used. The temperature at which egg proteins coagulate and the time required for coagulation depend in part on the proportion of egg in any mixture. Coagulation does not occur instantaneously, but rather proceeds gradually. At a moderate rate of heating, undiluted egg white begins to coagulate and change from a clear mass to an opaque substance at about 140°F (60°C). The egg white gradually becomes completely opaque and more firm as the temperature is increased above 140°F (60°C). At 158°F (70°C), the coagulated mass is fairly firm.

Egg yolk proteins require a slightly higher temperature for coagulation than those of egg white. Because little color change occurs in egg yolk at the beginning of coagulation, the exact temperature at which thickening starts is more difficult to judge than is the case with egg white. Egg white loses its transparency and becomes opaque white on coagulation. The beginning of coagulation and the thickening of undiluted egg yolk probably occur at about 149°F (65°C). At approximately 158°F (70°C), the yolk loses its fluidity.

The texture of coagulated egg yolk, when cooked intact, is crumbly and mealy but solid. When the yolk membrane is ruptured and the stirred yolk is heated; however, the texture of the resulting gel is firm and rubbery. This difference in texture of intact and stirred egg yolk may result from changes that occur in the intricate microstructure of egg yolk with stirring. The tiny discrete granules of the intact yolk may form a highly cross-linked protein network when disrupted [37]. To achieve complete coagulation, whole egg must be heated to the temperature required for yolk protein coagulation, as whole egg includes the yolk.

Dilution of egg increases the temperature at which coagulation occurs. Egg diluted with 1 cup of milk coagulates at approximately 176°F (80°C), although the exact temperature varies with the rate of heating and the presence or absence of other substances in the dispersion.

Time and Temperature. The rate of coagulation and the amount of coagulum formed in a definite time increase with increasing temperature. The character of the coagulum formed when egg white is heated at high temperatures is firm, even tough, as compared with the soft, tender, more evenly coagulated product obtained when coagulation takes place at lower temperatures.

The toughness and greater shrinkage of the protein coagulated at a high temperature are the basis for the recommended use of low or moderate temperatures for egg cookery. The temperatures used do not need to be as low as 158°F (70°C), although that temperature, maintained for a sufficient length of time, eventually brings about complete coagulation of egg proteins. If eggs are cooked in water, the water should not boil. Water at a temperature of about 185°F (85°C) will produce a texture that is tender, yet firm. Coagulation at this temperature takes place in a noticeably shorter time than is required at 158°F (70°C).

For an omelet cooked in a skillet over direct heat, the heat should be kept low so that the mass cooks slowly and can be heated uniformly throughout without toughening the bottom layers. The coagulation of a puffy omelet may be finished in a moderate oven. Oven temperatures from 300° to 350°F (149° to 177°C) have been found to be satisfactory for cooking eggs and egg dishes, although there are indications that somewhat higher temperatures are also satisfactory if time is carefully controlled. Placing egg dishes in a pan of water when baking them in the oven helps to protect the egg product from becoming overcooked.

Effect of Rate of Heating.   Rapidly heated egg mixtures such as custards coagulate at a higher temperature than similar mixtures that are slowly heated. The fact that the coagulation temperature with rapid heating is very close to the curdling temperature means that a rapidly cooked custard is more likely to curdle than one that is slowly heated. A slowly heated custard can, nevertheless, curdle if it is heated to too high a temperature.

Effect of Added Substances.   Egg mixtures containing sugar require a higher temperature for coagulation than mixtures containing no sugar. The addition of sugar increases the heat stability of the proteins.

Slightly acid egg mixtures, such as those with added dates or raisins, omelets made with tomato or orange juice, and Hollandaise sauce containing lemon juice, appear to coagulate more rapidly, at a somewhat lower temperature. The coagulum formed is also more firm than that of mixtures with somewhat less acidity. The hardness and cohesiveness of egg white gels have been reported to be minimal at pH 6 and increased as the pH was either decreased to 5 or increased to 9 [36]. Too much acid in egg mixtures may cause curdling. Certain salts, such as chlorides, phosphates, sulfates, and lactates, aid in gel formation in cooked egg mixtures.

Coagulation by Mechanical Beating

As egg whites are beaten, they first become foamy and then form soft moist peaks. With additional beating, the peaks become stiffer, and eventually, with overbeating, the foam becomes dry and may appear to be **flocculated** (Figure 24-10).

flocculated separated into small woolly or fluffy masses

Part of the protein in the thin films surrounding each of the air bubbles or cells that comprise the structure of a beaten egg white foam is coagulated in the beating process. This provides some rigidity and stabilizes the foam. If the protein becomes overcoagulated, however, the foam takes on a dry, lumpy appearance because of loss of flexibility in the films and the breaking of many air cells. Undesirable effects on both foam volume and stability can be expected when

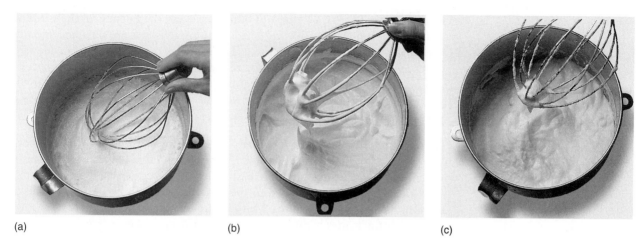

(a)   (b)   (c)

Figure 24-10
(a) Eggs properly whipped to soft peaks; (b) eggs properly whipped to stiff peaks; (c) spongy, overwhipped eggs. (Source: Reference 19)

whites are overbeaten. The foam is brittle and inelastic, and large amounts of liquid drain from it on standing. It does not blend well with other food ingredients.

For most uses in food preparation, including the making of soufflés, soft meringues, and puffy omelets and the beating of egg whites with sugar for angel food cakes, egg whites should be beaten to form moderately stiff peaks. The tips should fall over when the beater is withdrawn from the beaten whites. The foam should retain a shiny, smooth surface, and the mass should flow very slowly if the bowl is partially inverted. Air cells should be quite fine and of even size. Reconstituted dried egg whites, such as those in angel food cake mixes using a two-stage mixing method, are beaten to a very stiff stage, as indicated in the package directions.

Whole eggs can be beaten much stiffer than might be expected if beating is continued for a long enough time. As a result of the presence of the fat from the yolk, which retards foam formation, there is little danger of overbeating the whole egg.

Egg yolks increase slightly in volume when beaten. They change to a pale lemon color as air is incorporated and the mass may become thick and full of fine cells. It is difficult if not impossible to beat a small quantity of egg yolk thoroughly unless a small dish of narrow diameter and a small egg beater are used.

Because beaten eggs, particularly egg whites, are used in so many cooked dishes, they require proper handling to produce stable foams and retain air cells. Several factors affect the whipping quality of eggs.

Thin and Thick Whites. The foam produced from the beating of thin whites is more fluffy and has less body than the foam created from thick, viscous whites. Thick whites seem to produce a more stable foam even though thin whites may initially beat to a larger volume. The volume of cooked products, such as angel food cake and meringues, is greater when thick whites are used rather than thin whites.

Temperature. Eggs at room temperature whip more easily, quickly, and to a larger volume than eggs at refrigerator temperature. This may be due to the lower **surface tension** of the eggs at room temperature.

surface tension the tension or force at the surface of a liquid that produces a resistance to spreading or dispersing due to the attraction of the liquid molecules for each other

Type of Beater Used. The type of beater used and the fineness of the wires or blades of the beater can affect the size of the air cells that are obtained and the ease with which the eggs are beaten. Thick blades or wires do not divide egg whites as easily as fine wires, and the resulting air cells are therefore larger. All cells become smaller with longer beating regardless of the type of beater used. Egg whisks sometimes give a larger volume of beaten egg mass than rotary types of beaters, but the cells are also larger.

Type of Container in Which Eggs are Beaten. Bowls with small rounded bottoms and sloping sides are preferable to bowls with large flat bottoms because, in the former, the beater can more easily pick up the egg mass. The size of the bowl must obviously be adapted to the amount of egg to be beaten. If whisks are used for beating egg whites, a large plate or platter is preferable to a bowl for holding the whites because of the over-and-over strokes that are used.

Effect of Added Substances

Fat. Fat, in the form of refined cottonseed oil, has been shown to interfere with whipping when present to the extent of 0.5 percent or more. The presence of small amounts of yolk in egg white greatly retards foam formation. This effect is thought to be the result of the fat, probably the lipoproteins, in the egg yolk, which may form a complex with proteins in the white. The directions on packages of angel food cake mix indicate that plastic bowls should not be used for mixing because of the difficulty in removing all fat from the surface of the plastic.

Salt. The addition of a small amount of salt to egg whites (1 gram salt to 40 grams egg white) has been reported to decrease the volume and stability of the foam and to increase the whipping time [12]. Egg white foams are less elastic when they are beaten with salt than when no salt is added.

Acid. The addition of acid or acid salts to egg white decreases the alkalinity of the white and increases the stability of the egg white foam. The whipping time is increased. A stiff foam and a large foam volume result from addition of acid before or shortly after foaming has started. **Cream of tartar** is frequently added to egg whites before beating to increase the stability of the foam.

cream of tartar potassium acid tartrate, the partial salt of tartaric acid, an organic acid

Sugar. Sugar retards the denaturation and coagulation of egg proteins and increases the beating time required to attain maximum volume. It is therefore important to not add sugar to egg whites before beating is started, but rather very gradually, possibly 1 to 2 tablespoons at a time, after foaming first occurs. In fact, it is probably best, in the preparation of any sugar-containing egg white foam, to beat the whites to soft peaks before adding sugar, with intermittent beating between the additions of sugar. Otherwise, the beating time is considerably prolonged. The presence of sugar in an egg white foam stabilizes the foam as it forms, greatly decreasing the possibility of overbeating. The texture of the foam is also very fine, with many small air cells, and the surface has a shiny, satiny appearance.

Specific Methods of Egg Preparation

Poached Eggs. Poaching consists of cooking the edible portion of an egg in hot water, milk, cream, or other liquids. To guard against scorching when eggs are poached in milk or cream, the dish should be suspended over hot water. For adequate coagulation of egg proteins, the liquid in which the eggs are poached need not approach the boiling point. However, a temperature of about 185°F (85°C) will still maintain the desirable tender quality of the coagulated egg while requiring less time than when the egg is poached at 158° to 167°F (70° to 75°C). Because the addition of cold eggs to hot liquid immediately lowers the temperature of the liquid, it is possible to have the temperature of the liquid at the boiling point when the eggs are added. The heat can then be regulated to keep the liquid at a simmering temperature of about 185°F (85°C). If the water is not hot enough when the egg is added, the egg white will spread throughout the liquid rather than set quickly and hold its original shape.

The liquid in the pan used for poaching should be deep enough to cover the eggs in order that a film of coagulated white may form over the yolk. Salt and acid added to the cooking water are both aids in coagulation but are not necessary. Two teaspoons of vinegar and 1/2 to 1 teaspoon of salt per pint of water can be effective. Eggs poached in salted water are more opaque white and less shiny than eggs poached in unsalted water. They may also appear puckered or ruffled as they do when poached in boiling water. The time required for coagulation depends on the temperature of the water, but at a water temperature of 185°F (85°C), the time required is 5 to 8 minutes. The longer time will, of course, produce a greater degree of coagulation.

There is a wide range of individual preference regarding the desirable characteristics of poached eggs. Many people enjoy a poached egg that is rounded, with a film of coagulated white covering the yolk. The white is completely coagulated but jellylike and tender (Figure 24-5), and the yolk is thick enough to resist flowing. For safety, as discussed earlier in the chapter, the yolk should be thickened and not runny.

The freshness of eggs and thickness of whites have considerable influence on the poached product. For example, eggs with thin whites tend to spread out in thin layers and may fragment into pieces when placed in the hot liquid. The technique of adding the egg to the water is also important to the quality of the cooked egg. It is usually desirable to remove the egg from the shell and place it in a small flat dish from which it can easily and quickly be slipped into the poaching water which has been brought just to a boil, and then the heat is turned off.

Cooked in the Shell. Eggs may be cooked in the shell to varying degrees of firmness. The usual objective, in any case, is to produce a tender coagulated white and a yolk that is at least thickened and not runny. The temperature of the yolk should be at least 160°F (71°C) to destroy any salmonellae organisms that may be present. Water maintained at a boiling temperature for the entire cooking period has a definite toughening effect on the white. Either of the following two methods can be used to ensure satisfactory tenderness.

Method I. Place eggs in a single layer in a saucepan and add water until the eggs are covered. Cover and bring just to boiling, then turn off heat. For hard-cooked eggs allow the eggs to remain in the water for 15 minutes for large eggs. For soft-cooked eggs let stand in the hot water for 4 to 5 minutes. At the end of the designated time for either hard- or soft-cooked eggs, place the eggs in ice water until cool enough to handle [2].

Method II. Add eggs to water at a simmering but not boiling temperature of about 185°F (85°C). Maintain this temperature for at least 7 minutes for hard-cooked eggs.

Eggs prepared for those who are pregnant, elderly, very young, or ill should be thoroughly cooked. Foodservice operations serving these groups can use pasteurized egg products safely without having to thoroughly cook them.

The white of hard-cooked eggs should be firmly coagulated, yet tender. The yolk should be dry and mealy. If the yolk is waxy, it is not sufficiently cooked. The surface of the yolk should be yellow, with no dark green deposit.

One group of researchers [14] compared hard-cooked eggs prepared by two different methods.

Method I. Place the eggs in cold water in a covered pan, bring the water to boiling, remove the pan from the heat, and hold for 25 minutes.

Method II. Carefully place the eggs in boiling water, reduce the heat, and simmer (at 185°F or 85°C) eggs for 18 minutes.

In both methods, the eggs were submerged in cold running water for 5 minutes at the end of the cooking period. The researchers reported that method II produced eggs that were easier to peel and rated higher in all criteria than those prepared by starting with cold water. In another study, boiling for 20 minutes produced hard-cooked eggs that were firmer and exhibited stronger egg odor and more off-flavors than simmering or steaming methods of cooking [30].

Cooling hard-cooked eggs in cold water immediately after cooking facilitates the removal of the shell. Even so, very fresh eggs (less than 48 hours old) are difficult to peel without considerable white adhering to the shell. The rapid cooling of cooked eggs also aids in the prevention of a dark green deposit, ferrous sulfide (FeS), which tends to form on the outside of the coagulated yolk and detracts from its appearance. Most of the iron in an egg is present in the yolk. Sulfur occurs in about equal amounts in yolk and white, but the sulfur compounds in the white are more labile to heat than those in the yolk. Hydrogen sulfide (H_2S) is therefore easily formed from the sulfur compounds in the white during prolonged heating and forms even more readily when the pH of the egg is markedly alkaline, as in an older egg. Reaction of the iron in the yolk with the hydrogen sulfide from the white produces the greenish ferrous sulfide deposit.

Ferrous sulfide forms very slowly until the yolk reaches about 158°F (70°C) and seldom occurs in fresh eggs cooked 30 minutes at 185°F (85°C). The green color tends to form less in eggs that are cooled rapidly, because the hydrogen sulfide gas is drawn to the lowered pressure at the surface of the cooling egg and thus combines less readily with iron at the surface of the yolk. However, if an egg is cooked 30 minutes in boiling water, the ferrous sulfide will probably form regardless of cooling. Also, in older eggs that are very alkaline, the green color may be produced despite the precautions taken during cooking [3].

In summary, fresh eggs of high quality should be selected for the preparation of hard-cooked eggs. The temperature of the water in which the eggs are cooked should be maintained below the boiling point, and the time of cooking should be no longer than is required to coagulate both the white and the yolk. The eggs should be cooled as quickly as possible after cooking.

Fried Eggs. Because of the difficulty in controlling the temperature of both the fat and the pan, fried eggs can often be somewhat tough, and for this reason are among the preparations requiring the greatest skill. If excess fat is used during the frying of eggs or if the hot fat is dipped with a spoon and poured over the top surface of the eggs as they cook, the eggs may be too greasy to suit many people.

One suggested method of preparation is to use only enough fat to prevent the eggs from sticking to the pan but enough to give the desired flavor. The pan should be sufficiently hot to coagulate the egg white, but not hot enough to toughen it or to decompose the fat. A cover on the pan may be used to provide steam, which cooks the top surface of the egg. A small amount of water may be added to the pan just before covering. The water not only furnishes more steam but tends to prevent toughening or hardening of the edges of the eggs. If the pan is not covered, the egg should be turned over midway during cooking to cook the yolk sufficiently to destroy pathogens that might be present in the egg (Figure 24-11). If the underside of a fried egg is brown and the edges crisp and frilled, the pan and fat were probably too hot, unless, as is true for some people, crispness in a fried egg is preferred.

Scrambled Eggs.   The whites and yolks are mixed together in the preparation of scrambled eggs. If they are thoroughly mixed, the product has a uniform yellow color. Some people like the marbled effect that is produced by mixing yolks and whites only slightly. About 1 tablespoon of milk is added per egg, with salt and pepper. The mixture is then poured into a warm skillet containing a small amount of melted butter or margarine. As the mixture begins to set under moderate heat, an inverted pancake turner may be gently drawn across the bottom, forming large soft curds.

Because large numbers of broken-out eggs should not be pooled, for safety reasons, frozen or refrigerated pasteurized scrambled egg mixes are available. Scrambled eggs can be dressed up for lunch or supper by combining them with other ingredients (Figure 24-12).

Shirred Eggs.   Shirred eggs are cooked and served in the same dish. The dish is coated with butter or margarine, the eggs are broken into it, and the dish is

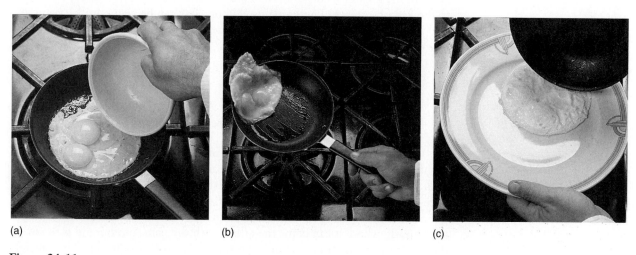

(a)   (b)   (c)

Figure 24-11
(a) Pouring eggs into a nonstick sauté pan; (b) eggs are flipped with a quick movement of the wrist; (c) eggs are slid out onto a plate.
(Source: Reference 19)

set directly on the range until the whites are coagulated. The dish is then transferred to a moderate oven to finish cooking. Care must be taken to not overcook and thus toughen shirred eggs.

Omelets.   The two basic types of omelets are plain or French, and foamy or puffy. The puffy omelet has a more spongy texture than the French omelet because of the greater incorporation of air. Small amounts of liquid may be added to the French omelet. The liquid used in omelets can be water, milk, cream, or acid juices such as tomato and orange. Omelets can be filled with cheese, a mixture of vegetables, or fruits (Figure 24-13).

Proportions for a French Omelet

4 eggs	1/2 tsp (3 g) salt
4 Tbsp (59 mL) liquid	fg pepper

Whole eggs are beaten enough to blend white and yolk, then diluted slightly with liquid and seasoned. The mixture is cooked in a lightly greased pan until it is coagulated, after which the omelet is folded (Figure 24-14). To produce more rapid coagulation, a spatula can be used to carefully lift the edges of the egg mass as it coagulates, thus allowing the liquid portion on top to flow underneath, where it can come in contact with the pan. Another aid is to cover the pan to furnish steam to cook the top surface of the omelet. The omelet should be cooked slowly, keeping the heat low to avoid toughening of the coagulated eggs. The omelet should be cooked uniformly throughout.

Figure 24-13
A variety of fillings can be used in a plain omelet. (Courtesy of the American Egg Board)

(a)

(b)

(c)

(d)

Figure 24-14
The preparation of a folded omelet is shown here. It is similar to a French omelet, except the fillings are added before the omelet is folded.
(a) Lifting the egg from the pan's edges to allow raw egg under the cooked eggs; (b) adding filling; (c) folding the omelet; (d) Placing omelet onto a plate. (Source: Reference 19)

Proportions for a Puffy Omelet

4 eggs	1/2 tsp (3 g) salt
2 to 4 Tbsp (30 to 59 mL) liquid	fg pepper
1/8 tsp cream of tartar	

The cream of tartar is added to the egg whites, which are beaten until moderately stiff. The liquid, salt, and pepper are added to the egg yolks, and the mixture is beaten until it is lemon colored and so thick that it piles. The beaten yolk mixture is folded into the beaten whites carefully to blend the mass evenly and yet avoid too much loss of air.

The lightly greased pan in which the omelet is cooked should be hot enough to start coagulation, but not hot enough to toughen the coagulated layer in contact with the pan or to brown it excessively. The omelet is cooked slowly until it is light brown underneath.

Several methods can be used to coagulate the top of the foamy omelet.

Method I. Placing a cover on the pan during part of the cooking period forms steam, which cooks the top layer of egg. The cover must not stick to the omelet, as the omelet is likely to collapse when the cover is removed. This method involves some risk, as a covered pan is hotter than an open pan and overheating may cause the omelet to collapse. If the cover is lifted occasionally and the omelet is cooked successfully by this method, the omelet is usually quite tender and moist, partly because it cooks in less time and partly because less evaporation occurs.

Method II. When the mass is coagulated to within 1/4 to 1/3 inch of the top, the omelet pan can be placed in a moderate oven to dry the top (Figure 24-15).

Method III. Following method I, the pan can be held in a broiler to dry the top. This method must be used with caution, as a broiler flame can easily overheat the mass and cause it to collapse.

Method IV. The omelet can be cooked in an oven at 300° to 350°F (149° to 177°C) for the entire time.

Crêpes. Crêpes are thin, tender pancakes containing a relatively high proportion of egg. They can be filled with a variety of items, including fish, meats, poultry, eggs, cheese, vegetables, and fruits (Figure 24-16). Crêpes can also be served with sweet, dessert-type fillings.

The thin crêpe batter is cooked on medium heat in a seasoned slope-sided omelet or crêpe pan. Enough batter is poured in to cover the bottom of the pan; then the pan is tipped or tilted to allow the batter to move quickly over the bottom. Any excess batter is poured off. The crêpe is cooked until it is lightly browned on the bottom and dry on the top.

Soufflés. The word *soufflé* is French for *puff*. A soufflé is thus a dish that puffs up spectacularly in the oven. Soufflés are similar to foamy omelets, except that they have a thick, white sauce base and contain additional ingredients such as grated cheese, vegetable pulp, or ground meats. Dessert soufflés are sweet and may contain lemon, strawberry, and chocolate.

In the preparation of a soufflé, egg yolks are added to the thick white sauce base. Then cheese or other ingredients are added. A stiffly beaten egg white

Cook the omelet slowly until it is lightly browned on the bottom.

After drying the top of the omelet in a moderate oven, test it for doneness by inserting a spatula in the center. The spatula should come out clean.

Make a shallow crease across the middle of the omelet.

Fold the omelet over and carefully transfer it to a serving platter.

Figure 24-15
Preparation of a puffy omelet (Courtesy of the Poultry and Egg National Board)

foam is folded into the white sauce base. The high proportion of egg in the soufflé provides structure as the egg proteins coagulate, and basic principles of egg cookery require moderate cooking temperatures. Soufflés are usually baked, although they can be steamed. When they are baked, the dish containing the soufflé mixture should be placed in a pan of hot water to protect against excessive heating. Soufflés will shrink after removal from the oven and should be served immediately.

Custards. A true custard consists only of eggs, milk, sugar, and flavoring. No starchy agent is added. Custards are of two types: the stirred or soft custard, which is given a creamy consistency by being stirred while it is cooking; and the

Figure 24-16
*Chopped hard-cooked eggs and as-
paragus spears provide the filling for
these delicious crepes, which are
topped with a cheese sauce.* (Courtesy
of the American Egg Board)

baked custard, which is allowed to coagulate without stirring, thereby producing a gel. There must be enough egg in the baked custard to produce a firm
mass when cooked, particularly if the custard is to be unmolded when served.
The proportion of egg to milk is often the same for baked and stirred custards;
however, less egg is used in stirred custard when a thin consistency is desired.

Custard dishes can be served as simple egg desserts or can be elegant
dishes. Flan, popular in Mexican cuisine, is similar to baked custard. It is a custard baked over a layer of caramelized sugar. Flans are generally unmolded and
the caramelized sugar flows over the top for a delicious and beautiful dessert.
Crème brûlée is another type of custard that can be prepared either as a baked
or a stirred custard. Crème brûlée is a very rich custard generally composed of
egg yolks and heavy cream rather than whole eggs and milk, as in other baked
custards. This custard is generally topped with brown or white sugar that is either caramelized under a broiler or with a torch. A description of basic baked
and stirred custards follows.

Proportions for Custards

1 c (237 mL) milk	2 Tbsp (25 g) sugar
1 to 1 1/2 eggs or 2 to 3 yolks	1/4 tsp vanilla or 1/16 tsp nutmeg

(To measure 1/2 egg, mix together white and yolk of whole egg; then divide
into two equal portions by measuring 1 Tbsp at a time.)

Baked Custard.   Because the egg is used for thickening, it is beaten only
enough to blend the white and yolk well. Sugar can be added to the egg or dissolved in the milk. Milk is usually scalded before being added to the egg mix-

ture. Scalding hastens the cooking and helps retain a mild, sweet flavor, but it does not produce a smoother custard. Flavoring must be added when the mixture is prepared for cooking.

The custard cups should be placed in a pan of hot water as a protection against overheating, even though a moderate oven temperature may be used (about 350°F or 177°C). Custards placed in a pan of very hot water can be baked in a 400°F (204°C) oven for a much shorter time than in a 350°F oven. However, care must be exercised to remove the custard from the oven as soon as it is coagulated to avoid undesirable overcooking.

The baked custard is done when the tip of a knife inserted halfway between the center and outside comes out clean (Figure 24-17). When a custard is overcooked, some clear liquid separates from the gel structure, that is, syneresis occurs. In addition, the custard may appear porous and contain holes, especially on the outer surfaces, when it is unmolded. The top surface may be concave and browned. In an overcooked custard, the egg proteins that form the mesh-like gel structure apparently shrink and squeeze out some of the liquid that was held in the mesh.

Soft or Stirred Custard. The mixture of egg, milk, and sugar is prepared in the same manner as for baked custard. The vanilla, because of its volatility, is added after the other ingredients are cooked. Custards that are cooked more slowly coagulate more completely at a lower temperature than custards that are cooked rapidly. There is less danger of curdling and both consistency and flavor are better in stirred custards cooked relatively slowly. The total cooking time, in a double boiler, should be 12 to 15 minutes, heating more rapidly at first and then more slowly while stirring thoroughly and rapidly during the entire process.

It is best to keep the water in the lower part of the double boiler under the boiling point, particularly after the custard becomes hot.

Constant stirring is necessary to prevent lumping. Stirring separates the coagulated particles, resulting in a creamy consistency regardless of the amount of egg used. The tendency is to cook a soft custard until it appears as thick as is desired, but caution should be exercised. The custard will be thicker when it is cold. When the custard coats the spoon well, it should be removed from the heat and cooled immediately by either pouring it into a cold dish or suspending it, in the pan used for cooking, in cold water.

Overheating a stirred custard results in curdling. A very slightly curdled custard may be improved if it is beaten with a rotary beater, but this treatment is of no value for excessively curdled custards. In an overcooked custard, the coagulated proteins shrink and separate out from the more liquid portion of the mixture, giving the appearance of curds. Also, the flavor of an overcooked custard tends to be strong and sulfury.

A stirred custard can be used to create some interesting and delicious desserts. For example, hard meringue shells can be filled with crushed or whole sweetened strawberries or other fruit and the custard poured over the fruit. This can then be crowned with a bit of whipped topping. Or, the custard can be flavored with caramelized sugar and poured into individual serving dishes. Small soft meringues that have been previously baked can be placed on top of the custard.

Meringues. Meringues are of two types: the soft meringue used for pies and puddings, and the hard meringue generally used as a crisp dessert base or as a cookie.

Figure 24-17

(a) A baked custard is done when the tip of the knife, inserted into the custard about halfway between the center and the outside, comes out clean. (Courtesy of Chris Meister)

(a)

(b) Unmolded baked custards may be served with a fruit sauce. (Courtesy of the Poultry and Egg National Board)

(b)

(c) This chocolate sponge custard topped with whipped cream and chocolate curls is not only delicious, but pleasing to the eyes as well. (Courtesy of the American Egg Board, www.aeb.org.)

(c)

Proportions for Soft Meringues

1 egg white	1/16 tsp cream of tartar (optional)
2 Tbsp (25 g) sugar	1/8 tsp flavoring (if desired)

To produce a soft meringue that is fine textured, tender, cuts easily without tearing, and shows neither syneresis nor **beading** on top of the baked meringue, each of the following items should be considered carefully.

1. When the egg whites are partially beaten (possibly to a soft foam), sugar is gradually added, 1/2 to 1 tablespoon at a time, and the beating is continued until the mixture is stiff but with soft peaks that still tip over.
2. The meringue should be placed on a *hot* filling.
3. The meringue should be baked at 350°F (177°C) for 12 to 15 minutes, depending on the depth of the meringue.

beading the appearance of tiny droplets of syrup on the surface of a baked meringue as it stands

Heating must be sufficient throughout the soft meringue to destroy any *Salmonella* organisms that may be present in the eggs. Meringues baked at moderate oven temperatures may be slightly sticky, as compared with those baked at high oven temperatures, but the moderate temperature produces an attractive, evenly browned product that is safe to eat. Two particular problems that may be encountered in making soft meringues are weeping, or leaking of liquid from the bottom of the meringue, and beading [11, 13]. Weeping or syneresis apparently results from undercooking the meringue. It can also occur as a result of underbeating the egg whites. Placing the meringue on a hot filling helps to achieve complete coagulation of the egg proteins. Beading is usually attributed to overcooking or overcoagulation of the egg white proteins. It can also result from a failure to dissolve the sugar sufficiently when it is beaten into the meringue.

Proportions for Hard Meringues

1 egg white	1/16 tsp cream of tartar
1/4 c (50 g) sugar	fg salt
1/8 tsp vanilla	

In the preparation of hard meringues, cream of tartar is added to the egg white, which is beaten until a soft foam begins to form. Flavoring may be added at this point. Sugar is added gradually and beating continued until the mass is very stiff. Portions of the meringue are dropped onto a baking sheet, which may be covered with heavy paper, and shaped into small shells. Meringues are baked at a low oven temperature (about 250°F or 121°C) for 50 to 60 minutes, depending on the size of the meringues, and then left in the oven with the heat turned off for another hour.

If a temperature lower than 250°F (121°C) can be maintained for a longer time, the effect is one of drying instead of baking the meringue and produces even better results. Well-insulated ovens that hold the heat for several hours can be preheated, and then turned off entirely.

Desirable hard meringues are crisp, tender, and white in appearance. It is important that they do not show gumminess or stickiness, which results from underbaking. This may occur either from an oven temperature that is too high or a baking time that is too short. When the baking temperature is too high, the meringues are browned on the outside before the interior is dry enough, and the residual moisture produces stickiness.

Microwave Cooking.   One thing that the microwave oven does *not* do successfully is cook an egg in its shell. Steam builds up inside the egg and it bursts. However, eggs can be satisfactorily cooked in several other ways by microwaves. They can be poached in liquid. The liquid is first brought to a boil in a custard cup. Then the broken-out egg is added and cooked for a short time on medium power. The egg should be cooked until the white is opaque but not set. During a standing period of 2 to 3 minutes, the cooking is completed. Broken-out eggs can also be cooked in individual custard cups without liquid, as shirred eggs are cooked. The yolk membrane should be first pierced with a toothpick to help prevent bursting from steam pent up during cooking.

Because the egg yolk contains more fat than the egg white, it attracts more energy and cooks faster. If an egg is microwaved until the white is completely coagulated, the yolk may toughen.

Scrambled eggs are prepared for the microwave by mixing melted butter, eggs, and milk and cooking on high power for about half the cooking time before breaking up the set parts and pushing them to the center of the dish. The eggs are stirred once or twice more while the cooking is completed. Again, standing time after cooking is important to finish the cooking without toughening the eggs. Scrambled eggs prepared by microwaves are fluffier and have more volume than conventionally scrambled eggs. Omelets, including fluffy omelets, can also be prepared in the microwave oven.

For fried eggs, a browning dish is necessary. The browning dish is preheated on high, and then the eggs are added. The browning dish absorbs enough energy and produces a hot enough surface to brown the eggs lightly. Egg dishes such as quiche can also be prepared using microwaves.

In hospital foodservice, microwaves are often used to reheat food at the point of serving; however, some questions have been raised concerning the lack of uniformity in heating, which results in lack of confidence in the ability of this heating process to sufficiently destroy microorganisms. It has been found, when reheating scrambled eggs in a microwave oven under actual foodservice operating conditions, that temperature variability in the eggs could be controlled within 9°F (5°C) if voltage to the oven and temperature of the food before heating were rigidly controlled [7]. Careful attention to these factors that affect heating is necessary to ensure safety of the food for service to clients.

EGG SUBSTITUTES

The food industry has responded to the desire of some consumers to have a low-cholesterol egg product by marketing egg substitutes in both liquid and dry forms. Most of the available egg substitute products contain no egg yolk, but have a high concentration of egg white (over 80 percent). To provide yolklike properties to the egg white mixture, various ingredients are used. These include, in different products, corn oil and nonfat dry milk; soy protein isolate, soybean oil, and egg white solids; and calcium caseinate, nonfat dry milk, and corn oil. A few products on the market contain small amounts of egg yolk. Most of the egg substitutes are free or almost free of cholesterol and contain considerably less fat, and the fat is more unsaturated, than in whole egg.

When compared with fresh whole eggs, egg substitutes may have somewhat less desirable flavor, aroma, and overall acceptability [9]. Custards made from egg substitute products, however, have been reported to have less sag and spread than those made with whole egg. One study found in custards prepared with nonfat, 70 percent lactose-reduced milk, that egg substitutes produced less desirable custards as compared to those made with whole eggs [38]. Yellow cakes prepared with egg substitutes were higher in volume than those made with whole eggs, but were less desirable in flavor and overall acceptability.

CHAPTER SUMMARY

- Eggs function in several roles in food preparation because of the ability to emulsify, foam, coagulate, and clarify some liquids.

- The white and the yolk are very different in composition. Essentially all of the fat is found in the yolk; the white is higher in water. In general, the yolk has a higher nutrient density than the white.

- The major protein in the egg white is ovalbumin. Lipoproteins are the major proteins in the yolk. The lipoproteins are responsible for the emulsifying properties of egg yolks.

- The fatty materials in egg yolk include trigycerides, phospholipids, and cholesterol. The egg white has no cholesterol. The cholesterol content of the egg may be reduced by changing the diet of the laying hens or through processing of the egg.

- The predominant yellow pigment of the egg yolk is xanthophyll. Yellow carotenoid pigments also are present and may be converted into vitamin A in the body, however the color of the yolk is not a reliable indicator of the vitamin A content of the yolk.

- The egg shell is porous and allows exchange of gases and loss of moisture from the egg. Egg shells may be brown or white, depending on the breed of the chicken. The natural bloom on the outside of the egg is washed off during processing to clean the eggs. Eggs are lightly oiled prior to packaging to replace the natural bloom.

- The egg white consists of thin and thick portions that may be observed when a fresh egg is broken out onto a flat surface. Chalazae are two strands of thickened white that anchor the yolk in the center of the egg. The yolk is composed of tiny spheres of protein granules and oil droplets. No difference in nutritive value is noted between infertile and fertilized eggs.

- As eggs age the proportion of thin white increases, the chalazae disintegrate, the yolk absorbs water from the white, the air cell increases in size, and alkalinity increases.

- Consumers can gauge the freshness of eggs by the expiration or Julian date on the egg carton as well as by observing the appearance of the egg upon cracking.

- Candling is the method used to determine the interior quality of the eggs that go into trade channels. USDA grades for eggs are based on their candled appearance. Grade AA and A eggs have a large proportion of thick white that stands up around a firm high yolk. USDA grading services are available on a fee-for-service basis.

- The Egg Products Inspection Act of 1970 assures the consumer that only wholesome, unadulterated, and truthfully labeled egg products are marketed. Under this act, frozen and dried egg products must be pasteurized.

- Eggs are sorted into six weight classes. Size relative to cost per dozen is an important factor to consider. In addition, recipes are generally formulated on the basis of the large size. Adjustments in recipes can be made for different sizes of eggs.

- The FDA and FSIS share federal responsibility for egg safety. Since the mid 1980's, *Salmonella enteritidis* has been frequently implicated in foodborne illness. Unbroken shell eggs may contain this bacterium or the eggs may become infected as contamination on the shell exterior moves through the shell pores into the interior.

- In 2000, FDA finalized regulations to require safe food handling instructions on cartons and to specify refrigeration temperature during storage and sale. At warm temperatures, microorganisms can increase rapidly, which is why eggs should always be properly refrigerated. Methods of enhancing the safety of shell eggs include rapid cryogenic cooling during processing, pasteurization, and irradiation.

- Raw eggs should not be consumed. Pasteurized eggs should be used in recipes such as Caesar dressing. Eggs should be cooked slowly over moderate heat until the whites are completely coagulated and the yolks are firm. Casseroles and other dishes containing eggs should be cooked to 160°F (71°C). When serving high-risk populations, the use of only pasteurized egg products is recommended.

- Egg-processing plants usually do egg breaking, separation, and pasteurization in preparation for freezing or drying. Pasteurization is required by the federal government for all processed eggs.

- The functional properties of raw egg whites are not altered by freezing and thawing. However, frozen egg yolks become viscous and gummy on thawing unless they are mixed with sugar, salt, or syrup before freezing.

- Spray-dried egg whites and egg yolks have long shelf lives. Drying is a satisfactory method for the preservation of eggs. Dried eggs can be reconstituted before use, or they can be sifted with dry ingredients and extra liquid can be added later to the recipe.

- Liquid eggs, broken out of the shell, are available as whole eggs, egg whites, egg yolks, or blended egg products such as scrambled egg mix. Like other processed eggs, these liquid egg products are pasteurized with standard methods or an ultrapasteurization process.

- Eggs are useful in food preparation in many ways. Both egg white and yolk proteins coagulate when heated and can therefore be used for thickening or gel formation. The temperature at which egg proteins coagulate depends in part on the proportion of egg in the mixture. Egg diluted with 1 cup of milk coagulates at approximately 176°F (80°C).

- Coagulation occurs not instantly, but gradually. Egg yolk protein requires a slightly higher temperature for coagulation as compared to egg whites. The toughness and greater shrinkage of egg proteins coagulated at a high temperature are the basis for the recommended use of low or moderate temperatures for egg cookery. Rapidly heated egg mixtures coagulate at a higher temperature than mixtures heated slowly. Mixtures containing sugar require higher temperatures for coagulation, whereas slightly acid mixtures appear to coagulate rapidly at slightly lower temperatures.

- Eggs whites coagulate with mechanical beating. First egg whites become foamy, then soft moist peaks form. Stiff peaks form with continued beating, but overbeating will result in a dry, lumpy foam. The foam produced from thin whites is more fluffy and has less body than one created from thick, viscous whites. Thick whites also appear to produce a more stable foam. Eggs whip more easily and quickly at room temperature. Both whole eggs and egg yolks may be beaten, but with different results than observed with egg whites.

- Fat interferes with the whipping of egg whites. Thus, contamination with egg yolk, or oil from the bowl or beaters should be avoided. Plastic bowls are generally not recommended because it is difficult to make a plastic bowl completely oil free.

- The addition of salt decreases the volume and stability of the foam, in addition to increasing whipping time. Sugar retards the denaturation and coagulation of the egg proteins and increases the beating time. Sugar is therefore added after the eggs have started to foam and is added gradually.

- Poached, hard-cooked or soft-cooked in the shell, fried, scrambled, shirred, omelets, crepes, custards, meringues, as well as many other egg dishes may be prepared.

- Microwave ovens may be used to prepare scrambled, fried, poached, and other egg dishes. However, microwave ovens are not recommended for hard- or soft-cooked eggs in the shell. Steam builds up in the egg and it bursts.

- Egg substitutes have been developed by industry to provide low-cholesterol egg products in both liquid and dried forms. Most of the egg substitutes contain no yolk, but have a high concentration of egg white with other ingredients to provide yolk-like properties to the egg white mixture.

KEY TERMS

emulsion	Maillard reaction
foam	viscosity
coagulate	surface activity
clarify	gel
protein efficiency ratio	denaturation
lipoproteins	disulfide linkages
atherogenic	flocculated
headspace	surface tension
5-log reduction	cream of tartar
syneresis	beading

STUDY QUESTIONS

1. **a.** Compare the chemical composition of whole egg, egg white, and egg yolk, indicating major differences.
   b. What major protein is found in egg white?
   c. What types of proteins predominate in egg yolk?

2. Describe the following parts of an egg and indicate the location for each.
   a. Cuticle or bloom
   b. Shell
   c. Outer membrane
   d. Inner membrane
   e. Air cell
   f. Thin white
   g. Thick white
   h. Chalazae
   i. Vitelline membrane
   j. Yolk

3. a. Compare the major characteristics of fresh and deteriorated eggs.
   b. How can freshness best be maintained in eggs during storage?

4. a. List the USDA consumer grades for eggs and describe the major characteristics of each grade.
   b. Describe the process by which eggs are graded.

5. a. Explain why the FDA has designated shell eggs as a potentially hazardous food.
   b. Give several suggestions for the safe handling and preparation of shell eggs.

6. a. Explain why eggs are usually pasteurized before freezing or drying.
   b. What special problem is usually encountered in the freezing of egg yolks and how can this problem be solved?

7. List several different uses for eggs in food preparation.

8. Egg proteins coagulate on heating and can therefore be used for thickening purposes in cooking. Describe the effect of each of the following factors on the temperature of coagulation.
   a. Source of egg protein (white or yolk)
   b. Rate of heating
   c. Dilution
   d. Addition of sugar
   e. Addition of acid

9. Describe the various changes or stages that occur as egg white is mechanically beaten to a very stiff, dry foam.

10. Describe the effect of each of the following on the volume and/or stability of egg white foam.
    a. Thickness of the white
    b. Temperature of the white
    c. Type of beater used
    d. Type of container used
    e. Addition of salt
    f. Addition of acid
    g. Addition of sugar

11. Describe and explain an appropriate procedure for preparing each of the following food items.
    a. Poached eggs
    b. Eggs cooked in the shell
    c. Fried eggs
    d. Scrambled eggs
    e. Omelets, plain or French and foamy or puffy
    f. Shirred and poached eggs cooked by microwaves

12. a. Describe appropriate procedures for preparing stirred custard and baked custard and explain why each step in the procedures is important.

b. Why should precautions be taken to avoid overheating custards during preparation? Explain.

13. Describe major differences in preparation and use of soft and hard meringues.

REFERENCES

1. American Egg Board. (2002, September). Egg industry fact sheet. Retrieved from http://www.aeb.org/eii/facts/industry-facts-06-2002.htm

2. American Egg Board. (1994, April). *Eggcyclopedia* (3rd ed.). Chicago: American Egg Board.

3. Baker, R. C., Darfler, J., & Lifshitz, A. (1967). Factors affecting the discoloration of hard-cooked egg yolks. *Poultry Science, 46,* 664.

4. Bringe, N. A., & Cheng, J. (1995). Low-fat, low-cholesterol egg yolk in food applications. *Food Technology, 49*(5), 94.

5. Bufano, N. S. (2000). Keeping eggs safe from farm to table. *Food Technology, 54*(8), 192.

6. Code of Federal Regulations. (1997, January 7). Inspection of eggs and egg products: Pasteurization of eggs. 7CFR59.570.

7. Cremer, M. L. (1981). Microwave heating of scrambled eggs in a hospital food-service system. *Journal of Food Science, 46,* 1573.

8. *Egg grading manual.* (1990). Agriculture Handbook No. 75. Washington, DC: U.S. Department of Agriculture.

9. Gardner, F. A., Beck, M. L., & Denton, J. H. (1982). Functional quality comparison of whole egg and selected egg substitute products. *Poultry Science, 61,* 75.

10. Giese, J. (1994). Ultrapasteurized liquid whole eggs earn 1994 IFT Food Technology Industrial Achievement Award. *Food Technology, 48*(9), 94.

11. Gillis, J. N., & Fitch, N. K. (1956). Leakage of baked soft meringue topping. *Journal of Home Economics, 48,* 703.

12. Hanning, F. (1945). Effect of sugar or salt upon denaturation produced by beating and upon the ease of formation and the stability of egg white foams. *Iowa State College Journal of Science, 20,* 10.

13. Hester, E. E., & Personius, C. J. (1949). Factors affecting the beading and leaking of soft meringues. *Food Technology, 3,* 236.

14. Irmiter, T. F., Dawson, L. E., & Reagan, J. G. (1970). Methods of preparing hard cooked eggs. *Poultry Science, 49,* 1232.

15. Itoh, T., Miyazaki, J., Sugawara, H., & Adachi, S. (1987). Studies on the characterization of ovomucin and chalaza of the hen's egg. *Journal of Food Science, 52,* 1518.

16. Kinner, J. A., & Moats, W. A. (1981). Effect of temperature, pH, and detergent on survival of bacteria associated with shell eggs. *Poultry Science, 60,* 761.

17. Kline, L., & Sugihara, T. F. (1966, August). Effects of pasteurization on egg products. *Baker's Digest, 40,* 40.

18. Kurisaki, J., Kaminogawa, S., & Yamauchi, K. (1980). Studies on freeze-thaw gelation of very low density lipoprotein from hen's yolk. *Journal of Food Science, 45,* 463.

19. Labensky, S. R. & Hause, A. M. (2003). *On cooking: A textbook of culinary fundamentals* (3rd ed.). New Jersey: Prentice Hall.

20. Lin, C. T. J., Morales, R. A., & Ralston, K. (1997). Raw and undercooked eggs: A danger of salmonellosis. *Food Review, 20*(1), 27.

21. Margoshes, B. A. (1990). Correlation of protein sulfhydryls with the strength of heat-formed egg white gels. *Journal of Food Science, 55,* 1753.

22. Matiella, J. E., & Hsieh, T. C. Y. (1991). Volatile compounds in scrambled eggs. *Journal of Food Science, 56*, 387.

23. Meehan, J. J., Sugihara, T. F., & Kline, L. (1962). Relationships between shell egg handling factors and egg product properties. *Poultry Science, 41*, 892.

24. Mermelstein, N. H. (2000). Cryogenic system rapidly cools eggs. *Food Technology, 54*(6), 100–103.

25. Mermelstein, N. H. (2001). Pasteurization of shell eggs. *Food Technology, 55*(12), 72–73, 79.

26. Mineki, M., & Kobayashi, M. (1997). Microstructure of yolk from fresh eggs by improved method. *Journal of Food Science, 62*, 757.

27. Neff, J. (1998). The great egg breakthrough. *Food Processing, 59*(1), 25.

28. Parsons, A. H. (1982). Structure of the eggshell. *Poultry Science, 61*, 2013.

29. Pszczola, D.E. (1999). Waking up breakfast foods. *Food Technology, 53*(3), 60–67.

30. Sheldon, B. W., & Kimsey, Jr., H. R. (1985). The effects of cooking methods on the chemical, physical, and sensory properties of hard-cooked eggs. *Poultry Science, 64*, 84.

31. U.S. Department of Agriculture. (1995). *How to buy eggs.* Home and Garden Bulletin No. 264.

32. U.S. Department of Agriculture, Food Safety Inspection Service. (2002, October). Focus on shell eggs. Retrieved December 30, 2002, from http://fsis.usda.gov/OA/pubs/shelleggs.htm

33. U.S. Food and Drug Administration, Center for Food Safety and Applied Nutrition. (2001, February). Food safety facts for consumers: Playing it safe with eggs. Retrieved December 29, 2002, from http://www.cfsan.fda.gov/~dms/fs-eggs.html

34. U.S. Health and Human Services. (2000, November). FDA finalizes safe handling labels and refrigeration requirements for marketing shell eggs. Retrieved December 29, 2002, from http://www.cfsan.fda.gov/~lrd/hhseggs.2html

35. Van Elswyk, M. E., Sams, A. R., & Hargis, P. S. (1992). Composition, functionality, and sensory evaluation of eggs from hens fed dietary menhaden oil. *Journal of Food Science, 57*, 342.

36. Woodward, S. A., & Cotterill, O. J. (1986). Texture and microstructure of heat-formed egg white gels. *Journal of Food Science, 51*, 333.

37. Woodward, S. A., & Cotterill, O. J. (1987). Texture and microstructure of cooked whole egg yolks and heat-formed gels of stirred egg yolk. *Journal of Food Science, 52*, 63.

38. Wu, V.T., Brochetti, D., and Duncan, S. E. (1998). Sensory characteristics and acceptability of lactose-reduced baked custards made with an egg substitute. *Journal of the American Dietetic Association, 98*, 1467–1469.

39. Zottola, E. A. (2001). Reflections on *Salmonella* and other "wee beasties" in foods. *Food Technology, 55*(9), 60.

Meat and Meat Cookery

25

 Meat is defined as the flesh of animals used for food. Cattle, swine, and sheep are the chief meat animals in the United States. Small amounts of rabbit and venison are also consumed in the United States; and in other parts of the world, horse, dog, llama, and camel are used as meat.

CONSUMPTION OF RED MEAT

Along with poultry and fish, meat plays an important role in meal planning, often being the focus of the menu around which the balance of the meal is planned. Changes have occurred, however, over the past two decades in the amounts of these protein-rich foods consumed by Americans. The current trend is toward the consumption of less red meat and more poultry (Figure 25-1) [81]. According to U.S. Department of Agriculture (USDA) food disappearance data, Americans ate, on an annual per capita basis, 148 pounds of red meat (beef, pork, and lamb) in 1975 but only 134 pounds in 1999. At the same time, the consumption of poultry increased from 47 pounds per person in 1975 to 95 pounds in 1999 [8]. Nevertheless, the total consumption of meat, poultry, and fish increased from 207 pounds per person per year in 1975 to 245 pounds in 1999.

Data from food consumption studies, collected by the USDA, show somewhat different trends from those described in the preceding paragraph. Total meat, poultry, and fish intake of women for 1 day was reported to be 184 grams (6.5 ounces) in 1977 to 1978 and 168 grams (5.9 ounces) in 1994 to 1995 [26]. Reported intakes for men were 280 grams (9.9 ounces) in 1977 to 1978 and 275 grams (9.7 ounces) in 1994 to 1995. An interesting trend in the food consumption studies was a 38 percent increase in the use of mixtures containing mainly meat, poultry, or fish (such as hamburgers, frozen dinners, and chili con carne) [10]. Consumption of separate cuts of beef and pork, such as steaks and roasts, decreased. Change in the consumption patterns of beef and chicken is partly related to the relatively higher beef price. Consumer health concerns regarding fat, and the greater offering of convenience products by the poultry industry, have influenced the trends [41]. In the past few years, however, a trend toward increased beef consumption by Americans has been noted. Steakhouse restaurants are doing a brisk business and some fully cooked convenience items, such as beef stew, Swiss steak and gravy, beef pot roast, and meat loaf, are now being marketed as comfort foods that consumers buy for home meal replacements.

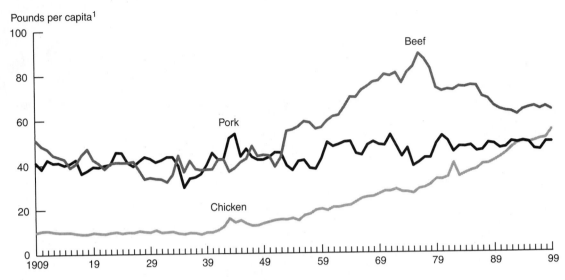

¹Boneless, trimmed weight. Excludes beef and pork organ meats.

Figure 25-1
Consumption of beef, pork, and chicken in the U.S.¹Boneless, trimmed weight. Excludes beef and pork organ meats.
(Source: USDA's Economic Research Service.)

COMPOSITION AND NUTRITIVE VALUE

Meat is composed chiefly of water, protein, fat, and mineral matter. It also contains, in much smaller amounts, vitamins, pigments, and enzymes. Liver contains carbohydrate as glycogen. The amount is variable, but usually ranges from 1 to 5 percent.

Fat, Protein, and Water

The percentage of fat in meats varies widely, depending on the breed or biological type of animal, its nutritional state, and the part of the carcass from which the cut is taken. Cuts of meat are usually trimmed of excess fat by meat handlers, and many Americans are increasingly using leaner meats. Fat trimming is, of course, costly to the meat industry; therefore, there is a concerted attempt to develop genetic lines or biological types of animals that produce lean carcasses [14]. The external fat layer that remains on meat is often not eaten, and thus can be considered waste [83].

Fats from different species and from different parts of the same animal differ to some extent in composition. The more brittle, hard fats of beef and mutton contain higher percentages of **saturated fatty acids.** Softer fats contain more **unsaturated fatty acids.** The high melting point of lamb fat causes it to congeal when served unless the meat is very hot. Lard extracted from the fatty tissue around the glandular organs has a somewhat higher melting point than that produced from back fat.

Lean uncooked muscle contains about 75 percent water and about 20 percent protein. In the muscle cells, much of the water is held by the proteins in a gel-type structure. The chief intracellular proteins that take part in the contraction process are myosin and actin. Other proteins, many of which are soluble in

saturated fatty acids fatty acids that have no double bonds between carbon atoms; they hold all of the hydrogen that they can attach

unsaturated fatty acids fatty acids that have one or more double bonds between carbon atoms; they could hold more hydrogen atoms if these bonds were broken

water, are present in small amounts. The cell proteins are of excellent nutritional quality. The gelatin formed from connective tissue by cooking has a much lower biologic value. Normal cooking procedures appear to have little effect on protein quality. Excessive heating, however, can decrease the biologic value of meat proteins.

It has been reported that when lean and lean-marbled-with-fat portions of cooked meat were analyzed together, they were found to contain 10 to 21 percent fat and 23 to 32 percent protein [53]. The lean portion or the lean-plus-

hyphae the threadlike parts that make up the mycelium or vegetative part of a fungus such as *Fusarium*

Hot Topics

Mycoprotein—From fungi?

Can we interest you in a new—that is, **really new**—food ingredient? It is really new in the sense that it has never been used in a food product before—before 1985, that is, when a British company began marketing the first Quorn™ food product, Savory Pie. Over the next few years, many new products were introduced in the U.K. and many other Western European countries and, beginning in 2001, in the United States. These products include burgers, nuggets, sausages, deli slices, cutlets, and prepared entrees such as fettucine Alfredo and lasagna. And all these food products are made without meat—called meat alternatives [110].

What is the origin of this interesting new food ingredient? From whence did it come and what is it called? Mycoprotein is the generic name and it is derived from the cells of *Fusarium venenatum*, a mushroom-like fungi originally discovered growing in a field in Buckinghamshire in the U.K. This particular organism was selected from more than 3,000 samples from all over the world. Stock cultures of this organism are available as PTA-2684.

Mycoprotein is produced in a fermentation process where all raw materials used are of food-grade quality and purity. Liquid and gaseous feeds, including a glucose source, are added to the fermenter and inoculated with the culture. After a batch growth, the process becomes a continuous feed of nutrients and simultaneous removal of fermenter product. The next step is to reduce the content of RNA in the fermenter product by rapidly heating it. This is done in order to mini-

mize the amount of uric acid that may be produced as the body metabolizes the RNA. The heating process also kills the fungal cells and renders the protein component insoluble [87].

Mycoprotein is physically made up of a filamentous or threadlike network created by the growth of **hyphae.** This structure is similar to that which exists in the fibers of natural meat. When the hyphae are mixed in binders (such as egg albumin), flavorings, and other ingredients, formed into any desired shape or size, and then heated, they gel or bind together and become similar to meat products. They also break down in the mouth during chewing in much the same way as meat products [87].

But how about nutritional value? All essential amino acids are present and the protein quality of mycoprotein is similar to that of soybean protein. The small amount of egg albumin and milk proteins used in fabricating the products enhances the protein quality. Mycoprotein is relatively low in fat, and the fat is more like vegetable fat than animal fat. Also, it contains an appreciable amount of fiber from the cell walls of the hyphae. In addition, millions of people have consumed these products with reported adverse reactions at a level below that reported for other foods in common use. Its nutritional contribution appears to be well worth investigating [66].

So, why not try this *really* new food ingredient? In the future you may find it not only in simulated meat products but also in dairy products as a fat replacer or in extruded snacks and breakfast cereals.

marble portions of cooked pork contained no more fat than similar portions of beef, veal, or lamb. It is evident that moderate amounts of lean red meat, as well as poultry and fish, can be included in a low-fat diet plan to lower blood lipid levels, thereby retaining the valuable contributions that red meats make to the diet in terms of protein, vitamins, and minerals.

Vitamins and Minerals

Lean meats are a good source of thiamin, riboflavin, and niacin, as well as other members of the B complex. Lean pork is particularly rich in thiamin. Liver and kidney are good dietary sources of riboflavin and are richer in niacin than most other tissues. All meats furnish tryptophan, the amino acid that serves as a **precursor** of niacin for the body. Liver is a variable but excellent source of vitamin A. Meat is an excellent source of iron, zinc, and phosphorus. Twenty-three percent of the iron in the U.S food supply is supplied by meat, poultry, fish, and meat alternatives [31]. Some copper and other trace minerals are also supplied by meat.

Some minerals dissolve in the juices or cooking water of meat, but these can be consumed in gravies. The loss of thiamin in cooking or processing meats appears to be related to the severity of heat treatment. The average retention of thiamin in cooked meats is about 65 percent. Riboflavin and niacin are more resistant to destruction in cooking than thiamin, and seem to be well retained (see Appendix C for the nutritive value of selected meats).

Pigments

The color of meat comes chiefly from the pigment *myoglobin*. In a well-bled animal, most of the red *hemoglobin* pigment of the blood is removed. Myoglobin and hemoglobin are similar in chemical structure. Both contain the protein globin and the iron-containing pigment heme, but myoglobin is smaller. Hemoglobin carries oxygen in the bloodstream, whereas myoglobin holds it in the muscle cells. The quantity of myoglobin in muscle increases with age; thus, beef has a darker color than veal. The color of meat also varies with the species of animal from which it is obtained. Pork muscle generally contains less myoglobin than beef muscle and appears lighter in color. Different muscles of the same animal also may differ in color.

When meat is first cut, the myoglobin is in a chemically reduced form and appears purplish red. Meat also is a purplish red when packaged in *cryovac*, which is a vacuum-sealed, airtight, plastic package. As meat combines with oxygen, or is oxygenated, the myoglobin changes to a bright red pigment called *oxymyoglobin*. Fresh cuts of meat seen in the market show oxymyoglobin on the surfaces that are exposed to air. After a certain period of storage, when **reducing substances** are no longer produced in the tissues, the meat may appear brownish because of the change of myoglobin or oxymyoglobin to an oxidized form, called *metmyoglobin* (see Figure 25-2). Fluorescent light accelerates the formation of metmyoglobin. If further **oxidation** changes take place in fresh meat, several greenish compounds may be produced from the breakdown of the heme pigment. The display life of fresh beef has been reported to be extended 2 to 5 days when supplements of vitamin E (alpha-tocopherol), an antioxidant, were fed to beef steers on a long-term basis. Lipid oxidation in the meat was also markedly reduced [5].

precursor a substance that "comes before"; the precursor of a vitamin is a substance that can be used by the body to make the vitamin

reducing substances chemical molecules that can supply hydrogen or electrons to prevent or reverse oxidation; the reduced state of iron is the ferrous form (Fe^{2+})

oxidation a chemical change that involves the addition of oxygen or the loss of electrons; the oxidized state (Fe^{3+}) of iron is the ferric form

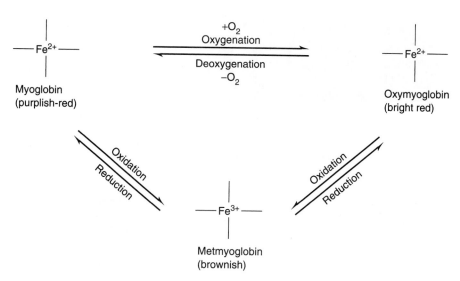

Figure 25-2
Some changes that occur in meat pigments.

STRUCTURE OF MEAT

As purchased from the market, meat is composed of muscle, connective tissue, fatty or adipose tissue, and bone. The connective tissue is distributed throughout muscle, binding cells and bundles of cells together. It also is present in tendons and ligaments. Depending on the grade and the cut, the amount of fatty tissue varies widely. Although the bone is not eaten, it is an important aid in identifying various cuts of meat.

Muscle Tissue

Muscle has a complex structure that is important to its function in the living animal, where it performs work by contracting and relaxing. Because the structure and function of muscle fibers, which are the basic structural units of muscle, affect the quality and cooking characteristics of meat, it is important to pay attention to the way muscles are put together.

The muscle fiber is a long threadlike cell that tapers slightly at both ends (Figure 25-3). It is tiny, averaging about 1/500th inch in diameter and 1 to 2 inches in length. Inside the fiber or cell is an intricate structure. It includes contractile material called *myofibrils*, surrounded by the **cytoplasmic** substance called *sarcoplasm* (Figure 25-4). There is also a system of tubules and **reticulum** around each myofibril that plays a key role in initiating muscle contraction. In addition, many **mitochondria** act as powerhouses to provide energy for the cell in the form of the high-energy compound adenosine triphosphate **(ATP)**.

cytoplasm pertaining to the protoplasm of a cell, exclusive of the nucleus

reticulum a netlike sheath

mitochondria sausage-shaped bodies in the cell cytoplasm that contain the enzymes necessary for energy metabolism

ATP adenosine triphosphate, a compound containing high-energy phosphate bonds in which the body cell traps energy from the metabolism of carbohydrate, fat, or protein; the energy in ATP is then used to do mechanical or chemical work in the body

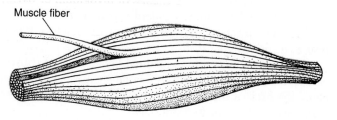

Muscle fiber

Figure 25-3
Tiny muscle fibers or cells are combined to form small bundles.

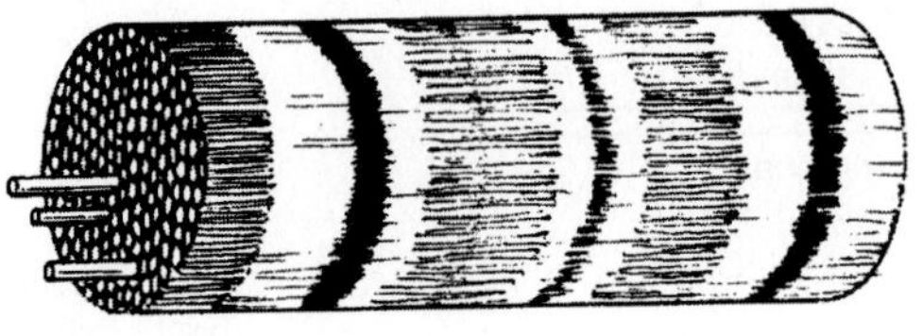

Figure 25-4
The muscle fiber or cell consists of many tiny myofibrils held together by the cell membrane. Each myofibril is made up of contractile proteins in a special ordered array, as shown in Figure 25-5.

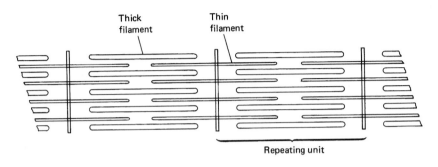

Figure 25-5
Thick and thin, rodlike components or filaments inside the myofibril are composed of protein molecules. Myosin is the protein found in the thick filaments; actin makes up the thin filaments. They are systematically arranged in a cylindrical shape. When muscle contracts, the thin filaments in each repeating unit push together, thus shortening the length of the muscle.

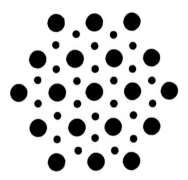

Figure 25-6
Transverse section through a cylindrical myofibril. The large dots represent the thick filaments composed of myosin molecules. The smaller dots represent the thin filaments composed of actin.

If you could look further into the structure of the tiny myofibrils, about 2,000 of which are present in each muscle cell, you would see special proteins. These proteins form thick filaments and thin filaments that are set in an orderly array (Figure 25-5). If you visualize a transverse section cut through the center of a myofibril, it would be similar to that shown in Figure 25-6. The thick filaments are composed primarily of the protein *myosin*, whereas the thin filaments are made up of another protein, *actin*.

It is thought that when a muscle contracts, the thick and thin filaments slide together, something like a telescope, thus shortening the length of the muscle. As the thick and thin filaments slide together, they apparently form cross-bridges with each other, thus making a new protein in the shortened myofibril called *actomyosin*. Energy for this process is provided from chemical changes in ATP.

The parallel alignment of the thick and thin filaments in all the myofibrils of a cell produces a pattern of dark and light lines and spaces when viewed under a microscope (see Figure 25-7). The thick filaments are present in the dark bands, and the thin filaments extend into the light bands. The striated pattern continues to repeat itself along the length of the myofibril.

Let us now return to the basic unit, the muscle fiber or cell, and see how these units are built into larger bundles and muscles. Each cell or fiber is surrounded by a fine membrane called the *sarcolemma*. Small bundles of the fibers, surrounded by thin sheaths of connective tissue to hold them together, form primary bundles (each containing twenty to forty fibers). The primary bundles are then bound together with sheets of connective tissue to form secondary bundles. Secondary bundles bound together by connective tissue form major muscles. The primary bundles comprise the grain of the meat, which may appear to be fine or coarse.

Each major muscle in the animal body has been named. Figure 25-8 shows two of the major muscles in a T-bone steak—the *longissimus dorsi*, which runs along the back of the animal, and the *psoas major* or *tenderloin* muscle, which is particularly valued for its tenderness.

Figure 25-7
Representation of a striated muscle showing light and dark bands on the myofibrils (enlarged about 20,000 diameters).

Connective Tissue

As indicated, muscle tissue does not occur without connective tissue, which binds the muscle cells together in various-size bundles. It also makes up the tendons and ligaments of an animal body. Generally, connective tissue has few cells, but a considerable amount of extracellular background material called *ground substance*. Running through and embedded in this matrix of ground substance are long, strong fibrils or fibers. Many of these fibrils contain the protein *collagen*. Collagen-containing connective tissue is white. Connective tissue that contains another protein, called *elastin*, is yellow. Although collagen fibers are flexible, they do not stretch as much and are not as elastic as elastin fibers. Very little elastin seems to be present in most muscles, particularly those of the loin and round regions, but a considerable amount of elastin may be present in the connective tissue of a few muscles, including some in the shoulder area. A third type of connective tissue fibril, *reticulin*, consists of very small fibers. This type of connective tissue forms a delicate network around the muscle cells.

In muscles that are used by an animal for locomotion, such as those in the legs, chest, and neck, connective tissue tends to develop more extensively. Less tender cuts of meat usually contain more connective tissue than tender cuts, although this is not the only factor affecting meat tenderness.

When connective tissue is heated with moisture, some collagen is **hydrolyzed** to produce the smaller gelatin molecule. This change accounts for much of the increase in tenderness that occurs in less tender cuts of meat cooked by moist heat. Heating causes only slight softening of elastin, however. If elastin is present in relatively large amounts, it should be trimmed out or tenderized by cutting or cubing (as in the preparation of minute steaks).

hydrolyze to break a molecular linkage utilizing a molecule of water

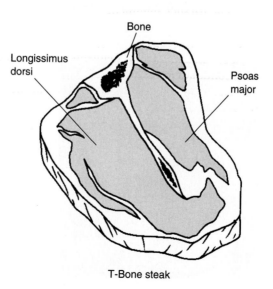

T-Bone steak

Figure 25-8
The major muscles in a T-bone steak.

Fatty Tissue

Special cells contain large amounts of fat for storage in the body. These cells are embedded in a network of connective tissue to form adipose or fatty tissue. Some hard fats, such as beef suet, have visible sheets of connective tissue separating layers or masses of fat cells. Fatty tissue is supplied with blood vessels and fatty deposits are found under the skin and around glandular organs. As an animal is fattened, fat cells are deposited between muscles, and finally there is intramuscular distribution to produce the **marbling** of muscle tissue (Figure 25-9).

The color of fatty tissue changes with age. In older animals, it becomes yellowish instead of white as **carotenoid pigments** accumulate.

marbling the distribution of fat throughout the muscles of meat animals

carotenoid pigments fat-soluble, yellow-orange pigments that are produced by plants; may be stored in the fatty tissues of animals

Bone

Long shafts of bone consist chiefly of compact bony tissue. A center canal is filled with yellow marrow. Other bones may be spongy in character and may contain red marrow, which has many blood vessels. Bones or pieces of bone that appear in retail cuts of meat aid in the identification of the cut, giving clues as to its location on the carcass.

CLASSIFICATION

Beef

Beef carcasses are classified on the basis of age and sex. A *steer* is a male castrated when young; a *heifer* is a young female that has not yet borne a calf; a *cow* is a female that has borne a calf; a *stag* is a male castrated after maturity; and a *bull* is a mature male that has not been castrated.

Steer carcasses are generally preferred by meat handlers because of their heavier weight and the higher proportion of meat to bone, but steer and heifer carcasses of the same grade are of equal quality. The quality of meat from cows is variable, depending on maturity, but is usually inferior to both steer and heifer meat. Stag meat is not normally marketed in the United States, and bull carcasses generally are used in processed meats.

Figure 25-9

This steak is well marbled. Fat is distributed throughout the muscle of this beef rib eye steak. (Courtesy of the Cattlemen's Beef Board through the National Cattlemen's Beef Association)

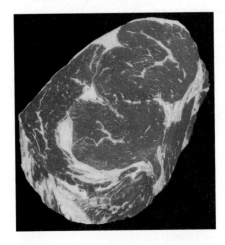

Veal

Veal is meat from immature bovines. In the wholesale market, veal carcasses are usually from animals of either sex that are at least 3 weeks but generally less than 20 weeks of age [72]. They are fed largely on milk or milk products. The term *calf* is applied to animals slaughtered between 5 months and about 10 months of age. The older animals have passed the good veal stage but do not yet possess the properties of good beef.

Lamb and Mutton

Sheep carcasses are classified as lamb, yearling mutton, and mutton according to the age of the animal. Lamb is obtained from young animals of either sex that are less than 12 months of age, although the exact age at which lamb changes to mutton is somewhat indefinite. Mutton carcasses are those that have passed the lamb stage. The usual test for a lamb carcass is the break joint. The feet of a lamb, when broken off sharply, separate from the leg above the regular joint. The break shows four distinct ridges that appear smooth, moist, and red with blood. In mutton, the break comes in the true joint, which is below the break joint.

Most of the meat from sheep is marketed as lamb. Relatively little older mutton is sold. The flesh of all carcasses in the mutton class is darker in color than lamb. It is also less tender and has a stronger flavor when it is from animals beyond 2 years of age.

Pork

Pork is the meat of swine. Good-quality pork is obtained from young animals usually 7 to 12 months of age. In young animals there is no distinction in quality or grade because of sex, whereas in older animals sex differences are pronounced. Most of the pork marketed in the United States comes from young animals.

POSTMORTEM CHANGES AND AGING

Before an animal is slaughtered, the muscles are soft and pliable. On death, as metabolism in the cells is interrupted, processes begin that lead to a stiffening of the carcass known as *rigor mortis*. Metabolic changes include the accumulation of lactic acid in the muscles, as oxygen is no longer available and circulating blood cannot remove end products of metabolism from the tissues. Therefore the pH decreases. The high-energy compound produced in metabolism in the living animal, ATP, also gradually disappears. The muscle becomes contracted as a result of these changes. The muscle proteins (actin and myosin), which form the thin and thick filaments of the myofibrils in the muscle cell, slide or telescope on each other and bond together, forming actomyosin, so that the muscle is no longer extensible.

The time required after the death of the animal for occurrence of the stiffening process is affected by various factors. Rigor mortis begins and is completed relatively slowly when the carcass is held under the usual refrigeration conditions. Both colder and warmer temperatures speed the development of rigor [36, 111]. The species of animal, its age, and its activity just before slaughter also affect the time of onset of rigor. In large animals, such as cattle, rigor begins more slowly and lasts longer than in smaller animals. It is usually

Multicultural Cuisine

Bison

Huge shaggy animals once roamed the land from Canada to Mexico, grazing the great plains and mountain areas. These animals—the scientific species *Bison*—were the center of life for many Native Americans, since from them they received food, shelter, and clothing. In some cases, spiritual comfort and inspiration were also attached to these creatures. Called buffalo, although not truly buffalo, they are of the bovine family—as are domestic cattle. Wild West stories relate the thrill of buffalo hunts and the terror when the herds stampeded. From an estimated 60 million animals in earlier times, by 1893 there were only slightly more than 300 bison left in the United States.

Today, however, the bison are coming back, with an estimated 350,000 head in North America [101]. In addition to bison found in public park lands, many are privately owned, raised on the open range, and grain-fed 90 to 120 days before they are slaughtered for food. Some 20,000 are slaughtered each year in the U.S., compared to approximately 125,000 cattle per day. Nevertheless, Americans consume approximately one million pounds of bison each month.

As meat, is bison different from beef? Bison is considerably lower in fat, when comparing lean cuts. A 3-ounce portion of roast bison contains about 22 grams protein, 2 grams fat, 66 mg cholesterol, and 145 calories. It is an excellent source of iron and B vitamins, as well as good quality protein. Some say that bison has a sweeter, richer flavor than beef.

What do you do with bison, once you have made the decision to try it? Well, you should handle bison meat as you would any other type of meat—always following safe food handling practices. Refrigerate it—properly packaged to prevent any leakage onto other foods—and use within 3 to 5 days—or freeze it. USDA inspection of bison is voluntary.

Since bison is very lean and lacks marbled fat, it should generally be cooked using low heat and long cooking times. Braising or other moist cooking methods are recommended for roasts and steaks, although broiling or pan frying may be used on thin-sliced bison. Ground bison should always be cooked to 160°F for safety reasons. Roasts, steaks, and chops should be loosely covered with foil and braised for 1 hour to a medium rare, medium, or well done stage, as preferred. Less tender cuts should be braised or stewed in a tightly covered pan [101].

As you continue your experiences with new foods, you might like to try "beefalo," a cross between bison and domestic cattle. It has taken years of research to develop this breed, since the natural result of bison-domestic bovine cross breeding is a sterile offspring. Beefalo is also an excellent high quality protein source with relatively low fat content. Enjoy your journey as you explore more red meat varieties.

---

resolved in 24 to 48 hours in beef. If meat is separated from the carcass immediately after slaughter and cooked rapidly before rigor has a chance to develop, it will be tender. If the cooking process is slow, however, rigor may develop during heating and increase toughness in the cooked meat [36, 43].

If the supply of glycogen in the muscle is low at the time of death, as is the case when much activity occurs just before slaughter, less lactic acid is produced from glycogen. The pH of the muscle remains relatively high, above 6.3. The muscle tissue is only slightly acid. In beef, the result is a dark color that is less acceptable in market channels. The muscle tissue also has an increased water-binding capacity and a sticky texture, although it is tender [25, 111].

If meat is allowed to hang under refrigeration for 1 or 2 days after slaughter, it will gradually begin to soften as rigor mortis passes. If it is held still longer, a process of ripening or aging occurs. This results in some increase in tenderness, improvement of flavor and juiciness, better browning in cooking of both lean and fat, and a loss of red interior color at a lower cooking temperature [44]. Aging too long may result in a strong flavor or development of an off-flavor and off-odor. A major reason for the increase in tenderness during aging appears to be a breakdown of proteins in the myofibrils by enzymes [47]. Aging of beef may also produce some change in **mucoprotein,** which is a component of connective tissue [62].

Meat is commonly aged at approximately 36°F (2°C). However, aging sides of beef at 60°F (16°C) produces changes in tenderness more rapidly than aging at the lower temperature. At the higher temperature, some means of retarding microbial growth is necessary. Aging of meat is a commercial process not accomplished in home kitchens.

Two different methods can be used for the postmortem aging of meat: Dry aging is aging meat "as is" under refrigeration, whereas wet aging involves packaging the meat in a vacuum bag and holding it under refrigeration. When these two methods of aging were compared for short-cut strip loins and ribs of beef, it was found that differences in palatability attributes of cooked steaks and roasts were slight. Scores for tenderness and overall palatability of steaks from wet aging, as judged by trained panelists, were somewhat higher, but both aging treatments provided very palatable products [78]. No significant differences in palatability were detected by consumer panelists. There was, however, one major difference between the two methods: a greater shrink and trim loss was associated with dry aging, making this process more costly and time consuming.

Beef is the only type of meat that is commonly aged, although some consumers also prefer lamb when it is aged. Beef is usually in market channels for a week to 10 days before the consumer purchases it. There may be little advantage to extending the aging period beyond 10 days [67].

Veal is not improved by aging, and the lack of fat on the carcass results in excessive surface drying. Pork is usually obtained from a young, tender animal; thus, toughness is not generally a problem. Aging of pork for more than 3 or 4 days may be complicated by the tendency for relatively rapid development of rancidity in the fat during holding.

mucoprotein a complex or conjugated protein containing a carbohydrate substance combined with a protein

FACTORS AFFECTING TENDERNESS

One of the most valued attributes of meat is tenderness. The grading of meat by USDA standards does not directly measure this characteristic, although the probability that a beef carcass will be tender is greater in a higher grade than it is in a lower grade. Pork and lamb, because they are marketed young, are usually tender.

Much more variation exists in beef, and much of the research on tenderness has been concerned with beef cuts. A system of sampling, cooking, and testing beef was developed in the U.S. Meat Animal Research Center in Nebraska that identifies beef carcasses with rib and loin cuts of above-average tenderness [37]. Under this system, a rib steak from a chilled carcass is cooked then measured for tenderness with an electronic testing machine that provides computer data (Figure 25-10). Research at the Meat Animal Research Center has shown that marbling accounts for only 10 percent of the variation in beef ribeye tenderness [37]. Thus, a system of more accurately predicting tenderness will be of value.

Figure 25-10
A food technologist uses a computer programmed to predict tenderness and beef carcass composition based on test results. (Courtesy of Agriculture Research Service, U.S. Department of Agriculture; photo by Keith Weller)

Taste panels, in studying the tenderness of meat, have described several components of tenderness that are apparent during the biting and chewing of meat. These include the ease with which teeth sink into the meat, or softness, the crumbliness of the muscle fibers, and the amount of connective tissue or the amount of residue remaining after the meat is chewed for a specified time. Each of these components of tenderness may be influenced by various factors operating in the production and preparation of beef and other meats, including, as we have discussed, aging of beef and changes in the muscle proteins producing actomyosin.

Connective Tissue

It is generally agreed that larger amounts of connective tissue in a cut of meat cause decreased tenderness. The least used muscles of an animal, particularly those in the rib and loin sections, contain less connective tissue than muscles that are used for locomotion (Figure 25-11). The muscles of the rib and loin, for example, are more tender than the muscles of the legs and shoulders.

Figure 25-11
This beef chuck 7 bone steak has more connective tissue than cuts from the rib and loin. (Courtesy of the Cattlemen's Beef Board through the National Cattlemen's Beef Association)

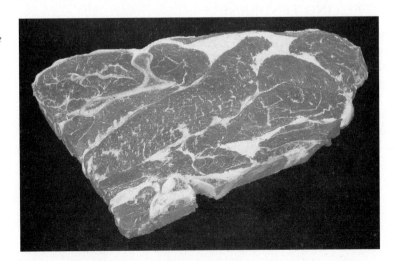

As animals mature and become older, more and stronger connective tissue usually forms in muscle tissues. The cross-links between collagen monomers that comprise the fibrils in connective tissue appear to become less soluble and more resistant to heat as an animal ages. This factor is important in explaining the difference in tenderness between younger and older animals. It has been reported that the decrease in tenderness with age depends on connective tissue strength. The tenderloin muscle, which is not used in locomotion and has little connective tissue, remained tender in animals up to 48 months of age, whereas other muscles with strong connective tissue tripled in toughness [90]. The case of veal is different, however. Although it is a very young animal, there is still a relatively high percentage of connective tissue in the muscles because of the lack of time for development of the muscle itself.

Fat and Marbling

The fattening of animals has long been thought to improve the tenderness of meat. It has been suggested that a layer of subcutaneous fat on a carcass delays chilling of the meat, thereby allowing postmortem metabolic changes that result in greater tenderness [22]. The USDA quality grade standards for beef include an estimation of the amount of marbling (the distribution of fat throughout the muscle). Small but statistically significant decreases in tenderness have been found in beef by expert judging panels as marbling decreased from moderately abundant to practically devoid [91]. Juiciness and flavor also decreased. Untrained consumers in San Francisco and Kansas City gave slightly lower scores for overall desirability of top loin beef steaks as the marbling level decreased. In the same study, consumers in Philadelphia rated the steaks with lesser marbling considerably lower than those well marbled, indicating regional differences [89]. Marbling would appear to have an impact on the eating quality of beef steaks, including tenderness, but sometimes this effect on tenderness may be small.

Ground beef is a popular meat product in the United States. When cooked ground beef patties made from raw meat containing 5, 10, 15, 20, 25, and 30 percent fat were compared, it was noted that the low-fat patties (5 and 10 percent) were firmer in texture, less juicy, and less flavorful than the patties with 20 to 30 percent fat [96]. Objective measurements with the Warner-Bratzler and Lee-Kramer shear instruments also showed decreasing tenderness with decreasing fat content.

Other Factors

Carcasses of beef are sometimes subjected to low-voltage electrical stimulation immediately after slaughter to increase tenderness. The beneficial effects may result from an increase in the rate of postmortem metabolism and a disruption of the myofibrils with accelerated enzymatic breakdown of the muscle proteins [28]. Electrical stimulation and 48 hours of aging were reported to have the same tenderizing effect on both steer and bull carcasses as a 6-day aging period [30].

The hereditary background of the animal, the management of its feeding, and the size of muscle fibers are other factors that affect meat tenderness. Many of these factors are undoubtedly interrelated, and more research is needed to clarify the whole picture of tenderness in meat. For example, pronounced differences in tenderness are apparent among various muscles of the beef carcass. The tenderloin or psoas major and the longissimus dorsi muscles in the rib and loin sections are the most tender; muscles of the round and chuck sections are less tender. These differences in tenderness cannot be completely explained by differences in connective tissue, fat content, or state of muscle contraction [63].

Tenderizing

Because of the lower cost of certain less tender cuts of meat in comparison with more tender pieces, attempts have been made to tenderize the less tender cuts. Grinding and cubing break up the connective tissue and make meat more tender.

proteinase an enzyme that hydrolyzes proteins to smaller peptides and amino acids

Tenderizing compounds containing various enzymes, usually **proteinases,** may be used to hydrolyze some of the proteins in meat. The enzymes include papain and chymopapain from the green papaya fruit, bromelin from pineapple, ficin from figs, and actinidin from kiwifruit. The compounds are applied to the surface of meats prior to cooking. A fork can be used to pierce the meat and allow the material to penetrate a little further. Most of these enzymes act primarily on the muscle cell proteins; bromelin is more active on the collagen of connective tissue. Care must be taken to control excessive action on the meat fibers and prevent the development of a mealy or mushy texture. Little enzymatic action occurs at room temperature, the optimal temperature for papaya enzyme activity being 140° to 160°F (60° to 70°C). This temperature is reached during cooking.

An enzyme mixture may be injected into the bloodstream of the animal just before slaughter. Theoretically, the enzyme is carried to all parts of the body and is evenly distributed throughout the various retail cuts. The enzyme remains inactive until the meat is heated in cooking. Cuts of meat that are usually classified as less tender can be cooked as tender cuts if the beef animals have received enzyme injections. If the enzyme has not been destroyed in cooking, continued tenderization should occur during standing time after cooking.

BUYING OF MEAT

American families tend to spend a substantial percentage of their food money on meats. If this amounts to as much as 38 to 40 percent of the food budget, it is quite possible that other important food items, such as milk, fruits, and vegetables, are being neglected. Meats are among the most expensive items of the diet. They are well liked, and many families place undue emphasis on the need for meat in every meal. Many consumers also lack information as to what determines the price and quality of meats.

Several laws have been passed and regulations have been published, at both the national and local levels, to protect and inform the consumer with respect to the purchasing of meat and poultry products. The aim of these regulations is to protect the public, not only from obvious abnormalities and animal disease, but also from the hazards of pathogenic microorganisms that may be present on carcasses or in processing plants.

The USDA has responsibility at the federal level for the inspection, grading, setting of standards, and labeling of all meat and poultry products. Partly because of recent outbreaks of foodborne illness involving meat and poultry, new rules for meat and poultry processors and new testing procedures for plants and federal inspectors were instituted in July 1996 [16]. In 2002, USDA strengthened food safety programs to further reduce the presence of *E. coli* O157:H7 [98, 34]. Many of the newer rules are aimed at preventing contamination rather than detecting it after the fact. However, safe food-handling techniques should always be used by those preparing potentially hazardous foods such as meat and poultry products as the final stage in preventing foodborne illness.

Federal agencies including the U.S. Department of Agriculture and the U.S. Department of Health and Human Services have worked to prevent bovine spongiform encephalopathy (BSE) from entering the United States. BSE, also sometimes called mad cow disease, has never been found in the United States. BSE was first reported in the United Kingdom in 1986 and since that time has been identified in several additional European countries [106, 107]. Since 1989, the U.S. prohibited the importation of cattle and edible animal products from countries with cases of BSE [75]. The importation of live ruminants and most ruminant products from all of Europe was banned starting in 1997 [106]. Additional preventative measures have included: (1) regulations prohibiting the use of most mammalian protein in feeds manufactured for **ruminants,** (2) FDA inspection of feed mills and rendering facilities, (3) USDA examination of all cattle before approval for food and prohibition of the use of all cattle with neurological diseases, and (4) USDA examination of cattle brains for presence of BSE; 11,700 cattle brains were examined in 2000 [75, 106, 107]. Although the risk of BSE occurring in the United States is believed to be low, research and the review of regulations are ongoing [64].

ruminant an animal with four stomachs. Cattle, sheep, goats, deer, and elk are ruminant animals.

Another area of regulation is the oversight of additives that can be used in meat products. Additives are regulated by the USDA, using guidelines from the U.S. Food and Drug Administration (FDA). During the 1950s, the practice of administering compounds with estrogenic activity to beef cattle developed and became fairly common. The purpose for their use was to increase weight gain in the animals with less feed, thus allowing a savings to the cattle industry and making earlier marketing possible. Diethylstilbestrol (DES), the most commonly used substance, generated considerable controversy over its safety, and eventually its use was prohibited by federal regulatory agencies. Certain other substances, however, have been approved for use to promote an increased rate of weight gain in calves and heifers. The conditions of their use are prescribed. Some substances are implanted **subcutaneously** in the ear of the animal and may include a mixture of progesterone and estradiol hormones.

subcutaneous under the skin

Techniques in biotechnology have been used to produce substances that improve production efficiency in meat- and milk-producing animals. Bovine somatotropin (bST), when given to dairy cows, increases milk production by at least 10 percent and increases the efficiency with which the cows use feed by about 10 percent. This hormone can be produced artificially with genetic technology (rbST). Porcine somatotropin (pST), administered to growing pigs, increases their growth rate and reduces carcass fat while increasing muscle growth. It also increases their weight gain per unit of feed consumed [27]. Consumer panelists found no difference in acceptability between loin and ham roasts from control or pST-treated animals [80].

The USDA has published standards of identity for some meat products, including corned beef hash; however, for most meat and poultry products, standards of composition have been set. These standards identify the minimum amount of meat or poultry required in a product's recipe. For example, meat pie must contain at least 25 percent meat, beef with gravy or beef with barbecue sauce must contain at least 50 percent beef, and chili con carne must have at least 40 percent meat. Frankfurters and similar cooked sausages must contain no more than 30 percent fat, 10 percent added water, and 2 percent corn syrup. Their labels must clearly indicate the products used in their formulation.

You should be aware of standards and required inspection procedures. Your responsibility to report any infractions that you observe is an important one, because enforcement of regulations at all levels is extremely difficult.

Labeling

The FDA handles labeling on approximately 70 percent of the food items found in supermarkets, and the USDA Food Safety and Inspection Service approves labels on the other 30 percent, which are meat and poultry products. Each meat or poultry label must contain the following information:

1. Product name
2. Name and address of producer or distributor
3. Inspection mark (round stamp)
4. List of ingredients, in order from highest to lowest amounts, and net weight
5. Establishment number indicating the plant where the product was processed
6. Handling instructions for products that require special handling to remain safe

In 1994, the USDA required a special label with safe handling instructions to appear on raw or partially cooked (not processed to be ready-to-eat) meat and poultry products (Figure 25-12). These instructions were designed to decrease the risk of foodborne illness attributable to unsafe handling, preparation, and storage of meat and poultry products, both at foodservice facilities and in private kitchens. The label is mandated for products packaged and labeled in USDA- or state-inspected processing plants and at retail stores. The language and format for the label is specified [54].

Nutrition labeling (discussed in Chapter 2) is mandated for processed meat and poultry products. The USDA has also defined the nutrient content claims that can be used on meat and poultry products. These include the following [35].

1. *Free:* only a tiny or insignificant amount of fat, cholesterol, sodium, sugar, and/or calories

Figure 25-12

The USDA requires safe handling instructions on packages of all raw or partially cooked meat and poultry products. (Courtesy of the American Meat Institute and the U.S. Department of Agriculture)

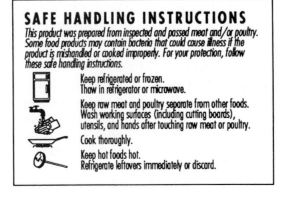

SAFE HANDLING INSTRUCTIONS

This product was prepared from inspected and passed meat and/or poultry. Some food products may contain bacteria that could cause illness if the product is mishandled or cooked improperly. For your protection, follow these safe handling instructions.

Keep refrigerated or frozen.
Thaw in refrigerator or microwave.

Keep raw meat and poultry separate from other foods. Wash working surfaces (including cutting boards), utensils, and hands after touching raw meat or poultry.

Cook thoroughly.

Keep hot foods hot.
Refrigerate leftovers immediately or discard.

2. *Low:* a product that could be eaten fairly often without exceeding dietary guidelines for fat, saturated fat, cholesterol, sodium, and/or calories; *low in fat* means no more than 3 grams of fat per serving

3. *Lean:* less than 10 grams of fat, 4 grams of saturated fat, and 95 milligrams of cholesterol per serving

4. *Extra lean:* less than 5 grams of fat, 2 grams of saturated fat, and 95 milligrams of cholesterol per serving (still not as lean as *low*)

5. *Reduced, less, fewer:* 25 percent less of a nutrient or calories

6. *Light (lite):* one-third fewer calories or one-half the fat or sodium of the original

7. *More:* at least 10 percent more of the Daily Value of a vitamin or mineral per serving

8. *Good source of:* 10 to 19 percent of the Daily Value for a particular vitamin, mineral, or fiber

Government Inspection

All meats entering interstate commerce must be inspected by qualified agents of the USDA Food Safety and Inspection Service. Traditionally the inspection system relied largely on sight, touch, and smell, which was appropriate in an era when the goal was to protect the public against obvious abnormalities and animal disease. Animals are inspected alive and at various stages of the slaughtering process. The brain tissue of dead cattle is microscopically examined for evidence of BSE [33]. The cleanliness and operating procedures of meat packing plants are also supervised. However, certain hazards cannot easily be observed, particularly contamination of the animals or processing plants with pathogenic microorganisms—bacteria, parasites, fungi, and viruses—that can cause human illness. Because of this danger of illness for the meat-consuming public, the USDA has modernized many aspects of the current inspection system to detect and reduce the microbial hazards, to better ensure that meat and meat products are safe for human consumption, and to ensure that labeling is proper and truthful.

The USDA has implemented a comprehensive strategy as it has modernized the inspection process; this strategy contains four essential elements [16].

1. All state and federally inspected meat and poultry slaughter and processing plants must have a Hazard Analysis and Critical Control Points (HACCP) plan (see Chapter 3).

2. Each of these meat and poultry plants must develop written sanitation standard operating procedures (SOPs) to show how they will meet daily sanitation requirements.

3. The federal agency tests for *Salmonella* on raw meat and poultry products to verify that pathogen reduction standards for *Salmonella* are being met.

4. Slaughter plants test for generic *E. coli* on carcasses to verify the process is under control with respect to preventing and removing fecal contamination.

In 2002, the regulations designed to reduce the incidence of *E. coli* O157:H7 were strengthened [98]. If meat carcasses pass the inspection process, the in-

Inspection stamp used on meat carcasses.

Seal used on prepared meat products.

Figure 25-13
Federal meat inspection stamps.
(Courtesy of the U.S. Department of Agriculture)

spector's stamp (Figure 25-13) is placed on each wholesale cut of the carcass. This stamp carries numbers to indicate the packer and identify the carcass. If the meat is unsound, it is not permitted to enter retail trade. The Federal Meat Inspection Act also requires that all meat imported into the United States comes under the same standards of inspection that are applied to meat produced in the United States.

The Wholesome Meat Act of 1967 requires that state governments have, for meat that is sold within state boundaries, local programs of meat inspection equal to those of the federal government. Otherwise, the federal government will assume the responsibility for inspection. State programs are periodically reviewed to see that satisfactory standards are maintained.

There is no practical means of inspecting for the presence of the small parasite *Trichinella spiralis*, which may be found in the muscle of pork carcasses. When consumed, this organism causes trichinosis. Regulations for the inspection of meat products containing pork that are usually eaten without cooking require treatment of such products in a way that destroys any live trichinae that may be in the pork muscle tissue. This process can be accomplished in one of three ways: heating uniformly to a temperature of 137°F (59°C), freezing for not less than 20 days at a maximum temperature of 5°F (−15°C), or curing under special methods prescribed by the USDA. Products such as dried and summer sausage, bologna, frankfurter-style sausage, cooked hams, and cooked pork in casings are among those requiring this treatment.

Much of the slaughtered meat and poultry goes into processed items, including sausages, ham, pizza, frozen dinners, and soups. The federal inspection program is also responsible for the safety of these products. An in-plant inspector monitors the processing operations (Figure 25-14).

Grades and Grading

A program separate from the inspection service is the USDA system of grading meat. Whereas inspection of meat for wholesomeness is mandatory for all meat as it is slaughtered, grading is voluntary. Although it is not required that meat be graded to be marketed, grading provides a national uniform language for use in the buying and selling of meat. Grades are also useful to the consumer in knowing what quality to expect from purchased meats. The grading program is administered by the USDA, but the cost of the service is borne by those meat packers who use it.

Quality grades have been established for beef, veal, lamb, and mutton (Figure 25-15). Grades for pork are not intended to identify differences in quality to consumers, as much of the pork is processed before it reaches the retail market. The grades for pork are more concerned with yield than with quality. Pork carcasses and cuts are graded for wholesale trade and for price control on a weight basis, with heavier weights grading lower than lighter weights. Pork, as marketed, is less variable in age and quality than carcasses from other animals.

For beef and lamb, *yield grades* (Figure 25-16) have been established for use with quality grades. Yield grades are based on cutability, which indicates the proportionate amount of salable retail cuts that can be obtained from a carcass. Yield Grade 1 is for the highest yield and Yield Grade 5 is for the lowest. A large proportion of edible meat is indicated by a relatively large rib-eye area, a thin layer of external fat, and a small amount of fat around the internal organs.

Figure 25-14
A USDA inspector is checking pork carcasses. (Courtesy of U.S. Department of Agriculture)

The dual system of grading, for both quality and yield, attempts to offer the consumer high-quality meat without excess fat. Both quality and yield grades must be used when beef and lamb are federally graded. Conformation, or shape and build of the animal, is reflected to some degree in the yield grade. A stocky, muscular build usually represents a relatively high proportion of salable meat and receives a high yield grade.

Factors considered in determining the quality grades are associated with palatability or eating quality [97]. Marbling and maturity are the two major considerations in evaluating the quality of beef. Marbling refers to the flecks of fat within the lean muscle. An optimum thickness of surface fat layer also appears to contribute to palatability [22, 94]. Some breeds of meat-producing cattle that are considerably lower in fat than the conventional types include zebu, beefalo, Chianina, and Limousin.

The maturity of an animal affects the lean meat texture—the grain generally becoming more coarse with increasing maturity. Fine-textured lean is usually slightly more tender than lean with a very coarse texture. A mature animal develops changes in connective tissue that contribute to decreased tenderness.

Characteristics of Quality. In good-quality beef, the lean has a bright red color after the cut surface is exposed to air for a few minutes (recall that meat will be a purple-red color before it is exposed to air). It is fine grained and smooth to the touch, and the fat is firm. The chine or backbone is soft, red, and

Figure 25-15
The meat grading program is administered by the U.S. Department of Agriculture but the cost of the service is borne by the meat packers. (Courtesy of the U.S. Department of Agriculture)

Federal inspectors/graders confer in a meat packing plant. Beef carcasses are hanging in the background.

U.S. federal meat quality grade stamps are placed within a shield.

spongy, and shows considerable cartilage. The lean of a poor carcass is darker red in color, is coarse grained, and lacks the smooth, satiny surfaces when cut. In a poor-quality carcass the fat is oily or soft in texture, and the bones are white, hard, brittle, and show little or no cartilage.

Good quality in veal is shown by the grayish-pink flesh and a texture that is fine grained and smooth to the touch. The interior fat of good-quality veal is firm and brittle. The bones are red, spongy, and soft and have an abundance of cartilage. Poor quality in veal is characterized by either a very pale or a dark color of the lean and little or no fat distributed throughout the carcass.

Good quality in lamb is shown by the pinkish-red color, fine grain, and smooth cut surfaces of the flesh. The fat of good lamb is firm, flaky, and brittle, and the bones are soft, red, and spongy and show cartilage. Poor quality in lamb is characterized by darker color of the lean, heavier fat layers, and a stronger flavor.

The flesh of good-quality pork is grayish pink and fine grained. The fat of pork should be very firm but not brittle as in other types of meats. The bones

(a)

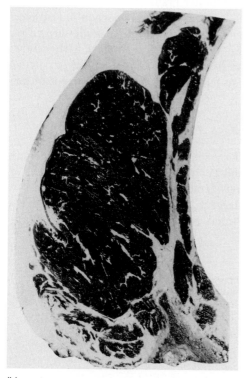 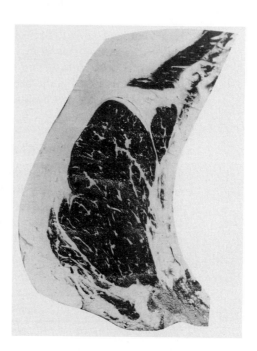

(b)

Figure 25-16
(a) U.S. yield grades identify carcass differences in cutability: the percentage yields of boneless, closely trimmed retail cuts from the high-value parts of the carcass. (Courtesy of the U.S. Department of Agriculture)
(b) Beef rib from Yield Grade 2 (left). Beef rib from Yield Grade 4 (right). (Courtesy of the U.S. Department of Agriculture)

are soft, red, and spongy. Pork of poor quality has an excess of fat distributed in the lean tissues and on the exterior. The color of the lean is darker, the grain is coarser, and the bones may appear less red and spongy. This is particularly true if the meat is from an animal beyond the optimal age limit.

Grading does not directly measure tenderness. Various studies have produced inconsistent results in relating USDA carcass grades to tenderness. Some researchers have reported that higher grades of beef showed significantly more tenderness than lower grades [78]. Others have not found significant differences, particularly between choice and select grades [93]. The variation in tenderness from one carcass to another within a grade appears to be great.

Quality Grades for Meat.   Table 25-1 shows USDA quality grades for beef, veal, lamb, and mutton. Utility and lower grades of meat are rarely, if ever, sold as cuts in retail stores, but instead are used in processed meat products. The appropriate USDA quality grade mark is applied to meat with a roller stamp that leaves its mark the full length of the carcass.

Because beef can vary so much in quality, it has eight designated grades, with USDA Prime beef being the highest quality. Only about 7 percent of marketed beef is likely to be graded Prime, and most of this beef is purchased for use in commercial foodservice. USDA Choice grade beef has slightly less marbling than prime but is still of very high quality. USDA Select grade lacks some of the juiciness and quality of the higher grades, but is usually relatively tender and palatable. USDA Standard beef has a high proportion of lean meat and little fat. It comes from young animals, as the top four grades are all restricted to beef from young animals, and is therefore usually fairly tender. USDA Commercial grade beef comes from mature animals and generally requires long cooking with moist heat to tenderize. It has the full flavor of mature beef.

Cuts of Meat and Identification

It is important in purchasing meat to have some knowledge about the retail cuts into which the carcasses are divided and to understand the relative quality characteristics of these cuts. Prices vary considerably among various cuts. Meat carcasses are first divided into relatively large primal or wholesale cuts, such as the square-cut chuck section of beef. Primal cuts are then further divided into

Table 25-1
USDA Quality Grades for Meat

Beef	Veal	Lamb	Mutton
Prime	Prime	Prime	Choice
Choice	Choice	Choice	Good
Select	Good	Good	Utility
Standard	Standard	Good	Cull
Commercial	Utility	Utility	
Utility			
Cutter			
Canner			

smaller retail cuts. Primal or wholesale and retail cuts of beef, pork, veal, and lamb are shown in Figures 25-17, 25-18, 25-19, and 25-20, respectively.

Division into cuts is made in relation to bone and muscle structure. Muscles that are found together in any one retail cut generally have similar characteristics of tenderness and texture. The shapes and sizes of bones and muscles in retail cuts act as guides to identification. Figures 25-21 and 25-22 show basic retail meat cuts that can be identified by their characteristic bone shapes. Because the skeletal structure is similar for all meat animals, the basic cuts are similar for beef, pork, veal, and lamb; however, each type of meat carcass is divided in a somewhat different manner.

Some meat cuts are known by different names in various parts of the country. For example, boneless beef top loin steaks are commonly called Delmonico, Kansas City, New York, or strip steaks; and flank steak may be called London broil or minute steak. A tri tip steak is the boneless, trimmed single muscle portion of the bottom butt of the sirloin. It is sometimes referred to as a triangle roast and ranges in weight from 1 1/2 to 2 pounds. The average thickness of the roast is about 2 inches. It is usually tender and can be roasted, broiled, or grilled.

An industrywide Cooperative Meat Identification Standards Committee, organized by the meat industry, has developed standards for the retail meat trade and provided a master list of recommended names for retail cuts of beef, pork, veal, and lamb. The list serves all regions of the United States. The recommended retail package label information includes the species or kind of meat, the primal cut name, and the specific retail name from the master list. A typical label reads "Beef Chuck—Blade Roast." When purchasing meat for food service, Institutional Meat Purchase Specifications (IMPS) provide standardized meat cuts by number. Photographs and written descriptions of the IMPS items are provided in the North America Meat Processors Association's *Meat Buyer's Guide* [72]. Photographs of selected beef and pork retail cuts are shown in Color Plates XX, XXI, XXII, XXIII, XXIV, XXVI, and XXVII.

Beef. Cuts of beef are sometimes classified by most tender, medium tender, and least tender cuts.

Most Tender Cuts	Medium Tender Cuts	Least Tender Cuts	
Rib	Chuck	Flank	
Short loin	Rump	Plate	Neck
Sirloin	Round	Brisket	Shanks

The rib and loin sections lie along the center of the back. Because that part of the body is affected little by the exercise of the animal, the meat is tender. The rib section yields the choicest roasts in the carcass.

The short loin and sirloin are cut into steaks as follows: top loin, nearest the rib, then T-bone, porterhouse, and sirloin. The tenderloin muscle, which lies on the underside of the backbone (between the backbone and kidney fat), forms one eye of meat in the loin steaks. It is very small or even nonexistent in the top loin steak area, but increases in size further back, having maximum size in the porterhouse steaks. The tenderloin may be bought as a boneless cut

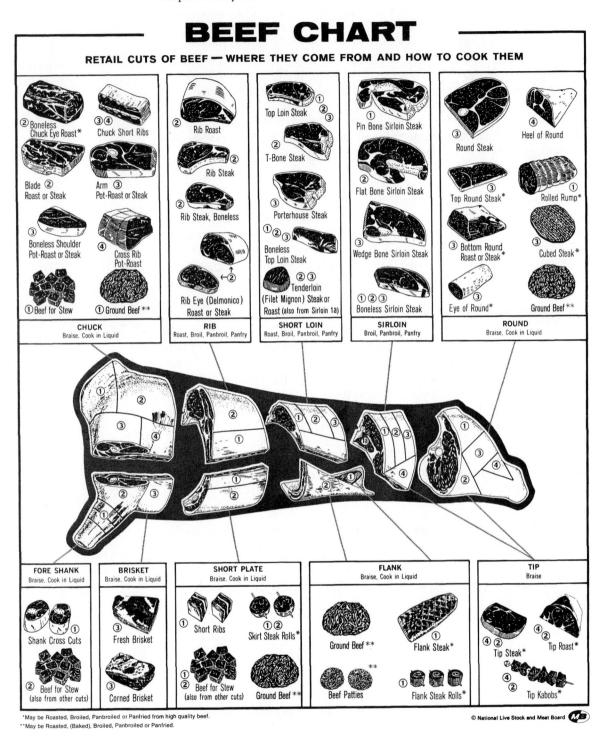

Figure 25-17
Primal and retail cuts of beef. (Courtesy of the National Live Stock and Meat Board)

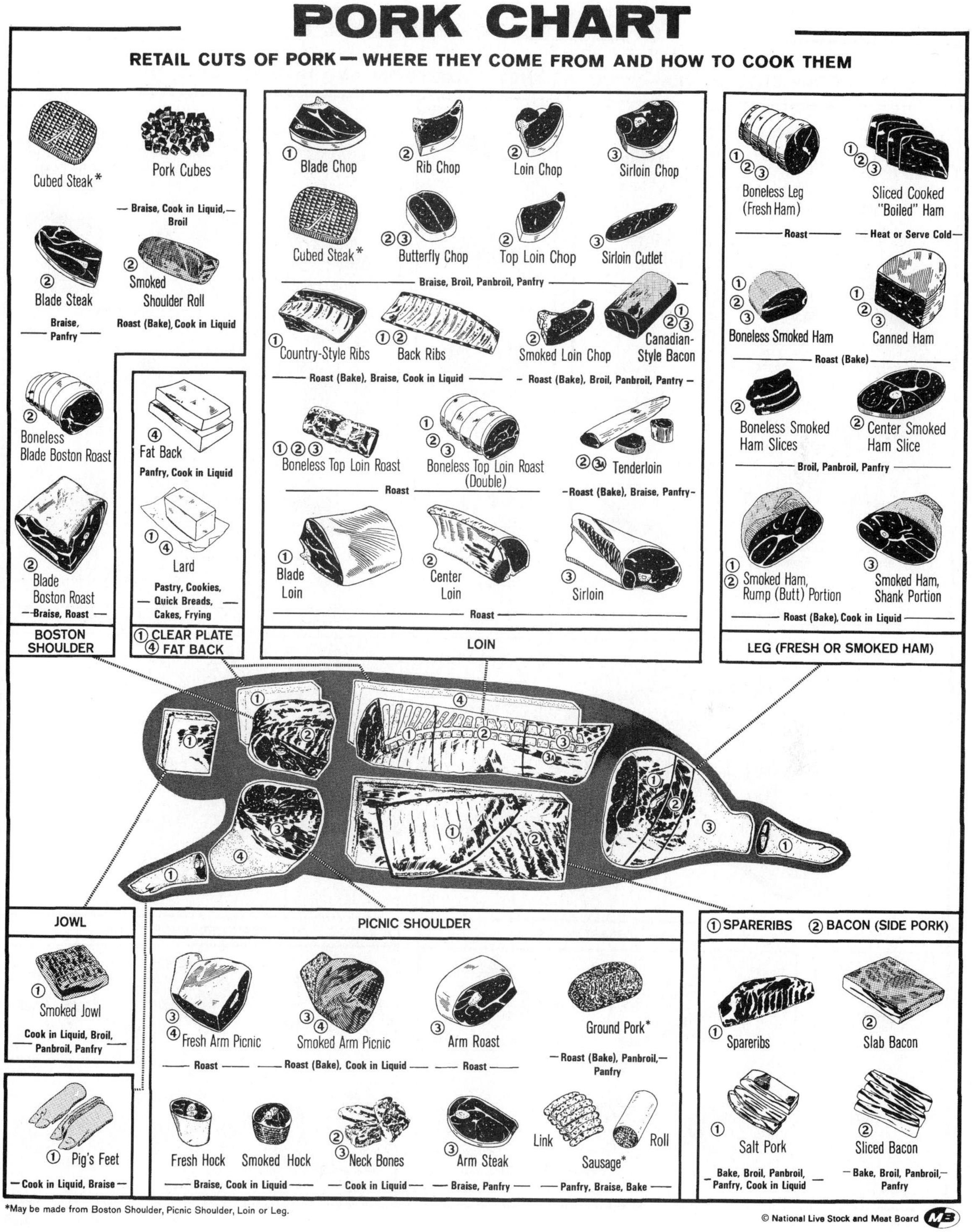

Figure 25-18
Primal and retail cuts of pork. (Courtesy of the National Live Stock and Meat Board)

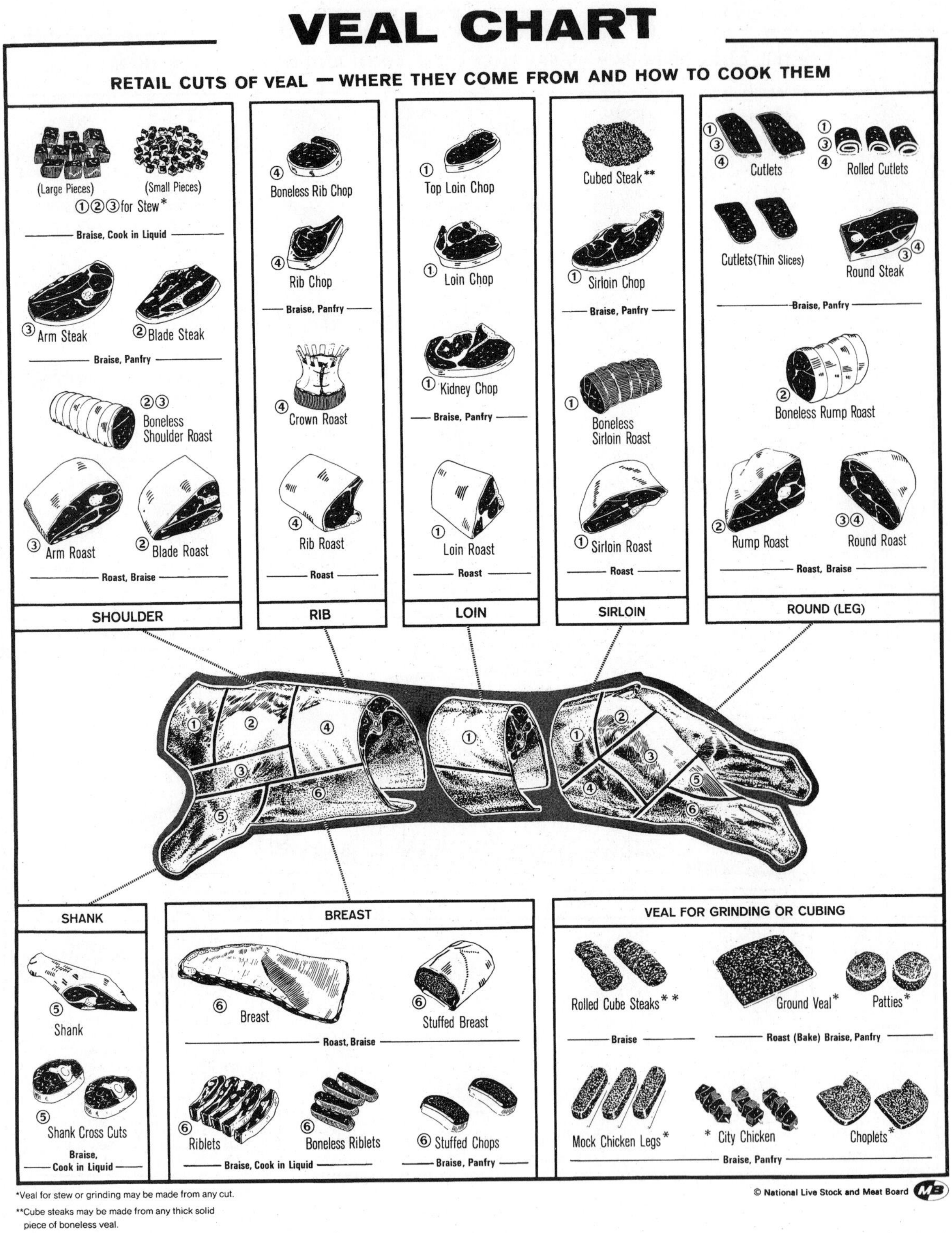

VEAL CHART

RETAIL CUTS OF VEAL — WHERE THEY COME FROM AND HOW TO COOK THEM

SHOULDER

(Large Pieces)   (Small Pieces)

① ② ③ for Stew*

— Braise, Cook in Liquid —

③ Arm Steak   ② Blade Steak

— Braise, Panfry —

② ③ Boneless Shoulder Roast

③ Arm Roast   ② Blade Roast

— Roast, Braise —

RIB

④ Boneless Rib Chop

④ Rib Chop

— Braise, Panfry —

④ Crown Roast

④ Rib Roast

— Roast —

LOIN

① Top Loin Chop

① Loin Chop

① Kidney Chop

— Braise, Panfry —

① Loin Roast

— Roast —

SIRLOIN

Cubed Steak**

① Sirloin Chop

— Braise, Panfry —

① Boneless Sirloin Roast

① Sirloin Roast

— Roast —

ROUND (LEG)

① ③ ④ Cutlets   ① ③ ④ Rolled Cutlets

Cutlets (Thin Slices)   ④ Round Steak

— Braise, Panfry —

② Boneless Rump Roast

② Rump Roast   ③ ④ Round Roast

— Roast, Braise —

SHANK

⑤ Shank

⑤ Shank Cross Cuts

— Braise, Cook in Liquid —

BREAST

⑥ Breast   ⑥ Stuffed Breast

— Roast, Braise —

⑥ Riblets   ⑥ Boneless Riblets   ⑥ Stuffed Chops

— Braise, Cook in Liquid —   — Braise, Panfry —

VEAL FOR GRINDING OR CUBING

Rolled Cube Steaks**   Ground Veal*   Patties*

— Braise —   — Roast (Bake) Braise, Panfry —

Mock Chicken Legs*   * City Chicken   Choplets*

— Braise, Panfry —

*Veal for stew or grinding may be made from any cut.

**Cube steaks may be made from any thick solid piece of boneless veal.

© National Live Stock and Meat Board

Figure 25-19

Primal and retail cuts of veal. (Courtesy of the National Live Stock and Meat Board)

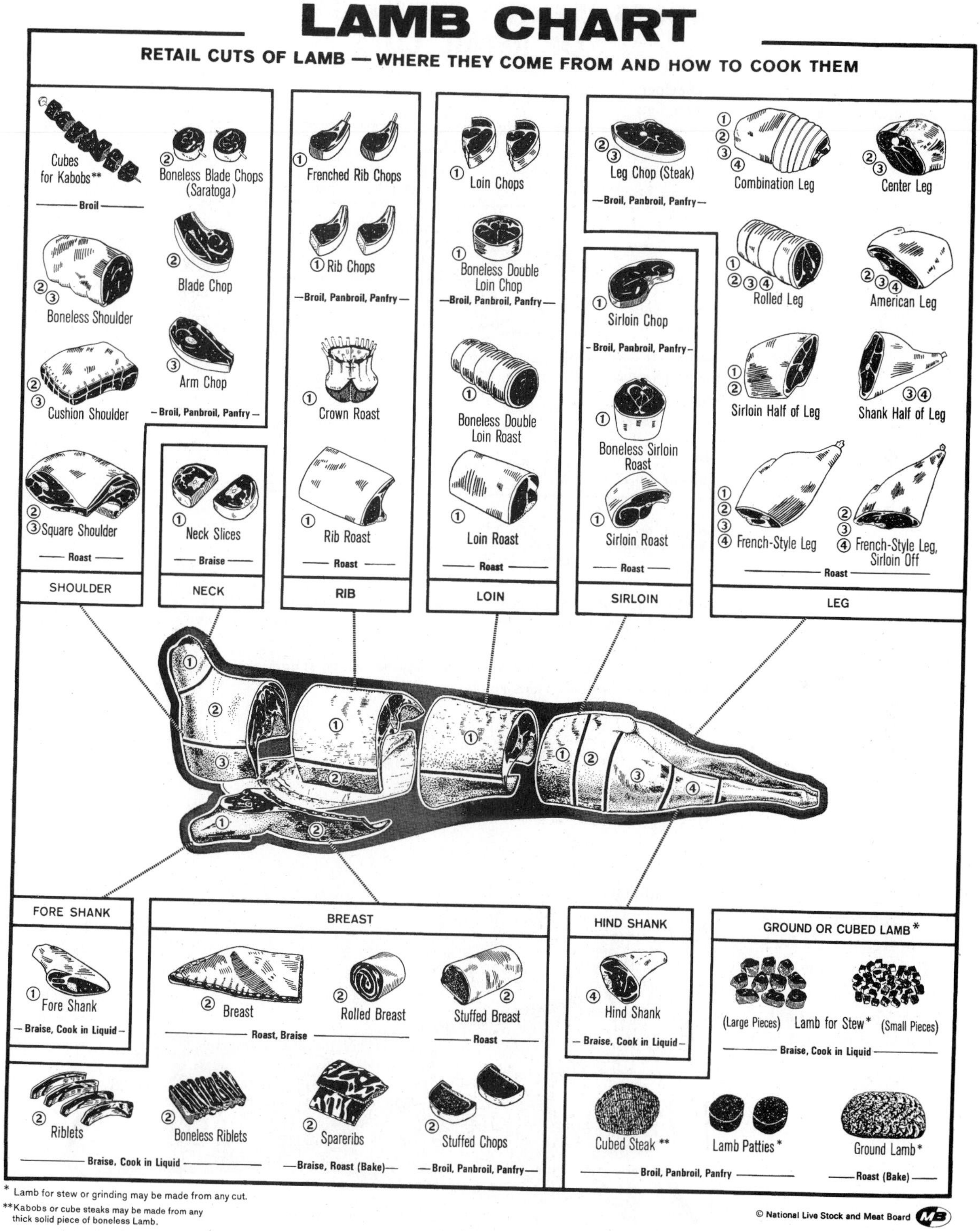

Figure 25-20
Primal and retail cuts of lamb. (Courtesy of the National Live Stock and Meat Board)

Figure 25-21
Basic bone shapes aid in meat cut identification. (From Uniform Retail Meat Identity Standards, Industrywide Cooperative Meat Identification Standards Committee, National Live Stock and Meat Board, 1973)

BONES IDENTIFY SEVEN GROUPS OF RETAIL CUTS
Shoulder Arm Cuts
Arm Bone
Shoulder Blade Cuts (Cross Sections of Blade Bone)
Blade Bone (near neck)
Blade Bone (center cuts)
Blade Bone (near rib)
Rib Cuts
Back Bone and Rib Bone
Short Loin Cuts
Back Bone (T-Shape) T-Bone
Hip (Sirloin) Cuts (Cross Sections of Hip Bone)
Pin Bone (near short loin)
Flat Bone* (center cuts)
Wedge Bone† (near round)
Leg or Round Cuts
Leg or Round Bone
Breast, or Brisket Cuts
Breast and Rib Bones
*Formerly part of "double bone" but today the back bone is usually removed leaving only the "flat bone" (sometimes called "pin bone") in the sirloin steak.
†On one side of sirloin steak, this bone may be wedge shaped while on the other side the same bone may be round.

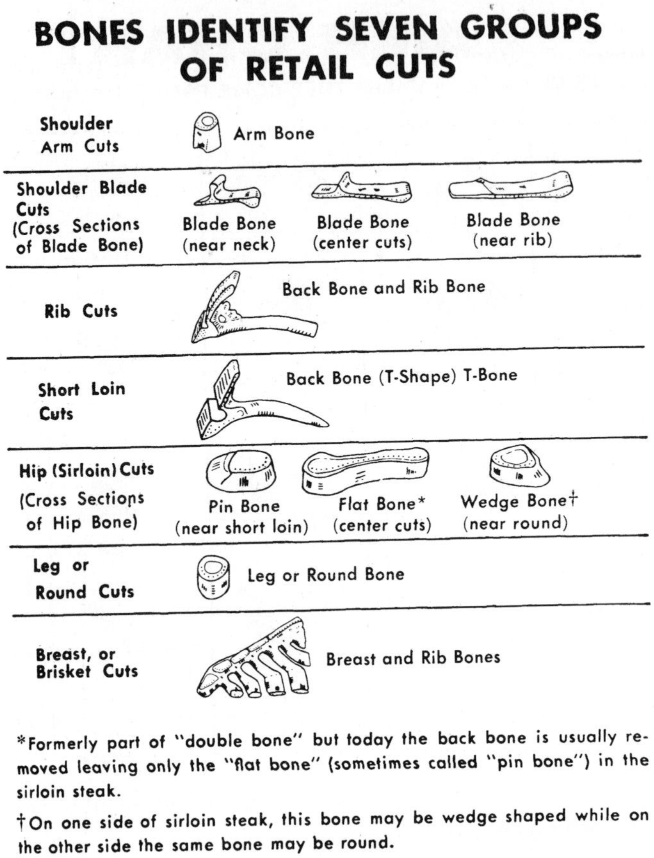

Figure 25-22
Seven basic retail cuts of meat. (From Uniform Retail Meat Identity Standards, Industrywide Cooperative Meat Identification Standards Committee, National Live Stock and Meat Board, 1973)

Blade Cuts
Blade bone
Rib Cuts
Rib bone
Loin Cuts
Backbone
T-bone
Sirloin Cuts
Hip bone
Blade Cuts
SHOULDER or CHUCK
Arm Cuts
RIB or HOTEL RACK
LOIN or SHORT LOIN
SIRLOIN or HIP
LEG or ROUND or HAM
SHANK
BRISKET
SHORT PLATE
FLANK
Rib bones
Breast bone
Arm bone
Arm Cuts
Breast
Brisket
Short Plate
Leg bone
Leg, Round and Ham Cuts

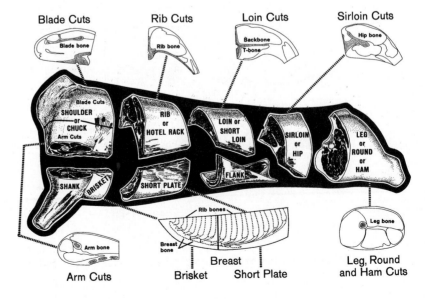

suitable for roasting or cutting into steaks. It is may not be removed from high-grade carcasses but instead from lower-grade carcasses. Because of its tenderness, tenderloin commands a high price.

The medium tender cuts are more easily made tender by moist-heat cookery than the least tender cuts. In the latter, the connective tissue is more developed.

Veal, Lamb, and Pork. Veal, lamb, and pork carcasses, being smaller than those of beef, are divided into fewer primal and retail cuts. The loin of pork is a long cut including both the rib and loin sections. The rib and loin sections of veal, lamb, and pork are cut into chops or roasts. The hind legs are also tender enough for roasts. The individual cuts are identical in general shape and characteristics to similar cuts from beef, but less variation exists in the tenderness of cuts from different sections of the animal. All cuts of young pork of good quality, both fresh and cured, are tender.

Lamb and veal are similar to beef in that neck, shoulder or chuck, breast, and shanks may require some moist heat in cooking for tenderness. Some cuts of lamb and veal are shown in Color Plate XXIV and XXV. Even the most tender cuts of veal may be improved by some application of moist heat to hydrolyze the collagen in connective tissue. The lack of fat marbling in veal may also affect its tenderness. Larding, which involves inserting strips of fat into lean meat, supplies fat and enhances the flavor. The leg, loin, and rib sections of good-quality veal may be satisfactorily roasted.

Restructured Meat. The market demand today for boneless steak meat that can be prepared rapidly cannot always be met with existing high-quality meat supplies at prices that are seen as reasonable by consumers. One way to help supply this potential market is with the production of restructured meats. *Restructuring* is changing the form of soft tissues, including lean, fat, and connective tissue [57]. The process generally begins with flaking, coarse grinding, dicing, or chopping the meat to reduce the particle size. Following this reduction process, it is mixed with small amounts of such substances as salt and phosphates to solubilize muscle proteins on the surface of the meat pieces and to aid in binding the particles together. The meat mass is then formed into the desired shape and size. Through restructuring, less valuable pieces of meat, including lean trimmings, are upgraded. They are used to produce boneless, uniformly sized steak or roast products that resemble fresh intact muscle in flavor, color, and texture [19]. For example, a Canadian *style* bacon is a restructured product, whereas Canadian bacon is a smoked and cured whole-muscle pork loin. Canadian bacon is more expensive, but if the intended use is for a sandwich, then Canadian *style* bacon may be perfectly acceptable.

The composition of restructured meats can be formulated to meet consumer demands, including low-fat items. The meat pieces used may be trimmed of connective tissue to varying degrees [84], and lean meat from grass-fed animals may be used [83].

Variety Meats Included in the category of variety meats are sweetbreads, brains, heart, tongue, tripe, liver, kidney, and oxtail (Figure 25-23). Sweetbreads are the thymus gland of the calf or young beef. This gland disappears as the animal matures. The thymus gland of lamb is sometimes used for sweetbreads but is too small to be of practical value.

Livers (top, beef; middle left, veal; middle right, lamb; bottom, pork)

Kidneys (top left, beef; top right, veal; lower left, lamb; lower right, pork)

Hearts (in order of size: beef, veal, pork, and lamb)

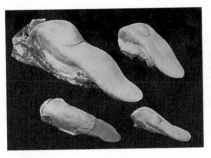

Tongues (in order of size: beef, veal, pork, and lamb)

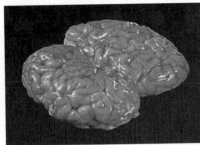

Brains

Sweetbreads

Figure 25-23
Variety meats. (Courtesy of the National Live Stock and Meat Board)

The thymus gland has two parts—the heart sweetbread and the throat, or neck, sweetbread. It is white and soft. Brains are also soft and delicate in flavor, and are very tender. However, because of concerns about BSE, brains are not marketed in countries with BSE and the continued sale in countries without BSE is under consideration. Tripe is the smooth lining from the first beef stomach, the honeycombed lining from the second stomach, and the pocket-shaped section from the end of the second stomach. The heart and tongue are much-exercised muscles and therefore are not tender. They, as well as tripe, require relatively long, slow cooking for tenderization. Liver is a fine-textured variety meat. Veal or calf liver, because of its tenderness and mild flavor, is usually preferred to other kinds of liver and for that reason is more expensive. Livers from all meat animals are high in nutritive value. Kidneys from beef and veal consist of irregular lobes and deep clefts. Kidneys from veal are more tender and delicate in flavor than those from beef.

Considerations in Buying Meat

Yield and Cost.   Considerable variation exists in the percentage of bone, muscle meat, and visible fat among retail cuts. Table 25-2 provides some information about the yield of boneless cooked meat from various cuts. Ground beef yields the largest number of 3-ounce servings per pound of beef; short ribs,

Kind and Cut of Meat	Number of 3 oz Servings	Volume, Chopped or Diced (cups)
Beef		
Brisket		
Bone-in	2	1–1½
Boneless, fresh or corned	3	1½–2
Chuck roast		
Arm		
Bone-in	2½–3	1½–2
Boneless	3½	2
Blade		
Bone-in	2½	1½
Boneless	3–3½	2
Club or T-bone steak, bone-in	2	—
Flank steak, boneless	3½	—
Ground beef	4	—
Porterhouse steak, bone-in	2–2½	—
Rib roast		
Bone-in	2½	1½
Boneless	3	1½–2
Round steak		
Bone-in	3–3½	—
Boneless	3½–4	—
Rump roast		
Bone-in	2½	1½
Boneless	3½	2
Short ribs, bone-in	1½	1
Sirloin steak		
Bone-in	2–2½	—
Boneless	2½–3	—
Veal		
Breast		
Bone-in	2	1–1½
Boneless	3	1½–2
Cutlet		
Bone-in	3½	—
Boneless	4	—
Leg roast		
Bone-in	2½	1½
Boneless	3½	2
Loin chops, bone-in	2½–3	—
Loin roast		
Bone-in	2½	1½
Boneless	3½	2
Rib chops, bone-in	2½	—
Rib roast		
Bone-in	2–2½	1–1½
Boneless	3½	2
Shoulder roast		
Bone-in	2½	1½
Boneless	3½	2

Table 25-2

*Yield of Boneless Cooked Meat from 1-Pound Retail Cuts of Beef and Veal**

*These figures allow no more than 10 percent fat on a cooked bone-in cut and no more than 15 percent fat on a cooked boneless cut.

Source: Used by permission of the U.S. Department of Agriculture.

bone-in, yield the smallest number of servings. In general, the cost per pound of an edible portion is greatest in those cuts that command the highest prices, and vice versa, but several exceptions occur because of differences in the percentage of bone and fat in the cuts. For example, at the same price per pound, the rump (bone-in) may cost almost double the price of round per pound of edible portions because only about 43 percent of the rump is edible as compared with about 76 percent of round. Also, the price per pound of short ribs would need to be quite low for this cut to be a very economical buy in terms of cooked lean meat yield. Therefore, it is important to recognize that cost per pound of meat as purchased is not the sole consideration. Waste is also a factor.

The usual amount to buy per serving is 4 ounces of meat with little or no bone, and 3/4 to 1 pound of meat with a high refuse content. One average pork chop is a serving, as is one to two lamb chops, depending on the size and thickness of the chops. In buying for foodservice operations, fresh or frozen meat may be ordered as preportioned individual servings.

Most of the less expensive cuts of meat are a more economical source of lean than expensive cuts. Retail prices are determined largely by such factors as tenderness, general appearance, and ease or convenience in cooking. The consumer tends to buy on the basis of these qualities to so great an extent that the loins and ribs, which constitute about one-fourth of the beef carcass, represent about one-half of the retail cost. Neither palatability nor food value corresponds directly to market price. Many of the less expensive, less tender cuts of meat have more flavor than tender cuts and, if properly cooked, are delicious. The food value is similar in both tender and less tender lean meat cuts. Thus, consumers have many opportunities to save money when selecting meat cuts.

Ground Beef.   A maximum fat content of 30 percent by weight has been set for beef ground in federally inspected plants. Most ground beef, however, is prepared in local supermarkets to maintain freshness. There, it is generally labeled to show the proportion of lean muscle tissue and fatty tissue that has been included.

Cooking yields of ground beef increase with decreasing fat content in the raw product, but tenderness and juiciness generally decrease [21]. Ground beef is the most commonly consumed form of red meat in the United States, accounting for approximately 42 percent of total beef consumption in 1990 [85]. Researchers continue to explore ways to produce a palatable product with low fat content [32]. Isolated soy protein has been added to lean ground beef, but it has had little or no success in increasing juiciness [55]. The addition of water, up to 10 percent, with or without added phosphate, has been reported to increase juiciness, tenderness, and overall palatability scores in low-fat ground beef patties (10 percent fat). The low-fat patties with added water scored equal in texture and flavor to those containing 22 percent fat [65]. Combinations of unhydrated dietary fiber (from sugarbeets, oats, or peas), potato starch, and **polydextrose** added to ground beef with 5 to 10 percent fat content produced cooked patties that were similar in texture to control patties containing 20 percent fat. However, the experimental patties were less juicy than the higher-fat product [95]. If the price differential between extra lean and regular ground beef is relatively great, regular ground beef may be purchased, cooked, drained of extra fat, and possibly also rinsed with hot water to substantially reduce its fat content [85]. However, if rinsed, the ground beef should be reheated up to 160°F (71°C).

polydextrose a bulking agent often used with nonnutritive sweeteners in manufactured foods

Ground chuck must come specifically from the chuck area of the carcass, and ground round must come only from the round. Because of marked differences in cost per pound for ground beef, ground chuck, and ground round, ground beef is often the best buy per pound of protein and per pound edible yield. Even though the fat content may be highest in ground beef, intermediate in ground chuck, and lowest in ground round, much of the fat in the ground beef is rendered out during cooking.

Irradiated ground beef may be purchased as one method of avoiding *E. coli* O157:H7 (Figure 25-24). The meat industry and the government are pursuing methods of reducing the risk of *E. coli* O157:H7 contaminated meat reaching the marketplace. Microbiological product testing has resulted in meat recalls. However, because a small number of organisms can cause disease, irradiation can provide a high level of safety [4, 76]. This extra level of protection may be especially important when serving populations at a high risk for foodborne illness such as children or when preparing ground beef in situations where careful and consistent temperature control may be difficult. In one study, consumers rated irradiated and control ground beef patties equally for overall liking, toughness, flavor, and texture. The irradiated beef patties were rated as juicier than the nonirradiated [108].

Figure 25-24
Irradiated ground beef can take the worry out of grilling hamburgers by significantly reducing the risk of E. coli O157:H7. (Courtesy of Agricultural Research Service, U.S. Department of Agriculture; photo by Stephen Ausmus)

Packaging. Centralized packaging of fresh red meat or *case-ready* meat may be much more prevalent in grocery stores in the future. Most supermarkets receive reduced-oxgygen barrier bags of primal cuts or chubs of coarsely ground beef that are opened and processed further prior to repackaging onto expanded polystyrene (EPS) trays that are then overwrapped with PVC film [13]. Centralized packaging would move the cutting and packaging steps from the supermarket meat departments into centralized operations. Costs can be reduced and the microbiological quality of the product may improve. One of the challenges is providing the cherry red color that consumers appear to demand for beef instead of the purple red color common in reduced oxygen packages. Although much of the pork and chicken sold in supermarkets is case-ready, consumers and supermarkets will need to decide if they are ready for centrally packaged, case-ready beef.

CURED MEATS

For centuries, curing has been an important method for preserving meat. At one time, salt (sodium chloride) in comparatively large amounts was the substance used in curing. Today, curing ingredients include sodium nitrite, sugar, and seasonings, in addition to salt. Nitrite reacts with myoglobin, the red pigment of meat, producing nitrosylmyoglobin, which later changes to the characteristic pink color of cured meats during the heating portion of the curing process. The heated pink pigment is *nitric oxide hemochrome.*

Nitrite is toxic when consumed in excessive amounts. In addition, it has been shown that certain cancer-producing substances, called *nitrosamines,* can be formed in food products or in the acid environment of the stomach by reactions between nitrite and **secondary amines.** The FDA has therefore limited the amount of nitrite that can be present in a finished cured product. However, nitrite, in addition to fixing color in cured meats, contributes to the development of characteristic flavor and inhibits the growth of the bacterium *Clostridium botulinum.* This organism has the ability, under suitable conditions, to produce a deadly toxin. Other ingredients, such as vitamins C and E, are now used with the lesser amounts of nitrite [17]. A 1997 report of analysis for nitrite in cured meats obtained from the marketplace indicated that the current residual nitrite level is approximately one-fifth the level of 25 years ago [18]. The risks from nitrites are considered to be very low at this time. In 2000, a review of data from a long-term rodent study concluded there was no evidence that nitrite is a carcinogen in male and female rats and male mice. The evidence for female mice was insufficient [3]. No doubt research on this subject will continue.

Salt in the curing mixture inhibits the growth of undesirable microorganisms during curing and adds flavor. Salt, in sufficient quantities with or without other curing agents, also causes the development of a heated pink pigment. This change in color can occur accidently and undesirably in products such as meatloaf if the salt content is high enough and the product is not cooked shortly after mixing. Raw, processed turkey breasts also may show this color defect if the salt used in processing was at too high a level. Both of these products will remain pink even if thoroughly cooked. In processed meats such as ham, or smoked turkey, this pink color is expected.

Some processed meats are being produced with lower salt content because of the interest in decreasing the sodium levels in the American diet. Phosphates

secondary amines derivatives of ammonia (NH_3) in which two of the hydrogen atoms are replaced by other carbon-containing chemical groups

$$\begin{matrix} R \\ \diagdown \\ & NH \\ \diagup \\ R \end{matrix}$$

may also be used in curing solutions to decrease shrinkage in meat by retaining moisture.

Ham, bacon, smoked pork-shoulder picnic, and Canadian bacon are commonly cured pork cuts. Corned beef is the cured brisket of beef. Frankfurters and a variety of sausages are also cured products. The desire to reduce the amount of fat in meats has extended to the cured meat-processing industry. **Comminuted** emulsion-type products such as wieners, sausages, and bologna can be produced with reduced fat levels. An increased level of water, with binders such as starch, cereal, soy flour, soy protein concentrate, and nonfat dry milk, can be used to produce texture and sensory properties similar to those of the higher-fat products [35].

During the curing process, the curing mixture may be rubbed dry on the outside of a cut of meat, or the meat may be submerged in a solution of the curing ingredients. The rate of diffusion of the ingredients into the meat is, however, slow. The curing ingredients are much more rapidly and uniformly distributed throughout the meat when they are injected internally. In meat cuts in which the vascular system is still intact, as in hams, briskets, and tongues, the curing solution may be pumped into the arteries. Brine may be injected with needles into other cuts such as bacon. Pumping the curing solution into meat increases the weight of the meat. Federal regulations require that a ham must be "shrunk" back to at least its original fresh weight by the time heating and/or smoking is completed. If not, the ham must be labeled "ham, water added" if it contains up to 10 percent added moisture. Hams labeled country-style are processed by using a dry cure, slow smoking, and a long drying process. They are firm textured, relatively low in moisture (about 85 percent of the original weight), and always require cooking before eating.

It is no longer necessary to cure ham primarily for preservation purposes, since refrigeration is readily available; thus, ham is cured with more interest in flavor and color. After the injection of curing solution, hams are heated or smoked. During this process they are heated to an internal temperature of 140°F (60°C), but they need additional cooking before serving. Hams labeled "fully cooked" are heated to an internal temperature of about 150°F (66°C). No additional cooking is required, but they may be cooked further if desired. Canned hams that have been processed at sterilizing temperatures are also available. All processed products containing pork must be treated so that any trichinae present are destroyed, as this organism causes trichinosis in humans.

More than 200 varieties of sausages and luncheon meats are marketed in the United States (Figure 25-25). These are made from chopped or ground meat with various seasonings and often contain curing ingredients. Sausages are usually molded in casings, either natural or manufactured, or in metal molds. Many casings are edible, but some, such as the casings used for summer sausage, are not edible and should be removed prior to use.

Amendments to the standards of identity for frankfurters and other similar cooked sausages allow low-fat processed meat products to be included. A maximum combination of 40 percent fat and added water is allowed, with the maximum fat content no more than 30 percent. The maximum allowable level of binders, individually or collectively, is 3.5 percent. Sausages containing more than 3.5 percent of the various binders or more than 2 percent of isolated soy protein or caseinate must be labeled "imitation" [32]. Frankfurters may contain up to 15 percent poultry without special labeling. Turkey is used in the produc-

comminute to reduce to small, fine particles

Figure 25-25
Agricultural research scientists study the source of flavor differences in deli meats, bologna, and sausages. Consumers have a wide variety of meats from which to choose. (Courtesy of the Agricultural Research Service, U.S. Department of Agriculture; photo by Scott Bauer)

tion of a variety of sausages, frankfurters, and luncheon meats, including bologna. Sausages can be classified as follows:

1. Uncooked
    a. Fresh pork sausage in bulk or encased as links
    b. Fresh bratwurst
    c. Bockwurst
2. Cooked
    a. Bologna (small, medium, and large)
    b. Frankfurters (wieners)
    c. Knockwurst
    d. Liver sausage or Braunschweiger
    e. Miscellaneous loaves
3. Semidry or dry
    a. Salami
    b. Cervelat
    c. Pepperoni

Cured meat pigments tend to be oxidized and to discolor when exposed to the lighting of display cases in supermarkets. Vacuum packaging in oxygen-impermeable material prevents oxygen from coming in contact with the meat. Such packaging increases the shelf life of processed products such as bacon and luncheon meats by controlling the oxidation of pigments and the development of oxidized off-flavors.

SAFE STORAGE AND PREPARATION OF MEATS

Storage and Handling

Fresh meats require a cold storage temperature that is at or below 40°F (4.5°C). To maintain the cold temperature of the product, meats should be placed in the refrigerator immediately upon delivery. Coolers for meat in foodservice operations should be set at 36°F (2°C) or colder. Most meats on the retail market are prepackaged for self-service. The films used for covering the packages of fresh meats are usually permeable to oxygen so that the color of the meat will remain bright red. Prepackaged meats can be placed in the refrigerator in their original packages, but should be used within a few days or frozen for longer storage. Fresh meat that has not been prepackaged should be removed from the market wrapping and stored loosely wrapped in waxed paper, plastic wrap, or aluminum foil.

Meats should not be placed above other foods in the refrigerator, particularly vegetables, unless they are held in a leak-proof container. If bacteria are present on meat and its drippings come in contact with other foods, cross-contamination can occur.

Moist meat surfaces are conducive to bacterial growth. Slight drying of the surface is preferable to bacterial action. Ground meats and variety meats are particularly perishable and should be cooked within 1 to 2 days after purchase if they are not frozen. Frozen ground meat should be defrosted in the refrigerator, in the microwave and cooked immediately after thawing, or in cold, running water—never at room temperature. When handling meat, everything should be kept clean—hands, utensils, counters, cutting boards, and sinks. In particular, wash, rinse, and sanitize utensils that have touched raw meat before using them for cooked meats.

Suggested storage times for some meats are given in Table 25-3. For freezing, meat should be wrapped tightly in moisture-/vapor-proof material (Figure 25-26). The meat may be divided into serving-size portions before freezing. It should be kept frozen at 0°F (−18°C) until used.

Preparation

Knowledge of and adherence to the recommended endpoint cooking temperatures of meat is necessary to prevent foodborne illness. All raw meats are more or less contaminated with a variety of bacteria, some of which may constitute

Table 25-3

Suggested Storage Periods to Maintain High Quality in Beef and Veal

	Storage Period	
Product	Refrigerator [35° to 40°F (2° to 4°C)]	Freezer [0°F (−18°C)]
Fresh meat		
Chops and cutlets	3–5 days	3–4 months
Ground beef or veal	1–2 days	2–3 months
Roasts		
Beef	3–5 days	8–12 months
Veal	3–5 days	4–8 months
Steaks	3–5 days	8–12 months
Stew meat	1–2 days	2–3 months
Variety meats	1–2 days	3–4 months
Cooked meat and meat dishes	1–2 days	2–3 months

Source: Used by permission of the U.S. Department of Agriculture.

Figure 25-26
Wrapping instructions for meat that is to be frozen. (Courtesy of National Cattlemen's Beef Association)

Wrapping Instructions

Choose a moisture/vapor-proof freezer wrap to seal out air and lock in moisture. Heavy duty, pliable wraps such as aluminum foil, freezer paper and plastic wrap are good choices for bulky, irregular-shaped beef cuts since they can be molded to the shape of the cut.

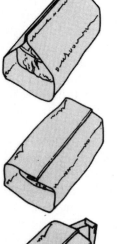

1. Place beef cut in center of wrapping material. When several cuts are packaged together, place a double thickness of freezer wrap between them for easier separation.

2. Bring edges of wrap together over beef. Fold over at least twice, pressing wrap closely to beef to force out air.

3. Smooth ends of wrap, creasing edges to form triangles. Double-fold ends toward package to seal out air.

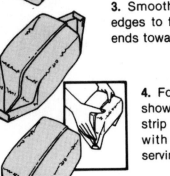

4. Fold ends under package as shown and seal with continuous strip of freezer tape. Label tape with name of cut, number of servings and date of freezing.

hazards, particularly if the food is mishandled or undercooked. In addition, flesh foods may contain parasites or the larvae of tapeworms when they are raw.

Ground beef must be cooked to at least 155°F (68°C) for 15 seconds in foodservice operations and 160°F (70°C) in home kitchens to destroy any *Escherichia coli* O157:H7 that may be present. The ground beef temperature guidelines also should be applied to beef products that have been punctured, such as blade tenderized or minute steaks. Beef steaks and roasts may be cooked to lower temperatures (145°F or 63°C) since these solid muscle meats will be heated to high enough temperatures to kill bacteria that could be present on the surface. Pork steaks and roasts must be cooked to 145°F (63°C) to destroy *Trichinela spiralis*. Ground pork, like ground beef, must be cooked to 155°F (68°C). Although the infection rate of pork with *Trichinela spiralis* has declined considerably over the years, cooking to recommended temperatures is still advisable. Lamb should be cooked to an endpoint temperature of 145°F (63°C). When cooking any meat in a microwave oven, an endpoint temperature 25°F (14°C) higher than in conventional cooking is recommended. All previously cooked products should be reheated to 165°F (74°C) [71]. See Chapter 3 for additional guidance on safe cooking temperatures.

Ground meat has special potential for harboring pathogens. *Escherichia coli* O157:H7 caused concern after several outbreaks of hemorrhagic colitis resulting in some deaths were traced to ground beef patties in the early 1990's. Efforts to control this organism, and other potential dangers, at all levels of production and processing include treatment of ground beef with ionizing radiation (which has been approved by the FDA) and testing for this pathogen during processing as part of the inspection process. Food-handling and preparation practices play important roles in preventing foodborne illness.

One important contributing factor in *E. coli* O157:H7 outbreaks associated with ground beef has been *undercooking* [15]. For safety, ground meat should always be cooked to the recommended internal temperature and checked with a properly calibrated thermometer. In the early 1990's, consumers were told to cook their ground beef until the juices ran clear; however, starting in 1997 the Food Safety Inspection Service (FSIS) began recommending the use of a food thermometer [82]. This change was made because research conducted at Kansas State University and later confirmed by the USDA's Agricultural Research Service found that some meat appears to be brown before reaching a safe endpoint temperature. Thus, color is not a reliable indicator of doneness.

One group of researchers found that nearly 50 percent of the patties tested showed premature browning [46]. This study supported other research [42], that found patties were more likely to brown before reaching a safe internal temperature if the ground beef contains predominately oxymyoglobin (cherry-red) or metmyoglobin (brown) pigments. Alternatively some lean ground beef or ground beef that contains spices and spice extractives may remain pink at temperatures well above 160°F (70°C).

COOKING MEAT

In preparing meat for cooking, the outer surfaces may require some trimming. Any dried or otherwise undesirable portions may be trimmed off, but it is not necessary to trim off government inspection and grade stamps. Safe vegetable dyes are used in the stamping process. Splinters of bone should be removed.

Meats generally are more appealing and palatable to most people when cooked. It is important in meat cookery to know the nature of the cut to be cooked and then to choose the proper method for cooking it. Because the meat from most young animals and from the least-exercised muscles of more mature animals is tender, it has a small amount of connective tissue and should be kept tender during cooking. Less tender meats require tenderization during cooking to make them palatable. Distinctive flavors are developed by some methods of cooking.

General Methods

Conventional cooking of meat is divided into dry-heat and moist-heat methods. Dry-heat cookery traditionally includes roasting or baking, broiling, and pan-broiling. Frying can also be included in this classification because fat, not moisture, comes in contact with the surface of the meat during cooking. These procedures are discussed in more detail under "Specific Cooking Methods." Cooking by microwaves is suitable, as are all dry-heat methods, for cooking tender cuts of meat. Microwave cooking at low power levels can also be used for less tender cuts of meat.

Moist-heat methods are braising, stewing or cooking in water, and pressure cooking (Figure 25-27). Simmering temperatures for stewing are sometimes specified on the assumption that the boiling temperature toughens meat; however, there is apparently little difference in the final tenderness of meats cooked in water at simmering or boiling temperatures. The term *fricassee* may be applied to braised meats cut into small pieces before cooking. The braising of large pieces of meat is sometimes called *pot-roasting*. When meats are braised, their surfaces may first be browned using dry heat by pan-broiling or frying.

For many years, dry-heat methods of cooking were generally applied only to tender cuts of meat, whereas moist-heat methods were thought to be necessary to tenderize all less tender pieces. However, roasting less tender cuts with dry heat can be satisfactorily accomplished using very low oven temperatures and long periods of time [50]. The flavors developed in beef during roasting and broiling seem to be favored by most people over those developed in braising or pot-roasting.

Beef loin, generally considered tender, and bottom round, generally considered less tender, do not respond alike to moist- and dry-heat methods of cooking. Some researchers [20] have found that loin steaks become tougher as they are cooked thoroughly and that moist heat does not seem to tenderize them. Bottom round steaks braised very well done are much more tender than loin steaks cooked in the same way. Although moist-heat methods seem to be unsuitable for some tender cuts of meat, dry-heat methods seem to be suitable for both tender and less tender cuts if the time of cooking is adapted. Apparently there is enough water in the meat itself to provide for the hydrolysis of connective tissue during cooking. Additional water, as in braising or stewing, is not necessary for this purpose.

Figure 25-27
This savory beef stew with roasted vegetables is prepared by lightly browning the beef in oil then simmering until tender. (Courtesy of the Cattlemen's Beef Board through the National Cattlemen's Beef Association)

Effect of Heat on Meat

Heat produces many changes in meat. Studies conducted using small pieces of meat that were heated more quickly and uniformly than large roasts have shown that a decrease in tenderness occurs when the meat reaches from 104° to 140°F (40° to 60°C). This is followed by a gradual increase in tenderness above 140°F (60°C) or even above 122°F (50°C) in young animals. The original toughening appears to be the result of a shortening of the fibers accompanied by hardening as the proteins **denature** and **coagulate**. The later tenderizing evidently results from the softening of connective tissue and the hydrolysis to gelatin of some collagen in this tissue [11, 52, 61].

The response of an individual muscle to heating apparently depends to some degree on the amount of connective tissue; however, the muscle fibers from different muscles may also react differently toward heat. In one study, researchers heated a tender muscle (longissimus dorsi) and less tender muscles (semitendinosus and semimembranosus) of beef to three different internal temperatures. They found that the tender muscle did not change in tenderness with increasing degrees of doneness, but the two less tender muscles increased in tenderness with higher internal temperatures [88]. The less tender muscles contained more connective tissue, which was evidently softened with increased temperatures. A different balance between the hardening of muscle fibers and the softening of connective tissue was achieved in the less tender muscles than in the tender muscle.

Fat melts when meat is heated, and the capacity of the muscle proteins to hold water is lessened, thus causing reduced juiciness and tenderness and increased weight loss. The volume of the meat decreases on cooking.

Significant visual color changes occur in heated meat between 140° and 150°F (60° and 65°C) and between 168° and 176°F (75° and 80°C) [12]. Redness decreases as internal temperature increases. The meat pigment myoglobin appears to be denatured around 140°F (60°C), and denaturation of other proteins seems to be complete by 176°F (80°C). However, as previously noted, a brown color is not a reliable indicator of the doneness of ground beef.

denaturation a change in a protein molecule, usually by unfolding of the amino acid chains, with a decrease in solubility

coagulation usually a change in proteins after denaturation, with new bonds being formed between protein chains, resulting in precipitation or gel formation

Cooking Losses

Cooking losses, including loss of weight and loss of nutrients, increase gradually with increasing internal temperatures [12]. Weight loss results from the formation of drippings, evaporation of water, and evaporation of other volatile substances. When meat is roasted in an open pan, considerable evaporation of water from the meat surface occurs, but nutrients and flavor substances are better retained in the meat than when the meat is cooked in water or steam. As water evaporates, minerals and extractives are deposited on the surface of the meat, which may account in part for the pronounced flavor of the outer brown layer of roasted meat.

Fat losses are less consistent than those of other constituents, probably because of the unequal distribution of fat throughout most pieces of meat. Fat on or near the surface is lost to a greater extent than fat in the interior because of the slowness of heat penetration. Not all fat that liquefies is lost, because some of it can and does penetrate to the interior. The fat layer on the outside of meat aids in decreasing water loss by preventing evaporation. Researchers have found that the degree of fat trim on raw beef loin steaks did not significantly affect the sensory characteristics of the cooked meat; however, the fat content of the cooked steak with the fat totally trimmed off was significantly less than the fat content of the steak with regular trim [1]. In cooking ground beef, either as patties or as crumbles, fat losses are greater when the fat content of the raw meat is higher [56]. Ground beef with 20 percent and 30 percent fat in the raw state was reported to yield cooked meats with similar fat contents, which were only slightly greater than the fat content of cooked ground beef that contained 10 percent fat in the raw state.

The final internal temperature to which meat is cooked influences total weight losses. Weight loss increases with increasing internal temperature. Total weight loss is usually greater in moist-heat than in dry-heat methods of cooking meat. Top round steaks showed total cooking losses of 27.5 percent when they were cooked by moist heat as compared with 20.6 percent when they were cooked by dry heat [70].

Although some losses of B vitamins, including thiamin, riboflavin, and niacin, occur during cooking, cooked meats are still good sources of these vitamins. Greater vitamin losses occur during braising and stewing than during roasting and broiling, but many are retained in the cooking liquid. Vitamin retention in meats during cooking in water is dependent on the cooking time, with greater losses occurring as cooking continues. Riboflavin and niacin are more resistant to destruction by heat than thiamin.

Shrinkage

Shrinkage in cooked meats begins at 122° to 140°F (50° to 60°C) because of the shortening of muscle fibers and coagulation of proteins. There is loss of water and melting of fat. The higher the interior temperature of the meat, the greater the shrinkage. Less shrinkage usually occurs in meats roasted at 300° to 350°F (149° to 177°C) than in meats roasted at higher oven temperatures. Meats roasted for the whole cooking time at a high oven temperature may shrink as much as 40 to 60 percent as compared with 15 or 20 percent at low temperatures. It is wise to consider excess shrinkage in economic terms, as fewer servings can be obtained from meats that have been allowed to shrink excessively during cooking. Particularly in quantity cookery, the yield of the meat can have a very noticeable impact on the number of servings available after cooking.

Basting

Pouring or spooning liquids such as meat drippings or a marinade over the surface of meat while it is roasting is called *basting*. The major purpose of basting is to keep the surface moist, but the use of a savory liquid also enhances the flavor of the cooked meat. If meats are placed in the roasting pan with the fat layer on top, the melted fat flows over the surface of the roast as it cooks and self-basting occurs.

Salting

When should meat be salted? There is debate about the answer to this question. Rubs have become popular in the preparation of many meat dishes. Rubs are a mixture of spices and herbs that may be used dry or wet to season meat [51]. Many of the rubs do include salt and it is clear that these rubs add a unique flavor to the dish even if it is a large roast that was seasoned with the rub before cooking (Figure 25-28).

Others prefer not to salt their meat before cooking. If the piece of meat is large, the salt will not penetrate a roast to a depth greater than 1/2 inch. Putting a lot of salt on the outer surface may result in too salty an outer layer or salty drippings. The outer layer then also becomes crusty. Therefore some find it unnecessary to salt a roast before cooking. Salt retards the browning of meat, and for that reason, salt may be applied to steaks and chops after they are cooked.

Meatloaves cannot be well seasoned unless salt is mixed with the meat before the loaf is shaped. To season small pieces of meat, as in stew, salt may be added to the cooking water. Total losses from the meat seem to be no greater in salted than in unsalted stews.

Although salting a raw or slightly cooked surface of meat draws juice to the surface, it has not been proven that salting meats before or during cooking

(a)　　　　　　　　　　　　　　　　(b)

Figure 25-28
(a) This Italian beef roast was rubbed with a mixture of basil, oregano, salt and pepper prior to roasting. (Courtesy of the Cattlemen's Beef Board through the National Cattlemen's Beef Association) *(b) A purchased Italian seasoning blend was rubbed on this pork loin roast before roasting.* (Courtesy of Pork Producers Council)

results in any greater total losses from the meat than would occur if meats were not salted.

Juiciness

Juiciness is a highly desirable characteristic in cooked meats. Depending on such factors as the quality of the meat, the amount of marbling, and aging, meats differ in their juiciness. Aged meats are usually the juiciest of meats. The meat from younger animals is often more juicy than that from older animals. The amount of fat in a piece of meat, particularly fat marbled throughout the muscle, may increase the apparent juiciness of meat as it is eaten. In comparing the sensory properties of ground beef patties with three different levels of fat, it was reported that juiciness, as well as tenderness, was associated with the higher amounts of fat [9].

The interior temperature to which meats are cooked affects juiciness, with meats cooked to the rare and medium-done stages being more juicy than well-done meats. In fact, it is difficult to cook meats to a brown interior color without a substantial loss of juiciness.

Meats that are cooked for a long time in moist heat to develop tenderness reach so high an interior temperature that they cannot fail to be dry. If meats are cooked in moisture and are served in the cooking liquid, as Swiss steak is, they may appear to be moist, but that moistness is not juiciness within the meat itself.

Tenderization

Proper cooking contributes to the development of the desirable trait of tenderness in less tender meat and to its preservation in already tender cuts. The tender cuts do not contain large amounts of connective tissue, which may need to be softened by long cooking. Therefore, overcooking of these cuts should be avoided.

Adequate tenderization of connective tissue generally occurs with either the application of moist heat or the use of dry heat for extremely long cooking periods at low temperatures. In either case, tenderization results from hydrolysis of the collagen in connective tissue to produce gelatin. A firming effect that may take place in muscle fibers subjected to long cooking is more than counterbalanced by the softening of connective tissue. However, if the meat is not carved across the grain, producing short muscle fiber segments, the long intact muscle fibers that are separated because of connective tissue disintegration may contribute to apparent toughness as the meat is eaten. Proper carving of meat thus contributes to tenderness as the meat is served.

Less tender cuts of beef can be tenderized to some extent by soaking the meat in an acid-containing marinade for 24 to 48 hours before cooking [40, 77]. The tenderizing effect is dependent upon the concentration of acid present. Marinated beef muscles with a pH of 3.25 have been found to be significantly more tender than those with a pH of 4.25 [77]. At the lower pH, the water-binding capacity of the muscle is increased, the total collagen content is reduced, and cooking losses are decreased. Meats should always be marinated in the refrigerator, not on the counter. Marinade used on raw meat or poultry should not be reused unless it is boiled first to destroy any bacteria.

Meat tenderizers increase the tenderness of meat through enzymatic hydrolysis of proteins in the tissue as the meat is heated [29]. (See "Factors Affecting Tenderness" earlier in this chapter.)

Specific Cooking Methods

Roasting or Baking. Historically, the term *roasting* was applied to the cooking of large cuts of meat before an open fire. Today the terms *roasting* and *baking* are often used synonymously and apply to the method of placing meat on a rack in an open pan and cooking by the dry heat of an oven. Baking is actually more commonly used with portion cuts and roasting with large pieces of meat (Figure 25-29).

The oven temperature generally recommended for roasting tender cuts of meat is 325°F (177°C). As the oven temperature is increased from 300° to 450°F (149° to 232°C), the cooking time for meats cooked to the same internal temperature is decreased, total cooking losses are increased, and the uniformity of doneness throughout the meat is decreased.

Adequate browning for good flavor and attractive appearance occurs at low constant oven temperatures, particularly if temperatures of 325° and 350°F (163° and 177°C) are used. A higher temperature can be used at the end of the roasting period merely for browning purposes, but is usually not necessary. A high temperature at the beginning does not seal in juices.

Meat can also be roasted in a convection oven in which the heated air is constantly recirculated by means of a fan. The cooking process is speeded up in convection ovens and the roasting time is therefore somewhat less than with a conventional oven.

In the past, roasting has been recommended only for cuts of meat that are expected to be tender, and moist-heat methods of cooking have been suggested for less tender cuts. However, studies have shown that less tender cuts of beef are tender and acceptable when roasted at oven temperatures of 225° to 250°F (107° to 121°C) [73]. They are more moist and juicy than similar cuts that are braised. The cooking time at the low temperature is considerably extended.

A meat thermometer or an instant read thermometer should preferably be used to determine the stage of doneness; the thermometer is inserted in the

Figure 25-29
This roast is being checked for doneness with an instant read thermometer. Notice the temperature is taken in the center of the roast. (Reference 51.)

thickest portion of the meat (Figure 25-29). Using a thermometer is the only accurate way to know the interior temperature or stage of doneness of the meat. Different types of food thermometers are available. Meat thermometers may remain in the roast while it is cooking. Instant read thermometers may be used to check the internal temperature at the end of the cooking period, but may not be left in the oven.

Meat can be cooked by minutes per pound (Table 25-4). These times are only estimates, however, because pieces of meat of the same weight may vary greatly in shape, thickness, and the proportion of meat to bone. Thus, it is desirable to check the temperature with a thermometer near the end of the anticipated cooking period. A standing rib roast cooks in less time than a rolled rib roast because the latter is made more compact by boning and rolling. Large roasts of the same general shape as small roasts require fewer minutes per pound.

The recommended internal temperatures for fresh beef or lamb cooked to various stages of doneness are as follows [102, 104]:

Medium rare	145°F (63°C)
Medium	160°F (71°C)
Well done	170°F (77°C)

The color of the meat's interior changes as the internal temperature increases and the muscle pigments are denatured and coagulated. Bright red or pink gradually changes to grayish pink and finally to grayish brown. The appearance may vary at a specific internal temperature, depending on the particular cut of meat being cooked and on the cooking procedure, especially the length of time required to reach the final temperature. For example, a beef roast may appear less well done when cooked to the same internal temperature at a high oven temperature than when cooked at a low temperature because of the shorter cooking time at the high temperature. Some unaged beef may still have some pink color at 170°F (77°C) and may require cooking a few degrees higher to reach a gray stage. A thermometer should, therefore, be used as a more accurate method to assess desired degree of doneness.

The cooking of fresh pork to a final internal temperature of 175° to 185°F (79° to 85°C) was recommended for many years to ensure destruction of the parasite *Trichinella spiralis*, which might be present in the pork muscle. Later studies, however, found that *Trichinella* was destroyed at a lower temperature. The USDA now recommends a final cooking temperature of 160°F (71°C) for medium-cooked pork and 170°F (77°C) for well-done pork in the home [105]. In foodservice operations, the minimum safe cooking temperature for fresh pork is 145°F (63°C) [71]. Generally, increased juiciness and decreased cooking losses occur at the lower internal temperatures. Flavor and tenderness appear to be comparable. One study of consumer preference for pork loins cooked to 160°F (71°C) or 185°F (85°C) found that 57 percent of the 516 participants preferred the pork cooked to 160°F (71°C), but 43 percent preferred the pork cooked to 185°F (85°C) [60]. Another study, however, indicated that the optimum endpoint temperature for fresh pork roasts, to maximize sensory characteristics, should be at least 160°F (71°C) but not exceed 170°F (77°C) [38]. Cured pork (ham) that requires cooking may be cooked to an internal temperature of 160°F (71°C), whereas precooked ham may be reheated to 140°F (60°C) [99].

Table 25-4

Approximate Roasting Time and Interior Temperature for Some Typical Meat Cuts*

Cut	Weight (lb)	Oven Temperature	Interior Endpoint Cooking Temperature of Meat	Approximate Time per Pound (minutes)
Beef				
Rib roast, bone in	5–6	325°F (163°C)	145°F (63°C) medium rare	23–25
			160°F (71°C) medium	27–30
			170°F (77°C) well done	32–34 (If boneless, add 5–8 minutes per pound)
Round or rump roast	2½–4	325°F (163°C)	145°F (63°C) medium rare	30–35
			160°F (71°C) medium	35–40
Tenderloin, whole	4–6	425°F (218°C)	145°F (63°C) medium rare	45–60 minutes total
Half			160°F (71°C) medium	35–45 minutes total
Veal				
Rib roast	4–5	325°F (163°C)	160°F (71°C) medium	25–27
			170°F (77°C) well done	29–31
Loin	3–4	325°F (163°C)	160°F (71°C) medium	34–36
			170°F (77°C) well done	38–40
Pork, Fresh				
Loin roast, bone-in or boneless	2–5	350°F (176°C)	160°F (71°C) medium	20–30
Boston butt	3–6	350°F (176°C)	160°F (71°C) medium	45
Tenderloin	½ to 1½	425°F (218°C)	160°F (71°C) medium	20–30 minutes total
Leg (fresh ham), Whole, bone-in	12–16	350°F (176°C)	160°F (71°C) medium	22–26
Pork, Cured and Fully Cooked				
Whole, bone in	10–14	325°F (163°C)	140°F (60°C)	15–18
Spiral cut, whole or half	7–9	325°F (163°C)	140°F (60°C)	14–18
Arm picnic shoulder, boneless	5–8	325°F (163°C)	140°F (60°C)	25–30
Lamb				
Lamb leg, bone in	5–7	325°F (163°C)	145°F (63°C) medium rare	20–25
			160°F (71°C) medium	25–30
			170°F (77°C) well done	30–35
Lamb leg, boneless rolled	4–7	325°F (163°C)	145°F (63°C) medium rare	25–30
			160°F (71°C) medium	30–35
			170°F (77°C) well done	35–40
Shoulder roast or shank leg half	3–4	325°F (163°C)	145°F (63°C) medium rare	30–35
			160°F (71°C) medium	40–45
			170°F (77°C) well done	45–50

*If higher or lower temperatures are used for roasting, the times will obviously be somewhat shorter or longer, respectively.

Source: U.S. Department of Agriculture, Food Safety Inspection Service.

Veal is usually cooked to an internal temperature of 160° to 170°F (71° to 77°C) [100]. For food safety purposes, a minimum endpoint temperature of 145°F (63°C) is acceptable when cooking veal steaks and roasts [71]. Veal, which has a tendency to become dry during cooking, can be successfully roasted in an open pan if low oven temperatures are used (Figure 25-30). Larding the roast improves both flavor and juiciness because of the additional fat.

When meat is wrapped in aluminum foil before roasting, it cooks in a moist-heat rather than a dry-heat atmosphere. The foil is thought to have an insulating effect on the meat and, for this reason, higher oven temperatures are sometimes recommended for foil-wrapped roasts in comparison with unwrapped roasts. However, this insulating effect may not be present at oven temperatures as low as 200°F (93°C) [6]. In a comparison of unwrapped and tightly foil-wrapped beef roasts cooked at an oven temperature of 300°F (149°C) to an internal temperature of 170°F (77°C), the foil-wrapped roasts were found to be less juicy and less tender, and they received lower flavor scores than the unwrapped roasts [39].

After a relatively large roast is removed from the oven, it continues to cook as heat continues to penetrate to the center. This effect may be referred to as *carry over* cooking. The rise in temperature may continue for 15 to 45 minutes

Figure 25-30
This veal roast with apricot thyme chutney is moist and flavorful.
(Courtesy of the Cattlemen's Beef Board through the National Cattlemen's Beef Association)

or longer and may be from 5° to 10°F (3° to 6°C), depending on the oven temperature at which the meat is roasted, the internal temperature at which the roast is removed from the oven, the size of the roast, and the composition of the meat.

The higher the oven temperature at which the roast is cooked, the greater the increase in internal temperature of the roast after removal from the oven. The lower the internal temperature of the roast when it is removed from the oven, the greater the rise in temperature after removal from the oven. Small, thin roasts may show little or no rise in temperature because of the rapid cooling from the surface.

Broiling and Pan-Broiling. In broiling, meats are cooked with a direct heat source, such as a gas flame, live coals, or an electric element, that emits radiant energy (Figure 25-31). Broiling is used for relatively thin cuts of meat such as steaks and chops. It is usually done using the broil setting on a range, with the door closed for a gas range and open for an electric range. Steam may accumulate in an electric oven with the door closed, and steam retards browning. A rack for holding the meat out of the drippings is essential, both to keep the meat from stewing in its juices and to prevent burning of the fat.

The source of heat used for broiling is usually constant, with variation in temperature achieved through regulating the distance of the surface of the meat from the source of radiant heat. The relatively high temperatures normally used in broiling do not seem to toughen the meat, possibly because cooking times are relatively short or because tender cuts of meat are used. Broiling may be used for relatively thin, less tender cuts of meat if they have been treated with meat tenderizers.

Figure 25-31
Grilling is a great choice for these pineapple and soy glazed rib eye steaks. (Courtesy of the Cattlemen's Beef Board through the National Cattlemen's Beef Association.)

If steaks are thick, they can be broiled using a thermometer that registers internal temperature. A thermocouple thermometer can be used to measure the internal temperature of thin foods at the end of cooking. Steaks may also be tested by pulling the fibers in the thickest portion apart to see the color of the juice. A cut is sometimes made next to the bone to determine interior color. The firmness of the meat may also be used as a guide to doneness. Rare meat will be soft, but well-done meat will be firm when pressed with a utensil. With experience, the firmness of meat can become a good indication of doneness for steaks. Table 25-5 gives the approximate broiling time for some typical cuts. Like the timetable for roasting, it is strictly a guide, not a precise statement of time. The distance of the meat surface from the broiling unit is usually 2 to 5 inches. Thicker cuts are placed farther from the heat source than thin cuts to allow more uniform cooking.

A variation of broiling is pan-broiling. In this case, heat is applied by means of direct contact with a hot surface such as a heavy pan or a grill. The surface of the pan is lightly oiled with a piece of fat meat to prevent the muscle tissue from sticking. As fat accumulates in the pan during cooking, it should be poured off to avoid frying the meat in its own fat.

Tender beef steaks, lamb chops, and ground beef patties are satisfactorily pan-broiled. Veal, because of its lack of fat, does not broil or pan-broil well. Pork chops are tender enough for dry-heat methods of cooking but should be brought to 145°F (63°C). Broiling and pan-broiling, as they are usually practiced, may not ensure that the centers of pork chops reach an appropriate stage of doneness, especially if the chops are very thick.

In one study, the degree of marbling and the level of fat trimmed from beef loin steaks did not significantly affect the sensory properties of the broiled

Table 25-5

Approximate Broiling Times for Some Typical Meat Cuts

Cut	Average Weight (lb)	Time (min)		
		Rare	Medium	Well Done
Beef				
Club steak (top loin)				
1 in.	1	14–17	18–20	22–25
1½ in.	1¼	25–27	30–35	35–40
Porterhouse				
1 in.	2	19–21	22–25	26–30
1½ in.	2½	30–32	35–38	40–45
Sirloin				
1 in.	3	20–22	23–25	26–30
1½ in.	4½	30–32	33–35	36–40
Ground beef patty, 1 in. thick by 3½ in. diameter	¼		18–22	24–28
Lamb				
Loin chops				
1 in.	³⁄₁₆		10–15	16–18
1½ in.	⁵⁄₁₆		16–18	19–22
Rib chops				
1 in.	⅛		10–15	16–18
1½ in.	¼		16–18	19–22
Ground lamb patty				
1 in. thick by 3½ in. diameter	¼		18–20	22–24

steaks [1]. The steaks did become increasingly less tender and juicy as they were cooked from the rare to the well-done stage.

Bacon is pan-broiled by placing the slices in a cold pan and heating them slowly while frequently turning until crisp. Much of the fat should be drained off, but the bacon browns more evenly when a small amount of fat is left in the pan.

Sautéing and Frying. Sautéing and frying are additional methods that may be used for cooking tender cuts of meat (Figure 25-32). Sautéing and frying are similar, but sautéeing uses less fat and a higher temperature as compared to frying. Also, pan fried foods are often lightly dredged in flour or crumbs. In pan-frying, only a small amount of fat (enough to form a layer of melted fat 1/4 to 1/2 inch deep) is used.

Foods also may be deep-fat fried. In deep-fat frying, the melted fat is deep enough to cover the food. Fried food requires draining on absorbent paper to remove excess fat. Meats may be dipped in flour or in egg and crumbs before frying to produce a brown crust on the meat. Frying can also be used to brown meats that are to be braised.

Microwave Cooking. An important advantage of the microwave oven for cooking meat is that it uses substantially less energy for the same degree of

Figure 25-32
Asian beef and broccoli with noodles is a dish that may be stir fried and ready to eat in about 30 minutes. (Courtesy of the Cattlemen's Beef Board through the National Cattlemen's Beef Association)

doneness than conventional methods, cooking in one-third to one-half the time [49]. Convection ovens also conserve energy because lower cooking temperatures and shorter cooking and preheating times are used.

Some early studies involving comparisons of meat cookery using microwave and conventional ovens often found greater cooking losses and somewhat less palatable products with microwave cooking, particularly when less tender cuts of meat were prepared [48, 58]. Today, microwave ovens with variable power settings allow cooking at different energy levels. Cooking top round roasts of beef, particularly from the frozen state, at simmer power levels produces more palatable products than cooking similar roasts at high power levels. Roasts cooked at the lower power level are often similar in palatability to roasts cooked in conventional ovens [24, 109].

Microwaves do not heat uniformly. It has been suggested that rapid microwave cooking of pork chops or roasts does not allow the uniform heating necessary to ensure destruction of all trichinae, should they be present, when the meat has an internal temperature (in the center) of 145°F (63°C), which is the minimum acceptable temperature for conventional cooking. The National Restaurant Association recommends that food cooked in the microwave oven be heated 25°F (14°C) higher than in conventional cooking. To ensure consistently well-done pork roasts cooked in a microwave oven, one researcher [112] has made the following recommendations:

1. Use a 50 percent or less power level.
2. Use selected roasts weighing 2 kilograms (4.4 pounds) or less—preferably boneless loin, center loin, or blade loin.
3. Allow roasts to stand after cooking, covered with foil, for 10 minutes or longer.
4. Measure the temperature at several locations in the roast.
5. When the roast is cut, make sure no pink or red meat is evident.

If general recommended procedures for microwave cooking of pork are followed, including proper turning of the meat during cooking and less than high power levels, the temperature throughout should be in excess of that required to destroy any trichinae that are present [7]. Drastic deviations from recommended cooking procedures by either conventional or microwave methods may result in less than safe final temperatures in pork.

Roasts that are about twice as long as they are wide cook well in a microwave oven. Boned and rolled roasts, such as rolled rib roasts, are excellent. Frequent turning and basting with a sauce ensure full flavor and color development of the surface. A rapid-reading thermometer may be inserted in the roast *after it is removed from the oven* to check the degree of doneness. Some special thermometers are available for use inside the microwave oven.

Small pieces of meat, particularly, do not brown when cooked in a microwave oven. Various browning elements and special browning grills have been developed by the manufacturers of microwave equipment to solve this problem. The use of browning devices increases fuel consumption by 50 percent or more over cooking by microwaves alone. Total cooking time is also increased [23].

After cooking in the microwave oven, roasts of meat should be set aside before carving. Heat is stored inside the product during cooking, and the standby time allows this heat to distribute itself throughout the meat to achieve proper doneness. Most roasts require a standby time of 30 to 50 minutes. Standing time is particularly important for less tender cuts of meat to ensure tenderization.

The flavor of microwaved meats may be somewhat different from that of meat cooked by conventional methods. After a comparison of several cooking methods for the preparation of ground beef patties of different fat content, some researchers indicated that they did not recommend microwave cooking of the patties as the method of choice for enhancing sensory properties [9]. Microwave cooking scored lower in this study than broiling or charbroiling on tenderness, juiciness, and flavor intensity.

Using nonwoven, melt-blown polypropylene pads is a simple and effective method of reducing fat in products such as bacon and sausages when they are cooked in a microwave oven [32]. These microwavable pads absorb the fat lost in the cooking process. Because the fat goes into the material and is removed from contact with the meat surface, a larger amount of fat can be withdrawn from the meat than is true with the use of paper towels as absorbants. The material also is hydrophobic and thus aids in retaining moisture in the food being cooked.

Main dishes containing meat often microwave well; they are prepared rapidly and generally result in a flavorful mixture. Microwaving is also particularly useful for reheating cooked meat and meat dishes, not only because it is rapid but also because it results in minimal **warmed-over flavor** and aroma [45]. Still another convenient use of the microwave oven is for the rapid thawing of frozen meats.

warmed-over flavor describes the rapid onset of lipid oxidation that occurs in cooked meats during refrigerated storage; oxidized flavors are detectable after only 48 hours

Braising. A moist-heat method of cooking, braising is usually applied to less tender cuts of meat, but may be used for a variety of meats (Figure 25-33). Browning of the meat surface can be accomplished by first frying, pan-broiling, or broiling. Meats can be braised without added water because steam from the water in the meat itself can provide the moisture needed to hydrolyze the collagen in connective tissue; however, a small amount of water may be added. It is better to add small quantities of water frequently rather than a large amount at one time to retain the brown surface, if the meat was browned before braising began. The pan or kettle is closely covered, and cooking is continued, with the liquid simmering or slowly boiling until the meat becomes tender.

Braising can be done either on the top of the range or in the oven. The cooking time is longer in the oven and more energy is expended. Because the pan is tightly covered, the meat is cooked in a moist atmosphere even though it is cooked in the oven. The time of cooking depends on the character of the meat and the size of the cut, but braised meat is always cooked well done. The term *pot-roasting* is often used to refer to the braising of large cuts of meat such as beef chuck roasts. Swiss steaks are braised beef steaks.

Cuts from the chuck and round of beef are commonly braised. Braising is recommended for veal and pork chops, although pork chops are also effectively cooked by roasting or baking.

Stewing. The method of cooking meats in liquid at simmering or slow-boiling temperatures is stewing (Figure 25-34). For brown stew, part or all of the meat may be browned before stewing to help develop flavor and color in the stew. If vegetables are used, they should be added just long enough before the stew is to be served so that they are not overcooked.

Figure 25-33
*These pork chops are browned lightly
in oil then simmered in salsa to create
this easy and tasty dish.* (Courtesy of
National Pork Producers)

Pressure Cooking. Cooking meat in a pressure saucepan is a moist-heat
method generally used for less tender cuts. Only a relatively short cooking time
is necessary because heating produces a temperature higher than that of the
usual boiling point of water, which is the temperature used for braising and
stewing. The retention of steam within the cooking vessel, which increases the
vapor pressure of the water, is responsible for the high temperature. Meats prepared in a pressure saucepan are commonly cooked to a well-done stage. A distinctive steamed flavor can usually be recognized.

Crockery Slow Cooking. Various types of crockery slow-cooking pots are
available and are often used for meat cookery. These electric appliances have a
low-temperature setting that allows meat and other foods to be cooked for long
periods without constant watching. For example, a beef roast can be placed in
the cooker with no added liquid, covered, and cooked on the lowest setting for
10 to 12 hours. Meat dishes with added liquid, such as beef stew or Swiss steak,
are also satisfactorily cooked in crockery slow cookers. The low setting usually
represents a temperature of about 200°F (93°C). The direct heat from the pot,
lengthy cooking, and steam created within the tightly covered container combine to destroy bacteria and make this method of cooking meat a safe one [103].
   Cooking in these covered pots is achieved by moist heat. The long cooking
period allows the breakdown of the connective tissue to gelatin in less tender
meats, thus increasing tenderness.

STEP 1. **Coat beef with seasoned flour, if desired. Brown on all sides in small amount of oil, if desired.**

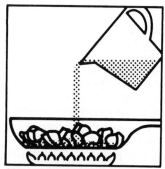

STEP 3. **Cover with liquid. Season with additional herbs, if desired.**

STEP 2. **Pour off excess drippings.**

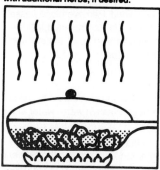

STEP 4. **Cover utensil and simmer on top of range or in oven until tender. Add vegetables to meat and liquid just long enough before serving to cook through, or until tender.**

Figure 25-34
Less tender meat may be tenderized by cooking in liquid. (Courtesy of the National Cattlemen's Beef Association)

Cooking Variety Meats

The choice of a cooking method for variety meats is influenced by the tenderness of the various parts. Heart, kidney, tongue, and tripe require cooking for tenderness and are braised or simmered. Older beef liver may also require tenderizing by braising. Brains, sweetbreads, and veal or calf liver are tender. They may be cooked by dry-heat methods such as broiling or frying. For variety, they may also be cooked by moist-heat methods. Brains and sweetbreads are delicate tissues that are made more firm and white when they are precooked for about 20 minutes at a simmering temperature in salted, acidulated water. After this preliminary treatment they can be prepared in various ways. Table 25-6 provides suggestions pertinent to the preparation of variety meats.

Cooking Frozen Meats

Frozen meats can be thawed and cooked or cooked without thawing first. The cooking temperature must be lower and the time of cooking increased if the meat is frozen when cooking begins. If pieces of frozen meat are large, the cooking time may be considerably longer than for similar thawed or fresh cuts. Frozen roasts require up to 1.5 times as long to cook as unfrozen roasts of the same size. If frozen meats are braised, they may be browned at the end of the braising period rather than at the beginning.

There are no appreciable differences in palatability or nutritive value in meats cooked from the thawed or frozen state. Thawed meats are cooked in the same way as fresh meats. Thawing of frozen meat, particularly large pieces of meat, should be done in the refrigerator for microbiologic safety.

Table 25-6
Variety Meats

Name	Preliminary Preparation	Cooking Methods
Liver	Liver from young animals should be sliced ½ in. thick for best results in retaining juiciness. Remove outside membrane, blood vessels, and excess connective tissue. Wash large pieces before removing membrane.	Broil or pan-broil young liver. Fry or bread young liver. Braise whole piece of older beef liver. Grind and make into liver loaf. (Liver is easier to grind if first coagulated in hot water.)
Kidney	Wash kidneys and remove outer membrane. Lamb kidneys may be split in half and veal kidneys cut into slices. Cook beef kidneys in water for tenderness, changing the water several times.	Young kidneys may be broiled, pan-broiled, made into stew or kidney pie, or ground and made into loaf. Beef kidneys, after being cooked for tenderness, may be cooked in the same way, except that they should not be broiled or pan-broiled.
Sweetbreads and brains	Soak in cold water to remove blood. Remove blood vessels and excess connective tissue. Parboil in salted, acidulated water to make firm and white using 1 tsp salt and 1 Tbsp vinegar per quart of water.	Sweetbreads may be creamed, dipped in egg and crumbs and fried in fat, combined with cooked chicken and creamed or scalloped, or dipped in melted fat and broiled. Brains may be breaded or broiled as suggested for sweetbreads or cut into small pieces and scrambled with eggs.
Heart	Heart is a muscular organ that is usually cooked by moist-heat methods for tenderness. Wash in warm water and remove large blood vessels.	Stuff with bread dressing and braise until tender. May be cooked in water seasoned with salt, onion, bay leaf, celery, and tomato and served hot or cold.
Tongue	Tongue is a muscular tissue that requires precooking in water for tenderness. After cooking, remove the skin and cut out the roots. Smoked or pickled tongue is usually soaked for several hours before cooking.	May be cooked in water, seasoned with salt, onion, bayleaf, and celery. If it is to be served cold, it is more moist when allowed to cool in the water. After it is cooked in water, the tongue may be covered with brown or tomato sauce and braised in the oven. The cooked tongue may be reheated in a sweet pickling solution. For this method, the tongue is best precooked in plain salted water.
Tripe	Fresh tripe is cooked before selling but requires further cooking in water until tender (1 or more hours).	Serve precooked tripe with well-seasoned tomato sauce. Dip in batter and fry in deep fat. Brush with flavorful fat and broil.

Meat Flavor

USDA quality grades for meat relate to palatability. In the evaluation of grade, such characteristics as marbling and firmness of the lean cut surface in relation to evidences of carcass maturity or age are considered. It is quite likely that USDA quality grades are related to flavor of the meat because grade indirectly assesses the extent to which flavor compounds are likely to be present in high or low concentrations [92]. For example, carcasses from older and leaner animals and from animals fed little or no grain are assigned low USDA quality grades. These animals are likely to yield meat of less desirable flavor than young, fatter animals fed large quantities of grain and graded higher.

The flavor of meat involves responses from taste and smell and also sensations from pressure-sensitive and heat-sensitive areas of the mouth. Flavor of meat is developed primarily by cooking; raw meat has little aroma and only a bloodlike taste. The flavor of boiled meats differs from that of roasted meats.

The chemistry of meat flavor is highly complex, as many compounds contribute to the characteristic flavor of the cooked product. Some of these flavor compounds are volatile and give rise to odor. One study of the volatile flavor components of fresh beef stew identified 132 different compounds [79].

Although volatile components are possibly the most important part of meat flavor, nonvolatile compounds stimulate taste buds and contribute to the overall flavor complex. The most important taste compounds are inorganic salts, producing a salty taste; sugars, producing a sweet taste; hypoxanthine, contributing some bitterness; organic acids, producing a sour taste; and some nitrogen-containing compounds including nucleotides, amino acids, and peptides. In addition to volatile and nonvolatile components of meat flavor, are other substances called *flavor potentiators* and *synergists*. Although these substances have no distinctive flavor of their own, they enhance the flavor of other compounds. Flavor potentiators in meat include some amino acids, such as glutamic acid, and certain 5′-nucleotides such as inosinic acid [69].

The feeding management of beef cattle affects the flavor of the meat, particularly the flavor of the fatty portions. Grass- or forage-fed steers have less desirable flavor, characterized as grassy, gamey, and milky-oily, than those animals finished on grain [59, 68]. Serving temperature also affects perceived meat flavor. Beef steaks tasted at 122°F (50°C) are more flavorful and juicy than similar samples tasted at 72°F (22°C) [74]. Not only the temperature, but also the time a meat product is held before serving, can affect flavor. Freshly cooked meat sauce with spaghetti was found to be more flavorful and generally more acceptable to a taste panel than a similar product held hot on a cafeteria counter for 90 minutes [2].

A knowledge of meat flavor components, both boiled and roasted, is helpful in attempting to duplicate meaty flavors in the laboratory. Simulated meat flavors are needed for flavoring meat analogues made from plant proteins. They are also useful in the preparation of various convenience foods.

SOUP STOCK

A stock is a flavored liquid used chiefly in the making of soups. Beef is the most commonly used meat for stock. Veal produces a very mild stock that may be desirable in some dishes. Lamb and mutton produce excellent broth, but they should be used only when lamb or mutton flavor is desired. The bones and meat from poultry make desirable broth. Stock may also be made from fish.

Seven principles should be followed to produce high quality stocks: (1) start with cold water, (2) simmer gently, (3) skim frequently, (4) strain carefully, (5) cool quickly, (6) store properly, and (7) degrease [51]. The more surface of the meat that is exposed to the water, the more flavor that is extracted when making stock. For the best stock, then, this means cutting the meat into small cubes or grinding it through a coarse grinder rather than cooking it in one piece. The meat may be soaked for 1/2 to 1 hour in cold water; then cooking is started and the water is allowed to simmer 3 to 4 hours. Cooking some bone and some fat with the lean meat is thought to improve the flavor.

Vegetables and seasonings should be added during the last hour of cooking to avoid the development of undesirable flavors resulting from the overcooking of some vegetables. When cooking is finished, the stock is poured through a colander to remove the meat, bone, and seasonings. When the stock is cool, the hard fat layer may be removed from the top.

The major difference between brown and white soup stock is that in the making of brown stock, about one-third of the meat cubes are first browned in a skillet. The vegetables also may be caramelized in the oven or on top of the range for additional flavor and color. The pan is *deglazed* by adding water to dissolve the brown matter from the pan. The browned meat and water are then added to the soup kettle in which the remaining cubes have been placed in cold water.

The meat left from making soup stock retains many of its nutrients. The flavor is lacking, but other flavors from vegetables and condiments may be added so that the meat can be utilized. For example, it can be cut into small pieces and served in the soup.

Bouillon is prepared by seasoning a soup stock. *Consommé* is an enriched or double-strength bouillon that has been clarified so that it is crystal clear. It can be made from any kind of stock, although beef is most commonly used. One egg white and one crushed shell per quart of broth accomplish clarification. The broth is heated to the boiling point and boiled for a few minutes, after which it is poured through several thicknesses of cheesecloth to strain out the coagulated egg with its adhering particles. The material that is removed from the soup stock by clarifying is chiefly coagulated protein.

GRAVY

Gravies or sauces are commonly used as accompaniments to enhance the flavor of meat. The drippings from fried, pan-broiled, or roasted meat and the cooking liquid from stewed or braised meats or poultry can be used to make gravy. Low temperatures for meat cookery usually produce a minimum of brown material. Particularly for the making of gravy, there should be no burned drippings. Gravies and some sauces may be served either thickened or unthickened. *Au jus* gravy goes naturally with roast beef and is unthickened. To thicken gravy, flour or another starch thickener can be added (1 1/2 to 2 tablespoons per cup of liquid) in one of two ways: as a smooth flour and water paste (slurry), or as dry flour stirred into the fat (roux). The latter method is usually preferable when the drippings contain little or no water. Excess fat in the pan should be removed before the flour is added. Once the approximate quantity of gravy desired is determined, 2 tablespoons of fat should be retained for each cup of gravy. When dry flour and fat in the drippings are blended together and cooked for a few minutes, they form a *roux*. Cold liquid can then be mixed gradually with the hot roux until a smooth gravy is formed. Heating is continued, with stirring, until the **starch gelatinizes** and the mixture thickens. Seasonings may then be added.

starch gelatinization the swelling of starch granules when heated with moisture

In the alternate method of making gravy, a cold slurry of liquid and a thickener, such as flour, are mixed with hot liquid that has been added to the drippings, with constant stirring until the gravy thickens. The liquid used in gravies is usually water, but milk, meat stock, tomato juice, wine, vegetable juice, or other liquids may be used. The richer and more flavorful the drippings, the better the gravy. Gravies should be tasted before serving to make certain that the proper blending of flavors has been achieved.

A great variety of sauces can be served with meats. Sauces may be made from drippings, but are often made without any meat components. White sauce (discussed in Chapter 13) may be the basis for some sauces served with meats. Tomato sauces go with meatballs and spaghetti, and mushroom sauce is often served with Swiss steak. Brushing broiled lamb chops with melted butter containing parsley, lemon juice, and white pepper produces a sauce called *maître d'hôtel butter.*

CARVING MEAT

Successful carving of meat partly depends on some knowledge of the anatomy of the cut to be carved. It is important to know something of the location of the joints and the direction in which the muscle fibers run. Insofar as possible, meats should be carved across the grain. Knives for carving should be well sharpened and of good-quality steel that will hold an edge well.

Carving should be done rapidly so that the meat stays warm. Neatness and economy of cutting are also important. If some parts of the meat are better than others, such parts should be divided among those at the table rather than given to the first ones served. Enough meat to serve all at the table should be carved before the host starts to serve the plates. The slices are arranged neatly on the platter. Before inviting guests to be served a second time, the host should be sure that some meat is carved and ready.

Diagrams showing the techniques for carving certain cuts of meat are shown in Figure 25-35.

Beef Steak

Steak is one of the easiest meats to carve. With the steak lying flat on the platter, the fork is inserted in a suitable position for holding the steak firmly. Steaks from the loin (top loin, T-bone, porterhouse, and sirloin) have the bone separated from the meat before the meat is carved. The knife is allowed to follow the bone closely until the meat is completely separated. The meat is then cut into pieces of a suitable size for serving. Porterhouse and T-bone steaks are usually carved so that each person receives some tenderloin and some outer muscle. In this case, steaks are cut with, rather than across, the fiber.

Standing Rib Roast

A standing rib roast is placed before the carver with the rib side to the left. The carver inserts a fork between two ribs. The knife passes from the outer edge toward the ribs in removing a slice of meat. Slices may vary in thickness, but 1/4 to 3/8 inch is desirable. After several slices have been carved, the knife is used to separate the slices from the bone. Each slice is then transferred to the platter.

Rolled Rib Roast

Horizontal slices are cut from the top of a rolled rib roast.

Pot Roasts

Insofar as possible, slices of pot roasts should be cut across the grain. Some cuts used for pot roasts may have fibers running in several directions, in which case it is difficult to carve across the fibers. If the muscles are separated first, cutting across the grain is easier.

Ham

The shank bone of the ham is placed toward the carver's right. The larger muscles of the ham are sliced by cutting straight down from the outer edge to the leg bone. After several slices have been carved, the knife is inserted in the last opening and is allowed to follow the bone, thus separating slices from the bone. Slices can then be lifted out.

Standing rib roast of beef

Beef porterhouse steak

Loin roast of pork

Blade pot roast of beef

Ham, rump portion

Figure 25-35
Techniques for carving various cuts of meat. (Courtesy of the National Live Stock and Meat Board)

Loin Roasts

A loin roast of pork is carved by cutting slices from the end of the roast. The roast is prepared at the market to make carving easy. The rib section has the backbone sawed loose from the ribs. The backbone is removed in the kitchen before the roast is placed on the platter. Cutting is done close along each side of the rib bone. One slice contains the rib, the next is boneless, and so on.

Leg of Lamb

The cushion of a leg of lamb, which is the most meaty portion, lies below the tail. The carver inserts a fork to bring the cushion into an upright position. Slices are then carved as from ham.

SOY PROTEINS AND MEAT PROCESSING

The addition of soy ingredients in ground beef products results in reduced shrinkage on cooking and thus higher yields, while generally allowing the product to retain acceptable sensory quality. Soy proteins may also be added for nutritional enhancement. Consumer-acceptable beef patties made with the addition of various soy products are sold on the retail market. Combining textured soy-protein concentrate with a powdered soy concentrate that has emulsifying properties has been reported to produce the highest cooking yields with the greatest nutrient retention in the most economical manner [86]. At high substitution levels, however, soy flavor may be detected. Strong-flavored ingredients such as onions, tomatoes, and chilies can mask the flavor of soy. Soy products may also be used in combination with other substances to improve the flavor and texture of low-fat ground beef products [55].

The soybean is a source of good-quality protein, particularly in combination with some animal protein. Convenience foods produced from these vegetable protein products are marketed frozen, dehydrated, freeze-dried, and canned. One example of this type of food is hickory-smoked strips, which can be used in place of bacon. Bacon-flavored bits for use in salads or combined with eggs and other foods are also made from soy protein. In the preparation of restructured meats, soy protein or wheat gluten products may be used to improve binding properties and to increase the cooking yield because of the higher retention of water.

Tofu or bean curd (see Chapter 20) also offers interesting opportunities to extend meat, fish, and poultry dishes. The texture of this product can vary from soft and creamy to extra firm, broadening its possible uses.

CHAPTER SUMMARY

- Meat is defined as the flesh of animals used for food. Cattle, swine, and sheep are the chief meat animals in the United States.
- Meat is composed chiefly of water, protein, fat, and mineral matter. It also contains, in much smaller amounts, vitamins, pigments, and enzymes. Lean meats are a good source of thiamin, riboflavin, niacin, iron, zinc, and phosphorus as well as other vitamins and minerals.
- The percentage of fat in meats varies widely, depending on the breed or biological type of animal, its nutritive state, and the part of the carcass from

which the cut is taken. Fats from different species and from different parts of the same animal differ in composition. More brittle fats contain higher percentages of saturated fatty acids.

- Lean uncooked muscle contains about 75 percent water and about 20 percent protein.

- The color of meat comes chiefly from the pigment myoglobin. When first cut, or in oxygen-reduced packaging, myoglobin is in the chemically reduced form and is a purplish red color. With the addition of oxygen, the myglobin changes to the bright red pigment called oxymyoglobin. With extended storage, an oxidized form of the pigment called metmyoglobin is produced. This oxidized form is a brown color.

- Structurally, meat is composed of muscle, connective tissue, fatty or adipose tissue, and bone. The muscle fiber is a long threadlike cell that tapers slightly at both ends. Inside this cell or fiber is an intricate structure including myofibrils and sarcoplasm. Inside the myfibrils are thick filaments composed of myosin and thin filaments made up of the protein actin.

- Connective tissue binds the muscle cells together in various-size bundles. Generally, connective tissue has few cells but a considerable amount of extracellular background material called ground substance. Running through this matrix of ground substance are fibrils that contain the protein collagen. Collagen-containing connective tissue is white. Connective tissue composed primarily of elastin is yellow. Reticulin is a third type of connective tissue.

- Collagen may be hydrolyzed when heated with moisture to produce gelatin. Elastin is not tenderized by moist heat; thus it must be trimmed out or tenderized by cutting, as is done in minute steaks.

- Marbling is the intramuscular distribution of fat. Fat is also deposited between muscles, under the skin, and around glandular organs.

- Bones that appear in retail cuts of meat aid in the identification of the cut.

- Beef carcasses are classified on the basis of age and sex. Veal is the meat from immature bovines that are at least 3 weeks but generally less than 20 weeks of age. Sheep carcasses are classified as lamb, yearling mutton, and mutton according to the age of the animal. Pork is the meat of swine. Good-quality pork is obtained from young animals usually 7–12 months of age.

- Before an animal is slaughtered, the muscles are soft and pliable. The stiffening of the carcass after death is known as rigor mortis. Meat is generally allowed to hang under refrigeration for 1 or 2 days after slaughter until the rigor mortis passes and the meat softens. If it is held longer, the process of ripening or aging occurs. Beef is the only type of meat that is commonly aged. Aging of meat can be accomplished by dry aging or wet aging.

- Tenderness is one of the most valued attributes of meat. Although higher grades of meat are an indicator of tenderness, grading does not directly measure this characteristic. Animals that are marketed young, such as lamb and pork, are usually tender.

- Tenderness in meat appears to be influenced by the age of the animal, the amounts of connective tissue in the cut of meat, and amount of marbling. The hereditary background of the animal, the management of its feeding, and the size of the muscle fibers are additional factors that influence meat tenderness.

- Processing methods such as electrical stimulation of the muscle and the use of tenderizing compounds containing enzymes may be used to tenderize meat.

- Several laws have been passed and regulations published to protect and inform the consumer with respect to the purchasing of meat and poultry products. The USDA has responsibility at the federal level for the inspection, grading, setting of standards, and labeling of all meat and poultry products. In 2002, the USDA further strengthened food safety programs to further reduce the presence of *E. coli*. Since the late 1980's, several steps have been taken by the U.S. federal agencies to prevent BSE from entering the United States. BSE has never been found in the United States.

- Additives used in meat products, biotechnology, standards of identify for meat products, and labeling are additional areas of governmental oversight.

- All meats entering interstate commerce must be inspected by the USDA Food Safety and Inspection Service. An inspector's stamp is placed on each wholesale cut of the carcass that passes inspection. The Wholesome Meat Act of 1967 requires that state governments have local programs of meat inspection equivalent to those of the federal government for meat sold within state boundaries.

- A program separate from the inspection service is the USDA system of grading meat. Whereas inspection of meat for wholesomeness is mandatory, grading is voluntary. Quality grades have been established and the appropriate USDA grade mark is applied to the meat carcass. Yield grades are based on cutability, which indicates the proportionate amount of salable retail cuts that can be obtained from a carcass.

- Good quality beef has a bright red color after the cut surface has been exposed to air. It is fine-grained, smooth to the touch, and the fat is firm. The chine or backbone is soft, red, and spongy. Good quality veal has a grayish-pink flesh and a texture that is fine-grained and smooth. Good quality lamb has a pinkish red color, fine grain, and smooth cut surfaces of the flesh. Good quality pork is grayish pink and fine grained. In good quality veal, lamb, and pork, the bones are soft, red, and spongy.

- An understanding of the division of the carcass into retail cuts is helpful in understanding the relative quality characteristics and the associated prices. The parts of the body that are affected little by the exercise of the animal will yield the most tender, as well as most expensive, cuts of meat.

- Restructured meat products may be made by flaking, coarse grinding, dicing, or chopping the meat, then binding the particles together into the desired shape and size.

- Variety meats include sweetbreads, brains, heart, tongue, tripe, liver, kidney, and oxtail.

- When purchasing meat, the yield and cost of the lean portion should be considered. A maximum fat content of 30 percent by weight has been set for ground beef ground in federally inspected plants. Ground beef labels generally provide the proportion of lean muscle tissue to fatty tissue.

- Irradiated ground beef may be purchased to reduce the risk of *E. coli*. Much of the beef currently available in supermarkets has been packaged on premise. Centralized packaging of fresh red meat may become more prevalent in the future.

- Many kinds of cured meats are available in the marketplace. Curing ingredients include sodium nitrite, salt, sugar, and seasonings. Nitrite and salt will react with myoglobin to produce the characteristic pink color of cooked cured meats. The curing process may be accomplished by rubbing a dry curing mixture on the meat, submerging the meat in a curing solution, or injecting the meat with the curing solution.

- Fresh meats must be stored at or below 40°F (4.5°C). Meats should not be placed above other foods in the refrigerator so as to prevent cross-contamination with other foods such as produce. Frozen meat should be defrosted in the refrigerator, in the microwave and cooked immediately, or under cold running water.

- Knowledge and adherence to the recommended endpoint cooking temperatures of meat is necessary to prevent foodborne illness. For food safety purposes, cook ground beef to 155°–160°F (68–70°C) and beef, pork or lamb steaks and roasts to 145°F (63°C). When cooking in a microwave oven, an endpoint temperature of 25°F (14°C) higher than used in conventional cooking is recommended. Thermometers should be used to test the internal temperature of meats to assess doneness. Some ground beef has been shown to be brown in color before the meat has reached a safe temperature.

- Meats generally are more appealing and palatable to people when cooked. Conventional cooking is divided into dry-heat and moist-heat methods.

- Heat produces many changes in meat. The proteins denature and coagulate, the fats melt, and significant color changes occur.

- Cooking losses, including loss of weight and loss of nutrients, increase gradually with increasing internal temperatures.

- Juiciness is a highly desirable characteristic in cooked meats. Aged meats, meats from younger animals, and well marbled meats are likely to be more juicy. Meats cooked to rare and medium rare done stages are generally more juicy as compared to well-done meats.

- In preparation of meats, tenderization may be achieved by the use of moist cooking methods if the cut of meat has significant amounts of collagen connective tissue, carving across the grain, or marinating in a mixture that contains acid.

- Commonly used cooking methods for meats include: roasting, baking, broiling, pan-broiling, sautéing, frying, microwave cooking, braising, and crockery slow cooking. Cooking charts are available to provide guidance in the amount of time necessary to roast, bake, or grill meat. Thermometers should be used to determine if the desired or safe endpoint cooking temperature has been reached. Roasted meats will continue to rise in temperature after removal from the oven.

- Frozen meats can be thawed and cooked or cooked without thawing first. The cooking temperature must be lower and the time of cooking increased by as much as 1.5 times if the meat was frozen when cooking started.

- The flavor of meat is developed primarily by cooking. The feeding management of beef cattle also affects the flavor of the meat.

- A stock is a flavored liquid used in the making of soups, sauces, and gravies. Beef is the meat commonly used for stock. Bouillon and consommé are made from stocks.

- Gravies may be made by thickening drippings with a slurry or with a roux, then adding liquid and cooking until the starch is gelatinized.
- Successful carving of meat depends on some knowledge of the anatomy of the cut to be carved. Neatness, economy of cutting, and consideration of the guests to be served are additional important components of carving.
- The soybean is a source of good-quality protein that may be used in combination ground beef and other meat products.

KEY TERMS

saturated fatty acids
unsaturated fatty acids
precursor
reducing substances
oxidation
cytoplasm
reticulum
mitochondria
ATP
hydrolyze
marbling
carotenoid pigments

mucoprotein
proteinase
ruminant
subcutaneous
polydextrose
secondary amines
comminute
denaturation
coagulation
warmed-over flavor
starch gelatinization
hyphae

STUDY QUESTIONS

1. a. List the major and minor components of meat.
   b. The protein content of meat varies with the amount of fat. How much protein is usually present in lean muscle?
   c. What vitamins and minerals does meat provide in significant amounts?
2. Explain why the color of meat may change from a purplish red to a bright red when exposed to air. Explain why meat may turn a brownish color when held too long. What is responsible for the typical cured meat color?
3. Meat is basically muscle tissue containing some fat and bone. Briefly describe what meat is like in structure, including each of the following components in your explanation.
   a. Muscle proteins—myosin and actin
   b. Myofibrils
   c. Muscle fibers
   d. Bundles of muscle fibers (making the grain of the meat)
   e. Muscles (such as tenderloin and rib eye)
   f. Connective tissue
   g. Connective tissue proteins—collagen and elastin
   h. Fat cells, fatty tissues, and marbling
   i. Bone
4. a. What is *rigor mortis* and why is it important in a study of meat?
   b. Why is beef aged? What changes occur during aging or ripening of meat?
5. List several factors that may affect tenderness of meat and discuss what effect each factor has on tenderness.

6. Meat and poultry labeling is the responsibility of the USDA.
   a. What must be included on a meat or poultry label?
   b. What nutrient content claims can be made?

7. Explain what the round inspection stamp on meat carcasses implies.

8. a. Why are meats graded and by whom are they graded? Is this a mandatory or voluntary program?
   b. Explain the difference between quality grades and yield grades for meat. What factors are considered in each?
   c. From the following list of quality grade names, indicate which apply to beef, which to veal, and which to lamb.

(1) Prime	(6) Choice
(2) Select	(7) Cutter
(3) Standard	(8) Canner
(4) Commercial	(9) Cull
(5) Utility	(10) Good

9. a. Name the primal or wholesale cuts of beef and pork.
   b. Name several retail cuts that come from each primal cut listed in question a.
   c. Which primal cuts of beef are usually tender? Which are less tender?
   d. Be able to identify pictures of each of the following retail cuts of meat.

Beef	Pork
Rib steak and roast	Rib chops
Top loin steak	Loin chops
T-bone steak	Blade steak
Porterhouse steak	Ham
Sirloin steak	
Round steak or roast	
Blade steak or roast	
Arm steak or roast	
Flank steak	
Brisket	
Short ribs	

10. What are *restructured meats?* What advantages do they offer?

11. Name several variety meats and discuss possible advantages for their use in meal planning.

12. a. Name several cuts of meat that are commonly cured.
    b. What ingredients are usually used in the curing process? Discuss advantages and disadvantages of the use of nitrite as a curing ingredient.

13. Describe appropriate storage conditions for meat in the kitchen.

14. How does heat generally affect muscle fibers? Connective tissue? Explain why this information is important in deciding how to cook tender and less tender cuts of meat.

15. When meat is cooked by any method it usually loses weight. Account for this weight or cooking loss.

16. Describe the usual procedures used in cooking meat by each of the following methods. Indicate whether each is a dry-heat or a moist-heat method. Also suggest several cuts of meat that may appropriately be cooked by each of the methods listed.

    a. Roasting
    b. Broiling
    c. Pan-broiling
    d. Frying

    e. Microwave cooking
    f. Braising
    g. Stewing
    h. Pressure cooking

17. In roasting, broiling, and pan-broiling, when should meats be salted and why?

18. Describe how frozen meats may be appropriately handled in preparation for cooking.

19. **a.** What oven temperatures are most satisfactory when roasting tender cuts of beef? Less tender cuts? Explain why these temperatures are appropriate.
    b. Why should a meat thermometer be used when roasting meat?
    c. Explain why ground beef should always be cooked well done.

20. What types of compounds appear to be important components of meat flavor?

21. Describe appropriate procedures for the preparation of the following.
    a. Soup stock
    b. Gravy

22. Describe several soybean protein products that are available for use in meat processing or as meat extenders in cooking.

REFERENCES

1. Akinwunmi, I., Thompson, L. D., & Ramsey, C. B. (1993). Marbling, fat trim, and doneness effects on sensory attributes, cooking loss, and composition of cooked beef steaks. *Journal of Food Science, 58,* 242.

2. Al-Obaidy, H. M., Khan, M. A., & Klein, B. P. (1984). Comparison between sensory quality of freshly prepared spaghetti with meat sauce before and after hot holding on a cafeteria counter. *Journal of Food Science, 49,* 1475.

3. Archer, D. L. (2001). Nitrite and the impact of advisory groups. *Food Technology, 55*(3), 26.

4. Archer, D. L. (2000). *E. coli* O157:H7—Searching for solutions. *Food Technology, 54*(10), 142.

5. Arnold, R. N., Scheller, K. K., Arp, S. C., Williams, S. N., & Schaefer, D. M. (1993). Dietary alpha-tocopheryl acetate enhances beef quality in Holstein and beef breed steers. *Journal of Food Science, 58,* 28.

6. Baity, M. R., Ellington, A. E., & Woodburn, M. (1969). Foil wrap in oven cooking. *Journal of Home Economics, 61,* 174.

7. Bakanowski, S. M., & Zoller, J. M. (1984). Endpoint temperature distributions in microwave and conventionally cooked pork. *Food Technology, 38*(2), 45.

8. Bente, L. & Gerrior, S. A. (2002). Selected food and nutrient highlights of the 20th century: U.S. food supply series. *Family Economics and Nutrition Review, 14*(1), 43–51.

9. Berry, B. W., & Leddy, K. F. (1984). Effects of fat level and cooking method on sensory and textural properties of ground beef patties. *Journal of Food Science, 48,* 1715.

10. Borrud, L., Enns, C. W., & Mickle, S. (1996). What we eat in America: USDA surveys food consumption changes. *Food Review, 19*(3), 14.

11. Bouton, P. E., Harris, P. V., & Ratcliff, D. (1981). Effect of cooking temperature and time on the shear properties of meat. *Journal of Food Science, 46*, 1082.

12. Bowers, J. A., Craig, J. A., Kropf, D. H., & Tucker, T. J. (1987). Flavor, color, and other characteristics of beef longissimus muscle heated to seven internal temperatures between 55° and 85°C. *Journal of Food Science, 52*, 533.

13. Brody, A. L. (2002). The case for—or against—case-ready fresh red meat in the United States. *Food Technology, 54*(8), 153–156.

14. Browning, M. A., Huffman, D. L., Egbert, W. R., & Jungst, S. B. (1990). Physical and compositional characteristics of beef carcasses selected for leanness. *Journal of Food Science, 55*, 9.

15. Buchanan, R. L., & Doyle, M. P. (1997). Foodborne disease significance of *Escherichia coli* O157:H7 and other enterohemorrhagic *E. coli. Food Technology, 51*(10), 69.

16. Buzby, J. C., & Crutchfield, S. R. (1997). USDA modernizes meat and poultry inspection. *Food Review, 20*(1),14.

17. Cassens, R. G. (1995). Use of sodium nitrite in cured meats today. *Food Technology, 49*(7), 72.

18. Cassens, R. G. (1997). Residual nitrite in cured meat. *Food Technology, 51*(2), 53.

19. Costello, C. A., Penfield, M. P., & Riemann, M. J. (1985). Quality of restructured steaks: Effects of days on feed, fat level, and cooking method. *Journal of Food Science, 50*, 685.

20. Cover, S., & Hostetler, R. L. (1960). *Beef tenderness.* Texas Agricultural Experiment Station Bulletin No. 947. College Station, TX: Texas Agricultural Experiment Station.

21. Cross, H. R., Berry, B. W., & Wells, L. H. (1980). Effects of fat level and source on the chemical, sensory, and cooking properties of ground beef patties. *Journal of Food Science, 45*, 791.

22. Dolezal, H. G., Smith, G. C., Savell, J. W., & Carpenter, Z. L. (1982). Comparison of subcutaneous fat thickness, marbling and quality grade for predicting palatability of beef. *Journal of Food Science, 47*, 397.

23. Drew, F., & Rhee, K. S. (1979). Microwave cookery of beef patties: Browning methods. *Journal of the American Dietetic Association, 74*, 652.

24. Drew, F., Rhee, K. S., & Carpenter, Z. L. (1980). Cooking at variable microwave power levels. *Journal of the American Dietetic Association, 77*, 455.

25. Egbert, W. R., & Cornforth, D. P. (1986). Factors influencing color of dark cutting beef muscle. *Journal of Food Science, 51*, 57.

26. Enns, C. W., Goldman, J. D., & Cook, A. (1997). Trends in food and nutrient intakes by adults: NFCS 1977–78, CSFII 1989–91, and CSFII 1994–95. *Family Economics and Nutrition Review, 10*(4), 2.

27. Etherton, T. D. (1993). The new bio-tech foods. *Food and Nutrition News, 65*(3), 13.

28. Fabiansson, S., & Libelius, R. (1985). Structural changes in beef longissimus dorsi induced by postmortem low voltage electrical stimulation. *Journal of Food Science, 50*, 39.

29. Fogle, D. R., Plimpton, R. F., Ockerman, H. W., Jarenback, L., & Persson, T. (1982). Tenderization of beef: Effect of enzyme, enzyme level, and cooking method. *Journal of Food Science, 47*, 1113.

30. Gariepy, C., Amiot, J., Pommier, S. A., Flipot, P. M., & Girard, V. (1992). Electrical stimulation and 48 hours aging of bull and steer carcasses. *Journal of Food Science, 57*, 541.

31. Gerrier, S. & Bente, L. (2001). Food supply nutrients and dietary guidance, 1970–1999. *Food Review, 24*(3), 39–46.

32. Giese, J. H. (1992). Developing low-fat meat products. *Food Technology, 46*(4), 100.

33. Giese, J. H. (2001). It's a mad, mad, mad, mad cow test. *Food Technology, 55*(6), 60–62.

34. Giese, J. H. (2002). Washington news. *Food Technology, 56*(10), 22.

35. Gravely, M. H. (1993). Understanding the new meat and poultry labels. *Food News for Consumers, 10*(1–2), 8.

36. Hamm, R. (1982). Postmortem changes in muscle with regard to processing of hot-boned beef. *Food Technology, 36*(11), 105.

37. Hardin, B. (1999). Predicting tenderness in beefsteaks. *Agricultural Research Magazine, 47*(11).

38. Heymann, H., Hedrick, H. B., Karrasch, M. A., Eggeman, M. K., & Ellersieck, M. R. (1990). Sensory and chemical characteristics of fresh pork roasts cooked to different endpoint temperatures. *Journal of Food Science, 55*, 613.

39. Hood, M. P. (1960). Effect of cooking method and grade on beef roasts. *Journal of the American Dietetic Association, 37*, 363.

40. Howat, P. M., Sievert, L. M., Myers, P. J., Koonce, K. L., & Bidner, T. D. (1983). Effect of marination upon mineral content and tenderness of beef. *Journal of Food Science, 48*, 662.

41. Huang, K. S. (1996). Price and income affect nutrients consumed from meats. *Food Review, 19*(1), 37.

42. Hunt, M. C., Sorheim, O., & Slinde, E. (1999). Color and heat denaturation of myoglobin forms. *Journal of Food Science, 60*, 1175–1196.

43. Jacobs, D. K., & Sebranek, J. G. (1980). Use of prerigor beef for frozen ground beef patties. *Journal of Food Science, 45*, 648.

44. Jennings, T. G., Berry, B. W., & Joseph, A. L. (1978). Influence of fat thickness, marbling, and length of aging on beef palatability and shelf-life characteristics. *Journal of Animal Science, 46*, 658.

45. Johnston, M. B., & Baldwin, R. E. (1980). Influence of microwave reheating on selected quality factors of roast beef. *Journal of Food Science, 45*, 1460.

46. Killinger, K. M., Hunt, M. C., Campbell, R. E., & Kropf, D. H. (2000). Factors affecting premature browning during cooking of store-purchased ground beef. *Journal of Food Science, 65*, 585–587.

47. Koohmaraie, M., Seideman, S. C., Schollmeyer, J. E., Dutson, T. R., & Babiker, A. S. (1988). Factors associated with the tenderness of three bovine muscles. *Journal of Food Science, 53*, 407.

48. Korschgen, B. M., Baldwin, R. E., & Snider, S. (1976). Quality factors in beef, pork, and lamb cooked by microwaves. *Journal of the American Dietetic Association, 69*, 635.

49. Korschgen, B. M., Berneking, J. M., & Baldwin, R. E. (1980). Energy requirements for cooking beef rib roasts. *Journal of Food Science, 45*, 1054.

50. Laakkonen, E., Wellington, G. H., & Sherbon, J. W. (1970). Low-temperature, long-time heating of bovine muscle. 1. Changes in tenderness, water-binding capacity, pH and amount of water-soluble components. *Journal of Food Science, 35*, 175.

51. Labensky, S. R. & Hause, A. M. (2003). *On cooking: A textbook of culinary fundamentals* (3rd ed.). Upper Saddle River, NJ: Prentice Hall.

52. Leander, R. C., Hedrick, H. B., Brown, M. F., & White, J. A. (1980). Comparison of structural changes in bovine longissimus and semitendinosus muscles during cooking. *Journal of Food Science, 45*, 1.

53. Leverton, R. M., & Odell, G. V. (1985). *The nutritive value of cooked meat.* Oklahoma Agricultural Experiment Station Miscellaneous Publication No. MP-49. Stillwater, OK: Oklahoma Agricultural Experiment Station.

54. Lin, J. C., & Kaufman, P. (1995). Food companies offer views of safe handling label for meat and poultry. *Food Review, 18*(3), 23.

55. Liu, M. N., Huffman, D. L., Egbert, W. R., McCaskey, T. A., & Liu, C. W. (1991). Soy protein and oil effects on chemical, physical and microbial stability of lean ground beef patties. *Journal of Food Science, 56,* 906.

56. Love, J. A., & Prusa, K. J. (1992). Nutrient composition and sensory attributes of cooked ground beef: Effects of fat content, cooking method, and water rinsing. *Journal of the American Dietetic Association, 92,* 1367.

57. Mandigo, R. W. (1986). Restructuring of muscle foods. *Food Technology, 40*(3), 85.

58. Marshall, N. (1960). Electronic cookery of top round of beef. *Journal of Home Economics, 52,* 31.

59. Maruri, J. L., & Larick, D. K., (1992). Volatile concentration and flavor of beef as influenced by diet. *Journal of Food Science, 57,* 1275.

60. McComber, D. R., Clark, R., & Cox, D. F. (1990). Consumer preference for pork loin roasts cooked to 160°F and 185°F. *Journal of the American Dietetic Association, 90,* 1718.

61. McDowell, M. D., Harrison, D. L., Pacey, C., & Stone, M. B. (1982). Differences between conventionally cooked top round roasts and semimembranous muscle strips cooked in a model system. *Journal of Food Science, 47,* 1603.

62. McIntosh, E. N. (1967). Effect of postmortem aging and enzyme tenderizers on mucoprotein of bovine skeletal muscle. *Journal of Food Science, 32,* 210.

63. McKeith, F. K., de Vol, D. L., Miles, R. S., Bechtel, P. J., & Carr, T. R. (1985). Chemical and sensory properties of thirteen major beef muscles. *Journal of Food Science, 50,* 869.

64. Mermelstein, N. H. (2002). Comprehensive BSE risk study released. *Food Technology, 56*(1), 75–76.

65. Miller, M. F., Andersen, M. K., Ramsey, C. B., & Reagan, J. O. (1993). Physical and sensory characteristics of low-fat ground beef patties. *Journal of Food Science, 58,* 461.

66. Miller, S. A. & Dwyer, J. T. (2001). Evaluating the safety and nutritional value of mycoprotein. *Food Technology, 55*(7), 42.

67. Mitchell, G. E., Giles, J. E., Rogers, S. A., Tan, L. T., Naidoo, R. J., & Ferguson, D. M. (1991). Tenderizing, aging, and thawing effects on sensory, chemical, and physical properties of beef steaks. *Journal of Food Science, 56,* 1125.

68. Mitchell, G. E., Reed, A. W., & Rogers, S. A. (1991). Influence of feeding regimen on the sensory qualities and fatty acid contents of beef steaks. *Journal of Food Science, 56,* 1102.

69. Moody, W. G. (1983). Beef flavor: A review. *Food Technology, 37*(5), 227.

70. Moore, L. J., Harrison, D. L., & Dayton, A. D. (1980). Differences among top round steaks cooked by dry or moist heat in a conventional or a microwave oven. *Journal of Food Science, 45,* 777.

71. National Restaurant Association Educational Foundation. (2002). *ServSafe coursebook* (2nd ed.). Chicago, IL: National Restaurant Association Education Foundation.

72. North American Meat Processors Association (NAMP). (1997). *The Meat Buyers Guide.* Restoin VA: NAMP.

73. Nielsen, M. M., & Hall, F. T. (1965). Dry-roasting of less tender beef cuts. *Journal of Home Economics, 57,* 353.

74. Olson, D. G., Caporaso, F., & Mandigo, R. W. (1980). Effects of serving temperature on sensory evaluation of beef steaks from different muscles and carcass maturities. *Journal of Food Science, 45,* 627.

75. Omaye, S. T. (2001). Preventing BSE in the U.S. *Food Technology, 55*(4), 26.

76. Omaye, S. T. (2001). Shiga-toxin—producing *Escherichia coli:* Another concern. *Food Technology, 55*(5), 26.

77. Oreskovich, D. C., Bechtel, P. J., McKeith, F. K., Novakofski, J., & Basgall, E. J. (1992). Marinade pH affects textural properties of beef. *Journal of Food Science, 57,* 305.

78. Parrish, F. C., Jr., Boles, J. A., Rust, R. E., & Olson, D. G. (1991). Dry and wet aging effects on palatability attributes of beef loin and rib steaks from three quality grades. *Journal of Food Science, 56,* 601.

79. Peterson, R. J., & Chang, S. S. (1982). Identification of volatile flavor compounds of fresh, frozen beef stew and a comparison of these with those of canned beef stew. *Journal of Food Science, 47,* 1444.

80. Prusa, K. J., Fedler, C. A., & Miller, L. F. (1993). National in-home consumer evaluation of pork roasts from pigs administered porcine somatotropin (pST). *Journal of Food Science, 58,* 480.

81. Putnam, J. J. (2000). Major trends in U.S. food supply, 1909–1999. *Food Review, 23*(1), 8–14.

82. Ralston, K. Starke, Y., Brent, P., & Riggins, T. (2000). Awareness of risks changing how hamburgers are cooked. *Food Review, 23*(2), 44–50.

83. Rathje, W. L., & Ho, E. E. (1987). Meat fat madness: Conflicting patterns of meat fat consumption and their public health implications. *Journal of the American Dietetic Association, 87,* 1357.

84. Recio, H. A., Savell, J. W., Branson, R. E., Cross, H. R., & Smith, G. C. (1987). Consumer ratings of restructured beef steaks manufactured to contain different residual contents of connective tissue. *Journal of Food Science, 52,* 1461.

85. Rhee, K. S. (1994). Reducing fat in ground meat cookery. *Food and Nutrition News, 66*(5), 37.

86. Rice, D. R., Neufer, P. A., & Sipos, E. F. (1989). Effects of soy protein blends, fat level, and cooking methods on the nutrient retention of beef patties. *Food Technology, 43*(4), 88.

87. Roger, G. (2001). Mycoprotein—a meat alternative new to the U.S. *Food Technology, 55*(7), 36.

88. Sanderson, M., & Vail, G. E. (1963). Fluid content and tenderness of three muscles of beef cooked to three internal temperatures. *Journal of Food Science, 28,* 590.

89. Savell, J. W., Branson, R. E., Cross, H. R., Stiffler, D. M., Wise, J. W., Griffin, D. B., & Smith, G. C. (1987). National consumer retail beef study: Palatability evaluations of beef loin steaks that differed in marbling. *Journal of Food Science, 52,* 517.

90. Shorthose, W. R., & Harris, P. V. (1990). Effect of animal age on the tenderness of selected beef muscles. *Journal of Food Science, 55,* 1.

91. Smith, G. C., Carpenter, Z. L., Cross, H. R., Murphey, C. E., Abraham, H. C., Savell, J. W., Davis, G. W., Berry, B. W., & Parrish, Jr., F. C. (1984). Relationship of USDA marbling groups to palatability of cooked beef. *Journal of Food Quality, 7,* 289.

92. Smith, G. C., Savell, J. W., Cross, H. R., & Carpenter, Z. L. (1983). The relationship of USDA quality grade to beef flavor. *Food Technology, 37*(5), 233.

93. Tatum, J. D., Smith, G. C., Berry, B. W., Murphey, C. E., Williams, F. L., & Carpenter, Z. L. (1980). Carcass characteristics, time on feed and cooked beef palatability attributes. *Journal of Animal Science, 50,* 833.

94. Tatum, J. D., Smith, G. C., & Carpenter, Z. L. (1982). Interrelationships between marbling, subcutaneous fat thickness and cooked beef palatability. *Journal of Animal Science, 54,* 777.

95. Troutt, E. S., Hunt, M. C., Johnson, D. E., Claus, J. R., Kastner, C. L., & Kropf, D. H. (1992). Characteristics of low-fat ground beef containing texture-modifying ingredients. *Journal of Food Science, 52,* 19.

96. Troutt, E. S., Hunt, M. C., Johnson, D. E., Claus, J. R., Kastner, C. L., Kropf, D. H., & Stroda, S. (1992). Chemical, physical, and sensory characterization of ground beef containing 5 to 30 percent fat. *Journal of Food Science, 57,* 25.

97. U.S. Department of Agriculture. (1995, July). How to buy meat. Home and Garden Bulletin Number 265.

98. U.S. Department of Agriculture. (2002, September). News release: USDA strengthens food safety policies. Release No. 0405.02. Retrieved September 26, 2002, from http://www.usda.gov/news/releases/2002/09/0405.htm

99. U.S. Department of Agriculture, Food Safety Inspection Service. (1995, March). Focus on: Ham. Retrieved January 9, 2003, from http://www.fsis.usda.gov/OA/pubs/ham.htm

100. U.S. Department of Agriculture, Food Safety Inspection Service. (1998, May). Safety of veal . . . from farm to table. Retrieved January 9, 2003, from http://www.fsis.usda.gov/OA/pubs/veal.htm

101. U.S. Department of Agriculture, Food Safety Inspection Service. (2000, May). Focus on: Bison. Retrieved January 9, 2003 from http://www.fsis.usda.gov/OA/pubs/focusbison.htm

102. U.S. Department of Agriculture, Food Safety Inspection Service. (2000, May). Focus on: Lamb . . . from farm to table. Retrieved January 9, 2003, from http://www.fsis.usda.gov/OA/pubs/focuslamb.htm

103. U.S. Department of Agriculture, Food Safety Inspection Service. (2000, July). Focus on: Slow cooker safety. Retrieved January 9, 2003, from http://www.fsis.usda.gov/OA/pubs/slocookr.htm

104. U.S. Department of Agriculture, Food Safety Inspection Service. (2002, June). Focus on: Beef . . . from farm to table. Retrieved January 9, 2003, from http://www. fsis.usda.gov/OA/pubs/focusbeef.htm

105. U.S. Department of Agriculture, Food Safety Inspection Service. (2002, September). Safety of fresh pork . . . from farm to table. Retrieved January 9, 2003, from http://www.fsis.usda.gov/OA/pubs/pork.htm

106. U.S. Department of Health and Human Services. (2001, August). Federal agencies take special precautions to keep "mad cow disease" out of the United States. Retrieved June 23, 2002, from http://www.hhs.gov/news/press/2001pres/01fsbse.html

107. U.S. Food and Drug Administration. (2002, February). Keeping the U.S. free of "mad cow disease"—FDA's actions to keep out disease that's stalked Europe. Retrieved November 15, 2002, from http://www.fda.gov/opacom/factsheets/justthefacts/8BSE.html

108. Vickers, Z. M. & Wang, J. (2002). Liking of ground beef patties is not affected by irradiation. *Journal of Food Science, 67,* 380–383.

109. Voris, H. H., & van Duyne, F. O. (1979). Low wattage microwave cooking of top round roasts: Energy consumption, thiamin content and palatability. *Journal of Food Science, 44,* 1447.

110. Wilson, D. (2001). Marketing mycoprotein: The Quorn Foods story. *Food Technology, 55*(7), 48.

111. Yu, L. P., & Lee, Y. B. (1986). Effects of postmortem pH and temperature on bovine muscle structure and meat tenderness. *Journal of Food Science, 51,* 774.

112. Zimmermann, W. J. (1983). An approach to safe microwave cooking of pork roasts containing *Trichinella spiralis*. *Journal of Food Science, 43,* 1715.

Poultry

 The term *poultry* is used to describe all domesticated birds that are intended for human consumption, including chickens, turkeys, ducks, geese, guinea fowl, squab (young pigeons), and pigeons. Chickens and turkeys are by far the most commonly consumed poultry items in the United States. Poultry is marketed throughout the year in a wide variety of forms, many of which are convenience foods.

CONSUMPTION

Poultry production is adaptable to most areas of the world, and it provides a good-quality protein food at a relatively modest cost to supplement the diets of many people. Much of the poultry in the United States is produced with the application of modern management practices. Thousands of birds are sometimes raised under one roof.

As measured by food supply data, red meat remains the most commonly consumed meat in the United States at 134 pounds per person in 1999 [2]; however, poultry consumption has increased considerably over the years. Between 1975 and 1999, annual per capita poultry consumption doubled; 95 pounds of poultry were consumed in 1999 as compared to 47 pounds in 1975. The popularity of poultry has been influenced by the consumer's perception that it is low fat, inexpensive, and convenient to prepare as compared to other meat [29].

PROCESSING

Many improvements in technology have occurred in poultry-processing plants over the past decade and, particularly in large plants, many of the processes are automated. This type of equipment includes a picking machine with rotating drums and rubber fingers that remove feathers from the slaughtered and scalded birds, a carousel eviscerator that slides metal spoons into the birds and pulls out the viscera, and a carousel fat remover that removes abdominal fat [10]. Cutting machines cut up broilers in the processing plant while saw lines are used to cut birds into more sophisticated cuts than automated machines can manage. Boneless parts may be breaded and frozen in the processing plant. A wide variety of poultry products are processed, many of them going to foodservice operations.

salmonella bacteria, some strains of which can cause illness in humans; because the micro-organisms themselves produce the gastrointestinal symptoms, the illness is called a food infection

Slaughtered, eviscerated poultry are washed with chlorinated water and chilled immediately, usually by immersion of the carcasses in chilled water at less than 36°F (2°C) to control the growth of microorganisms. USDA inspectors monitor the processes and test for **Salmonella** organisms as a measure of the plant's effectiveness in controlling contamination. The USDA has modernized its inspection procedures for poultry, as it has for meat [4].

A certain number of chickens will leave processing plants with some detectable salmonellae bacteria. Some of these bacteria may be firmly attached to or entrapped in poultry skin when they first arrive at the processing plant. The USDA's Food Safety and Inspection Service has approved the use of trisodium phosphate (TSP) to reduce the incidence of these microorganisms on the birds. After inspection and chilling, the chicken may be dipped into a TSP solution. This treatment can reduce to less than 5 percent the number of birds containing salmonellae. It does not affect the flavor, texture, or appearance of the chicken.

Polyphosphates may be used in meat and poultry products to improve water binding, texture, color, and flavor. These characteristics are enhanced in ground turkey by the addition of polyphosphates [5, 20].

The use of ionizing radiation for the treatment of raw poultry and poultry products to control and reduce the population of pathogens such as *Salmonella*, *Campylobacter*, and *Listeria monocytogenes* has been approved by the USDA and by the Food and Drug Administration (FDA). Irradiation can be used to treat fresh or frozen, uncooked whole poultry carcasses or parts. Packages must bear an irradiation logo and the statement "Treated with radiation" or "Treated by irradiation." The shelf life of irradiated chicken has been reported to be as long as 15 days compared with about 6 days for unirradiated carcasses, as evidenced by the bacterial counts [19]. As with meat, raw or partially cooked poultry products must carry a safe handling label (see Figure 25-12).

COMPOSITION AND NUTRITIVE VALUE

The composition and nutritive value of poultry do not differ substantially from those of other meats, except that chicken and turkey breast, particularly, are lower in fat and cholesterol and higher in niacin than other lean meats with separable fat removed [31].

capon a male bird castrated when young

The fat of poultry is deposited in the muscle tissue, in thick layers under the skin, and in the abdominal cavity. **Capons** have more fat and a more uniform distribution of fat in the flesh than chickens that have not been castrated. The fat of all types of poultry has a softer consistency and lower melting point than the fat of other meats. Goose and duck are higher in fat than chicken or turkey. Fat of mature birds has a pronounced flavor. Geese, particularly, have a distinctive flavor, which may be objectionable in old birds. The composition of chicken and turkey is given in Appendix C.

The amount of fat in ground chicken influences cooked yield and quality characteristics [37]. In one study, as fat content increased from 5 to 10 percent, cooking losses and moisture/protein ratios of grilled patties increased. Lower-fat patties were harder, springier, less cohesive, and chewier than patties containing higher fat levels.

The light meat of poultry, particularly the breast, has shorter, more tender fibers that are less firmly bound together with connective tissue than those of dark meat. As in mammals, the amount of connective tissue in poultry varies with age; it is more abundant in old birds, especially males.

CLASSIFICATION AND MARKET FORMS

The market forms of poultry have changed over the years, from the early 1960's when whole dressed chicken accounted for over 80 percent of chicken sales to the present day when the largest share of chicken is marketed as cut-up parts, some of them boneless and skinless. The proliferation of fast-food chains that sell chicken fillet sandwiches and chicken nuggets has contributed to these changing market trends.

Poultry is classified on the basis of age and weight in Table 26-1. Ready-to-cook chickens, chilled or frozen, are marketed whole, halved, quartered, and in individual pieces such as breasts, thighs, drumsticks, and wings. Boneless, and sometimes skinless, parts and ground raw chicken are also sold. Also available is boned, canned chicken. Many different precooked frozen convenience items are available, for example, chicken cannelloni, chicken enchiladas, Mandarin chicken with vegetables (in a savory plum sauce), chicken with fettucini (with mushrooms and spinach in a cream sauce), sweet and sour chicken with rice, and glazed chicken breast (light style), as well as many different brands of fried chicken parts and chicken dinners. Restructured chicken, formed into boneless breaded pieces from chunks of chicken meat, is a popular finger food for dipping into sauces. A complete list of available convenience foods containing chicken would be very long indeed.

No longer just for holidays, turkey has become popular year-round. Since 1975, turkey consumption has increased by 180 percent. In 2001, the per capita consumption of turkey in the United States was 17.5 pounds, with about 70 percent of the turkey consumption at times other than holidays [27]. Turkey is marketed as frozen whole birds and as frozen breasts, which are essentially oven ready, and also as ground raw turkey and fully cooked turkey breast deli meats. Frozen boneless raw turkey roasts and boneless cooked turkey rolls are convenience items that are available in all white meat, all dark meat, or a combination. Canned boned turkey and many frozen turkey products, such as turkey pies, main-dish items, and turkey dinners, are also available.

Type	Description	Age	Weight (lb)
Young chicken			
Broiler-fryer	Either sex; tender	9–12 weeks	2–2½
Roaster	Either sex; tender	3–5 months	3–5
Capon	Castrated male; tender	<8 months	4–8
Rock Cornish game hen	Cross of Cornish chicken with another breed; either sex; immature; tender	5–7 weeks	<2
Older chicken			
Baking hen	Female; tender	>10 months	3–6
Stewing hen or fowl	Mature female; less tender	>10 months	3–6
Young turkey			
Fryer-roaster	Either sex, tender	10–12 weeks	4–8
Young hen	Female; tender	5–7 months	8–15
Young tom	Male; tender	5–7 months	>12
Ducks	Either sex; tender	7–8 weeks	3–7
Geese	Either sex; tender	<11 weeks	6–12

Table 26-1
Poultry Classification

Figure 26-1
(a) A federal inspector examines the poultry in the production room. (Courtesy of the U.S. Department of Agriculture)

(b) An Agricultural Research Service engineer is developing a computer directed scanning system to speed the inspection of the nearly 8 billion chickens processed annually through federally inspected plants in the United States. (Courtesy of U.S. Agriculture Research Service, photo by Keith Weller)

BUYING POULTRY

Changes in the efficiency of production and processing of poultry have greatly increased the supply of poultry meat on a year-round basis. Prices for poultry have become competitive with other meat products, and poultry is a popular item with the American consumer. Often, poultry is being chosen in preference to red meats.

Poultry has a relatively high proportion of waste from the raw carcass to the cooked bird. The yield of cooked weight for young chickens has been reported to be 65 percent of the raw weight for those that were baked and 73 percent for those that were simmered [22]. Skin, fat, and bone accounted for about

Hot Topics

Scientists and chickens—Partners?

It takes a tough scientist to make a tender (and juicy) chicken! Thus says the Agricultural Research Service of the USDA [11]. Brenda Lyon is a food scientist at their research center in Athens, Georgia, where she focuses on the relationships between sensory attributes (eating quality) of poultry meat and production practices (growing and processing the birds).

For over 20 years Lyon has studied the characteristics of poultry meat—and there are a lot of characteristics. We like our chicken to be tender and moist, but there are many components that affect these characteristics. The amount of force it takes to cut through a piece of poultry—called shear value—can be easily measured with a machine. But human subjects, with their senses of smell, taste, touch, and sight, are essential in evaluating aroma, appearance, juiciness, texture, and so on. And it doesn't stop there. For example, characteristics such as mouthfeel, springiness, chewiness, compaction of the meat after chewing, and ease of swallowing all play a part in creating a sensory texture profile.

Now, if you are to be a sensory evaluator in these research projects, you will need to be intensively trained in order to identify the various characteristics of poultry meat and assign intensity values to them. Just how tender is tender; how juicy is juicy—on a scale monitored by a computer?

In Lyon's lab she is a tough trainer. She sets up individual workstations equipped with special lights and filtered air and a computer mouse for recording your evaluation on a line scale from 0 to 15. Each attribute must be assessed and results of the study are statistically analyzed.

What is the ultimate goal of this food technology research? It is to assist the poultry producers in bringing to the marketplace a product that consumers will buy, will be nourished by, and will enjoy. Processes developed to handle poultry must ultimately pass the sensory panel test for eating quality.

As an example, it has been found that the amount of time the breast muscles remain on the bone after processing affects the texture and tenderness of the boned meat. It seems that the best timing for acceptable tenderness is 4 to 6 hours postmortem. Rigor mortis occurs and is dissipated by this time period. Sensory panels found that meat left on the bone for less than 4 hours was tougher than meat left on the bone longer. This 4 to 6 hour period must be integrated into the inspection, chilling, and cutting processes in a poultry plant. Reducing the chilling time to accommodate the deboning process interfered with rigor mortis and made the cooked breast meat tough. The sensory panels were key in determining the real effects of the production processes.

Thus the food scientist and the poultry processor need to work together as partners in order to produce the kind of chicken we all enjoy. Eating quality is the ultimate deciding factor in whether or not a process is successful.

Food technologists discuss the fiber orientation of a chicken breast sample. (Courtesy of ARS USDA, photo by Peggy Greb)

Figure 26-2
U.S. Department of Agriculture inspection mark for poultry. (Courtesy of the U.S. Department of Agriculture)

Figure 26-3
The U.S. Department of Agriculture grade shield denotes that poultry has been graded for quality. Poultry must first be inspected for wholesomenes, however. (Courtesy of the U.S. Department of Agriculture)

50 percent of the weight of the cooked chicken. Thus, the yield of cooked edible meat from the raw chicken carcass was about 35 percent. Losses vary with the temperature and method of cooking and with the percentage of fat. The high fat content of ducks and geese results in particularly high cooking losses.

Inspection

Federal legislation passed in 1968, the Wholesome Poultry Products Act, is similar to the Meat Inspection Act. It requires that all poultry marketed in the United States be inspected for sanitary processing and freedom from disease. This inspection is performed either by agents of the federal government or by adequate state systems. The inspection process in a poultry-production plant is illustrated in Figure 26-1. The handling of both poultry and meat inspection at the federal level is the responsibility of the Food Safety and Inspection Service of the USDA.

The traditional inspection system for poultry has been modernized by the USDA in recent years. The newer plan focuses on prevention and requires that all poultry-processing plants operate under a Hazard Analysis and Critical Control Points (HACCP) plan. The processor must also have written sanitation standard operating procedures (SOPs) for daily operation and must test for certain microorganisms. Pathogen reduction is a major goal of the program.

Figure 26-2 shows the USDA inspection mark. Poultry bearing the official mark, sometimes printed on a tag attached to the wing (Figure 26-4), must come from a healthy flock, be processed under specified sanitary conditions, contain only approved additives, and be properly packaged and labeled. Prepared poultry products, such as canned, boned poultry, frozen dinners and pies, and specialty items, must also be produced with USDA inspection.

Labeling

In 1997, a new labeling rule went into effect to define the terms *fresh* and *frozen* as applied to poultry products. Fresh poultry must have never been below 26°F (−3°C). Raw poultry held at 0°F (−18°C) or below must be labeled as frozen or previously frozen. A third category of poultry is referred to as *hard chilled* or *previously hard chilled.* Hard chilled poultry has been held below 26°F (−3°C) but above 0°F (−18°C). Poultry that has been hard chilled is not required to have any descriptive label on the product, but it should not be labeled as fresh or frozen, as neither of these categories applies [33, 35].

Under new regulations effective in 2002, poultry products must label the percentage of absorbed or retained water in any raw poultry product as a result of carcass washing, chilling, or other post-slaughter processing unless the amount of water retained can be demonstrated to be unavoidable due to meeting food safety requirements [36]. Poultry has been traditionally chilled using water immersion instead of using air chilling, as is common in the processing of meats. The immersion of the product in water during processing may result in water retention. This new regulation came into effect as a result of a suit brought by poultry consumers and red meat producers alleging that poultry products containing absorbed water were adulterated (in an economic sense) and misbranded under the Poultry Products Inspection Act.

The 1990 Nutrition Education and Labeling Act mandates nutrition labels on processed poultry products. As with meat, merchandisers can choose to provide nutrition information on raw, single-ingredient poultry products such as raw chicken legs. This information may appear on labels, posters, pamphlets, or videos in the store. The nutrient content claims that are allowed for poultry are the same as for meat, and are discussed in Chapter 2.

The other requirements for a poultry label include the product name, the name and address of the producer or distributor, the inspection mark, the ingredients and net weight, the establishment number identifying the plant where the product was processed, and the handling instructions. After the product leaves the processing plant it comes under the jurisdiction of the FDA, which is responsible for preventing the sale of adulterated food, including poultry. Additional information and terms that may appear on a poultry label are provided in Table 26-2.

Grading

In addition to inspecting for wholesomeness, the USDA has developed standards for quality grades. These grades—A, B, and C—are placed on the label in a shield-shaped mark (see Figures 26-3 and 26-4). Signs of quality that are evaluated in grading include conformation or shape of the bird, fleshing, distribution and amount of fat, and freedom from pinfeathers, skin and flesh blemishes, cuts, and bruises.

Many states participate in a grading program, and in such states the official stamp reads, "Federal–State Graded." Grading of poultry is not mandatory but consumers profit by its use. It provides an assurance of quality and class as stated, permits selection of the desired quality for the intended use, and helps in evaluating variable prices. Differences between Grades A and B can be noted by an examination of Figure 26-5.

Figure 26-4
The wing tag may include the class name—in this case, Frying Chicken—in addition to the inspection mark and the grade mark. (Courtesy of the U.S. Department of Agriculture)

Table 26-2
Poultry Labeling Terms

Basted or self-basted	Poultry products that are injected or marinated with a solution containing butter or other edible fat, stock or water plus spices, flavor enhancers, and other approved substances. Bone-in poultry products may have a maximum added weight of 3 percent and boneless poultry products may have an added weight of 8 percent.
Chemical free	This term is *not allowed* on labels.
Free range or Free roaming	The poultry has been allowed access to outside.
Halal or Zabiah Halal	Products prepared in federally inspected plants and handled according to Islamic rule under Islamic authority.
Kosher	Products prepared in federally inspected plants and handled under rabbinical supervison.
Mechanically separated poultry	Effective 1996, poultry product that has been separated from the bone through a sieve or similar device under pressure must be labeled as *mechanically separated chicken or turkey.*
No hormones	Hormones are not allowed in the raising of poultry; therefore if this statement is used on a label it must be followed by the statement *"Federal regulations prohibit the use of hormones."*
No antibiotics	This term may be used if sufficient evidence has been provided that the poultry was raised without antibiotics.
Oven prepared	Product is fully cooked and ready to eat.
Oven ready	Product is ready to cook.

Source: Food Safety and Inspection Service, U.S. Department of Agriculture [35].

Figure 26-5
Grading for quality is not required by law, but many firms choose to have their poultry graded. U.S. Grade A (left) and U.S. Grade B (right) young turkeys are shown. (Courtesy of the U.S. Department of Agriculture)

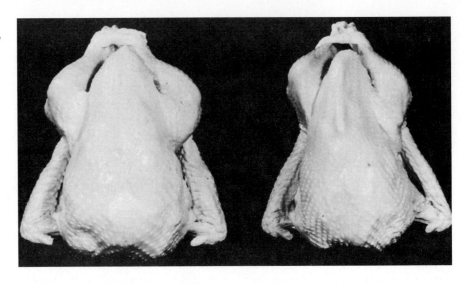

Characteristics of Age

Most poultry sold in retail markets are young, tender birds. In a young bird, the end of the breastbone is pliable and the wing offers little resistance when bent into an upright position. The skin of a young bird is pliable and soft and tears easily. An older bird has a hard, calcified breastbone and may show an abundance of long hairs. Greater weight is not necessarily an indication of age, as some breeds of poultry grow very large. In young birds, sex differences are not significant; however, with increase in age, male birds are inferior in flavor to female birds.

Poultry should be purchased with the intended use in mind. The class name sometimes suggests the cooking method, for example, broiler-fryers and roasters.

Amount to Buy

Table 26-3 gives the estimated number of servings from a pound of ready-to-cook poultry. Whole chickens usually cost slightly less per pound than those already cut into individual pieces. Figure 26-6 shows procedures to follow in cutting up chickens.

So that individual preferences for various poultry parts may be satisfied, pieces of all one kind, such as chicken breasts or drumsticks, are often packaged together and marketed. As Table 26-3 indicates, more poultry is needed per serving when such pieces as wings or thighs are purchased than when breasts, which contain less bone, are bought. The cost per serving should be compared, in these cases, rather than the cost per pound.

STORAGE AND HANDLING

Chilled, raw poultry is a highly perishable product and should be stored at a refrigerator temperature of 40°F (4°C) or below. Even at refrigerator temperatures, storage time is usually limited to a few days, although irradiation may increase the shelf life. The transparent wrap on prepackaged poultry is designed for refrigerator storage after purchase. In fact, repackaging chicken for short-

Table 26-3

Number of Servings from a Pound of Ready-to-Cook Poultry

Kind and Class	Approximate Servings of Cooked Meat		Approximate Yield of Cooked, Diced Meat (c)
	Size of Serving	Number of Servings	
Chicken			
Whole			
Broiler-fryer	3 oz without bone	2	1¼
Roaster	3 oz without bone	2¼	1½
Stewing hen	3 oz without bone	2	1¼
Pieces			
Breast halves (about 5¾ oz each)	1, about 2¾ oz without bone	2¾	
Drumsticks (about 3 oz each)	2, about 2½ oz without bone	2½	
Thighs (about 3¾ oz each)	2, about 3 oz without bone	2¼	
Wings (about 2¾ oz each)	4, about 2¾ oz without bone	1½	
Breast quarter (about 11 oz each)	1, about 4½ oz without bone	1½	
Leg quarter (about 10¾ oz each)	1, about 4¼ oz without bone	1½	
Turkey			
Whole	3 oz without bone	2¼	1¼
Pieces			
Breast	3 oz without bone	2¾	1¾
Thigh	3 oz without bone	2¾	
Drumstick	3 oz without bone	2½	
Wing	3 oz without bone	1¾	
Ground	3 oz	3¾	
Boneless turkey roast	3 oz	3¼	
Duckling	3 oz without bone	1	
Goose	3 oz without bone	1¾	

(Courtesy of the U.S. Department of Agriculture)

term storage in the refrigerator may actually increase the bacterial count as a result of the additional handling [12].

Because some poultry may be contaminated with salmonellae or Campylobacter when brought into the kitchen, special precautions in handling are necessary. A retail study conducted in Minnesota found that 88 percent of the poultry sampled from local supermarkets tested positive for Campylobacter [15]. All surfaces, such as countertops and cutting boards, that come into contact with raw poultry during its preparation for cooking should be thoroughly cleaned and sanitized before other foods are placed on them. One tablespoon of household bleach in 1 quart of water may be used to sanitize cutting boards and other work surfaces. Cutting boards made of wood, which may be difficult to adequately sanitize, should not be used for cutting up raw poultry. These precautions are necessary to avoid cross-contamination of cooked poultry and other foods prepared on the same surfaces as raw poultry that may be infected with salmonellae. *Salmonella* food poisoning is discussed in Chapter 3.

Poultry should always be cooked to a well-done stage to destroy any food-poisoning organisms that may be present. Although 165°F (74°C) is the acceptable minimum endpoint cooking temperature for poultry [26], higher temperatures of 170°F (77°C) to 180°F (82°C) are often recommended to ensure that an acceptable temperature has been reached throughout the bird [34, 25]. When a bird is stuffed, the temperature of the stuffing must be checked

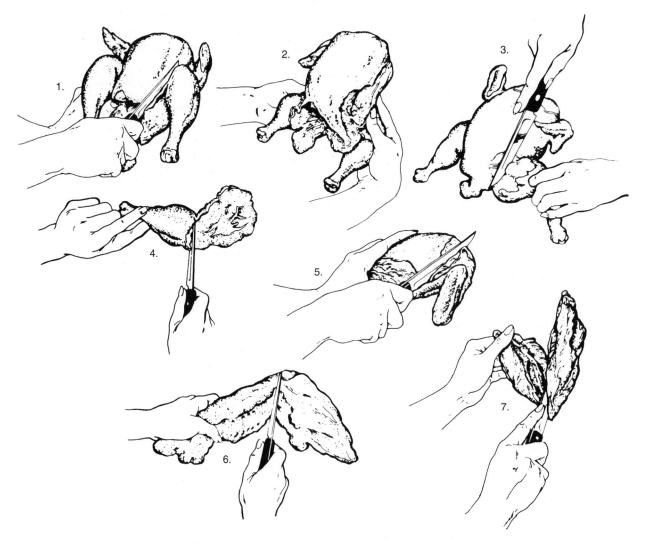

Figure 26-6A
Cutting up chicken. (Courtesy of the National Broiler Council)
1. Place chicken, breast-side up, on cutting board. Cut skin between thighs and body.
2. Grasping one leg in each hand, lift chicken and bend legs until bones break at hip joints.
3. Remove leg-thigh from body by cutting (from tail toward shoulder) between the joints, close to bones in back of bird. Repeat other side.
4. To separate thighs and drumsticks, locate knee joint by bending thigh and leg together. With skin-side down, cut through joints of each leg.
5. With chicken on back, remove wings by cutting inside of wing just over joint. Pull wing from body and cut from top down, through joint.
6. Separate breast and back by placing chicken on neck-end or back and cutting (toward board) through joints along each side of rib cage.
7. Breast may be left whole or, to cut into halves, place skin-side down on board and cut wishbone in two at V of bone.

with a thermometer to ensure an endpoint temperature of 165°F (74°C) or higher has been reached.

Cooked poultry products are ideal for the growth and/or toxin production of any microorganisms with which they may have been contaminated during handling and serving; therefore, maintaining proper temperature control is essential. Poultry products should always be refrigerated promptly and used within a few days. If it is anticipated that cooked poultry will be kept longer than this time, it should be placed in a moisture/vapor-proof wrapping or con-

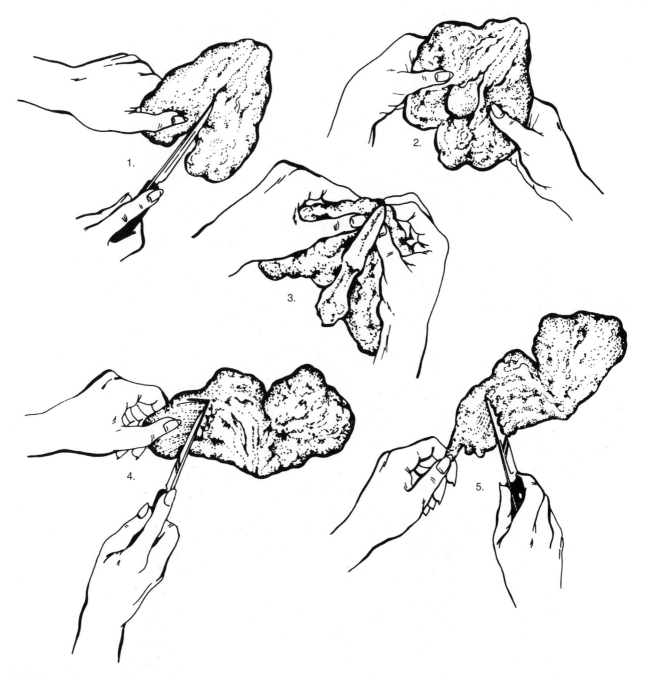

Figure 26-6B

Boning a whole chicken breast.

1. Place skin-side down on cutting board with widest part nearest you. With point of knife, cut through white cartilage at neck end of keel bone.
2. Pick up breast and bend back, exposing keel bone.
3. Loosen meat from bone by running thumbs around both sides; pull out bone and cartilage.
4. Working with one side of breast, insert tip of knife under long rib bone inside thin membrane and cut or pull meat from rib cage. Turn breast and repeat on other side.
5. Working from ends of wishbone, scrape all flesh away and cut bone from meat. (If white tendons remain on either side of breast, loosen with knife and pull out.)

tainer and frozen. Longer storage periods are possible when raw or cooked poultry is frozen. Better flavor and texture are maintained in the uncooked than in the cooked frozen product when they are to be stored for a few months.

Poultry products, like other highly perishable foods, should be thawed one of three ways: (1) under refrigeration, (2) in clean, cold water that is changed every 30 minutes, (3) or in the microwave and then cooked immediately. Thawing on the kitchen counter or in warm water are unsafe practices.

Processed poultry products are popular for use in the foodservice industry because they are uniform in weight, shape, yield, composition, and cooking requirements. Some of these are distributed in a precooked form that requires only refrigeration rather than freezing. The raw poultry product may be vacuum packaged in a multilaminate film, cooked, and then marketed in the same package. When vacuum packaged, uncured precooked turkey breast rolls were evaluated for microbiologic stability past 30 days of storage at 40°F (4°C), no colonies of **psychrotrophic** aerobic **bacteria** were detected; however, some **mesophilic** anaerobic **bacteria** were present. These findings indicate that precautions should be taken when serving these precooked poultry products to ensure that they are not temperature abused. Thus, they should not be held at higher than refrigerator temperatures for any period that would allow bacteria to multiply, and they must always be refrigerated [30].

psychrotrophic bacteria bacteria that grow best at cold temperatures (cold-loving bacteria)

mesophilic bacteria bacteria that grow best at moderate temperatures

COOKING POULTRY

The fundamental principles of cooking poultry do not differ from those for other meats. Dry-heat methods (broiling, frying, baking, and roasting) are applicable to young, tender birds. Moist-heat methods should be applied to older, less tender birds to make them tender and palatable. Most of the poultry sold on the market today is young and tender and can be cooked by dry-heat methods. As with meat, poultry should not be washed in water before cooking.

Microwave cooking of poultry is not recommended. Microwave energy is not as effective as conventional cooking for destruction of microorganisms in whole turkeys, in chicken halves, and probably in pieces. In one study, turkeys that had been inoculated with food-poisoning bacteria before cooking were baked in the microwave oven. Roasting to an internal breast temperature of 170°F (77°C) did not completely eliminate the microorganisms [1]. Although the turkeys in this study contained abnormally high numbers of bacteria, it is possible that pathogenic microorganisms present in more usual numbers will survive. In another study, cooking chicken halves in the microwave oven to an internal temperature of 185°F (85°C) was not sufficient to destroy, in more than 50 percent of the chickens, all *Salmonella* organisms with which the birds had been inoculated [21]. Therefore, the microwave oven is not recommended for the cooking of poultry.

Roasting

All kinds of young, tender poultry can be roasted or baked (Figure 26-7) Color Plates XXVIII and XXIX. One problem associated with roasting whole poultry arises from the necessity of cooking all parts of the bird in one cooking operation even though some parts are more tender than others. The breast may be overcooked and dry by the time the legs and thighs are cooked to the desired degree of doneness.

Figure 26-7
A roasted chicken can be presented on a platter before carving for the diners. (Courtesy of the National Chicken Council and U.S. Poultry and Egg Association)

To determine the stage of doneness of large-size poultry, particularly turkeys, a thermometer can be inserted in the thickest part of the thigh muscle or in the breast muscle. Internal thigh temperatures of 180° to 185°F (82° to 85°C) appear to produce a desired degree of doneness without an objectionable decrease in juiciness [3, 16]. Pop-up timers, which are internal temperature-indicating devices, are sometimes placed in the breasts of turkeys during processing and are usually set for 185°F (85°C). Even with a pop-up timer, it is suggested that the temperature be checked with a thermometer in several places. A minimum endpoint temperature of 165°F (74°C) throughout the bird and the stuffing, if stuffed, is necessary for food safety purposes [26].

Variable oven temperatures, within a moderate range, appear to be satisfactory for roasting turkeys. Palatability scores for the tenderness and juiciness of both light and dark meat were found to be similar for turkeys roasted at three different oven temperatures—300°, 325°, and 350°F (149°, 163°, and 177°C) [13]. Drippings and total cooking losses were also similar at the three temperatures. However, the USDA recommends that the oven temperature for roasting poultry be no lower than 325°F (163°C).

An aluminum foil tent is sometimes used to cover the breast of turkeys during roasting to prevent overbrowning. Alternatively, the whole bird can be wrapped in foil, although lower palatability for foil-wrapped turkeys versus open pan–roasted birds has been reported [9]. Palatability is probably similar for birds roasted with the breast either up or down in the roasting rack.

General recommendations for roasting turkey might be an oven temperature of 325°F (163°C) and an internal temperature in the thigh muscle of 180° to 185°F (82° to 85°C). Table 26-4 gives approximate cooking times for unstuffed turkeys. The internal temperature of turkey meat, both whole birds and light or dark meat roasts, appears to be a good guide in cooking. The yield and juiciness of cooked meat decrease as the internal temperature increases from

Table 26-4

Timetable for Roasting Fresh or Thawed Turkey

Purchased Weight (lb)	Approximate Roasting Time @ 325°F (Hours)*
8 to 12	2¾ to 3
12 to 14	3 to 3¾
14 to 18	3¾ to 4¼
18 to 20	4¼ to 4½
20 to 24	4½ to 5

*These times are approximate and should always be used in conjunction with a properly placed thermometer.

(Courtesy of the U.S. Department of Agriculture)

104° to 194°F (40° to 90°C). At the same time, the scores for odor, flavor, and mealiness increase with increasing temperature [17].

Some general rules for ensuring safety in the preparation of turkey should be followed. Cook a fresh turkey within 2 days or freeze it. Defrost frozen turkeys in the refrigerator, allowing 24 hours per 5 pounds. Within 2 hours of cooking, cut turkey off the bones. Refrigerate in shallow containers and use leftover turkey within 4 days.

Stuffing a bird before roasting is not generally recommended. Bacteria can survive in stuffing which has not reached the safe temperature of 165°F (74°C), possibly resulting in foodborne illness. Even if the turkey meat has reached the proper internal temperature of 180°F (82°C), the stuffing may not have reached a temperature in all parts sufficient to destroy pathogenic bacteria. Some turkeys purchased frozen have been stuffed at a processing plant under USDA inspection. These turkeys should be safe when cooked from the frozen state. Manufacturer's directions should be followed. The temperature in the center of the stuffing should reach 165°F (74°C). This temperature should be measured with a thermometer.

Oil is sometimes injected into the breast just below the skin during the processing of turkeys to produce a self-basting effect during cooking. According to one study [24], the moistness of the breast meat was not affected by self-basting, but a higher proportion of fat appeared in the drippings. In another study [6], however, oil-basted turkeys were considered significantly more juicy and tender than unbasted birds. Injecting fat into the major muscles of the breast has produced a decrease in moisture and an increase in fat in the cooked meat. An analysis of the extracted fat indicated that the fat increase was representative of the injected fat [23].

The yield of cooked meat, fat, and skin from roasted or braised turkeys has been reported [8] to be about 55 percent of the ready-to-cook weight. The cooked lean meat without fat and skin was 46 percent of raw weight for turkeys and 41 percent for chickens.

Broiling

For broiling, young tender birds are cut into halves, quarters, or smaller pieces. Small young chickens and small fryer-roaster turkey pieces are appropriately broiled.

The pieces are placed on a slotted grid or rack on the broiler pan. Joints may be snapped so that pieces lie flat. With the broiler rack placed 5 to

6 inches from the flame or heating element, chicken pieces broiled for 20 to 25 minutes on each side should be cooked well done. Turkey pieces require 30 to 35 minutes on each side. Tongs should be used to turn the poultry pieces during broiling.

The flavor and color of broiled poultry may be enhanced by basting during broiling or by applying a coating or breading mixture before cooking. Coating greatly reduces cooking losses not only with broiling but also with other cooking methods [28].

Frying

Pieces of young chickens are frequently fried. In fact, fried chicken is a popular fast food. The pieces are first coated by being rolled in seasoned flour mixtures, batters, or egg and crumbs [7, 32]. Slow, careful cooking is necessary when pan-frying to prevent overbrowning before the birds are done. Usually, 40 to 60 minutes is required to cook the flesh thoroughly, part of this time with the frying pan covered.

When they are fried in deep fat, pieces of chicken may be steamed almost done before being dipped in flour, batter, or egg and crumbs and then browned in the heated fat. Deep-fat fried chicken may also be coated and fried from the raw state. It is cooked at 325° to 350°F (165° to 175°C) for 20 to 30 minutes, depending on the size of the chicken piece. Pressure deep-fat fryers have been developed especially for the frying of poultry in the food-processing and food-service industries.

The amounts of batter and breading used on food products have increased in recent years, and breading losses are a problem in the food industry. To improve adhesion of batters to poultry patties or nuggets, hydrocolloids such as xanthan or guar gums may be added to the batter. The increased apparent viscosity of the hydrocolloid-containing batters is positively correlated with batter adhesion [18].

Young chickens may be oven fried at about 400°F (204°C). The pieces are first coated and then placed in a baking pan containing a small amount of oil. The chicken is turned midway through the baking process.

Braising

The method of braising involves cooking poultry in steam in a covered container. The term *fricassee* is often applied to cut pieces of chicken that are braised. Usually, the pieces are browned by first frying them in a small amount of fat. Then, moisture is added and the poultry is simmered in a covered skillet until tender and well done. The pieces of poultry can also first be cooked until they are tender and then fried until brown. A sauce or gravy made from the pan liquor is often served over the poultry pieces. Braising tenderizes older, less tender poultry but is also an appropriate method for cooking young birds.

Stewing

For stewing, birds are usually cut into pieces, although whole birds may be cooked in water seasoned with spices and herbs and vegetables. The poultry should be simmered in a relatively large amount of water until tender.

Cooking Skinless Poultry

Poultry carries a layer of fat just under the skin. For those who are following a low-fat diet regimen, it is usually recommended that the skin not be eaten. Individual pieces of poultry such as chicken may have the skin removed either before or after cooking. In the cooking of skinless poultry, a method should be chosen that avoids drying of the skinless surface during the cooking process. For example, skinless pieces of chicken may be dipped in milk or oil and then rolled in fine bread or cereal crumbs, placed in an oiled baking pan, and baked. The crumbs form a crisp coating that acts as a skin. Skinless chicken breasts can also be used to prepare a dinner all in one pot, with potatoes and other vegetables cooked with the seasoned chicken in a covered casserole. Boneless chicken can be poached in chicken stock until tender, cooled, cut into cubes, and combined with celery, sliced mushrooms, garlic, ginger root, and soy sauce to make an Oriental chicken mixture that is served over rice.

Discoloration of Poultry Bones

The bones of frozen young birds are often very dark in color after the birds are cooked. Freezing and thawing break down the blood cells of bone marrow and cause a deep red color to appear [14, 34]. During cooking, the red color changes to brown, although this color change does not affect flavor. Cooking directly from the frozen state has been shown to result in less darkening than rapid or slow thawing [14].

CHAPTER SUMMARY

- The term poultry is used to describe all domesticated birds that are intended for human consumption, including chickens, turkeys, ducks, geese, guinea fowl, squab (young pigeons), and pigeons.
- Between 1975 and 1999, the consumption of poultry in the United States doubled. Turkey consumption has increased 180 percent since 1975, and is now popular year around.
- Many improvements in technology have occurred in poultry processing plants. Many of the processes such as feather removal and evisceration are automated. USDA inspectors monitor the process and test for *Salmonella* organisms.
- Irradiation can be used to reduce the population of pathogens such as *Salmonella, Campylobacter,* and *Listeria monocytogenes.* USDA and FDA have approved the use of irradiation on poultry. Packages must be labeled to inform the consumer that the product has been irradiated.
- The composition and nutritive value of poultry do not differ substantially from those of other meats, except that chicken and turkey breast, particularly, are lower in fat and cholesterol and higher in niacin than other lean meats with separable fat removed. The fat of poultry is deposited in the muscle tissue, in thick layers under the skin, and in the abdominal cavity.
- The market forms of poultry have changed over the years. The largest share of chicken is currently marketed as cut-up parts, some of them boneless and skinless.
- Poultry is classified on the basis of age and weight.

- Poultry has a relatively high proportion of waste from the raw carcass to the cooked bird. Skin, fat, and bone account for about 50 percent of the weight of cooked chicken. Cooking losses vary with the cooking temperature and method, and with the percentage of fat in the bird.

- The Wholesome Poultry Products Act, passed in 1968, requires that all poultry marketed in the United States be inspected for sanitary processing and freedom from disease. All poultry-processing plants are required to operate under an HACCP plan due to updates in the traditional inspection system in recent years. Wholesome birds are identified with the USDA inspection mark.

- In 1997, the terms *fresh* and *frozen* were defined as applied to poultry products. Poultry may not be labeled as fresh if it has been held below 26°F (−3°C). Effective in 2002, labels on raw poultry products must provide the percentage of absorbed or retained water in the product.

- The 1990 Nutrition Education and Labeling Act mandates nutrition labels on processed poultry products. Other requirements for a poultry label include the product name, the name and address of the producer or distributor, the inspection mark, the ingredients and net weight, the establishment number identifying the plant where the product was processed, and the handling instructions.

- In addition to inspecting for wholesomeness, the USDA has developed standards for quality grades. These grades—A, B, and C—are placed on the label in a shield-shaped mark. Several signs of quality are evaluated in determination of the grade.

- Most poultry sold in retail markets are young tender birds. In a young bird, the end of the breastbone is pliable and the wing offers little resistance when bent into an upright position. The skin of a young bird is pliable, soft, and tears easily.

- Chilled, raw poultry is highly perishable and may be contaminated with microorganisms. Thus, poultry should be stored under refrigeration and not allowed to drip into other food products so as to avoid cross-contamination. Cutting boards and other work surfaces should be cleaned and sanitized after contact with raw poultry.

- Poultry should be cooked to a minimum endpoint temperature of 165°F (74°C) to destroy foodborne pathogens. Higher endpoint temperatures are often recommended to ensure the product is at the minimum required safe temperature throughout.

- Cooked or fresh poultry products should be used within a few days or frozen. Only safe methods for thawing of frozen poultry should be used.

- Processed poultry products may be precooked and vacuum packed. These products must be held under refrigeration.

- The fundamental principles of cooking poultry do not differ from those of other meats. Dry-heat methods are appropriate for young, tender birds. Moist heat methods should be applied to older, less tender birds. Microwave cooking of poultry is not recommended since inconsistent destruction of microorganisms has been found with this cooking method.

- When roasting birds, a safe level of doneness throughout the bird must be obtained. When thawing a whole turkey, 24 hours per 5 pounds of bird is generally required. Stuffing a bird before roasting is generally not recommended. However, if a bird is stuffed, the center of the stuffing must reach a minimum of 165°F (74°C).

- Broiling, frying, braising, and stewing are additional ways in which poultry may be cooked.
- Poultry bones may be discolored and dark when very young birds have been frozen. This color does not affect flavor. Cooking directly from the frozen state may result in less darkening of the bones.

KEY TERMS

salmonella   psychrotrophic bacteria
capon   mesophilic bacteria

STUDY QUESTIONS

1. Poultry may be divided into several groups with respect to type, age, and sex.
   a. Describe each of the following classes of chickens and turkeys.

Chickens	Turkeys
Broiler-fryer	Fryer-roaster
Roaster	Young hen
Capon	Young tom
Rock Cornish hen	
Baking hen	
Stewing hen or fowl	

   b. Suggest satisfactory methods of cooking each type of poultry listed in question a. Why is each method appropriate?

2. a. What does the round USDA inspection mark mean when placed on poultry?
   b. List the USDA grades that may be used on poultry and describe the qualities that are considered in grading.

3. Explain why it is so important to handle poultry properly, both in the raw and in the cooked state.

4. Describe an appropriate method for roasting turkeys and explain why you would suggest this procedure.

5. Describe general procedures for broiling, frying, braising, and stewing poultry. Why is the microwave cooking of poultry not recommended?

6. Discuss the information and the terminology that is found on the labels of poultry products.

REFERENCES

1. Aleixo, J. A. G., Swaminathan, B., Jamesen, K. S., & Pratt, D. E. (1985). Destruction of pathogenic bacteria in turkeys roasted in microwave ovens. *Journal of Food Science, 50,* 873.

2. Bente, L. & Gerrior, S. A. (2002). Selected food and nutrient highlights of the 20th century: U.S. food supply series. *Family Economics and Nutrition Review, 14*(1), 43–51.

3. Bramblett, V. D., & Fugate, K. W. (1967). Choice of cooking temperature for stuffed turkeys. Part I, Palatability factors. *Journal of Home Economics, 59,* 180.

4. Buzby, J. C., & Crutchfield, S. R. (1997). USDA modernizes meat and poultry inspection. *Food Review, 20*(1), 14.

5. Chambers, L., Chambers IV, E., & Bowers, J. R. (1992). Consumer acceptability of cooked stored ground turkey patties with differing levels of phosphate. *Journal of Food Science, 57,* 1026.

6. Cornforth, D. P., Brennand, C. P., Brown, R. J., & Godfrey, D. (1982). Evaluation of various methods for roasting frozen turkeys. *Journal of Food Science, 47,* 1108.

7. Cunningham, F. E., & Tiede, L. M. (1981). Influence of batter viscosity on breading of chicken drumsticks. *Journal of Food Science, 46,* 1950.

8. Dawson, E. H., Gilpin, G. L., & Harkin, A. M. (1960). Yield of cooked meat from different types of poultry. *Journal of Home Economics, 52,* 445.

9. Deethardt, D., Burrill, L. M., Schneider, K., & Carlson, C. W. (1971). Foil-covered versus open-pan procedure for roasting turkey. *Journal of Food Science, 36,* 624.

10. Demetrakakes, P. (1997). Speeding pullets. *Food Processing, 58*(9), 67.

11. Durham, S. (2002). It takes a tough scientist to make a tender (and juicy) chicken. *Agricultural Research Magazine, 50*(2).

12. Gardner, F. A., Hopkins, W., & Denton, J. H. (1980). A comparison of consumer methods of storing chicken broilers at home. *Poultry Science, 59,* 743.

13. Goertz, G. E., & Stacy, S. (1960). Roasting half and whole turkey hens. *Journal of the American Dietetic Association, 37,* 458.

14. Hatch, V., & Stadelman, W. J. (1972). Bone darkening in frozen chicken broilers and ducklings. *Journal of Food Science, 37,* 850.

15. Hingley, A. (1999). *Campylobacter*: Low-profile bug is food poisoning leader. *FDA Consumer, 33*(5).

16. Hoke, I. M., & Kleve, M. K. (1966). Heat penetration, quality, and yield of turkeys roasted to different internal thigh temperatures. *Journal of Home Economics, 58,* 381.

17. Hoke, I. M., McGeary, B. K., & Kleve, M. K. (1967). Effect of internal and oven temperatures on eating quality of light and dark meat turkey roasts. *Food Technology, 21,* 773.

18. Hsia, H. Y., Smith, D. M., & Steffe, J. F. (1992). Rheological properties and adhesion characteristics of flour-based batters for chicken nuggets as affected by three hydrocolloids. *Journal of Food Science, 57,* 16.

19. Lamuka, P. O., Sunki, G. R., Chawan, C. B., Rao, D. R., & Shackelford, L. A. (1992). Bacteriological quality of freshly processed broiler chickens as affected by carcass pretreatment and gamma irradiation. *Journal of Food Science, 57,* 330.

20. Li, W., Bowers, J. A., Craig, J. A., & Perng, S. K. (1993). Sodium tripolyphosphate stability and effect in ground turkey meat. *Journal of Food Science, 58,* 501.

21. Lindsay, R. E., Krissinger, W. A., & Fields, B. F. (1986). Microwave vs. conventional oven cooking of chicken: Relationship of internal temperature to surface contamination by *Salmonella*. *Journal of the American Dietetic Association, 86,* 373.

22. Meiners, C., Crews, M. G., & Ritchey, S. J. (1982). Yield of chicken parts: Proximate composition and mineral content. *Journal of the American Dietetic Association, 81,* 435.

23. Moran, E. T., Jr. (1992). Injecting fats into breast meat of turkey carcasses differing in finish and retention after cooking. *Journal of Food Science, 57,* 1071.

24. Moran, E. T., Jr., & Larmond, E. (1981). Carcass finish and breast internal oil basting effects on oven and microwave prepared small toms: Cooking characteristics, yields, and compositional changes. *Poultry Science, 60,* 1229.

25. National Chicken Council. (n.d.). Chicken: Consumer's guide to buying, preparing, storing, serving, enjoying. Washington, DC: National Chicken Council.

26. National Restaurant Association Educational Foundation. (2002). *ServSafe coursebook* (2nd ed.). Chicago, IL: National Restaurant Association Educational Foundation.

27. National Turkey Federation. (2002). Consumer Statistics. Retrieved January 17, 2003, from http://www.eatturkey.com/consumer/stats/stats.html

28. Proctor, V. A., & Cunningham, F. E. (1983). Composition of broiler meat as influenced by cooking methods and coating. *Journal of Food Science, 48,* 1696.

29. Putnam, J. J. & Allshouse, J. E. (1999). Food consumption, prices, and expenditures, 1970–1997. Food and Rural Economics Division, Economic Research Service, U.S. Department of Agriculture. Statistical Bulletin No. 965.

30. Smith, D. M., & Alvarez, V. B. (1988). Stability of vacuum cook-in-bag turkey breast rolls during refrigerated storage. *Journal of Food Science, 53,* 46.

31. Stadelman, W. J. (1978). Tenderness, flavor, and nutritive value of chickens. *Food Technology, 32*(5), 80.

32. Suderman, D. R., & Cunningham, F. E. (1980). Factors affecting adhesion of coating to poultry skin, effect of age, method of chilling, and scald temperature on poultry skin ultrastructure. *Journal of Food Science, 45,* 444.

33. U.S. Food Safety Inspection Service. (1999, October). The poultry label says "fresh." Retrieved January 14, 2003, from http://fsis.usda.gov/OA/pubs/freshlabel.htm

34. U.S. Food Safety Inspection Service. (2000, September). Focus on: Chicken. Retrieved January 3, 2003, from www.fsis.usda.giv/OA/pubs/chicken.pdf

35. U.S. Food Safety Inspection Service. (2001, January). Meat and poultry labeling terms. Retrieved January 14, 2003, from http://fsis.usda.gov/OA/pubs/lablterm.htm

36. U.S. Food Safety Inspection Service. (2001, April). USDA rule on retained water in meat and poultry. Retrieved January 14, 2003, from http://fsis.usda.gov/oa/background/waterretention.html

37. Young, L. L., Garcia, J. M., Lillard, H. S., Lyon, C. E., & Papa, C. M. (1991). Fat content effects on yield, quality, and microbiological characteristics of chicken patties. *Journal of Food Science, 56,* 1527.

Seahood

Seafood

27

There are thousands of different species of fish worldwide, about 300 of these being within the United States or in the coastal waters surrounding it. Fish live in fresh water or in the seas and oceans. However, most people are familiar with only a few species of fish and shellfish; thus, numerous species are probably underutilized. Seafood comes to the United States from all over the world, sometimes traveling long distances before being processed, sold, or eaten [9]. About two-thirds of the seafood in the United States is imported [4]. Nevertheless, the United States fishing fleet is the fourth largest in the world and represents about 23,000 large vessels and more than 100,000 smaller craft [17].

In 2001, the most popular fish in the United States was shrimp at 3.4 pounds consumed per capita (Figure 27-1). Tuna was the second most popular fish, after having previously held the number one spot. The remaining top ten species consumed in the United States in decending order are: salmon, Alaska pollock, catfish, cod, clams, crabs, flatfish, and tilapia. Tilapia is a farm-raised fresh water fish that edged out scallops to be in the top ten [18].

COMPOSITION AND NUTRITIVE VALUE

The gross composition of seafood is similar to that of lean meat (see Appendix C). As are meats and poultry, seafoods are valuable sources of good-quality protein, with fish averaging 18 to 20 percent of this important nutrient. Because many fish are lower in fat and cholesterol than moderately fat beef, public health groups have suggested that the average American would do well from a health standpoint to substitute more fish for red meats in the diet. However, the annual per capita consumption of fish in the United States increased only by 3 pounds per person from 1975 to 1999 [1]. The 15 pound consumption figure from 1999 was actually less than the 1987 peak for annual per capita seafood consumption of 16.1 pounds [1, 27].

Another nutritional reason for eating fish on a regular basis is that the fat in most fish is highly unsaturated. Included among the unsaturated fats in fish oil are the omega-3 **polyunsaturated fatty acids (PUFA),** the most important of which is *eicosapentaenoic acid (EPA)* (see Chapter 9). The fat in many common fish contains 8 to 12 percent EPA and 30 to 45 percent total **omega-3 PUFA** [6] (see Table 27-1), which makes fish an important source of these nutrients, the intake of which is apparently related to a decreased risk of coronary heart

polyunsaturated fatty acids fatty acids with two or more double bonds between carbon atoms

omega-3 PUFA a group of polyunsaturated fatty acids that have the first double bond on the third carbon atom from the end of the carbon chain; also called *n-3* fatty acids

755

Figure 27-1
Shrimp can be prepared many ways. In this dish it is sautéed and served with lemon and orange sections over angel hair pasta. (Courtesy of © Sunkist Growers, Inc., All rights reserved)

disease. Menhaden oil, a rich source of omega-3 PUFAs, has been affirmed by the U.S. Food and Drug Administration (FDA) as generally recognized as safe (GRAS) [22]. It is available commercially for use in baked goods, salad dressings, as a cooking oil, or as a health supplement.

 All shellfish have some carbohydrate in the form of **glycogen.** Lobster has less than 1 percent, but abalone, clams, mussels, oysters, and scallops have from 3 to 5 percent. The sweet taste of various shellfish is due to the glucose formed by enzyme action from the glycogen. Shrimp are high in cholesterol as compared to beef, chicken, and other seafood products. However, shrimp are very low fat.

glycogen a complex carbohydrate—a polysaccharide—used for carbohydrate storage in the liver and muscles of the body; sometimes called *animal starch*

Table 27-1
ω-3 (n-3) Fatty Acids in Some Fish

Fish	Total Oil (wt %)	Total (*n*-3) Fatty Acids (wt % of total oil)
Sea bass	2.9	33.7
Butterfish	2.3	22.2
Atlantic cod	1.1	53.1
Pacific cod	0.9	45.9
Flounder	1.5	37.5
Haddock	1.1	44.3
Halibut	3.1	28.3
Herring	11.2	23.6
Pink salmon	4.2	39.9
Sardines	9.7	43.4
Red snapper	1.2	32.9
Rainbow trout	1.8	30.1
Tuna	7.5	37.6

Source: Reference 6.

Seafoods are important sources of minerals, with oysters being particularly rich in zinc, iron, and copper. Oysters, clams, and shrimp also contain a somewhat higher percentage of calcium than other fish and meats, which are notably low in calcium. Marine fish are a dependable source of iodine. Oysters, clams, and lobster are the highest in iodine of all seafood. Shrimp ranks next, with crab and other ocean fish last in order.

Fat fish contain more vitamin A than lean varieties. Canned salmon is a fair source of vitamin A and a good source of riboflavin and niacin. The presence in raw fish of the enzyme thiaminase, which destroys thiamin, may make the vitamin unavailable if fish is held in the raw state.

Fish protein concentrate or fish flour is produced from dehydrated and defatted whole fish. It appears to be an excellent, concentrated source of high-quality protein and may be used to supplement the breads and cereal products consumed by humans in some parts of the world. The FDA has approved the use of fish protein concentrate made from whole fish as a food additive under prescribed conditions. The making of acceptable crackers containing up to 12 percent fish protein concentrate has been reported [24]. Fish protein concentrate has also been used to enrich noodles.

CLASSIFICATION AND MARKET FORMS

Two major categories for the classification of fish are vertebrate fish with fins, and shellfish or invertebrates. Fish are covered with scales and may be further divided into two types: flat and round fish. Round fish swim vertically, whereas flat fish swim in a horizontal position. Fish with vertebrae are further classified on

Table 27-2

Some Species of Fish

Species	Weight Range (lb)	Usual Market Form	Suggested Preparation Method
Lean saltwater fish			
Bluefish	1–7	Whole and drawn	Broil, bake, fry
Cod	3–20	Steaks and fillets	Broil, bake, fry, steam
Flounder	¼–5	Whole, dressed, and fillets	Broil, bake, fry
Haddock	1½–7	Drawn and fillets	Broil, bake, steam
Hake	2–5	Whole, dressed, and fillets	Broil, bake, fry
Halibut	8–75	Steaks	Broil, bake, steam
Rosefish	½–1¼	Fillets	Bake
Snapper, red	2–15	Drawn, steaks and fillets	Bake, steam
Whiting	½–1½	Whole, dressed, and fillets	Bake, fry
Fat saltwater fish			
Butterfish	¼–1	Whole and dressed	Broil, bake, fry
Herring	¾–1	Whole	Bake, fry
Mackerel	¾–3	Whole, drawn, and fillets	Broil, bake
Salmon	3–30	Drawn, dressed, steaks, and fillets	Broil, bake, steam
Shad	1½–7	Whole and fillets	Bake
Lean freshwater fish			
Brook trout	¾–8	Whole	Broil, bake, fry
Yellow pike	1½–10	Whole, dressed, and fillets	Broil, bake, fry
Fat freshwater fish			
Catfish	1–10	Whole, dressed, and skinned	Bake, fry
Lake trout	1½–10	Drawn, dressed, and fillets	Bake, fry
Whitefish	2–6	Whole, dressed, and fillets	Broil, bake

the basis of their fat content as *lean* or *fat*, lean fish having less than 5 percent fat in their edible flesh. Examples of lean and fat fish are found in Table 27-2.

Shellfish are also of two types: mollusks and crustaceans. The mollusks have a soft structure and are either partially or wholly enclosed in a hard shell that is largely of mineral composition. Mollusks may be further subdivided into univalves (abalone), bivalves (clams, oysters, and mussels), and cephalopods (squid and octopus). Crustaceans are covered with a crustlike shell and have segmented bodies. Common examples are lobster, crab, shrimp, and crayfish.

The kinds of fish available for food vary widely in different localities. They include both saltwater and freshwater varieties, which differ considerably in flavor and quality. Saltwater fish usually have more distinctive flavors than freshwater fish, and oily fish have more flavor than the lean varieties. Many markets, even those located far from fishing waters, now sell live fish and shellfish.

Several varieties of fish, fresh or frozen, are marketed in various forms, Figure 27-2 showing some of these. Whole or round fish are marketed just as they come from the water. Drawn fish have had only the entrails removed, and dressed fish are scaled and eviscerated and usually have the head, tail, and fins removed. Steaks are cross-cut sections of the larger sizes of dressed fish. Fillets

---

Hot Topics

Future fish—Are they here now?

From bacteria to plants and, now, to animals—scientists have been moving the technology of genetic modification. Fish make attractive candidates for genetic engineering research. First, they produce eggs in large quantities, and these eggs are released and develop outside the body, where scientists can easily work with them. Also, commercial aquaculture—where fish are grown in farms—is a rapidly growing sector of food production on a global basis. Many developing countries, including China and Vietnam, are exporting aquacultured products. And aquaculture production has lowered market costs for salmon, tilapia, and catfish [4].

In the near future, will you be buying genetically modified salmon or trout for your Saturday night dinner? It is not clear just when or if this will happen. But AquaBounty Farms of Waltham, Massachusetts has already developed a salmon that is modified to grow twice as fast as its wild counterpart, by adding a growth hormone gene. Other fish are also being studied. And AquaBounty Farms has submitted a pre-market application to the FDA, the agency responsible for regulating genetically modified fish under federal policy developed in the mid-1980's [20].

This brings us to the subject of regulation—of genetically modified food products, that is. There are many pros and cons in this area. Some of these have been presented for discussion and debate by the Pew Initiative on Food and Biotechnology, a group funded by the Pew Charitable Trust that attempts to be an independent and objective source of credible information on agricultural biotechnology for both the public and the policymakers.

This group suggests that the application of genetic engineering to animals—including fish—could provide numerous benefits to mankind. But, they say, it is unclear if regulators presently have the tools they need to adequately evaluate these new products. A new and clearly articulated road map may be needed to adequately assess the risk and benefits while keeping the public well informed. Innovation may be getting somewhat ahead of the ability to manage it [21]. What will the future bring? Stay tuned!

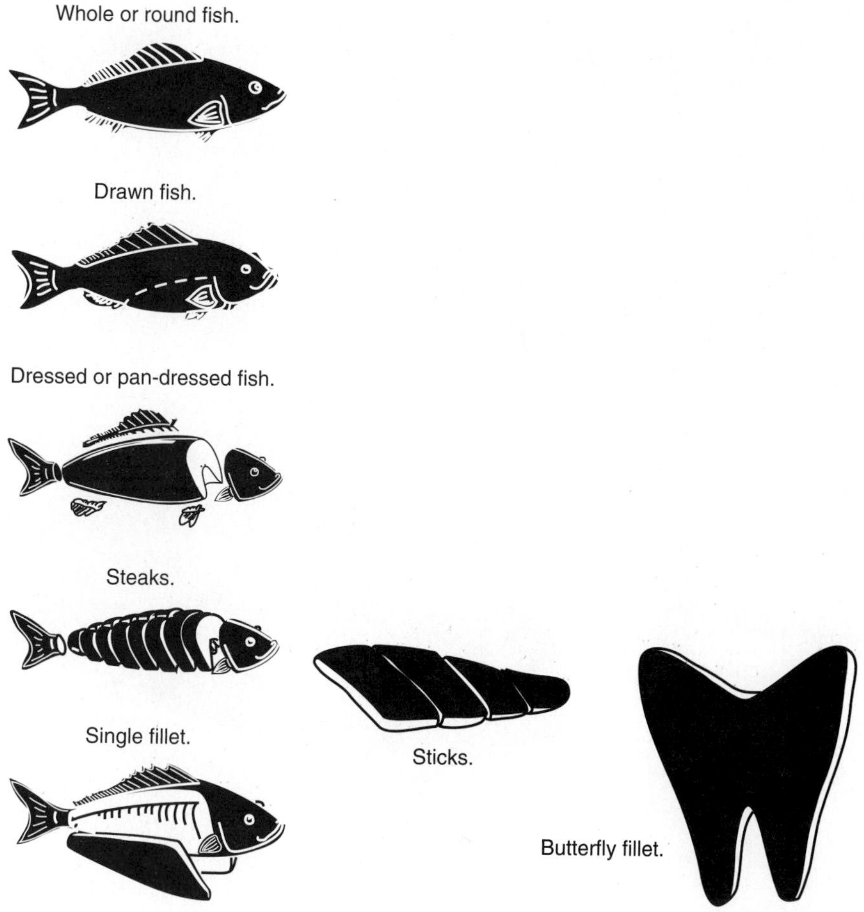

Figure 27-2
Market forms of fish. (Courtesy of the Bureau of Commercial Fisheries, U.S. Department of the Interior)

Whole or round fish.

Drawn fish.

Dressed or pan-dressed fish.

Steaks.

Single fillet.

Sticks.

Butterfly fillet.

are sides of the fish cut lengthwise away from the backbone. A butterfly fillet is the two sides of a fillet. Sticks are uniform pieces of fish cut lengthwise or crosswise from fillets or steaks; however, some breaded, frozen fish sticks may be made from minced fish. Figure 27-3 shows several forms of fish. Shellfish is marketed in the shell, shucked (removed from the shell), headless (shrimp and some lobster), or already cooked.

Many convenience items containing fish are available. In addition to frozen, breaded, precooked fish fillets and sticks are a variety of frozen items including creamed fish, fish Florentine, fish soups, fish pies, and fish dinners.

SHELLFISH

The shellfish most commonly marketed in the United States are clams, crab, lobster, oysters, scallops, and shrimp. Clams, oysters, shrimp, and spiny lobster are shown in Color Plate XXX.

Shrimp include the common or white shrimp, which is greenish gray when caught; the brown or Brazilian shrimp, which is brownish red when raw; the pink or coral shrimp; and the Alaska and California varieties, which vary in color and are relatively small. Despite the differences in color in the raw state, cooked shrimp differ little in appearance and flavor. Raw shrimp in the shell are

A drawn fish, with entrails removed.

Filleting a fish.

A whole Red Grouper and fillets.

Steaks cut from tuna loin.

Catfish with fillet, steak, and sticks.

Broiled Florida fish fillets accompanied by fresh seasoned vegetables.

Figure 27-3
Fish may be prepared in various forms. (Courtesy of Florida Department of Agriculture and Consumer Services, Bureau of Seafood and Aquaculture)

often called *green shrimp*. Shrimp are usually sold with the head and thorax removed.

Shrimp are designated, according to the number required to weigh a pound, as Jumbo, Large, Large Medium, Medium, and Small. The largest size has 15 or fewer shrimp to the pound; the smallest size has 60 or more to the pound. Breaded shrimp, which have been peeled, cleaned, and breaded for frying, are available (Figure 27-4). Prawns are shrimplike crustaceans that are usually relatively large in size.

Oysters can be purchased live in the shell, fresh or frozen shucked (removed from the shell), or canned. Live oysters have a tightly closed shell. Gaping shells indicate that they are dead and therefore no longer usable. Shucked oysters should be plump and have a natural creamy color, with clear liquor. Eastern shucked oysters are usually packed in the following commercial sizes: Counts or Extra Large, Extra Selects or Large, Selects or Medium, Standards or Small, and Standards or Very Small. For the Pacific area the designations vary somewhat: size 1 is extra large; size 2, large; size 3, medium; and size 4, small.

The true lobster, or Northern lobster, is found near the shores of Europe and North America in the cold waters of the North Atlantic Ocean. The spiny or rock lobster is nearly worldwide in its distribution. The spiny lobster may be distinguished by the absence of large, heavy claws and the presence of many prominent spines on its body and legs. Figure 27-5 shows both of these lobsters.

Lobsters are a dark bluish green when taken from the water, but change to a "lobster red" during cooking. Lobsters and crabs must be alive at the time of cooking to ensure freshness. The tail should curl under the body when the live lobster is picked up. Whole lobsters and crabs cooked in the shell are available. They should be bright red in color and have a fresh odor. Frozen lobster tails can be purchased in some markets. The cooked meat, picked from the shells of lobsters and crabs, is marketed fresh, frozen, and canned.

Blue crabs, constituting about three-fourths of all crabs marketed in the United States, come from the Atlantic and Gulf coasts. Dungeness crabs are found on the Pacific Coast from Alaska to Mexico. Both types of crabs are

Figure 27-4
Breaded shrimp ready for frying.
(Courtesy of the Florida Department of Agriculture and Consumer Services. Bureau of Seafood and Aquaculture)

Figure 27-5
Two types of lobster. (Courtesy of the Bureau of Commercial Fisheries, U.S. Department of the Interior)

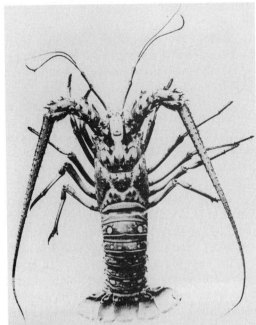

Northern lobster.

Spiny or rock lobster.

shown in Figure 27-6. Fresh-cooked meat from blue crabs may be packed in several grades: lump meat, or solid lumps of white meat from the body of the crab; flake meat, or small pieces of white meat from the rest of the body; lump and flake meat combined; and claw meat, which has a brownish tinge. Fresh-cooked meat from both the body and claws of Dungeness crabs has a pinkish tinge and is packed as one grade.

Blue crab.

Dungeness crab.

Figure 27-6
The two most common types of crabs available in the United States. (Courtesy of the Bureau of Commercial Fisheries, U.S. Department of the Interior)

Scallops are mollusks similar to oysters and clams except that they swim freely through the water by snapping their shells together. The oversize adductor muscle that closes the shell is the only part of the scallop eaten by Americans. Europeans eat the entire scallop.

Several species of clams are used for food. They are marketed live in the shell, fresh or frozen shucked, or canned. Tightly closed shells indicate that they are alive and therefore usable. Shucked clams should be plump, with clear liquor, and free from shell particles (see Color Plate XXX).

Fish Roe

Roe is the mass of eggs from finfish and consists of sacs of connective tissue enclosing thousands of small eggs. It is important that the sacs remain intact, because the eggs cannot otherwise be held together. Although roe is of minor importance in the marketing of fish, available only during spawning season and very perishable, fresh fish roe is well liked by some people. The most highly prized for flavor is shad roe, although in the Great Lakes area, whitefish roe is also popular. Roe from most fish that are commonly consumed can be eaten.

A method of cooking that intensifies flavor is preferable for fish roe. It is usually parboiled for 2 to 5 minutes, after which it is dipped in cornmeal or in egg and crumbs and fried. Parboiling aids in thorough cooking of the roe without its hardening by being fried too long.

Caviar is sturgeon roe preserved in brine. It is expensive and is used mainly for making appetizers.

FISH PRODUCTS

Many value-added fish products are available from which consumers and food service establishments can choose. The largest seafood plant in the United States is located in Alaska. This plant is capable of processing 125 million pounds of seafood per year [16]. Salmon, halibut, and cod portions are prepared with a variety of glazes and coatings. In addition, salmon burgers and breaded products are processed and packaged for sale. Fish may be marinated by injection into the fillets or by vacuum tumbling to add distinctive flavors such as garlic or honey-sesame ginger.

Minced Fish Products

Included in the technological advances made in the U.S. seafood industry is the production of deboned, minced raw fish from lesser-known species and fillet trimmings. Minced fish has given rise to new families of food products. For example, frozen minced fish blocks are cut into fish sticks and portions. These products can be found on the market in a variety of forms, including crunchy breaded pieces, seafood nuggets, and fish loaf with creamy sauce [14, 23].

A raw material called *surimi* (from the Japanese) offers opportunities for the production of several food items. To prepare surimi, minced fish is first washed to remove fat, blood, pigments, and other undesirable substances, leaving only the myofibrillar proteins of the fish flesh. This material is then frozen with the addition of **cryoprotectants,** such as sucrose and sorbitol or possibly maltodextrins and polydextrose, because the myofibrillar proteins of fish are labile to denaturation on freezing [13].

Further processing and fiberizing produce an elastic and chewy texture in the product that can be made to resemble that of shellfish [10]. Surimi-based

cryoprotectants substances that offer protection to such sensitive molecules as proteins during freezing and frozen storage

Figure 27-7
Surimi is made by a special process from mechanically deboned fish flesh. It is used for a variety of fabricated seafood products and can be a tasty addition to an entrée salad.
(Courtesy of Florida Department of Agriculture and Consumer Services, Bureau of Seafood and Aquaculture)

fiberized simulated crab legs are shown in Figure 27-7. Japanese techniques in the production of surimi have been Americanized, and several plants are producing surimi and its analogue products in the United States. Novel snack foods are also produced from surimi [8].

Cured Fish

Although fish may be cured for preservation purposes, the cure often imparts a distinctive flavor of its own that is appreciated for variety. Some hardening and toughening of the outer surface occur when fish is salted, dried, or smoked. Common examples of cured fish are salt cod, mackerel (see Color Plate XXXI), finnan haddie, and kippered herring. Finnan haddie is haddock that has been cured in brine to which carotene pigment has been added and later smoked. It is preferred lightly cured but does not keep long with a light cure. If finnan haddie is to be kept for some time or shipped long distances, the cure must be stronger. Kippered herring is also lightly brined and smoked. It is often canned to preserve its typical flavor rather than being cured in a heavier brine.

Canned Fish

The principal kinds of canned fish are salmon, tuna, sardines, shrimp, crab, lobster, and clams.

Salmon packing is one of the big industries of the Pacific Northwest. Five principal varieties of salmon are packed, depending on the locality. The five varieties in order of consumer preference are (1) red salmon or sockeye; (2) chinook; (3) coho, medium red or silverside; (4) pink; and (5) chum. The fish with red flesh and high oil content are preferred by consumers, although they are the most expensive. The red-fleshed varieties are somewhat higher in vitamin A content.

In the United States, only six species of tuna may be labeled "tuna" when canned: yellowfin, skipjack, albacore, bluefin, Oriental tuna, and little tuna. The related species of bonito and Pacific yellowtail cannot legally be marketed as tuna. Albacore may be labeled "white meat"; the other species are labeled "light meat" tuna. Three different styles of packing for canned tuna are fancy or solid pack, chunk style, and flake or grated style. Each style can be packed in either oil or water. The normal color of precooked or canned tuna is pinkish. Some fish do not develop the pink color, but take on a tan or tannish-green color and then are rejected. These fish are referred to in the industry as *green* tuna.

Tuna is now being sold in flexible retort packaging as an alternative method of providing the consumer with "canned" tuna. The flexible pouches are not packed in oil or water and thus the product is ready to use without draining (see Chapter 2 and Figure 2-9a).

AQUACULTURE

Aquaculture, or fish farming, is not new. It was apparently practiced in China as early as 2000 B.C. Fish farming can be done on land that is unsuitable for other food-producing purposes, such as swamplands or poorly drained lands. Fish convert feed into body tissue more efficiently than farm animals; they have a lower dietary energy requirement. Also, the percentage of edible, lean tissue in fish is higher than that in beef, pork, and poultry because fish contain less bone, adipose tissue, and connective tissue [7].

Extremely rapid growth has occurred in this industry since the mid 1980's. Aquaculture production has increased to 40 million metric tons in 1998 from only 10 million metric tons in 1984 [4]. Aquaculture is now a viable and profitable enterprise worldwide. Developing countries, especially, are increasing their production of aquaculture products [4]. Aquaculture will no doubt continue to grow because of increasing demand for seafood, diminishing supplies, and increasing costs of sea-caught fish and shellfish [7].

SELECTION, HANDLING, AND STORAGE

Freshness

Fresh finfish have firm flesh, a stiff body, and tight scales. The gills are red, and the eyes are bright and unsunken. Pressure on the body does not leave an indentation in the flesh (see Color Plate XXX) except in the case of fish that has been frozen and thawed. The exterior of fresh fish has little or no slime. Fresh seafood should not smell "fishy," but rather like a "fresh ocean breeze." Stale fish, on the other hand, are flabby, and the eyes are dull and sunken. The scales are easily brushed off, the gills are no longer bright red, and the odor is stale or sour.

Frozen fish should be solidly frozen when purchased, with no discoloration or brownish tinge in the flesh. It should have little or no odor and should be wrapped in a moisture/vapor-proof material.

Mollusks in the shell should always be alive when they are purchased. The shells of live mollusks will be tightly closed or will close when tapped lightly or iced. Any mollusks that do not close tightly should be thrown away. Seafood should be bought only from reputable dealers.

Inspection and Grading

The U.S. Food and Drug Administration (FDA) maintains an Office of Seafood as part of its regulatory responsibilities. Since December 1997, seafood processors, repackers, and warehouses—both domestic and foreign exporters to this country—have been required to follow a Hazard Analysis and Critical Control Points (HACCP) system (see Chapter 3). The HACCP system focuses on identifying and preventing hazards that could cause foodborne illness rather than relying on random sampling of finished seafood products and occasional plant inspections. Seafood retailers are encouraged to institute an HACCP system, although they are not required to do so. In 2001, the FDA announced additional measures to intensify the focus on seafood processors whose products could present the greatest risk to consumers. Noncompliant firms will be inspected more frequently and laboratory testing will be more extensive with enforcement action when necessary [25].

The FDA also sets standards for seafood contaminants such as pesticide residues and mercury; administers the National Shellfish Sanitation Program with shellfish-producing states and other countries; and analyzes fish and fishery products for toxins, chemicals, and other hazards in agency laboratories [9]. In addition, the National Oceanic Atmospheric Administration (NOAA) in the U.S. Department of Commerce operates a voluntary seafood inspection and grading program. A fee for the voluntary service is paid by the processor. Fish products meeting the official standards may carry U.S. inspection and grade labels.

Quality grades are determined largely on the basis of appearance, uniformity, absence of defects, character (mainly texture), and flavor and odor of the product. Grades for breaded items also consider the amount of edible fish as compared with the amount of breading and the presence of bone in fish sticks. For most items, specific grades are U.S. Grade A, U.S. Grade B, and Substandard.

Seafood Safety

When properly handled and thoroughly cooked, fish is safe to eat. Seafood, however, is the most perishable of flesh foods and does present potential hazards if not produced and handled properly. The Centers for Disease Control and Prevention (CDC) reported, in 1995, thirty-four incidences of food poisoning in people who had eaten oysters harvested from certain southern U.S. waters. The flulike illness that resulted from eating the oysters was blamed on a virus similar to the Norwalk virus. This virus is usually introduced into fishing areas by human sewage. Data reporting foodborne illness associated with fish and shellfish undoubtedly underestimate the number of actual cases of seafood-related illness, as many incidences go unreported.

In many of the cases reported to the CDC the cause was "unknown" or "unconfirmed," although the evidence indicated that a majority of these unconfirmed cases, mostly those from shellfish, were probably due to viruses, particularly the Norwalk virus. The problem with viruses is usually linked to human populations and waste disposal [12]. Mollusks generally live where rivers and seas meet, in protected bays and inlets. Many cities are located near these areas and the waters are more likely to be polluted than off-shore waters.

Another major cause of illness from eating seafood is from bacteria of the *Vibrio* species. These bacteria naturally occur in marine environments and may be a major component of the intestinal flora in marine fish. From 1988 to 1995, the CDC received reports of over 300 *Vibrio vulnificus* infections from the Gulf Coast states, and about 30–40 *Vibrio parahaemolyticus* infections are reported each year. Both of these infections are from eating shellfish. *Vibrios* are easily destroyed by even modest levels of heat. In fact, disease from both viruses and bacteria in seafood may be prevented by thorough cooking. *Shellfish, especially mollusks, should not be eaten raw.* Finfish dishes, such as sushi, can be safe for most people to eat if they are made with very fresh fish, commercially frozen at very low temperatures, and then thawed before eating. These steps kill any parasites that may be present. Parasites, which may be another cause of illness, are also killed by thorough cooking. People with diabetes, liver disease, or immune disorders should not eat even raw finfish, because freezing does not kill bacteria.

So-called natural toxins, probably derived through the food chain as certain tropical fish and shellfish feed on toxigenic materials, can cause illness. Ciguatera fish poisoning is caused by fish, usually from tropical or subtropical waters, that have eaten toxic substances in the food chain. Certain algae blooms, called red tides, can produce toxins in shellfish that consume them. Waters are monitored for these blooms, and when they appear, the waters are closed to fishing. Scombroid poisoning occurs when the scombroid species of fish are temperature-abused, thereby resulting in the production of the toxin histamine by bacteria associated with these fish.

Chemicals such as mercury may also be present in some fish in hazardous amounts [5]. The FDA released a consumer advisory for pregnant women in 2001 about the risks of mercury in fish [26]. In this advisory, the avoidance of shark, swordfish, king mackerel, and tilefish by pregnant women is suggested to reduce mercury exposure. Furthermore, a general recommendation of eating only an average of 12 ounces of fish per week was provided. Additional research into mercury contamination of fish, the potential protective role of selenium, and environmental clean-up is needed [19].

Storage

Fresh fish are extremely perishable and spoil rapidly. After fish are caught, they are stored in flaked ice (cubed ice may bruise the fish), or in a frozen salt solution to achieve a somewhat lower temperature, until the fish are ready for sale [11].

As bacteria decompose fish tissue, a volatile substance called trimethylamine is released. Measurement of trimethylamine, for which relatively simple, rapid methods exist, gives an indication of the microbiologic quality of fish [28]. Off-flavors in seafood can also occur as a result of environmental conditions. Sensory evaluation by trained panelists may be used to detect the presence and intensity of these off-flavors [2].

In addition to the delicate structure of fish, which makes bacterial invasion easy, it has been shown that rapid spoilage is partly the result of the high degree of activity of the enzymes present in fish. The low temperatures of the natural environment of some fish may account for the unusual activity of the body enzymes.

Fresh fish should be kept at a temperature near 32°F (0°C) if possible. In any case, it must be placed in the coldest part of the refrigerator until it is cooked and should be stored in the same wrapper it had in the market. Live mollusks should be refrigerated in containers covered loosely with a clean, damp cloth. Live shellfish should not be stored in airtight containers or in water. Fresh fish must be used no later than 2 days after purchase. For long-term storage, fish must be frozen. Rapid freezing is desirable to prevent the formation of large ice crystals that can damage cells and contribute to large drip loss on thawing. Equipment for very rapid freezing is available commercially [15].

Researchers are developing methods of packaging fish for sale in supermarkets to enhance safety and shelf life. Packaging structures may incorporate antimicrobial compounds or package surfaces may provide spoilage indicators that measure substances such as ammonia, trimethylamine, and dimethylamine [3]. Modified atmosphere packaging retains seafood quality, although the avoidance of time-temperature abuse is critical. Labels that change colors when a product has been subjected to time and temperature abuse are being tested [3].

WASTE

The refuse of fish is rather high, commonly around 50 percent by weight. In general, the smaller the fish, the higher the percentage of refuse. The waste is composed chiefly of scales, head, and bones, although in some cases the skin, being tough, is also waste. In shellfish, the shell constitutes the chief waste and in some instances runs as high as 60 to 80 percent of the total weight. For example, a lobster weighing 1 1/4 pounds will yield only about 1/4 pound of edible flesh. The percentage of waste in large lobsters is somewhat less but is still quite high. In addition to the shell, clams have a tough portion that must be discarded. The scallop, as it is eaten in the United States, is only the muscle that operates the opening and closing of the shell.

PREPARATION

Cooking Finfish

Frozen seafood should be thawed in the refrigerator in its own container. Allow about a day for defrosting. Individual steaks or fillets may be cooked either thawed or frozen. If they have been thawed, they may be cooked as fresh fish.

To lend variety to menus, fish may be cooked by either dry- or moist-heat methods. Fish have very little connective tissue, and it is of a kind that is easily hydrolyzed. The structure of fish is delicate and tender, even in the raw state; therefore, the use of moist heat for tenderization purposes is not necessary. In fact, a big problem in fish cookery is retention of the form of the fish, which is done by careful handling. If fish is cooked in water, it is usually necessary to tie the piece of fish in cheesecloth or wrap it in parchment paper to prevent it from falling apart during cooking. Because extractives are low in fish, a method that develops flavor, such as frying, broiling, and baking, is often preferred.

Although overcooking is to be avoided, fish must be cooked until thoroughly done. Fish is unpalatable to many people when it is rare and may also be unsafe; for example, fish from some localities may be a source of tapeworm. Fish is fully cooked when the flakes separate easily. It should be tested with a fork in a thick portion, as the outer, thin edges cook more readily than the thicker muscles. A minimum safe temperature of 145°F (63°C) is recommended. About 10 minutes of cooking time per 1 inch of thickness is generally suggested for fish fillets.

If two or more fish fillets have been frozen in a package, it is necessary to partially defrost them to separate them for cooking. For partially or wholly frozen fish, the cooking temperature must be lower and the time of cooking longer than for defrosted fish to permit thawing as the fish cooks. Otherwise, ice may remain in the center of the cut even when the outside is thoroughly cooked.

Broiling

Fish to be broiled may be in the form of fillets, steaks, or boned or unboned whole fish (head removed). Unboned whole fish is cut through the ribs along the backbone, allowing it to lie flat. If the skin has been left intact, the fish is placed skin-side down on the broiler rack. It may later be turned, but turning large pieces of fish is difficult and tends to break the fish apart. Using a rela-

(a)   (b)   (c)

Figure 27-8
1. Brushing the fillets with butter
2. Topping snapper with the tomato concassée
3. The fish after baking.

tively low broiling temperature to prevent overbrowning and basting the top surface with fat to keep it moist usually make it possible for fish to be broiled until done without turning (Figure 27-8).

Baking

Fish fillets may be used for baking, but often whole fish, stuffed and sewed or skewered to prevent loss of stuffing, is baked. The fish are usually placed in a shallow, open pan and basted to keep the skin from becoming hard and dry. A moderately heated oven produces the most satisfactory results, especially if the fish are stuffed. Stuffed pompano fillets are shown in Color Plate XXXI.

Frying

Small whole fish, fillets, or steaks may be fried (Figure 27-9). Pieces of a suitable size for serving are usually dipped in water, milk, or egg mixed with milk, then in a dry ingredient, such as cornmeal, flour, or fine crumbs. If the fish is to

Figure 27-9
These Florida Mullet fillets were breaded in cornmeal and fried in oil until golden brown. Mashed potatoes, fresh sliced tomatoes, and okra are tasty accompaniments. (Courtesy of Florida Department of Agriculture and Consumer Services, Bureau of Seafood and Aquaculture)

be deep-fat fried, the temperature of the fat should not exceed 385° to 395°F (196° to 202°C) so that the fish will be fully cooked by the time it is browned.

Steaming and Simmering

Fish may be cooked by steaming or simmering. These are closely related methods of cookery, varying in the amount of the cooking liquid used. Fish to be steamed may be placed on a rack over a boiling liquid with a tight cover on the pan, and cooked until done. Steaming may also be done in the oven in a covered pan, or the fish may be wrapped tightly in aluminum foil. The foil retains moisture, and the fish cooks in an atmosphere of steam. Finnan haddie, which is a cured fish, retains its characteristic flavor particularly well when it is steamed and served with melted butter.

Fish that are simmered are covered with a liquid and cooked just below the boiling point. The fish hold their form better if tied in cheesecloth, wrapped in parchment paper, or placed in a wire basket in the water. Large, firm-fleshed fish are better cooked by this method, as the flesh does not fall apart as readily as less firm or fatty fish. Adding 3 tablespoons of vinegar, lemon juice, or white wine and 1 1/2 tablespoons of salt per quart of water seasons fish well. Fish cooked in moist heat are usually served with a sauce.

Microwave Cooking

Fish can be prepared in a variety of ways using the microwave oven, including soups and chowders, appetizers, and main dishes. Generally, fillets or steaks are arranged in a baking dish, with the thickest portions toward the outside of the dish. They may be brushed with melted butter or lemon juice, covered with waxed paper, and microwaved on medium-high or high. The dish should be rotated halfway during the cooking period unless a turntable is available.

Cooking Shellfish

Shellfish, the flesh of which appears to differ in structure from that of finfish, are much firmer and are easily toughened by high temperatures. Whether the differences are due to the amount and kind of connective tissue is not certain. Nevertheless, in cooking most shellfish, high temperatures and long cooking should be avoided. Moist-heat methods are generally satisfactory, but if the shellfish are cooked in a liquid medium, as in the making of oyster stew, a simmering temperature of 181° to 185°F (82° to 85°C) should be used.

Live lobsters are parboiled in salted water (2 teaspoons salt per quart of water). The water should be boiling when the lobster is added, but kept at a simmering temperature once it has been added. Simmering for about 12 minutes is recommended depending on the size of the lobster. Overcooking toughens the flesh. After parboiling, the flesh is removed from the shell and prepared in any desired manner. The pink coral on the outside adds attractiveness to the lobster meat and should not be discarded. The edible meat is in the claws, which must be cracked to remove the meat, and in the tail. The whole tail may be separated from the body and the segmented shell removed.

Simmering is the basic method of cooking raw shrimp. Depending on the size, the time of cooking is 3 to 5 minutes or until the shrimp begin to curl and turn pink. Shrimp can be simmered, the shell removed, and then the sand vein along the back taken out. The sand vein is the intestinal tract located just under the outer curved surface. Alternatively, the shrimp can first be peeled and then simmered. Either way, 1 1/2 pounds of raw shrimp yield about 3/4 pound of cooked ready-to-eat shrimp. The sand vein often remains in canned shrimp and must be removed before this product is used. Large shrimp are often deep-fat fried. Color Plate XXXI shows sweet-and-sour shrimp served over rice.

CHAPTER SUMMARY

- There are thousands of different species of fish worldwide. Shrimp, tuna, and salmon are among the most popular fish in the United States.

- The gross composition of seafood is similar to that of lean meat. Many fish are lower in fat and cholesterol as compared to other meats. The fat in fish is highly unsaturated. Included among the unsaturated fats in fish are the omega-3 polyunsaturated fatty acids that have been associated with health benefits.

- Two major categories of fish are vertebrate fish with fins and shellfish. Fish may be further classified as flat or round fish, lean or fat. Shellfish are sub-divided into mollusks and crustaceans. Mollusks may be univalves, bivalves, or cephalopods.

- Fish may be marketed as whole fish, drawn, dressed, steaks, or fillets. Fish may be fresh or frozen. Shellfish is generally marketed in the shell, shucked, headless, or precooked.

- Several varieties of shrimp may be purchased. Green shrimp are raw shrimp in the shell. Shrimp are sold by the count per pound.

- Oysters, clams, and mussels shells must be closed or snap shut if alive and suitable for use. Bivalves that have died will have gaping shells and they should be discarded.

- Lobsters are of two types: the true lobster or Northern lobster, and the spiny or rock lobster. The spiny lobster is distinguished by the absence of large, heavy claws.

- Blue crabs come from the Atlantic and Gulf coasts. Dungeness crabs are found on the Pacific Coast.

- Roe is the mass of eggs from finfish and consists of sacs of connective tissue enclosing thousands of eggs. Caviar is sturgeon roe preserved in brine.

- Many value-added fish products are available for purchase. Minced fish products are used in the production of fish sticks and portions. Surimi is a minced fish product that is processed to produce simulated crab legs.

- Fish may be cured. Salted, dried, and smoked fish will have some hardening and toughening of the outer surface.

- The principal kinds of canned fish are salmon, tuna, sardines, shrimp, crab, lobster, and clams. There are five varieties of salmon and six species of tuna that are commonly canned.

- Aquaculture, or fish farming, is not new. However, rapid growth in this in-dustry has occurred since the mid 1980's. Developing countries, especially, are increasing their production of aquaculture products.

- Fresh finfish have firm flesh, a stiff body, and tight scales. The gills are red, and the eyes are bright and unsunken. Fresh seafood does not smell fishy, but rather like a fresh ocean breeze. Frozen fish should be solidly frozen, with no discoloration or brownish tinge in the flesh. Mollusks in the shell should always be alive when purchased.

- The FDA maintains an Office of Seafood as part of its regulatory responsibility. Seafood processors, packers, and warehouses are required to follow an HACCP system and are inspected by the FDA. The FDA also sets standards for seafood contaminates, administers the National Shellfish Sanitation Program, and analyzes fish and fishery products for hazards.

- The National Oceanic Atmospheric Administration in the U.S. Department of Commerce operates a voluntary system of seafood inspection and grading that is paid for by the processor. Quality grades are determined largely on the basis of appearance, uniformity, absence of defects, character, flavor, and odor of the product.

- Seafood is the most perishable of flesh foods and needs to be produced and handled properly. Bacteria, viruses, natural toxins, and chemical toxins can result in foodborne illnesses associated with the consumption of seafood. FDA released a consumer advisory about the risks of mercury in fish.

- Fresh fish are very perishable. After fish are caught they are stored in flaked ice until ready for sale. Rapid spoilage of fish is in part the result of the high degree of activity of the enzymes present in fish. If fish are not to be used within 2 days of purchase, they should be frozen. Rapid freezing is desirable to prevent the formation of large ice crystals.

- The refuse of fish is high, commonly around 50 percent by weight. The waste is composed chiefly of scales, head, and bones. In shellfish, the shell is the chief waste and can run as high as 60–80 percent of the total weight.

- Frozen seafood should be thawed in the refrigerator or if individual steaks or fillets, cooked from the frozen state.

- Fish may be cooked by dry or moist heat methods since it has very little connective tissue. Overcooking should be avoided. Fish is fully cooked when the flakes separate easily. A minimum safe temperature of 145°F (63°C) is recommended.

- Fish may be broiled, baked, fried, steamed, simmered, poached, or cooked in the microwave. Sauces or flavored liquids used during cooking can enhance the flavor.

- Shellfish are much firmer and are easily toughened by high temperatures. Therefore, shrimp, lobster, and clams are often simmered. The water should be boiling when lobster is added, but retained at simmering for cooking.

KEY TERMS

polyunsaturated fatty acids   glycogen
omega-3 PUFA   cryoprotectants

STUDY QUESTIONS

1. How do fish and shellfish differ? Suggest subclassifications for both fish and shellfish and give several examples from each group.

2. a. Describe five market forms in which fish may be sold.
   b. In what forms may minced fish appear on the retail market?
   c. What is surimi and how is it used in the seafood industry?

3. Why has there been an emphasis in recent years on increasing the consumption of fish in the American diet?

4. **a.** Describe characteristics of fresh fish.
   b. Suggest appropriate procedures for handling and storing fish and explain why these procedures are necessary.
   c. Explain why shellfish should never be eaten raw.
   d. What are some possible causes of illness when seafood is not properly handled or prepared?

5. Describe or identify the following:
   a. Green shrimp
   b. Northern lobster
   c. Spiny or rock lobster
   d. Scallops
   e. Fish roe
   f. Finnan haddie
   g. Tuna

6. List five principal varieties of salmon.

7. Explain why it is appropriate to cook fish with either dry- or moist-heat methods.

8. Describe satisfactory procedures for cooking fish by each of the following methods:
   a. Broiling
   b. Baking
   c. Frying
   d. Steaming
   e. Microwaves

9. What chief precaution should be taken when cooking shellfish and why?

REFERENCES

1. Bente, L. & Gerrior, S. A. (2002). Selected food and nutrient highlights of the 20th century: U.S. food supply series. *Family Economics and Nutrition Review, 14*(1), 43–51.

2. Bett, K. L., & Dionigi, C. P. (1997). Detecting seafood off-flavors: Limitations of sensory evaluation. *Food Technology 51*(8), 70.

3. Brody, A. L. (2001). Is something fishy about packaging? *Food Technology, 55*(4), 97–98.

4. Flick, G. J. (2002). U.S. aquaculture is fighting an upstream battle. *Food Technology, 56*(9), 124.

5. Foulke, J. (1994). Mercury in fish. *FDA Consumer, 28*(7), 5.

6. Hearn, T. L., Sgoutas, S. A., Hearn, J. A., & Sgoutas, D. S. (1987). Polyunsaturated fatty acids and fat in fish flesh for selecting species for health benefits. *Journal of Food Science, 52*, 1209.

7. Institute of Food Technologists' Expert Panel on Food Safety and Nutrition. (1991). Foods from aquaculture. *Food Technology, 45*(9), 87.

8. Karmas, E., & Lauber, E. (1987). Novel products from underutilized fish using combined processing technology. *Journal of Food Science, 52*, 7.

9. Kurtzweil, P. (1997). Critical steps toward safer seafood. *FDA Consumer, 31*(7), 10.

10. Lee, C. M. (1984). Surimi process technology. *Food Technology, 38*(11), 69.

11. Lee, C. M., & Toledo, R. T. (1984). Comparison of shelf life and quality of mullet stored at zero and subzero temperature. *Journal of Food Science, 49*, 317.

12. Liston, J. (1990). Microbial hazards of seafood consumption. *Food Technology, 44*(12), 56.

13. MacDonald, G. A., & Lanier, T. (1991). Carbohydrates as cryoprotectants for meats and surimi. *Food Technology, 45*(3), 150.

14. Martin, R. E. (1988). Seafood products, technology, and research in the U.S. *Food Technology, 42*(3), 58.

15. Mermelstein, N. H. (1998). Freezing seafood. *Food Technology, 52*(2), 72.

16. Mermelstein, N. H. (2002). Processing in the largest U.S. seafood plant. *Food Technology, 56*(2), 69.

17. National Fisheries Institute, Inc. (2003). About our industry: Harvesting. Retrieved January 20, 2003, from http://www.nfi.org/?a=about&b=Harvesting

18. National Fisheries Institute, Inc. (2003). News releases: Shrimp, salmon, tilapia rise in popularity. Retrieved January 20, 2003, from http://www.nfi.org/?a=news&b=News%20Releases&year=2002&x=41

19. Omaye, S. T. (2001). Shark-fin soup and methylmercury: To eat or not to eat. *Food Technology, 55*(10), 26.

20. Pew Initiative on Food and Biotechnology. (2003). Biotech and the deep blue sea. Retrieved February 1, 2003, from http://pewagbiotech.org/buzz/display/php3?storyID=47

21. Pew Initiative on Food and Biotechnology. (2003). Future fish: Issues in science and regulation of transgenic fish. Retrieved February 1, 2003, from http://pewagbiotech.org/research/fish

22. Pszczola, D. E. (1998). Discovering treasures of the deep. *Food Technology, 52*(4), 74.

23. Regenstein, J. M. (1986). The potential for minced fish. *Food Technology, 40*(3), 101.

24. Sidwell, V. D., & Stillings, B. R. (1972). Crackers fortified with fish protein concentrate (FPC). *Journal of the American Dietetic Association, 61*, 276.

25. U.S. Food and Drug Administration. (2001, February). FDA's seafood HACCP program: Mid-course correction. Retrieved June 23, 2002, from http://www.cfsan.fda.gov/~comm/shaccpl.html

26. U.S. Food and Drug Administration. (2001, March). An important message for pregnant women and women of childbearing age who may become pregnant about the risks of mercury in fish. Retrieved January 21, 2003, from http://cfsan.fda.gov/~dms/admehg.html

27. Williams, R., & Zorn, D. J. (1994). New inspection program for the nation's seafood. *Food Review, 17*(2), 32.

28. Wong, K., & Gill, T. A. (1987). Enzymatic determination of trimethylamine and its relationship to fish quality. *Journal of Food Science, 52*, 1.

Beverages

28

A wide variety of commercially produced beverages is on the market. This market continues to diversify, with beverage production increasingly being targeted to specific market segments. Beverages have been formulated for such groups as children, older people, physically active individuals, and persons with special dietary needs. Alcoholic beverages, water, and drinkable yogurts were reported by ACNielsen to be among the top nine fastest growing categories of food and beverages in the global marketplace in 2001 [1].

Some beverages that do not fit traditional definitions have been grouped as New Age or **functional** beverages and are moving into the mainstream. Energy drinks, some isotonic (sport) beverages, herbal and green teas, fortified waters, and some caffeinated drinks are part of this group. People in their twenties and thirty-somethings, teenagers, and preteens are the targets for New Age beverages, including so-called smart drinks that claim to be able to keep you going through the day's work and into the night. Smart drinks contain substances such as herbal extracts (ginseng, ginkgo leaf, and ma huang), **guarana,** amino acids, vitamins, minerals, and other ingredients that allegedly stimulate energy and alertness. Some of these ingredients are untested and their short- and long-term effects are controversial. The Food and Drug Administration (FDA) has relaxed its oversight in this area since passage of the Dietary Supplement Health and Education Act [15, 16].

Consumers are buying bottled water in increasing quantities. Bottled water represents a $5.2 billion market that is growing near 30 percent per year [19]. Per capita consumption was 3.4 gallons per annum in 1983, 8 gallons in 1990, and 10 gallons in 1994. Between 1977 and 1997, the per capita annual consumption of bottled water increased by 908 percent [31]. In 2001, Americans drank a record 5 billion gallons of bottled water [4]. **Spring water, mineral water,** and **purified water,** as well as a variety of transparent, sweetened, flavored sparkling water drinks with exotic-sounding flavor names, are sold [3, 14, 30]. *Enhanced waters* containing functional ingredients such as vitamins, calcium, or super oxygenation may become the next big trend in bottled waters [19].

CARBONATED BEVERAGES

Between 1977 and 1997 the per capita annual consumption of soft drinks in the United States increased 61 percent. In 1997, the average American consumed 53 gallons of carbonated soft drinks [31]. Carbonated soft drinks are still the

---

functional foods any food that has a positive impact on an individual's health, physical performance, or state of mind in addition to its normal nutritive value; sometimes called nutraceuticals

guarana a South American berry with alleged aphrodisiac qualities; the seeds of the berry contain caffeine

spring water derived from an underground formation from which water flows naturally to the surface of the earth

mineral water ground water containing at least 250 ppm total dissolved solids (TDS); more than 1500 ppm TDS must be labeled as high mineral content

purified water chemically pure; treated bottled water produced by distillation, deionization, reverse osmosis, or other suitable processes

most widely consumed beverage in the United States. Carbonation is the process of saturating the beverage with carbon dioxide, giving unique zest to the drink. The carbonation also provides protection against bacterial spoilage during storage [12].

The first step in the production of carbonated soft drinks is the preparation of a syrup for sweetening. To this are added flavoring, coloring, acid, and a preservative, with continuous mixing and blending. Finally, the syrup is diluted to the finished beverage level, which is carbonated in a pressurized carbon dioxide vessel, or carbo-cooler. The carbonated beverage is then pumped to the filler, which meters the liquid into a sterile container, and the container is then closed [12]. Many carbonated drinks are made without sugar, using alternative sweeteners such as **aspartame.** They are often labeled "diet" drinks. Refer to Chapter 11 for more information about high-intensity, alternative sweeteners.

Sparkling water beverages contain carbon dioxide, a low level of sweetener, which is often fructose, and flavoring. Enticing names such as *summer strawberry, wild mountain berry, Mexican lime, fiesta orange,* and *orchard peach* are often attached to these flavored waters. Club soda is carbonated water with sodium bicarbonate and potassium carbonate added. The original seltzer is simply carbonated water, but seltzers are also sold with sweetener and flavor ingredients added.

Many carbonated beverages contain caffeine, including cola drinks, pepper products, and many citrus products. It has been reported that private-label store brands generally contain less caffeine than national-brand canned drinks. Carbonated fountain beverages from restaurants were also found to contain higher caffeine levels than their canned counterparts, although the fountain items showed more variability [13]. Caffeine content of some carbonated drinks is shown in Table 28-1.

aspartame an alternative sweetener whose trade name is Nutrasweet®

Table 28-1
Caffeine Content of Selected Foods and Beverages

	Caffeine (mg)
Coffee (5 oz cup)	
Drip method	110–150
Percolated	64–124
Instant	40–108
Decaffeinated	2–5
Instant decaffeinated	2
Tea (5 oz cup)	
1-minute brew (black)	21–33
3-minute brew (black)	35–46
5-minute brew (black)	39–50
Instant	12–28
Iced tea (12 oz can)	22–36
Chocolate products	
Hot cocoa (6 oz cup)	2–8
Milk chocolate (1 oz)	1–15
Soft drinks (12 oz can)	
Tab	49.1 ± 2.1
RC Cola	42.7 ± 1.3
Pepsi	32.1 ± 0.4
Coca-Cola	29.7 ± 0.7
Dr. Pepper	42.4 ± 0.6
Mountain Dew	54.5 ± 1.2
Sunkist Orange	42.7 ± 0.5

Source: References 5, 13, 36.

SPORTS OR ISOTONIC BEVERAGES

Sports beverages are designed to prevent dehydration during vigorous exercise and to give a quick energy burst. They should have the same osmotic pressure as human blood to allow for rapid absorption. Typically they have a low level of carbonation and a carbohydrate content of 6 to 8 percent (compared with soft drinks, which have 10 to 12 percent). The sweeteners added to sports drinks are usually glucose, maltodextrins, and sucrose. For electrolyte replacement, sports drinks contain such ingredients as monopotassium phosphate, sodium chloride, sodium citrate, and potassium chloride [12]. The ideal beverage for fluid replacement in athletes during training and competition appears to be one that tastes good, does not cause gastrointestinal discomfort when consumed in large volumes, promotes rapid fluid absorption and maintenance of extracellular fluid volume, and provides energy to working muscles [7].

NONCARBONATED FRUIT BEVERAGES

Fruit beverages contain fruit or juice (1.5 to 70 percent) and water, as well as sweeteners, flavoring, coloring, and preservatives. These are not fruit juices, although fruit may be a predominant ingredient. They can be either low calorie or high calorie. Acidulants are normally added. They contribute to flavor and may act as preservatives to restrict microbial growth by lowering the **pH.** The addition of flavoring substances strengthens and deepens the flavor of the fruit juice in the drink. The trend in recent years has been toward an increased demand for flavors obtained from natural sources. A line of concentrated pink grapefruit flavors derived from pink grapefruit grown in the Mediterranean is available, for example. Interest in tropical fruit flavors is also growing. New Age juice drinks often feature combinations of exotic fruit flavors, such as mango/passion fruit, kiwi/strawberry, and pear/clove [11, 12]. Juice drinks may also contain various vegetable gums, cellulose derivatives, and starch in small amounts to add body and affect the mouthfeel of the beverage [29].

Fruit beverages are susceptible to microbial spoilage and **fermentation.** They therefore require protection by **pasteurization** or added preservatives. Pasteurization is accomplished by heat or microfiltration, with the product

pH a numerical scale from 1 to 14 indicating the degree of acidity; 1 is most acid; 7 is neutral; and 14 is most alkaline

fermentation the transformation of organic molecules, such as sugar, into smaller ones by the action of microorganisms

pasteurization the process of heating to a temperature below the boiling point of water but high enough to destroy pathogenic microorganisms

(a)

(b)

Figure 28-1
(a) Bananas, orange juice, strawberries, sherbet, and a lemon-lime carbonated beverage are blended for this smoothie.
(b) The fruit garnish may be as tasty as the fruit beverage. (Courtesy of Dole Food Company, Inc.)

aseptic free from disease-producing microorganisms; filling a container that has been previously sterilized without recontaminating either product or container is an aseptic process

often being heated in-line and then placed in **aseptic** packaging. The approval of hydrogen peroxide as a packaging sterilant in 1984 made possible the packaging of many beverages in laminated boxes, which are available in various sizes. Alternatively, the beverage may be pasteurized by filling the package, closing, and then heating it. A hot-filling method, involving filling the package with the hot product and turning the package so that all sides contact the product, may also be used [12].

Fruit smoothies have become a popular beverage that may be prepared in the home or purchased when eating out. Smoothies are a frozen blended beverage composed of fruit, fruit juices, yogurt, or other dairy ingredients. In the commerial market a variety of healthy or functional ingredients may be added to create a unique beverage [28]. Fruit smoothies are shown in Figure 28-1.

ALCOHOLIC BEVERAGES

The French have a saying, "A meal without wine is a day without sunshine." A meal accompanied by wine must be eaten slowly because the wine must be sipped; and there should be long pauses between sips so that the bouquet of the wine can linger on the palate. Wine may aid the digestive processes by the simple fact that it prevents eating in a hurry.

Epidemiologic studies of important factors in the development of coronary heart disease have revealed that French subjects who have intakes of saturated fatty acids and risk factors similar to U.S. subjects show a much lower incidence of death from heart disease. The intake of wine was different between the two groups studied and showed a negative correlation with coronary heart disease. Components in wine, in addition to alcohol, may be important factors. It has been suggested that antioxidant substances in wine are responsible for some of these effects, as may be similar substances found in fruits and vegetables [22].

The process of making wine involves the chemistry of fermentation, as does the making of all alcoholic beverages. The process of fermentation is simple in that yeast acts on sugar, converting it into alcohol and carbon dioxide gas [23]. If, at this point, the mixture is not protected from the air, then the alcohol turns into acetic acid, producing vinegar. The complete process of making wine, however, is complicated, and involves the selection of the right kinds of grapes and consideration of where they are grown. The grapes are crushed and their pulp and juice fermented. The wine is slowly aged in closed oak casks and sampled periodically for quality. Some impurities may be removed from the wine before it is bottled by a process called *fining*. The neck of the wine bottle is closed with a cork. When the bottle is tilted on its side, the cork is moistened by the wine and permits only a minuscule amount of air to enter the bottle; a larger amount of air would quickly turn the liquid to vinegar. The wine then continues to age slowly.

Some upscale frozen food items now on the market, such as mushroom ravioli with wild mushroom sauce and eggplant Parmesan with tomato basil sauce, include wine as an ingredient. Wine flavorings have potential for frozen sauces, vegetables, and entrees [26].

COFFEE

The coffee plant is apparently native to Ethiopia and other parts of tropical Africa. It was introduced into the Middle Eastern countries in the 15th century, and, later, both the growing of the plant and the custom of coffee drinking spread throughout the eastern hemisphere. Coffee was introduced into Java by the Dutch in the 17th century and later into South America. Since that time, Brazil has become the largest coffee-producing country in the world. Central America, Colombia, Hawaii, and Puerto Rico also have climatic conditions favorable to the growth of a fine grade of mild coffee.

The Coffee Plant

The coffee plant grows 6 to 20 feet high, depending on the species, the country in which it is grown, and the local custom of pruning. There are many varieties of coffee, but only a few are grown for commercial use. The original species native to Ethiopia and the one most commonly grown is *Coffea arabica*, but when grown in different soils, altitudes, and climates, this species takes on different characteristics. Arabica, which is now grown chiefly in Central and South America, has a fine full flavor and aroma. A second hardy variety commonly grown in Africa is *Coffea robusta*. Robusta coffee shrubs are best suited to low elevations (about 1,000 feet), and the beans are not as flavorful or as acid tasting as those from arabica coffee plants.

The evergreen coffee plant bears white flowers, from which the fruit develops. When ripe, the fruit resembles a small cherry with the dark red pulp covering two oval beans, growing with the flat sides together (Figure 28-2). The bean or seed is the part used to make the coffee beverage.

Preparation and Blending of Beans

In the curing process that prepares the coffee beans for market, the cherries may be either dried for 2 to 3 weeks in the sun, or soaked, depulped, washed, and dried by machine. One curing process—the washed coffee process—makes use of **pectic enzymes** on selectively picked cherries to replace spontaneous fermentation.

pectic enzymes enzymes such as pectinase that hydrolyze the large pectin molecules

The skin, pulp, parchment, and silverskin are all removed, leaving the cleaned beans, which are light green or blue-green. The green beans are then classified into six different sizes and graded. Unripened and discolored beans, sticks, small stones, and other foreign matter are eliminated. Next the beans are packed into jute or fiber bags and shipped to various markets. Green coffee may be stored for prolonged periods with no adverse effects.

Each variety of coffee has its own flavor and other characteristics. Coffee that is available to the consumer may be a blend of as many as five or six different varieties of coffee beans. The blends are controlled for flavor, aroma, color, and strength or body of the beverage from the roasted bean. Blending is done by "creative artists" of the coffee world, who choose beans that combine to produce desirable brews and yet are not too expensive. Once a blend combination has been developed, it is continuously produced so that one brand of coffee always has the same flavor and aroma.

Roasting

Green coffee beans have little flavor and aroma until they are roasted. Roasting is the main odor and taste determinate for a given green bean coffee blend; thus a precise control of time and temperature is required to reach the desired flavor profile [33]. Naturally occurring sugars, plant acids (including **chlorogenic acid**), proteins, and other minor nitrogen-containing compounds react at roasting temperatures to form a majority of the desirable flavor constituents [20].

chlorogenic acid polyphenolic organic acid

(a) Ripening coffee berries.

(b) Coffee berries may be dried in the sun.

(c) Green coffee beans.

(d) Bags of green coffee beans ready for shipment.

Figure 28-2
(Courtesy of Specialty Coffee Association of America)

The beans expand to 1.5 times their original size and become more porous. The dull green changes to brown. Coffee roasts are classified according to the color of the roasted bean into light roast, medium roast, dark roast, and Italian or French roast, which is very dark. Other names may be given to the various roasts such as *cinnamon*, *high*, *New York*, *Chicago*, and *New Orleans*.

Moisture is lost during roasting, carbon dioxide gas is formed, and sugar is decomposed. Changes in the sugar, possibly in combination with other substances, contribute much to the color of the beverage produced from the roasted beans. Modern roasting equipment allows careful control of time and temperature so that the flavor is constant from batch to batch.

Carbon dioxide gas appears to be lost gradually from roasted coffee on standing, but is better retained in the bean than in ground coffee. Carbon dioxide is a desirable constituent of coffee from the standpoint of both the keeping quality and the retention of flavor and aroma substances. Flavor and aroma substances may be in some way tied up with the gas, or the presence of the gas may tend to prevent undesirable oxidation reactions on certain coffee constituents. At any rate, the loss of carbon dioxide is closely associated with loss of flavor and aroma.

Composition of Coffee

The constituents of coffee that are of significance in the making of the beverage include acids, volatile substances, bitter substances, and caffeine. Caffeine is desired by those who seek stimulation from the beverage. It is not desirable for others who enjoy the flavor, but not the stimulating effect, of coffee.

Organic Acids.   Several organic acids are present in aqueous coffee extracts, including acetic, pyruvic, caffeic, chlorogenic, malic, citric, and tartaric acids. The predominant acid is chlorogenic, which is somewhat sour and slightly bitter. It has been suggested that, in general, the more acid tasting the coffee, the better the aroma and flavor [36]. Coffee acidity is apparently affected by many factors, including variety, altitude at which the plant is grown, processing of the fruit, age of the beans, and the degree of roasting of the beans.

Volatile Substances.   Almost 700 volatile compounds have been identified as contributing to the aroma of coffee [32]. The most desirable aroma comes from a delicate balance in composition of volatiles. Sulfur compounds and **phenolic compounds** are among the main contributors to the characteristic aroma. Many of the flavor substances in a coffee beverage are lost or changed by heat. Therefore, an extended heating period at a high temperature can remove or destroy the desirable aroma and flavor. Long heating even at a low temperature may have the same effect. Reheating a coffee beverage has been shown to decrease organoleptic acceptance by a judging panel at the same time that a loss of volatile substances was shown by gas chromatographic techniques [35].

phenolic compound an organic compound containing in its structure an unsaturated ring of carbon atoms with an −OH group

Bitter Substances.   Bitterness in coffee becomes more pronounced as the **polyphenol** content increases. Polyphenol solubility apparently increases with temperature, and a boiling temperature releases polyphenols readily from the coffee bean. Caffeine contributes to bitterness. Coffee also contains other substances that produce distinctly bitter tastes.

polyphenol a phenol compound with more than one −OH group attached to the unsaturated ring of carbon atoms; some produce bitterness in coffee and tea

Caffeine.   Pharmacologists classify caffeine as a mild stimulant of the central nervous system and consider it one of the world's most widely used drugs [21]. Caffeine is one of a group of chemical compounds called *methylxanthines*, which occur naturally in the parts of many species of plants, including coffee beans, tea leaves, cocoa beans, and cola nuts. Theobromine, a somewhat milder stimulant than caffeine, is also a methylxanthine and is found in chocolate and cocoa.

Table 28-1 gives the caffeine content of some common foods and beverages. Although caffeine is added to some soft drinks, manufacturers of soft drinks also market caffeine-free cola beverages. Decaffeinated coffee and tea are produced as well.

Decaffeinated Coffee

Some people want the flavor of the coffee beverage but not the stimulating effect of the caffeine it contains. Most of the caffeine can be removed from the green coffee beans to yield decaffeinated coffee. Several processes are available for use in accomplishing decaffeination. These extraction processes primarily employ (1) water, (2) steam, (3) carbon dioxide, (4) ethyl acetate, (5) methylene chloride, or (6) coffee oils. The FDA regulates the level of solvent residue that may remain in the decaffeinated bean. Much of the decaffeination of coffee beans is presently being done in Europe.

Although decaffeinated coffee generally has good flavor, there is a slight loss of the usual coffee flavor during processing.

Instant Coffee Products

Instant or soluble coffee is convenient. It is composed of dry, powdered, water-soluble solids produced by dehydrating very strong, brewed coffee, which is often percolated under vacuum to minimize the loss of flavor substances. Some carbohydrate may be added. The flavor of instant coffee is similar to that of freshly brewed coffee, but the aroma is usually somewhat lacking in comparison with the fresh-brewed beverage. The quality of soluble coffee flavor can be improved by capturing desirable aroma compounds in coffee oil and adding them back to the coffee powder [15].

Some soluble coffees are freeze-dried. In this process the strong, brewed coffee is first frozen and then dried by vaporization in a vacuum. Like instant coffees produced by other methods, the freeze-dried products are reconstituted by adding boiling water according to directions on the package. Soluble coffees should be kept packaged in water- and airtight containers because they are **hygroscopic,** tending to absorb moisture.

hygroscopic tending to attract or absorb moisture from the atmosphere

Instant coffee beverage is available in dry form, containing instant coffee, flavorings, and coffee creamer. Gourmet flavors to be added to brewed coffee are also marketed. The wide assortment of flavored and instant coffee products offered to the consumer can make choosing one a real challenge.

Specialty Coffee Beverages

How Americans drink coffee has changed over the years. The growth of premium, upscale coffee shops such as Starbucks has resulted in the popularity of a wide variety of coffee beverages, many of which are based on espresso [17]. *Espresso* coffee is prepared from a French roast coffee and heated by steam. Expresso is a strongly flavored, rich beverage prepared with special equipment (Figure 28-3). *Expresso machiatto* is expresso with a small amount of steamed

Figure 28-3
An espresso coffee machine (Courtesy of KRUPS North America)

milk. *Cappuccino* is prepared with one-third expresso, one-third steamed milk, and one-third foamed milk (Figure 28-4). *Caffè latte* is composed of one-third expresso and two-thirds steamed milk without the foam. A strong coffee with steamed milk is called *café au lait* [25]. Additionally, a variety of flavored coffees such as hazelnut and French vanilla may be purchased or coffee beverages may be prepared from sweet, icy blended coffees.

Instant cappuccino may contain sugar, hydrogenated fat, corn syrup solids, coffee, nonfat milk solids, sodium caseinate, and emulsifiers. It may also contain additives to aid the dissolving process (dipotassium phosphate) and to prevent caking (silicon dioxide). Flavors such as hazelnut, almond, and chocolate may be added. Iced cappuccino coffee is marketed in bottles to be served cold. Freeze-dried espresso coffee is also marketed as an instant product.

Coffee Substitutes

Parched ground cereals and/or roots are used as coffee substitutes. Their flavor is due largely to various products formed during the heating process. **Chicory** is sometimes added to coffee substitutes for a somewhat bitter taste. Chicory can also be blended with coffee. This mixture is preferred over coffee alone by some people. A darker color results from the addition of chicory, but the characteristic coffee flavor and aroma are decreased. The coffee substitutes do not generally produce a stimulating effect as does the caffeine in coffee.

chicory a plant whose root is roasted and ground for use as a coffee substitute

Storage and Staling

An important factor affecting the quality of the coffee beverage is the freshness of the coffee used. Coffee is best when it is freshly roasted. It deteriorates on standing. Because ground coffee becomes flat or stale more rapidly than coffee in the bean, and because coffee exposed to air changes more rapidly than coffee not so exposed, the chief cause of staleness has been assumed to be the oxidation of certain coffee constituents. The oxidation theory seems to be inade-

Cappuccino.

Caffé latte.

Figure 28-4
Cappuccino and Caffé Latte have become popular coffee beverages.
(Reference 25)

quate, however, in explaining all the changes brought about in stale coffee. The fat of coffee apparently does not become rancid in the short time required for coffee to become stale.

Moisture has a pronounced effect in decreasing the storage life of coffee. Tests on volatile substances extracted from coffee show that if the substances are sealed in a vacuum tube, changes are retarded; if the substances are exposed to air, changes occur rapidly; and if the substances are exposed to moisture, the changes are still more pronounced.

The effect of oxygen on roasted coffee is rapid during the first 3 weeks and is thought to affect mainly the flavor constituents. After 3 weeks, the oxygen probably combines with the oils of the coffee, which results in the development of true rancidity several months later.

Proper sealing of roasted—especially ground—coffee is fundamental. The vacuum type of package from which air is removed before sealing affords more protection than other types of packages. Flavor deterioration in vacuum-packed coffee depends on the extent to which air is removed from the container. Another development involves the use of carbon dioxide gas under pressure in cans after the air is removed. It has been suggested that vacuum-packed roasted and ground coffee in cans at a moisture content of 5 percent or less can be expected to have a storage life of at least 2 years [2]. Because of the rapid loss of flavor after grinding and exposure to air, many markets have facilities for grinding coffee at the time of purchase.

After a container of vacuum-packed coffee is opened, it should be stored, tightly covered, in a cool place, preferably at a temperature as low as 40°F (4°C), to retard staling. Contact with moist air should be kept to a minimum.

Preparation of Coffee Beverage

Grind and Quality. Coffee may be ground to differing degrees of fineness. Any grind, however, contains particles of many sizes. Ground coffees differ basically in the proportion of each size of particles. A *regular grind* contains a higher proportion of coarse particles than a *drip* or *medium grind*; a *fine grind* contains no coarse particles. It is also possible to pulverize coffee, but neither institutional nor home type brewing equipment is designed for pulverized coffee. Its use in such equipment would result in a bitter-tasting beverage.

Consistency in the grind is important in maintaining consistent quality. As the percentage of large particles in the coffee grind is increased, the brewed beverage is weaker. A foodservice manager should know if the supplier actually measures the grinds and is consistent in the grind provided.

Good grades of coffee are characterized by a sharp, more desirable flavor as compared with the flat, neutral flavor of poor grades. A middle grade of coffee, purchased and used fresh, yields a better beverage than a high grade that is stale. Poor grade coffee, although less expensive, may not result in the anticipated cost savings because a larger amount of coffee may be required for an acceptable flavor as compared to a high quality coffee.

Methods. Instant coffee has gained wide acceptance because of its convenience, but it has not replaced brewed coffee. Good coffee may be brewed by several methods (Figure 28-5). In each method, important factors include control of the water temperature and control of the time that the coffee is in contact with the water. The temperature of the water should be at least 185°F (85°C) to extract a desirable amount of soluble solids; however, it should not be

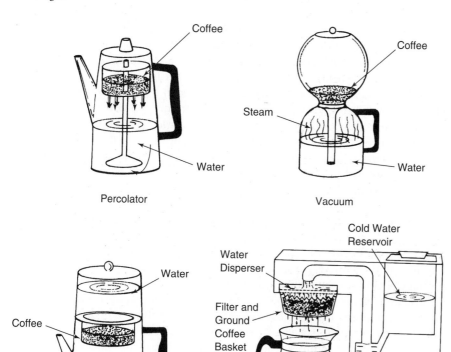

Figure 28-5
Types of coffeemakers.

Percolator

Vacuum

Drip

Automatic Drip-filter Coffee Maker

hotter than 203°F (95°C) to avoid extraction of excessive amounts of bitter substances and loss of many volatile flavor substances.

The amount of coffee used in relation to the water determines the initial strength of the brew. Measures of 1 to 3 tablespoons of coffee per cup (8 ounces) of water yields brews ranging from weak to very strong. Use of 1 1/3 to 1 1/2 tablespoons of coffee per cup of water gives a medium-strength brew.

Filtration.   In the drip or filtration method, the water filters through the coffee into the lower compartment of the coffeemaker. In institutional foodservice, an urn is used to make drip or filtered coffee. The upper part of a drip coffeemaker is perforated and holds the coffee grounds, and the lower compartment receives the filtered beverage. The perforations of the upper compartment are covered with thin filter paper or cheesecloth to prevent the passage of coffee grounds into the beverage. If the perforations are too small, the rate of filtration is too slow to yield a desirable beverage.

The drip method probably extracts less of the bitter substances than other methods. If it is not allowed to boil and is not kept hot too long, coffee made by the drip method retains more of the flavor constituents than coffee made by other methods. Probably all methods extract a high percentage of the caffeine.

Another type of pot for the filtration method is the vacuum coffeemaker. The upper compartment, which holds the coffee, has an open tube that extends almost to the bottom of the lower compartment. Coffee is usually prevented from passing into the lower compartment by a cloth-covered disk, which is held in place over the tube opening. In some models, a glass rod that fits the tube opening is used instead of the disk. Water is placed in the lower compartment and the pot is heated until most of the water rises into the upper compartment. The pot is then removed from the source of heat until the water filters through the coffee and passes back into the lower compartment. The upper compartment is removed, and the beverage is carefully reheated to a desirable temperature for serving. The chief difficulties in the use of this method are that the coffee may not be hot when served, and that, in being kept hot it may boil, thus losing much of the flavor and aroma.

Percolation. When coffee is percolated, heated water is forced upward through a tube into the coffee compartment. The water filters through the coffee several times before the beverage is of desirable strength. The water is probably not at the boiling point when it is in contact with the coffee, but the beverage is close to the boiling point when it is ready to be served. Unless the construction of the pot is good and the time of percolating is carefully controlled, much of the flavor and aroma may be lost by this method. The time required varies with the speed of percolation and with the quantity of coffee made. Usually 6 to 8 minutes is adequate to make 4 to 6 cups of coffee.

Steeping. Although steeped coffee is sometimes described as *boiled*, the beverage made by heating the coffee and water together is more desirable in flavor if it is not allowed to boil. Steeping (extracting flavor below the boiling point) extracts much less of the bitter substances from coffee than boiling. Coffee boiled for 1 minute is distinctly more bitter than coffee heated from 185° to 203°F (85° to 95°C). This method may be convenient for use on picnics and camping excursions. If egg white is mixed with the coffee before the water is added, the temperature must rise high enough to coagulate the dilute solution of egg to clarify the beverage. Boiled coffee made with egg is more bland than that made without egg because of the combination of egg albumin with the polyphenol compounds. The length of steeping varies with the temperature of the water that is mixed with the coffee and with the fineness of the coffee grind. Hot water is preferable because less time is required to make the beverage than when cold water is used. Short infusion periods usually yield better flavored coffee than longer periods.

Iced Coffee

An iced beverage that possesses the maximum flavor is made by pouring a freshly made, strong coffee infusion over crushed ice in a glass. Strong infusions, whether combined hot or cold with ice, are made with a larger-than-usual amount of coffee per cup of water rather than by longer-than-usual infusion periods. Long infusion periods decrease flavor and aroma and increase bitterness. Iced coffee is also available in bottles to be refrigerated and served cold.

Other Factors

The Coffee Pot. Some metals form compounds with caffeine and probably with other constituents of coffee. Metallic pots impart a metallic flavor to coffee. Pots made of glass, earthenware, or enamelware are good choices. Stainless steel is resistant to attack and, therefore, its effect on the flavor of coffee is negligible. Chrome and nickel plating show no staining or corrosion when used in a coffee pot.

A clean coffee pot is essential to making a good coffee beverage. The pot should be washed with hot soapy water or scoured as necessary to remove the oily film that collects on the inside. Thorough rinsing is essential. A pot that retains a stale coffee odor is not a clean pot and will mar the flavor of the best-made coffee. Regular cleaning schedules should be employed for coffee-making equipment used in foodservice establishments.

Water. The water used to brew coffee should be free of any undesirable elements picked up in pipelines, boilers, or water tanks. You should never brew coffee with water you would not drink. Soft water or water of low hardness gives coffee a more desirable flavor than very hard or alkaline water. Water having a high carbonate or bicarbonate content and water that has passed through an ion-exchange softening system (and thus is high in sodium ions) will not filter through coffee in a drip or vacuum pot as rapidly as naturally soft water. This means an increase in both the time of contact with the coffee and the amount of material extracted, which can be objectionable.

Temperature. The optimum temperature for brewing a good coffee beverage is probably 185° to 203°F (85° to 95°C). Boiling produces a distinctly bitter beverage. Polyphenol substances are more soluble at boiling than at 203°F (95°C). The longer the heating period, even at lower temperatures, the higher the percentage of bitter substances dissolved and the greater the loss of flavor substances. Nearly all the caffeine is dissolved at 185° to 203°F (85° to 95°C) and the flavor substances are not lost as much as at higher temperatures. Boiling water may be used to start the preparation of coffee, because the temperature drops once the water comes in contact with the coffee and the pot.

TEA

A legend tells us that one day in 2737 B.C. the Chinese emperor Shen Nung was boiling drinking water over an open fire. He believed that drinking boiled water was a healthy practice. Some leaves from a nearby *Camellia sinensis* plant floated into the pot. The emperor drank the mixture and declared that it gave him vigor of body, contentment of mind, and determination of purpose. Today that potion—tea beverage—is widely consumed throughout the world. As a consumed liquid, it is second only to water. The U.S. population drank 2.25 billion gallons of tea in 1994, as a hot, iced, spiced, or flavored beverage, with or without sugar, honey, milk, cream, or lemon [34]. The annual per capita consumption of tea is currently about 7 gallons and appears to be on the rise, with increasing research results suggesting health benefits associated with tea consumption [18].

Countries that produce the largest volumes of tea are India and China. Other regions of production include Kenya, Sri Lanka, Turkey, Indonesia, Japan, South America, and Bangladesh. Teas vary according to the age of the leaf, the season of plucking, the soil, and climatic conditions, as well as the method of processing.

Figure 28-6
Tea shoots, showing buds and leaves.
(Copyright © *Tea and Coffee Trade Journal*)

The Tea Plant

Tea comes from the leaves of *Camellia sinensis*, a white-flowered evergreen (Figure 28-6). The plant is pruned and cultivated to produce many young shoots. Pluckings may extend over a period of several months (Figure 28-7).

After processing, tea leaves are sorted into sizes by a screening procedure. Grades refer to the leaf size and have nothing to do with the quality or flavor of

Figure 28-7
Picking tea leaves, two leaves and a bud at a time. The work is done chiefly by women who carry light bamboo baskets strapped to their backs. (Courtesy of the U.S. Food and Drug Administration. From *FDA Consumer*, 30:23[2]. 1996)

tea. The largest leaves are orange pekoe, pekoe, and pekoe souchong. The smaller or broken leaves are classified as broken orange pekoe, broken pekoe souchong, broken orange pekoe fannings, and fines (also called "dust")[34].

Processing

Three principal types of tea, differentiated by the method of leaf processing, are black, green, and oolong.

Black Tea.　Nearly 95 percent of the tea consumed in the United States is black tea. In the traditional method of its manufacture, the leaves are first withered, a process in which excess moisture is removed. They are then rolled in special machines which release enzymes and juices from the leaves. Next, the leaves ferment in a room with controlled temperature and humidity. Finally, they are dried in ovens. A nontraditional method may be used by some processors to speed production by using machines that finely chop the leaves, thereby shortening the time for withering and fermenting [34].

Green Tea.　Only about 4 percent of the tea consumed in the United States is green tea. Green tea is produced by first steaming the leaves to inactivate the enzymes and then rolling and drying. The leaf retains much of its original green color, especially the finer leaves. Older leaves often are a blackish gray color. The beverage made from green tea is greenish yellow and is distinctly bitter and astringent. It has little aroma and flavor as compared with black tea because the preliminary steaming destroys the enzymes that produce flavor substances during the fermentation of black tea.

Oolong Tea.　Oolong tea is a partially fermented tea. The fermentation period is too short to change the color of the leaf completely; it is only partially blackened. The flavor and aroma of this beverage are intermediate between those produced from green and black teas.

Composition

The stimulating characteristic of tea comes from its caffeine content. The tea beverage contains less than half as much caffeine as coffee (see Table 28-1). The actual content of caffeine depends on the method of brewing. Longer brewing results in higher caffeine content.

Tea has been reported to contain a significant amount of folacin [6]. A person could obtain up to 25 percent of the Recommended Dietary Allowance (RDA) for folacin by drinking 5 cups of tea per day. Tea appears to have a negative effect on iron absorption when consumed with a meal [9].

The flavor of tea is influenced by the presence of considerable quantities of polyphenolic substances, which are particularly responsible for **astringency.** Some of the polyphenols are changed in the **oxidation** process that takes place when black tea is fermented. They contribute to the characteristic aroma and flavor of this tea. Degradation of other substances, including **linolenic acid,** amino acids, and **carotenes,** during the manufacture of black tea may also contribute to flavor and aroma.

astringency the puckering, drawing, or shrinking sensation produced by certain compounds in food

oxidation a chemical change that involves the addition of oxygen; for example, polyphenols are oxidized to produce different flavor and color compounds

linolenic acid polyunsaturated fatty acid

carotenes yellow-orange, fat-soluble pigments

Market Forms

A wide variety of teas are available on the market. Much of the tea sold for consumer use is in the form of tea bags for convenient brewing. Many scented and flavored teas are marketed. These teas contain such flavorings as oils of peppermint, strawberry, orange, or lemon; spices such as cinnamon or cloves; blackberry leaves; almond; and licorice root.

As with coffee, decaffeinated tea is available. The decaffeinated product is also sold with various flavors added, such as blackberry and almond.

Instant teas are dried products prepared from brewed teas. These teas are particularly useful for preparing iced tea. To serve, simply disperse the tea in cold water and add ice. Instant tea mixes may contain sugar, citric acid, maltodextrins, and flavoring such as lemon. Low-calorie tea products sweetened with aspartame or saccharin are also available.

A variety of herbal teas are on the market. They contain dried leaves of various plants other than tea. Often they are a mixture of several dried plant materials such as strawberry leaves, apples, hibiscus flowers, rose hips, peppermint, ginger, nutmeg, cinnamon, chamomile, and alfalfa. Various flavors may also be added. Herbal teas contain no caffeine but often contain substances that have soothing, stimulating, or euphoric effects. Some potential health hazards are associated with their misuse. For example, long-term use of ginseng may produce hypertension, nervousness, sleeplessness, and edema. So-called dieter's teas may contain senna, aloe, buckthorn, and other plant-derived laxatives that, when consumed in excessive amounts, can cause diarrhea, vomiting, nausea, stomach cramps, chronic constipation, fainting, and perhaps death [24].

Preparation of Tea Beverage

Soft water is preferable to hard alkaline water for making tea, just as it is for making coffee. The polyphenol substances in tea may interact with certain salts in hard water to produce an undesirable precipitate. Water should be freshly boiled with enough oxygen still in it to prevent the flat taste that results from the loss of dissolved gases by boiling.

Metallic pots impart a metallic taste to the tea beverage. Glass, earthenware, enamelware, or other vitrified ware is recommended for making tea.

Temperatures slightly under boiling are less likely to volatilize flavor and aroma substances than boiling temperature. Boiling water is quickly reduced in temperature, however, when poured over tea leaves. Flavor substances and caffeine are readily extracted by short infusion periods. The aim in making tea is to extract the maximum flavor with a minimum of polyphenol compounds, which are bitter. Strong beverages of good flavor require more of the beverage-making constituents than long infusion periods.

The usual proportion of tea per cup of water is about 1 teaspoon. However, when steeping periods are prolonged or when the quantity of beverage made is larger, as little as 1/2 to 2/3 teaspoon produces a better beverage.

Tea Bags. In 1994, according to the Tea Council of the U.S.A., approximately 60 percent of the tea brewed in the United States was made with the use of tea bags; slightly more than 1 percent was brewed from loose tea; 25 percent used iced tea mixes; and the remainder was made from instant tea [34]. The tea bag dominates the tea market.

The tea bag is placed in boiling or almost boiling water and remains in contact with the water until the desired strength is achieved, after which it is removed. Many foodservice establishments serve those who order tea with a pot of hot water and the tea bags on the side.

Steeping. To steep tea, the measured tea is placed in a preheated pot, and boiling water is poured into the pot. The pot is then covered and allowed to stand in a warm place until the desired strength is obtained. Steeping periods usually range from 2 to 4 minutes, depending on the temperature and the strength desired. If the maximum quantity of tea is used, 4 minutes may produce a somewhat bitter beverage.

Iced Tea. Iced tea, a favorite drink in the United States, is best made from a larger proportion of tea to water than is normally used for hot tea, because melting ice dilutes the beverage. Lengthy steeping to brew a beverage strong enough to stand dilution extracts too many polyphenol substances. It is believed that a cloudy beverage may result from a complex formed between caffeine and some of the polyphenol substances. This complex may form more readily in iced tea than in hot tea. Its formation is encouraged when larger amounts of polyphenol substances are present. Diluting strong infusions while they are hot helps to prevent cloudiness.

Tea is lightened by the addition of lemon because the oxidized polyphenolic compounds change color in an acid medium. These substances tend to be dark in an alkaline medium.

For sweetening iced tea with sugar, an extrafine granulation that is quickly soluble is desirable. If mint flavor is desired in iced tea, the mint leaves can be crushed and added to the tea leaves before the boiling water is added, or a sprig of mint can be served in the glass of iced tea.

In addition to regular, decaffeinated, sweetened, and low-calorie instant iced tea mixes, bottled iced tea drinks with a variety of flavors also are marketed. Commercial iced tea drinks may contain water, high fructose corn syrup, tea, citric acid, and flavoring.

Iced tea dispensers may be used in foodservice establishments. Care should be taken to dismantle, clean, and sanitize these dispensers at least once a day, as is recommended by the FDA, to avoid microbial buildup in the tubing connections.

COCOA AND CHOCOLATE

The cacao tree (*Theobroma cacao*) requires very exacting growing conditions and is cultivated only in an area within 20 degrees of the equator. Much of the world cacao crop now comes from West Africa; however, cocoa originated in Latin America, where Brazil and Ecuador are still large producers.

The cultivated cacao tree is deliberately kept pruned to a height of about 19 feet (6 meters) so that the fruits can be harvested with a long stick. The fruits grow directly on the stem or thick branches of the tree. Full-grown fruits are about 8 inches (20 centimeters) long and 4 inches (10 centimeters) across in an oblong shape. Botanically, the leathery fruits are giant berries. Each berry, or pod, contains 30 to 40 seeds or beans occurring in rows and embedded in a white or pinkish pulp (Figure 28-8).

(a)   (b)

Figure 28-8
(a) Cocoa pods have a hard semiwoody shell. One pod carries anywhere from 20 to 50 beans. (b) Cocoa beans ready for export. (Courtesy of Chocolate Manufacturers Association)

Processing

Cocoa and chocolate are made by grinding the seeds of the cacao tree. To decrease the bitter taste, the seeds are first fermented. The ripe pods are cut from the tree and chopped open. The seeds, surrounded by the gelatinous pulp, are piled into large heaps or put into special boxes and covered with a layer of leaves. Fermentation then begins; the fruit pulp is digested as the temperature rises. This process is completed within 5 to 7 days; the cocoa flavor has begun to develop. The bean has become dark brown and its shell thinner. Now the beans can be dried easily, preferably outdoors in the sun. After they are dried, the beans are bagged and shipped to the cocoa processor.

There are many varieties of cacao beans, and the great variation in flavor, color, and other characteristics that exists in cocoa and chocolate products is explained, to a large extent, by the characteristics of the various seeds used to make these products. Usually, there is some blending of the beans of different varieties.

The processor cleans the beans and removes impurities and irregularities; the beans are then roasted to further develop flavor characteristics. The beans next go to a winnowing machine, which cracks them and separates the shell from the bean. The cracked kernels are called *nibs*. The nibs go to grinders and various mills that reduce the particle sizes so that they cannot be detected on the tongue. Heat from this process melts the fat, converting the nibs into a suspension of cocoa solids in cocoa butter called *chocolate liquor* [10].

For the making of cocoa, the liquid mass is pumped into presses from which much of the cocoa butter is squeezed out under high pressure. The remaining solids are formed into a cocoa cake, which is further processed. Eventually it is broken up to form a powder.

Cocoas may be divided into two main classes: natural processed and Dutch processed. Some chocolate is also Dutch processed. Dutch processing consists of treating the nibs with alkali, the object being to increase the reddish color and the solubility. The latter effect is accomplished only to a slight degree.

Dutch-processed cocoa is distinctly darker than natural-processed cocoa. It also has a reddish tinge. The characteristic chocolate flavor is changed by the alkali treatment. The pH of Dutch-processed cocoa is 6.0 to 8.8, and that of natural-processed cocoa is usually 5.2 to 6.0. The color of such products as chocolate cake may range from cinnamon brown to deep mahogany red as the pH changes from acid to alkaline (see Chapter 18).

If chocolate is to be produced from the roasted nibs, the ground liquid mass is refined to a smooth, velvety texture and then subjected to a process called *conching*. This process involves heating the liquid chocolate at a carefully controlled temperature while constantly stirring. The mixture is aerated, some volatile acids and moisture are driven off, and flavor is developed. Additional cocoa butter, emulsifiers, sugar, milk solids, and flavorings may be added at this stage before the liquid mass is molded. Chocolate must be carefully tempered at a controlled temperature while it cools to ensure that a desirable texture results from the proper type of crystallization of the fat in the finished product.

Chocolate liquor can be solidified without the addition of sugar to form unsweetened chocolate, mixed with sugar and fat to produce sweet chocolate, or processed with sugar and milk to produce milk chocolate.

Several instant cocoa mixtures are on the market. They contain sugar, flavorings, emulsifiers, and sometimes nonfat dry milk. The beverage is made simply by adding the dry mixture to hot or cold milk, or to water if nonfat milk or whey is an ingredient in the dry mix. Instant cocoa mixes sweetened with aspartame and/or saccharin are also produced for the low-calorie market.

Composition

Fat. According to the FDA standard of identity, bitter chocolate contains not less than 50 percent and not more than 58 percent by weight of cocoa fat or cocoa butter. The high fat content of chocolate produces a beverage richer than that made from cocoa. Cocoas vary in fat content. Breakfast cocoa is a relatively high-fat cocoa and must contain at least 22 percent cocoa fat.

When cocoa is substituted for chocolate, particularly in baked products, approximately 3 tablespoons of cocoa plus 1 tablespoon of fat are considered to be equivalent to 1 ounce of chocolate.

The fat of chocolate contributes much to its eating quality because it has a sharp melting point that is close to body temperature. This results in rapid melting of the chocolate in the mouth with a smooth, velvety feel and the release of flavor substances.

Starch. Cocoa contains about 11 percent starch and chocolate about 8 percent starch. In preparing a beverage from cocoa and chocolate, a method that cooks the starch results in a more homogeneous beverage in which there is less tendency for the cocoa or chocolate to settle out than a method in which no heat is applied.

The thickening effect of starch must be taken into account when cocoa and chocolate are used in flour mixtures, and the amount of flour must be adjusted accordingly. If cocoa is substituted for chocolate directly, on the basis of weight, it thickens more than chocolate.

Flavor and Color. Chocolate, like many foods, contains a large number of flavor molecules; many have not been chemically identified. Volatile compounds make up a large part of the flavor bouquet. Marked changes in the flavor of chocolate and cocoa occur when these products are heated to high temperatures, especially in the absence of water. Bitter, disagreeable flavors develop, and scorching occurs easily.

Both flavor and color are affected by the phenolic compounds present in the cocoa bean. These substances undergo oxidation to form various reddish-brown compounds that are insoluble in water. Some of the astringent phenolic compounds in the fresh unfermented bean have an extremely bitter taste. These undergo a change during fermentation, but are present to a small extent in the fermented bean.

Theobromine and Caffeine.   Considerably more theobromine than caffeine is found in cocoa and chocolate. Both substances are methylxanthines, but theobromine is a milder stimulant than caffeine. The theobromine and caffeine contents of various foods containing cocoa or chocolate are listed in Table 28-2.

NUTRITIVE VALUE OF CHOCOLATE BEVERAGES

Because cocoa and chocolate beverages are usually made with milk, they have a food value similar to milk in proportion to the amount of milk used. Unlike tea leaves and coffee grounds, which are strained from the beverages, cocoa and chocolate remain in the beverage, thus adding fat and starch to the milk and increasing the caloric value.

BLOOM

A grayish-white haze called *bloom* may sometimes develop on the surface of chocolate. Preventing bloom is an important consideration for both manufacturers and retailers of chocolate. There are two types of bloom. One type arises from changes in the fat crystals with an accumulation of large fat crystals or agglomerates of fat crystals on the surface of the chocolate. These reflect light, creating the appearance that is called bloom. Another type of bloom results from the action of moisture on the sugar ingredients in the chocolate [27].

Bloom may occur for a variety of reasons, including incorrect cooling methods, warm or fluctuating storage temperatures, the addition of fats that are incompatible with cocoa butter, and abrasion or finger marking, particularly under warm conditions. The use of proper tempering temperatures and time

Table 28-2
Theobromine and Caffeine Content of Cocoa Products

	Theobromine (mg/serving)	Caffeine (mg/serving)
Dark sweet chocolate, 1 oz	123.5	15.1
Milk chocolate, 1 oz	38.1	5.4
Chocolate fudge topping, 2 Tbsp	62.7	3.5
Brownies, 1 oz	29.4	2.8
Chocolate chip cookies, one serving	17.6	2.1
Chocolate cake with chocolate frosting, 1/12 cake	161.2	15.8
Chocolate pudding, 1/2 cup	87.5	7.0

Source: Reference 8.

periods during the manufacturing process and the use of emulsifiers and modifiers retard bloom formation.

STORAGE

The avoidance of high storage temperatures is essential in maintaining the quality of chocolate and avoiding the development of bloom. Moisture is also detrimental and encourages lumping in cocoas. Both chocolate and cocoa are best stored at a temperature no higher than 65° to 70°F (18° to 21°C) and 50 to 65 percent relative humidity. The mouthfeel of solid sweetened chocolate may be granular when bloom develops. Milk chocolate absorbs flavors and odors and should be stored where this cannot occur.

Melting Chocolate

When chocolate is melted, care must be used to avoid overheating, which may produce a firm, lumpy mass that does not blend with other ingredients. A low to moderate temperature should be applied to chocolate that has been shaved or chopped into pieces. Heating the chocolate over hot water lessens the danger of overheating. However, care should be taken to avoid getting water into the melting chocolate as it can cause it to seize (suddenly harden), thereby becoming stiff rather than smooth throughout. Chocolate can also be easily melted in the microwave oven. The use of chocolate in coating confections is discussed in Chapter 11.

Methods for Making Cocoa Beverage

The quick method, in which hot liquid is poured over a cocoa-sugar mixture in the cup, does not cook the starch sufficiently to prevent the cocoa from settling out. Preparation of the beverage by either a syrup or a paste method produces more desirable body and flavor than usually results from the quick method. With instant cocoa mixes, the addition of a stabilizer or emulsifier may help keep the particles dispersed.

Syrup Method

Cocoa	Chocolate
2 tsp to 1 Tbsp cocoa	1/3 oz chocolate, shaved fine
2 tsp to 1 Tbsp sugar	1 to 1 1/2 Tbsp sugar
1/4 cup water	1/3 cup water

Make a syrup by boiling the ingredients in either of these two lists for 1 minute. Evaporation reduces the volume. Add 3/4 cup hot milk. The syrup can be made in quantity and stored in the refrigerator.

Paste Method

1/2 Tbsp corn starch	1 oz chocolate (or 3 Tbsp cocoa)
1/3 cup water	2 Tbsp sugar

Boil for 1 or 2 minutes. Combine with 2 cups hot milk. The purpose of the cornstarch is to produce a beverage with more body and to most satisfactorily prevent any tendency of the cocoa to settle. Because milk is a prominent constituent of cocoa or chocolate beverages, scum formation may occur. It can be retarded by covering the pan or by beating the mixture to produce a light foam. High temperatures, which may scorch both milk and chocolate, should be avoided (see Chapter 23).

CHAPTER SUMMARY

- A wide variety of commercially produced beverages is on the market. Bottled water has increased in consumer popularity in recent years. Carbonated soft drinks are the most widely consumed beverage in the United States.

- Sparkling water beverages contain carbon dioxide, a low level of sweetener, and flavoring. Club soda is carbonated water with sodium bicarbonate and potassium carbonate added. Seltzer is simply carbonated water; however, seltzers also may be sold with sweetener and flavoring ingredients added.

- Sports drinks are designed to prevent dehydration during vigorous exercise and to give a quick energy burst. Sweeteners and electrolytes are added to these beverages.

- Fruit beverages contain fruit or juice (1.5 to 70 percent) and water, as well as sweeteners, flavoring, coloring, and preservatives. These are not fruit juices, although fruit may be a predominant ingredient. Fruit beverages are pasteurized and may have added preservatives. Fruit smoothies are a frozen blended beverage composed of fruit, fruit juices, yogurt, or other dairy ingredients.

- Wine may be an accompaniment with a meal or an ingredient in a dish. The process of making wine involves the chemistry of fermentation. In the process of fermentation, yeast acts on sugar, converting it into alcohol and carbon dioxide gas.

- *Coffea arabica* and *Coffea robusta* are two comon coffee plants. Arabica is grown chiefly in Central and South America and has a fine full flavor and aroma. Robusta is best suited to low elevations. It is grown in Africa and is not as flavorful or acidic as compared to arabica.

- In the preparation of coffee beans for market, the cherries are dried either by machine or in the sun. Cleaned beans are light-green or blue-green in color. Beans are roasted to develop flavor and aroma. Coffee roasts are classified according to the color of the roasted bean.

- The consitutents of coffee that are of significance in the making of the beverage include acids, volatile substances, bitter substances, and caffeine. Decaffeinated coffee may be prepared through extraction processes employing (1) water, (2) steam, (3) carbon dioxide, (4) ethyl acetate, (5) methylene chloride, or (6) coffee oils.

- Instant coffee is composed of dry, powdered, water-soluble solids produced by dehydrating very strong, brewed coffee.

- A number of specialty coffee beverages including espresso, cappuccino, and others have become popular with the American public.

- Freshness is an important factor affecting the quality of the coffee beverage. Ground coffee becomes flat more rapidly than coffee in the bean. Vacuum packaging protects coffee freshness.

- Coffee may be ground to differing degrees of fineness. Consistency in the grind is important in maintaining quality.

- Coffee may be brewed using filtration, percolation, or steeping methods. The temperature of the water should be at least 185°F (85°C). Boiling produces a distinctly bitter beverage. The use of 1 1/3 to 1/2 tablespoons of coffee per cup of water gives a medium-strength brew.

- Pots made of glass, earthenware, enamelware, or stainless steel are good choices for coffee pots. A clean coffee pot is essential to avoid stale coffee odor and flavor.

- Soft water, or water of low hardness, gives coffee a more desirable flavor than very hard or alkaline water. However, water that has passed through an ion-exchange softening system is less desirable as compared to naturally soft water.

- Tea comes from the plant *Camellia sinensis*. Three principal types of tea, differentiated by the method of leaf processing, are black, green, and oolong. Black tea is fermented, oolong is partially fermentated, whereas green tea is steamed, rolled, and dried without fermentation.

- The flavor of tea is influenced by polyphenolic substances. In the manufacture of black tea, the degradation of linolenic acid, amino acids, and carotenes may also contribute to flavor and aroma.

- Tea is marketed in many forms, including tea bags, scented and flavored, decaffeinated, instant, or as loose leaf. Herbal teas contain leaves of various plants other than tea.

- Soft water is preferable to hard alkaline water for making tea. Water should be freshly boiled. Glass, earthenware, enamelware or other vitrified ware is recommended to avoid metallic tastes from metallic pots. The usual proportion of tea per cup of water is about 1 teaspoon.

- Iced tea is best made from a larger proportion of tea to water than is used for hot tea to allow for dilution from melting ice. A cloudy beverage may result from a complex formed between caffeine and some of the polyphenol substances. Diluting strong infusions while they are hot helps to prevent cloudiness.

- The cacao tree (*Theobroma cacao*) requires very exact growing conditions. It is cultivated in an area within 20 degrees of the equator.

- Cocoa and chocolate are made by grinding the seeds of the cacao tree. The seeds are fermented, then the beans are dried. Processors clean the beans and then roast further to develop the flavor. The beans are then cracked to separate the shell from the bean. The cracked kernels are called nibs. The nibs are then ground. Heat in this process converts the nibs into a suspension of cocoa solids in cocoa butter called chocolate liquor. To make cocoa, the liquid mass is pumped into presses producing cocoa butter and cocoa cake. The cocoa cake is further processed into cocoa. Cocoa may be divided into two classes: natural processed and Dutch processed.

- If chocolate is produced from the nibs, the ground liquid mass is refined into a smooth, velvety texture and subjected to a process called conching. Additional cocoa butter, emulsifiers, sugar, milk solids, and flavoring may be added at this stage.

- FDA standards of identity specify the percent of cocoa fat or cocoa butter by weight for types of chocolate such as bitter chocolate.

- When cocoa is substituted for chocolate, approximately 3 tablespoons of cocoa plus 1 tablespoon of fat are equivalent to 1 ounce of chocolate.

- Cocoa contains about 11 percent starch and chocolate about 8 percent starch. In the preparation of beverages from chocolate, or when baking, the starch content should be considered.

- Volatile compounds make up a large part of the flavor bouquet. Heating to high temperatures, especially in the absence of water, will result in bitter, disagreeable flavors.

- Theobromine, a milder stimulant than caffeine, is found in cocoa and chocolate. Small quantitites of caffeine also are present in cocoa and chocolate.

- Bloom may develop on the surface of chocolate as a result of incorrect cooling temperatures, warm or fluctuating cooling temperatures, the addition of incompatible fats, and abrasion or finger marking.

- The avoidance of high storage temperatures is essential in maintaining the quality of chocolate and avoiding the development of bloom. The mouth-feel of solid sweetened chocolate may be granular when bloom develops.

- Overheating should be avoided when melting chocolate to prevent the development of a firm, lumpy mass that does not blend well with other ingredients.

- A syrup or paste method may be used in the preparation of hot cocoa beverages.

KEY TERMS

functional foods	pectic enzymes
guarana	chlorogenic acid
spring water	phenolic compound
mineral water	polyphenol
purified water	hygroscopic
aspartame	chicory
pH	astringency
fermentation	oxidation
pasteurization	linolenic acid
aseptic	carotenes

STUDY QUESTIONS

1. **a.** Describe trends in beverage consumption in the United States.
   b. How are carbonated soft drinks usually processed?
   c. What roles do sports drinks play in the beverage market?
   d. How do fruit drinks differ from fruit juices?
   e. How is wine produced?

2. From what is coffee made and how is it processed to make it ready for use in preparing a beverage?

3. List the constituents of coffee that contribute to its quality as a beverage and describe the contributions each constituent makes.

4. Describe conditions that will aid in preserving freshness in coffee, both in the bean and in the ground.

5. **a.** Describe three methods for preparing coffee.
   b. What types of material are preferable for coffee pots?
   c. How does the type of water used affect coffee quality?
   d. Why should coffee not be boiled? Explain.

    e. How is instant coffee produced?

6. Describe differences in processing and characteristics of black, green, and oolong teas.

7. a. Describe two appropriate procedures for the preparation of tea.

    b. Discuss several factors that are important in the preparation of tea and of iced tea of good quality.

    c. What cautions should be kept in mind when using various herbal teas?

8. What is the source of chocolate and cocoa and how are they processed?

9. a. How do natural-processed and dutch-processed cocoa differ?

    b. How do chocolate and breakfast cocoa differ in fat and in starch content?

    c. How might cocoa be appropriately substituted for chocolate in a recipe?

10. Describe *bloom* on chocolate and give possible explanations for its development.

11. How should chocolate and cocoa be stored and why?

12. Suggest a satisfactory method for preparing cocoa beverage and explain why this is a good method.

REFERENCES

1. ACNielsen. (2002, May). What's hot around the globe: Insights on growth in food and beverages. Executive News Report from ACNielson Global Services.

2. Adinolfi, J. (1981). How long is coffee's shelf life? *Food Technology, 35*(6), 42.

3. Anonymous. (1997). The making of water. *Food Testing and Analysis, 3*(2), 25.

4. Bullers, A. C. (2002). Bottled water: Better than tap? *FDA Consumer Magazine, 36*(4).

5. Bunker, M. L., & McWilliams, M. (1979). Caffeine content of common beverages. *Journal of the American Dietetic Association, 74,* 28.

6. Chen, T., Lui, C. K. F., & Smith, C. H. (1983). Folacin content of tea. *Journal of the American Dietetic Association, 82,* 627.

7. Coleman, E. (1991). Sports drink research. *Food Technology, 45*(3), 104.

8. Craig, W. J., & Nguyen, T. T. (1984). Caffeine and theobromine levels in cocoa and carob products. *Journal of Food Science, 49,* 302.

9. Disler, P. B., Lynch, S. R., Charlton, R. W., Torrance, J. D., and Bothwell, T. H. (1975). The effect of tea on iron absorption. *Gut, 16,* 193.

10. Dziezak, J. S. (1989). Ingredients for sweet success. *Food Technology, 43*(10), 94.

11. Giese, J. (1995). Developments in beverage additives. *Food Technology, 49*(9), 64.

12. Giese, J. H. (1992). Hitting the spot: Beverages and beverage technology. *Food Technology, 46*(7), 70.

13. Grand, A. N., & Bell, L. N. (1997). Caffeine content of fountain and private-label store brand carbonated beverages. *Journal of the American Dietetic Association, 97,* 179.

14. Hollingsworth, P. (1993). Clear conscience. *Food Technology, 47*(5), 44.

15. Hollingsworth, P. (1997). Beverages: Redefining New Age. *Food Technology, 51*(8), 44.

16. Hollingsworth, P. (2000). Functional beverage juggernaut faces tighter regulations. *Food Technology, 54*(11), 50–54.

17. Hollingsworth, P. (2002). Burgers or biscotti? The fast-food market is changing. *Food Technology, 56*(9), 20.

18. Hollingsworth, P. (2002). It's tea time. *Food Technology, 56*(7), 16.

19. Hollingsworth, P. (2002). Profits pouring from bottled water. *Food Technology, 56*(5), 18.

20. Hughes, W. J., & Thorpe, T. M. (1987). Determination of organic acids and sucrose in roasted coffee by capillary gas chromatography. *Journal of Food Science, 52,* 1078.

21. Institute of Food Technologists' Expert Panel on Food Safety and Nutrition. (1987). Evaluation of caffeine safety. *Food Technology, 41*(6), 105.

22. Kinsella, J. E., Frankel, E., German, B., & Kanner, J. (1993). Possible mechanisms for the protective role of antioxidants in wine and plant foods. *Food Technology, 47*(4), 85.

23. Kolpan, S., Smith, B. H., & Weiss, M. A. (2002). *Exploring wine: The Culinary Institute of America's complete guide to the wines of the world* (2nd ed.). New York: John Wiley & Sons, Inc.

24. Kurtzweil, P. (1997). Dieter's brews make tea time a dangerous affair. *FDA Consumer, 31*(5), 6.

25. Labensky, S. R. & Hause, A. M. (2003). *On cooking: A textbook of culinary fundamentals* (3rd ed.). Upper Saddle River, NJ: Prentice Hall.

26. Neff, J. (1997). Wining and dining. *Food Processing, 58*(3), 55.

27. Pszczola, D. E. (1997). The bloom is off the chocolate. *Food Technology, 51*(3), 28.

28. Pszczola, D.E. (1999). Sipping into the mainstream. *Food Technology, 53*(11), 78–92.

29. Pszczola, D.E. (2001). How ingredients help solve beverage problems. *Food Technology, 55*(10), 61–74.

30. Putnam, J. J. (1991). Food consumption, 1970–90. *Food Review, 14*(3), 2.

31. Putnam, J. J. & Allshouse, J. E. (1999). Food consumption, prices, and expenditures, 1970–97. Food and Rural Economics Division, Economic Research, U.S. Department of Agriculture. Statistical Bulletin No. 965.

32. Sakano, T., Yamamura, K., Tamon, H., Miyahara, M., & Okazaki, M. (1996). Improvement of coffee aroma by removal of pungent volatiles using A-type zeolite. *Journal of Food Science, 61,* 473.

33. Schenker, S., Heinemann, C., Huber, M., Pompizzi, R., Perren, R., & Escher, F. (2002). Impact of roasting conditions on the formation of aroma compounds in coffee beans. *Journal of Food Science, 67,* 60–66.

34. Segal, M. (1996). Tea, a story of serendipity. *FDA Consumer, 30*(2), 22.

35. Segall, S., Silver, C., & Bacino, S. (1970). The effect of reheating upon the organoleptic and analytical properties of beverage coffee. *Food Technology, 24*(11), 54.

36. Sivetz, M. (1972). How acidity affects coffee flavor. *Food Technology, 26*(5), 70.

Food Preservation and Packaging

29

Food preservation has been practiced for thousands of years, but marked changes have occurred in the processes applied as civilization has developed and technology increased. In early historic times, people learned to dry their supplies of fresh meat and fish in the sun and to store food for the cold winter months. Later they discovered how to smoke and salt these products to extend the time that the foods remained edible.

In the early years of American history, particularly on the frontiers, a precise schedule of work was necessary to harvest crops of fruits, vegetables, and grains at just the right time. Much labor was expended in preserving excesses of these crops, often in root cellars and granaries, for later use when nothing could be grown. When animals were slaughtered, they had to be processed quickly. To decrease the likelihood of rapid spoilage, the processing was usually done in cool weather. Canning had not yet been discovered in the very early days of America—that came later, beginning in France about 1810. During these early periods, much time was required by members of a household, particularly the housewife, for preparing and preserving food.

Today is very different from the early days in America, but is continually changing. The basic food preservation methods used in previous years are still utilized. Added to them, however, is a whole arsenal of technology for ensuring the availability of a large variety of high-quality foods throughout the year. The future is likely to bring the development of new nonthermal preservation methods that use such technologies as pulsed electric field and ultra-high-pressure processing [34, 35, 38]. Ultra-high-pressure processing is in use for the pasteurization of guacamole, meats, and seafood, but research continues into high-pressure sterilization [39, 47] Combinations of different preservation processes or techniques also may be used to obtain stable, nutritious, and tasty foods that are mildly but reliably preserved for short-term storage.

Much of the processing and initial treatment for the preservation of foods in Western countries is done by the food industry. Consumers, as well as food-service managers, are becoming very used to purchasing canned, frozen, fermented, dried, portioned, and packaged foods for only short-term storage in their kitchens. The freezer and the microwave oven form a duo that is widely used for the final storage and then rapid heating of the processed and preserved foods that are purchased.

Despite these trends in commercial preservation and packaging of foods, there are still many places in America, particularly in rural areas and smaller

801

towns, where home gardens are popular and the excess produce is canned, frozen, or dried for future use. Thus, a brief discussion of home canning and freezing techniques is provided in Chapter 30. In this chapter, some other developed techniques for food preservation and packaging are described. The basic causes of food spoilage and general methods of food preservation are also discussed.

CAUSES OF FOOD SPOILAGE

When foods spoil, they become inedible or hazardous to eat because of chemical and physical changes that occur within the food. The two major causes of food spoilage are the growth of microorganisms, including bacteria, yeasts, and molds, and the action of **enzymes** that occur naturally in the food. Additional causes of food spoilage are nonenzymatic reactions such as oxidation and **desiccation**, mechanical damage such as bruising, and damage from insects and rodents.

    Although microorganisms can cause food spoilage, they also have important advantageous roles in food preservation and processing. For example, certain cheeses, such as Roquefort and Camembert, are ripened by molds; other cheeses are ripened by bacteria. Production of some Oriental foods, including soy sauce, requires fermentation by molds. Yeast is an essential ingredient in bread and many other baked products. The brewing industry also relies on yeast. Buttermilk, yogurt, sauerkraut, and fermented pickles owe their special desirable flavors to bacterial action. (Some basic characteristics of molds, yeasts, and bacteria are described in Chapter 3.)

    Enzymes are present in any food that has been living tissue, such as meat, fish, fruits, and vegetables. They are also present in milk and eggs. Unless undesirable enzyme action is controlled or the enzymes are destroyed (often by heating), they may be responsible for unwanted chemical changes in preserved foods. (General characteristics of enzymes are discussed in Chapter 9.)

    Proper packaging of food plays an important role in controlling food spoilage resulting from desiccation, bruising, and damage by insects and rodents. Oxidation of fats may also be retarded to some degree by appropriate packaging, as well as by the control of environmental conditions and the addition of antioxidants. Biodegradable polymer films offer alternative packaging without the environmental problems produced by plastic packaging [30].

    Edible films or coatings, composed of lipids, resins, polysaccharides, proteins, or combinations of these substances, are used on a variety of food products. On fresh fruits and vegetables, for example, they act as moisture barriers, as barriers for oxygen and carbon dioxide to control respiration in the tissues, or to control postharvest decay [1, 30]. They may be used as vehicles for incorporating antioxidants onto the surface of foods such as nuts and to prevent clumping and sticking in dried raisins [19]. New technologies are bringing dramatic changes to the world of food packaging, some of which are discussed later in this chapter.

GENERAL METHODS OF FOOD PRESERVATION

All methods used for preserving foods are based on the general principle of preventing or retarding the causes of spoilage—microbial decomposition, enzymatic and nonenzymatic chemical reactions, and damage from mechanical

enzymes protein molecules produced by living cells that act as organic catalysts and change the rate of a reaction without being used up in the process

desiccation the process of drying as moisture is lost

causes, insects, and rodents. When the growth of microorganisms is only retarded or inhibited, preservation is temporary. When spoilage organisms are completely destroyed and the food is protected so that no other microorganisms are permitted to reinfect it, more permanent preservation is achieved.

No method of food preservation improves the original quality of a food product. If a preserved food is to be of satisfactory quality, then the starting material must be fresh, flavorful produce at an optimal stage of ripeness or maturity.

Preservation by Temperature Control

Either cold or hot temperatures can be used to preserve foods. Cold temperatures produce an environment unfavorable to microbial growth, whereas sufficiently high temperatures destroy spoilage agents.

Cold Temperatures.   Cold temperatures mainly inhibit the growth of microorganisms, although some destruction of microbial cells occurs at very low temperatures. With chilling, the length of time that the food remains wholesome varies with the temperature employed and with the type of food being chilled. It also depends on the type of packaging, including modified-atmosphere packaging and vacuum cooking–packaging, which extend the effective period of refrigerated storage for food. Refrigerated foods with extended shelf life have generally received precooking or minimal processing and include such items as meat, seafood, egg, and vegetable salads; fresh pasta and pasta sauces; soups; and entrees, as well as precut fruits and vegetables. The chief microbiological concern for these products is the growth of **psychrotropic** and **mesophilic** pathogens that might occur during extended refrigerated storage or temperature abuse [33].

> **psychrotropic microorganisms**
> organisms that can grow at refrigerator temperatures
>
> **mesophilic microorganisms**
> organisms that grow at moderate temperatures

In most refrigerators, maintenance of a temperature of 41° (5°C), or slightly lower, preserves many foods for only a few days. In cold-storage warehouses, the time is increased. Here the temperature is lower and the humidity is controlled, both conditions favoring preservation. Control and monitoring of gases in the atmosphere of the cold-storage facility (controlled-atmosphere storage) are also used in some cases to retard ripening or maturation changes that decrease the storage life of fresh produce. Apples are often stored in controlled atmosphere storage to maintain quality for extended periods after harvest.

Freezing can preserve foods for long, but not indefinite, periods of time provided that the quality of the food is initially good and the temperature of storage is well below the actual freezing temperature of the food. For the highest retention of both flavor and nutritive value in frozen foods, the freezer should be maintained at no higher than 0°F (−18°C) [25]. Care must be exercised in the marketing of frozen foods to ensure that they are held at freezing temperatures at all times as they move through the various market channels to the consumer.

The action of enzymes already present in the tissues is retarded at freezing temperatures. In certain products such as vegetables, however, enzyme action may still produce undesirable effects on flavor and texture during freezer storage. The enzymes, therefore, must be destroyed by heating the vegetables in hot water or steam, a process called *blanching*, before they are frozen. The market for refrigerated and frozen foods is large. The success of the microwave oven and its penetration into the majority of American homes have stimulated this market, particularly in the area of ready-to-eat foods.

spore an encapsulated, resistant form of a microorganism

botulism a disease resulting from consumption of a deadly toxin produced by the anaerobic bacterium *Clostridium botulinum*

retort pressure canning equipment used in commercial canning operations to process low-acid foods at high temperatures

pasteurization a mild heat treatment that destroys many, but not all, vegetative microorganisms

sterilization the complete destruction of microorganisms in a medium

Thermal Processing. Hot temperatures preserve by destroying both microorganisms and enzymes. Yeasts, molds, and enzymes are readily destroyed at the boiling temperature of water. The heating must be maintained long enough to permit all parts of the food to reach the necessary temperature, however. Heat penetration is sometimes slow in such foods as partially ripe pears or peaches. Bacteria are less readily destroyed than yeasts, molds, and enzymes, the vegetative or active cells being more readily destroyed than **spore** forms. Many bacterial spores, including spores of *Clostridium botulinum*, are highly resistant to heat, especially in a low-acid environment. Care must be exercised in the heat processing of canned food to ensure destruction of bacterial spores. The leading cause of **botulism** in the United States is the consumption of inadequately processed home canned foods, usually low-acid vegetables or meats. *Clostridium botulinum* also may be found in home-prepared garlic-seasoned oils that have been improperly handled.

Canning as a method of food preservation involves essentially the complete destruction of microorganisms and their spores, as well as enzymes, by the use of high temperatures, followed by sealing of the container to prevent recontamination of the food (Figure 29-1). The food in this case is essentially sterilized.

Retort pouches or packages have been developed as flexible packaging for thermoprocessed foods. Lightweight pouches that have a relatively thin cross section when filled with food improve the quality of sterilized packaged food because of the decreased time required for complete heat penetration. Energy savings also result. The weight of the packages is much less than that of metal cans and lids. The ease of transporting is thus increased, but the expense is decreased [52]. Tuna in retort packaging made its debut in 2000 [9]. Chapter 2 discusses the use of retort packaged foods in military rations.

Pasteurization of food products involves the use of temperatures lower than those required for **sterilization**. Foods that are often pasteurized include milk, fruit juices, and eggs that are to be frozen or dried. All pathogenic microorganisms, but not all other microorganisms present, are destroyed by pas-

Figure 29-1
Bottled green beans are sealed so that recontamination by microorganisms cannot occur. (Courtesy of the Ball Brothers Company)

teurization, which results in a more limited or temporary preservation period than sterilization and canning.

Preservation by Moisture Control

Drying.   One of the oldest methods of preserving foods involves the removal of moisture until the product is dry. As practically applied, the food is dried in the sun or by air currents and artificial heat until the moisture content of the food is reduced to a level that inhibits the growth of microorganisms. The actual percentage of moisture varies, but is usually under 30 percent. Some dehydrated foods such as dried potato slices contain only 2 to 3 percent moisture. Many commercially dried fruits with an intermediate moisture content, about 15 to 35 or 40 percent, have water activity low enough for preservation yet are pleasant to eat directly without rehydration [18]. Osmotic drying is used in some commercial products such as *craisins*. In osmotic drying, a strong syrup is used to draw water from the food and then the food is finish-dried with air [11].

Some foods can be easily dried at home, including most garden vegetables, fruits, and garden herbs such as parsley and oregano. Drying can be done in driers especially designed for this purpose, in the oven, or, in sunny climates, in trays placed in the sun. Vegetables, with few exceptions, should be **blanched** before drying to stop the action of enzymes that produce undesirable changes in texture and flavor during storage. Dried vegetables that have been blanched also dry more easily and retain more vitamins. Light-colored fruits, such as apples, apricots, and peaches, are of better quality when they are sulfured before drying to prevent darkening as a result of the action of oxidizing enzymes. This process involves exposing the fruit to the fumes of burning sulfur or, alternatively, dipping in a weak bisulfite solution.

blanch to immerse in hot water or steam for a short time and then cool quickly in cold water

Freeze-Drying.   In the process of freeze-drying, the food product is first frozen, and then placed in a vacuum chamber to which a small amount of heat is applied. Under the reduced pressure of the vacuum, the ice in the frozen food changes directly to water vapor (sublimes) and is carried away by the circulating heated air. The moisture content of the food is thus reduced. The food remains frozen through most of the drying period; it does not get warm as does food that is subjected to ordinary drying processes. Fresh flavors and textures are therefore better preserved by freeze-drying than by sun-drying or other procedures of artificial drying without vacuum. It is also possible, on a commercial basis, to use microwaves rather than a conventional heat source in the freeze-drying process [51].

The time for freeze-drying depends on the product and its thickness, usually requiring 10 to 20 hours. The moisture content of the final product is 1 to 4 percent. Oxidation during freeze-drying is curbed by the low oxygen tension maintained and sometimes by the breaking of the vacuum with an inert gas rather than air.

By conventional drying methods, the satisfactory drying of meat is limited to ground or extremely thin strips. By freeze-drying, steaks and chops 1/2 to 1 inch thick can be processed. Roasts require a longer drying period, thus presenting cost and technical problems. The freeze-drying of food is a relatively expensive process.

Two advantages of freeze-dried foods, from a food industry perspective, are (1) transportation and storage costs are reduced (the weight of the dried product is about one-third that of the original food), and (2) refrigeration is not required. As an example of these advantages, Sir Edmund Hillary took 300 pounds of freeze-dried items on his Himalayan mountain-climbing expedition. The products reconstituted to 1,200 pounds and included ham, chicken, chops, steaks, fruits, and vegetables. Although refrigeration is not required, freeze-dried products do tend to deteriorate with long storage unless they are properly packaged.

Some fruits are successfully freeze-dried to 5 to 8 percent moisture levels. Apricots are light in color, hydrate rapidly, and have a fresh flavor. Some strawberries have been held for long periods without a change in flavor. The browning of fruits that are freeze-dried can be prevented by treatment with sulfur dioxide. Freeze-dried coffee, dried by both conventional and microwave methods, is marketed. Freeze-dried fish salad mixes are available for institutional use. A number of freeze-dried foods for individual use are sold in sporting goods outlets and are used by campers and hikers.

Freeze-dried meats are similar to fresh meats in flavor and color, but they may be somewhat tougher and drier. Tenderness is improved if the meat is hydrated in 2 percent brine or if proteolytic enzymes are added to the hydrating liquid.

Use of Preservatives

Adding chemical preservatives to a food product is another method of inhibiting the growth of undesirable microorganisms. Common preservatives, sometimes called *household preservatives*, include acids, salt, sugar, spices, and smoke. It is the phenols in wood smoke that seem to exert the major preservative action. Vinegar contains acetic acid and is commonly used, along with salt, to pickle vegetables (Figure 29-2). In pickle and sauerkraut fermentations, lactic and other organic acids are produced over time by friendly bacteria present on the vegetables. Not only does the acid prevent unwanted microbial growth, but additional flavor substances are produced by the desirable bacteria. Sugar in

Figure 29-2
A mixture of salt, vinegar, and water is poured over cucumbers and dill in the preparation of dill pickles.
(Courtesy of the U.S. Department of Agriculture)

Figure 29-3
A good-quality jelly is stiff enough to hold its shape yet is delicate and tender. The jelly is preserved by its content of approximately 65 percent sugar.

large amounts is used in the production of jellies, jams, and preserves (Figure 29-3). It acts as a preservative by binding the moisture necessary for microbial growth and activity.

Spices inhibit bacterial growth to some degree but vary in their effectiveness. Ground cinnamon and cloves are more valuable than nutmeg and allspice in quantities that can be used without marring flavor. However, spices themselves are often responsible for introducing bacteria into foods. Oils of spice are sterile and have a more inhibitory effect on microbial growth than ground spices.

Numerous preservatives are used as food additives and must be approved for use by the U.S. Food and Drug Administration (FDA). Thorough testing for safety is required before approval is given. (Food additives are discussed in Chapter 4.) Sodium benzoate, used in very small amounts in some margarines, and sodium propionate, used to retard molding in bread, are examples of preservatives that may be added to foods. An antioxidant is a special type of preservative that inhibits the spoilage of fats that may occur from a nonenzymatic oxidative process. The FDA has approved nisin, or *bacteriocin*, a polypeptide antibacterial substance, for use in some pasteurized cheese spreads. It is active only against gram-positive bacteria and is approved for use to inhibit the growth of *Clostridium botulinum* spores. The bacterium *Streptococcus lactis* produces this antibiotic [13, 20].

Preservation by Ionizing Radiation

Research on the application of ionizing radiation to food for the purpose of destroying pathogenic and other microorganisms began in the early 1950s. This technology was essentially ready to be commercialized within a few years; however, the passage of the Food Additives Amendment in 1958 delayed its implementation. This amendment classified sources of radiation as food additives and required pre-market review and acceptance by the FDA. This process has consumed many years and it was only in 1992 that the first irradiated foods were produced commercially in the United States [40]. Foods treated with ionizing radiation are commonly called *irradiated foods*.

Energy exists in the form of waves and is defined by its wavelength. Shorter wavelengths have higher energy. Ionizing radiation has high enough energy to change atoms in the irradiated food by removing an electron to form an **ion.**

ion an electrically charged atom or group of atoms; the electrical charge results when a neutral atom or group of atoms loses or gains one or more electrons; loss of electrons results in a positively charged ion

radioactive giving off radiant energy in the form of particles or rays, such as alpha, beta, and gamma rays, by the disintegration of atomic nuclei (the central part of atoms)

However, it does not have enough energy to split atoms in the food and cause it to become **radioactive**. The amount of radiation energy absorbed is measured in units of grays (or kilograys, meaning 1,000 grays, kGy). One gray equals 1 joule of absorbed energy per kilogram. In the past, the term *rad* was commonly used; it stands for *radiation absorbed dose*. One gray equals 100 rads. The sources of radiation allowed for food processing include cobalt-60 and cesium-137 as sources of gamma rays, accelerated electrons, and machine-generated X rays (see Figure 7-4 for the electromagnetic spectrum showing these rays in relation to visible light and microwaves). At the dosages allowed, the radiation cannot make food radioactive [14].

Irradiation of food serves many purposes. Low doses, less than 1 kilogray, inhibit sprouting of tubers, delay ripening of some fruits and vegetables, control insects in fruits and stored grains, and reduce the problems of parasites in products of animal origin. Medium doses, 1 to 10 kilograys, control pathogenic microorganisms responsible for foodborne illness and extend the shelf life of refrigerated foods. Doses greater than 10 kilograys are not used for foods other than spices and dried vegetable seasonings. High doses *could* be used to destroy all microorganisms without the effects on food produced by heat sterilization [14]; however, these dosages are not allowed at the present time except for frozen, packaged meat that is used solely in the National Aeronautics and Space Administration space flight programs. The irradiation of fresh or frozen poultry was approved by the FDA in 1990 and that of uncooked chilled or frozen meat, for the purpose of controlling pathogenic microorganisms such as salmonellae and *E. coli* O157:H7, was approved in December 1997 [40].

Table 29-1 lists food products that have been approved for irradiation by the FDA. Irradiated foods marketed for consumers must be labeled with an of-

Table 29-1
Food Irradiation in the United States

Product	Purpose of Irradiation	Dose Permitted (kGy)	Date of Rule
Wheat and wheat powder	Disinfestation of insects	0.2–0.5	8/21/63
White potatoes	Extend shelf life	0.05–0.15	11/1/65
Spices and dry vegetable seasoning	Decontamination or disinfestation of insects	30 (max.)	7/5/83
Dry or dehydrated enzyme preparations	Control of insects and microorganisms	10 (max.)	6/10/85
Pork carcasses or fresh noncut processed cuts	Control of *Trichinella spiralis*	0.3 (min.) 1.0 (max.)	7/22/85
Fresh fruits	Delay maturation	1	4/18/86
Dry or dehydrated aromatic vegetable substances	Decontamination	30	4/18/86
Poultry, fresh or frozen	Control of illness causing microorganisms such as *Salmonella*	3	5/2/90
Meat, frozen, packaged*	Sterilization	44 min.	3/8/95
Animal feed and pet food	*Salmonella* control	2–25	9/28/95
Meat, uncooked, chilled	Microbial control	4.5 max.	12/2/97
Meat, uncooked, frozen	Microbial control	7 max.	12/2/97

*For meats used solely in the National Aeronautics and Space Administration space flight programs.
Source: References 2, 40.

ficial logo (Figure 29-4) and the statement "treated with radiation" or "treated by irradiation." Consumer acceptance is important for commercial application of food irradiation. A few stores across the United States have successfully marketed irradiated foods [44]. Early studies of consumer acceptance have indicated that an education program is effective in increasing both consumers' knowledge and their positive attitude toward food irradiation [42, 45]. It is important for consumers to know that irradiation of food can effectively reduce or eliminate pathogens and spoilage microorganisms while maintaining wholesomeness and sensory quality [40, 32]. Major food companies such as poultry processors, meat packers, and grocery chains are beginning to offer irradiated meats more frequently because these products are more available due to the completion of an electron-beam plant [36]. However, hesitation remains since processors and retailers are unsure of consumer attitudes toward irradiated food [21].

Radiation preservation of food is considered to be a cold process because there is only a slight rise in the temperature of the food being irradiated. The dose of radiation that a food receives depends on the time of exposure to the source of radiation—often the man-made **radioisotope** cobalt-60, which generates **gamma rays**. Usually the cobalt-60 is contained in a lead-lined chamber and the food is conveyed into and out of the chamber on a moving belt. The speed of the conveyor belt determines the amount of exposure. The dose of radiation that a food receives must be sufficient to produce the desired effect but not enough to exceed legal limits [46]. When food is irradiated with electron beams, commercial electricity is used to accelerate electrons [36].

The irradiation of food does not generally cause major changes in flavor, texture, color, and composition, but some chemical reactions do occur in the food. The FDA must ensure that none of the compounds that may be produced are harmful. Some of the reactions in irradiated food are similar to those occurring in food when it is heated by conventional means [46]. Most of the research reported on irradiated foods indicates that nutrient retention in these foods is comparable to that of heat-processed foods [24].

Figure 29-4
An irradiated food on the retail market should bear the international symbol along with either of the statements "treated with radiation" or "treated by irradiation."

radioisotope an artificially created radioactive isotope of a chemical element that is normally nonradioactive

gamma rays one of three kinds of rays emitted by radioactive substances

PACKAGING OF FOOD

Major changes have occurred in food packaging over the past 20 or 30 years. Some trends in this area include packages that adapt to preserve desirable environments around fresh, chilled, or prepared foods in the supermarket; increased aseptic packaging; a wider variety of packaging materials from which to choose; and the movement for environmentally friendly packaging [43]. Innovations in food packaging, along with new food-processing technologies, have resulted in greater convenience for the consumer, less flavor loss during processing, and savings on materials and energy costs.

Functions of Food Packaging

The main function of a food package is to contain the food product, then to protect it from contamination and spoilage until it reaches the consumer. In addition, the food package also acts as a form of communication in its labeling function. In containing the food, it separates it into units of a particular size and weight, which allows ease in handling and convenience and serves as a marketing tool. Appropriate packaging minimizes reactions that affect the stability or the shelf life of the food products. Water vapor and oxygen are always present in the environment around foods and can affect the stability of packaged food products. The package may provide a barrier to these gases. It acts in some cases to keep moisture in the food and thus prevent desiccation or drying. In other cases, it prevents moisture from entering the package and being absorbed by the food. Certain packages control migration of atmospheric oxygen. The permeability of the package to light may also affect the stability of the food.

Packaging materials should be carefully chosen. As gases and moisture migrate into and out of the food, fatty acids may be rearranged and volatile flavor compounds changed, affecting total flavor impact [3]. Direct contact of food with packaging materials may also result in migration of volatile compounds from the package into the packaged food, possibly influencing flavor adversely. The loss of desirable content constituents in the plastic packaging is referred to as *scalping* [8]. Plastic materials such as polyethylene and polypropylene in particular have been implicated in flavor sorption into the plastic [8].

Deterioration from microbial decomposition depends on the presence of microorganisms in the food and on the environmental conditions conducive to their growth in the packaged product. Both temperature and moisture content can affect the microbes' potential for growth and activity. Proper packaging keeps microbial contamination at a minimum.

Food packaging may also allow energy and cost savings when the product is reheated and served in its original package. This is often of particular benefit in foodservice operations. The results of a survey of foodservice administrators revealed that many respondents perceived food-packaging information as being useful and beneficial in making decisions concerning food procurement [12].

The shelf life of packaged food products is affected by physical or mechanical factors. For example, damage to the package in shipping, insect infestation, and failure of the package seal may all affect food quality and stability.

Regulatory Requirements

The FDA considers the compatibility of food and its packaging to be a safety issue. The package is a potential source of chemical substances for the food product. Migration of substances from packaging materials does occur and cannot be completely eliminated; thus, the packaging materials are legally considered to be food additives and require premarket safety evaluation and approval by the FDA [26]. Testing is extensive and thorough to ensure safety.

Packaging Materials

thermoforming the application of heat in the formation of a product

aseptic packaging packaging a product that is free of microorganisms; product and package are sterilized separately before packaging

A variety of packaging materials are available for use with different food products (Figure 29-5). Plastics, manufactured by a number of **thermoforming** technologies, have taken over an increasingly larger share of the container market. The packaging industry is the largest user of plastics. Fewer glass and metal containers were utilized as plastics became more popular. Glass containers have made a comeback in recent years, however, being used for sliced peaches, pears, and mixed fruit in mason-style jars, for example [50]. These products, as well as ready-to-eat soups, have a home-style appearance and hearken back to the days when grandmothers spent summers cooking and preserving fruits and vegetables from the garden. Also, the producers of some canned fruits and soups are marketing unique flavors and combinations to expand the market for canned products. Several items, including **aseptic-packaged,** hot-filled, dry-filled–no process, frozen, and retorted foods, are the result of innovations in packaging

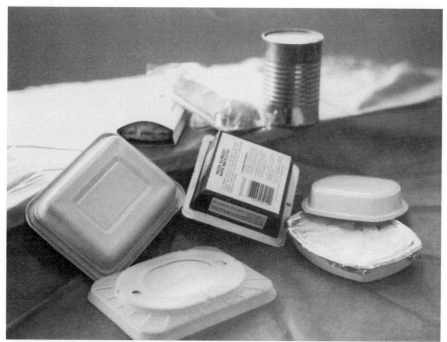

Figure 29-5
Many types of food packaging are used today. (Photographs by Chris Meister except photograph of institutional-size retort pouches, which is reprinted from Adams, J. P., W. R. Peterson, and W. S. Otwell. Processing of seafood in institutional-sized retort pouches. *Food Technology*, 37: 123(4), 1983. Copyright© by Institute of Food Technologists.)

1. The tray at the left is a retortable package used for shelf-stable meat and vegetable dishes. The light plastic cover in front can be placed on the tray after it is opened. The box in the center is a paperboard container for individual servings of frozen foods. It can be heated in either a microwave or a conventional oven. At the top is a microwave sleeve in which a pastry-type product can be microwaved to preserve crispness. The metal can at the top right is made of only two pieces and is seamless. At the lower right are examples of microwavable plastic trays used for many frozen entrees.

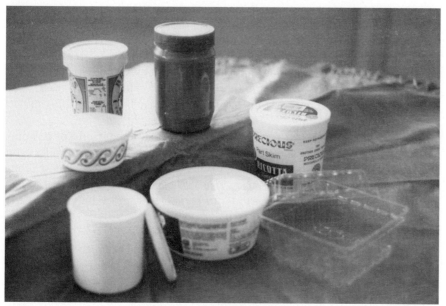

2. A variety of light plastic materials are used to package such items as ready-made frostings, soft margarines, frozen desserts, peanut butter, soft cheeses, baked products, and whipped toppings.

Figure 29-5
Continued

3. Retail and institutional-size retort pouches and cans of comparable capacity.

materials [10]. Stand-up flexible pouches have gained in popularity as one way to reduce the amount of packaging materials [5].

Paper. Paperboard trays, transparent to microwave energy, were developed for use in microwave ovens, but they can also withstand up to 400°F (204°C) in conventional ovens. A heat-resistant plastic resin is applied to solid, bleached sulfate board, which is formed into trays of various shapes and sizes. These containers can be used for **shelf-stable foods,** refrigerated foods, and frozen foods [12]. Orange juice and milk cartons of paperboard may have resealable caps for easier opening and pouring.

> **shelf-stable foods** foods that can be stored at room temperature

Rectangular paperboard cartons, laminated with aluminum and/or polyethylene, can be used for the aseptic packaging of products such as fruit juices and drinks [31]. These containers are made in various sizes. An assortment of products, including dry cereals, cake mixes, rice mixes, macaroni and cheese, and so on, are packed in paperboard cartons. In some cases, inner linings hold the product.

Plastics. Plastics are **organic polymers** with variable chemical compositions and physical properties. Many different fabrication processes are used to produce the many types and shapes of both rigid and flexible packages used by the packaging industry. Most applications involve several types of resins. Structural polymers such as polyethylene and polypropylene provide mechanical properties at low cost. Barrier polymers such as polyvinylidene chloride (PVDC) and ethylene vinyl alcohol (EVOH) provide protection against transfer of gases such as oxygen through the package. Adhesive resins bond the structural and barrier resins together. In flexible packaging, heat-seal resins provide closure

> **organic polymers** large carbon-containing molecules made up of many small molecules linked together

for the package [16]. Polyethylene terephthalate (PET) is a durable packaging material with good barrier properties and impact resistance. PET containers are widely used for carbonated beverages, pourable dressings, edible oils, peanut butter, and other products [28].

Plastic films have been used in *skin packaging* for many years (see Figure 29-6). In skin packaging, the individual products are placed on a substrate, such

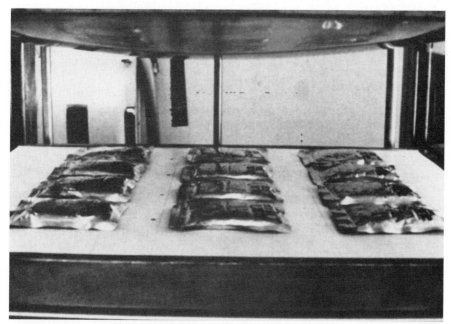

Film (top) is lowered over the pouches on a substrate pad.

A vacuum tightly draws the film over the pouches and seals the film to the substrate, which may then be cut into individual packages.

Figure 29-6
Skin packaging can be used to protect retort pouches in handling and shipping. (Reprinted from Friedman, D. Skin packaging retort pouches. *Food Technology, 39:* 106(5), 1985. Copyright© by Institute of Food Technologists.)

as a large piece of corrugated board or box board, that has been previously treated with a special coating. The plastic film is preheated, draped over the product and the board, and tightly drawn down around each individual product. The coating on the substrate fuses with the heated film to secure the product between the film and the substrate. After cooling, the substrate is cut into individual packages. The use of skin packaging has been suggested as a means to give rigidity and physical support to flexible retort pouches so that potential damage to the pouch is lessened during shipping [17].

Metals.   Today's metal cans may be flat rectangles, tall and thin, squat, pot-bellied, and many other configurations. The bodies may be three- or two-piece and fabricated from steel or aluminum [9]. Likewise, many different styles of closure may be used.

The traditional metal can is made of steel with a thin coating of tin. It generally is cylindrical and is made of three pieces. The two ends are attached to the cylinder, which has a soldered seam. Tin-free steel cans have now been developed and the side seam may be cemented or welded instead of soldered, decreasing concern about potential lead contamination. The National Food Processors Association has recommended that food manufacturers cease the production, packing, and distribution of foods in lead-soldered containers. Two-piece cans, with the base and cylinder in one piece, are manufactured; these cans have fewer seams, are more durable, lighter in weight, stack better on shelves, and can be produced more inexpensively than the traditional three-piece cans. The two-piece can may also be shaped as a tray to allow more rapid heat penetration during processing and thus to reduce heating time [12].

Aluminum cans are produced for such products as beverages. Aluminum foil, both alone and with other laminated materials, is also used for packaging foods.

Combinations of Materials.   A combination of two or more materials can provide improved functional properties for food packages. Several films can be laminated together, each layer contributing specific characteristics. For example, containers for aseptic packaging may be fabricated with aluminum foil as a barrier material and polypropylene or polyethylene as heat-sealing and food contact surfaces. Because foil needs to be protected from mechanical damage, paperboard is often utilized as the outer layer of this laminate. These packages act as barriers to moisture, oxygen, light, and microorganisms, and they have the necessary strength and heat sealability [48]. Individually portioned fruit drinks are often marketed in such packages.

The flexible retort pouch is another example of a package using a combination of materials. It typically consists of three laminated materials held together by adhesives. The outer layer is polyester, which provides strength; the middle layer is aluminum foil, which provides a barrier to moisture, gas, and light; and the inner layer is polyolefin (polyethylene or polypropylene), which provides a good heat seal.

The retort pouch is thin and permits sterilizing temperatures to be reached more quickly throughout it than the traditional can. Thus, the processed product is fresher and firmer. The sealed pouch, which can be stored on the shelf, may be heated in boiling water in preparation for serving. The pouch is easily opened by cutting with scissors or tearing across the top [12].

The retort pouch was promoted during the 1960's through the 1980's, but failed to gain widespread use except for military rations (see Chapter 2). However, since the introduction of tuna in retort packaging in 2000, commercial acceptance along with the recognition of superior quality is expected to result in greater use of retort pouches [9].

Edible Films and Coatings. An edible film is defined as a thin layer of edible material formed on a food as a coating or placed (pre-formed) on or between food components [30]. Edible coatings and films are not meant to replace nonedible, synthetic packaging materials for prolonged storage of foods. They can, however, act as adjuncts for improving overall food quality and extending shelf life. They may inhibit migration of moisture, oxygen, carbon dioxide, aromas, lipids, and so on; carry food ingredients such as antioxidants, antimicrobials, or flavor; and/or improve mechanical integrity or handling characteristics of the food. The desired characteristics of the edible film depend on the food product and its primary type of deterioration. For example, if the food is a manufactured product high in polyunsaturated fat, a film extremely resistant to the entrance of oxygen would be desirable to avoid the early development of rancidity. If the product is a fresh fruit or vegetable, however, the film would need to retard moisture loss but allow some permeability of oxygen and carbon dioxide gases as the plant cells continue to respire [29].

Potential edible films include polysaccharides such as starch, high amylose starch, methyl cellulose, **alginate, carrageenan,** and low-methoxyl pectin; proteins such as collagen, gelatin, wheat gluten, zein from corn, soy protein isolate, whey proteins, and casein; edible waxes; and combinations of these substances [30]. As fabricated foods become more prevalent, the use of edible films and coatings is likely to increase.

alginate and carrageenan
vegetable gums produced from seaweed

Packaging Waste Management

As we evolve into a "throw-away" society, we are producing waste from packaging, as well as from other sources, at a faster rate than we are finding solutions to deal with it. Landfills are quickly being filled up. Industries and legislatures alike are facing the challenge of handling solid waste in an economical and environmentally attractive manner. Some strategies include source reduction, or eliminating unnecessary packaging and using lighter-weight materials; reusable plastic containers and pallets; recycling, which provides another source of raw materials and decreases the waste going to landfills; incineration, burning waste properly without causing air pollution; and landfilling—the least desirable method but the most commonly used. The success of these strategies will depend on communication between industry and government, the creation of markets for recycled goods, the development of effective disposal systems, and public support of recycling programs.

Aseptic Packaging

Aseptic processing involves sterilization of the food product, sterilization of the package or container in which the food will be placed, filling the sterilized container with the sterilized food in an environment in which sterility is maintained, and sealing the container to prevent subsequent contamination [7]. Aseptic processing was developed in the 1940's. Since 1981, when the use of hydrogen peroxide for the sterilization of packaging materials was approved by the FDA, this process has rapidly gained popularity in the United States. In 1995, about 10 billion retail and institutional aseptic packages entered U.S. distribution channels [4]. Superheated steam or dry hot air may be used to sterilize aseptic packages, as well as hydrogen peroxide in combination with heat or ultraviolet light [27]. Hydrogen peroxide together with heat or ultraviolet radiation treatment is commonly used for the sterilization of paper-based packaging. Magnetic resonance imaging (MRI) inspection of aseptically packaged foods has been developed as a technique for the 100 percent inspection of products, at production line speeds, to assure product quality and safety [37].

Food products to be aseptically packaged are pumped through heat exchangers of various types, then into a holding tube, and finally into a cooling section before being packaged. Aseptic packaging of low-acid foods containing particulates requires demonstration of sterility at the center of the food particles, based on a defined microbiological procedure and a mathematical model. Destruction of any *Clostridium botulinum* spores present must be ensured. An aseptic process filing for a low-acid particulate product, specifically potato soup, was accepted by the FDA in 1997 [41]. These types of products have been sold in other countries for several years.

Aseptic sterilization and packaging has several advantages over in-container sterilization, the process used in conventional canning. Processing conditions are independent of container size and, therefore, very large containers can be used. The process is highly automated, resulting in higher productivity. It is also more energy efficient and less expensive. Packaging costs are lower for many container types. Aseptic processing yields higher-quality foods than traditional procedures requiring longer heating. Transport and storage costs are also less than those for frozen foods, as refrigeration is unnecessary [48].

Modified-Atmosphere Packaging

Modified-atmosphere packaging (MAP) may be defined as the enclosure of food products in gas-barrier materials, in which the gaseous environment has been changed or modified (Figure 29-7). The modification may slow respiration rates of fresh produce, reduce microbial spoilage, and retard deterioration due to enzymatic reactions with the end result of extending the shelf life of the food [22, 49]. The gaseous atmosphere within the package usually contains a reduced amount of oxygen and increased amounts of carbon dioxide and nitrogen. MAP is most commonly applied to fresh-cut produce, which in 1995 approached 10 percent of retail produce sales [4]; however, sandwiches, pastas

Clostridium botulinum a spore-forming, anaerobic bacterium that can produce a very potent toxin that causes botulism

Figure 29-7
Pre-cut lettuce is often sold in modified atmosphere packaging.
(Courtesy of USDA, photograph by Ken Hammond.)

and sauces, prepared poultry, and lunch kits also use MAP. MAP may be of two types: high gas permeable or low gas permeable. Respiring products such as fresh produce are packaged in high gas permeable MAP; pasta and other prepared dishes are placed in low gas permeable MAP [6].

Modification of the gas mixture may be accomplished by two different methods: vacuum packaging and gas packaging. Vacuum packaging involves packaging the product in a film with low oxygen permeability, removing air from the package, and sealing it **hermetically.** Oxygen in the headspace is reduced to less than 1 percent. Carbon dioxide, if it is produced from tissue and microbial respiration, eventually increases to 10 to 20 percent within the headspace. Low oxygen and elevated carbon dioxide extend the shelf life of fresh meat by inhibiting the growth of aerobic microorganisms. The meat must be kept refrigerated. Although this works well for fresh and processed meat products, it cannot be used for crushable items such as pizza, pasta, and baked products [49].

The technique in gas packaging involves removing air from the package and replacing it with a mixture of nitrogen, oxygen, and carbon dioxide. The pressure of gas inside the package is maintained approximately equal to the external pressure. Nitrogen is an inert gas that does not affect the food and has no antimicrobial properties. It is used chiefly as a filler to prevent package collapse in products that can absorb carbon dioxide. Oxygen is generally avoided except for products that continue to respire after packaging, such as fruits and vegetables. It is also used with fresh meat to maintain the red color associated with good-quality meat. Carbon dioxide is bacteriostatic and fungistatic. Its effect depends on several factors, including the microbial load, gas concentration, temperature, and packaging film permeability. Table 29-2 gives some examples of gas mixtures for selected foods [49].

Gas packaging is being used to extend the shelf life of fresh pasta, cheese, peanuts, pecans, prepared salads, sandwiches, and certain gourmet foods. In addition to increased shelf life, the advantages of MAP in these cases include increased market area, lower production and storage costs, and fresh appearance. Some disadvantages of MAP are the initial high cost of equipment and the potential growth of organisms of public health significance. When temperature abuse is a factor and carbon dioxide is thus less effective, there is a danger of the growth of microorganisms capable of causing illness [34]. A safety concern with MAP is whether it will inhibit microorganisms that might warn consumers of

hermetic completely sealed so as to keep air or gas from getting in or out

Product	Temperature (°C)	Gas Concentration (%)		
		Oxygen	**Carbon Dioxide**	**Nitrogen**
Fresh meat	0–2	70	20	10
Cured meat	1–3	0	50	50
Cheese	1–3	0	60	40
Apples	4–6	2	1	97
Tomatoes	5–10	4	4	92
Baked products	Room temperature	0	60	40
Pizza	Room temperature	0	60	40

Source: Reference 49.

Table 29-2

Gas Mixtures for Selected Food Products

spoilage while either allowing or promoting the growth of pathogens. It is essential to ensure that such organisms as *Clostridium botulinum* do not grow in these products [23]; thus, *they must be kept properly refrigerated at all times* [15].

Sous vide is a French term meaning "under vacuum." Sous vide processing technology involves the slow, controlled cooking of foods in sealed, evacuated, heat-stable pouches or trays so that the natural flavors are retained, followed by quick chilling, and cold storage at 32° to 37°F (0° to 3°C). These refrigerated products with extended shelf life can be reheated in a boiling water bath or in a microwave oven. The major microbiological hazard associated with this processing technology is the potential growth and toxin production of *Clostridium botulinum*. Other organisms of public health concern include pathogenic strains of *E. coli*, *Salmonella*, *Staphylococcus*, *Listeria*, and *Yersinia* species. These organisms should all be destroyed during the heating process; however, a hazard analysis and critical control points (HACCP) approach at all stages of sous vide processing and handling is essential to promote a reasonable degree of confidence in product safety [49]. The risks involved in temperature abuse continue into the kitchen. Refrigerator temperatures should always be 40°F (4°C) or lower.

CHAPTER SUMMARY

- Food preservation has been practiced for thousands of years. Technological advances have permitted the preservation of a wide variety of foods in convenient packaging.

- Spoiled foods are inedible or hazardous to eat. The two major causes of food spoilage are the growth of microorganisms and the action of naturally occurring enzymes. Some microorganisms have advantageous roles in food preservation and processing. Additional causes of food spoilage are nonenzymatic reactions, mechanical damage, and damage from insects and rodents.

- Proper packaging of food plays an important role in controlling food spoilage.

- No method of preservation improves the original quality of the food product. Therefore, the starting material must be fresh and flavorful.

- Food preservation may be accomplished by temperature control, thermal processing, freeze-drying, use of preservatives, or ionizing radiation.

- Cold temperatures inhibit the growth of microorganisms. Refrigerated foods should be at a temperature at or below 41°F (5°C). Frozen foods should be maintained at or below 0°F (−18°C). Vegetables are generally blanched before they are frozen to destroy enzymes naturally present.

- Hot temperatures preserve by destroying both microorganisms and enzymes. Many bacterial spores are highly resistant to heat; thus, care must be taken in the heat processing of canned foods. Pasteurization of food products involves the use of temperatures lower than those required for sterilization.

- One of the oldest methods of preserving foods involves the removal of moisture until the product is dry. The percentage of moisture in dried foods is usually under 30 percent. Vegetables may be blanched and fruits may be sulfured before drying.

- In the process of freeze-drying, the food product is first frozen then placed in a vacuum chamber, to which a small amount of heat is applied. Fresh flavors and textures are better preserved by freeze-drying than by sun-drying or other drying procedures.

- Acids, salt, sugar, spices, and smoke are common food preservatives. Numerous other preservatives may be used as food additives. The FDA approves these preservatives. Sodium benzoate and sodium propionate are examples of preservatives that may be added to food.

- Ionizing radiation has been researched as a method of preservation since the early 1950's. The FDA approves products that may be irradiated. Irradiated foods are labeled with an official logo. The sources of radiation allowed for food processing include gamma rays, accelerated electrons, and machine-generated X rays. At the dosages allowed, the radiation cannot make food radioactive.

- Major changes have occurred in food packaging over the past 20–30 years. The main function of the food package is to contain the food product, then to protect it from contamination and spoilage. The FDA considers the compatibility of food and the packaging to be a safety issue. Migration of substances from packaging materials does occur and thus the packaging materials are legally considered to be food additives.

- A variety of packaging materials are available for food products. Paper, plastics, metals, and edible films are all examples of possible packaging materials. The management of packaging waste may include source reduction, resusable containers, and recycling.

- Aseptic packaging involves the sterilization of the food product, sterilization of the package or container, filling the sterilized container with the sterilized food in an environment in which sterility is maintained, and sealing the container to present subsequent contamination. Aseptic processing yields higher-quality foods than traditional procedures requiring longer heating.

- Modified-atmosphere packaging (MAP) may be defined as the enclosure of food products in gas barrier materials, in which the gaseous environment has been changed or modified. Fresh-cut produce, pasta, and other prepared dishes may be packaged using MAP.

- Sous vide is a French term meaning "under vacuum." Sous vide technology involves the slow, controlled heating of foods in sealed, evacuated, heat-stable pouches or trays, followed by quick chilling and cold storage.

KEY TERMS

enzymes	radioactive
desiccation	radioisotope
psychrotropic microorganisms	gamma rays
mesophilic microorganisms	thermoforming
spore	aseptic packaging
botulism	shelf-stable foods
retort	organic polymers
pasteurization	alginate and carrageenan
sterilization	*Clostridium botulinum*
blanch	hermetic
ion	

STUDY QUESTIONS

1. Describe several basic causes of food spoilage.

2. Why are enzymes of some concern in preserving foods? Explain.

3. For each of the following general principles of food preservation, describe a specific method of preserving food.
   a. Use of low temperatures
   b. Use of high temperatures
   c. Reduction of moisture
   d. Addition or development of acid
   e. Addition of large amounts of sugar

4. a. What is meant by *ionizing radiation?*
   b. Describe several uses of low-dose ionizing radiation in the preservation of foods, both short and long term.
   c. Why might some members of the public be concerned about the safety of irradiated foods? How can these concerns be addressed?

5. a. Describe several functions of food packages.
   b. Why does the FDA consider food-packaging materials to be food additives?
   c. Briefly describe and give examples of how each of the following materials can be used in packaging.
      1. Paper
      2. Plastics
      3. Metals
      4. Combinations of materials
      5. Edible films and coatings

6. What is *aseptic packaging* and what advantages does it have for food products?

7. a. Describe what is meant by *modified-atmosphere packaging.*
   b. What types of foods may benefit from a modified atmosphere and why? Explain.
   c. What two methods may be employed for the modification of the gaseous atmosphere in a package? Describe them.
   d. Describe the sous vide processing of food. What precautions must be exercised in its processing and handling?

REFERENCES

1. Baldwin, E. A., Nisperos, M. O., Hagenmaier, R. D., & Baker, R. A. (1997). Use of lipids in coatings for food products. *Food Technology, 51*(6), 56.

2. Blumenthal, D. (1990). Food irradiation. Department of Health and Human Services Publication No. (FDA) 91–2241.

3. Blumenthal, M. M. (1997). How food packaging affects food flavor. *Food Technology, 51*(1), 71.

4. Brody, A. L. (1996). Integrating aseptic and modified atmosphere packaging to fulfill a vision of tomorrow. *Food Technology, 50*(4), 56.

5. Brody, A. L. (2000). Has the stand-up flexible pouch come of age? *Food Technology, 54*(7), 94–95.

6. Brody, A. L. (2000). Smart packaging becomes Intellipac™. *Food Technology, 54*(6), 104–107.

7. Brody, A. L. (2000). The when and why of aseptic packaging. *Food Technology, 54*(9), 101–102.

8. Brody, A. L. (2002). Flavor scalping: Quality loss due to packaging. *Food Technology, 56*(6), 124–125.

9. Brody, A. L. (2002). Food canning in the 21st century. *Food Technology, 56*(3), 75–78.

10. Cabes, L. J., Jr. (1985). Plastic packaging used in retort processing: Control of key parameters. *Food Technology, 39*(12), 57.

11. Clark, J. P. (2002). Drying still being actively researched. *Food Technology, 56*(9), 97–101.

12. Clausen, S., Barclay, M. J. A., & Wolf-Novak, L. C. (1986). Food packaging: A consideration for procurement. *Journal of the American Dietetic Association, 86,* 362.

13. Delves-Broughton, J. (1990). Nisin and its uses as a food preservative. *Food Technology, 44*(11), 100.

14. Derr, D. D. (1993). Food irradiation: What is it? Where is it going? *Food and Nutrition News, 65*(1), 5.

15. Doyle, M. P. (1998). Extending the shelf life of refrigerated foods: For better or worse? *Food Technology, 52*(2), 20.

16. Eidman, R. A. L. (1989). Advances in barrier plastics. *Food Technology, 43*(12), 91.

17. Friedman, D. (1985). Skin packaging retort pouches. *Food Technology, 39*(5), 105.

18. Gee, M., Farkas, D., & Rahman, A. R. (1977). Some concepts for the development of intermediate moisture foods. *Food Technology, 31*(4), 58.

19. Giese, J. (1993). Packaging, storage, and delivery of ingredients. *Food Technology, 47*(8), 54.

20. Giese, J. (1994). Antimicrobials: Assuring food safety. *Food Technology, 48*(6), 102.

21. Henkel, J. (1998). Irradiation: A safe measure for safer food. *FDA Consumer, 32*(3), 12.

22. Hintlian, C. B., & Hotchkiss, J. H. (1986). The safety of modified atmosphere packaging: A review. *Food Technology, 40*(12), 70.

23. Hotchkiss, J. H. (1988). Experimental approaches to determining the safety of food packaged in modified atmospheres. *Food Technology, 42*(9), 55.

24. Institute of Food Technologists' Expert Panel on Food Safety and Nutrition. (1983). Radiation preservation of foods. *Food Technology, 37*(2), 55.

25. Institute of Food Technologists' Expert Panel on Food Safety and Nutrition. (1986). Effects of food processing on nutritive values. *Food Technology, 40*(12), 109.

26. Institute of Food Technologists' Expert Panel on Food Safety and Nutrition. (1988). Migration of toxicants, flavors, and odor-active substances from flexible packaging materials to food. *Food Technology, 42*(7), 95.

27. Ito, K. A., & Stevenson, K. E. (1984). Sterilization of packaging materials using aseptic systems. *Food Technology, 38*(3), 60.

28. Kern, C. L., Jr. (1989). High-performance polyester for food and beverage packaging. *Food Technology, 43*(12), 93.

29. Kester, J. J., & Fennema, O. R. (1986). Edible films and coatings: A review. *Food Technology, 40*(12), 47.

30. Krochta, J. M., & De Mulder-Johnston, C. (1997). Edible and biodegradable polymer films: Challenges and opportunities. *Food Technology, 51*(2), 61.

31. Lisiecki, R., Spisak, A., Pawloski, C., & Stefanovic, S. (1990). Aseptic package addresses a variety of needs. *Food Technology, 44*(6), 126.

32. Lusk, J. L., Fox, J. A., & McIlvain, C. L. (1999). Consumer acceptance of irradiated meat. *Food Technology, 53*(3), 56–59.

33. Marth, E. H. (1998). Extended shelf life refrigerated foods: Microbiological quality and safety. *Food Technology, 52*(2), 57.

34. Mermelstein, N. H. (1997). High-pressure processing reaches the U.S. market. *Food Technology, 51*(6), 95.

35. Mermelstein, N. H. (1998). Interest in pulsed electric field processing increases. *Food Technology, 52*(1), 81.

36. Mermelstein, N. H. (1999). Electron-beam pasteurization plant near completion. *Food Technology, 53*(8), 88–89.

37. Mermelstein, N. H. (1999). Magnetic resonance imaging provides 100 percent inspection. *Food Technology, 53*(11), 94–97.

38. Mertens, B., & Knorr, D. (1992). Developments of nonthermal processes for food preservation. *Food Technology, 46*(5), 124.

39. Meyer, R. S., Cooper, K. L., Knorr, D., & Lelieveld, H. L. M. (2000). High-pressure sterilization of foods. *Food Technology, 54*(11), 67–72.

40. Olson, D. G. (1998). Irradiation of food. *Food Technology, 52*(1), 56.

41. Palaniappan, S., & Sizer, C. E. (1997). Aseptic process validated for foods containing particulates. *Food Technology, 51*(8), 60.

42. Pohlman, A. J., Wood, O. B., & Mason, A. C. (1994). Influence of audiovisuals and food samples on consumer acceptance of food irradiation. *Food Technology, 48*(12), 46.

43. Pszczola, D. E. (1995). Packaging takes an active approach. *Food Technology, 49*(8), 104.

44. Pszczola, D. E. (1997). 20 ways to market the concept of food irradiation. *Food Technology, 51*(2), 46.

45. Resurreccion, A. V. A., & Galvez, F. C. F. (1999). Will consumers buy irradiated beef? *Food Technology, 53*(3), 52–55.

46. Rogan, A., & Glaros, G. (1988). Food irradiation: The process and implications for dietitians. *Journal of the American Dietetic Association, 88*, 833.

47. Sizer, C. E., Balasubramaniam, V. M., & Ting, E. (2002). Validating high pressure processes for low-acid foods. *Food Technology, 56*(2), 36–42.

48. Smith, J. P., Ramaswamy, H. S., & Simpson, B. K. (1990). Developments in food packaging technology. Part 1: Processing/cooking considerations. *Trends in Food Science & Technology, 1*(5), 107.

49. Smith, J. P., Ramaswamy, H. S., & Simpson, B. K. (1990). Developments in food packaging technology. Part 2: Storage aspects. *Trends in Food Science & Technology, 1*(5), 111.

40. Steinriede, K. (1998). Clear advantages: Glass makes a comeback as consumers crave nostalgia. *Food Processing, 61*(3), 90.

51. Sunderland, J. E. (1982). An economic study of microwave freeze-drying. *Food Technology, 36*(2), 50.

52. Tuomy, J. M., & Young, R. (1982). Retort-pouch packaging of muscle foods for the Armed Forces. *Food Technology, 36*(2), 68.

Food Preservation by Freezing and Canning

FREEZING

Clarence Birdseye, a food technology pioneer, began development of the frozen food industry in the 1920s with the production of frozen fish. He applied his engineering skills to develop plate freezers and blast freezers not unlike those used today. Although interrupted by World War II, the infant frozen food industry grew rapidly during the late 1940's and 1950's [5]. Equipment for rapid freezing and widespread availability of freezers in both home and institutional kitchens contributed importantly to this growth. Since the early days, there have been many improvements in freezing technology. Researchers have studied the freezing process itself in an attempt to understand and minimize the effects on food quality at each stage in the production of frozen foods [18]. A large assortment of frozen foods is marketed. The sweeping success of the microwave oven has also contributed to growth in the frozen food industry in recent years. Many frozen ready-to-eat entrées, meals, and snacks, accompanied by instructions for reheating in the microwave oven, are available.

The frozen food industry continues to work at improving the quality of frozen foods. For example, research concerning the properties and possible applications of "antifreeze" proteins as agents to prevent the growth of large ice crystals during frozen storage may in the future be applied to certain frozen foods. Antifreeze proteins are **glycoproteins** found in fish from southern polar oceans, but they also can now be synthesized chemically or by genetic engineering [10].

Other areas of research include air-impingement, pressure shift, and extrusion freezing methods [15]. Air-impingement freezing uses thin, high-velocity jets of air directed at the food to accomplish fast cooling rates producing reduced moisture loss and small ice crystals [7, 15]. Pressure-shift freezing uses an increase of pressure to depress the freezing point of water, thereby allowing the product to be cooled to −4°F (−20°C) without the water freezing. When the pressure is released, the water rapidly freezes and small, uniform ice crystals are formed. Extrusion freezing is being studied as a way to freeze ice cream to −4°F (−20°C) directly from the freezer. Traditionally, ice cream is frozen to 19°F (−7°C), then placed in a hardening room to complete the freezing process. Extrusion freezing has been shown to produce a more uniform crystal size [15].

Producers of frozen foods are concerned with maintaining quality as the food moves through the transport and distribution systems, where it must

glycoproteins proteins composed of amino acid chains with a carbohydrate moiety, such as a galactose derivative, attached at certain points

always be held at low temperatures [4]. Various devices called *time-temperature indicators (TTIs)* have been developed as means of monitoring and controlling critical temperatures during the storage, handling, and distribution of frozen and refrigerated foods [5, 21].

The extent to which home freezing is practiced depends on individual circumstances and objectives. Produce, for example, must be available at advantageous prices in the market or from home gardens to make freezing an economical practice. In any case, however, the freezer contributes to efficient management in meal planning and preparation, and it has the advantage of allowing quantity buying with less frequent purchasing. It also provides convenience in the temporary storage of prepared foods made in larger quantities than are to be consumed immediately.

The Freezing Process

Freezing is the change in physical state from liquid to solid that occurs when heat is removed from a substance. When foods are frozen, they undergo a phase change of liquid water into solid ice. The water molecules reduce their motion and form an organized pattern of crystals. The three stages in the freezing process are as follows:

1. The temperature of the food is lowered to freezing.
2. Ice crystals begin to form as the liquid reaches the freezing point; the temperature required varies with the product to be frozen. For water, the freezing temperature is 32°F (0°C). As ice crystals form from water, the remaining water becomes more concentrated with solute, lowering the freezing point still further. This process is continuous, but the zone of maximum crystal formation in frozen foods is 25° to 31°F (−4° to −0.5°C).
3. After ice formation ceases, the temperature of the frozen product is gradually lowered to the necessary storage temperature.

In a frozen food product, the activity of microorganisms is negligible. Enzymatic processes may continue, although at a reduced rate. Fast freezing and low storage temperatures are favorable for holding enzyme action at a minimum and for the best retention of nutrients. Most vegetables are **blanched** before freezing to destroy enzymes so that enzymatic action does not produce off-flavors and undesirable texture changes during frozen storage. When the secondary changes in flavor and texture resulting from blanching are unacceptable, such as in freezing strawberries or other fresh fruits, chemicals such as vitamin C (ascorbic acid) may be added to control some of the enzymatic reactions [18]. After thawing, the growth of microorganisms may occur at a rapid rate.

The first commercial method of freezing foods was the slow freezing process sometimes called *sharp freezing*. In this method, foods are placed in refrigerated rooms ranging from 25° to −20°F (−4° to −29°C), and large pieces of food or large containers of food require many hours or days to freeze. There are also quick-freezing methods. When lower temperatures are used, −25° to −40°F (−32° to −40°C), the time of freezing is greatly reduced over that required in sharp freezing. Other factors that aid in hastening the freezing process are small masses of foods, contact with freezing coils or metal plates, and rapidly moving currents of frigid air. Figure 30-1 shows the relative differ-

blanch to heat for a few minutes by immersing in boiling water, surrounding with steam, or applying microwaves

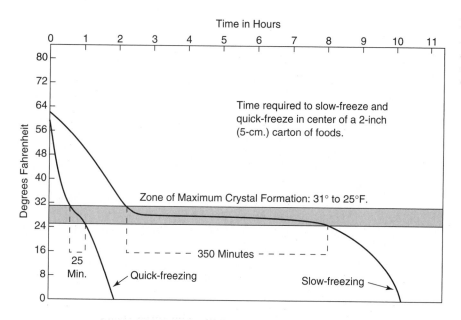

Figure 30-1
Diagram showing some differences between quick and slow freezing.
(Courtesy of Frosted Foods Sales Corporation)

ences in time of freezing by quick- and slow-freezing methods. The freezing of food in most home freezers is a relatively slow process.

The process of freezing rapidly at very low temperatures (−76°F or −60°C or lower) is called *cryogenic freezing*. In cryogenic freezers, which use liquid nitrogen or carbon dioxide, the food is cooled so quickly that many tiny ice crystals form simultaneously, producing a much smaller number of large crystals. Tiny ice crystals have a less damaging effect on plant and animal cells than large crystals.

Changes During Freezing, Storage, and Thawing

Changes may occur in many foods that are to be frozen as they are held before freezing. Careful handling, transportation, and storage procedures must be used before and during preparation for freezing if quality loss is to be minimized [18]. Crops should be harvested at the optimal stage of maturity and the produce frozen before the sugar content is reduced or undesirable enzyme activity develops. Such care greatly increases the chances that high-quality frozen produce will result. Many changes still occur in the freezing of food, holding it in frozen storage, and thawing it.

Formation of Ice Crystals.   Ice crystal formation, changes in ice crystals during frozen storage, and later thawing all affect the texture of many frozen foods. The effects of freezing depend partly on the nature and state of the material that is frozen. Vegetable and fruit tissues, in particular, decrease in firmness with freezing and thawing. Whether plant tissues are blanched may affect the way ice crystals form in the tissues. For example, in unblanched tissue, the cell walls are intact and the exchange of water through **osmosis** is possible. If the freezing rate is slow, significant amounts of water may translocate from within cells into the extracellular medium. The formation of ice crystals in extracellular spaces causes injury to the cells. On thawing, not all the moisture is reabsorbed by the cells.

osmosis the movement of water through a semipermeable membrane; as ice crystals form extracellularly, the concentration of solute in this area is increased and water then moves out of the cell in an attempt to equalize the solute concentration

With rapid freezing, more and smaller ice crystals are formed within cells. These also cause damage to cell structures, although the damage is less when the crystals are small. The loss of water held in the cells (turgor) as the cells are ruptured during freezing is probably responsible for much of the loss of firmness in frozen and thawed plant tissues.

As the temperature is reduced during freezing and more ice crystals form, the concentration of dissolved substances in the unfrozen medium increases and the viscosity of this unfrozen portion increases. At some temperature, depending on the composition of the system, the viscosity of the unfrozen matrix becomes so high that molecular motion is greatly inhibited. Unfrozen water molecules can then no longer migrate to join ice crystals. Other reaction rates become slowed. The temperature at which this transformation takes place is called the *glass transition temperature* (T_g). The transition state can be detected by observing changes in various dielectric, mechanical, and thermodynamic properties [20]. Frozen storage stability is greatest at or below T_g temperature. This information can be valuable in optimizing storage conditions for particular frozen products as researchers develop methods of modifying T_g [18].

Enzyme Action. Enzymes are present in all living tissue. Respiration, catalyzed by many enzymes, continues in fruits and vegetables after they are severed from the growing plant. These metabolic reactions reduce sugar content, which accounts for the loss of sweetness in such vegetables as peas and corn. Other enzymatic changes also occur. Unless the enzymes responsible for undesirable chemical changes are destroyed before foods are frozen, the foods may show various undesirable color, flavor, and texture changes during freezing, storage, and thawing. Freezing inhibits enzyme action somewhat, but it does not destroy the enzymes.

Vegetables are blanched before freezing to inactivate enzymes that may cause browning, destruction of chlorophyll and carotenoid pigments, or development of unpleasant flavors during storage [3, 17]. In addition, blanching shrinks the vegetable tissues so that they pack more easily, expels air so that the potential for oxidation is lessened, and decreases the microbial load. From the standpoint of both overcooking and loss of soluble nutrients, however, the blanching operation should be as short as possible.

Light-colored fruits, such as peaches and apples, are particularly susceptible to **enzymatic oxidative browning** in both the fresh and frozen states. The addition of sugar or syrup to the fruit before freezing aids in the retention of color, although darkening may occur if the fruits are held too long. Sugar also aids in preventing marked flavor changes and loss of the natural aroma. The addition of vitamin C to the syrup is effective in preventing browning; it acts as an **antioxidant**. Citric and other organic acids also may be effective for some fruits by lowering the pH enough to interfere with the activity of the browning enzymes.

Nonenzymatic Oxidation. The process of **nonenzymatic oxidation** of fatty materials in frozen foods may occur. Residual oxygen is usually present in frozen foods and the fat of pork is particularly susceptible to oxidation and the development of rancidity. Bacon does not keep well in frozen storage. Antioxidants may be added to some products commercially to control unwanted oxidation.

Desiccation. If food products to be frozen are not properly packaged with **moisture/vapor-proof material**, they tend to lose moisture by **sublimation.**

---

enzymatic oxidative browning the discoloration produced in some light-colored substances in plant tissue by the enzyme polyphenol oxidase when the tissue is cut or injured

antioxidant a substance that interferes with the oxidation process

nonenzymatic oxidation an oxidation reaction that occurs spontaneously and is not catalyzed by enzymes, for example, oxidation of fats that results in rancidity

moisture/vapor-proof materials materials that are relatively impermeable to water vapor and other gases; they are desirable for wrapping frozen foods to minimize the loss of moisture, particularly from sublimation

sublimation a solid, such as ice, goes directly to the vapor state (water vapor) without going through the liquid state; in the freezer, sublimed water may collect as frost

Some of the ice changes directly to water vapor without going through the liquid state, and the water vapor collects to form frost inside the package and/or inside the freezing compartment. **Desiccation** or dehydration thus occurs.

desiccation drying out

The term *freezer burn* as applied to frozen foods refers to dehydration resulting in discoloration, change in texture, and off-flavors. This condition is often observed in frozen poultry and other flesh foods as brownish dehydrated areas. It may also occur in other foods. Proper packaging is important in the control of freezer burn.

Activity of Microorganisms. Usually present in frozen foods, microorganisms' activity is negligible as long as the storage temperature remains below 16° to 10°F (−9° to −12°C). The microorganisms become active at warmer temperatures. They may begin to multiply rapidly as soon as defrosting occurs. It is important that frozen foods be held at optimal, nonfluctuating storage temperatures and be used as soon as they are defrosted.

Selection of Foods for Freezing

Success in freezing depends to a considerable degree on the kinds and varieties of foods selected for freezing. Local agricultural experiment stations are usually able to furnish advice concerning the kinds and varieties of locally grown fruits and vegetables that are best adapted to freezing preservation. The fruits that are least changed in freezing preservation include red tart cherries, cranberries, currants, gooseberries, blueberries, and raspberries. Strawberries and peaches yield frozen products superior to those preserved by other methods. Loganberries, boysenberries, blackberries, dewberries, pineapples, melons, apples, and plums also yield good frozen products.

Although citrus fruits do not freeze well, their juices freeze quite satisfactorily, as do apple cider and other fruit juices. Some fruit juices are concentrated by partial freezing, the ice crystals being removed by straining. Some vegetables do not freeze satisfactorily, including green onions, lettuce and other salad greens, radishes, and raw tomatoes.

Fruits and vegetables should be frozen at the proper stage of maturity. Vegetables should be harvested while they are young and tender, and fruits should be at their optimal stage of ripeness for best flavor, color, and texture. Meats and poultry to be frozen should be of high quality. Fish deteriorates so rapidly that it is best frozen as soon as possible after it is caught.

Techniques for Freezing

Fruits. Detailed instructions for the freezing of fruits and vegetables are provided in the Cooperative Extension Service, University of Georgia/Athens, Bulletin 989 [2] and the *Ball Blue Book* [1]. Figure 30-2 shows a procedure for the freezing of sliced peaches.

Mixing juicy fruits with dry sugar draws out the juices to form a syrup. Alternatively, the fruit can be covered with a sugar syrup. Most fruits require sugar or syrup treatment to protect against enzymatic changes during freezing and storage. Blanching changes the fresh flavor and texture characteristics of fruits and is thus not commonly used. Blueberries and cranberries yield satisfactory products when frozen without sugar or syrup or scalding. Strawberries can be frozen whole, but they retain their best color and flavor in sliced form in sugar or syrup packs.

1. Select mature peaches that are firm-ripe, with no green color in the skins. Allow 1 to 1 1/2 pounds for each pint to be frozen. Wash the peaches carefully and drain.

2. Pit the peaches and peel them by hand for the most attractive product. Peaches peel more quickly if they are dipped first in boiling then in cold water, but they may have ragged edges after thawing.

3. Pour about 1/2 cup of cold syrup into each pint container. Slice the peaches directly into the container.

4. Add syrup to cover the peaches. Leave 1/2 inch of headspace at the top of wide-mouth containers like these, to allow for expansion of the fruit during freezing.

5. Put a small piece of crumpled waxed paper on top of the fruit to keep it down in the syrup. The syrup should always cover the fruit to keep the top pieces from changing color and flavor.

6. Wipe all sealing edges clean for a good seal. Screw the lid on tight. Label with the name of the fruit and the date of freezing. Put the sealed containers in the coldest part of the freezer. Leave a little space between containers so that air can circulate freely. Store the frozen fruit at 0°F (−18°C) or below.

Figure 30-2
Steps involved in the freezing of peaches at home. (Courtesy of the U.S. Department of Agriculture)

When syrups are used, they are prepared and chilled prior to packing. Vitamin C may be added to the syrup to control browning of the fruit—approximately 1/2 teaspoon of crystalline vitamin C per quart of syrup. Commercial products containing vitamin C are also available for use in retarding the browning of frozen fruit. Syrup concentrations usually vary from about 30 to 70 percent sugar, although lower concentrations may be preferred from both a flavor and nutritive standpoint.

Vegetables. Most vegetables yield products of the best quality and flavor when frozen on the day they are harvested. If immediate freezing is impossible, adequate refrigeration is necessary for the interim. The speed at which the vegetables go from garden to freezer is one of the most important factors affecting quality in frozen products. The stage of maturity is also important. For those vegetables that change rapidly in maturity, such as peas, corn, snap beans, lima beans, soybeans, and asparagus, 1 or 2 days may mean the difference between a young tender vegetable and one that is tough and of poor quality.

Figure 30-3 shows the steps involved in the freezing of snap beans. Washing, draining, and sorting of the vegetable usually precede trimming and cutting. To avoid undesirable enzymatic changes, which adversely affect color, flavor, and texture during freezing and frozen storage, most vegetables require blanching to inactivate enzymes. Blanching can be done in boiling water, in steam, or by the application of microwaves. Water-soluble constituents are better retained in steam blanching, but efficient steaming equipment is sometimes difficult to obtain for home use. What is necessary is a tightly closed container that holds enough rapidly boiling water to form steam and a rack to hold the vegetable above the water level. If boiling water is used, the water should be of such a volume that the boiling does not stop when the vegetable is placed in the water. Wire racks are ideal containers to hold the vegetable. At least 1 gallon of water per pound of vegetable is needed, and more might be desirable.

Important as the blanching process is, it should not be overdone. The shortest possible time needed to inactivate enzymes should be used to avoid both actual cooking and the loss of water-soluble nutrients. Small quantities of a vegetable are blanched at one time so that all pieces will be quickly, thoroughly, and uniformly heated. After blanching, the vegetable must be cooled *quickly* in cold running water or ice water to about 50°F (10°C). Chilling is necessary to avoid overheating and to maintain quality. Required times are equal for chilling and blanching.

Prompt freezing is very important in the freezing preservation of foods, particularly vegetables. The sooner vegetables are frozen after blanching, the better the product is likely to be.

Meat, Fish, and Poultry. Meats to be frozen are usually cut into pieces of a suitable size for cooking. The pieces may be steaks, chops, roasts, ground meat, cubes for stews, or other forms. Removal of the bone conserves freezer space. Fish can be boned and packed as fillets or steaks. Poultry can be dressed and left whole for roasting or cut into pieces. Giblets are usually wrapped in parchment and placed inside of whole roasters and broilers. Only high-quality fresh meat products should be frozen.

Careful wrapping or packaging with recommended packaging materials is essential in protecting the products from oxidation and desiccation. More information on the freezing of meat, fish, and poultry is found in the *Ball Blue Book* [1] and in bulletins obtained from county agricultural extension agents [2].

Eggs.   Frozen egg whites seem to lose none of the quality needed for culinary uses; however, yolks become gummy and gelled on thawing because of an irreversible change involving the lipoproteins. To be usable, a stabilizer such as sugar, syrup, or salt must be added to yolks. Mixed whole eggs usually have a small amount of stabilizer added because they contain the yolk, but they have been successfully frozen without a stabilizer.

When freezing eggs at home, about 1 tablespoon of sugar or corn syrup or 1/2 teaspoon of salt can be blended with 1 cup of egg yolk before freezing. The use of a small container that makes possible the thawing of only the amount of egg needed is recommended. Defrosted eggs usually have a relatively high bacterial count and deteriorate rapidly after defrosting.

Prepared Foods.   On the market are many different frozen prepared foods and meals that require only reheating. Packaging technologies that allow direct heating in the microwave oven or boiling in the bag in which the product was frozen contribute to the wide variety of available choices. Prepared foods that require only thawing, including a variety of baked products, are usually brought into the kitchen for short-term storage only.

Many prepared foods can also be frozen in the kitchen for convenience and efficiency. Various casseroles, main dish items, and plated meals can be prepared in quantity and frozen for future use.

Programs to provide meals for homebound elderly people often involve the preparation and delivery of single meals 1 to 5 days a week. Some programs, however, have elected to offer supplementary meals. Plated meals prepared on-site, but not served immediately, may be frozen, decreasing cost and waste in preparation. Freezing practices in such programs have been investigated in a study of time-temperature relationships during the freezing of packaged meals. Similar meals were frozen in a refrigerator-freezer unit, an upright freezer, and a walk-in freezer [22]. Meals packaged in individually divided foil containers were positioned either individually or stacked three deep on the freezer shelf. The temperature during the freezing process was recorded in the center meal.

These investigators reported that the temperature in the refrigerator-freezer was 12°F (−11°C), in the upright freezer it was −15°F (−26°C), and in the walk-in freezer it was −9°F (−23°C). The time that the meals spent in the danger zone, 45° to 140°F (7° to 60°C), after placement in the freezer, was longer in the refrigerator-freezer than in the other freezing units and was much longer in all the freezers for the stacked meals than for the single layer. The time in the danger zone was about half as long for pot roast as for oven-baked chicken. It was concluded that freezers that maintain temperatures above 0°F (−18°C) may have difficulty freezing meals within a 2-hour period. It was also concluded that stacked meals take considerably longer to exit the danger zone than those that are placed in a single layer. Employees who work in feeding programs for the elderly may need to be trained in the proper handling of food to be frozen [22].

Baked products can be frozen either before or after baking. The storage life of unbaked batters and doughs is usually less than that of the baked products. If frosted or iced cakes are to be frozen, they might be frozen first without wrap-

1. Select young, tender, stringless beans that snap when broken. Allow 2/3 to 1 pound for 1 pint of frozen vegetable. Wash thoroughly.

2. Cut the beans into 1- or 2-inch pieces, or slice them lengthwise.

3. Put the beans in the blanching basket, lower the basket into boiling water, and cover. Heat 3 minutes. Keep heat high under the water.

4. Plunge the basket of heated beans into cold water to stop the cooking. It takes about as long to cool vegetables as to heat them. When the beans are cool, remove them from the water and drain.

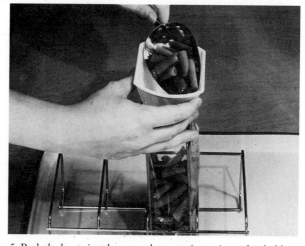

5. Pack the beans into bags or other containers. A stand to hold the bags makes filling easier. A funnel helps keep the sealing edges clean. Seal and freeze.

Figure 30-3
Steps involved in the freezing of snap beans at home. (Courtesy of the U.S. Department of Agriculture)

ping to prevent the wrapping material from sticking to the frosting, and then wrapped and returned to the freezer.

Frozen bread doughs can be made from the usual formulations, provided that the level of yeast is increased to 4 or 5 percent. A short fermentation period is desirable before freezing. If a satisfactory product is to result, sufficient yeast viability must be maintained during freezing and freezer storage to produce adequate amounts of carbon dioxide gas.

Certain foods do not freeze well at home, although commercial processes and materials may produce satisfactory results [14]. For example, cooked egg whites toughen and become rubbery, mayonnaise tends to separate as the emulsion breaks, starch-thickened sauces tend to weep as starch retrogradation occurs, and fried foods often change in flavor when reheated.

Containers

Containers for freezing foods can be made of glass, metal, plastic materials, paper or fiber board, and certain moisture/vapor-proof transparent materials and should have tight-fitting lids or closures. A container that is ideal for freezer use has been described as one that is both airtight to prevent oxidation and moisture/vapor-proof to prevent dehydration. Of course, liquid tightness is necessary for use with liquid foods, such as sugar and syrup packs for fruits.

Freezer space is usually such that cube-shaped containers permit the most efficient use of storage space. It is obvious that rigidity in a container prevents crushing of the products. If containers are of such a material as to permit thorough cleaning, they may be reused. Moisture/vapor-proof bags are satisfactory if little handling is required.

Pliable moisture/vapor-proof bags should have as much air as possible removed from them and should be twisted and tightly closed. Immersing the lower part of the bag and its contents in water while packaging such irregularly shaped items as whole poultry may aid in removing air by the pressure of the water on the bag. Boil-in-the-bag containers are available for home use in freezing prepared foods. These bags may be heat-sealed before freezing.

The size of the container used is important because many frozen foods should not be held after defrosting (see Table 30-1). Containers larger than 1/2 gallon or 5 pounds are not recommended because of the slow rate of freezing.

For dry packs, the cartons can be almost completely filled before freezing. Syrup packs, or juicy products such as sliced strawberries mixed with sugar, should have about 10 percent headspace to allow for expansion of the contents during freezing.

Use and Management of the Home Freezer

A freezer can be a convenience in many ways, but careful planning should go into its selection and use. The needs in each situation differ, and freezer use should be adapted to individual conditions and preferences. A freezer is a con-

Table 30-1
Size of Container in Relation to Number of Servings

Servings	Size of Container
1 or 2	1/2 pt
4	1 pt
8	1 qt

siderable investment and should be kept full or nearly full at all times to minimize the cost per unit of food stored. For example, as the stock of frozen garden vegetables and fruits diminishes, it may be possible to buy larger quantities of commercially frozen products at a savings; however, the quality of frozen foods is not maintained indefinitely—it decreases with time. Suggested maximum storage periods for maintaining good quality in commercially frozen foods that are stored in kitchen freezers are provided in Table 30-2.

Table 30-2
Suggested Maximum Home-Storage Periods to Maintain Good Quality in Commercially Frozen Foods

Food	Approximate Holding Period at 0°F (−18°C) (months)	Food	Approximate Holding Period at 0°F (−18°C) (months)	Food	Approximate Holding Period at 0°F (−18°C) (months)
Fruits and vegetables		Pies (unbaked)		Cooked chicken and	
Fruits		Apple	8	turkey	
Cherries	12	Boysenberry	8	Chicken or turkey	6
Peaches	12	Cherry	8	dinners (sliced	
Raspberries	12	Peach	8	meat and gravy)	
Strawberries	12			Chicken or turkey pies	12
Fruit juice concentrates		*Meat*		Fried chicken	4
Apple	12	Beef		Fried chicken dinners	4
Grape	12	Hamburger	3		
Orange	12	or chopped		*Fish*	
Vegetables		(thin) steaks		Fillets	
Asparagus	8	Roasts	12	Cod, flounder,	6
Beans	8	Steaks	12	haddock, halibut,	
Cauliflower	8	Lamb		pollack	
Corn	8	Patties (ground	3	Mullet, ocean perch,	3
Peas	8	meat)		sea trout, striped	
Spinach	8	Roasts	12	bass	
		Pork, cured	2	Pacific Ocean perch	2
Frozen desserts		Pork, fresh		Salmon steaks	2
Ice cream	1	Chops	4	Sea trout, dressed	3
Sherbet	1	Roasts	8	Striped bass, dressed	3
		Sausage	2	Whiting, drawn	4
Baked goods		Veal			
Bread and yeast rolls		Cutlets, chops	4	*Shellfish*	
White bread	3	Roasts	8	Clams, shucked	3
Cinnamon rolls	2	Cooked meat		Crabmeat	
Plain rolls	3	Meat dinners	3	Dungeness	3
Cakes		Meat pie	3	King	10
Angel	2	Swiss steak	3	Oysters, shucked	4
Chiffon	2			Shrimp	12
Chocolate layer	4	*Poultry*			
Fruit	12	Chicken		*Cooked fish and shellfish*	
Pound	6	Cut up	9	Fish with cheese sauce	3
Yellow	6	Livers	3	Fish with lemon butter	3
Danish pastry	3	Whole	12	sauce	
Doughnuts		Duck, whole	6	Fried fish dinner	3
Cake type	3	Goose, whole	6	Fried fish sticks, scallops,	3
Yeast raised	3	Turkey		or shrimp	
		Cut up	6	Shrimp creole	3
		Whole	12	Tuna pie	3

Source: Courtesy of the U.S. Department of Agriculture.

Time can be saved by doubling or tripling recipes when they are being prepared if they are suitable for freezing. The frozen products can be conveniently served on busy days. Advance planning in meal preparation and entertaining may be simplified with the use of a freezer. An accurate inventory of frozen foods should be kept.

All foods should be stored no higher than 0°F (-18°C) to maintain palatability and nutritive value. Accurate and effective temperature control is therefore important. If a freezer stops running and remains off for an extended period, several alternatives are possible to keep the food from spoiling. If it is available, enough dry ice may be added to the freezer to maintain below-freezing temperatures for a few days. Or, the food may be put into insulated boxes or wrapped in newspapers and blankets and rushed to a freezer-locker plant. If the freezer will be off only a few hours, it should simply be kept tightly closed.

Sometimes frozen foods are partially or completely thawed before it is discovered that the freezer is not operating. Although partial thawing and refreezing reduce the quality of most foods, partially thawed foods that still contain ice crystals or foods that are still cold (about 40°F or 4°C) can usually be safely refrozen. Ground meats, poultry, and seafood should not be refrozen if they have thawed completely, because bacteria multiply rapidly in these foods. Each package of meat, vegetable, or cooked food should be carefully examined. If the food is thawed or the color or odor is questionable, the food should be discarded because it may be dangerous.

CANNING

Canning involves, first, the application to foods of temperatures high enough to destroy essentially all microorganisms present, both vegetative cells and spores, and second, the sealing of the heated product in sterilized airtight containers to prevent recontamination. The degree of heat and the length of heating vary with the type of food and the kinds of microorganisms likely to occur. Fruits and tomatoes that are sufficiently acid are successfully canned at the temperature of boiling water. The time of boiling depends on the degree of acidity, the consistency of the product, the method of preparation, and other factors. Vegetables, including some low-acid tomatoes, and meats, which are relatively low in acid, must be heated to temperatures higher than that of boiling water at atmospheric pressure. This method involves the use of a pressure canner. Because bacterial spores that may be present are more resistant to heat under conditions of low acidity, the time of heating necessary to destroy them at the temperature of boiling water would likely be several hours. The food would be rather unpalatable after such a prolonged cooking period. Moist heat evidently destroys microorganisms by coagulating proteins and destroys enzymes in a similar manner.

Historical Highlights

The history of canning begins in about 1795, when the French government offered a prize for the development of a new method of preserving food from one harvest to the next. Nicolas Appert, a Parisian confectioner, worked many years on such a process and finally, in 1809, he successfully preserved some foods by sealing them with corks in glass bottles and heating them for various lengths of time [8]. Appert received financial support from the French government, including an initial cash award (12,000 francs) for his accomplishment.

With contributions from many workers along the way, the canning industry gradually developed until today cans of food are being filled, sealed, and processed by the millions. The tin canister was first developed in England in about 1810. Peter Durand, a broker, was granted a patent in London, possibly as an agent or middleman for a French inventor, Phillipe de Girard [9]. Canned foods were produced in England for the British navy in the early 1800's. The retort for pressure canning was developed in Philadelphia around 1874 [11]. Pasteur's work with microorganisms in about 1860 began a study of the true causes of food spoilage, and the process of canning was approached on a scientific basis at the turn of the 20th century.

Various types of batch and continuous **retorts** are used in commercial canning [12] (Figure 30-4). Some retorts agitate or rotate the cans during processing to increase the rate of heat penetration and to aid in heat distribution. Commercial canning also includes methods that employ higher temperatures and shorter time periods than are used in traditional commercial canning. **Aseptic canning** (discussed in Chapter 29) is also practiced, preserving a

retort commercial equipment used for pressure canning

aseptic canning a process in which the food material and the container are sterilized separately, and the container is filled without recontamination

Figure 30-4
Various types of commercial retorts are available. (Reprinted from Kimball, R. N., and T. L. Heyliger. Verifying the operation of steam retorts. *Food Technology,* 44(12), pp. 102–103, 1990. Copyright© by Institute of Food Technologists.)

Batch agitating retorts, such as the Orbitort, produce product agitation by rotating the containers.

Continuous rotary sterilizers provide continuous handling of containers at up to 600 cans per minute.

fresher flavor for many food products. The variety of equipment available for commercial canning provides the industry with the flexibility it needs to develop and produce unique food products and to select various packaging options. Semi-rigid and flexible packages, such as the **retort pouch,** can be readily handled to produce shelf-stable foods. In all cases of commercial canning, careful written documentation of temperature distribution during processing must be maintained [16].

Although much of our canned food is now produced commercially, some people still can or bottle foods at home for various reasons, including palatability, economy, and the satisfaction derived from do-it-yourself projects. For those who must restrict their intake of salt and sugar, products may be canned without the addition of these substances. Canning tomatoes from backyard gardens appears to be one of the more popular home food preservation activities.

retort pouches flexible laminated packages made of special materials that withstand high-temperature processing in a commercial pressure canner called a *retort*

Methods for Home Canning

High-quality products should always be selected for canning and recommended procedures followed to ensure safe products that do not spoil on storage. Detailed steps to be followed in home canning are given in the Cooperative Extension Service, University of Georgia/Athens, Bulletin 989 [2], the *Ball Blue Book* [1], and the *USDA Complete Guide to Home Canning* [23].

Packing. Only glass jars are generally available for home canning. Foods can be packed into the jars either raw or hot in preparation for the canning processing step (Figure 30-5).

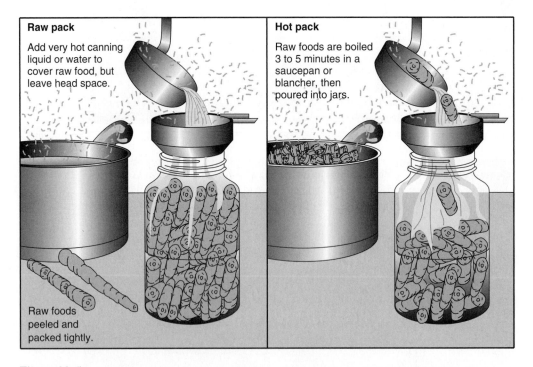

Figure 30-5
Bottles can be filled by either the raw-pack or the hot-pack method, as illustrated. (Courtesy of the U.S. Department of Agriculture)

In the *raw-pack method* of canning, the uncooked food is packed into the container and the container is filled with boiling liquid. Some headspace should be left in the top of the container before sealing; usually 1/2 to 1 inch is suggested. This space allows for the expansion of the jar contents during heating. Glass jars are only partially sealed before processing at the necessary temperature for the recommended time.

In the *hot-pack method* of canning, the food is heated in syrup, water, steam, or extracted juice before being packed into containers. With this method, the temperature of the food should be at least 170°F (77°C) when packed in the container.

The raw-pack method may have an advantage over the hot-pack method in that large pieces of fruit, such as peach halves, or fragile berries can be placed in jars so that they present an attractive appearance and are closely packed. The hot-pack method may be advantageously used for some foods because it helps to drive out air, wilts or shrinks plant tissues, allows closer packing, and slightly shortens the processing time. The initial temperature of the food is relatively high and heat penetration is more rapid when the food is packed hot. Pears, apples, and pineapples have a more attractive translucent appearance when prepared by the hot-pack rather than by the raw-pack method. Also, more fruit can be fit into the container.

Processing. The processing of canned fruits, vegetables, and meats is done after these foods have been packed into containers by either the hot- or raw-pack method as described previously. The processing may be accomplished in a boiling water bath for acid fruits and acid tomatoes. For vegetables, meat, fish, and poultry, which are low in acid, the use of a pressure canner is essential. A higher temperature is required with these products for the complete destruction of bacterial spores. Of particular concern is the destruction of the spores of *Clostridium botulinum*. These spores can vegetate and, under the anaerobic conditions that are found in the sealed cans, may produce a deadly toxin that causes **botulism** when consumed, even in tiny amounts. In low-acid foods such as vegetables and meats, the temperature of boiling water is not sufficient to ensure spore destruction. A pressure canner, in which higher temperatures can be attained, must be used in the canning of these products.

Boiling Water Bath. Processing by means of a boiling water bath requires a large boiling water canner (Figure 30-6). The canner must be deep enough so that at least 1 inch of briskly boiling water will be above the tops of the jars during processing. A fitted lid covers the canner. A rack keeps jars 1 inch or less above the bottom, thus avoiding breakage and allowing even circulation of heat underneath the jars. Unless the bath has a removable holder for jars, a lifter of some kind is necessary for placing jars into and removing them from the boiling water.

The canner should be filled halfway with water. For raw-packed foods, preheat the water to 140°F (60°C); for hot-packed foods, 180°F (82°C). Load the filled jars, fitted with lids, into the canner rack and use the handles to lower the rack into the water, or fill the canner one jar at a time. Add more boiling water so that the water level is at least 1 inch above the jar tops. Heat on high until the water boils vigorously. Cover the canner and lower the heat to maintain a gentle boil (212°F, 100°C) throughout the processing period [1, 23].

botulism a serious illness resulting from consumption of food containing the toxin produced by *Clostridium botulinum* bacterial spores that are not destroyed in processing and vegetate on storage in an anaerobic environment

Figure 30-6
The boiling water should extend two inches above the jars in a boiling water canner. A rack in the canner promotes proper water circulation around the jars and allows for easy removal of the jars. (Courtesy of Alltrista Consumer Products Company, Marketers of Ball brand and Kerr brand home canning products.)

Some varieties of tomatoes now being grown in the United States, including Garden State, Ace, 55VF, and Cal Ace, are lower in acid content than those commonly produced in previous years. These tomatoes are likely to have pH values above 4.6 and are considered to be low-acid foods. If they are to be canned as acid foods in a boiling water canner, they must be acidified with lemon juice or citric acid to a pH of less than 4.6. Two tablespoons of bottled lemon juice or ½ teaspoon citric acid per quart of tomatoes will ensure a safe level of acidity [1, 23]. Properly acidified tomatoes can be processed in a boiling water canner. Alternatively, low-acid tomatoes, not treated with lemon juice or citric acid, must be processed in a pressure canner, as are other vegetables and meat products.

Pressure Canning.   If temperatures higher than 212°F (100°C) are necessary for processing, a pressure canner must be used. The boiling point of a liquid such as water varies with the atmospheric pressure over its surface. As the atmospheric pressure is decreased with higher altitudes, the boiling point of the liquid is decreased. In a pressure canner, the water vapor or steam that is produced when the water is heated to its normal boiling point is captured inside the canner with its tightly sealed cover, thus increasing the pressure over the surface of the water in the pressure canner. This raises the boiling point of the water and temperatures higher than the usual boiling point of water can thus be achieved.

Pressure canners in the past were constructed of heavy metal with clamp-on or turn-on lids. They had a dial gauge to indicate pressure. Most pressure canners of today are lightweight, thin-walled kettles with turn-on lids (Figure 30-7). Their essential features are a *rack* to hold jars off the bottom, a *vent port* (steam vent or petcock) that is left open for a few minutes to drive out air and fill the compartment with steam and then closed with a *counterweight* or *weighted gauge*, and a *safety fuse* or *valve* through which steam may escape if too high a pressure develops within the canner (Figure 30-8). The pressure canner is used primarily to provide a high temperature for the destruction of heat-resistant microorganisms and their spores in a shorter time than is possible at the boiling temperature of water.

To operate the pressure canner, put 2 to 3 inches of water in the canner and then place filled jars on the rack, using a jar lifter. Space the jars to permit circulation of steam. Fasten the canner lid securely, making sure that the gasket is clean and in place. Leave the petcock open or the weight off the vent port and heat on high until steam flows from the port or petcock. Allow a steady stream of steam to exit from the canner for 10 minutes before closing the petcock or placing the weight on the vent port. The steam drives air out of the canner as completely as possible, or *exhausts* the canner. If the air is not removed, the air in the canner contributes a partial pressure along with the steam and the temperature inside the canner will not be as high as when all the pressure comes from steam. The food may therefore be underprocessed. Canners are not equipped with thermometers that show the exact interior temperature, so it is important that the canner be properly exhausted. Table 30-3 shows temperatures that are obtainable in a pressure canner at different pressures, provided that no air remains in the canner.

Pressure will build up during the first 3 to 5 minutes after closing the vent port. Start the timing process when the pressure gauge shows the desired pressure or when the weighted gauge begins to wiggle or rock. Regulate the source

(a)

(b)

Figure 30-7
A pressure canner is necessary to obtain temperatures higher than 212°F (100°C).
(a) This pressure canner is shown with jars of canned food. (Courtesy of National Presto Industries, Inc.)
(b) Pressure canners are heated on top of the range to achieve the necessary pressure for the canning of low-acid foods such as green beans. (Courtesy of Alltrista Consumer Products Company, Makers of Ball brand and Kerr brand home canning products.)

of heat to maintain a steady pressure on the gauge. Rapid and large fluctuations in pressure during processing will cause liquid to be lost from the jars. Weighted gauges should jiggle periodically or rock slowly throughout the process. They allow the release of tiny amounts of steam each time they move and thus control the pressure precisely. Constant watching is not required.

When the processing time is completed, turn off the heat and remove the canner from the heat source, if possible. Let the canner depressurize. *Do not*

Figure 30-8
Essential parts of a pressure canner.
Also note the water level in the can-
ner. (Courtesy of the U.S. Department of Agriculture)

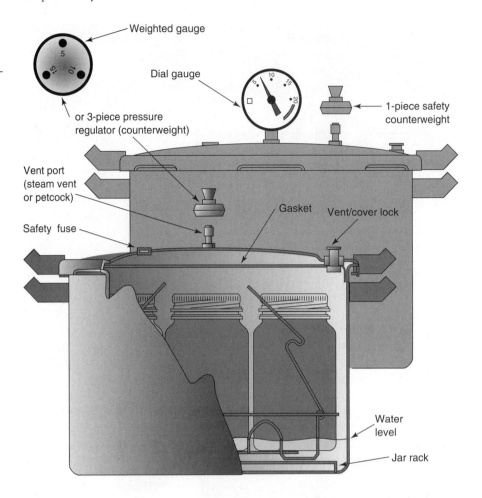

force the cooling process. Cooling the canner with cold water or opening the vent
port or petcock before the canner is depressurized will cause loss of liquid from
the jars and the seals may fail. After the canner is depressurized, remove the
weight from the vent port or open the petcock, unfasten the lid, and open the
canner carefully.

Immediately after processing in either the boiling water canner or the pressure canner, jars that were not tightly closed before processing, as is proper
when using self-sealing lids, should now be tightly closed. Sealing occurs automatically with cooling. A vacuum is gradually produced as the jars cool.

Table 30-3
Temperatures Obtainable at Differ-
ent Pressures in a Pressure Cooker

	Temperature	
Pressure (lb)	°F	°C
5	228	109
10	240	116
15	250	121
20	259	126
25	267	131

The temperature most commonly used for home canning of low-acid foods is 240°F (116°C), corresponding to a pressure of 10 pounds per square inch. However, it has been reported that a higher pressure (15 pounds) and thus a shorter processing time also gives satisfactory results in terms of texture, color, and flavor of vegetables. Asparagus, peas, and strained squash were the vegetables tested [13].

Internal canner temperatures are lower at higher altitudes. Adjustments must therefore be made to compensate. If the pressure canner has a pressure gauge, the canner should be checked for accuracy at the beginning of each season. Checking is often done locally through the county cooperative extension service or the home service department of a utility company. The amount and direction of error in the pressure gauge should be noted on a tag tied to the canner. An adjustment should then be made when the canner is used. Weighted-gauge canners cannot be adjusted for altitude. Therefore, at altitudes above 1,000 feet, they must be operated at canner pressures of 10 instead of 5 pounds per square inch or 15 instead of 10 pounds, as indicated in the *Ball Blue Book* [1] and USDA Home Canning Guide [23].

Containers for Canning

Containers for commercially canned foods are usually made of tin-plated steel (tin cans), aluminum, or glass. Tin-free steel cans have also been produced. Tin cans are of two types: plain and lacquered. The latter may be coated with the bright, or R, lacquer suitable for all red-colored foods containing anthocyanin pigment and for pumpkin and squash. If anthocyanins are canned in plain tin they fade and become bluish. Pumpkin and squash tend to corrode plain tin. The dull, or C, lacquer is best not used with acid foods or with meats that contain much fat, as both acid and fat may cause the lacquer to peel. This makes the food unsightly, although it is harmless. The dull, or C, lacquer is used for corn, succotash, and other sulfur-containing foods to prevent dark deposits of tin or iron sulfide on the food and on the can. Tin sulfide, which is brown, and iron sulfide, which is black, are not harmful but detract from the appearance of the food.

Commercial canning in metal has several advantages over glass: Breakage is eliminated, cans are always sealed before processing, heat penetration is more rapid than with glass, the cans may be rapidly cooled after processing by being plunged into cold water, and the cans are generally less expensive. Special flexible packages, such as retort pouches, may also be used for commercial canning to produce shelf-stable foods not requiring refrigeration. These packages are less expensive to process and ship, after the initial expense by the food processor for the necessary processing equipment or modification of conventional equipment [19, 24]

The jars generally available in the United States for home canning are heat-resistant glass jars with self-sealing lids (Figure 30-9). The self-sealing closure for a canning jar has a composition ring in the lid that becomes soft when heated and then hardens, forming a seal on the edge of the jar top when it becomes cold. New lids are required for self-sealing jars each time the jars are used, but the screw bands may be reused over a long period. The lids are placed in simmering, but not boiling water, for at least 10 minutes prior to use according to the manufacturer's directions [1].

For low-acid vegetables and for meats, jars no larger than quart size are recommended because of the danger of poor heat penetration in larger jars.

Figure 30-9
The most commonly used closure for canning jars is the metal screw band and metal self-sealing lid. Sealing occurs on the top edge of the jar.
(Courtesy of the U.S. Department of Agriculture)

The pint size is usually advised for corn, shell beans, and lima beans, in which heat penetration is slow.

Heat Penetration

Heat penetration during canning is affected by such factors as the size of the container, the material from which the container is made, the initial temperature of the food when the processing is started, the temperature used for processing, the fullness of the pack, and the character of the food. Heat penetration is more rapid in smaller containers and in tin than in glass. Starchy vegetables and closely packed leafy vegetables transmit heat poorly. Colloidal starch solutions retard heat penetration more than concentrated sugar solutions. Heat penetration is more rapid if the food is hot when the processing is started and if a higher temperature is used for processing. In general, the higher the processing temperature, the shorter the required heating time.

Obtaining a Partial Vacuum

A partial vacuum in the sealed jar is important in the canning of food because it helps to maintain an effective seal and it inhibits oxidative changes. A partial vacuum is created when the air within the jar exerts less pressure outward than the atmosphere exerts on the outside of the jar. This vacuum is produced as a result of several events that occur during the canning process. First, food is heated. The application of heat causes internal gases to expand. When the food is heated in a glass canning jar, the gases escape through the partially sealed lid. Formation of an effective vacuum depends largely on this process of *venting*.

After processing is completed and the jar is removed from the canner, sealing occurs. With self-sealing devices, the complete sealing takes place automatically as the softened sealing compound hardens on cooling. During cooling, the contents of the jar contract, leaving a space in the top that is less dense than the atmosphere pressing down on the outside of the lid. Thus, a partial vacuum is formed to aid in keeping the seal tight.

Obtaining an Effective Seal

A good seal is essential in canned foods. All jars should be examined for nicks or rough places on the sealing surfaces that might interfere with a good seal. Lids must fit well. Care should be taken to remove small bits of food from the top of the jar before closing the container, because they interfere with the formation of a complete seal.

After the jars have cooled for 12 to 24 hours, the screw bands may be removed and the jars tested for a complete seal. If the center of the lid is either flat or bulging, it is probably not sealed. It should be concave, that is, pulled down slightly in the center. Try to gently lift the lid off with your fingertips. If the lid does not flex up and down and the lid is tightly attached, then the lid has a good seal [1].

Handling after Processing

Proper handling and storage of canned food are important in maintaining its quality. When glass jars with self-sealing lids are thoroughly cool and have sealed, the screw bands should be removed and rinsed clean so that they can be used again. If they are left on the jars they may stick or rust, making removal difficult. The outside of the jars should be wiped clean of any residual syrup or other material. Containers should be labeled to show the contents and date of processing.

Canned foods should be stored in a cool, dry, dark place. At cool storage temperatures the eating quality and nutritive value are better maintained. Glass jars, particularly, should be stored in a dark place because light causes fading and discoloration of plant pigments. Properly canned foods may be safely stored for several years, but the quality of the food gradually decreases, especially if storage temperatures are relatively high. Therefore, use of canned foods within a year is generally recommended.

If low-acid vegetables, including low-acid tomatoes, have not been canned according to the recommendations of the USDA, they should be boiled for 10 minutes after opening the can and before tasting any of the food contained in it. For altitudes at and above 1,000 feet, 1 additional minute should be added per 1,000 feet. This recommendation is for safety in case *Clostridium botulinum* organisms have survived and produced toxin in the sealed jar [1]. Botulism has occurred most commonly from the use of home-canned products.

All canned products should be inspected before use to ensure the vacuum seal is present. Check for signs of mold, gassiness, cloudiness, spurting liquid when the jar is opened, seepage, yeast growth, fermentation, sliminess, and disagreeable odors [1]. All of these signs are indications of spoilage and the food should not be used.

CHAPTER SUMMARY

- Clarence Birdseye began development of the frozen food industry in the 1920's. There have been many improvements to freezing technology over the years. Air-impingement, pressure shift, and extrusion freezing methods are current areas of research. Time-temperature indicators have been developed to monitor critical temperatures during the storage, handling and distribution of frozen and refrigerated foods.

- Freezing is the change in physical state from liquid to solid that occurs when heat is removed from a substance. There are three stages in the freezing process.

- Most vegetables are blanched before freezing to destroy enzymes that can produce undesirable changes. In fruits, vitamin C may be added to control the enzymatic reactions because it acts as an antioxidant. The addition of sugar or syrup to fruit before freezing aids in the retention of color and the maintenance of natural flavors and aromas.

- Cryogenic freezing is the process of freezing rapidly at very low temperatures. When food is frozen quickly, tiny ice crystals are formed. Tiny ice crystals have a less damaging effect on plant and animal cells than the large crystals formed during slow freezing.

- The loss of water held in cells as the cells are ruptured during freezing is probably responsible for much of the loss of firmness in frozen and thawed plant tissues.

- If foods to be frozen are not properly packaged they tend to lose moisture by sublimation. Desiccation or dehydration thus occurs. Freezer burn, as applied to frozen foods, refers to dehydration resulting in discoloration, change in texture, and off-flavors.

- The activity of microorganisms is negligible as long as the storage temperature remains below 16° to 10°F (−9° to −12°C). The microorganisms, however, become active at warmer temperatures and begin to multiply rapidly as soon as defrosting occurs.

- Specific techniques for the freezing of fruits, vegetables, meat, fish, poultry, eggs, and prepared foods are recommended for optimum quality. Containers for the freezing of foods may be made of a variety of materials. These containers should be airtight and moisture/vapor-proof.

- If a freezer stops running and remains off for an extended period, dry ice may be added to maintain freezing temperatures or the food may be packaged and transported to another a freezer-locker plant. Freezers that are off for only a few hours should remain tightly closed.

- Although partial thawing and then refreezing of foods reduces quality, foods that still contain ice crystals may be refrozen. Meats, poultry, and seafood should not be refrozen if complete thawing has occurred. Any questionable food product should be discarded.

- Canning involves, first, the application to foods of temperatures high enough to destroy essentially all microorganisms present, and second, the sealing of the heated product in sterilized, airtight containers. The degree of heat and length of heating vary with the type of food and kinds of microorganisms likely to occur.

- Foods are often canned commercially; however, some still can foods at home for various reasons.

- Only glass jars manufactured for home canning should be used. Food may be packed into the jars using the raw-pack or hot-pack methods.

- Following packing, foods are processed using a boiling water bath or pressure canning. The boiling water bath requires the use of a large boiling water canner. Only high acid foods may be processed using the boiling water bath.

- Pressure canning is required for all low acid foods because these foods must be heated to 240°F (116°C), which may only be achieved in a pressure canner. Some varieties of tomatoes may be low acid and therefore it is recommended that all tomatoes be properly acidified with the addition of lemon juice or citric acid if processed using a boiling water canner, or alternatively are processed using a pressure canner.

- The time of processing varies by altitude. Therefore, when canning, the altitude in your area should be checked and the proper time and pressure guidelines followed.

- Upon the completion of the processing in a pressure canner, the heat should be turned off and the canner should be allowed to depressurize without using cold water or opening the vent port or petcock to speed the cooling process. After the canner is depressurized, remove the weight or open the petcock, unfasten the lid, and open the canner carefully.

- Immediately after processing in either the boiling water canner or the pressure canner, all jars should be tightly closed. Sealing of the jars occurs automatically with cooling.

- Containers for commercially canned foods are usually made of tin-plated steel, aluminum, or glass. Tin cans may be of two types: plain and lacquered. Jars for home canning are glass.

- In home canned foods, the jars should be tested for a complete seal after the jars have cooled for 12–24 hours. The lid should be concave and it should not lift off with your fingertips.

- Canned foods should be stored in a dry, dark place, at cool storage temperatures to maintain optimum quality. Although properly canned foods may be safely stored for years, the quality declines over time. Thus, use of canned foods within a year is recommended.

- All canned products should be inspected before use to ensure the vacuum seal is still present and to check for signs of spoilage. Low-acid foods, for which the canning process may not have been done according to guidelines, should be boiled for 10 minutes after opening the can and before tasting any of the food. At altitudes above 1,000 feet, additional boiling time is necessary.

KEY TERMS

glycoproteins   sublimation
blanch   desiccation
osmosis   retort
enzymatic oxidative browning   aseptic canning
antioxidant   retort pouches
nonenzymatic oxidation   botulism
moisture/vapor-proof materials

STUDY QUESTIONS

1. Discuss differences in methods used, rate and time of freezing, and size of resulting ice crystals between slow freezing and quick freezing.

2. Describe several undesirable changes that may occur during freezing, frozen storage, or thawing of frozen foods.

3. a. Explain why vegetables should be blanched before freezing.
   b. Give several suggestions for carrying out the blanching process to ensure that it will accomplish its purpose satisfactorily.

4. What is *freezer burn* and how can it be prevented in frozen foods?

5. How does freezing control the causes of food spoilage and thus preserve foods?

6. Discuss several points that should be considered in selecting foods for freezing.

7. What are two important roles, in addition to sweetening, that are played by sugar or syrup packs in freezing fruits?

8. What general procedures should be followed in the freezing of meat, fish, and poultry?

9. What differences exist between the procedures for freezing egg whites and egg yolks? Why are these different procedures necessary?

10. a. Why should containers and wrappers used on frozen foods be moisture/vapor-proof?
    b. Why should headspace be left in containers when freezing foods?

11. List several things that should be considered if you are to make the most effective use of your freezer.

12. Describe some pertinent events in the history of canning that are associated with each of the following names and dates.
   a. Appert, 1809
   b. 1810
   c. 1874
   d. Pasteur, 1860's

13. Distinguish between the raw-pack and the hot-pack methods of packing canned foods and discuss advantages of each.

14. Explain why fruits and high-acid tomatoes can be safely canned in a boiling water bath, but vegetables and meat products must be canned in a pressure canner. What might botulism have to do with your explanation?

15. a. Describe the essential parts of a pressure canner and explain their functions.
   b. Why is it important to completely *exhaust* a pressure canner before closing the petcock and building pressure?
   c. Suggest a possible explanation for the loss of liquid from jars processed in a pressure canner.

16. a. Of what materials are "tin" cans usually made? Why are their inside surfaces sometimes lacquered with R or C enamel?
   b. Describe self-sealing lids commonly used on bottled produce and explain how they work.
   c. What steps should be taken to ensure that an effective seal is formed in bottled produce?

17. List several factors that may affect the rate of heat penetration as canned foods are processed.

18. Explain how a partial vacuum is formed in canned foods. Why is it important that this occurs?

REFERENCES

1. Alltrista Corporation. (2001). *Ball Blue Book: Guide to home canning, freezing, and dehydration.* Muncie, IN: Alltrista Corporation.

2. Andress, E. L. & Harrison, J. A. (1999). *So easy to preserve* (4th ed.). Athens, GA: Cooperative Extension Service, The University of Georgia/Athens. Bulletin 989.

3. Barrett, D. M., & Theerakulkait, C. (1995). Quality indicators in blanched, frozen, stored vegetables. *Food Technology, 49*(1) 62.

4. Bramsnaes, F. (1981). Maintaining the quality of frozen foods during distribution. *Food Technology, 35*(4), 38.

5. Brody, A. L. (1996). Chills: A chronology of IFT's refrigerated & frozen foods division. *Food Technology, 48*(12), 50.

6. Brody, A. L. (2001). What's active about intelligent packaging. *Food Technology, 55*(6), 75–78.

7. Clark, J. P. (2002). Developments in food freezing. *Food Technology, 56*(10), 76–77.

8. Corcos, A. (1975). A note on the early life of Nicolas Appert. *Food Technology, 29*(5), 114.

9. Cowell, N. D. (1995). Who introduced the tin can?—A new candidate. *Food Technology, 49*(12), 61.

10. Feeney, R. E., & Yeh, Y. (1993). Antifreeze proteins: Properties, mechanism of action, and possible applications. *Food Technology, 47*(1), 82.

11. Goldblith, S. A. (1972). Controversy over the autoclave. *Food Technology, 26*(12), 62.

12. Kimball, R. N., & Heyliger, T. L. (1990). Verifying the operation of steam retorts. *Food Technology, 44*(12), 100.

13. Lazaridis, H. N., & Sander, E. H. (1988). Home-canning of food: Effect of a higher process temperature (121° C) on the quality of low-acid foods. *Journal of Food Science, 53*, 985.

14. Luallen, T. E. (1994). The use of starches in frozen food formulation. *Food Technology, 48*(5), 39.

15. Mermelstein, N. H. (2001). What's happening in freezing research. *Food Technology, 55*(10), 81–83.

16. Park, D. J., Cabes, Jr., L. J., & Collins, K. M. (1990). Determining temperature distribution in rotary, full-immersion, hot-water sterilizers. *Food Technology, 44*(12), 113.

17. Poulsen, K. P. (1986). Optimization of vegetable blanching. *Food Technology, 40*(6), 122.

18. Reid, D. S. (1990). Optimizing the quality of frozen foods. *Food Technology, 44*(7), 78.

19. Roop, R. A., & Nelson, P. E. (1982). Processing retort pouches in conventional sterilizers. *Journal of Food Science, 47*, 303.

20. Roos, Y. H., Karel, M., & Kokini, J. L. (1996). Glass transitions in low moisture and frozen foods: Effects on shelf life and quality. *Food Technology, 50*(11), 95.

21. Taoukis, P. S., Fu, B., & Labuza, T. P. (1991). Time-temperature indicators. *Food Technology, 45*(10), 70.

22. Thole, C., & Gregoire, M. B. (1992). Time-temperature relationships during freezing of packaged meals in feeding programs for the elderly. *Journal of the American Dietetic Association, 92*, 350.

23. U.S. Department of Agriculture. (1994, September). *Complete guide to home canning.* Agriculture Information Bulletin No. 539.

24. Williams, J. R., Steffe, J. F., & Black, J. R. (1981). Economic comparison of canning and retort pouch systems. *Journal of Food Science, 47*, 284.

Weights and Measures

SYMBOLS FOR MEASUREMENTS

tsp	= teaspoon	cc	= cubic centimeter
Tbsp	= tablespoon	mL	= milliliter
fg	= few grains	L	= liter
fl oz	= fluid ounce	oz	= ounce
c	= cup	lb	= pound
pt	= pint	μg	= microgram
qt	= quart	mg	= milligram
gal	= gallon	g	= gram
		kg	= kilogram
		mm	= millimeter
		cm	= centimeter
		m	= meter

EQUIVALENTS

		Common Use
1 gram	= 0.035 ounce	
1 ounce	= 28.35 grams	30 grams
4 ounces	= 113.40 grams	125 grams
8 ounces	= 226.80 grams	250 grams
1 kilogram	= 2.2 pounds	
1 kilogram	= 1,000 grams	
1 pound	= 0.454 kilogram	
1 pound	= 453.59 grams	450 grams
1 liter	= 1.06 quarts	
1 liter	= 1,000 milliliters	
1 quart	= 0.946 liter	0.95 liter
1 quart	= 946.4 milliliters	950 milliliters
1 cup	= 236.6 milliliters	240 milliliters
1/2 cup	= 118 milliliters	120 milliliters
1 fluid oz	= 29.57 milliliters	30 milliliters
1 tablespoon	= 14.8 milliliters	15 milliliters
1 teaspoon	= 4.9 milliliters	5 milliliters
1 inch	= 2.54 centimeters	2.5 centimeters
1 centimeter	= 0.4 inch	
1 yard	= 0.914 meter	

SOME INGREDIENT SUBSTITUTIONS

For:	Substitute:
1 tablespoon flour (thickener)	½ tablespoon cornstarch, potato starch, or arrowroot starch, or 1 tablespoon quick-cooking tapioca
1 cup sifted all-purpose flour	1 cup unsifted all-purpose flour minus 2 tablespoons
1 cup sifted cake flour	7/8 cup or 1 cup minus 2 tablespoons sifted all-purpose flour
1 cup sifted self-rising flour	1 cup sifted all-purpose flour plus 1½ teaspoons baking powder and ½ teaspoon salt
1 cup honey	1¼ cups sugar plus ¼ cup liquid
1 cup corn syrup	1 cup sugar plus ¼ cup liquid
1 cup butter	1 cup margarine or ⅞ cup hydrogenated shortening or ⅞ cup lard
1 ounce baking chocolate	3 tablespoons cocoa plus 1 tablespoon fat
1 ounce semisweet chocolate	½ ounce baking chocolate plus 1 tablespoon sugar
1 cup buttermilk	1 cup plain yogurt
1 teaspoon baking powder	¼ teaspoon baking soda plus ⅝ teaspoon cream of tartar or ¼ teaspoon baking soda plus ½ tablespoon vinegar or lemon juice

STANDARD CAN SIZES

Can Size	Contents (c)	Average Net Weight
8 oz	1	8 oz
Picnic	1¼	11 oz
No. 300	1¾	15 oz
No. 303	2	16 oz
No. 2	2½	1 lb 4 oz
No. 2½	3½	1 lb 13 oz
No. 3 cylinder	5¾	46 fl oz
No. 10	13	6 lb 10 oz

Source: American Home Economics Association. (1993). *Handbook of Food Preparation* (9th ed.). Washington, D.C.: American Home Economics Association.

METRIC CONVERSIONS

		Multiply by
Length	inches to centimeters	2.5
	feet to centimeters	30
	yards to meters	0.9
Volume or Capacity	teaspoons to milliliters	5
	tablespoons to milliliters	15
	fluid ounces to milliliters	30
	cups to liters	0.24
	cups to milliliters	237
	quarts to liters	0.95
	gallons to liters	3.8
Mass or Weight	ounces to grams	28
	pounds to grams	454
	pounds to kilograms	0.45

COMMON MEASUREMENTS
USED IN FOOD PREPARATION

3 tsp	= 1 Tbsp		10⅔ Tbsp	= 2/3 c
16 Tbsp	= 1 c		2 c	= 1 pt
4 Tbsp	= 1/4 c		4 c	= 1 qt
8 Tbsp	= 1/2 c		4 qt	= 1 gal
12 Tbsp	= 3/4 c		2 Tbsp	= 1 fl oz or 1/8 c
5⅓ Tbsp	= 1/3 c		8 fl oz	= 1 c or 1/2 pt

APPROXIMATE NUMBER OF CUPS IN
A POUND OF SOME COMMON FOODS

2¼ c granulated sugar   2 c butter or margarine
4 c all-purpose flour   4 c grated cheese

WEIGHTS AND MEASURES FOR
SOME FOOD INGREDIENTS

All-purpose flour, sifted	1 lb	= 4 c	115 g per c
Whole wheat flour, stirred	1 lb	= 3⅓ c	132 g per c
SAS-phosphate baking powder	14 oz	= 2½ c	3.2 g per tsp
Baking soda	1 lb	= 2⅓ c	4 g per tsp
Granulated sugar	1 lb	= 2¼ c	200 g per c
Brown sugar, packed	1 lb	= 2¼ c	200 g per c
Salt	1 lb	= 1½ c	288 g per c
Margarine	1 lb	= 2 c	224 g per c
Hydrogenated fat	1 lb	= 2⅓ c	188 g per c
Oil	1 lb	= 2⅙ c	210 g per c
Eggs, fresh whole	1 lb	= 1¾ c	248 g per c

B Temperature Control

OVEN TEMPERATURES

Temperatures for cooking can be most accurately controlled when a thermostat or a thermometer is used. Ovens generally have thermostat-controlled heat. They may be checked occasionally with a portable oven thermometer if there is some question about the accuracy of the thermostatic control.

Temperature Range for Ovens

Very low	250–275°F	121–135°C
Low	300–325°F	149–163°C
Moderate	350–375°F	177–191°C
Hot	400–425°F	204–218°C
Very hot	450–500°F	232–260°C

THERMOMETERS FOR OTHER USES

Thermometers are available for reading the temperature of deep fats, sugar syrups, and meats. In taking the temperature of hot fats or of boiling sugar syrups, the bulb of the thermometer should be fully submerged but should not touch the bottom of the utensil. In reading the scale, the eye should be level with the top of the mercury column.

Meat thermometers have a short scale, up to about 212° F (100° C). The bulb is small, and the thermometer is inserted so that the bulb rests in the center of the roast or the muscle being roasted.

CONVERTING FAHRENHEIT AND CELSIUS TEMPERATURES

Formulas

$$1.8 \times °C = °F - 32$$

or

$$°C = (°F - 32) \times 5/9$$
$$°F = (°C \times 9/5) + 32$$

The first formula given for temperature conversion can be used either for changing Celsius to Fahrenheit or Fahrenheit to Celsius simply by inserting the known temperature in the appropriate place in the formula and then solving the equation for the unknown.

Conversion Table			
°F	°C	°F	°C
50	10.0	200	93.3
60	15.6	210	98.9
70	21.1	212	100.0
80	26.7	215	101.7
90	32.2	220	104.4
100	37.8	230	110.0
110	43.3	235	112.8
120	48.9	240	115.6
130	54.4	245	118.3
140	60.0	248	120.0
150	65.6	250	121.1
160	71.1	252	122.2
170	76.7	255	123.9
180	82.2	260	126.7
190	87.8	270	132.2

Nutritive Value
of Selected Foods

Table C-1

Vegetables

Vegetable	Approximate Measure	Food Weight (g)	Energy (kcal)	Water (%)	Protein (g)	Carbohydrate (g)	Calcium (mg)	Iron (mg)	Vitamin A Value (IU)	Vitamin A Value (RE)	Thiamin (mg)	Riboflavin (mg)	Ascorbic acid (mg)
Leaves													
Cabbage, raw, finely shredded	1 c	70	15	93	1	4	33	0.4	90	9	0.04	0.02	33
Lettuce, raw, crisphead	½ head	135	20	96	1	3	26	0.7	450	45	0.06	0.04	5
Spinach, frozen cooked	1 c	190	55	90	6	10	277	2.9	14,790	1,479	0.11	0.32	23
Vegetable-fruits													
Peppers, green, sweet, raw	1 pod	74	20	93	1	3	3	0.6	390	39	0.06	0.04	95
Squash, winter, baked, cubes	1 c	205	80	89	2	18	29	0.7	7,290	729	0.17	0.05	20
Tomatoes, raw	1	123	25	94	1	5	9	0.6	1,390	139	0.07	0.06	22
Flowers and stems													
Asparagus, cooked from raw, cut	1 c	180	45	92	5	8	43	1.2	1,490	149	0.18	0.22	49
Broccoli, cooked from raw, cut	1 c	155	45	90	5	9	71	1.8	2,180	218	0.13	0.32	97
Cauliflower, cooked from raw	1 c	125	30	93	2	6	34	0.5	20	2	0.08	0.07	69
Celery, raw, outer stalk	1 stalk	40	5	95	Trace	1	14	0.2	50	5	0.01	0.01	3

Vegetable	Approximate Measure	Food Weight (g)	Energy (kcal)	Water (%)	Protein (g)	Carbohydrate (g)	Calcium (mg)	Iron (mg)	Vitamin A Value (IU)	Vitamin A Value (RE)	Thiamin (mg)	Riboflavin (mg)	Ascorbic acid (mg)
Bulbs, roots, tubers													
Beets, cooked, diced	1 c	170	55	91	2	11	19	1.1	20	2	0.05	0.02	9
Carrots, cooked from raw, sliced	1 c	156	70	87	2	16	48	1.0	38,300	3,830	0.05	0.09	4
Potatoes, peeled after boiling	1	135	115	77	2	27	11	0.4	0	0	0.14	0.03	18
Sweet potatoes, boiled, peeled	1	151	160	73	2	37	32	0.8	25,750	2,575	0.08	0.21	26
Seeds and pods													
Snap beans, cooked from frozen	1 c	135	35	92	2	8	61	1.1	710	71	0.06	0.10	11
Corn, sweet, cooked from raw	1 ear	77	85	70	3	19	2	0.5	170	17	0.17	0.06	5
Peas, green, cooked from frozen	1 c	160	125	80	8	23	38	2.5	1,070	107	0.45	0.16	16
Peas, split, dry, cooked	1 c	200	230	70	16	42	22	3.4	80	8	0.30	0.18	0
Beans, dry, cooked Pinto	1 c	180	265	65	15	49	86	5.4	Trace	Trace	0.33	0.16	0

Source: Nutritive Value of Foods, Home and Garden Bulletin No. 72. Washington, DC: U.S. Department of Agriculture, 1991.

Table C-2
Fruits and Fruit Juices

Fruit	Approximate Measure	Food Weight (g)	Energy (kcal)	Water (%)	Protein (g)	Carbohydrate (g)	Vitamin A Value (IU)	(RE)	Ascorbic Acid (mg)
Apples, raw,									
unpeeled	1 medium	138	80	84	Trace	21	70	7	8
Apricots, raw	3 apricots	106	50	86	1	12	2,770	277	11
Avocados, raw,									
California	1 avocado	173	305	73	4	12	1,060	106	14
Bananas, raw,									
without peel	1 banana	114	105	74	1	27	90	9	10
Blueberries, raw	1 c	145	80	85	1	20	150	15	19
Cantaloupe, raw	½ medium	267	95	90	2	22	8,610	861	113
Grapefruit, medium									
White	½	120	40	91	1	10	10	1	41
Pink or red	½	120	40	91	1	10	310	31	41
Grapefruit juice, frozen concentrate diluted with 3 parts water	1 c	247	100	89	1	24	20	2	83
Grapes, raw,									
Thompson	10 grapes	50	35	81	Trace	9	40	4	5
Oranges, raw	1 orange	131	60	87	1	15	270	27	70
Orange juice,									
fresh	1 c	248	110	88	2	26	500	50	124
canned, unsweetened	1 c	249	105	89	1	25	440	44	85
frozen concentrate, diluted with 3 parts water	1 c	249	110	88	2	27	190	19	97
Peaches, raw	1 medium	87	35	88	1	10	470	47	6
Pears, raw	1 pear	166	100	84	1	25	30	3	7
Pineapple, raw,									
diced	1 c	155	75	87	1	19	40	4	24
Raspberries,									
red, raw	1 c	123	60	87	1	14	160	16	31
Strawberries, raw,									
capped	1 c	149	45	92	1	10	40	4	84
Tangerines, raw	1 medium	84	35	88	1	9	770	77	26
Watermelon, raw, wedge, with rind and seeds	4 × 8 in.	482	155	92	3	35	1,760	176	46

Source: Nutritive Value of Foods, Home and Garden Bulletin No. 72. Washington, DC: U.S. Department of Agriculture, 1991.

Table C-3
Meat, Fish, and Poultry

Meat	Approximate Measure (oz)	Weight (g)	Food Energy (kcal)	Water (%)	Protein (g)	Fat (g)	Iron (mg)	Thiamin (mg)
Beef, cooked								
Cuts braised, simmered, or pot roasted								
Lean and fat	3	85	325	43	22	26	2.5	0.06
Lean only	2.2	62	170	53	19	9	2.3	0.05
Ground beef, broiled								
Lean	3	85	230	56	21	16	1.8	0.04
Regular	3	85	245	54	20	18	2.1	0.03
Roast, oven-cooked								
Relatively fat, such as rib								
Lean and fat	3	85	315	46	19	26	2.0	0.06
Lean only	2.2	61	150	57	17	9	1.7	0.05
Relatively lean, such as eye of round								
Lean and fat	3	85	205	57	23	12	1.6	0.07
Lean only	2.6	75	135	63	22	5	1.5	0.07
Lamb, cooked								
Leg, roasted								
Lean and fat	3	85	205	59	22	13	1.7	0.09
Lean only	1.6	73	140	64	20	6	1.5	0.08
Liver, beef, fried	3	85	185	56	23	7	5.3	0.18
Pork, fresh, cooked								
Chop, loin, broiled								
Lean and fat	3.1	87	275	50	24	19	0.7	0.87
Roast, rib								
Lean and fat	3	85	270	51	21	20	0.8	0.50
Lean only	2.5	71	175	57	20	10	0.7	0.45
Veal, cooked, bone removed								
Roast, rib, medium fat	3	85	230	55	23	14	0.7	0.11
Poultry								
Chicken, breast, fried, batter-dipped								
Flesh with skin	4.9	140	365	52	35	18	1.8	0.16
Chicken, drumstick, fried, batter-dipped								
Flesh with skin	2.5	72	195	53	16	11	1.0	0.08
Chicken, canned, boneless	5	142	235	69	31	11	2.2	0.02
Turkey, roasted, flesh only								
Dark meat	3	85	160	63	24	6	2.0	0.05
Light meat	3	85	135	66	25	3	1.1	0.05
Fish								
Haddock, breaded, fried	3	85	175	61	17	9	1.0	0.06
Tuna, canned in oil								
Drained solids	3	85	165	61	24	7	1.6	0.04
Tuna, canned in water								
Solids and liquid	3	85	135	63	30	1	0.6	0.03
Flounder, baked	3	85	80	78	17	1	0.3	0.05
Salmon, baked	3	85	140	67	21	5	0.5	0.18

Source: Nutritive Value of Foods, Home and Garden Bulletin No. 72. Washington, DC: U.S. Department of Agriculture, 1991.

Table C-4

Dairy Products

Product	Approximate Measure	Food Weight (g)	Energy (kcal)	Water (%)	Protein (g)	Fat (g)	Carbohydrate (g)	Calcium (mg)	Vitamin A (IU)	(RE)
Fluid milk										
Whole, 3.3% fat	1 c	244	150	88	8	8	11	291	310	76
Nonfat (skim)	1 c	245	85	91	8	Trace	12	302	500	149
Reduced fat, 2% fat, nonfat milk solids added, less than 10 g of protein per cup	1 c	245	125	89	9	5	12	313	500	140
Buttermilk	1 c	245	100	90	8	2	12	285	80	20
Canned										
Evaporated, unsweetened whole	1 c	252	340	74	17	19	25	657	610	136
Condensed, sweetened	1 c	306	980	27	24	27	166	868	1,000	248
Dry, nonfat, instant	1 c	68	245	4	24	Trace	35	837	1,610 (added)	483
Yogurt, plain (from partially skimmed milk with added milk solids)	1 c	227	145	85	12	4	16	415	150	36
Cream										
Half-and-half	1 c	242	315	81	7	28	10	254	1,050	259
Light, coffee or table	1 c	240	470	74	6	46	9	231	1,730	437
Heavy whipping	1 c	238	820	58	5	88	7	154	3,500	1,002
Cheese										
Cheddar	1 oz	28	115	37	7	9	Trace	204	300	86
Creamed cottage, 4% fat (curd not pressed down), large curd	1 c	225	235	79	28	10	6	135	370	108

Source: Nutritive Value of Foods, Home and Garden Bulletin No. 72, Washington, DC: U.S. Department of Agriculture, 1991.

Table C-5
Cereal Products

Product	Approximate Measure	Weight (g)	Food Energy (kcal)	Water (%)	Protein (g)	Carbohydrate (g)	Iron (mg)	Thiamin (mg)	Riboflavin (mg)	Niacin (mg)
Wheat										
Bread, whole wheat	1 slice	25	70	29	3	13	1.0	0.08	0.06	1.1
Bread, white, enriched	1 slice	25	65	37	2	12	0.7	0.12	0.08	0.9
Bulgur, uncooked	1 c	170	600	10	19	129	9.5	0.48	0.24	7.7
Cream of Wheat, quick, enriched, cooked	1 c	244	140	86	4	29	10.9	0.24	0.07	1.5
Flour, whole wheat	1 c	120	400	12	16	85	5.2	0.66	0.14	5.2
Flour, all-purpose, enriched	1 c	125	455	12	13	95	5.5	0.80	0.50	6.6
Flour, cake or pastry, enriched	1 c	96	350	12	7	76	4.2	0.58	0.38	5.1
Raisin Bran	1 oz	28	90	8	3	21	3.5	0.28	0.34	3.9
Shredded Wheat	1 oz	28	100	5	3	23	1.2	0.07	0.08	1.5
Wheaties	1 oz	28	100	5	3	23	4.5	0.37	0.43	5.0
Macaroni, cooked enriched	1 c	130	190	64	7	39	2.1	0.23	0.13	1.8
Noodles (egg), enriched, cooked	1 c	160	200	70	7	37	2.6	0.22	0.13	1.9

Product	Approximate Measure	Weight (g)	Food Energy (kcal)	Water (%)	Protein (g)	Carbohydrate (g)	Iron (mg)	Thiamin (mg)	Riboflavin (mg)	Niacin (mg)
Corn										
Cornmeal, whole-ground, dry	1 c	122	435	12	11	90	2.2	0.46	0.13	2.4
Cornmeal, degermed, enriched, cooked	1 c	240	120	88	3	26	1.4	0.14	0.10	1.2
Corn tortillas	1	30	65	45	2	13	0.6	0.05	0.03	0.4
Cornflakes										
plain	1 oz	28	110	3	2	24	1.8	0.37	0.43	5.0
sugar covered	1 oz	28	110	3	1	25	1.8	0.37	0.43	5.0
Oats										
Oatmeal or rolled oats, cooked	1 c	234	145	85	6	25	1.6	0.26	0.05	0.3
Rice										
white, enriched, cooked regular	1 c	205	225	73	4	50	1.8	0.23	0.02	2.1
instant	1 c	165	180	73	4	40	1.3	0.21	0.02	1.7
brown	1 c	195	230	70	5	50	1.0	0.18	0.04	2.7

Source: Nutritive Value of Foods, Home and Garden Bulletin No. 72, Washington, DC: U.S. Department of Agriculture, 1991.

Glossary

TERMS USED IN COOKERY

Baste. To spoon liquid over food as it cooks. The liquid may be drippings from the food itself.

Beat. To make a mixture smooth using a brisk motion that has an up-and-down movement.

Blanch. To apply boiling water or steam for a few minutes.

Blend. To mix two or more ingredients thoroughly.

Boil. To cook in water at a boiling temperature.

Braise. To cook meat or poultry slowly in a covered utensil in a small amount of liquid or in steam.

Bread. To roll in bread crumbs before cooking.

Broil. To cook by direct exposure to radiant heat.

Brown. To produce a brown surface on a food by the use of relatively high heat.

Caramelize. To heat sugar until a brown color and characteristic flavor develop.

Chop. To cut into pieces using a sharp knife or other tool.

Clarify. To clear a liquid of all solid particles.

Cream. To mix one or more foods, usually fat and sugar, until smooth and creamy.

Crumb. To coat or top with crumbs, such as topping a casserole dish.

Cut in. To distribute solid fat throughout dry ingredients using two knives or a pastry blender.

Dice. To cut into small cubes.

Dot. To place small particles at intervals on a surface, as to dot with butter.

Dredge. To sprinkle or coat with flour or other fine substance.

Fold. To combine by using two motions, cutting vertically through the mixture and turning the mixture over and over.

Fricassee. To cook by braising; usually applied to fowl, rabbit, or veal cut into pieces.

Fry. To cook in fat. Pan-frying is to cook to doneness in a small amount of fat; deep-fat frying is to cook submerged in hot fat.

Grind. To reduce to small particles by cutting or crushing mechanically.

Knead. To manipulate by pressure alternated with folding and stretching, as in kneading a dough.

Lard. To place fat on top or insert strips of fat in uncooked lean meat or fish to give flavor and prevent drying of the surface.

Leaven. To make lighter by use of a gaseous agent such as air, water vapor, or carbon dioxide.

Level off. To move the level edge of a knife or spatula across the top edge of a container, scraping away the excess material.

Marinate. To let lie in a prepared liquid for a period for tenderizing and seasoning purposes.

Melt. To liquefy by use of heat.

Mince. To divide into very small pieces by chopping or cutting.

Mix. To combine ingredients.

Oven spring. The rapid increase in volume of yeast bread during the first few minutes of baking.

Pan-broil. To cook uncovered on a hot surface, pouring off fat as it accumulates.

Panning. The cooking of a vegetable in a tightly covered skillet, using a small amount of fat but no added water.

Pare. To cut off an outside covering such as skins of vegetables.

Peel. To remove outside coverings.

Poach. To cook in a hot liquid. The food is carefully handled to retain its form as in poaching an egg.

Pot-roast. To cook large pieces of meat by braising.

Proofing. The final rising period before baking for yeast doughs that have been molded.

Render. To melt fat and remove from connective tissue using low heat.

Retort pouch. A flexible laminated package that withstands high-temperature processing in a commercial pressure canner called a *retort*.

Roast. To cook, uncovered, by use of dry heat.

Roux. A thickening agent made by heating a blend of flour and fat. It may be white or brown and is used in making sauces and gravies.

Sauté. To cook quickly in a small amount of hot fat; a partial cooking process.

Scald. To heat milk or other liquids just below the boiling point.

Sear. To coagulate or brown the surface of meat by the application of intense heat for a brief period.

Sift. To separate the fine parts of a material from the coarse parts by use of a sieve.

Simmer. To cook in liquid at about 185°F (85°C). The liquid may show slight movement or bubbling, but the bubbles tend to form slowly and to break below the surface.

Steam. To cook in direct contact with steam in a closed container. Indirect steaming may be done in the closed top of a double boiler.

Steep. To extract flavor or color at a temperature below the boiling point of water.

Stew. To simmer in a small to moderate quantity of liquid.

Stir. To mix food materials with a circular motion.

Toast. To brown by means of dry heat.

Truss. To secure the wings and legs of a bird with pins or twine.

Whip. To rapidly beat such mixtures as gelatin dishes, eggs, and cream to incorporate air and increase volume.

TERMS USED IN FOOD SCIENCE

Acid. Sour-tasting compound containing hydrogen that may be ionized or replaced by positive elements to form salts.

Acrolein. Irritating substance formed by the decomposition of glycerol at high temperatures.

Alkali. Substance having the ability to neutralize an acid.

Amino acid. Organic molecule containing both an amino

$$O$$
$$\|$$

group ($-NH_2$) and an acid group ($-C-OH$); the basic building block of proteins.

Amylase. Enzyme that breaks down or hydrolyzes starch.

Amylopectin. Highly branched-chain fraction of starch.

Amylose. Straight-chain fraction of starch.

Antioxidant. Substance that retards oxidative rancidity in fats by becoming oxidized itself and stopping a chain reaction.

Aroma. Distinctive, pleasant fragrance or odor.

Astringent. Shrinking or contracting of tissues in the mouth to produce a puckery effect.

Boiling point. Temperature at which the atmospheric pressure is equal to the vapor pressure of a liquid and an equilibrium is established.

Brownian movement. The pushing to and fro of comparatively large molecules, such as those in a colloidal dispersion, by the rapidly moving small molecules of the dispersing medium (usually water in food products).

Buffer. Substance that resists change in acidity or alkalinity.

Carbohydrates. Organic compounds containing carbon, hydrogen, and oxygen; simple sugars and polymers of simple sugars.

Catalyst. Substance that affects the rate of a chemical reaction without being used up in the reaction.

Chymosin. Enzyme from the stomach that clots milk; previously called *rennin.*

Coagulation. Usually refers to a change in or denaturation of a protein that results in hardening or precipitation. Often accomplished by heat or mechanical agitation.

Colloid. Usually refers to the state of subdivision of dispersed particles; intermediate between very small particles in true solution and large particles in suspension. Proteins and pectins are usually colloidal.

Crystallization. Process of forming crystals that result from chemical elements solidifying with an orderly internal structure.

Denaturation. Changing of a protein molecule, usually by the unfolding of the chains, to a less soluble state.

Dextrinization. Breakdown of starch molecules to dextrins by dry heat.

Dextrins. Polysaccharides resulting from the partial hydrolysis of starch.

Disaccharide. Carbohydrate made up of two simple sugars (monosaccharides) linked together. Table sugar (sucrose) is a disaccharide.

Disperse. To distribute or spread throughout some other substance.

Dispersed phase. Separated or particle component in a dispersion.

Dispersion. System composed of dispersed particles in a dispersion medium.

Dispersion medium. Continuous medium in which particles are dispersed.

Emulsifier. Surface-active agent that acts as a bridge between two immiscible liquids and allows an emulsion to form.

Emulsion. Dispersion of one liquid in another with which it is usually immiscible.

Enzyme. Organic catalyst produced by living cells that changes the rate of a reaction without being used up in the reaction.

Ester. Chemical combination of an alcohol and an organic acid. Fats are esters of glycerol and three fatty acids.

Fatty acids. Organic acids made up of chains of carbon atoms with a carboxyl group ($-\overset{\overset{\text{O}}{\|}}{\text{C}}-\text{OH}$) on one end; three fatty acids combine with glycerol to make a triglyceride.

Fermentation. Transformation of organic substances into smaller molecules by the action of a microorganism; yeast ferments glucose to carbon dioxide and alcohol.

Foam. Dispersion of a gas in a liquid.

Gel. Colloidal dispersion that shows some rigidity and keeps the shape of the container in which it has been placed.

Gelatinization. Swelling and consequent thickening of starch granules when heated in water.

Gluten. Elastic, tenacious substance formed from the insoluble proteins of wheat flour during dough development.

Glycerol. Three-carbon organic compound (an alcohol) that combines with fatty acids to produce fats (triglycerides).

Gram. Basic unit of weight in the metric system; 28.35 grams equal 1 ounce and 453.59 grams equal 1 pound.

Gustatory. Having to do with the sense of taste.

Homogenize. To break up particles into small, uniform-size pieces. Fat in milk may be homogenized.

Hydration. Process of absorbing water.

Hydrogenation. Process in which hydrogen is combined chemically with an unsaturated compound such as an oil. Hydrogenation of oil produces a plastic shortening.

Hydrolysis. Chemical reaction in which a molecular linkage is broken and a molecule of water is utilized. Starch is hydrolyzed to produce glucose; water is a necessary component of the reaction.

Hydrophilic. Attracted to water.

Hygroscopic. Tending to absorb water readily.

Immiscible. Not capable of being mixed.

Inversion. Breakdown of sucrose to its component monosaccharides, glucose and fructose.

Irradiation. Process in which food is exposed to radiant energy.

Kilocalorie. Amount of heat required to raise the temperature of 1 kilogram (1,000 grams) of water 1°C; a unit of energy.

Kinetic energy. Energy created by the very rapid movement of small molecules or ions in a liquid.

Lecithin. Fatty substance containing two fatty acids esterified to glycerol along with phosphoric acid and a nitrogen-containing compound; a phospholipid.

Maillard reaction. Browning reaction involving combination of an amino group ($-NH_2$) from a protein and an aldehyde group ($-\overset{\overset{\text{H}}{|}}{\text{C}}=\text{O}$) from a sugar, which then leads to the formation of many complex substances.

Minerals. Inorganic substances; noncarbon compounds; ash.

Monoglyceride. Glycerol esterified to one fatty acid.

Monosaccharides. Simple sugars, for example, glucose, fructose, and galactose.

Olfactory. Having to do with the sense of smell.

Opaque. Not reflecting or giving out light; not clear.

Organic. Pertaining to carbon compounds.

Osmosis. Movement of water through a semipermeable membrane from an area of low concentration of solute to an area of higher concentration to equalize the osmotic pressure created by differences in concentration.

Oxidases. Enzymes that catalyze oxidation reactions.

Oxidation. Gain in oxygen or loss of electrons.

Pasteurization. Mild heat treatment to destroy vegetative microorganisms; not complete destruction of microbes.

Pectin. Polysaccharide composed of galacturonic acid subunits, partially esterified with methyl alcohol, and capable of forming a gel.

pH. Expression of degree of acidity. On a scale from 1 to 14, 7 is neutral, 1 is most acid, and 14 is most alkaline or least acid.

Photosynthesis. Formation of carbohydrates in living plants from water and carbon dioxide by the action of sunlight on the green chlorophyll pigment of the leaves.

Plasticity. Ability to be molded or shaped.

Polyphenols. Organic compounds that include as part of their chemical structures an unsaturated ring with more than one −OH group on it. These compounds are implicated in certain types of oxidative enzymatic browning in foods.

Polysaccharides. Complex carbohydrates containing many simple sugars (monosaccharides) linked together. Starch and pectins are polysaccharides.

Polyunsaturated fatty acid. Fatty acid that has two or more double bonds between carbon atoms. A polyunsaturated fat is one that contains a relatively high proportion of polyunsaturated fatty acids.

Reduction. Gain of hydrogen or gain of electrons.

Rennet. Crude extract from calf stomach containing the enzyme chymosin (previously called *rennin*).

Retrograde. Close association of amylose molecules in a starch gel during aging.

Saturated fatty acid. Fatty acid that has no double bonds between its carbon atoms and thus holds all of the hydrogen it can hold. A saturated fat is one that contains a relatively high proportion of saturated fatty acids.

Saturated solution. Solution containing all of the solute that it can dissolve at that temperature.

Sol. Pourable colloidal dispersion that has not yet set into a gel.

Solubility. Amount of a substance that will dissolve in a specified quantity of another substance.

Solute. Substance to be dissolved in another substance (called the *solvent*).

Solution. Mixture resulting when a solute is dissolved in a solvent.

Solvent. Substance that will dissolve another substance (called the *solute*).

Spore. Encapsulated, resistant form of a microorganism.

Sterilize. To destroy microorganisms by heating with steam or dry heat or by boiling in liquid for 20 to 30 minutes.

Substrate. Substance on which an enzyme acts or the medium on which microorganisms grow.

Supersaturated solution. Solution that has dissolved more solute or dispersed substance than it can ordinarily hold at a particular temperature. The solution is formed by being heated and slowly cooled without disturbance.

Syneresis. Separation or weeping of liquid from a gel.

Tactile. Having to do with the sense of touch.

Toxin. A poison, usually a protein, formed by microorganisms.

Translucent. Shining or glowing through; partly transparent.

Viscosity. Resistance to flow.

Volatile. Readily forming a vapor or gaseous phase.

Volatilization. Process of becoming volatile.

Whey. Liquid portion of milk remaining after the curd, which is chiefly the protein casein, is precipitated.

Index

Abbreviations, 124t, 849
Accredited certifiers, 114, 115
Acculturation, 3
Acesulfame-K, 272
Acid coagulation, 598–599
Acid hydrolysis, 262
Acidophilus milks, 596
Acids
    as additives, 108t, 109
    fatty, 202–205, 221
    gelatin and, 575
    organic, 535
Adsorption, 246
Aftertaste, 20
Agglomerates, 297
Agglutination, 87
Air, heat transfer by, 150
Albumins, 364
Alcohols
    in beverages, 778
    as flavoring, 183–184
    regulation of, 116
    sugar, 274–275
    in vegetables, 489
Aldehydes, 489
Alginate, 815
Alimentary paste. *See* Pasta
Alitame, 274
Alkalies, 108t, 109, 263
Allergies, 88–89
Altitude, baking and, 377–378
Amaranth flour, 367
Amino acids, 187, 207–208, 571
Amino groups, 201
Amphiphilic molecules, 247
Amylases, 311, 342, 368, 415
Amylopectin, 421–422

Amylose, 312, 338, 421, 570
Anaphylactic shock, 88–89
Anaphylactoid reactions, 89
Angel food cake, 439, 441–444
Animal parasites, 83–84
Anthocyanins, 487
Anthoxanthins, 487
Anticaking agents, 108t, 109
Antimicrobial agents, 108t, 109
Antioxidants, 488, 826
    as additives, 108t, 109
    in lard, 230
    rancidity and, 235
Appearance, of food, 12
Appetite, 11
Apples, 537, 538t, 540t
Aquaculture, 765
Aroma, 14
Aromatic compounds, 535
Aromatic products, 176
Aseptic canning, 835–836
Aseptic packaging, 11, 590, 778, 810,
    815–816
Aseptic storage, 548–549
Asparagus, 491, 492
Aspartame, 271–272, 533, 535, 604, 776
Aspics, 576, 578
Astringency, 789
Atherogenic foods, 628
ATP (adenosine triphosphate), 667
Avocados, 537, 540

Bacteria, 68–69
Baking
    cakes, 438–439
    cookies, 449–450
    freezing foods and, 830, 832

fruits, 555
high-altitude, 377–378
meat, 707–711
microwave, 158–159
pastry, 461–463
seafood, 769
vegetables, 496
Baking powder, 369–371
Bananas, 537, 539–540
Barley, 342
Basting, 704
Batalains, 487
Batters and doughs, 357–382
    classification of, 374
    definition of, 374
    dry flour mixes for, 376–377
    eggs in, 373
    fats in, 371–372
    flour in, 357–367
    high-altitude baking of, 377–378
    ingredients in, 357–374
    leavening agents in, 367–371
    liquids in, 373
    mixing, 374–376
    structure of, 376
    sweeteners in, 373–374
Bavarian creams, 577
Beef, 670
    broiling, 711–713
    carving, 721
    cuts of, 685–686, 691
    ground, 694–695, 700, 701
    quality of, 681–682
    roasting times for, 709t
Berries, 538t, 540–541
Beta-amylase, 267
Beta-glucans, 199, 200

Beverages, 775–800
  alcoholic, 778
  carbonated, 7, 9, 775–776
  cocoa and chocolate, 791–796
  coffee, 778–787
  fruit juices, 547–549
  noncarbonated fruit, 777–778
  sports/isotonic, 777
  tea, 787–791
Biotechnology, 11, 88, 89–90, 107, 478–479
Birdseye, Clarence, 45
Birefringence, 313
Biscuit method, 375
Biscuits, 393–395
Bison, 672
Blanching, 142, 805, 824, 829
Bleaching agents, 108t, 109
Bloom, chocolate, 794–795
Body, 301
Boiling
  in home canning, 837–838
  vegetables, 498–499
Boiling points, 276–278
Botulinum toxin, 506
Botulism, 72t, 80–82, 506, 804, 837
Bound water, 189
Bovine spongiform encephalopathy (BSE), 677
Braising, 150–151, 715, 749
Bran, 332, 334, 341
Bread
  flour for, 362–363
  machines, 409
  quick, 383–398
  yeast, 399–427
Breakfast cereals, 342–346
  cooking, 345–346
  purchasing, economics of, 343, 345
  ready-to-cook and instant, 342–343
  ready-to-eat, 343
Brittles, 284
Broiling
  fruits, 555
  meat, 711–713
  poultry, 748–749
  seafood, 768–769
Browning, 201
  enzymatic oxidative, 109, 487–488, 826
  microwave cooking and, 161, 166
  of milk, 598
  nonenzymatic, 261–262
Brown roux, 317
Buckwheat, 342, 367
Buffers, 108t, 109, 210

Bulbs, 473, 477
Bulgur, 336
Bulking agents, 108t, 110, 275–276, 298
Bureau of Alcohol, Tobacco, and Firearms, 116
Butter, 227–228, 584–585
Buttermilk, 369, 370–371, 595–596
Butyric acid, 233

Cabbage, 489
Caffeine, 776, 782, 794
Cakes, 429–445
  angel food, 439–444
  baking shortened, 438–439
  conventional method for, 375–376
  flour for, 363
  high-altitude baking of, 377–378
  ingredients in shortened, 430–436
  mixing shortened, 436–437
  preparation of pans for, 437–438, 443
  shortened, 429–439
  sponge, 444–445
  types and characteristics of shortened, 429–430
  unshortened, 439–445
Calories, 143
  kilocalories, 193
Campylobacter jejuni, 72t, 74–75
Candling, 631–632
Candy making, 276–279
  candy classifications and, 279–288
  chocolate dipping, 286–288
  confectionery industry, 288
  crystalline candies, 279–283
  fudge, 282–283
  noncrystalline candies, 283–285
  temperatures and tests for, 280t
Canned foods
  fish, 764–765
  fruits, 551
  vegetables, 506
Canning, 45, 804–805, 834–843
  boiling water bath, 837–838
  botulism and, 81–82
  containers for, 841–842
  handling after processing, 842–843
  heat penetration in, 842
  history of, 834–836
  lacquered tin-coated cans in, 85, 487
  methods for home, 836–841
  obtaining effective seal in, 842
  obtaining partial vacuum in, 842
  packing in, 836–837
  pressure, 151–152, 838–841
  processing in, 837

Can sizes, 850
Capons, 736
Caproic acid, 233
Caramelization, 201, 261–262, 373
Caramels, 284–285
Carbohydrates, 194–201
  chemical classification of, 195–201
  as fat replacers, 245
  in milk products, 585–586
Carbon dioxide production, 368–370
Carbonyl groups, 201
Carcinogenic process, 271
Carcinogens, 106–107, 271
Carotenes, 789
Carotenoid pigments, 361, 473, 486–487, 530, 670
Carotenoids, 109
Carrageenan, 815
Casein, 213, 582, 583
Caseinate, 102
Catalysts, 317
Catalyze, 201
Cellulase, 549
Cellulose, 199–200
Centers for Disease Control and Prevention, 57, 114, 116
Cereal grains, 331–356
  in breakfast cereals, 342–346
  common, 336–342
  consumption of, 331–332
  nutritive value and enrichment of, 334–336, 860–861t
  structure and composition of, 332–334
Certified colors, 102
Changes of state, 142–145
Cheese, 604–618
  cold-pack, 608
  composition and nutritive value of, 607–608
  in cooked foods, 616, 618
  grading, 607
  process, 608, 615
  ripening, 605–607
  storing, 615–616
  types of, 608–615
Chelates, 235
Cherries, 538t, 541
Chicken. *See* Poultry
Chicory, 783
Chili peppers, 174
Chlorophyll, 485–486
Chocolate, 288
  beverages, 791–795
  bloom on, 794–795
  cakes, 435

composition of, 793–794
dipping, 286–288
processing, 792–793
storing, 795–796
Cholesterol, 205, 229, 628
Cis configuration, 226
Cis-trans configuration, 204–205
Citrus fruits, 541–542
Clams, 763
Clarifying liquids, 627
Clostridium botulinum, 80–82, 490, 804, 816, 818, 837, 843
Clostridium perfringens, 72t, 79–80
Coagulation, 210–211, 373, 627, 703
of eggs, 641–644
of milk, 597, 598–600
Cocoa
beverages, 791–795
composition of, 793–794
processing, 792–793
storing, 795–796
Coconuts, 538t, 545
Codex Alimentarius Commission, 87, 117
Coffee, 778–787
composition of, 781–782
decaffeinated, 782
iced, 786
instant, 782
preparing, 784–786
roasting, 779, 781
specialty, 782–783
substitutes for, 783
Coffeecakes, 393
Collagen, 571–572
Colloidal dispersions, 214–215, 583
Colloidal substances, 311
Color
additives, 106, 108t, 109
blanching and, 142
in eggs, 629
in fruits, 532–533
in meats, 666–667
of milk, 586
of vegetables, 485–488
Comminuted products, 697
Complex carbohydrates, 189
Computerized checkout systems, 42
Condensation, 145
Conduction, 145–147
Confectionery industry, 288
Consumption surveys, 31–33
Continuing Survey of Food Intakes by Individuals (CSFII), 32
Controlled atmosphere storage, 484
Convection currents, 147–149

Convenience foods, 830, 832 36, 11
availability and use of, 42–50
cost of, 48–49
eating quality of, 49
nutritive value of, 49–50
Convenience stores, 37
Cookies, 429, 445–450
baking, 449–450
ingredients for, 445, 447–448
mixing and handling, 448–449
types of, 445
Cooking, effects of on food, 141–142
Cooking utensils
conduction by, 146–147
for microwave cooking, 164–166
Corn, 337–338
Corn flour, 366
Cornmeal, 366
Corn starch pudding, 324–325
Corn syrups, 267
Cost of foods, 34–42, 48–49
Covalent bonds, 191
Crab, 761–762
Cream, 601–604
churning, 227–228
types of, 601–602
whipping, 602–603
Cream of tartar, 262, 369, 442–443, 644
Cream puffs, 385–387
Crêpes, 650
Critical control points, 59–61
Critical temperature, 585
Crockery slow cooking, 716
Crop production, 35
Cross-contamination, 61, 63
Crudités, 568
Crumb crusts, 463–465
Cryoprotectants, 763
Crystalline substances, 172
Crystallization, 215, 261
in candies, 281–282
cocrystallization, 265–267
in frozen desserts, 300
Cuisine, 3, 117, 174. *See also* Multicultural cuisine
Culture, 1–4
Cured fish, 764
Custards, 307, 651–653, 654
Cyclamates, 273–274
Cytoplasm, 667

Daily Reference Values (DRVs), 40
Daily values, 39–40
Deep-fat fryers, 152, 237

Deep-fat frying, 236–238, 239t, 498
De-esterification, 494
Defrosting, 167
Dehydrated foods, 46. *See also* Dried foods
Dehydrogenases, 212
Delaney clause, 105, 106–107
Demographics, 3
Denaturation, 210–211, 641, 703
Density, 123, 161, 585
Department of Agriculture (USDA), 110–114, 187
Desiccation, 802, 827
Desserts
gelatin, 576–577
starch-thickened, 324–325
Desserts, frozen, 295–310
characteristics of, 300–301
commercial ice cream, 296–297
light, 297–299
nutritive value of, 300
preparing, 301–307
types of, 299–300
Dextrinization, 385
Dextrins, 198–199, 267, 317
Diabetes, 270, 449
Dielectric properties, 167–168
Dietary guidelines, 5–8, 9, 221–222
Diffusion, 552
Diglycerides, 231, 371
Dipolar molecules, 161, 192
Disaccharides, 196–197, 261, 317
Disappearance data, 30–31, 259, 331
Disodium 5'-guanylate, 176
Disodium 5'-inosinate, 176
Dispersions, 213–215
Disulfide bonds, 364–365
Disulfide linkages, 641
Dough conditioners, 413, 415
Doughs. *See* Batters and doughs
Dried foods, 549–550, 639–640, 805–806
Duck. *See* Poultry
Durbin, Dick, 112
Durum wheat, 336, 348–349

Éclairs, 385–387
Economics, 29–50
consumer food waste and, 33–34
convenience foods and, 42–50
factors influencing food costs, 34–42
in food choice, 10–11
food purchasing and, 50–51
food use trends and, 29–33
in purchasing breakfast cereals, 343, 345

Edible films, 802, 815
Egg custards, 307, 651–653
Eggs, 627–662
  in angel food cake, 441–442, 443
  in batters and doughs, 373
  beating, 642–644
  in cakes, 431–432
  composition and nutritive value of,
    627–629
  cooking, 641–642
  cooking in the shell, 645–646
  cooking temperatures for, 64
  in crêpes, 650
  in food preparation, 640–656
  food safety and, 73
  freezing, 830
  frying, 646–647
  in meringues, 653, 655–656
  in omelets, 648–650
  poaching, 644–645
  preserving and processing, 638–640
  quality of, 630–638
  scrambling, 647
  shirring, 647–648
  in soufflés, 650–651
  structure of, 629–630
  substitutes for, 656–657
Embryo (grain), 334
Emulsifiers
  as additives, 108t, 109
  in batters and doughs, 371
  in butter, 227
  in cakes, 433–434
  as fat replacers, 245
  in frozen desserts, 303
  in milk homogenization, 591
Emulsifying agents, 221, 222
Emulsions, 19, 187, 221, 246–247
  additives in, 109
  breaking and re-forming, 252
  eggs in, 627
  in foods, 246–247
  mayonnaise, 251–252
  in milk, 584
  permanent, 247
  salad dressings, 247–252, 570
  temporary, 247
  on vegetables, 484
Encapsulated flavorings, 182–183
Endosperms, 334, 360
Enrichment, 335–336, 364
Enteropathogenic bacteria, 75
Environmental contaminants, 85
Environmental Protection Agency
    (EPA), 114

Enzymatic oxidative browning, 109,
    487–488, 826
Enzymatic reactions, 18
Enzyme coagulation, 599–600
Enzymes, 211–213, 802
  gelatin and, 576
  hydrolysis of, 263
Epidemiological studies, 271
Equipment, 132–137
  hand tools, 135–136
  knives, 132–135
  portioning and measuring tools,
    135–136
Escherichia coli, 59, 72t, 75–76, 701
Espagnole sauce, 317
Essential oils, 109, 535
Esters, 244, 271–272, 489
Ethnicity, 2–4. *See also* Multicultural
    cuisine
Ethylene, 536
Evaporated milk, 593, 603
Extracts, flavor, 181–183

Factor method, 131–132
Fair Packaging and Labeling Act, 99
Family, food choices and, 1–2
Farmers' markets, 37
Farm-value shares, 35
Fat replacers, 108t, 110, 243–246, 317,
    372
Fats, 221–258
  in batters and doughs, 371–372
  buying, 242–243
  in cakes, 432–433
  consumption of, 221–222
  cooking low fat, 243
  deterioration of, 233–235
  in eggs, 628
  in emulsions, 246–247
  in food preparation, 206
  frying with, 236–242
  heat transfer by, 152
  measuring solid, 128
  in meats, 664–666
  in milk, 584–585
  nutritive value of, 221–224
  phospholipids, 205
  processing and refining of, 226–233
  properties of, 224–225
  replacers for, 243–246
  in salad dressings, 247–252
  saturated/unsaturated, 224–225
  sterols, 205–206
  triglycerides, 202–205
  visible and invisible, 221

in yeast breads, 407
Fatty acids, 202–205, 221
  omega-6 and omega-3, 224
  saturated, 372, 584–585, 664
  trans, 226–227, 243
  unsaturated, 664
Federal Fungicide, Rodenticide, and
    Insecticide Act, 86
Federal Register, 100
Federal Trade Commission (FTC),
    116
Fermentation, 68, 368
  fruit beverage, 777–778
  of milk, 594–596
  of monosodium glutamate, 174–175
  of soy products, 516
  sugar in, 262
  yeast bread, 401, 411
Ferric iron, 509
Ferrous metals, 150
Fiber, 199, 362
  breads with high, 419
  cooking and, 494
  in fruits, 530
  in vegetables, 471–472
Filled milk, 596
Fill of container standards, 101
Fish. *See also* Seafood
  cooking temperatures for, 64
  food safety and, 73
  inspections of, 116
  jellies, 576
  nutritive value of, 858t
5'-ribonucleotides, 171, 175–176
Flakiness, 455–457
Flavonoid pigments, 485
Flavor, 12, 14–18, 171
  additives, 108t, 109
  enhancers, 174–176
  extracts, 181–183
  fats in, 225
  of fruits, 533, 535
  meat, 718–719
  of milk, 586
  profiles, 19
  raw starch, 319
  reversion, 234–235
  taste and odor in, 14–17
  types of, 17–18
  of vegetables, 489–490
Flavorings, 171
  alcohol, 183–184
  vegetables and fruits as, 183
  yeast bread, 415
Flocculation, 642, 643

Flour, 357–367
  all-purpose, 363
  bleaching and maturing, 361
  bleaching and maturing agents in, 108t, 109
  bread, 362–363
  cake, 363, 442
  in cakes, 434–435
  corn, 366
  dry mixes with, 376–377
  durum, 350
  enriched/fortified, 335–336, 364
  gluten, 363–364, 364–366
  grades of, 361
  instantized, 322, 363
  measuring, 127–128
  milling, 359–361
  pastry, 363
  rye, 366
  self-rising, 363
  soy, 366–367
  types of, 362–364
  wheat classes for, 359
  whole wheat, 362
  in yeast breads, 405–406
Flowers, edible, 179–181, 183, 473, 476
Foams, 206, 575, 576–577, 627
Fondant, 279–282, 285–286
Food
  availability of, 9–10
  buying, 50–51
  composition of, 187–220
  costs, 34–42
  disappearance data, 30–31
  functional, 44
  handling, 61–67
  high risk or potentially hazardous, 61
  objective evaluation of, 20–22
  trends in use of, 29–33
  waste of, 33–34
Food additives, 99, 102–110
  commonly used, 107–110
  definition of, 103
  fat replacers, 243–246
  justifiable uses of, 103–104
  legislation on, 104–107, 106
  in meat, 677
  preservatives, 806–807
Food Additives Amendment (1958), 106
Food allergies, 88–89
Food and Agriculture Organization (FAO), 117

Food and Drug Administration (FDA), 99–110, 104–107
Food and Drug Administration Modernization Act (1997), 40
Foodborne illness
  animal parasites in, 83–84
  environmental contaminants and, 85
  food handling and, 61–67
  Hazard Analysis and Critical Control Points system and, 58–61
  ionizing radiation and, 67
  mycotoxins in, 82–83
  naturally occurring toxic substances and, 87–88
  pesticide residues and, 85–87
  preventing, 57–67
  Salmonella, 71–74
  viruses in, 84–85
Food choices, 1–12
  cultural factors in, 2–3
  economic/marketplace factors in, 9–11
  emotional/psychological effects of, 12
  family/social factors in, 1–2
  nutrition/health and, 5–9
  religion and, 3–4
  technology and, 11–12
Food consumption surveys, 31–33
Food cooperatives (co-ops), 37
Food Guide Pyramid, 6–7, 8, 9
Food infections, 67–68, 71–78
Food intolerances, 89
Food intoxications, 67, 78–79
FoodNet, 69, 112, 114
Food poisoning, 78–79. *See also* Foodborne illness
Food processing, 11–12, 36, 226–233, 508–509, 548–549
Food purchasing
  economics and, 50–51
  fats, 242–243
  fresh fruits, 537–546
  meat, 676–696, 692–696
  poultry, 738–742
  seafood, 765
  vegetables, 479–482
Food Quality Protection Act (1996), 86, 105
Food regulations/standards, 99–122
  Centers for Disease Control and Prevention, 114, 116
  EPA, 114
  FDA, 99–110

  Federal Trade Commission, 116
  of fill of container, 101
  of identity, 100–101
  international, 117
  of minimum quality, 101
  organic foods, 113–114, 115
  sanitation requirements, 101–102
  state and local agency, 116
  USDA, 110–114
Food safety, 57–97
  agency for, 112
  of eggs, 635–6383
  foodborne infections and intoxications and, 69–90
  fresh fruits and vegetables, 566
  of meat, 699–701
  microorganism characteristics and, 67–69
  of milk, 588–590
  preventing foodborne illness, 57–67
  salad ingredients, 564–565
  of seafood, 766–767
Food Safety and Inspection Service, 39
Food Safety Council, 57
Food security, 10–11
Food Systems Engineering Facility (FSEF), 48
FORC-G, 112
Fortified products, 335–336, 591
Freeze-drying, 550, 805–806
Freezers, home, 832–834
Freezing, 823–834
  changes during, 825–827
  containers for, 832
  food preservation by, 803
  food selection for, 827
  frozen desserts, 303–304
  home freezer use/management and, 832–834
  milk, 600–601
  mixtures, 190, 303–304
  process for, 824–825
  techniques for, 827–832
French dressing, 250
French fries, 507–509
Frozen foods, 45
  desserts, 295–310
  eggs, 639
  fruits, 551
  meats, 717
  poultry, discoloration of bones in, 749
  vegetables, 505–506
  yeast doughs, 416
Fructose, 195

Fruits, 529–560
　beverages from, 777–778
　canned, 551
　color in, 532–533
　composition and nutritive value of, 529–532, 857
　cooking, 552–555
　dried, 549–550
　as flavorings, 183
　flavor of, 533, 535
　freezing, 8270829
　frozen, 551
　in gelatin, 576
　juices of, 547–549
　preparing, 551–555
　ripening changes in, 535–537
　in salads, 561–570
　selecting, 537–546
　storing, 546–547
　vegetable-fruits, 473, 475
Frying, 236–242
　care of fat in, 242
　deep-fat, 236–238
　fat absorption in, 240–241
　fat selection for, 241–242
　fats' interaction with food in, 238–239
　fat turnover and, 240
　meats, 713
　pan, 236
　poultry, 749
　seafood, 769–770
　vegetables, 496
Fudge, 282–283, 285
Functional foods, 44, 775

Galactose, 195
Galacturonic acid, 200, 571
Gamma rays, 809
Garnishes, 569–570
Gastroenteritis, 74, 84
Gelatin, 570–577
　hydration, swelling, and dispersion of, 574
　manufacture of, 571–572, 573
　nutritive value of, 572, 574
　salads and desserts, 576–577
　unmolding, 577
　uses of, 572
Gelatinization, 318
　in cream puff batter, 385
　starch, 373, 493, 720
Gelation, 574–576
Gels, 206, 215, 570–577, 640
　starch in, 312, 320–321
　structure and characteristics of, 570–571

Generic products, 38
Genetic engineering, 88, 89–90, 340, 478–479, 758
Germ (grain), 334
Germination, 311
Glazing, 555
Globulins, 364
Glucoamylase, 267
Glucose, 195, 311
Glucose isomerase, 267
Gluten, 221, 363, 364–366
　flour, 363–364
Glycogen, 199, 756
Glycoproteins, 823
Goitrogens, 87
Good manufacturing practices (GMPs), 99, 102, 566
Goose. See Poultry
Grading, 99
　cheese, 607
　eggs, 631–633
　flour, 361
　meat, 680–684
　milk, 588–589
　potatoes, 508
　poultry, 741–742
　seafood, 765–766
　standards, 111–113
　symbols of, 113
　vegetables, 480–482, 483
Grains, 82–83, 331–356
Grapes, 542–543
GRAS status, 70, 229, 269–270
Gravy, 720
Grilling, 496
Guarana, 775
Gums, vegetable, 195, 200–201, 311

Hand tools, 135
Handwashing, 62
Hard conversion, 125
Hazard analysis, 58–61
Hazard Analysis and Critical Control Points (HACCP) system, 58–61, 110–111
Headspace, 631
Health, 5–8, 10, 288, 333. See also Nutrition
Health claims, 40
Healthy People 2010: National Health Promotion and Disease Prevention Objectives, 5–8
Heat
　effects of on meat, 703–704
　effects of on starch, 317–320
　fat changes under, 238–239

　latent, 143, 145
　microwave action in, 159–161
　sensible, 143
Heat susceptors, 156
Heat transfer, 141–154
　changes of state and, 142–145
　by conduction, 145–147
　by convection, 147–149
　effects of cooking food and, 141–142
　by induction, 150
　media for, 150–152
　by radiation, 149–150
　thermometer scales and, 145
　types of, 145–150
Hedonic scales, 20, 276
Hemicelluloses, 199, 200
Hemorrhagic colitis, 75
Hepatitis, 84
Herbs, 176–183
　classification and use of, 176–177, 180–181t
　fresh, 179, 182
　history of, 176
　storage of, 177–179
Hermetic packaging, 506, 817
Hexoses, 195–196
High-fructose corn syrups (HFCSs), 267
High risk or potentially hazardous foods, 61
Home meal replacement, 2
Homogenization, 246, 297, 590–591
Honey, 268–269
Humectants, 108t, 109, 245
Hydration capacity, 406
Hydrocolloids, 163–164, 200, 311
Hydrogenated shortenings, 230–231
Hydrogenation, 226–227
Hydrogen bonds, 192–193, 207
Hydrolysis, 191, 195, 494, 584–585, 669
　acid, 262
　enzyme, 263
　in germination, 311
　rancidity and, 233
　of starch, 317
Hygroscopic products, 782
Hyphae, 665

Ice cream, 295–296, 299t. See also Desserts, frozen
　commercial processing of, 296–297
　freezers, 304–307
Ice milk, 297
Identity, standards of, 100–101, 228
Idiosyncratic illnesses, 89
Imitation food products, 101, 596

Immisibility, 246
Impingement ovens, 438–439
Induction coils, 150
Inspections, 99, 110–114
    of meat, 679–680
    poultry, 740
    seafood, 116, 765–766
Inulin, 288, 362
Invisible fat, 221
Ionizing radiation, 67
Ions, 189, 807
Isoflavones, 512
Isomerization, 487
Isotonic beverages, 777

Jaundice, 84

Ketones, 489
Kilocalories, 193
Kinetic motion, 215
Kiwifruit, 538t, 545
Kneading, 409–411
Knives, 132–135

Labeling, 39–42
    descriptors in, 43t
    information in, 102
    meat, 678–679
    nutrition information in, 7–8, 39–42
    open-date, 38
    organic foods, 113–114, 115
    poultry, 740–741
Labile flavor components, 17
Lacquered tin-coated cans, 85, 487
Lactobacillus acidophilus, 594
Lacto-ovo vegetarians, 4
Lactose, 197
Lamb, 671
    broiling, 712t
    carving, 723
    cooking, 700–701
    cuts of, 689, 691
    quality of, 682
    roasting times for, 709t
Lard, 230, 243
Latent heat, 143, 145, 190
LDL cholesterol, 229
Leavening agents, 367–371
    in cakes, 434
    fats and, 372
Legumes, 477–478, 509–511, 512
Lettuce, 564–569
Lignin, 199
Linoleic acid, 224, 234–235
Linolenic acid, 234–235, 789
Lipase, 341

Lipids, 221. *See* Fats
Lipoproteins, 373, 628
Lipoxygenase, 513
Liquids
    in cakes, 435
    measuring, 129
    in yeast breads, 406–407
Listeria monocytogenes, 77
Listeriosis, 72t
Lobster, 761–762, 770

Maillard reaction, 201, 284, 385, 407, 415, 462, 593, 640
Maltase, 368
Maltodextrins, 298
Maltose, 197, 311, 368
Mangoes, 538t, 545
Maple syrup, 268
Marbling, 670, 675
Margarine, 228–229
Marinades, 515, 569
Marketing, 36–42
Mass, 124
Maturing agents, 108t, 109
Mayonnaise, 251–252
Meals, Ready-to-Eat, 48
Measuring equipment, 126–127, 135–136. *See also* Weights and measures
Meats, 663–734
    braising, 715
    broiling and pan-broiling, 711–713
    carving, 721–723
    classification of, 670–671
    composition and nutritive value of, 664–667, 858t
    consumption of red, 663–664
    cooking, 701–719
    cooking temperatures for, 64
    crockery slow cooking, 716
    cured, 696–698
    cuts of, 684–692
    freezing, 829–830
    in gelatin, 576
    grading, 680–684
    gravy, 720
    inspections of, 679–680
    microwave cooking, 713–715
    postmortem changes and aging of, 671–673
    preparing, 699–701
    pressure cooking, 716
    processing, soy proteins in, 723
    purchasing, 676–696
    roasting or baking, 707–711
    in salads, 567

    sautéing and frying, 713
    soup stock from, 719–720
    stewing, 715
    storing, 699
    structure of, 667–670
    tempering, 157–158
    tenderness of, 673–676, 706–707
Melons, 538t, 543
Melting points, 224–225, 261–262
Meniscus, 129
Meringues, 653, 655–656
Mesophilic bacteria, 746, 803
Metabolic activity, 402
Metabolic food disorders, 89
Methyl esters, 571
Metric system, 123–125, 851
Micelles, 583
Microbiology, 58
Microcrystalline cellulose, 163–164
Microencapsulation, 70
Microfiltration, 548
Microorganisms, 67–69
Microwave cooking, 155–170
    action of microwaves in, 159–161
    advantages of, 161–162
    browning in, 166
    of cakes, 439
    combining with conventional cooking, 167
    defrosting with, 167
    of eggs, 656
    food industry use of, 157–159
    food safety and, 73
    foodservice use of, 157
    heating meals in, 167–168
    home use of, 156–157
    limitations of, 162–164
    of meats, 713–715
    packaging materials and cooking utensils for, 164–166
    of pastry, 463
    of seafood, 769–770
    standing time in, 167
    starch mixtures, 325–326
    stirring and turning in, 166–167
    vegetables, 501, 505
    yeast bread, 416
Military rations, 48
Milk, 581–625
    acid coagulation of, 598–599
    cheese and, 604–618
    composition and properties of, 582–588
    concentrated fluid, 593
    consumption of, 581–682
    cream and, 601–604

Milk (*cont.*)
  cultured milk products, 594–596
  dry, 594
  effects of heat on, 597–598
  enzyme coagulation of, 599–600
  filled and imitation, 596
  fluid, 591–593
  in food preparation, 597
  food safety and, 73–74
  freezing, 600–601
  homogenization of, 246
  making sour, 371
  nutritive value of, 859t
  phenolic compound coagulation of,
    600
  processing, 590–591
  products, types of, 591–601
  salts coagulation of, 600
  sanitation and quality of, 588–590
  soy, 515
Milkfat, 302
Miller Pesticide Amendment (1954),
    105
Mineral water, 775
Minimum quality standards, 101
Mitochondria, 667
Mixes, 50, 376–377
Modified-atmosphere packaging, 506,
    816–818
Moisture/vapor-proof materials,
    826–827, 832
Molasses, 267–268
Molds, 68
Mollusks, 84
Monoglycerides, 231, 371
Monosaccharides, 195–196, 261, 317
Monosodium glutamate (MSG),
    174–175, 175–176
Mucoprotein, 673
Muffin method, 375, 436
Muffins, 389–393
  characteristics of, 390
  ingredients for, 389–390
  mixing, 390–391
  variations for, 391–392
Multicultural cuisine, 4, 178
  dairy products in, 605
  pasta in, 352
  sandwiches, 400
  soups in, 323
Mutton, 671
Mycoprotein, 665
Mycotoxins, 82–83

National Oceanic and Atmospheric
    Administration (NOAA), 116

Nectarines, 538t, 544
Neotame, 273
Noncariogenic sweeteners, 275
Nonenzymatic oxidation, 826
Nonfat milk solids, 302
Nonvolatile flavor components, 17
Nonvolatile substances, 189
Nut breads, 393
Nutraceuticals, 44
Nutrient-content claims, 40
Nutrient Database for Standard Refer-
    ence, Release 15 (SR15), 187
Nutrients as additives, 108t, 109
Nutrition
  in cereal grains, 334–336, 860–861t
  in cheese, 607–608
  convenience foods and, 49–50
  daily values in, 39–40
  in eggs, 627–629
  in fats, 221–224
  food choice in, 5–8
  in frozen desserts, 300
  in fruits, 529–532, 857
  in gelatin, 572, 574
  labeling, 7–8, 39–42
  in meats, 664–667, 858t
  in milk, 587–588, 859t
  in poultry, 736
  in seafood, 755–757
  in selected foods, 854–861
  in sugars, 260
  in vegetables, 469–478, 855–856
Nutrition Labeling and Education Act
    (1990), 7–8, 39, 99

Oats, 341
Objective evaluations, 20–22
Odor, 14–17
Oils, refined, 231–233. *See also* Fats
Olestra, 244
Olfactory center, 12, 15
Oligofructose, 288
Oligosaccharides, 197, 317
Omega-3 fatty acids, 224, 755–756
Omega-6 polyunsaturated fatty acids
    (PUFAs), 224
Omelets, 648–650
Onions, 489–490
Open-date labeling, 38
Organic acids, 489, 535, 781
Organic foods, 113–115
Organic polymers, 812
Osmosis, 825
Ovalbumin, 213
Ovaries, 529
Oven spring, 411

Overrun, 301
Overweight, 10, 270
Oxidase, 211
Oxidases, 487–488
Oxidation, 486, 666, 789, 826
Oxidation reactions, 211, 323–324,
    361
Oxidative rancidity, 233–235

Packaging, 809–818
  aseptic, 11, 590, 778, 810, 815–816
  food costs and, 36
  in food preservation, 802
  functions of, 809–810
  hermetic, 506
  materials for, 810–815
  meat, 696
  metal, 814
  for microwave cooking, 164–166
  modified-atmosphere, 506, 816–818
  paper, 812
  plastic, 812–814
  regulatory requirements in, 810
  sous vide, 11
  waste management and, 815
Palatability, 11
Pan-broiling, 711–713
Pancakes, 387–388
Panfrying, 236
Panning, 496–497
Papayas, 538t, 545–546
Papillae, 14–15
Pasta, 331, 336, 348–352
  history of, 348–349
  manufacture of, 349–351
  preparing, 351–352
Pasteurization, 58, 141, 297, 804
  of eggs, 639
  of fruit beverages, 549, 777–778
  microwave, 158
  of milk, 589–590
Pastry, 455–467
  baking, 461–463
  characteristics of plain, 455–458
  crumb, cookie, and sweet crusts,
    463–465
  flakiness, 455–457
  ingredients in plain, 458
  mixing techniques for, 458–459
  phyllo dough, 465
  puff, 465
  rolling, 459–461
  tenderness, 457–458
Pastry method, 375
Pathogenic bacteria, 70
Pathogenic microorganisms, 141

Peaches, 538t, 544
Pearled grains, 341–342
Pears, 538t, 544
Pectic substances, 199, 200
Pectin esterase, 549
Pentosans, 362
Pentoses, 195
Pepper, 173–174
Peptide chains, 364–365
Peptide linkages, 206–207
Peptides, 187, 274
Pesticides, 85–87, 105, 492
pH, 68, 109, 191t, 318, 487
  of fruit beverages, 777
  of milk, 586–587
  of starches, 320
Phenolic compounds, 487–488, 535, 600, 781
Phenylketonuria (PKU), 272
Phospholipids, 205, 221, 584
Phyllo dough, 465
Phytochemicals, 296, 333, 471, 530
Phytoestrogens, 333, 516
Pie crusts, 462–463
Pies. *See also* Pastry
Pilaf, 348
Pineapple, 538t, 544–545
Pizza dough, 420
Plant exudates, 201
Plastic fats, 128, 225, 371–372
Plasticity, 128, 225
Plums, 538t, 544
Poaching, 150–151
Poison squad, 104–105
Polarized light, 313
Polarized molecules, 161
Polar materials, 242
Polar nature, 192
Polydextrose, 276, 298, 447
Polymerization, 262
Polymers, 200, 239, 471, 570
  organic, 812
Polyols, 274–275
Polyphenol, 781
Polysaccharides, 311, 471
Polyunsaturated fats, 372
Polyunsaturated fatty acids, 224–225, 755–756
Popovers, 383–385
Pork, 671
  carving, 721, 723
  cuts of, 687, 689, 691
  quality of, 682–683
  roasting times for, 709t
Potassium bromate, 406
Potatoes, 491, 507–509

Poultry, 735–754
  boning, 744–745
  buying, 738–742
  classification and market forms of, 737
  composition and nutritive value of, 736, 858t
  consumption of, 735
  cooking, 64, 746–750
  food safety and, 73
  freezing, 829–830
  processing, 735–736
  Salmonella and, 72–73
  storing and handling, 742–746
Prebiotics, 197, 362
Precipitates, 597
Precursors, 17, 402, 473, 666
Preservation, 801–809. *See also* Packaging
  by canning, 834–843
  causes of spoilage and, 802
  by freezing, 823–834
  by ionizing radiation, 807–809
  by moisture control, 805–806
  with preservatives, 806–807
  by temperature control, 803–805
Preservatives, 806–807
Pressure cooking
  canning by, 151–152, 838–841
  meats, 716
  vegetables, 500–501
Probiotics, 70, 595
Proofing, 158, 401, 411–412
Pro-oxidants, 234
Protease inhibitors, 87
Proteases, 415, 583
Proteinase, 676
Protein efficiency ratios (PERs), 628
Protein hydrolysates, 102
Proteins, 206–213, 582–584, 597, 628
  as fat replacers, 245–246
  food sources of, 209–210
  plant, 511–517
  properties and reactions of, 210–213
  quality of, 208–209
  soy, 513–517
  structure of, 206–208
Protozoa, 83–84
Prunes, 550
P/S ratios, 224–225
Psychotrophic microorganisms, 746, 803
Puddings, 324–325
Puff pastry, 465
PulseNet, 112, 114, 116
Pungency, 12

Pure Food and Drug Act (1906), 104–105
Purified water, 775
Putrefactive fermentation, 70

Quick breads, 383–398
  biscuits, 393–395
  cream puffs and éclairs, 385–387
  muffins, 389–393
  nut breads, coffeecakes, and fried breads, 393
  pancakes, 387–388
  popovers, 383–385
  waffles, 389
Quick-mix method, 436–437
Quick service restaurants, 8

Radiation
  heat transfer by, 149–150
  irradiation of food, 107, 695, 807–809
Radioactivity, 808
Radioisotopes, 809
Rancidity, 109, 226, 233–235, 591
Raw starch flavor, 319
Recipes, 129–132
  descriptive standardization of, 131–132
  styles of, 130–131
Recombinant DNA technology, 88
Reducing substances, 419, 666
Reducing sugars, 267
Reduction reactions, 212
Reference Daily Intakes (RDIs), 40, 42t
Refrigeration, 65–67, 803. *See also* Freezing
Rehydration, 141
Religion, food choices and, 3–4
Respiration, 484
Restructured meat, 691
Reticulum, 667
Retort pouches, 44, 804, 814–815, 836
Retorts, 835
Retrogradation, 320–321
Reverse osmosis, 548
Rice, 338–341, 346–348, 367
Ripening, 282, 535–537, 605–607
Risks, 58–61
Roasting, 707–711, 746–748, 779, 781
Roe, 763
Root vegetables, 473, 477, 491
Roux, 317, 322
Ruminants, 204, 677
Rye, 341–342
Rye flour, 366

Saccharin, 270–271
Salad dressings, 247–252, 570
    classification of, 247–250
    reduced-fat, 250–251
Salads, 561–570
    gelatin, 576–577
    ingredients in, 563–564
    nutritive value of, 563
    preparing, 564–570
    uses of, 561–563
Salmonella, 59, 71–74, 163, 635–638,
        736, 743
Salmonellosis, 71, 72t
Salts, 172–173, 535
    coagulation by, 600
    gelatin and, 576
    iodized, 172
    on meat, 704–706
    in yeast breads, 407
Sandwiches, 400
Saturated fats, 224–225
Saturated fatty acids, 372, 584, 664
Saturated solutions, 303
Sauces
    espagnole, 317
    gravy, 720
    white, 322
Sautéing, 496–498, 555, 713
Scallops, 763
Scones, 395
Scoville Heat Units, 174
Seafood, 755–774
    aquaculture and, 765
    classification and market forms of,
        757–759
    composition and nutritive value of,
        755–757
    fish products, 763–765
    food safety and, 766–767
    freezing, 829–830
    preparing, 768–771
    selecting, 765–766
    shellfish, 759, 761–763
    storing, 767
    waste, 768
Seafood Inspection Program, 116
Seasonings, 171–186
    flavor enhancers, 174–176
    flavor extracts, 181–183
    herbs and spices, 176–183
    pepper, 173–174
    salt, 172–173
Secondary amines, 696
Seeds, 477–478
Semolina, 348
Senescence, 482, 484

Sensory factors, 1
    in evaluation of food, 19–20
    flavor, 12, 14–18
    in food appearance, 12
    in food choices, 12–20
    texture, 18–19
Septicemia, 77
Sequestering agents, 235
Sequestrants, 108t, 109
Serving sizes, 7t, 470
Shelf-stable foods, 812
Shellfish, 758, 759, 761–763, 770–771
Shigella, 77–78
Shopping aids, 38
Shred, 401
Shrimp, 761, 770–771
Slurries, 321
Smoke points, 230, 241
Sodium bicarbonate, 368–369, 370–371
Soft conversion, 125
Solanine, 87
Solubility, 261
Solutes, 215
Solutions and dispersions, 213–215,
        261, 276–278, 303
Solvents, 189, 215
Sorbitol, 245, 298
Sorghum, 267–268
Soufflés, 618, 650–651
Soups
    cream, 323–324
    stocks for, 719–720
Sous vide packaging, 11, 818
Soybeans, 513–517, 723
Soy flour, 366–367
Space program, 46–48
Spanish creams, 577
Specialty stores, 37
Specifications, 113
Specific heat, 143, 161
Speed scratch foods, 50
Spices, 176–183
    classification and use of, 176–177,
        180–181t
    history of, 176
    pepper, 173–174
    quality of, 179
    storage of, 177–179
Spoilage, 802. *See also* Preservation
Sponge, 404–405, 409
    cake method, 436
    gelatin, 576–577
Sponge cake, 444–445
Spores, 68, 80, 81, 804
Sports beverages, 777
Spring water, 775

Stabilizers, 108t, 109, 303
Staling, 421–422, 783–784
Standard legal meanings, 114, 115
Standard operating procedures (SOPs),
        60
Standing time, 167
Staphylococcus, 72t, 78–79
Starches, 198–199, 311–330
    composition and structure of,
        312–317
    cookery with, 321–326
    effects of heat on, 317–320
    as fat replacers, 317
    gelatinization of, 373, 493, 720
    gel formation and retrogradation of,
        320–321
    hydrolysis of, 317
    improved native, 316
    instant, 316
    modified, 312, 314–316
    sources of, 311–312
Starch granules, 142, 199, 313, 315
Starter, bread, 404–405
Steaming, 151–152, 499–500, 769–770
Steeping, 337–338
Sterilization, 58, 158, 804
Sterols, 205–206, 221, 229, 584
Stewing, 150–151, 715, 749
Stir-frying, 496–498
Stirring and turning, 166–167, 319–320
Storage
    of cheese, 615–616
    of chocolate, 795–796
    of coffee, 783–784
    of dried fruits, 550
    of eggs, 637–638
    food safety and, 73–74
    of fresh fruits, 546–547
    of frozen foods, 832–834
    of meat, 699, 700
    of milk, 590
    of poultry, 742–743
    of seafood, 767
    of vegetables, 482, 484
Stores, types of food, 37–38
Subcutaneous substances, 677
Sublimation, 826–827
Substitutions, ingredient, 850
Succulent vegetables, 530
Sucralose, 273
Sucrose, 196–197, 265–267, 278–279
Sugars
    in batters and doughs, 373–374
    brown, 265
    bulking agents, 275–276
    in cakes, 430–431, 442

cocrystallized sucrose, 265–267
consumption of, 259–260
cookery with, 276–279
crystalline forms of, 264–267
disaccharides, 196–197
gelatin and, 576
granulated, 264–265
honey, 268–269
measuring, 128–129
molasses and sorghum, 267–268
monosaccharides, 195–196
nutritive value of, 260
oligosaccharides, 197
polysaccharides, 198–201
powdered, 265
properties of, 261–264
substitutions between, 269t
sweeteners vs., in baking, 449
sweetness of, 263–264
syrups, 267, 268
in yeast breads, 407
Sulfhydryl compounds, 488
Supercenters, 37
Supercritical fluid extraction, 585
Supermarkets, 37–38
Supersaturated solutions, 261
Surface activity, 640
Surface cleaning, 62
Surface tension, 239, 602, 643
Surimi, 763
Sweetened condensed milk, 593
Sweeteners, 259–260, 269–274. *See also*
    Sugars
    as additives, 108t, 110
    baking with, 449
    in batters and doughs, 373–374
    in frozen desserts, 302–303
Syneresis, 571, 639
Synergists, 235
Synthetic compounds, 18
Syrups, 129, 280t. *See also* Canning

Tactile receptors, 12
Taffy, 285
Tallow, 241
Tart crusts, 465
Taste, 14–17
Taste buds, 14–15
Taste pores, 14
Taste receptors, 14
Tea, 787–791
    composition of, 789
    market forms of, 790
    preparing, 790–791
    processing, 789
    types of, 789

Temperature
    bacteria growth and, 66
    control, 852–853
    converting between scales, 852–853
    critical, 585
    for deep-fat frying, 239t
    effects of on milk, 597–598
    food preservation and, 803–805
    food safety and, 63–65
    gelatin and, 575
Temperature danger zone, 65–67
Tempering, 157–158, 324–325
Tenderness
    meat, 673–676, 676, 706–707
    pastry, 457–458
Texture, 18–19, 142, 301
Thaumatin, 274
Thermoforming, 810
Thermometers, 64–65, 144, 145, 278,
    852–853
Thickeners, 108t, 109
Tofu, 515, 517
Tortillas, 337–338
Trade policies, 35–36
Trans configuration, 226
Trans fatty acids, 226–227, 243
Translucency, 318
Triacylglycerols, 202–205
Trichinella spiralis, 83–84, 163, 680
Triglycerides, 202–205, 221, 244, 371,
    584
Triticale, 342, 367
Tubers, 311, 312, 473, 477, 491
Turkey. *See* Poultry
Turnover, fat, 240

Ultrafiltration, 548, 583–584
Ultrahigh-temperature (UHT) milk,
    592–593
Umami, 175
Unit pricing, 38
Unsaturated fats, 224–225
Unsaturated fatty acids, 664
UPC (Universal Product Code) sym-
    bols, 42, 43
USDA. *See* Department of Agri-
    culture

Vacuum-drying, 549
Vaporization, 145
Vapor pressure, 143, 189, 276–277
Variety meats, 691–692, 717, 718
Veal, 671
    cuts of, 688, 689, 691
    quality of, 682
    roasting times for, 709t, 710

Vegans, 4
Vegetable gums, 195, 200–201, 311
Vegetables, 469–527
    biotechnology and, 478–479
    canned, 506
    color of, 485–488
    composition and nutritive value of,
        469–478, 855–856t
    cooking, 492–505
    cooking losses in, 493–494
    cooking times for, 502–504t
    dried legumes, 509–511
    as flavorings, 183
    flavor of, 489–490
    freezing, 829
    frozen, 505–506
    in gelatin, 576
    grades of, 480–482, 483
    leaf, 472–473, 474
    partially processed, 506–507
    potatoes, 507–509
    preparing, 485–506
    protein in, 511–517
    in salads, 561–570
    selecting, 479–482
    storing, 482, 484
    vegetable-fruits, 473, 475
    vegetarian diets and, 511–517
Vegetarians, 4, 511–517
Vibrio parahaemolyticus, 78
Viruses, 84–85
Viscosity, 318, 601, 640
Visible fats, 221
Vitamins, 494–495, 530, 532, 548, 666.
    See also Nutrition

Waffles, 389
Warmed-over flavor, 715
Waste, 33–34, 472t, 768, 815
Water
    bottled, 775
    in coffee, 787
    content of foods, 188–194
    in food preparation, 189–191
    hardness of, 193–194
    heat capacity of, 143
    heat transfer by, 150–151
    nature of, 191–193
Water-holding capacity, 188–189
Waxy maize, 316
Weights and measures, 123–129,
    849–851
    measuring equipment, 126–127
    metric system, 123–125
    of staple foods, 127–129
Welsh rabbit, 618

Wheat, 336–337
    classes of, 359
    cracked, 366
    flour, 357–367
    germ, 366
    milling, 359–361
Whey protein isolate, 583–584
Whipped cream, 602–603
White sauces, 322
Wholesale clubs, 37
Wiley, Harvey, 104–105

Winterization, 227
World Health Organization, 117
World Trade Organization, 117

Yeast, 68, 402–405, 405
    autolysates, 176
    fermentation, 18
Yeast breads, 399–427
    artisan, 419–420
    baking, 415–416
    characteristics of, 401–402

commercial processes for, 413–415
fermentation and proofing, 411–412
ingredients for, 402–407
mixing and handling, 407–411
rolls, 416–417
staling, 421–422
whole-grain and variety, 417–420
Yersinia enterocolitica, 76–77
Yersiniosis, 72t, 76–77
Yield grades, 680–681
Yogurt, 595